MORNINGSTAR®
ETFs150™

Annual Sourcebook
2007 Edition

Introduction by
Dan Culloton,
Editor

Library of Congress Cataloging-in-Publication Data:

ISBN-13 978-0-471-78666-5
ISBN-10 0-471-78666-7

Printed in the United States of America

10 9 8 7 6 5 4 3 2 1

Table of Contents

Don't blink. You might miss the launch of a new exchange-traded fund, or two, or three, or a couple dozen. Lest you harbor doubts that ETFs were the hottest trend in the mutual fund business, consider this: Established and upstart firms flooded the market with an unprecedented number of new ETFs and ETF-like vehicles in 2006. Never before have the choices for ETF investors been as plentiful; consequently never before has the need for a guidebook like this been greater.

Morningstar has made a lot of changes in the past year to stay ahead of the curve in the rapidly changing and growing ETF universe, and you'll see that reflected in the pages of the *Morningstar ETFs 150*. Right off the bat, you'll notice the book offers commentary and analysis on more ETFs—150 versus last year's 100. This year's edition also features the Morningstar Rating for ETFs, both on a newly redesigned report page for each ETF and with an expanded array of tables and charts. Because many of the new ETFs launched in the past year track alternative asset classes that may be unfamiliar to you, we've also included articles on how to use ETFs and some that explore whether esoteric investments, such as commodities, belong in your portfolio.

As always, the goal of this book is to help you cut through the abundance of hype and information about ETFs to make informed, responsible investing decisions. Toward that end our tables and charts this year draw from the entire ETF universe and rank the funds by a variety of useful measures, such as expenses, trading volume, average valuation ratios, and star ratings.

Our analyst staff provides in-depth research and commentary on about half of the burgeoning list of ETFs. We focus on the largest, most actively traded ETFs first; throw in funds that offer low-cost, diversified alternatives to traditional funds in their categories, and, finally, add ETFs that employ methods that beg for closer examination and explication, such as those tracking fundamentally weighted and dividend-weighted indexes.

The heart of this book remains the individual ETF reports. For each member of the ETFs 150, we provide a one-page report that includes all the data you need to do your due diligence, including 10-years worth of performance history, a snapshot of the ETF's risk profile, details about the construction methodology of its benchmark, and an indication if the fund is trading above or below the fair value of its underlying holdings. Tying all of the data on the report page together is Morningstar's Take—our analyst's critical evaluation of whether a particular ETF is worth buying.

Whether you're an experienced ETF investor or checking them out for the first time, *Morningstar ETFs 150* has the data and analysis to help you make better ETF choices. Good luck.

Dan Culloton, Editor *Morningstar ETFs 150*

Year in Review

The best and worst new ETFs.

by Sonya Morris, CPA, Editor, Morningstar ETFInvestor

A torrent of new ETFs debuted in 2006. More than 150 new offerings were launched, almost doubling the choices available to ETF investors. Here's a rundown of some of the newest ETFs on the market.

Overlooked but Promising

While many of the newest ETFs venture into unusual asset classes or track esoteric benchmarks, a number of plain-vanilla sector funds were introduced in 2006. I was pleased to see that Barclays expanded their lineup of global sector ETFs in 2006. These days, most industries are global in nature and if a sector looks attractive, I want to be able to invest in the leading firms in the industry, no matter where they happen to be headquartered. These new ETFs include many dominant foreign players. For example, iShares S&P Global Consumer Staples includes Nestle and Unilever among its top holdings. Similarly, Toyota and Sony play prominent roles in iShares S&P Global Consumer Discretionary. Although none of these new sector ETFs looks particularly attractive from a valuation perspective at the moment, I'll be keeping them on my radar screen.

The Jury's Still Out

Several ETFs debuted have abandoned the traditional cap-weighting index methodology for systems that the providers view as superior.

PowerShares pioneered the fundamental weighting concept in the ETF world when it introduced PowerShares FTSE RAFI 1000. The firm expanded its RAFI lineup in 2006 by adding a slew of sector ETFs based on RAFI fundamental weighting methodology. The RAFI approach is still relatively new, and it remains to be seen how it will work at the sector-specific level. The older RAFI indexes look compelling from a historical, back-tested perspective, but I'm concerned that the methodology's bias toward smaller, value-oriented stocks skews the results. If large-growth stocks come back—as I suspect they might—it could put the RAFI funds at a disadvantage. I'll be intrigued if it appears that these ETFs are able to ferret out cheap, wide-moat stocks, but I'd like to see how these ETFs perform in the real world and

in different market environments before getting comfortable with them.

In 2006, an entire fund complex, WisdomTree Investments, was launched based on the concept of weighting stocks by cash dividends paid. By the end of 2006, there were 30 WisdomTree ETFs on the market and more are on the way. Some WisdomTree ETFs hold promise, particularly for yield-hungry sorts. But some of these ETFs court substantial sector-specific risk and they may not be as tax efficient as competing ETFs.

Not So New and Improved

Rydex rolled out a collection of pure style indexes using the new S&P/Citigroup style methodology, but rather than weighting the stocks by market capitalization, the stocks are ranked based on the "style score" awarded by the S&P/Citigroup system. In addition, unlike the other S&P/Citigroup style indexes offered by Barclays under the iShares brand, these ETFs eliminate duplication between indexes. Many style indexes—not just S&P's—allow some overlap between the growth and value indexes because some stocks exhibit characteristics of both groups. For example, you'll find General Electric and Exxon Mobil in both the S&P 500/Citigroup Value Index and Growth Index. In contrast, the pure style indexes hone in on those stocks that exclusively exhibit either growth or value traits. While this is an improvement in index construction, in practice it doesn't seem to make much of a difference. For example, it's logical to assume that the pure value ETF would own more value stocks than its rivals. However, the data doesn't bear that out. Rydex S&P 500 Pure Value's valuation characteristics don't look much different from the competition. For instance, its price/earnings ratio is right near the middle of the pack. Until I see evidence that these funds are delivering as advertised, I can't recommend them.

The Time's Not Right

Rydex also rolled out a collection of equal-weighted sector indexes. Cap-weighted indexes are dominated by the largest stocks in their universe, but equal-weighted indexes are more democratic; every stock in the index holds equal sway. That could be a good thing if smaller stocks look attractive, but that's not the case right now. Equal-weighted indexes have benefited in recent years by the strong small-cap rally, which is beginning to look a little long in the tooth. Given their long run, it wouldn't be surprising to see small-caps take a breather. If that happens, these new ETFs could struggle to keep up with their cap-weighted peers. Someday, small-cap stocks will look cheap again, and I'll revisit these ETFs then. But even under those circumstances, I think the odds are good that a cheap, plain-vanilla small-cap ETF could do the job better.

Special Asset Classes Not So Special After All

One broad theme that dominated 2006 was the emergence of ETFs that venture beyond equities. The majority of these new funds focus on commodities. Several commodities have experienced bull markets (though some began to sputter as 2006 progressed), and as a result, some of these ETFs delivered promising early returns. Consequently, investors flocked to these new offerings.

The most popular newbie ETF in 2006 was iShares Silver Trust. Although this ETF might offer a measure of diversification to a portfolio given its lack of correlation with stocks and bonds, it's not a necessary holding by any stretch. Some argue that silver and gold are good inflation hedges, but I think investing in stocks for the long haul is a far better hedge against rising prices. In short, I think you can skip this ETF altogether.

My pick for commodity exposure is the iPath Dow Jones-AIG Commodity Index, which also debuted in 2006. It offers diversified exposure to a broad basket of commodities, and the ETN structure offers certain tax advantages.

I'm not a fan of single-commodity ETFs, particularly those that track the price of oil. Betting on the direction of the price of oil is the investor's equivalent of playing with fire. And in late November, Claymore handed investors a match when it launched two new exchange-traded securities—Claymore MacroShares Oil Down Tradeable Shares and Claymore MacroShares Oil Up Tradeable Shares. Most investors should steer well clear of these new vehicles. If the recent volatility of the price of oil isn't enough to warn you off, the price tag on these securities should be. The expense ratios clock in at a hefty 1.60%, which is expensive even for a conventional front-load mutual fund. These two are my picks for the worst new funds of the year.

A Poor 'Alternative'

Another specialized area that's garnering a lot of attention is private equity. M&A activity really picked up in 2006. That's partly been fueled by private-equity firms, which are in the business of acquiring companies. Pension funds and other institutional investors have poured cash into private-equity firms in recent years. Thanks to that trend and relatively cheap debt financing, private-equity firms have plenty of financial resources to fund acquisitions. Several deals have been inked already, and there likely will be more. If these acquisitions pan out as expected, these private-equity firms and their shareholders stand to benefit.

In late October, PowerShares launched the first private-equity ETF, PowerShares Listed Private Equity Portfolio, giving small investors the chance to gain access to this hot market. Many private-equity firms aren't publicly traded, so the index provider, Red Rocks Capital Partners, had to make some compromises in constructing this ETF's benchmark. For instance, some of the index constituents aren't pure private-equity firms. In fact, some get the bulk of their revenue from other operations. Witness such holdings as Triarc, which is the franchiser for the Arby's restaurant chain; CIT Group leases heavy equipment, and Pinnacle West Capital gets 75% of its revenue from Arizona Public Service, a utility company.

I have other reservations about this ETF as well. Just because private-equity firms are doing a lot of deals at the moment, doesn't necessarily mean that they are smart ones. In fact, it's just these sorts of overheated environments that can result in bad deals.

Finally, even though this ETF has been pitched as an alternative asset class, I'm not sure I buy that. Many of the stocks included in this index can be found in other broad benchmarks. And when it comes down to it, private-equity firms still own just that—equity. I think this ETF looks more like a micro-cap fund than a special asset class of its own. But whatever you call it, I would avoid it like the plague. ▥

Sonya Morris, CPA, is editor of Morningstar ETFInvestor, a monthly newsletter that showcases Morningstar's latest thinking on the ETF market. Please visit http://www.morningstar.com/Products/Store_ETFInvestor.html for more information and to order Morningstar ETFInvestor. Before becoming editor of ETFInvestor, she spearheaded Morningstar's coverage of Vanguard funds and wrote Morningstar's monthly newsletter, the Vanguard Fund Family Report. Morris holds bachelor's degrees in finance and English from University of Illinois at Urbana-Champaign and a master's degree in English from Northwestern University.

How to Use This Book

Tips for getting the most out of your *Morningstar ETFs 150*.

by Dan Culloton, Editor,
Morningstar ETFs 150

When it comes to selecting conventional funds, Morningstar has long advocated eschewing past performance trends and instead focusing on fundamental analysis. Though exchange-traded funds are different from their traditional counterparts, the same rule applies. Successful ETF investing begins not by checking last year's leaders' lists, but with research into expenses, index methodology, and the competence of the advisor.

True, looking at the best-performing ETFs for any given time period can provide important clues about market trends, and that's why this book includes plenty of rankings. (See Pages 192-224.) But to truly understand an ETF and the role it might play in a portfolio, investors have to drill down into its holdings, understand how its index is built and how its manager tracks it, and evaluate the ETF's risk level.

Toward that end, this edition of Morningstar ETFs 150 is full of all the data and analysis you need to make informed decisions. Read on as we walk through some of the best tools for doing just that. (The Glossary that begins on Page 227 provides you with specific definitions of all of the data points in the book.)

Morningstar's Take

The text box in the lower left-hand quadrant of each individual ETF page is the analysis, or "Morningstar's Take." Reading the analysis is an essential first step as you attempt to determine whether an ETF is appropriate for your goals and risk tolerance. In it, the analyst sums up all of an ETF's salient points by assessing its historical risk/reward profile relative to its peer group and competing conventional mutual funds, discussing how the ETF's benchmark is constructed, and noting and evaluating any recent changes to that methodology. And because Morningstar analysts speak regularly with ETF sponsors and advisors, and have Morningstar's extensive database at their fingertips, the analysis can provide glimpses into individual ETFs that you won't find anywhere else.

Morningstar Rating

In the center of the ETF page you'll find the Morningstar rating for ETFs. Morningstar rates investments from 1 to 5 stars based on how well they've performed (after adjusting for risk and accounting for all relevant sales charges) in comparison to similar investments. Within each Morningstar Category, the top 10% of investments receive 5 stars, the next 22.5% 4 stars, the middle 35% 3 stars, the next 22.5% 2 stars, and the bottom 10% receive 1 star. Investments are rated for up to three time periods—three, five, and 10 years—and these ratings are combined to produce an overall rating. Investments with less than three years of history are not rated. Ratings are objective, based entirely on a mathematical evaluation of past performance. They are good for getting a sense of an ETFs risk-adjusted returns, but not necessarily picking ETFs that will outperform in the future.

Morningstar Price/Fair Value Measure

This gives investors a way to use Morningstar stock research to evaluate ETF portfolios. In addition to its staff of more than two dozen mutual fund analysts, Morningstar has 90 in-house equity analysts researching and estimating fair values for more than 1,800 stocks. The price/fair value ratio basically taps that research to offer a bottom-up assessment of whether an ETF portfolio is cheap or expensive by gauging if its holdings, on average, are trading above or below their Morningstar fair value estimates. First we calculate the market value of all the holdings in the ETF for which we have fair value estimates. Then we use the fair value estimates of those stocks to calculate what we believe is the fair value of the same portfolio.

Lastly, we compare the two numbers and calculate a ratio of the market value compared to the fair value. A reading higher than 1 means the ETF is overvalued; lower than 1 indicates it's undervalued. Because Morningstar does not estimate a fair value for every stock an ETF might own, the relevance of the results of the price/fair value depends on how many stocks in a given portfolio have received a fair value estimate and the percentage of that portfolio's assets these stocks represent. You can see how pertinent the measure is by looking at the "Coverage Rate," which shows the percentage of the ETF's market capitalization covered by Morningstar equity analysts. Our stock coverage is pretty compre-hensive for the vast majority of domestic large-cap ETFs.

You'll find the price/fair value measure in the upper left-hand corner of the ETF page beneath the ETF's name and ticker.

Style Boxes/Morningstar Categories

The Morningstar style box, the nine-square grid that appears toward the bottom right-hand corner of each individual fund page, is designed to give you a visual snapshot of the type of securities an ETF owns. For stock funds, the style box shows you the size of companies in which an ETF invests, as well as whether it focuses on growth- or value-oriented securities. For bond ETFs, the style box depicts an ETF's sensitivity to interest rates as well as the average credit quality of the bonds in the portfolio. Armed with three years' worth of style boxes, we determine an ETF's Morningstar Category placement, which reflects how the ETF has invested its assets over the past three years. (The Morningstar Category appears in the top right-hand corner of each ETF page.)

As a general rule of thumb, large-blend or large-value ETFs make the best core stock holdings, because they invest in the well-established companies that tend to dominate the market and because they're not as volatile as their large-growth counterparts. For those seeking a core bond-ETF holding, the intermediate-term bond category will generally be the best hunting ground. Such ETFs are typically well diversified across government and corporate bonds and have some (although not extreme) sensitivity to interest-rate changes. There aren't many fixed-income ETFs to choose from currently, but that could change in the future.

Just as Morningstar's style boxes and categories can help you make smart ETF selections, they can also help you determine how to put the ETFs together into a well-diversified package. While you need not buy an ETF in every single Morningstar Category, building a portfolio of ETFs with varying investment styles is a sensible diversification strategy.

Sector Weightings

Sector weightings, which appear in the bottom right-hand corner of each stock ETF page, pick up where an ETF's investment style box leaves off. Eyeballing an ETF's sector weightings is an essential step on the road to understanding how an ETF will behave and how you might use it to build a diversified portfolio. After all, ETFs may land in different Morningstar Categories, but if their sector compositions are similar, it's possible that their performances will be, too.

Methodology

In this area Morningstar's analyst sums up the ETF's investment process, which for index ETFs means how their benchmarks are constructed and how the ETFs' advisors go about tracking the bogies. How does the fund's index define the asset class it is trying to measure? How does it weight its constituents? How often does it rebalance? What method does the manager use to mimic the index's returns—exact replication or representative sampling? The strategy section tries to address all of these questions and could help you differentiate between ETFs that purport to track the same areas of the market.

Tables and Charts

For those of you who love lists Pages 192-224 include an impressive array of ETF data and rankings. In general, selecting ETFs from a list of short-term leaders is a poor investment strategy. But eyeballing the lists of top-performing ETFs over longer time frames—over the past five and 10 years, for example—can provide you with great ideas for further research. This year we've also included tables ranking ETFs by their ratings, as well as their valuation and growth metrics. These can give you an idea of ETFs' risk adjusted performance histories, and whether their underlying portfolios look cheap or expensive based on various measures, such as price/cash flow. Happy hunting. ▓

The Morningstar Stock-ETF Page

In this six-page walk-through, we briefly describe how each section of the page is relevant to your ETF research and offer some tips on using these features to better analyze ETFs. More-detailed discussions of the elements presented in this section appear in the Glossary.

A Investment Value Graph

B Morningstar Fair Value

C Management

D Methodology

E Performance

F Tax Analysis

G Morningstar's Take

H Operations

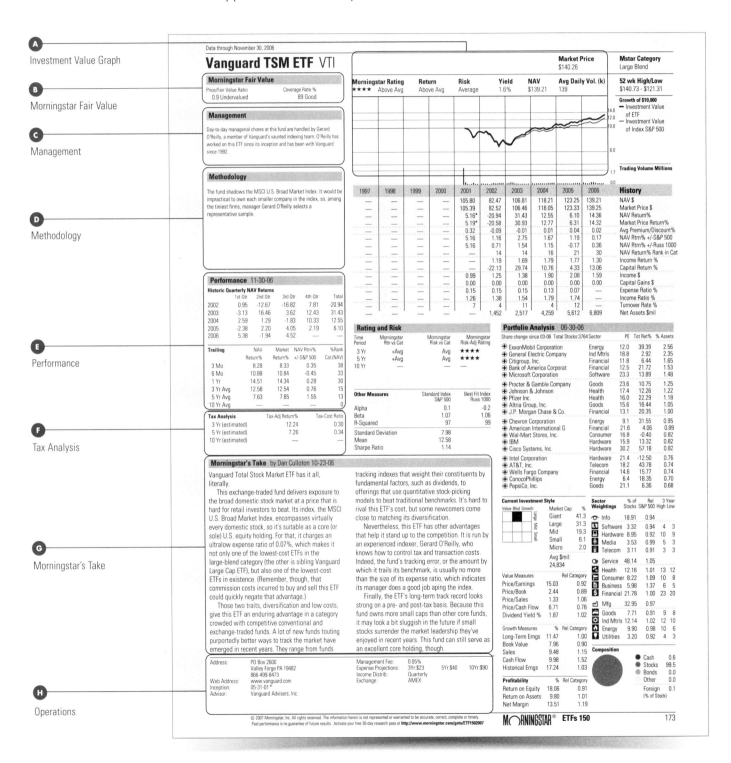

A **Investment Value Graph**

The Investment Value graph line shows an ETF's performance trend, derived from the ETF's historical growth of $10,000. It provides a visual depiction of how an ETF has amassed its returns, including the performance swings its shareholders have endured along the way. The growth of $10,000 begins at the date of the ETF's inception, or if the ETF has been in existence for more than 10 years, then growth of $10,000 begins at the first year listed on the graph. Also, featured in the graph is the performance of an index (S&P 500 or MSCI EAFE, for example), which allows investors to compare the performance of the ETF with the performance of the benchmark index.

B **Morningstar Fair Value**

This ratio in the upper left side of the page offers a bottom-up assessment of whether an ETF portfolio is cheap or expensive by gauging if its holdings, on average, are trading above or below their Morningstar fair value estimates. The process draws on the research of Morningstar's in-house equity analysts. A measure higher than 1.0 means the ETF is overvalued. A reading lower than 1.0 means the offering is undervalued. The Coverage Rate is the percentage of stocks in an ETF under coverage by Morningstar stock analysts.

C **Management**

The portfolio manager is the individual or individuals responsible for the overall investment operations of the ETF, including the buying and selling required for index ETFs to track their benchmarks. In many cases managers are also involved in selecting benchmarks for new ETFs. To help investors know who is running an ETF, we detail the ETF's management with a brief biography.

D **Methodology**

While the Morningstar Category gives investors an idea of the kind of investments an ETF makes; it does not fully capture the nuances of the ETFs methodology for capturing the returns of the market segment it claims to represent. In this section, Morningstar's analysts explain how an ETF's benchmark selects securities for inclusion, how often it rebalances, when it decides to kick issues out, how it controls turnover, and how risky a given index may be. On the equity side, the strat-

egy description often focuses on what size and type of company on which an ETF's index focuses. For style-based ETFs this includes a discussion of how the index defines growth and value stocks. With bond ETFs, the strategy section explains how the ETF goes about matching the duration, credit quality, and maturity of its benchmark index.

E **Performance**

The quarterly returns show the performance investors have seen over each calendar quarter in the past five years. This section is a good spot to quickly test your risk tolerance. Find the largest quarterly loss; if it makes you uneasy, you should probably look for less-volatile ETFs. The trailing returns section illustrates performance over short and long periods. We compare returns against appropriate benchmarks and peers: 1 is the best percentile; 100 is the worst.

F **Tax Analysis**

This section lists an ETF's tax-adjusted returns and the percentage-point reduction in annualized returns that results from taxes, called the tax-cost ratio. For context, each figure is then given a percentile rank in the ETF's category (1 is the best percentile; 100 is the worst). Examine the two returns figures together because high tax-adjusted returns do not necessarily mean the ETF is tax-efficient. Also, an ETF could be very tax efficient, but if returns are poor to begin with, an investor will still pocket a low sum.

G **Moningstar's Take**

Our analysts interpret the data on the page and interview the ETF's manager to explain the methodologies guiding investment decisions. They then succinctly detail how and why an ETF has succeeded or failed, and what role—if any—it should play in your portfolio.

H **Operations**

Here we list where to write or call to obtain investment information from the ETF. We also list the ETF's management fee, income distribution frequency, inception date, and exchange on which it trades.

The Morningstar Stock-ETF Page (continued)

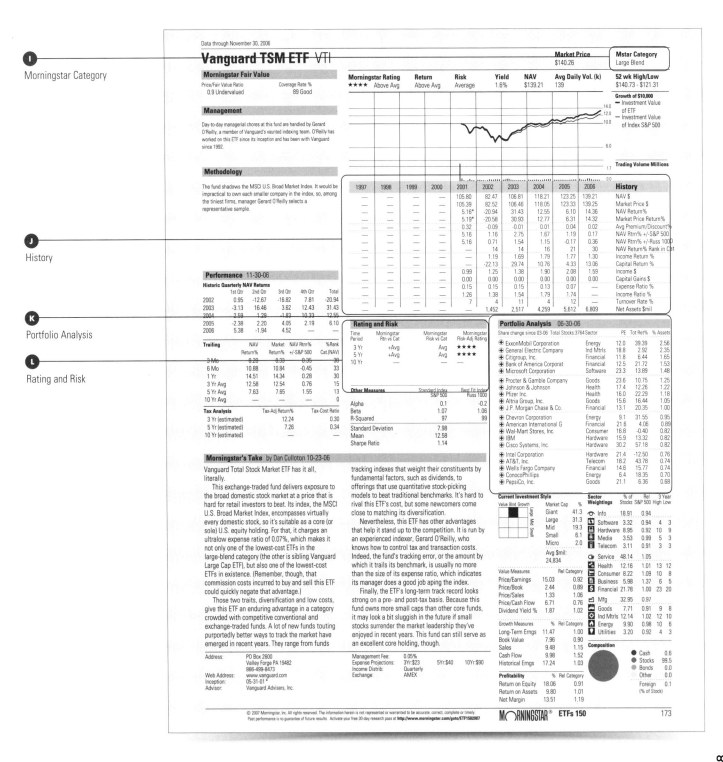

I — Morningstar Category

J — History

K — Portfolio Analysis

L — Rating and Risk

ⓘ Morningstar Category

The Morningstar Category is the first stage of digging into the ETF's portfolio. We sort ETFs into peer groups based on the types of securities the ETFs hold. Each category is assigned using a fundamental analysis of an ETF's portfolio over a three-year period. It is important to analyze the types of securities an ETF holds. Portfolio analysis, and an ETF's category, can tell you a lot about an ETF's performance and future volatility. For example, investors can expect bumpier rides with ETFs in the small-cap growth category—those that focus on small, rapidly growing companies— than with large-cap value ETFs, which focus on well-established companies that are trading cheaply. In addition to portfolio analysis, the Morningstar categories also can help you diversify and evaluate the role an ETF might play in your portfolio. For example, you might head to the more-volatile categories (the small-cap groups or emerging markets) if you decided to spice up your large-cap-laden portfolio. Or you might want to tone down a growth-oriented portfolio with a value ETF or two.

ⓙ History

Use this table to spot trends over the past 10 years. Pay particular attention to the following statistics.

Expense Ratio

This percentage tells you how much it costs to own the ETF each year. Generally ETFs are much cheaper than traditional mutual funds with expense ratios that are a fraction of that of the average conventional mutual fund. The average expense ratio is 0.41% for domestic-stock ETFs, 0.52% for international ETFs, and 0.29% for fixed-income ETFs.

Turnover Rate

Virtually all ETFs are index funds and should have low turnover relative to conventional mutual funds. However, turnover still matters. Depending on how they are constructed, the benchmarks of smaller-cap and style base-indexes can have higher turnover as stocks that get larger or smaller, or cheaper or more expensive migrate in and out of the benchmarks. To keep up with the changes, ETFs may have to sell securities. Higher turnover drives up an ETF's costs because more broker-age commissions are being paid. Higher-turnover ETFs also could be less tax-efficient, although the unique structure of ETFs allows them to avoid many gains. Still,

if an ETF has a high turnover rate, check the ETF's tax efficiency. And watch for significant year-to-year changes in the turnover rate: It could indicate a change in the ETF's benchmark.

ⓚ Portfolio Analysis

Analyzing an ETF's portfolio will give you an understanding of the ETF's performance and potential volatility. First, note the ETF's total holdings: The ETF with fewer stocks will get more kick from its best performers, but if just a few holdings falter, the ETF will lag. All things being equal, an ETF with 50 or fewer stocks will be more volatile than an ETF holding twice as many issues. Next, check the percentage of assets devoted to each security. An ETF following a concentrated index will have large hunks of the ETF's assets (more than 5% per stock) invested in its top holdings. Now identify each stock's sector to gain insight into where an ETF's top holdings are concentrated and where its vulnerabilities lie. Then check the stocks' P/E ratios; high P/Es are another indication of possible future volatility. Each stock's year-to-date returns tell you which securities in which sectors are driving the performance of the ETF.

ⓛ Rating and Risk

This section breaks down the ETF's risk, returns, and overall star rating over the three-, five-, and 10-year time periods. The return versus category section shows how the ETF's returns compare with those of ETFs and conventional open-end mutual funds in its peer group. We rate the top 10% ETFs high, the next 22.5% above average, and the middle 35% average. We call the next 22.5% ETFs below average, and the bottom 10% low. Similarly, the Risk versus Category section ranks a fund's historical volatility versus that of its peer group, with those funds that have exhibited a lot of downside volatility faring worse than those that have not. The rationale here is highly volatile funds are risky, but those offerings that tend to lose a lot of money are most worrisome to investors. The historical star ratings offer some clues regarding the consistency of a fund's historical risk-adjusted performance. Those with 5-star three-, five-, and 10-year results have often put up consistently strong risk-adjusted results while those with poor marks have often languished year after year. Funds with markedly different short- and long-term results may have extreme strategies that produce feast-or-famine

The Morningstar Stock-ETF Page (continued)

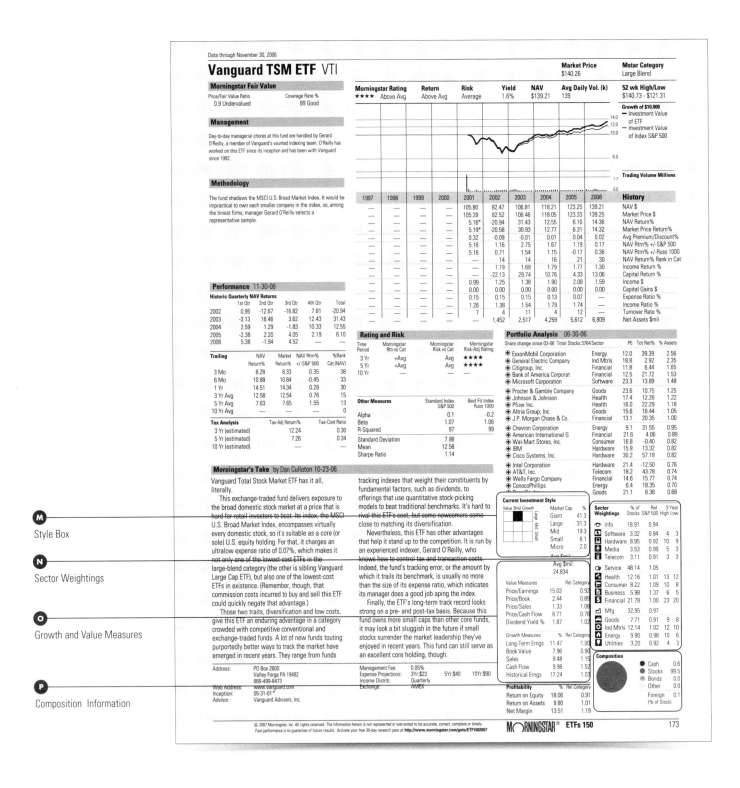

M Style Box

N Sector Weightings

O Growth and Value Measures

P Composition Information

returns or they may have experienced a manager change that has materially affected performance.

Alpha, Beta, and R-squared are three Modern Portfolio Theory statistics that measure how much you can expect an ETF to follow a market index and whether the ETF has added or subtracted value versus that benchmark. We compare all domestic- and international-equity ETFs with the S&P 500 and a Best Fit Index (the index with which the ETF has the highest correlation).

Alpha

Alpha measures excess returns per unit of risk. The higher the alpha the better. A positive alpha indicates the ETF performed better in the past than its beta would predict. A negative alpha indicates the ETF performed worse. Below these statistics, standard deviation measures risk as volatility by showing the range within which an ETF's monthly returns have landed. The larger the number, the wider the range and more volatile the ETF has been. To set an ETF's standard deviation in context, compare it with others in the ETF's category. The mean represents the annualized total return for an ETF over the trailing three years.

Beta

Beta measures an ETF's volatility relative to its benchmark. A beta of more than 1.0 means the ETF is more volatile than the index and should outperform it when the index is rising and underperform it when the index is falling. A beta of less than 1.0 works the opposite way. The iShares Dow Jones Real Estate Index's beta of 0.98 versus the Dow Jones Wilshire REIT Index means it's just as volatile as that bogy. The ETF's beta of 0.43 versus the S&P 500 means its less volatile than the broad market.

R-squared

For beta and alpha to be reliable measures of risk and reward, an ETF must have a high correlation with its index, as measured by R-squared. R-squared indicates how marketlike an ETF is. A high R-squared (between 85 and 100) indicates the ETF's performance patterns have been in line with the index's. An ETF with a low R-squared (70 or less) doesn't act much like the index. Index ETFs should have R-squared of 100 when compared against their own or similar indexes, but the measure can vary when they are compared against a different bogy. The iShares Dow Jones Real Estate Index, for example, has an R-squared of 99 versus the Dow Jones

Wilshire REIT Index, but an R-squared of 9 versus the S&P 500. That means the ETF is more like the REIT index.

Sharpe Ratio

The Sharpe ratio is a risk-adjusted performance measure. The higher the Sharpe ratio (1.0 is pretty good), the better the ETF's risk-adjusted performance has been.

Ⓜ Style Box

For stock ETFs, Morningstar assigns style-box classifications based on portfolios' scores for Growth Measures, Value Measures, and average weighted market cap. For example, ETFs that invest predominantly in large-cap, fast-growing firms with high valuations typically land in large growth. By contrast, ETFs that specialize in smaller, slower-growing firms with modest valuations are assigned to the small-value style box.

Ⓝ Sector Weightings

Learn which sectors of the economy the ETF invests in to gauge how diversified the ETF is. An ETF that has more than 25% of assets concentrated in one sector is almost certain to carry more risk than a more-diversified offering. Knowing the ETF's weightings can help you maintain a well-diversified portfolio. Weightings are displayed relative to the S&P 500 for domestic-stock ETFs and to the category for international-stock ETFs. (We show relative subsector breakdowns for ETFs in our specialty categories.) The last two columns of the section give an ETF's historical range of the percentage of assets held in each sector.

Ⓞ Growth and Value Measures

This section lists an ETF portfolio's current averages for various portfolio statistics, including price/earnings, price/cash flow, and historical earnings growth. To provide perspective, we compare these measures with the ETF's category average.

Ⓟ Composition Information

This section shows the percentage of assets devoted to cash, stocks, bonds, and other, along with what percentage of stock assets are invested in foreign securities. All ETFs should be nearly fully invested, though they typically will carry a trace of cash for settlement purposes.

The Morningstar Bond-ETF Page

In this two-page walk-through, we spotlight sections that are unique to the bond-ETF page and offer some advice on using the page to select a bond ETF. More-detailed discussions of the elements presented in this section appear in the Glossary.

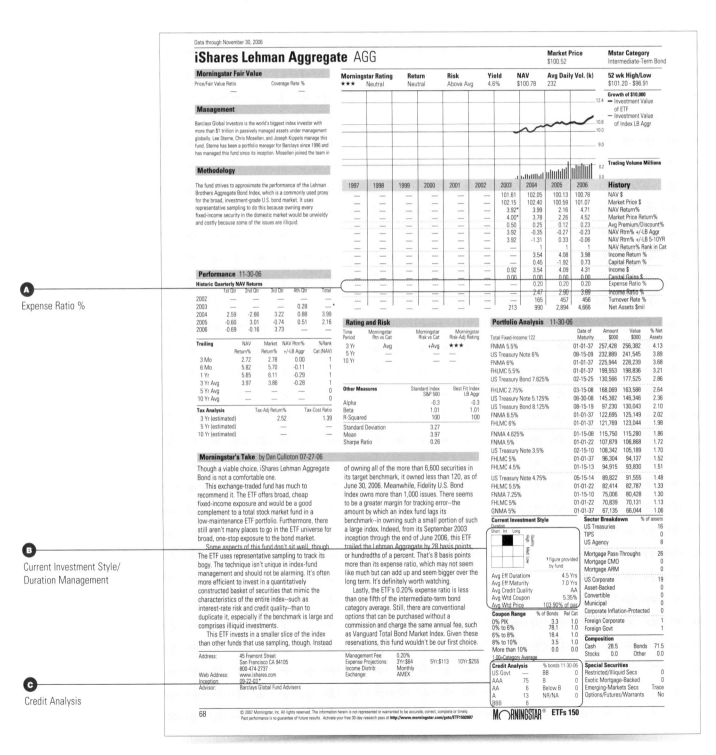

A — Expense Ratio %

B — Current Investment Style/ Duration Management

C — Credit Analysis

Ⓐ Expense Ratio %

It's critical to look for bond ETFs with low expenses. Expenses can eat into total returns and income payments.

Ⓑ Current Investment Style / Duration

The bond style box is based on an ETF's credit quality and its duration. Check the ETF's average credit quality and average effective duration in the column next to the style box. Credit quality is an important aspect of any bond ETF, as it measures the creditworthiness of the ETF's holdings. An ETF with an average credit quality of AAA, for example, is less likely to get stung by defaults than an ETF with an average credit quality of BBB. Duration is equally important, as it measures an ETF's overall interest-rate risk. The longer an ETF's duration, the more sensitive the ETF is to shifts in interest rates. When rates fall, ETFs with longer durations benefit; when interest rates climb, shorter-duration ETFs are beneficial. First-time bond-ETF buyers, especially those looking to cushion their stock-heavy portfolios, probably should stick with ETFs in the intermediate-term range (3.5 to six years). Intermediate-term bond funds have offered yields and returns similar to long-term bond funds but with less volatility.

Ⓒ Credit Analysis

Average credit quality provides a snapshot of a portfolio's overall credit quality, while the Credit Analysis section shows the percentage of fixed-income securities that fall within each credit-quality rating, as assigned by Standard & Poor's or Moody's. The lower a bond's rating, the greater its default risk and the higher its yield. Bonds rated BBB and above are considered investment-grade issues; those rated BB and below are high-yield, commonly called junk bonds. Pay particularly close attention to an ETF's weightings in below B and nonrated bonds. Often these issues are riskier bonds that are in danger of defaulting or that have already defaulted. They are also typically less liquid than higher-quality bonds. That's why it's a good idea to diversify with a good mix of high- and low-quality bonds. (Lean more toward the high-quality side.)

ETFs 101

The nuts and bolts of ETFs and how Morningstar views them.

**by Dan Culloton, Editor,
Morningstar ETFs 150**

If you've paid any attention at all to investing and mutual funds in the past couple of years you've probably heard of exchange-traded funds. That doesn't necessarily mean you've become familiar enough with them to know how to use them to your advantage in your portfolio. Here's a quick primer on ETFs and some suggestions for analyzing them and working them into your investment mix.

The Basics

ETFs are essentially mutual funds that can be bought and sold throughout the day like stocks on an exchange through a broker. Consequently, unlike conventional mutual funds, ETF share prices are determined throughout the day by supply and demand instead of once per day at 4 p.m. Eastern Standard Time. Anything you can do with a stock you can do with an ETF: You can sell them short (or sell borrowed shares with the intention of buying them back at a lower price and pocketing the difference), write options on many of them, and set market, limit, and stop-loss orders on them.

How They Work

Most individual investors never deal directly with an ETF they way they would with a traditional mutual fund. Individuals and financial planners buy and sell ETFs among themselves via a broker. In this way they are similar to closed-end funds. But the similarities end there. Closed-end fund shares can trade at large premiums or discounts to the net asset values of their underlying portfolios. ETF discounts and premiums tend to be much smaller, though, because ETFs can do something closed-end funds can't: continuously create and redeem shares in-kind. This means the ETFs exchange fund shares for baskets of their underlying securities and vice versa.

The in-kind creation/redemption process creates an arbitrage opportunity for large institutional investors and market makers, known as authorized participants (APs), who deal directly with the ETF. This helps keep ETF premiums and discounts narrow. When ETF shares trade at a discount to the NAVs of their underlying holdings the APs buy the ETF shares and sell the underlying securities. If the ETF shares trade at a premium the APs buy the underlying securities and sell the ETF shares.

Advantages

As you might guess, ETFs' flexibility is one of their key attractions. Many institutional and individual investors have been drawn to the ability to pick their own entry and exit prices, as well as the chance to use fund portfolios in various trading and hedging strategies. Another advantage is transparency. Because all ETFs currently are index funds, it's easy to know what you own. ETFs also come in more exotic flavors. While conventional mutual funds still greatly outnumber ETFs, funds that drill down into specific sectors, industries, regions, countries, and asset classes make up a greater percentage of the ETF universe. They offer relatively inexpensive access to investments, such as currencies, precious metals, or emergent industries, that heretofore have been the sole province of larger institutional and wealthy investors.

From Morningstar's (typically long-term) viewpoint, though, low expenses and tax efficiency are the most attractive features of ETFs. They are able to offer much lower expense ratios than conventional mutual funds, because they're index funds that typically don't hire professional (and often expensive) researchers and stock-pickers in an effort to beat the market. Furthermore, because investors purchase ETFs via a broker on the open market instead of from the fund companies, the ETFs don't have all the record-keeping and shareholder-servicing costs that conventional mutual funds incur.

When it comes to taxes, the ETF structure has a lot of advantages, too. Index funds in general tend to be more tax efficient than actively managed funds because they don't trade as often. The in-kind creation/redemption mechanism also gives ETFs additional tools to sidestep capital gains, though. Because no one redeems their fund shares for cash, ETFs don't have to sell securities to pay off departing shareholders. Furthermore, ETFs can use in-kind redemptions to flush low cost basis shares out of the portfolio, thereby reducing the chance of realizing capital gains when the ETFs have to sell securities to keep up with changes in their benchmarks.

ETF Creation/Redemption Process

Disadvantages

There are hidden costs to ETFs though. They can be more costly to use than conventional mutual funds after you factor in commissions. You can find discount brokerages, but even then transaction costs can pile up quickly and negate ETFs' expense advantage if you trade frequently or make regular monthly investments. Many brokerages also saddle account holders with additional account maintenance, inactivity, and minimum balance fees. And don't forget the bid/ask spread, or the difference between the price you offer to pay for an ETF share and what the market is willing to give you. ETFs spreads often are fairly tight, but it's still an additional cost you don't incur with traditional funds.

Lastly, ETFs, especially very narrow ones, are prone to be misused. Many of the more specialized offerings are concentrated, volatile, and more expensive. Indeed, the average non-sector ETF has an expense ratio of 0.39%, while the average sector ETF costs 0.49%. Sector ETFs also tend to be more volatile as measured by standard deviation. Many sector and regional ETFs seem of marginal use in building a diversified portfolio.

How to Use ETFs

The ability to trade, short, and buy ETFs on margin is alluring, but these are speculative tactics that require accurate short-term market calls, which few, if any, can get right consistently over the long term. Similarly, market-timing and sector-rotation strategies don't get any easier just because you use ETFs to implement them.

Core and explore approaches, which involve using diversified funds or ETFs as your portfolio cornerstones and deploying more specialized ETFs around its edges to enhance returns, seem reasonable. But they require strict discipline and attention to detail lest you sabotage yourself with increased complexity and costs.

As is usually the case it's best to keep it simple. Resort to ETFs when the conventional mutual fund options

in a given category tend to be limited, expensive, and run by managers with short tenures. For example, in some of the small-cap categories, conventional funds with decent expenses, managers, strategies, and track records often close soon after investors discover them. ETFs can be a viable alternative in this area. Of course the simplest way to use ETFs is for a lump sum, buy-and-hold investment. For example, if you've decided to go aggressive and put 80% of your money in stocks and 20% in bonds, you could use the Vanguard Total Stock Market ETF for the equity portion and the iShares Lehman Aggregate Bond, which tracks virtually the entire bond market, for your helping of fixed income. If you're an even more adventurous sort, you could throw in the iShares MSCI EAFE Index, which tracks most of the major developed markets outside of the United States, or even a smidgen of the Vanguard Emerging Markets Stock ETF.

ETFs also have become popular tax-management tools. Some investors and financial planners use them to maintain exposure to areas of the market while they realize tax losses. You can sell your losing funds and use up to $3,000 of net investment losses to offset income in the current year and capital gains indefinitely. (There's no limit to the amount of losses you can use to offset capital gains). The problem is you can't buy that fund back within 31 days without running afoul of IRS rules. That's where ETFs can come in; you can use them to maintain exposure to the style or market segment while you wait. For example, in December 2006 many Japan Funds—even decent ones—were in the red over the year-to-date. You could have sold, booked a loss to offset gains elsewhere in your portfolio, and then bought an ETF, such as iShares MSCI Japan EWJ.

Analyze This

As you sort through the burgeoning list of ETFs, don't forget to pay attention to fundamentals. There is no reason you shouldn't apply many of the same standards you would with a conventional fund to ETFs. Understanding a fund's management, expenses, taxes, strategy, risk/reward profile, and long-term record should lead you to decent options. ▐

2007 Morningstar ETFs 150

17

The Stars Come Out for ETFs

A primer on Morningstar's ETF Star Rating.

by Dan Culloton, Editor,
Morningstar ETFs 150

In an effort to shed a little light on the choice between exchange-traded funds and conventional mutual funds, Morningstar introduced star ratings for ETFs in March 2006. You can find them for the first time on individual ETF reports in this edition of the ETFs 150 book, on Morningstar.com, and in other Morningstar products. We think the ratings will provide investors with a familiar tool to gauge ETFs' risk-adjusted returns and compare them with those of conventional mutual funds, as well as other ETFs.

Star Gazing

Like the star rating for traditional funds, the Morningstar Rating for ETFs is a purely objective, mathematically derived measure based on funds' past risk/return profiles. For the most part, this is the same star rating you're probably familiar with, though we made some accommodations for the unique nature of ETFs. We're adjusting ETF returns for brokerage commissions, just like we adjust traditional open-end fund returns for sales charges. We treat ETF commissions like front- and back-end loads of 0.2%. (That assumes investors paid a $20 commission on a $10,000 investment, or $40 to buy and sell.) Investors can pay lower or higher brokerage fees when trading ETFs, but they can't avoid them, so we deemed it appropriate to factor commissions into the rating.

Because many ETF categories remain too thinly populated to make meaningful comparisons, we rate ETFs against the conventional open-end funds in their respective categories as well as other ETFs in their peer groups. Thus, an investor can readily compare how a conventional index fund such as Vanguard 500 Index compares with its ETF competitors, such as the SPDR. Comparability is also one of the reasons we're using ETFs' NAV total returns—as opposed to their market price total returns—as the basis for the ratings. ETF market prices, which are set throughout the day by supply and demand, tend to stick pretty close to their NAVs, which are set at the end of the trading day. Furthermore, market prices can be stale for ETFs that don't trade often, making the ETFs' NAV return a better indicator of performance in those cases.

Constant as a Star

Beyond those notable differences, it's the same old rating. Funds have to be three years old to be rated, and we adjust ETF returns for both excess return over the risk-free rate of return and for risk. The Morningstar risk adjustment is based on expected utility theory, which assumes that investors are more concerned about potential losses than unexpected gains and are willing to sacrifice some of their returns for more certainty. Accordingly, we measure the amount of variation in the ETFs' monthly returns, penalizing funds more for downside variation. Each month, we first rank all the open-end funds by category using risk-adjusted returns. Then we see where ETFs' risk-adjusted returns fall on the bell curves for their respective categories.

The Results So Far

By and large, the ETF ratings are consistent with those of their conventional counterparts. At the end of July 2006, for instance, more than 60% of the ETFs with records long enough to earn ratings end up in the 3- to 4-star range. Given that they are all index funds that strive to match the return and risk profile of their asset classes, that's appropriate. The oldest and largest ETF, the SPDR, gets 3 stars overall. Its largest traditional and ETF rivals, Vanguard 500 and iShares S&P 500 Index received 4 and 3 stars, respectively. (The Vanguard fund has a longer track record than the iShares' and has slightly outperformed the SPDR over the trailing 10 years.) Meanwhile, Nasdaq 100 Trust, the most actively traded ETF, earns 1 star, which befits the tech-heavy portfolio's boom-or-bust nature. The largest international ETF, iShares MSCI EAFE, received 4 stars, which matches the three-year ratings (the ETF is less than five years old, so it only has a three-year rating) of traditional open-end rivals, such as Fidelity Spartan International Index and Vanguard Total International Stock Index.

Don't Get Star Struck

Be careful how you use these new ratings, though. The ETF ratings are based on historical returns, so they are a better indicator of where ETFs have been than where they are going. They're a useful tool for identifying funds worthy of further research but shouldn't be considered buy or sell signals. ▥

Mutual Funds vs. ETFs

Is a conventional or exchange-traded fund right for you?

by Dan Culloton, Editor,
Morningstar ETFs 150

ETFs have a lot to offer investors. They're versatile, cheap, and their underlying portfolios are protected from the impact of investor trading. Beware, though: Many ETFs are too narrowly focused and concentrated to be of much use to the average investor. Moreover, transaction costs can add up quickly and erode returns. Let's take a closer look at some of these pros and cons.

ETF Strengths

Low expenses are an obvious benefit. Because ETF sponsors deal directly with just a few, very large investors, they save money on many administrative costs. For example, they don't need call centers to handle scores of calls from retail investors and don't have to take care of hundreds of small accounts. On average, ETFs have large expense ratio advantages over the typical passive and actively managed mutual funds in many Morningstar categories.

ETFs also can be tax friendly. ETFs are not immune from capital gains distributions. They have to sell stocks to adjust for changes to their underlying benchmarks. But their structure allows them to greatly minimize their tax impact. Currently most ETFs are index funds, which usually trade less than the average actively managed fund and therefore generate fewer capital gains.

Types of ETF	Average Expense Ratio %
U.S. Equity ETF	**0.41**
Traditional Actively Managed U.S. Equity Fund	1.50
Traditional U.S. Equity Index Fund	0.76
International ETF	**0.52**
Traditional Actively Managed International Equity Fund	1.70
Traditional International Equity Index Fund	1.03
Fixed-Income ETF	**0.29**
Traditional Actively Managed Fixed-Income Fund	1.09
Traditional Fixed-Income Index Fund	0.38

Data as of October 31, 2006

ETFs' tax efficiency is also helped by the fact that only large institutional investors (known as authorized participants) are allowed to trade directly with the fund—everyone else buys or sells shares from each other over an exchange—so the ETF portfolio is largely insulated from the need to sell securities (and possibly realize capital gains) to raise cash to meet redemptions from small investors. Further, when an authorized participant redeems a block of ETF shares, the ETF manager gives it a basket of the underlying securities owned by the ETF, not cash. This allows the ETF manager to continually offload its lowest-cost-basis shares of securities, thus reducing the fund's potential capital gains exposure. It also shields the fund from having to sell securities—and potentially realize capital gains—to raise cash to meet redemptions from these large investors.

ETFs also offer greater trading flexibility than mutual funds. Mutual fund share prices are set once a day at the close of trading and any purchases or sales placed after their prices are set (typically, 4 p.m. Eastern Time) are supposed to be executed at the next day's price. In contrast, ETF investors can buy or sell their shares without limit throughout the trading day, and ETFs, like stocks, are priced continuously, enabling ETF investors to know the price of the fund at the time they are trading. As proponents of long-term investing, we don't view this intraday trading ability as an advantage, but some may find it useful.

Just as they can with stocks, investors also can set market, limit, stop loss, or stop buy orders on ETFs. They also can sell them short (sell borrowed shares with the intention of buying them back at lower prices and pocketing the difference), buy them on margin, and buy and write options on ETF shares. These are tricky tactics that can do more harm than good in the hands of novice investors. Many professionals argue, however, that such trading techniques allow them to hedge their portfolios against sudden losses.

Finally, the fact that ETFs are not susceptible to the kind of trading abuses uncovered in the mutual fund industry in 2003 has won a few converts among scandal-weary investors. Simply put, because ETF prices are set throughout the day by the market, there is no opportunity for late trading or NAV arbitrage.

ETF Drawbacks

Despite their advantages, there is nothing about ETFs that guarantees they'll perform better than traditional mutual funds. Because most ETFs are index funds, they simply try to mimic the returns of their benchmark indexes, like their conventional index fund counterparts. When the indexes do well, so should the ETFs that track them. When the benchmarks do poorly, so will their corresponding ETFs. Low costs and diversification give ETFs a very good shot at beating the average comparable actively managed fund over the long term, but you could say the same for many regular, no-load index mutual funds. Furthermore, ETFs have a number of features that can trip investors up.

Commission costs are ETFs' biggest nemesis. Brokerage costs can range from a few dollars at some cut-rate online brokers to as much as $30 per trade at full-service brokerages. Even at the discount brokers, though, transaction costs can pile up quickly and negate ETFs' expense advantage for investors who trade frequently or make regular investments. Many brokerages also saddle account holders with additional account maintenance, inactivity, and minimum balance fees.

Yes, online brokerage fees have fallen. Nevertheless, given roughly equal expense ratios, most long-term investors are still better off with the traditional open-end index fund. For example, assuming an online brokerage commission of $12 (the current average according to Consumer Reports) and a return of 7%, someone who makes an initial investment of $10,000 in Fidelity Spartan 500 and subsequent monthly contri-butions of $250 would have $2,000 more in his or her account at the end of 10 years thanks to cost savings and compounding than if he or she followed the same plan with iShares S&P 500.

Gaps also can open between ETF prices and NAVs. Unlike traditional open-end mutual funds, ETFs don't always trade exactly at the net asset values of their portfolios. Some infrequently traded, highly specialized ETFs can trade at discounts or premiums to their NAVs, often to their shareholders' disadvantage.

Dividends can be a drag. Some older ETFs that are organized as unit investment trusts instead of open-end funds cannot reinvest the dividends they receive from their holdings and must hold them as cash until they are distributed quarterly. That can provide a cushion in down markets, but also restrain the fund when stocks rise. Also, some brokerages don't let investors auto-matically reinvest dividends in their ETF portfolios, and those that do may charge a fee for the service.

ETFs are ripe for misuse. Some of the broadly diversified, low-cost ETFs can be decent core holdings, but many of the more specialized offerings are concentrated and narrowly focused and therefore are extremely volatile. Indeed many sector and region ETFs seem of marginal use in building a diversified portfolio. They often are marketed to those who wish to speculate on certain industry groups or geographic areas, which, at best, can be extremely costly and difficult to do successfully over the long term.

Not all index managers are created equal. There is evidence that skilled open-end index fund managers, such as Vanguard's indexing team lead by Gus Sauter, can outperform their underlying index and be very competitive with ETFs tracking the same bogy, despite the ETFs' lower costs. For example, through July 31, 2006, the Vanguard 500's trailing five-year gain of 2.7% was within 2 or 3 basis points, or hundredths of a percent, of the returns of the S&P 500 SPDR and the iShares S&P 500 Index. That's not bad when you consider the Vanguard 500's expense ratio is nearly twice that of those ETF competitors. Clearly an index fund manager's ability to minimize tracking error, the amount by which an index fund trails its benchmark, matters.

Finally, though they are cheap, ETFs aren't always the cheapest option. It's possible to find traditional mutual funds with expense ratios as low as or lower than those of ETFs and that can be bought without the commission or bid-ask spread that you must pay to trade ETFs. There are several no-load mutual funds in Morningstar's database that are still open to new investors and have expense ratios as low or lower than the median ETF levy of 0.36%. Most of them are (not surprisingly) from Vanguard and include offerings that also can compete with the vaunted tax efficiency of ETFs, such as Vanguard's series of quantitatively run tax-managed funds. There are some worthy offerings from other shops, too, such as Fidelity Spartan 500, Fidelity Spartan U.S. Equity, Fidelity Spartan International, and Bridgeway Blue-Chip 35 Index. Once you factor in the brokerage commissions you have to pay to trade ETFs, these funds are often as cheap as or cheaper than ETFs.

What's Right for You?

Given their advantages and disadvantages, when should an investor consider an ETF? We think ETFs are excellent options for lump-sum investments that you plan to hold for a long time. ETFs also can be compelling in categories where the traditional mutual fund options are scarce, expensive, or run by managers with little experience. ETFs also are viable alternatives for investors who want to minimize taxes or make opportunistic bets on particular segments of the market. In the latter case, investors should limit such bets to a small portion of a diversified portfolio.

Should you decide on an ETF, not just any one will do. When selecting an ETF, investors should consider the same fundamental factors that are key to choosing conventional mutual funds:

Expenses

Like conventional index funds ETFs aim to match the gross returns of a given market segment and then rely on low costs to differentiate themselves. So for ETFs, the lower the expense ratio the better. Keep in mind, however, that with any ETF, you will need to pay brokerage commissions when you buy and sell shares of the fund. I can't emphasize enough that if you trade even a few times a year, these extra costs can easily wipe out any expense ratio advantage the ETF has over a regular index mutual fund. To make ETFs work you have to keep your trading level low and hold your shares for a reasonably long period of time. If this doesn't apply to you, you may well be better off with a mutual fund from a total cost perspective, regardless of ETFs' low annual expense ratios.

For example, assume you put $10,000 investments in four core equity funds—Selected American Shares , Vanguard 500, SDPR , and iShares S&P 500 Index . If you paid no commission on the mutual funds and a $12 brokerage fee on the ETFs, made additional investments of $100 monthly, and got a 7% annualized return over 10 years, the Vanguard fund would have the lowest total cost even though it has a higher expense ratio than the ETFs. Indeed, in this scenario, even the more expensive actively managed fund Selected American would have lower total costs than the ETFs.

ETF Name	Expense Ratio %	Return %	Total Cost $
Vanguard 500	0.18	6.81	389.70
Selected American	0.60	6.36	1,272.89
iShares S&P 500	0.09	6.10	1,672.15
SPDR	0.10	6.10	1,672.15

Source: Morningstar Cost Analyzer

Taxes and Turnover

ETFs have the potential to be more tax-efficient than traditional mutual funds. As I stated earlier, however, it's theoretically possible for ETFs to issue capital gains. An ETF that tracks an index that frequently changes its constituents, such as some of the style- or market-cap-based benchmarks, can realize gains and transaction costs as it changes its portfolio to keep up with its benchmark. So treat ETF turnover like expenses: the lower the better.

The Benchmark

You want to make sure the ETF is tracking a diversified index that does a good job of capturing the gross returns of the asset class it hopes to measure. If it's too narrow, top-heavy, or concentrated in one or more industries, the benchmark could fail to accurately represent its market segment.

Management

Look for management firms with a lot of experience running index funds. Seasoned skippers know how to reduce tracking error and turnover, and thereby enhance the total return and tax efficiency of their offerings. ⅢⅢ

Sector ETFs: Use at Your Own Risk

by Dan Culloton, Editor,
Morningstar ETFs 150

Exchange-traded funds seem to encourage myopia.
As the variety of ETFs widen, the individual funds themselves are narrowing.

Most of the new ETFs launched in 2006 were sector or industry funds that hone in on ever thinner slices of the stock market, such as home builders, oil equipment makers, biotechs, aerospace and defense companies, and even nanotech and water industry stocks. At the end of October 2006 nearly half of all ETFs are sector or industry or specialized funds and there are many more on the way. The percentage of conventional stock mutual funds that focus on a single sector or industry, by contrast, is about 10%.

This is an exciting development if you believe that there is a new game afoot in investing; that individual security or manager selection doesn't matter as much as asset allocation, and that ETFs allow you to slice and dice your way to superior returns without all that pesky research or stock specific risk. I think, however, that sector ETFs are a bit trickier to use effectively than advocates of the slice and dice approach to investing would have you believe.

The history of sector offerings in the conventional mutual fund universe shows investors, professional and novice alike, tend to misuse them. They chase hot returns and then dump the funds when they cool off or prove to be more volatile than expected. Sure, sector ETFs offer a lot of flexibility and variety, but investors who think they can ignore fundamentals and risk profiles do so at their own risk. Here are some factors to which you should pay attention before adding sector ETFs to your portfolio.

The Narrower the Fund, The Higher the Price

Adding sector ETFs to your mix of holdings is likely to increase your total costs, which counteracts one of the key advantages of ETFs—their low expense ratios. Sector ETFs are more expensive than more diversified ETFs. The average non-sector ETF has an expense ratio of 0.39% while the average sector ETF cost 0.49%. Even if you assembled a collection of relatively inexpensive sector ETFs—say an equal-weighted portfolio of 10 Vanguard domestic sector ETFs—and never traded you would still surrender more to costs than if you bought more diversified ETFs. The average expense ratio of 0.26% for the equal weighted sector portfolio would be more than three times that of Vanguard Total Stock Market ETF, and more than twice that of an equal weighted portfolio of Vanguard Large Cap, Mid Cap and Small Cap ETFs.

Throw in some more expensive sector ETFs, such as PowerShares WilderHill Clean Energy and its 0.71% expense ratio, as well as trading costs incurred during periodic rebalancings or sector rotations, and the hurdle between you and outperformance gets even higher. You have to add a lot of value on a consistent basis to make this approach pay.

There's Still Plenty of Stock Risk

Think your sector or industry ETF is immune from the kind of blow-ups that often hit individual stocks? Think again. Many sector ETFs are dangerously concentrated in a handful of names, largely because they're composed of slices of market cap weighted equity indexes.

For example, Energy Select SPDRs keeps more than a third of its assets in two holdings, ExxonMobil and Chevron. Meanwhile, the Materials Select SPDR has more than fifth of its money in E.I. DuPont De Nemours E.I. and Dow Chemical . Consequently, these top-heavy ETFs can be more volatile than the typical stock in their sectors. In August and September of 2006, for instance, the average energy stock in Morningstar's database fell 6.9%, but the Energy SPDR dropped 8.4%. From the start of May to the end of July this past year the average industrial materials stock fell 7%, but the Materials SPDR offered no more protection, falling 7.2%.

Some ETFs try to mitigate such variability by tracking indexes that keep all their holdings equal or modify the weightings of their constituents to keep a few stocks from dominating. That still doesn't immunize the funds against volatility, though, especially if the ETFs track tightly focused indexes. PowerShares Dynamic Energy Exploration and PowerShares Dynamic Oil & Gas Services control the size of their holdings, but are extremely limited in scope with just 30 stocks each. As the energy sector fell in August and September these ETFs plunged 11.5% and 10.1%, respectively. That's worse than the average actively managed conventional natural resources fund faired over the same period (it lost 9%). One losing period does not a loser make, but it does demonstrate that such parochial funds have nowhere to hide when the sky falls on their corner of the market.

Know What You Own

Just because an ETF purports to track consumer or technology stocks, doesn't mean they track the ones you want. You'd think that at this point in market history we might have arrived at clear universal standards for what companies belong in what sectors. Alas, that is not the case. The stocks included in a sector ETF depend on how the index it tracks is constructed.

If you buy the Technology Select Sector SPDR, for instance you also get a big helping of telecom services stocks, such as Verizon and AT&T, while rivals like iShares Dow Jones US Technology and Vanguard Information Technology ETF play it pretty straight with hardware and software stocks.

Consider also Wal-Mart. Even though it is the world's largest retailer, Wal-Mart shows up in the Consumer Staples Select Sector SPDR and the Vanguard Consumer Staples ETF, alongside the makers of tangible goods like Procter & Gamble. Meanwhile, Wal-Mart also is the biggest holding in the iShares Dow Jones U.S. Consumer Services ETF, which owns lots of merchants including Target, Lowe's and Home Depot. By the way if you are really keen on having exposure to those two home improvement retailers, don't by PowerShares Dynamic Retail. They're not there; they're in PowerShares Dynamic Building and Construction.

Confused? I don't blame you. It's clear that if you don't pay attention you can easily foul up your asset allocation plan when you start mixing sector and industry ETFs, owning too much of one stock and not enough of another, and paying too much for it all. Even when it seems like your fund's holdings should be obvious, it's still important to know what you own. ▥

The Cheap, the Dear, and the Fairly Valued

Funds our analysts would and wouldn't buy in today's market.

by Dan Culloton, Editor, Morningstar ETFs 150

The universe of domestic-stock ETFs wasn't offering up too many screaming buys or sells at the end of 2006, according to Morningstar equity analysts. From a valuation perspective, though, funds focused on homebuilders still looked attractive, while real estate offerings looked rich.

This is how the market looked in December 2006 through the lens of Morningstar's ETF Price/Fair Value measure. The ratio is derived from the individual stock research of Morningstar's nearly 90 equity analysts. The measure basically tries to offer a bottom-up assessment of whether an ETF portfolio is cheap or expensive by gauging if its holdings, on average, are trading above or below the fair value estimates Morningstar's equity analysts have set for them.

We arrive at the ratio by calculating the current market value of all the holdings in the ETFs for which we have fair value estimates. Then we use the fair value estimates of those stocks to calculate what we believe is the fair value of the same portfolios. Finally, we compare the two numbers and come up with a ratio that should give you an idea of whether the ETFs' underlying portfolios are undervalued, fairly valued, or overvalued. A reading of more than 1 means an ETF's portfolio is expensive, by our analysts' estimates; less than 1 indicates it's less so; and one means it's priced just about right.

The price/fair value measure can help you find diversified ETFs that look attractive. You also can use it to find sector ETFs that might be ripe for more-speculative bets, though it's best to limit those to a small portion of an already diversified portfolio. The measure isn't useful, however for funds that own a lot of stocks Morningstar analysts don't cover. So for this article, I focused on the more than 140 ETFs in which companies on Morningstar's equity coverage list make up at least 80% of the market capitalization of the underlying portfolios.

All's Fair

In general, our analysis indicates that there's not much on sale as of late December 2006. Near the end of the year the broad U.S. market looked fairly valued. All-encompassing ETFs such as Vanguard Total Stock Market ETF, StreetTracks Total Market ETF, and iShares Russell 3000 Index all had price/fair values of 0.99. That's not terribly surprising given that the domestic-stock market posted double-digit returns in 2006, and segments of it, such as small-cap stocks, have enjoyed a multiyear tear.

Even some ETFs that looked attractive earlier in the year, such as large-cap growth ETFs, have seen their price/fair values climb closer to 1. That doesn't necessarily mean that large-cap growth has missed its chance for resurgence relative to other categories. In fact, I still think the next few years are bound to be better for this group, at least when compared with the areas of the market that have been the hottest in recent years. The opportunity, however, is less glaring now, according to Morningstar stock analysts. So, if you are interested in making a long-term bet on a growth-stock revival, stack the odds of success in your favor by choosing a broadly diversified, very low-cost option, such as Vanguard Growth ETF. It spreads its bets over hundreds of issues and charges an 0.11% expense ratio.

Broad Market ETFs ETF Name	Coverage Rate %	Price/ Fair Value
Vanguard Total Stock Market ETF VTI	89.5	0.99
StreetTracks Total Market ETF TMW	89.92	0.99
iShares Russell 3000 Index IWV	90.36	0.99
SPDRs SPY	97.4	0.97
iShares S&P 500 IVV	97.4	0.97

Data as of Dec. 20, 2006

Home Improvement

In any market, though, something always looks cheap. And in December, ETFs targeting home-builders, such as iShares Dow Jones Home Construction and SPDR Homebuilders, had the lowest price/fair value ratios of all the ETFs I examined. The performance charts for these young ETFs induce vertigo. They dropped off a cliff shortly after launching in the first half of the year as

Undervalued ETFs ETF Name	Coverage Rate %	Price/ Fair Value
iShares Dow Jones US Home Construction ITB	80.16	0.82
SPDR Homebuilders XHB	80.61	0.85
iShares Dow Jones US Oil & Gas Exploration IEO	84.9	0.87
iShares Goldman Sachs Networking IGN	86.22	0.91
streetTRACKS KBW Bank ETF KBE	100	0.92

Data as of Dec. 20, 2006

concerns about rising interest rates, slowing home sales, and debt-burdened consumers gathered. They bounced back in the last six months of 2006, but many of these funds' top holdings, such as Ryland Group and Hovnanian Enterprises, were trading below Morningstar analysts' estimates of their fair values as the year drew to a close.

With the economy slowing and home inventories building, the potential for more trouble for home builders is palpable. But Morningstar stock analysts' estimates of these stocks' values already account for significant sales decreases over the next year and a half, and some of them still looked cheap in December. Plus our analysts argue many of the companies in this area have better balance sheets and more experienced and disciplined managers than they have in the past.

There is great risk here, but also the possibility of reward. That's why if you want to buy one of these ETFs as an opportunistic play on an out-of-favor industry, you should keep it to a very small portion of a diversified portfolio and be prepared to take some lumps. These funds will insulate you from some of the stock-specific risk of buying one or two stocks because they both have more than 20 holdings. They still are both extremely concentrated, though, so handle with care. My colleague and editor of the Morningstar ETFInvestor newsletter, Sonya Morris, recommends iShares Dow Jones Home Construction as an opportunistic play.

Oil Slick

The only other ETF with a price/fair value ratio under 0.90 in December was iShares Dow Jones US Oil & Gas Exploration, but I'd be even more cautious with this fund than with the home builders. The thesis for this ETF is deceptively simple. Oil prices, despite slipping in 2006, are still high. Voracious, growing economies like those in China, India, and the United States need to find more and more fossil fuels, and the energy industry

has underinvested in exploration and production for years. Even if prices were to slip further there still would be a need to find and produce more oil and gas to meet demand.

A bet on this ETF, however, is still in large part a bet on the direction of oil prices, which are notoriously fickle and hard even for seasoned professional investors to predict. This ETF's short track record exemplifies that. So far, it lost money in two of the four rolling three-month periods it has been around, falling 9% between July and September 2006 and more than 7% between August and October 2006. More than oscillating oil prices makes this ETF risky, though. It is also very top-heavy, with more than 40% of its assets in its five biggest holdings, including 11% in Occidental Petroleum alone. The portfolio is filled with risky companies, such as Valero Energy, that strive in fiercely competitive businesses in which it is hard to build an enduring competitive advantage. This is one opportunity I'd let pass.

For similar reasons, I'd avoid iShares Dow Jones US Oil Equipment Index. The fund faces the same uncertainty about energy prices and is prey to the same concentration risk as its sibling. (This one has more than a fifth of its assets in oil field service giant Schlumberger alone.) On top of that, at least 70% of portfolio's market capitalization is trading above what Morningstar equity analysts think it's worth. No thanks.

Unreal Real Estate

As they have been for most of the year, real estate ETFs were conspicuous on the overvalued end of the price/fair value rankings. Vanguard REIT Index, StreetTracks Dow Jones Wilshire REIT, iShares Dow Jones Real Estate Index, and iShares Cohen & Steers Realty Majors all had price/fair values between 1.3 and 1.4. This, of course, has not kept the funds, which have enjoyed a multiyear rally, from continuing to defy expectations (my own included) of an imminent retreat. All of them were on pace for annual returns of more than 30% in December.

Overvalued ETFs ETF Name	Coverage Rate %	Price/ Fair Value
Market Vectors Gold Miners GDX	81.19	1.66
iShares Cohen & Steers Realty Majors ICF	99.11	1.39
iShares Dow Jones US Oil Equipment IEZ	86.42	1.39
StreetTracks DJ Wilshire REIT RWR	91.86	1.37
Vanguard Real Estate Index VNQ	85.49	1.34

Data as of Dec. 20, 2006

I still think, however, that it will be hard for these offerings to duplicate what they have done over the past six years. Not only do these funds look richly valued according to Morningstar equity analysts, but also according to other measures. Average valuations—such as price/earnings, price/book, price/sales, and price/cash flow—for all of the portfolios were higher than those of the broad domestic stock market, as defined by the Morningstar U.S. Market Index. REIT yields, after a multiyear rally, also offer no more compensation to investors than less-risky 10-year Treasury issues. So, investors take on a lot of price risk here and really don't get paid for it.

There are good reasons to set aside a small portion of your portfolio for real estate. Given the sector's valuations, though, I'd tread cautiously, if at all.

All That Glitters

Real estate ETFs were not the most overvalued funds I found in December, though. That dubious honor goes to one dubious fund: Market Vectors Gold Miners, whose portfolio of gold mining stocks had a Price/Fair Value of nearly 1.7, probably the highest I have ever seen. Precious metals stocks have enjoyed a memorable run in the last six years (the average gold and silver industry stock in Morningstar's database more than tripled in six years ending Nov. 30, 2006). So it's not earth shattering to learn that after such a powerful rally nearly all of the stocks Morningstar stock analysts cover in this portfolio are trading well above their fair value estimates.

But that's not what really scares me about this fund. The ETF's holdings are an unattractive lot. Their profitability swings with the volatile price of gold and gold miners are notorious for their poor returns on invested capital, which measures whether a company's management is putting its capital to good use. Gold miners

also are subject other socioeconomic risks because they often have to dig in emerging markets, such as Peru and Ghana. All this makes gold mining stocks more volatile than the price of the metal itself. Furthermore, this fund is expensive for an ETF with a management fee of 0.50% and keeps more than a fourth of its assets in two stocks, Barrick Gold and Newmont Mining.

Like real estate there are arguments for maintaining some exposure to gold as part of a long-term asset allocation plan. An ETF like this looks unacceptably risky now, though, with gold prices trading near 25-year highs and mining stocks trading at premiums. ⅢⅢ

Using ETFs in a Fund Portfolio

How to best exploit ETFs' low costs and flexibility.

by Dan Culloton, Editor,
Morningstar ETFs 150

Legendary college Ohio State University football coach Woody Hayes famously explained his aversion to passing by saying, "Three things can happen on a forward pass, and two of them are bad." A similar aphorism applies to ETFs: You can do a lot of things with them, but many of them can be counterproductive.

You can trade ETFs, short them, buy them on margin, and buy and write options on them. But that doesn't mean you should. These tactics are exciting and potentially potent tools, but they're also fraught with complexity and risk.

Day traders love ETFs because the funds enable quick bets on whole markets, sectors, industries, and geographic regions. Frequent trading and market timing is a tough way to make a living, though. Studies by Morningstar and others have shown that, over the long haul, market-timing strategies lose to a buy-and-hold approach most of the time. Factor in brokerage fees and capital gains taxes, and market timing looks even more perilous.

The ability to sell ETFs short also is oversold. Short selling, or betting a security's price will decline by selling borrowed shares with the intent of buying them back at lower prices, offers finite upside but infinite downside risks.

Here's a simple example: You think HypotheticalShares Small Cap Growth ETF is overpriced at $50 per share, so you decide to short it. On your behalf, your broker borrows 100 shares of the ETF from another investor and then sells the shares, netting you about $5,000. If you were right about the ETF and it falls to $20 per share, you can buy 100 shares for just $2,000 and return them to your broker; keeping $3,000 (the $5,000 sale minus the $2,000 purchase) minus whatever you have to pay for the broker's services.

If you're mistaken, however, and its shares soar from $50 to $150, you're in trouble. You have to buy back the shares, and it'll cost you $15,000. You've lost $10,000, but theoretically, you could lose more if you are not able to cover your short position because there is no limit on how high HypotheticalShares Small Growth's market price can rise.

Judicious short selling can control a portfolio's volatility, but it's a risky strategy if not used properly and so is buying stocks or ETFs on margin. When buying on margin, an investor puts up a certain percentage of the purchase price (at least half, according to current regulations) and borrows the rest from a broker. That can magnify both your returns and losses. For example, the now infamous hedge fund Long-Term Capital Management posted eye-popping gains when the market was soaring but suffered spectacular losses that imperiled the global financial system when markets turned south in September 1998. Its successes and near catastrophic failure were fueled, in part, by excessive borrowing.

You can also buy and write options on ETFs. Options give their owners the right, but not the obligation, to buy or sell a specific item at a specific price (the "strike price") over a specific time span. The owner can choose when to exercise an option, or he or she can choose not to exercise the option at all. The option then expires worthless, and the investor's only loss is what he or she paid for the option. Thus, options have less downside risk than other financial derivatives such as futures, which are contractual agreements to buy something at a specific time and price in the future.

There are two types of options: calls and puts. Anyone can buy or sell them on exchanges, such as the Chicago Board of Options Exchange. A call option gives you the right (but not the obligation) to buy an ETF at a specified price (the strike price); you would buy calls if you think an ETF's price will rise above the strike price. A call option is said to be "in the money" if the ETF's market price is above the strike price.

A put option gives you the right (but not the obligation) to sell a stock at a specified price; you would buy puts if you think an ETF's price will go down. A put option is in the money if the market price of the ETF underlying the option is below the strike price.

Calls and puts may not be as risky as futures because you're not obligated to do anything; your greatest loss will be the loss of the cost of the call or put. But options are leveraged on the upside. For example, buying call options requires far less outlay than buying stocks would.

Yet calls and puts are inappropriate for most investors, too. Why? Because few investors make money with options. In fact, 80% of all options expire worthless. Even if you're buying puts to protect your portfolio, you're still betting on the direction of a stock's price or the market during a specific time period. That's not investing; it's gambling. And for the majority of investors, it's not profitable.

Buying and Holding ETFs

Trading ETFs is expensive and most likely wasteful. Shorting them, leveraging them, or writing options on them is risky, so how can an investor use ETFs?

Try buying and holding. Because you must pay a brokerage commission every time you buy (or sell) shares in an ETF, they are poor vehicles for investors making regular purchases. However, broadly diversified ETFs are hard to beat as an option for lump sum investing.

The first step is to determine an appropriate asset allocation for your goals. One way to do that is to consult with a financial advisor. Another is to use online portfolio allocation tools such as Morningstar's Asset Allocator, or those provided by online brokers such as Amerivest and Sharebuilder.

Now it's time to choose ETFs. The easiest way is to stick with broadly diversified offerings. For example, if you've decided to go aggressive and put 80% of your money in stocks and 20% in bonds, you could use a U.S. total stock market ETF, such as the iShares Russell 3000 Index or Vanguard Total Stock Market ETF. For your fixed income allocation, you could use the iShares Lehman Aggregate Bond, which tracks virtually the entire bond market. For international exposure, you could employ the iShares MSCI EAFE Index, which tracks most of the major developed markets outside of the United States. If you want exposure to emerging economies, throw in a smidgen of the Vanguard Emerging Markets Stock ETF. Many investors devote about 20% to 30% of their total stock portfolios to international stocks, but

you may want to go higher or lower depending on your goals and risk tolerance.

The growing number of ETFs allows you to further break down both the international and domestic portions of your portfolio by style, market cap, country, and sector. Remember, however, that the more ETFs you own, the more commissions you will incur. It's better to keep it simple.

The All-Sector Fund Portfolio

Not everyone wants to keep it simple, though. Investors who want near-total control over their sector exposure can use ETFs like building blocks.

Want to dedicate certain portions of your portfolio to technology, utilities, and a variety of other sectors? If you invest in diversified stock funds, trying to maintain those allocations would be nearly impossible. Maybe your growth fund has 40% of its assets in technology today, but the manager's favor might shift to health-care or communications stocks tomorrow. Instead, you could buy a group of sector ETFs and control your sector weights.

There are a couple of serious drawbacks to the all-sector-ETF portfolio, though. For starters, it's expensive. You'd pay more in commissions maintaining your target allocations than you would buying a diversified offering that did it for you. Worse yet, an all-sector-fund portfolio can be tax inefficient. As you tweak your portfolio, you could incur capital gains along the way. It's also worth noting that many sector ETFs are highly concentrated in their top holdings, so you may not be getting as much diversification as you think.

Portfolio Enhancers

If you already have a well-rounded portfolio but want to emphasize a particular part of the market such as communications companies or dividend-paying stocks, you could use a sector or style ETF. You also could use Morningstar's price/fair value measure for ETFs to help identify opportunities. The measure tries to offer a bottom-up assessment of whether an ETF portfolio is cheap or expensive by gauging if its holdings, on average, are trading above or below Morningstar stock analysts' fair value estimates. Regard "plays" such as these as speculative investments, though, and limit them to 5% or 10% of your portfolio. That way, you'll limit the damage if that sector or style disappoints.

Tax Strategies

Some investors and financial planners use tax swaps to try to reduce the tax collector's cut. One form of swap consists of looking at your fund lineup for offerings that are about to make big distributions and then selling those funds before they make their payouts. Once distribution season is over, you swap into another fund with a similar mandate, thereby maintaining your asset allocation. (You can't buy the same fund back within 31 days without running into IRS regulations.) ETFs can be useful in this role. For example, you could sell Fidelity Low-Priced Stock before it makes a distribution and then buy Vanguard Small Cap ETF.

If you try this, don't forget about your own tax position in a fund: If you have a taxable gain in the fund—that is, if it has appreciated since you purchased it—you'll be forced to pay taxes on that gain and the swap could end up costing you more than its worth. Keep transaction costs in mind too. Brokerage fees or conventional fund redemption charges may make the swap counterproductive.

Tax swaps can be much more effective if you're holding a losing investment. You can sell your loser and use up to $3,000 of net investment losses to offset income in the current year and capital gains indefinitely (there is no limit on the amount of losses you can use to offset capital gains) and then swap into a similar ETF. For example, at the end of 2006 many specialty technology funds—even decent ones—were in the red over the past year. If you find yourself in that position, you can sell, book a loss to offset gains elsewhere in your portfolio, and then buy an ETF such as Vanguard Information Technology ETF. ▮▮

Using ETFs in a Stock Portfolio

Using exchange-traded funds to diversify your holdings.

by Dan Culloton, Editor,
Morningstar ETFs 150

Disclosure: Barclays Global Investors (BGI), which is owned by Barclays, currently licenses Morningstar's 16 style-based indexes for use in BGI's iShares exchange-traded funds. iShares are not sponsored, issued, or sold by Morningstar. Morningstar does not make any representation regarding the advisability of investing in iShares that are based on Morningstar indexes.

Some investors buy funds and others buy stocks, and never the twain shall meet. That has been the conventional wisdom, but the rising popularity of exchange-traded funds, especially among those who prefer to pick their own equities, proves what we at Morningstar have known for a long time: Investing doesn't have to be a choice between investing directly in stocks or indirectly through mutual funds. Investors can—and many should—do both. The trick is determining how your portfolio can benefit most from each type of investment.

Its pretty clear why stock investors are warming to ETFs. Their low costs and ability to be bought and sold throughout the day enables stock pickers to diversify their portfolios on the fly, stay fully invested while they research new ideas, hedge their bets, and employ tax management strategies. Be careful, though. As we mentioned in our article on building ETF and fund portfolios, the more exotic the strategy, the higher potential costs and risks. That's why we favor using ETFs to provide stability and diversity to a stock portfolio. Here are a few of the many ways to use ETFs in a stock portfolio.

ETFs as Stabilizers

Adding a broad equity ETF to your holdings can smooth your portfolio's flight path. The chance of an individual stock taking a big plunge is greater than that of a diversified ETF. For example in the 12 months ending Oct. 31, 2006, more than one fifth of the nearly 6,400 domestic stocks in Morningstar's database fell by more than 20%, while none of more than 240 domestic-equity ETFs dropped that hard. If you only have enough money to buy a couple of stocks and funds, a broad market ETF such as the iShares S&P 500 or the Vanguard Total Stock Market ETF could be a cheap and easy way to help control portfolio volatility.

ETFs as Trailblazers

Many stock investors favor household names such as software titan Microsoft, industrial conglomerate General Electric, or health-care giant Johnson &

Johnson. It's pretty easy to find annual reports, financial data, and other research on those mega-cap stocks.

But what about micro-caps such as International Shipholding or foreign companies such as Japan's Nippon Telegraph & Telephone? Such off-the-beaten-path securities aren't within most stock investors' comfort zones. Nor are such stocks easy to analyze, buy, or sell. That's where an ETF can help. Some funds, such as the First Trust Dow Jones Select MicroCap ETF, invest in tiny stocks, others invest around the globe, and still others focus on markets such as real estate, which have their own quirks. These ETFs can give stock investors affordable, diversified exposure to hard-to-reach areas like these without forcing them to learn a whole new set of analytical skills.

ETFs as Balancers

Just like personalities, everyone has an investment style. Perhaps you have a health-care industry job and thus are familiar with and own a number of pharmaceutical and biotechnology stocks. Or maybe you're a Warren Buffett devotee and stick to dominant, easy-to-understand businesses such as Home Depot and Coca-Cola. Or you could be a true believer in the broadband revolution with a portfolio full of tech and wireless stocks.

No matter how convinced you are that time will prove your predilections are prescient, there will be periods when your style falters, at least temporarily. Biotech underwent a fierce correction in early 2000. Investors who stashed their money in Buffett-like businesses found it tough to profit in 1999. And new economy tech and telecom stocks have eaten the dust of old economy energy and utility shares in the past five years.

The market is constantly shifting. No one style remains in favor forever. However, there is an alternative to frantically trying to master value, or growth, investing, or whatever styles you don't use and happen to be in favor of at the moment. You could use an ETF designed to track the territory with which you're not familiar; that way, your portfolio will have some protection when your style slumps.

Take the health-care worker with a portfolio full of biotech names, for instance. A diversified stock ETF is a natural first choice, adding some variety in one swoop. A value ETF, such as iShares Russell 3000 Value or Vanguard Value ETF, probably won't have much biotech exposure, so you could get diversity with little overlap with what you already own.

ETFs for Tax Swaps

Similar to mutual funds, you can use ETFs to maintain exposure to a portion of the market while harvesting tax losses to use as offsets to any realized gains or up to $3,000 in ordinary income. Say you're holding Dell with an unrealized loss (a loss on paper only) but still like the computer maker's long-term prospects. If you sell the stock to book the losses, you can't buy back the shares, or any "substantially similar" security, for 31 days or you'll violate the IRS' "wash sale rules" that prohibit using the loss to cancel out gains. To maintain some exposure to Dell and other tech stocks, you could move into a technology sector ETF, such as the Technology SPDR. The SPDR is similar enough to keep your asset allocation in line but different enough to keep you out of trouble with the IRS. Of course, as with all tax-related decisions, it's a good idea to consult with a professional tax advisor before attempting a tactic like this. As always, you should also pay attention to transaction costs. They can wipe out any benefit if you aren't careful. ▥

Should You Add Commodities to Your Investment Mix?

Pros and cons to consider before buying a commodity ETF.

by Karen Wallace,
Fund Analyst

Anyone who has been paying even a little attention to the financial markets over the past few years has probably noticed the stunning gains in commodities markets. Investors are increasingly seeking out investments in commodities, and more mutual funds than ever before in the marketplace provide exposure to these types of investments. Let's preface this discussion by stating that, as a general rule, Morningstar seldom endorses performance chasing, or jumping into a hot asset class. All too often, it simply works out badly for investors. One of the biggest mistakes investors routinely make is flocking to hot-performing investments because they expect the good times will keep on rolling, when all too often the opposite happens. By the time investors buy into that sizzling fund, it's ready to cool off, usually because the type of securities it buys are more expensive than they once were and therefore have a lot less room to move up in price. That said, the potential portfolio diversification benefit from commodities could be a compelling reason for a risk-tolerant investor to allocate a small portion of his or her portfolio to the asset class. However, before you do so, take time to consider the pros and cons.

What Are the Potential Benefits?

Commodities tend to bear a low or, depending on which data and time periods you look at, even negative correlation to other types of financial assets (namely, stocks and bonds). Essentially, this means that when stocks are rising, commodities tend to retreat, and vice versa. The low correlation between commodities and stocks is a trend that is well established over long periods; in fact, many correlation studies span 30 years or longer. In addition, commodities exposure can also help offset the deleterious effects of inflation. Put simply, inflation weighs down stocks and bonds, over both short- and long-term periods. For example, when Federal Reserve Chairman Ben Bernanke says inflation is a near-term economic concern, his remarks are usually followed by a decline in the share prices of stocks and bonds. That's because investors expect higher interest rates, which, in turn, could crimp stock and bond prices. These are usually just short-term sell-offs, so investors

usually jump back into the markets when the near-term inflation picture looks rosier. A bigger concern is the long-term effects of inflation. Over the long-term, inflation can eat into an investor's nominal return. (Real return is the nominal return of an investment minus inflation). Let's say you invested $1,000 in a 10-year Treasury note that pays a 6% yield. At the end of 10 years, your nominal return would be $1,600, or your principal, $1,000, plus $600 in yield. Now, factor in the costs of inflation: Let's say inflation increased 4% over a period of 10 years. That means that at the end of 10 years, your real return would be only $1,200, or $1,600 minus the $400 eaten by inflation.

Commodities, however, often benefit from inflation over the short term and long term, because when the price of goods and services increases, the prices of the comodities needed to produce the goods and services will subsequently increase. And when prices are increasing, producers are compelled to supply more, so more commodities are needed to meet increased demand for raw goods. Of course, there are exceptions: Gold markets also benefit from inflation, but not because gold has any practical use in manufacturing. When the economy struggles in times of geopolitical uncertainty or when monetary problems erupt, gold prices have historically risen, sometimes dramatically, as consumers and institutions demand and hoard more, perceiving it as a "safe haven" or a true store of value.

What Are the Risks?

Make no mistake that despite their potential benefits, commodities are not a silver bullet. Commodities are one of the most volatile asset classes available. PIMCO Commodity RealReturn, a fund that invests in derivative instruments that seek to replicate the performance of the Dow Jones-AIG Commodity Index, has a standard deviation of 16.17. For context, that's more than twice as volatile as an S&P 500 Index fund and more than four times as volatile as a fund that tracks the Lehman Brothers Aggregate Bond Index. Put simply, that means that just as surely as the commodity markets can put up stunning gains, they can take some heart-wrenching stumbles. For example, the Dow Jones-AIG Commodity Index lost 27% in 1998. Before diving into commodities today, it's important to determine whether you would truly hold onto that commodities investment if prices dropped over the next few years. If you sold instead of sitting tight, you'd wind up looking like that performance chaser who bought high and sold low.

However, volatility is not necessarily a bad thing, especially in the context of a diversified portfolio. Commodities' returns tend to be negatively correlated with other asset classes, so when commodities funds are on the upswing, they can significantly offset losses in other parts of a portfolio. Because the gains and losses are so magnified, we wouldn't recommend allocating any more than 10% of a portfolio to commodities; closer to 5% seems reasonable to us. In addition, it's a misconception that the asset classes will always move in opposite directions. Many investors sat up and took notice of commodities in 2002, when the Dow Jones-AIG Commodities Index soared almost 26% and the S&P 500 Index sank more than 22%.

Despite that one year of markedly divergent performance, commodities and stocks have been moving in the same direction lately. In 2003 and 2004, the Dow Jones-AIG Commodities Index returned 24% and 9%, respectively, but the S&P 500 outpaced the Index's return by a few percentage points in both years. It certainly stings investors less when both asset classes are gaining rather than losing ground, but the latter also happens. In 2001 the Dow Jones-AIG Commodities Index lost more than 19%, while the S&P 500 lost around 12%.

Finally, to get the full benefit of diversification, investors should maintain the viewpoint that a small allocation to commodities over a long period, maybe 10 years or longer, depending on one's investment timeline, is best. That means riding out the highs and not running for the hills during the lows. With that in mind, let's turn our focus to some of the ways investors can invest in commodities.

The Basic Features of Commodities Investments
Investing in commodities is usually done through futures contracts, which are traded on an exchange and guarantee the delivery of a certain commodity at a pre-determined price on a future date. These contracts can be settled by delivering the physical commodity itself, or they can be settled in cash, which means that there is a cash payment between the buyer and seller in the amount of profit or loss rather than the physical delivery

of a commodity. Because trading commodities futures can be a complex business and requires sizable amounts of cash, individual investors have not traditionally invested in commodities markets. In fact, unlike some other traditional inflation hedges such as real estate investment trusts, you are unlikely to find commodity futures in traditional mutual funds.

For a while now, institutional investors have been onto the potential diversification benefits that commodities offer, and small investors are increasingly jumping on the bandwagon. That's because more investments are giving investors direct exposure to commodities than ever before. Here are the basics on how they work. There are three ways these investments make money: spot-price movements, roll yield, and collateral income. The mechanics behind how these elements work are very complex, but here's a brief overview: A commodities investor benefits if there a commodity's spot price increases, which is the price one would pay to buy the commodity in the market today. Investors can also benefit from the roll yield. Roll yield adds to a fund's returns when the commodity's futures price is lower than its current spot price, as is often the case. As the futures contract approaches its delivery date, the contract's value converges with the new spot price. It then rolls over into a new contract with a lower futures price. The investor then picks up the yield between the lower futures price and the higher spot price. Finally, investors also benefit from collateral income. The funds don't have to devote much money to buying actual barrels of crude oil or bushels of wheat. They use some form of a derivative contract, mainly structured notes (where the fund agrees to exchange a set payment for the total return of the index at a later date), to mimic the returns of the index. That only requires a small amount of assets, so the funds have cash left over to buy bonds. Those bonds can add incremental return.

Finally, before getting into the specific types of investments available, it's important to understand the basic differences between the two major benchmarks for commodities: Dow Jones-AIG Commodity Index and Goldman Sachs Commodity Index. That's because most of the commodity investments available to retail investors track one or the other of these indexes. Both indexes are diversified across a broad spectrum of commodities, but the big difference between them boils down to energy. The Goldman Sachs Commodity

Index has a lot more energy exposure than the Dow Jones-AIG Commodity Index. Both indexes attempt to weight each individual commodity within the index proportionally with the production of that commodity in the world economy. For example, energy is currently a major player in both indexes. However, to reduce volatility and keep a single commodity or sector from dominating the index, the Dow Jones-AIG Commodity Index puts maximum and minimum thresholds (33% and 2%, respectively) on related groups of commodities (for example, energy or precious metals), while the Goldman Sachs Commodity Index does not; its energy weighting is currently about 68%.

Mutual Funds

For commodity exposure, going with one of the open-end mutual funds in the space is good. Not only is the process of buying a mutual fund simpler and more convenient than trading futures, but commodities mutual funds offer exposure to a diversified collection of commodities (many track either the Dow Jones-AIG Commodity Index or Goldman Sachs Commodity Index). Among the few open-end mutual funds that invest in commodities, we particularly like PIMCO Commodity RealReturn, a fund that invests in derivative instruments that seek to replicate the performance of the Dow Jones-AIG Commodity Index. Because the fund can gain full exposure to the index with only a portion of assets, the remaining assets are invested in Treasury Inflation-Protected Securities (TIPS). One detractor is this fund's 1.24% expense ratio, which we think is too high, considering the fund's $12 billion asset base.

But investors beware: These types of funds tend to pay out their income in the form of taxable distributions to shareholders. For this reason, we would recommend that investors hold them in a tax-advantaged account. In addition, it's worth noting that this yield fluctuates wildly depending on how commodities have been performing. For example the fund had a 17.6% yield in mid-2006, but it has dropped to 2.8% recently. So if you're enticed by the fund's high yield, beware that it is sure to erode in periods when commodity prices are flat or negative.

Exchange-Traded Funds

Exchange-traded funds, or ETFs, may appeal to speculators trying to take advantage of the price swings in the commodities market because shares trade on an exchange, just like a stock. But ETFs are also useful for long-term investors because they often have expense advantages over traditional mutual funds. That said, if one is dollar-cost averaging into commodities—that is, building the position slowly with regular investments over time—then one has to be mindful of brokerage fees because they could eventually erode any expense advantage over a traditional mutual fund.

The first commodity ETF, PowerShares DB Commodity Index, debuted on the American Stock Exchange in February 2006. This fund may have the first-mover advantage, but the index it tracks is not as diversified or robust as the more widely followed Dow Jones-AIG Commodity Index or even the Goldman Sachs Commodity Index. The Deutsche Bank Liquid Commodity Index, which is the index the fund tracks, follows only six commodities: sweet light crude, heating oil, aluminum, gold, wheat, and corn. We think it leaves out some important commodities such as natural gas and cattle.

In July 2006, Barclays launched the iShares Goldman Sachs Commodity-Indexed Trust GSG. Its 0.75% expense ratio is competitive with those of the aforementioned funds. One thing to keep in mind here is the Goldman Sachs Commodity Index's huge weighting in energy-related commodities, which have dominated the world economy over the past few years. If you want a more diversified array of commodities, this isn't for you. In addition, for the same reasons that traditional mutual funds are not tax-efficient, ETFs aren't either. They are best held in a tax-deferred account.

Exchange-Traded Notes

If tax-friendliness is a major concern, you might want to check into Barclays' new exchange-traded notes, or ETNs, that link to the Goldman Sachs Total Return Index, the Dow Jones-AIG Commodity Index Total Return, or the Goldman Sachs Crude Oil Total Return Index. Basically, these funds are structured notes, which are really just 30-year debt securities with an ending value that is tied to the total return of one of the indexes minus fees. At 0.75%, they are reasonably priced, and they trade on the New York Stock Exchange, so they are convenient to buy and sell. Investors are taking on some credit risk because they are essentially buying a debt instrument backed by Barclays Bank, whose debt is rated AA. What's more, the ETNs look like they are going to be far more tax-friendly than conventional mutual funds or ETFs because they don't make distributions. Instead, investors pay capital gains tax depending on when they bought and sold (we dig into the nuts and bolts of these securities on Page 36).

Conclusion

More types of investments than ever before allow investors direct access to commodities. And given the red-hot performance of the commodities markets lately, it's likely that the number of available products competing for shelf space will only continue to increase. Of all the available options, we prefer the PIMCO fund. Aside from the fact that it tracks a well-diversified commodities index, it also adds value with its TIPS. What's more, PIMCO has experience in the structured notes market. That said, we think the ETNs are the ones to watch, primarily because of their tax-friendly nature and cheaper expenses. However, they haven't been out long enough to judge, and we don't know enough about them to pound the table for these securities. But we are keeping them on our watch list. In short, handle these red-hot assets with care. It's our strong bias that investors will have a more rewarding experience if they pick a sensible and reasonably priced fund to have and to hold for the long term, preferably in a tax-deferred account. Additionally, dollar-cost averaging into the fund is a wise way to buy in. ▐▌

Are Exchange-Traded Notes
a Gimmick?

by Dan Culloton, Editor,
Morningstar ETFs 150

Many of the so-called new ideas pitched in the last few years by exchange-traded fund families are actually old notions repackaged as ETFs. For every ETF that tracks a fundamentally weighted or heretofore inaccessible asset class, there are several more sector and industry funds; slicing the stock market into ever-narrower segments is not the most imaginative investment strategy.

It's noteworthy when an ETF purveyor comes up with a truly innovative idea. Barclays Global Investors' (BGI) new iPath exchange-traded notes are among those envelope-pushing concepts worth examining. It's a debt security that can be bought, sold, and shorted like a stock and can be used to gain access to asset classes that are otherwise hard to invest in, such as commodities and some types of bonds. The first two iPath ETNs tracked broad commodity indexes, although Barclays is sure to roll out more ETNs tracking other benchmarks and asset classes. (Indeed, in August the firm launched an ETN that tracks the Goldman Sachs Crude Oil Total Return Index.) There are still many questions about how these securities, which have been trading for about a month, will behave and be taxed over the long term, but here's an early read on them.

Familiar Features

ETNs are not funds but 30-year debt securities. Nevertheless, ETF investors will recognize many of the notes' features. They track indexes, and investors can buy and sell them on the New York Stock Exchange through a broker at market prices that are set throughout the day by supply and demand. They also have an arbitrage mechanism that theoretically should keep their market prices close to the intrinsic value of their benchmarks. Large institutional investors who can amass 50,000 notes can redeem them directly back to Barclays once per week (usually on Thursday). The bank says that should give them the opportunity to take advantage of any premiums or discounts. The first two ETNs—iPath GSCI Total Return Index and iPath Dow Jones-AIG Commodity Index Total Return—also aren't hard to grasp. They offer exposure to broad

commodities benchmarks—the Goldman Sachs Commodity Index and Dow Jones-AIG Commodity Index, respectively. The GSCI includes 24 commodities weighted by their production value. Meanwhile, the Dow Jones-AIG bogy tracks 19 products ranked both by their liquidity and their production value. The Dow Jones-AIG benchmark also caps the weights of individual commodities and commodity groups so nothing dominates the benchmark. That makes it more appealing from a diversification standpoint. For example, the Dow Jones-AIG has a 33% cap on its assets in energy (mostly oil and natural gas), while the GSCI has roughly 68% of its money there. Not surprisingly, Barclays says so far, the iPath Dow Jones-AIG has been the more popular of the two. Barclays also has launched ETNs tracking the price of Oil—the iPath Goldman Sachs Crude Oil Total Return Index—and has filed for a number of other ETNs as well.

Expenses and Taxes

ETF investors who are familiar with low expense ratios will like the price tag. Note that holders pay a 0.75% annual fee, which makes ETNs more expensive than most ETFs but cheaper than conventional commodity funds, such as PIMCO Commodity Real Return, which charges 1.24% and is the only other broad-based commodity ETF currently on the market. Additionally, the PowerShares DB Commodity Index estimated expenses at 1.30% when it launched, but shortly after the ETN's launch the PowerShares DB Commodity fund reduced its management fee to 0.75%. Finally ETNs, like their ETF cousins, potentially offer big tax advantages because they don't make income or capital gains distributions. We say potential tax advantages because the rules here are not entirely clear. Barclays says investors have to pay capital gains taxes only when they sell their notes in the secondary market or accept payment when the securities mature. The firm, however, admits that the IRS has never actually opined on how this kind of structured product should be taxed. Indeed, the ETNs' prospectuses concede their federal tax consequences are uncertain and acknowledge the IRS could rule that ETNs need to be taxed differently. This is not a far-fetched notion. In December 2005, the IRS banned commodity funds from using a special derivative contract called a swap, which sent funds like PIMCO Commodity Real Return scrambling to find alternate ways of tracking its asset classes.

If Barclays' interpretation is right (and the bank's lawyers are as confident as they are), it would give ETNs a huge advantage over traditional funds and ETFs such as Deutsche Bank Commodity Index, which use futures to track commodities. When those offerings roll over their futures contracts, forty percent of the capital gains realized are subject to the higher short-term capital gains rate.

Investing on a Promise

It's clear ETNs are quite different beasts. They aren't open-end mutual funds like most ETFs but are instead senior unsecured debt issued by Barclays Bank PLC, a sister company of BGI. When you buy an ETF or traditional mutual fund, you get a share of the stocks, bonds, derivatives, or cash in the underlying portfolio. When you buy an ETN, you get a promise that Barclays will pay you what you would have gained or lost if you invested directly in the index that the ETN tracks (minus commission costs and the ETNs' fees). You can take your payoff at the end of your holding period by selling your notes in the secondary market or hanging on until the security matures, which in the case of the first two ETNs is 2036.

The structure shields investors from tracking error, or the difference between the return of an index fund and those of its index. When Barclays creates a bunch of ETNs and sells them, it takes the proceeds and gives them to another subsidiary, investment bank Barclays Capital, which puts the money to work hedging the bank's obligations to pay off ETN owners. Barclays Capital can do this by buying and selling futures or other derivatives that track the commodities in the indexes or by doing the same with the actual products themselves. Ideally, Barclays Capital will succeed in capturing the return (and possibly more) of the indexes. However, the bank has a contractual obligation to pay investors the return of the index net of fees.

Credit Risk

In exchange for close tracking, however, investors take on credit risk. No specific assets are backing the ETNs, which seems scarier than it is because Barclays Bank has a solid credit rating (AA, or "very strong," from Standard & Poor's and Aa1, or "very low credit risk," from Moody's). No company is too big to fail (a single rogue trader in Singapore brought down the venerable Barings Bank in 1995), but Barclays, which has

$1.5 trillion in assets and a 300-year history, qualifies as a high-quality issuer. Furthermore, even if Barclays were to go bankrupt, when all of the bank's creditors line up in court to stake their claims, the ETNs would move to the head of the queue because of their senior status.

Eyeing ETNs

There are still a lot of questions about ETNs. The possibility of an adverse IRS ruling or a default, while remote, might keep some investors up at night. Furthermore, the iPath notes don't have much of a track record, so it's difficult to tell how closely their market prices will stick to their index values. The premiums and discounts of ETFs tend to be narrow because large institutional investors who create and redeem shares in-kind directly with the fund can jump on arbitrage opportunities as they appear throughout the day. It remains to be seen if ETNs' arbitrage mechanism, which allows only for weekly institutional-size redemptions, will be as efficient at minimizing premiums and discounts. It's hard to feel completely comfortable with ETNs before seeing them in action in the real world for a while. Nevertheless, for long-term investors seeking commodity exposure, these newfangled vehicles could prove to be viable options. ▥

Report Pages

This section offers a full-page report on each of the 150 ETFs.

PowerShares DB Com Idx Fd DBC

Market Price $23.02	**Mstar Category** Specialty-Natural Res	

Morningstar Fair Value

Price/Fair Value Ratio —   Coverage Rate % —

Management

This ETF falls under the quickly growing PowerShares umbrella, which was started in 2002. The fund invests all of its assets in a master fund managed by Deutsche Bank Commodity Services, LLC.

Methodology

This ETF tracks the Deutsche Bank Commodity Index, which is composed of crude oil, heating oil, aluminum, gold, corn and wheat. The index leaves out raw goods such as natural gas, livestock, copper, and nickel among others. Competing indexes have a broader basket of 20 or more raw goods. Deutsche Bank argues that the six raw goods represented here are the most liquid, are correlated with other commodities in their respective sectors, and are thus the best representation. It primarily relies on futures contracts for exposure to commodities.

Performance 12-31-06

Historic Quarterly NAV Returns

	1st Qtr	2nd Qtr	3rd Qtr	4th Qtr	Total
2002	—	—	—	—	—
2003	—	—	—	—	—
2004	—	—	—	—	—
2005	—	—	—	—	—
2006	—	5.76	-5.60	5.19	—*

Trailing	NAV Return%	Market Return%	NAV Rtrn% +/-S&P 500	%Rank Cat.(NAV)
3 Mo	5.19	5.19	-1.51	21
6 Mo	-0.70	-0.42	-13.44	18
1 Yr	—	—	—	—
3 Yr Avg	—	—	—	—
5 Yr Avg	—	—	—	—
10 Yr Avg	—	—	—	—

Tax Analysis	Tax-Adj Return%	Tax-Cost Ratio
3 Yr (estimated)	—	—
5 Yr (estimated)	—	—
10 Yr (estimated)	—	—

		Morningstar Rating — Not Rated	Return — Not Rated	Risk — Not Rated	Yield —	NAV $24.55	Avg Daily Vol. (k) 239	52 wk High/Low $26.94 - $22.31

Growth of $10,000
- Investment Value of ETF
- Investment Value of Index S&P 500

Trading Volume Millions

	1997	1998	1999	2000	2001	2002	2003	2004	2005	2006	History
	—	—	—	—	—	—	—	—	—	24.55	NAV $
	—	—	—	—	—	—	—	—	—	24.58	Market Price $
	—	—	—	—	—	—	—	—	—	4.45*	NAV Return%
	—	—	—	—	—	—	—	—	—	—	Market Price Return%
	—	—	—	—	—	—	—	—	—	0.24	Avg Premium/Discount%
	—	—	—	—	—	—	—	—	—	4.45	NAV Rtrn% +/-S&P 500
	—	—	—	—	—	—	—	—	—	4.45	NAV Rtrn% +/-GS NATR RES
	—	—	—	—	—	—	—	—	—	—	NAV Return% Rank in Cat
	—	—	—	—	—	—	—	—	—	—	Income Return %
	—	—	—	—	—	—	—	—	—	—	Capital Return %
	—	—	—	—	—	—	—	—	—	0.61	Income $
	—	—	—	—	—	—	—	—	—	0.00	Capital Gains $
	—	—	—	—	—	—	—	—	—	—	Expense Ratio %
	—	—	—	—	—	—	—	—	—	—	Income Ratio %
	—	—	—	—	—	—	—	—	—	—	Turnover Rate %
	—	—	—	—	—	—	—	—	—	712	Net Assets $mil

Rating and Risk

Time Period	Morningstar Rtn vs Cat	Morningstar Risk vs Cat	Morningstar Risk-Adj Rating
3 Yr	—	—	—
5 Yr	—	—	—
10 Yr	—	—	—

Other Measures	Standard Index S&P 500	Best Fit Index
Alpha	—	—
Beta	—	—
R-Squared	—	—
Standard Deviation	—	
Mean	—	
Sharpe Ratio	—	

Portfolio Analysis 09-30-06

Share change since 00-00 Total Stocks:0	Sector	PE	Tot Ret%	% Assets
☼ Light Sweet Crude Oil		—	—	29.44
☼ Heating Oil		—	—	16.07
☼ Aluminum		—	—	11.59
☼ Wheat		—	—	10.77
☼ Corn		—	—	10.42
☼ Gold		—	—	10.18

Current Investment Style

Value Blnd Growth — Large Mid Small

	Market Cap	%
	Giant	—
	Large	—
	Mid	—
	Small	—
	Micro	—
	Avg $mil: —	

Value Measures		Rel Category
Price/Earnings	—	—
Price/Book	—	—
Price/Sales	—	—
Price/Cash Flow	—	—
Dividend Yield %	—	—

Growth Measures	%	Rel Category
Long-Term Erngs	—	—
Book Value	—	—
Sales	—	—
Cash Flow	—	—
Historical Erngs	—	—

Profitability	%	Rel Category
Return on Equity	—	—
Return on Assets	—	—
Net Margin	—	—

Industry Weightings	% of Stocks	Rel Cat
Oil & Gas	—	—
Oil/Gas Products	—	—
Oil & Gas Srv	—	—
Pipelines	—	—
Utilities	—	—
Hard Commd	—	—
Soft Commd	—	—
Misc. Indstrl	—	—
Other	—	—

Composition

● Cash	11.5	
● Stocks	0.0	
● Bonds	0.0	
● Other	88.5	
Foreign	0.0	
(% of Stock)		

Morningstar's Take by Karen Dolan 12-31-06

Investors should be wary of PowerShares DB Commodity Index's limitations.

Most commodity funds follow either the Goldman Sachs Commodity Index or the Dow Jones AIG Commodity Index. This ETF tracks the lesser-known Deutsche Bank Commodity Index, which is composed of crude oil, heating oil, aluminum, gold, corn, and wheat. That's far fewer commodities than found in competing indexes, and we think it leaves some important ones out. Livestock, for example, are not represented at all, and key energy components, such as natural gas, are also excluded. Deutsche Bank argues that the six raw goods in the index are the most liquid, are correlated with other commodities in their sectors, and are thus the best representation.

All commodity funds, this one included, are extremely volatile. Though this ETF only dates back to 2005, data on its index goes back to 1988. In five of six down years since then, the index lost more than 10% of its value. The best stretch of performance began in 2002 and extends to the present, heightening our worry that we're closer to a peak than a trough. In any case, investors should be careful because we doubt the next few years will see a repeat of the strong performance experienced in the past four years.

Though bumpy when viewed in isolation, commodities' funds volatility makes them useful in a portfolio. Commodities' returns bear little correlation with stocks and bonds, so they can reduce the overall volatility of one's holdings.

Even for investors committed to the long-term diversification benefits, buying commodities slowly over time and limiting overall exposure to a small portion of one's portfolio is the best way to build a position, especially on the heels of such a strong rally. Yet, ETFs' brokerage commissions make them costly to buy or sell in small increments. Overall, we question whether most investors have the patience to be successful with commodities, and we're unconvinced that this index is superior.

Address:	301 West Roosevelt Road
	Wheaton, IL 60187
	877-369-4617
Web Address:	www.dbfunds.db.com
Inception:	02-03-06*
Advisor:	DB Commodity Services, LLC

Management Fee:	0.75%		
Expense Projections:	3Yr: —	5Yr: —	10Yr: —
Income Distrib:	None		
Exchange:	AMEX		

 M⊙RNINGSTAR® ETFs 150

DIAMONDS Trust DIA

	Market Price $124.07	Mstar Category Large Value

Morningstar Fair Value

Price/Fair Value Ratio
0.89 Undervalued

Coverage Rate %
100 Good

Management

SSgA Funds Management is this ETF's advisor. The ETF group at SSgA is headed by John Tucker. He joined the firm in 1988.

Methodology

This exchange-traded fund mimics the composition and performance of the Dow Jones Industrial Average, a 30-member index maintained by the editors of The Wall Street Journal. The selection committee looks for nonutility stocks with exceptional reputations and wide interest from individual and institutional investors. The committee has tried to add new economy stocks such as Microsoft in recent years, but, by and large, the Dow is made up of true-blue mega-cap firms, with a focus on industrial stocks. The index is price-weighted.

Morningstar Rating ★★ Below Avg	Return Below Avg	Risk Average	Yield 2.0%	NAV $124.45	Avg Daily Vol. (k) 6,568	52 wk High/Low $124.93 - $106.47

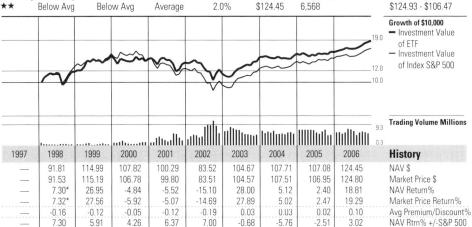

Growth of $10,000
- Investment Value of ETF
- Investment Value of Index S&P 500

Trading Volume Millions

	1997	1998	1999	2000	2001	2002	2003	2004	2005	2006	History
	—	91.81	114.99	107.82	100.29	83.52	104.67	107.71	107.08	124.45	NAV $
	—	91.53	115.19	106.78	99.80	83.51	104.57	107.51	106.95	124.80	Market Price $
	—	7.30*	26.95	-4.84	-5.52	-15.10	28.00	5.12	2.40	18.81	NAV Return%
	—	7.32*	27.56	-5.92	-5.07	-14.69	27.89	5.02	2.47	19.29	Market Price Return%
	—	-0.16	-0.12	-0.05	-0.12	-0.19	0.03	0.03	0.02	0.10	Avg Premium/Discount%
	—	7.30	5.91	4.26	6.37	7.00	-0.68	-5.76	-2.51	3.02	NAV Rtrn% +/-S&P 500
	—	7.30	19.60	-11.85	0.07	0.42	-2.03	-11.37	-4.65	-3.44	NAV Rtrn% +/-Russ 1000 Vl
	—	—	2	2	7	7	7	8	11	14	NAV Return% Rank in Cat
	—	—	1.57	1.37	1.46	1.75	2.33	2.12	2.94	2.39	Income Return %
	—	—	25.38	-6.21	-6.98	-16.85	25.67	3.00	-0.54	16.42	Capital Return %
	—	1.35	1.43	1.57	1.56	1.74	1.93	2.20	3.13	2.53	Income $
	—	0.00	0.00	0.00	0.00	0.00	0.00	0.00	0.00	0.00	Capital Gains $
	—	—	0.18	0.17	0.17	0.18	0.18	0.18	0.18	—	Expense Ratio %
	—	—	1.37	1.34	1.51	1.85	2.12	1.89	2.27	—	Income Ratio %
	—	—	35	24	13	1	9	14	8	—	Turnover Rate %
	—	—	—	—	—	4,728	6,778	8,022	7,634	6,733	Net Assets $mil

Performance 12-31-06

Historic Quarterly NAV Returns

	1st Qtr	2nd Qtr	3rd Qtr	4th Qtr	Total
2002	4.20	-10.73	-17.44	10.55	-15.10
2003	-3.69	13.05	3.72	13.35	28.00
2004	-0.47	1.20	-2.94	7.53	5.12
2005	-1.27	-1.67	3.39	2.02	2.40
2006	4.19	0.90	5.29	7.34	18.81

Trailing	NAV Return%	Market Return%	NAV Rtrn% +/-S&P 500	%Rank Cat.(NAV)
3 Mo	7.34	7.60	0.64	16
6 Mo	13.02	12.96	0.28	16
1 Yr	18.81	19.29	3.02	14
3 Yr Avg	8.55	8.68	-1.89	8
5 Yr Avg	6.81	6.97	0.62	7
10 Yr Avg	—	—	—	—

Tax Analysis	Tax-Adj Return%	Tax-Cost Ratio
3 Yr (estimated)	7.63	0.85
5 Yr (estimated)	5.95	0.81
10 Yr (estimated)	—	—

Rating and Risk

Time Period	Morningstar Rtn vs Cat	Morningstar Risk vs Cat	Morningstar Risk-Adj Rating
3 Yr	Low	Avg	★
5 Yr	-Avg	Avg	★★
10 Yr	—	—	—

Other Measures	Standard Index S&P 500	Best Fit Index S&P 500
Alpha	-1.3	-1.3
Beta	0.93	0.93
R-Squared	83	83
Standard Deviation	7.14	
Mean	8.55	
Sharpe Ratio	0.75	

Morningstar's Take by Dan Culloton 12-31-06

Dow watching is more fun than Dow investing.

Diamonds Trust, an exchange-traded fund tracking the Dow Jones Industrial Average, grabbed attention in 2006 as its benchmark rallied to new historic highs. While this ETF merits some of the notice, it has its limits.

The fund isn't bad. It's filled with dividend-paying companies with fortified competitive positions. A couple of them, such as Wal-Mart and Alcoa, even looked attractively valued at the end of 2006, according to Morningstar equity analysts. And it's one of the cheapest large-value funds available to retail investors.

The idiosyncrasies of the ETF's benchmark restrict its utility, though. It's best to think of the Dow as a concentrated, ultralow-turnover, actively managed portfolio run by the editors of The Wall Street Journal. They do a good job selecting widely held, market-leading companies, but the average isn't a good representation of the market. It's more than 80% mega cap; heavy on industrial, consumer goods, and hardware stocks; and light on energy, financial, and utilities firms.

Indeed, this ETF often has been out of step with its category and broader value indexes. Its five-year returns at the end of 2006 lagged those of typical large-value fund and indexes. Even in 2006, when the Dow set new records, this fund edged the category and trailed the large-value indexes.

That could change if giant stocks build on the momentum they gathered in the latter half of 2006. But such trends are hard to predict and this portfolio isn't as attractively valued as it was before the Dow started reaching new peaks. More than half its holdings are now fairly valued, by Morningstar equity analyst's reckoning. Some of the fund's average valuation measures, such as price/earnings, price/book, and price/cash flow, are also high relative its peers.

This isn't as risky as many concentrated funds, but you still might want a wider margin of safety before investing here.

Portfolio Analysis 12-31-06

Share change since 11-06 Total Stocks:30

	Sector	PE	Tot Ret%	% Assets
⊖ IBM	Hardware	16.8	19.77	6.23
⊖ Boeing Company	Ind Mtrls	41.1	28.38	5.70
⊖ Altria Group, Inc.	Goods	15.9	19.87	5.50
⊖ 3M Company	Ind Mtrls	16.8	2.98	5.00
⊖ ExxonMobil Corporation	Energy	11.7	39.07	4.91
⊖ American International G	Financial	17.1	6.05	4.59
⊖ Johnson & Johnson	Health	17.4	12.44	4.23
⊖ Procter & Gamble Company	Goods	24.2	13.36	4.12
⊖ United Technologies	Ind Mtrls	17.6	13.65	4.01
⊖ Caterpillar Inc.	Ind Mtrls	12.0	7.86	3.93
⊖ American Express Company	Financial	21.2	19.09	3.89
⊖ Citigroup, Inc.	Financial	13.3	19.55	3.57
⊖ E.I. du Pont de Nemours	Ind Mtrls	18.6	18.64	3.12
⊖ J.P. Morgan Chase & Co.	Financial	13.7	25.60	3.10
⊖ Coca-Cola Company	Goods	21.5	23.10	3.09
⊖ Wal-Mart Stores, Inc.	Consumer	16.6	0.13	2.96
⊖ Honeywell International,	Ind Mtrls	18.7	24.14	2.90
⊖ McDonald's Corporation	Consumer	19.2	34.63	2.84
⊖ Merck & Co., Inc.	Health	18.8	42.66	2.80
⊖ Hewlett-Packard Company	Hardware	18.9	45.21	2.64

Current Investment Style

Value Blnd Growth — Large Mid Small

Market Cap	%
Giant	86.1
Large	13.9
Mid	0.0
Small	0.0
Micro	0.0

Avg $mil: 111,318

Value Measures		Rel Category
Price/Earnings	15.87	1.11
Price/Book	3.18	1.32
Price/Sales	1.24	0.93
Price/Cash Flow	10.29	1.33
Dividend Yield %	2.23	0.86

Growth Measures	%	Rel Category
Long-Term Erngs	10.69	1.06
Book Value	7.05	0.98
Sales	4.86	0.57
Cash Flow	10.55	1.23
Historical Erngs	16.23	1.05

Profitability	%	Rel Category
Return on Equity	20.34	1.17
Return on Assets	10.86	1.09
Net Margin	12.19	0.89

Sector Weightings	% of Stocks	Rel S&P 500	3 Year High Low	
↻ Info	19.00	0.95		
🔲 Software	1.92	0.56	2	2
💻 Hardware	10.19	1.10	11	9
🎙 Media	2.20	0.58	2	2
📶 Telecom	4.69	1.34	5	3
☞ Service	32.30	0.70		
🏥 Health	8.71	0.72	10	7
🛒 Consumer	8.40	1.10	9	8
💼 Business	0.00	0.00	0	0
💲 Financial	15.19	0.68	16	10
🏭 Mfg	48.69	1.44		
🏠 Goods	14.72	1.72	20	13
⚙ Ind Mtrls	29.04	2.43	35	29
🔥 Energy	4.93	0.50	5	3
💡 Utilities	0.00	0.00	0	0

Composition

- ● Cash 0.3
- ● Stocks 99.8
- ● Bonds 0.0
- ○ Other 0.0
- Foreign 0.0 (% of Stock)

Address:	PDR Services, 86 Trinity Place New York NY 10006 800-843-2639	Management Fee:	0.07%
		Expense Projections:	3Yr: — 5Yr: — 10Yr: —
Web Address:	www.amex.com	Income Distrib:	Monthly
Inception:	01-20-98*	Exchange:	AMEX
Advisor:	PDR Services, SSgA Funds Management Inc		

M⊙RNINGSTAR® ETFs 150

Energy SPDR XLE

	Market Price $55.44	Mstar Category Specialty-Natural Res

Morningstar Fair Value

Price/Fair Value Ratio	Coverage Rate %
1.07 Overvalued	100 Good

Management

State Street Global Advisors serves as advisor to the trust. Michael Feehily, head of U.S. Equity in SSgA's global structured products group, and John Tucker, head of SSgA's ETF management effort, lead a team that runs all of SSgA's ETFs. They both have 15 years or more of experience at SSgA.

Methodology

This exchange-traded offering owns the oil and gas and energy-services companies in the S&P 500. (Power companies fall into the Utilities Select Sector SPDR.) This provides an initial screen for quality, as holdings meet the standards of the S&P's selection committee. Constituents usually have to be leading U.S. companies that meet S&P's profitability criteria. Unfortunately, the criteria eliminate large international oil companies, including Royal Dutch Petroleum, BP, and Total SA. This leaves the fund concentrated on the likes of ExxonMobil.

Morningstar Rating ★★★ Neutral	Return Neutral	Risk Below Avg	Yield 1.2%	NAV $58.75	Avg Daily Vol. (k) 18,952	52 wk High/Low $61.57 - $50.19

Growth of $10,000
— Investment Value of ETF
— Investment Value of Index S&P 500

Trading Volume Millions

	1997	1998	1999	2000	2001	2002	2003	2004	2005	2006	History
	—	23.20	27.18	33.27	26.70	22.30	27.62	36.29	50.28	58.75	NAV $
	—	23.34	27.09	33.19	26.70	22.33	27.55	36.32	50.31	58.63	Market Price $
	—	14.08*	19.07	24.30	-18.33	-14.81	26.32	33.47	40.20	18.40	NAV Return%
	—	14.02*	17.95	24.41	-18.14	-14.69	25.82	33.93	40.17	18.08	Market Price Return%
	—	0.60	-0.04	-0.03	-0.03	0.01	0.04	-0.01	0.01	0.02	Avg Premium/Discount%
	—	14.08	-1.97	33.40	-6.44	7.29	-2.36	22.59	35.29	2.61	NAV Rtrn% +/-S&P 500
	—	14.08	-8.15	8.49	-2.74	-1.55	-7.69	8.90	3.72	1.58	NAV Rtrn% +/-GS NATR RES
	—	—	1	1	2	4	4	4	6	9	NAV Return% Rank in Cat
	—	—	1.94	1.78	1.50	1.82	2.17	1.87	1.58	1.44	Income Return %
	—	—	17.13	22.52	-19.83	-16.63	24.15	31.60	38.62	16.96	Capital Return %
	—	0.00	0.45	0.48	0.49	0.48	0.48	0.51	0.57	0.72	Income $
	—	0.00	0.00	0.00	0.00	0.00	0.00	0.00	0.00	0.00	Capital Gains $
	—	—	0.56	0.41	0.28	0.27	0.28	0.27	0.26	—	Expense Ratio %
	—	—	1.73	1.71	1.56	1.82	2.06	1.70	1.36	—	Income Ratio %
	—	—	20	31	17	39	7	10	10	—	Turnover Rate %
	—	—	—	—	—	289	635	1,572	2,896	3,808	Net Assets $mil

Performance 12-31-06

Historic Quarterly NAV Returns

	1st Qtr	2nd Qtr	3rd Qtr	4th Qtr	Total
2002	8.64	-8.79	-18.90	6.02	-14.81
2003	0.67	8.18	0.30	15.65	26.32
2004	6.66	7.80	11.56	4.05	33.47
2005	18.48	4.11	20.96	-6.04	40.20
2006	8.49	4.59	-5.30	10.19	18.40

Trailing	NAV Return%	Market Return%	NAV Rtrn% +/-S&P 500	%Rank Cat.(NAV)
3 Mo	10.19	10.02	3.49	21
6 Mo	4.35	3.98	-8.39	18
1 Yr	18.40	18.08	2.61	9
3 Yr Avg	30.37	30.39	19.93	4
5 Yr Avg	18.98	18.93	12.79	4
10 Yr Avg	—	—	—	—

Tax Analysis	Tax-Adj Return%	Tax-Cost Ratio
3 Yr (estimated)	29.75	0.48
5 Yr (estimated)	18.30	0.57
10 Yr (estimated)	—	—

Rating and Risk

Time Period	Morningstar Rtn vs Cat	Morningstar Risk vs Cat	Morningstar Risk-Adj Rating
3 Yr	+Avg	-Avg	★★★★
5 Yr	Avg	-Avg	★★★
10 Yr	—	—	—

Other Measures	Standard Index S&P 500	Best Fit Index GS NATR RES
Alpha	18.8	3.6
Beta	0.95	1.01
R-Squared	11	94
Standard Deviation	19.76	
Mean	30.37	
Sharpe Ratio	1.28	

Morningstar's Take by Dan Culloton 12-31-06

Energy Select Sector SPDR offers cheap exposure to oil and gas giants, but it's not worth the risk.

This ETF has its strong points. With an expense ratio of 0.26%, it's one of the lowest-cost natural-resource funds retail investors can buy. Furthermore, its holdings are apt to be established, high-quality firms because its benchmark draws its constituents from the S&P 500 and the committee that assembles that broader index requires its denizens to be profitable.

Nevertheless, there are limits to this ETF's utility. Its primary drawback is its concentration. It keeps more than a fourth of its assets in two holdings: ExxonMobil and Chevron. Those are leading energy companies with defensible market positions, but their shares and those of the rest of this fund's holdings still move in tandem with fickle oil and gas prices. Due to its concentration and commodity links, this ETF can be more volatile than the typical stock in its sector. In August and September of 2006, for instance, the average

energy stock in Morningstar s database fell 6.9% as oil prices fell, but the Energy SPDR dropped 8.4%. So you may not be diversifying away as much stock-specific risk as you think here.

Another limitation is this fund's lack of foreign stocks. Some of the sector's biggest players, such as London-based BP and France's Total SA, are absent from this portfolio. That has hurt the ETF relative to its more global peers.

The fund's strong run of recent years also may not be sustainable. Increased demand from China, India, and the U.S., depleted reserves, and the need for new exploration and production could buoy this fund's holdings, or it might already be priced into the stocks after a multiyear rally. According to Morningstar's stock analysts, more than half of this ETF's holdings were, at best, fairly valued at the end of 2006. Given the unpredictable nature of oil and gas prices, as well as energy stocks themselves; and this ETF's concentration, a larger margin of safety is in order.

Portfolio Analysis 12-31-06

Share change since 11-06 Total Stocks:31	Sector	PE	Tot Ret%	% Assets
⊕ ExxonMobil Corporation	Energy	11.7	39.07	22.82
⊕ Chevron Corporation	Energy	9.3	33.75	13.16
⊕ ConocoPhillips	Energy	6.9	26.53	9.87
⊕ Schlumberger, Ltd.	Energy	24.0	31.07	4.23
⊕ Occidental Petroleum Cor	Energy	8.6	24.32	3.83
⊕ Marathon Oil Corporation	Energy	6.5	54.68	3.15
⊖ Halliburton Company	Energy	12.0	1.11	2.98
⊕ Valero Energy Corporatio	Energy	6.5	-0.33	2.92
⊕ Devon Energy Corporation	Energy	9.4	8.06	2.87
⊖ Baker Hughes Inc.	Energy	10.8	23.67	2.42
⊕ Transocean, Inc.	Energy	29.3	16.07	2.37
⊕ Apache Corporation	Energy	7.9	-2.30	2.24
⊕ Anadarko Petroleum Corp.	Energy	5.5	-7.44	2.07
⊕ XTO Energy, Inc.	Energy	9.2	12.16	1.91
⊕ Williams Companies, Inc.	Energy	65.3	14.41	1.77
⊕ Hess Corporation	Ind Mtrls	7.8	19.01	1.70
⊕ EOG Resources	Energy	10.1	-14.62	1.67
⊕ Weatherford Internationa	Energy	16.9	16.56	1.61
⊕ Chesapeake Energy Corp.	Energy	6.3	-7.74	1.49
⊕ El Paso Corporation	Energy	—	27.07	1.40

Current Investment Style

Value Blend Growth — Large/Mid/Small

Market Cap	%
Giant	50.8
Large	36.9
Mid	12.2
Small	0.0
Micro	0.0

Avg $mil: 65,523

Value Measures		Rel Category
Price/Earnings	10.57	0.85
Price/Book	2.48	0.97
Price/Sales	0.88	0.64
Price/Cash Flow	6.54	0.90
Dividend Yield %	1.41	1.26

Growth Measures	%	Rel Category
Long-Term Erngs	11.15	0.77
Book Value	17.71	1.28
Sales	22.31	1.38
Cash Flow	28.15	0.94
Historical Erngs	51.90	1.03

Profitability	%	Rel Category
Return on Equity	27.49	1.19
Return on Assets	13.36	1.21
Net Margin	14.52	0.98

Industry Weightings	% of Stocks	Rel Cat
Oil & Gas	56.4	1.8
Oil/Gas Products	15.8	1.5
Oil & Gas Srv	21.2	0.7
Pipelines	4.5	4.4
Utilities	0.0	0.0
Hard Commd	0.0	0.0
Soft Commd	0.0	0.0
Misc. Indstrl	0.0	0.0
Other	2.0	0.3

Composition

● Cash	0.1
● Stocks	99.9
● Bonds	0.0
● Other	0.0
Foreign	0.0
(% of Stock)	

Address:	c/o State Street Bk&Tr, 225 Franklin St Boston MA 02210 800-843-2639
Web Address:	www.spdrindex.com
Inception:	12-22-98 *
Advisor:	SSgA Funds Management Inc

Management Fee:	0.05%		
Expense Projections:	3Yr:$77	5Yr:$136	10Yr:$307
Income Distrib:	Quarterly		
Exchange:	AMEX		

Financial SPDR XLF

	Market Price	Mstar Category
	$36.61	Specialty-Financial

Morningstar Fair Value

Price/Fair Value Ratio	Coverage Rate %
0.90 Undervalued	96 Good

Management

State Street Global Advisors serves as advisor to the trust. Michael Feehily, head of U.S. Equity in SSgA's global structured products group, and John Tucker, head of SSgA's ETF management effort, lead a team that runs all of SSgA's ETFs. They both have 15 years or more of experience at SSgA.

Methodology

This fund contains all the financial companies in the S&P 500 Index, which screens its components for profitability, industry leadership, and certain trading criteria. The index is limited to U.S. companies, which eliminates some big international players. The fund holds more than 80 stocks, giving it a certain level of diversification, but it is top-heavy: Nearly half of its assets are in its largest 10 positions. The S&P 500 committee rebalances the index every quarter and on certain occasions.

Morningstar Rating	Return	Risk	Yield	NAV	Avg Daily Vol. (k)	52 wk High/Low
★★	Below Avg	Below Avg	2.3%	$36.77	5,646	$37.12 - $31.32
	Below Avg	Average				

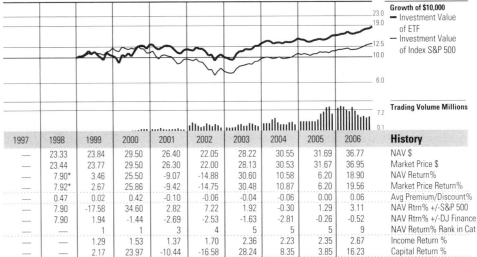

Growth of $10,000
— Investment Value of ETF
— Investment Value of Index S&P 500

Trading Volume Millions

1997	1998	1999	2000	2001	2002	2003	2004	2005	2006	History
—	23.33	23.84	29.50	26.40	22.05	28.22	30.55	31.69	36.77	NAV $
—	23.44	23.77	29.50	26.30	22.00	28.13	30.53	31.67	36.95	Market Price $
—	7.90*	3.46	25.50	-9.07	-14.88	30.60	10.58	6.20	18.90	NAV Return%
—	7.92*	2.67	25.86	-9.42	-14.75	30.48	10.87	6.20	19.56	Market Price Return%
—	0.47	0.02	0.42	-0.10	-0.06	-0.04	-0.06	0.00	0.06	Avg Premium/Discount%
—	7.90	-17.58	34.60	2.82	7.22	1.92	-0.30	1.29	3.11	NAV Rtrn% +/-S&P 500
—	7.90	1.94	-1.44	-2.69	-2.53	-1.63	-2.81	-0.26	-0.52	NAV Rtrn% +/-DJ Finance
—		1	1	3	4	5	5	5	9	NAV Return% Rank in Cat
—	—	1.29	1.53	1.37	1.70	2.36	2.23	2.35	2.67	Income Return %
—	—	2.17	23.97	-10.44	-16.58	28.24	8.35	3.85	16.23	Capital Return %
—	0.00	0.30	0.36	0.40	0.45	0.52	0.63	0.71	0.84	Income $
—	0.00	0.00	0.00	0.00	0.00	0.00	0.00	0.00	0.00	Capital Gains $
—	—	0.57	0.44	0.27	0.27	0.28	0.26	0.26	—	Expense Ratio %
—	—	1.14	1.45	1.43	1.70	2.09	2.14	2.30	—	Income Ratio %
—	—	6	7	9	11	6	9	9	—	Turnover Rate %
—	—	—	—	—	451	802	1,140	1,872	2,301	Net Assets $mil

Performance 12-31-06

Historic Quarterly NAV Returns

	1st Qtr	2nd Qtr	3rd Qtr	4th Qtr	Total
2002	3.40	-7.49	-17.11	7.36	-14.88
2003	-5.16	18.37	4.12	11.74	30.60
2004	4.79	-2.43	0.31	7.82	10.58
2005	-6.42	4.25	0.67	8.15	6.20
2006	3.18	-0.16	7.91	6.96	18.90

Trailing	NAV Return%	Market Return%	NAV Rtrn% +/-S&P 500	%Rank Cat.(NAV)
3 Mo	6.96	7.55	0.26	14
6 Mo	15.42	15.79	2.68	13
1 Yr	18.90	19.56	3.11	9
3 Yr Avg	11.77	12.07	1.33	4
5 Yr Avg	9.19	9.38	3.00	4
10 Yr Avg	—	—	—	—

Tax Analysis	Tax-Adj Return%	Tax-Cost Ratio
3 Yr (estimated)	10.87	0.81
5 Yr (estimated)	8.35	0.77
10 Yr (estimated)	—	—

Rating and Risk

Time Period	Morningstar Rtn vs Cat	Morningstar Risk vs Cat	Morningstar Risk-Adj Rating
3 Yr	Avg	Avg	★★★
5 Yr	-Avg	Avg	★★
10 Yr	—	—	—

Other Measures	Standard Index S&P 500	Best Fit Index DJ Finance
Alpha	2.6	-0.9
Beta	0.82	0.98
R-Squared	46	97
Standard Deviation	8.32	
Mean	11.77	
Sharpe Ratio	1.01	

Portfolio Analysis 12-31-06

Share change since 11-06 Total Stocks:88	Sector	PE	Tot Ret%	% Assets
⊖ Citigroup, Inc.	Financial	13.3	19.55	9.64
⊖ Bank of America Corporat	Financial	12.4	20.68	8.44
⊖ American International G	Financial	17.1	6.05	6.56
⊖ J.P. Morgan Chase & Co.	Financial	13.7	25.60	5.90
⊖ Wells Fargo Company	Financial	14.7	16.82	4.23
⊖ Wachovia Corporation	Financial	13.0	12.02	3.82
⊖ Morgan Stanley	Financial	12.3	45.93	3.03
⊖ Goldman Sachs Group, Inc	Financial	12.1	57.41	2.99
⊖ Merrill Lynch & Company,	Financial	14.1	39.27	2.90
⊖ American Express Company	Financial	21.2	19.09	2.57
⊖ US Bancorp	Financial	14.1	26.29	2.24
⊖ Fannie Mae	Financial	—	24.34	2.04
⊖ Freddie Mac	Financial	24.0	7.06	1.65
⊖ Metropolitan Life Insura	Financial	15.8	21.67	1.58
⊖ Washington Mutual, Inc.	Financial	13.5	9.62	1.51
⊖ Lehman Brothers Holdings	Financial	12.2	22.74	1.46
⊖ Prudential Financial, In	Financial	16.1	18.70	1.44
⊖ Allstate Corporation	Financial	8.7	23.38	1.43
⊖ St. Paul Travelers Compa	Financial	12.0	22.90	1.31
⊕ Capital One Financial Co	Financial	10.3	-10.97	1.11

Current Investment Style

Value Blnd Growth — Large/Mid/Small

Market Cap	%
Giant	54.5
Large	39.6
Mid	6.0
Small	0.0
Micro	0.0

Avg $mil: 59,736

Value Measures		Rel Category
Price/Earnings	13.11	0.97
Price/Book	2.16	1.05
Price/Sales	2.56	0.98
Price/Cash Flow	7.86	1.00
Dividend Yield %	2.43	1.05

Growth Measures	%	Rel Category
Long-Term Erngs	10.81	1.01
Book Value	6.85	0.84
Sales	6.89	0.90
Cash Flow	—	—
Historical Erngs	14.07	0.92

Profitability	%	Rel Category
Return on Equity	16.38	1.03
Return on Assets	15.98	1.16
Net Margin	21.97	1.03

Industry Weightings	% of Stocks	Rel Cat
Intl Banks	26.7	1.5
Banks	18.9	0.9
Real Estate	5.6	1.8
Sec Mgmt	14.7	1.2
S & Ls	2.8	0.4
Prop & Reins	13.8	0.8
Life Ins	6.2	1.2
Misc. Ins	2.4	0.8
Other	8.9	0.7

Composition

● Cash	0.2	
● Stocks	99.8	
● Bonds	0.0	
● Other	0.0	
Foreign	0.0	
(% of Stock)		

Morningstar's Take by Dan Culloton 12-31-06

Few funds can match Financial Select Sector SPDR for cheap exposure to big financial-services stocks.

Like other members of the Select Sector exchange-traded fund family, this one carves out a sector's stocks from the S&P 500 Index and groups them together in one package. Unlike some of its siblings, though, this ETF does so without getting too top-heavy. With nearly half of its assets in its top 10 holdings, this is no milquetoast ETF, to be sure. But among Select Sector SPDRs and sector ETFs in general, that passes for well-diversified.

The ETF's portfolio also is full of sector bellwethers with strong competitive advantages and, at least at the end of 2006, undervalued shares. According to Morningstar stock analysts, some this fund's biggest holdings, J.P. Morgan Chase, Wells Fargo, Bank of America, and American Express, were trading below their fair-value estimates and were designated as wide economic-moat stocks.

Indeed, because this fund's benchmark is an offspring of the S&P 500, you know its nearly 90 holdings are established domestic firms because the S&P index selection committee requires constituents to be profitable and headquartered in the U.S. That explains the fund's bias toward the sector's established giants (where it keeps more than half of its assets) and illuminates its lagging performance relative to other traditional financial-services funds that have the liberty to own more small-cap and international stocks in recent years.

You probably don't need more financial exposure if you have a large-cap fund. And if you think you do, it is possible to get even broader and slightly cheaper exposure to the financial-services sector via Vanguard Financials ETF. This ETF's 0.26% expense ratio is very low relative to the typical conventional sector mutual fund but is still a hair higher than its Vanguard rival, which owns more mid- and small-cap stocks. Still, for exposure to large financial stocks, this will do.

Address:	c/o State Street Bk&Tr, 225 Franklin St, Boston MA 02210, 800-843-2639
Web Address:	www.spdrindex.com
Inception:	12-22-98*
Advisor:	SSgA Funds Management Inc

Management Fee:	0.05%	
Expense Projections:	3Yr:$81	5Yr:$141	10Yr:$320
Income Distrib:	Quarterly	
Exchange:	AMEX	

MORNINGSTAR® ETFs 150

First Trust DJ S MicroCap FDM

	Market Price $23.52	Mstar Category Small Blend

Morningstar Rating	Return	Risk	Yield	NAV	Avg Daily Vol. (k)	52 wk High/Low
— Not Rated	Not Rated	—	0.2%	$23.92	11	$24.23 - $20.20

Morningstar Fair Value

Price/Fair Value Ratio — Coverage Rate % —

Management

This is one of several ETFs managed by First Trust Advisors. The advisor manages about 10 ETFs, ranging from large-cap offerings that invest in widely followed companies to niche industry and micro-cap ETFs. A five-person investment committee, led by Daniel Lindquist, makes all decisions regarding this fund.

Methodology

This ETF is designed to match the return of the Dow Jones Select MicroCap index before all expenses. The index tracks small-company stocks traded on the New York Stock Exchange, Nasdaq, and American Stock Exchange, as defined by the smallest two market-cap deciles of NYSE-traded stocks. Its screening process is also more selective, though this ETF failed to top its peers in the up-and-down market of 2006.

Growth of $10,000
- Investment Value of ETF
- Investment Value of Index S&P 500

Trading Volume Millions

History	1997	1998	1999	2000	2001	2002	2003	2004	2005	2006
NAV $	—	—	—	—	—	—	—	—	20.73	23.92
Market Price $	—	—	—	—	—	—	—	—	20.72	23.95
NAV Return%	—	—	—	—	—	—	—	—	14.88*	15.70
Market Price Return%	—	—	—	—	—	—	—	—	15.82*	15.89
Avg Premium/Discount%	—	—	—	—	—	—	—	—	-0.24	-0.08
NAV Rtrn% +/-S&P 500	—	—	—	—	—	—	—	—	14.88	-0.09
NAV Rtrn% +/-Russ 2000	—	—	—	—	—	—	—	—	14.88	-2.67
NAV Return% Rank in Cat	—	—	—	—	—	—	—	—	—	8
Income Return %	—	—	—	—	—	—	—	—	—	0.27
Capital Return %	—	—	—	—	—	—	—	—	—	15.43
Income $	—	—	—	—	—	—	—	—	0.02	0.06
Capital Gains $	—	—	—	—	—	—	—	—	0.00	0.00
Expense Ratio %	—	—	—	—	—	—	—	—	0.60	—
Income Ratio %	—	—	—	—	—	—	—	—	0.51	—
Turnover Rate %	—	—	—	—	—	—	—	—	6	—
Net Assets $mil	—	—	—	—	—	—	—	—	39	17

Performance 12-31-06

Historic Quarterly NAV Returns

	1st Qtr	2nd Qtr	3rd Qtr	4th Qtr	Total
2002	—	—	—	—	—
2003	—	—	—	—	—
2004	—	—	—	—	—
2005	—	—	—	2.82	—*
2006	10.85	-4.62	-1.06	10.60	15.70

Trailing	NAV Return%	Market Return%	NAV Rtrn% +/-S&P 500	%Rank Cat.(NAV)
3 Mo	10.60	10.88	3.90	12
6 Mo	9.43	9.86	-3.31	10
1 Yr	15.70	15.89	-0.09	8
3 Yr Avg	—	—	—	—
5 Yr Avg	—	—	—	—
10 Yr Avg	—	—	—	—

Tax Analysis	Tax-Adj Return%	Tax-Cost Ratio
3 Yr (estimated)	—	—
5 Yr (estimated)	—	—
10 Yr (estimated)	—	—

Rating and Risk

Time Period	Morningstar Rtn vs Cat	Morningstar Risk vs Cat	Morningstar Risk-Adj Rating
3 Yr	—	—	—
5 Yr	—	—	—
10 Yr	—	—	—

Other Measures	Standard Index S&P 500	Best Fit Index
Alpha	—	—
Beta	—	—
R-Squared	—	—
Standard Deviation	—	
Mean	—	
Sharpe Ratio	—	

Portfolio Analysis 11-30-06

Share change since 10-06 Total Stocks:296

	Sector	PE	Tot Ret%	% Assets
⊖ W.R. Grace & Company	Ind Mtrls	NMF	110.64	0.83
⊕ Northstar Realty Finance	Financial	13.7	79.48	0.73
⊖ Mid-State Bancshares	Financial	23.0	39.39	0.64
⊖ Manhattan Associates, In	Software	41.8	46.88	0.62
⊖ Oxford Industries, Inc.	Goods	17.5	-8.01	0.61
⊖ Heidrick & Struggles Int	Business	23.4	32.17	0.60
⊖ Open Solutions, Inc.	Business	40.5	64.22	0.60
⊖ Middleby Corporation	Ind Mtrls	23.8	21.01	0.59
⊖ Trizetto Group, Inc.	Software	61.2	8.12	0.59
⊕ Amedisys, Inc.	Health	21.0	3.76	0.59
⊖ Chattem, Inc.	Health	22.8	37.62	0.58
⊖ The Geo Group, Inc.	Business	57.5	145.44	0.58
⊖ Skechers USA, Inc.	Goods	23.6	117.43	0.57
⊖ McGrath RentCorp	Consumer	18.8	12.67	0.57
⊖ Triquint Semiconductor	Hardware	50.0	1.12	0.56
⊖ Standard Microsystems Co	Hardware	27.2	-2.47	0.56
⊖ Andersons, Inc.	Ind Mtrls	22.9	97.72	0.55
⊖ Insituform Technologies	Business	38.0	33.51	0.55
⊖ ElkCorp	Ind Mtrls	19.0	22.87	0.54
⊖ Brush Engineered Materia	Ind Mtrls	28.9	112.39	0.54

Current Investment Style

Value Blend Growth — Large / Mid / Small

Market Cap	%
Giant	0.0
Large	0.0
Mid	0.0
Small	43.0
Micro	57.0

Avg $mil: 536

Value Measures		Rel Category
Price/Earnings	18.52	1.05
Price/Book	2.09	1.01
Price/Sales	0.96	0.93
Price/Cash Flow	6.28	0.97
Dividend Yield %	1.29	0.81

Growth Measures	%	Rel Category
Long-Term Erngs	14.38	1.08
Book Value	7.31	1.34
Sales	10.09	4.44
Cash Flow	11.48	1.27
Historical Erngs	9.80	0.82

Profitability	%	Rel Category
Return on Equity	12.01	1.04
Return on Assets	7.24	1.10
Net Margin	8.33	0.85

Sector Weightings	% of Stocks	Rel S&P 500	3 Year High Low
⟳ Info	14.07	0.70	
Software	4.24	1.23	— —
Hardware	5.88	0.64	— —
Media	1.80	0.47	— —
Telecom	2.15	0.61	— —
⟨ Service	55.62	1.20	
Health	7.58	0.63	— —
Consumer	11.83	1.55	— —
Business	16.60	3.92	— —
Financial	19.61	0.88	— —
Mfg	30.31	0.90	
Goods	8.04	0.94	— —
Ind Mtrls	17.53	1.47	— —
Energy	3.95	0.40	— —
Utilities	0.79	0.23	— —

Composition

	%
Cash	0.0
Stocks	100.0
Bonds	0.0
Other	0.0
Foreign	0.0

(% of Stock)

Morningstar's Take by Andrew Gunter 12-31-06

First Trust Dow Jones Select MicroCap doesn't convince us.

This ETF is interesting, if nothing else. As a competitor in the small-blend category, it holds close to 300 stocks whose typical market cap is tiny--just $501 million as of Nov. 30, 2006. Smaller stocks tend to trade much less frequently than larger ones; thus, this fund holds some of the most illiquid names in the domestic stock universe.

This fund's bogy, the Dow Jones Select MicroCap index, lends it that unusual look. It tracks firms traded on three exchanges (NYSE, Nasdaq, AMEX) whose market caps fall within the bottom two deciles of NYSE-traded companies. Most of its small-cap competitors follow the more widely tracked Russell 2000 or S&P 600 indexes. And while all indexes have some set of standards a company must meet to become a constituent, those of this ETF's bogy are more subjective than usual. The index provider screens firms by their quarter-over-quarter per-share profit growth, by

several trailing price ratios and by operating profit margins.

Such a methodology has both benefits and drawbacks. The growth rate of this fund's holdings, as measured by growth in book value, revenue, and cash flow, exceeds that of its typical rival. But more stringent screening standards may cause this ETF to miss good opportunities in firms whose growth is in its infancy. And the quality screens don't necessarily decrease volatility, either. In the sharp market decline of 2006's second quarter, this ETF lost as much as the average small-blend rival (a peer group of both ETFs and actively managed funds).

This fund's 0.60% expense ratio is the final nail in its coffin. Vanguard and iShares offer attractive alternatives with wider small-cap exposure at just a fraction of this ETF's price.

Address:	1001 Warrenville Road, Ste 300 Lisle, IL, 60532 800-621-1675	Management Fee:	0.50%	
		Expense Projections:	3Yr:$379 5Yr: — 10Yr: —	
Web Address:	www.ftportfolios.com	Income Distrib:	Semi-Annually	
Inception:	09-30-05*	Exchange:	AMEX	
Advisor:	First Trust Advisor L.P.			

Health Care Sel SPDR XLV

Market Price $33.69	**Mstar Category** Specialty-Health

Morningstar Fair Value

Price/Fair Value Ratio	Coverage Rate %
0.92 Undervalued	97 Good

Management

State Street Global Advisors serves as advisor to the trust. Michael Feehily, head of U.S. Equity in SSgA's global structured products group, and John Tucker, head of SSgA's ETF management effort, lead a team that runs all of SSgA's ETFs. They both have 15 years or more of experience at SSgA.

Methodology

This ETF owns the health-care companies in the S&P 500. The bogy includes companies from a number of industries, including health equipment and supplies, hospitals and health-care providers, medical devices, health insurers, biotechnology, and drugs. Because the index draws its constituents from the broader S&P 500, it has an inherent quality screen. S&P 500 holdings have to meet the standards of the S&P's selection committee, and this includes profitability and status as a leading U.S. company. Unfortunately, the criteria eliminate large foreign-based health-care companies.

Morningstar Rating ★★★ Neutral	**Return** Neutral	**Risk** Below Avg	**Yield** 1.3%	**NAV** $33.50
Avg Daily Vol. (k) 1,185				
52 wk High/Low $33.95 - $29.56				

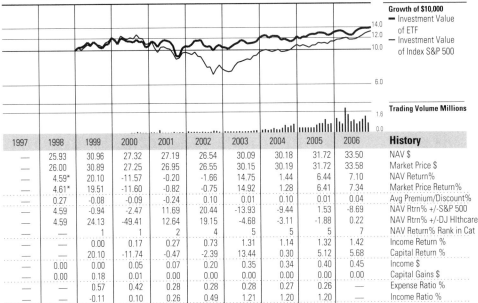

Growth of $10,000
- Investment Value of ETF
- Investment Value of Index S&P 500

Trading Volume Millions

	1997	1998	1999	2000	2001	2002	2003	2004	2005	2006	History
	—	25.93	30.96	27.32	27.19	26.54	30.09	30.18	31.72	33.50	NAV $
	—	26.00	30.89	27.25	26.95	26.55	30.15	30.19	31.72	33.58	Market Price $
	—	4.59*	20.10	-11.57	-0.20	-1.66	14.75	1.44	6.44	7.10	NAV Return%
	—	4.61*	19.51	-11.60	-0.82	-0.75	14.92	1.28	6.41	7.34	Market Price Return%
	—	0.27	-0.08	-0.09	-0.24	0.10	0.01	0.10	0.01	0.04	Avg Premium/Discount%
	—	4.59	-0.94	-2.47	11.69	20.44	-13.93	-9.44	1.53	-8.69	NAV Rtrn% +/-S&P 500
	—	4.59	24.13	-49.41	12.64	19.15	-4.68	-3.11	-1.88	0.22	NAV Rtrn% +/-DJ Hlthcare
	—	—	1	1	2	4	5	5	5	7	NAV Return% Rank in Cat
	—	—	0.00	0.17	0.27	0.73	1.31	1.14	1.32	1.42	Income Return %
	—	—	20.10	-11.74	-0.47	-2.39	13.44	0.30	5.12	5.68	Capital Return %
	—	0.00	0.00	0.05	0.07	0.20	0.35	0.34	0.40	0.45	Income $
	—	0.00	0.18	0.01	0.00	0.00	0.00	0.00	0.00	0.00	Capital Gains $
	—	—	0.57	0.42	0.28	0.28	0.28	0.27	0.26	—	Expense Ratio %
	—	—	-0.11	0.10	0.26	0.49	1.21	1.20	1.20	—	Income Ratio %
	—	—	15	22	28	103	6	7	3	—	Turnover Rate %
	—	—	—	—	—	158	454	1,053	1,787	1,843	Net Assets $mil

Performance 12-31-06

Historic Quarterly NAV Returns

	1st Qtr	2nd Qtr	3rd Qtr	4th Qtr	Total
2002	8.50	-6.93	-7.29	5.04	-1.66
2003	0.94	9.86	-4.51	8.37	14.75
2004	-0.49	2.61	-5.51	5.14	1.44
2005	-0.68	4.08	1.50	1.44	6.44
2006	1.14	-5.12	10.10	1.37	7.10

Trailing	NAV Return%	Market Return%	NAV Rtrn% +/-S&P 500	%Rank Cat.(NAV)
3 Mo	1.37	1.53	-5.33	14
6 Mo	11.61	11.82	-1.13	13
1 Yr	7.10	7.34	-8.69	7
3 Yr Avg	4.96	4.97	-5.48	4
5 Yr Avg	5.47	5.70	-0.72	4
10 Yr Avg	—	—	—	—

Tax Analysis	Tax-Adj Return%	Tax-Cost Ratio
3 Yr (estimated)	4.50	0.44
5 Yr (estimated)	5.04	0.41
10 Yr (estimated)	—	—

Rating and Risk

Time Period	Morningstar Rtn vs Cat	Morningstar Risk vs Cat	Morningstar Risk-Adj Rating
3 Yr	-Avg	-Avg	★★
5 Yr	+Avg	-Avg	★★★★
10 Yr	—	—	

Other Measures	Standard Index S&P 500	Best Fit Index DJ Hlthcare
Alpha	-2.2	-1.6
Beta	0.60	1.04
R-Squared	22	98
Standard Deviation	8.76	
Mean	4.96	
Sharpe Ratio	0.23	

Portfolio Analysis 12-31-06

Share change since 11-06 Total Stocks:55	Sector	PE	Tot Ret%	% Assets
⊖ Johnson & Johnson	Health	17.4	12.44	12.48
⊖ Pfizer Inc.	Health	15.1	15.22	12.18
⊖ Merck & Co., Inc.	Health	18.8	42.66	6.18
⊖ Amgen, Inc.	Health	28.0	-13.38	5.20
⊖ UnitedHealth Group, Inc.	Health	21.0	-13.49	4.76
⊕ Wyeth	Health	17.0	12.88	4.50
⊕ Abbott Laboratories	Health	23.6	26.88	4.14
⊕ Medtronic, Inc.	Health	23.7	-6.29	4.04
⊕ Bristol-Myers Squibb Com	Health	23.3	19.93	3.40
⊕ Eli Lilly & Company	Health	17.4	-5.16	3.35
⊕ WellPoint, Inc.	Health	17.2	-1.38	3.27
⊖ Schering-Plough Corporat	Health	36.9	14.63	2.31
⊕ Baxter International Inc	Health	24.0	24.81	2.01
⊕ Gilead Sciences, Inc.	Health	41.1	23.51	1.95
⊖ Cardinal Health, Inc.	Health	20.9	-5.81	1.72
⊖ Caremark RX, Inc.	Health	23.8	10.89	1.59
⊖ Aetna, Inc.	Health	14.6	-8.34	1.51
⊕ Celgene Corporation	Health	—	77.56	1.40
⊖ Boston Scientific Corpor	Health	—	-29.85	1.33
⊖ Zimmer Holdings, Inc.	Health	24.6	16.22	1.24

Current Investment Style

Value Blnd Growth — Large Mid Small

	Market Cap	%
	Giant	56.8
	Large	32.3
	Mid	10.9
	Small	0.0
	Micro	0.0
	Avg $mil:	
	51,039	

Value Measures		Rel Category
Price/Earnings	18.27	0.89
Price/Book	3.52	0.99
Price/Sales	1.78	0.60
Price/Cash Flow	15.37	1.05
Dividend Yield %	1.50	1.49

Growth Measures	%	Rel Category
Long-Term Erngs	11.81	0.83
Book Value	11.51	1.45
Sales	9.68	0.80
Cash Flow	3.40	0.30
Historical Erngs	10.59	0.71

Profitability	%	Rel Category
Return on Equity	19.50	1.38
Return on Assets	10.45	1.80
Net Margin	15.00	1.33

Industry Weightings	% of Stocks	Rel Cat
Biotech	12.1	0.4
Drugs	54.0	1.7
Mgd Care	14.1	1.3
Hospitals	0.6	0.5
Other HC Srv	0.3	0.2
Diagnostics	1.2	0.9
Equipment	14.8	1.1
Good/Srv	2.7	0.8
Other	0.4	0.1

Composition

● Cash	0.0
● Stocks	100.0
● Bonds	0.0
● Other	0.0
Foreign	0.0
(% of Stock)	

Morningstar's Take by Dan Culloton 12-31-06

Health Care Select Sector SPDR offers simple and cheap exposure to large-cap health-care stocks, but it's still fraught with risk.

A good many of the large-cap pharmaceutical and medical-device stocks in this exchange-traded fund were looking undervalued at the end of 2006. The ranks of the undervalued included established, profitable companies such as Johnson & Johnson, Amgen, and Medtronic. This isn't surprising given the fact that some of this fund's top holdings have been hit with patent problems, thin product pipelines, regulatory uncertainty, and product recalls. For those looking for exposure to undervalued large-cap health-care stocks, this ETF might fit the bill.

This fund's focus, however, cuts both ways. The price of having one of the biggest average market capitalizations in the health-care category is concentration. The ETF has about 50 holdings and keeps more than a fourth of its assets in just two stocks: Pfizer and Johnson & Johnson. Those are profitable companies with strong positions in their industries, but the challenges they and other health-care stocks face are very real. For example, Merck still faces years of litigation in the wake of its decision to yank its Vioxx painkiller from the market due to potentially deadly side effects. Pfizer, which is struggling to replace blockbuster drugs that are about to lose patent protection, recently ceased development of a cholesterol drug for which it had high hopes.

The concentration and uncertainty make this fund more risky than its relatively low risk measures would indicate. It has lost money in about half of the 32 calendar quarters since its inception. The typical health-care fund has shed money in 38% of those same periods.

Similarly priced funds could offer a smoother ride. Vanguard Health Care ETF, for example, is more diversified and has a slightly lower expense ratio. In the year ending Nov. 30, 2006, the Vanguard offering's standard deviation was lower.

Address:	c/o State Street Bk&Tr, 225 Franklin St Boston MA 02210 800-843-2639
Web Address:	www.spdrindex.com
Inception:	12-22-98*
Advisor:	SSgA Funds Management Inc

Management Fee:	0.05%		
Expense Projections:	3Yr:$77	5Yr:$136	10Yr:$307
Income Distrib:	Quarterly		
Exchange:	AMEX		

MORNINGSTAR® ETFs 150

iShares C&S Realty ICF

	Market Price $100.43	Mstar Category Specialty-Real Estate

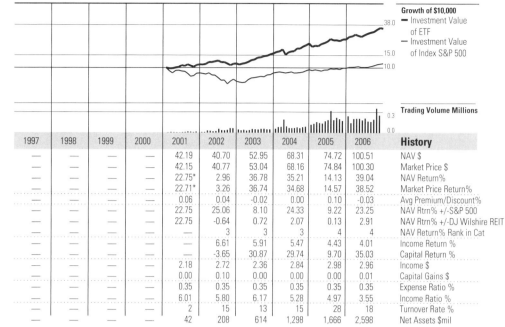

Morningstar Rating ★★★★ Above Avg	Return Above Avg	Risk High	Yield 3.0%	NAV $100.51	Avg Daily Vol. (k) 361	52 wk High/Low $104.50 - $77.92

Growth of $10,000
— Investment Value of ETF
— Investment Value of Index S&P 500

38.0
15.0
10.0

0.3 Trading Volume Millions

Morningstar Fair Value

Price/Fair Value Ratio	Coverage Rate %
1.24 Overvalued	99 Good

Management

Patrick O'Connor and S. Jane Leung lead the team that manage this and several other iShares ETFs fund. O'Connor has been on the team since the fund's inception and Leung since September 2006. Both have been with the ETF's advisor Barclays Global Investors for five or more years.

Methodology

This exchange-traded fund tracks the Cohen & Steers Realty Majors Index. The benchmark includes office, industrial, apartments, and retail REITs that meet the liquidity and quality standards of real estate investment firm Cohen & Steers' investment committee--usually about 30 stocks. Index constituents can't exceed 8% of assets. The bogy is rebalanced quarterly.

1997	1998	1999	2000	2001	2002	2003	2004	2005	2006	History
—	—	—	—	42.19	40.70	52.95	68.31	74.72	100.51	NAV $
—	—	—	—	42.15	40.77	53.04	68.16	74.84	100.30	Market Price $
—	—	—	—	22.75*	2.96	36.78	35.21	14.13	39.04	NAV Return%
—	—	—	—	22.71*	3.26	36.74	34.68	14.57	38.52	Market Price Return%
—	—	—	—	0.06	0.04	-0.02	0.00	0.10	-0.03	Avg Premium/Discount%
—	—	—	—	22.75	25.06	8.10	24.33	9.22	23.25	NAV Rtrn% +/-S&P 500
—	—	—	—	22.75	-0.64	0.72	2.07	0.13	2.91	NAV Rtrn% +/-DJ Wilshire REIT
—	—	—	—	—	3	3	3	4	4	NAV Return% Rank in Cat
—	—	—	—	—	6.61	5.91	5.47	4.43	4.01	Income Return %
—	—	—	—	—	-3.65	30.87	29.74	9.70	35.03	Capital Return %
—	—	—	—	2.18	2.72	2.36	2.84	2.98	2.96	Income $
—	—	—	—	0.00	0.10	0.00	0.00	0.00	0.01	Capital Gains $
—	—	—	—	0.35	0.35	0.35	0.35	0.35	0.35	Expense Ratio %
—	—	—	—	6.01	5.80	6.17	5.28	4.97	3.55	Income Ratio %
—	—	—	—	2	15	13	15	28	18	Turnover Rate %
—	—	—	—	42	208	614	1,298	1,666	2,598	Net Assets $mil

Performance 12-31-06

Historic Quarterly NAV Returns

	1st Qtr	2nd Qtr	3rd Qtr	4th Qtr	Total
2002	7.87	4.63	-8.82	0.05	2.96
2003	1.43	11.73	10.88	8.85	36.78
2004	13.03	-5.98	9.19	16.52	35.21
2005	-7.39	14.80	4.28	2.94	14.13
2006	15.69	-1.53	10.36	10.60	39.04

Trailing	NAV Return%	Market Return%	NAV Rtrn% +/-S&P 500	%Rank Cat.(NAV)
3 Mo	10.60	10.34	3.90	5
6 Mo	22.06	21.76	9.32	5
1 Yr	39.04	38.52	23.25	4
3 Yr Avg	28.98	28.81	18.54	3
5 Yr Avg	24.75	24.72	18.56	3
10 Yr Avg	—	—	—	—

Tax Analysis	Tax-Adj Return%	Tax-Cost Ratio
3 Yr (estimated)	27.15	1.42
5 Yr (estimated)	22.67	1.67
10 Yr (estimated)	—	—

Rating and Risk

Time Period	Morningstar Rtn vs Cat	Morningstar Risk vs Cat	Morningstar Risk-Adj Rating
3 Yr	+Avg	High	★★★★
5 Yr	+Avg	High	★★★★
10 Yr	—	—	—

Other Measures	Standard Index S&P 500	Best Fit Index DJ Wilshire REIT
Alpha	14.9	0.8
Beta	1.30	1.02
R-Squared	27	99
Standard Deviation	17.22	
Mean	28.98	
Sharpe Ratio	1.39	

Morningstar's Take by Dan Culloton 12-31-06

We're still worried about iShares Cohen & Steers Realty Majors.

We've been calling this ETF unattractive and overvalued for more than a year and have been wrong. The fund not only defied expectations for more modest returns, but also put up a more than 30% gain that ranked in the upper echelons of the real estate category (including both ETFs and traditional funds) in 2006.

Nevertheless, we still think the risk of disappointment is high here. It will be hard for this fund to repeat what it has done over the past six years. Not only does this portfolio look richly valued according to Morningstar equity analysts (25 of the 30 REITs in this ETF were trading above their fair value estimates at the end of 2006), but also according to other measures.

The portfolio's average valuations--such as price/earnings, price/book, price/sales, and price/cash flow--were higher than those of the broad domestic stock market, as defined by the

Morningstar U.S. Market Index and the category average. REIT yields, after a multiyear rally, also offer no more compensation to investors than less-risky 10-year Treasury issues.

Even if its holdings weren't looking pricey, this fund would be risky. It's concentrated, with just 30 office, industrial, apartment, and retail REITs and nearly 60% of its money in its top 10 holdings. That has made the offering more volatile than 94% all other real estate funds, exchange traded or otherwise, over the three- and five-year periods ending Nov. 30, 2006.

Finally, this fund, while cheap, isn't the cheapest real estate ETF available. StreetTracks Dow Jones Wilshire REIT and Vanguard REIT Index and its ETF share class have lower expense ratios. You can even by the conventional Vanguard index fund without a commission.

Real estate can diversify a portfolio, but given the sector's valuations and this ETF's risks, you'd best leave this one alone.

Address:	45 Fremont Street San Francisco CA 94105 800-474-2737
Web Address:	www.ishares.com
Inception:	01-29-01 *
Advisor:	Barclays Global Fund Advisers

Management Fee:	0.35%		
Expense Projections:	3Yr:$113	5Yr:$197	10Yr:$443
Income Distrib:	Annually		
Exchange:	NYSE		

Portfolio Analysis 12-31-06

Share change since 11-06 Total Stocks:30

	Sector	PE	Tot Ret%	% Assets
⊖ Simon Property Group, In	Financial	59.2	36.97	7.87
⊖ Vornado Realty Trust	Financial	38.2	51.13	7.04
⊖ Equity Office Properties	Financial	—	64.28	6.71
⊖ Equity Residential	Financial	NMF	34.64	6.09
⊖ ProLogis Trust	Financial	34.3	34.02	6.08
⊖ Public Storage, Inc.	Financial	46.2	47.46	5.44
⊖ Boston Properties, Inc.	Financial	15.1	62.75	5.31
⊖ Archstone-Smith Trust	Financial	60.0	43.93	5.04
⊖ General Growth Propertie	Financial	—	15.09	4.80
⊖ Host Hotels & Resorts, I	Financial	53.4	33.95	4.76
⊖ Kimco Realty Corporation	Financial	30.8	44.91	4.30
⊖ AvalonBay Communities, I	Financial	67.7	49.69	4.03
⊖ Developers Diversified R	Financial	41.1	39.65	2.93
⊖ Macerich Company	Financial	—	33.91	2.50
⊖ SL Green Realty Corporat	Financial	58.2	77.73	2.42
⊖ Regency Centers Corporat	Financial	57.1	37.58	2.37
⊕ Health Care Property	Financial	33.5	53.18	2.35
⊖ Duke Realty Corporation	Financial	75.7	28.98	2.31
⊖ AMB Property Corporation	Financial	30.9	23.30	1.94
⊖ Liberty Property Trust	Financial	19.4	20.84	1.71

Current Investment Style

Value Blnd Growth — Large Mid Small

Market Cap	%
Giant	0.0
Large	59.2
Mid	39.9
Small	0.9
Micro	0.0

Avg $mil: 10,079

Value Measures	Rel Category
Price/Earnings	20.74	1.21
Price/Book	3.63	1.29
Price/Sales	6.47	1.70
Price/Cash Flow	19.77	1.21
Dividend Yield %	3.38	1.03

Growth Measures	%	Rel Category
Long-Term Erngs	6.87	0.88
Book Value	0.18	0.05
Sales	8.11	0.70
Cash Flow	—	—
Historical Erngs	2.65	0.28

Profitability	%	Rel Category
Return on Equity	12.23	0.86
Return on Assets	10.88	0.98
Net Margin	28.78	1.29

Sector Weightings	% of Stocks	Rel S&P 500	3 Year High Low
ⓘ Info	0.00	0.00	
▣ Software	0.00	0.00	0 0
▣ Hardware	0.00	0.00	0 0
▣ Media	0.00	0.00	0 0
▣ Telecom	0.00	0.00	0 0
⌽ Service	100.00	2.16	
▣ Health	0.00	0.00	0 0
▣ Consumer	0.00	0.00	0 0
▣ Business	0.00	0.00	0 0
▣ Financial	100.00	4.49	100 100
⌐ Mfg	0.00	0.00	
▣ Goods	0.00	0.00	0 0
▣ Ind Mtrls	0.00	0.00	0 0
▣ Energy	0.00	0.00	0 0
▣ Utilities	0.00	0.00	0 0

Composition

		%
●	Cash	0.2
●	Stocks	99.8
●	Bonds	0.0
●	Other	0.0
	Foreign	0.0
	(% of Stock)	

iShares COMEX Gold Trust IAU

Market Price $60.94						**Mstar Category** Specialty-Precious Metals	

Morningstar Fair Value

Price/Fair Value Ratio	Coverage Rate %
—	—

Morningstar Rating	Return	Risk	Yield	NAV	Avg Daily Vol. (k)	52 wk High/Low
— Not Rated	Not Rated	Not Rated	—	$63.03	171	$71.27 - $52.36

Management

Barclays Global Investors NA is the sponsor of the trust, The Bank of New York is the trustee of the trust, and The Bank of Nova Scotia is the custodian of the trust.

Growth of $10,000
— Investment Value of ETF
— Investment Value of Index MSCI EAFE

Methodology

This fund issues shares equal to roughly one tenth of an ounce of gold, at current market prices.

Trading Volume Millions

1997	1998	1999	2000	2001	2002	2003	2004	2005	2006	History
—	—	—	—	—	—	—	—	51.52	63.03	NAV $
—	—	—	—	—	—	—	—	51.73	63.25	Market Price $
—	—	—	—	—	—	—	—	22.26*	22.35	NAV Return%
—	—	—	—	—	—	—	—	22.48*	22.27	Market Price Return%
—	—	—	—	—	—	—	—	0.09	0.30	Avg Premium/Discount%
—	—	—	—	—	—	—	—	22.26	-3.99	NAV Rtrn% +/-MSCI EAFE
—	—	—	—	—	—	—	—	22.26	-12.21	NAV Rtrn% +/-MSCI W Me&M
—	—	—	—	—	—	—	—		2	NAV Return% Rank in Cat
—	—	—	—	—	—	—	—	—	0.00	Income Return %
—	—	—	—	—	—	—	—	—	22.35	Capital Return %
—	—	—	—	—	—	—	—	0.00	0.00	Income $
—	—	—	—	—	—	—	—	0.00	0.00	Capital Gains $
—	—	—	—	—	—	—	—	—	—	Expense Ratio %
—	—	—	—	—	—	—	—	—	—	Income Ratio %
—	—	—	—	—	—	—	—	—	—	Turnover Rate %
—	—	—	—	—	—	—	—	368	908	Net Assets $mil

Performance 12-31-06

Historic Quarterly NAV Returns

	1st Qtr	2nd Qtr	3rd Qtr	4th Qtr	Total
2002	—	—	—	—	—
2003	—	—	—	—	—
2004	—	—	—	—	—
2005	—	1.56	7.49	10.16	—*
2006	12.40	5.34	-2.52	6.01	22.35

Trailing	NAV Return%	Market Return%+/-MSCI EAFE	NAV Rtrn%	%Rank Cat.(NAV)
3 Mo	6.01	6.27	-4.34	4
6 Mo	3.33	3.30	-11.36	4
1 Yr	22.35	22.27	-3.99	2
3 Yr Avg	—	—	—	—
5 Yr Avg	—	—	—	—
10 Yr Avg	—	—	—	—

Tax Analysis	Tax-Adj Return%	Tax-Cost Ratio
3 Yr (estimated)	—	—
5 Yr (estimated)	—	—
10 Yr (estimated)	—	—

Rating and Risk

Time Period	Morningstar Rtn vs Cat	Morningstar Risk vs Cat	Morningstar Risk-Adj Rating
3 Yr	—	—	—
5 Yr	—	—	—
10 Yr	—	—	—

Other Measures	Standard Index S&P 500	Best Fit Index
Alpha	—	—
Beta	—	—
R-Squared	—	—
Standard Deviation	—	
Mean	—	
Sharpe Ratio	—	

Portfolio Analysis 12-31-06

Share change since 11-06 Total Stocks:0

	Sector	Country	% Assets
⊕ Gold Bullion	—	—	100.00

Morningstar's Take by Karen Wallace 12-31-06

IShares COMEX Gold Trust has merits as a long-term holding, but we wouldn't use it to speculate on gold prices.

Gold's rise over the past six years has piqued many investors' interests. In fact, this fund and its similarly structured rival, StreetTRACKS Gold Shares, have arguably fueled gold's rise. Together they have attracted more than $10 billion in assets since they launched just over a year ago.

This ETF offers direct exposure to gold price fluctuations in a more liquid and convenient format than taking physical delivery of the metal itself. Unlike most precious metals funds, this one does not invest in the stocks of gold producers. Rather, each share of the trust represents one tenth of an ounce of gold bullion at current market prices, less the fund's 0.40% expense ratio. (Another important difference: This investment is taxed differently than other gold-linked investments, so it's a good idea to consult your tax advisor before buying in.)

Rolling three-month returns since the fund's inception shows that it has been less volatile than the average fund that invests in the stocks of gold producers over the same time period. (This makes sense because the price of bullion tends not to be as volatile as gold producers' stock prices.)

But that's not to say that this is a tame investment: Gold prices have historically fluctuated wildly. If we were to see another period of flat to falling gold prices, as we saw in much of the 1990s, this fund would languish. In addition, the amount of gold represented by each share will continue to decrease due to the sales necessary to pay the sponsor's fee and trust expenses.

A gold investment makes the most sense as part of a long-term asset-allocation plan. A speculator buying into this fund now, with gold trading near 25-year highs, could be in for a disappointment. Many factors could negatively impact gold prices going forward, including a strengthening dollar and increased selling by speculators. Handle this fund with care.

Address:	45 Fremont Street San Francisco CA 94105 800-474-2737	Management Fee:	0.40%
		Expense Projections:	3Yr: — 5Yr: — 10Yr: —
		Income Distrib:	Annually
Web Address:	www.ishares.com	Exchange:	AMEX
Inception:	01-21-05*		
Advisor:	Barclays Global Fund Advisers		

Current Investment Style

Value Blnd Growth	Market Cap	%
	Giant	—
	Large	—
	Mid	—
	Small	—
	Micro	—
	Avg $mil:	

Value Measures	Rel Category
Price/Earnings	—
Price/Book	—
Price/Sales	—
Price/Cash Flow	—
Dividend Yield %	—

Growth Measures	% Rel Category
Long-Term Erngs	—
Book Value	—
Sales	—
Cash Flow	—
Historical Erngs	—

Composition

Cash	0.0	Bonds	0.0
Stocks	0.0	Other	100.0
Foreign	(% of Stock)		0.0

Sector Weightings	% of Stocks	Rel MSCI EAFE	3 Year High Low
☎ Info	0.00	0.00	
▣ Software	—	0.00	— —
▣ Hardware	—	0.00	— —
▣ Media	—	0.00	— —
▣ Telecom	—	0.00	— —
☞ Service	—	0.00	— —
▣ Health	—	0.00	— —
▣ Consumer	—	0.00	— —
▣ Business	—	0.00	— —
$ Financial	—	0.00	— —
⊡ Mfg	0.00	0.00	
▣ Goods	—	0.00	— —
▣ Ind Mtrls	—	0.00	— —
▣ Energy	—	0.00	— —
▣ Utilities	—	0.00	— —

Regional Exposure			% Stock
UK/W. Europe	0	N. America	0
Japan	0	Latn America	0
Asia X Japan	0	Other	100

Country Exposure	% Stock

MORNINGSTAR® ETFs 150

iShares DJ Sel Dividend DVY

	Market Price	Mstar Category
	$70.39	Large Value

Morningstar Fair Value

Price/Fair Value Ratio	Coverage Rate %
0.96 Fairly valued	87 Good

Management

Patrick O Connor and S. Jane Leung lead the team that manage this and several other iShares ETFs fund. O Connor has been on the team since the fund's inception and Leung since September 2006. Both have been with the ETF s advisor Barclays Global Investors for five or more years.

Methodology

Dow Jones created its Select Dividend Index for this fund. The benchmark screens the 1,600-member Dow Jones Total Market Index for 100 stocks that have three-month average daily trading volumes of 200,000 shares, have increased and never cut their dividends over the last five years, and that have paid out less than 60% of their earnings. The index screens out REITs because they do not qualify for the dividend tax cut passed in 2003. Dow Jones weights constituent stocks based on their indicated annual dividend and rebalances annually in December.

Morningstar Rating	Return	Risk	Yield	NAV	Avg Daily Vol. (k)	52 wk High/Low
★★★★ Above Avg	Above Avg	Average	3.1%	$70.76	366	$71.44 - $61.42

Growth of $10,000
- ─ Investment Value of ETF
- ─ Investment Value of Index S&P 500

18.2 / 16.0 / 14.2 / 11.0 / 10.0

Trading Volume Millions
0.6 / 0.3

	1997	1998	1999	2000	2001	2002	2003	2004	2005	2006	History
	—	—	—	—	—	—	53.80	61.34	61.30	70.76	NAV $
	—	—	—	—	—	—	53.84	61.40	61.26	70.73	Market Price $
	—	—	—	—	—	—	14.95*	17.90	2.98	19.41	NAV Return%
	—	—	—	—	—	—	14.93*	17.93	2.81	19.44	Market Price Return%
	—	—	—	—	—	—	0.10	0.11	0.03	0.02	Avg Premium/Discount%
	—	—	—	—	—	—	14.95	7.02	-1.93	3.62	NAV Rtrn% +/-S&P 500
	—	—	—	—	—	—	14.95	1.41	-4.07	-2.84	NAV Rtrn% +/-Russ 1000 VI
	—	—	—	—	—	—	—	8	11	14	NAV Return% Rank in Cat
	—	—	—	—	—	—	—	3.59	3.05	3.68	Income Return %
	—	—	—	—	—	—	—	14.31	-0.07	15.73	Capital Return %
	—	—	—	—	—	—	0.29	1.91	1.85	2.22	Income $
	—	—	—	—	—	—	0.00	0.00	0.00	0.00	Capital Gains $
	—	—	—	—	—	—	—	0.40	0.40	0.40	Expense Ratio %
	—	—	—	—	—	—	—	3.43	3.39	3.35	Income Ratio %
	—	—	—	—	—	—	—	2	20	14	Turnover Rate %
	—	—	—	—	—	—	460	5,009	7,252	7,770	Net Assets $mil

Performance 12-31-06

Historic Quarterly NAV Returns

	1st Qtr	2nd Qtr	3rd Qtr	4th Qtr	Total
2002	—	—	—	—	—
2003	—	—	—	—	—*
2004	3.58	1.47	4.01	7.85	17.90
2005	-1.59	3.78	1.62	-0.78	2.98
2006	2.90	1.66	6.25	7.44	19.41

Trailing	NAV Return%	Market Return%	NAV Rtrn% +/-S&P 500	%Rank Cat.(NAV)
3 Mo	7.44	7.26	0.74	16
6 Mo	14.15	13.96	1.41	16
1 Yr	19.41	19.44	3.62	14
3 Yr Avg	13.18	13.14	2.74	8
5 Yr Avg	—	—	—	—
10 Yr Avg	—	—	—	—

Tax Analysis	Tax-Adj Return%	Tax-Cost Ratio
3 Yr (estimated)	11.91	1.12
5 Yr (estimated)	—	—
10 Yr (cstimated)	—	—

Rating and Risk

Time Period	Morningstar Rtn vs Cat	Morningstar Risk vs Cat	Morningstar Risk-Adj Rating
3 Yr	+Avg	Avg	★★★★
5 Yr	—	—	—
10 Yr	—	—	—

Other Measures	Standard Index S&P 500	Best Fit Index Russ 1000 VI
Alpha	4.1	0.0
Beta	0.76	0.85
R-Squared	63	74
Standard Deviation	6.64	
Mean	13.18	
Sharpe Ratio	1.43	

Portfolio Analysis 12-31-06

Share change since 11-06 Total Stocks:115	Sector	PE	Tot Ret%	% Assets
⊕ Altria Group, Inc.	Goods	15.9	19.87	4.12
⊕ Bank of America Corporat	Financial	12.4	20.68	3.12
⊕ Regions Financial Corpor	Financial	13.8	14.92	2.80
⊕ PNC Financial Services G	Financial	8.6	23.60	2.72
⊕ Pinnacle West Capital	Utilities	21.9	27.04	2.72
⊕ DTE Energy Holding Compa	Utilities	12.6	17.58	2.71
⊕ FPL Group	Utilities	17.7	35.49	2.69
⊕ FirstEnergy Corporation	Utilities	16.6	27.31	2.57
⊕ Merck & Co., Inc.	Health	18.8	42.66	2.49
⊕ AT&T, Inc.	Telecom	19.2	51.59	2.29
⊕ Kinder Morgan, Inc.	Energy	20.7	19.22	2.14
⊕ Comerica Incorporated	Financial	11.8	7.78	2.05
⊕ Unitrin, Inc.	Financial	11.2	15.59	2.02
⊕ Lincoln National Corp.	Financial	13.2	28.58	1.97
⊕ KeyCorp	Financial	13.0	21.03	1.92
⊕ Bristol-Myers Squibb Com	Health	23.3	19.93	1.69
⊕ National City Corporatio	Financial	12.2	13.67	1.67
⊕ Chevron Corporation	Energy	9.3	33.75	1.61
⊕ People's Bank	Financial	46.0	47.71	1.59
⊕ Nicor Inc.	Utilities	15.8	24.33	1.58

Current Investment Style

Value Blnd Growth — Large Mid Small

Market Cap	%
Giant	21.2
Large	32.3
Mid	39.5
Small	6.9
Micro	0.1

Avg $mil: 14,886

Value Measures		Rel Category
Price/Earnings	14.95	1.05
Price/Book	2.12	0.88
Price/Sales	1.21	0.91
Price/Cash Flow	9.36	1.21
Dividend Yield %	3.51	1.36

Growth Measures	%	Rel Category
Long-Term Erngs	8.16	0.81
Book Value	4.52	0.63
Sales	6.83	0.80
Cash Flow	-3.29	NMF
Historical Erngs	5.42	0.35

Profitability	%	Rel Category
Return on Equity	14.09	0.81
Return on Assets	9.06	0.91
Net Margin	14.81	1.08

Sector Weightings	% of Stocks	Rel S&P 500	3 Year High Low	
↻ Info	3.09	0.15		
🖥 Software	0.00	0.00	0	0
💻 Hardware	0.00	0.00	0	0
🎙 Media	0.53	0.14	1	0
☎ Telecom	2.56	0.73	4	2
☞ Service	49.61	1.07		
⚕ Health	5.73	0.48	6	1
Consumer	1.44	0.19	3	1
Business	1.31	0.31	3	1
$ Financial	41.13	1.85	45	37
⊐ Mfg	47.30	1.40		
Goods	10.86	1.27	12	10
Ind Mtrls	8.59	0.72	10	6
Energy	4.59	0.47	10	5
Utilities	23.26	6.65	23	20

Composition

● Cash	0.4	
● Stocks	99.6	
● Bonds	0.0	
● Other	0.0	
Foreign (% of Stock)	0.0	

Morningstar's Take by Dan Culloton 12-31-06

IShares Dow Jones Select Dividend Index is no longer the default choice for dividends.

This exchange-traded fund has competition. The ETF still offers exposure to a big basket of dividend-paying stocks as well as one of the highest yields among large-cap value index funds. That, plus the fact that is was the first dividend-focused ETF on the market, has helped it grow to more than $7 billion in assets.

Success hasn't spoiled this fund yet (its results have been competitive with other large-value and dividend-centric index funds), but it has raised challenges. Cheaper rivals have emerged. This ETF's 0.40% expense ratio is low compared with conventional actively managed funds, but higher than the typical large-value index fund and other, newer dividend-focused ETFs.

Not only are some of the newcomers, such as WisdomTree Total Dividend and Vanguard High Dividend Yield ETF, cheaper, but they also are more diversified. This ETF had more than 60% of its assets in financial and utility stocks in 2006, exposing it to considerable sector risk. WisdomTree and Vanguard's offerings spread their money across more stocks and sectors.

Finally, capacity could become an issue at this fund. This ETF's benchmark gives some small stocks with high yields a lot of weight. As the ETF has swelled in size it has had to buy bigger and bigger chunks of such companies. In late 2006 it owned more than 5% of the outstanding shares of Nicor, Universal, and Citizens Banking, and more than 4% of the outstanding shares of a few others, such as top five holding Pinnacle West. A low turnover index fund such as this does not have to worry as much as a more active fund does about affecting the prices of the stocks it owns as it moves in and out of them. Still, as the fund grows it could have a harder time establishing and maintaining positions in smaller high-yield stocks without some impact. You won't shoot an airball with this ETF, but it's no slam dunk, either.

Address:	45 Fremont Street	Management Fee:	0.40%		
	San Francisco CA 94105	Expense Projections:	3Yr:$128	5Yr:$224	10Yr:$505
	800-474-2737	Income Distrib:	Quarterly		
Web Address:	www.ishares.com	Exchange:	NYSE		
Inception:	11-03-03*				
Advisor:	Barclays Global Fund Advisers				

MORNINGSTAR® ETFs 150

iShares DJ US Energy IYE

			Market Price	Mstar Category
			$96.00	Specialty-Natural Res

Morningstar Fair Value

Price/Fair Value Ratio	Coverage Rate %
1.05 Fairly valued	99 Good

Morningstar Rating	Return	Risk	Yield	NAV	Avg Daily Vol. (k)	52 wk High/Low
★★★ Neutral	Neutral	Below Avg	1.1%	$101.85	106	$107.12 - $85.25

Management

Patrick O'Connor and S. Jane Leung lead the team that manage this and several other iShares ETFs fund. O'Connor has been on the team since the fund's inception and Leung since September 2006. Both have been with the ETF s advisor Barclays Global Investors for five or more years.

Methodology

This exchange-traded fund tracks a subset of the Dow Jones U.S. Total Market Index: The Dow Jones U.S. Oil & Gas Index. The bogy includes the oil- and gas-company stocks from the broader-market benchmark. The index includes more than 80 stocks, but this fund typically owns fewer than that because it uses representative sampling to track the benchmark. The fund is extremely concentrated, with most of its assets in its top holdings.

Growth of $10,000
— Investment Value of ETF
— Investment Value of Index S&P 500

Trading Volume Millions

	1997	1998	1999	2000	2001	2002	2003	2004	2005	2006	History
	—	—	—	54.63	47.56	39.57	49.46	64.30	85.52	101.85	NAV $
	—	—	—	54.97	47.70	39.41	49.45	64.30	85.76	101.85	Market Price $
	—	—	—	12.65*	-11.83	-15.47	27.12	31.72	34.29	20.47	NAV Return%
	—	—	—	12.65*	-12.12	-16.06	27.60	31.74	34.67	20.14	Market Price Return%
	—	—	—	0.31	0.30	0.08	0.15	0.07	0.07	0.01	Avg Premium/Discount%
	—	—	—	12.65	0.06	6.63	-1.56	20.84	29.38	4.68	NAV Rtrn% +/-S&P 500
	—	—	—	12.65	3.76	-2.21	-6.89	7.15	-2.19	3.65	NAV Rtrn% +/-GS NATR RES
	—	—	—	—	2	4	4	4	6	9	NAV Return% Rank in Cat
	—	—	—	—	1.14	1.46	1.86	1.54	1.24	1.26	Income Return %
	—	—	—	—	-12.97	-16.93	25.26	30.18	33.05	19.21	Capital Return %
	—	—	—	0.27	0.62	0.69	0.73	0.76	0.79	1.07	Income $
	—	—	—	0.00	0.00	0.00	0.00	0.00	0.00	0.00	Capital Gains $
	—	—	—	—	0.60	0.60	0.60	0.60	0.60	0.60	Expense Ratio %
	—	—	—	—	0.94	1.32	1.79	1.42	1.16	1.00	Income Ratio %
	—	—	—	—	20	18	9	2	3	2	Turnover Rate %
	—	—	—	41	74	105	223	498	812	901	Net Assets $mil

Performance 12-31-06

Historic Quarterly NAV Returns

	1st Qtr	2nd Qtr	3rd Qtr	4th Qtr	Total
2002	6.95	-8.97	-17.55	5.30	-15.47
2003	0.12	9.41	0.23	15.79	27.12
2004	5.84	7.74	11.74	3.37	31.72
2005	17.20	2.70	18.79	-6.07	34.29
2006	8.02	4.72	-3.29	10.13	20.47

Trailing	NAV Return%	Market Return%	NAV Rtrn% +/-S&P 500	%Rank Cat.(NAV)
3 Mo	10.13	10.08	3.43	21
6 Mo	6.50	6.28	-6.24	18
1 Yr	20.47	20.14	4.68	9
3 Yr Avg	28.69	28.69	18.25	4
5 Yr Avg	18.02	17.95	11.83	4
10 Yr Avg	—	—	—	—

Tax Analysis	Tax-Adj Return%	Tax-Cost Ratio
3 Yr (estimated)	28.17	0.40
5 Yr (estimated)	17.46	0.47
10 Yr (estimated)	—	—

Rating and Risk

Time Period	Morningstar Rtn vs Cat	Morningstar Risk vs Cat	Morningstar Risk-Adj Rating
3 Yr	Avg	-Avg	★★★
5 Yr	-Avg	-Avg	★★★
10 Yr	—	—	—

Other Measures	Standard Index S&P 500	Best Fit Index GS NATR RES
Alpha	17.4	3.0
Beta	0.94	0.97
R-Squared	11	93
Standard Deviation	19.10	
Mean	28.69	
Sharpe Ratio	1.25	

Morningstar's Take by Dan Culloton 12-31-06

IShares Dow Jones U.S. Energy Index has lowered its expense ratio, but not its risks.

This exchange-traded fund dropped its expense ratio by 20% to 0.48% in 2006. That's a substantial discount that makes it significantly less expensive than the typical conventional mutual fund in the natural-resources category. There remain, however, a few funds in this peer group with lower levies, such as the Energy SPDR and Vanguard Energy Index and its ETF share class.

Despite its improved competitive position, this still shouldn't be your first choice for energy stock exposure. It's one of the most concentrated funds retail investors can buy in the natural-resources category, stashing nearly 70% of its assets in its top 10 holdings. More than 50% of the fund's money resides in oil patch titans ExxonMobil and Chevron alone. Those are well-established, profitable companies with defensible market positions, but their shares and those of the rest of this fund's holdings still move in tandem with fickle

oil and gas prices. Due to its concentration and commodity links, this fund can be volatile. Its standard deviation, a measure of volatility, is lower than the category average, but the fund has shown it can lose money in a hurry. It has fallen in a third of the 26 calendar quarters since its mid-2000 inception, and that's during a period that has been generally favorable toward energy stocks.

This ETF has other shortcomings. It's hampered by its domestic focus: Some of the industry's biggest players, such as BP, Total, and Royal Dutch, are excluded because they are based on foreign shores. Energy stocks, like those in other sectors, are influenced more by their global industries than their home addresses. From that perspective, this ETF's sibling, iShares S&P Global Energy, is more attractive.

Before you consider that or any other energy fund, though, consider how much exposure you already have to the sector. Chances are you already have plenty.

Portfolio Analysis 12-31-06

Share change since 11-06 Total Stocks:74	Sector	PE	Tot Ret%	% Assets
⊕ ExxonMobil Corporation	Energy	11.7	39.07	24.59
⊕ Chevron Corporation	Energy	9.3	33.75	17.90
⊕ Schlumberger, Ltd.	Energy	24.0	31.07	6.01
⊕ ConocoPhillips	Energy	6.9	26.53	5.48
⊕ Occidental Petroleum Cor	Energy	8.6	24.32	4.34
⊕ Devon Energy Corporation	Energy	9.4	8.06	2.80
⊕ Baker Hughes Inc.	Energy	10.8	23.67	2.77
⊕ Marathon Oil Corporation	Energy	6.5	54.68	2.59
⊕ Valero Energy Corporatio	Energy	6.5	-0.33	2.33
⊕ Halliburton Company	Energy	12.0	1.11	2.25
⊕ Transocean, Inc.	Energy	29.3	16.07	2.12
⊕ Apache Corporation	Energy	7.9	-2.30	2.11
⊕ Anadarko Petroleum Corp.	Energy	5.5	-7.44	2.09
⊕ EOG Resources	Energy	10.1	-14.62	1.66
⊕ Hess Corporation	Ind Mtrls	7.8	19.01	1.35
⊕ Williams Companies, Inc.	Energy	65.3	14.41	1.28
⊕ Kinder Morgan, Inc.	Energy	20.7	19.22	1.21
⊕ Murphy Oil Corporation	Energy	13.6	-4.82	1.09
⊕ Weatherford Internationa	Energy	16.9	16.56	0.98
⊕ XTO Energy, Inc.	Energy	9.2	12.16	0.97

Current Investment Style

Value Blnd Growth — Large Mid Small

Market Cap	%
Giant	54.1
Large	32.5
Mid	12.9
Small	0.6
Micro	0.0
Avg $mil:	67,332

Value Measures		Rel Category
Price/Earnings	10.91	0.87
Price/Book	2.57	1.00
Price/Sales	0.97	0.71
Price/Cash Flow	6.72	0.93
Dividend Yield %	1.42	1.27

Growth Measures	%	Rel Category
Long-Term Erngs	11.19	0.78
Book Value	17.64	1.27
Sales	22.18	1.37
Cash Flow	29.03	0.97
Historical Erngs	48.64	0.97

Profitability	%	Rel Category
Return on Equity	27.78	1.20
Return on Assets	13.91	1.26
Net Margin	15.20	1.03

Industry Weightings	% of Stocks	Rel Cat
Oil & Gas	60.5	1.9
Oil/Gas Products	13.6	1.3
Oil & Gas Srv	22.9	0.8
Pipelines	2.9	2.8
Utilities	0.0	0.0
Hard Commd	0.1	0.0
Soft Commd	0.0	0.0
Misc. Indstrl	0.0	0.0
Other	0.0	0.0

Composition

● Cash	0.1	
● Stocks	99.9	
● Bonds	0.0	
○ Other	0.0	
Foreign	0.0	
(% of Stock)		

Address:	45 Fremont Street San Francisco CA 94105 800-474-2737	
Web Address:	www.ishares.com	
Inception:	06-12-00*	
Advisor:	Barclays Global Fund Advisers	

Management Fee:	0.48%		
Expense Projections:	3Yr:$154	5Yr:$269	10Yr:$604
Income Distrib:	Quarterly		
Exchange:	NYSE		

MORNINGSTAR® ETFs 150

iShares DJ Fin Sectr IYF

	Market Price	Mstar Category
	$117.27	Specialty-Financial

Morningstar Fair Value

Price/Fair Value Ratio	Coverage Rate %
0.92 Undervalued	94 Good

Management

Patrick O'Connor and Jane Leung of Barclays Global Fund Advisors lead the charge in running this and many other ETFs. IShares portfolio management group is responsible for billions in assets. Most of the managers have at least five or more years of experience with Barclays as well as prior industry experience.

Methodology

This exchange-traded fund tracks the Dow Jones U.S. Financials Index. The index covers only U.S.-based companies and is unlikely to encounter liquidity problems because it invests mainly in large- and mid-cap companies. It is market-capitalization weighted and is reconstituted on a quarterly basis.

Morningstar Rating	Return	Risk	Yield	NAV	Avg Daily Vol. (k)	52 wk High/Low
★★★ Neutral	Neutral	Average	1.9%	$117.80	21	$118.73 - $100.55

Growth of $10,000
- Investment Value of ETF
- Investment Value of Index S&P 500

Trading Volume Millions

	1997	1998	1999	2000	2001	2002	2003	2004	2005	2006	History
	—	—	—	87.00	79.79	68.44	88.24	97.66	101.16	117.80	NAV $
	—	—	—	87.00	80.49	68.21	88.04	97.68	101.09	117.67	Market Price $
	—	—	—	9.93*	-7.07	-12.81	31.37	12.74	5.82	18.79	NAV Return%
	—	—	—	9.91*	-6.25	-13.86	31.51	13.01	5.72	18.74	Market Price Return%
	—	—	—	0.56	0.01	0.06	-0.03	-0.03	-0.01	0.00	Avg Premium/Discount%
	—	—	—	9.93	4.82	9.29	2.69	1.86	0.91	3.00	NAV Rtrn% +/-S&P 500
	—	—	—	9.93	-0.69	-0.46	-0.86	-0.65	-0.64	-0.63	NAV Rtrn% +/-DJ Finance
	—	—	—	—	3	4	5	5	5	9	NAV Return% Rank in Cat
	—	—	—	—	1.20	1.50	2.15	1.95	2.12	2.18	Income Return %
	—	—	—	—	-8.27	-14.31	29.22	10.79	3.70	16.61	Capital Return %
	—	—	—	1.44	1.04	1.19	1.46	1.71	2.05	2.19	Income $
	—	—	—	0.39	0.00	0.00	0.00	0.00	0.00	0.00	Capital Gains $
	—	—	—	—	0.60	0.60	0.60	0.60	0.60	0.60	Expense Ratio %
	—	—	—	—	1.46	1.49	1.94	2.08	2.23	2.26	Income Ratio %
	—	—	—	—	11	4	28	7	7	6	Turnover Rate %
	—	—	—	22	96	140	229	303	389	548	Net Assets $mil

Performance 12-31-06

Historic Quarterly NAV Returns

	1st Qtr	2nd Qtr	3rd Qtr	4th Qtr	Total
2002	3.99	-6.49	-15.92	6.63	-12.81
2003	-4.76	17.93	4.60	11.81	31.37
2004	5.29	-2.63	1.08	8.78	12.74
2005	-6.58	4.99	0.59	7.26	5.82
2006	4.22	-0.56	7.29	6.83	18.79

Trailing	NAV Return%	Market Return%	NAV Rtrn% +/-S&P 500	%Rank Cat.(NAV)
3 Mo	6.83	6.65	0.13	14
6 Mo	14.62	14.32	1.88	13
1 Yr	18.79	18.74	3.00	9
3 Yr Avg	12.32	12.37	1.88	4
5 Yr Avg	10.17	9.95	3.98	4
10 Yr Avg	—	—	—	—

Tax Analysis	Tax-Adj Return%	Tax-Cost Ratio
3 Yr (estimated)	11.54	0.69
5 Yr (estimated)	9.43	0.67
10 Yr (estimated)	—	—

Rating and Risk

Time Period	Morningstar Rtn vs Cat	Morningstar Risk vs Cat	Morningstar Risk-Adj Rating
3 Yr	Avg	Avg	★★★
5 Yr	Avg	Avg	★★★
10 Yr	—	—	—

Other Measures	Standard Index S&P 500	Best Fit Index DJ Finance
Alpha	2.6	-0.6
Beta	0.89	1.00
R-Squared	54	100
Standard Deviation	8.33	
Mean	12.32	
Sharpe Ratio	1.06	

Morningstar's Take by Andrew Gunter 12-31-06

iShares Dow Jones U.S. Financial Sector ETF is a reasonable choice by most measures.

Investors considering a financial-services-focused ETF should first consider this statistic: The typical large-cap core offering benchmarked to the Russell 1000 or S&P 500 indexes already devotes more than 20% of assets to financial stocks alone. For good reason then, this sector's ETFs haven't been wildly popular (combined they hold barely more than $5 billion in assets); passive investors don't generally need such a fund.

But for those who follow the market closely and believe financial stocks are poised to rally, this ETF merits a second look. Its benchmark, the Dow Jones U.S. Financials Index, offers nice, mixed exposure to banks, insurers, and other, smaller industries within this vast sector. It allots about 45% of assets to banks, but that's reasonable given their place as the anchor of the sector. Insurance comes next, with about 22% of assets divided across various types of insurers, followed by general financial

institutions and real-estate companies.

This ETF also offers solid mid-cap exposure. Its index dedicates nearly 20% of assets to such fare, significantly more than the 7% exposure found in a similar ETF from State Street Global Advisors. To be sure, many midsize regional banks and thrifts are viewed as richly priced today, but we think the State Street ETF's $56 billion market cap ties its returns too closely to a select group of mega-caps such as Citigroup and American International Group.

That's not to say this ETF is perfect, however. If the banking industry stumbles, this fund won't escape the carnage. And a rival offering from Vanguard offers more exposure to small-cap stocks and has an expense ratio of just 0.26%. Still, as sector ETFs go, this offering should satisfy most investors' thirst for an extra dose of financials stocks.

Portfolio Analysis 12-31-06

Share change since 11-06 Total Stocks:310	Sector	PE	Tot Ret%	% Assets
⊕ Citigroup, Inc.	Financial	13.3	19.55	8.26
⊖ Bank of America Corporat	Financial	12.4	20.68	7.16
⊕ J.P. Morgan Chase & Co.	Financial	13.7	25.60	5.01
⊖ American International G	Financial	17.1	6.05	4.87
⊕ Wells Fargo Company	Financial	14.7	16.82	3.35
⊖ Wachovia Corporation	Financial	13.0	12.02	3.25
⊖ Merrill Lynch & Company,	Financial	14.1	39.27	2.45
⊖ Morgan Stanley	Financial	12.3	45.93	2.34
⊕ Goldman Sachs Group, Inc	Financial	12.1	57.41	2.16
⊕ American Express Company	Financial	21.2	19.09	1.95
⊖ US Bancorp	Financial	14.1	26.29	1.90
⊕ Fannie Mae	Financial	—	24.34	1.72
⊕ Freddie Mac	Financial	24.0	7.06	1.40
⊕ Washington Mutual, Inc.	Financial	13.5	9.62	1.28
⊖ Lehman Brothers Holdings	Financial	12.2	22.74	1.23
⊖ Prudential Financial, In	Financial	16.1	18.70	1.22
⊖ Allstate Corporation	Financial	8.7	23.38	1.21
⊕ St. Paul Travelers Compa	Financial	12.0	22.90	1.11
⊕ Capital One Financial Co	Financial	10.3	-10.97	0.94
⊖ SunTrust Banks, Inc.	Financial	14.4	19.81	0.89

Current Investment Style

Value Blnd Growth — Large / Mid / Small

Market Cap	%
Giant	44.4
Large	33.9
Mid	18.1
Small	3.5
Micro	0.0
Avg $mil:	35,995

Value Measures		Rel Category
Price/Earnings	13.43	0.99
Price/Book	2.15	1.05
Price/Sales	2.58	0.99
Price/Cash Flow	8.26	1.05
Dividend Yield %	2.55	1.10

Growth Measures	%	Rel Category
Long-Term Erngs	10.63	1.00
Book Value	6.54	0.81
Sales	6.88	0.90
Cash Flow	2.85	0.61
Historical Erngs	12.44	0.82

Profitability	%	Rel Category
Return on Equity	15.76	0.99
Return on Assets	15.23	1.10
Net Margin	21.97	1.03

Industry Weightings	% of Stocks	Rel Cat
Intl Banks	22.9	1.3
Banks	18.4	0.9
Real Estate	11.3	3.7
Sec Mgmt	13.3	1.1
S & Ls	3.6	0.5
Prop & Reins	13.8	0.8
Life Ins	5.3	1.0
Misc. Ins	2.6	0.8
Other	8.8	0.7

Composition

	%
Cash	0.0
Stocks	100.0
Bonds	0.0
Other	0.0
Foreign (% of Stock)	0.4

Address:	45 Fremont Street San Francisco CA 94105 800-474-2737
Web Address:	www.ishares.com
Inception:	05-22-00*
Advisor:	Barclays Global Fund Advisers

Management Fee:	0.48%		
Expense Projections:	3Yr:$154	5Yr:$269	10Yr:$604
Income Distrib:	Quarterly		
Exchange:	NYSE		

iShares DJ Fin Svcs IYG

Market Price	Mstar Category
$133.53	Specialty-Financial

Morningstar Fair Value

Price/Fair Value Ratio	Coverage Rate %
0.89 Undervalued	94 Good

Management

Patrick O'Connor and Jane Leung of Barclays Global Fund Advisors lead the charge in running this and many other ETFs. IShares portfolio management group is responsible for billions in assets. Most of the managers have at least five or more years of experience with Barclays as well as prior industry experience.

Methodology

This exchange-traded fund tracks the Dow Jones U.S. Financial Services Index. The index covers only U.S.-based companies, and its large-cap focus ensures that this ETF will run into few, if any, liquidity problems. The index draws its constituents from many industries, though it's tilted heavily toward the country's largest banks. It is market-capitalization weighted and is reconstituted on a quarterly basis.

	Morningstar Rating	Return	Risk	Yield	NAV	Avg Daily Vol. (k)	52 wk High/Low
★★★	Neutral	Neutral	Above Avg	1.9%	$133.75	102	$135.17 – $113.22

Growth of $10,000
— Investment Value of ETF
— Investment Value of Index S&P 500

Trading Volume Millions

1997	1998	1999	2000	2001	2002	2003	2004	2005	2006	History
—	—	—	98.46	91.01	78.33	103.02	112.97	114.38	133.75	NAV $
—	—	—	98.81	91.74	78.35	103.22	113.15	114.45	133.69	Market Price $
—	—	—	9.08*	-6.38	-12.41	34.04	11.92	3.45	19.32	NAV Return%
—	—	—	9.07*	-5.96	-13.09	34.26	11.88	3.35	19.19	Market Price Return%
—	—	—	0.06	0.05	0.05	0.08	0.04	0.06	0.06	Avg Premium/Discount%
—	—	—	9.08	5.51	9.69	5.36	1.04	-1.46	3.53	NAV Rtrn% +/-S&P 500
—	—	—	9.08	0.00	-0.06	1.81	-1.47	-3.01	-0.10	NAV Rtrn% +/-DJ Finance
—	—	—	—	3	4	5	5	5	9	NAV Return% Rank in Cat
—	—	—	—	1.16	1.62	2.22	2.12	2.09	2.22	Income Return %
—	—	—	—	-7.54	-14.03	31.82	9.80	1.36	17.10	Capital Return %
—	—	—	0.93	1.14	1.47	1.72	2.17	2.35	2.52	Income $
—	—	—	0.13	0.00	0.00	0.00	0.00	0.00	0.00	Capital Gains $
—	—	—	—	0.60	0.60	0.60	0.60	0.60	0.60	Expense Ratio %
—	—	—	—	1.33	1.46	1.90	2.08	2.20	2.29	Income Ratio %
—	—	—	—	5	3	41	7	7	9	Turnover Rate %
—	—	—	25	59	55	124	119	177	274	Net Assets $mil

Performance 12-31-06

Historic Quarterly NAV Returns

	1st Qtr	2nd Qtr	3rd Qtr	4th Qtr	Total
2002	4.94	-7.86	-15.85	7.64	-12.41
2003	-4.10	19.41	4.74	11.75	34.04
2004	4.21	-3.22	1.37	9.47	11.92
2005	-6.80	3.37	-1.00	8.46	3.45
2006	4.53	-0.07	7.43	6.32	19.32

Trailing	NAV Return%	Market Return%	NAV Rtrn% +/-S&P 500	%Rank Cat.(NAV)
3 Mo	6.32	6.26	-0.38	14
6 Mo	14.22	14.05	1.48	13
1 Yr	19.32	19.19	3.53	9
3 Yr Avg	11.37	11.28	0.93	4
5 Yr Avg	10.15	9.97	3.96	4
10 Yr Avg	—	—	—	—

Tax Analysis	Tax-Adj Return%	Tax-Cost Ratio
3 Yr (estimated)	10.57	0.72
5 Yr (estimated)	9.38	0.70
10 Yr (estimated)	—	—

Rating and Risk

Time Period	Morningstar Rtn vs Cat	Morningstar Risk vs Cat	Morningstar Risk-Adj Rating
3 Yr	Avg	Avg	★★★
5 Yr	Avg	+Avg	★★★
10 Yr	—	—	—

Other Measures	Standard Index S&P 500	Best Fit Index DJ Finance
Alpha	2.5	-1.5
Beta	0.78	1.00
R-Squared	38	93
Standard Deviation	8.71	
Mean	11.37	
Sharpe Ratio	0.92	

Portfolio Analysis 12-31-06

Share change since 11-06 Total Stocks:148	Sector	PE	Tot Ret%	% Assets
⊖ Citigroup, Inc.	Financial	13.3	19.55	12.34
⊖ Bank of America Corporat	Financial	12.4	20.68	10.70
⊖ J.P. Morgan Chase & Co.	Financial	13.7	25.60	7.48
⊖ Wells Fargo Company	Financial	14.7	16.82	5.00
⊖ Wachovia Corporation	Financial	13.0	12.02	4.85
⊖ Merrill Lynch & Company,	Financial	14.1	39.27	3.67
⊖ Morgan Stanley	Financial	12.3	45.93	3.50
⊖ Goldman Sachs Group, Inc	Financial	12.1	57.41	3.23
⊖ American Express Company	Financial	21.2	19.09	2.91
⊖ US Bancorp	Financial	14.1	26.29	2.83
⊖ Fannie Mae	Financial	—	24.34	2.56
⊖ Freddie Mac	Financial	24.0	7.06	2.09
⊖ Washington Mutual, Inc.	Financial	13.5	9.62	1.91
⊖ Lehman Brothers Holdings	Financial	12.2	22.74	1.85
⊖ Capital One Financial Co	Financial	10.3	-10.97	1.40
⊖ SunTrust Banks, Inc.	Financial	14.4	19.81	1.33
⊖ Bank of New York Company	Financial	18.8	26.85	1.32
⊖ Regions Financial Corpor	Financial	13.8	14.92	1.22
⊖ Countrywide Financial Co	Financial	9.8	26.22	1.17
⊖ BB&T Corporation	Financial	14.0	8.92	1.05

Current Investment Style

Value Blnd Growth — Large/Mid/Small

Market Cap	%
Giant	59.1
Large	27.6
Mid	10.4
Small	2.8
Micro	0.0

Avg $mil: 54,024

Value Measures		Rel Category
Price/Earnings	13.52	1.00
Price/Book	2.22	1.08
Price/Sales	3.42	1.32
Price/Cash Flow	7.79	0.99
Dividend Yield %	2.65	1.15

Growth Measures	%	Rel Category
Long-Term Erngs	10.77	1.01
Book Value	7.76	0.96
Sales	7.16	0.93
Cash Flow	1.41	0.30
Historical Erngs	12.39	0.81

Profitability	%	Rel Category
Return on Equity	17.51	1.11
Return on Assets	17.11	1.24
Net Margin	24.90	1.17

Industry Weightings	% of Stocks	Rel Cat
Intl Banks	34.5	1.9
Banks	27.8	1.3
Real Estate	0.0	0.0
Sec Mgmt	20.0	1.6
S & Ls	5.4	0.8
Prop & Reins	0.2	0.8
Life Ins	0.0	0.0
Misc. Ins	0.0	0.0
Other	12.1	0.9

Composition

● Cash	0.1	
● Stocks	99.9	
● Bonds	0.0	
Other	0.0	
Foreign	0.1	
(% of Stock)		

Morningstar's Take by Andrew Gunter 12-31-06

IShares Dow Jones US Financial Services is caught in no-man's land.

First, we should note that most investors' diversified portfolios already get plenty of exposure to financial-services companies. The firms comprise the S&P 500 Index's largest constituent sector at about 21% of assets, and large-cap core funds typically invest heavily in them. But as strictly opportunistic plays, we understand how investors might want to use a niche exchange-traded fund covering U.S. financials firms. These funds allow investors who follow broader market trends to tilt their portfolio a bit toward their predicted market sweet spot.

Investors should be aware, however, of what this ETF buys. Its bogy, the Dow Jones U.S. Financial Services Index, actually forces the ETF to invest nearly twice as many assets in banking stocks as in all the sector's other industries combined. Ultimately, that outsized bet on banks amounts to a sink-or-swim proposition for investors

based on just one industry. Indeed, the fund's 10 biggest holdings are a who's who among U.S. global and super-regional banks: Citigroup and Bank of America both represent more than 10% of assets each, and several others aren't far behind.

This ETF isn't an industry-specific one either, though, so it's not a pure play on large, domestically based banks. The fund will no doubt suffer when bank stocks are down, but when they're rallying, it could still get dragged down by its positions in brokers, asset managers, and insurers. Its index allots about 33% of assets to such companies, whose stocks don't necessarily move in lock step with those of banks. The fund isn't well diversified in its sector, and yet its positions in nonbanking firms could ruin an otherwise good industry bet.

The financial-services sector has so many industries that we think it's worth investors' time to understand the nuances of each of its ETFs. We don't like what we see here.

Address:	45 Fremont Street	Management Fee:	0.48%		
	San Francisco CA 94105	Expense Projections:	3Yr:$154	5Yr:$269	10Yr:$604
	800-474-2737	Income Distrib:	Quarterly		
Web Address:	www.ishares.com	Exchange:	NYSE		
Inception:	06-12-00*				
Advisor:	Barclays Global Fund Advisers				

MORNINGSTAR® ETFs 150

iShares DJ Health IYH

	Market Price	**Mstar Category**
	$66.89	Specialty-Health

Morningstar Fair Value

Price/Fair Value Ratio	Coverage Rate %
0.93 Undervalued	94 Good

Management

Barclays Global Investors runs this fund. It is the world's largest advisor of indexed assets. It also is the sponsor of the world's largest ETF family. Patrick O'Connor, the head of Barclay's U.S. iShares portfolio management group leads a team of a half dozen managers in running this and 57 other ETFs.

Methodology

This exchange-traded fund tracks a subset of the Dow Jones U.S. Total Market Index that includes the health-care stocks in that broad market benchmark. That usually includes nearly 200 companies. Still, the fund's bogy is market-cap weighted and extremely concentrated, with most of its assets in its top holdings. The free-float-adjusted, market-capitalization-weighted index is rebalanced quarterly.

Morningstar Rating	**Return**	**Risk**	**Yield**	**NAV**	**Avg Daily Vol. (k)**	**52 wk High/Low**
★★★ Neutral	Neutral	Below Avg	0.9%	$66.42	149	$67.17 - $58.85

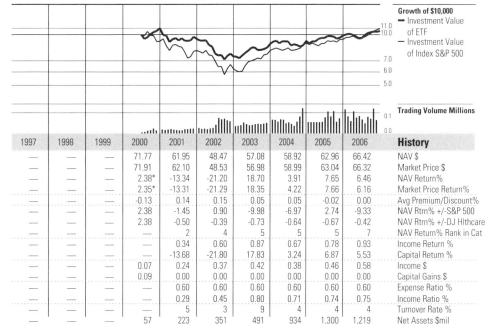

Growth of $10,000
— Investment Value of ETF
— Investment Value of Index S&P 500

Trading Volume Millions

History	1997	1998	1999	2000	2001	2002	2003	2004	2005	2006
NAV $	—	—	—	71.77	61.95	48.47	57.08	58.92	62.96	66.42
Market Price $	—	—	—	71.91	62.10	48.53	56.98	58.99	63.04	66.32
NAV Return%	—	—	—	2.38*	-13.34	-21.20	18.70	3.91	7.65	6.46
Market Price Return%	—	—	—	2.35*	-13.31	-21.29	18.35	4.22	7.66	6.16
Avg Premium/Discount%	—	—	—	-0.13	0.14	0.15	0.05	0.05	-0.02	0.00
NAV Rtrn% +/-S&P 500	—	—	—	2.38	-1.45	0.90	-9.98	-6.97	2.74	-9.33
NAV Rtrn% +/-DJ Hlthcare	—	—	—	2.38	-0.50	-0.39	-0.73	-0.64	-0.67	-0.42
NAV Return% Rank in Cat	—	—	—	—	2	4	5	5	5	7
Income Return %	—	—	—	—	0.34	0.60	0.87	0.67	0.78	0.93
Capital Return %	—	—	—	—	-13.68	-21.80	17.83	3.24	6.87	5.53
Income $	—	—	—	0.07	0.24	0.37	0.42	0.37	0.46	0.58
Capital Gains $	—	—	—	0.09	0.00	0.00	0.00	0.00	0.00	0.00
Expense Ratio %	—	—	—	—	0.60	0.60	0.60	0.60	0.60	0.60
Income Ratio %	—	—	—	—	0.29	0.45	0.80	0.71	0.74	0.75
Turnover Rate %	—	—	—	—	5	3	9	4	4	4
Net Assets $mil	—	—	—	57	223	351	491	934	1,300	1,219

Performance 12-31-06

Historic Quarterly NAV Returns

	1st Qtr	2nd Qtr	3rd Qtr	4th Qtr	Total
2002	-1.80	-16.70	-7.65	4.30	-21.20
2003	1.29	11.23	-3.05	8.67	18.70
2004	0.67	2.53	-4.78	5.73	3.91
2005	-0.62	4.85	1.84	1.44	7.65
2006	1.37	-4.91	8.71	1.59	6.46

Trailing	NAV Return%	Market Return%	NAV Rtrn% +/-S&P 500	%Rank Cat.(NAV)
3 Mo	1.59	1.46	-5.11	14
6 Mo	10.44	10.24	-2.30	13
1 Yr	6.46	6.16	-9.33	7
3 Yr Avg	6.00	6.00	-4.44	4
5 Yr Avg	2.18	2.10	-4.01	4
10 Yr Avg	—	—	—	—

Tax Analysis	Tax-Adj Return%	Tax-Cost Ratio
3 Yr (estimated)	5.71	0.27
5 Yr (estimated)	1.90	0.27
10 Yr (estimated)	—	—

Rating and Risk

Time Period	Morningstar Rtn vs Cat	Morningstar Risk vs Cat	Morningstar Risk-Adj Rating
3 Yr	-Avg	-Avg	★★★
5 Yr	Avg	-Avg	★★★
10 Yr	—	—	—

Other Measures	Standard Index S&P 500	Best Fit Index DJ Hlthcare
Alpha	-1.4	-0.5
Beta	0.62	1.00
R-Squared	26	100
Standard Deviation	8.34	
Mean	6.00	
Sharpe Ratio	0.36	

Morningstar's Take by Christopher Davis 12-31-06

IShares Dow Jones U.S. Healthcare isn't awful, but ultimately it's not the best choice.

Like most exchange-traded funds, this offering gets a huge leg up from low costs. At 0.48% annually, its expense ratio is less than a third of the health-care category norm. Still, among ETFs, it's not the cheapest option. Rival Vanguard Health Care ETF is the leader in that respect, with a skimpy 0.26% annual price tag.

The fund, which tracks all the health-care stocks in the Dow Jones U.S. Total Stock Market Index, has some advantages over other health-care ETFs. It's a bit less concentrated in larger names than iShares S&P Global Healthcare, for instance. The fund's mid-cap stake, at 17% of assets, is twice that of its iShares sibling. And it's a touch more diversified by industry, with a bit less in drug stocks and more in biotech.

While comparing favorably to some rivals, the fund still suffers from the same pitfalls as most sector-focused ETFs. For one, the portfolio is heavily weighted in its largest holdings--the top 10 stocks account for 55% of assets. There's nothing wrong with concentration, but the biggest names include big pharma firms such as Pfizer and Johnson & Johnson, widely owned companies that investors likely own if they have diversified portfolios. These drug stocks also make up a disproportionate share of the fund's holdings. Indeed, they make up half of the portfolio's assets, 60% above the health-care category norm. That means the fund will likely lead the way when pharma rallies, but it's not well suited to make a broad bet on health care. Finally, because the fund's bogy only includes U.S.-based firms, it has no exposure to foreign drug companies. With the health-care industry becoming increasingly global, that's a big flaw.

All in all, we think investors who want a health-care fund are better off with active management. Affordable mutual-fund options like T. Rowe Price Health Sciences would be a better choice.

Address:	45 Fremont Street San Francisco CA 94105 800-474-2737
Web Address:	www.ishares.com
Inception:	06-12-00*
Advisor:	Barclays Global Fund Advisers

Management Fee:	0.48%		
Expense Projections:	3Yr:$154	5Yr:$269	10Yr:$604
Income Distrib:	Quarterly		
Exchange:	NYSE		

Portfolio Analysis 12-31-06

Share change since 11-06 Total Stocks:160	Sector	PE	Tot Ret%	% Assets
⊖ Johnson & Johnson	Health	17.4	12.44	11.06
⊖ Pfizer Inc.	Health	15.1	15.22	10.79
⊖ Merck & Co., Inc.	Health	18.8	42.66	5.48
⊖ Amgen, Inc.	Health	28.0	-13.38	4.60
⊖ Abbott Laboratories	Health	23.6	26.88	4.33
⊖ UnitedHealth Group, Inc.	Health	21.0	-13.49	4.18
⊖ Wyeth	Health	17.0	12.88	3.92
⊖ Medtronic, Inc.	Health	23.7	-6.29	3.57
⊖ Bristol-Myers Squibb Com	Health	23.3	19.93	2.97
⊖ Eli Lilly & Company	Health	17.4	-5.16	2.91
⊖ WellPoint, Inc.	Health	17.2	-1.38	2.82
⊖ Genentech, Inc.	Health	47.2	-12.29	2.17
⊖ Schering-Plough Corporat	Health	36.9	14.63	2.01
⊖ Baxter International Inc	Health	24.0	24.81	1.76
⊖ Gilead Sciences, Inc.	Health	41.1	23.51	1.71
⊖ Caremark RX, Inc.	Health	23.8	10.89	1.41
⊖ Boston Scientific Corpor	Health	—	-29.85	1.35
⊖ Aetna, Inc.	Health	14.6	-8.34	1.30
⊕ Celgene Corporation	Health	—	77.56	1.24
⊖ Zimmer Holdings, Inc.	Health	24.6	16.22	1.09

Current Investment Style

Value Blend Growth — Large Mid Small

	Market Cap	%
	Giant	53.0
	Large	26.3
	Mid	16.6
	Small	3.7
	Micro	0.3
	Avg $mil:	37,547

Value Measures		Rel Category
Price/Earnings	18.97	0.92
Price/Book	3.55	1.00
Price/Sales	2.35	0.79
Price/Cash Flow	16.15	1.10
Dividend Yield %	1.35	1.34

Growth Measures	%	Rel Category
Long-Term Erngs	12.25	0.86
Book Value	11.75	1.48
Sales	10.80	0.90
Cash Flow	2.75	0.24
Historical Erngs	11.15	0.75

Profitability	%	Rel Category
Return on Equity	18.57	1.31
Return on Assets	9.68	1.67
Net Margin	14.51	1.28

Industry Weightings	% of Stocks	Rel Cat
Biotech	16.0	0.5
Drugs	49.1	1.6
Mgd Care	13.1	1.2
Hospitals	1.2	1.0
Other HC Srv	1.2	0.8
Diagnostics	1.5	1.1
Equipment	16.3	1.2
Good/Srv	1.5	0.4
Other	0.1	0.0

Composition

		%
●	Cash	0.1
●	Stocks	99.9
●	Bonds	0.0
	Other	0.0
	Foreign	0.0
	(% of Stock)	

iShares DJ RE Index IYR

	Market Price	Mstar Category
	$83.50	Specialty-Real Estate

Morningstar Fair Value

Price/Fair Value Ratio	Coverage Rate %
1.21 Overvalued	89 Good

Management

Patrick O'Connor and S. Jane Leung lead the team that manages this and several other iShares ETFs. O'Connor has been on the team since the fund's inception and Leung since September 2006. Both have been with the ETF's advisor, Barclays Global Investors, for five or more years.

Methodology

This fund tracks the Dow Jones U.S. Real Estate Index, which includes the REITs and the real estate operating and holding companies in the Dow Jones U.S. Financials Index. It is market-cap-weighted and adjusted for insider ownership, cross ownership, and other factors that could limit the number of stock shares that actually trade. The fund's advisor uses representative sampling to mirror the benchmark's return, which means the offering owns most but not every single stock in the index.

Morningstar Rating	Return	Risk	Yield	NAV	Avg Daily Vol. (k)	52 wk High/Low
★★ Below Avg	Below Avg	Above Avg	3.4%	$83.83	1,973	$86.85 - $66.92

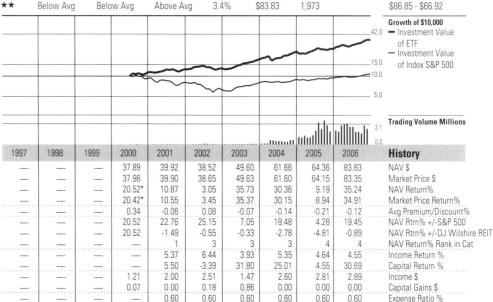

Growth of $10,000
— Investment Value of ETF
— Investment Value of Index S&P 500

Trading Volume Millions

	1997	1998	1999	2000	2001	2002	2003	2004	2005	2006	History
	—	—	—	37.89	39.92	38.52	49.60	61.66	64.36	83.83	NAV $
	—	—	—	37.98	39.90	38.65	49.63	61.60	64.15	83.35	Market Price $
	—	—	—	20.52*	10.87	3.05	35.73	30.36	9.19	35.24	NAV Return%
	—	—	—	20.42*	10.55	3.45	35.37	30.15	8.94	34.91	Market Price Return%
	—	—	—	0.34	-0.06	0.08	-0.07	-0.14	-0.21	-0.12	Avg Premium/Discount%
	—	—	—	20.52	22.76	25.15	7.05	19.48	4.28	19.45	NAV Rtrn% +/-S&P 500
	—	—	—	20.52	-1.49	-0.55	-0.33	-2.78	-4.81	-0.89	NAV Rtrn% +/-DJ Wilshire REIT
	—	—	—	—	1	3	3	3	4	4	NAV Return% Rank in Cat
	—	—	—	—	5.37	6.44	3.93	5.35	4.64	4.55	Income Return %
	—	—	—	—	5.50	-3.39	31.80	25.01	4.55	30.69	Capital Return %
	—	—	—	1.21	2.00	2.51	1.47	2.60	2.81	2.89	Income $
	—	—	—	0.07	0.18	0.18	0.86	0.00	0.00	0.00	Capital Gains $
	—	—	—	—	0.60	0.60	0.60	0.60	0.60	0.60	Expense Ratio %
	—	—	—	—	6.37	5.97	6.40	5.58	5.35	3.92	Income Ratio %
	—	—	—	—	30	10	21	20	16	19	Turnover Rate %
	—	—	—	38	96	166	382	1,295	1,046	1,714	Net Assets $mil

Performance 12-31-06

Historic Quarterly NAV Returns

	1st Qtr	2nd Qtr	3rd Qtr	4th Qtr	Total
2002	7.99	4.36	-9.07	0.55	3.05
2003	0.15	12.66	9.20	10.17	35.73
2004	12.02	-6.57	8.25	15.05	30.36
2005	-7.71	14.28	1.93	1.57	9.19
2006	14.83	-1.51	8.68	10.03	35.24

Trailing	NAV Return%	Market Return%	NAV Rtrn% +/-S&P 500	%Rank Cat.(NAV)
3 Mo	10.03	9.45	3.33	5
6 Mo	19.58	19.60	6.84	5
1 Yr	35.24	34.91	19.45	4
3 Yr Avg	24.40	24.13	13.96	3
5 Yr Avg	21.91	21.78	15.72	3
10 Yr Avg	—	—	—	—

Tax Analysis	Tax-Adj Return%	Tax-Cost Ratio
3 Yr (estimated)	22.53	1.50
5 Yr (estimated)	19.97	1.59
10 Yr (estimated)	—	—

Rating and Risk

Time Period	Morningstar Rtn vs Cat	Morningstar Risk vs Cat	Morningstar Risk-Adj Rating
3 Yr	Avg	+Avg	★★
5 Yr	-Avg	+Avg	★★
10 Yr	—	—	—

Other Measures	Standard Index S&P 500	Best Fit Index DJ Wilshire REIT
Alpha	11.0	-1.8
Beta	1.30	0.97
R-Squared	30	99
Standard Deviation	16.36	
Mean	24.40	
Sharpe Ratio	1.23	

Morningstar's Take by Dan Culloton 12-31-06

Don't lose your head.

The iShares Dow Jones U.S. Real Estate Index has enjoyed a terrific run in absolute terms. As 2006 drew to a close, it was on pace for better than a 30% annual return. Its five-year annualized gain looked strong, too, though it lagged that of the typical conventional mutual fund in the real estate category.

Real estate funds like this one have been defying predictions of slower returns for years. So, it's tempting to shrug off warnings and project the sector's strong returns into the future. That would be a mistake, though. It will be hard for these offerings to duplicate what they have done over the past six years. Not only do these funds look richly valued according to Morningstar equity analysts (more than half of this fund's holdings were trading above their fair value estimates at the end of December), but also according to other measures. Average valuations--such as price/earnings--for this portfolio were higher than those of the broad

domestic stock market. This fund's yield also offers no more compensation to investors than less-risky 10-year Treasury issues.

That said, there are strong arguments for making a long-term strategic allocation to real estate, and this fund has attributes that make it a good candidate for such a role. The fund, which tracks an index of REITs and real estate operating and holding companies in the Dow Jones U.S. Financials Index, is well-diversified for a sector fund. It also lowered its expense ratio from 0.60% to 0.48% in 2006, making it more attractive.

Nevertheless, there are cheaper index options in the category that can be bought without a brokerage commission, namely Vanguard REIT Index. The Vanguard option looks particularly attractive relative to this one because, given the risks in the sector, it's a better idea to dollar cost average into it, and the commission costs you pay to buy ETFs would eat into your long-term results. Those costs will sting more when the sector cools.

Address:	45 Fremont Street San Francisco CA 94105 800-474-2737	Management Fee:	0.48%
Web Address:	www.ishares.com	Expense Projections:	3Yr:$154 5Yr:$269 10Yr:$604
Inception:	06-12-00*	Income Distrib:	Quarterly
Advisor:	Barclays Global Fund Advisers	Exchange:	NYSE

Portfolio Analysis 12-31-06

Share change since 11-06 Total Stocks:86	Sector	PE	Tot Ret%	% Assets
⊖ Simon Property Group, In	Financial	59.2	36.97	5.88
⊖ Equity Office Properties	Financial	—	64.28	4.89
⊖ Vornado Realty Trust	Financial	38.2	51.13	4.26
⊖ ProLogis Trust	Financial	34.3	34.02	4.00
⊖ Equity Residential	Financial	NMF	34.64	3.90
⊖ Archstone-Smith Trust	Financial	60.0	43.93	3.43
⊖ Boston Properties, Inc.	Financial	15.1	62.75	3.42
⊖ Public Storage, Inc.	Financial	46.2	47.46	3.39
⊖ General Growth Propertie	Financial	—	15.09	3.22
⊖ Host Hotels & Resorts, I	Financial	53.4	33.95	3.20
⊖ Kimco Realty Corporation	Financial	30.8	44.91	2.62
⊖ AvalonBay Communities, I	Financial	67.7	49.69	2.60
⊖ Plum Creek Timber Compan	Financial	23.6	15.65	1.96
⊖ Realogy Corporation	Financial	—	—	1.91
⊖ Developers Diversified R	Financial	41.1	39.65	1.90
⊖ CB Richard Ellis Group,	Financial	30.3	69.24	1.68
⊖ Macerich Company	Financial	—	33.91	1.66
⊖ Apartment Investment & M	Financial	—	55.18	1.62
⊖ SL Green Realty Corporat	Financial	58.2	77.73	1.56
⊖ Duke Realty Corporation	Financial	75.7	28.98	1.55

Current Investment Style

Value Blnd Growth — Large Mid Small

	Market Cap	%
	Giant	0.0
	Large	40.8
	Mid	52.3
	Small	6.9
	Micro	0.0

Avg $mil: 6,885

Value Measures		Rel Category
Price/Earnings	19.01	1.10
Price/Book	3.08	1.10
Price/Sales	3.56	0.94
Price/Cash Flow	17.10	1.05
Dividend Yield %	3.68	1.13

Growth Measures	%	Rel Category
Long-Term Erngs	7.02	0.90
Book Value	-1.17	NMF
Sales	10.29	0.89
Cash Flow	0.61	0.08
Historical Erngs	4.90	0.51

Profitability	%	Rel Category
Return on Equity	11.46	0.80
Return on Assets	9.82	0.88
Net Margin	24.01	1.08

Sector Weightings	% of Stocks	Rel S&P 500	3 Year High Low	
↻ Info	0.00	0.00		
🖪 Software	0.00	0.00	0	0
🖥 Hardware	0.00	0.00	0	0
🎤 Media	0.00	0.00	0	0
📱 Telecom	0.00	0.00	0	0
☞ Service	99.70	2.16		
🩺 Health	0.00	0.00	0	0
🛒 Consumer	0.00	0.00	0	0
💼 Business	0.00	0.00	0	0
💲 Financial	99.70	4.48	100	96
🏭 Mfg	0.30	0.01		
📦 Goods	0.00	0.00	0	0
⚙ Ind Mtrls	0.30	0.03	4	0
🔋 Energy	0.00	0.00	0	0
💡 Utilities	0.00	0.00	0	0

Composition

	%
● Cash	0.1
● Stocks	99.9
● Bonds	0.0
● Other	0.0
Foreign (% of Stock)	1.2

MORNINGSTAR® ETFs 150

iShares DJ Tech IYW

	Market Price	Mstar Category
	$55.65	Specialty-Technology

Morningstar Fair Value

Price/Fair Value Ratio	Coverage Rate %
0.84 Undervalued	95 Good

Management

Patrick O'Connor and S. Jane Leung lead the team that manages this and several other iShares ETFs. O'Connor has been on the team since the fund's inception and Leung since September 2006. Both have been with the ETF's advisor, Barclays Global Investors, for five or more years.

Methodology

This exchange-traded fund tracks a subset of the Dow Jones U.S. Total Market Index that includes the technology stocks in that broad market benchmark. That usually amounts to the shares of about 260 companies. The fund's bogy is market-cap weighted, so it's still concentrated on its top holdings.

Morningstar Rating	Return	Risk	Yield	NAV	Avg Daily Vol. (k)	52 wk High/Low
★★★ Neutral	Neutral	Average	0.1%	$54.43	323	$56.10 - $43.91

Growth of $10,000
- Investment Value of ETF
- Investment Value of Index S&P 500

Trading Volume Millions

	1997	1998	1999	2000	2001	2002	2003	2004	2005	2006	History
	—	—	—	74.57	53.15	32.41	48.66	48.52	49.76	54.43	NAV $
	—	—	—	74.56	53.20	32.50	48.51	48.46	49.72	54.45	Market Price $
	—	—	—	-10.62*	-28.72	-39.02	50.14	1.15	2.72	9.56	NAV Return%
	—	—	—	-10.61*	-28.65	-38.91	49.26	1.34	2.77	9.68	Market Price Return%
	—	—	—	0.44	0.30	0.21	0.04	0.04	-0.06	0.01	Avg Premium/Discount%
	—	—	—	-10.62	-16.83	-16.92	21.46	-9.73	-2.19	-6.23	NAV Rtrn% +/-S&P 500
	—	—	—	-10.62	-13.13	-5.69	-2.00	-10.58	-4.64	4.88	NAV Rtrn% +/-ArcaEx Tech 100
	—	—	—		4	8	8	8	9	14	NAV Return% Rank in Cat
	—	—	—	—	0.00	0.00	0.00	1.43	0.15	0.15	Income Return %
	—	—	—	—	-28.72	-39.02	50.14	-0.28	2.57	9.41	Capital Return %
	—	—	—	0.00	0.00	0.00	0.00	0.70	0.07	0.08	Income $
	—	—	—	0.00	0.00	0.00	0.00	0.00	0.00	0.00	Capital Gains $
	—	—	—	—	0.60	0.60	0.60	0.60	0.60	0.60	Expense Ratio %
	—	—	—	—	-0.47	-0.41	-0.22	-0.22	1.78	-0.04	Income Ratio %
	—	—	—	—	11	8	15	5	9	7	Turnover Rate %
	—	—	—	112	154	152	363	468	513	678	Net Assets $mil

Performance 12-31-06

Historic Quarterly NAV Returns

	1st Qtr	2nd Qtr	3rd Qtr	4th Qtr	Total
2002	-6.85	-27.25	-26.68	22.72	-39.02
2003	-0.31	19.56	11.39	13.08	50.14
2004	-2.63	1.67	-10.75	14.49	1.15
2005	-7.54	2.22	6.33	2.22	2.72
2006	4.94	-9.12	8.24	6.13	9.56

Trailing	NAV Return%	Market Return%	NAV Rtrn% +/-S&P 500	%Rank Cat.(NAV)
3 Mo	6.13	6.06	-0.57	18
6 Mo	14.88	14.80	2.14	18
1 Yr	9.56	9.68	-6.23	14
3 Yr Avg	4.41	4.53	-6.03	8
5 Yr Avg	0.83	0.82	-5.36	8
10 Yr Avg	—	—	—	

Tax Analysis	Tax-Adj Return%	Tax-Cost Ratio
3 Yr (estimated)	4.20	0.20
5 Yr (estimated)	0.71	0.12
10 Yr (estimated)	—	—

Rating and Risk

Time Period	Morningstar Rtn vs Cat	Morningstar Risk vs Cat	Morningstar Risk-Adj Rating
3 Yr	Avg	-Avg	★★★
5 Yr	Avg	Avg	★★★
10 Yr	—	—	—

Other Measures	Standard Index S&P 500	Best Fit Index ArcaEx Tech 100
Alpha	-11.2	-3.4
Beta	1.93	1.07
R-Squared	72	92
Standard Deviation	15.60	
Mean	4.41	
Sharpe Ratio	0.15	

Morningstar's Take by Dan Culloton 12-31-06

This exchange-traded fund is better, but not yet the best.

The iShares Dow Jones U.S. Technology Index helped its case considerably in 2006 by getting cheaper. Its expense ratio dropped from 0.60% to 0.48%, which is dramatically lower than the typical conventional tech mutual fund. The ETF is still not the lowest-cost option for broad tech-sector exposure. Technology Select Sector SPDRs and Vanguard Information Technology ETF are both much cheaper.

Yet this fund has advantages over at least one of its more affordable rivals. The ETF, which tracks tech stocks in the Dow Jones U.S. Total Market Index, owns more stocks than the Technology Select Sector SPDR and doesn't mix in telecom service providers, such as AT&T, like the SPDR does. That gives investors in this offering a straighter shot of hardware and software stocks.

The diversification doesn't dull this ETF's edge, though. It's one of the more concentrated technology index funds with more than 55% of its assets in its top 10 holdings. Microsoft and Cisco Systems take up more than a third of the ETF's assets alone. That leaves the portfolio more reliant on large-cap tech bellwethers than most funds in this category. Such a stance could prove to be a boon if large-cap tech stocks, which have been out of favor in recent years, regain the market's favor, but it also can be a drag when such issues are on the outs. Indeed there appears to be some upside here. Many of the fund's big holdings, including Microsoft, Dell, and EMC, were trading below Morningstar equity analysts' estimates of their worth at the end of December. The same could be said of more diversified options, such as Vanguard Information Technology ETF, though.

So while this ETF offers investors relatively cheap, easy, and pure exposure to technology stocks (many of which look undervalued), there are cheaper and more diversified options.

Address:	45 Fremont Street San Francisco CA 94105 800-474-2737
Web Address:	www.ishares.com
Inception:	05-15-00*
Advisor:	Barclays Global Fund Advisers

Management Fee:	0.48%		
Expense Projections:	3Yr:$154	5Yr:$269	10Yr:$604
Income Distrib:	Quarterly		
Exchange:	NYSE		

Portfolio Analysis 12-31-06

Share change since 11-06 Total Stocks:221

	Sector	PE	Tot Ret%	% Assets
⊖ Microsoft Corporation	Software	23.7	15.83	12.69
⊖ Cisco Systems, Inc.	Hardware	28.8	59.64	8.07
⊖ IBM	Hardware	16.8	19.77	7.10
⊖ Intel Corporation	Hardware	20.3	-17.18	5.72
⊖ Hewlett-Packard Company	Hardware	18.9	45.21	5.48
⊖ Google, Inc.	Business	58.6	11.00	4.99
⊖ Apple Computer, Inc.	Hardware	37.4	18.01	3.49
⊖ Oracle Corporation	Software	25.6	40.38	3.35
⊖ Qualcomm, Inc.	Hardware	26.2	-11.32	3.03
⊖ Dell, Inc.	Hardware	17.7	-16.23	2.44
⊖ Motorola, Inc.	Hardware	13.0	-8.17	2.41
⊖ Texas Instruments, Inc.	Hardware	16.8	-9.82	2.07
⊖ Yahoo, Inc.	Media	32.3	-34.81	1.60
⊖ Corning Inc.	Hardware	25.6	-4.83	1.42
⊖ EMC Corporation	Hardware	30.7	-3.08	1.41
⊖ Applied Materials	Hardware	19.0	3.89	1.24
⊖ Adobe Systems Inc.	Software	49.0	11.26	1.15
⊖ Symantec Corporation	Software	49.6	19.14	0.95
⊖ Sun Microsystems, Inc.	Hardware	—	29.36	0.92
⊖ Xerox Corporation	Ind Mtrls	13.4	15.70	0.79

Current Investment Style

Value Blnd Growth — Large Mid Small

	Market Cap	%
	Giant	56.4
	Large	20.2
	Mid	18.1
	Small	4.6
	Micro	0.6
	Avg $mil:	43,007

Value Measures		Rel Category
Price/Earnings	21.74	0.87
Price/Book	3.67	1.16
Price/Sales	2.42	0.90
Price/Cash Flow	11.33	1.08
Dividend Yield %	0.71	1.13

Growth Measures	%	Rel Category
Long-Term Erngs	14.35	0.95
Book Value	5.36	0.77
Sales	10.22	1.09
Cash Flow	14.95	0.77
Historical Erngs	25.59	0.83

Profitability	%	Rel Category
Return on Equity	20.98	1.23
Return on Assets	11.74	1.23
Net Margin	16.43	1.18

Industry Weightings	% of Stocks	Rel Cat
Software	24.2	1.1
Hardware	23.9	2.1
Networking Eq	11.1	1.5
Semis	17.4	1.0
Semi Equip	3.2	0.7
Comp/Data Sv	5.8	0.6
Telecom	1.5	0.5
Health Care	0.0	0.0
Other	13.0	0.7

Composition

	%
● Cash	0.1
● Stocks	99.9
● Bonds	0.0
● Other	0.0
Foreign	0.0
(% of Stock)	

iShares DJ Telecom IYZ

	Market Price	Mstar Category
	$29.01	Specialty-Communications

Morningstar Fair Value

Price/Fair Value Ratio	Coverage Rate %
1.00 Fairly valued	88 Good

Management

Patrick O'Connor and S. Jane Leung lead the team that manages this and several other iShares ETFs. O'Connor has been on the team since the fund's inception and Leung since September 2006. Both have been with the ETF's advisor, Barclays Global Investors, for five or more years.

Methodology

This exchange-traded fund tracks a subset of the Dow Jones U.S. Total Market Index that includes the telecom service provider stocks in that broad market benchmark. That usually amounts to the shares of fewer than two dozen companies. The fund's bogy is market-cap weighted and extremely concentrated, with most of its assets in its top holdings.

Morningstar Rating	Return	Risk	Yield	NAV	Avg Daily Vol. (k)	52 wk High/Low
★★★ Neutral	Neutral	Below Avg	2.0%	$29.62	380	$29.66 - $23.11

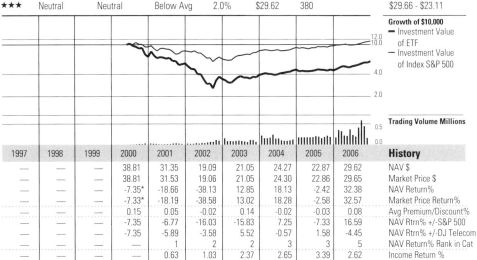

Growth of $10,000
■ Investment Value of ETF
— Investment Value of Index S&P 500

Trading Volume Millions

	1997	1998	1999	2000	2001	2002	2003	2004	2005	2006	History
	—	—	—	38.81	31.35	19.09	21.05	24.27	22.87	29.62	NAV $
	—	—	—	38.81	31.53	19.06	21.05	24.30	22.86	29.65	Market Price $
	—	—	—	-7.35*	-18.66	-38.13	12.85	18.13	-2.42	32.38	NAV Return%
	—	—	—	-7.33*	-18.19	-38.58	13.02	18.28	-2.58	32.57	Market Price Return%
	—	—	—	0.15	0.05	-0.02	0.14	-0.02	-0.03	0.08	Avg Premium/Discount%
	—	—	—	-7.35	-6.77	-16.03	-15.83	7.25	-7.33	16.59	NAV Rtrn% +/-S&P 500
	—	—	—	-7.35	-5.89	-3.58	5.52	-0.57	1.58	-4.45	NAV Rtrn% +/-DJ Telecom
	—	—	—	—	1	2	2	3	3	5	NAV Return% Rank in Cat
	—	—	—	—	0.63	1.03	2.37	2.65	3.39	2.62	Income Return %
	—	—	—	—	-19.29	-39.16	10.48	15.48	-5.81	29.76	Capital Return %
	—	—	—	0.22	0.24	0.32	0.45	0.55	0.81	0.59	Income $
	—	—	—	0.59	0.00	0.00	0.00	0.00	0.00	0.00	Capital Gains $
	—	—	—	—	0.60	0.60	0.60	0.60	0.60	0.60	Expense Ratio %
	—	—	—	—	0.80	1.05	2.27	2.27	2.97	3.63	Income Ratio %
	—	—	—	—	43	43	23	22	10	25	Turnover Rate %
	—	—	—	45	58	104	144	352	497	948	Net Assets $mil

Performance 12-31-06

Historic Quarterly NAV Returns

	1st Qtr	2nd Qtr	3rd Qtr	4th Qtr	Total
2002	-16.22	-27.17	-24.69	34.65	-38.13
2003	-10.86	22.40	-7.32	11.60	12.85
2004	3.35	-1.26	7.17	8.01	18.13
2005	-4.98	2.71	1.50	-1.49	-2.42
2006	13.54	-0.58	8.80	7.78	32.38

Trailing	NAV Return%	Market Return%	NAV Rtrn% +/-S&P 500	%Rank Cat.(NAV)
3 Mo	7.78	7.69	1.08	6
6 Mo	17.27	17.02	4.53	5
1 Yr	32.38	32.57	16.59	5
3 Yr Avg	15.13	15.17	4.69	2
5 Yr Avg	1.28	1.18	-4.91	2
10 Yr Avg	—	—	—	—

Tax Analysis	Tax-Adj Return%	Tax-Cost Ratio
3 Yr (estimated)	14.05	0.94
5 Yr (estimated)	0.42	0.85
10 Yr (estimated)	—	—

Rating and Risk

Time Period	Morningstar Rtn vs Cat	Morningstar Risk vs Cat	Morningstar Risk-Adj Rating
3 Yr	-Avg	Low	★★★
5 Yr	-Avg	-Avg	★★★
10 Yr	—	—	—

Other Measures	Standard Index S&P 500	Best Fit Index DJ Telecom
Alpha	6.3	1.4
Beta	0.72	0.82
R-Squared	31	93
Standard Deviation	8.89	
Mean	15.13	
Sharpe Ratio	1.28	

Portfolio Analysis 12-31-06

Share change since 11-06 Total Stocks:25	Sector	PE	Tot Ret%	% Assets
⊕ AT&T, Inc.	Telecom	19.2	51.59	22.70
⊕ Verizon Communications	Telecom	16.1	34.88	18.80
⊕ Sprint Nextel Corporatio	Telecom	29.1	-10.44	7.89
⊕ Alltel Corp.	Telecom	17.6	19.54	5.09
⊕ BellSouth Corporation	Telecom			4.95
⊕ Centurytel, Inc.	Telecom	14.4	32.52	4.38
⊕ NII Holdings, Inc.	Telecom	47.0	47.53	4.24
⊕ Qwest Communications Int	Telecom	—	48.14	3.93
⊖ BCE Inc.	Telecom	15.0	19.09	2.95
⊕ Citizens Communications	Telecom	17.1	26.56	2.80
⊕ Embarq Corporation	Telecom	—	—	2.77
⊕ United States Cellular C	Telecom	36.8	40.87	2.73
⊕ Telephone and Data Syste	Telecom	20.2	52.10	2.66
⊕ Leucadia National Corpor	Ind Mtrls	57.0	19.92	2.47
⊕ Telephone and Data Syste	Telecom	—	—	2.29
⊕ NTL, Inc.	Telecom	—	6.08	2.18
⊕ American Tower Corporati	Telecom	—	37.56	1.17
⊕ Windstream Corporation	Telecom	—	37.36	1.14
⊕ Level 3 Communications,	Telecom	—	95.12	0.96
⊕ Leap Wireless Internatio	Telecom	79.3	57.00	0.91

Current Investment Style

Value Blnd Growth — Large Mid Small

Market Cap	%
Giant	48.4
Large	19.7
Mid	30.4
Small	1.5
Micro	0.0

Avg $mil: 33,623

Value Measures		Rel Category
Price/Earnings	14.10	0.81
Price/Book	1.35	0.74
Price/Sales	1.76	1.02
Price/Cash Flow	5.88	0.80
Dividend Yield %	2.76	0.98

Growth Measures	%	Rel Category
Long-Term Erngs	7.95	0.82
Book Value	19.47	1.86
Sales	2.63	0.71
Cash Flow	4.98	1.00
Historical Erngs	12.26	1.10

Profitability	%	Rel Category
Return on Equity	11.61	0.83
Return on Assets	3.82	0.74
Net Margin	8.40	1.11

Industry Weightings	% of Stocks	Rel Cat
Telecom Srv	71.4	2.1
Wireless Srv	25.7	0.9
Network Eq	0.0	0.0
Semis	0.0	0.0
Big Media	0.0	0.0
Cable TV	0.0	0.0
Other Media	0.0	0.0
Soft/Hardwr	0.0	0.0
Other	2.9	0.3

Composition

● Cash	0.2
● Stocks	99.8
● Bonds	0.0
● Other	0.0
Foreign	3.0
(% of Stock)	

Morningstar's Take by Dan Culloton 12-31-06

A lower expense ratio doesn't lift this exchange-traded fund's appeal.

The iShares Dow Jones Telecom Index got cheaper in 2006, but not cheap enough. The fund's expense ratio dropped from 0.60% to 0.48%, making it one of the lowest-cost options in a category that can get expensive (the average conventional mutual fund's levy in this area approaches 1.5%). That is a big improvement and extends this ETF's low-cost advantage over the vast majority of its peers. It still is not the cheapest index fund in its peer group, though. That distinction goes to Vanguard Telecom Services ETF.

Neither of the funds, however, is very attractive. They both track concentrated indexes. This one's bogy has little more than two dozen stocks and stores a huge helping of its assets in its top two holdings--AT&T and Verizon Communications. When the market smiles on those stocks, as it did in 2006, it smiles on this fund, too. The ETF's heavily reliance on a couple of holdings, though,

leaves it vulnerable to wide performance swings over short periods. It has lost money in about half of the rolling three-month periods since its 2000 inception.

The fund is coming off a year of very strong performance, but that may be more of a reason to be cautious. Few of the ETF's holdings are attractively priced, according Morningstar equity analysts. Most were trading at or above their fair value estimates at the end of December, including large holdings, such as AT&T and NII Holdings. And telecom stocks are the kinds of investments that need a healthy margin of safety because they strive in highly competitive, rapidly changing industries that can require heavy capital spending. Indeed, some of the average quality measures of this portfolio, such as debt/capital ratio and returns on assets and equity, look worse than the category average and the broad market overall.

There is too much issue, price, and business risk here for this fund to be attractive.

Address:	45 Fremont Street San Francisco CA 94105 800-474-2737	
Web Address:	www.ishares.com	
Inception:	05-22-00*	
Advisor:	Barclays Global Fund Advisers	

Management Fee:	0.48%		
Expense Projections:	3Yr:$154	5Yr:$269	10Yr:$604
Income Distrib:	Quarterly		
Exchange:	NYSE		

MORNINGSTAR® ETFs 150

iShares DJ Total Mkt IYY

Market Price $68.50	**Mstar Category** Large Blend	

Morningstar Fair Value

Price/Fair Value Ratio	Coverage Rate %
0.92 Undervalued	93 Good

Management

Patrick O'Connor and S. Jane Leung lead the team that manages this and several other iShares ETFs. O'Connor has been on the team since the fund's inception and Leung since September 2006. Both have been with the ETF's advisor, Barclays Global Investors, for five or more years.

Methodology

This fund tracks the Dow Jones U.S. Total Market Index, which includes about 95% of the domestic-stock market capitalization. It is market-cap-weighted and adjusted for insider ownership, cross ownership, and other factors that could limit the number of stock shares that actually trade. The fund's advisor uses representative sampling to mirror the benchmark's return, which means the offering owns most, but not every, stock in the index.

Morningstar Rating ★★★★ Above Avg	Return Above Avg	Risk Above Avg	Yield 1.5%	NAV $68.72	Avg Daily Vol. (k) 26	52 wk High/Low $69.51 - $59.56

Growth of $10,000
- Investment Value of ETF
- Investment Value of Index S&P 500

Trading Volume Millions

1997	1998	1999	2000	2001	2002	2003	2004	2005	2006	History
—	—	—	61.42	53.39	41.00	52.71	57.94	60.53	68.72	NAV $
—	—	—	61.53	53.57	41.02	52.71	58.00	60.51	68.69	Market Price $
—	—	—	1.75*	-12.13	-22.17	30.42	11.78	6.14	15.31	NAV Return%
—	—	—	1.75*	-11.99	-22.40	30.36	11.90	6.00	15.30	Market Price Return%
—	—	—	0.13	0.02	0.10	0.12	0.04	0.01	-0.02	Avg Premium/Discount%
—	—	—	1.75	-0.24	-0.07	1.74	0.90	1.23	-0.48	NAV Rtrn% +/-S&P 500
—	—	—	1.75	0.32	-0.52	0.53	0.38	-0.13	-0.15	NAV Rtrn% +/-Russ 1000
—	—	—	—	12	14	14	16	21	30	NAV Return% Rank in Cat
—	—	—	—	0.94	1.13	1.64	1.76	1.63	1.67	Income Return %
—	—	—	—	-13.07	-23.30	28.78	10.02	4.51	13.64	Capital Return %
—	—	—	0.24	0.57	0.60	0.67	0.92	0.94	1.01	Income $
—	—	—	0.01	0.00	0.00	0.00	0.00	0.00	0.00	Capital Gains $
—	—	—	—	0.20	0.20	0.20	0.20	0.20	0.20	Expense Ratio %
—	—	—	—	0.98	1.15	1.57	1.49	1.81	1.63	Income Ratio %
—	—	—	—	5	5	14	5	6	5	Turnover Rate %
—	—	—	37	104	143	335	435	472	539	Net Assets $mil

Performance 12-31-06

Historic Quarterly NAV Returns

	1st Qtr	2nd Qtr	3rd Qtr	4th Qtr	Total
2002	0.37	-13.57	-17.07	8.18	-22.17
2003	-3.09	16.12	3.16	12.35	30.42
2004	2.15	1.46	-1.93	9.98	11.78
2005	-2.12	2.10	3.92	2.20	6.14
2006	4.95	-1.83	4.71	6.89	15.31

Trailing	NAV Return%	Market Return%	NAV Rtrn% +/-S&P 500	%Rank Cat.(NAV)
3 Mo	6.89	6.92	0.19	44
6 Mo	11.93	11.61	-0.81	38
1 Yr	15.31	15.30	-0.48	30
3 Yr Avg	11.01	11.00	0.57	15
5 Yr Avg	6.79	6.71	0.60	13
10 Yr Avg	—	—	—	—

Tax Analysis	Tax-Adj Return%	Tax-Cost Ratio
3 Yr (estimated)	10.39	0.56
5 Yr (estimated)	6.21	0.54
10 Yr (estimated)	—	—

Rating and Risk

Time Period	Morningstar Rtn vs Cat	Morningstar Risk vs Cat	Morningstar Risk-Adj Rating
3 Yr	+Avg	Avg	★★★★
5 Yr	+Avg	+Avg	★★★★
10 Yr	—	—	—

Other Measures	Standard Index S&P 500	Best Fit Index Russ 1000
Alpha	0.0	-0.3
Beta	1.08	1.04
R-Squared	99	100
Standard Deviation	7.48	
Mean	11.01	
Sharpe Ratio	1.02	

Portfolio Analysis 12-31-06

Share change since 11-06 Total Stocks:1632

Sector	PE	Tot Ret%	% Assets
ExxonMobil Corporation	Energy	11.7	39.07	2.95
General Electric Company	Ind Mtrls	19.8	9.35	2.55
Citigroup, Inc.	Financial	13.3	19.55	1.83
Microsoft Corporation	Software	23.7	15.83	1.73
Bank of America Corporat	Financial	12.4	20.68	1.59
Procter & Gamble Company	Goods	24.2	13.36	1.35
Johnson & Johnson	Health	17.4	12.44	1.26
Pfizer Inc.	Health	15.1	15.22	1.23
Altria Group, Inc.	Goods	15.9	19.87	1.17
J.P. Morgan Chase & Co.	Financial	13.7	25.60	1.11
Cisco Systems, Inc.	Hardware	28.8	59.64	1.10
American International G	Financial	17.1	6.05	1.08
Chevron Corporation	Energy	9.3	33.75	1.07
IBM	Hardware	16.8	19.77	0.97
AT&T, Inc.	Telecom	19.2	51.59	0.91
Wal-Mart Stores, Inc.	Consumer	16.6	0.13	0.79
Intel Corporation	Hardware	20.3	-17.18	0.78
Hewlett-Packard Company	Hardware	18.9	45.21	0.75
Wells Fargo Company	Financial	14.7	16.82	0.74
ConocoPhillips	Energy	6.9	26.53	0.73

Current Investment Style

Value Blnd Growth — Large Mid Small

Market Cap	%
Giant	42.6
Large	32.8
Mid	20.4
Small	4.1
Micro	0.2

Avg $mil: 33,361

Value Measures		Rel Category
Price/Earnings	16.21	0.98
Price/Book	2.66	0.97
Price/Sales	1.47	1.16
Price/Cash Flow	9.17	0.97
Dividend Yield %	1.70	0.95

Growth Measures	%	Rel Category
Long-Term Erngs	11.64	1.01
Book Value	8.56	1.00
Sales	5.48	0.66
Cash Flow	10.84	1.43
Historical Erngs	17.58	1.05

Profitability	%	Rel Category
Return on Equity	18.99	0.99
Return on Assets	10.52	1.09
Net Margin	13.83	1.24

Sector Weightings	% of Stocks	Rel S&P 500	3 Year High	Low
↻ Info	19.58	0.98		
Software	3.55	1.03	4	3
Hardware	9.05	0.98	12	9
Media	3.57	0.94	4	4
Telecom	3.41	0.97	3	3
⊆ Service	47.49	1.03		
Health	11.96	0.99	14	12
Consumer	8.22	1.07	9	8
Business	5.34	1.26	6	4
Financial	21.97	0.99	22	20
Mfg	32.92	0.97		
Goods	8.02	0.94	9	8
Ind Mtrls	11.66	0.98	12	11
Energy	9.56	0.98	10	6
Utilities	3.68	1.05	4	3

Composition

Cash	0.1
Stocks	99.9
Bonds	0.0
Other	0.0
Foreign (% of Stock)	0.2

Morningstar's Take by Dan Culloton 12-31-06

This fund has most of what you need in a core holding, but it still shouldn't be your first choice.

IShares Dow Jones Total Market Index has a number of appealing traits: It offers broad exposure to the domestic stock market in one swoop for a low price relative to conventional core stock options. It's diversified across stocks and sectors, so it's unlikely to be any more volatile than the market. Turnover is extremely low, which keeps down transaction and tax costs, though there is little to worry about on the latter front with this fund due to its tax-efficient ETF structure. The fund has never distributed a capital gain, but it has paid out some income. A team of experienced indexers also runs this ETF. It has faithfully mimicked its index, the Dow Jones Total Market Index, trailing the benchmark's returns by no more than its expense ratio on an annualized basis since inception--a sign of capable management.

Nevertheless, this fund isn't the best option for one main reason: Expenses. Sure, this ETF's expense ratio is much cheaper than the vast majority of conventional large-blend funds. But it is not the cheapest. While competitive with rivals such as streetTRACKS Total Market ETF, this ETF's expense ratio of 0.20% is nearly three times that of the lowest-cost options: Vanguard Total Stock Market ETF and one share class of conventional mutual fund Fidelity Spartan Total Market (which can be bought without a commission).

Why split hairs? Because the best predictor of long-term outperformance among index funds that track similar benchmarks (and there is not that much difference among total stock market indexes) is usually the size of their expense ratios. Indeed over the last five years, the annualized returns of this ETF have trailed those of the cheaper Vanguard Total Stock Market ETF (though they have been better than the category average).

This fund can get the job done, but if you want the biggest bang for your buck, consider some of the less-expensive options first.

Address:	45 Fremont Street San Francisco CA 94105 800-474-2737
Web Address:	www.ishares.com
Inception:	06-12-00*
Advisor:	Barclays Global Fund Advisers

Management Fee:	0.20%		
Expense Projections:	3Yr:$64	5Yr:$113	10Yr:$255
Income Distrib:	Quarterly		
Exchange:	NYSE		

iShares DJ Utilities IDU

| | Market Price $88.40 | Mstar Category Specialty-Utilities |

Morningstar Fair Value

Price/Fair Value Ratio	Coverage Rate %
1.03 Fairly valued	94 Good

Management

Patrick O'Connor and S. Jane Leung lead the team that manages this and several other iShares ETFs. O'Connor has been on the team since the fund's inception and Leung since September 2006. Both have been with the ETF's advisor Barclays Global Investors for five or more years.

Methodology

This fund tracks the Dow Jones U.S. Utilities Index, which includes the power, gas, water, and other utility stocks from the Dow Jones U.S. Total Market Index. It's market-cap-weighted and adjusted for insider ownership, cross ownership, and other factors that could limit the number of stock shares that actually trade. The fund's advisor uses representative sampling to mirror the benchmark's return, which means the offering owns most, but not all, the stocks in the index.

| Morningstar Rating ★★★ Neutral | Return Neutral | Risk Average | Yield 2.5% | NAV $89.82 | Avg Daily Vol. (k) 28 | 52 wk High/Low $91.33 - $74.13 |

Growth of $10,000
- Investment Value of ETF
- Investment Value of Index S&P 500

Trading Volume Millions

	1997	1998	1999	2000	2001	2002	2003	2004	2005	2006	History
	—	—	—	88.90	63.58	47.95	57.47	68.66	76.47	89.82	NAV $
	—	—	—	88.78	63.97	48.06	57.59	68.70	76.46	89.87	Market Price $
	—	—	—	7.21*	-26.42	-21.62	24.11	23.26	14.63	20.71	NAV Return%
	—	—	—	7.22*	-25.87	-21.92	24.08	23.07	14.54	20.79	Market Price Return%
	—	—	—	0.15	-0.05	0.11	0.04	-0.02	-0.04	0.02	Avg Premium/Discount%
	—	—	—	7.21	-14.53	0.48	-4.57	12.38	9.72	4.92	NAV Rtrn% +/-S&P 500
	—	—	—	7.21	-0.15	1.76	-5.28	-6.98	-10.51	4.08	NAV Rtrn% +/-DOWJNS UTIL
	—	—	—	—	2	2	2	2	3	5	NAV Return% Rank in Cat
	—	—	—	—	2.32	3.29	3.81	3.42	3.22	2.94	Income Return %
	—	—	—	—	-28.74	-24.91	20.30	19.84	11.41	17.77	Capital Return %
	—	—	—	1.12	2.05	2.07	1.80	1.94	2.19	2.23	Income $
	—	—	—	0.14	0.00	0.00	0.00	0.00	0.00	0.00	Capital Gains $
	—	—	—	—	0.60	0.60	0.60	0.60	0.60	0.60	Expense Ratio %
	—	—	—	—	2.59	2.89	4.15	3.41	3.10	2.82	Income Ratio %
	—	—	—	—	11	8	15	7	7	5	Turnover Rate %
	—	—	—	36	73	276	486	560	704	786	Net Assets $mil

Performance 12-31-06

Historic Quarterly NAV Returns

	1st Qtr	2nd Qtr	3rd Qtr	4th Qtr	Total
2002	4.54	-10.20	-20.04	4.42	-21.62
2003	-3.68	19.33	-0.24	8.24	24.11
2004	5.01	-1.00	6.00	11.85	23.26
2005	4.62	9.24	6.88	-6.16	14.63
2006	-0.51	5.31	5.54	9.15	20.71

Trailing	NAV Return%	Market Return%	NAV Rtrn% +/-S&P 500	%Rank Cat.(NAV)
3 Mo	9.15	9.09	2.45	7
6 Mo	15.20	15.19	2.46	5
1 Yr	20.71	20.79	4.92	5
3 Yr Avg	19.48	19.41	9.04	2
5 Yr Avg	10.66	10.53	4.47	2
10 Yr Avg	—	—	—	—

Tax Analysis	Tax-Adj Return%	Tax-Cost Ratio
3 Yr (estimated)	18.27	1.01
5 Yr (estimated)	9.39	1.15
10 Yr (estimated)	—	—

Rating and Risk

Time Period	Morningstar Rtn vs Cat	Morningstar Risk vs Cat	Morningstar Risk-Adj Rating
3 Yr	Avg	+Avg	★★★
5 Yr	Avg	Avg	★★★
10 Yr	—	—	—

Other Measures	Standard Index S&P 500	Best Fit Index DOWJNS UTIL
Alpha	12.5	-0.1
Beta	0.37	0.80
R-Squared	8	88
Standard Deviation	8.68	
Mean	19.48	
Sharpe Ratio	1.73	

Morningstar's Take by Dan Culloton 12-31-06

This exchange-traded fund still looks pricey.

The iShares Dow Jones Utilities Index is far cheaper than the average conventional sector mutual fund. The ETF dropped its expense ratio from 0.60% to 0.48% in 2006, giving it an even larger expense advantage over its traditional peers. This fund is still not the cheapest utilities ETF, though. The expense ratios for the Utilities Select Sector SPDR and Vanguard Utilities ETF still are about 45% lower than this fund's levy.

This ETF also is riskier than it may appear. The fund owns more than 70 utilities stocks culled from the Dow Jones U.S. Total Market Index. But the offering also is concentrated with 30% of its assets in its top five holdings. It also is more focused on electric utilities than the average conventional utilities fund. This ETF keeps more than 85% of its money in electricity providers. Meanwhile the average traditional utilities fund devotes more than a fifth of its money to telecom stocks.

There can be a cost associated with that divergence. For most of 2006, this ETF lagged far behind the typical conventional utilities fund as telecom stocks such as AT&T and Verizon rallied. The fund's five-year annualized trailing returns of more than 11% through Dec. 22, 2006, are strong on an absolute basis, but average among peers.

Furthermore, this fund's holdings didn't look very compelling from a valuation perspective at year-end. After three years of double-digit returns, the average utility stock is no bargain. Some of this portfolio's average valuation measures, such as price/prospective earnings, were above the category average and higher than those of the S&P 500 in December 2006. According to Morningstar's equity analysts, most of the ETF's holdings were trading at or above their fair value estimates, including TXU, whose stock looks pricey despite slipping in 2006's fourth quarter. There's not much of an upside or a margin of safety here.

Address:	45 Fremont Street San Francisco CA 94105 800-474-2737
Web Address:	www.ishares.com
Inception:	06-12-00*
Advisor:	Barclays Global Fund Advisers

Management Fee:	0.48%		
Expense Projections:	3Yr:$154	5Yr:$269	10Yr:$604
Income Distrib:	Quarterly		
Exchange:	NYSE		

Portfolio Analysis 12-31-06

Share change since 11-06 Total Stocks:75

	Sector	PE	Tot Ret%	% Assets
⊖ Duke Energy Corporation	Utilities	14.6	30.15	7.30
⊖ Exelon Corporation	Utilities	—	19.78	7.27
⊖ Dominion Resources, Inc.	Utilities	18.3	12.56	5.18
⊖ Southern Company	Utilities	17.8	11.69	4.80
⊖ TXU Corporation	Utilities	13.0	11.19	4.38
⊖ FPL Group	Utilities	17.7	35.49	3.54
⊖ FirstEnergy Corporation	Utilities	16.6	27.31	3.37
⊖ Entergy Corporation	Utilities	19.9	38.40	3.36
⊖ American Electric Power	Utilities	18.6	19.58	2.94
⊖ Public Service Enterpris	Utilities	21.4	5.72	2.92
⊖ PG & E Corporation	Utilities	16.8	31.58	2.86
⊖ AES Corporation	Utilities	35.0	39.23	2.53
⊖ PPL Corporation	Utilities	15.4	26.06	2.39
⊖ Edison International	Utilities	13.5	7.02	2.38
⊖ Sempra Energy	Utilities	10.9	28.10	2.25
⊖ Progress Energy, Inc.	Utilities	16.7	18.07	2.16
⊕ Consolidated Edison Comp	Utilities	17.5	9.14	2.16
⊖ Constellation Energy Gro	Utilities	17.4	22.70	2.15
⊖ Ameren Corporation	Utilities	21.3	10.14	1.92
⊖ Xcel Energy, Inc.	Utilities	17.0	30.53	1.62

Current Investment Style

Value Blnd Growth — Large Mid Small

Market Cap	%
Giant	0.0
Large	66.0
Mid	30.3
Small	3.7
Micro	0.0

Avg $mil: 12,543

Value Measures		Rel Category
Price/Earnings	17.29	0.98
Price/Book	2.18	1.00
Price/Sales	1.20	0.94
Price/Cash Flow	11.41	1.14
Dividend Yield %	2.94	0.92

Growth Measures	%	Rel Category
Long-Term Erngs	7.23	0.88
Book Value	1.96	0.57
Sales	7.02	1.50
Cash Flow	-12.74	NMF
Historical Erngs	4.97	0.68

Profitability	%	Rel Category
Return on Equity	10.84	0.86
Return on Assets	3.09	0.85
Net Margin	7.72	0.92

Industry Weightings	% of Stocks	Rel Cat
Telecom Srv	0.0	0.0
Electric Utls	85.5	1.4
Nat Gas Utls	10.2	1.1
Wireless Srv	0.0	0.0
Energy	3.4	0.4
Media	0.0	0.0
Network Eq	0.0	0.0
Water	0.6	0.9
Other	0.3	0.1

Composition

	%
Cash	0.2
Stocks	99.8
Bonds	0.0
Other	0.0
Foreign	0.0
(% of Stock)	

Morningstar® ETFs 150

iShares FTSE/Xinhua China FXI

	Market Price	Mstar Category
	$104.20	Pacific/Asia ex-Japan Stk

Morningstar Fair Value

Price/Fair Value Ratio — Coverage Rate % —

Management

The fund is managed by Barclays Global Investors, one of the world's largest and most experienced managers of index-tracking portfolios.

Methodology

This fund tracks the FTSE/Xinhua China 25 Index. The bogy tracks the stocks of 25 large and liquid Chinese companies whose shares trade on the Hong Kong Stock Exchange and are available to international investors (some share classes of Chinese companies restrict foreign investment). The index is rebalanced quarterly.

Morningstar Rating	Return	Risk	Yield	NAV	Avg Daily Vol. (k)	52 wk High/Low
— Not Rated	— Not Rated	— Not Rated	1.2%	$111.14	1,247	$116.40 - $66.00

Growth of $10,000
- Investment Value of ETF
- Investment Value of Index MSCI EAFE

Trading Volume Millions

	1997	1998	1999	2000	2001	2002	2003	2004	2005	2006	History
	—	—	—	—	—	—	—	54.91	61.44	111.14	NAV $
	—	—	—	—	—	—	—	55.47	61.62	111.45	Market Price $
	—	—	—	—	—	—	—	40.58*	14.15	83.19	NAV Return%
	—	—	—	—	—	—	—	41.38*	13.31	83.17	Market Price Return%
	—	—	—	—	—	—	—	0.65	0.44	0.48	Avg Premium/Discount%
	—	—	—	—	—	—	—	40.58	0.61	56.85	NAV Rtrn% +/-MSCI EAFE
	—	—	—	—	—	—	—	40.58	-3.71	54.72	NAV Rtrn% +/-MSCIAC FExJ
	—	—	—	—	—	—	—	—	9	9	NAV Return% Rank in Cat
	—	—	—	—	—	—	—	—	2.28	2.12	Income Return %
	—	—	—	—	—	—	—	—	11.87	81.07	Capital Return %
	—	—	—	—	—	—	—	0.00	1.25	1.31	Income $
	—	—	—	—	—	—	—	0.00	0.00	0.00	Capital Gains $
	—	—	—	—	—	—	—	—	0.74	0.74	Expense Ratio %
	—	—	—	—	—	—	—	—	2.97	2.62	Income Ratio %
	—	—	—	—	—	—	—	—	13	45	Turnover Rate %
	—	—	—	—	—	—	—	568	1,352	5,696	Net Assets $mil

Performance 12-31-06

Historic Quarterly NAV Returns

	1st Qtr	2nd Qtr	3rd Qtr	4th Qtr	Total
2002	—	—	—	—	—
2003	—	—	—	—	—*
2004	—	—	—	—	—*
2005	-0.97	5.42	11.53	-1.97	14.15
2006	19.94	3.61	6.51	38.41	83.19

Trailing	NAV Return%	Market Return%	NAV Rtrn% +/-MSCI EAFE	%Rank Cat.(NAV)
3 Mo	38.41	38.74	28.06	9
6 Mo	47.42	46.96	32.73	9
1 Yr	83.19	83.17	56.85	9
3 Yr Avg	—	—	—	—
5 Yr Avg	—	—	—	—
10 Yr Avg	—	—	—	—

Tax Analysis	Tax-Adj Return%	Tax-Cost Ratio
3 Yr (estimated)	—	—
5 Yr (estimated)	—	—
10 Yr (estimated)	—	—

Rating and Risk

Time Period	Morningstar Rtn vs Cat	Morningstar Risk vs Cat	Morningstar Risk-Adj Rating
3 Yr	—	—	—
5 Yr	—	—	—
10 Yr	—	—	—

Other Measures	Standard Index S&P 500	Best Fit Index
Alpha	—	—
Beta	—	—
R-Squared	—	—
Standard Deviation	—	
Mean	—	
Sharpe Ratio	—	

Portfolio Analysis 12-31-06

Share change since 11-06 Total Stocks:25	Sector	Country	% Assets
⊕ PetroChina	Energy	Hong Kong	8.78
⊕ China Life Insurance	Financial	Hong Kong	8.63
⊕ Indl And Commrcl Bk Of C	Financial	China	8.44
⊕ China Mobile	Telecom	Hong Kong	7.85
⊕ Bank of China	Financial	Hong Kong	5.80
⊕ Ping An Insurance Grp Co	Financial	Hong Kong	4.83
⊕ Bank of Communications	Financial	Hong Kong	4.65
⊕ China Telecom	Telecom	Hong Kong	4.41
⊕ China Construction Bank	Financial	Hong Kong	4.23
⊕ China Shenhua Energy	Energy	Hong Kong	4.16
⊕ Sinopec	Business	Hong Kong	4.09
⊕ China Unicom Ltd	Telecom	Hong Kong	4.02
⊕ Bank of China (Hong Kong	Financial	Hong Kong	3.67
⊕ China Merchants Hldgs (I	Ind Mtrls	Hong Kong	3.55
⊕ CNOOC Ltd	Energy	Hong Kong	3.48
⊕ Citic Pacific	Ind Mtrls	Hong Kong	2.89
⊕ China Netcom Grp	Telecom	Hong Kong	2.69
⊕ China Resources Enterpri	Financial	Hong Kong	2.49
⊕ Zijin Mining Industry	Ind Mtrls	Hong Kong	2.21
⊕ Huaneng Power Int'l	Utilities	China	2.04

Current Investment Style

Value Blnd Growth — Large Mid Small

Market Cap	%
Giant	78.0
Large	22.0
Mid	0.0
Small	0.0
Micro	0.0
Avg $mil:	45,990

Value Measures	Rel Category
Price/Earnings	17.83	1.17
Price/Book	2.79	1.35
Price/Sales	1.97	1.09
Price/Cash Flow	7.10	0.77
Dividend Yield %	2.87	0.74

Growth Measures	%	Rel Category
Long-Term Erngs	12.09	0.91
Book Value	11.68	1.62
Sales	22.88	1.47
Cash Flow	18.92	1.51
Historical Erngs	22.57	1.32

Composition

Cash	0.2	Bonds	0.0
Stocks	99.8	Other	0.0
Foreign (% of Stock)			100.0

Sector Weightings

	% of Stocks	Rel MSCI EAFE	3 Year High	Low
↻ Info	19.00	1.61		
Software	0.00	0.00	2	0
Hardware	0.00	0.00	2	0
Media	0.00	0.00	0	0
Telecom	19.00	3.41	24	19
☞ Service	50.18	1.06		
Health	0.00	0.00	0	0
Consumer	0.00	0.00	0	0
Business	6.06	1.20	15	6
Financial	44.12	1.47	44	20
Mfg	30.82	0.75		
Goods	0.00	0.00	4	0
Ind Mtrls	10.22	0.66	12	9
Energy	17.33	2.42	27	17
Utilities	3.27	0.62	7	3

Regional Exposure % Stock

UK/W. Europe	0	N. America	0
Japan	0	Latn America	0
Asia X Japan	100	Other	0

Country Exposure % Stock

Hong Kong	89
China	11

Morningstar's Take by William Samuel Rocco 12-31-06

Investors who ignore iShares FTSE/Xinhua China 25 Index's risks do so at their own peril.

This two-year-old exchange-traded fund has already attracted more assets than the other 45 mutual funds and ETFs in the Pacific/Asia ex-Japan category, but its popularity is no surprise. It provides undiluted exposure to a rapidly growing and trendy economic powerhouse. Its index consists of 25 of the largest and most-liquid Chinese companies that trade in Hong Kong, so it allows investors to gain access to well-established mainland firms while avoiding the various challenges that come with most other Chinese companies. This ETF also is quite attractively priced for a China offering. And it has posted big gains so far.

But fans of the Middle Kingdom need to understand that this and other China vehicles, like all single-country emerging-markets funds, are dangerous due to their geographic focus, sector concentration, and other hazards. Indeed, though

this ETF has encountered pretty favorable conditions thus far, the six China offerings that have been around 10 years or more have all suffered double-digit losses in 15 or more rolling three-month periods over the past decade and plunged 30% or more during their worst three-month periods.

Moreover, though the emphasis on large and liquid names does reduce certain dangers, this ETF is far more focused than the other China funds from both a sector perspective and an issue perspective, and concentration boosts volatility. Thus, we expect this young ETF to be just as volatile as other China funds over time. And China aficionados should note that impressive economic growth and clout don't always translate into superior fund performance. Despite the success of the Chinese economy, China funds lag the average Pacific/Asia ex-Japan offering over the trailing three-, five-, and 10-year periods.

This ETF should be approached warily.

Address:	45 Fremont Street San Francisco CA 94105 800-474-2737
Web Address:	www.ishares.com
Inception:	10-05-04 *
Advisor:	Barclays Global Fund Advisers

Management Fee:	0.74%
Expense Projections:	3Yr:$237 5Yr:$411 10Yr:$918
Income Distrib:	Annually
Exchange:	NYSE

MORNINGSTAR® ETFs 150

iShares GS Nat Res IGE

	Market Price	Mstar Category
	$95.60	Specialty-Natural Res

Morningstar Fair Value

Price/Fair Value Ratio	Coverage Rate %
1.09 Overvalued	92 Good

Management

Managerial duties at this ETF are handled by Patrick O'Connor and S. Jane Leung. O'Connor has managed ETFs and index funds at Barclays Global Advisors, this fund's advisor, since 1999. Leung has been a portfolio manager at Barclays since 2001.

Methodology

This ETF mimics the Goldman Sachs Natural Resources Sector Index, a benchmark of U.S.-traded natural-resources stocks. Unlike many competing funds, this ETF includes a passel of nonenergy stocks in areas such as metals, mining, basic materials, and paper and forest products. The index ranks stocks by market capitalization and is reconstituted semiannually.

Morningstar Rating	Return	Risk	Yield	NAV	Avg Daily Vol. (k)	52 wk High/Low
★★★ Neutral	Neutral	Below Avg	1.1%	$101.35	75	$107.40 - $88.00

Growth of $10,000
- Investment Value of ETF
- Investment Value of Index S&P 500

Trading Volume Millions

	1997	1998	1999	2000	2001	2002	2003	2004	2005	2006	History
	—	—	—	—	47.48	40.67	53.47	65.64	88.20	101.35	NAV $
	—	—	—	—	47.80	40.70	53.41	65.64	88.33	101.60	Market Price $
	—	—	—	—	17.32*	-13.00	33.63	24.24	35.79	16.30	NAV Return%
	—	—	—	—	17.37*	-13.54	33.39	24.40	35.98	16.41	Market Price Return%
	—	—	—	—	1.54	-0.36	0.05	0.09	0.08	0.05	Avg Premium/Discount%
	—	—	—	—	17.32	9.10	4.95	13.36	30.88	0.51	NAV Rtrn% +/-S&P 500
	—	—	—	—	17.32	0.26	-0.38	-0.33	-0.69	-0.52	NAV Rtrn% +/-GS NATR RES
	—	—	—	—	—	4	4	4	6	9	NAV Return% Rank in Cat
	—	—	—	—	—	1.47	1.83	1.34	1.31	1.31	Income Return %
	—	—	—	—	—	-14.47	31.80	22.90	34.48	14.99	Capital Return %
	—	—	—	—	0.19	0.70	0.74	0.71	0.85	1.15	Income $
	—	—	—	—	0.00	0.00	0.00	0.00	0.00	0.00	Capital Gains $
	—	—	—	—	—	0.50	0.50	0.50	0.50	0.50	Expense Ratio %
	—	—	—	—	—	1.51	1.92	1.33	1.20	1.12	Income Ratio %
	—	—	—	—	—	12	7	7	8	7	Turnover Rate %
	—	—	—	—	—	20	112	374	1,094	1,505	Net Assets $mil

Performance 12-31-06

Historic Quarterly NAV Returns

	1st Qtr	2nd Qtr	3rd Qtr	4th Qtr	Total
2002	9.53	-7.27	-20.14	7.27	-13.00
2003	-1.86	12.30	2.06	18.81	33.63
2004	3.35	4.53	9.86	4.68	24.24
2005	12.23	3.64	20.51	-3.13	35.79
2006	8.92	4.33	-6.48	9.43	16.30

Trailing	NAV Return%	Market Return%	NAV Rtrn% +/-S&P 500	%Rank Cat.(NAV)
3 Mo	9.43	9.54	2.73	21
6 Mo	2.34	2.72	-10.40	18
1 Yr	16.30	16.41	0.51	9
3 Yr Avg	25.19	25.34	14.75	4
5 Yr Avg	17.93	17.83	11.74	4
10 Yr Avg	—	—	—	—

Tax Analysis	Tax-Adj Return%	Tax-Cost Ratio
3 Yr (estimated)	24.69	0.40
5 Yr (estimated)	17.37	0.47
10 Yr (estimated)	—	—

Morningstar's Take by Sonya Morris 12-31-06

IShares Goldman Sachs Natural Resources hasn't distinguished itself from the competition.

This exchange-traded fund is one of the oldest and most popular natural-resources ETFs. In fact, it's one of only three ETFs in the category that has accumulated a five-year track record. From an absolute perspective, its long-term returns are alluring, but when compared with its category rivals (both ETFs and conventional funds), this fund's performance fails to impress. Its three- and five-year trailing returns rank in the category's bottom quartile.

This fund has trailed its peers largely because--as its name suggests--its portfolio is spread over a wide variety of natural-resources stocks. Consequently, it's had exposure to some underperforming paper, forest products, and aluminum stocks such as Bowater, Smurfit-Stone Container, and Alcoa. Meanwhile, most of its rivals have been focused almost exclusively on the red-hot energy sector.

Granted, because this fund is more diversified, it has been slightly less volatile than its peers. Its three-year standard deviation of returns is lower than three quarters of its rivals. Nevertheless, this ETF should not be mistaken for a low-risk option. Indeed, shareholders here have recently gotten a taste of this fund's downside. During the third quarter of 2006, it lost 6.5% of its value. And that's not as bad as it can get here. During the third quarter of 2002, this ETF plunged more than 20%. So even though this fund has a slightly wider wingspan than the competition, it's not immune to the volatility that is part and parcel of natural-resources investing.

Given the strong performance from most energy and natural-resources stocks over the past few years, it wouldn't be surprising to see them take a breather, giving investors another reason to approach this ETF with caution.

Address:	45 Fremont Street San Francisco CA 94105 800-474-2737
Web Address:	www.ishares.com
Inception:	10-22-01*
Advisor:	Barclays Global Fund Advisers

Management Fee:	0.48%		
Expense Projections:	3Yr:$154	5Yr:$269	10Yr:$604
Income Distrib:	Quarterly		
Exchange:	AMEX		

Rating and Risk

Time Period	Morningstar Rtn vs Cat	Morningstar Risk vs Cat	Morningstar Risk-Adj Rating
3 Yr	-Avg	-Avg	★★
5 Yr	-Avg	-Avg	★★★
10 Yr	—	—	—

Other Measures	Standard Index S&P 500	Best Fit Index GS NATR RES
Alpha	13.9	-0.4
Beta	1.05	1.00
R-Squared	14	100
Standard Deviation	18.99	
Mean	25.19	
Sharpe Ratio	1.11	

Portfolio Analysis 12-31-06

Share change since 11-06 Total Stocks:132	Sector	PE	Tot Ret%	% Assets
⊕ ExxonMobil Corporation	Energy	11.7	39.07	9.14
⊕ Chevron Corporation	Energy	9.3	33.75	9.04
⊕ BP PLC ADR	Energy	10.9	7.94	7.01
⊕ ConocoPhillips	Energy	6.9	26.53	6.81
⊕ Schlumberger, Ltd.	Energy	24.0	31.07	4.28
⊕ Occidental Petroleum Cor	Energy	8.6	24.32	2.25
⊕ EnCana Corporation	Energy	11.9	2.55	2.20
⊕ Suncor Energy, Inc.	Energy	35.8	25.42	2.11
⊕ Marathon Oil Corporation	Energy	6.5	54.68	1.86
⊕ Halliburton Company	Energy	12.0	1.11	1.84
⊕ Valero Energy Corporatio	Energy	6.5	-0.33	1.83
⊕ Devon Energy Corporation	Energy	9.4	8.06	1.69
⊕ Canadian Natural Resourc	Energy	33.0	7.84	1.67
⊕ Barrick Gold Corporation	Ind Mtrls	42.1	10.95	1.52
⊕ Alcoa, Inc.	Ind Mtrls	12.6	3.49	1.50
⊕ Phelps Dodge Corp.	Ind Mtrls	12.9	76.29	1.44
⊕ Transocean, Inc.	Energy	29.3	16.07	1.42
⊕ Baker Hughes Inc.	Energy	10.8	23.67	1.38
⊕ Petro-Canada	Energy	15.4	3.18	1.20
⊕ Anadarko Petroleum Corp.	Energy	5.5	-7.44	1.14

Current Investment Style

Value Blnd Growth — Large Mid Small

Market Cap	%
Giant	44.2
Large	35.4
Mid	19.0
Small	1.3
Micro	0.0

Avg $mil: 36,376

Value Measures		Rel Category
Price/Earnings	11.75	0.94
Price/Book	2.52	0.98
Price/Sales	1.06	0.77
Price/Cash Flow	6.72	0.93
Dividend Yield %	1.32	1.18

Growth Measures	%	Rel Category
Long-Term Erngs	12.18	0.85
Book Value	14.52	1.05
Sales	19.73	1.22
Cash Flow	26.17	0.88
Historical Erngs	45.23	0.90

Profitability	%	Rel Category
Return on Equity	23.36	1.01
Return on Assets	10.94	0.99
Net Margin	14.19	0.96

Industry Weightings	% of Stocks	Rel Cat
Oil & Gas	50.0	1.6
Oil/Gas Products	11.5	1.1
Oil & Gas Srv	22.0	0.7
Pipelines	2.8	2.7
Utilities	0.0	0.0
Hard Commd	7.8	0.9
Soft Commd	3.6	1.6
Misc. Indstrl	0.0	0.0
Other	2.2	0.3

Composition

● Cash	0.1
● Stocks	99.9
● Bonds	0.0
● Other	0.0
Foreign	25.3
(% of Stock)	

MORNINGSTAR® ETFs 150

iShares Semiconductor IGW

	Market Price $61.30	Mstar Category Specialty-Technology

Morningstar Fair Value

Price/Fair Value Ratio	Coverage Rate %
0.86 Undervalued	90 Good

Management

Barclays Global Fund Advisors is the advisor. The firm is the world's largest manager of indexed portfolios. IShares portfolio management group is responsible for billions in assets. Most of the managers have at least five or more years of experience with Barclays as well as prior industry experience.

Methodology

This ETF tracks the Goldman Sachs Semiconductor Index, which is a subset of the Goldman Sachs Technology Index. The index rebalances twice a year and caps top positions at 8.5% of assets. Although the index does include foreign chip companies that are listed on U.S. exchanges, it lacks a global focus.

Morningstar Rating ★★ Below Avg	Return Below Avg	Risk High	Yield 0.2%	NAV $61.03	Avg Daily Vol. (k) 291	52 wk High/Low $68.52 - $50.92

Growth of $10,000
- Investment Value of ETF
- Investment Value of Index S&P 500

Trading Volume Millions

History

	1997	1998	1999	2000	2001	2002	2003	2004	2005	2006	
	—	—	—	—	66.55	34.56	62.94	53.85	61.01	61.03	NAV $
	—	—	—	—	66.50	34.68	62.75	53.80	60.97	61.01	Market Price $
	—	—	—	—	-1.28*	-48.07	82.13	-14.44	13.35	0.20	NAV Return%
	—	—	—	—	-1.29*	-47.85	80.95	-14.26	13.38	0.23	Market Price Return%
	—	—	—	—	-0.13	-0.09	-0.07	-0.02	-0.03	0.00	Avg Premium/Discount%
	—	—	—	—	-1.28	-25.97	53.45	-25.32	8.44	-15.59	NAV Rtrn% +/-S&P 500
	—	—	—	—	-1.28	-14.74	29.99	-26.17	5.99	-4.48	NAV Rtrn% +/-ArcaEx Tech 100
	—	—	—	—	8	8	8	9	14		NAV Return% Rank in Cat
	—	—	—	—	0.00	0.01	0.00	0.05	0.16		Income Return %
	—	—	—	—	-48.07	82.12	-14.44	13.30	0.04		Capital Return %
	—	—	0.00	0.00	0.00	0.00	0.00	0.03	0.10		Income $
	—	—	0.00	0.00	0.00	0.00	0.00	0.00	0.00		Capital Gains $
	—	—	—	—	0.50	0.50	0.50	0.50	0.50	0.50	Expense Ratio %
	—	—	—	—	-0.29	-0.20	-0.20	-0.09	0.07		Income Ratio %
	—	—	—	—	8	11	6	10	6		Turnover Rate %
	—	—	—	—	20	24	173	307	415	305	Net Assets $mil

Performance 12-31-06

Historic Quarterly NAV Returns

	1st Qtr	2nd Qtr	3rd Qtr	4th Qtr	Total
2002	7.44	-32.77	-38.49	16.88	-48.07
2003	1.19	25.25	19.00	20.76	82.13
2004	-1.83	-4.05	-19.11	12.28	-14.44
2005	-5.14	3.27	12.64	2.73	13.35
2006	6.69	-10.97	6.25	-0.72	0.20

Trailing	NAV Return%	Market Return%	NAV Rtrn% +/-S&P 500	%Rank Cat.(NAV)
3 Mo	-0.72	-0.75	-7.42	18
6 Mo	5.49	5.38	-7.25	18
1 Yr	0.20	0.23	-15.59	14
3 Yr Avg	-0.95	-0.86	-11.39	8
5 Yr Avg	-1.67	-1.67	-7.86	8
10 Yr Avg	—	—	—	—

Tax Analysis	Tax-Adj Return%	Tax-Cost Ratio
3 Yr (estimated)	-0.98	0.03
5 Yr (estimated)	-1.69	0.02
10 Yr (estimated)	—	—

Rating and Risk

Time Period	Morningstar Rtn vs Cat	Morningstar Risk vs Cat	Morningstar Risk-Adj Rating
3 Yr	Low	+Avg	★
5 Yr	-Avg	High	★★
10 Yr	—	—	—

Other Measures	Standard Index S&P 500	Best Fit Index ArcaEx Tech 100
Alpha	-20.4	-9.5
Beta	2.69	1.48
R-Squared	65	81
Standard Deviation	23.00	
Mean	-0.95	
Sharpe Ratio	-0.07	

Morningstar's Take by Karen Dolan 12-31-06

We see no good reason to invest in iShares Goldman Sachs Semiconductor.

As far as different industries go, we think it's particularly difficult to find value in the semiconductor industry. That's because the semiconductor business is capital intensive and very cyclical as companies contend with vicious competition and intense pricing pressure, making it hard for firms to consistently earn more than their cost of capital. That cyclicality leads to a great deal of volatility in this ETF's returns. On mulitple occasions, it has both gained and lost more than 30% of its value in a three-month stretch.

Given its bumpy nature, most investors have little to gain and much to lose by trying to pick entry and exit points here. What's more, investors likely already have exposure to many of the companies that grace this ETFs portfolio such as Intel, Morotola, and Texas Instruments. Those three stocks alone consume more than 24% of assets here. Notably, though, the fund does own a broader basket of semiconductor stocks than competing semiconductor ETFs, most of which key in on 20 or so holdings.

Even for those investors who follow the market closely and think semiconductors are a screaming buy right now, this ETF doesn't offer a complete package. It leaves out an important subset of Taiwanese chip companies such as Taiwan Semiconductor Manufacturing and other foreign behemoths such as South Korea-based Samsung.

We might be a little more forgiving if we thought this ETF's holdings looked attractive from a valuation standpoint. Only a dozen or so of the fund's 55 stocks are good buys according to Morningstar's equity analysts. Likewise, a full 70% of the fund's assets are invested in stocks that have a no- or narrow-moat rating by Morningstar equity analysts, which is a result of the challenging industry landscape. Combined, the current valuations and industry characteristics decrease the likelihood of success here.

Address:	45 Fremont Street San Francisco CA 94105 800-474-2737	Management Fee:	0.48%		
		Expense Projections:	3Yr:$154	5Yr:$269	10Yr:$604
Web Address:	www.ishares.com	Income Distrib:	Annually		
Inception:	07-10-01 *	Exchange:	AMEX		
Advisor:	Barclays Global Fund Advisers				

Portfolio Analysis 12-31-06

Share change since 11-06 Total Stocks:56	Sector	PE	Tot Ret%	% Assets
⊖ Intel Corporation	Hardware	20.3	-17.18	8.55
⊖ Texas Instruments, Inc.	Hardware	16.8	-9.82	8.46
⊖ Motorola, Inc.	Hardware	13.0	-8.17	8.38
⊖ Applied Materials	Hardware	19.0	3.89	6.90
⊖ STMicroelectronics NV	Hardware	63.5	2.98	4.51
⊖ Broadcom Corporation	Hardware	39.3	2.79	4.10
⊖ NVIDIA Corporation	Hardware	36.5	102.46	3.53
⊖ ASML Holding NV	Hardware	30.8	22.66	3.24
⊖ Analog Devices, Inc.	Hardware	22.2	-6.66	3.05
⊖ Marvell Technology Group	Hardware	35.5	-31.57	3.04
⊖ Advanced Micro Devices	Hardware	19.4	-33.50	3.02
⊖ Micron Technology, Inc.	Hardware	24.5	4.88	2.84
⊖ KLA-Tencor Corporation	Hardware	28.4	1.88	2.68
⊖ Maxim Integrated Product	Hardware	22.4	-14.06	2.66
⊖ SanDisk Corporation	Hardware	23.5	-31.50	2.62
⊖ Linear Technology	Hardware	21.2	-14.44	2.46
⊖ MEMC Electronic Material	Hardware	30.8	76.54	2.35
⊖ Xilinx, Inc.	Hardware	22.5	-4.28	2.17
⊖ National Semiconductor	Hardware	16.6	-12.17	2.06
⊖ Lam Research Corporation	Hardware	21.6	41.87	1.96

Current Investment Style

Value Blnd Growth — Large Mid Small

Market Cap	%
Giant	8.6
Large	48.3
Mid	35.3
Small	7.9
Micro	0.0
Avg $mil:	
13,414	

Value Measures	Rel Category
Price/Earnings	20.30	0.81
Price/Book	3.04	0.96
Price/Sales	2.70	1.01
Price/Cash Flow	9.79	0.93
Dividend Yield %	0.92	1.46

Growth Measures	%	Rel Category
Long-Term Erngs	15.67	1.04
Book Value	4.77	0.69
Sales	10.90	1.16
Cash Flow	25.32	1.31
Historical Erngs	35.04	1.14

Profitability	%	Rel Category
Return on Equity	16.95	1.00
Return on Assets	11.91	1.25
Net Margin	15.63	1.12

Industry Weightings	% of Stocks	Rel Cat
Software	0.0	0.0
Hardware	0.0	0.0
Networking Eq	0.0	0.0
Semis	73.8	4.1
Semi Equip	16.7	3.4
Comp/Data Sv	0.0	0.0
Telecom	0.0	0.0
Health Care	0.0	0.0
Other	9.5	0.5

Composition

	%
● Cash	0.1
● Stocks	99.9
● Bonds	0.0
● Other	0.0
Foreign (% of Stock)	8.0

iShares GS Tech IGM

	Market Price $52.33	Mstar Category Specialty-Technology

Morningstar Fair Value

Price/Fair Value Ratio
0.83 Undervalued

Coverage Rate %
95 Good

Management

Patrick O'Connor and S. Jane Leung lead the team that manage this and several other iShares ETFs. O'Connor has been on the team since the fund's inception and Leung since September 2006. Both have been with the ETF's advisor, Barclays Global Investors, for five or more years.

Methodology

Management attempts to track the performance of the Goldman Sachs Technology Index, which covers six tech subsectors ranging from software to semiconductors to the Internet. The index's holdings are weighted by market cap, but some position sizes are limited to improve diversification. Even so, it is dominated by the stocks with the largest market caps. The index rebalances semiannually.

Morningstar Rating ★★★ Neutral	Return Neutral	Risk Average	Yield 0.1%	NAV $51.35	Avg Daily Vol. (k) 64	52 wk High/Low $52.68 - $41.18

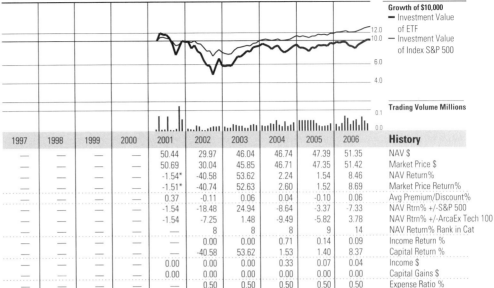

Growth of $10,000
- Investment Value of ETF
- Investment Value of Index S&P 500

Trading Volume Millions

	1997	1998	1999	2000	2001	2002	2003	2004	2005	2006	History
	—	—	—	—	50.44	29.97	46.04	46.74	47.39	51.35	NAV $
	—	—	—	—	50.69	30.04	45.85	46.71	47.35	51.42	Market Price $
	—	—	—	—	-1.54*	-40.58	53.62	2.24	1.54	8.46	NAV Return%
	—	—	—	—	-1.51*	-40.74	52.63	2.60	1.52	8.69	Market Price Return%
	—	—	—	—	0.37	-0.11	0.06	0.04	-0.10	0.06	Avg Premium/Discount%
	—	—	—	—	-1.54	-18.48	24.94	-8.64	-3.37	-7.33	NAV Rtrn% +/-S&P 500
	—	—	—	—	-1.54	-7.25	1.48	-9.49	-5.82	3.78	NAV Rtrn% +/-ArcaEx Tech 100
	—	—	—	—	—	8	8	8	9	14	NAV Return% Rank in Cat
	—	—	—	—	—	0.00	0.00	0.71	0.14	0.09	Income Return %
	—	—	—	—	—	-40.58	53.62	1.53	1.40	8.37	Capital Return %
	—	—	—	—	0.00	0.00	0.00	0.33	0.07	0.04	Income $
	—	—	—	—	0.00	0.00	0.00	0.00	0.00	0.00	Capital Gains $
	—	—	—	—	—	0.50	0.50	0.50	0.50	0.50	Expense Ratio %
	—	—	—	—	—	-0.30	-0.18	-0.20	0.81	0.04	Income Ratio %
	—	—	—	—	—	8	11	5	7	5	Turnover Rate %
	—	—	—	—	73	39	147	194	280	352	Net Assets $mil

Performance 12-31-06

Historic Quarterly NAV Returns

	1st Qtr	2nd Qtr	3rd Qtr	4th Qtr	Total
2002	-7.41	-27.84	-27.18	22.13	-40.58
2003	-0.63	22.20	11 77	13.71	53.62
2004	-1.30	1.69	-11.15	14.64	2.24
2005	-8.83	1.42	6.85	2.78	1.54
2006	4.23	-9.32	7.29	6.96	8.46

Trailing	NAV Return%	Market Return%	NAV Rtrn% +/-S&P 500	%Rank Cat.(NAV)
3 Mo	6.96	6.95	0.26	18
6 Mo	14.75	14.73	2.01	18
1 Yr	8.46	8.69	-7.33	14
3 Yr Avg	4.03	4.22	-6.41	8
5 Yr Avg	0.55	0.48	-5.64	8
10 Yr Avg	—	—	—	—

Tax Analysis	Tax-Adj Return%	Tax-Cost Ratio
3 Yr (estimated)	3.92	0.11
5 Yr (estimated)	0.48	0.07
10 Yr (estimated)	—	—

Rating and Risk

Time Period	Morningstar Rtn vs Cat	Morningstar Risk vs Cat	Morningstar Risk-Adj Rating
3 Yr	Avg	-Avg	★★★
5 Yr	Avg	Avg	★★★
10 Yr	—	—	—

Other Measures	Standard Index S&P 500	Best Fit Index ArcaEx Tech 100
Alpha	-12.2	-3.9
Beta	2.03	1.12
R-Squared	75	94
Standard Deviation	16.12	
Mean	4.03	
Sharpe Ratio	0.12	

Portfolio Analysis 12-31-06

Share change since 11-06 Total Stocks:232	Sector	PE	Tot Ret%	% Assets
⊕ Microsoft Corporation	Software	23.7	15.83	8.83
⊕ Cisco Systems, Inc.	Hardware	28.8	59.64	6.93
⊕ IBM	Hardware	16.8	19.77	6.11
⊕ Intel Corporation	Hardware	20.3	-17.18	4.88
⊕ Hewlett-Packard Company	Hardware	18.9	45.21	4.71
⊕ Google, Inc.	Business	58.6	11.00	4.30
⊕ Oracle Corporation	Software	25.6	40.38	3.72
⊕ Apple Computer, Inc.	Hardware	37.4	18.01	3.02
⊕ Qualcomm, Inc.	Hardware	26.2	-11.32	2.61
⊕ Dell, Inc.	Hardware	17.7	-16.23	2.38
⊕ Motorola, Inc.	Hardware	13.0	-8.17	2.08
⊕ Texas Instruments, Inc.	Hardware	16.8	-9.82	1.79
⊕ eBay, Inc.	Consumer	40.6	-30.43	1.75
⊕ Yahoo, Inc.	Media	32.3	-34.81	1.45
⊕ Corning Inc.	Hardware	25.6	-4.83	1.22
⊕ EMC Corporation	Hardware	30.7	-3.08	1.21
⊕ Automatic Data Processin	Business	25.1	9.11	1.13
⊕ Applied Materials	Hardware	19.0	3.89	1.06
⊕ Adobe Systems Inc.	Software	49.0	11.26	1.00
⊕ Research in Motion, Ltd.	Hardware	65.2	93.58	0.98

Current Investment Style

Value Blnd Growth — Large/Mid/Small

	Market Cap	%
	Giant	48.5
	Large	26.7
	Mid	20.1
	Small	4.7
	Micro	0.0
	Avg $mil: 34,734	

Value Measures		Rel Category
Price/Earnings	21.99	0.88
Price/Book	3.63	1.15
Price/Sales	2.33	0.87
Price/Cash Flow	11.09	1.06
Dividend Yield %	0.62	0.98

Growth Measures	%	Rel Category
Long-Term Erngs	14.69	0.97
Book Value	5.60	0.81
Sales	10.33	1.10
Cash Flow	16.07	0.83
Historical Erngs	24.17	0.79

Profitability	%	Rel Category
Return on Equity	21.31	1.25
Return on Assets	11.36	1.19
Net Margin	15.86	1.14

Industry Weightings	% of Stocks	Rel Cat
Software	23.0	1.1
Hardware	22.2	1.9
Networking Eq	10.3	1.4
Semis	15.8	0.9
Semi Equip	2.5	0.5
Comp/Data Sv	9.4	1.0
Telecom	0.4	0.1
Health Care	0.1	0.0
Other	16.2	0.9

Composition

●	Cash	0.1
●	Stocks	99.9
●	Bonds	0.0
	Other	0.0
	Foreign (% of Stock)	3.5

Morningstar's Take by Dan Culloton 12-31-06

This exchanged-traded fund isn't our first choice for technology stock exposure.

IShares Goldman Sachs Technology Index offers diversified exposure to U.S. software, hardware, Internet, and related stocks. Like a lot of other market-cap-weighted tech indexes, it has a lot of money in bellwethers such as Microsoft, Cisco Systems, and Google. Consequently, the sector's biggest players have a lot of influence on this fund. Even though the ETF owns more than 200 stocks and its benchmark caps individual position sizes, it packs nearly half its assets in its top 10.

For most of its life, the ETF's large-cap leanings have been a drag. Its long-term returns lag those of the typical conventional and exchange-traded tech fund, largely because many of them own more small-cap stocks, and in recent years smaller has generally meant better returns. That won't last forever. Indeed, large-cap and technology stocks mounted a comeback in the second half of the year, helping this fund's absolute and relative returns.

It's hard to predict if that tech and big-cap resurgence has legs. If it does, this ETF should continue to improve. But so will a lot of other technology funds that cover the same territory for less. This fund's expense ratio dropped a couple of basis points, or hundredths of a percent, to 0.48% in 2006. That's below average for the average tech ETF and far lower than the more than 1.2% charged by the typical conventional sector fund. This ETF's levy is more than twice the cost of the cheapest tech ETFs available, including Vanguard Information Technology ETF.

In terms of risk/reward profile, this ETF really doesn't offer anything different than its cheaper rivals. Its predilection for large caps has not made it significantly less volatile than the typical tech fund, and its risk-adjusted returns have not stood out either. So, while this fund offers decent exposure to large-cap tech stocks, there are better long-term holdings, such as Vanguard Information Technology ETF and its conventional cousin.

Address:	45 Fremont Street San Francisco CA 94105 800-474-2737	Management Fee:	0.48%	
		Expense Projections:	3Yr:$154	5Yr:$269 10Yr:$604
Web Address:	www.ishares.com	Income Distrib:	Quarterly	
Inception:	03-13-01 *	Exchange:	AMEX	
Advisor:	Barclays Global Fund Advisers			

 MORNINGSTAR® ETFs 150

iShares iBoxx$ Corp Bd LQD

	Market Price	Mstar Category
	$107.17	Long-Term Bond

Morningstar Fair Value

Price/Fair Value Ratio	Coverage Rate %
—	—

Management

Three managers are in charge of the six fixed-income ETFs offered by Barclays Global Investors, although Lee Sterne and Christopher Mosellen are the heads of this fund. Recently, Trevor Whelan was also added as a backup.

Methodology

The fund's benchmark, the iBoxx $ Liquid Investment Grade Index, uses sampling techniques to mimic the corporate-bond market. The index includes bonds from companies that meet Goldman Sachs' definition of liquid, long-term corporate debt. The issuers must have headquarters in the U.S., Canada, Western Europe, or Japan; have investment-grade ratings; have at least $500 million in outstanding debt; be less than five years old; and have at least three years until maturity. The managers can also differ from the index by up to 10% to add value on the margins.

Morningstar Rating	Return	Risk	Yield	NAV	Avg Daily Vol. (k)	52 wk High/Low
★★ Below Avg	Below Avg	Average	5.1%	$106.21	105	$108.70 - $102.24

Growth of $10,000
- Investment Value of ETF
- Investment Value of Index LB Aggr

Trading Volume Millions

	1997	1998	1999	2000	2001	2002	2003	2004	2005	2006	History
	—	—	—	—	—	107.99	110.38	111.53	107.50	106.21	NAV $
	—	—	—	—	—	109.69	110.57	111.53	107.69	106.68	Market Price $
	—	—	—	—	—	5.75*	7.43	5.91	1.00	3.96	NAV Return%
	—	—	—	—	—	5.83*	5.93	5.72	1.16	4.22	Market Price Return%
	—	—	—	—	—	0.92	0.24	0.25	0.09	0.12	Avg Premium/Discount%
	—	—	—	—	—	5.75	3.33	1.57	-1.43	-0.37	NAV Rtrn% +/-LB Aggr
	—	—	—	—	—	5.75	1.56	-2.65	-4.33	1.25	NAV Rtrn% +/-LB LongTerm
	—	—	—	—	—		1	1	1	1	NAV Return% Rank in Cat
	—	—	—	—	—	—	5.20	4.81	4.70	5.12	Income Return %
	—	—	—	—	—	—	2.23	1.10	-3.70	-1.16	Capital Return %
	—	—	—	—	—	2.48	5.48	5.19	5.13	5.37	Income $
	—	—	—	—	—	0.00	0.00	0.00	0.00	0.00	Capital Gains $
	—	—	—	—	—	—	0.15	0.15	0.15	0.15	Expense Ratio %
	—	—	—	—	—	—	5.38	5.38	4.71	4.75	Income Ratio %
	—	—	—	—	—	—	20	20	32	71	Turnover Rate %
	—	—	—	—	—	1,857	2,307	2,520	2,419	2,719	Net Assets $mil

Performance 12-31-06

Historic Quarterly NAV Returns

	1st Qtr	2nd Qtr	3rd Qtr	4th Qtr	Total
2002	—	—	—	3.33	—*
2003	2.60	5.26	-0.82	0.29	7.43
2004	3.71	-4.26	5.04	1.55	5.91
2005	-1.52	4.03	-1.66	0.25	1.00
2006	-1.46	-0.55	4.79	1.24	3.96

Trailing	NAV Return%	Market Return%	NAV Rtrn% +/-LB Aggr	%Rank Cat.(NAV)
3 Mo	1.24	1.56	0.00	1
6 Mo	6.09	6.72	1.00	1
1 Yr	3.96	4.22	-0.37	1
3 Yr Avg	3.60	3.68	-0.10	1
5 Yr Avg	—	—	—	—
10 Yr Avg	—	—	—	—

Tax Analysis	Tax-Adj Return%	Tax-Cost Ratio
3 Yr (estimated)	1.87	1.67
5 Yr (estimated)	—	—
10 Yr (estimated)	—	—

Rating and Risk

Time Period	Morningstar Rtn vs Cat	Morningstar Risk vs Cat	Morningstar Risk-Adj Rating
3 Yr	-Avg	Avg	★★
5 Yr	—	—	—
10 Yr	—	—	—

Other Measures	Standard Index S&P 500	Best Fit Index LB Credit
Alpha	-0.3	-0.3
Beta	1.48	1.18
R-Squared	98	100
Standard Deviation	4.86	
Mean	3.60	
Sharpe Ratio	0.09	

Morningstar's Take by Lawrence Jones 12-31-06

iShares GS $ InvesTop Corporate Bond gets the job done, but we have some concerns.

This ETF has a new name. With the sale of its underlying index, the fund will now be called the iShares iBoxx $ Investment Grade Corporate Bond Fund, though its fundamental principles remain the same. The index that it matches takes a 100-bond sample of the most liquid, long-term bonds in the corporate universe. The bonds are selected to mimic the universe's sector profile and maturity position.

We're concerned about a few facets of the fund's strategy, though. For one, it seems quite concentrated, considering that there are more than 500 bonds in its universe. If a problem arises with one of the fund's bonds, it would have a big impact on results. Moreover, unlike some other ETFs, there is a hands-on aspect here. The fund's advisor, Barclays Global Investors, may devote 10% of assets to bonds that aren't in the benchmark to try to reflect index additions and deletions. Although

the managers haven't yet used this flexibility, doing so would add an uncertain active hand to the mix.

So far, the fund has tracked its index reasonably well. Since the fund's July 2002 inception, it has gained 6.10% per year on an NAV basis, right in line with its index's gain through Nov. 30, 2006. A better reflection of an investor's results is an ETF's market-price return, which is impacted by demand for its shares. (Investors trade ETF shares at market prices and buy and sell mutual fund shares at NAV.) The fund's since-inception market return is in line with its NAV return, but meaningful deviations have occurred over shorter periods. And based on the fund's history, we think investors should expect similar variations in the future.

The biggest advantage here is costs. At 0.15%, the ETF easily beats its closest mutual fund rival on fees. Still, that's not enough for us to get excited about it.

Dieter Bardy contributed to this analysis.

Address:	45 Fremont Street San Francisco CA 94105 800-474-2737
Web Address:	www.ishares.com
Inception:	07-22-02 *
Advisor:	Barclays Global Fund Advisers, Rydex Inv

Management Fee:	0.15%		
Expense Projections:	3Yr:$48	5Yr:$85	10Yr:$192
Income Distrib:	Monthly		
Exchange:	AMEX		

Portfolio Analysis 12-31-06

Total Fixed-Income:100	Date of Maturity	Amount $000	Value $000	% Net Assets
Mohawk Inds 6.125%	01-15-16	32,512	32,336	1.20
Hsbc Hldgs 6.5%	05-02-36	26,880	28,896	1.07
JPMORGAN CHASE CAP XVIII	08-17-36	26,880	28,896	1.07
United Tech 4.375%	05-01-10	29,440	28,716	1.07
Intl Lease Fin Mtn Be 5.	03-24-11	28,160	28,288	1.05
Comcast 5.9%	03-15-16	28,160	28,260	1.05
Txu Engy 7%	03-15-13	26,880	28,187	1.05
Citigroup 6.125%	08-25-36	26,880	28,044	1.04
Embarq 7.995%	06-01-36	26,880	28,005	1.04
GOLDMAN SACHS GROUP	05-01-36	26,880	27,910	1.04
Merrill Lynch 6.05%	05-16-16	26,880	27,860	1.04
ORACLE	01-15-11	28,160	27,857	1.04
CATERPILLAR	08-15-36	26,880	27,807	1.03
CAPITAL ONE FINL	09-01-16	26,880	27,749	1.03
MARSH & MCLENNAN COS	09-15-10	28,160	27,664	1.03
Hm Depot 5.4%	03-01-16	28,160	27,566	1.02
Embarq 6.738%	06-01-13	26,880	27,565	1.02
WELLS FARGO BK NATL ASSN	08-26-36	26,880	27,564	1.02
ANADARKO PETE	09-15-36	26,880	27,411	1.02
Shell Intl Fin Bv 5.625%	06-27-11	26,880	27,398	1.02

Current Investment Style

Duration: Short Int Long
Quality: High Med Low

1 figure provided by fund

Avg Eff Duration1	6.7 Yrs
Avg Eff Maturity	10.9 Yrs
Avg Credit Quality	A
Avg Wtd Coupon	5.54%
Avg Wtd Price	100.09% of par

Coupon Range	% of Bonds	Rel Cat
0% PIK	0.0	0.0
0% to 6%	79.2	1.0
6% to 8%	20.8	1.0
8% to 10%	0.0	0.0
More than 10%	0.0	0.0

1.00=Category Average

Credit Analysis		% bonds 12-31-06	
US Govt	—	BB	0
AAA	5	B	0
AA	24	Below B	0
A	46	NR/NA	0
BBB	25		

Sector Breakdown
	% of assets
US Treasuries	0
TIPS	0
US Agency	0
Mortgage Pass-Throughs	0
Mortgage CMO	0
Mortgage ARM	0
US Corporate	98
Asset-Backed	0
Convertible	0
Municipal	0
Corporate Inflation-Protected	0
Foreign Corporate	2
Foreign Govt	0

Composition
Cash	0.4	Bonds	99.6
Stocks	0.0	Other	0

Special Securities
Restricted/Illiquid Secs	0
Exotic Mortgage-Backed	—
Emerging-Markets Secs	0
Options/Futures/Warrants	No

iShares KLD Sel Soc Idx KLD

Market Price $58.88		**Mstar Category** Large Blend	

Price/Fair Value Ratio: 0.89 Undervalued
Coverage Rate %: 95 Good

Management

Patrick O'Connor and Lisa Chen are responsible for the day-to-day management of this fund, along with several other iShares index funds. They work for Barclays Global Fund Advisors, the fund's advisor and an indirect subsidiary of Barclays Bank.

Methodology

This fund tracks the KLD Select Social Index, which includes 230 mostly large-cap companies drawn from the Russell 1000 and S&P 500 indexes. This index is designed to have risk and return characteristics similar to the Russell 1000 while limiting itself to companies with positive social and environmental characteristics. It overweights stocks with good social scores relative to their weight in the Russell 1000 and underweights or cuts those with low scores. KLD uses similar social criteria for the Domini 400 Social Index, which has historically been the basis for Domini Social Equity.

Performance 12-31-06

Historic Quarterly NAV Returns

	1st Qtr	2nd Qtr	3rd Qtr	4th Qtr	Total
2002	—	—	—	—	—
2003	—	—	—	—	—
2004	—	—	—	—	—
2005	—	2.38	2.49	2.57	—*
2006	3.63	-1.85	5.06	5.60	12.85

Trailing	NAV Return%	Market Return%	NAV Rtrn% +/-S&P 500	%Rank Cat.(NAV)
3 Mo	5.60	5.56	-1.10	44
6 Mo	10.95	10.80	-1.79	38
1 Yr	12.85	12.84	-2.94	30
3 Yr Avg	—	—	—	—
5 Yr Avg	—	—	—	—
10 Yr Avg	—	—	—	—

Tax Analysis	Tax-Adj Return%	Tax-Cost Ratio
3 Yr (estimated)	—	—
5 Yr (estimated)	—	—
10 Yr (estimated)	—	—

	Morningstar Rating	Return	Risk	Yield	NAV	Avg Daily Vol. (k)	52 wk High/Low
—	Not Rated	Not Rated	—	1.5%	$59.02	5	$59.84 - $51.84

Growth of $10,000
— Investment Value of ETF
— Investment Value of Index S&P 500

13.0
10.7
10.0

Trading Volume Millions
0.03
0.0

1997	1998	1999	2000	2001	2002	2003	2004	2005	2006	History
—	—	—	—	—	—	—	—	53.14	59.02	NAV $
—	—	—	—	—	—	—	—	53.17	59.05	Market Price $
—	—	—	—	—	—	—	—	10.89*	12.85	NAV Return%
—	—	—	—	—	—	—	—	10.92*	12.84	Market Price Return%
—	—	—	—	—	—	—	—	-0.09	0.04	Avg Premium/Discount%
—	—	—	—	—	—	—	—	10.89	-2.94	NAV Rtrn% +/-S&P 500
—	—	—	—	—	—	—	—	10.89	-2.61	NAV Rtrn% +/-Russ 1000
—	—	—	—	—	—	—	—	—	30	NAV Return% Rank in Cat
—	—	—	—	—	—	—	—	—	1.68	Income Return %
—	—	—	—	—	—	—	—	—	11.17	Capital Return %
—	—	—	—	—	—	—	—	0.61	0.89	Income $
—	—	—	—	—	—	—	—	0.00	0.00	Capital Gains $
—	—	—	—	—	—	—	—	0.50	0.50	Expense Ratio %
—	—	—	—	—	—	—	—	1.16	1.32	Income Ratio %
—	—	—	—	—	—	—	—	3	46	Turnover Rate %
—	—	—	—	—	—	—	—	117	68	Net Assets $mil

Rating and Risk

Time Period	Morningstar Rtn vs Cat	Morningstar Risk vs Cat	Morningstar Risk-Adj Rating
3 Yr	—	—	—
5 Yr	—	—	—
10 Yr	—	—	—

Other Measures	Standard Index S&P 500	Best Fit Index
Alpha	—	—
Beta	—	—
R-Squared	—	—
Standard Deviation	—	
Mean	—	
Sharpe Ratio	—	

Portfolio Analysis 12-31-06

Share change since 11-06 Total Stocks:216	Sector	PE	Tot Ret%	% Assets
⊖ IBM	Hardware	16.8	19.77	5.13
⊖ American Express Company	Financial	21.2	19.09	5.06
⊖ Johnson & Johnson	Health	17.4	12.44	4.12
⊖ Wells Fargo Company	Financial	14.7	16.82	3.35
⊖ Microsoft Corporation	Software	23.7	15.83	2.86
⊖ General Mills, Inc.	Goods	19.2	19.94	2.82
⊕ St. Paul Travelers Compa	Financial	12.0	22.90	2.03
⊕ 3M Company	Ind Mtrls	16.8	2.98	1.90
⊖ Bristol-Myers Squibb Com	Health	23.3	19.93	1.86
⊖ Cisco Systems, Inc.	Hardware	28.8	59.64	1.78
Freddie Mac	Financial	24.0	7.06	1.78
⊕ Procter & Gamble Company	Goods	24.2	13.36	1.72
⊕ Bank of America Corporat	Financial	12.4	20.68	1.71
⊕ Texas Instruments, Inc.	Hardware	16.8	-9.82	1.61
⊖ Progress Energy, Inc.	Utilities	16.7	18.07	1.60
⊖ Nike, Inc. B	Goods	19.3	15.84	1.57
⊕ Gap, Inc.	Consumer	18.8	12.45	1.43
⊖ Hewlett-Packard Company	Hardware	18.9	45.21	1.42
⊖ Molson Coors Brewing Com	Goods	22.6	16.31	1.41
⊕ Pfizer Inc.	Health	15.1	15.22	1.24

Current Investment Style

Value Blnd Growth — Large Mid Small

Market Cap	%
Giant	43.4
Large	37.5
Mid	19.1
Small	0.1
Micro	0.0

Avg $mil: 37,481

Value Measures		Rel Category
Price/Earnings	16.90	1.02
Price/Book	2.95	1.07
Price/Sales	1.82	1.43
Price/Cash Flow	6.55	0.69
Dividend Yield %	1.64	0.92

Growth Measures	%	Rel Category
Long-Term Erngs	11.54	1.00
Book Value	8.19	0.96
Sales	8.25	0.99
Cash Flow	16.33	2.16
Historical Erngs	15.42	0.92

Profitability	%	Rel Category
Return on Equity	20.92	1.09
Return on Assets	12.50	1.30
Net Margin	15.19	1.36

Sector Weightings	% of Stocks	Rel S&P 500	3 Year High Low
Info	25.84	1.29	
Software	4.53	1.31	— —
Hardware	16.28	1.76	— —
Media	2.86	0.75	— —
Telecom	2.17	0.62	— —
Service	45.41	0.98	
Health	12.70	1.05	— —
Consumer	6.70	0.88	— —
Business	2.52	0.60	— —
Financial	23.49	1.05	— —
Mfg	28.76	0.85	
Goods	9.81	1.15	— —
Ind Mtris	10.42	0.87	— —
Energy	5.94	0.61	— —
Utilities	2.59	0.74	— —

Composition

● Cash	0.1	
● Stocks	99.9	
● Bonds	0.0	
● Other	0.0	
Foreign	0.0	
(% of Stock)		

Morningstar's Take by David Kathman 12-31-06

IShares KLD Select Social Index does a respectable job of filling a niche, though it's not the cheapest socially responsible option.

This exchange-traded fund tracks the KLD Select Social Index, which aims to mimic the characteristics of the Russell 1000 Index in a socially responsible way. It avoids companies involved with alcohol, tobacco, gambling, military weapons, and nuclear power, and prefers those with good relationships with employees, shareholders, and the environment. The screens are very similar to those in Domini Social Equity, which has historically tracked an S&P 500-like index maintained by KLD, but which has been actively managed by Wellington (though subject to the same social screens) since November 2006.

Though the index behind this fund is very similar to the Russell 1000, the screening criteria do result in some differences. Most notably, this fund is significantly underweight in energy stocks, mostly because of its environmental and anti-nuclear

criteria, and significantly overweight in technology stocks. That energy underweighting has been the biggest factor in the fund's underperformance versus the index since its January 2005 inception, though in the future it's likely to outperform in most growth-led markets.

This is the only exchange-traded fund that pursues a diversified socially responsible strategy, and for that reason it may have some appeal for ETF investors. However, for those with a bit of flexibility, there are a number of open-end mutual funds that are similar to this fund but sport expense ratios cheaper than this fund's 0.50% price tag. Specifically, Vanguard FTSE Social Index, at 0.25%, and TIAA-CREF Social Choice Equity, at 0.27%, are worth considering for socially conscious investors for whom price is a major issue.

Address:	45 Fremont Street
	San Francisco CA 94105
	800-474-2737
Web Address:	www.ishares.com
Inception:	01-24-05*
Advisor:	Barclays Global Fund Advisers

Management Fee:	0.50%
Expense Projections:	3Yr:$160 5Yr:$280 10Yr:$628
Income Distrib:	Annually
Exchange:	AMEX

MORNINGSTAR® ETFs 150

iShares Lehman 1-3 T SHY

	Market Price	Mstar Category
	$80.05	Short Government

Morningstar Rating	Return	Risk	Yield	NAV	Avg Daily Vol. (k)	52 wk High/Low
★★★ Neutral	Neutral	Average	4.1%	$79.86	814	$80.49 - $79.33

Morningstar Fair Value

Price/Fair Value Ratio — Coverage Rate % —

Management

Joseph Kippels and Lee Sterne are primarily responsible for the day-to-day operations of this and three other ETFs. They are employed by Barclays Global Fund Advisors, a subsidiary of Barclays Global Investors.

Methodology

The fund tries to match the returns and yield of its index, the Lehman Brothers U.S. Treasury: 1-3 Year Index. The index includes U.S. Treasury bonds that have between one and three years until maturity; at least $250 million in par outstanding. On the margins, the managers can also differ from the index by up to 10% if these investments better help track the index.

Growth of $10,000
- Investment Value of ETF
- Investment Value of Index LB Aggr

13.0 / 12.2 / 10.6 / 10.0

Trading Volume Millions 0.6 / 0.1

	1997	1998	1999	2000	2001	2002	2003	2004	2005	2006	History
	—	—	—	—	—	82.21	82.35	81.42	80.16	79.86	NAV $
	—	—	—	—	—	82.27	82.47	81.43	80.21	79.96	Market Price $
	—	—	—	—	—	2.29*	1.78	0.80	1.48	3.83	NAV Return%
	—	—	—	—	—	2.31*	1.86	0.66	1.53	3.89	Market Price Return%
	—	—	—	—	—	0.06	0.07	0.04	-0.09	0.01	Avg Premium/Discount%
	—	—	—	—	—	2.29	-2.32	-3.54	-0.95	-0.50	NAV Rtrn% +/-LB Aggr
	—	—	—	—	—	2.29	-0.38	-0.74	-0.72	-0.18	NAV Rtrn% +/-LB 1-5 YR GOVT
	—	—	—	—	—	—	1	1	1	1	NAV Return% Rank in Cat
	—	—	—	—	—	—	1.61	1.94	3.05	4.20	Income Return %
	—	—	—	—	—	—	0.17	-1.14	-1.57	-0.37	Capital Return %
	—	—	—	—	—	0.64	1.31	1.58	2.45	3.30	Income $
	—	—	—	—	—	0.00	0.00	0.00	0.00	0.00	Capital Gains $
	—	—	—	—	—	—	0.15	0.15	0.15	0.15	Expense Ratio %
	—	—	—	—	—	—	1.80	1.63	2.11	3.36	Income Ratio %
	—	—	—	—	—	—	44	21	106	83	Turnover Rate %
	—	—	—	—	—	896	1,326	2,247	4,401	5,662	Net Assets $mil

Performance 12-31-06

Historic Quarterly NAV Returns

	1st Qtr	2nd Qtr	3rd Qtr	4th Qtr	Total
2002	—	—	—	0.82	—*
2003	0.57	0.68	0.40	0.12	1.78
2004	1.00	-1.16	0.98	-0.01	0.80
2005	-0.33	1.12	0.03	0.66	1.48
2006	0.35	0.61	1.96	0.87	3.83

Trailing	NAV Return%	Market Return%	NAV Rtrn% +/-LB Aggr	%Rank Cat.(NAV)
3 Mo	0.87	0.93	-0.37	1
6 Mo	2.84	2.85	-2.25	1
1 Yr	3.83	3.89	-0.50	1
3 Yr Avg	2.03	2.02	-1.67	1
5 Yr Avg	—	—	—	—
10 Yr Avg	—	—	—	—

Tax Analysis	Tax-Adj Return%	Tax-Cost Ratio
3 Yr (estimated)	0.95	1.06
5 Yr (estimated)	—	—
10 Yr (estimated)	—	—

Rating and Risk

Time Period	Morningstar Rtn vs Cat	Morningstar Risk vs Cat	Morningstar Risk-Adj Rating
3 Yr	Avg	Avg	★★★
5 Yr	—	—	—
10 Yr	—	—	—

Other Measures	Standard Index S&P 500	Best Fit Index LB 1-5 YR GOVT
Alpha	-1.4	-0.6
Beta	0.34	0.66
R-Squared	87	99
Standard Deviation	1.27	
Mean	2.03	
Sharpe Ratio	-1.00	

Portfolio Analysis 12-31-06

Total Fixed-Income:29	Date of Maturity	Amount $000	Value $000	% Net Assets
US Treasury Note 3.75%	05-15-08	666,460	656,316	11.67
US Treasury Note 3%	02-15-08	445,961	436,417	7.76
US Treasury Note	08-15-09	397,040	398,247	7.08
US Treasury Note 4.125%	08-15-08	355,918	352,088	6.26
US Treasury Note 2.625%	05-15-08	277,928	269,660	4.80
US Treasury Note 4.875%	05-15-09	248,150	248,723	4.42
US Treasury Note 4.75%	11-15-08	248,859	248,588	4.42
US Treasury Note 3.25%	01-15-09	252,404	244,913	4.36
US Treasury Note 2.625%	03-15-09	249,568	238,520	4.24
US Treasury Note 4.5%	02-15-09	222,626	221,288	3.94
US Treasury Note 4.625%	11-15-09	212,700	212,051	3.77
US Treasury Note 4%	06-15-09	195,684	192,314	3.42
US Treasury Note 4.375%	01-31-08	173,705	172,552	3.07
US Treasury Note 3.125%	09-15-08	161,652	157,163	2.79
US Treasury Note 3.375%	12-15-08	155,980	151,873	2.70
US Treasury Note 3.125%	10-15-08	148,890	144,606	2.57
US Treasury Note 4.625%	03-31-08	138,255	137,678	2.45
US Treasury Note 4.625%	02-29-08	134,710	134,148	2.39
US Treasury Note 3.625%	07-15-09	129,038	125,643	2.23
US Treasury Note 4.375%	11-15-08	120,530	119,565	2.13

Current Investment Style

Duration: Short / Int / Long
Quality: High / Med / Low

¹ figure provided by fund

Avg Eff Duration¹	1.8 Yrs
Avg Eff Maturity	1.9 Yrs
Avg Credit Quality	AAA
Avg Wtd Coupon	3.36%
Avg Wtd Price	98.56% of par

Coupon Range	% of Bonds	Rel Cat
0% PIK	11.7	1.0
0% to 6%	100.0	1.0
6% to 8%	0.0	0.0
8% to 10%	0.0	0.0
More than 10%	0.0	0.0
1.00=Category Average		

Credit Analysis	% bonds 12-31-06		
US Govt	—	BB	0
AAA	100	B	0
AA	0	Below B	0
A	0	NR/NA	0
BBB	0		

Sector Breakdown % of assets

US Treasuries	100
TIPS	0
US Agency	0
Mortgage Pass-Throughs	0
Mortgage CMO	0
Mortgage ARM	0
US Corporate	0
Asset-Backed	0
Convertible	0
Municipal	0
Corporate Inflation-Protected	0
Foreign Corporate	0
Foreign Govt	0

Composition

Cash	0.4	Bonds	99.6
Stocks	0.0	Other	0.0

Special Securities

Restricted/Illiquid Secs	0
Exotic Mortgage-Backed	—
Emerging-Markets Secs	0
Options/Futures/Warrants	No

Morningstar's Take by Annie Sorich 12-31-06

IShares Lehman 1-3 Year Treasury is a decent option, although not the best for individual investors with a short time horizon.

This ETF has carved out a spot for itself. It's the sole ETF in the short-term government category, making it the only way for pure-ETF investors to get exposure to the short-term Treasury market.

Following the Lehman 1-3 Year Treasury Index isn't as difficult as tracking other fixed-income indexes, which tend to harbor thousands of holdings. This index usually only holds around three dozen bonds, and even then, there aren't many differences among U.S. Treasury issues other than maturity and coupon, meaning it's not necessary to hold every bond in order to replicate the characteristics of the index. The ETF holds most of the underlying issues and tracks the index's returns closely: It has a three-year R-squared of 1.00, indicating that the investments' returns are related. This fund's performance has also measured up to that of the index. Since its inception in July 2006, it

gained an annualized 2.33% versus 2.46% for the index through the end of November 2006. The differential reflects the fund's expenses.

Although this ETF executes its mandate, we're not convinced it's for everyone. It's designed to be a place for investors with short-term goals to stash some cash. If, however, one's time horizon truly is short, it's important to consider the transaction costs associated with ETFs. Each time an investor buys or sells an ETF, he or she may pay a commission, which can knock out the expense advantage of these low-cost investments. It therefore might make more sense to hunt for a short-term bond mutual fund, a Certificate of Deposit, or a low-cost money market fund.

Although this fund achieves its objective, we urge investors to investigate their options before parking cash here.

Address:	45 Fremont Street San Francisco CA 94105 800-474-2737
Web Address:	www.ishares.com
Inception:	07-22-02 *
Advisor:	Barclays Global Fund Advisers

Management Fee:	0.15%		
Expense Projections:	3Yr:$48	5Yr:$85	10Yr:$192
Income Distrib:	Monthly		
Exchange:	AMEX		

iShares Lehman 20+ TLT

	Market Price	Mstar Category
	$89.37	Long Government

Morningstar Fair Value

Price/Fair Value Ratio	Coverage Rate %
—	—

Management

Lee Sterne and Joseph Kippels of Barclays Global Investors man this fund's controls. Sterne has been a portfolio manager for the advisor since 1996, and has helmed this offering since its July 22, 2002, inception. Kippels joined Barclays in 2005 and has been on board here since June 2006.

Methodology

This exchange-traded fund attempts to mimic the behavior of the Lehman Brothers 20+ Year Treasury Bond Index. The index, and the fund, own about a dozen long-term Treasury issues. The fund's return has trailed the index's by less than the amount of its expense ratio over time. As Treasury bonds are issued by the U.S. government, investors need not worry about credit risk, but the tradeoff is that interest-rate risk is a major concern.

Morningstar Rating	Return	Risk	Yield	NAV	Avg Daily Vol. (k)	52 wk High/Low
★★★★ Above Avg	Above Avg	Average	4.5%	$88.42	987	$92.57 - $82.65

Growth of $10,000
■ Investment Value of ETF
— Investment Value of Index LB Aggr

Trading Volume Millions

	1997	1998	1999	2000	2001	2002	2003	2004	2005	2006	History
	—	—	—	—	—	88.35	85.34	88.57	91.78	88.42	NAV $
	—	—	—	—	—	88.57	85.45	88.55	91.90	88.43	Market Price $
	—	—	—	—	—	6.51*	1.75	8.88	8.44	0.83	NAV Return%
	—	—	—	—	—	6.51*	1.62	8.71	8.61	0.71	Market Price Return%
	—	—	—	—	—	0.13	0.11	0.02	-0.18	-0.20	Avg Premium/Discount%
	—	—	—	—	—	6.51	-2.35	4.54	6.01	-3.50	NAV Rtrn% +/-LB Aggr
	—	—	—	—	—	6.51	-0.86	0.94	1.83	-1.23	NAV Rtrn% +/-LB LTGvtBd
	—	—	—	—	—	—	2	2	2	2	NAV Return% Rank in Cat
	—	—	—	—	—	—	5.26	4.96	4.82	4.44	Income Return %
	—	—	—	—	—	—	-3.51	3.92	3.62	-3.61	Capital Return %
	—	—	—	—	—	1.94	4.53	4.14	4.18	3.99	Income $
	—	—	—	—	—	0.00	0.00	0.00	0.00	0.00	Capital Gains $
	—	—	—	—	—	—	0.15	0.15	0.15	0.15	Expense Ratio %
	—	—	—	—	—	—	4.92	4.84	4.71	4.42	Income Ratio %
	—	—	—	—	—	—	7	31	18	25	Turnover Rate %
	—	—	—	—	—	504	282	585	817	1,432	Net Assets $mil

Performance 12-31-06

Historic Quarterly NAV Returns

	1st Qtr	2nd Qtr	3rd Qtr	4th Qtr	Total
2002	—	—	—	-0.40	—*
2003	1.09	5.53	-3.29	-1.39	1.75
2004	5.79	-5.75	7.15	1.90	8.88
2005	1.43	9.22	-3.37	1.30	8.44
2006	-4.71	-1.78	7.34	0.37	0.83

Trailing	NAV Return%	Market Return%	NAV Rtrn% +/-LB Aggr	%Rank Cat.(NAV)
3 Mo	0.37	0.41	-0.87	2
6 Mo	7.74	8.14	2.65	2
1 Yr	0.83	0.71	-3.50	2
3 Yr Avg	5.99	5.94	2.29	2
5 Yr Avg	—	—	—	—
10 Yr Avg	—	—	—	—

Tax Analysis	Tax-Adj Return%	Tax-Cost Ratio
3 Yr (estimated)	4.28	1.61
5 Yr (estimated)	—	—
10 Yr (estimated)	—	—

Rating and Risk

Time Period	Morningstar Rtn vs Cat	Morningstar Risk vs Cat	Morningstar Risk-Adj Rating
3 Yr	+Avg	Avg	★★★★
5 Yr	—	—	—
10 Yr	—	—	—

Other Measures	Standard Index S&P 500	Best Fit Index LB LTGvtBd
Alpha	1.8	0.1
Beta	2.63	1.18
R-Squared	91	99
Standard Deviation	8.98	
Mean	5.99	
Sharpe Ratio	0.33	

Portfolio Analysis 12-31-06

Total Fixed-Income:10	Date of Maturity	Amount $000	Value $000	% Net Assets
US Treasury Bond 4.5%	02-15-36	244,458	232,656	16.43
US Treasury Bond 6.125%	11-15-27	171,720	199,386	14.08
US Treasury Bond 6.25%	05-15-30	145,314	173,297	12.24
US Treasury Bond 5.375%	02-15-31	153,252	164,347	11.60
US Treasury Bond 5.25%	02-15-29	135,594	142,374	10.05
US Treasury Bond 6.125%	08-15-29	99,630	116,568	8.23
US Treasury Bond 5.5%	08-15-28	106,272	114,927	8.11
US Treasury Bond 6.375%	08-15-27	83,430	99,355	7.01
US Treasury Bond 6.625%	02-15-27	78,246	95,419	6.74
US Treasury Bond 5.25%	11-15-28	68,850	72,288	5.10

Morningstar's Take by Paul Herbert 12-31-06

IShares Lehman 20+ Year Treasury Bond is a useful vehicle, but investors should mind the risks of its habitat.

There's some obvious appeal to this ETF. Owning long-dated Treasury bonds, or funds that hold them, makes sense for long-term investors who don't want to deal with the risks and complexities of mortgage-backed or corporate securities.

And this fund in particular has some advantages over its mutual fund rivals. First, it's straightforward. Like the index it mimics, it is made up of plain-vanilla U.S. Treasury bonds with 20 years or more to maturity. Second, it's cheap. Though you'll have to pay a commission to buy it, its 0.15% expense ratio is the lowest in the long-government group. Third, low fees let it offer one of the fattest 12-month yields in its group.

However, investors should remember that long-dated bonds are very sensitive to changes in long-term interest rates. That relationship has been amicable during the fund's nearly five-year history.

The yield on the 20-year Treasury bond has fallen by about 50 basis points, or 0.50%, since the fund's July 2004 inception. This decline has helped the fund to outpace shorter-term sibling iShares Lehman 7-10 Year Treasury Bond by about 3 percentage points. (Bonds' prices rise when their yields fall.)

But during periods when yields on long-term bonds have risen, such as in 1999 and for brief periods in Spring 2004 and earlier in 2006, investors have been treated to meaningful losses. Due to such swings, the typical intermediate-government fund has delivered nearly three fourths the return of the typical long-government fund, with less than 35% of the risk (as measured by standard deviation) for the 10-year period through Nov. 2006.

These stats should serve as a warning to performance chasers. Long-term investors, however, have enough reasons to consider this fund further.

Address:	45 Fremont Street San Francisco CA 94105 800-474-2737
Web Address:	www.ishares.com
Inception:	07-22-02*
Advisor:	Barclays Global Fund Advisers

Management Fee:	0.15%		
Expense Projections:	3Yr:$48	5Yr:$85	10Yr:$192
Income Distrib:	Monthly		
Exchange:	AMEX		

Current Investment Style

Duration: Short Int Long
Quality: High Med Low

1 figure provided by fund

Avg Eff Duration	13.3 Yrs
Avg Eff Maturity	23.1 Yrs
Avg Credit Quality	AAA
Avg Wtd Coupon	5.65%
Avg Wtd Price	110.35% of par

Coupon Range	% of Bonds	Rel Cat
0% PIK	0.0	0.0
0% to 6%	51.5	0.9
6% to 8%	48.5	1.9
8% to 10%	0.0	0.0
More than 10%	0.0	0.0
1.00=Category Average		

Credit Analysis	% bonds 12-31-06		
US Govt	—	BB	0
AAA	100	B	0
AA	0	Below B	0
A	0	NR/NA	0
BBB	0		

Sector Breakdown % of assets

US Treasuries	100
TIPS	0
US Agency	0
Mortgage Pass-Throughs	0
Mortgage CMO	0
Mortgage ARM	0
US Corporate	0
Asset-Backed	0
Convertible	0
Municipal	0
Corporate Inflation-Protected	0
Foreign Corporate	0
Foreign Govt	0

Composition

Cash	0.4	Bonds	99.6
Stocks	0.0	Other	0.0

Special Securities

Restricted/Illiquid Secs	0
Exotic Mortgage-Backed	—
Emerging-Markets Secs	0
Options/Futures/Warrants	No

MORNINGSTAR® ETFs 150

iShares Lehman 7-10 IEF

Market Price $82.75	**Mstar Category** Long Government	

Management

Joseph Kippels and Lee Sterne are primarily responsible for the day-to-day operations of this and three other ETFs. They are employed by Barclays Global Fund Advisors, a subsidiary of Barclays Global Investors.

Methodology

The fund tries to match the returns and yield of its index, the Lehman Brothers U.S. Treasury 7-10 Year Index. The index includes U.S. Treasury bonds that have between seven and 10 years until maturity and at least $250 million in par outstanding. On the margins, the managers can also differ from the index by up to 10% if these investments better help track the index.

Morningstar Rating ★★ Below Avg	Return Below Avg	Risk Low	Yield 4.2%	NAV $82.35	Avg Daily Vol. (k) 290	52 wk High/Low $84.23 - $79.68

Growth of $10,000
— Investment Value of ETF
— Investment Value of Index LB Aggr

Trading Volume Millions

History	1997	1998	1999	2000	2001	2002	2003	2004	2005	2006
NAV $	—	—	—	—	—	86.05	84.56	85.06	83.71	82.35
Market Price $	—	—	—	—	—	86.15	84.70	84.95	83.91	82.44
NAV Return%	—	—	—	—	—	4.13*	2.05	4.43	2.27	2.65
Market Price Return%	—	—	—	—	—	4.15*	2.10	4.13	2.64	2.52
Avg Premium/Discount%	—	—	—	—	—	0.12	0.09	0.03	-0.13	-0.02
NAV Rtrn% +/-LB Aggr	—	—	—	—	—	4.13	-2.05	0.09	-0.16	-1.68
NAV Rtrn% +/-LB LTGvtBd	—	—	—	—	—	4.13	-0.56	-3.51	-4.34	0.59
NAV Return% Rank in Cat	—	—	—	—	—	—	2	2	2	2
Income Return %	—	—	—	—	—	—	3.81	3.82	3.89	4.25
Capital Return %	—	—	—	—	—	—	-1.76	0.61	-1.62	-1.60
Income $	—	—	—	—	—	1.78	3.22	3.18	3.25	3.49
Capital Gains $	—	—	—	—	—	0.00	0.00	0.00	0.00	0.00
Expense Ratio %	—	—	—	—	—	—	0.15	0.15	0.15	0.15
Income Ratio %	—	—	—	—	—	—	3.79	3.59	3.75	4.02
Turnover Rate %	—	—	—	—	—	—	54	74	121	94
Net Assets $mil	—	—	—	—	—	594	397	638	1,164	1,787

Performance 12-31-06

Historic Quarterly NAV Returns

	1st Qtr	2nd Qtr	3rd Qtr	4th Qtr	Total
2002	—	—	—	0.14	—*
2003	1.04	3.21	-1.12	-1.03	2.05
2004	4.17	-4.39	4.51	0.33	4.43
2005	-1.13	4.77	-1.82	0.56	2.27
2006	-2.03	-0.38	4.61	0.54	2.65

Trailing	NAV Return%	Market Return%	NAV Rtrn% +/-LB Aggr	%Rank Cat.(NAV)
3 Mo	0.54	0.63	-0.70	2
6 Mo	5.18	5.30	0.09	2
1 Yr	2.65	2.52	-1.68	2
3 Yr Avg	3.11	3.09	-0.59	2
5 Yr Avg	—	—	—	—
10 Yr Avg	—	—	—	—

Tax Analysis	Tax-Adj Return%	Tax-Cost Ratio
3 Yr (estimated)	1.70	1.37
5 Yr (estimated)	—	—
10 Yr (estimated)	—	—

Rating and Risk

Time Period	Morningstar Rtn vs Cat	Morningstar Risk vs Cat	Morningstar Risk-Adj Rating
3 Yr	-Avg	Low	★★
5 Yr	—	—	—
10 Yr	—	—	—

Other Measures	Standard Index S&P 500	Best Fit Index LB Govt
Alpha	-0.8	0.0
Beta	1.58	1.48
R-Squared	97	99
Standard Deviation	5.24	
Mean	3.11	
Sharpe Ratio	0.00	

Portfolio Analysis 12-31-06

Total Fixed-Income:13	Date of Maturity	Amount $000	Value $000	% Net Assets
US Treasury Bond 11.25%	02-15-15	301,413	433,161	24.54
US Treasury Note 4.125%	05-15-15	315,518	303,071	17.17
US Treasury Note 4.875%	08-15-16	191,611	193,991	10.99
US Treasury Note 4.75%	05-15-14	133,021	133,380	7.56
US Treasury Note 4.625%	11-15-16	124,775	123,995	7.02
US Treasury Bond 9.25%	02-15-16	86,800	115,664	6.55
US Treasury Note 4.25%	08-15-14	94,395	91,652	5.19
US Treasury Note 4.5%	02-15-16	88,970	87,586	4.96
US Treasury Note 4.25%	11-15-14	88,102	85,497	4.84
US Treasury Note 5.125%	05-15-16	71,610	73,794	4.18
US Treasury Bond 7.25%	05-15-16	53,599	63,736	3.61
US Treasury Note 4.5%	11-15-15	28,644	28,213	1.60
US Treasury Bond 9.875%	11-15-15	17,360	23,798	1.35

Morningstar's Take by Annie Sorich 12-31-06

IShares Lehman 7-10 Year Treasury offers a cheap way to get longer-term treasury exposure.

This is one of two ETFs in the long-term government-bond category. The other is its sibling, iShares Lehman 20+ Year Treasury Bond, which tracks U.S. Treasuries with even longer maturities. This fund stands as a pure-ETF investor's only option in garnering exposure to medium-term U.S. Treasuries.

Following the Lehman 7-10 Year Treasury Index isn't as difficult as tracking other fixed-income indexes, which tend to harbor thousands of holdings. This index usually holds around 20 bonds, and the fund itself had only 13 bonds in its portfolio through Dec. 20, 2006. The managers use a representative sampling technique, meaning they attempt to mirror the qualities of the index with fewer underlying holdings. This ETF has managed to mimic the index with as few as seven holdings in the past, because often there aren't many differences between U.S. Treasury bonds, other than maturities and coupons.

In addition, because the fund only invests in U.S. Treasuries (many of its mutual fund rivals in the same category hold some mortgage and agency debt), credit risk isn't an issue. These circumstances, however, do not make this fund a risk-free investment. In fact, bond funds with longer durations are often the most volatile fixed-income group. This fund's duration (a measure of interest-rate sensitivity) currently is 6.7 years, meaning if interest rates rise 1%, the fund might drop 6.7% in value. Although interest rates are stagnant now, dramatic swings in performance are not uncommon in this category.

Investors with long time horizons looking for this particular snapshot of U.S. Treasury exposure have found their niche. With an expense ratio of just 0.15% of assets, the ETF's low fees should keep it competitive.

Current Investment Style		
Duration: Short Int Long	Quality High Med Low	1 figure provided by fund

Avg Eff Duration	6.7 Yrs
Avg Eff Maturity	8.6 Yrs
Avg Credit Quality	AAA
Avg Wtd Coupon	6.12%
Avg Wtd Price	113.31% of par

Coupon Range	% of Bonds	Rel Cat
0% PIK	11.0	2.0
0% to 6%	63.8	1.1
6% to 8%	3.6	0.1
8% to 10%	7.9	2.0
More than 10%	24.6	2.0
1.00=Category Average		

Credit Analysis	% bonds 12-31-06		
US Govt	—	BB	0
AAA	100	B	0
AA	0	Below B	0
A	0	NR/NA	0
BBB	0		

Sector Breakdown	% of assets
US Treasuries	100
TIPS	0
US Agency	0
Mortgage Pass-Throughs	0
Mortgage CMO	0
Mortgage ARM	0
US Corporate	0
Asset-Backed	0
Convertible	0
Municipal	0
Corporate Inflation-Protected	0
Foreign Corporate	0
Foreign Govt	0

Composition			
Cash	0.4	Bonds	99.6
Stocks	0.0	Other	0.0

Special Securities	
Restricted/Illiquid Secs	0
Exotic Mortgage-Backed	0
Emerging-Markets Secs	0
Options/Futures/Warrants	No

Address:	45 Fremont Street San Francisco CA 94105 800-474-2737	Management Fee:	0.15%	
Web Address:	www.ishares.com	Expense Projections:	3Yr:$48	5Yr:$85 10Yr:$192
Inception:	07-22-02*	Income Distrib:	Monthly	
Advisor:	Barclays Global Fund Advisers	Exchange:	AMEX	

iShares Lehman Aggregate AGG

	Market Price $100.11	Mstar Category Intermediate-Term Bond

Morningstar Rating ★★★ Neutral	Return Neutral	Risk Above Avg	Yield 4.7%	NAV $99.45	Avg Daily Vol. (k) 316	52 wk High/Low $101.20 - $96.91

Morningstar Fair Value

Price/Fair Value Ratio —   Coverage Rate % —

Management

Lee Sterne, Chris Mosellen, and Joseph Kippels of Barclays Global Investors manage this fund. Sterne has been a portfolio manager for Barclays since 1996 and has managed this fund since its inception. Mosellen joined the team in 2003, and Kippels in 2005.

Methodology

The fund strives to approximate the performance of the Lehman Brothers Aggregate Bond Index, which is a commonly used proxy for the broad, investment-grade U.S. bond market. It uses representative sampling to do this because owning every fixed-income security in the domestic market would be unwieldy and costly because some of the issues are illiquid.

Growth of $10,000
- Investment Value of ETF
- Investment Value of Index LB Aggr

Trading Volume Millions

1997	1998	1999	2000	2001	2002	2003	2004	2005	2006	History
—	—	—	—	—	—	101.61	102.05	100.13	99.45	NAV $
—	—	—	—	—	—	102.15	102.40	100.59	99.70	Market Price $
—	—	—	—	—	—	3.63*	3.99	2.16	4.13	NAV Return%
—	—	—	—	—	—	3.70*	3.78	2.26	3.90	Market Price Return%
—	—	—	—	—	—	0.50	0.25	0.12	0.23	Avg Premium/Discount%
—	—	—	—	—	—	3.63	-0.35	-0.27	-0.20	NAV Rtrn% +/-LB Aggr
—	—	—	—	—	—	3.63	-1.31	0.33	0.32	NAV Rtrn% +/-LB 5-10YR
—	—	—	—	—	—	—	1	1	1	NAV Return% Rank in Cat
—	—	—	—	—	—	—	3.54	4.08	4.77	Income Return %
—	—	—	—	—	—	—	0.45	-1.92	-0.64	Capital Return %
—	—	—	—	—	—	0.92	3.54	4.09	4.68	Income $
—	—	—	—	—	—	0.00	0.00	0.00	0.00	Capital Gains $
—	—	—	—	—	—	—	0.20	0.20	0.20	Expense Ratio %
—	—	—	—	—	—	—	2.47	2.90	3.89	Income Ratio %
—	—	—	—	—	—	—	165	457	456	Turnover Rate %
—	—	—	—	—	—	213	990	2,894	4,913	Net Assets $mil

Performance 12-31-06

Historic Quarterly NAV Returns

	1st Qtr	2nd Qtr	3rd Qtr	4th Qtr	Total
2002	—	—	—	—	— *
2003	—	—	—	0.28	— *
2004	2.59	-2.66	3.22	0.88	3.99
2005	-0.60	3.01	-0.74	0.51	2.16
2006	-0.69	-0.16	3.73	1.24	4.13

Trailing	NAV Return%	Market Return%	NAV Rtrn% +/-LB Aggr	%Rank Cat.(NAV)
3 Mo	1.24	1.14	0.00	1
6 Mo	5.02	5.23	-0.07	1
1 Yr	4.13	3.90	-0.20	1
3 Yr Avg	3.42	3.31	-0.28	1
5 Yr Avg	—	—	—	—
10 Yr Avg	—	—	—	—

Tax Analysis	Tax-Adj Return%	Tax-Cost Ratio
3 Yr (estimated)	1.96	1.41
5 Yr (estimated)	—	—
10 Yr (estimated)	—	—

Rating and Risk

Time Period	Morningstar Rtn vs Cat	Morningstar Risk vs Cat	Morningstar Risk-Adj Rating
3 Yr	Avg	+Avg	★★★
5 Yr	—	—	—
10 Yr	—	—	—

Other Measures	Standard Index S&P 500	Best Fit Index LB Aggr
Alpha	-0.3	-0.3
Beta	1.01	1.01
R-Squared	100	100
Standard Deviation	3.28	
Mean	3.42	
Sharpe Ratio	0.06	

Portfolio Analysis 12-31-06

Total Fixed-Income:125	Date of Maturity	Amount $000	Value $000	% Net Assets
FNMA 5.5%	01-01-37	274,664	271,402	4.12
US Treasury Note 6%	08-15-09	248,482	256,004	3.89
FNMA 6%	01-01-37	241,072	242,654	3.69
FHLMC 5.5%	01-01-37	212,914	210,519	3.20
US Treasury Bond 7.625%	02-15-25	139,308	184,371	2.80
FHLMC 2.75%	03-15-08	179,322	174,402	2.65
FNMA 6.5%	01-01-37	167,960	171,057	2.60
US Treasury Note 5.125%	06-30-08	155,116	155,605	2.36
US Treasury Bond 8.125%	08-15-19	103,740	135,643	2.06
FHLMC 6%	01-01-37	129,922	130,836	1.99
FNMA 4.625%	01-15-08	123,500	122,816	1.87
US Treasury Note 3.5%	02-15-10	105,716	102,003	1.55
FHLMC 5%	01-01-37	102,752	99,108	1.51
FHLMC 4.5%	01-15-13	101,270	98,867	1.50
US Treasury Note 4.75%	05-15-14	95,836	96,095	1.46
US Treasury Note 4.75%	11-15-08	88,920	88,823	1.35
FHLMC 5.5%	01-01-22	87,932	87,822	1.33
FNMA 7.25%	01-15-10	80,028	85,114	1.29
FNMA 5%	01-01-22	82,992	81,566	1.24
FHLMC 5%	01-01-22	75,582	74,236	1.13

Current Investment Style

Duration: Short Int Long
Quality: High Med Low

¹ figure provided by fund

Avg Eff Duration¹	4.4 Yrs
Avg Eff Maturity	6.9 Yrs
Avg Credit Quality	AAA
Avg Wtd Coupon	5.34%
Avg Wtd Price	102.69% of par

Coupon Range	% of Bonds	Rel Cat
0% PIK	3.2	1.0
0% to 6%	78.0	1.0
6% to 8%	18.6	1.0
8% to 10%	3.4	1.0
More than 10%	0.0	0.0

1.00=Category Average

Credit Analysis		% bonds 12-31-06	
US Govt	—	BB	0
AAA	75	B	0
AA	6	Below B	0
A	13	NR/NA	0
BBB	6		

Sector Breakdown % of assets

US Treasuries	18
TIPS	0
US Agency	8
Mortgage Pass-Throughs	26
Mortgage CMO	0
Mortgage ARM	0
US Corporate	19
Asset-Backed	0
Convertible	0
Municipal	0
Corporate Inflation-Protected	0
Foreign Corporate	1
Foreign Govt	1

Composition

Cash	26.2	Bonds	73.8
Stocks	0.0	Other	0.0

Special Securities

Restricted/Illiquid Secs	0
Exotic Mortgage-Backed	0
Emerging-Markets Secs	Trace
Options/Futures/Warrants	No

Morningstar's Take by Dan Culloton 12-31-06

Although a viable choice, iShares Lehman Aggregate Bond is not a comfortable one.

This exchange-traded fund has much to recommend it. The ETF offers broad, cheap fixed-income exposure and would be a good complement to a total stock market fund in a low-maintenance ETF portfolio. Furthermore, there still aren't many places to go in the ETF universe for broad, one-stop exposure to the bond market.

Some aspects of this fund don't sit well, though. The ETF uses representative sampling to track its bogy. The technique isn't unique in index-fund management and should not be alarming. It's often more efficient to invest in a quantitatively constructed basket of securities that mimic the characteristics of the entire index--such as interest-rate risk and credit quality--than to duplicate it, especially if the benchmark is large and comprises illiquid investments.

This ETF invests in a smaller slice of the index than other funds that use sampling, though. Instead

of owning all of the more than 6,600 securities in its target benchmark, it held less than 125 as of Nov. 30, 2006. Meanwhile, Fidelity U.S. Bond Index own more than 1,300 issues as of the same date. There seems to be a greater margin for tracking error--the amount by which an index fund lags its benchmark--in owning such a small portion of such a large index. Indeed, from its September 2003 inception through the end of November 2006, this ETF trailed the Lehman Aggregate by 28 basis points, or hundredths of a percent. That's 8 basis points more than its expense ratio, which may not seem like much but can add up and seem bigger over the long term. It's definitely worth watching.

Lastly, the ETF's 0.20% expense ratio is less than one third of the intermediate-term bond category average. Still, there are conventional options that can be purchased without a commission and charge the same annual fee, such as Vanguard Total Bond Market Index. Given these reservations, this fund wouldn't be our first choice.

Address:	45 Fremont Street	Management Fee:	0.20%		
	San Francisco CA 94105	Expense Projections:	3Yr:$64	5Yr:$113	10Yr:$255
	800-474-2737	Income Distrib:	Monthly		
Web Address:	www.ishares.com	Exchange:	AMEX		
Inception:	09-22-03*				
Advisor:	Barclays Global Fund Advisers				

 **M**ORNINGSTAR® ETFs 150

iShares Lehman TIPS Bond TIP

	Market Price	Mstar Category
	$99.02	Inflation-Protected Bond

Morningstar Rating	Return	Risk	Yield	NAV	Avg Daily Vol. (k)	52 wk High/Low
★★★ Neutral	Neutral	Above Avg	4.3%	$98.79	229	$103.41 - $98.43

Morningstar Fair Value

Price/Fair Value Ratio —   Coverage Rate % —

Management

Two managers are in charge of this ETF and work on a handful of others offered by Barclays Global Investors. Lee Sterne and Joseph Kippels are responsible for the day-to-day management of this fund. Sterne has been a portfolio manager at BGI since 1996 and Kippels joined in 2005.

Methodology

The fund's index, the Lehman Brothers U.S. Treasury Inflation Notes Index, holds all TIPs that currently trade: 21 individual issues, as of Nov. 30, 2006. The index includes bonds that have at least one year until maturity and that have at least $250 million par outstanding. The managers can also differ from the index by up to 5%, in order to add value on the margins.

Growth of $10,000
■ Investment Value of ETF
— Investment Value of Index LB Aggr

1997	1998	1999	2000	2001	2002	2003	2004	2005	2006	History
—	—	—	—	—	—	101.61	105.64	102.80	98.79	NAV $
—	—	—	—	—	—	101.71	105.81	102.82	98.80	Market Price $
—	—	—	—	—	—	3.84*	8.21	2.65	0.29	NAV Return%
—	—	—	—	—	—	3.84*	8.27	2.49	0.28	Market Price Return%
—	—	—	—	—	—	0.10	0.18	0.06	0.04	Avg Premium/Discount%
—	—	—	—	—	—	3.84	3.87	0.22	-4.04	NAV Rtrn% +/-LB Aggr
—	—	—	—	—	—	3.84	-0.25	-0.19	-0.12	NAV Rtrn% +/-LB US Treas TIPS
—	—	—	—	—	—	—	1	1	1	NAV Return% Rank in Cat
—	—	—	—	—	—	—	4.15	5.41	4.23	Income Return %
—	—	—	—	—	—	—	4.06	-2.76	-3.94	Capital Return %
—	—	—	—	—	—	0.12	4.14	5.58	4.27	Income $
—	—	—	—	—	—	0.00	0.00	0.00	0.00	Capital Gains $
—	—	—	—	—	—	0.20	0.20	0.20	0.20	Expense Ratio %
—	—	—	—	—	—	—	-0.25	3.60	4.12	Income Ratio %
—	—	—	—	—	—	—	2	32	13	Turnover Rate %
—	—	—	—	—	—	142	1,511	3,310	4,001	Net Assets $mil

Performance 12-31-06

Historic Quarterly NAV Returns

	1st Qtr	2nd Qtr	3rd Qtr	4th Qtr	Total
2002	—	—	—	—	—
2003	—	—	—	—	—*
2004	5.07	-3.14	3.79	2.44	8.21
2005	-0.37	2.98	-0.02	0.06	2.65
2006	-2.30	0.44	3.60	-1.35	0.29

Trailing	NAV Return%	Market Return%	NAV Rtrn% +/-LB Aggr	%Rank Cat.(NAV)
3 Mo	-1.35	-1.33	-2.59	1
6 Mo	2.20	2.51	-2.89	1
1 Yr	0.29	0.28	-4.04	I
3 Yr Avg	3.66	3.63	-0.04	1
5 Yr Avg	—	—	—	
10 Yr Avg	—	—	—	

Tax Analysis	Tax-Adj Return%	Tax-Cost Ratio
3 Yr (estimated)	2.03	1.57
5 Yr (estimated)	—	—
10 Yr (estimated)	—	—

Rating and Risk

Time Period	Morningstar Rtn vs Cat	Morningstar Risk vs Cat	Morningstar Risk-Adj Rating
3 Yr	Avg	+Avg	★★★
5 Yr	—	—	—
10 Yr	—	—	—

Other Measures	Standard Index S&P 500	Best Fit Index LB Govt
Alpha	-0.1	0.5
Beta	1.41	1.32
R-Squared	76	78
Standard Deviation	5.21	
Mean	3.66	
Sharpe Ratio	0.10	

Portfolio Analysis 12-31-06

Total Fixed-Income:20	Date of Maturity	Amount $000	Value $000	% Net Assets
US Treasury Bond 3.875%	04-15-29	237,268	298,936	7.54
US Treasury Bond 2.375%	01-15-25	290,654	289,538	7.31
US Treasury Note 0.875%	04-15-10	300,422	284,884	7.19
US Treasury Note 3%	07-15-12	252,411	259,845	6.56
US Treasury Bond 3.625%	04-15-28	206,276	249,336	6.29
US Treasury Note 1.875%	07-15-13	243,983	235,866	5.95
US Treasury Note 2%	01-15-14	238,093	231,400	5.84
US Treasury Note 2%	07-15-14	220,810	214,427	5.41
US Treasury Note 1.625%	01-15-15	216,695	204,066	5.15
US Treasury Note 3.625%	01-15-08	201,450	203,560	5.14
US Treasury Note 2.375%	04-15-11	193,630	192,904	4.87
US TREASURY NOTE	07-15-15	190,442	182,586	4.61
US Treasury Note	01-15-16	180,867	174,732	4.41
US Treasury Note 3.5%	01-15-11	157,864	164,327	4.15
US Treasury Note 3.875%	01-15-09	158,559	162,955	4.11
US Treasury Note 4.25%	01-15-10	154,557	162,696	4.11
US Treasury Bond 2%	01-15-26	170,979	160,750	4.06
US Treasury Note 2.5%	07-15-16	131,596	132,654	3.35
US Treasury Note 3.375%	01-15-12	86,578	90,405	2.28
US Treasury Bond 3.375%	04-15-32	53,440	64,591	1.63

Current Investment Style

Duration: Short Int Long
Quality: High Med Low

1 figure provided by fund

Avg Eff Duration	5.0 Yrs
Avg Eff Maturity	9.8 Yrs
Avg Credit Quality	AAA
Avg Wtd Coupon	2.55%
Avg Wtd Price	102.67% of par

Coupon Range	% of Bonds	Rel Cat
0% PIK	3.4	1.0
0% to 6%	100.0	1.0
6% to 8%	0.0	0.0
8% to 10%	0.0	0.0
More than 10%	0.0	0.0

1.00=Category Average

Credit Analysis	% bonds 12-31-06		
US Govt	—	BB	0
AAA	100	B	0
AA	0	Below B	0
A	0	NR/NA	0
BBB	0		

Sector Breakdown
% of assets
US Treasuries	0
TIPS	100
US Agency	0
Mortgage Pass-Throughs	0
Mortgage CMO	0
Mortgage ARM	0
US Corporate	0
Asset-Backed	0
Convertible	0
Municipal	0
Corporate Inflation-Protected	0
Foreign Corporate	0
Foreign Govt	0

Composition
Cash	0.1	Bonds	100.0
Stocks	0.0	Other	0.0

Special Securities
Restricted/Illiquid Secs	0
Exotic Mortgage-Backed	—
Emerging-Markets Secs	0
Options/Futures/Warrants	No

Morningstar's Take by Karen Dolan 12-31-06

iShares Lehman TIPS Bond is a decent way to get pure TIPS exposure, and the only way to do so in ETF form.

This is the only ETF around that focuses on Treasury Inflation-Protected Securities, and it does a good job providing plain-vanilla exposure. The portfolio here is straightforward. As of Nov. 30, 2006, it had a stake in all 21 available issues. Though the TIPS market still has a fairly narrow number of outstanding securities, it has grown to a rather significant size in recent years. Ten years ago, U.S. TIPS didn't exist, but by the end of November 2006 there were roughly $400 billion of them outstanding, representing about 10% of all outstanding treasury debt. Thus, TIPS have become much more than just a small sliver of available government bonds.

TIPS offer something that investors can't get from other treasury securities: Protection against inflation. The bonds' face values change with inflation, and the absolute value of corresponding fixed coupon payments adjusts accordingly. TIPS are ultimately set up to keep up with inflation and provide some extra yield.

Although the fund is a good option for investors who prefer the trading flexibility of ETFs, attractive mutual fund options exist as well. For example, Vanguard Inflation-Protected Securities provides similar plain-vanilla exposure and charges the same amount. The Vanguard fund is a better option for investors planning to make regular investments or withdrawals because brokerage commissions add up fast and can make the ETF quite costly.

In addition, there are some actively managed options as well. For example, we've long admired PIMCO's expertise in the TIPs arena, but we haven't liked the price tag on its retail shares. We found a way to get around that in late 2005 when Harbor Real Return was launched. PIMCO subadvises that fund and investors can access it at a bargain price. If plain-vanilla TIPS exposure is what you seek, though, this ETF fills the bill.

Address:	45 Fremont Street San Francisco CA 94105 800-474-2737	Management Fee:	0.20%
		Expense Projections:	3Yr:$64 5Yr:$113 10Yr:$255
Web Address:	www.ishares.com	Income Distrib:	Monthly
Inception:	12-04-03*	Exchange:	NYSE
Advisor:	Barclays Global Fund Advisers		

iShares MSCI EAFE Growth EFG

	Market Price $67.46	**Mstar Category** Foreign Large Growth

Morningstar Fair Value

Price/Fair Value Ratio —   Coverage Rate % —

Management

The fund's advisor, Barclays Global Fund Advisors, is one of the world's largest and most experienced managers of index-tracking portfolios.

Methodology

This ETF tracks the MSCI EAFE Growth Index, a free-float-adjusted market-capitalization index designed to track developed stock markets outside Canada and the United States. The fund's portfolio is dominated by large-cap companies, and it is skewed toward "growth" stocks, which MSCI classifies using an eight-factor model. MSCI also employs "buffer zones" to limit migration between growth and value camps. The fund does not hedge its foreign currency exposure.

Morningstar Rating	Return	Risk	Yield	NAV	Avg Daily Vol. (k)	52 wk High/Low
— Not Rated	Not Rated	Not Rated	1.0%	$67.94	74	$68.63 - $56.06

Growth of $10,000
- Investment Value of ETF
- Investment Value of Index MSCI EAFE

(Chart values: 15.3, 14.0, 12.8, 10.7, 10.0)

Trading Volume Millions (0.07, 0.0)

1997	1998	1999	2000	2001	2002	2003	2004	2005	2006	History
—	—	—	—	—	—	—	—	56.31	67.94	NAV $
—	—	—	—	—	—	—	—	56.60	68.23	Market Price $
—	—	—	—	—	—	—	—	23.90*	21.88	NAV Return%
—	—	—	—	—	—	—	—	24.28*	21.78	Market Price Return%
—	—	—	—	—	—	—	—	0.36	0.40	Avg Premium/Discount%
—	—	—	—	—	—	—	—	23.90	-4.46	NAV Rtrn% +/-MSCI EAFE
—	—	—	—	—	—	—	—	23.90	-3.83	NAV Rtrn% +/-MSCI Wd xUS
—	—	—	—	—	—	—	—	—	1	NAV Return% Rank in Cat
—	—	—	—	—	—	—	—	—	1.22	Income Return %
—	—	—	—	—	—	—	—	—	20.66	Capital Return %
—	—	—	—	—	—	—	—	0.23	0.69	Income $
—	—	—	—	—	—	—	—	0.00	0.00	Capital Gains $
—	—	—	—	—	—	—	—	—	0.40	Expense Ratio %
—	—	—	—	—	—	—	—	—	2.25	Income Ratio %
—	—	—	—	—	—	—	—	—	35	Turnover Rate %
—	—	—	—	—	—	—	—	45	408	Net Assets $mil

Performance 12-31-06

Historic Quarterly NAV Returns

	1st Qtr	2nd Qtr	3rd Qtr	4th Qtr	Total
2002	—	—	—	—	—
2003	—	—	—	—	—
2004	—	—	—	—	—
2005	—	—	—	4.24	—*
2006	9.00	0.21	2.16	9.22	21.88

Trailing	NAV Return%	Market Return%+/-MSCI EAFE	NAV Rtrn% +/-MSCI EAFE	%Rank Cat.(NAV)
3 Mo	9.22	9.11	-1.13	1
6 Mo	11.58	11.53	-3.11	1
1 Yr	21.88	21.78	-4.46	1
3 Yr Avg	—	—	—	—
5 Yr Avg	—	—	—	—
10 Yr Avg	—	—	—	—

Tax Analysis	Tax-Adj Return%	Tax-Cost Ratio
3 Yr (estimated)	—	—
5 Yr (estimated)	—	—
10 Yr (estimated)	—	—

Rating and Risk

Time Period	Morningstar Rtn vs Cat	Morningstar Risk vs Cat	Morningstar Risk-Adj Rating
3 Yr	—	—	—
5 Yr	—	—	—
10 Yr	—	—	—

Other Measures	Standard Index S&P 500	Best Fit Index
Alpha	—	—
Beta	—	—
R-Squared	—	—
Standard Deviation	—	
Mean	—	
Sharpe Ratio	—	

Morningstar's Take by Gregg Wolper 12-31-06

iShares MSCI EAFE Growth Index Fund can be a solid addition to a larger portfolio.

This fund's portfolio is a subset of iShares MSCI EAFE Index. Using a number of measures to determine whether individual stocks lean more toward the value or growth realm, MSCI offers investors this fund and a companion focused on value stocks (iShares MSCI Value Index) for those who would rather not just accept the regular EAFE menu. It wouldn't necessarily be prudent to choose one of these subset funds merely because you expect value or growth to outperform in the future. Such predictions are tough to make correctly. But one of these funds could provide balance for an international portfolio that is heavily tilted the other way. Another strength is that this fund has a much lower cost than actively managed foreign funds.

It's also encouraging that this portfolio isn't as narrowly focused as a growth-targeted ETF could be. For example, energy and industrial materials are traditionally considered as value territory, but this fund has nearly the same energy weighting as the broad EAFE Index and a higher materials stake. Yet it does meet a typical growth investor's expectations in some sectors. Most notably, its stakes in health-care and the software and hardware sectors are all higher than EAFE s, and the financials position is well below. Country weightings, meanwhile, are very close to those of EAFE.

That s not to say you should invest all your money here. Like the EAFE fund, it has no exposure to emerging markets or small companies, and it excludes Canada. And with many foreign markets and currencies having been very strong recently, this fund's returns since its August 2005 inception have been exceptionally high. (Don t expect it to keep up that pace though.) Finally, its 0.40% expense ratio, although low in comparison to actively managed funds, isn t as inexpensive as some EAFE-tracking index funds and ETFs.

Portfolio Analysis 12-31-06

Share change since 11-06 Total Stocks:546

	Sector	Country	% Assets
⊖ GlaxoSmithKline	Health	U.K.	2.36
⊖ Novartis	Health	Switzerland	2.10
⊖ Roche Holding	Health	Switzerland	1.98
⊖ Total SA	Energy	France	1.57
⊕ Telefonica	Telecom	Spain	1.43
⊖ Siemens	Hardware	Germany	1.31
⊖ AstraZeneca	Health	U.K.	1.31
⊖ Nokia	Hardware	Finland	1.28
⊖ Anglo American	Ind Mtrls	U.K.	1.11
⊖ BHP Billiton, Ltd.	Ind Mtrls	Australia	1.09
⊖ Mitsubishi UFJ Financial	Financial	Japan	1.09
⊖ Mizuho Financial Grp	Financial	Japan	1.05
⊖ Sumitomo Mitsui Financia	Financial	Japan	0.98
⊕ Tesco	Consumer	U.K.	0.97
⊖ Ericsson AB (publ)	Hardware	Sweden	0.94
☼ Canon	Goods	Japan	0.91
☼ Rio Tinto	Ind Mtrls	U.K.	0.86
☼ Suez	Utilities	France	0.82
⊕ Diageo	Goods	U.K.	0.82
⊕ RWE	Utilities	Germany	0.76

Current Investment Style

Value Blnd Growth (Large / Mid / Small)

Market Cap	%
Giant	47.5
Large	38.8
Mid	13.6
Small	0.1
Micro	0.0
Avg $mil:	25,727

Value Measures		Rel Category
Price/Earnings	17.16	1.00
Price/Book	2.93	1.00
Price/Sales	1.33	1.00
Price/Cash Flow	9.70	1.00
Dividend Yield %	2.41	1.00

Growth Measures	%	Rel Category
Long-Term Erngs	14.69	1.00
Book Value	8.54	1.00
Sales	5.52	1.00
Cash Flow	8.92	1.00
Historical Erngs	25.41	1.00

Composition

Cash	0.1	Bonds	0.0
Stocks	99.6	Other	0.3
Foreign	(% of Stock)		100.0

Sector Weightings

	% of Stocks	Rel MSCI EAFE	3 Year High Low
↻ Info	13.27	1.12	
Software	1.13	2.02	— —
Hardware	6.21	1.61	— —
Media	2.29	1.25	— —
Telecom	3.64	0.65	— —
Service	43.42	0.92	
Health	10.51	1.48	— —
Consumer	7.73	1.56	— —
Business	6.78	1.34	— —
Financial	18.40	0.61	— —
Mfg	43.33	1.06	
Goods	14.60	1.11	— —
Ind Mtrls	20.78	1.35	— —
Energy	3.43	0.48	— —
Utilities	4.52	0.86	— —

Regional Exposure % Stock

UK/W. Europe	70	N. America	0
Japan	22	Latn America	0
Asia X Japan	8	Other	0

Country Exposure % Stock

U.K.	24	Germany	7
Japan	22	Switzerland	7
France	10		

Address:	45 Fremont Street San Francisco CA 94105 800-474-2737
Web Address:	www.ishares.com
Inception:	08-01-05*
Advisor:	Barclays Global Fund Advisers

Management Fee:	0.40%		
Expense Projections:	3Yr:$128	5Yr:$224	10Yr:$505
Income Distrib:	Annually		
Exchange:	NYSE		

MORNINGSTAR® ETFs 150

iShares MSCI EAFE EFA

Market Price $72.37	**Mstar Category** Foreign Large Blend	

Morningstar Fair Value

Price/Fair Value Ratio —   Coverage Rate % —

Management

The fund's advisor, Barclays Global Fund Advisors, is the world's largest manager of index-tracking portfolios.

Methodology

This exchange-traded offering is a passive fund that simply attempts to match the performance of the MSCI EAFE Index. The benchmark is a free-float-adjusted market-capitalization index designed to track the developed world's stock markets outside Canada and the U.S. The index includes equities from Australia, Western Europe, Hong Kong, Japan, New Zealand, and Singapore. It uses a representative sampling method of tracking the index, so it doesn't own the thousands of securities in the benchmark. Rather it invests in a portion of the bogy that is quantitatively constructed to match the index.

Morningstar Rating ★★★★ Above Avg	Return Above Avg	Risk Average	Yield 2.1%	NAV $72.95	Avg Daily Vol. (k) 4,851

52 wk High/Low $74.33 - $59.46

Growth of $10,000
— Investment Value of ETF
— Investment Value of Index MSCI EAFE

Trading Volume Millions

1997	1998	1999	2000	2001	2002	2003	2004	2005	2006	History
—	—	—	—	39.76	32.92	45.03	53.11	59.12	72.95	NAV $
—	—	—	—	39.77	33.00	45.59	53.42	59.43	73.22	Market Price $
—	—	—	—	12.36*	-15.61	38.45	19.75	13.39	26.00	NAV Return%
—	—	—	—	12.43*	-15.42	39.79	18.95	13.32	25.81	Market Price Return%
—	—	—	—	0.30	0.12	0.32	0.58	0.24	0.29	Avg Premium/Discount%
—	—	—	—	12.36	0.33	-0.14	-0.50	-0.15	-0.34	NAV Rtrn% +/-MSCI EAFE
—	—	—	—	12.36	0.19	-0.97	-0.63	-1.08	0.29	NAV Rtrn% +/-MSCI Wd xUS
—	—	—	—	1	2	2	2	2	2	NAV Return% Rank in Cat
—	—	—	—	—	1.58	1.59	1.78	2.09	2.59	Income Return %
—	—	—	—	—	-17.19	36.86	17.97	11.30	23.41	Capital Return %
—	—	—	—	0.08	0.63	0.52	0.80	1.11	1.53	Income $
—	—	—	—	0.00	0.00	0.00	0.00	0.00	0.00	Capital Gains $
—	—	—	—	—	0.35	0.35	0.35	0.36	0.35	Expense Ratio %
—	—	—	—	—	1.87	2.31	2.34	2.57	2.77	Income Ratio %
—	—	—	—	—	8	8	7	8	7	Turnover Rate %
—	—	—	—	—	2,192	5,404	13,639	22,739	37,076	Net Assets $mil

Performance 12-31-06

Historic Quarterly NAV Returns

	1st Qtr	2nd Qtr	3rd Qtr	4th Qtr	Total
2002	1.06	-2.18	-19.69	6.30	-15.61
2003	-8.18	19.16	8.10	17.06	38.45
2004	4.21	0.20	-0.32	15.05	19.75
2005	-0.18	-1.14	10.44	4.05	13.39
2006	9.29	0.73	3.86	10.21	26.00

Trailing	NAV Return%	Market Return%+/-	NAV Rtrn% +/-MSCI EAFE	%Rank Cat.(NAV)
3 Mo	10.21	10.36	-0.14	7
6 Mo	14.46	14.34	-0.23	6
1 Yr	26.00	25.81	-0.34	2
3 Yr Avg	19.60	19.25	-0.33	2
5 Yr Avg	14.86	14.93	-0.12	1
10 Yr Avg	—	—	—	

Tax Analysis	Tax-Adj Return%	Tax-Cost Ratio
3 Yr (estimated)	18.85	0.63
5 Yr (estimated)	14.16	0.61
10 Yr (estimated)	—	—

Rating and Risk

Time Period	Morningstar Rtn vs Cat	Morningstar Risk vs Cat	Morningstar Risk-Adj Rating
3 Yr	Avg	-Avg	★★★★
5 Yr	+Avg	Avg	★★★★
10 Yr	—	—	—

Other Measures	Standard Index S&P 500	Best Fit Index MSCI EAFE
Alpha	-0.2	-0.2
Beta	0.99	0.99
R-Squared	100	100
Standard Deviation	9.42	
Mean	19.60	
Sharpe Ratio	1.63	

Morningstar's Take by Gregg Wolper 12-31-06

There's good news from iShares MSCI EAFE Index but also reasons to think twice before joining the crowd in this fund.

With $34 billion in assets, this offering is one of the biggest exchange-traded funds of any kind and one of the largest international funds--including conventional mutual funds--as well. In some ways, it's understandable why that would be so. The MSCI EAFE Index is the most recognized benchmark for non-U.S. stocks, and it provides instant diversification among many countries in several regions, as well as many different sectors. Big institutions, which pay minimal trading costs, might prefer this ETF, which can be traded intraday, to owning similar mutual funds. Moreover, the fund has tracked its benchmark closely.

Now there's another reason to pay attention: The fund recently instituted breakpoints in its management fee, so its advisor will earn less in percentage terms on assets over $30 billion. Breakpoints give shareholders the benefit of the economies of scale when assets rise.

However, those reasons alone aren't enough to make this an obvious pick. For one thing, EAFE is a limited index. It essentially has no exposure to small-cap stocks and also ignores all companies in emerging markets. True, keeping out small caps and emerging markets holds down the potential for volatility, and the typical foreign large-blend mutual fund has a similar lack of small caps and a mid-cap weighting about the same as this offering's 12% stake. But those funds also average about 10% of assets in emerging markets.

A second caveat here is cost. This fund's asset size would have to rise significantly for the new breakpoints to have much effect, and in the meantime, it's more expensive than several mutual fund EAFE-trackers. In short, this fund is a reasonable option but not the standout its massive popularity might imply.

Address:	45 Fremont Street San Francisco CA 94105 800-474-2737
Web Address:	www.ishares.com
Inception:	08-14-01 *
Advisor:	Barclays Global Fund Advisers

Management Fee:	0.35%		
Expense Projections:	3Yr:$113	5Yr:$197	10Yr:$443
Income Distrib:	Annually		
Exchange:	AMEX		

Portfolio Analysis 12-31-06

Share change since 11-06 Total Stocks:816

	Sector	Country	% Assets
BP	Energy	U.K.	1.69
HSBC Hldgs	Financial	U.K.	1.58
Toyota Motor	Goods	Japan	1.48
Total SA	Energy	France	1.21
GlaxoSmithKline	Health	U.K.	1.16
Vodafone Grp	Telecom	U.K.	1.13
Nestle	Goods	Switzerland	1.09
Novartis	Health	Switzerland	1.03
Royal Dutch Shell	Energy	U.K.	1.01
Roche Holding	Health	Switzerland	0.97
Royal Bank Of Scotland G	Financial	U.K.	0.96
UBS AG	Financial	Switzerland	0.95
Banco Santander Central	Financial	Spain	0.87
Mitsubishi UFJ Financial	Financial	Japan	0.82
Telefonica	Telecom	Spain	0.74
Royal Dutch Shell	Energy	U.K.	0.74
Sanofi-Synthelabo	Health	France	0.72
Barclays	Financial	U.K.	0.71
BNP Paribas	Financial	France	0.71
Eni	Energy	Italy	0.68

Current Investment Style

Value Blnd Growth — Large Mid Small

Market Cap	%
Giant	55.3
Large	33.3
Mid	11.3
Small	0.1
Micro	0.0

Avg $mil: 32,619

Value Measures		Rel Category
Price/Earnings	14.99	1.07
Price/Book	2.18	1.00
Price/Sales	1.11	1.14
Price/Cash Flow	8.79	1.16
Dividend Yield %	3.05	0.81

Growth Measures	%	Rel Category
Long-Term Erngs	11.94	1.05
Book Value	8.58	1.12
Sales	5.61	0.95
Cash Flow	4.79	1.96
Historical Erngs	21.44	1.12

Composition

Cash	0.2	Bonds	0.0
Stocks	99.6	Other	0.2
Foreign (% of Stock)			100.0

Sector Weightings	% of Stocks	Rel MSCI EAFE	3 Year High	Low
Info	11.71	0.99		
Software	0.56	1.00	1	1
Hardware	3.74	0.97	5	4
Media	1.86	1.02	2	2
Telecom	5.55	1.00	8	5
Service	47.01	1.00		
Health	6.99	0.98	8	7
Consumer	5.06	1.02	5	4
Business	5.08	1.00	5	5
Financial	29.88	0.99	30	26
Mfg	41.26	1.01		
Goods	13.07	1.00	15	13
Ind Mtrls	15.69	1.02	16	12
Energy	7.29	1.02	9	7
Utilities	5.21	0.99	5	5

Regional Exposure % Stock

UK/W. Europe	69	N. America	0
Japan	23	Latn America	0
Asia X Japan	8	Other	0

Country Exposure % Stock

U.K.	24	Germany	7
Japan	23	Switzerland	7
France	10		

Mᴏʀɴɪɴɢsᴛᴀʀ® ETFs 150

iShares MSCI EAFE Value EFV

	Market Price $71.03	Mstar Category Foreign Large Value

Morningstar Fair Value

Price/Fair Value Ratio — Coverage Rate % —

	Morningstar Rating — Not Rated	Return Not Rated	Risk —	Yield 1.7%	NAV $71.58	Avg Daily Vol. (k) 131	52 wk High/Low $72.48 - $57.20

Management

The fund's advisor, Barclays Global Fund Advisors, is one of the world's largest and most experienced managers of index-tracking portfolios.

Growth of $10,000
— Investment Value of ETF
— Investment Value of Index MSCI EAFE

Methodology

This exchange-traded fund tracks the MSCI EAFE Value Index, a free-float-adjusted market-capitalization index designed to track developed stock markets outside of Canada and the United States. The fund's portfolio is dominated by large-cap companies. This fund is skewed toward "value" stocks, which MSCI classifies using an eight-factor model. MSCI also employs "buffer zones" to limit migration between growth and value camps. The fund does not hedge its foreign currency exposure.

Trading Volume Millions

1997	1998	1999	2000	2001	2002	2003	2004	2005	2006	History
—	—	—	—	—	—	—	—	56.00	71.58	NAV $
—	—	—	—	—	—	—	—	56.32	72.20	Market Price $
—	—	—	—	—	—	—	—	28.97*	29.96	NAV Return%
—	—	—	—	—	—	—	—	29.75*	30.34	Market Price Return%
—	—	—	—	—	—	—	—	0.48	0.47	Avg Premium/Discount%
—	—	—	—	—	—	—	—	28.97	3.62	NAV Rtrn% +/-MSCI EAFE
—	—	—	—	—	—	—	—	28.97	4.25	NAV Rtrn% +/-MSCI Wd xUS
—	—	—	—	—	—	—	—	—	3	NAV Return% Rank in Cat
—	—	—	—	—	—	—	—	—	2.13	Income Return %
—	—	—	—	—	—	—	—	—	27.83	Capital Return %
—	—	—	—	—	—	—	—	0.25	1.19	Income $
—	—	—	—	—	—	—	—	0.00	0.00	Capital Gains $
—	—	—	—	—	—	—	—	—	0.40	Expense Ratio %
—	—	—	—	—	—	—	—	—	4.34	Income Ratio %
—	—	—	—	—	—	—	—	—	31	Turnover Rate %
—	—	—	—	—	—	—	—	90	687	Net Assets $mil

Performance 12-31-06

Historic Quarterly NAV Returns

	1st Qtr	2nd Qtr	3rd Qtr	4th Qtr	Total
2002	—	—	—	—	—
2003	—	—	—	—	—
2004	—	—	—	—	—
2005	—	—	—	3.69	—*
2006	9.70	1.14	5.42	11.11	29.96

Trailing	NAV Return%	Market Return%	NAV Rtrn% +/-MSCI EAFE	%Rank Cat.(NAV)
3 Mo	11.11	11.48	0.76	3
6 Mo	17.14	17.25	2.45	3
1 Yr	29.96	30.34	3.62	3
3 Yr Avg	—	—	—	—
5 Yr Avg	—	—	—	—
10 Yr Avg	—	—	—	—

Tax Analysis	Tax-Adj Return%	Tax-Cost Ratio
3 Yr (estimated)	—	—
5 Yr (estimated)	—	—
10 Yr (estimated)	—	—

Rating and Risk

Time Period	Morningstar Rtn vs Cat	Morningstar Risk vs Cat	Morningstar Risk-Adj Rating
3 Yr	—	—	—
5 Yr	—	—	—
10 Yr	—	—	—

Other Measures	Standard Index S&P 500	Best Fit Index
Alpha	—	—
Beta	—	—
R-Squared	—	—
Standard Deviation	—	
Mean	—	
Sharpe Ratio	—	

Portfolio Analysis 12-31-06

Share change since 11-06 Total Stocks:522

	Sector	Country	% Assets
☼ BP	Energy	U.K.	3.41
⊕ HSBC Hldgs	Financial	U.K.	3.24
⊕ Toyota Motor	Goods	Japan	3.01
⊕ Vodafone Grp	Telecom	U.K.	2.26
⊕ Nestle	Goods	Switzerland	2.22
⊖ Royal Dutch Shell	Energy	U.K.	2.04
⊖ Royal Bank Of Scotland G	Financial	U.K.	1.92
⊕ Banco Santander Central	Financial	Spain	1.77
⊕ Royal Dutch Shell	Energy	U.K.	1.50
☼ Sanofi-Synthelabo	Health	France	1.46
⊕ Barclays	Financial	U.K.	1.44
⊕ BNP Paribas	Financial	France	1.42
⊕ Eni	Energy	Italy	1.38
⊕ Allianz	Financial	Germany	1.37
⊕ E.ON	Utilities	Germany	1.31
⊕ HBOS	Financial	U.K.	1.31
⊕ ING Groep	Financial	Netherlands	1.29
⊖ Credit Suisse Grp	Financial	Switzerland	1.26
⊖ UBS AG	Financial	Switzerland	1.23
⊕ Deutsche Bank AG	Financial	Germany	1.08

Current Investment Style

Value Blnd Growth — Large/Mid/Small

Market Cap	%
Giant	63.7
Large	26.3
Mid	9.7
Small	0.3
Micro	0.0
Avg $mil	41,245

Value Measures		Rel Category
Price/Earnings	13.25	0.96
Price/Book	1.73	0.78
Price/Sales	0.96	0.66
Price/Cash Flow	7.82	1.08
Dividend Yield %	3.66	1.35

Growth Measures	%	Rel Category
Long-Term Erngs	9.71	0.93
Book Value	8.85	1.23
Sales	6.06	0.63
Cash Flow	1.52	0.25
Historical Erngs	19.21	0.94

Composition

Cash	0.1	Bonds	0.0
Stocks	99.7	Other	0.2
Foreign (% of Stock)			100.0

Sector Weightings	% of Stocks	Rel MSCI EAFE	3 Year High	Low
↻ Info	10.23	0.87	—	—
🖳 Software	0.04	0.07	—	—
💻 Hardware	1.53	0.40	—	—
🎙 Media	1.38	0.75	—	—
📱 Telecom	7.28	1.31	—	—
⊖ Service	50.97	1.08		
Health	3.55	0.50	—	—
🛒 Consumer	2.05	0.41	—	—
📋 Business	3.51	0.69	—	—
💲 Financial	41.86	1.39	—	—
☐ Mfg	38.80	0.95		
🏭 Goods	11.51	0.88	—	—
❖ Ind Mtrls	10.63	0.69	—	—
◔ Energy	10.96	1.53	—	—
♀ Utilities	5.70	1.09	—	—

Regional Exposure	% Stock
UK/W. Europe 68	N. America 0
Japan 23	Latn America 0
Asia X Japan 8	Other 1

Country Exposure	% Stock
U.K. 23	Germany 7
Japan 23	Switzerland 7
France 10	

Morningstar's Take by Gregg Wolper 12-31-06

Although it has some limitations, iShares MSCI EAFE Value Index Fund could be a nice choice for some investors.

This fund's portfolio is a subset of the holdings of much bigger sibling iShares MSCI EAFE Index. Using a number of measures to determine whether individual stocks lean more toward the value or growth realm, MSCI offers investors this fund and a companion focused on growth stocks (iShares MSCI Growth Index) for those who'd rather not just accept the regular EAFE menu. While it can be treacherous to choose one of these subset funds merely because you expect value or growth to outperform in the future--such predictions are tough to make correctly--one of these funds could provide balance for an international portfolio that is heavily tilted the other way. Another strength: This fund has a much lower cost than actively managed foreign funds.

It's also encouraging to note that unlike some other ETFs that divide the foreign markets into narrower slices, with a few exceptions this one is not heavily skewed toward particular countries or sectors. Its country weightings look much like those of MSCI EAFE. And it is not overly tilted toward the energy or industrial-materials sectors, as one might suspect a value fund could be. Its 40% financials stake is rather high, though, as is its utilities weighting, which at just below 9% is nearly twice the EAFE norm.

That's not to say this fund is an all-purpose vehicle. Like the EAFE fund, it has no exposure to emerging markets or small companies and excludes Canada. Also, value stocks (and European currencies) have been strong recently; don't expect a 25% gain every year, as this fund has posted for the year to date through November. Finally, its 0.40% expense ratio, though cheap compared with actively managed funds, isn't as inexpensive as some EAFE-tracking index funds and ETFs.

Address:	45 Fremont Street San Francisco CA 94105 800-474-2737	Management Fee:	0.40%
		Expense Projections:	3Yr:$128 5Yr:$224 10Yr:$505
Web Address:	www.ishares.com	Income Distrib:	Annually
Inception:	08-01-05*	Exchange:	NYSE
Advisor:	Barclays Global Advisors		

MORNINGSTAR® ETFs 150

iShares MSCI Emerg Mkts EEM

	Market Price	Mstar Category
	$108.55	Diversified Emerging Mkts

Morningstar Fair Value

Price/Fair Value Ratio —   Coverage Rate % —

Management

Barclays Global Fund Advisors is the advisor. The firm is the world's largest manager of indexed portfolios.

Methodology

This fund tracks the MSCI Emerging Markets Index. The fund doesn't own all of the stocks in the index; rather, it uses quantitative tools to help it own a representative sample of the stocks in the index.

Morningstar Rating	Return	Risk	Yield	NAV	Avg Daily Vol. (k)	52 wk High/Low
★★★ Neutral	Neutral	Above Avg	1.4%	$114.09	5,054	$115.14 - $81.95

Growth of $10,000
— Investment Value of ETF
— Investment Value of Index MSCI EAFE

Trading Volume Millions

	1997	1998	1999	2000	2001	2002	2003	2004	2005	2006	History
NAV $	—	—	—	—	—	—	53.95	66.91	88.52	114.09	
Market Price $	—	—	—	—	—	—	54.64	67.28	88.25	114.38	
NAV Return%	—	—	—	—	—	—	40.15*	25.53	33.78	30.71	
Market Price Return%	—	—	—	—	—	—	40.81*	24.63	32.62	31.43	
Avg Premium/Discount%	—	—	—	—	—	—	0.53	0.25	0.07	0.10	
NAV Rtrn% +/-MSCI EAFE	—	—	—	—	—	—	40.15	5.28	20.24	4.37	
NAV Rtrn% +/-MSCI EmrMkt	—	—	—	—	—	—	40.15	3.08	3.47	1.53	
NAV Return% Rank in Cat	—	—	—	—	—	—	—	3	3	4	
Income Return %	—	—	—	—	—	—	—	1.49	1.48	1.78	
Capital Return %	—	—	—	—	—	—	—	24.04	32.30	28.93	
Income $	—	—	—	—	—	—	0.27	0.80	0.99	1.57	
Capital Gains $	—	—	—	—	—	—	0.00	0.00	0.00	0.00	
Expense Ratio %	—	—	—	—	—	—	0.78	0.76	0.77	0.77	
Income Ratio %	—	—	—	—	—	—	1.58	2.10	2.40	1.77	
Turnover Rate %	—	—	—	—	—	—	10	8	9	12	
Net Assets $mil	—	—	—	—	—	—	1,076	3,894	10,264	15,694	

Performance 12-31-06

Historic Quarterly NAV Returns

	1st Qtr	2nd Qtr	3rd Qtr	4th Qtr	Total
2002	—	—	—	—	—
2003	—	—	14.19	19.41	—*
2004	7.67	-7.92	6.87	18.48	25.53
2005	1.73	4.96	18.30	5.91	33.78
2006	12.19	-5.77	3.85	19.06	30.71

Trailing	NAV Return%	Market Return%	NAV Rtrn% +/-MSCI EAFE	%Rank Cat.(NAV)
3 Mo	19.06	19.86	8.71	4
6 Mo	23.64	23.52	8.95	4
1 Yr	30.71	31.43	4.37	4
3 Yr Avg	29.96	29.51	10.03	3
5 Yr Avg	—	—	—	
10 Yr Avg	—	—	—	

Tax Analysis	Tax-Adj Return%	Tax-Cost Ratio
3 Yr (estimated)	29.40	0.43
5 Yr (estimated)	—	—
10 Yr (estimated)	—	—

Rating and Risk

Time Period	Morningstar Rtn vs Cat	Morningstar Risk vs Cat	Morningstar Risk-Adj Rating
3 Yr	Avg	+Avg	★★★
5 Yr	—	—	—
10 Yr	—	—	—

Other Measures	Standard Index S&P 500	Best Fit Index MSCI EmrMkt
Alpha	-1.7	1.7
Beta	1.71	1.02
R-Squared	79	98
Standard Deviation	18.22	
Mean	29.96	
Sharpe Ratio	1.37	

Portfolio Analysis 12-31-06

Share change since 11-06 Total Stocks:270

Sector		Country	% Assets
⊕ Gazprom OAO (ADR)	Energy	U.K.	4.53
⊕ Samsung Electnc GDR 144A	Goods	Korea	4.47
⊕ Taiwan Semiconductor Man	Hardware	Taiwan	3.54
⊕ Posco ADR	Ind Mtrls	Korea	2.96
⊕ Kookmin Bank ADR	Financial	Korea	2.61
⊕ Lukoil ADR	Energy	Russia	2.14
⊕ United Microelectronics	Hardware	Taiwan	2.00
⊕ Korea Electric Power ADR	Utilities	Korea	1.95
⊕ Chunghwa Telecom Company	Telecom	Taiwan	1.95
⊕ Siliconware Precision In	Hardware	Taiwan	1.90
⊕ China Mobile	Telecom	Hong Kong	1.84
⊕ Petroleo Brasileiro S.A.	Energy	Brazil	1.60
⊕ America Movil S.A. de C.	Telecom	Mexico	1.41
⊕ Banco Itau Holding Finan	Financial	Brazil	1.38
⊕ CEZ	Utilities	Czech Republic	1.37
⊖ Petroleo Brasileiro S.A.	Energy	Brazil	1.36
⊖ Banco Bradesco SA ADR	Financial	Brazil	1.35
⊕ Infosys Technologies, Lt	Software	India	1.28
⊕ China Life Insurance	Financial	Hong Kong	1.22
⊕ Companhia Vale Do Rio Do	Ind Mtrls	Brazil	1.21

Current Investment Style

Value Blnd Growth — Large Mid Small

Market Cap	%
Giant	46.7
Large	32.9
Mid	17.6
Small	2.4
Micro	0.3

Avg $mil: 15,830

Value Measures		Rel Category
Price/Earnings	14.84	1.09
Price/Book	2.70	1.04
Price/Sales	1.32	1.10
Price/Cash Flow	10.17	1.11
Dividend Yield %	2.73	0.71

Growth Measures		Rel Category
Long-Term Erngs	15.51	1.05
Book Value	11.96	1.02
Sales	19.97	1.17
Cash Flow	13.49	1.07
Historical Erngs	26.95	1.05

Composition

Cash	0.3	Bonds	0.0
Stocks	99.7	Other	0.1
Foreign (% of Stock)			99.6

Sector Weightings	% of Stocks	Rel MSCI EAFE	3 Year High Low	
☍ Info	26.04	2.20		
Software	2.90	5.18	4	2
Hardware	9.22	2.39	12	8
Media	1.31	0.72	1	1
Telecom	12.61	2.26	16	10
☖ Service	30.21	0.64		
Health	2.06	0.29	4	2
Consumer	4.17	0.84	5	3
Business	2.63	0.52	5	1
Financial	21.35	0.71	21	14
☐ Mfg	43.76	1.07		
Goods	7.80	0.59	15	8
Ind Mtrls	15.73	1.02	21	14
Energy	15.45	2.16	17	11
Utilities	4.78	0.91	5	3

Regional Exposure	% Stock		
UK/W. Europe	5	N. America	0
Japan	0	Latn America	20
Asia X Japan	51	Other	24

Country Exposure	% Stock		
South Korea	15	Brazil	10
Hong Kong	11	South Africa	10
Taiwan	11		

Morningstar's Take by Gregg Wolper 12-31-06

The main concern with iShares MSCI Emerging Markets Index Fund has little to do with the fund's structure or cost.

Investors know that strong rallies don't go on forever, but it's tempting to ignore that knowledge when an investment that has provided mouth-watering returns shows no sign of slowing down. That's why it makes sense to begin here by noting that, in spite of a sharp drop for one month in spring 2006, emerging-markets returns have been on a powerful roll for three years now. This index-tracking ETF gained 25% in 2004, 33% in 2005, and for the year to date through Dec. 8, 2006, it is up nearly 27%. Rallies can continue for lengthy periods, and it's possible the next year or two will be as prosperous as the past three have been. But buying this fund with the expectation that such a high level of returns will continue--and without being prepared for the possibility of a deep loss--would be treacherous indeed. Not only do all rallies reverse at some point, but emerging-markets reversals can be particularly severe.

For those mindful of the risks who do want to increase their emerging-markets exposure, this ETF has both advantages and disadvantages. On the positive side, it provides straightforward exposure to a wide variety of the bigger emerging-markets stocks from around the world--just what an investor wants a basic investment of this type to give. With an expense ratio of 0.75%, it's much cheaper than actively managed emerging-markets funds, some of which cost more than double that figure.

On a less attractive note, however, a rival, Vanguard Emerging Markets ETF, offers very similar exposure now that it has recently included Russia in its portfolio--and that fund's expense ratio is less than half of this one's. The existence of that solid, cheaper alternative makes it tough to recommend this choice.

Address:	45 Fremont Street San Francisco CA 94105 800-474-2737
Web Address:	www.ishares.com
Inception:	04-07-03*
Advisor:	Barclays Global Fund Advisers

Management Fee:	0.75%			
Expense Projections:	3Yr:$240	5Yr:$417	10Yr:$930	
Income Distrib:	Annually			
Exchange:	AMEX			

iShares EMU Index EZU

	Market Price	Mstar Category
	$102.19	Europe Stock

Morningstar Fair Value

Price/Fair Value Ratio —

Coverage Rate % —

Management

The fund's advisor, Barclays Global Fund Advisors, is one of the world's largest and most experienced managers of index-tracking portfolios.

Methodology

This exchange-traded offering is a passive fund that simply attempts to match the performance of the MSCI EMU Index. The benchmark is a free float-adjusted market-capitalization index designed to track the stocks in member nations of the European Monetary Union. It includes companies based in Austria, Belgium, Finland, France, Germany, Greece, Ireland, Italy, the Netherlands, Portugal, and Spain, but excludes the United Kingdom, Switzerland, and others. It uses a representative sampling method of tracking the index.

Morningstar Rating	Return	Risk	Yield	NAV	Avg Daily Vol. (k)	52 wk High/Low
★★ Below Avg	Below Avg	Above Avg	1.8%	$103.05	112	$104.63 - $79.15

Growth of $10,000
- Investment Value of ETF
- Investment Value of Index MSCI EAFE

Trading Volume Millions

	1997	1998	1999	2000	2001	2002	2003	2004	2005	2006	History
	—	—	—	73.22	55.78	43.28	60.81	72.31	77.23	103.05	NAV $
	—	—	—	73.25	55.99	43.50	61.25	72.60	77.65	103.35	Market Price $
	—	—	—	5.29*	-22.96	-21.60	42.39	21.06	8.61	35.84	NAV Return%
	—	—	—	5.34*	-22.70	-21.49	42.68	20.67	8.76	35.50	Market Price Return%
	—	—	—	0.62	0.59	0.16	0.30	0.57	0.12	0.15	Avg Premium/Discount%
	—	—	—	5.29	-1.54	-5.66	3.80	0.81	-4.93	9.50	NAV Rtrn% +/-MSCI EAFE
	—	—	—	5.29	-3.06	-3.22	3.85	0.18	-0.81	2.12	NAV Rtrn% +/-MSCI Eur
	—	—	—	—	12	12	15	15	15	16	NAV Return% Rank in Cat
	—	—	—	—	0.56	0.81	1.83	2.14	1.83	2.40	Income Return %
	—	—	—	—	-23.52	-22.41	40.56	18.92	6.78	33.44	Capital Return %
	—	—	—	0.01	0.41	0.45	0.79	1.30	1.32	1.85	Income $
	—	—	—	0.00	0.26	0.00	0.00	0.00	0.00	0.00	Capital Gains $
	—	—	—	—	0.84	0.84	0.84	0.79	0.58	0.54	Expense Ratio %
	—	—	—	—	1.13	1.44	2.08	2.29	2.50	3.23	Income Ratio %
	—	—	—	—	24	3	7	11	8	8	Turnover Rate %
	—	—	—	—	—	143	234	456	718	2,221	Net Assets $mil

Performance 12-31-06

Historic Quarterly NAV Returns

	1st Qtr	2nd Qtr	3rd Qtr	4th Qtr	Total
2002	-0.32	-4.30	-28.17	14.42	-21.60
2003	-10.24	26.00	2.51	22.81	42.39
2004	-0.59	2.43	0.18	18.68	21.06
2005	-0.10	-1.22	7.83	2.06	8.61
2006	12.72	1.34	6.36	11.81	35.84

Trailing	NAV Return%	Market Return%	NAV Rtrn% +/-MSCI EAFE	%Rank Cat.(NAV)
3 Mo	11.81	11.71	1.46	19
6 Mo	18.92	19.48	4.23	19
1 Yr	35.84	35.50	9.50	16
3 Yr Avg	21.33	21.16	1.40	15
5 Yr Avg	14.80	14.78	-0.18	12
10 Yr Avg	—	—	—	—

Tax Analysis	Tax-Adj Return%	Tax-Cost Ratio
3 Yr (estimated)	20.59	0.61
5 Yr (estimated)	14.18	0.54
10 Yr (estimated)	—	—

Rating and Risk

Time Period	Morningstar Rtn vs Cat	Morningstar Risk vs Cat	Morningstar Risk-Adj Rating
3 Yr	Avg	Avg	★★★
5 Yr	Avg	+Avg	★★
10 Yr	—	—	—

Other Measures	Standard Index S&P 500	Best Fit Index MSCI Eur
Alpha	0.5	-1.2
Beta	1.05	1.10
R-Squared	84	95
Standard Deviation	10.92	
Mean	21.33	
Sharpe Ratio	1.56	

Portfolio Analysis 11-30-06

Share change since 10-06 Total Stocks:288

	Sector	Country	% Assets
⊕ Total SA	Energy	France	3.70
⊕ Banco Santander Central	Financial	Spain	2.56
⊕ Telefonica	Telecom	Spain	2.14
⊕ BNP Paribas	Financial	France	2.13
⊕ Sanofi-Synthelabo	Health	France	2.13
⊕ Eni	Energy	Italy	2.04
⊕ Nokia	Hardware	Finland	1.99
⊕ ING Groep	Financial	Netherlands	1.96
⊕ BBVA	Financial	Spain	1.95
⊕ Allianz	Financial	Germany	1.92
⊕ Siemens	Hardware	Germany	1.90
⊕ E.ON	Utilities	Germany	1.88
⊕ Deutsche Bank AG	Financial	Germany	1.66
⊕ UniCredito Italiano Grp	Financial	Italy	1.59
⊕ AXA	Financial	France	1.51
⊕ Societe Generale Grp	Financial	France	1.49
⊕ ABN AMRO Holding	Financial	Netherlands	1.29
⊕ DaimlerChrysler AG	Goods	Germany	1.25
⊕ Suez	Utilities	France	1.19
⊕ RWE	Utilities	Germany	1.18

Current Investment Style

Value Blnd Growth — Large / Mid / Small

Market Cap	%
Giant	57.5
Large	32.1
Mid	10.1
Small	0.4
Micro	0.0

Avg $mil: 35,946

Value Measures		Rel Category
Price/Earnings	13.27	0.98
Price/Book	2.02	0.90
Price/Sales	0.96	0.85
Price/Cash Flow	7.31	0.87
Dividend Yield %	3.47	1.00

Growth Measures	%	Rel Category
Long-Term Erngs	9.92	0.89
Book Value	8.94	1.05
Sales	5.03	0.66
Cash Flow	0.53	0.20
Historical Erngs	18.70	0.83

Composition

Cash	0.3	Bonds	0.0
Stocks	99.3	Other	0.4
Foreign	(% of Stock)		100.0

Sector Weightings	% of Stocks	Rel MSCI EAFE	3 Year High	Low
↻ Info	16.74	1.42		
▣ Software	1.34	2.39	2	1
▣ Hardware	5.18	1.34	9	5
▣ Media	2.47	1.35	3	2
▣ Telecom	7.75	1.39	11	7
☞ Service	44.47	0.94		
▣ Health	3.17	0.45	5	3
▣ Consumer	3.54	0.72	4	3
▣ Business	4.54	0.90	5	3
⑤ Financial	33.22	1.10	34	27
◻ Mfg	38.78	0.95		
▣ Goods	10.82	0.82	12	10
▣ Ind Mtrls	12.02	0.78	12	9
▣ Energy	7.54	1.05	13	7
▣ Utilities	8.40	1.60	8	6

Regional Exposure	% Stock
UK/W. Europe 100	N. America 0
Japan 0	Latn America 0
Asia X Japan 0	Other 0

Country Exposure	% Stock
France	29	Italy	12
Germany	22	Netherlands	10
Spain	13		

Morningstar's Take by Gregg Wolper 12-31-06

IShares MSCI EMU Index isn't appropriate as a currency play, and it's tough to find any other reason to like it.

This offering has an unusual construction. It targets Europe, but not all of it; rather, it focuses only on those countries that have adopted the euro as their currency. That takes in 11 countries, including most of the big nations in the European Union, such as Germany, France, and Italy.

However, the fund has two very notable exceptions. One won't find any companies from the United Kingdom or Switzerland in this portfolio, because those countries have not adopted the euro. Yet the former is the biggest stock market in Europe by far and includes global leaders in many areas, including BP and GlaxoSmithKline. And Switzerland's market cap is much larger than one might guess judged by its population or political profile. It is the home of heavyweight financial firms UBS and Credit Suisse and pharmaceutical giants Roche and Novartis, to name just the most

obvious examples. To show just how drastic a difference the omission of those countries makes, just look at the composition of Vanguard European Stock ETF: It has 35% of assets in the U.K. and 10% in Switzerland (tied with Germany for the third-largest country weighting). The iShares fund also omits Sweden, which makes up 3.5% of the Vanguard portfolio.

So why would anyone want this fund? One reason would be a conviction that the euro area's markets will, for some reason, outperform those of Europe as a whole. Space doesn't allow a full discussion of that idea, but in short, it's not a given, to say the least. Second, U.S.-based investors from euro countries may want to invest in a fund focused specifically on the euro. Even so, there are much more direct ways to make currency investments if that's what one wants. Think more than twice before buying this fund.

Address:	45 Fremont Street San Francisco CA 94105 800-474-2737	Management Fee:	0.54%
		Expense Projections:	3Yr:$173 5Yr:$302 10Yr:$677
Web Address:	www.ishares.com	Income Distrib:	Annually
Inception:	07-25-00*	Exchange:	NYSE
Advisor:	Barclays Global Fund Advisers		

MORNINGSTAR® ETFs 150

iShares Japan Index EWJ

	Market Price	Mstar Category
	$14.15	Japan Stock

Morningstar Fair Value

Price/Fair Value Ratio —   Coverage Rate % —

Management

This fund is run by a team from Barclays Global Investors. Firm veterans Patrick O'Connor and S. Jane Leung head the team, and Barclays Global Investors is one of the largest and most experienced managers of indexed assets in the world, with more than $1 trillion in assets under management

Methodology

This passively run offering provides mainstream exposure to Japan. It's designed to track the MSCI Japan Index, a market-cap-weighted index that aims to replicate the top 85% of the publicly available stock universe in Japan. This ETF's biggest holdings are well-known powerhouses like Toyota, Mitsubishi UFJ Financial Group, Canon, and Sony. It has a relatively large average market cap to go along with its relatively neutral sector and style stances.

Morningstar Rating	Return	Risk	Yield	NAV	Avg Daily Vol. (k)	52 wk High/Low
★★★ Neutral	Neutral	Below Avg	0.7%	$14.12	16,006	$15.55 - $12.29

Growth of $10,000
— Investment Value of ETF
— Investment Value of Index MSCI EAFE

Trading Volume Millions

	1997	1998	1999	2000	2001	2002	2003	2004	2005	2006	History
	10.00	10.34	16.15	11.17	7.83	7.01	9.50	10.86	13.48	14.12	NAV $
	9.88	10.25	16.31	11.06	7.71	6.95	9.64	10.92	13.52	14.21	Market Price $
	-23.63	3.53	57.89	-28.57	-29.90	-10.47	35.54	14.78	24.65	5.49	NAV Return%
	-24.32	3.87	60.85	-29.98	-30.29	-9.86	38.73	13.74	24.33	5.85	Market Price Return%
	0.03	-0.07	0.31	0.53	0.37	-0.08	0.61	0.24	0.00	-0.13	Avg Premium/Discount%
	-25.41	-16.40	30.86	-14.38	-8.48	5.47	-3.05	-5.47	11.11	-20.85	NAV Rtrn% +/-MSCI EAFE
	0.04	-1.52	-3.64	-0.40	-0.51	-0.19	-0.37	-1.08	-0.87	-0.75	NAV Rtrn% +/-MSCI JP NDT
	1	1	1	1	1	2	2	2	2	3	NAV Return% Rank in Cat
	0.00	0.00	0.43	0.00	0.00	0.00	0.02	0.45	0.53	0.74	Income Return %
	-23.63	3.53	57.46	-28.58	-29.90	-10.47	35.52	14.33	24.12	4.75	Capital Return %
	0.00	0.00	0.04	0.00	0.00	0.00	0.00	0.05	0.06	0.10	Income $
	0.01	0.01	0.11	0.45	0.00	0.00	0.00	0.00	0.00	0.00	Capital Gains $
	—	—	0.94	0.88	0.84	0.84	0.84	0.64	0.57	0.54	Expense Ratio %
	—	—	-0.27	-0.32	-0.11	-0.12	0.03	0.28	0.59	0.48	Income Ratio %
	—	—	—	22	21	2	2	5	6	8	Turnover Rate %
	120	310	979	650	474	542	2,890	6,624	13,042	13,787	Net Assets $mil

Performance 12-31-06

Historic Quarterly NAV Returns

	1st Qtr	2nd Qtr	3rd Qtr	4th Qtr	Total
2002	3.32	4.45	-12.19	-5.53	-10.47
2003	-7.56	11.42	21.47	8.34	35.54
2004	14.63	-3.95	-7.65	12.88	14.78
2005	-2.58	-3.69	18.94	11.69	24.65
2006	6.38	-4.60	-0.88	4.87	5.49

Trailing	NAV Return%	Market Return%+/-MSCI EAFE	NAV Rtrn%	%Rank Cat.(NAV)
3 Mo	4.87	5.69	-5.48	6
6 Mo	3.95	4.92	-10.74	6
1 Yr	5.49	5.85	-20.85	3
3 Yr Avg	14.71	14.39	-5.22	2
5 Yr Avg	12.87	13.36	-2.11	2
10 Yr Avg	1.36	1.45	-6.35	1

Tax Analysis	Tax-Adj Return%	Tax-Cost Ratio
3 Yr (estimated)	14.50	0.18
5 Yr (estimated)	12.74	0.12
10 Yr (estimated)	1.21	0.15

Rating and Risk

Time Period	Morningstar Rtn vs Cat	Morningstar Risk vs Cat	Morningstar Risk-Adj Rating
3 Yr	Avg	-Avg	★★★
5 Yr	Avg	-Avg	★★★
10 Yr	-Avg	-Avg	★★★

Other Measures	Standard Index S&P 500	Best Fit Index MSCI JP NDT
Alpha	-5.1	-0.7
Beta	1.08	1.00
R-Squared	46	100
Standard Deviation	14.93	
Mean	14.71	
Sharpe Ratio	0.78	

Portfolio Analysis 11-30-06

Share change since 10-06 Total Stocks:347

	Sector	Country	% Assets
⊖ Toyota Motor	Goods	Japan	6.20
⊖ Mitsubishi UFJ Financial	Financial	Japan	3.97
⊖ Mizuho Financial Grp	Financial	Japan	2.52
⊖ Sumitomo Mitsui Financia	Financial	Japan	2.28
⊖ Takeda Chemical Industri	Health	Japan	2.04
⊖ Canon	Goods	Japan	2.01
⊖ Honda Motor	Goods	Japan	1.96
⊖ Sony	Goods	Japan	1.43
⊖ Matsushita Electric Indu	Ind Mtrls	Japan	1.41
⊖ The Tokyo Electric Power	Utilities	Japan	1.31
⊖ Nomura Hldgs	Financial	Japan	1.10
⊖ Nissan Motor	Goods	Japan	0.98
⊖ NTT DoCoMo	Telecom	Japan	0.98
⊖ Nippon Steel	Ind Mtrls	Japan	0.97
⊖ Shin-Etsu Chemical	Ind Mtrls	Japan	0.95
⊖ Millea Hldgs	Financial	Japan	0.95
⊖ Mitsubishi Estate	Financial	Japan	0.95
⊖ JFE Hldgs	Ind Mtrls	Japan	0.94
⊖ Seven & I Holdings	Consumer	Japan	0.92
⊖ Nippon Telegraph & Telep	Telecom	Japan	0.91

Current Investment Style

Value Blnd Growth — Large Mid Small

Market Cap	%
Giant	51.6
Large	36.9
Mid	11.5
Small	0.0
Micro	0.0

Avg $mil: 19,642

Value Measures		Rel Category
Price/Earnings	18.06	1.09
Price/Book	1.68	1.07
Price/Sales	0.93	1.09
Price/Cash Flow	8.44	1.05
Dividend Yield %	1.44	0.83

Growth Measures	%	Rel Category
Long-Term Erngs	10.01	0.86
Book Value	12.16	1.18
Sales	3.89	0.76
Cash Flow	0.66	33.00
Historical Erngs	24.25	1.26

Composition

Cash	0.2	Bonds	0.0
Stocks	99.8	Other	0.0
Foreign (% of Stock)			100.0

Sector Weightings	% of Stocks	Rel MSCI EAFE	3 Year High	Low
↻ Info	9.44	0.80		
Software	0.44	0.79	1	0
Hardware	5.72	1.48	8	5
Media	0.77	0.42	1	1
Telecom	2.51	0.45	4	2
⊂ Service	39.76	0.84		
Health	5.96	0.84	6	3
Consumer	4.52	0.91	6	4
Business	6.82	1.35	8	7
Financial	22.46	0.75	24	16
↥ Mfg	50.81	1.24		
Goods	22.85	1.74	28	22
Ind Mtrls	22.73	1.47	24	19
Energy	0.76	0.11	1	1
Utilities	4.47	0.85	6	4

Regional Exposure % Stock

UK/W. Europe	0	N. America	0
Japan	100	Latn America	0
Asia X Japan	0	Other	0

Country Exposure % Stock

Japan	100

Morningstar's Take by William Samuel Rocco 12-31-06

IShares MSCI Japan Index has real strengths, but it's hard to use.

This ETF is attractively priced relative to its rivals. Its expense ratio has declined over time and is currently 0.59%. That's less than half what the median Japan offering levies and in line with what most other Japan ETFs charge. And the only two Japan funds that are markedly less expensive, the ETF and mutual fund versions of Vanguard Pacific Stock, devote small but significant portions of their assets to non-Japanese issues and thus may not satisfy hard-core Japan fans.

Meanwhile, this ETF provides pure and mainstream exposure to Japan. It's designed to replicate the MSCI Japan Index, a market-cap-weighted index that aims to capture the top 85% of the publicly available stock universe in Japan. As a result, this ETF's biggest holdings are well-known powerhouses like Toyota, Mitsubishi UFJ Financial Group, Canon and Sony, and its average market cap is more than twice the category norm.

Moreover, this exchange-traded fund has been a solid performer. It has tracked the returns of its index reasonably well over time (after accounting for fees). Though it regularly lagged its peers in the 1990s, it has fared better in the 2000s and its five-year annualized returns are 1 percentage point better than the Japan-category norm. And it has suffered less overall volatility than its typical peer.

All this is no doubt heartening for Japan fans, but such individuals need to recognize that this ETF can be tough to fit into their portfolios. Most foreign large-cap offerings keep around 20% of their assets in Japan and favor the same blue chips as this ETF does. Thus, investors who already have a core foreign holding will likely be doubling up on Japanese names they already own if they purchase this ETF. And while that's certainly an issue with many Japan offerings, it's a particular problem here.

Address:	45 Fremont Street San Francisco CA 94105 800-474-2737	Management Fee:	0.54%
		Expense Projections:	3Yr:$173 5Yr:$302 10Yr:$677
		Income Distrib:	Annually
Web Address:	www.ishares.com	Exchange:	NYSE
Inception:	03-12-96		
Advisor:	Barclays Global Fund Advisers		

iShares MSCI ex-Japn EPP

	Market Price	Mstar Category
	$122.79	Pacific/Asia ex-Japan Stk

Morningstar Fair Value

Price/Fair Value Ratio —   Coverage Rate % —

Management

Barclays Global Fund Investors, the world's largest manager of passively run indexed assets, operates this fund. Barclays offers nearly 100 exchange-traded funds, including individual country ETFs based on the major countries covered by this portfolio.

Methodology

This ETF tracks the MSCI's Pacific Free ex-Japan Index. Thus, it spreads its assets across four developed markets: Australia, Hong Kong, Singapore, and New Zealand. The index is market-cap-weighted, so this ETF has a pronounced large-cap bias, and it normally devotes around 66% of its assets to Australia, 21% of its assets to Hong Kong, 10% of its assets to Singapore, and 2% of its assets to New Zealand.

Morningstar Rating	Return	Risk	Yield	NAV	Avg Daily Vol. (k)	52 wk High/Low
★★★★ Above Avg	Above Avg	Low	4.2%	$124.86	147	$127.68 - $99.82

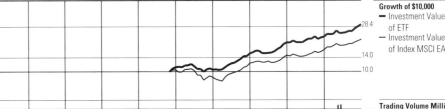

Growth of $10,000
— Investment Value of ETF
— Investment Value of Index MSCI EAFE

Trading Volume Millions

1997	1998	1999	2000	2001	2002	2003	2004	2005	2006	History
—	—	—	—	54.55	50.55	72.10	89.70	98.55	124.86	NAV $
—	—	—	—	54.17	50.79	72.48	90.17	98.67	125.24	Market Price $
—	—	—	—	22.95*	-5.73	45.73	28.68	14.03	32.07	NAV Return%
—	—	—	—	22.99*	-4.64	45.77	28.63	13.55	32.30	Market Price Return%
—	—	—	—	0.07	0.87	1.10	0.34	0.19	0.08	Avg Premium/Discount%
—	—	—	—	22.95	10.21	7.14	8.43	0.49	5.73	NAV Rtrn% +/-MSCI EAFE
—	—	—	—	22.95	5.32	4.96	14.45	-3.83	3.60	NAV Rtrn% +/-MSCIAC FExJ
—	—	—	—	7	7	7	7	9	9	NAV Return% Rank in Cat
—	—	—	—	—	1.62	2.99	4.18	4.12	5.27	Income Return %
—	—	—	—	—	-7.35	42.74	24.50	9.91	26.80	Capital Return %
—	—	—	—	0.27	0.88	1.51	3.01	3.70	5.20	Income $
—	—	—	—	0.00	0.00	0.00	0.00	0.00	0.00	Capital Gains $
—	—	—	—	—	0.50	0.50	0.50	0.50	0.50	Expense Ratio %
—	—	—	—	—	2.87	3.47	3.68	4.09	3.67	Income Ratio %
—	—	—	—	—	5	8	8	16	8	Turnover Rate %
—	—	—	—	157	490	996	1,675	2,497	Net Assets $mil

Performance 12-31-06

Historic Quarterly NAV Returns

	1st Qtr	2nd Qtr	3rd Qtr	4th Qtr	Total
2002	3.94	-1.82	-11.75	4.67	-5.73
2003	0.65	14.86	10.76	13.80	45.73
2004	6.13	-4.78	9.47	16.33	28.68
2005	0.52	4.57	9.26	-0.72	14.03
2006	6.41	2.35	3.99	16.62	32.07

Trailing	NAV Return%	Market Return%	NAV Rtrn%+/-MSCI EAFE	%Rank Cat.(NAV)
3 Mo	16.62	17.66	6.27	9
6 Mo	21.27	21.66	6.58	9
1 Yr	32.07	32.30	5.73	9
3 Yr Avg	24.67	24.56	4.74	7
5 Yr Avg	21.63	21.85	6.65	7
10 Yr Avg	—	—	—	—

Tax Analysis	Tax-Adj Return%	Tax-Cost Ratio
3 Yr (estimated)	23.07	1.28
5 Yr (estimated)	20.35	1.05
10 Yr (estimated)	—	—

Rating and Risk

Time Period	Morningstar Rtn vs Cat	Morningstar Risk vs Cat	Morningstar Risk-Adj Rating
3 Yr	+Avg	Low	★★★★
5 Yr	Avg	Low	★★★★
10 Yr	—	—	—

Other Measures	Standard Index S&P 500	Best Fit Index MSCI Pac xJp
Alpha	2.6	0.2
Beta	1.11	1.00
R-Squared	72	100
Standard Deviation	12.30	
Mean	24.67	
Sharpe Ratio	1.61	

Portfolio Analysis 12-31-06

Share change since 11-06 Total Stocks:176

	Sector	Country	% Assets
⊕ BHP Billiton, Ltd.	Ind Mtrls	Australia	6.44
⊖ National Australia Bank	Financial	Australia	4.66
⊖ Commonwealth Bank of Aus	Financial	Australia	4.56
⊖ Australia & New Zealand	Financial	Australia	3.72
⊖ Westpac Banking	Financial	Australia	3.19
⊖ Westfield Grp	Financial	Australia	2.24
⊖ Woolworths Ltd	Consumer	Australia	2.01
⊖ Hutchison Whampoa Ltd	Telecom	Hong Kong	1.99
⊖ Cheung Kong (hldgs) Ltd	Financial	Hong Kong	1.71
⊖ QBE Insurance Grp Ltd	Financial	Australia	1.64
⊕ Rio Tinto Ltd	Ind Mtrls	Australia	1.54
⊖ DBS Grp Hldgs Ltd	Financial	Singapore	1.52
⊕ Brambles	Business	Australia	1.46
⊖ Sun Hung Kai Properties	Financial	Hong Kong	1.45
⊕ Macquarie Bank Ltd	Financial	Australia	1.43
⊖ Singapore Telecommunicat	Telecom	Singapore	1.39
⊖ AMP Ltd	Financial	Australia	1.37
⊕ Woodside Petroleum Ltd	Energy	Australia	1.34
⊖ United Overseas Bank Ltd	Financial	Singapore	1.33
⊕ CLP Holdings Limited	Utilities	Hong Kong	1.22

Current Investment Style

Value Blnd Growth — Large Mid Small

Market Cap	%
Giant	50.0
Large	40.0
Mid	9.9
Small	0.0
Micro	0.0

Avg $mil: 14,696

Value Measures		Rel Category
Price/Earnings	15.66	1.03
Price/Book	2.28	1.10
Price/Sales	2.13	1.13
Price/Cash Flow	11.11	1.21
Dividend Yield %	4.59	1.18

Growth Measures	%	Rel Category
Long-Term Erngs	11.86	0.89
Book Value	3.41	0.47
Sales	11.97	0.77
Cash Flow	14.17	1.13
Historical Erngs	20.41	1.20

Composition

Cash	0.3	Bonds	0.0
Stocks	99.7	Other	0.0
Foreign (% of Stock)			100.0

Sector Weightings	% of Stocks	Rel MSCI EAFE	3 Year High Low
ⓘ Info	7.99	0.68	
🖥 Software	0.30	0.54	0 0
💻 Hardware	0.50	0.13	1 0
🎬 Media	1.49	0.81	4 1
📶 Telecom	5.70	1.02	8 4
🛎 Service	63.94	1.35	
🏥 Health	2.17	0.30	2 1
🛒 Consumer	7.02	1.42	7 5
💼 Business	7.09	1.40	7 5
$ Financial	47.66	1.58	49 45
🏭 Mfg	28.06	0.69	
📦 Goods	3.44	0.26	4 3
⚙ Ind Mtrls	18.00	1.17	21 18
🔥 Energy	2.81	0.39	3 2
💡 Utilities	3.81	0.73	5 3

Regional Exposure	% Stock		
UK/W. Europe	0	N. America	0
Japan	0	Latn America	0
Asia X Japan	100	Other	0

Country Exposure	% Stock		
Australia	66	New Zealand	2
Hong Kong	21		
Singapore	11		

Morningstar's Take by William Samuel Rocco 12-31-06

IShares MSCI Pacific ex-Japan doesn't provide what many investors might expect.

This ETF stands out from its rivals from a country perspective. Most Pacific/Asia ex-Japan offerings invest in eight to 10 countries and pay significant attention to the region's many emerging markets, but this ETF invests in just four countries, and they're all developed markets. Further, while many, but not all, of its rivals ignore Australia, it keeps around 66% of its assets there.

This ETF also differs from its rivals in other respects. It typically has nearly twice as much exposure to financial stocks as the average Pacific/Asia ex-Japan offering, because Australia, Hong Kong, and Singapore are full of banking, real estate, and other financial issues. It has far less exposure to hardware stocks than its average rival for the opposite reason. And it's heavy on industrial materials names because Australia is. What's more, it tracks a market-cap-weighted index of larger stocks from the region's biggest markets, so it has a relatively hefty median market cap.

The overall portfolio is relatively conservative as well as rather distinctive, and that's reflected in the risk/reward profile. This ETF has been less volatile than nearly all other Pacific/Asia ex-Japan offerings so far. And it has posted decent overall returns since opening in late 2001, while outperforming in a rough 2002 and posting mixed results in the ensuing rallies.

All this may be appealing to reserved fans of the region, particularly once this ETF's low costs are taken into account, but such investors should consider two more things before jumping aboard. Australia has outpaced many of its neighbors in recent years, largely due to the strength of its metals stocks, so this ETF has enjoyed favorable conditions thus far. And though it will reap indirect benefits, this ETF won't directly profit from future growth in China, India, and other emerging markets in the region like most of its rivals will.

Address:	45 Fremont Street San Francisco CA 94105 800-474-2737	Management Fee:	0.50%
		Expense Projections:	3Yr:$160 5Yr:$280 10Yr:$628
		Income Distrib:	Annually
Web Address:	www.ishares.com	Exchange:	AMEX
Inception:	10-25-01 *		
Advisor:	Barclays Global Fund Advisers		

 MORNINGSTAR® ETFs 150

iShares NASD Biotech IBB

	Market Price	Mstar Category
	$78.91	Specialty-Health

Morningstar Fair Value

Price/Fair Value Ratio	Coverage Rate %
0.88 Undervalued	72 Fair

Management

Barclays Global Investors runs this fund. It is the world's largest advisor of indexed assets. It also is the sponsor of the world's largest ETF family.

Methodology

The fund uses representative sampling to track the Nasdaq Biotechnology Index. Companies that meet the FTSE definition of biotech are commonly those that do most of their research and development on drugs and diagnostic tools with "living material" and derive most of their revenue from these products. The stocks also must have a market cap of $200 million, trading volume of 100,000 shares, and six months of trading history. They cannot be in bankruptcy or have a withdrawn audit opinion.

Morningstar Rating	Return	Risk	Yield	NAV	Avg Daily Vol. (k)	52 wk High/Low
★ Lowest	Lowest	High	—	$77.90	961	$85.41 - $67.94

Growth of $10,000
- Investment Value of ETF
- Investment Value of Index S&P 500

Trading Volume Millions

	1997	1998	1999	2000	2001	2002	2003	2004	2005	2006	History
	—	—	—	—	90.94	49.62	72.24	75.40	77.46	77.90	NAV $
	—	—	—	—	91.05	49.35	71.95	75.40	77.24	77.76	Market Price $
	—	—	—	—	-4.09*	-45.44	45.59	4.37	2.73	0.57	NAV Return%
	—	—	—	—	-4.12*	-45.80	45.80	4.79	2.44	0.67	Market Price Return%
	—	—	—	—	-0.19	-0.04	-0.03	-0.12	0.03	-0.12	Avg Premium/Discount%
	—	—	—	—	-4.09	-23.34	16.91	-6.51	-2.18	-15.22	NAV Rtrn% +/-S&P 500
	—	—	—	—	-4.09	-24.63	26.16	-0.18	-5.59	-6.31	NAV Rtrn% +/-DJ Hlthcare
	—	—	—	—	4	5	5	5	5	7	NAV Return% Rank in Cat
	—	—	—	—	—	0.00	0.00	0.00	0.00	0.00	Income Return %
	—	—	—	—	—	-45.44	45.59	4.37	2.73	0.57	Capital Return %
	—	—	—	—	0.00	0.00	0.00	0.00	0.00	0.00	Income $
	—	—	—	—	0.00	0.00	0.00	0.00	0.00	0.00	Capital Gains $
	—	—	—	—	0.50	0.50	0.50	0.50	0.50	0.50	Expense Ratio %
	—	—	—	—	-0.50	-0.46	-0.43	-0.43	-0.40	-0.37	Income Ratio %
	—	—	—	—	9	17	48	36	14	15	Turnover Rate %
	—	—	—	—	214	486	708	1,493	1,607	1,605	Net Assets $mil

Performance 12-31-06

Historic Quarterly NAV Returns

	1st Qtr	2nd Qtr	3rd Qtr	4th Qtr	Total
2002	-15.02	-34.06	-8.83	6.80	-45.44
2003	2.96	31.16	7.07	0.68	45.59
2004	7.13	-2.87	-6.86	7.70	4.37
2005	-15.31	6.14	13.60	0.60	2.73
2006	6.21	-11.61	1.38	5.67	0.57

Trailing	NAV Return%	Market Return%	NAV Rtrn% +/-S&P 500	%Rank Cat.(NAV)
3 Mo	5.67	5.39	-1.03	14
6 Mo	7.12	6.96	-5.62	13
1 Yr	0.57	0.67	-15.22	7
3 Yr Avg	2.55	2.62	-7.89	4
5 Yr Avg	-3.05	-3.11	-9.24	4
10 Yr Avg	—	—	—	—

Tax Analysis	Tax-Adj Return%	Tax-Cost Ratio
3 Yr (estimated)	2.55	0.00
5 Yr (estimated)	-3.05	0.00
10 Yr (estimated)	—	—

Rating and Risk

Time Period	Morningstar Rtn vs Cat	Morningstar Risk vs Cat	Morningstar Risk-Adj Rating
3 Yr	Low	+Avg	★
5 Yr	Low	High	★
10 Yr	—	—	—

Other Measures

	Standard Index S&P 500	Best Fit Index Merrill Lynch Convert
Alpha	-10.2	-5.9
Beta	1.53	1.89
R-Squared	46	58
Standard Deviation	15.42	
Mean	2.55	
Sharpe Ratio	0.03	

Morningstar's Take by Christopher Davis 12-31-06

IShares Nasdaq Biotechnology is affordable, but its risks greatly limit its appeal.

Investing in biotechnology-focused investments is a costly proposition. There are 15 funds and ETFs solely or mostly focused on the industry, charging roughly 1.5% per year for their services on average. By contrast, this exchange-traded fund's annual levy is just 0.50%, giving it a big head start over the competition.

The fund's considerable expense advantage has often been overwhelmed by high volatility and big losses. Indeed, in the 58 rolling one-year periods since its February 2001 inception, the fund has suffered losses in nearly half of them, the biggest being its 50% slide from July 2001 through June 2002. To be sure, much of that stretch includes the wrenching bear market. But the fund has also run into trouble more recently. It slumped 15% from March through July 2006 as biotech stocks faltered, versus a 6% loss for the typical health-care offering. All told, the fund's standard deviation (a

measure of volatility) is among the highest in the health-care category.

Of course, a bumpy ride goes with the biotech territory. Whenever investors flee from riskier fare, biotech stocks take it on the chin. That's because many are small firms whose fates are tied to a handful of marketable or still-unavailable products. It's true the fund's bogy, the Nasdaq Biotechnology Index, screens out stocks with market caps below $200 million and don't trade a lot, which keeps out the most speculative fare. Still, at $4.1 billion, its average market cap is about 80% below the typical health-care fund's. Moreover, biotech stocks usually aren't cheap, either--witness this fund's well above-market price multiples. There's also plenty of stock-specific risk, with top holding Amgen soaking up 14% of assets.

Of course, the potential for reward at this ETF is great, but most investors can live without the risk. If you must own it, hold it in limited doses.

Address:	45 Fremont Street San Francisco CA 94105 800-474-2737	Management Fee:	0.48%
		Expense Projections:	3Yr:$154 5Yr:$269 10Yr:$604
Web Address:	www.ishares.com	Income Distrib:	Annually
Inception:	02-05-01 *	Exchange:	AMEX
Advisor:	Barclays Global Fund Advisers		

Portfolio Analysis 12-31-06

Share change since 11-06 Total Stocks:173

	Sector	PE	Tot Ret%	% Assets
⊖ Amgen, Inc.	Health	28.0	-13.38	14.19
⊖ Gilead Sciences, Inc.	Health	41.1	23.51	5.78
⊖ Celgene Corporation	Health	—	77.56	5.29
⊖ Teva Pharmaceutical Indu	Health	19.6	-27.22	3.66
⊖ Biogen Idec, Inc.	Health	NMF	8.64	3.64
⊖ Genzyme Corporation	Health	46.6	-13.00	3.21
⊖ Vertex Pharmaceuticals	Health	—	35.24	2.49
⊖ Sepracor, Inc.	Health	NMF	19.34	1.84
⊖ Shire PLC ADR	Health	39.3	59.84	1.71
⊖ MedImmune, Inc.	Health	—	-7.57	1.61
⊖ Medarex, Inc.	Health	—	6.79	1.42
⊖ Abraxis BioScience, Inc.	Health	54.7	-29.52	1.33
⊖ Amylin Pharmaceuticals	Health	—	-9.64	1.25
⊖ New River Pharmaceutical	Health	—	110.91	1.12
⊖ Cephalon, Inc.	Health	28.3	8.76	1.11
⊖ Gen-Probe, Inc.	Health	45.9	7.34	1.09
⊕ Regeneron Pharmaceutical	Health	—	26.23	1.04
⊖ Endo Pharmaceutical Hold	Health	16.9	-8.86	1.03
⊖ Biomarin Pharmaceutical,	Health	—	52.04	1.02
⊖ OSI Pharmaceuticals, Inc	Health	—	24.75	1.02

Current Investment Style

Value Blnd Growth — Large Mid Small

Market Cap	%
Giant	14.2
Large	23.3
Mid	19.6
Small	27.8
Micro	15.1

Avg $mil: 4,050

Value Measures

		Rel Category
Price/Earnings	23.80	1.15
Price/Book	3.90	1.10
Price/Sales	5.74	1.93
Price/Cash Flow	16.96	1.16
Dividend Yield %	0.01	0.01

Growth Measures

	%	Rel Category
Long-Term Erngs	18.21	1.28
Book Value	-0.03	NMF
Sales	18.41	1.53
Cash Flow	22.99	2.02
Historical Erngs	32.05	2.16

Profitability

	%	Rel Category
Return on Equity	-1.88	NMF
Return on Assets	-7.09	NMF
Net Margin	7.94	0.70

Industry Weightings

	% of Stocks	Rel Cat
Biotech	83.6	2.5
Drugs	12.0	0.4
Mgd Care	0.0	0.0
Hospitals	0.0	0.0
Other HC Srv	0.0	0.0
Diagnostics	1.6	1.3
Equipment	1.6	0.1
Good/Srv	1.2	0.3
Other	0.0	0.0

Composition

● Cash	0.0
● Stocks	100.0
● Bonds	0.0
● Other	0.0
Foreign	9.2
(% of Stock)	

iShares NYSE 100 Index NY

	Market Price	Mstar Category
	$74.31	Large Value

Morningstar Fair Value

Price/Fair Value Ratio	Coverage Rate %
0.90 Undervalued	98 Good

Management

This ETF is advised by Barclays Global Fund Advisors. Patrick O'Connor and S. Jane Leung are responsible for its daily management. O'Connor has managed index funds at Barclays since 1999. Leung's tenure at the firm began in 2001.

Methodology

This ETF's benchmark is the NYSE 100, a collection of the 100 largest stocks (as measured by market capitalization) listed on the New York Stock Exchange. It's loaded with financially sturdy blue chips, but it has certain idiosyncrasies because it excludes stocks listed on other exchanges.

Morningstar Rating	Return	Risk	Yield	NAV	Avg Daily Vol. (k)	52 wk High/Low
— Not Rated	Not Rated		1.6%	$74.91	20	$75.56 - $64.79

Growth of $10,000
- Investment Value of ETF
- Investment Value of Index S&P 500

	1997	1998	1999	2000	2001	2002	2003	2004	2005	2006	History
	—	—	—	—	—	—	—	64.27	65.14	74.91	NAV $
	—	—	—	—	—	—	—	64.40	65.23	74.94	Market Price $
	—	—	—	—	—	—	—	9.90*	3.52	16.96	NAV Return%
	—	—	—	—	—	—	—	9.78*	3.45	16.85	Market Price Return%
	—	—	—	—	—	—	—	-0.02	0.05	0.09	Avg Premium/Discount%
	—	—	—	—	—	—	—	9.90	-1.39	1.17	NAV Rtrn% +/-S&P 500
	—	—	—	—	—	—	—	9.90	-3.53	-5.29	NAV Rtrn% +/-Russ 1000 Vl
	—	—	—	—	—	—	—	—	11	14	NAV Return% Rank in Cat
	—	—	—	—	—	—	—	—	2.14	1.86	Income Return %
	—	—	—	—	—	—	—	—	1.38	15.10	Capital Return %
	—	—	—	—	—	—	—	0.84	1.36	1.20	Income $
	—	—	—	—	—	—	—	0.00	0.00	0.00	Capital Gains $
	—	—	—	—	—	—	—	0.20	0.20	0.20	Expense Ratio %
	—	—	—	—	—	—	—	1.89	2.03	1.83	Income Ratio %
	—	—	—	—	—	—	—	3	7	6	Turnover Rate %
	—	—	—	—	—	—	—	26	29	345	Net Assets $mil

Performance 12-31-06

Historic Quarterly NAV Returns

	1st Qtr	2nd Qtr	3rd Qtr	4th Qtr	Total
2002	—	—	—	—	—
2003	—	—	—	—	—
2004	—	0.58	-1.13	7.32	—*
2005	-1.43	0.37	2.50	2.08	3.52
2006	3.60	-0.25	6.27	6.51	16.96

Trailing	NAV Return%	Market Return%	NAV Rtrn% +/-S&P 500	%Rank Cat.(NAV)
3 Mo	6.51	6.43	-0.19	16
6 Mo	13.19	13.05	0.45	16
1 Yr	16.96	16.85	1.17	14
3 Yr Avg	—	—	—	—
5 Yr Avg	—	—	—	—
10 Yr Avg	—	—	—	—

Tax Analysis	Tax-Adj Return%	Tax-Cost Ratio
3 Yr (estimated)	—	—
5 Yr (estimated)	—	—
10 Yr (estimated)	—	—

Rating and Risk

Time Period	Morningstar Rtn vs Cat	Morningstar Risk vs Cat	Morningstar Risk-Adj Rating
3 Yr	—	—	—
5 Yr	—	—	—
10 Yr	—	—	—

Other Measures	Standard Index S&P 500	Best Fit Index
Alpha	—	—
Beta	—	—
R-Squared	—	—
Standard Deviation	—	
Mean	—	
Sharpe Ratio	—	

Portfolio Analysis 12-31-06

Share change since 11-06 Total Stocks:100	Sector	PE	Tot Ret%	% Assets
⊖ ExxonMobil Corporation	Energy	11.7	39.07	6.16
⊖ General Electric Company	Ind Mtrls	19.8	9.35	5.34
⊖ Citigroup, Inc.	Financial	13.3	19.55	3.82
⊖ Bank of America Corporat	Financial	12.4	20.68	3.31
⊖ Procter & Gamble Company	Goods	24.2	13.36	2.81
⊖ Johnson & Johnson	Health	17.4	12.44	2.64
⊖ Pfizer Inc.	Health	15.1	15.22	2.58
⊖ Altria Group, Inc.	Goods	15.9	19.87	2.45
⊖ J.P. Morgan Chase & Co.	Financial	13.7	25.60	2.32
⊖ American International G	Financial	17.1	6.05	2.25
⊖ Chevron Corporation	Energy	9.3	33.75	2.23
⊖ IBM	Hardware	16.8	19.77	2.02
⊖ AT&T, Inc.	Telecom	19.2	51.59	1.89
⊖ Wal-Mart Stores, Inc.	Consumer	16.6	0.13	1.65
⊖ Hewlett-Packard Company	Hardware	18.9	45.21	1.56
⊖ Wells Fargo Company	Financial	14.7	16.82	1.55
⊖ ConocoPhillips	Energy	6.9	26.53	1.53
⊖ Wachovia Corporation	Financial	13.0	12.02	1.50
⊖ Verizon Communications	Telecom	16.1	34.88	1.49
⊖ Coca-Cola Company	Goods	21.5	23.10	1.43

Current Investment Style

Value Blnd Growth — Large/Mid/Small (Giant highlighted)

Market Cap	%
Giant	74.4
Large	25.6
Mid	0.0
Small	0.0
Micro	0.0

Avg $mil: 105,476

Value Measures		Rel Category
Price/Earnings	14.58	1.02
Price/Book	2.63	1.09
Price/Sales	1.63	1.23
Price/Cash Flow	9.79	1.27
Dividend Yield %	2.17	0.84

Growth Measures	%	Rel Category
Long-Term Erngs	10.63	1.06
Book Value	10.74	1.49
Sales	11.95	1.40
Cash Flow	11.00	1.28
Historical Erngs	18.34	1.18

Profitability	%	Rel Category
Return on Equity	20.78	1.19
Return on Assets	11.63	1.17
Net Margin	14.62	1.07

Sector Weightings	% of Stocks	Rel S&P 500	3 Year High Low
Info	13.99	0.70	
Software	0.00	0.00	0 0
Hardware	5.66	0.61	6 5
Media	3.01	0.79	5 3
Telecom	5.32	1.52	5 4
Service	47.69	1.03	
Health	14.65	1.21	18 14
Consumer	5.58	0.73	7 5
Business	1.85	0.44	3 2
Financial	25.61	1.15	26 24
Mfg	38.31	1.13	
Goods	9.81	1.15	11 10
Ind Mtrls	12.35	1.03	14 12
Energy	13.88	1.42	15 8
Utilities	2.27	0.65	2 1

Composition

	%
Cash	0.1
Stocks	99.9
Bonds	0.0
Other	0.0
Foreign	0.0
(% of Stock)	

Morningstar's Take by Sonya Morris 12-31-06

Although it's not the worst choice in the world, iShares NYSE 100 Index isn't the model core holding.

This ETF tracks the NYSE 100 Index, which includes the 100 largest stocks, as measured by market capitalization, listed on the New York Stock Exchange. That gives this fund certain peculiarities that have implications for its performance. For example, because it concentrates on market giants, its aggregate market cap is one of the highest in the large-value category. On the plus side, that means this portfolio is loaded with global industry leaders that possess significant competitive advantages. In fact, 43 of the ETF's 100 holdings have been awarded wide-moat ratings by Morningstar equity analysts. On the other hand, because this ETF emphasizes the market's biggest names, it is likely to lag when smaller stocks rule the roost, as has been the case for the past few years. This fund's average annual returns since its March 2004 inception trail almost 90% of its large-value rivals.

That said, there are signs that market winds may be shifting, and mega-cap stocks have looked stronger in recent months. Unfortunately, this ETF's foibles have kept it from fully capitalizing on that trend. Because it excludes stocks not listed on the NYSE, it has a light tech weighting, since many of those stocks are listed on the Nasdaq. Consequently, this fund has been at a competitive disadvantage to other similar ETFs. For example, iShares S&P 100 Index, which also focuses on big blue chips, has gotten a lift lately from a number of Nasdaq-listed stocks such as Microsoft, Cisco Systems, and Comcast. Consequently, iShares S&P 100 has outperformed this fund in 2006.

Granted, this ETF has certain charms. With an expense ratio of 0.20%, it offers cheap exposure to financially solid industry leaders. But its benchmark's biases make it a less-than-ideal choice for a core holding.

Address:	45 Fremont Street	Management Fee:	0.20%	
	San Francisco CA 94105	Expense Projections:	3Yr:$64	5Yr:$113 10Yr:$255
	800-474-2737	Income Distrib:	Quarterly	
Web Address:	www.ishares.com	Exchange:	NYSE	
Inception:	03-29-04 *			
Advisor:	Barclays Global Fund Advisers			

MORNINGSTAR® ETFs 150

iShares R1000 Growth IWF

Market Price $55.43	**Mstar Category** Large Growth

Morningstar Fair Value

Price/Fair Value Ratio
0.88 Undervalued

Coverage Rate %
96 Good

Management

Barclays Global Fund Advisors is the advisor. The firm is the world's largest manager of indexed portfolios. Patrick O'Connor and S. Jane Leung are responsible for the daily management of this ETF. O'Connor has managed index funds at Barclays since 1999. Leung's tenure at the firm began in 2001.

Methodology

This exchange-traded fund tracks the Russell 1000 Growth Index, which is a subset of the Russell 1000 Index of the largest 1,000 publicly traded U.S. stocks. As such, the portfolio spans hundreds of individual names and the full panoply of industries. This fund and its bogy focus on large-cap stocks in the Russell 1000 with higher book values and forecast earnings growth.

Morningstar Rating ★★★ Neutral	Return Neutral	Risk Average	Yield 0.9%	NAV $55.10	Avg Daily Vol. (k) 1,346	52 wk High/Low $55.84 - $47.92

Growth of $10,000
— Investment Value of ETF
— Investment Value of Index S&P 500

Trading Volume Millions

	1997	1998	1999	2000	2001	2002	2003	2004	2005	2006	History
	—	—	—	64.52	50.99	36.45	46.77	49.09	51.11	55.10	NAV $
	—	—	—	64.62	50.94	36.55	46.80	49.15	51.01	55.03	Market Price $
	—	—	—	-4.60*	-20.64	-27.99	29.46	6.10	5.08	8.86	NAV Return%
	—	—	—	-4.62*	-20.84	-27.73	29.19	6.16	4.75	8.94	Market Price Return%
	—	—	—	0.08	0.01	0.02	0.01	0.12	0.02	0.01	Avg Premium/Discount%
	—	—	—	-4.60	-8.75	-5.89	0.78	-4.78	0.17	-6.93	NAV Rtrn% +/-S&P 500
	—	—	—	-4.60	-0.22	-0.11	-0.29	-0.20	-0.18	-0.21	NAV Rtrn% +/-Russ 1000Gr
	—	—	—	—	6	6	6	7	10	13	NAV Return% Rank in Cat
	—	—	—	—	0.32	0.58	1.02	1.10	0.93	1.00	Income Return %
	—	—	—	—	-20.96	-28.57	28.44	5.00	4.15	7.86	Capital Return %
	—	—	—	0.09	0.21	0.29	0.37	0.51	0.45	0.51	Income $
	—	—	—	0.11	0.00	0.00	0.00	0.00	0.00	0.00	Capital Gains $
	—	—	—	0.20	0.20	0.20	0.20	0.20	0.20	0.20	Expense Ratio %
	—	—	—	0.26	0.52	0.92	0.87	1.27	0.96	Income Ratio %
	—	—	—	—	11	22	13	9	14	18	Turnover Rate %
	—	—	—	106	502	744	1,455	3,071	5,399	7,675	Net Assets $mil

Performance 12-31-06

Historic Quarterly NAV Returns

	1st Qtr	2nd Qtr	3rd Qtr	4th Qtr	Total
2002	-2.63	-18.70	-15.07	7.10	-27.99
2003	-1.11	14.22	3.86	10.35	29.46
2004	0.74	1.90	-5.26	9.10	6.10
2005	-4.12	2.41	3.96	2.94	5.08
2006	3.04	-3.95	3.89	5.87	8.86

Trailing	NAV Return%	Market Return%	NAV Rtrn% +/-S&P 500	%Rank Cat.(NAV)
3 Mo	5.87	5.82	-0.83	15
6 Mo	9.99	9.33	-2.75	15
1 Yr	8.86	8.94	-6.93	13
3 Yr Avg	6.67	6.60	-3.77	7
5 Yr Avg	2.50	2.49	-3.69	6
10 Yr Avg	—	—	—	

Tax Analysis	Tax-Adj Return%	Tax-Cost Ratio
3 Yr (estimated)	6.30	0.35
5 Yr (estimated)	2.17	0.32
10 Yr (estimated)	—	—

Rating and Risk

Time Period	Morningstar Rtn vs Cat	Morningstar Risk vs Cat	Morningstar Risk-Adj Rating
3 Yr	Avg	-Avg	★★★
5 Yr	Avg	Avg	★★★
10 Yr	—	—	—

Other Measures	Standard Index S&P 500	Best Fit Index Russ 1000Gr
Alpha	-4.5	-0.2
Beta	1.15	1.00
R-Squared	89	100
Standard Deviation	8.42	
Mean	6.67	
Sharpe Ratio	0.43	

Portfolio Analysis 12-31-06

Share change since 11-06 Total Stocks:683

	Sector	PE	Tot Ret%	% Assets
⊕ Microsoft Corporation	Software	23.7	15.83	3.72
⊕ General Electric Company	Ind Mtrls	19.8	9.35	2.64
⊕ Johnson & Johnson	Health	17.4	12.44	2.43
⊕ Cisco Systems, Inc.	Hardware	28.8	59.64	2.34
⊕ IBM	Hardware	16.8	19.77	1.92
⊕ Intel Corporation	Hardware	20.3	-17.18	1.65
⊕ Wal-Mart Stores, Inc.	Consumer	16.6	0.13	1.60
⊕ PepsiCo, Inc.	Goods	21.4	7.86	1.45
⊕ Google, Inc.	Business	58.6	11.00	1.35
⊕ Altria Group, Inc.	Goods	15.9	19.87	1.14
⊕ Amgen, Inc.	Health	28.0	-13.38	1.13
⊕ Home Depot, Inc.	Consumer	13.7	1.01	1.10
⊕ UnitedHealth Group, Inc.	Health	21.0	-13.49	1.02
⊕ Apple Computer, Inc.	Hardware	37.4	18.01	1.01
⊕ Boeing Company	Ind Mtrls	41.1	28.38	1.00
⊕ Hewlett-Packard Company	Hardware	18.9	45.21	0.98
⊕ Oracle Corporation	Software	25.6	40.38	0.96
⊕ American Express Company	Financial	21.2	19.09	0.92
⊕ Coca-Cola Company	Goods	21.5	23.10	0.91
⊕ Medtronic, Inc.	Health	23.7	-6.29	0.91

Morningstar's Take by Sonya Morris 12-31-06

IShares Russell 1000 Growth Index just doesn't stand out from the competition.

This exchange-traded fund provides broad exposure to large-growth stocks at a very low price. But investors can get almost the same thing at an even lower price. Vanguard Growth ETF has very similar style and sector characteristics as this fund's, yet its 0.11% expense ratio is almost half this ETF's 0.20% levy. What's more, the conventional share class of Vanguard Growth Index charges just 0.22%. True, that's slightly more expensive than this ETF, but investors don't have to pay brokerage commissions to invest in it, which makes it a better deal for those who plan to make periodic purchases over time.

This ETF's performance also fails to impress. Its three- and five-year trailing returns lag 60% of its large-growth rivals. Some investors might be willing to accept such subpar results if this fund were less volatile than the competition. But that hasn't been the case here. According to its five-year standard deviation of returns (a statistical measure of volatility), this ETF hasn't been significantly less turbulent than its peers.

Furthermore, competing index providers have done a better job of keeping up with indexing best practices. For example, Standard & Poor's, MSCI, and Dow Jones Wilshire all employ more-complex style methodologies that use several variables to identify growth and value stocks. In contrast, Russell relies on only two measures--price/book ratios and analysts' estimates for long-term earnings growth--to accomplish the same task.

Granted, this ETF has some appealing traits. It provides exposure to a broad swath of large-growth stocks at a reasonable price. And it's run by a capable management team that has done a good job of tracking its benchmark over time. But those strengths aren't enough to make up for its weaknesses.

In short, we think investors have better choices than this ETF.

Address:	45 Fremont Street San Francisco CA 94105 800-474-2737
Web Address:	www.ishares.com
Inception:	05-22-00*
Advisor:	Barclays Global Fund Advisers

Management Fee:	0.20%		
Expense Projections:	3Yr:$64	5Yr:$113	10Yr:$255
Income Distrib:	Quarterly		
Exchange:	NYSE		

Current Investment Style

Value Blnd Growth — Large Mid Small

Market Cap	%
Giant	41.4
Large	36.2
Mid	21.9
Small	0.5
Micro	0.0

Avg $mil: 34,261

Value Measures		Rel Category
Price/Earnings	19.54	0.94
Price/Book	3.75	1.15
Price/Sales	1.78	1.01
Price/Cash Flow	12.34	1.10
Dividend Yield %	1.16	1.35

Growth Measures	%	Rel Category
Long-Term Erngs	13.68	0.91
Book Value	9.54	1.19
Sales	11.73	1.00
Cash Flow	12.11	0.83
Historical Erngs	19.33	0.68

Profitability	%	Rel Category
Return on Equity	22.34	1.11
Return on Assets	11.22	1.13
Net Margin	13.46	1.07

Sector Weightings	% of Stocks	Rel S&P 500	3 Year High Low	
↻ Info	26.64	1.33		
▦ Software	6.49	1.88	7	6
▣ Hardware	15.62	1.69	18	15
🎤 Media	3.66	0.97	4	3
▮ Telecom	0.87	0.25	1	1
⊂ Service	46.94	1.02		
▨ Health	17.45	1.45	26	17
▤ Consumer	12.87	1.68	15	12
⬡ Business	8.09	1.91	8	5
$ Financial	8.53	0.38	10	6
⬓ Mfg	26.40	0.78		
⬢ Goods	8.17	0.96	11	8
◈ Ind Mtrls	12.90	1.08	14	6
⬡ Energy	4.10	0.42	5	1
⬡ Utilities	1.23	0.35	1	0

Composition

● Cash	0.1	
● Stocks	99.9	
● Bonds	0.0	
● Other	0.0	
Foreign	0.0	
(% of Stock)		

iShares R1000 Index IWB

	Market Price $76.63	Mstar Category Large Blend

Morningstar Fair Value

Price/Fair Value Ratio
0.91 Undervalued

Coverage Rate %
96 Good

Management

Barclays Global Fund Advisors is the advisor. The firm is the market leader when it comes to index funds. Daily managerial chores at this ETF are handled by Patrick O'Connor and S. Jane Leung. O'Connor has managed index funds at Barclays since 1999. Leung's tenure at the firm began in 2001.

Methodology

This exchange-traded fund tracks the Russell 1000 Index, a collection of the largest 1,000 publicly traded U.S. stocks. As such, the portfolio spans hundreds of individual names and the full panoply of industries. Unlike conventional index mutual funds, shares in ETFs are bought and sold throughout the day on the secondary market (similar to closed-end funds). So, management does not have to buy or sell shares depending on the flow of assets into the fund.

Morningstar Rating ★★★★ Above Avg	Return Above Avg	Risk Average	Yield 1.6%	NAV $76.85	Avg Daily Vol. (k) 266	52 wk High/Low $77.57 - $66.57

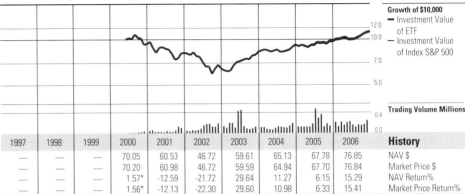

Growth of $10,000
— Investment Value of ETF
— Investment Value of Index S&P 500

Trading Volume Millions

	1997	1998	1999	2000	2001	2002	2003	2004	2005	2006	History
	—	—	—	70.05	60.53	46.72	59.61	65.13	67.78	76.85	NAV $
	—	—	—	70.20	60.98	46.72	59.59	64.94	67.70	76.84	Market Price $
	—	—	—	1.57*	-12.59	-21.72	29.64	11.27	6.15	15.29	NAV Return%
	—	—	—	1.56*	-12.13	-22.30	29.60	10.98	6.33	15.41	Market Price Return%
	—	—	—	-0.05	0.10	-0.02	0.08	0.01	0.02	-0.03	Avg Premium/Discount%
	—	—	—	1.57	-0.70	0.38	0.96	0.39	1.24	-0.50	NAV Rtrn% +/-S&P 500
	—	—	—	1.57	-0.14	-0.07	-0.25	-0.13	-0.12	-0.17	NAV Rtrn% +/-Russ 1000
	—	—	—	—	12	14	14	16	21	30	NAV Return% Rank in Cat
	—	—	—	—	0.99	1.20	1.82	1.90	2.01	1.79	Income Return %
	—	—	—	—	-13.58	-22.92	27.82	9.37	4.14	13.50	Capital Return %
	—	—	—	0.45	0.69	0.72	0.85	1.12	1.30	1.21	Income $
	—	—	—	0.00	0.00	0.00	0.00	0.00	0.00	0.00	Capital Gains $
	—	—	—	—	0.15	0.15	0.15	0.15	0.15	0.15	Expense Ratio %
	—	—	—	—	1.01	1.23	1.66	1.62	1.87	1.72	Income Ratio %
	—	—	—	—	9	8	5	5	5	7	Turnover Rate %
	—	—	—	238	393	691	1,860	1,869	2,413	3,051	Net Assets $mil

Performance 12-31-06

Historic Quarterly NAV Returns

	1st Qtr	2nd Qtr	3rd Qtr	4th Qtr	Total
2002	0.71	-13.49	-16.89	8.10	-21.72
2003	-2.97	15.66	2.96	12.20	29.64
2004	1.87	1.37	-1.82	9.75	11.27
2005	-1.92	2.02	3.93	2.08	6.15
2006	4.46	-1.69	5.02	6.90	15.29

Trailing	NAV Return%	Market Return%	NAV Rtrn% +/-S&P 500	%Rank Cat.(NAV)
3 Mo	6.90	6.84	0.20	44
6 Mo	12.26	12.18	-0.48	38
1 Yr	15.29	15.41	-0.50	30
3 Yr Avg	10.84	10.85	0.40	15
5 Yr Avg	6.68	6.52	0.49	13
10 Yr Avg	—	—	—	—

Tax Analysis	Tax-Adj Return%	Tax-Cost Ratio
3 Yr (estimated)	10.14	0.63
5 Yr (estimated)	6.04	0.60
10 Yr (estimated)	—	—

Rating and Risk

Time Period	Morningstar Rtn vs Cat	Morningstar Risk vs Cat	Morningstar Risk-Adj Rating
3 Yr	+Avg	Avg	★★★★
5 Yr	+Avg	Avg	★★★★
10 Yr	—	—	—

Other Measures	Standard Index S&P 500	Best Fit Index Russ 1000
Alpha	0.2	-0.1
Beta	1.03	1.00
R-Squared	99	100
Standard Deviation	7.13	
Mean	10.84	
Sharpe Ratio	1.04	

Morningstar's Take by Sonya Morris 12-31-06

IShares Russell 1000 Index offers reliable exposure to large caps, but it faces challenges from cheaper rivals.

As far as large-cap benchmarks go, this ETF's bogy runs a distant second to the S&P 500, which is the most popular proxy for the large-cap universe by far. Indeed, far more indexing assets are tied to the S&P 500 than to the Russell 1000. That's somewhat curious because the Russell 1000 Index is more reflective of the large-blend peer group, particularly when it comes to size characteristics. To illustrate, this ETF's average market cap is just a shade higher than the typical large-blend fund, while the S&P 500's is more than a third higher than the category norm.

That positioning has worked in this ETF's favor of late. Over the past five years, this ETF has generated 0.5% more in annual returns on average than its rival, iShares S&P 500 Index. The market's biggest stocks have struggled over the past few years, and that has been a drag on the mega-cap-heavy S&P 500. But market winds could be shifting, as blue chips have shown renewed strength of late; consequently, the iShares S&P 500 has outperformed this fund so far in 2006. That said, investors shouldn't make too much of these performance differences. Since these ETFs have so much of their portfolios in common, we'd expect them to perform very similarly over longer stretches of time.

Accordingly, investors have good reason to opt for the cheapest fund. That's where the case for this ETF falls short. Its expense ratio of 0.15% is certainly reasonable, but there are cheaper options, including its chief rival, iShares S&P 500, which charges just 0.09%. But the toughest competition comes from Vanguard Large Cap Index, which at 0.07% is the cheapest ETF around. And that fund's size and sector characteristics are almost identical to this offering's. So while this ETF is a decent enough option, it's not our first choice for cheap, large-cap exposure.

Address:	45 Fremont Street San Francisco CA 94105 800-474-2737
Web Address:	www.ishares.com
Inception:	05-15-00*
Advisor:	Barclays Global Fund Advisers

Management Fee:	0.15%		
Expense Projections:	3Yr:$48	5Yr:$85	10Yr:$192
Income Distrib:	Quarterly		
Exchange:	NYSE		

Portfolio Analysis 12-31-06

Share change since 11-06 Total Stocks:987	Sector	PE	Tot Ret%	% Assets
⊕ ExxonMobil Corporation	Energy	11.7	39.07	3.26
⊕ General Electric Company	Ind Mtrls	19.8	9.35	2.72
⊕ Citigroup, Inc.	Financial	13.3	19.55	1.95
⊕ Microsoft Corporation	Software	23.7	15.83	1.86
⊕ Bank of America Corporat	Financial	12.4	20.68	1.71
⊕ Procter & Gamble Company	Goods	24.2	13.36	1.48
⊕ Johnson & Johnson	Health	17.4	12.44	1.38
⊕ Pfizer Inc.	Health	15.1	15.22	1.34
⊕ Altria Group, Inc.	Goods	15.9	19.87	1.26
⊕ J.P. Morgan Chase & Co.	Financial	13.7	25.60	1.18
⊕ Cisco Systems, Inc.	Hardware	28.8	59.64	1.17
⊕ Chevron Corporation	Energy	9.3	33.75	1.15
⊕ American International G	Financial	17.1	6.05	1.11
⊕ IBM	Hardware	16.8	19.77	1.06
⊕ AT&T, Inc.	Telecom	19.2	51.59	0.98
⊕ Wells Fargo Company	Financial	14.7	16.82	0.84
⊕ ConocoPhillips	Energy	6.9	26.53	0.84
⊕ Intel Corporation	Hardware	20.3	-17.18	0.83
⊕ Hewlett-Packard Company	Hardware	18.9	45.21	0.81
⊕ Wal-Mart Stores, Inc.	Consumer	16.6	0.13	0.80

Current Investment Style

Value Blnd Growth — Large / Mid / Small

Market Cap	%
Giant	45.1
Large	34.4
Mid	20.2
Small	0.3
Micro	0.0

Avg $mil: 39,953

Value Measures		Rel Category
Price/Earnings	16.19	0.97
Price/Book	2.69	0.98
Price/Sales	1.49	1.17
Price/Cash Flow	9.31	0.98
Dividend Yield %	1.73	0.97

Growth Measures	%	Rel Category
Long-Term Erngs	11.44	0.99
Book Value	8.75	1.02
Sales	10.17	1.23
Cash Flow	11.09	1.47
Historical Erngs	17.84	1.06

Profitability	%	Rel Category
Return on Equity	19.38	1.01
Return on Assets	10.79	1.12
Net Margin	14.04	1.26

Sector Weightings	% of Stocks	Rel S&P 500	3 Year High Low
⟲ Info	19.74	0.99	
▣ Software	3.46	1.00	4 3
▣ Hardware	8.93	0.97	12 9
▣ Media	3.77	0.99	4 4
▣ Telecom	3.58	1.02	4 3
⟲ Service	47.88	1.04	
▣ Health	12.20	1.01	15 12
▣ Consumer	8.33	1.09	9 8
▣ Business	4.94	1.17	5 4
▣ Financial	22.41	1.01	22 20
⟲ Mfg	32.39	0.96	
▣ Goods	8.10	0.95	9 8
▣ Ind Mtrls	11.46	0.96	12 10
▣ Energy	9.05	0.92	10 6
▣ Utilities	3.78	1.08	4 3

Composition

		%
●	Cash	0.1
●	Stocks	99.9
●	Bonds	0.0
●	Other	0.0
	Foreign	0.0
	(% of Stock)	

MORNINGSTAR® ETFs 150

iShares R1000 Value IWD

	Market Price	Mstar Category
	$81.59	Large Value

Morningstar Fair Value

Price/Fair Value Ratio	Coverage Rate %
0.94 Undervalued	95 Good

Management

Barclays Global Fund Advisors is the advisor. The firm is the world's largest manager of indexed portfolios. Patrick O'Connor, the head of Barclays' U.S. iShares portfolio management group, leads a team of half-a-dozen managers in running this and about 60 other ETFs.

Methodology

This fund tracks the Russell 1000 Value Index, which is a subset of the Russell 1000 Index of large-cap stocks that measures the performance of companies whose shares have lower price/book ratios and forecasted growth according to the Institutional Brokers Estimate System. Russell uses a purely quantitative method to construct the index. The index reconstitutes just once a year, at the end of May.

Morningstar Rating	Return	Risk	Yield	NAV	Avg Daily Vol. (k)	52 wk High/Low
★★★★ Above Avg	Above Avg	Average	2.0%	$82.60	1,008	$83.14 - $70.22

Growth of $10,000
- Investment Value of ETF
- Investment Value of Index S&P 500

22.8
17.0
12.0
10.0
5.0

Trading Volume Millions
0.9

History

	1997	1998	1999	2000	2001	2002	2003	2004	2005	2006	
	—	—	—	59.88	55.57	45.94	58.30	66.38	69.22	82.60	NAV $
	—	—	—	60.03	55.40	46.05	58.37	66.37	69.03	82.70	Market Price $
	—	—	—	8.18*	-5.73	-15.68	29.70	16.28	6.92	22.00	NAV Return%
	—	—	—	8.20*	-6.26	-15.22	29.54	16.12	6.64	22.48	Market Price Return%
	—	—	—	0.36	-0.02	-0.01	0.00	0.05	-0.05	0.03	Avg Premium/Discount%
	—	—	—	8.18	6.16	6.42	1.02	5.40	2.01	6.21	NAV Rtrn% +/-S&P 500
	—	—	—	8.18	-0.14	-0.16	-0.33	-0.21	-0.13	-0.25	NAV Rtrn% +/-Russ 1000 VI
	—	—	—	—	7	7	7	8	11	14	NAV Return% Rank in Cat
	—	—	—	—	1.45	1.78	2.44	2.25	2.58	2.47	Income Return %
	—	—	—	—	-7.18	-17.46	27.26	14.03	4.34	19.53	Capital Return %
	—	—	—	0.44	0.87	0.98	1.11	1.30	1.70	1.69	Income $
	—	—	—	0.00	0.00	0.00	0.00	0.00	0.00	0.00	Capital Gains $
	—	—	—	—	0.20	0.20	0.20	0.20	0.20	0.20	Expense Ratio %
	—	—	—	—	1.64	1.82	2.29	2.29	2.42	2.38	Income Ratio %
	—	—	—	—	9	16	20	12	15	7	Turnover Rate %
	—	—	—	153	639	1,123	2,326	4,710	6,185	9,177	Net Assets $mil

Performance 12-31-06

Historic Quarterly NAV Returns

	1st Qtr	2nd Qtr	3rd Qtr	4th Qtr	Total
2002	4.04	-8.58	-18.76	9.11	-15.68
2003	-4.92	17.20	2.01	14.10	29.70
2004	2.98	0.84	1.51	10.31	16.28
2005	0.09	1.63	3.85	1.20	6.92
2006	5.88	0.56	6.15	7.94	22.00

Trailing	NAV Return%	Market Return%	NAV Rtrn% +/-S&P 500	%Rank Cat.(NAV)
3 Mo	7.94	7.97	1.24	16
6 Mo	14.58	14.41	1.84	16
1 Yr	22.00	22.48	6.21	14
3 Yr Avg	14.90	14.89	4.46	8
5 Yr Avg	10.65	10.74	4.46	7
10 Yr Avg	—	—	—	—

Tax Analysis	Tax-Adj Return%	Tax-Cost Ratio
3 Yr (estimated)	13.99	0.79
5 Yr (estimated)	9.79	0.78
10 Yr (estimated)	—	—

Rating and Risk

Time Period	Morningstar Rtn vs Cat	Morningstar Risk vs Cat	Morningstar Risk-Adj Rating
3 Yr	+Avg	Avg	★★★★
5 Yr	+Avg	Avg	★★★★
10 Yr	—	—	—

Other Measures	Standard Index S&P 500	Best Fit Index Russ 1000 VI
Alpha	4.6	-0.1
Beta	0.91	1.00
R-Squared	87	100
Standard Deviation	6.76	
Mean	14.90	
Sharpe Ratio	1.64	

Portfolio Analysis 12-31-06

Share change since 11-06 Total Stocks:611

Share	Sector	PE	Tot Ret%	% Assets
⊕ ExxonMobil Corporation	Energy	11.7	39.07	6.16
⊕ Citigroup, Inc.	Financial	13.3	19.55	3.90
⊕ Bank of America Corporat	Financial	12.4	20.68	3.43
⊕ General Electric Company	Ind Mtrls	19.8	9.35	2.80
⊕ Pfizer Inc.	Health	15.1	15.22	2.67
⊕ J.P. Morgan Chase & Co.	Financial	13.7	25.60	2.36
⊕ Procter & Gamble Company	Goods	24.2	13.36	2.36
⊕ Chevron Corporation	Energy	9.3	33.75	2.30
⊕ AT&T, Inc.	Telecom	19.2	51.59	1.96
⊕ American International G	Financial	17.1	6.05	1.93
⊕ ConocoPhillips	Energy	6.9	26.53	1.67
⊕ Verizon Communications	Telecom	16.1	34.88	1.53
⊕ Wells Fargo Company	Financial	14.7	16.82	1.43
⊕ Wachovia Corporation	Financial	13.0	12.02	1.39
⊕ Altria Group, Inc.	Goods	15.9	19.87	1.38
⊕ BellSouth Corporation	Telecom	—	—	1.20
⊕ Time Warner, Inc.	Media	19.1	26.37	1.14
⊕ Morgan Stanley	Financial	12.3	45.93	1.10
⊕ Merrill Lynch & Company,	Financial	14.1	39.27	0.99
⊕ Merck & Co., Inc.	Health	18.8	42.66	0.93

Current Investment Style

Value Blnd Growth — Large Mid Small

Market Cap	%
Giant	48.9
Large	32.5
Mid	18.5
Small	0.2
Micro	0.0

Avg $mil: 46,597

Value Measures		Rel Category
Price/Earnings	13.78	0.97
Price/Book	2.10	0.87
Price/Sales	1.28	0.96
Price/Cash Flow	7.20	0.93
Dividend Yield %	2.32	0.90

Growth Measures	%	Rel Category
Long-Term Erngs	9.87	0.98
Book Value	8.35	1.16
Sales	9.11	1.07
Cash Flow	10.23	1.19
Historical Erngs	16.88	1.09

Profitability	%	Rel Category
Return on Equity	16.38	0.94
Return on Assets	10.35	1.04
Net Margin	14.64	1.07

Sector Weightings	% of Stocks	Rel S&P 500	3 Year High	Low
↻ Info	12.82	0.64		
🖥 Software	0.41	0.12	1	0
💻 Hardware	2.22	0.24	6	2
🎙 Media	3.89	1.03	6	4
📶 Telecom	6.30	1.79	6	5
⊂ Service	48.79	1.06		
🩺 Health	6.93	0.57	8	3
🛒 Consumer	3.76	0.49	5	3
📋 Business	1.77	0.42	3	2
💲 Financial	36.33	1.63	37	31
🔩 Mfg	38.38	1.14		
🏭 Goods	8.03	0.94	9	6
⚙ Ind Mtrls	10.01	0.84	16	9
🔥 Energy	14.01	1.43	16	10
⚡ Utilities	6.33	1.81	7	6

Composition

● Cash	0.1	
● Stocks	99.9	
● Bonds	0.0	
● Other	0.0	
Foreign	0.0	
(% of Stock)		

Morningstar's Take by Sonya Morris 12-31-06

Is iShares Russell 1000 Value Index behind the times?

This ETF's benchmark includes all the value-oriented stocks in the Russell 1000 Index. The index employs a methodology that identifies value stocks using just two metrics--price/book value ratio and the average analyst's forecast for long-term earnings growth.

That approach differs from competing indexes, which use several variables to separate stocks into value and growth camps. Index providers have begun using more-sophisticated style methodologies because simplistic approaches can result in distortions, particularly during market extremes. For example, during the bull market of the late 1990s, Standard & Poor's, Russell's chief rival, relied solely on price/book ratios to identify growth and value stocks. Because some growth-oriented names took acquisition-related write-offs that distorted their book values, the S&P 500 Value Index wound up pulling more growth

names than the category norm. That proved to be a major liability in the 2000-02 bear market. Over the long haul, the performance difference between this fund and other diversified large-value index funds shouldn't be dramatic, but we prefer more-complex methodologies that we think will give a more accurate picture of the large-value realm.

This ETF has other weaknesses as well. Most importantly, it doesn't stand up to its peers when it comes to costs. True, at 0.2%, its expense ratio is one of the lowest around. But broad large-value exposure can be had more cheaply from both Vanguard Value ETF and iShares S&P 500 Value Index. What's more, conventional mutual fund Vanguard Value Index is just a shade more expensive at 0.21%, but you don't have to pay brokerage commissions when you trade it, making it a better deal for those who plan to make periodic purchases or sales. So while you could certainly do worse than this ETF, there are competing funds that provide similar exposure for less.

Address:	45 Fremont Street San Francisco CA 94105 800-474-2737
Web Address:	www.ishares.com
Inception:	05-22-00*
Advisor:	Barclays Global Fund Advisers

Management Fee:	0.20%		
Expense Projections:	3Yr:$64	5Yr:$113	10Yr:$255
Income Distrib:	Quarterly		
Exchange:	NYSE		

iShares R2000 Growth IWO

| | Market Price $77.91 | Mstar Category Small Growth |

Morningstar Fair Value
Price/Fair Value Ratio — Coverage Rate % —

| Morningstar Rating ★★★ Neutral | Return Neutral | Risk Above Avg | Yield 0.3% | NAV $78.77 | Avg Daily Vol. (k) 1,617 | 52 wk High/Low $81.29 - $67.09 |

Management

Barclays Global Fund Advisors is the advisor. Daily managerial chores are handled by Patrick O'Connor and S. Jane Leung. O'Connor has managed index funds at Barclays since 1999. Leung's tenure at the firm began in 2001.

Growth of $10,000
— Investment Value of ETF
— Investment Value of Index S&P 500

Methodology

This fund tracks the Russell 2000 Growth Index, a subset of the Russell 2000 Index that measures the performance of companies whose shares have higher price/book ratios and forecasted growth according to the I/B/E/S. Russell uses a purely quantitative method to construct the index. It holds nearly 1,300 stocks. The index reconstitutes just once a year, at the end of each May.

Trading Volume Millions

1997	1998	1999	2000	2001	2002	2003	2004	2005	2006	History
—	—	—	64.27	57.84	40.16	59.28	67.48	69.86	78.77	NAV $
—	—	—	64.19	57.60	39.85	59.26	67.30	69.66	78.58	Market Price $
—	—	—	-0.16*	-9.82	-30.29	48.19	14.13	4.04	13.13	NAV Return%
—	—	—	-0.20*	-10.08	-30.54	49.29	13.86	4.02	13.18	Market Price Return%
—	—	—	-0.09	-0.14	-0.20	-0.09	-0.13	-0.11	-0.19	Avg Premium/Discount%
—	—	—	-0.16	2.07	-8.19	19.51	3.25	-0.87	-2.66	NAV Rtrn% +/-S&P 500
—	—	—	-0.16	-0.59	-0.03	-0.35	-0.18	-0.11	-0.22	NAV Rtrn% +/-Russ 2000 Gr
—	—	—	—	3	3	3	3	5	6	NAV Return% Rank in Cat
—	—	—	—	0.17	0.30	0.50	0.27	0.49	0.36	Income Return %
—	—	—	—	-9.99	-30.59	47.69	13.86	3.55	12.77	Capital Return %
—	—	—	0.02	0.11	0.17	0.20	0.16	0.33	0.25	Income $
—	—	—	0.04	0.00	0.00	0.00	0.00	0.00	0.00	Capital Gains $
—	—	—	—	0.25	0.25	0.25	0.25	0.25	0.25	Expense Ratio %
—	—	—	—	0.14	0.22	0.58	0.38	0.37	0.45	Income Ratio %
—	—	—	—	9	28	41	37	22	38	Turnover Rate %
—	—	—	106	414	608	1,515	2,203	2,620	2,954	Net Assets $mil

Performance 12-31-06

Historic Quarterly NAV Returns

	1st Qtr	2nd Qtr	3rd Qtr	4th Qtr	Total
2002	-1.99	-15.70	-21.47	7.45	-30.29
2003	-3.91	24.06	10.39	12.61	48.19
2004	5.54	0.09	-6.04	14.98	14.13
2005	-6.84	3.47	6.28	1.55	4.04
2006	14.32	-7.31	-1.79	8.71	13.13

Trailing	NAV Return%	Market Return%	NAV Rtrn% +/-S&P 500	%Rank Cat.(NAV)
3 Mo	8.71	8.65	2.01	7
6 Mo	6.76	7.11	-5.98	7
1 Yr	13.13	13.18	-2.66	6
3 Yr Avg	10.34	10.26	-0.10	3
5 Yr Avg	6.77	6.81	0.58	3
10 Yr Avg	—	—	—	—

Tax Analysis	Tax-Adj Return%	Tax-Cost Ratio
3 Yr (estimated)	10.20	0.13
5 Yr (estimated)	6.63	0.13
10 Yr (estimated)	—	—

Rating and Risk

Time Period	Morningstar Rtn vs Cat	Morningstar Risk vs Cat	Morningstar Risk-Adj Rating
3 Yr	Avg	+Avg	★★★
5 Yr	Avg	+Avg	★★★
10 Yr	—	—	—

Other Measures	Standard Index S&P 500	Best Fit Index Russ 2000 Gr
Alpha	-6.0	-0.1
Beta	1.99	1.00
R-Squared	75	100
Standard Deviation	15.78	
Mean	10.34	
Sharpe Ratio	0.50	

Morningstar's Take by Sonya Morris 12-31-06

IShares Russell 2000 Growth Index hasn't gotten the job done.

The goal of indexing is to keep expenses and trading costs low in order to edge past actively managed rivals. While this fund delivers on the first count--its 0.25% expense ratio is well below the small-growth category norm--it has failed to generate peer-topping results; its five-year annualized returns are decidedly mediocre. What's more, competing index funds have fared much better. For example, iShares S&P SmallCap 600 Growth Index's five-year trailing returns rank in the category's top 15%.

Part of this fund's underperformance can likely be traced to its benchmark's vulnerability to front-running. Russell reconstitutes its indexes at the same time every year, and the adjustments are largely predictable. That allows speculators to trade in advance of the changes, bidding up the price of the stocks index managers must buy on or near the reconstitution day. A recent study estimated that

this phenomenon cost Russell 2000 indexers between 1.3% and 1.8% in returns per year. Because this fund's benchmark is a subset of that index, it also likely experiences reconstitution costs.

The fund's underwhelming record can also be partially attributed to a particularly poor showing during the 2000-02 bear market. That's partly due to the fund's noteworthy stake in smaller, more speculative stocks. Specifically, it allocates 18.5% of its portfolio to the market's tiniest names, which tend to experience lower lows and higher highs than larger, more-established fare. As a result, shareholders here have experienced their share of turbulence. This fund's standard deviation of returns (a statistical measure of volatility) ranks among the category's highest third.

In sum, this fund's risk/reward profile just doesn't add up. Investors seeking small-growth exposure should look elsewhere.

Portfolio Analysis 12-31-06				
Share change since 11-06 Total Stocks:1292	Sector	PE	Tot Ret%	% Assets
⊕ Hologic, Inc.	Health	57.7	24.68	0.38
⊕ Herman Miller, Inc.	Goods	23.6	30.34	0.37
⊕ Acuity Brands, Inc.	Ind Mtrls	22.2	66.05	0.36
⊕ ValueClick, Inc.	Business	47.3	30.48	0.35
⊕ Varian Semiconductor Equ	Hardware	27.4	55.43	0.34
⊕ Time Warner Telecom, Inc.	Telecom	—	102.34	0.34
⊕ ICOS Corporation	Health	NMF	22.29	0.34
⊕ Digital River, Inc.	Business	38.5	87.59	0.34
⊕ Equinix, Inc.	Business	—	85.53	0.33
⊕ Veritas DGC, Inc.	Energy	35.1	141.28	0.32
⊕ FLIR Systems, Inc.	Ind Mtrls	28.7	42.54	0.32
⊕ Micros Systems, Inc.	Software	33.8	9.06	0.31
⊕ General Cable Corporatio	Ind Mtrls	23.6	121.88	0.31
⊕ American Commercial Line	Business	—	—	0.31
⊕ OSI Pharmaceuticals, Inc.	Health	—	24.75	0.30
⊕ BE Aerospace	Ind Mtrls	14.0	16.73	0.30
⊕ Psychiatric Solutions, I	Health	45.8	27.75	0.30
⊕ Immucor, Inc.	Health	44.3	87.70	0.30
⊕ Sotheby's Holdings, Inc.	Consumer	18.8	70.12	0.30
⊕ JetBlue Airways Corporat	Business	—	-7.67	0.30

Current Investment Style

Value Blnd Growth — Large/Mid/Small

	Market Cap	%
	Giant	0.0
	Large	0.0
	Mid	13.8
	Small	67.5
	Micro	18.8

Avg $mil: 1,027

Value Measures		Rel Category
Price/Earnings	21.56	1.02
Price/Book	3.09	1.04
Price/Sales	1.50	1.01
Price/Cash Flow	7.62	1.08
Dividend Yield %	0.45	1.45

Growth Measures	%	Rel Category
Long-Term Erngs	17.50	1.00
Book Value	7.57	0.63
Sales	-3.37	NMF
Cash Flow	17.63	0.83
Historical Erngs	18.70	0.93

Profitability	%	Rel Category
Return on Equity	11.62	0.79
Return on Assets	5.04	0.63
Net Margin	7.91	0.82

Sector Weightings	% of Stocks	Rel S&P 500	3 Year High Low
Info	19.92	1.00	
Software	6.19	1.79	10 6
Hardware	10.26	1.11	16 10
Media	1.32	0.35	2 1
Telecom	2.15	0.61	2 2
Service	52.97	1.15	
Health	18.06	1.50	24 18
Consumer	11.32	1.48	12 9
Business	14.34	3.39	14 11
Financial	9.25	0.42	12 9
Mfg	27.11	0.80	
Goods	6.18	0.72	6 3
Ind Mtrls	15.11	1.27	15 10
Energy	5.65	0.58	8 3
Utilities	0.17	0.05	0 0

Composition

	%
● Cash	0.1
● Stocks	99.8
● Bonds	0.0
● Other	0.0
Foreign (% of Stock)	0.2

Address:	45 Fremont Street San Francisco CA 94105 800-474-2737	Management Fee:	0.25%
Web Address:	www.ishares.com	Expense Projections:	3Yr:$80 5Yr:$141 10Yr:$318
Inception:	07-24-00*	Income Distrib:	Quarterly
Advisor:	Barclays Global Fund Advisers	Exchange:	NYSE

MORNINGSTAR® ETFs 150

iShares R2000 Index IWM

	Market Price $77.15	Mstar Category Small Blend

Morningstar Rating ★★★ Neutral	Return Neutral	Risk Above Avg	Yield 1.1%	NAV $78.13	Avg Daily Vol. (k) 44,709	52 wk High/Low $79.38 - $66.65

Morningstar Fair Value

Price/Fair Value Ratio —   Coverage Rate % —

Management

Barclays Global Fund Advisors is the advisor. Patrick O'Connor and S. Jane Leung are responsible for the daily management of this ETF. O'Connor has managed index funds at Barclays since 1999. Leung's tenure at the firm began in 2001.

Methodology

This fund tracks the Russell 2000 Index, which measures the performance of the 2,000 smallest companies in the Russell 3000 Index. The bogy represents about 7% of the U.S. stock market's total capitalization. The index reconstitutes just once a year. The fund uses representative sampling to track the bogy.

Growth of $10,000
- Investment Value of ETF
- Investment Value of Index S&P 500

Trading Volume Millions

	1997	1998	1999	2000	2001	2002	2003	2004	2005	2006	History
	—	—	—	48.14	48.53	38.12	55.47	64.89	66.86	78.13	NAV $
	—	—	—	47.88	48.17	37.91	55.40	64.75	66.72	78.03	Market Price $
	—	—	—	9.19*	1.97	-20.51	46.94	18.15	4.46	18.17	NAV Return%
	—	—	—	9.17*	1.78	-20.37	47.58	18.05	4.46	18.27	Market Price Return%
	—	—	—	-0.16	-0.30	-0.40	-0.08	-0.13	-0.06	-0.08	Avg Premium/Discount%
	—	—	—	9.19	13.86	1.59	18.26	7.27	-0.45	2.38	NAV Rtrn% +/-S&P 500
	—	—	—	9.19	-0.52	-0.03	-0.31	-0.18	-0.09	-0.20	NAV Rtrn% +/-Russ 2000
	—	—	—	—	2	2	2	2	4	8	NAV Return% Rank in Cat
	—	—	—	1.09	1.03	1.16	1.08	1.36	1.25		Income Return %
	—	—	—	0.88	-21.54	45.78	17.07	3.10	16.92		Capital Return %
	—	—	—	0.34	0.52	0.50	0.44	0.59	0.88	0.83	Income $
	—	—	—	0.08	0.00	0.00	0.02	0.00	0.00	0.00	Capital Gains $
	—	—	—	0.20	0.20	0.20	0.20	0.20	0.20	0.20	Expense Ratio %
	—	—	—	1.39	1.25	1.28	1.08	1.20	1.19		Income Ratio %
	—	—	—	39	20	30	26	17	20		Turnover Rate %
	—	—	—	395	2,067	2,127	4,515	6,988	7,432	12,392	Net Assets $mil

Performance 12-31-06

Historic Quarterly NAV Returns

	1st Qtr	2nd Qtr	3rd Qtr	4th Qtr	Total
2002	3.95	-8.38	-21.35	6.12	-20.51
2003	-4.52	23.34	9.01	14.46	46.94
2004	6.21	0.47	-2.89	14.02	18.15
2005	-5.36	4.30	4.66	1.11	4.46
2006	13.90	-5.07	0.40	8.85	18.17

Trailing	NAV Return%	Market Return%	NAV Rtrn% +/-S&P 500	%Rank Cat.(NAV)
3 Mo	8.85	8.83	2.15	12
6 Mo	9.29	9.59	-3.45	10
1 Yr	18.17	18.27	2.38	8
3 Yr Avg	13.41	13.40	2.97	2
5 Yr Avg	11.24	11.38	5.05	2
10 Yr Avg	—	—	—	—

Tax Analysis	Tax-Adj Return%	Tax-Cost Ratio
3 Yr (estimated)	12.95	0.41
5 Yr (estimated)	10.80	0.40
10 Yr (estimated)	—	—

Rating and Risk

Time Period	Morningstar Rtn vs Cat	Morningstar Risk vs Cat	Morningstar Risk-Adj Rating
3 Yr	Avg	+Avg	★★★
5 Yr	Avg	+Avg	★★★
10 Yr	—	—	—

Other Measures	Standard Index S&P 500	Best Fit Index Russ 2000
Alpha	-2.0	-0.1
Beta	1.76	1.00
R-Squared	75	100
Standard Deviation	13.93	
Mean	13.41	
Sharpe Ratio	0.74	

Portfolio Analysis 12-31-06

Share change since 11-06 Total Stocks:1969

Sector	PE	Tot Ret%	% Assets
⊕ Veritas DGC, Inc.	Energy	35.1	141.28	0.22
⊕ Alexandria Real Estate E	Financial	45.0	28.54	0.21
⊕ Time Warner Telecom, Inc	Telecom	—	102.34	0.21
⊕ Phillips-Van Heusen Corp	Goods	19.3	55.45	0.20
⊕ Realty Income Corporatio	Financial	26.9	36.01	0.20
⊕ Polycom, Inc.	Hardware	49.9	102.03	0.20
⊕ Varian Semiconductor Equ	Hardware	27.4	55.43	0.19
⊕ Big Lots, Inc.	Consumer	44.1	90.84	0.19
⊕ Nationwide Health Proper	Financial	30.5	50.74	0.19
⊕ Hologic, Inc.	Health	57.7	24.68	0.18
⊕ JetBlue Airways Corporat	Business	—	-7.67	0.18
⊕ Herman Miller, Inc.	Goods	23.6	30.34	0.18
⊕ Acuity Brands, Inc.	Ind Mtrls	22.2	66.05	0.17
⊕ Waddell & Reed Financial	Financial	63.6	34.04	0.17
⊕ NBTY, Inc.	Health	25.7	155.82	0.17
⊕ ValueClick, Inc.	Business	47.3	30.48	0.17
⊕ Westar Energy, Inc.	Utilities	14.5	26.11	0.17
⊕ Brocade Communications S	Software	48.3	101.72	0.16
⊕ Sybase Inc.	Software	22.7	12.99	0.16
⊕ General Cable Corporatio	Ind Mtrls	23.6	121.88	0.16

Current Investment Style

Value Blnd Growth — Large Mid Small

Market Cap	%
Giant	0.0
Large	0.0
Mid	12.9
Small	68.7
Micro	18.4

Avg $mil: 1,027

Value Measures		Rel Category
Price/Earnings	18.83	1.07
Price/Book	2.18	1.05
Price/Sales	1.07	1.04
Price/Cash Flow	7.05	1.09
Dividend Yield %	1.30	0.82

Growth Measures	%	Rel Category
Long-Term Erngs	13.39	1.01
Book Value	5.24	0.96
Sales	-2.17	NMF
Cash Flow	7.29	0.81
Historical Erngs	11.45	0.96

Profitability	%	Rel Category
Return on Equity	10.18	0.88
Return on Assets	5.53	0.84
Net Margin	9.37	0.95

Sector Weightings

	% of Stocks	Rel S&P 500	3 Year High Low
⌒ Info	17.34	0.87	
🅺 Software	4.75	1.38	6 4
🖥 Hardware	8.53	0.92	11 7
🎙 Media	1.83	0.48	2 1
📶 Telecom	2.23	0.64	2 2
☞ Service	54.32	1.18	
⚕ Health	11.13	0.92	14 11
🛒 Consumer	9.87	1.29	10 9
💼 Business	11.10	2.62	11 10
💲 Financial	22.22	1.00	23 20
⎚ Mfg	28.35	0.84	
🏭 Goods	6.24	0.73	6 4
⚙ Ind Mtrls	14.43	1.21	17 14
🔋 Energy	4.79	0.49	7 4
💡 Utilities	2.89	0.83	3 2

Composition

- Cash 0.2
- Stocks 99.8
- Bonds 0.0
- Other 0.0
- Foreign 0.2 (% of Stock)

Morningstar's Take by Sonya Morris 12-31-06

Investors have better choices than iShares Russell 2000 Index.

This ETF has failed to distinguish itself from a variety of perspectives. First of all, in spite of the tax advantages conferred by its ETF structure, this isn't the most tax-efficient small-cap fund around. A handful of conventional small-blend funds, including Analyst Pick Vanguard Tax-Managed Small Cap, have lower tax-cost ratios than this fund's, and rival ETFs, such as iShares S&P SmallCap 600, have also done a better job of limiting the taxman's bite.

This ETF doesn't stand out from a pretax perspective either: Its five-year annualized returns trail roughly 60% of its peers, and its performance doesn't look much better when evaluated over rolling periods. Some contend that indexing doesn't fare as well in the small-cap space, but rival ETFs have done a much better job of keeping up with the competition. For instance, iShares S&P SmallCap 600 generated five-year annualized returns that

rank in the category's top 40%.

Some investors might be willing to tolerate this ETF's lackluster results if it offered them a smoother ride than competing small-cap funds, but that hasn't been the case. As measured by its five-year standard deviation of returns (a statistical measure of volatility), this ETF has been more turbulent than almost three quarters of its rivals. That's partly due to the fact that this fund dedicates less of its assets to mid-caps and more to the tiniest stocks in the market, as evidenced by its below-average aggregate market cap. Smaller companies tend to be riskier and less financially stable than larger, more-established firms, and as a result, their stocks often experience more ups and downs.

This fund doesn't completely lack appeal. It provides exposure to a broad swath of small-cap stocks at a low price, but investors don't have to look hard to find superior alternatives.

Address:	45 Fremont Street San Francisco CA 94105 800-474-2737	Management Fee:	0.20%
		Expense Projections:	3Yr:$64 5Yr:$113 10Yr:$255
Web Address:	www.ishares.com	Income Distrib:	Quarterly
Inception:	05-22-00*	Exchange:	NYSE
Advisor:	Barclays Global Fund Advisers		

 Morningstar® ETFs 150

iShares R2000 Value IWN

			Market Price $79.01			Mstar Category Small Value

Morningstar Fair Value

Price/Fair Value Ratio —   Coverage Rate % —

Morningstar Rating ★★★ Neutral	Return Neutral	Risk Above Avg	Yield 1.6%	NAV $80.05	Avg Daily Vol. (k) 1,493	52 wk High/Low $81.12 - $67.62

Management

Barclays Global Fund Advisors is the advisor. Patrick O'Connor and S. Jane Leung are responsible for the daily management of this ETF. O'Connor has managed index funds at Barclays since 1999. Leung's tenure at the firm began in 2001.

Growth of $10,000
— Investment Value of ETF
— Investment Value of Index S&P 500

33.2 / 26.0 / 14.0 / 10.0 / 5.0

Trading Volume Millions
1.2 / 0.0

Methodology

This fund tracks the Russell 2000 Value Index, which is a subset of the Russell 2000 Index that measures the performance of companies whose shares have lower price/book ratios and lower forecasted growth according to the I/B/E/S. Russell uses a purely quantitative method to construct the index, and this fund's advisor, Barclays Global Fund Advisors, uses representative sampling to track the index. It holds more than 1,300 stocks. The index reconstitutes just once a year, at the end of each May.

1997	1998	1999	2000	2001	2002	2003	2004	2005	2006	History
—	—	—	38.61	42.93	37.34	53.58	64.40	66.10	80.05	NAV $
—	—	—	38.54	42.93	37.17	53.47	64.32	65.93	80.04	Market Price $
—	—	—	15.95*	13.42	-11.52	45.60	22.02	4.49	23.18	NAV Return%
—	—	—	15.95*	13.62	-11.92	45.96	22.11	4.36	23.48	Market Price Return%
—	—	—	-0.05	0.02	-0.30	-0.14	0.00	-0.13	-0.07	Avg Premium/Discount%
—	—	—	15.95	25.31	10.58	16.92	11.14	-0.42	7.39	NAV Rtrn% +/-S&P 500
—	—	—	15.95	-0.60	-0.09	-0.43	-0.23	-0.22	-0.30	NAV Rtrn% +/-Russ 2000 VL
—	—	—	—	3	3	3	3	5	6	NAV Return% Rank in Cat
—	—	—	—	2.05	1.65	1.16	1.66	1.81	1.94	Income Return %
—	—	—	—	11.37	-13.17	44.44	20.36	2.68	21.24	Capital Return %
—	—	—	0.29	0.79	0.70	0.43	0.88	1.16	1.27	Income $
—	—	—	0.01	0.00	0.00	0.23	0.00	0.00	0.00	Capital Gains $
—	—	—	—	0.25	0.25	0.25	0.25	0.25	0.25	Expense Ratio %
—	—	—	—	2.40	2.07	1.85	1.64	1.84	1.80	Income Ratio %
—	—	—	—	9	26	45	16	23	14	Turnover Rate %
—	—	—	162	560	790	1,607	2,908	3,014	4,375	Net Assets $mil

Performance 12-31-06

Historic Quarterly NAV Returns

	1st Qtr	2nd Qtr	3rd Qtr	4th Qtr	Total
2002	9.51	-2.20	-21.22	4.86	-11.52
2003	-5.13	22.62	7.64	16.28	45.60
2004	6.85	0.85	0.11	13.11	22.02
2005	-4.03	5.01	3.05	0.62	4.49
2006	13.42	-2.75	2.50	8.96	23.18

Trailing	NAV Return%	Market Return%	NAV Rtrn% +/-S&P 500	%Rank Cat.(NAV)
3 Mo	8.96	9.12	2.26	7
6 Mo	11.68	11.76	-1.06	7
1 Yr	23.18	23.48	7.39	6
3 Yr Avg	16.24	16.31	5.80	3
5 Yr Avg	15.14	15.13	8.95	3
10 Yr Avg	—	—	—	—

Tax Analysis	Tax-Adj Return%	Tax-Cost Ratio
3 Yr (estimated)	15.57	0.58
5 Yr (estimated)	14.51	0.55
10 Yr (estimated)	—	—

Rating and Risk

Time Period	Morningstar Rtn vs Cat	Morningstar Risk vs Cat	Morningstar Risk-Adj Rating
3 Yr	+Avg	+Avg	★★★★
5 Yr	+Avg	+Avg	★★★
10 Yr	—	—	—

Other Measures	Standard Index S&P 500	Best Fit Index Russ 2000 VL
Alpha	1.9	-0.2
Beta	1.54	1.00
R-Squared	72	100
Standard Deviation	12.49	
Mean	16.24	
Sharpe Ratio	1.02	

Portfolio Analysis 12-31-06

Share change since 11-06 Total Stocks:1308

	Sector	PE	Tot Ret%	% Assets
⊕ Realty Income Corporatio	Financial	26.9	36.01	0.39
⊕ Big Lots, Inc.	Consumer	44.1	90.84	0.37
⊕ Nationwide Health Proper	Financial	30.5	50.74	0.36
⊕ Alexandria Real Estate E	Financial	45.0	28.54	0.34
⊕ Westar Energy, Inc.	Utilities	14.5	26.11	0.32
⊕ Highwoods Properties	Financial	—	50.55	0.31
⊕ Jack In The Box, Inc.	Consumer	20.1	74.75	0.31
⊕ KKR Financial Corporatio	Financial	—		0.30
⊕ PNM Resources, Inc.	Utilities	28.0	31.23	0.30
⊕ Sybase Inc.	Software	22.7	12.99	0.30
⊕ First Industrial Realty	Financial	—	30.08	0.30
⊕ Nicor Inc.	Utilities	15.8	24.33	0.29
⊕ AptarGroup, Inc.	Goods	21.3	14.89	0.29
⊕ Gaylord Entertainment	Consumer	—	16.84	0.29
⊕ Rent-A-Center, Inc.	Consumer	14.9	56.47	0.29
⊕ NBTY, Inc.	Health	25.7	155.82	0.29
⊕ Piedmont Natural Gas Com	Utilities	20.6	15.05	0.29
⊕ Knight Capital Group, In	Business	14.0	93.83	0.28
⊕ Lear Corporation	Ind Mtrls	—	4.93	0.28
⊕ Post Properties, Inc.	Financial	NMF	18.95	0.28

Current Investment Style

Value Blnd Growth — Large/Mid/Small

Market Cap	%
Giant	0.0
Large	0.0
Mid	12.2
Small	69.9
Micro	17.9

Avg $mil: 1,028

Value Measures		Rel Category
Price/Earnings	16.96	1.12
Price/Book	1.74	1.02
Price/Sales	0.84	1.14
Price/Cash Flow	6.64	1.10
Dividend Yield %	2.09	1.01

Growth Measures	%	Rel Category
Long-Term Erngs	10.84	1.01
Book Value	4.28	0.92
Sales	7.47	1.75
Cash Flow	1.23	0.34
Historical Erngs	8.26	0.87

Profitability	%	Rel Category
Return on Equity	8.87	0.84
Return on Assets	5.99	0.91
Net Margin	10.66	1.07

Sector Weightings	% of Stocks	Rel S&P 500	3 Year High	Low
⟳ Info	14.93	0.75		
Software	3.41	0.99	4	1
Hardware	6.92	0.75	9	4
Media	2.31	0.61	2	1
Telecom	2.29	0.65	3	1
☞ Service	55.56	1.20		
Health	4.70	0.39	5	4
Consumer	8.52	1.11	11	8
Business	8.11	1.92	10	7
Financial	34.23	1.54	36	30
Mfg	29.51	0.87		
Goods	6.30	0.74	6	5
Ind Mtrls	13.82	1.16	19	13
Energy	3.98	0.41	7	4
Utilities	5.41	1.55	6	4

Composition

● Cash	0.1	
● Stocks	99.8	
● Bonds	0.0	
● Other	0.0	
Foreign	0.3	(% of Stock)

Morningstar's Take by Sonya Morris 12-31-06

IShares Russell 2000 Value Index may be too hot to handle right now.

Small-value stocks have staged a scorching multiyear rally, and this ETF has gone along for the ride. It's generated impressive absolute long-term returns, and it has also managed to outperform a good chunk of the competition. The fund's three- and five-year trailing returns rank in the small-value category's top third.

That's a much better showing than its sibling ETFs, iShares Russell 2000 and iShares Russell 2000 Growth. Those funds have suffered from a performance drag that's partly due to the Russell 2000 Index's vulnerability to front-running. Russell reconstitutes its indexes at the same time every year, and the adjustments are largely predictable. That allows arbitragers to game the system, and in the process, they bid up the price of the stocks index managers must buy to remain consistent with their funds' benchmarks. Studies have shown that such front-running takes a bite out of the Russell

2000's returns.

Since this fund is a subset of the Russell 2000, it's likely also suffered some degree of reconstitution costs, but it's still been able to outpace the competition thanks in part to a sizable stake in REITs. The fund dedicates a hefty 9.7% of its portfolio to that market segment, which has enjoyed a stellar run in recent years.

However, small-value stocks--and REITs in particular--are looking overheated, and it wouldn't be surprising to see them cool off. If they do, expect this fund to take a breather. Index funds generally don't compete well when market winds change: Unlike their actively managed rivals, they must remain fully invested at all times and can't hold cash or invest outside their style boundaries to blunt the blow of a downturn. So now's not the best time to jump into this ETF with both feet. And dollar-cost averaging is impractical with ETFs, since you must pay a brokerage commission with each trade.

Address:	45 Fremont Street San Francisco CA 94105 800-474-2737	Management Fee: Expense Projections: Income Distrib:	0.25% 3Yr:$80 Quarterly	5Yr:$141 10Yr:$318
Web Address: Inception: Advisor:	www.ishares.com 07-24-00* Barclays Global Fund Advisers	Exchange:	NYSE	

M⚛RNINGSTAR® ETFs 150

Data through December 31, 2006

iShares R3000 Growth IWZ

	Market Price $45.12	**Mstar Category** Large Growth

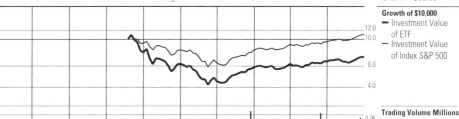

Morningstar Rating ★★★ Neutral	**Return** Neutral	**Risk** Average	**Yield** 0.8%	**NAV** $44.90	**Avg Daily Vol. (k)** 58	**52 wk High/Low** $45.47 - $39.06

Morningstar Fair Value

Price/Fair Value Ratio	Coverage Rate %
0.89 Undervalued	91 Good

Management

This ETF is advised by Barclays Global Fund Advisors, the world's largest manager of indexed portfolios. Patrick O'Connor and S. Jane Leung run the fund on a day-to-day basis. O'Connor has been a portfolio manager at Barclays since 1999, and Leung since 2001.

Methodology

This fund tracks the Russell 3000 Growth Index, which includes all the growth stocks in the Russell 3000 Index, a benchmark that spans virtually the entire domestic stock market. Russell uses price/book ratios and forecasted growth according to the Institutional Brokers Estimate System to identify growth stocks. Russell uses a purely quantitative method to construct the index, which reconstitutes just once a year, at the end of each May.

Growth of $10,000
- Investment Value of ETF
- Investment Value of Index S&P 500

Trading Volume Millions

	1997	1998	1999	2000	2001	2002	2003	2004	2005	2006	History
	—	—	—	51.23	40.85	29.14	37.79	39.88	41.48	44.90	NAV $
	—	—	—	51.78	40.89	29.22	37.80	39.80	41.45	45.01	Market Price $
	—	—	—	-5.69*	-19.96	-28.15	30.66	6.65	4.92	9.19	NAV Return%
	—	—	—	-5.66*	-20.73	-28.02	30.34	6.41	5.06	9.54	Market Price Return%
	—	—	—	0.10	0.14	0.24	0.21	0.01	0.00	0.01	Avg Premium/Discount%
	—	—	—	-5.69	-8.07	-6.05	1.98	-4.23	0.01	-6.60	NAV Rtrn% +/-S&P 500
	—	—	—	-5.69	0.46	-0.27	0.91	0.35	-0.34	0.12	NAV Rtrn% +/-Russ 1000Gr
	—	—	—	—	6	6	6	7	10	13	NAV Return% Rank in Cat
	—	—	—	—	0.29	0.58	0.86	1.08	0.87	0.90	Income Return %
	—	—	—	—	-20.25	-28.73	29.80	5.57	4.05	8.29	Capital Return %
	—	—	—	0.03	0.15	0.24	0.25	0.41	0.35	0.37	Income $
	—	—	—	0.00	0.00	0.00	0.00	0.00	0.00	0.00	Capital Gains $
	—	—	—	—	0.25	0.25	0.25	0.25	0.25	0.25	Expense Ratio %
	—	—	—	—	0.20	0.47	0.83	0.78	1.12	0.86	Income Ratio %
	—	—	—	—	3	18	15	11	16	20	Turnover Rate %
	—	—	—	26	49	58	128	132	214	294	Net Assets $mil

Performance 12-31-06

Historic Quarterly NAV Returns

	1st Qtr	2nd Qtr	3rd Qtr	4th Qtr	Total
2002	-2.60	-18.49	-15.53	7.13	-28.15
2003	-1.33	14.86	4.33	10.50	30.66
2004	1.07	1.74	-5.36	9.58	6.65
2005	-4.37	2.47	4.16	2.79	4.92
2006	4.02	-4.28	3.37	6.09	9.19

Trailing	NAV Return%	Market Return%	NAV Rtrn% +/-S&P 500	%Rank Cat.(NAV)
3 Mo	6.09	6.43	-0.61	15
6 Mo	9.67	9.88	-3.07	15
1 Yr	9.19	9.54	-6.60	13
3 Yr Avg	6.91	6.98	-3.53	7
5 Yr Avg	2.78	2.81	-3.41	6
10 Yr Avg	—	—	—	—

Tax Analysis	Tax-Adj Return%	Tax-Cost Ratio
3 Yr (estimated)	6.56	0.33
5 Yr (estimated)	2.47	0.30
10 Yr (estimated)	—	—

Rating and Risk

Time Period	Morningstar Rtn vs Cat	Morningstar Risk vs Cat	Morningstar Risk-Adj Rating
3 Yr	Avg	Avg	★★★
5 Yr	Avg	Avg	★★★
10 Yr	—	—	—

Other Measures	Standard Index S&P 500	Best Fit Index Russ 1000Gr
Alpha	-4.7	-0.1
Beta	1.23	1.05
R-Squared	90	99
Standard Deviation	8.90	
Mean	6.91	
Sharpe Ratio	0.44	

Portfolio Analysis 12-31-06

Share change since 11-06 Total Stocks:1975	Sector	PE	Tot Ret%	% Assets
⊕ Microsoft Corporation	Software	23.7	15.83	3.41
⊕ General Electric Company	Ind Mtrls	19.8	9.35	2.42
⊕ Johnson & Johnson	Health	17.4	12.44	2.23
⊕ Cisco Systems, Inc.	Hardware	28.8	59.64	2.15
⊕ IBM	Hardware	16.8	19.77	1.76
⊕ Intel Corporation	Hardware	20.3	-17.18	1.52
⊕ Wal-Mart Stores, Inc.	Consumer	16.6	0.13	1.46
⊕ PepsiCo, Inc.	Goods	21.4	7.86	1.33
⊕ Google, Inc.	Business	58.6	11.00	1.24
⊕ Altria Group, Inc.	Goods	15.9	19.87	1.05
⊕ Amgen, Inc.	Health	28.0	-13.38	1.04
⊕ Home Depot, Inc.	Consumer	13.7	1.01	1.01
⊕ UnitedHealth Group, Inc.	Health	21.0	-13.49	0.93
⊕ Apple Computer, Inc.	Hardware	37.4	18.01	0.93
⊕ Boeing Company	Ind Mtrls	41.1	28.38	0.91
⊕ Hewlett-Packard Company	Hardware	18.9	45.21	0.90
⊕ Oracle Corporation	Software	25.6	40.38	0.88
⊕ American Express Company	Financial	21.2	19.09	0.84
⊕ Coca-Cola Company	Goods	21.5	23.10	0.84
⊕ Medtronic, Inc.	Health	23.7	-6.29	0.83

Current Investment Style

Value Blnd Growth — Large/Mid/Small

Market Cap	%
Giant	37.9
Large	33.2
Mid	21.2
Small	6.1
Micro	1.6

Avg $mil: 25,549

Value Measures		Rel Category
Price/Earnings	19.68	0.95
Price/Book	3.70	1.13
Price/Sales	1.75	0.99
Price/Cash Flow	11.82	1.06
Dividend Yield %	1.10	1.28

Growth Measures	%	Rel Category
Long-Term Erngs	13.88	0.93
Book Value	9.36	1.17
Sales	4.81	0.41
Cash Flow	12.44	0.85
Historical Erngs	19.24	0.68

Profitability	%	Rel Category
Return on Equity	21.48	1.07
Return on Assets	10.71	1.07
Net Margin	13.02	1.03

Sector Weightings	% of Stocks	Rel S&P 500	3 Year High Low	
☎ Info	26.07	1.30		
🖥 Software	6.46	1.87	8	6
💻 Hardware	15.18	1.64	18	14
📺 Media	3.46	0.91	4	3
☏ Telecom	0.97	0.28	1	1
⊏ Service	47.45	1.03		
⚕ Health	17.50	1.45	25	17
🛒 Consumer	12.74	1.67	14	12
📋 Business	8.61	2.04	9	5
💲 Financial	8.60	0.39	10	6
📐 Mfg	26.47	0.78		
🏭 Goods	8.00	0.94	11	8
⚙ Ind Mtrls	13.08	1.10	14	7
◊ Energy	4.24	0.43	5	1
⚡ Utilities	1.15	0.33	1	0

Composition

● Cash	0.1	
● Stocks	99.9	
● Bonds	0.0	
● Other	0.0	
Foreign	0.0	
(% of Stock)		

Morningstar's Take by Sonya Morris 12-31-06

IShares Russell 3000 Growth doesn't stand out from the crowd.

This ETF does have some distinctive features. It has a wider wingspan than most competing large-growth funds. That's because its benchmark includes all the growth stocks (as defined by Russell) in the Russell 3000 Index, which spans virtually the entire domestic stock market. So, this ETF dedicates 28% to mid- and small-cap stocks, compared with 18% for its typical rival.

That positioning should have worked to this ETF's advantage of late because the market has shone on smaller fare over the past few years. But that hasn't been the case. Its three-year trailing returns are only a few percentage points ahead of the large-cap dominated iShares S&P 500 Growth, which only allocates 10% to small- and mid-size firms.

That result could be because Russell indexes are vulnerable to front-running. Because they reconstitute on the same day each year, traders can anticipate the changes to the indexes and bid up the prices of the stocks index fund managers must buy on the day the changes become effective. Studies have shown that this phenomenon can take a bite out of shareholders' returns.

This ETF suffers from other weaknesses as well. Russell relies solely on price/book ratios and forecasted earnings growth to divide stocks into growth and value camps. Most competing index providers use more variables. As such, this ETF may not reflect its universe as well as competing funds that track more sophisticated benchmarks.

Finally, while this offering is reasonably priced at 0.25%, it's not the cheapest large-growth ETF around. A handful of rivals, including iShares Russell 1000 Growth ETF and Vanguard Growth ETF, can be had for less.

Granted, you could certainly do worse than this ETF, and it's an adequate core growth holding, but it's not among our top picks.

Address:	45 Fremont Street San Francisco CA 94105 800-474-2737	Management Fee:	0.25%
		Expense Projections:	3Yr:$80 5Yr:$141 10Yr:$318
Web Address:	www.ishares.com	Income Distrib:	Quarterly
Inception:	07-24-00*	Exchange:	NYSE
Advisor:	Barclays Global Fund Advisers		

MORNINGSTAR® ETFs 150

Data through December 31, 2006

iShares R3000 Index IWV

	Market Price $81.69	Mstar Category Large Blend

Morningstar Fair Value

Price/Fair Value Ratio	Coverage Rate %
0.91 Undervalued	91 Good

Management

Barclays Global Fund Advisors is the advisor to this ETF. Patrick O'Connor and S. Jane Leung run the fund on a daily basis. O'Connor has managed index funds at Barclays since 1999. Leung's tenure at the firm began in 2001.

Methodology

This index offering mirrors the Russell 3000 Index, which is made up of the 3,000 largest U.S.-based companies. Thus, its huge portfolio holds a broadly diversified mix of large-, mid-, and small-cap names. The index reconstitutes just once a year, at the end of each May.

Morningstar Rating ★★★★ Above Avg	Return Above Avg	Risk Above Avg	Yield 1.4%	NAV $81.93	Avg Daily Vol. (k) 399	52 wk High/Low $82.76 - $70.98

Growth of $10,000
■ Investment Value of ETF
— Investment Value of Index S&P 500

Trading Volume Millions

History	1997	1998	1999	2000	2001	2002	2003	2004	2005	2006
NAV $	—	—	—	72.65	63.45	48.93	62.98	69.21	72.01	81.93
Market Price $	—	—	—	72.44	63.50	48.96	62.96	69.15	72.02	82.04
NAV Return%	—	—	—	2.59*	-11.78	-21.63	30.77	11.76	5.97	15.52
Market Price Return%	—	—	—	2.61*	-11.46	-21.64	30.65	11.70	6.08	15.66
Avg Premium/Discount%	—	—	—	0.16	0.10	-0.19	0.02	-0.01	0.02	0.04
NAV Rtrn% +/-S&P 500	—	—	—	2.59	0.11	0.47	2.09	0.88	1.06	-0.27
NAV Rtrn% +/-Russ 1000	—	—	—	2.59	0.67	0.02	0.88	0.36	-0.30	0.06
NAV Return% Rank in Cat	—	—	—	—	12	14	14	16	21	30
Income Return %	—	—	—	—	0.88	1.36	1.81	1.77	1.86	1.64
Capital Return %	—	—	—	—	-12.66	-22.99	28.96	9.99	4.11	13.88
Income $	—	—	—	0.34	0.64	0.86	0.88	1.11	1.28	1.17
Capital Gains $	—	—	—	0.01	0.00	0.00	0.00	0.00	0.00	0.00
Expense Ratio %	—	—	—	—	0.20	0.20	0.20	0.20	0.20	0.20
Income Ratio %	—	—	—	—	1.09	1.20	1.53	1.54	1.81	1.62
Turnover Rate %	—	—	—	—	3	6	5	4	5	5
Net Assets $mil	—	—	—	312	1,485	1,236	1,316	1,754	1,955	2,814

Performance 12-31-06

Historic Quarterly NAV Returns

	1st Qtr	2nd Qtr	3rd Qtr	4th Qtr	Total
2002	0.92	-13.09	-17.22	7.94	-21.63
2003	-3.08	16.16	3.37	12.36	30.77
2004	2.17	1.30	-1.92	10.09	11.76
2005	-2.23	2.22	3.96	1.99	5.97
2006	5.27	-2.02	4.60	7.08	15.52

Trailing	NAV Return%	Market Return%	NAV Rtrn% +/-S&P 500	%Rank Cat.(NAV)
3 Mo	7.08	7.14	0.38	44
6 Mo	12.00	12.22	-0.74	38
1 Yr	15.52	15.66	-0.27	30
3 Yr Avg	11.01	11.07	0.57	15
5 Yr Avg	6.99	7.01	0.80	13
10 Yr Avg	—	—	—	—

Tax Analysis	Tax-Adj Return%	Tax-Cost Ratio
3 Yr (estimated)	10.36	0.59
5 Yr (estimated)	6.37	0.58
10 Yr (estimated)	—	—

Rating and Risk

Time Period	Morningstar Rtn vs Cat	Morningstar Risk vs Cat	Morningstar Risk-Adj Rating
3 Yr	+Avg	Avg	★★★★
5 Yr	+Avg	+Avg	★★★★
10 Yr	—	—	—

Other Measures	Standard Index S&P 500	Best Fit Index Russ 1000
Alpha	-0.1	-0.4
Beta	1.09	1.06
R-Squared	98	99
Standard Deviation	7.59	
Mean	11.01	
Sharpe Ratio	1.00	

Portfolio Analysis 12-31-06

Share change since 11-06 Total Stocks:2956

Sector	PE	Tot Ret%	% Assets
⊕ ExxonMobil Corporation	Energy	11.7	39.07	2.98
⊕ General Electric Company	Ind Mtrls	19.8	9.35	2.48
⊕ Citigroup, Inc.	Financial	13.3	19.55	1.78
⊕ Microsoft Corporation	Software	23.7	15.83	1.70
⊕ Bank of America Corporat	Financial	12.4	20.68	1.56
⊕ Procter & Gamble Company	Goods	24.2	13.36	1.35
⊕ Johnson & Johnson	Health	17.4	12.44	1.26
⊕ Pfizer Inc.	Health	15.1	15.22	1.22
⊕ Altria Group, Inc.	Goods	15.9	19.87	1.15
⊕ J.P. Morgan Chase & Co.	Financial	13.7	25.60	1.08
⊕ Cisco Systems, Inc.	Hardware	28.8	59.64	1.07
⊕ Chevron Corporation	Energy	9.3	33.75	1.05
⊕ American International G	Financial	17.1	6.05	1.01
⊕ IBM	Hardware	16.8	19.77	0.97
⊕ AT&T, Inc.	Telecom	19.2	51.59	0.89
⊕ Wells Fargo Company	Financial	14.7	16.82	0.77
⊕ ConocoPhillips	Energy	6.9	26.53	0.76
⊕ Intel Corporation	Hardware	20.3	-17.18	0.76
⊕ Hewlett-Packard Company	Hardware	18.9	45.21	0.74
⊕ Wal-Mart Stores, Inc.	Consumer	16.6	0.13	0.73

Current Investment Style

Value Blnd Growth — Large Mid Small

Market Cap	%
Giant	41.2
Large	31.4
Mid	19.6
Small	6.3
Micro	1.6

Avg $mil: 29,002

Value Measures		Rel Category
Price/Earnings	16.37	0.99
Price/Book	2.64	0.96
Price/Sales	1.44	1.13
Price/Cash Flow	9.07	0.96
Dividend Yield %	1.70	0.95

Growth Measures	%	Rel Category
Long-Term Erngs	11.56	1.00
Book Value	8.41	0.98
Sales	6.26	0.75
Cash Flow	10.80	1.43
Historical Erngs	17.43	1.04

Profitability	%	Rel Category
Return on Equity	18.60	0.97
Return on Assets	10.34	1.07
Net Margin	13.65	1.22

Sector Weightings

	% of Stocks	Rel S&P 500	3 Year High Low	
↗ Info	19.54	0.98		
Software	3.57	1.03	4	3
Hardware	8.90	0.96	12	9
Media	3.61	0.95	4	3
Telecom	3.46	0.99	3	3
☎ Service	48.43	1.05		
Health	12.11	1.00	14	12
Consumer	8.46	1.11	9	8
Business	5.47	1.29	6	4
Financial	22.39	1.01	22	20
Mfg	32.04	0.95		
Goods	7.94	0.93	9	8
Ind Mtrls	11.71	0.98	12	11
Energy	8.68	0.89	9	6
Utilities	3.71	1.06	4	3

Composition

● Cash	0.1
● Stocks	99.9
● Bonds	0.0
● Other	0.0
Foreign	0.0
(% of Stock)	

Morningstar's Take by Sonya Morris 12-31-06

IShares Russell 3000's not bad, but you can do better.

This ETF provides exposure to virtually the entire U.S. stock market, making it a handy one-stop domestic core fund. But that's nothing unusual. A number of ETFs and conventional funds do the same thing, including Vanguard Total Stock Market ETF, streetTracks Total Market ETF, and Fidelity Spartan Total Market Index. These funds have the vast majority of their holdings in common. And while not all of them have been around for 10 years, data on their benchmarks show they have produced similar returns and experienced similar levels of volatility over the past decade. Accordingly, these funds compete on expenses.

Unfortunately, that's where this ETF falls short. Granted, it's darn cheap at 0.20%, but it's not the cheapest of the bunch. That honor goes to Vanguard Total Stock Market ETF, which charges just 0.07%, so it's the ETF to choose for lump sums. But if you plan to make periodic investments over

time, Fidelity Spartan Total Market Index is the fund to beat. With its 0.10% expense ratio, it's only slightly more expensive than the Vanguard offering. Plus, you won't have to pay brokerage commissions each time you make a purchase as you would with an ETF.

It's worth noting that this ETF and other total stock market index funds have enjoyed an advantage over their large-blend peers in recent years. Unlike rivals that concentrate exclusively on the market's largest stocks, these funds span the market-cap spectrum and thus own a slug of mid- and small-cap stocks, which have been in favor in recent years. But when that trend reverses, this fund's relative performance could suffer.

While that's reason to temper your expectations for total stock market index funds, it's not the main argument against this ETF. Expenses are this fund's Achilles' heel. In a very competitive marketplace, investors can go elsewhere to get virtually the same exposure at half the price.

Address:	45 Fremont Street	Management Fee:	0.20%		
	San Francisco CA 94105	Expense Projections:	3Yr:$64	5Yr:$113	10Yr:$255
	800-474-2737	Income Distrib:	Quarterly		
Web Address:	www.ishares.com	Exchange:	NYSE		
Inception:	05-22-00*				
Advisor:	Barclays Global Fund Advisers				

MORNINGSTAR® ETFs 150

iShares R3000 Value IWW

	Market Price	Mstar Category
	$106.48	Large Value

Morningstar Fair Value

Price/Fair Value Ratio	Coverage Rate %
0.94 Undervalued	91 Good

Management

Barclays Global Fund Advisors is this ETF's advisor. The firm is the world's largest manager of indexed portfolios. Patrick O'Connor, the head of Barclays' U.S. iShares portfolio management group, leads a team of a half dozen managers in running this and about 60 other ETFs. iShares' domestic portfolio-management group is responsible for about

Methodology

This ETF tracks the Russell 3000 Value Index, which is a subset of the Russell 3000 Index of the broad stock market. The index measures the performance of Russell 3000 companies whose shares have below-average price/book ratios and forecasted growth according to Institutional Brokers Estimate System. Russell uses a purely quantitative method to construct the index. It holds about half the stocks in the Russell 3000. The index reconstitutes just once a year, at the end of May, and rebalances in June.

Morningstar Rating	Return	Risk	Yield	NAV	Avg Daily Vol. (k)	52 wk High/Low
★★★★ Above Avg	Above Avg	Average	1.9%	$107.81	37	$108.59 - $91.59

Growth of $10,000
— Investment Value of ETF
— Investment Value of Index S&P 500

	1997	1998	1999	2000	2001	2002	2003	2004	2005	2006	History
	—	—	—	75.95	71.22	59.16	75.72	86.56	90.21	107.81	NAV $
	—	—	—	76.62	71.70	59.05	75.76	86.66	90.28	107.79	Market Price $
	—	—	—	9.14*	-4.61	-15.35	30.76	16.64	6.63	22.01	NAV Return%
	—	—	—	9.13*	-4.81	-16.07	31.08	16.71	6.59	21.90	Market Price Return%
	—	—	—	0.09	0.06	0.07	0.11	0.02	0.06	-0.02	Avg Premium/Discount%
	—	—	—	9.14	7.28	6.75	2.08	5.76	1.72	6.22	NAV Rtrn% +/-S&P 500
	—	—	—	9.14	0.98	0.17	0.73	0.15	-0.42	-0.24	NAV Rtrn% +/-Russ 1000 Vl
	—	—	—	—	7	7	7	8	11	14	NAV Return% Rank in Cat
	—	—	—	1.60	1.71	2.43	2.16	2.36	2.31	Income Return %
	—	—	—	-6.21	-17.06	28.33	14.48	4.27	19.70	Capital Return %
	—	—	—	0.55	1.21	1.21	1.43	1.62	2.03	2.07	Income $
	—	—	—	0.09	0.00	0.00	0.00	0.00	0.00	0.00	Capital Gains $
	—	—	—	0.25	0.25	0.25	0.25	0.25	0.25	Expense Ratio %
	—	—	—	1.67	1.79	2.20	2.19	2.33	2.26	Income Ratio %
	—	—	—	4	15	16	13	16	7	Turnover Rate %
	—	—	—	19	64	89	148	325	433	674	Net Assets $mil

Trading Volume Millions 0.06 / 0.0

Performance 12-31-06

Historic Quarterly NAV Returns

	1st Qtr	2nd Qtr	3rd Qtr	4th Qtr	Total
2002	4.41	-8.07	-18.93	8.79	-15.35
2003	-4.94	17.54	2.43	14.25	30.76
2004	3.26	0.83	1.37	10.51	16.64
2005	-0.31	1.89	3.78	1.15	6.63
2006	6.52	0.22	5.80	8.02	22.01

Trailing	NAV Return%	Market Return%	NAV Rtrn% +/-S&P 500	%Rank Cat.(NAV)
3 Mo	8.02	7.91	1.32	16
6 Mo	14.29	14.20	1.55	16
1 Yr	22.01	21.90	6.22	14
3 Yr Avg	14.92	14.89	4.48	8
5 Yr Avg	10.93	10.78	4.74	7
10 Yr Avg	—	—	—	—

Tax Analysis	Tax-Adj Return%	Tax-Cost Ratio
3 Yr (estimated)	14.07	0.74
5 Yr (estimated)	10.11	0.74
10 Yr (estimated)	—	—

Rating and Risk

Time Period	Morningstar Rtn vs Cat	Morningstar Risk vs Cat	Morningstar Risk-Adj Rating
3 Yr	+Avg	Avg	★★★★
5 Yr	+Avg	Avg	★★★★
10 Yr	—	—	—

Other Measures	Standard Index S&P 500	Best Fit Index Russ 1000 Vl
Alpha	4.3	-0.6
Beta	0.96	1.04
R-Squared	88	99
Standard Deviation	7.09	
Mean	14.92	
Sharpe Ratio	1.56	

Portfolio Analysis 12-31-06

Share change since 11-06 Total Stocks:1919

Sector		PE	Tot Ret%	% Assets
⊕ ExxonMobil Corporation	Energy	11.7	39.07	5.60
⊕ Citigroup, Inc.	Financial	13.3	19.55	3.55
⊕ Bank of America Corporat	Financial	12.4	20.68	3.12
⊕ General Electric Company	Ind Mtrls	19.8	9.35	2.55
⊕ Pfizer Inc.	Health	15.1	15.22	2.43
⊕ J.P. Morgan Chase & Co.	Financial	13.7	25.60	2.15
⊕ Procter & Gamble Company	Goods	24.2	13.36	2.14
⊕ Chevron Corporation	Energy	9.3	33.75	2.09
⊕ AT&T, Inc.	Telecom	19.2	51.59	1.78
⊕ American International G	Financial	17.1	6.05	1.76
⊕ ConocoPhillips	Energy	6.9	26.53	1.52
⊕ Verizon Communications	Telecom	16.1	34.88	1.39
⊕ Wells Fargo Company	Financial	14.7	16.82	1.30
⊕ Wachovia Corporation	Financial	13.0	12.01	1.26
⊕ Altria Group, Inc.	Goods	15.9	19.87	1.25
⊕ BellSouth Corporation	Telecom	—	—	1.09
⊕ Time Warner, Inc.	Media	19.1	26.37	1.04
⊕ Morgan Stanley	Financial	12.3	45.93	1.00
⊕ Merrill Lynch & Company,	Financial	14.1	39.27	0.90
⊕ Merck & Co., Inc.	Health	18.8	42.66	0.85

Current Investment Style

Value Blnd Growth — Large Mid Small

Market Cap	%
Giant	44.4
Large	29.5
Mid	17.9
Small	6.5
Micro	1.6

Avg $mil: 32,935

Value Measures		Rel Category
Price/Earnings	14.01	0.98
Price/Book	2.07	0.86
Price/Sales	1.22	0.92
Price/Cash Flow	7.14	0.92
Dividend Yield %	2.30	0.89

Growth Measures	%	Rel Category
Long-Term Erngs	9.92	0.99
Book Value	7.93	1.10
Sales	8.90	1.04
Cash Flow	9.45	1.10
Historical Erngs	16.26	1.05

Profitability	%	Rel Category
Return on Equity	15.71	0.90
Return on Assets	9.96	1.00
Net Margin	14.28	1.04

Sector Weightings	% of Stocks	Rel S&P 500	3 Year High	Low
↗ Info	13.00	0.65		
🖥 Software	0.68	0.20	1	1
💻 Hardware	2.64	0.29	6	3
🎤 Media	3.75	0.99	5	4
📶 Telecom	5.93	1.69	6	5
⊂ Service	49.40	1.07		
🩺 Health	6.73	0.56	7	3
Consumer	4.19	0.55	5	4
Business	2.34	0.55	4	2
Financial	36.14	1.62	37	31
🏭 Mfg	37.59	1.11		
Goods	7.87	0.92	9	6
Ind Mtrls	10.35	0.87	16	10
Energy	13.11	1.34	15	10
Utilities	6.26	1.79	7	6

Composition

● Cash	0.1	
● Stocks	99.9	
● Bonds	0.0	
● Other	0.0	
Foreign	0.0	
(% of Stock)		

Morningstar's Take by Sonya Morris 12-31-06

It has its shortcomings, but iShares Russell 3000 Value is a serviceable choice for one-stop value exposure.

This ETF boasts a fine performance record. Its three- and five-year trailing returns rank in the large-value category's top 20%. However, that showing has been influenced by its benchmark's structure. Because the Russell 3000 Value Index provides exposure to virtually all the value stocks (as defined by Russell) in the U.S. stock market, this ETF holds more smaller stocks than its rivals. Specifically, it dedicates 26% of its portfolio to mid- and small-cap stocks, compared with the category norm of 16%. Because the market has favored smaller value-oriented stocks in recent years, this fund's performance has gotten a boost, helping it outpace many of its large-cap-focused peers.

Interestingly, though, this ETF hasn't done much better than its sibling, iShares Russell 1000 Value (which also holds an above-average stake in small stocks). That suggests that the smallest 2,000

stocks haven't contributed much to this fund's strong relative record. That could be attributed to the Russell indexes' susceptibility to front-running. Russell reconstitutes its indexes at the same time every year. Because the changes are largely predictable, traders game the system by scooping up additions to the index in advance of the change, driving up the price that fund managers must pay on the day the changes go into effect. Front-running impacts smaller, less liquid stocks the most, and studies have shown that it has eroded the returns of the Russell 2000 Index over time.

That's definitely a drawback, but we still think this is an acceptable choice for those who'd like broad exposure to U.S. value stocks in one holding. Those worried about front-running issues could sidestep the problem by buying the cheaper iShares Russell 1000 Value and pairing it with a small-cap holding that isn't prone to front running.

Address:	45 Fremont Street San Francisco CA 94105 800-474-2737	Management Fee:	0.25%
		Expense Projections:	3Yr:$80 5Yr:$141 10Yr:$318
		Income Distrib:	Quarterly
Web Address:	www.ishares.com	Exchange:	NYSE
Inception:	07-24-00*		
Advisor:	Barclays Global Fund Advisers		

iShares Russell Microcap IWC

	Market Price	Mstar Category
	$57.74	Small Blend

Morningstar Fair Value

Price/Fair Value Ratio	Coverage Rate %
—	—

Management

Patrick O'Connor and S. Jane Leung lead the team that manages this and several other iShares ETFs. O'Connor has been on the team since the fund's inception and Leung since September 2006. Both have been with the ETF's advisor, Barclays Global Investors, for five or more years.

Methodology

Management tracks the Russell Microcap Index, which includes the 1,000 smallest stocks from the Russell 2000 Index, plus the next 1,000 smallest stocks from outside the benchmark. It excludes stocks from the OTC bulletin board and Pink Sheets. The fund uses a representative sampling to track the index, which rebalances annually in June.

Morningstar Rating	Return	Risk	Yield	NAV	Avg Daily Vol. (k)	52 wk High/Low
— Not Rated	Not Rated	—	0.5%	$58.56	80	$59.18 - $50.09

Growth of $10,000
- Investment Value of ETF
- Investment Value of Index S&P 500

Trading Volume Millions

	1997	1998	1999	2000	2001	2002	2003	2004	2005	2006	History
	—	—	—	—	—	—	—	—	51.31	58.56	NAV $
	—	—	—	—	—	—	—	—	51.15	58.45	Market Price $
	—	—	—	—	—	—	—	—	12.67*	14.75	NAV Return%
	—	—	—	—	—	—	—	—	12.52*	14.89	Market Price Return%
	—	—	—	—	—	—	—	—	-0.23	-0.14	Avg Premium/Discount%
	—	—	—	—	—	—	—	—	12.67	-1.04	NAV Rtrn% +/-S&P 500
	—	—	—	—	—	—	—	—	12.67	-3.62	NAV Rtrn% +/-Russ 2000
	—	—	—	—	—	—	—	—	—	8	NAV Return% Rank in Cat
	—	—	—	—	—	—	—	—	—	0.59	Income Return %
	—	—	—	—	—	—	—	—	—	14.16	Capital Return %
	—	—	—	—	—	—	—	—	0.10	0.30	Income $
	—	—	—	—	—	—	—	—	0.00	0.00	Capital Gains $
	—	—	—	—	—	—	—	—	—	0.60	Expense Ratio %
	—	—	—	—	—	—	—	—	—	0.56	Income Ratio %
	—	—	—	—	—	—	—	—	—	6	Turnover Rate %
	—	—	—	—	—	—	—	—	103	258	Net Assets $mil

Performance 12-31-06

Historic Quarterly NAV Returns

	1st Qtr	2nd Qtr	3rd Qtr	4th Qtr	Total
2002	—	—	—	—	—
2003	—	—	—	—	—
2004	—	—	—	—	—
2005	—	—	—	1.05	—*
2006	14.06	-7.42	-1.03	9.80	14.75

Trailing	NAV Return%	Market Return%	NAV Rtrn% +/-S&P 500	%Rank Cat.(NAV)
3 Mo	9.80	9.72	3.10	12
6 Mo	8.67	8.95	-4.07	10
1 Yr	14.75	14.89	-1.04	8
3 Yr Avg	—	—	—	—
5 Yr Avg	—	—	—	—
10 Yr Avg	—	—	—	—

Tax Analysis	Tax-Adj Return%	Tax-Cost Ratio
3 Yr (estimated)	—	—
5 Yr (estimated)	—	—
10 Yr (estimated)	—	—

Rating and Risk

Time Period	Morningstar Rtn vs Cat	Morningstar Risk vs Cat	Morningstar Risk-Adj Rating
3 Yr	—	—	—
5 Yr	—	—	—
10 Yr	—	—	—

Other Measures	Standard Index S&P 500	Best Fit Index
Alpha	—	—
Beta	—	—
R-Squared	—	—
Standard Deviation	—	
Mean	—	
Sharpe Ratio	—	

Morningstar's Take by Annie Sorich 12-31-06

Despite its curb appeal, investors don't need iShares Russell Microcap Index.

To many investors, micro-cap stocks sound sexy. Ranging in market cap from $50 to $500 million, these stocks are often not covered by analysts at big investment banks, making these stocks potential hidden gems. But the quest for a diamond in the rough comes with noteworthy risks.

Even though it's only been around for a year, this exchange-traded fund (which tracks the Russell Microcap Index minus its most illiquid members) is clearly not immune from risks inherent to the micro-cap sphere. It performed as expected--like a roller coaster. While it gained 14% over the three-month period between January and March 2006, it lost more than 10% from May through July 2006. Such undulations are par for the course in this asset class. Smaller companies often rely on only a few products or services, and as a result, their stocks often experience more ups and downs. This may be bearable for risk-tolerant long-term

investors, but the added volatility may make this ETF too difficult to use for those with shorter time horizons (less than 10 years) or weaker stomachs.

One way investors can damp the effects of such price volatility is by investing small amounts on a regular basis (also known as dollar-cost averaging), thereby avoiding making a large investment at the wrong time. Unfortunately, this is impractical with ETFs because brokerage commissions must be paid with every trade, quickly eroding any cost savings that come from ETFs' lower expense ratios.

Thankfully, those interested in dollar-cost averaging have a viable alternative in a conventional mutual fund, Bridgeway Ultra-Small Company Market. With an expense ratio of 0.65%, it's only 5 basis points more expensive than this ETF, and it has a time-tested, tax-efficient investment strategy. We think dollar-cost averaging into a proven fund makes more sense in this turbulent asset class.

Address:	45 Fremont Street	Management Fee:	0.60%		
	San Francisco CA 94105	Expense Projections:	3Yr:$192	5Yr:$335	10Yr:$750
	800-474-2737	Income Distrib:	Quarterly		
Web Address:	www.ishares.com	Exchange:	NYSE		
Inception:	08-12-05*				
Advisor:	Barclays Global Fund Advisers				

Portfolio Analysis 12-31-06

Share change since 11-06 Total Stocks:1447	Sector	PE	Tot Ret%	% Assets
⊕ EnergySouth, Inc.	Energy	22.9	53.83	0.29
⊕ City Bank	Financial	23.4	57.99	0.28
⊕ Integra Bank Corporation	Financial	16.7	32.53	0.28
⊕ IBERIABANK Coporation	Financial	24.9	18.17	0.27
⊕ Stratasys	Software	32.0	25.59	0.27
⊕ Independent Bank (MA) Co	Financial	16.5	28.80	0.26
⊕ Coastal Financial Corpor	Financial	20.0	45.43	0.26
⊕ Charter Communications,	Media	—	150.82	0.26
⊕ One Liberty Properties,	Financial	25.6	45.25	0.26
⊕ World Acceptance Corpora	Financial	21.6	64.74	0.25
⊕ SAVVIS, Inc.	Telecom	—	217.42	0.25
⊕ Provident New York Banco	Financial	30.6	38.18	0.25
⊕ Capital Trust, Inc. A	Financial	14.1	85.85	0.24
⊕ Columbia Banking System,	Financial	17.5	25.20	0.24
⊕ TierOne Corporation	Financial	13.4	8.38	0.24
⊕ Coca-Cola Bottling Compa	Goods	37.6	62.18	0.23
⊕ Healthcare Services Grou	Business	34.5	42.74	0.23
⊕ KNBT Bancorp, Inc.	Financial	22.0	4.68	0.23
⊕ Align Technology, Inc.	Health	—	115.92	0.23
⊕ L-1 Identity Solutions,	Business	—	-14.08	0.23

Current Investment Style

Value Blnd Growth — Large Mid Small

Market Cap	%
Giant	0.0
Large	0.0
Mid	0.0
Small	20.5
Micro	79.5
Avg $mil: 357	

Value Measures		Rel Category
Price/Earnings	19.99	1.13
Price/Book	1.96	0.95
Price/Sales	1.03	1.00
Price/Cash Flow	6.80	1.05
Dividend Yield %	1.37	0.86

Growth Measures	%	Rel Category
Long-Term Erngs	14.50	1.09
Book Value	1.65	0.30
Sales	5.98	2.63
Cash Flow	4.78	0.53
Historical Erngs	5.12	0.43

Profitability	%	Rel Category
Return on Equity	4.11	0.36
Return on Assets	1.23	0.19
Net Margin	6.79	0.69

Sector Weightings

	% of Stocks	Rel S&P 500	3 Year High Low
⊙ Info	19.26	0.96	
Software	5.73	1.66	— —
Hardware	9.27	1.00	— —
Media	1.69	0.45	— —
Telecom	2.57	0.73	— —
⊆ Service	59.36	1.28	
Health	16.67	1.38	— —
Consumer	7.65	1.00	— —
Business	11.09	2.62	— —
Financial	23.95	1.08	— —
⊡ Mfg	21.38	0.63	
Goods	5.70	0.67	— —
Ind Mtrls	10.89	0.91	— —
Energy	3.92	0.40	— —
Utilities	0.87	0.25	— —

Composition

● Cash	0.1	
● Stocks	99.7	
● Bonds	0.0	
○ Other	0.1	
Foreign	0.3	
(% of Stock)		

MORNINGSTAR® ETFs 150

iShares R. Midcap Gr IWP

	Market Price	Mstar Category
	$103.48	Mid-Cap Growth

Morningstar Fair Value

Price/Fair Value Ratio	Coverage Rate %
0.94 Undervalued	90 Good

Management

Barclays Global Investors is the advisor to all iShares ETFs, including this fund. Daily managerial chores are handled by Patrick O'Connor and S. Jane Leung. O'Connor has managed index funds at Barclays since 1999, and Leung joined the managerial ranks in 2001.

Methodology

The fund tracks the Russell Midcap Growth Index, which consists of the smallest 800 stocks in the Russell 1000 Index (essentially the smallest of the big). The Russell Midcap Growth Index includes mid-cap stocks that show higher book values and forecasted earnings growth. It represents about 40% of the Russell Midcap's market capitalization. The index reconstitutes just once a year.

Morningstar Rating	Return	Risk	Yield	NAV	Avg Daily Vol. (k)	52 wk High/Low
★★★ Neutral	Neutral	Average	0.7%	$103.12	102	$105.46 - $88.86

Growth of $10,000
- Investment Value of ETF
- Investment Value of Index S&P 500

Trading Volume Millions

	1997	1998	1999	2000	2001	2002	2003	2004	2005	2006	History
	—	—	—	—	71.61	51.82	73.63	84.53	94.06	103.12	NAV $
	—	—	—	—	71.86	51.70	73.70	84.50	93.96	103.07	Market Price $
	—	—	—	—	6.89*	-27.55	42.38	15.15	11.82	10.44	NAV Return%
	—	—	—	—	6.88*	-27.97	42.85	15.00	11.74	10.51	Market Price Return%
	—	—	—	—	0.43	0.16	0.07	0.09	0.01	-0.01	Avg Premium/Discount%
	—	—	—	—	6.89	-5.45	13.70	4.27	6.91	-5.35	NAV Rtrn% +/-S&P 500
	—	—	—	—	6.89	-0.14	-0.33	-0.33	-0.28	-0.22	NAV Rtrn% +/-Russ MG
	—	—	—	—	2	2	3	4	6	NAV Return% Rank in Cat
	—	—	—	—	—	0.09	0.26	0.32	0.52	0.76	Income Return %
	—	—	—	—	—	-27.64	42.12	14.83	11.30	9.68	Capital Return %
	—	—	—	—	0.02	0.06	0.14	0.23	0.44	0.72	Income $
	—	—	—	—	0.00	0.00	0.00	0.00	0.00	0.00	Capital Gains $
	—	—	—	—	—	0.25	0.25	0.25	0.25	0.25	Expense Ratio %
	—	—	—	—	—	0.08	0.20	0.27	0.38	0.64	Income Ratio %
	—	—	—	—	—	5	31	10	27	14	Turnover Rate %
	—	—	—	—	25	104	409	820	1,312	1,593	Net Assets $mil

Performance 12-31-06

Historic Quarterly NAV Returns

	1st Qtr	2nd Qtr	3rd Qtr	4th Qtr	Total
2002	-1.83	-18.29	-17.21	9.10	-27.55
2003	-0.06	18.69	7.09	12.09	42.38
2004	4.76	0.99	-4.40	13.84	15.15
2005	-1.74	3.37	6.50	3.37	11.82
2006	7.59	-4.75	0.83	6.89	10.44

Trailing	NAV Return%	Market Return%	NAV Rtrn% +/-S&P 500	%Rank Cat.(NAV)
3 Mo	6.89	6.91	0.19	8
6 Mo	7.78	7.71	-4.96	7
1 Yr	10.44	10.51	-5.35	6
3 Yr Avg	12.46	12.40	2.02	3
5 Yr Avg	7.97	7.88	1.78	2
10 Yr Avg	—	—	—	—

Tax Analysis	Tax-Adj Return%	Tax-Cost Ratio
3 Yr (estimated)	12.25	0.19
5 Yr (estimated)	7.83	0.13
10 Yr (estimated)	—	—

Rating and Risk

Time Period	Morningstar Rtn vs Cat	Morningstar Risk vs Cat	Morningstar Risk-Adj Rating
3 Yr	+Avg	-Avg	★★★★
5 Yr	Avg	Avg	★★★
10 Yr	—	—	—

Other Measures	Standard Index S&P 500	Best Fit Index Russ MG
Alpha	-1.2	-0.3
Beta	1.49	1.00
R-Squared	81	100
Standard Deviation	11.35	
Mean	12.46	
Sharpe Ratio	0.81	

Portfolio Analysis 12-31-06

Share change since 11-06 Total Stocks:539

Sector	PE	Tot Ret%	% Assets
⊕ Celgene Corporation	Health	—	77.56	0.99
⊕ Harley-Davidson, Inc.	Goods	18.6	38.81	0.88
⊕ J.C. Penney Company, Inc	Consumer	17.6	40.59	0.84
⊕ Allergan, Inc.	Health	—	11.33	0.83
⊕ Coach, Inc.	Goods	31.4	28.85	0.76
⊕ Forest Laboratories, Inc	Health	22.6	24.39	0.76
⊕ Yum Brands, Inc.	Consumer	20.6	26.76	0.74
⊕ International Game Tech.	Consumer	34.5	52.07	0.72
⊕ American Tower Corporati	Telecom	—	37.56	0.72
⊕ Electronic Arts, Inc.	Software	86.8	-3.73	0.71
⊕ Avon Products	Goods	31.2	18.45	0.69
⊕ Network Appliance, Inc.	Hardware	55.3	45.48	0.68
⊕ AES Corporation	Utilities	35.0	39.23	0.67
⊕ Hilton Hotels Corporatio	Consumer	30.4	45.62	0.62
⊕ Paychex, Inc.	Business	30.0	5.62	0.61
⊕ St. Jude Medical, Inc.	Health	34.5	-27.17	0.61
⊕ TJX Companies	Consumer	16.7	24.05	0.60
⊕ NVIDIA Corporation	Hardware	36.5	102.46	0.60
⊕ Northern Trust Corporati	Financial	20.9	19.11	0.58
⊕ Amazon.com, Inc.	Consumer	58.0	-16.31	0.57

Current Investment Style

Value Blnd Growth		Market Cap	%
(Large Mid Small)		Giant	0.5
		Large	26.5
		Mid	71.3
		Small	1.7
		Micro	0.0
		Avg $mil:	
		7,013	

Value Measures		Rel Category
Price/Earnings	20.47	1.04
Price/Book	3.60	1.05
Price/Sales	1.62	0.95
Price/Cash Flow	11.91	1.08
Dividend Yield %	0.81	1.65

Growth Measures	%	Rel Category
Long-Term Erngs	15.06	0.96
Book Value	10.99	0.94
Sales	11.67	1.01
Cash Flow	13.96	0.82
Historical Erngs	20.99	0.91

Profitability	%	Rel Category
Return on Equity	21.01	1.04
Return on Assets	9.56	0.92
Net Margin	10.82	0.95

Sector Weightings	% of Stocks	Rel S&P 500	3 Year High	Low
℧ Info	18.95	0.95		
▣ Software	4.44	1.29	8	4
▣ Hardware	10.15	1.10	17	10
▣ Media	2.11	0.56	4	2
▣ Telecom	2.25	0.64	2	1
☞ Service	51.93	1.12		
▣ Health	14.87	1.23	22	14
▣ Consumer	16.47	2.15	19	15
▣ Business	11.44	2.70	13	11
▣ Financial	9.15	0.41	9	6
▣ Mfg	29.14	0.86		
▣ Goods	8.54	1.00	9	5
▣ Ind Mtrls	11.20	0.94	11	11
▣ Energy	8.10	0.83	11	4
▣ Utilities	1.30	0.37	1	0

Composition

- Cash 0.1
- Stocks 99.9
- Bonds 0.0
- Other 0.0
- Foreign 0.1 (% of Stock)

Morningstar's Take by Sonya Morris 12-31-06

Competition just got tougher for iShares Russell Midcap Growth.

This ETF provides low cost exposure to mid-cap growth stocks, but it's no longer the cheapest game in town. In August 2006, Vanguard launched Vanguard Mid-Cap Growth ETF, which charges an expense ratio of 0.13%. That's almost half the cost of this ETF, which levies a 0.25% fee. That difference might seem small, but in the world of indexing every percentage point counts. When evaluating index funds that essentially cover the same ground (as these two funds do), we've found the expense ratio to be one of the best predictors of future performance. That gives the new Vanguard fund a notable edge over this ETF.

What's more, we think the Vanguard fund stands a better chance of more accurately reflecting the mid-growth universe over time. That's because Russell relies on only two quantitative measures--price/book ratios and consensus analysts' forecasts for long-term earnings

growth--to distinguish growth stocks from value stocks. In contrast, most other index providers (including MSCI, which constructs the Vanguard fund's benchmark) use several metrics to determine a stock's style.

This ETF also doesn't mirror its universe when it comes to size. It holds more large-cap stocks and fewer smaller names than the typical mid-growth fund. As a result, its aggregate market cap is almost 30% larger than the category norm. As a result, this fund may experience more overlap with large-cap funds than competing offerings.

Because of these quirks, this ETF isn't our first choice for mid-growth exposure. That said, this fund has its strong points that provide justification for owning it. It offers broad mid-growth exposure at a very reasonable price. Plus, it has also amassed a competitive track record. Its average annual returns over the past five years surpass more than 60% of its rivals.

Address:	45 Fremont Street San Francisco CA 94105 800-474-2737	Management Fee:	0.25%
		Expense Projections:	3Yr:$80 5Yr:$141 10Yr:$318
		Income Distrib:	Quarterly
Web Address:	www.ishares.com	Exchange:	AMEX
Inception:	07-17-01*		
Advisor:	Barclays Global Fund Advisers		

iShares R. Midcap IWR

	Market Price $99.83	Mstar Category Mid-Cap Blend

Morningstar Fair Value

Price/Fair Value Ratio	Coverage Rate %
0.97 Fairly valued	91 Good

Management

Barclays Global Investors runs the show here. This fund is one of more than 175 exchange-traded funds that the firm runs under the "iShares" banner. Patrick O'Connor and S. Jane Yeung run the ETF on a day-to-day basis. O'Conner has managed index funds at Barclays since 1999, and Leung joined the managerial ranks in 2001.

Methodology

The strategy here is simple: Match the risk-adjusted performance of the Russell Midcap Index. To that end, management assembles a basket of securities corresponding to the benchmark and rebalances the portfolio as necessary. The Russell index spans the smallest 800 names in the Russell 1000 Index (which, in turn, represents the 1,000 largest publicly traded stocks in the U.S.). Unlike the S&P Midcap 400 Index, which is derived using a mix of qualitative and quantitative factors, the Russell bogy's methodology is wholly quantitative.

Morningstar Rating	Return	Risk	Yield	NAV	Avg Daily Vol. (k)	52 wk High/Low
★★★★ Above Avg	Above Avg	Average	1.3%	$99.93	166	$101.62 - $86.86

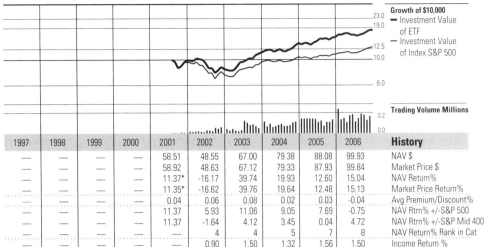

Growth of $10,000
— Investment Value of ETF
— Investment Value of Index S&P 500

Trading Volume Millions

1997	1998	1999	2000	2001	2002	2003	2004	2005	2006	History
—	—	—	—	58.51	48.55	67.00	79.38	88.08	99.93	NAV $
—	—	—	—	58.92	48.63	67.12	79.33	87.93	99.84	Market Price $
—	—	—	—	11.37*	-16.17	39.74	19.93	12.60	15.04	NAV Return%
—	—	—	—	11.35*	-16.62	39.76	19.64	12.48	15.13	Market Price Return%
—	—	—	—	0.04	0.06	0.08	0.02	0.03	-0.04	Avg Premium/Discount%
—	—	—	—	11.37	5.93	11.06	9.05	7.69	-0.75	NAV Rtrn% +/-S&P 500
—	—	—	—	11.37	-1.64	4.12	3.45	0.04	4.72	NAV Rtrn% +/-S&P Mid 400
—	—	—	—	—	4	4	5	7	8	NAV Return% Rank in Cat
—	—	—	—	—	0.90	1.50	1.32	1.56	1.50	Income Return %
—	—	—	—	—	-17.07	38.24	18.61	11.04	13.54	Capital Return %
—	—	—	—	0.35	0.53	0.72	0.88	1.23	1.31	Income $
—	—	—	—	0.00	0.00	0.00	0.00	0.00	0.00	Capital Gains $
—	—	—	—	—	0.20	0.20	0.20	0.20	0.20	Expense Ratio %
—	—	—	—	—	1.40	1.50	1.39	1.48	1.49	Income Ratio %
—	—	—	—	—	7	15	7	15	9	Turnover Rate %
—	—	—	—	18	165	415	1,131	1,696	2,763	Net Assets $mil

Performance 12-31-06

Historic Quarterly NAV Returns

	1st Qtr	2nd Qtr	3rd Qtr	4th Qtr	Total
2002	4.22	-9.56	-17.56	7.89	-16.17
2003	-2.41	18.19	6.37	13.89	39.74
2004	5.09	1.41	-0.89	13.54	19.93
2005	-0.23	4.18	5.90	2.29	12.60
2006	7.59	-2.62	2.05	7.60	15.04

Trailing	NAV Return%	Market Return%	NAV Rtrn% +/-S&P 500	%Rank Cat.(NAV)
3 Mo	7.60	7.48	0.90	10
6 Mo	9.81	9.59	-2.93	9
1 Yr	15.04	15.13	-0.75	8
3 Yr Avg	15.82	15.71	5.38	5
5 Yr Avg	12.72	12.54	6.53	4
10 Yr Avg	—	—	—	—

Tax Analysis	Tax-Adj Return%	Tax-Cost Ratio
3 Yr (estimated)	15.27	0.47
5 Yr (estimated)	12.21	0.45
10 Yr (estimated)	—	—

Rating and Risk

Time Period	Morningstar Rtn vs Cat	Morningstar Risk vs Cat	Morningstar Risk-Adj Rating
3 Yr	+Avg	Avg	★★★★
5 Yr	+Avg	Avg	★★★★
10 Yr	—	—	—

Other Measures	Standard Index S&P 500	Best Fit Index Mstar Mid Core
Alpha	2.9	2.4
Beta	1.30	0.87
R-Squared	84	98
Standard Deviation	9.74	
Mean	15.82	
Sharpe Ratio	1.23	

Morningstar's Take by Sonya Morris 12-31-06

The market's favor won't always shine on iShares Russell MidCap, but it's still a justifiable long-term holding.

This ETF tracks the Russell MidCap Index, a subset of the Russell 1000 Index, a popular large-cap benchmark. To fit this index into the mid-cap slot, Russell tosses out the largest 200 companies in the Russell 1000. Nevertheless, this ETF still includes a slug of large-cap stocks. At present, 30% of its portfolio is dedicated to large-cap names, which is 10 percentage points more than its typical mid-blend rival. That could cause portfolio construction problems for those who intend to pair this with a large-cap fund. Those seeking more targeted mid-cap exposure may want to give streetTracks DJ Wilshire Mid Cap a closer look, because virtually all of its portfolio is packed into the mid-cap space.

But although this ETF may stretch a bit further up the market-cap ladder than much of the competition, there's justification for owning it. It provides broad exposure to a large slug of midsize businesses. And it sports a very low expense ratio of 0.20%. (The only competing ETF that's cheaper is Vanguard Mid Cap ETF, which charges 0.13%.)

This ETF also owns a competitive track record. Its five-year trailing returns outrank 80% of its category rivals. That said, this ETF has led a charmed life. Mid- and small-cap stocks have been in favor during most of its limited life span. Shareholders here shouldn't expect this ETF to continue to benefit from such tail winds. The small- and mid-cap rally has gone on for much longer than most analysts have expected, and it wouldn't be surprising to see them cool off in the relatively near future. So, while shareholders here own a respectable mid-cap ETF, they'd be wise to temper their near-term expectations and remain focused on the long haul.

Address:	45 Fremont Street San Francisco CA 94105 800-474-2737
Web Address:	www.ishares.com
Inception:	07-17-01*
Advisor:	Barclays Global Fund Advisers

Management Fee:	0.20%		
Expense Projections:	3Yr:$64	5Yr:$113	10Yr:$255
Income Distrib:	Quarterly		
Exchange:	NYSE		

Portfolio Analysis 12-31-06

Share change since 11-06 Total Stocks:784	Sector	PE	Tot Ret%	% Assets
⊕ Celgene Corporation	Health	—	77.56	0.53
⊕ Entergy Corporation	Utilities	19.9	38.40	0.47
⊕ Harley-Davidson, Inc.	Goods	18.6	38.81	0.47
⊕ Thermo Fisher Scientific	Health	37.7	50.32	0.46
⊕ J.C. Penney Company, Inc	Consumer	17.6	40.59	0.45
⊕ Allergan, Inc.	Health	—	11.33	0.44
⊕ Equity Office Properties	Financial	—	64.28	0.44
⊕ American Electric Power	Utilities	18.6	19.58	0.41
⊕ Kroger Company	Consumer	17.1	23.31	0.41
⊕ Coach, Inc.	Goods	31.4	28.85	0.41
⊕ Forest Laboratories, Inc	Health	22.6	24.39	0.41
⊕ PG & E Corporation	Utilities	16.8	31.58	0.41
⊕ Xerox Corporation	Ind Mtrls	13.4	15.70	0.40
⊕ PACCAR, Inc.	Ind Mtrls	11.5	46.88	0.40
⊕ Yum Brands, Inc.	Consumer	20.6	26.76	0.39
⊕ Air Products and Chemica	Ind Mtrls	21.4	21.17	0.39
⊕ International Game Tech.	Consumer	34.5	52.07	0.39
⊕ American Tower Corporati	Telecom	—	37.56	0.39
⊕ Safeway Inc.	Consumer	21.1	47.22	0.38
⊕ Williams Companies, Inc.	Energy	65.3	14.41	0.38

Current Investment Style

Value Blnd Growth — Large/Mid/Small

Market Cap	%
Giant	0.3
Large	29.1
Mid	69.4
Small	1.2
Micro	0.0

Avg $mil: 7,009

Value Measures		Rel Category
Price/Earnings	17.97	1.08
Price/Book	2.61	1.02
Price/Sales	1.22	1.09
Price/Cash Flow	7.95	0.87
Dividend Yield %	1.35	0.99

Growth Measures	%	Rel Category
Long-Term Erngs	11.95	0.98
Book Value	7.97	1.09
Sales	8.52	1.21
Cash Flow	10.35	1.05
Historical Erngs	15.93	0.83

Profitability	%	Rel Category
Return on Equity	17.00	0.99
Return on Assets	8.56	1.00
Net Margin	11.63	1.10

Sector Weightings	% of Stocks	Rel S&P 500	3 Year High Low
↻ Info	14.41	0.72	
▣ Software	2.81	0.81	4 2
▣ Hardware	7.07	0.77	11 7
▣ Media	2.29	0.60	3 2
▣ Telecom	2.24	0.64	2 1
☞ Service	50.53	1.09	
♥ Health	9.70	0.80	11 9
▣ Consumer	12.54	1.64	14 11
▣ Business	8.55	2.02	9 7
$ Financial	19.74	0.89	22 19
⌐ Mfg	35.07	1.04	
▣ Goods	9.15	1.07	9 7
❖ Ind Mtrls	11.66	0.98	12 11
◆ Energy	6.49	0.66	9 5
▣ Utilities	7.77	2.22	8 6

Composition

		%
●	Cash	0.1
●	Stocks	99.9
●	Bonds	0.0
○	Other	0.0
	Foreign	0.0
	(% of Stock)	

MORNINGSTAR® ETFs 150

iShares R. Midcap VI IWS

Market Price $145.93	**Mstar Category** Mid-Cap Value	

Morningstar Fair Value

Price/Fair Value Ratio	Coverage Rate %
0.99 Fairly valued	91 Good

Management

Barclays Global Fund Advisors is the advisor. The firm is the world's largest manager of indexed portfolios. Patrick O'Connor and S. Jane Leung share managerial duties here. O'Connor began managing index funds at Barclays in 1999. Leung's tenure at the firm began in 2001.

Methodology

This fund tries to match the performance of the Russell Midcap Value Index. The index is a subset of the smallest 800 names in the Russell 1000 Index (which, in turn, represents the 1,000 largest publicly traded stocks in the United States). Unlike the S&P Midcap 400 Index, which is derived using a mix of qualitative and quantitative factors, the Russell bogy's methodology is wholly quantitative. This fund focuses on Russell Midcap stocks with lower price/book ratios and forecasted growth according to the Institutional Brokers Estimate System.

Morningstar Rating	Return	Risk	Yield	NAV	Avg Daily Vol. (k)	52 wk High/Low
★★★★★ Highest	Highest	Average	1.8%	$146.56	152	$148.39 - $126.48

Growth of $10,000
— Investment Value of ETF
— Investment Value of Index S&P 500

Trading Volume Millions

	1997	1998	1999	2000	2001	2002	2003	2004	2005	2006	History
	—	—	—	—	77.62	68.87	93.11	112.83	124.59	146.56	NAV $
	—	—	—	—	77.93	68.55	93.30	112.81	124.42	146.43	Market Price $
	—	—	—	—	14.14*	-9.69	37.70	23.26	12.68	19.95	NAV Return%
	—	—	—	—	14.12*	-10.47	38.62	22.98	12.54	20.00	Market Price Return%
	—	—	—	—	0.13	0.05	0.20	0.00	0.00	-0.02	Avg Premium/Discount%
	—	—	—	—	14.14	12.41	9.02	12.38	7.77	4.16	NAV Rtrn% +/-S&P 500
	—	—	—	—	14.14	-0.05	-0.37	-0.45	0.03	-0.27	NAV Rtrn% +/-Russ MV
	—	—	—	—	—	2	2	2	4	6	NAV Return% Rank in Cat
	—	—	—	—	—	1.70	2.14	1.87	2.17	2.17	Income Return %
	—	—	—	—	—	-11.39	35.56	21.39	10.51	17.78	Capital Return %
	—	—	—	—	0.67	1.31	1.46	1.73	2.43	2.68	Income $
	—	—	—	—	0.00	0.00	0.00	0.00	0.00	0.00	Capital Gains $
	—	—	—	—	—	0.25	0.25	0.25	0.25	0.25	Expense Ratio %
	—	—	—	—	—	1.91	2.24	2.05	2.20	2.18	Income Ratio %
	—	—	—	—	—	6	24	10	20	11	Turnover Rate %
	—	—	—	—	35	96	275	1,055	2,012	3,049	Net Assets $mil

Performance 12-31-06

Historic Quarterly NAV Returns

	1st Qtr	2nd Qtr	3rd Qtr	4th Qtr	Total
2002	7.84	-4.73	-17.84	7.00	-9.69
2003	-4.11	17.79	5.88	15.14	37.70
2004	5.27	1.68	1.62	13.31	23.26
2005	0.83	4.70	5.34	1.31	12.68
2006	7.55	-0.60	3.47	8.43	19.95

Trailing	NAV Return%	Market Return%	NAV Rtrn% +/-S&P 500	%Rank Cat.(NAV)
3 Mo	8.43	8.29	1.73	8
6 Mo	12.19	12.02	-0.55	7
1 Yr	19.95	20.00	4.16	6
3 Yr Avg	18.54	18.43	8.10	2
5 Yr Avg	15.68	15.57	9.49	2
10 Yr Avg	—	—	—	—

Tax Analysis	Tax-Adj Return%	Tax-Cost Ratio
3 Yr (estimated)	17.76	0.66
5 Yr (estimated)	14.92	0.66
10 Yr (estimated)	—	—

Rating and Risk

Time Period	Morningstar Rtn vs Cat	Morningstar Risk vs Cat	Morningstar Risk-Adj Rating
3 Yr	High	Avg	★★★★★
5 Yr	High	Avg	★★★★★
10 Yr	—	—	—

Other Measures	Standard Index S&P 500	Best Fit Index Russ MV
Alpha	6.3	-0.1
Beta	1.15	1.00
R-Squared	81	100
Standard Deviation	8.74	
Mean	18.54	
Sharpe Ratio	1.63	

Morningstar's Take by Sonya Morris 12-31-06

It's not perfect, but there's a case to be made for iShares Russell MidCap Value.

This ETF's benchmark, the Russell MidCap Value Index, includes all the value-oriented stocks in the Russell MidCap Index. Although that benchmark excludes the 200 largest stocks in the Russell 1000, this ETF still includes a substantial number of large-cap stocks. In fact, its aggregate market cap is twice that of its mid-value ETF rivals.

That's had implications for this ETF's performance. Because it includes a big slug of larger firms, which are generally more financially stable than smaller businesses, this fund has experienced less volatility than its peers, as measured by its long-term standard deviation of returns (a statistical measure of volatility). Although smaller fry have outperformed larger stocks in recent years, this ETF's large-cap stake hasn't held it back. Its average annual returns since its inception surpass more than 80% of the competition.

Still, this ETF has its warts. Although its 0.25% expense ratio is very low, it's still not the cheapest way to gain mid-value exposure. In August of 2006, Vanguard launched Vanguard Mid-Cap Value ETF, which charges just 0.13% in expenses, making it almost half the price of this fund.

Moreover, Russell relies solely on analysts' earnings growth forecasts and price/book ratios to separate stocks into growth and value camps, while competing index providers use more sophisticated methodologies, which could help them better reflect the composition of the mid-value universe.

Finally, this ETF's big large-cap stake could result in portfolio-construction headaches for those trying to pair this with a large-cap fund.

In spite of these drawbacks, investors could do far worse than this ETF. It's cheap and it owns a competitive track record. Plus, it's run by an experienced management team.

Address:	45 Fremont Street San Francisco CA 94105 800-474-2737
Web Address:	www.ishares.com
Inception:	07-17-01 *
Advisor:	Barclays Global Fund Advisers

Management Fee:	0.25%
Expense Projections:	3Yr:$80 5Yr:$141 10Yr:$318
Income Distrib:	Quarterly
Exchange:	NYSE

Portfolio Analysis 12-31-06

Share change since 11-06 Total Stocks:481

	Sector	PE	Tot Ret%	% Assets
⊕ Entergy Corporation	Utilities	19.9	38.40	1.02
⊕ Equity Office Properties	Financial	—	64.28	0.93
⊕ American Electric Power	Utilities	18.6	19.58	0.89
⊕ PG & E Corporation	Utilities	16.8	31.58	0.87
⊕ Xerox Corporation	Ind Mtrls	13.4	15.70	0.87
⊕ Safeway Inc.	Consumer	21.1	47.22	0.82
⊕ KeyCorp	Financial	13.0	21.03	0.81
⊕ ProLogis Trust	Financial	34.3	34.02	0.79
⊕ Vornado Realty Trust	Financial	38.2	51.13	0.79
⊕ Edison International	Utilities	13.5	7.02	0.78
⊕ Equity Residential	Financial	NMF	34.64	0.78
⊕ Kroger Company	Consumer	17.1	23.31	0.77
⊕ Sempra Energy	Utilities	10.9	28.10	0.77
⊕ Gannett Co., Inc.	Media	12.5	1.92	0.76
⊕ ConAgra Foods, Inc.	Goods	36.0	38.10	0.74
⊕ Air Products and Chemica	Ind Mtrls	21.4	21.17	0.74
⊕ Liberty Capital A	Consumer	—	—	0.73
⊕ PPL Corporation	Utilities	15.4	26.06	0.72
⊕ Ford Motor Company	Goods	—	0.57	0.72
⊖ Cigna Corporation	Health	13.6	17.89	0.71

Current Investment Style

Value Blnd Growth / Large Mid Small

Market Cap	%
Giant	0.2
Large	32.0
Mid	67.2
Small	0.6
Micro	0.0

Avg $mil: 6,996

Value Measures		Rel Category
Price/Earnings	15.75	1.05
Price/Book	1.99	1.04
Price/Sales	0.94	1.06
Price/Cash Flow	5.78	0.78
Dividend Yield %	1.98	1.11

Growth Measures	%	Rel Category
Long-Term Erngs	9.36	0.99
Book Value	6.34	1.11
Sales	6.65	0.80
Cash Flow	7.80	5.74
Historical Erngs	12.47	1.13

Profitability	%	Rel Category
Return on Equity	12.44	0.95
Return on Assets	7.41	0.98
Net Margin	12.57	1.08

Sector Weightings	% of Stocks	Rel S&P 500	3 Year High Low	
↻ Info	9.21	0.46		
Software	0.95	0.28	2	1
Hardware	3.54	0.38	8	3
Media	2.50	0.66	3	1
Telecom	2.22	0.63	2	1
☞ Service	48.91	1.06		
Health	3.79	0.31	5	4
Consumer	8.03	1.05	11	7
Business	5.22	1.23	6	4
Financial	31.87	1.43	33	27
Mfg	41.88	1.24		
Goods	9.85	1.15	10	6
Ind Mtrls	12.19	1.02	16	12
Energy	4.66	0.48	9	5
Utilities	15.18	4.34	15	11

Composition

		%
● Cash		0.1
● Stocks		99.9
● Bonds		0.0
● Other		0.0
Foreign		0.0
(% of Stock)		

iShares S&P 100 Ind. OEF

	Market Price	**Mstar Category**
	$65.87	Large Blend

Morningstar Fair Value

Price/Fair Value Ratio	Coverage Rate %
0.87 Undervalued	100 Good

Management

Patrick O'Connor and S. Jane Leung lead the team that manages this and several other iShares ETFs. O'Connor has been on the team since the fund's inception and Leung since September 2006. Both have been with the ETF's advisor, Barclays Global Investors, for five or more years.

Methodology

This exchange-traded offering is a passive fund that simply attempts to match the performance of the S&P 100 Index. The benchmark is a market-capitalization-weighted index designed to track large liquid companies in the S&P 500 that also have options trading on the Chicago Board of Options Exchange. The bogy's sector exposures are similar to that of the S&P 500 and constituents have to meet the S&P index committee's profitability and index representation guidelines. The fund uses a representative sampling method of tracking the index.

Morningstar Rating ★★	**Return**	**Risk**	**Yield**	**NAV**	**Avg Daily Vol. (k)**	**52 wk High/Low**
Below Avg	Below Avg	Average	1.6%	$66.08	701	$66.80 - $56.25

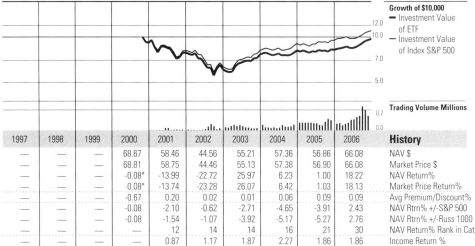

Growth of $10,000
- Investment Value of ETF
- Investment Value of Index S&P 500

Trading Volume Millions

	1997	1998	1999	2000	2001	2002	2003	2004	2005	2006	History
	—	—	—	68.67	58.46	44.56	55.21	57.36	56.86	66.08	NAV $
	—	—	—	68.81	58.75	44.46	55.13	57.38	56.90	66.08	Market Price $
	—	—	—	-0.08*	-13.99	-22.72	25.97	6.23	1.00	18.22	NAV Return%
	—	—	—	-0.08*	-13.74	-23.28	26.07	6.42	1.03	18.13	Market Price Return%
	—	—	—	-0.67	0.20	0.02	0.01	0.06	0.09	0.09	Avg Premium/Discount%
	—	—	—	-0.08	-2.10	-0.62	-2.71	-4.65	-3.91	2.43	NAV Rtrn% +/-S&P 500
	—	—	—	-0.08	-1.54	-1.07	-3.92	-5.17	-5.27	2.76	NAV Rtrn% +/-Russ 1000
	—	—	—	—	12	14	14	16	21	30	NAV Return% Rank in Cat
	—	—	—	—	0.87	1.17	1.87	2.27	1.86	1.86	Income Return %
	—	—	—	—	-14.86	-23.89	24.10	3.96	-0.86	16.36	Capital Return %
	—	—	—	0.15	0.59	0.68	0.83	1.25	1.06	1.05	Income $
	—	—	—	0.00	0.00	0.00	0.00	0.00	0.00	0.00	Capital Gains $
	—	—	—	0.20	0.20	0.20	0.20	0.20	0.20	0.20	Expense Ratio %
	—	—	—	—	1.03	1.12	1.63	1.62	2.41	1.96	Income Ratio %
	—	—	—	—	5	13	4	5	6	12	Turnover Rate %
	—	—	—	185	161	178	378	608	685	3,182	Net Assets $mil

Performance 12-31-06

Historic Quarterly NAV Returns

	1st Qtr	2nd Qtr	3rd Qtr	4th Qtr	Total
2002	-0.81	-14.88	-16.56	9.68	-22.72
2003	-3.08	14.72	2.08	10.98	25.97
2004	0.45	0.90	-2.99	8.05	6.23
2005	-1.85	-0.23	2.04	1.07	1.00
2006	3.64	-0.88	7.50	7.05	18.22

Trailing	NAV Return%	Market Return%	NAV Rtrn% +/-S&P 500	%Rank Cat.(NAV)
3 Mo	7.05	7.05	0.35	44
6 Mo	15.08	14.93	2.34	38
1 Yr	18.22	18.13	2.43	30
3 Yr Avg	8.25	8.30	-2.19	15
5 Yr Avg	4.31	4.20	-1.88	13
10 Yr Avg	—	—	—	

Tax Analysis	Tax-Adj Return%	Tax-Cost Ratio
3 Yr (estimated)	7.52	0.67
5 Yr (estimated)	3.66	0.62
10 Yr (estimated)	—	—

Rating and Risk

Time Period	Morningstar Rtn vs Cat	Morningstar Risk vs Cat	Morningstar Risk-Adj Rating
3 Yr	-Avg	-Avg	★★
5 Yr	-Avg	+Avg	★★
10 Yr	—	—	—

Other Measures	Standard Index S&P 500	Best Fit Index S&P 500
Alpha	-1.3	-1.3
Beta	0.90	0.90
R-Squared	92	92
Standard Deviation	6.54	
Mean	8.25	
Sharpe Ratio	0.77	

Portfolio Analysis 12-31-06

Share change since 11-06 Total Stocks:100	Sector	PE	Tot Ret%	% Assets
⊖ ExxonMobil Corporation	Energy	11.7	39.07	6.10
⊖ General Electric Company	Ind Mtrls	19.8	9.35	5.23
⊖ Citigroup, Inc.	Financial	13.3	19.55	3.73
⊖ Microsoft Corporation	Software	23.7	15.83	3.52
⊖ Bank of America Corporat	Financial	12.4	20.68	3.27
⊖ Procter & Gamble Company	Goods	24.2	13.36	2.78
⊖ Johnson & Johnson	Health	17.4	12.44	2.61
⊖ Pfizer Inc.	Health	15.1	15.22	2.55
⊖ American International G	Financial	17.1	6.05	2.54
⊖ Altria Group, Inc.	Goods	15.9	19.87	2.45
⊖ J.P. Morgan Chase & Co.	Financial	13.7	25.60	2.29
⊖ Cisco Systems, Inc.	Hardware	28.8	59.64	2.26
⊖ Chevron Corporation	Energy	9.3	33.75	2.19
⊖ IBM	Hardware	16.8	19.77	2.00
⊖ AT&T, Inc.	Telecom	19.2	51.59	1.87
⊖ Wells Fargo Company	Financial	14.7	16.82	1.64
☼ ConocoPhillips	Energy	6.9	26.53	1.62
⊖ Intel Corporation	Hardware	20.3	-17.18	1.59
⊖ Wal-Mart Stores, Inc.	Consumer	16.6	0.13	1.55
⊖ Hewlett-Packard Company	Hardware	18.9	45.21	1.54

Current Investment Style

Value Bnd Growth — Large Mid Small

Market Cap	%
Giant	82.5
Large	16.6
Mid	0.9
Small	0.0
Micro	0.0

Avg $mil: 114,320

Value Measures		Rel Category
Price/Earnings	15.42	0.93
Price/Book	2.76	1.00
Price/Sales	1.65	1.30
Price/Cash Flow	10.17	1.08
Dividend Yield %	2.07	1.16

Growth Measures	%	Rel Category
Long-Term Erngs	10.72	0.93
Book Value	8.20	0.96
Sales	9.97	1.20
Cash Flow	8.72	1.15
Historical Erngs	17.42	1.04

Profitability	%	Rel Category
Return on Equity	21.00	1.09
Return on Assets	11.86	1.23
Net Margin	14.97	1.34

Sector Weightings	% of Stocks	Rel S&P 500	3 Year High Low
↻ Info	21.74	1.09	
Software	4.46	1.29	6 4
Hardware	9.24	1.00	13 9
Media	3.93	1.04	5 3
Telecom	4.11	1.17	4 4
⊂ Service	41.50	0.90	
Health	10.81	0.90	14 11
Consumer	4.43	0.58	7 4
Business	3.66	0.87	4 1
Financial	22.60	1.01	23 19
Mfg	36.77	1.09	
Goods	10.18	1.19	12 10
Ind Mtrls	12.93	1.08	15 13
Energy	12.03	1.23	12 6
Utilities	1.63	0.47	2 1

Composition

	%
● Cash	0.1
● Stocks	99.9
● Bonds	0.0
● Other	0.0
Foreign	0.0
(% of Stock)	

Morningstar's Take by Dan Culloton 12-31-06

With or without a large-cap rally, iShares S&P 100 Index has utility.

This ETF offers a straight shot of big, frequently traded stocks. Its benchmark is a subset of the S&P 500 Index. So, the ETF focuses on the bluest of blue chips, such as Microsoft, General Electric, and Procter & Gamble. For most of this fund's life that predilection has been a handicap, as small caps have ruled the market roost. In the second half of 2006, though, the big boys woke up and this fund finally outperformed smaller-cap indexes, such as the Russell 2000.

There is no way for certain to know if this is the start of the long-awaited large-cap revival. Either way this fund has its good points. Its advisor, Barclays Global Investors, is an experienced indexer and has tracked this fund's bogy accurately. While the fund isn't the cheapest ETF in the large-blend category, its 0.20% expense ratio is lower than that of its typical conventional mutual fund peer. Although the ETF owns more technology, consumer goods, and industrial stocks than the broad market, and keeps more than a third of its holdings in its top 10 positions, it's fairly well diversified. That, as well as the preponderance of established, profitable stocks in the portfolio, has kept a lid on volatility. The fund has one of the lowest standard deviations in its peer group.

There are risks. The fund lost money in half of the 14 rolling five-year periods from its inception through Nov. 30. Most of those losses coincided with a bear market that was harder on large-cap stocks than others, though. Furthermore, even after 2006's second half surge, about a third of this ETF s holdings were trading under Morningstar equity analysts' fair value estimates. So, there may be upside left.

This fund wouldn't work as a sole core holding due to its lack of mid- and small-cap stocks. But it's a viable alternative for those looking for exposure to mega-cap companies.

Address:	45 Fremont Street San Francisco CA 94105 800-474-2737	Management Fee:	0.20%
		Expense Projections:	3Yr:$64 5Yr:$113 10Yr:$255
Web Address:	www.ishares.com	Income Distrib:	Quarterly
Inception:	10-23-00*	Exchange:	CBOE
Advisor:	Barclays Global Fund Advisers		

 MORNINGSTAR® ETFs 150

iShares S&P 1500 Index ISI

	Market Price $125.46	Mstar Category Large Blend

Morningstar Fair Value

Price/Fair Value Ratio	Coverage Rate %
0.91 Undervalued	94 Good

Management

Barclays Global Fund Advisors is the advisor. The firm is the world's largest manager of indexed portfolios. Patrick O'Connor and S. Jane Leung lead a team of managers in running this and Barclays' other domestic and foreign ETFs.

Methodology

This exchange-traded fund tracks the S&P Composite 1500 Index, which combines the S&P 500, the S&P Midcap 400, and the S&P Smallcap 600 to create a market portfolio representing 85% of U.S. market capitalization. The index screens for profitability and liquidity, but ultimately index constituents are determined by the S&P committee, which makes decisions on a case-by-case basis.

Morningstar Rating	Return	Risk	Yield	NAV	Avg Daily Vol. (k)
— Not Rated	Not Rated	Not Rated	1.5%	$125.84	21

52 wk High/Low $127.14 – $109.25

Growth of $10,000
- Investment Value of ETF
- Investment Value of Index S&P 500

14.0
11.0
10.0

Trading Volume Millions

0.02

	1997	1998	1999	2000	2001	2002	2003	2004	2005	2006	History
	—	—	—	—	—	—	—	106.96	111.02	125.84	NAV $
	—	—	—	—	—	—	—	107.07	110.98	125.78	Market Price $
	—	—	—	—	—	—	—	9.87*	5.47	15.13	NAV Return%
	—	—	—	—	—	—	—	9.79*	5.32	15.12	Market Price Return%
	—	—	—	—	—	—	—	-0.09	-0.03	0.02	Avg Premium/Discount%
	—	—	—	—	—	—	—	9.87	0.56	-0.66	NAV Rtrn% +/-S&P 500
	—	—	—	—	—	—	—	9.87	-0.80	-0.33	NAV Rtrn% +/-Russ 1000
	—	—	—	—	—	—	—	—	21	30	NAV Return% Rank in Cat
	—	—	—	—	—	—	—	—	1.62	1.68	Income Return %
	—	—	—	—	—	—	—	—	3.85	13.45	Capital Return %
	—	—	—	—	—	—	—	1.64	1.72	1.85	Income $
	—	—	—	—	—	—	—	0.00	0.00	0.00	Capital Gains $
	—	—	—	—	—	—	—	—	0.20	0.20	Expense Ratio %
	—	—	—	—	—	—	—	—	1.73	1.61	Income Ratio %
	—	—	—	—	—	—	—	—	5	6	Turnover Rate %
	—	—	—	—	—	—	—	59	133	189	Net Assets $mil

Performance 12-31-06

Historic Quarterly NAV Returns

	1st Qtr	2nd Qtr	3rd Qtr	4th Qtr	Total
2002	—	—	—	—	—
2003	—	—	—	—	—
2004	—	1.68	-1.89	9.56	—*
2005	-2.03	1.68	3.76	2.04	5.47
2006	4.82	-1.75	4.77	6.71	15.13

Trailing	NAV Return%	Market Return%	NAV Rtrn% +/-S&P 500	%Rank Cat.(NAV)
3 Mo	6.71	6.61	0.01	44
6 Mo	11.80	11.65	-0.94	38
1 Yr	15.13	15.12	-0.66	30
3 Yr Avg	—	—	—	—
5 Yr Avg	—	—	—	—
10 Yr Avg	—	—	—	—

Tax Analysis	Tax-Adj Return%	Tax-Cost Ratio
3 Yr (estimated)	—	—
5 Yr (estimated)	—	—
10 Yr (estimated)	—	—

Rating and Risk

Time Period	Morningstar Rtn vs Cat	Morningstar Risk vs Cat	Morningstar Risk-Adj Rating
3 Yr	—	—	—
5 Yr	—	—	—
10 Yr	—	—	—

Other Measures	Standard Index S&P 500	Best Fit Index
Alpha	—	—
Beta	—	—
R-Squared	—	—
Standard Deviation	—	
Mean	—	
Sharpe Ratio	—	

Portfolio Analysis 12-31-06

Share change since 11-06 Total Stocks:1499

	Sector	PE	Tot Ret%	% Assets
⊖ ExxonMobil Corporation	Energy	11.7	39.07	3.10
⊕ General Electric Company	Ind Mtrls	19.8	9.35	2.66
⊖ Citigroup, Inc.	Financial	13.3	19.55	1.90
⊕ Microsoft Corporation	Software	23.7	15.83	1.79
⊖ Bank of America Corporat	Financial	12.4	20.68	1.66
Procter & Gamble Company	Goods	24.2	13.36	1.41
⊖ Johnson & Johnson	Health	17.4	12.44	1.33
⊖ Pfizer Inc.	Health	15.1	15.22	1.29
⊕ American International G	Financial	17.1	6.05	1.29
⊕ Altria Group, Inc.	Goods	15.9	19.87	1.24
J.P. Morgan Chase & Co.	Financial	13.7	25.60	1.16
⊖ Cisco Systems, Inc.	Hardware	28.8	59.64	1.15
⊖ Chevron Corporation	Energy	9.3	33.75	1.11
⊖ IBM	Hardware	16.8	19.77	1.01
⊖ AT&T, Inc.	Telecom	19.2	51.59	0.95
⊕ Wells Fargo Company	Financial	14.7	16.82	0.83
ConocoPhillips	Energy	6.9	26.53	0.82
Intel Corporation	Hardware	20.3	-17.18	0.81
Wal-Mart Stores, Inc.	Consumer	16.6	0.13	0.78
Hewlett-Packard Company	Hardware	18.9	45.21	0.78

Current Investment Style

Value Blnd Growth — Large Mid Small

Market Cap	%
Giant	45.0
Large	33.7
Mid	17.2
Small	3.8
Micro	0.3

Avg $mil: 36,755

Value Measures		Rel Category
Price/Earnings	16.06	0.97
Price/Book	2.65	0.96
Price/Sales	1.45	1.14
Price/Cash Flow	9.26	0.98
Dividend Yield %	1.71	0.96

Growth Measures	%	Rel Category
Long-Term Erngs	11.57	1.00
Book Value	8.57	1.00
Sales	6.06	0.73
Cash Flow	10.67	1.41
Historical Erngs	17.75	1.06

Profitability	%	Rel Category
Return on Equity	19.20	1.00
Return on Assets	10.74	1.12
Net Margin	13.83	1.24

Sector Weightings	% of Stocks	Rel S&P 500	3 Year High Low
⌖ Info	19.23	0.96	
🖥 Software	3.47	1.01	5 3
💽 Hardware	9.08	0.98	12 9
🎙 Media	3.48	0.92	4 3
📞 Telecom	3.20	0.91	3 3
☞ Service	46.79	1.01	
⚕ Health	11.90	0.99	14 12
🛒 Consumer	8.11	1.06	10 8
💼 Business	5.15	1.22	6 4
💲 Financial	21.63	0.97	22 19
🏭 Mfg	33.99	1.01	
🏠 Goods	8.28	0.97	10 8
⚙ Ind Mtrls	12.27	1.03	13 11
🔥 Energy	9.64	0.98	11 6
💡 Utilities	3.80	1.09	4 3

Composition

● Cash	0.1	
● Stocks	99.9	
● Bonds	0.0	
● Other	0.0	
Foreign	0.0	
(% of Stock)		

Morningstar's Take by Marta Norton 12-31-06

IShares S&P 1500 Index is a decent choice, but it's not our favorite.

This exchange-traded fund is meant for investors who want exposure to nearly the entire domestic-stock universe in one fell swoop. It tracks the S&P 1500 Index, which rolls up the S&P 500, the S&P MidCap 400, and the S&P SmallCap 600 into a complete domestic-equity portfolio.

That sounds pretty straightforward, but Standard & Poor's has a few quirks that it passes along to this ETF. Unlike its rivals' benchmarks, all S&P indexes are assembled and maintained by a committee, which, among other things, admits only profitable companies. In theory, that should help the ETF keep a lid on volatility by limiting its exposure to speculative stocks. And in fact, the fund's returns have fluctuated less than those of its ETF rivals over its short tenure. Its lighter stake in smaller-cap companies helps in that regard, since small caps are often in the early stages of business development and are prone to more fits and starts

than their larger peers.

Still, although the fund's higher-quality approach makes for a smoother ride, its portfolio still overlaps heavily with those of its peers. Indeed, the vast majority of its stocks can be found in Vanguard Total Stock Market ETF's portfolio and in open-end competitor Fidelity Spartan Total Market Index's portfolio. Given the common exposure, expenses are the most important determinant of relative success. And on that score, there's no contest. The Vanguard ETF charges only 0.07%, which gives it a head start over this ETF and its 0.20% expense ratio. The open-end Fidelity competitor can also be had for less: It costs only 0.10%. These small differences in fees add up. Since the fund's early 2004 inception, it's trailed both rivals.

This ETF does an adequate job of fulfilling its mandate, and investors could certainly do worse. That said, its expenses keep it from being our first choice.

Address:	45 Fremont Street San Francisco CA 94105 800-474-2737
Web Address:	www.ishares.com
Inception:	01-20-04*
Advisor:	Barclays Global Fund Advisers

Management Fee:	0.20%		
Expense Projections:	3Yr:$64	5Yr:$113	10Yr:$255
Income Distrib:	Quarterly		
Exchange:	NYSE		

MORNINGSTAR® ETFs 150

93

iShares SP 500 Growth IVW

	Market Price $64.86	Mstar Category Large Growth

Morningstar Fair Value

Price/Fair Value Ratio	Coverage Rate %
0.88 Undervalued	98 Good

Management

Barclays Global Fund Advisors is the advisor. The firm is the world's largest manager of indexed portfolios. Patrick O'Connor and S. Jane Leung handle this ETF's day-to-day management. O'Connor has managed index funds at Barclays since 1999. Leung's tenure at the firm began in 2001.

Methodology

This fund tracks the S&P 500/Citigroup Growth Index. The bogy relies on seven growth and valuation measures to classify stocks. The factors are dividend yield; price-book, -sales and -cash flow; and five-year earnings, sales, and internal growth rates. A third of the index's market capitalization ends up in each value, core, or growth bucket, but stocks in the middle zone can end up in both style indexes in proportion to their style scores. The overlap should reduce turnover caused by stocks moving from one style to another. The index includes no buffer zones between market-cap ranges. It rebalances annually in December.

Morningstar Rating ★★★ Neutral	Return Neutral	Risk Below Avg	Yield 1.2%	NAV $64.93	Avg Daily Vol. (k) 327	52 wk High/Low $65.95 - $56.67

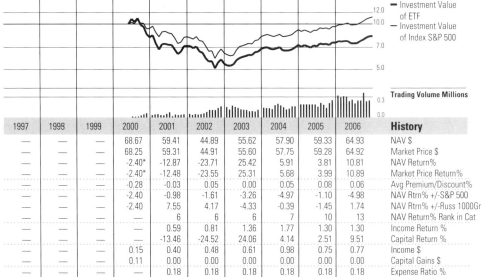

Growth of $10,000
— Investment Value of ETF
— Investment Value of Index S&P 500

Trading Volume Millions

	1997	1998	1999	2000	2001	2002	2003	2004	2005	2006	History
	—	—	—	68.67	59.41	44.89	55.62	57.90	59.33	64.93	NAV $
	—	—	—	68.25	59.31	44.91	55.60	57.75	59.28	64.92	Market Price $
	—	—	—	-2.40*	-12.87	-23.71	25.42	5.91	3.81	10.81	NAV Return%
	—	—	—	-2.40*	-12.48	-23.55	25.31	5.68	3.99	10.89	Market Price Return%
	—	—	—	-0.28	-0.03	0.05	0.00	0.05	0.08	0.06	Avg Premium/Discount%
	—	—	—	-2.40	-0.98	-1.61	-3.26	-4.97	-1.10	-4.98	NAV Rtrn% +/-S&P 500
	—	—	—	-2.40	7.55	4.17	-4.33	-0.39	-1.45	1.74	NAV Rtrn% +/-Russ 1000Gr
	—	—	—	—	6	6	6	7	10	13	NAV Return% Rank in Cat
	—	—	—	—	0.59	0.81	1.36	1.77	1.30	1.30	Income Return %
	—	—	—	—	-13.46	-24.52	24.06	4.14	2.51	9.51	Capital Return %
	—	—	—	0.15	0.40	0.48	0.61	0.98	0.75	0.77	Income $
	—	—	—	0.11	0.00	0.00	0.00	0.00	0.00	0.00	Capital Gains $
	—	—	—	—	0.18	0.18	0.18	0.18	0.18	0.18	Expense Ratio %
	—	—	—	—	0.45	0.82	1.19	1.22	1.93	1.28	Income Ratio %
	—	—	—	—	31	28	17	14	22	12	Turnover Rate %
	—	—	—	130	398	637	1,296	2,157	3,242	4,360	Net Assets $mil

Performance 12-31-06

Historic Quarterly NAV Returns

	1st Qtr	2nd Qtr	3rd Qtr	4th Qtr	Total
2002	-0.84	-16.29	-14.13	7.03	-23.71
2003	-0.85	12.09	2.70	9.88	25.42
2004	-0.03	2.63	-4.80	8.44	5.91
2005	-1.89	0.08	3.74	1.92	3.81
2006	2.58	-3.50	6.01	5.60	10.81

Trailing	NAV Return%	Market Return%	NAV Rtrn% +/-S&P 500	%Rank Cat.(NAV)
3 Mo	5.60	5.58	-1.10	15
6 Mo	11.94	11.90	-0.80	15
1 Yr	10.81	10.89	-4.98	13
3 Yr Avg	6.80	6.81	-3.64	7
5 Yr Avg	3.11	3.14	-3.08	6
10 Yr Avg	—	—	—	

Tax Analysis	Tax-Adj Return%	Tax-Cost Ratio
3 Yr (estimated)	6.27	0.50
5 Yr (estimated)	2.64	0.46
10 Yr (estimated)	—	—

Rating and Risk

Time Period	Morningstar Rtn vs Cat	Morningstar Risk vs Cat	Morningstar Risk-Adj Rating
3 Yr	Avg	Low	★★★
5 Yr	Avg	-Avg	★★★
10 Yr	—	—	—

Other Measures	Standard Index S&P 500	Best Fit Index S&P 500
Alpha	-3.7	-3.7
Beta	1.05	1.05
R-Squared	93	93
Standard Deviation	7.54	
Mean	6.80	
Sharpe Ratio	0.49	

Portfolio Analysis 12-31-06

Share change since 11-06 Total Stocks:310	Sector	PE	Tot Ret%	% Assets
⊕ ExxonMobil Corporation	Energy	11.7	39.07	7.21
⊕ Procter & Gamble Company	Goods	24.2	13.36	3.28
⊕ Johnson & Johnson	Health	17.4	12.44	3.09
⊕ American International G	Financial	17.1	6.05	3.00
⊖ Cisco Systems, Inc.	Hardware	28.8	59.64	2.68
⊖ General Electric Company	Ind Mtrls	16.8	9.35	2.48
⊕ IBM	Hardware	16.8	19.77	2.36
⊖ Microsoft Corporation	Software	23.7	15.83	2.34
⊖ Wal-Mart Stores, Inc.	Consumer	16.6	0.13	1.83
⊖ Pfizer Inc.	Health	15.1	15.22	1.69
⊕ PepsiCo, Inc.	Goods	21.4	7.86	1.65
⊕ Google, Inc.	Business	58.6	11.00	1.59
⊖ Altria Group, Inc.	Goods	15.9	19.87	1.46
⊖ Chevron Corporation	Energy	9.3	33.75	1.35
⊕ Home Depot, Inc.	Consumer	13.7	1.01	1.32
⊕ Amgen, Inc.	Health	28.0	-13.38	1.28
⊕ American Express Company	Financial	21.2	19.09	1.18
⊕ UnitedHealth Group, Inc.	Health	21.0	-13.49	1.16
⊕ Oracle Corporation	Software	25.6	40.38	1.10
⊕ Wyeth	Health	17.0	12.88	1.10

Current Investment Style

Value Blnd Growth — Large Mid Small

	Market Cap	%
	Giant	55.4
	Large	33.6
	Mid	11.0
	Small	0.0
	Micro	0.0
	Avg $mil: 59,192	

Value Measures		Rel Category
Price/Earnings	17.27	0.83
Price/Book	3.39	1.04
Price/Sales	1.72	0.97
Price/Cash Flow	11.65	1.04
Dividend Yield %	1.26	1.47

Growth Measures	%	Rel Category
Long-Term Erngs	12.45	0.83
Book Value	14.14	1.77
Sales	14.34	1.22
Cash Flow	13.43	0.92
Historical Erngs	20.33	0.72

Profitability	%	Rel Category
Return on Equity	23.33	1.16
Return on Assets	12.10	1.21
Net Margin	14.13	1.12

Sector Weightings	% of Stocks	Rel S&P 500	3 Year High Low	
↻ Info	19.07	0.95		
🖥 Software	4.95	1.43	9	5
📶 Hardware	11.46	1.24	19	11
🎙 Media	2.66	0.70	3	1
📱 Telecom	0.00	0.00	1	0
⊂ Service	44.76	0.97		
🩺 Health	17.62	1.46	24	17
🛒 Consumer	11.29	1.48	13	11
💼 Business	5.40	1.28	6	4
💲 Financial	10.45	0.47	11	2
🏭 Mfg	36.16	1.07		
🏗 Goods	12.31	1.44	16	12
⚙ Ind Mtrls	9.24	0.77	16	6
🔋 Energy	13.79	1.41	14	1
💧 Utilities	0.82	0.23	1	0

Composition

● Cash	0.1	
● Stocks	99.9	
● Bonds	0.0	
○ Other	0.0	
Foreign (% of Stock)	0.0	

Morningstar's Take by Sonya Morris 12-31-06

The time may be ripe for iShares S&P 500 Growth.

This ETF is tethered to the S&P 500/Citigroup Growth Index, which uses a variety of metrics to identify the growth stocks in the S&P 500. Because the base index focuses on the largest 500 domestic stocks, this ETF has a definite mega-cap bias. It dedicates 55% of its portfolio to giant stocks, compared with 39% for its typical large-growth rival. Accordingly, its aggregate market cap is almost twice the category norm.

For the past several years, big blue chips have looked rather sleepy compared with mid- and small-cap stocks, which have enjoyed a stellar, multiyear rally. Consequently, mega-cap stocks are looking cheap relative to their smaller brethren. So, this ETF's valuation statistics look compelling. Its aggregate price/cash flow and price/earnings ratios are among the lowest of all large-growth ETFs, and more of its assets are dedicated to stocks rated 4 and 5 stars by Morningstar equity analysts. It wouldn't be surprising to see market winds shift in favor of the market's biggest names. This ETF is well positioned to benefit from such a trend.

Even though the near-term prospects for this ETF may be brightening, the case in its favor isn't a slam dunk. While its 0.18% expense ratio is extremely low, it is still possible to get large-growth exposure for less from Vanguard Growth ETF, which charges just 0.11%. Furthermore, that fund's traditional mutual fund twin, Vanguard Growth Index, is a tad more expensive at 0.22%, but investors don't have to pay brokerage commissions to trade it as they do with ETFs, which makes it a better choice for those who plan to make periodic investments over time.

But while this ETF might not be the cheapest fund in its class, investors could certainly do a lot worse. It's a justifiable choice for those seeking broad and inexpensive large-growth exposure.

Address:	45 Fremont Street San Francisco CA 94105 800-474-2737	Management Fee:	0.18%
		Expense Projections:	3Yr:$58 5Yr:$101 10Yr:$230
Web Address:	www.ishares.com	Income Distrib:	Quarterly
Inception:	05-22-00*	Exchange:	NYSE
Advisor:	Barclays Global Fund Advisers		

MORNINGSTAR® ETFs 150

iShares S&P 500 IVV

	Market Price $141.38	Mstar Category Large Blend

Morningstar Fair Value

Price/Fair Value Ratio	Coverage Rate %
0.91 Undervalued	97 Good

Management

Barclays Global Fund Advisors is the advisor. The firm is the world's largest manager of indexed portfolios. Patrick O'Connor and S. Jane Leung are responsible for the daily management of this ETF. O'Connor has managed index funds at Barclays since 1999. Leung's tenure at the firm began in 2001.

Methodology

This fund owns all the stocks in the Standard & Poor's 500 Index, which includes more than 80% of the market's capitalization of U.S. stocks, but leaves out most mid- and virtually all small-cap equities.

	Morningstar Rating ★★★ Neutral	Return Neutral	Risk Average	Yield 1.7%	NAV $141.92	Avg Daily Vol. (k) 980	52 wk High/Low $143.25 - $122.75

Growth of $10,000
— Investment Value of ETF
— Investment Value of Index S&P 500

Trading Volume Millions

	1997	1998	1999	2000	2001	2002	2003	2004	2005	2006	History
	—	—	—	132.14	115.00	88.18	111.46	121.24	124.87	141.92	NAV $
	—	—	—	131.34	114.33	88.35	111.22	121.00	124.67	142.00	Market Price $
	—	—	—	1.21*	-11.96	-22.15	28.53	10.77	4.83	15.69	NAV Return%
	—	—	—	1.22*	-11.94	-21.55	28.00	10.79	4.87	15.94	Market Price Return%
	—	—	—	-0.03	-0.07	-0.15	0.03	0.07	-0.01	0.06	Avg Premium/Discount%
	—	—	—	1.21	-0.07	-0.05	-0.15	-0.11	-0.08	-0.10	NAV Rtrn% +/-S&P 500
	—	—	—	1.21	0.49	-0.50	-1.36	-0.63	-1.44	0.23	NAV Rtrn% +/-Russ 1000
	—	—	—	—	12	14	14	16	21	30	NAV Return% Rank in Cat
	—	—	—	1.01	1.30	1.87	1.90	1.78	1.91	Income Return %
	—	—	—	-12.97	-23.45	26.66	8.87	3.05	13.78	Capital Return %
	—	—	—	0.77	1.33	1.48	1.64	2.10	2.15	2.37	Income $
	—	—	—	0.07	0.00	0.00	0.00	0.00	0.00	0.00	Capital Gains $
	—	—	—	0.09	0.09	0.09	0.09	0.09	0.10	Expense Ratio %
	—	—	—	1.06	1.27	1.67	1.66	2.02	1.78	Income Ratio %
	—	—	—	5	3	5	3	6	7	Turnover Rate %
	—	—	—	2,319	3,611	5,075	7,874	11,784	14,229	17,982	Net Assets $mil

Performance 12-31-06

Historic Quarterly NAV Returns

	1st Qtr	2nd Qtr	3rd Qtr	4th Qtr	Total
2002	0.25	-13.41	-17.26	8.39	-22.15
2003	-3.16	15.34	2.61	12.14	28.53
2004	1.66	1.70	-1.89	9.20	10.77
2005	-2.15	1.35	3.58	2.05	4.83
2006	4.19	-1.46	5.64	6.67	15.69

Trailing	NAV Return%	Market Return%	NAV Rtrn% +/-S&P 500	%Rank Cat.(NAV)
3 Mo	6.67	6.70	-0.03	44
6 Mo	12.68	12.40	-0.06	38
1 Yr	15.69	15.94	-0.10	30
3 Yr Avg	10.34	10.44	-0.10	15
5 Yr Avg	6.09	6.23	-0.10	13
10 Yr Avg	—	—	—	—

Tax Analysis	Tax-Adj Return%	Tax-Cost Ratio
3 Yr (estimated)	9.65	0.63
5 Yr (estimated)	5.45	0.60
10 Yr (estimated)	—	—

Rating and Risk

Time Period	Morningstar Rtn vs Cat	Morningstar Risk vs Cat	Morningstar Risk-Adj Rating
3 Yr	Avg	-Avg	★★★
5 Yr	Avg	Avg	★★★
10 Yr	—	—	—

Other Measures	Standard Index S&P 500	Best Fit Index S&P 500
Alpha	-0.1	-0.1
Beta	1.00	1.00
R-Squared	100	100
Standard Deviation	6.91	
Mean	10.34	
Sharpe Ratio	1.01	

Portfolio Analysis 12-31-06

Share change since 11-06 Total Stocks:500

	Sector	PE	Tot Ret%	% Assets
⊖ ExxonMobil Corporation	Energy	11.7	39.07	3.51
⊖ General Electric Company	Ind Mtrls	19.8	9.35	3.01
⊖ Citigroup, Inc.	Financial	13.3	19.55	2.15
⊖ Microsoft Corporation	Software	23.7	15.83	2.03
⊖ Bank of America Corporat	Financial	12.4	20.68	1.88
⊖ Procter & Gamble Company	Goods	24.2	13.36	1.60
⊖ Johnson & Johnson	Health	17.4	12.44	1.50
⊖ Pfizer Inc.	Health	15.1	15.22	1.47
⊖ American International G	Financial	17.1	6.05	1.46
⊖ Altria Group, Inc.	Goods	15.9	19.87	1.41
⊖ J.P. Morgan Chase & Co.	Financial	13.7	25.60	1.32
⊖ Cisco Systems, Inc.	Hardware	28.8	59.64	1.30
⊖ Chevron Corporation	Energy	9.3	33.75	1.26
⊖ IBM	Hardware	16.8	19.77	1.15
⊖ AT&T, Inc.	Telecom	19.2	51.59	1.08
⊖ Wells Fargo Company	Financial	14.7	16.82	0.94
⊖ ConocoPhillips	Energy	6.9	26.53	0.93
⊖ Intel Corporation	Hardware	20.3	-17.18	0.92
⊖ Wal-Mart Stores, Inc.	Consumer	16.6	0.13	0.89
⊖ Hewlett-Packard Company	Hardware	18.9	45.21	0.89

Current Investment Style

Value Blend Growth — Large Mid Small

Market Cap	%
Giant	51.0
Large	38.2
Mid	10.7
Small	0.1
Micro	0.0

Avg $mil: 53,062

Value Measures		Rel Category
Price/Earnings	15.95	0.96
Price/Book	2.71	0.99
Price/Sales	1.52	1.20
Price/Cash Flow	9.34	0.99
Dividend Yield %	1.79	1.00

Growth Measures	%	Rel Category
Long-Term Erngs	11.41	0.99
Book Value	8.55	1.00
Sales	9.93	1.20
Cash Flow	10.72	1.42
Historical Erngs	17.90	1.07

Profitability	%	Rel Category
Return on Equity	19.78	1.03
Return on Assets	11.05	1.15
Net Margin	14.26	1.28

Sector Weightings	% of Stocks	Rel S&P 500	3 Year High Low	
⟳ Info	19.99	1.00		
Software	3.45	1.00	5	3
Hardware	9.24	1.00	12	9
Media	3.79	1.00	4	3
Telecom	3.51	1.00	4	3
⊆ Service	46.21	1.00		
Health	12.05	1.00	14	12
Consumer	7.66	1.00	9	7
Business	4.24	1.00	5	4
Financial	22.26	1.00	22	20
Mfg	33.80	1.00		
Goods	8.56	1.00	10	8
Ind Mtrls	11.95	1.00	13	12
Energy	9.80	1.00	11	6
Utilities	3.49	1.00	4	3

Composition

	%
● Cash	0.1
● Stocks	99.9
● Bonds	0.0
● Other	0.0
Foreign	0.0
(% of Stock)	

Morningstar's Take by Sonya Morris 12-31-06

IShares S&P 500 Index is a respectable option, but it faces tough competition from its rivals.

2006 was a good year for index funds. This ETF and the other funds that track the S&P 500 Index trumped more than three quarters of their large-blend rivals for the year. However, investors shouldn't make too much of that result. A calendar year is a relatively short period of time, and indexing is a long-term strategy that relies on low costs and broad diversification to edge past the actively managed competition over the long haul.

That's why expense ratios loom large in selecting index funds. Since large-cap index funds all fish from the same pond, costs can be the primary distinguishing feature. This ETF competes well on that front. At 0.09%, it's the cheapest fund that tracks the S&P 500 Index. But even with that tiny price tag, the case for this ETF isn't a slam dunk. A traditional mutual fund, E*Trade S&P 500, also charges just 0.09% in expenses, and Fidelity Spartan 500 Index is only a tad more expensive at

0.10%. These conventional funds have another cost advantage--unlike ETFs, you don't have to pay brokerage commissions each time you trade them, which makes them more appropriate for those who plan to make periodic investments over time.

But even if you're determined to go the ETF route, there are competing funds that give this ETF a run for its money. For instance, Vanguard Large Cap ETF costs just 0.07%, making it the cheapest ETF on the market. Granted, it dips a bit lower on the market-cap ladder than this ETF, but the two have 475 stocks in common, which means they'll likely perform similarly over the long haul.

But even though this ETF faces stiff competition from its rivals, shareholders here don't exactly own a lemon. This fund still provides broad exposure to domestic large caps at a very low price.

Address:	45 Fremont Street San Francisco CA 94105 800-474-2737	Management Fee:	0.09%		
		Expense Projections:	3Yr:$30	5Yr:$53	10Yr:$121
Web Address:	www.ishares.com	Income Distrib:	Quarterly		
Inception:	05-15-00*	Exchange:	NYSE		
Advisor:	Barclays Global Fund Advisers				

iShares SP 500 Value IVE

	Market Price	Mstar Category
	$76.45	Large Value

Morningstar Rating	Return	Risk	Yield	NAV	Avg Daily Vol. (k)	52 wk High/Low
★★★ Neutral	Neutral	Above Avg	1.9%	$76.92	321	$77.51 - $65.78

Morningstar Fair Value

Price/Fair Value Ratio	Coverage Rate %
0.94 Undervalued	97 Good

Management

Barclays Global Fund Advisors is the advisor. Patrick O'Connor and S. Jane Leung are responsible for the daily management of this ETF. O'Connor has managed index funds at Barclays since 1999. Leung's tenure at the firm began in 2001.

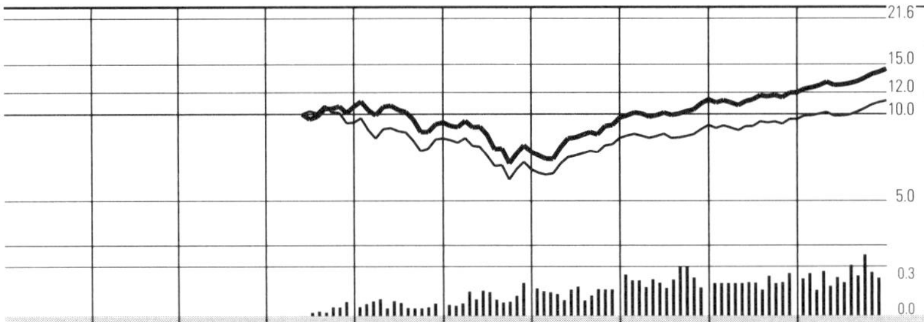

Methodology

This fund tracks the S&P MidCap 400/Citigroup Value Index. The bogy relies on seven growth and valuation measures to classify stocks. The factors are dividend yield; price-book, -sales and -cash flow; and five-year earnings, sales, and internal growth rates. A third of the index's market capitalization ends up in each value, core, or growth bucket, but stocks in the middle zone can end up in both style indexes in proportion to their style scores. The overlap should reduce turnover caused by stocks moving from one style to another. The index includes no buffer zones between market-cap ranges. It rebalances annually in December.

Growth of $10,000
- Investment Value of ETF
- Investment Value of Index S&P 500

Trading Volume Millions

	1997	1998	1999	2000	2001	2002	2003	2004	2005	2006	History
	—	—	—	63.63	55.28	42.93	55.42	62.91	65.11	76.92	NAV $
	—	—	—	63.38	55.28	42.90	55.33	62.88	65.05	76.89	Market Price $
	—	—	—	5.66*	-11.85	-20.98	31.51	15.51	5.67	20.59	NAV Return%
	—	—	—	5.65*	-11.50	-21.04	31.38	15.64	5.63	20.65	Market Price Return%
	—	—	—	0.05	-0.01	-0.02	0.06	0.07	0.02	0.02	Avg Premium/Discount%
	—	—	—	5.66	0.04	1.12	2.83	4.63	0.76	4.80	NAV Rtrn% +/-S&P 500
	—	—	—	5.66	-6.26	-5.46	1.48	-0.98	-1.38	-1.66	NAV Rtrn% +/-Russ 1000 VI
	—	—	—	—	7	7	7	8	11	14	NAV Return% Rank in Cat
	—	—	—	—	1.31	1.50	2.08	1.85	2.10	2.27	Income Return %
	—	—	—	—	-13.16	-22.48	29.43	13.66	3.57	18.32	Capital Return %
	—	—	—	0.45	0.83	0.83	0.89	1.02	1.31	1.47	Income $
	—	—	—	0.15	0.00	0.00	0.00	0.00	0.00	0.00	Capital Gains $
	—	—	—	—	0.18	0.18	0.18	0.18	0.18	0.18	Expense Ratio %
	—	—	—	—	1.51	1.56	2.01	1.91	1.95	2.12	Income Ratio %
	—	—	—	—	9	17	22	5	5	7	Turnover Rate %
	—	—	—	232	525	702	1,477	2,931	3,015	4,530	Net Assets $mil

Performance 12-31-06

Historic Quarterly NAV Returns

	1st Qtr	2nd Qtr	3rd Qtr	4th Qtr	Total
2002	1.26	-10.67	-20.45	9.81	-20.98
2003	-5.54	18.76	2.49	14.38	31.51
2004	3.29	0.76	1.00	9.88	15.51
2005	-2.44	2.54	3.41	2.15	5.67
2006	5.82	0.58	5.23	7.66	20.59

Trailing	NAV Return%	Market Return%	NAV Rtrn% +/-S&P 500	%Rank Cat.(NAV)
3 Mo	7.66	7.68	0.96	16
6 Mo	13.30	13.10	0.56	16
1 Yr	20.59	20.65	4.80	14
3 Yr Avg	13.75	13.80	3.31	8
5 Yr Avg	8.87	8.86	2.68	7
10 Yr Avg	—	—	—	—

Tax Analysis	Tax-Adj Return%	Tax-Cost Ratio
3 Yr (estimated)	12.98	0.68
5 Yr (estimated)	8.14	0.67
10 Yr (estimated)	—	—

Rating and Risk

Time Period	Morningstar Rtn vs Cat	Morningstar Risk vs Cat	Morningstar Risk-Adj Rating
3 Yr	+Avg	Avg	★★★★
5 Yr	Avg	+Avg	★★★
10 Yr	—	—	—

Other Measures	Standard Index S&P 500	Best Fit Index Russ 1000 VI
Alpha	3.4	-0.9
Beta	0.94	0.97
R-Squared	92	93
Standard Deviation	6.82	
Mean	13.75	
Sharpe Ratio	1.47	

Morningstar's Take by Sonya Morris 12-31-06

iShares S&P 500/Citigroup Value Index may not be the best choice, but it's still a decent option.

This ETF tracks the S&P 500/Citigroup Value Index, which includes the value stocks in the S&P 500 Index, as measured by several different style metrics. Unlike most other indexes--which are quantitatively derived--the methodology for the S&P 500 has subjective elements. For instance, IPOs become eligible for inclusion in most indexes as soon as they are launched or upon every quarter; however, the S&P committee decides the appropriate time to add an IPO to their indexes. In fact, Google had been public for almost two years before it was admitted to the S&P 500.

Some might argue that by introducing an element of human judgment, S&P has strayed from pure objective indexing, and we generally prefer indexes that are constructed entirely by quantitative means. But although this fund's benchmark may be influenced by the occasional judgment call, it's not fatally flawed. Over time, we think it will

adequately reflect the characteristics of its universe. In fact, it should do its job even better over the coming years thanks to a recent upgrade to a more sophisticated style methodology that should help it do a better job of identifying value stocks.

Accordingly, we think this ETF is an acceptable choice for those seeking to fill out the large-value slot of their portfolio. However, you can get similar exposure for less from Vanguard Value Index ETF, which charges an expense ratio of 0.11% compared with this fund's 0.19% levy. What's more, the conventional mutual fund share class of the Vanguard fund charges a slightly higher fee of 0.21%, but it can be had without the additional cost of brokerage commissions.

That said, shareholders here have no reason to jump over to the Vanguard fund, particularly if this ETF is held in a taxable account. They still own a fund that provides broad large-value exposure at a very low price.

Address:	45 Fremont Street San Francisco CA 94105 800-474-2737
Web Address:	www.ishares.com
Inception:	05-22-00*
Advisor:	Barclays Global Fund Advisers

Management Fee:	0.18%		
Expense Projections:	3Yr:$58	5Yr:$101	10Yr:$230
Income Distrib:	Quarterly		
Exchange:	NYSE		

Portfolio Analysis 12-31-06

Share change since 11-06 Total Stocks:351	Sector	PE	Tot Ret%	% Assets
⊕ Citigroup, Inc.	Financial	13.3	19.55	4.19
⊕ Bank of America Corporat	Financial	12.4	20.68	3.67
⊕ General Electric Company	Ind Mtrls	19.8	9.35	3.52
⊕ J.P. Morgan Chase & Co.	Financial	13.7	25.60	2.57
⊕ AT&T, Inc.	Telecom	19.2	51.59	2.10
⊕ Wells Fargo Company	Financial	14.7	16.82	1.84
⊕ ConocoPhillips	Energy	6.9	26.53	1.81
☼ Microsoft Corporation	Software	23.7	15.83	1.74
⊕ Hewlett-Packard Company	Hardware	18.9	45.21	1.73
⊕ Verizon Communications	Telecom	16.1	34.88	1.67
⊕ Wachovia Corporation	Financial	13.0	12.02	1.66
⊕ Merck & Co., Inc.	Health	18.8	42.66	1.44
⊕ Altria Group, Inc.	Goods	15.9	19.87	1.37
⊕ Time Warner, Inc.	Media	19.1	26.37	1.33
⊕ Morgan Stanley	Financial	12.3	45.93	1.32
⊕ BellSouth Corporation	Telecom	—	—	1.32
⊕ Merrill Lynch & Company,	Financial	14.1	39.27	1.26
☼ Pfizer Inc.	Health	15.1	15.22	1.25
⊕ Chevron Corporation	Energy	9.3	33.75	1.18
⊕ Intel Corporation	Hardware	20.3	-17.18	0.98

Current Investment Style

Value Blnd Growth — Large Mid Small

Market Cap	%
Giant	46.9
Large	42.6
Mid	10.4
Small	0.1
Micro	0.0

Avg $mil: 47,790

Value Measures		Rel Category
Price/Earnings	14.84	1.04
Price/Book	2.27	0.94
Price/Sales	1.37	1.03
Price/Cash Flow	7.53	0.97
Dividend Yield %	2.30	0.89

Growth Measures	%	Rel Category
Long-Term Erngs	10.51	1.05
Book Value	5.54	0.77
Sales	7.08	0.83
Cash Flow	8.34	0.97
Historical Erngs	15.92	1.03

Profitability	%	Rel Category
Return on Equity	16.26	0.94
Return on Assets	10.01	1.00
Net Margin	14.38	1.05

Sector Weightings	% of Stocks	Rel S&P 500	3 Year High Low	
↻ Info	20.86	1.04		
Software	2.03	0.59	2	0
Hardware	7.15	0.77	8	4
Media	4.83	1.27	7	4
Telecom	6.85	1.95	7	5
⊑ Service	47.53	1.03		
Health	6.68	0.55	8	3
Consumer	4.17	0.55	7	4
Business	3.14	0.74	4	3
Financial	33.54	1.51	39	32
Mfg	31.61	0.94		
Goods	4.97	0.58	5	3
Ind Mtrls	14.52	1.22	18	9
Energy	6.02	0.61	13	6
Utilities	6.10	1.74	6	5

Composition

● Cash	0.1	
● Stocks	99.9	
● Bonds	0.0	
● Other	0.0	
Foreign	0.0	
(% of Stock)		

 MORNINGSTAR® ETFs 150

iShares S&P Euro-350 IEV

	Market Price $103.23	**Mstar Category** Europe Stock

Morningstar Fair Value

Price/Fair Value Ratio — Coverage Rate % —

Management

The fund's advisor, Barclays Global Fund Advisors, is one of the world's largest and most experienced managers of index-tracking portfolios.

Methodology

This exchange-traded offering is a passive fund that attempts to match the performance of the S&P Europe 350 Index. The benchmark is a market-capitalization index designed to track leading stocks from across the developed countries of Europe. It has a very small mid-cap stake and essentially no small caps. It uses a representative sampling method of tracking the index.

Morningstar Rating ★★★ Neutral	**Return** Neutral	**Risk** Below Avg	**Yield** 2.0%	**NAV** $104.32	**Avg Daily Vol. (k)** 146	**52 wk High/Low** $106.72 - $82.55

Growth of $10,000
— Investment Value of ETF
— Investment Value of Index MSCI EAFE

Trading Volume Millions

History	1997	1998	1999	2000	2001	2002	2003	2004	2005	2006
NAV $	—	—	—	75.09	59.12	47.34	64.04	75.13	80.15	104.32
Market Price $	—	—	—	76.69	59.09	47.48	64.15	75.25	80.77	104.87
NAV Return%	—	—	—	6.29*	-20.05	-18.12	37.70	19.44	9.17	32.77
Market Price Return%	—	—	—	6.36*	-21.77	-17.84	37.50	19.42	9.77	32.44
Avg Premium/Discount%	—	—	—	2.12	0.94	0.37	0.30	0.74	0.29	0.45
NAV Rtrn% +/-MSCI EAFE	—	—	—	6.29	1.37	-2.18	-0.89	-0.81	-4.37	6.43
NAV Rtrn% +/-MSCI Eur	—	—	—	6.29	-0.15	0.26	-0.84	-1.44	-0.25	-0.95
NAV Return% Rank in Cat	—	—	—	—	12	12	15	15	15	16
Income Return %	—	—	—	—	1.25	1.80	2.35	2.11	2.50	2.60
Capital Return %	—	—	—	—	-21.30	-19.92	35.35	17.33	6.67	30.17
Income $	—	—	—	0.18	0.93	1.06	1.11	1.35	1.88	2.08
Capital Gains $	—	—	—	0.00	0.00	0.00	0.00	0.00	0.00	0.00
Expense Ratio %	—	—	—	—	0.60	0.60	0.60	0.60	0.60	0.60
Income Ratio %	—	—	—	—	1.12	1.49	2.11	2.17	2.26	2.47
Turnover Rate %	—	—	—	—	24	4	6	5	5	7
Net Assets $mil	—	—	—	86	195	428	647	1,082	1,270	2,384

Performance 12-31-06

Historic Quarterly NAV Returns

	1st Qtr	2nd Qtr	3rd Qtr	4th Qtr	Total
2002	-0.14	-4.15	-22.88	10.93	-18.12
2003	-9.42	22.08	3.51	20.29	37.70
2004	0.55	1.86	1.08	15.37	19.44
2005	0.21	-0.88	7.64	2.10	9.17
2006	10.43	2.72	5.65	10.78	32.77

Trailing	NAV Return%	Market Return%	NAV Rtrn% +/-MSCI EAFE	%Rank Cat.(NAV)
3 Mo	10.78	10.75	0.43	19
6 Mo	17.04	17.10	2.35	19
1 Yr	32.77	32.44	6.43	16
3 Yr Avg	20.07	20.18	0.14	15
5 Yr Avg	14.31	14.42	-0.67	12
10 Yr Avg	—	—	—	—

Tax Analysis	Tax-Adj Return%	Tax-Cost Ratio
3 Yr (estimated)	19.23	0.70
5 Yr (estimated)	13.49	0.72
10 Yr (estimated)	—	—

Rating and Risk

Time Period	Morningstar Rtn vs Cat	Morningstar Risk vs Cat	Morningstar Risk-Adj Rating
3 Yr	Avg	Low	★★★
5 Yr	-Avg	Avg	★★★
10 Yr	—	—	—

Other Measures	Standard Index S&P 500	Best Fit Index MSCI Eur
Alpha	1.2	-0.4
Beta	0.93	0.98
R-Squared	87	100
Standard Deviation	9.46	
Mean	20.07	
Sharpe Ratio	1.67	

Portfolio Analysis 12-31-06

Share change since 11-06 Total Stocks:344

	Sector	Country	% Assets
⊕ BP	Energy	U.K.	2.55
⊕ HSBC Hldgs	Financial	U.K.	2.45
⊖ Total SA	Energy	France	2.04
⊕ Novartis	Health	Switzerland	1.85
⊕ GlaxoSmithKline	Health	U.K.	1.78
⊕ Vodafone Grp	Telecom	U.K.	1.71
⊕ Nestle	Goods	Switzerland	1.67
⊕ UBS AG	Financial	Switzerland	1.54
⊕ Royal Dutch Shell	Energy	U.K.	1.52
⊕ Roche Holding	Health	Switzerland	1.46
⊕ Royal Bank Of Scotland G	Financial	U.K.	1.46
⊕ Banco Santander Central	Financial	Spain	1.37
⊕ Telefonica	Telecom	Spain	1.25
⊕ ING Groep	Financial	Netherlands	1.13
⊕ Royal Dutch Shell	Energy	U.K.	1.13
⊕ E.ON	Utilities	Germany	1.11
⊕ Barclays	Financial	U.K.	1.08
⊕ Sanofi-Synthelabo	Health	France	1.06
⊕ UniCredito Italiano Grp	Financial	Italy	1.06
⊕ BNP Paribas	Financial	France	1.05

Current Investment Style

Value Blnd Growth — Large Mid Small

Market Cap	%
Giant	61.3
Large	33.1
Mid	5.6
Small	0.0
Micro	0.0

Avg $mil: 49,533

Value Measures		Rel Category
Price/Earnings	13.48	0.99
Price/Book	2.31	1.03
Price/Sales	1.10	0.97
Price/Cash Flow	8.46	1.00
Dividend Yield %	3.44	0.99

Growth Measures	%	Rel Category
Long-Term Erngs	11.08	0.99
Book Value	8.18	0.96
Sales	6.15	0.81
Cash Flow	5.95	2.22
Historical Erngs	21.01	0.94

Composition

Cash	0.2	Bonds	0.0
Stocks	99.7	Other	0.1
Foreign	(% of Stock)		100.0

Sector Weightings	% of Stocks	Rel MSCI EAFE	3 Year High	Low
↻ Info	13.03	1.10		
▣ Software	0.58	1.04	1	1
▣ Hardware	3.57	0.92	5	3
▣ Media	2.07	1.13	3	2
▣ Telecom	6.81	1.22	9	6
☞ Service	47.68	1.01		
▣ Health	8.21	1.15	10	8
▣ Consumer	4.18	0.84	5	3
▣ Business	3.07	0.61	3	3
▣ Financial	32.22	1.07	32	28
▣ Mfg	39.28	0.96		
▣ Goods	11.17	0.85	12	11
▣ Ind Mtrls	11.80	0.76	12	9
▣ Energy	9.99	1.40	13	10
▣ Utilities	6.32	1.21	6	5

Regional Exposure % Stock

UK/W. Europe	100	N. America	0
Japan	0	Latn America	0
Asia X Japan	0	Other	0

Country Exposure % Stock

U.K.	35	Switzerland	11
France	16	Spain	7
Germany	11		

Morningstar's Take by Gregg Wolper 12-31-06

iShares S&P Europe 350 has some nice traits but also a noteworthy disadvantage.

This fund offers broad exposure to big companies in the most developed markets of Europe. Unlike some new rivals in the Europe ETF realm, it isn't notably skewed in its country or sector weightings. That can be seen as a plus; after all, a Europe fund tilted heavily toward one country or sector, or practically excluding some significant ones, doesn't provide the coverage many investors expect from such a straightforward, passively managed investment. This fund's country and sector weightings aren't all that different from those of exchange-traded Vanguard Europe or its older mutual fund version Vanguard European Stock Index, which both follow the MSCI Europe Index.

The fact that it resembles them isn't a shortcoming in and of itself. However, given that investors have those alternatives, it does mean this fund has to compete with them on the cost front--and it comes up short. Its expense ratio of 0.60% is more than triple that of the Vanguard exchange-traded version and more than double the Vanguard mutual fund's ratio. That cost disadvantage can make it tough for this fund's returns to keep up with those of Vanguard Europe or Vanguard European Stock Index.

There are two more reasons to think twice before jumping into this or the Vanguard ones. First, investors who already own a broad international fund are likely to have substantial exposure to the stocks featured in this portfolio. Second, Europe funds have racked up exceptionally high returns lately, owing partly to the strength of the euro against the dollar, which increases U.S.-based funds' returns. This fund has a three-year annualized gain of 22.3%. While there is no telling how long the rally will run, it wouldn't be prudent to expect that level of gain year after year from this fund.

Address:	45 Fremont Street San Francisco CA 94105 800-474-2737	Management Fee:	0.60%
		Expense Projections:	3Yr:$192 5Yr:$335 10Yr:$750
Web Address:	www.ishares.com	Income Distrib:	Annually
Inception:	07-25-00*	Exchange:	NYSE
Advisor:	Barclays Global Fund Advisers		

MORNINGSTAR® ETFs 150

iShares S&P Glb 100 | IOO

	Market Price $73.67	Mstar Category World Stock

Morningstar Fair Value

Price/Fair Value Ratio	Coverage Rate %
0.86 Undervalued	55 Poor

Management

This fund is run by a team from Barclays Global Investors. Firm veterans Patrick O'Connor and S. Jane Leung head the team, and Barclays Global Investors is one of the largest and most experienced managers of indexed assets in the world, with more than $1 trillion in assets under management.

Methodology

This ETF is a passive fund that simply attempts to match the performance of the S&P Global 100 Index. The benchmark is a market-capitalization-weighted index designed to track multinational companies with market caps greater than $5 billion, regardless of their country of origin. The bogy includes companies from 15 developed countries, but it's really concentrated on firms from two nations: the United States and the United Kingdom, which comprise roughly 60% of the index's country exposure (Western European nations and Japan account for most of the balance). The fund uses representative sampling.

Performance 12-31-06

Historic Quarterly NAV Returns

	1st Qtr	2nd Qtr	3rd Qtr	4th Qtr	Total
2002	-2.69	-12.30	-18.56	9.40	-23.96
2003	-4.61	15.58	3.83	14.02	30.53
2004	0.62	0.96	-2.15	10.21	9.55
2005	-0.95	-1.17	6.05	0.81	4.66
2006	4.51	0.38	6.15	7.61	19.84

Trailing	NAV Return%	Market Return%+/-MSCI EAFE	NAV Rtrn% 	%Rank Cat.(NAV)
3 Mo	7.61	7.34	-2.74	6
6 Mo	14.23	14.04	-0.46	2
1 Yr	19.84	19.91	-6.50	2
3 Yr Avg	11.17	10.84	-8.76	2
5 Yr Avg	6.40	6.29	-8.58	2
10 Yr Avg	—	—	—	—

Tax Analysis	Tax-Adj Return%	Tax-Cost Ratio
3 Yr (estimated)	10.48	0.62
5 Yr (estimated)	5.82	0.55
10 Yr (estimated)	—	—

	Morningstar Rating ★★ Below Avg	Return Below Avg	Risk Below Avg		Yield 1.8%	NAV $74.04	Avg Daily Vol. (k) 33	52 wk High/Low $75.68 - $62.41

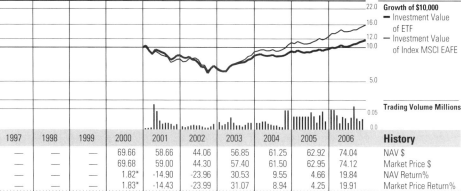

Growth of $10,000
— Investment Value of ETF
— Investment Value of Index MSCI EAFE

Trading Volume Millions

	1997	1998	1999	2000	2001	2002	2003	2004	2005	2006	History
	—	—	—	69.66	58.66	44.06	56.85	61.25	62.92	74.04	NAV $
	—	—	—	69.68	59.00	44.30	57.40	61.50	62.95	74.12	Market Price $
	—	—	—	1.82*	-14.90	-23.96	30.53	9.55	4.66	19.84	NAV Return%
	—	—	—	1.83*	-14.43	-23.99	31.07	8.94	4.25	19.91	Market Price Return%
	—	—	—	0.03	0.24	-0.02	0.29	0.47	0.09	0.22	Avg Premium/Discount%
	—	—	—	1.82	6.52	-8.02	-8.06	-10.70	-8.88	-6.50	NAV Rtrn% +/-MSCI EAFE
	—	—	—	1.82	1.90	-4.07	-2.58	-5.17	-4.83	-0.23	NAV Rtrn% +/-MSCI World
	—	—	—	—	2	2	2	2	2	2	NAV Return% Rank in Cat
	—	—	—	—	0.90	0.94	1.47	1.80	1.96	2.16	Income Return %
	—	—	—	—	-15.80	-24.90	29.06	7.75	2.70	17.68	Capital Return %
	—	—	—	0.02	0.63	0.55	0.65	1.03	1.20	1.36	Income $
	—	—	—	0.00	0.00	0.00	0.00	0.00	0.00	0.00	Capital Gains $
	—	—	—	—	0.40	0.40	0.40	0.40	0.40	0.40	Expense Ratio %
	—	—	—	—	0.88	1.08	1.60	1.63	2.24	2.05	Income Ratio %
	—	—	—	—	5	4	5	4	4	6	Turnover Rate %
	—	—	—	118	47	46	122	279	374	607	Net Assets $mil

Rating and Risk

Time Period	Morningstar Rtn vs Cat	Morningstar Risk vs Cat	Morningstar Risk-Adj Rating
3 Yr	-Avg	-Avg	★★
5 Yr	-Avg	Avg	★★
10 Yr	—	—	—

Other Measures	Standard Index S&P 500	Best Fit Index MSCI World
Alpha	-3.3	-2.3
Beta	0.71	0.93
R-Squared	79	90
Standard Deviation	7.57	
Mean	11.17	
Sharpe Ratio	1.03	

Morningstar's Take by William Samuel Rocco 12-31-06

Investors should be sure that they consider the big picture at iShares S&P Global 100.

This exchange-traded fund certainly is attractively priced. It is the cheapest by far of the few world-stock ETFs and funds that focus on giants caps. And its 0.40% expense ratio is very low for a member of the world-stock category and very fetching in absolute terms.

Meanwhile, its portfolio should appeal to those seeking exposure to the world's leading blue chips. It apes the S&P Global 100 Index, which is a market-cap-weighted collection of developed-markets mega caps that's dominated by huge, well-known stocks such as ExxonMobil, General Electric, and Citigroup. Thus, this ETF sports an average weighted market of roughly $123 billion, which is nearly 5 times the world-stock norm and one of the biggest of any offering around.

Meanwhile, this ETF has been a solid performer in certain respects. It has done a decent job of replicating the returns of its benchmark (after takings costs into account). And it has posted respectable results relative to the one other world-stock ETF and the one world-stock mutual fund with similar purviews that have been around as long as it has.

But this ETF has been a subpar performer relative to the world-stock category overall. Although it has gained more than the category norm in 2006, as many blue chips have thrived, it has returned much less than the group averages over the trailing three- and five-year periods, because smaller caps have led the way during most of the 2000s.

This ETF is a solid option for those seeking a pure play on the world's biggest stocks, but such investors should note that it will suffer whenever smaller caps shine. They should also make sure that owning this ETF won't overexpose them to certain areas, because it provides a lot of exposure to the U.S.; the financial, goods, and energy sectors; and a number of well-known names.

Portfolio Analysis 12-31-06

Share change since 11-06 Total Stocks:101	Sector	Country	% Assets
⊖ ExxonMobil Corporation	Energy	United States	5.00
⊖ General Electric Company	Ind Mtrls	United States	4.29
⊖ Citigroup, Inc.	Financial	United States	3.06
⊖ Microsoft Corporation	Software	United States	2.89
⊖ BP	Energy	U.K.	2.43
⊖ HSBC Hldgs	Financial	U.K.	2.36
⊖ Procter & Gamble Company	Goods	United States	2.27
⊖ Johnson & Johnson	Health	United States	2.14
⊖ Pfizer Inc.	Health	United States	2.09
⊖ American International G	Financial	United States	2.08
⊖ Toyota Motor	Goods	Japan	2.06
⊖ Altria Group, Inc.	Goods	United States	2.01
⊖ Total SA	Energy	France	1.96
⊖ J.P. Morgan Chase & Co.	Financial	United States	1.87
⊖ Chevron Corporation	Energy	United States	1.79
⊖ Novartis	Health	Switzerland	1.76
⊖ GlaxoSmithKline	Health	U.K.	1.69
⊖ IBM	Hardware	United States	1.64
⊖ Vodafone Grp	Telecom	U.K.	1.63
⊖ Nestle	Goods	Switzerland	1.59

Current Investment Style

Value Blnd Growth — Large / Mid / Small

Market Cap	%
Giant	94.4
Large	5.6
Mid	0.0
Small	0.0
Micro	0.0

Avg $mil: 125,226

Value Measures		Rel Category
Price/Earnings	14.29	0.89
Price/Book	2.46	0.92
Price/Sales	1.31	1.06
Price/Cash Flow	9.51	0.98
Dividend Yield %	2.79	1.16

Growth Measures	%	Rel Category
Long-Term Erngs	10.57	0.85
Book Value	9.11	0.97
Sales	7.81	1.06
Cash Flow	7.42	0.87
Historical Erngs	20.18	0.98

Composition

Cash	0.1	Bonds	0.0
Stocks	99.8	Other	0.1
Foreign (% of Stock)			52.3

Sector Weightings	% of Stocks	Rel MSCI EAFE	3 Year High Low	
☉ Info	18.07	1.53		
🅢 Software	2.89	5.16	4	3
🅗 Hardware	9.04	2.34	13	9
🅤 Media	2.17	1.19	2	2
🅕 Telecom	3.97	0.71	5	3
☜ Service	38.19	0.81		
🅗 Health	11.26	1.58	14	11
🅒 Consumer	2.59	0.52	3	2
🅑 Business	0.00	0.00	0	0
🅢 Financial	24.34	0.81	24	20
🖽 Mfg	43.74	1.07		
🅖 Goods	17.96	1.37	18	17
🅘 Ind Mtrls	9.85	0.64	11	10
🅔 Energy	14.14	1.98	16	11
🅤 Utilities	1.79	0.34	2	1

Regional Exposure % Stock

UK/W. Europe	45	N. America	48
Japan	6	Latn America	0
Asia X Japan	2	Other	0

Country Exposure % Stock

United States	48	Germany	6
U.K.	12	Switzerland	6
France	9		

Address:	45 Fremont Street San Francisco CA 94105 800-474-2737	Management Fee:	0.40%
		Expense Projections:	3Yr:$128 5Yr:$224 10Yr:$505
Web Address:	www.ishares.com	Income Distrib:	Annually
Inception:	12-05-00*	Exchange:	NYSE
Advisor:	Barclays Global Fund Advisers		

MORNINGSTAR® ETFs 150

iShares SP Glb Enrgy IXC

	Market Price	**Mstar Category**
	$104.15	Specialty-Natural Res

Morningstar Rating	Return	Risk	Yield	NAV	Avg Daily Vol. (k)	52 wk High/Low
★★★ Neutral	Neutral	Low	1.6%	$110.90	31	$116.60 - $94.52

Growth of $10,000
- Investment Value of ETF
- Investment Value of Index S&P 500

28.4
14.0
10.0

Trading Volume Millions
0.1

	1997	1998	1999	2000	2001	2002	2003	2004	2005	2006	**History**
	—	—	—	—	49.54	45.87	58.26	73.23	93.23	110.90	NAV $
	—	—	—	—	49.47	45.70	58.84	73.15	93.62	111.47	Market Price $
	—	—	—	—	18.71*	-5.59	28.39	27.88	28.79	20.89	NAV Return%
	—	—	—	—	18.83*	-5.80	30.14	26.47	29.47	20.99	Market Price Return%
	—	—	—	—	0.12	-0.36	0.66	0.86	0.28	0.24	Avg Premium/Discount%
	—	—	—	—	18.71	16.51	-0.29	17.00	23.88	5.10	NAV Rtrn% +/-S&P 500
	—	—	—	—	18.71	7.67	-5.62	3.31	-7.69	4.07	NAV Rtrn% +/-GS NATR RES
	—	—	—	—	—	4	4	4	6	9	NAV Return% Rank in Cat
	—	—	—	—	—	1.84	1.35	2.18	1.50	1.93	Income Return %
	—	—	—	—	—	-7.43	27.04	25.70	27.29	18.96	Capital Return %
	—	—	—	—	0.07	0.91	0.62	1.27	1.10	1.80	Income $
	—	—	—	—	0.00	0.00	0.00	0.00	0.00	0.00	Capital Gains $
	—	—	—	—	—	0.65	0.65	0.65	0.65	0.65	Expense Ratio %
	—	—	—	—	—	1.17	1.89	1.92	2.00	1.46	Income Ratio %
	—	—	—	—	—	5	9	4	5	5	Turnover Rate %
	—	—	—	—	14	52	238	601	688		Net Assets $mil

Morningstar Fair Value

Price/Fair Value Ratio	Coverage Rate %
1.07 Overvalued	64 Poor

Management

Barclays Global Fund Advisors is the advisor. Patrick O'Connor and S. Jane Leung are responsible for the daily management of this ETF. O'Connor has managed index funds at Barclays since 1999. Leung's tenure at the firm began in 2001.

Methodology

This exchange-traded fund tracks the S&P Global Energy Sector Index. The bogy is a market-capitalization-weighted, float-adjusted index that includes the largest and most liquid energy stocks in the world. The index covers seven distinct regions and 29 countries, capturing approximately 70% of the world market capitalization. Profitability is a major consideration for inclusion in the index. A committee oversees this index and makes all decisions on an as-needed basis.

Performance 12-31-06

Historic Quarterly NAV Returns

	1st Qtr	2nd Qtr	3rd Qtr	4th Qtr	Total
2002	10.15	-2.09	-17.74	6.42	-5.59
2003	-3.05	11.54	0.26	18.43	28.39
2004	3.11	6.03	9.56	6.77	27.88
2005	13.21	4.27	17.72	-7.32	28.79
2006	8.91	4.15	-3.29	10.20	20.89

Trailing	NAV Return%	Market Return%	NAV Rtrn% +/-S&P 500	%Rank Cat.(NAV)
3 Mo	10.20	10.39	3.50	21
6 Mo	6.57	7.01	-6.17	18
1 Yr	20.89	20.99	5.10	9
3 Yr Avg	25.80	25.60	15.36	4
5 Yr Avg	19.27	19.42	13.08	4
10 Yr Avg	—	—	—	—

Tax Analysis	Tax-Adj Return%	Tax-Cost Ratio
3 Yr (estimated)	25.15	0.52
5 Yr (estimated)	18.63	0.54
10 Yr (estimated)	—	—

Rating and Risk

Time Period	Morningstar Rtn vs Cat	Morningstar Risk vs Cat	Morningstar Risk-Adj Rating
3 Yr	Avg	-Avg	★★★
5 Yr	Avg	Low	★★★
10 Yr	—	—	—

Other Measures	Standard Index S&P 500	Best Fit Index GS NATR RES
Alpha	15.2	1.7
Beta	0.90	0.92
R-Squared	12	96
Standard Deviation	17.80	
Mean	25.80	
Sharpe Ratio	1.20	

Morningstar's Take by Sonya Morris 12-31-06

IShares S&P Global Energy Sector has some positive features, but they're not enough to compensate for its risks.

As energy ETFs go, this fund has some appealing attributes. While it's not the cheapest ETF in the natural-resources category, its 0.48% expense ratio (according to its most recent prospectus) is reasonable, particularly compared with actively managed rivals. Furthermore, this fund is one of the few energy-focused ETFs that has a global reach: Half of its portfolio is invested overseas. That's a big advantage over its rivals, who omit major oil companies like BP and Royal Dutch Shell from their holdings because they restrict their portfolios to domestic stocks. This fund also distinguishes itself from its peers by concentrating on the biggest names in the industry. In fact, its aggregate market cap is the highest in the category.

That's worked against the fund during the sector's most recent ascent, since smaller stocks tend to benefit most from rising commodity prices.

Consequently, its average annual returns since its November 2001 inception trail more than 67% of its rivals. And while this ETF's focus on industry stalwarts means it won't be quite as turbulent as competing funds that favor smaller industry players, it still won't be immune to the volatility that is endemic to the energy sector. Plus, with almost half of its portfolio stashed in the top five holdings, this ETF could take a tumble if any of its top names fall on hard times.

What's more, this fund faces heightened price risk at the moment. After a stellar rally, energy stocks can't be considered particularly cheap right now. According to Morningstar equity analysts, all of this ETF's top 10 holdings are trading either at or above their fair values.

Finally, when it comes down to it, the vast majority of investors don't need this ETF, or any energy-focused fund for that matter. Most investors get plenty of exposure to the sector from their other diversified funds.

Address:	45 Fremont Street San Francisco CA 94105 800-474-2737
Web Address:	www.ishares.com
Inception:	11-12-01*
Advisor:	Barclays Global Fund Advisers

Management Fee:	0.48%		
Expense Projections:	3Yr:$154	5Yr:$269	10Yr:$604
Income Distrib:	Annually		
Exchange:	AMEX		

Portfolio Analysis 12-31-06

Share change since 11-06 Total Stocks:63

	Sector	PE	Tot Rtn%	% Assets
⊖ ExxonMobil Corporation	Energy	11.7	39.07	18.53
⊕ BP	Energy	—	—	8.81
⊕ Total SA	Energy	—	—	6.96
⊖ Chevron Corporation	Energy	9.3	33.75	6.48
⊕ Royal Dutch Shell	Energy	—	—	5.15
⊕ ConocoPhillips	Energy	6.9	26.53	4.81
⊕ Royal Dutch Shell	Energy	—	—	3.82
⊖ Eni	Energy	—	—	3.50
⊖ Schlumberger, Ltd.	Energy	24.0	31.07	3.02
⊕ BG Grp	Energy	—	—	2.19
⊖ Occidental Petroleum Cor	Energy	8.6	24.32	1.71
⊖ EnCana Corporation	Energy	11.9	2.55	1.55
⊖ Suncor Energy, Inc.	Energy	35.8	25.42	1.51
⊖ Petroleo Brasileiro S.A.	Energy	—	—	1.48
⊖ Marathon Oil Corporation	Energy	6.5	54.68	1.31
⊖ Halliburton Company	Energy	12.0	1.11	1.28
⊕ Valero Energy Corporatio	Energy	6.5	-0.33	1.26
⊖ Devon Energy Corporation	Energy	9.4	8.06	1.21
⊖ Canadian Natural Resourc	Energy	33.0	7.84	1.19
⊖ PetroChina Company, Ltd.	Energy	15.4	79.05	1.15

Current Investment Style

Value Blnd Growth — Large Mid Small

Market Cap	%
Giant	74.9
Large	21.3
Mid	3.8
Small	0.0
Micro	0.0

Avg $mil: 97,649

Value Measures		Rel Category
Price/Earnings	10.88	0.87
Price/Book	2.68	1.05
Price/Sales	0.96	0.70
Price/Cash Flow	6.76	0.93
Dividend Yield %	1.88	1.68

Growth Measures	%	Rel Category
Long-Term Erngs	10.37	0.72
Book Value	14.82	1.07
Sales	16.47	1.02
Cash Flow	25.42	0.85
Historical Erngs	40.83	0.81

Profitability	%	Rel Category
Return on Equity	27.94	1.21
Return on Assets	12.97	1.18
Net Margin	13.30	0.90

Industry Weightings	% of Stocks	Rel Cat
Oil & Gas	65.3	2.1
Oil/Gas Products	11.4	1.1
Oil & Gas Srv	18.5	0.6
Pipelines	2.7	2.7
Utilities	0.0	0.0
Hard Commd	0.9	0.1
Soft Commd	0.0	0.0
Misc. Indstrl	0.0	0.0
Other	1.3	0.1

Composition

● Cash	0.2
● Stocks	99.8
● Bonds	0.0
Other	0.0
Foreign	48.8
(% of Stock)	

Mᴏʀɴɪɴɢsᴛᴀʀ® ETFs 150

Data through December 31, 2006

iShares SP Glb Fincl IXG

Market Price	$89.00
Mstar Category	Specialty-Financial

Morningstar Fair Value

Price/Fair Value Ratio — Coverage Rate % —

Management

Lisa Chen of Barclays Global Fund Advisors leads the charge in running this and all of Barclays' other global ETFs. IShares portfolio management group is responsible for billions in assets. Most of the managers have at least five or more years of experience with Barclays as well as prior industry experience.

Methodology

The exchange-traded fund tracks the S&P Global Financials Sector Index, a subset of the S&P Global 1200 Index. The ETF's index draws the financial stocks out of the Global 1200, which includes the largest and most-liquid stocks in the world. So, this ETF has a distinct bias for large caps. The fund's index is market-capitalization weighted and float-adjusted. Profitability is a major consideration for inclusion in the index. A committee oversees this index and makes all decisions on an as-needed basis.

Morningstar Rating ★★★★	Above Avg	**Return** Above Avg	**Risk** Above Avg	**Yield** 1.4%	**NAV** $89.32

Avg Daily Vol. (k) 24

52 wk High/Low $90.55 - $73.02

Growth of $10,000
— Investment Value of ETF
— Investment Value of Index S&P 500

Trading Volume Millions

	1997	1998	1999	2000	2001	2002	2003	2004	2005	2006	History
	—	—	—	—	52.35	43.03	57.96	66.56	73.13	89.32	NAV $
	—	—	—	—	52.30	42.86	58.34	66.95	73.53	90.55	Market Price $
	—	—	—	—	13.28*	-16.73	37.83	16.39	11.65	23.80	NAV Return%
	—	—	—	—	13.58*	-16.98	39.26	16.31	11.60	24.83	Market Price Return%
	—	—	—	—	0.73	-0.82	0.72	0.55	0.21	0.44	Avg Premium/Discount%
	—	—	—	—	13.28	5.37	9.15	5.51	6.74	8.01	NAV Rtrn% +/-S&P 500
	—	—	—	—	13.28	-4.38	5.60	3.00	5.19	4.38	NAV Rtrn% +/-DJ Finance
	—	—	—	—	—	4	5	5	5	9	NAV Return% Rank in Cat
	—	—	—	—	—	1.09	3.05	1.54	1.80	1.66	Income Return %
	—	—	—	—	—	-17.82	34.78	14.85	9.85	22.14	Capital Return %
	—	—	—	—	0.04	0.57	1.31	0.90	1.20	1.21	Income $
	—	—	—	—	0.00	0.00	0.00	0.00	0.00	0.00	Capital Gains $
	—	—	—	—	—	0.65	0.65	0.65	0.65	0.65	Expense Ratio %
	—	—	—	—	—	1.44	2.04	2.14	2.11	2.17	Income Ratio %
	—	—	—	—	—	2	8	8	5	7	Turnover Rate %
	—	—	—	—	13	17	63	110	308		Net Assets $mil

Performance 12-31-06

Historic Quarterly NAV Returns

	1st Qtr	2nd Qtr	3rd Qtr	4th Qtr	Total
2002	1.85	-4.44	-21.18	8.55	-16.73
2003	-7.09	21.96	5.52	15.27	37.83
2004	3.97	-2.04	0.97	13.19	16.39
2005	-3.52	0.98	6.23	7.87	11.65
2006	7.79	-0.38	6.65	8.11	23.80

Trailing	NAV Return%	Market Return%	NAV Rtrn% +/-S&P 500	%Rank Cat.(NAV)
3 Mo	8.11	8.94	1.41	14
6 Mo	15.29	16.55	2.55	13
1 Yr	23.80	24.83	8.01	9
3 Yr Avg	17.18	17.45	6.74	4
5 Yr Avg	13.05	13.37	6.86	4
10 Yr Avg	—	—	—	—

Tax Analysis	Tax-Adj Return%	Tax-Cost Ratio
3 Yr (estimated)	16.59	0.50
5 Yr (estimated)	12.42	0.56
10 Yr (estimated)	—	—

Rating and Risk

Time Period	Morningstar Rtn vs Cat	Morningstar Risk vs Cat	Morningstar Risk-Adj Rating
3 Yr	High	Avg	★★★★★
5 Yr	+Avg	+Avg	★★★★
10 Yr	—	—	—

Other Measures	Standard Index S&P 500	Best Fit Index MSCI World
Alpha	6.0	4.2
Beta	1.01	0.90
R-Squared	70	80
Standard Deviation	8.36	
Mean	17.18	
Sharpe Ratio	1.58	

Morningstar's Take by Andrew Gunter 12-31-06

We think iShares S&P Global Financials could benefit investors in small doses.

This fund is one of only two financial-services-category ETFs that invest in foreign-based companies. A team from Barclays Global Fund Advisors runs this portfolio to mimic the returns of its benchmark, the S&P Global Financials Sector Index. The fund's lone rival that buys foreign-based financials stocks is a new WisdomTree ETF, but in reality these two funds are far more different than they are alike.

The first benefit specific to this ETF is its truly global benchmark. It invests about 40% of its assets in North American firms, nearly that much in European firms, and more than 15% of assets in Asia-based companies. Its top 20 positions, for example, include several banks each from Europe, the United States, and Japan. In contrast, WisdomTree's ETF invests solely in companies based outside the United States. So this remains the only ETF around that provides investors with truly global exposure.

This offering also follows an ETF industry norm by using a market-cap-weighted index. That means investors get adequate exposure to faster-growing businesses including asset managers and investment banks (though four of the fund's top five positions are multinational conglomerate banks). All told, we think the fund adequately diversifies assets not only across geographical lines, but across industry ones as well.

These positive attributes still don't make this ETF a core holding, though. Investors already get significant financials exposure in diversified funds, so this ETF receives the same cautious outlook we often reserve for sector funds: They merit only a small slice of assets from investors who follow financial markets closely and who wish to opportunistically tilt a portfolio or cover a gap in one. For investors in that position, this fund should do the job nicely.

Address:	45 Fremont Street San Francisco CA 94105 800-474-2737
Web Address:	www.ishares.com
Inception:	11-12-01*
Advisor:	Barclays Global Fund Advisers

Management Fee:	0.48%
Expense Projections:	3Yr:$154 5Yr:$269 10Yr:$604
Income Distrib:	Annually
Exchange:	AMEX

Portfolio Analysis 12-31-06

Share change since 11-06 Total Stocks:233

	Sector	PE	Tot Ret%	% Assets
Citigroup, Inc.	Financial	13.3	19.55	3.98
⊖ Bank of America Corporat	Financial	12.4	20.68	3.32
⊖ HSBC Hldgs	Financial			2.88
American International G	Financial	17.1	6.05	2.61
J.P. Morgan Chase & Co.	Financial	13.7	25.60	2.42
Royal Bank Of Scotland G	Financial			1.77
⊖ UBS AG	Financial		29.62	1.75
Banco Santander Central	Financial			1.74
Mitsubishi UFJ Financial	Financial			1.72
⊖ Wells Fargo Company	Financial	14.7	16.82	1.61
Wachovia Corporation	Financial	13.0	12.02	1.56
ING Groep	Financial			1.36
Barclays	Financial			1.32
Morgan Stanley	Financial	12.3	45.93	1.29
Goldman Sachs Group, Inc	Financial	12.1	57.41	1.28
Allianz	Financial			1.27
⊖ BNP Paribas	Financial			1.25
Credit Suisse Grp	Financial			1.23
UniCredito Italiano Grp	Financial			1.22
BBVA	Financial			1.22

Current Investment Style

Value Blnd Growth — Large Mid Small

Market Cap	%
Giant	64.7
Large	31.5
Mid	3.8
Small	0.0
Micro	0.0
Avg $mil:	51,895

Value Measures		Rel Category
Price/Earnings	12.99	0.96
Price/Book	1.96	0.96
Price/Sales	1.58	0.61
Price/Cash Flow	7.98	1.02
Dividend Yield %	2.86	1.24

Growth Measures	%	Rel Category
Long-Term Erngs	9.89	0.93
Book Value	9.30	1.15
Sales	11.53	1.51
Cash Flow	-5.44	NMF
Historical Erngs	18.27	1.20

Profitability	%	Rel Category
Return on Equity	17.34	1.09
Return on Assets	7.83	0.57
Net Margin	22.58	1.06

Industry Weightings	% of Stocks	Rel Cat
Intl Banks	29.1	1.6
Banks	18.6	0.9
Real Estate	5.0	1.6
Sec Mgmt	14.1	1.1
S & Ls	2.7	0.4
Prop & Reins	13.2	0.8
Life Ins	5.8	1.1
Misc. Ins	2.4	0.8
Other	9.2	0.7

Composition

● Cash	0.3	
● Stocks	99.8	
● Bonds	0.0	
Other	0.0	
Foreign	59.8	(% of Stock)

MORNINGSTAR® ETFs 150

iShares SP Glb Hlth IXJ

	Market Price $57.51	Mstar Category Specialty-Health

Morningstar Fair Value

Price/Fair Value Ratio	Coverage Rate %
0.92 Undervalued	63 Poor

Management

Patrick O'Connor and S. Jane Leung lead the team that manages this and several other iShares ETFs. O'Connor has been on the team since the fund's inception and Leung since September 2006. Both have been with the ETF's advisor, Barclays Global Investors, for five or more years.

Methodology

The exchange-traded fund tracks the S&P Global Healthcare Sector Index, which is a subset of the S&P Global 1200 Index. The ETF's index draws health-care stocks out of the Global 1200, which includes the largest and most liquid stocks in the world. So, this ETF has a distinct bias for large caps. The fund's index is market-capitalization weighted and float-adjusted. Profitability is a major consideration for inclusion in the index. A committee oversees this index and makes all decisions on an as-needed basis.

Morningstar Rating ★★★ Neutral	Return Neutral	Risk Low	Yield 0.8%	NAV $57.11	Avg Daily Vol. (k) 72	52 wk High/Low $58.52 - $51.13

Growth of $10,000
- Investment Value of ETF
- Investment Value of Index S&P 500

14.0
12.0
10.0
7.0

0.1
Trading Volume Millions
0.0

1997	1998	1999	2000	2001	2002	2003	2004	2005	2006	History
—	—	—	—	49.34	40.27	47.10	48.76	52.20	57.11	NAV $
—	—	—	—	49.50	40.38	47.68	49.21	52.20	57.39	Market Price $
—	—	—	—	3.53*	-17.89	17.73	4.31	7.80	10.34	NAV Return%
—	—	—	—	3.63*	-17.93	18.85	3.98	6.81	10.88	Market Price Return%
—	—	—	—	0.34	0.19	0.69	0.78	0.23	0.29	Avg Premium/Discount%
—	—	—	—	3.53	4.21	-10.95	-6.57	2.89	-5.45	NAV Rtrn% +/-S&P 500
—	—	—	—	3.53	2.92	-1.70	-0.24	-0.52	3.46	NAV Rtrn% +/-DJ Hlthcare
—	—	—	—	—	4	5	5	5	7	NAV Return% Rank in Cat
—	—	—	—	—	0.50	0.75	0.77	0.75	0.93	Income Return %
—	—	—	—	—	-18.39	16.98	3.54	7.05	9.41	Capital Return %
—	—	—	—	0.01	0.25	0.30	0.36	0.37	0.49	Income $
—	—	—	—	0.00	0.00	0.00	0.00	0.00	0.00	Capital Gains $
—	—	—	—	—	0.65	0.65	0.65	0.65	0.65	Expense Ratio %
—	—	—	—	—	0.62	0.96	1.25	1.12	1.02	Income Ratio %
—	—	—	—	—	1	4	6	10	5	Turnover Rate %
—	—	—	—	—	26	52	190	457	737	Net Assets $mil

Performance 12-31-06

Historic Quarterly NAV Returns

	1st Qtr	2nd Qtr	3rd Qtr	4th Qtr	Total
2002	-0.57	-12.49	-9.32	4.07	-17.89
2003	-1.14	10.98	-2.81	10.41	17.73
2004	-0.93	2.31	-2.74	5.81	4.31
2005	-1.29	3.95	3.38	1.63	7.80
2006	2.82	-1.17	7.11	1.38	10.34

Trailing	NAV Return%	Market Return%	NAV Rtrn% +/-S&P 500	%Rank Cat.(NAV)
3 Mo	1.38	1.31	-5.32	14
6 Mo	8.59	8.91	-4.15	13
1 Yr	10.34	10.88	-5.45	7
3 Yr Avg	7.45	7.19	-2.99	4
5 Yr Avg	3.70	3.73	-2.49	4
10 Yr Avg	—	—	—	—

Tax Analysis	Tax-Adj Return%	Tax-Cost Ratio
3 Yr (estimated)	7.17	0.26
5 Yr (estimated)	3.44	0.25
10 Yr (estimated)	—	—

Rating and Risk

Time Period	Morningstar Rtn vs Cat	Morningstar Risk vs Cat	Morningstar Risk-Adj Rating
3 Yr	Avg	Low	★★★
5 Yr	Avg	Low	★★★
10 Yr	—	—	

Other Measures	Standard Index S&P 500	Best Fit Index DJ Hlthcare
Alpha	0.8	1.4
Beta	0.50	0.82
R-Squared	21	87
Standard Deviation	7.40	
Mean	7.45	
Sharpe Ratio	0.58	

Morningstar's Take by Christopher Davis 12-31-06

Take a pass on iShares S&P Global Healthcare Sector.

This exchange-traded fund's main attraction is the globe-trotting nature of the benchmark it tracks. While no other diversified health-care ETF invests overseas, its top holdings include European pharmaceutical heavyweights such as GlaxoSmithKline and Novartis. The fund's foreign stake also trumps the comparatively modest weighting the typical mutual fund keeps abroad. Indeed, non-U.S. stocks account for 35% of assets, versus 15% for the health-care category average.

If only the fund were as diversified in other respects. Large caps comprise more than 90% of the portfolio and its average market cap weighs in at an immense $61.8 billion, the second-highest of any health-care ETF and more than three times the category average. Drug stocks also play an outsized role, which gives other health-care industries the short shrift. Biotech stocks, for instance, soak up a mere 7% of assets, a fraction of the category norm.

That means the fund will fare well when large caps and pharma lead the way, but that makes it less suited to make a broad bet on the health-care sector.

We'd be a little more sanguine on the fund if its holdings were especially attractive, but that's not the case. Although Johnson and Johnson and Novartis look very cheap to Morningstar's equity analysts, most of the offering's largest positions are fairly valued. As a result, the fund's potential for above-average gains is limited, in our view.

Further dampening our enthusiasm for the fund is its cost. To be sure, its 0.48% annual expense ratio is far below the average no-load health-care fund's, but it's pricey relative to ETF competitors like Vanguard Health Care ETF and Health Care Select SPDR.

All in all, we think health-care investors can do better than this offering.

Portfolio Analysis 12-31-06

Share change since 11-06 Total Stocks:79	Sector	PE	Tot Ret%	% Assets
⊖ Johnson & Johnson	Health	17.4	12.44	8.09
⊖ Pfizer Inc.	Health	15.1	15.22	7.89
⊖ Novartis	Health	—	—	6.64
⊖ GlaxoSmithKline	Health	—	—	6.41
⊖ Roche Holding	Health	—	—	5.32
⊖ Merck & Co., Inc.	Health	18.8	42.66	4.00
⊖ Sanofi-Synthelabo	Health	—	—	3.79
⊖ AstraZeneca	Health	—	—	3.48
⊖ Amgen, Inc.	Health	28.0	-13.38	3.37
Abbott Laboratories	Health	23.6	26.88	3.16
⊖ UnitedHealth Group, Inc.	Health	21.0	-13.49	3.06
⊖ Wyeth	Health	17.0	12.88	2.90
⊖ Medtronic, Inc.	Health	23.7	-6.29	2.60
⊕ Takeda Chemical Industri	Health	—	—	2.30
⊖ Bristol-Myers Squibb Com	Health	23.3	19.93	2.19
⊖ Eli Lilly & Company	Health	17.4	-5.16	2.17
⊖ WellPoint, Inc.	Health	17.2	-1.38	2.06
⊖ Schering-Plough Corporat	Health	36.9	14.63	1.48
Baxter International Inc	Health	24.0	24.81	1.28
Gilead Sciences, Inc.	Health	41.1	23.51	1.26

Current Investment Style

Value Bind Growth — Large Mid Small

Market Cap	%
Giant	67.3
Large	25.1
Mid	7.6
Small	0.0
Micro	0.0

Avg $mil: 60,241

Value Measures		Rel Category
Price/Earnings	18.13	0.88
Price/Book	3.55	1.00
Price/Sales	2.15	0.72
Price/Cash Flow	14.23	0.97
Dividend Yield %	1.72	1.70

Growth Measures	%	Rel Category
Long-Term Erngs	11.49	0.81
Book Value	11.59	1.46
Sales	10.09	0.84
Cash Flow	9.59	0.84
Historical Erngs	9.59	0.65

Profitability	%	Rel Category
Return on Equity	22.38	1.58
Return on Assets	10.92	1.88
Net Margin	15.87	1.40

Industry Weightings	% of Stocks	Rel Cat
Biotech	12.1	0.4
Drugs	54.6	1.8
Mgd Care	13.8	1.2
Hospitals	0.5	0.4
Other HC Srv	0.2	0.2
Diagnostics	1.1	0.9
Equipment	14.6	1.1
Good/Srv	2.7	0.7
Other	0.4	0.1

Composition

	%
● Cash	0.1
● Stocks	99.9
● Bonds	0.0
● Other	0.0
Foreign	35.3

(% of Stock)

Address:	45 Fremont Street San Francisco CA 94105 800-474-2737
Web Address:	www.ishares.com
Inception:	11-13-01 *
Advisor:	Barclays Global Fund Advisers

Management Fee:	0.48%		
Expense Projections:	3Yr:$154	5Yr:$269	10Yr:$604
Income Distrib:	Annually		
Exchange:	AMEX		

ETFs 150

101

iShares SP Glb Tech IXN

	Market Price $58.89	Mstar Category Specialty-Technology

Morningstar Fair Value

Price/Fair Value Ratio	Coverage Rate %
0.82 Undervalued	73 Fair

Management

Barclays Global Fund Advisors is the advisor. The firm is the world's largest manager of indexed portfolios. Lisa Chen leads the charge in running this and all of Barclays' other global ETFs. iShares portfolio management group is responsible for billions in assets. Most managers have at least five years of experience.

Methodology

The exchange-traded fund tracks the S&P Global Information Technology Sector Index, which is a subset of the S&P Global 1200 Index. The ETF's index draws the tech stocks out of the Global 1200, which includes the largest and most liquid stocks in the world. So, this ETF has a distinct bias for large caps. The fund's index is market-capitalization weighted and float-adjusted. Profitability is a major consideration for inclusion in the index. A committee oversees this index and makes all decisions on an as-needed basis.

Performance 12-31-06

Historic Quarterly NAV Returns

	1st Qtr	2nd Qtr	3rd Qtr	4th Qtr	Total
2002	-5.87	-25.33	-26.21	19.72	-37.91
2003	-2.28	20.20	11.93	11.82	47.02
2004	1.29	-0.29	-9.99	13.09	2.80
2005	-6.79	1.49	5.96	3.66	3.90
2006	4.99	-8.49	7.19	6.25	9.43

Trailing	NAV Return%	Market Return%	NAV Rtrn% +/-S&P 500	%Rank Cat(NAV)
3 Mo	6.25	5.96	-0.45	18
6 Mo	13.90	14.20	1.16	18
1 Yr	9.43	9.81	-6.36	14
3 Yr Avg	5.34	5.30	-5.10	8
5 Yr Avg	1.30	1.19	-4.89	8
10 Yr Avg	—	—	—	—

Tax Analysis	Tax-Adj Return%	Tax-Cost Ratio
3 Yr (estimated)	5.16	0.17
5 Yr (estimated)	1.20	0.10
10 Yr (estimated)	—	—

Morningstar Rating ★★★ Neutral	Return Neutral	Risk Below Avg	Yield 0.2%	NAV $57.97	Avg Daily Vol. (k) 23	52 wk High/Low $59.25 - $47.20

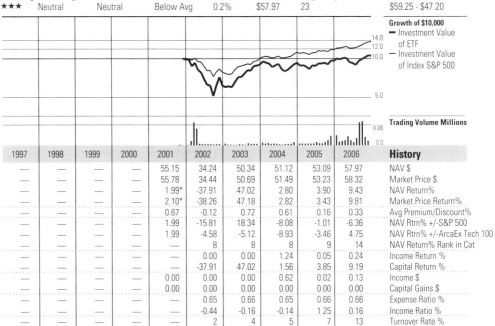

Growth of $10,000
- Investment Value of ETF
- Investment Value of Index S&P 500

Trading Volume Millions

	1997	1998	1999	2000	2001	2002	2003	2004	2005	2006	History
	—	—	—	—	55.15	34.24	50.34	51.12	53.09	57.97	NAV $
	—	—	—	—	55.78	34.44	50.69	51.49	53.23	58.32	Market Price $
	—	—	—	—	1.99*	-37.91	47.02	2.80	3.90	9.43	NAV Return%
	—	—	—	—	2.10*	-38.26	47.18	2.82	3.43	9.81	Market Price Return%
	—	—	—	—	0.67	-0.12	0.72	0.61	0.16	0.33	Avg Premium/Discount%
	—	—	—	—	1.99	-15.81	18.34	-8.08	-1.01	-6.36	NAV Rtrn% +/-S&P 500
	—	—	—	—	1.99	-4.58	-5.12	-8.93	-3.46	4.75	NAV Rtrn% +/-ArcaEx Tech 100
	—	—	—	—	—	8	8	8	9	14	NAV Return% Rank in Cat
	—	—	—	—	—	0.00	0.00	1.24	0.05	0.24	Income Return %
	—	—	—	—	—	-37.91	47.02	1.56	3.85	9.19	Capital Return %
	—	—	—	—	0.00	0.00	0.00	0.62	0.02	0.13	Income $
	—	—	—	—	0.00	0.00	0.00	0.00	0.00	0.00	Capital Gains $
	—	—	—	—	—	0.65	0.66	0.65	0.66	0.66	Expense Ratio %
	—	—	—	—	—	-0.44	-0.16	-0.14	1.25	0.16	Income Ratio %
	—	—	—	—	—	2	4	5	7	13	Turnover Rate %
	—	—	—	—	—	5	20	36	85	177	Net Assets $mil

Rating and Risk

Time Period	Morningstar Rtn vs Cat	Morningstar Risk vs Cat	Morningstar Risk-Adj Rating
3 Yr	Avg	-Avg	★★★
5 Yr	Avg	-Avg	★★★
10 Yr	—	—	—

Other Measures	Standard Index S&P 500	Best Fit Index ArcaEx Tech 100
Alpha	-9.7	-2.3
Beta	1.82	0.98
R-Squared	76	92
Standard Deviation	14.35	
Mean	5.34	
Sharpe Ratio	0.21	

Portfolio Analysis 12-31-06

Share change since 11-06 Total Stocks:117

	Sector	PE	Tot Ret%	% Assets
⊕ Microsoft Corporation	Software	23.7	15.83	9.38
⊕ Cisco Systems, Inc.	Hardware	28.8	59.64	6.08
⊕ IBM	Hardware	16.8	19.77	5.35
⊕ Intel Corporation	Hardware	20.3	-17.18	4.26
⊕ Hewlett-Packard Company	Hardware	18.9	45.21	4.13
⊕ Google, Inc.	Business	58.6	11.00	3.59
⊕ Samsung Electnc GDR 144A	Goods	—	—	3.14
⊕ Nokia	Hardware	—	—	3.02
⊕ Apple Computer, Inc.	Hardware	37.4	18.01	2.64
⊕ Oracle Corporation	Software	25.6	40.38	2.53
⊕ Canon	Goods	—	—	2.49
⊕ Taiwan Semiconductor Man	Hardware	19.2	18.75	2.38
⊕ Qualcomm, Inc.	Hardware	26.2	-11.32	2.26
⊕ Ericsson AB (publ)	Hardware	—	—	2.19
⊕ Dell, Inc.	Hardware	17.7	-16.23	2.05
⊕ Motorola, Inc.	Hardware	13.0	-8.17	1.82
⊕ SAP	Software	—	—	1.71
⊕ Texas Instruments, Inc.	Hardware	16.8	-9.82	1.59
⊕ eBay, Inc.	Consumer	40.6	-30.43	1.28
⊕ Alcatel	Hardware	—	—	1.21

Current Investment Style

Value Blnd Growth / Large Mid Small

Market Cap	%
Giant	59.7
Large	29.2
Mid	10.9
Small	0.2
Micro	0.0

Avg $mil: 48,647

Value Measures		Rel Category
Price/Earnings	21.62	0.86
Price/Book	3.55	1.12
Price/Sales	2.07	0.77
Price/Cash Flow	12.22	1.16
Dividend Yield %	0.96	1.52

Growth Measures	%	Rel Category
Long-Term Erngs	15.43	1.02
Book Value	6.27	0.90
Sales	7.89	0.84
Cash Flow	12.71	0.66
Historical Erngs	23.28	0.76

Profitability	%	Rel Category
Return on Equity	21.03	1.24
Return on Assets	11.97	1.25
Net Margin	16.33	1.17

Industry Weightings	% of Stocks	Rel Cat
Software	23.1	1.1
Hardware	24.7	2.1
Networking Eq	11.9	1.6
Semis	15.2	0.8
Semi Equip	2.2	0.5
Comp/Data Sv	9.0	1.0
Telecom	0.0	0.0
Health Care	0.0	0.0
Other	13.9	0.7

Composition

● Cash	0.2
● Stocks	99.4
● Bonds	0.0
○ Other	0.4
Foreign	29.0
(% of Stock)	

Morningstar's Take by Karen Dolan 12-31-06

Better days may lie ahead for technology stocks, but be wary of iShares S&P Global Technology's limits.

Tech stocks are arguably due for a comeback. After all, they've been the worst-performing group for the better part of the past six years. While prices of tech stocks have indeed come down, they've dropped from unjustifiably high levels. And although most tech firms that survived the bear market boast stronger balance sheets and more efficient operations, they still face a rough competitive landscape where pricing pressures and short product cycles pose a constant threat. With that backdrop, we have a hard time seeing the attractivenes of tech-focused funds.

This ETF provides broad exposure to the tech sector by investing in well-known tech stocks from around the world. It tracks the S&P Global Information Technology Sector Index, a benchmark assembled out of the S&P Global 1200. The bogy is maintained by a committee that rebalances as needed and screens for profitability and liquidity, which helps it avoid more volatile, speculative stocks. The resulting fund holds roughly 90% of its assets in large-cap stocks such as behemoths Microsoft and Cisco Systems. The resulting portfolio is far tamer than its rivals' but lacks the spark that funds with more mid- and small-cap tech exposure can provide in an upturn.

Despite its limitations, the current portfolio here does have some redeeming qualities right now. According to stock research conducted by Morningstar's 90 equity analysts, 78% of the fund's assets reside in stocks deemed good buys or holds.

For those investors who follow the market closely and agree that tech stocks are a good buy right now, other ETFs are more attractive from a cost perspective. The fund's 0.48% expense ratio is reasonable, but cheaper options exist including the U.S.-focused Vanguard Information Technology ETF and Technology Select Sector SPDR.

Address:	45 Fremont Street San Francisco CA 94105 800-474-2737
Web Address:	www.ishares.com
Inception:	11-12-01*
Advisor:	Barclays Global Fund Advisers

Management Fee:	0.48%		
Expense Projections:	3Yr:$154	5Yr:$269	10Yr:$604
Income Distrib:	Annually		
Exchange:	AMEX		

MORNINGSTAR® ETFs 150

iShares SP Glb Tele IXP

	Market Price $63.72	Mstar Category Specialty-Communications

Morningstar Rating ★★★ Neutral	Return Neutral	Risk Below Avg	Yield 2.4%	NAV $62.87	Avg Daily Vol. (k) 29	52 wk High/Low $64.62 - $47.94

Morningstar Fair Value

Price/Fair Value Ratio —   Coverage Rate % —

Management

Barclays Global Fund Advisors is the manager of this fund and is the world's largest manager of indexed portfolios. Patrick O'Connor and S. Jane Leung have been in charge of this portfolio since February and September 2006, respectively.

Methodology

The exchange-traded fund tracks the S&P Global Telecommunications Sector Index, which is a subset of the S&P Global 1200 Index. The ETF's index draws the telecom stocks out of the Global 1200, which includes the largest and most liquid stocks in the world. So, this ETF has a distinct bias for large caps. The fund's index is market-capitalization weighted and float-adjusted. Profitability is a major consideration for inclusion in the index. A committee oversees this index and makes all decisions on an as-needed basis.

Growth of $10,000
— Investment Value of ETF
— Investment Value of Index S&P 500

Trading Volume Millions

History

	1997	1998	1999	2000	2001	2002	2003	2004	2005	2006	
	—	—	—	—	51.66	36.49	45.11	52.86	48.32	62.87	NAV $
	—	—	—	—	51.66	36.74	45.53	53.49	48.66	63.31	Market Price $
	—	—	—	—	6.20*	-28.16	25.44	18.67	-6.27	33.26	NAV Return%
	—	—	—	—	6.34*	-27.68	25.74	18.96	-6.74	33.25	Market Price Return%
	—	—	—	—	0.19	-0.02	0.52	0.76	0.33	0.55	Avg Premium/Discount%
	—	—	—	—	6.20	-6.06	-3.24	7.79	-11.18	17.47	NAV Rtrn% +/-S&P 500
	—	—	—	—	6.20	6.39	18.11	-0.03	-2.27	-3.57	NAV Rtrn% +/-DJ Telecom
	—	—	—	—	—	2	2	3	3	5	NAV Return% Rank in Cat
	—	—	—	—	—	1.24	1.77	1.48	2.33	3.13	Income Return %
	—	—	—	—	—	-29.40	23.67	17.19	-8.60	30.13	Capital Return %
	—	—	—	—	0.02	0.64	0.65	0.67	1.23	1.51	Income $
	—	—	—	—	0.00	0.00	0.00	0.00	0.00	0.00	Capital Gains $
	—	—	—	—	0.65	0.65	0.65	0.65	0.65	0.65	Expense Ratio %
	—	—	—	—	0.61	1.78	1.54	2.24	2.72	Income Ratio %
	—	—	—	—	—	2	9	7	13	11	Turnover Rate %
	—	—	—	—	—	11	16	40	56	185	Net Assets $mil

Performance 12-31-06

Historic Quarterly NAV Returns

	1st Qtr	2nd Qtr	3rd Qtr	4th Qtr	Total
2002	-13.20	-19.85	-19.45	28.20	-28.16
2003	-8.47	20.81	-2.16	15.94	25.44
2004	2.19	-2.62	2.63	16.20	18.67
2005	-5.41	-0.70	4.21	-4.24	-6.27
2006	5.53	2.39	9.25	12.89	33.26

Trailing	NAV Return%	Market Return%	NAV Rtrn% +/-S&P 500	%Rank Cat.(NAV)
3 Mo	12.89	12.37	6.19	6
6 Mo	23.33	23.50	10.59	5
1 Yr	33.26	33.25	17.47	5
3 Yr Avg	14.02	13.92	3.58	2
5 Yr Avg	5.96	6.10	-0.23	2
10 Yr Avg	—	—	—	—

Tax Analysis	Tax-Adj Return%	Tax-Cost Ratio
3 Yr (estimated)	13.21	0.71
5 Yr (estimated)	5.26	0.66
10 Yr (estimated)	—	—

Rating and Risk

Time Period	Morningstar Rtn vs Cat	Morningstar Risk vs Cat	Morningstar Risk-Adj Rating
3 Yr	-Avg	Low	★★
5 Yr	Avg	-Avg	★★★
10 Yr	—	—	—

Other Measures	Standard Index S&P 500	Best Fit Index MSCI EASExJ
Alpha	4.0	-1.1
Beta	0.91	0.69
R-Squared	46	52
Standard Deviation	9.31	
Mean	14.02	
Sharpe Ratio	1.13	

Portfolio Analysis 12-31-06

Share change since 11-06 Total Stocks:44	Sector	PE	Tot Ret%	% Assets
⊕ Vodafone Grp	Telecom	—	—	11.02
⊕ AT&T, Inc.	Telecom	19.2	51.59	10.36
⊕ Verizon Communications	Telecom	16.1	34.88	8.20
⊕ Telefonica	Telecom	—	—	7.89
⊕ BellSouth Corporation	Telecom	—	—	6.48
⊕ Deutsche Telekom	Telecom	—	—	4.13
⊕ Sprint Nextel Corporatio	Telecom	29.1	-10.44	4.13
⊕ Nippon Telegraph & Telep	Telecom	—	—	3.95
⊕ BT Grp	Telecom	—	—	3.70
⊕ France Telecom	Telecom	—	—	3.66
⊕ China Mobile	Telecom	—	—	3.20
⊕ America Movil SA ADR	Telecom	28.0	55.53	2.96
⊕ Telecom Italia	Telecom	—	—	2.51
⊕ Koninklijke KPN	Telecom	—	—	2.19
⊕ NTT DoCoMo	Telecom	—	—	1.99
⊖ Alltel Corp.	Telecom	17.6	19.54	1.71
⊕ BCE Inc.	Telecom	15.0	19.09	1.66
⊕ Telstra Corporation, Ltd	Telecom	—	—	1.49
⊕ BOUYGUES	Telecom	—	—	1.32
⊕ Rogers Communications, I	Telecom	—	41.45	1.20

Current Investment Style

Value Blnd Growth — Large / Mid / Small

	Market Cap	%
	Giant	76.3
	Large	20.9
	Mid	2.9
	Small	0.0
	Micro	0.0
	Avg $mil: 62,980	

Value Measures		Rel Category
Price/Earnings	15.22	0.87
Price/Book	1.55	0.85
Price/Sales	1.59	0.92
Price/Cash Flow	5.26	0.72
Dividend Yield %	4.37	1.55

Growth Measures	%	Rel Category
Long-Term Erngs	9.03	0.93
Book Value	4.77	0.46
Sales	2.32	0.63
Cash Flow	3.80	0.77
Historical Erngs	12.36	1.11

Profitability	%	Rel Category
Return on Equity	16.23	1.17
Return on Assets	3.77	0.73
Net Margin	2.70	0.36

Industry Weightings	% of Stocks	Rel Cat
Telecom Srv	78.9	2.4
Wireless Srv	21.1	0.8
Network Eq	0.0	0.0
Semis	0.0	0.0
Big Media	0.0	0.0
Cable TV	0.0	0.0
Other Media	0.0	0.0
Soft/Hardwr	0.0	0.0
Other	0.0	0.0

Composition

● Cash	0.2
● Stocks	99.8
● Bonds	0.0
● Other	0.0
Foreign (% of Stock)	66.2

Morningstar's Take by Andrew Gogerty 12-31-06

We'd steer clear of iShares S&P Global Telecommunications.

Most investors gain little from investing in a sector-focused offering. Their returns tend to be considerably more volatile--especially in the telecom market--than diversified funds, which increases the chance that investors will pile in and out of the sector at the wrong time. Companies in this sector also face significant headwinds such as short product cycles and intense competition in nearly every industry. In addition, the regional Bell operating companies such as AT&T, BellSouth (which is slated to merge with AT&T in the coming months) Verizon Communications, and Qwest Communications International--which dominate this portfolio--are forced to make massive capital outlays to offer the same services as rival cable companies. Moreover, although the fund has a global footprint, more than 40% of the fund's assets are stashed in its top-five holdings, including a 30% stake in just AT&T and Verizon combined. As such, this fund isn't an all-weather choice but rather will sink or swim based its top holdings. AT&T and Verizon's strong gains have propelled returns in 2006.

Still, this fund isn't without merit. It invests in the telecom stocks contained in the S&P Global 1200 Index, a global benchmark of the largest, most widely traded stocks. As such, the fund's 60% plus stake in non-U.S. companies makes it somewhat more diversified than its peers--which typically keep at least 90% of their assets in the U.S. Moreover, the fund's tilt toward large, established companies avoids the sector's smaller fare, which may have less-certain futures. Not surprisingly, this offering has been relatively less volatile (as measured by standard deviation of returns) compared with the typical conventional telecom fund.

But overall this ETF is best avoided. A top-heavy portfolio in a volatile, cutthroat area of the market is not an endearing combination.

Address:	45 Fremont Street San Francisco CA 94105 800-474-2737	Management Fee:	0.48%	
		Expense Projections:	3Yr:$154	5Yr:$269 10Yr:$604
		Income Distrib:	Annually	
Web Address:	www.ishares.com	Exchange:	AMEX	
Inception:	11-12-01*			
Advisor:	Barclays Global Fund Advisers			

iShares SP 400 Growth IJK

	Market Price	Mstar Category
	$80.01	Mid-Cap Growth

Morningstar Fair Value

Price/Fair Value Ratio	Coverage Rate %
0.93 Undervalued	84 Good

Management

Barclays Global Fund Advisors is the advisor. Patrick O'Connor and S. Jane Leung lead the team that manage this and several other iShares ETFs. Both have been with the ETF's advisor Barclays Global Investors for five or more years.

Methodology

This fund tracks the S&P MidCap 400/Citigroup Growth Index. The bogy relies on seven growth and valuation measures to classify stocks: dividend yield; price/book; price/sales and price/cash flow; and five-year earnings, sales, and internal growth rates. A third of the index's market capitalization ends up in each value, core or growth bucket, but stocks in the middle can end up in both style indexes in proportion to their style scores. The overlap should reduce turnover caused by stocks shifting styles.

Morningstar Rating	Return	Risk	Yield	NAV	Avg Daily Vol. (k)	52 wk High/Low
★★★★ Above Avg	Above Avg	Below Avg	0.4%	$79.77	68	$82.26 ~ $70.70

Growth of $10,000
- Investment Value of ETF
- Investment Value of Index S&P 500

	1997	1998	1999	2000	2001	2002	2003	2004	2005	2006	History
	—	—	—	61.95	56.79	45.66	59.42	67.25	75.73	79.77	NAV $
	—	—	—	61.94	56.98	45.69	59.35	67.20	75.62	79.71	Market Price $
	—	—	—	2.96*	-8.22	-19.40	30.66	13.71	13.31	5.75	NAV Return%
	—	—	—	2.94*	-7.92	-19.61	30.42	13.76	13.23	5.82	Market Price Return%
	—	—	—	-0.08	0.10	0.09	0.05	0.04	-0.03	-0.08	Avg Premium/Discount%
	—	—	—	2.96	3.67	2.70	1.98	2.83	8.40	-10.04	NAV Rtrn% +/-S&P 500
	—	—	—	2.96	11.93	8.01	-12.05	-1.77	1.21	-4.91	NAV Rtrn% +/-Russ MG
	—	—	—	—	1	2	2	3	4	6	NAV Return% Rank in Cat
	—	—	—	—	0.09	0.21	0.46	0.49	0.65	0.40	Income Return %
	—	—	—	—	-8.31	-19.61	30.20	13.22	12.66	5.35	Capital Return %
	—	—	—	0.00	0.05	0.12	0.21	0.29	0.44	0.31	Income $
	—	—	—	0.23	0.00	0.00	0.00	0.00	0.00	0.00	Capital Gains $
	—	—	—	—	0.25	0.25	0.25	0.25	0.25	0.25	Expense Ratio %
	—	—	—	—	0.06	0.15	0.31	0.45	0.56	0.60	Income Ratio %
	—	—	—	—	67	50	58	37	34	24	Turnover Rate %
	—	—	—	93	250	352	612	1,083	1,787	1,751	Net Assets $mil

Performance 12-31-06

Historic Quarterly NAV Returns

	1st Qtr	2nd Qtr	3rd Qtr	4th Qtr	Total
2002	3.39	-13.10	-14.61	5.05	-19.40
2003	-3.07	15.95	5.92	9.76	30.66
2004	4.50	0.71	-3.48	11.94	13.71
2005	-0.13	3.60	4.32	4.98	13.31
2006	6.29	-4.43	-1.71	5.92	5.75

Trailing	NAV Return%	Market Return%	NAV Rtrn% +/-S&P 500	%Rank Cat.(NAV)
3 Mo	5.92	5.84	-0.78	8
6 Mo	4.10	4.11	-8.64	7
1 Yr	5.75	5.82	-10.04	6
3 Yr Avg	10.86	10.88	0.42	3
5 Yr Avg	7.49	7.40	1.30	2
10 Yr Avg	—	—	—	—

Tax Analysis	Tax-Adj Return%	Tax-Cost Ratio
3 Yr (estimated)	10.67	0.17
5 Yr (estimated)	7.33	0.15
10 Yr (estimated)	—	—

Rating and Risk

Time Period	Morningstar Rtn vs Cat	Morningstar Risk vs Cat	Morningstar Risk-Adj Rating
3 Yr	Avg	-Avg	★★★
5 Yr	Avg	-Avg	★★★★
10 Yr	—	—	—

Other Measures	Standard Index S&P 500	Best Fit Index S&P Mid 400
Alpha	-1.6	-2.0
Beta	1.32	1.00
R-Squared	75	97
Standard Deviation	10.44	
Mean	10.86	
Sharpe Ratio	0.73	

Portfolio Analysis 12-31-06

Share change since 11-06 Total Stocks:247	Sector	PE	Tot Ret%	% Assets
⊖ Expeditors International	Business	32.9	20.54	1.57
⊖ CH Robinson Worldwide, I	Business	28.4	11.88	1.29
⊖ Sepracor, Inc.	Health	NMF	19.34	1.22
⊕ Everest Re Group, Ltd.	Financial		-1.62	1.16
⊕ American Eagle Outfitter	Consumer	20.7	105.48	1.14
⊖ Noble Energy, Inc.	Energy	11.9	22.48	1.13
⊖ Abercrombie & Fitch Comp	Consumer	16.5	8.01	1.11
⊖ Varian Medical Systems,	Health	26.4	-5.50	1.11
⊕ Precision Castparts Corp	Ind Mtrls	24.0	51.40	1.08
⊖ Newfield Exploration Com	Energy	13.8	-8.23	1.07
⊖ Southwestern Energy Comp	Energy	33.4	-2.48	1.07
⊕ W.R. Berkley Corporation	Financial	10.4	9.20	1.06
⊕ Amphenol Corporation	Hardware	24.4	40.57	0.98
⊕ Dun & Bradstreet Corpora	Business	23.1	23.64	0.92
⊕ Equitable Resources, Inc	Energy	22.4	16.51	0.91
⊖ Pioneer Natural Resource	Energy	11.8	-22.11	0.88
⊖ Jacobs Engineering Group	Business	24.9	20.14	0.87
⊕ Polo Ralph Lauren Corpor	Goods	24.8	38.77	0.86
⊕ Leucadia National Corpor	Ind Mtrls	57.0	19.92	0.83
⊖ Western Digital Corporat	Hardware	10.7	9.94	0.82

Morningstar's Take by Sonya Morris 12-31-06

IShares S&P MidCap 400 Growth Index is an acceptable choice, but it faces a formidable new challenger.

The competitive landscape for mid-growth ETFs changed in August 2006 when Vanguard launched Vanguard Mid-Growth ETF. That new fund boasts an ultralow expense ratio of 0.13%, making it the cheapest retail mid-growth fund on the market and undercutting this ETF's low 0.25% price tag. Indexing is a game of inches, so while that price difference might seem small, it represents a sizable advantage for the new Vanguard ETF.

But while the new competition weakens the case for this fund, we think there's still justification for owning it, particularly for those seeking to dampen volatility. Unlike other index providers, S&P screens its index constituents for profitability. A firm must have four straight quarters of profitable results before it's admitted to the S&P universe. That helps screen out more speculative and more turbulent fare. As a result, this ETF has been less

volatile than the competition, based on its standard deviation of returns (a statistical measure of volatility). It also fared better during the bear market than rival funds. But even though it's been able to limit volatility, this fund hasn't given up anything it terms of returns. Its five-year trailing returns are better than 60% of its mid-growth peers.

The argument for this ETF is also strengthened by S&P's recently improved style methodology. Previously, S&P relied solely on price/book ratios to distinguish between growth and value stocks. Now it uses a more sophisticated system that employs multiple measures of style. That should help this fund more accurately reflect its universe over time.

Granted, this ETF's competitive position has gone down a notch since the introduction of the cheaper Vanguard fund. Nevertheless, it's still a serviceable--if imperfect--choice for mid-growth exposure.

Address:	45 Fremont Street
	San Francisco CA 94105
	800-474-2737
Web Address:	www.ishares.com
Inception:	07-24-00*
Advisor:	Barclays Global Fund Advisers

Management Fee:	0.25%			
Expense Projections:	3Yr:$80	5Yr:$141	10Yr:$318	
Income Distrib:	Quarterly			
Exchange:	NYSE			

Current Investment Style

Value Blnd Growth — Large/Mid/Small

Market Cap	%
Giant	0.0
Large	0.0
Mid	89.8
Small	10.2
Micro	0.0

Avg $mil: 3,768

Value Measures		Rel Category
Price/Earnings	16.97	0.86
Price/Book	2.95	0.86
Price/Sales	1.56	0.91
Price/Cash Flow	10.81	0.98
Dividend Yield %	0.61	1.24

Growth Measures	%	Rel Category
Long-Term Erngs	14.44	0.92
Book Value	13.61	1.16
Sales	15.18	1.31
Cash Flow	15.58	0.92
Historical Erngs	22.25	0.97

Profitability	%	Rel Category
Return on Equity	19.29	0.96
Return on Assets	10.58	1.02
Net Margin	11.80	1.03

Sector Weightings	% of Stocks	Rel S&P 500	3 Year High Low	
↻ Info	13.18	0.66		
🖩 Software	3.69	1.07	5	3
🖥 Hardware	8.19	0.89	11	7
🎚 Media	1.21	0.32	4	1
📶 Telecom	0.09	0.03	1	0
☞ Service	59.30	1.28		
🏥 Health	16.94	1.40	21	15
🛒 Consumer	17.01	2.22	23	16
🏢 Business	14.98	3.54	19	12
💲 Financial	10.37	0.47	13	9
⌐ Mfg	27.53	0.81		
🏭 Goods	5.43	0.64	8	4
⚙ Ind Mtrls	10.66	0.89	11	3
🔋 Energy	10.85	1.11	16	5
💡 Utilities	0.59	0.17	1	0

Composition

		%
● Cash		0.1
● Stocks		99.9
● Bonds		0.0
○ Other		0.0
	Foreign	0.0
	(% of Stock)	

MORNINGSTAR® ETFs 150

iShares SP MidCap400 IJH

	Market Price	Mstar Category
	$80.19	Mid-Cap Blend

Morningstar Rating	Return	Risk	Yield	NAV	Avg Daily Vol. (k)	52 wk High/Low
★★★ Neutral	Neutral	Average	1.2%	$80.25	249	$82.02 - $71.24

Morningstar Fair Value

Price/Fair Value Ratio	Coverage Rate %
0.96 Fairly valued	81 Fair

Management

Barclays Global Fund Advisors, the world's largest manager of indexed portfolios, serves as advisor to this ETF. Patrick O'Connor and S. Jane Leung are responsible for this ETF's daily management. O'Connor has been a portfolio manager at Barclays since 1999. Leung began managing funds at the firm in 2001.

Methodology

This index-based offering mirrors the holdings and performance of the S&P MidCap 400 Index, which represents the universe of midsize U.S. companies. The resulting portfolio is a broadly diverse mix of mid-caps. The benchmark is compiled and maintained by the S&P index committee. The bogy includes domestic stocks with market caps between $1 billion and $4 billion. Constituents must have a record of at least four profitable quarters and good liquidity to be eligible.

Growth of $10,000
- Investment Value of ETF
- Investment Value of Index S&P 500

Trading Volume Millions

	1997	1998	1999	2000	2001	2002	2003	2004	2005	2006	History
	—	—	—	51.56	50.78	42.99	57.60	66.36	73.76	80.25	NAV $
	—	—	—	51.64	50.58	42.93	57.53	66.16	73.80	80.17	Market Price $
	—	—	—	9.78*	-0.68	-14.70	35.36	16.29	12.48	10.13	NAV Return%
	—	—	—	9.76*	-1.24	-14.47	35.37	16.09	12.88	9.96	Market Price Return%
	—	—	—	0.05	-0.07	-0.03	-0.03	-0.02	-0.01	0.00	Avg Premium/Discount%
	—	—	—	9.78	11.21	7.40	6.68	5.41	7.57	-5.66	NAV Rtrn% +/-S&P 500
	—	—	—	9.78	-0.07	-0.17	-0.26	-0.19	-0.08	-0.19	NAV Rtrn% +/-S&P Mid 400
	—	—	—	—	2	4	4	5	7	8	NAV Return% Rank in Cat
	—	—	—	0.78	0.71	1.17	1.00	1.26	1.29		Income Return %
	—	—	—	—	-1.46	-15.41	34.19	15.29	11.22	8.84	Capital Return %
	—	—	—	0.24	0.40	0.36	0.50	0.57	0.83	0.95	Income $
	—	—	—	0.15	0.00	0.00	0.00	0.00	0.00	0.00	Capital Gains $
	—	—	—	0.20	0.20	0.20	0.20	0.20	0.20	Expense Ratio %
	—	—	—	0.86	0.87	0.98	1.02	1.21	1.19		Income Ratio %
	—	—	—	—	32	14	12	11	10	9	Turnover Rate %
	—	—	—	217	462	1,221	1,411	2,323	3,389	4,189	Net Assets $mil

Performance 12-31-06

Historic Quarterly NAV Returns

	1st Qtr	2nd Qtr	3rd Qtr	4th Qtr	Total
2002	6.64	-9.36	-16.57	5.77	-14.70
2003	-4.47	17.58	6.52	13.14	35.36
2004	5.01	0.93	-2.13	12.11	16.29
2005	-0.44	4.34	4.84	3.28	12.48
2006	7.67	-3.22	-1.12	6.90	10.13

Trailing	NAV Return%	Market Return%	NAV Rtrn% +/-S&P 500	%Rank Cat.(NAV)
3 Mo	6.90	6.66	0.20	10
6 Mo	5.70	5.63	-7.04	9
1 Yr	10.13	9.96	-5.66	8
3 Yr Avg	12.94	12.95	2.50	5
5 Yr Avg	10.71	10.78	4.52	4
10 Yr Avg	—	—	—	—

Tax Analysis	Tax-Adj Return%	Tax-Cost Ratio
3 Yr (estimated)	12.50	0.39
5 Yr (estimated)	10.31	0.36
10 Yr (estimated)	—	—

Rating and Risk

Time Period	Morningstar Rtn vs Cat	Morningstar Risk vs Cat	Morningstar Risk-Adj Rating
3 Yr	Avg	Avg	★★★
5 Yr	Avg	Avg	★★★
10 Yr	—	—	—

Other Measures	Standard Index S&P 500	Best Fit Index S&P Mid 400
Alpha	0.1	-0.1
Beta	1.35	1.00
R-Squared	80	100
Standard Deviation	10.34	
Mean	12.94	
Sharpe Ratio	0.92	

Morningstar's Take by Sonya Morris 12-31-06

Investors have better options than iShares S&P MidCap 400.

This ETF tracks the S&P MidCap 400 Index, which includes midsize companies that have market capitalizations between $1 billion and $4 billion. A committee of economists and index analysts oversees the construction of Standard & Poor's indexes. And unlike competing index providers, the S&P committee considers subjective factors when constructing the benchmarks. For instance, they require that a company post four straight quarters of profitable results to be admitted to an index.

That should help keep more speculative stocks out of this fund, which should theoretically help damp volatility. But that hasn't been the case for this ETF. According to its standard deviation of returns (a statistical measure of volatility), this ETF hasn't been any less volatile than competing mid-blend ETFs.

More importantly, this ETF has underperformed its competitors. Its five-year average returns, while slightly better than the typical mid-blend fund, fall well short of iShares Russell Mid-Cap Index and Vanguard Mid Capitalization Index.

This ETF doesn't stack up when expenses are considered either. Its 0.20% expense ratio is certainly low, but it's not the cheapest way to gain mid-cap exposure. Vanguard's Mid-Cap ETF gets that honor with its tiny 0.13% price tag. Furthermore, its conventional fund twin, Vanguard Mid Capitalization Index, charges just 0.22% in fees. Although that's slightly more expensive than this ETF, investors don't have to pay a brokerage commission to invest in it. That can make it cheaper in the long run for those who plan to make regular investments over time.

All told, while this fund provides broad mid-cap exposure at a low price, there are competing funds that do the same thing for less.

Portfolio Analysis 12-31-06

Share change since 11-06 Total Stocks:400	Sector	PE	Tot Ret%	% Assets
⊕ Precision Castparts Corp	Ind Mtrls	24.0	51.40	0.95
⊕ Expeditors International	Business	32.9	20.54	0.78
⊕ Noble Energy, Inc.	Energy	11.9	22.48	0.77
⊕ Ensco International, Inc	Energy	11.6	13.12	0.68
⊕ Lam Research Corporation	Hardware	21.6	41.87	0.65
⊕ CH Robinson Worldwide, I	Business	28.4	11.88	0.64
⊕ Microchip Technology, In	Hardware	26.2	4.37	0.63
⊕ Developers Diversified R	Financial	41.1	39.65	0.62
⊕ Sepracor, Inc.	Health	NMF	19.34	0.60
⊕ MEMC Electronic Material	Hardware	30.8	76.54	0.59
⊕ Everest Re Group, Ltd.	Financial	—	-1.62	0.57
⊕ Manpower, Inc.	Business	20.6	62.53	0.57
⊕ American Eagle Outfitter	Consumer	20.7	105.48	0.56
⊕ Macerich Company	Financial	—	33.91	0.56
⊕ Varian Medical Systems,	Health	26.4	-5.50	0.55
⊕ Harris Corporation	Hardware	23.5	7.57	0.55
⊕ Abercrombie & Fitch Comp	Consumer	16.5	8.01	0.55
⊕ Newfield Exploration Com	Energy	13.8	-8.23	0.53
⊕ Cooper Cameron Corporati	Energy	22.5	28.14	0.53
⊕ Southwestern Energy Comp	Energy	33.4	-2.48	0.53

Current Investment Style

Value Blnd Growth — Large Mid Small

	Market Cap	%
	Giant	0.0
	Large	0.0
	Mid	86.5
	Small	13.4
	Micro	0.1
	Avg $mil: 3,405	

Value Measures		Rel Category
Price/Earnings	16.70	1.00
Price/Book	2.30	0.89
Price/Sales	1.10	0.98
Price/Cash Flow	9.47	1.03
Dividend Yield %	1.28	0.93

Growth Measures	%	Rel Category
Long-Term Erngs	12.51	1.03
Book Value	8.18	1.11
Sales	11.56	1.65
Cash Flow	8.00	0.81
Historical Erngs	16.84	0.88

Profitability	%	Rel Category
Return on Equity	15.15	0.88
Return on Assets	8.52	1.00
Net Margin	10.96	1.03

Sector Weightings	% of Stocks	Rel S&P 500	3 Year High Low	
⌐ Info	13.57	0.68		
Software	2.86	0.83	3	3
Hardware	8.48	0.92	10	7
Media	1.54	0.41	3	1
Telecom	0.69	0.20	1	0
⌐ Service	52.42	1.13		
Health	10.85	0.90	12	10
Consumer	11.76	1.54	17	11
Business	12.27	2.90	13	10
Financial	17.54	0.79	19	16
⌐ Mfg	34.01	1.01		
Goods	5.31	0.62	8	4
Ind Mtrls	12.76	1.07	13	7
Energy	8.29	0.85	12	8
Utilities	7.65	2.19	8	6

Composition

● Cash	0.1	
● Stocks	99.9	
● Bonds	0.0	
● Other	0.0	
Foreign (% of Stock)	0.0	

Address:	45 Fremont Street San Francisco CA 94105 800-474-2737	Management Fee:	0.20%		
		Expense Projections:	3Yr:$64	5Yr:$113	10Yr:$255
		Income Distrib:	Quarterly		
Web Address:	www.ishares.com	Exchange:	NYSE		
Inception:	05-22-00*				
Advisor:	Barclays Global Fund Advisers				

iShares SP 400 Value IJJ

	Market Price	Mstar Category
	$78.88	Mid-Cap Value

Morningstar Fair Value

Price/Fair Value Ratio	Coverage Rate %
0.98 Fairly valued	79 Fair

Management

Barclays Global Fund Advisors is the advisor. The firm is the world's largest manager of indexed portfolios. Patrick O'Connor and S. Jane Leung are in charge of this ETF's daily management. Both are experienced index fund managers.

Methodology

This fund tracks the S&P MidCap 400/Citigroup Value Index. The bogy relies on seven growth and valuation measures to classify stocks. The factors are dividend yield; price-book, -sales, and -cash flow; and five-year earnings, sales, and internal growth rates. A third of the index's market capitalization ends up in each value, core, or growth bucket, but stocks in the middle zone can end up in both style indexes in proportion to their style scores. The overlap should reduce turnover caused by stocks moving from one style to another.

Morningstar Rating	Return	Risk	Yield	NAV	Avg Daily Vol. (k)	52 wk High/Low
★★★★ Above Avg	Above Avg	Average	1.8%	$79.22	88	$80.74 - $70.22

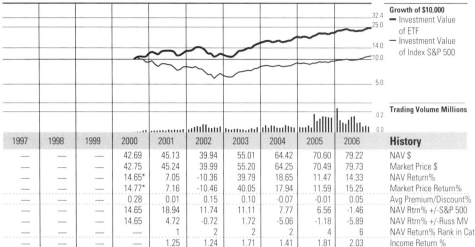

Growth of $10,000
— Investment Value of ETF
— Investment Value of Index S&P 500

Trading Volume Millions

	1997	1998	1999	2000	2001	2002	2003	2004	2005	2006	History
	—	—	—	42.69	45.13	39.94	55.01	64.42	70.60	79.22	NAV $
	—	—	—	42.75	45.24	39.99	55.20	64.25	70.49	79.73	Market Price $
	—	—	14.65*	14.65*	7.05	-10.36	39.79	18.65	11.47	14.33	NAV Return%
	—	—	14.77*	14.77*	7.16	-10.46	40.05	17.94	11.59	15.25	Market Price Return%
	—	—	—	0.28	0.01	0.15	0.10	-0.07	-0.01	0.05	Avg Premium/Discount%
	—	—	—	14.65	18.94	11.74	11.11	7.77	6.56	-1.46	NAV Rtrn% +/-S&P 500
	—	—	—	14.65	4.72	-0.72	1.72	-5.06	-1.18	-5.89	NAV Rtrn% +/-Russ MV
	—	—	—	1	2	2	2	2	4	6	NAV Return% Rank in Cat
	—	—	—	—	1.25	1.24	1.71	1.41	1.81	2.03	Income Return %
	—	—	—	—	5.80	-11.60	38.08	17.24	9.66	12.30	Capital Return %
	—	—	—	0.25	0.53	0.56	0.68	0.77	1.16	1.42	Income $
	—	—	—	0.07	0.00	0.00	0.00	0.00	0.00	0.00	Capital Gains $
	—	—	—	—	0.25	0.25	0.25	0.25	0.25	0.25	Expense Ratio %
	—	—	—	—	1.58	1.43	1.50	1.47	1.78	1.68	Income Ratio %
	—	—	—	—	17	13	11	11	10	21	Turnover Rate %
	—	—	—	47	298	607	996	1,726	2,513	2,571	Net Assets $mil

Performance 12-31-06

Historic Quarterly NAV Returns

	1st Qtr	2nd Qtr	3rd Qtr	4th Qtr	Total
2002	9.79	-5.91	-18.51	6.49	-10.36
2003	-5.86	19.11	7.09	16.42	39.79
2004	5.46	1.14	-0.83	12.17	18.65
2005	-0.76	5.04	5.36	1.50	11.47
2006	9.00	-2.08	-0.63	7.80	14.33

Trailing	NAV Return%	Market Return%	NAV Rtrn% +/-S&P 500	%Rank Cat.(NAV)
3 Mo	7.80	8.36	1.10	8
6 Mo	7.12	8.08	-5.62	7
1 Yr	14.33	15.25	-1.46	6
3 Yr Avg	14.78	14.90	4.34	2
5 Yr Avg	13.64	13.72	7.45	2
10 Yr Avg	—	—	—	—

Tax Analysis	Tax-Adj Return%	Tax-Cost Ratio
3 Yr (estimated)	14.13	0.57
5 Yr (estimated)	13.02	0.55
10 Yr (estimated)	—	—

Rating and Risk

Time Period	Morningstar Rtn vs Cat	Morningstar Risk vs Cat	Morningstar Risk-Adj Rating
3 Yr	Avg	+Avg	★★★
5 Yr	+Avg	Avg	★★★★
10 Yr	—	—	—

Other Measures	Standard Index S&P 500	Best Fit Index S&P Mid 400
Alpha	1.6	1.5
Beta	1.37	1.01
R-Squared	80	97
Standard Deviation	10.54	
Mean	14.78	
Sharpe Ratio	1.06	

Portfolio Analysis 12-31-06

Share change since 11-06 Total Stocks:284	Sector	PE	Tot Ret%	% Assets
⊕ Developers Diversified R	Financial	41.1	39.65	1.22
⊕ Manpower, Inc.	Business	20.6	62.53	1.13
⊕ Macerich Company	Financial	—	33.91	1.10
⊕ Telephone and Data Syste	Telecom	20.2	52.10	1.01
⊕ Wisconsin Energy Corpora	Utilities	17.3	24.21	0.99
⊕ Lyondell Chemical Compan	Energy	10.2	11.52	0.96
⊕ Regency Centers Corporat	Financial	57.1	37.58	0.96
⊕ Old Republic Internation	Financial	10.8	13.90	0.96
⊕ AMB Property Corporation	Financial	30.9	23.30	0.93
⊕ Fidelity National Financ	Financial	—	—	0.93
⊕ Pepco Holdings, Inc.	Utilities	16.9	21.37	0.89
⊕ A.G. Edwards, Inc.	Financial	17.1	37.15	0.85
⊕ Oneok, Inc.	Utilities	10.1	67.75	0.85
⊕ Scana Corporation	Utilities	15.0	7.60	0.84
⊖ Precision Castparts Corp	Ind Mtrls	24.0	51.40	0.83
⊕ Associated Banc-Corp	Financial	14.2	10.95	0.81
⊕ Liberty Property Trust	Financial	19.4	20.84	0.79
⊕ Alliant Energy Corporati	Utilities	52.5	39.41	0.78
⊕ Northeast Utilities	Utilities	33.9	47.76	0.77
⊕ United Dominion Realty	Financial	—	41.79	0.76

Current Investment Style

Value Blnd Growth — Large Mid Small

Market Cap	%
Giant	0.0
Large	0.0
Mid	83.3
Small	16.6
Micro	0.1

Avg $mil: 3,084

Value Measures		Rel Category
Price/Earnings	16.44	1.10
Price/Book	1.90	0.99
Price/Sales	0.85	0.96
Price/Cash Flow	8.43	1.14
Dividend Yield %	1.93	0.78

Growth Measures	%	Rel Category
Long-Term Erngs	10.75	1.14
Book Value	5.27	0.92
Sales	9.80	1.18
Cash Flow	2.53	1.86
Historical Erngs	12.31	1.12

Profitability	%	Rel Category
Return on Equity	11.14	0.85
Return on Assets	6.49	0.86
Net Margin	10.11	0.87

Sector Weightings	% of Stocks	Rel S&P 500	3 Year High Low
ⓘ Info	13.90	0.70	
Software	2.04	0.59	3 2
Hardware	8.74	0.95	10 7
Media	1.84	0.49	3 2
Telecom	1.28	0.36	1 1
Service	45.62	0.99	
Health	4.81	0.40	7 4
Consumer	6.64	0.87	14 6
Business	9.59	2.27	10 6
Financial	24.58	1.10	27 21
Mfg	40.48	1.20	
Goods	5.19	0.61	9 5
Ind Mtrls	14.90	1.25	18 9
Energy	5.75	0.59	12 6
Utilities	14.64	4.18	15 10

Composition

● Cash	0.1
● Stocks	99.9
● Bonds	0.0
● Other	0.0
Foreign	0.0
(% of Stock)	

Morningstar's Take by Sonya Morris 12-31-06

Has iShares S&P MidCap 400 Value recent makeover paid off?

At the end of 2005, this ETF's benchmark, the S&P Mid-Cap 400 Value Index, upgraded its style methodology. Previously, Standard & Poor's relied solely on price/book ratios to separate value stocks from growth stocks. That resulted in some distortions in the late-1990s when some firms' book values got out of whack because of accounting issues related to acquisitions. To address that problem, S&P adopted a new, more sophisticated methodology.

The jury's still out on the effectiveness of the new system. At present, this ETF's sector composition isn't entirely reflective of its universe. For example, both its hardware and utility weightings are roughly twice that the category norm, and its allocation to industrial stocks is 80% higher than its typical peer. But when it comes down to it, what constitutes a value or a growth stock is subjectively defined. It's nearly impossible

for a quantitative methodology to perfectly reflect its universe in all market conditions. We still think the new style metrics are an improvement and are in keeping with indexing best practices. Moreover, this ETF's low costs, which come courtesy of a tiny 0.25% expense ratio and low turnover approach, should give it a fighting chance to grind past its typical active rival.

It's worth nothing, however, that there's now a competing ETF with an even lower price tag. In August 2006, Vanguard launched Vanguard Mid-Cap Value ETF, which charges just 0.13%. That's almost half the cost of this fund and a big advantage in the world of indexing where every percentage point counts.

Still, we don't think shareholders of this ETF should necessarily jump over to the cheaper fund, particularly if tax consequences are involved. The Vanguard ETF is new and unproven, and this ETF still provides a cheap way to fill out the mid-value slot of your portfolio.

Address:	45 Fremont Street San Francisco CA 94105 800-474-2737	Management Fee:	0.25%
		Expense Projections:	3Yr:$80 5Yr:$141 10Yr:$318
		Income Distrib:	Quarterly
Web Address:	www.ishares.com	Exchange:	NYSE
Inception:	07-24-00*		
Advisor:	Barclays Global Fund Advisers		

MORNINGSTAR® ETFs 150

iShares SP 600 Growth IJT

	Market Price	Mstar Category
	$126.47	Small Growth

Morningstar Fair Value

Price/Fair Value Ratio — Coverage Rate % —

Management

Barclays Global Fund Advisors is the advisor. The firm is the world's largest manager of indexed portfolios. Patrick O'Connor and S. Jane Leung run the fund on a day-to-day basis. O'Connor has managed index funds at Barclays since 1999. Leung's tenure at the firm began in 2001.

Methodology

At the end of 2005, this ETF adopted a new benchmark, the S&P SmallCap 600/Citigroup Growth Index. The bogy relies on seven growth and valuation measures to classify stocks. The factors are dividend yield; price-book, -sales and -cash flow; and five-year earnings, sales, and internal growth rates. A third of the index's market capitalization ends up in each value, core, or growth bucket, but stocks in the middle zone can end up in both style indexes in proportion to their style scores. The overlap should reduce turnover caused by stocks moving from one style to another.

Performance 12-31-06

Historic Quarterly NAV Returns

	1st Qtr	2nd Qtr	3rd Qtr	4th Qtr	Total
2002	3.53	-8.99	-14.68	5.06	-15.55
2003	-3.63	16.85	7.79	12.92	37.05
2004	5.65	4.37	-3.08	13.80	21.61
2005	-1.77	3.71	6.56	0.39	8.99
2006	11.28	-5.17	-2.49	7.19	10.30

Trailing	NAV Return%	Market Return%	NAV Rtrn% +/-S&P 500	%Rank Cat.(NAV)
3 Mo	7.19	7.21	0.49	7
6 Mo	4.52	4.58	-8.22	7
1 Yr	10.30	10.55	-5.49	6
3 Yr Avg	13.50	13.45	3.06	3
5 Yr Avg	11.09	11.12	4.90	3
10 Yr Avg	—	—	—	—

Tax Analysis	Tax-Adj Return%	Tax-Cost Ratio
3 Yr (estimated)	13.33	0.15
5 Yr (estimated)	10.95	0.13
10 Yr (estimated)	—	—

Morningstar Rating	Return	Risk	Yield	NAV	Avg Daily Vol. (k)	52 wk High/Low
★★★★★ Highest	Highest	Low	0.3%	$128.05	50	$132.09 - $113.40

Growth of $10,000
— Investment Value of ETF
— Investment Value of Index S&P 500

Trading Volume Millions

	1997	1998	1999	2000	2001	2002	2003	2004	2005	2006	History
	—	—	—	78.24	77.09	64.96	88.67	107.43	116.41	128.05	NAV $
	—	—	—	78.41	76.95	65.10	88.72	107.10	116.07	127.96	Market Price $
	—	—	—	7.35*	-1.38	-15.55	37.05	21.61	8.99	10.30	NAV Return%
	—	—	—	7.34*	-1.77	-15.21	36.84	21.17	9.00	10.55	Market Price Return%
	—	—	—	0.07	0.22	0.07	0.10	-0.06	-0.08	-0.13	Avg Premium/Discount%
	—	—	—	7.35	10.51	6.55	8.37	10.73	4.08	-5.49	NAV Rtrn% +/-S&P 500
	—	—	—	7.35	7.85	14.71	-11.49	7.30	4.84	-3.05	NAV Rtrn% +/-Russ 2000 Gr
	—	—	—	3	3	3	3	3	5	6	NAV Return% Rank in Cat
	—	—	—	—	0.08	0.20	0.48	0.41	0.60	0.29	Income Return %
	—	—	—	—	-1.46	-15.75	36.57	21.20	8.39	10.01	Capital Return %
	—	—	—	0.00	0.06	0.16	0.31	0.36	0.65	0.34	Income $
	—	—	—	0.62	0.00	0.00	0.00	0.00	0.00	0.00	Capital Gains $
	—	—	—	0.25	0.25	0.25	0.25	0.25	0.25	Expense Ratio %
	—	—	—	0.00	0.14	0.34	0.39	0.45	0.53	Income Ratio %
	—	—	—	—	77	49	57	37	45	30	Turnover Rate %
	—	—	—	35	112	513	625	1,064	1,280	1,248	Net Assets $mil

Rating and Risk

Time Period	Morningstar Rtn vs Cat	Morningstar Risk vs Cat	Morningstar Risk-Adj Rating
3 Yr	+Avg	-Avg	★★★★
5 Yr	+Avg	Low	★★★★★
10 Yr	—	—	—

Other Measures	Standard Index S&P 500	Best Fit Index Mstar Small Core
Alpha	-0.7	-2.4
Beta	1.58	0.96
R-Squared	69	94
Standard Deviation	13.04	
Mean	13.50	
Sharpe Ratio	0.79	

Morningstar's Take by Sonya Morris 12-31-06

There's a case to be made for iShares S&P 600 Growth.

When it comes to indexing, cost is king because index funds use their low expense ratios to attempt to gain an edge over their actively managed rivals. This ETF certainly competes in that regard. It boasts an expense ratio of 0.25%, which is a full percentage point cheaper than the typical small-cap fund. Nevertheless, its price is undercut by Vanguard Small Cap Growth ETF, which levies a tiny 0.12% fee. That gives the Vanguard fund a notable edge, and for that reason, we think it's a preferable choice. But there's still justification for owning this ETF, particularly for investors who like to sidestep some of the volatility that comes with investing in small-growth stocks.

The committee that oversees the construction of Standard & Poor's indexes, including this ETF's benchmark, the S&P Small Cap 600/Citigroup Growth Index, applies financial-viability screens, which are intended to keep more-speculative fare

out of the index. For instance, to be admitted to an S&P index, a firm must have produced four straight quarters of profits. The committee also won't admit an IPO to an index until it has seasoned for a period of time. And that time period can vary based on the committee's judgment. For instance, Google had traded publicly for almost two years before it was added to the S&P 500.

While we generally prefer index methodologies that are more transparent and quantitatively based, S&P's caution has helped quell volatility at this ETF. Based on its three-year standard deviation of returns (a statistical measure of volatility), this fund has been less volatile than 85% of its peers. Yet it hasn't sacrificed returns to achieve that result. Its long-term returns rank in the category's top 20%.

Granted, this ETF is likely to lag when racier stocks are in favor, but given its low price tag, we think it will be competitive over the long haul.

Address:	45 Fremont Street San Francisco CA 94105 800-474-2737
Web Address:	www.ishares.com
Inception:	07-24-00*
Advisor:	Barclays Global Fund Advisers

Management Fee:	0.25%		
Expense Projections:	3Yr:$80	5Yr:$141	10Yr:$318
Income Distrib:	Quarterly		
Exchange:	NYSE		

Portfolio Analysis 12-31-06

Share change since 11-06 Total Stocks:350

	Sector	PE	Tot Ret%	% Assets
⊕ Manitowoc Company, Inc.	Business	28.6	137.42	1.28
⊖ Frontier Oil Corporation	Energy	8.4	53.75	1.12
⊖ Global Payments, Inc.	Business	27.9	-0.49	1.11
⊖ NVR, Inc.	Consumer	6.7	-8.12	1.08
⊖ Cerner Corporation	Software	37.3	0.10	1.04
⊖ Helix Energy Solutions G	Energy	11.3	-12.59	1.03
⊖ Cabot Oil & Gas Corporat	Energy	8.6	34.90	1.02
⊕ Trimble Navigation Ltd.	Hardware	28.3	42.94	0.98
⊖ Respironics Inc.	Health	26.8	1.83	0.97
⊖ Philadelphia Consolidate	Financial	13.4	38.26	0.90
⊕ Idexx Laboratories	Health	29.5	10.17	0.88
⊖ Hologic, Inc.	Health	57.7	24.68	0.87
⊖ Pediatrix Medical Group,	Health	24.8	10.42	0.84
⊖ NBTY, Inc.	Health	25.7	155.82	0.83
⊖ Unit Corporation	Energy	7.1	-11.96	0.79
⊖ Landstar System, Inc.	Business	17.4	-8.30	0.77
⊖ East West Bancorp, Inc.	Financial	16.0	-2.41	0.77
⊕ FactSet Research Systems	Business	34.4	37.91	0.75
⊖ Oceaneering Internationa	Energy	19.1	59.50	0.75
⊖ FLIR Systems, Inc.	Ind Mtrls	28.7	42.54	0.74

Current Investment Style

Value Blnd Growth — Large Mid Small

	Market Cap	%
	Giant	0.0
	Large	0.0
	Mid	33.8
	Small	61.6
	Micro	4.6
	Avg $mil:	1,474

Value Measures		Rel Category
Price/Earnings	18.19	0.86
Price/Book	2.81	0.94
Price/Sales	1.49	1.01
Price/Cash Flow	8.61	1.22
Dividend Yield %	0.32	1.03

Growth Measures	%	Rel Category
Long-Term Erngs	15.59	0.89
Book Value	16.88	1.40
Sales	1.30	0.14
Cash Flow	20.93	0.99
Historical Erngs	22.80	1.13

Profitability	%	Rel Category
Return on Equity	17.78	1.21
Return on Assets	10.33	1.30
Net Margin	11.49	1.18

Sector Weightings	% of Stocks	Rel S&P 500	3 Year High Low
⊙ Info	13.76	0.69	
🖳 Software	7.64	2.21	9 7
🖵 Hardware	4.88	0.53	10 3
🎙 Media	0.00	0.00	0 0
☎ Telecom	1.24	0.35	1 1
☞ Service	52.11	1.13	
🩺 Health	16.32	1.35	21 16
🛍 Consumer	12.83	1.68	15 11
📊 Business	12.06	2.85	13 9
💲 Financial	10.90	0.49	14 9
◩ Mfg	34.14	1.01	
🏭 Goods	7.90	0.92	8 5
⚙ Ind Mtrls	13.66	1.14	20 13
🔥 Energy	12.44	1.27	13 3
💡 Utilities	0.14	0.04	1 0

Composition

● Cash		0.1
● Stocks		99.9
● Bonds		0.0
● Other		0.0
Foreign (% of Stock)		0.0

iShares SP Small 600 IJR

	Market Price $65.21	Mstar Category Small Blend

Morningstar Fair Value

Price/Fair Value Ratio — Coverage Rate % —

Management

Barclays Global Fund Advisors is the advisor. The firm is the world's largest manager of indexed portfolios. On a daily basis, this ETF is comanaged by Patrick O'Connor and S. Jane Leung . O'Connor began managing index funds at Barclays in 1999. Leung's tenure at the firm began in 2001.

Methodology

The fund tracks the S&P SmallCap 600 Index. To join the bogy, stocks have to be U.S. companies with market caps between $300 million and $1 billion, good liquidity, and at least four profitable quarters. S&P defines profits as GAAP net income excluding discontinued operations and extraordinary items.

Morningstar Rating	Return	Risk	Yield	NAV	Avg Daily Vol. (k)	52 wk High/Low
★★★ Neutral	Neutral	Average	0.8%	$66.01	845	$67.22 - $57.54

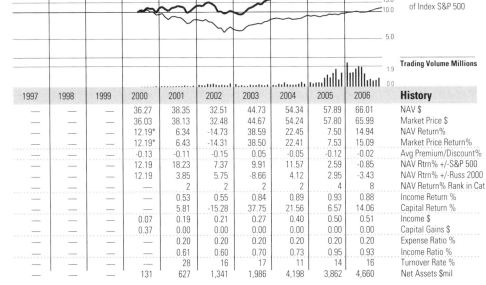

Growth of $10,000
■ Investment Value of ETF
— Investment Value of Index S&P 500

Trading Volume Millions

1997	1998	1999	2000	2001	2002	2003	2004	2005	2006	History
—	—	—	36.27	38.35	32.51	44.73	54.34	57.89	66.01	NAV $
—	—	—	36.03	38.13	32.48	44.67	54.24	57.80	65.99	Market Price $
—	—	—	12.19*	6.34	-14.73	38.59	22.45	7.50	14.94	NAV Return%
—	—	—	12.19*	6.43	-14.31	38.50	22.41	7.53	15.09	Market Price Return%
—	—	—	-0.13	-0.11	-0.15	0.05	-0.05	-0.12	-0.02	Avg Premium/Discount%
—	—	—	12.19	18.23	7.37	9.91	11.57	2.59	-0.85	NAV Rtrn% +/-S&P 500
—	—	—	12.19	3.85	5.75	-8.66	4.12	2.95	-3.43	NAV Rtrn% +/-Russ 2000
—	—	—	—	2	2	2	2	4	8	NAV Return% Rank in Cat
—	—	—	—	0.53	0.55	0.84	0.89	0.93	0.88	Income Return %
—	—	—	—	5.81	-15.28	37.75	21.56	6.57	14.06	Capital Return %
—	—	—	0.07	0.19	0.21	0.27	0.40	0.50	0.51	Income $
—	—	—	0.37	0.00	0.00	0.00	0.00	0.00	0.00	Capital Gains $
—	—	—	—	0.20	0.20	0.20	0.20	0.20	0.20	Expense Ratio %
—	—	—	—	0.61	0.60	0.70	0.73	0.95	0.93	Income Ratio %
—	—	—	—	28	16	17	11	14	16	Turnover Rate %
—	—	—	131	627	1,341	1,986	4,198	3,862	4,660	Net Assets $mil

Performance 12-31-06

Historic Quarterly NAV Returns

	1st Qtr	2nd Qtr	3rd Qtr	4th Qtr	Total
2002	6.94	-6.56	-18.62	4.86	-14.73
2003	-5.83	19.80	7.05	14.76	38.59
2004	6.18	3.56	-1.41	12.95	22.45
2005	-2.10	3.89	5.34	0.34	7.50
2006	12.80	-4.60	-0.93	7.82	14.94

Trailing	NAV Return%	Market Return%	NAV Rtrn% +/-S&P 500	%Rank Cat.(NAV)
3 Mo	7.82	7.93	1.12	12
6 Mo	6.82	6.74	-5.92	10
1 Yr	14.94	15.09	-0.85	8
3 Yr Avg	14.80	14.85	4.36	2
5 Yr Avg	12.33	12.45	6.14	2
10 Yr Avg	—	—	—	—

Tax Analysis	Tax-Adj Return%	Tax-Cost Ratio
3 Yr (estimated)	14.47	0.29
5 Yr (estimated)	12.02	0.28
10 Yr (estimated)	—	—

Rating and Risk

Time Period	Morningstar Rtn vs Cat	Morningstar Risk vs Cat	Morningstar Risk-Adj Rating
3 Yr	+Avg	Avg	★★★★
5 Yr	Avg	Avg	★★★
10 Yr	—	—	—

Other Measures	Standard Index S&P 500	Best Fit Index Mstar Small Core
Alpha	0.5	-1.3
Beta	1.58	0.97
R-Squared	71	98
Standard Deviation	12.86	
Mean	14.80	
Sharpe Ratio	0.89	

Morningstar's Take by Sonya Morris 12-31-06

iShares S&P Small Cap 600 has its charms, but it faces a tough challenge from a cheaper rival.

Some contend that indexing doesn't work in small-cap territory. They argue that the small-cap market is less efficient, resulting in mispricings that active managers can exploit to their advantage. You couldn't prove that by this ETF though. Its five-year trailing returns outclass 60% of its small-blend rivals. Plus, it's delivered those results without adding any undue volatility.

Accordingly, we think there's a case to be made for owning this ETF. It provides broad exposure to small caps at a very low price. In fact, its low price advantage is even more pronounced in the relatively expensive small-blend category. Its tiny expense ratio of 0.20% is well below the category norm of 1.07%. That gives it a huge head start over the average actively managed category fund.

However, even though this ETF is cheap, there's a way to get the same exposure for even less. Vanguard Tax Managed Small Cap attempts to

mimic the S&P Small-Cap 600 Index, which is also this ETF's benchmark. Yet the Vanguard fund charges a lower expense ratio of 0.14%. What's more, investors don't have to pay brokerage commissions to invest in that fund, as they do with this ETF.

The Vanguard fund has also been more tax-efficient than this ETF, despite the fact that an ETF's structure gives them certain tax advantages over traditional mutual funds. Vanguard Tax-Managed Small Cap's five-year tax-adjusted returns are slightly better than this ETFs, and its three-year tax-cost ratio (which expresses tax costs in the form of an expense ratio) of 0.11% is less than half this ETF's 0.29% result.

Accordingly, the Vanguard fund is our first choice for indexlike small-cap exposure. But even so, shareholders here certainly don't own a lemon. This ETF provides a low-cost way to fill out the small-cap slot of your portfolio.

Address:	45 Fremont Street San Francisco CA 94105 800-474-2737	Management Fee:	0.20%	
		Expense Projections:	3Yr:$64 5Yr:$113 10Yr:$255	
Web Address:	www.ishares.com	Income Distrib:	Quarterly	
Inception:	05-22-00*	Exchange:	NYSE	
Advisor:	Barclays Global Fund Advisers			

Portfolio Analysis 12-31-06

Share change since 11-06 Total Stocks:599

	Sector	PE	Tot Ret%	% Assets
⊕ Manitowoc Company, Inc.	Business	28.6	137.42	0.63
⊕ Energen Corporation	Energy	14.7	30.75	0.58
⊕ Frontier Oil Corporation	Energy	8.4	53.75	0.54
⊕ Global Payments, Inc.	Business	27.9	-0.49	0.54
⊕ Veritas DGC, Inc.	Energy	35.1	141.28	0.53
⊖ NVR, Inc.	Consumer	6.7	-8.12	0.52
⊕ Cimarex Energy Company	Energy	6.4	-14.79	0.52
⊕ Southern Union Company	Energy	—	20.09	0.52
⊕ Essex Property Trust	Financial	NMF	44.29	0.52
⊕ Cerner Corporation	Software	37.3	0.10	0.51
⊕ Helix Energy Solutions G	Energy	11.3	-12.59	0.50
⊕ Cabot Oil & Gas Corporat	Energy	8.6	34.90	0.50
⊕ UGI Corporation	Utilities	16.5	36.31	0.49
⊕ Trimble Navigation Ltd.	Hardware	28.3	42.94	0.48
⊕ Atmos Energy Corporation	Utilities	17.5	27.57	0.48
⊕ Phillips-Van Heusen Corp	Goods	19.3	55.45	0.48
⊕ Respironics Inc.	Health	26.8	1.83	0.47
⊕ Shaw Group	Ind Mtrls	50.8	15.16	0.46
⊕ Carpenter Technology Cor	Ind Mtrls	12.1	46.55	0.45
⊕ Corn Products Internatio	Goods	22.7	45.73	0.44

Current Investment Style

Value Blnd Growth — Large Mid Small

Market Cap	%
Giant	0.0
Large	0.0
Mid	25.5
Small	66.0
Micro	8.5

Avg $mil: 1,272

Value Measures		Rel Category
Price/Earnings	17.43	0.99
Price/Book	2.24	1.08
Price/Sales	1.03	1.00
Price/Cash Flow	7.60	1.17
Dividend Yield %	0.84	0.53

Growth Measures	%	Rel Category
Long-Term Erngs	13.93	1.05
Book Value	9.62	1.76
Sales	-2.89	NMF
Cash Flow	15.15	1.67
Historical Erngs	17.27	1.45

Profitability	%	Rel Category
Return on Equity	14.17	1.23
Return on Assets	8.19	1.24
Net Margin	10.11	1.03

Sector Weightings	% of Stocks	Rel S&P 500	3 Year High Low	
↻ Info	13.35	0.67		
🖥 Software	4.91	1.42	5	5
💻 Hardware	7.05	0.76	8	6
🎙 Media	0.09	0.02	0	0
📶 Telecom	1.30	0.37	1	1
⊕ Service	48.53	1.05		
🏥 Health	10.48	0.87	14	10
🛒 Consumer	10.45	1.37	14	10
💼 Business	11.34	2.68	12	9
💲 Financial	16.26	0.73	17	14
⚒ Mfg	38.13	1.13		
🏠 Goods	7.83	0.92	8	6
⚙ Ind Mtrls	17.93	1.50	21	18
🔋 Energy	8.59	0.88	10	6
🔌 Utilities	3.78	1.08	4	3

Composition

● Cash		0.1
● Stocks		99.9
● Bonds		0.0
○ Other		0.0
Foreign		0.1
(% of Stock)		

MORNINGSTAR® ETFs 150

iShares SP 600 Value IJS

	Market Price	Mstar Category
	$74.51	Small Value

Morningstar Fair Value

Price/Fair Value Ratio —   Coverage Rate % —

Management

This ETF is advised by Barclays Global Fund Advisors, the ETF market leader and the world's largest manager of indexed portfolios. It's run on a day-to-day basis by Patrick O'Connor and S. Jane Leung. O'Connor assumed a managerial role at Barclays beginning in 1999, while Leung's tenure at the firm began in 2001.

Methodology

This fund tracks the S&P SmallCap 600/Citigroup Value Index. The bogy relies on seven growth and valuation measures to classify stocks. The factors are dividend yield; price-book, -sales and -cash flow; and five-year earnings, sales, and internal-growth rates. A third of the index's market capitalization ends up in each value, core, or growth bucket, but stocks in the middle zone can end up in both style indexes in proportion to their style scores. The overlap should reduce turnover caused by stocks moving from one style to another. It rebalances annually in December.

	Morningstar Rating	Return	Risk	Yield	NAV	Avg Daily Vol. (k)	52 wk High/Low
	★★★ Neutral	Neutral	Above Avg	1.1%	$75.42	130	$76.52 - $64.82

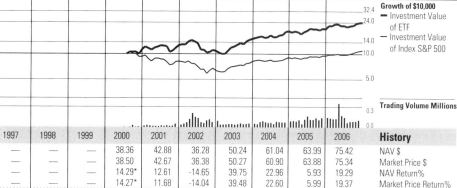

Growth of $10,000
■ Investment Value of ETF
— Investment Value of Index S&P 500

Trading Volume Millions

1997	1998	1999	2000	2001	2002	2003	2004	2005	2006	History
—	—	—	38.36	42.88	36.28	50.24	61.04	63.99	75.42	NAV $
—	—	—	38.50	42.67	36.38	50.27	60.90	63.88	75.34	Market Price $
—	—	—	14.29*	12.61	-14.65	39.75	22.96	5.93	19.29	NAV Return%
—	—	—	14.27*	11.68	-14.04	39.48	22.60	5.99	19.37	Market Price Return%
—	—	—	-0.04	-0.01	0.03	0.11	-0.01	-0.20	-0.14	Avg Premium/Discount%
—	—	—	14.29	24.50	7.45	11.07	12.08	1.02	3.50	NAV Rtrn% +/-S&P 500
—	—	—	14.29	-1.41	-3.22	-6.28	0.71	1.22	-4.19	NAV Rtrn% +/-Russ 2000 VL
—	—	—	—	3	3	3	3	5	6	NAV Return% Rank in Cat
—	—	—	—	0.77	0.81	1.05	1.35	1.07	1.35	Income Return %
—	—	—	—	11.84	-15.46	38.70	21.61	4.86	17.94	Capital Return %
—	—	—	0.13	0.29	0.35	0.38	0.68	0.65	0.86	Income $
—	—	—	0.17	0.00	0.00	0.00	0.00	0.00	0.00	Capital Gains $
—	—	—	—	0.25	0.25	0.25	0.25	0.25	0.25	Expense Ratio %
—	—	—	—	0.98	0.92	0.99	0.95	1.36	1.20	Income Ratio %
—	—	—	—	17	14	14	12	13	16	Turnover Rate %
—	—	—	42	283	704	864	1,618	1,606	1,961	Net Assets $mil

Performance 12-31-06

Historic Quarterly NAV Returns

	1st Qtr	2nd Qtr	3rd Qtr	4th Qtr	Total
2002	10.19	-4.39	-22.54	4.59	-14.65
2003	-8.01	22.65	6.30	16.52	39.75
2004	6.58	2.83	0.21	11.97	22.96
2005	-2.44	4.05	4.11	0.24	5.93
2006	14.21	-4.10	0.53	8.35	19.29

Trailing	NAV Return%	Market Return%	NAV Rtrn% +/-S&P 500	%Rank Cat.(NAV)
3 Mo	8.35	8.37	1.65	7
6 Mo	8.92	9.13	-3.82	7
1 Yr	19.29	19.37	3.50	6
3 Yr Avg	15.82	15.76	5.38	3
5 Yr Avg	13.13	13.22	6.94	3
10 Yr Avg	—	—	—	—

Tax Analysis	Tax-Adj Return%	Tax-Cost Ratio
3 Yr (estimated)	15.36	0.40
5 Yr (estimated)	12.71	0.37
10 Yr (estimated)	—	—

Rating and Risk

Time Period	Morningstar Rtn vs Cat	Morningstar Risk vs Cat	Morningstar Risk-Adj Rating
3 Yr	+Avg	+Avg	★★★★
5 Yr	Avg	+Avg	★★
10 Yr	—	—	—

Other Measures	Standard Index S&P 500	Best Fit Index Mstar Small Core
Alpha	1.4	-0.4
Beta	1.57	0.97
R-Squared	69	97
Standard Deviation	12.93	
Mean	15.82	
Sharpe Ratio	0.96	

Portfolio Analysis 12-31-06

Share change since 11-06 Total Stocks:448

	Sector	PE	Tot Ret%	% Assets
⊕ UGI Corporation	Utilities	16.5	36.31	0.97
⊕ Atmos Energy Corporation	Utilities	17.5	27.57	0.94
⊕ Shaw Group	Ind Mtrls	50.8	15.16	0.90
⊕ URS Corporation	Business	19.4	13.93	0.74
⊕ Kansas City Southern, In	Business	16.6	18.62	0.74
⊕ Colonial Properties Trus	Financial	21.3	18.27	0.73
⊕ Whitney Holding Corporat	Financial	17.5	22.11	0.72
⊕ Piedmont Natural Gas Com	Utilities	20.6	15.05	0.68
⊕ South Financial Group, I	Financial	32.8	-0.90	0.67
⊕ Massey Energy Company	Energy	—	-38.29	0.62
⊕ Anixter International	Ind Mtrls	13.1	38.80	0.62
⊖ Veritas DGC, Inc.	Energy	35.1	141.28	0.62
⊕ Essex Property Trust	Financial	NMF	44.29	0.61
⊕ Emcor Group, Inc.	Business	24.8	68.37	0.61
⊕ Phillips-Van Heusen Corp	Goods	19.3	55.45	0.60
⊖ Carpenter Technology Cor	Ind Mtrls	12.1	46.55	0.60
⊖ Lennox International, In	Business	14.0	10.33	0.59
⊖ Standard Pacific Corp.	Consumer	4.8	-26.78	0.58
⊕ Kilroy Realty Corporatio	Financial	NMF	29.67	0.58
⊕ Belden CDT, Inc.	Hardware	27.5	60.98	0.57

Current Investment Style

Value Blnd Growth — Large/Mid/Small

Market Cap	%
Giant	0.0
Large	0.0
Mid	17.7
Small	70.0
Micro	12.3

Avg $mil: 1,107

Value Measures		Rel Category
Price/Earnings	16.76	1.10
Price/Book	1.88	1.10
Price/Sales	0.79	1.07
Price/Cash Flow	6.78	1.12
Dividend Yield %	1.34	0.65

Growth Measures	%	Rel Category
Long-Term Erngs	12.38	1.16
Book Value	5.95	1.27
Sales	-4.56	NMF
Cash Flow	10.06	2.74
Historical Erngs	12.95	1.36

Profitability	%	Rel Category
Return on Equity	10.68	1.02
Return on Assets	6.16	0.93
Net Margin	8.82	0.89

Sector Weightings	% of Stocks	Rel S&P 500	3 Year High Low	
↻ Info	12.92	0.65		
Software	2.37	0.69	3	1
Hardware	9.06	0.98	9	6
Media	0.16	0.04	0	0
Telecom	1.33	0.38	1	0
☞ Service	45.18	0.98		
Health	5.01	0.42	8	4
Consumer	8.15	1.07	14	8
Business	10.66	2.52	12	9
Financial	21.36	0.96	23	17
Mfg	41.90	1.24		
Goods	7.66	0.90	8	5
Ind Mtrls	21.99	1.84	27	19
Energy	4.94	0.50	9	4
Utilities	7.31	2.09	8	5

Composition

●	Cash	0.1
●	Stocks	99.9
●	Bonds	0.0
○	Other	0.0
	Foreign	0.3
	(% of Stock)	

Morningstar's Take by Sonya Morris 12-31-06

Although it has its strengths, the time might not be right for iShares S&P 600 Value.

Small-value stocks have enjoyed a scorching rally. They've been one of the top-performing domestic-asset classes in recent years. However, it's unrealistic to expect such strong outperformance to continue unabated. Market leadership shifts from time to time, and it wouldn't be surprising to see this category cool off.

If that indeed transpires, this ETF and other category index funds could find it harder to keep up with their actively managed rivals. That's because index funds must remain fully invested in their selected universe. They have no place to hide when their category falls on hard times. Meanwhile, active managers can "cheat" by drifting up the market-cap ladder or holding cash. As a result, index funds don't perform well during inflection points in their universes. The year 2002 provides a case in point. During that year, the typical small-value fund lost 9.6%, while the average

category index fund lost 14.2%.

Furthermore, given this category's overheated conditions, now's not the time to jump into a small-value fund with both feet. It makes sense to ease into the category by investing a set amount on a regular basis (a practice that is often referred to as dollar-cost averaging). That argues in favor of traditional mutual funds because investors don't have to pay a brokerage commission each time they invest in them, as they do with ETFs. There's a competing mutual fund that offers similar exposure to small-value stocks at a slightly lower price: Vanguard Small Value Index charges an expense ratio of 0.23%, compared with this ETF's 0.25% levy.

Investors could certainly do worse than this ETF. But given current market conditions, shareholders here have good reason to temper their expectations. This ETF can't deliver double-digit returns indefinitely.

Address:	45 Fremont Street San Francisco CA 94105 800-474-2737	Management Fee:	0.25%		
		Expense Projections:	3Yr:$80	5Yr:$141	10Yr:$318
		Income Distrib:	Quarterly		
Web Address:	www.ishares.com	Exchange:	NYSE		
Inception:	07-24-00*				
Advisor:	Barclays Global Fund Advisers				

iShares Silver Trust SLV

	Market Price	Mstar Category
	$124.25	Specialty-Precious Metals

Morningstar Fair Value

Price/Fair Value Ratio	Coverage Rate %
—	—

Management

Barclay's Bank is this ETF's sponsor, but the Bank of New York serves as the fund's trustee and handles its day-to-day administration. The custodian of the silver bullion is JPMorgan Chase, and the physical metal is stored in its London branch.

Methodology

Unlike most ETFs, this fund does not track an index. Instead, the fund directly owns silver bullion, and its price will reflect the market price of silver less the expenses of the fund.

Morningstar Rating	Return	Risk	Yield	NAV	Avg Daily Vol. (k)	52 wk High/Low
— Not Rated	Not Rated		—	$128.57	493	$148.60 - $96.25

Growth of $10,000
- Investment Value of ETF
- Investment Value of Index MSCI EAFE

13.2
12.0
10.7
10.0
8.0

Trading Volume Millions

0.4
0.3

	1997	1998	1999	2000	2001	2002	2003	2004	2005	2006	History
	—	—	—	—	—	—	—	—	—	128.57	NAV $
	—	—	—	—	—	—	—	—	—	128.64	Market Price $
	—	—	—	—	—	—	—	—	—	2.41*	NAV Return%
	—	—	—	—	—	—	—	—	—	-6.86*	Market Price Return%
	—	—	—	—	—	—	—	—	—	1.84	Avg Premium/Discount%
	—	—	—	—	—	—	—	—	—	2.41	NAV Rtrn% +/-MSCI EAFE
	—	—	—	—	—	—	—	—	—	2.41	NAV Rtrn% +/-MSCI W Me&M
	—	—	—	—	—	—	—	—	—	—	NAV Return% Rank in Cat
	—	—	—	—	—	—	—	—	—	—	Income Return %
	—	—	—	—	—	—	—	—	—	—	Capital Return %
	—	—	—	—	—	—	—	—	—	0.00	Income $
	—	—	—	—	—	—	—	—	—	0.00	Capital Gains $
	—	—	—	—	—	—	—	—	—	—	Expense Ratio %
	—	—	—	—	—	—	—	—	—	—	Income Ratio %
	—	—	—	—	—	—	—	—	—	—	Turnover Rate %
	—	—	—	—	—	—	—	—	—	1,562	Net Assets $mil

Performance 12-31-06

Historic Quarterly NAV Returns

	1st Qtr	2nd Qtr	3rd Qtr	4th Qtr	Total
2002	—	—	—	—	—
2003	—	—	—	—	—
2004	—	—	—	—	—
2005	—	—	—	—	—*
2006	—	—	7.82	11.55	—*

Trailing	NAV Return%	Market Return%+/-MSCI EAFE	NAV Rtrn%	%Rank Cat.(NAV)
3 Mo	11.55	12.34	1.20	4
6 Mo	20.27	15.49	5.58	4
1 Yr	—	—	—	—
3 Yr Avg	—	—	—	—
5 Yr Avg	—	—	—	—
10 Yr Avg	—	—	—	—

Tax Analysis	Tax-Adj Return%	Tax-Cost Ratio
3 Yr (estimated)	—	—
5 Yr (estimated)	—	—
10 Yr (estimated)	—	—

Rating and Risk

Time Period	Morningstar Rtn vs Cat	Morningstar Risk vs Cat	Morningstar Risk-Adj Rating
3 Yr	—	—	—
5 Yr	—	—	—
10 Yr	—	—	—

Other Measures	Standard Index S&P 500	Best Fit Index
Alpha	—	—
Beta	—	—
R-Squared	—	—
Standard Deviation	—	
Mean	—	
Sharpe Ratio	—	

Portfolio Analysis 12-31-06

Share change since 11-06 Total Stocks:0	Sector	Country	% Assets
⊕ Silver Bullion			100.00

Morningstar's Take by Sonya Morris 12-31-06

Don't follow the crowd.

iShares Silver Trust proved to be one of the most popular ETFs of 2006. Demand was stoked by the bull market in silver prices, as well as the early success of gold ETFs. But shareholders here got an early and unpleasant surprise. In only its second full month of existence, this ETF plunged 18.5% in June 2006, offering an early lesson in the risks of precious-metals investing. Indeed, this ETF's volatility has been on full display lately. After rallying 13.2% in November, it tanked in December, losing 6% for the month. And there could be more downside risk here, with silver trending near 25-year highs.

There's a limited argument for investing in this ETF and similar funds that provide exposure to gold. Precious-metal prices are not highly correlated with stocks, so they can add a measure of diversification to a portfolio. But to benefit from that, investors must be able to overlook the volatility that these funds can experience and remain focused on the long term.

Some turn to gold and silver ETFs as hedges against inflation, and it's true that gold and silver prices have generally tracked inflation over time. But precious metals haven't returned much more than inflation over the long haul. Gold and silver generally perform best when economic conditions are at their worst. For example, both thrived in the 1970s when the economy suffered from rampant inflation. But an investor who had simply stuck with stocks through that period would have ended up much wealthier. Plus, unlike gold, silver experiences some industrial demand, so it's not entirely immune from economic cycles and may not be a foolproof inflation hedge.

Finally, this ETF has special--and unattractive--tax treatment. Silver is taxed as a collectible, and long-term gains are taxed at a maximum rate of 28%, rather than the lower 15% rate afforded gains on equities.

We'd take a pass on this ETF.

Address:	iShares Funds
	United States
	800-474-2737
Web Address:	www.ishares.com
Inception:	04-28-06*
Advisor:	Barclays Global Investors

Management Fee:	0.50%		
Expense Projections:	3Yr: —	5Yr: —	10Yr: —
Income Distrib:	Annually		
Exchange:	AMEX		

Current Investment Style

Value Blnd Growth — Large Mid Small

Market Cap	%
Giant	—
Large	—
Mid	—
Small	—
Micro	—

Avg $mil:

Value Measures	Rel Category
Price/Earnings	—
Price/Book	—
Price/Sales	—
Price/Cash Flow	—
Dividend Yield %	—

Growth Measures	%	Rel Category
Long-Term Erngs	—	—
Book Value	—	—
Sales	—	—
Cash Flow	—	—
Historical Erngs	—	—

Composition

Cash	0.0	Bonds	0.0
Stocks	0.0	Other	100.0
Foreign (% of Stock)			0.0

Sector Weightings

	% of Stocks	Rel MSCI EAFE	3 Year High	Low
⊙ Info	0.00	0.00		
Software	—	0.00		
Hardware	—	0.00		
Media	—	0.00		
Telecom	—	0.00		
☞ Service	0.00	0.00		
Health	—	0.00		
Consumer	—	0.00		
Business	—	0.00		
Financial	—	0.00		
⊐ Mfg	0.00	0.00		
Goods	—	0.00		
Ind Mtrls	—	0.00		
Energy	—	0.00		
Utilities	—	0.00		

Regional Exposure % Stock

UK/W. Europe	0	N. America	0
Japan	0	Latn America	0
Asia X Japan	0	Other	100

Country Exposure % Stock

MORNINGSTAR ETFs 150

MidCap SPDR Trust MDY

	Market Price $146.45	Mstar Category Mid-Cap Blend

Morningstar Fair Value

Price/Fair Value Ratio
0.96 Fairly valued

Coverage Rate %
81 Fair

Management

A management team at the Bank of New York, the fund's trustee, is in charge here.

Methodology

This fund seeks to duplicate as closely as possible the holdings and returns of the S&P MidCap 400 Index. The result is a broadly diversified portfolio of mid-cap stocks. The fund is structured as a unit investment trust, which inhibits it from reinvesting dividends immediately. That can lead to a cash drag on this fund relative to its rivals that have an open-end structure.

Morningstar Rating ★★★★ Above Avg	Return Above Avg	Risk Average	Yield 1.2%	NAV $146.46	Avg Daily Vol. (k) 2,673	52 wk High/Low $150.09 - $130.04

Growth of $10,000
— Investment Value of ETF
— Investment Value of Index S&P 500

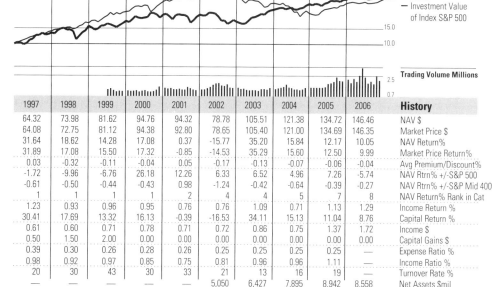

Trading Volume Millions

	1997	1998	1999	2000	2001	2002	2003	2004	2005	2006	History
	64.32	73.98	81.62	94.76	94.32	78.78	105.51	121.38	134.72	146.46	NAV $
	64.08	72.75	81.12	94.38	92.80	78.65	105.40	121.00	134.69	146.35	Market Price $
	31.64	18.62	14.28	17.08	0.37	-15.77	35.20	15.84	12.17	10.05	NAV Return%
	31.89	17.08	15.50	17.32	-0.85	-14.53	35.29	15.60	12.50	9.99	Market Price Return%
	0.03	-0.32	-0.11	-0.04	0.05	-0.17	-0.13	-0.07	-0.06	-0.04	Avg Premium/Discount%
	-1.72	-9.96	-6.76	26.18	12.26	6.33	6.52	4.96	7.26	-5.74	NAV Rtrn% +/-S&P 500
	-0.61	-0.50	-0.44	-0.43	0.98	-1.24	-0.42	-0.64	-0.39	-0.27	NAV Rtrn% +/-S&P Mid 400
	1	1	1	1	2	4	4	5	7	8	NAV Return% Rank in Cat
	1.23	0.93	0.96	0.95	0.76	0.76	1.09	0.71	1.13	1.29	Income Return %
	30.41	17.69	13.32	16.13	-0.39	-16.53	34.11	15.13	11.04	8.76	Capital Return %
	0.61	0.60	0.71	0.78	0.71	0.72	0.86	0.75	1.37	1.72	Income $
	0.50	1.50	2.00	0.00	0.00	0.00	0.00	0.00	0.00	0.00	Capital Gains $
	0.39	0.30	0.26	0.28	0.26	0.25	0.25	0.25	0.25	—	Expense Ratio %
	0.98	0.92	0.97	0.85	0.75	0.81	0.96	0.96	1.11	—	Income Ratio %
	20	30	43	30	33	21	13	16	19	—	Turnover Rate %
	—	—	—	—	—	5,050	6,427	7,895	8,942	8,558	Net Assets $mil

Performance 12-31-06

Historic Quarterly NAV Returns

	1st Qtr	2nd Qtr	3rd Qtr	4th Qtr	Total
2002	5.35	-9.36	-16.59	5.76	-15.77
2003	-4.51	17.53	6.52	13.10	35.20
2004	5.00	0.89	-2.17	11.78	15.84
2005	-0.47	4.19	4.78	3.23	12.17
2006	7.60	-3.21	-1.15	6.90	10.05

Trailing	NAV Return%	Market Return%	NAV Rtrn% +/-S&P 500	%Rank Cat.(NAV)
3 Mo	6.90	6.72	0.20	10
6 Mo	5.67	5.85	-7.07	9
1 Yr	10.05	9.99	-5.74	8
3 Yr Avg	12.66	12.67	2.22	5
5 Yr Avg	10.24	10.59	4.05	4
10 Yr Avg	13.07	13.12	4.65	1

Tax Analysis	Tax-Adj Return%	Tax-Cost Ratio
3 Yr (estimated)	12.27	0.35
5 Yr (estimated)	9.87	0.34
10 Yr (estimated)	12.47	0.53

Rating and Risk

Time Period	Morningstar Rtn vs Cat	Morningstar Risk vs Cat	Morningstar Risk-Adj Rating
3 Yr	Avg	Avg	★★★
5 Yr	Avg	Avg	★★★
10 Yr	+Avg	Avg	★★★★

Other Measures	Standard Index S&P 500	Best Fit Index S&P Mid 400
Alpha	-0.1	-0.4
Beta	1.34	1.00
R-Squared	80	100
Standard Deviation	10.30	
Mean	12.66	
Sharpe Ratio	0.90	

Portfolio Analysis 11-30-06

Share change since 08-06 Total Stocks:400	Sector	PE	Tot Ret%	% Assets
⊖ Precision Castparts Corp	Ind Mtrls	24.0	51.40	0.91
⊖ Expeditors International	Business	32.9	20.54	0.86
⊖ Noble Energy, Inc.	Energy	11.9	22.48	0.84
⊖ Ensco International, Inc	Energy	11.6	13.12	0.71
⊖ CH Robinson Worldwide, I	Business	28.4	11.88	0.68
⊖ Lam Research Corporation	Hardware	21.6	41.87	0.67
⊖ Microchip Technology, In	Hardware	26.2	4.37	0.65
⊖ Developers Diversified R	Financial	41.1	39.65	0.63
⊖ Southwestern Energy Comp	Energy	33.4	-2.48	0.63
⊖ MEMC Electronic Material	Hardware	30.8	76.54	0.59
⊖ Newfield Exploration Com	Energy	13.8	-8.23	0.58
⊖ Varian Medical Systems,	Health	26.4	-5.50	0.57
⊖ Everest Re Group, Ltd.	Financial	—	-1.62	0.57
⊖ Manpower, Inc.	Business	20.6	62.53	0.55
⊖ Macerich Company	Financial	—	33.91	0.55
⊖ Sepracor, Inc.	Health	NMF	19.34	0.54
⊖ Amphenol Corporation	Hardware	24.4	40.57	0.54
⊖ Cooper Cameron Corporati	Energy	22.5	28.14	0.54
⊖ American Eagle Outfitter	Consumer	20.7	105.48	0.54
⊖ Abercrombie & Fitch Comp	Consumer	16.5	8.01	0.53

Morningstar's Take by Sonya Morris 12-31-06

Old-timer MidCap SPDRs is losing ground to younger upstarts.

This is the granddaddy of all mid-cap ETFs. It was launched back in 1995, giving it the longest track record of any mid-cap ETF. In that time, it has gathered almost $8.6 billion in assets, making it one of the largest mid-blend funds around. It also sees about 5 times the trading volume of its closest mid-blend ETF competitor. But as is often the case in investing, it's not always wise to follow the crowd. This ETF has rivals that can do the same job better and for less.

The first knock against this fund is its structure. Unlike other ETFs, it is organized as a unit investment trust (as is its sibling SPDRs SPY). Under that structure, it must hold dividends as cash until it makes quarterly distributions to shareholders. That cash horde can be a drag on returns, putting this ETF at a disadvantage to its rivals. It's easy to see the difference when you compare this ETF's results with iShares S&P MidCap 400, which tracks the

same benchmark as this fund. The iShares offering's three-year trailing returns are much closer to its benchmark's and almost half a percentage point greater than this ETF's.

It gets even more difficult to make a case for this ETF when expenses are considered. Although its 0.25% expense ratio is certainly low, iShares S&P MidCap 400 is cheaper at 0.20%. There's no reason to pay up for this fund when you can get identical exposure from a cheaper ETF that tracks the index more closely.

What's more, there are cheaper options still for those willing to consider other mid-cap benchmarks. Vanguard's Mid Cap ETF boasts a tiny 0.13% expense ratio. And its conventional fund twin, Vanguard Mid Capitalization Index, is also cheaper than this ETF, and it can be had without paying brokerage commissions, making it a more appropriate choice for those who'd like to dollar-cost average.

Current Investment Style

Value Blnd Growth | Large Mid Small

	Market Cap	%
	Giant	0.0
	Large	0.0
	Mid	86.7
	Small	13.2
	Micro	0.0
	Avg $mil: 3,441	

Value Measures		Rel Category
Price/Earnings	16.65	1.00
Price/Book	2.33	0.91
Price/Sales	1.12	1.00
Price/Cash Flow	9.60	1.05
Dividend Yield %	1.26	0.92

Growth Measures	%	Rel Category
Long-Term Erngs	12.45	1.02
Book Value	8.15	1.11
Sales	11.51	1.64
Cash Flow	5.54	0.56
Historical Erngs	17.10	0.89

Profitability	%	Rel Category
Return on Equity	15.30	0.89
Return on Assets	8.42	0.98
Net Margin	11.12	1.05

Sector Weightings	% of Stocks	Rel S&P 500	3 Year High Low	
⟲ Info	13.56	0.68		
🖥 Software	2.87	0.83	3	3
🖴 Hardware	8.54	0.92	10	8
🎬 Media	1.50	0.40	3	1
☏ Telecom	0.65	0.19	1	1
☞ Service	52.02	1.13		
🩺 Health	10.86	0.90	12	10
Consumer	11.61	1.52	15	11
Business	12.37	2.92	13	9
Financial	17.18	0.77	20	17
Mfg	34.42	1.02		
Goods	5.22	0.61	7	4
Ind Mtrls	12.66	1.06	13	8
Energy	8.95	0.91	12	8
Utilities	7.59	2.17	8	6

Composition

● Cash	0.0	
● Stocks	100.0	
● Bonds	0.0	
● Other	0.0	
Foreign	0.0	
(% of Stock)		

Address:	PDR Services, 86 Trinity Place New York NY 10006 800-843-2639	Management Fee:	0.10%
		Expense Projections:	3Yr: — 5Yr: — 10Yr: —
Web Address:	www.amex.com/mdy/index.html	Income Distrib:	Quarterly
Inception:	05-04-95	Exchange:	AMEX
Advisor:	PDR Services, SSgA Funds Management Inc		

Nasdaq 100 Trust QQQQ

	Market Price $44.10	Mstar Category Large Growth

Morningstar Fair Value

Price/Fair Value Ratio	Coverage Rate %
0.84 Undervalued	95 Good

Morningstar Rating ★ Lowest	Return Lowest	Risk High	Yield 0.1%	NAV $43.17	Avg Daily Vol. (k) 98,951	52 wk High/Low $44.65 - $35.70

Management

The fund began trading publicly in 1999. A management team with Bank of New York, the fund's trustee, executes trades.

Growth of $10,000
- Investment Value of ETF
- Investment Value of Index S&P 500

Trading Volume Millions

Methodology

The fund, known popularly as Cubes or Qubes, tracks the Nasdaq 100 Index. The index was created in 1985 to represent the 100 largest (in terms of market cap) nonfinancial stocks in the Nasdaq Composite Index. Each company in the fund is reviewed in the fall of every year and must meet two market-capitalization criteria: It must be among the top 150 companies in the larger index, and it must have been among the top 100 in the index during the last annual review. Companies failing one or both of these criteria are replaced. Unlike the S&P 500, the index has no profitability requirement.

1997	1998	1999	2000	2001	2002	2003	2004	2005	2006	History
—	—	92.61	58.40	40.36	24.47	36.49	39.94	40.46	43.17	NAV $
—	—	91.38	58.38	38.91	24.37	36.46	39.91	40.41	43.16	Market Price $
—	—	-1.92*	-36.94	-30.89	-39.37	49.18	10.51	1.64	6.82	NAV Return%
—	—	-1.95*	-36.11	-33.35	-37.37	49.67	10.53	1.58	6.93	Market Price Return%
—	—	-0.20	0.08	-0.05	-0.08	0.00	0.03	-0.02	0.01	Avg Premium/Discount%
—	—	-1.92	-27.84	-19.00	-17.27	20.50	-0.37	-3.27	-8.97	NAV Rtrn% +/-S&P 500
—	—	-1.92	-14.52	-10.47	-11.49	19.43	4.21	-3.62	-2.25	NAV Rtrn% +/-Russ 1000Gr
—	—	1	6	6	6	7	10	13	NAV Return% Rank in Cat
—	—	—	0.00	0.00	0.00	0.06	1.04	0.34	0.13	Income Return %
—	—	—	-36.94	-30.89	-39.37	49.12	9.47	1.30	6.69	Capital Return %
—	—	0.00	0.00	0.00	0.00	0.01	0.38	0.14	0.05	Income $
—	—	0.00	0.00	0.00	0.00	0.00	0.00	0.00	0.00	Capital Gains $
—	—	—	0.18	0.18	0.18	0.20	0.20	0.20	—	Expense Ratio %
—	—	—	-0.16	-0.13	-0.13	-0.03	0.07	1.19	—	Income Ratio %
—	—	—	23	22	13	13	7	15	—	Turnover Rate %
—	—	—	—	—	17,034	25,632	22,196	20,311	17,957	Net Assets $mil

Performance 12-31-06

Historic Quarterly NAV Returns

	1st Qtr	2nd Qtr	3rd Qtr	4th Qtr	Total
2002	-10.41	-27.68	-20.84	18.21	-39.37
2003	3.51	17.96	8.47	12.63	49.18
2004	-2.00	5.43	-6.82	14.79	10.51
2005	-8.51	0.78	7.28	2.76	1.64
2006	3.53	-7.59	5.01	6.32	6.82

Trailing	NAV Return%	Market Return%	NAV Rtrn% +/-S&P 500	%Rank Cat.(NAV)
3 Mo	6.32	6.30	-0.38	15
6 Mo	11.65	11.46	-1.09	15
1 Yr	6.82	6.93	-8.97	13
3 Yr Avg	6.26	6.28	-4.18	7
5 Yr Avg	1.65	2.39	-4.54	6
10 Yr Avg	—	—	—	—

Tax Analysis	Tax-Adj Return%	Tax-Cost Ratio
3 Yr (estimated)	6.08	0.17
5 Yr (estimated)	1.54	0.11
10 Yr (estimated)	—	—

Rating and Risk

Time Period	Morningstar Rtn vs Cat	Morningstar Risk vs Cat	Morningstar Risk-Adj Rating
3 Yr	Avg	High	★★
5 Yr	-Avg	High	★
10 Yr	—	—	—

Other Measures	Standard Index S&P 500	Best Fit Index Mstar Large Growth
Alpha	-8.9	3.5
Beta	1.83	1.48
R-Squared	77	92
Standard Deviation	14.35	
Mean	6.26	
Sharpe Ratio	0.27	

Morningstar's Take by Sonya Morris 12-31-06

In spite of its popularity, Nasdaq 100 Trust Shares holds little appeal for long-term investors.

As measured by average daily trading volume, this exchange-traded fund, which is commonly known as the Cubes, is the most popular ETF by far. On average, more than 110 million shares of this fund change hands every day. That's much higher than its closest competitor, the SPDRs.

Speculators are drawn to this fund because its portfolio features many racy technology stocks. In fact, the tech sector consumes 60% of this ETF's portfolio, while the typical large-growth fund dedicates just 25% to that sector. Because its assets are concentrated primarily in one corner of the market, it's experienced the kind of turbulence that attracts short-term traders but that long-term investors may find difficult to stomach. This ETF's five-year standard deviation of returns (a statistical measure of volatility) is among the highest in the large-growth category. To illustrate the kinds of ups and downs long-term shareholders here have

experienced, after plunging 36.8% during the third quarter of 2001, the fund roared back the following quarter with a 41.6% advance. But this ETF's added risks haven't resulted in extra returns. Its five-year trailing returns lag more than 60% of its peers.

Finally, this fund's quirky profile makes it hard to fit into a diversified portfolio. Even though it's dominated by tech stocks, it's not a pure tech play. In fact, 40% of its portfolio is dedicated to other areas of the market, including health care and consumer services. Yet it's not diversified enough to be used as a core large-growth fund. For example, it has no financial exposure, while the typical large-growth fund allocates 13% of assets to that sector. And even the raciest of growth funds has some energy and industrials exposure, areas that this ETF barely registers.

All told, we think this fund is too hard to pigeonhole and too volatile to use well.

Address:	Nasdaq Global Fds, 9513 Key West Ave Rockville MD 20850 800-843-2639	Management Fee:	0.06%
		Expense Projections:	3Yr:$6 5Yr:$11 10Yr:$26
Web Address:	www.nasdaq.com/QQQQ	Income Distrib:	Annually
Inception:	03-10-99*	Exchange:	XNMS
Advisor:	Nasdaq Global Funds Inc		

Portfolio Analysis 11-30-06

Share change since 09-06 Total Stocks:100	Sector	PE	Tot Ret%	% Assets
⊖ Apple Computer, Inc.	Hardware	37.4	18.01	7.16
⊖ Microsoft Corporation	Software	23.7	15.83	6.61
⊖ Qualcomm, Inc.	Hardware	26.2	-11.32	4.79
⊖ Google, Inc.	Business	58.6	11.00	4.25
⊖ Cisco Systems, Inc.	Hardware	28.8	59.64	3.85
⊖ Intel Corporation	Hardware	20.3	-17.18	2.83
⊖ Oracle Corporation	Software	25.6	40.38	2.73
⊖ Amgen, Inc.	Health	28.0	-13.38	2.54
⊖ Comcast Corporation A	Media	45.0	63.31	2.54
⊖ Starbucks Corporation	Consumer	49.9	18.03	2.44
⊖ eBay, Inc.	Consumer	40.6	-30.43	2.24
⊖ Gilead Sciences, Inc.	Health	41.1	23.51	1.95
⊖ Sears Holdings Corporati	Consumer	19.8	45.36	1.81
⊖ Research in Motion, Ltd.	Hardware	65.2	93.58	1.70
⊖ Adobe Systems Inc.	Software	49.0	11.26	1.50
⊖ Dell, Inc.	Hardware	17.7	-16.23	1.50
⊖ Genzyme Corporation	Health	46.6	-13.00	1.39
⊖ Symantec Corporation	Software	49.6	19.14	1.37
⊕ Celgene Corporation	Health	—	77.56	1.35
⊖ Teva Pharmaceutical Indu	Health	19.6	-27.22	1.30

Current Investment Style

Value Blnd Growth — Large Mid Small

Market Cap	%
Giant	41.7
Large	30.9
Mid	27.4
Small	0.0
Micro	0.0

Avg $mil: 30,780

Value Measures		Rel Category
Price/Earnings	26.09	1.26
Price/Book	4.16	1.27
Price/Sales	2.86	1.62
Price/Cash Flow	15.49	1.38
Dividend Yield %	0.45	0.52

Growth Measures	%	Rel Category
Long-Term Erngs	16.66	1.11
Book Value	9.17	1.15
Sales	21.75	1.85
Cash Flow	21.03	1.44
Historical Erngs	27.46	0.97

Profitability	%	Rel Category
Return on Equity	18.73	0.93
Return on Assets	10.68	1.07
Net Margin	15.68	1.25

Sector Weightings	% of Stocks	Rel S&P 500	3 Year High Low
⊙ Info	59.95	3.00	
Software	17.94	5.20	20 17
Hardware	34.89	3.78	38 34
Media	5.55	1.46	7 5
Telecom	1.57	0.45	3 1
⊂ Service	37.52	0.81	
Health	13.55	1.12	15 13
Consumer	14.26	1.86	15 13
Business	9.71	2.30	10 4
Financial	0.00	0.00	0 0
Mfg	2.55	0.08	
Goods	0.00	0.00	0 0
Ind Mtrls	2.24	0.19	2 2
Energy	0.31	0.03	0 0
Utilities	0.00	0.00	0 0

Composition

	%
Cash	0.0
Stocks	100.0
Bonds	0.0
Other	0.0
Foreign (% of Stock)	4.1

MORNINGSTAR® ETFs 150

PowerShares Div Achievers PFM

	Market Price	Mstar Category
	$17.06	Large Value

Morningstar Fair Value

Price/Fair Value Ratio	Coverage Rate %
0.90 Undervalued	96 Good

Management

PowerShares Capital Management, founded in 2002, manages this fund. John W. Southard Jr. is the lead portfolio manager. He was a senior analyst of Chicago Investment Analytics, a quantitative research firm. He also worked as an analyst and portfolio manager at a unit investment trust firm.

Methodology

This ETF tracks Mergent's Broad Dividend Achievers Index, which holds companies that have increased their dividend payouts for 10 or more consecutive years. The index weights components with a modified market capitalization methodology and employs additional liquidity and investability screens. It is rebalanced quarterly and reconstituted annually.

Morningstar Rating	Return	Risk	Yield	NAV	Avg Daily Vol. (k)	52 wk High/Low
— Not Rated	Not Rated		2.1%	$16.81	24	$17.19 - $14.98

Growth of $10,000
— Investment Value of ETF
— Investment Value of Index S&P 500

Trading Volume Millions

1997	1998	1999	2000	2001	2002	2003	2004	2005	2006	History
—	—	—	—	—	—	—	—	15.05	16.81	NAV $
—	—	—	—	—	—	—	—	15.04	17.13	Market Price $
—	—	—	—	—	—	—	—	12.48*	14.27	NAV Return%
—	—	—	—	—	—	—	—	14.15*	16.48	Market Price Return%
—	—	—	—	—	—	—	—	0.06	0.33	Avg Premium/Discount%
—	—	—	—	—	—	—	—	12.48	-1.52	NAV Rtrn% +/-S&P 500
—	—	—	—	—	—	—	—	12.48	-7.98	NAV Rtrn% +/-Russ 1000 Vl
—	—	—	—	—	—	—	—	—	14	NAV Return% Rank in Cat
—	—	—	—	—	—	—	—	—	2.39	Income Return %
—	—	—	—	—	—	—	—	—	11.88	Capital Return %
—	—	—	—	—	—	—	—	0.08	0.36	Income $
—	—	—	—	—	—	—	—	0.00	0.00	Capital Gains $
—	—	—	—	—	—	—	—	—	0.67	Expense Ratio %
—	—	—	—	—	—	—	—	—	1.81	Income Ratio %
—	—	—	—	—	—	—	—	—	8	Turnover Rate %
—	—	—	—	—	—	—	—	109	50	Net Assets $mil

Performance 12-31-06

Historic Quarterly NAV Returns

	1st Qtr	2nd Qtr	3rd Qtr	4th Qtr	Total
2002	—	—	—	—	—
2003	—	—	—	—	—
2004	—	—	—	—	—
2005	—	—	—	2.12	—*
2006	2.96	0.15	6.72	3.84	14.27

Trailing	NAV Return%	Market Return%	NAV Rtrn% +/-S&P 500	%Rank Cat.(NAV)
3 Mo	3.84	5.47	-2.86	16
6 Mo	10.82	12.33	-1.92	16
1 Yr	14.27	16.48	-1.52	14
3 Yr Avg	—	—	—	—
5 Yr Avg	—	—	—	—
10 Yr Avg	—	—	—	—

Tax Analysis	Tax-Adj Return%	Tax-Cost Ratio
3 Yr (estimated)	—	—
5 Yr (estimated)	—	—
10 Yr (estimated)	—	—

Rating and Risk

Time Period	Morningstar Rtn vs Cat	Morningstar Risk vs Cat	Morningstar Risk-Adj Rating
3 Yr	—	—	—
5 Yr	—	—	—
10 Yr	—	—	—

Other Measures	Standard Index S&P 500	Best Fit Index
Alpha	—	—
Beta	—	—
R-Squared	—	—
Standard Deviation	—	
Mean	—	
Sharpe Ratio	—	

Morningstar's Take by Federico Cepeda 12-31-06

PowerShares Dividend Achievers could achieve more if it were cheaper.

Like any index fund, this exchange-traded fund has certain advantages. There won't be any strategy shifts here, because the fund tracks the Broad Dividend Achievers Index. This index looks for companies whose dividends have increased for at least 10 consecutive years and considers liquidity and profitability measures as a way to filter out financially unhealthy firms. The fund is tax-friendly and low-turnover and provides exposure to companies with high yields, which can serve as an excellent source of income.

This ETF, however, carries serious drawbacks. Expenses are much higher than the 0.31% average for ETFs in the Morningstar's large-value category. Even some actively managed funds in the category, such as Vanguard Dividend Growth, charge much less than this passive offering. Especially when you're investing for income, expenses can be a key determinant of future returns.

Also, the index this ETF tracks is flawed. Although the fund spreads its assets among 317 holdings, it isn't well diversified: 23% of its assets are clustered in its top five holdings. And the fund's fate is linked to the prospects of just a few sectors. Roughly 60% of assets are devoted to stocks in the financials, consumer goods, and health-care sectors. This concentration could be risky for those who seek a dependable source of income. If only two of such sectors perform poorly, almost half of the portfolio will drop in value.

There are other ways for investors to access this fund's strengths while sidestepping its weaknesses. For investors looking for ETFs, Vanguard Value ETF sports a higher yield, at 2.42%, broad diversification, and a slim 0.11% expense ratio. For traditional mutual funds, look to Morningstar's Analyst Picks list in the large-value category.

Portfolio Analysis 11-30-06

Share change since 10-06 Total Stocks:312	Sector	PF	Tot Rtn%	% Assets
⊕ ExxonMobil Corporation	Energy	11.7	39.07	5.62
⊕ General Electric Company	Ind Mtrls	19.8	9.35	5.24
⊕ Citigroup, Inc.	Financial	13.3	19.55	4.43
⊕ Bank of America Corporat	Financial	12.4	20.68	4.38
⊕ Pfizer Inc.	Health	15.1	15.22	3.62
⊕ Procter & Gamble Company	Goods	24.2	13.36	3.60
⊕ Johnson & Johnson	Health	17.4	12.44	3.48
⊕ Wal-Mart Stores, Inc.	Consumer	16.6	0.13	3.47
⊕ American International G	Financial	17.1	6.05	3.30
⊕ Altria Group, Inc.	Goods	15.9	19.87	3.18
⊕ Chevron Corporation	Energy	9.3	33.75	2.87
⊕ IBM	Hardware	16.8	19.77	2.53
⊕ AT&T, Inc.	Telecom	19.2	51.59	2.38
⊕ Wells Fargo Company	Financial	14.7	16.82	2.14
⊕ Coca-Cola Company	Goods	21.5	23.10	1.98
PepsiCo, Inc.	Goods	21.4	7.86	1.84
⊕ Merck & Co., Inc.	Health	18.8	42.66	1.75
Home Depot, Inc.	Consumer	13.7	1.01	1.41
Abbott Laboratories	Health	23.6	26.88	1.29
United Technologies	Ind Mtrls	17.6	13.65	1.17

Current Investment Style

Value Blnd Growth — Large Mid Small

Market Cap	%
Giant	63.3
Large	24.5
Mid	10.0
Small	1.9
Micro	0.2
Avg $mil:	69,980

Value Measures		Rel Category
Price/Earnings	15.07	1.06
Price/Book	2.81	1.17
Price/Sales	1.68	1.26
Price/Cash Flow	10.83	1.40
Dividend Yield %	2.44	0.94

Growth Measures	%	Rel Category
Long-Term Erngs	10.22	1.02
Book Value	11.83	1.65
Sales	11.21	1.31
Cash Flow	-1.83	NMF
Historical Erngs	11.18	0.72

Profitability	%	Rel Category
Return on Equity	21.04	1.21
Return on Assets	11.77	1.18
Net Margin	15.43	1.13

Sector Weightings	% of Stocks	Rel S&P 500	3 Year High Low
☎ Info	6.53	0.33	
📟 Software	0.00	0.00	— —
💻 Hardware	2.77	0.30	— —
🎙 Media	0.89	0.23	— —
📶 Telecom	2.87	0.82	— —
⊕ Service	53.00	1.15	
🏥 Health	13.46	1.12	— —
🛒 Consumer	9.29	1.21	— —
📋 Business	1.46	0.35	— —
💲 Financial	28.79	1.29	— —
⚒ Mfg	40.46	1.20	
🏭 Goods	15.41	1.80	— —
⚙ Ind Mtrls	14.64	1.23	— —
🔥 Energy	8.90	0.91	— —
💡 Utilities	1.51	0.43	— —

Composition

● Cash	0.3
● Stocks	99.7
● Bonds	0.0
● Other	0.0
Foreign	0.0
(% of Stock)	

Address:	301 West Roosevelt Road Wheaton, IL 60187 800-843-2639	Management Fee:	0.40%
		Expense Projections:	3Yr:$301 5Yr: — 10Yr: —
Web Address:	www.powershares.com	Income Distrib:	Quarterly
Inception:	09-15-05*	Exchange:	AMEX
Advisor:	PowerShares Capital Management LLC		

PowerShares Dyn Lg Growth PWB

Market Price $16.73	**Mstar Category** Large Growth	

Morningstar Fair Value

Price/Fair Value Ratio	Coverage Rate %
0.88 Undervalued	93 Good

Management

John W. Southard Jr. is the lead portfolio manager. He is a former senior analyst of Chicago Investment Analytics, a quantitative research firm bought by Charles Schwab in 2000. He also worked as an analyst and portfolio manager at a unit investment trust firm, First Trust Portfolios of Lisle, Ill.

Methodology

This ETF tracks the Amex Large Cap Growth Intellidex, which uses a 25-factor quantitative model to select 50 stocks from the 2000 largest U.S. companies listed on major U.S. exchanges. The factors employed include both technical (price and volume trends) and fundamental (P/E ratios and growth rates) data points. The index follows rules to make sure its sector weights stay close to those of its selection universe. It also caps position sizes and employs a stratified weighting scheme to keep large stocks from dominating the portfolio. The Intellidex reconstitutes quarterly.

Performance 12-31-06

Historic Quarterly NAV Returns

	1st Qtr	2nd Qtr	3rd Qtr	4th Qtr	Total
2002	—	—	—	—	—
2003	—	—	—	—	—
2004	—	—	—	—	—
2005	—	1.99	3.90	2.74	—*
2006	4.10	-6.47	2.60	5.59	5.47

Trailing	NAV Return%	Market Return%	NAV Rtrn% +/-S&P 500	%Rank Cat.(NAV)
3 Mo	5.59	5.62	-1.11	15
6 Mo	8.33	8.21	-4.41	15
1 Yr	5.47	5.56	-10.32	13
3 Yr Avg	—	—	—	—
5 Yr Avg	—	—	—	—
10 Yr Avg	—	—	—	—

Tax Analysis	Tax-Adj Return%	Tax-Cost Ratio
3 Yr (estimated)	—	—
5 Yr (estimated)	—	—
10 Yr (estimated)	—	—

Morningstar Rating
— Not Rated

Return
Not Rated

Risk
—

Yield
0.1%

NAV
$16.71

Avg Daily Vol. (k)
73

52 wk High/Low
$16.89 - $14.70

Growth of $10,000
- Investment Value of ETF
- Investment Value of Index S&P 500

Trading Volume Millions

	1997	1998	1999	2000	2001	2002	2003	2004	2005	2006	History
	—	—	—	—	—	—	—	—	15.86	16.71	NAV $
	—	—	—	—	—	—	—	—	15.86	16.72	Market Price $
	—	—	—	—	—	—	—	—	6.36*	5.47	NAV Return%
	—	—	—	—	—	—	—	—	6.29*	5.56	Market Price Return%
	—	—	—	—	—	—	—	—	0.04	0.05	Avg Premium/Discount%
	—	—	—	—	—	—	—	—	6.36	-10.32	NAV Rtrn% +/-S&P 500
	—	—	—	—	—	—	—	—	6.36	-3.60	NAV Rtrn% +/-Russ 1000Gr
	—	—	—	—	—	—	—	—	—	13	NAV Return% Rank in Cat
	—	—	—	—	—	—	—	—	—	0.13	Income Return %
	—	—	—	—	—	—	—	—	—	5.34	Capital Return %
	—	—	—	—	—	—	—	—	0.00	0.02	Income $
	—	—	—	—	—	—	—	—	0.00	0.00	Capital Gains $
	—	—	—	—	—	—	—	—	0.63	0.64	Expense Ratio %
	—	—	—	—	—	—	—	—	0.13	-0.04	Income Ratio %
	—	—	—	—	—	—	—	—	2	73	Turnover Rate %
	—	—	—	—	—	—	—	—	97	206	Net Assets $mil

Rating and Risk

Time Period	Morningstar Rtn vs Cat	Morningstar Risk vs Cat	Morningstar Risk-Adj Rating
3 Yr	—	—	—
5 Yr	—	—	—
10 Yr	—	—	—

Other Measures	Standard Index S&P 500	Best Fit Index
Alpha	—	—
Beta	—	—
R-Squared	—	—
Standard Deviation	—	
Mean	—	
Sharpe Ratio	—	

Portfolio Analysis 11-30-06

Share change since 10-06 Total Stocks:50	Sector	PE	Tot Ret%	% Assets
⊕ Schlumberger, Ltd.	Energy	24.0	31.07	3.53
⊕ UnitedHealth Group, Inc.	Health	21.0	-13.49	3.52
⊖ Comcast Corporation A	Media	45.0	63.31	3.45
⊖ Walt Disney Company	Media	20.9	44.26	3.41
✲ Hewlett-Packard Company	Hardware	18.9	45.21	3.38
⊖ Boeing Company	Ind Mtrls	41.1	28.38	3.37
⊖ Time Warner, Inc.	Media	19.1	26.37	3.37
✲ Procter & Gamble Company	Goods	24.2	13.36	3.35
⊖ News Corporation, Ltd. A	Media	—	—	3.34
⊕ PepsiCo, Inc.	Goods	21.4	7.86	3.34
⊖ Oracle Corporation	Software	25.6	40.38	3.33
⊖ American Express Company	Financial	21.2	19.09	3.33
⊖ Amgen, Inc.	Health	28.0	-13.38	3.31
✲ Cisco Systems, Inc.	Hardware	28.8	59.64	3.13
✲ Microsoft Corporation	Software	23.7	15.83	3.08
⊕ Halliburton Company	Energy	12.0	1.11	1.50
⊕ WellPoint, Inc.	Health	17.2	-1.38	1.50
⊕ Baker Hughes Inc.	Energy	10.8	23.67	1.50
⊕ Cardinal Health, Inc.	Health	20.9	-5.81	1.49
⊖ McGraw-Hill Companies, I	Media	29.1	33.44	1.48

Current Investment Style

Value Blnd Growth — Large / Mid / Small

Market Cap	%
Giant	48.5
Large	51.5
Mid	0.0
Small	0.0
Micro	0.0

Avg $mil: 46,238

Value Measures		Rel Category
Price/Earnings	19.97	0.96
Price/Book	3.77	1.15
Price/Sales	1.74	0.98
Price/Cash Flow	12.14	1.08
Dividend Yield %	0.73	0.85

Growth Measures	%	Rel Category
Long-Term Erngs	16.04	1.07
Book Value	5.41	0.68
Sales	10.33	0.88
Cash Flow	18.95	1.30
Historical Erngs	19.78	0.70

Profitability	%	Rel Category
Return on Equity	21.17	1.05
Return on Assets	11.94	1.20
Net Margin	14.28	1.14

Sector Weightings

Sector Weightings	% of Stocks	Rel S&P 500	3 Year High Low
☁ Info	33.64	1.68	
▨ Software	7.71	2.23	— —
▣ Hardware	9.39	1.02	— —
▦ Media	16.54	4.36	— —
▤ Telecom	0.00	0.00	— —
▨ Service	41.18	0.89	
▥ Health	15.36	1.27	— —
▨ Consumer	8.27	1.08	— —
▨ Business	5.64	1.33	— —
▨ Financial	11.91	0.53	— —
▨ Mfg	25.18	0.75	
▨ Goods	8.05	0.94	— —
▨ Ind Mtrls	7.69	0.64	— —
▨ Energy	6.53	0.67	— —
▨ Utilities	2.91	0.83	— —

Composition

● Cash	0.1
● Stocks	99.9
● Bonds	0.0
● Other	0.0
Foreign	0.0
(% of Stock)	

Morningstar's Take by Federico Cepeda 12-31-06

PowerShares Dynamic Large Cap Growth is an unproven and uneconomic option among index funds.

Actually, purists may argue that this exchange-traded fund is not even an index fund. It aims to match the returns of the Amex Large Cap Growth Intellidex, whose strategy lies between active and passive investing. The index uses computers to screen for certain qualities that, Amex believes, indicate the greatest potential for capital appreciation.

The index is based on a complex quantitative model. It uses 25 selection criteria that measure risk, momentum, current valuation, and fundamental growth prospects. This index then ranks stocks based on their scores on each of those fields. The process is repeated quarterly.

The problem is that the Intellidex methodology is unknown and unproven. Because it is proprietary, we don't know how Amex uses its criteria to evaluate stocks. And the fund's lack of a long track record adds more doubts to the effectiveness of the process.

What's more, because the index remakes itself quarterly, it will have much higher turnover than its peers. Its 73% turnover for the year to date is more than 3 times its category average. High turnover means frequent transaction costs that nibble on the fund's returns. It also generates higher tax liability. Low turnover and tax efficiency are two of the great advantages of ETFs. But investors here will not benefit from them.

And expenses are too high. Though PowerShares believes the fund's process justifies charging the highest fees of any ETF in the large-growth category, those fees constitute a high hurdle for returns to overcome. We'd point out that Vanguard Growth ETF provides exposure to large-growth firms, has the lowest expenses in the category, and its 23% turnover rate is more in line with long-term, tax-efficient investing.

Address:	301 West Roosevelt Road, Wheaton, IL 60187 / 800-983-0903
Web Address:	www.powershares.com
Inception:	03-04-05*
Advisor:	PowerShares Capital Management LLC
Management Fee:	0.50%
Expense Projections:	3Yr:$245 5Yr:$434 10Yr:$980
Income Distrib:	Quarterly
Exchange:	AMEX

MORNINGSTAR® ETFs 150

Data through December 31, 2006

PowerShares Dyn Lg Value PWV

Market Price $19.63	**Mstar Category** Large Value	

Morningstar Fair Value

Price/Fair Value Ratio	Coverage Rate %
0.95 Undervalued	99 Good

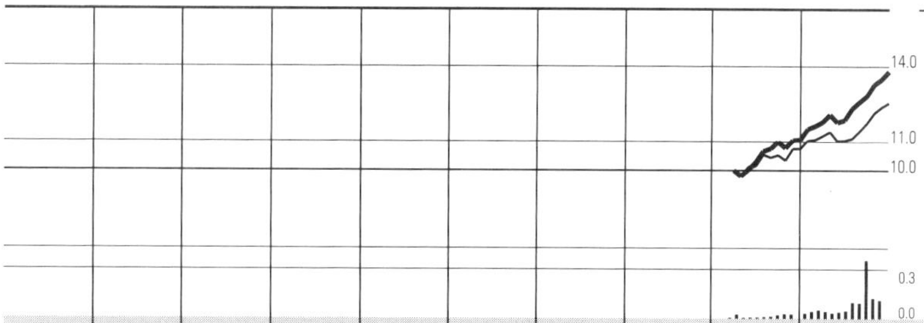

Management

John W. Southard Jr. is the lead portfolio manager. He is a former senior analyst of Chicago Investment Analytics, a quantitative research firm bought by Charles Schwab in 2000. He also worked as an analyst and portfolio manager at a unit investment trust firm, First Trust Portfolios of Lisle, Ill.

Methodology

This ETF tracks the AMEX Large Cap Value Intellidex, which uses a 25-factor quantitative model to select 50 stocks from the 2,000 largest U.S. companies listed on major U.S. exchanges. The factors employed include both technical (that is, price and volume trends) and fundamental (P/E ratios and growth rates) data points. The index follows rules to make sure its sector weights stay close to those of its selection universe. It also caps position sizes and employs a stratified weighting scheme to keep large stocks from dominating the portfolio. The Intellidex reconstitutes quarterly.

	Morningstar Rating	Return	Risk	Yield	NAV	Avg Daily Vol. (k)	52 wk High/Low
	— Not Rated	Not Rated	Not Rated	1.4%	$19.75	164	$19.90 - $16.32

Growth of $10,000
- Investment Value of ETF
- Investment Value of Index S&P 500

Trading Volume Millions

	1997	1998	1999	2000	2001	2002	2003	2004	2005	2006	History
	—	—	—	—	—	—	—	—	16.11	19.75	NAV $
	—	—	—	—	—	—	—	—	16.12	19.77	Market Price $
	—	—	—	—	—	—	—	—	17.44*	24.42	NAV Return%
	—	—	—	—	—	—	—	—	17.40*	24.44	Market Price Return%
	—	—	—	—	—	—	—	—	0.12	0.17	Avg Premium/Discount%
	—	—	—	—	—	—	—	—	17.44	8.63	NAV Rtrn% +/-S&P 500
	—	—	—	—	—	—	—	—	17.44	2.17	NAV Rtrn% +/-Russ 1000 VI
	—	—	—	—	—	—	—	—	—	14	NAV Return% Rank in Cat
	—	—	—	—	—	—	—	—	—	1.66	Income Return %
	—	—	—	—	—	—	—	—	—	22.76	Capital Return %
	—	—	—	—	—	—	—	—	0.21	0.27	Income $
	—	—	—	—	—	—	—	—	0.00	0.00	Capital Gains $
	—	—	—	—	—	—	—	—	0.63	0.65	Expense Ratio %
	—	—	—	—	—	—	—	—	1.99	1.75	Income Ratio %
	—	—	—	—	—	—	—	—	—	29	Turnover Rate %
	—	—	—	—	—	—	—	—	50	383	Net Assets $mil

Performance 12-31-06

Historic Quarterly NAV Returns

	1st Qtr	2nd Qtr	3rd Qtr	4th Qtr	Total
2002	—	—	—	—	—
2003	—	—	—	—	—
2004	—	—	—	—	—
2005	—	2.72	6.71	0.66	—*
2006	5.82	0.69	7.90	8.22	24.42

Trailing	NAV Return%	Market Return%	NAV Rtrn% +/-S&P 500	%Rank Cat.(NAV)
3 Mo	8.22	7.93	1.52	16
6 Mo	16.77	16.73	4.03	16
1 Yr	24.42	24.44	8.63	14
3 Yr Avg	—	—	—	—
5 Yr Avg	—	—	—	—
10 Yr Avg	—	—	—	—

Tax Analysis	Tax-Adj Return%	Tax-Cost Ratio
3 Yr (estimated)	—	—
5 Yr (estimated)	—	—
10 Yr (estimated)	—	—

Rating and Risk

Time Period	Morningstar Rtn vs Cat	Morningstar Risk vs Cat	Morningstar Risk-Adj Rating
3 Yr	—	—	—
5 Yr	—	—	—
10 Yr	—	—	—

Other Measures	Standard Index S&P 500	Best Fit Index
Alpha	—	—
Beta	—	—
R-Squared	—	—
Standard Deviation	—	
Mean	—	
Sharpe Ratio	—	

Morningstar's Take by Federico Cepeda 12-31-06

PowerShares Dynamic Large Cap Value--yet another expensive PowerShares ETF.

The track record of this exchange-traded fund is short but impressive. Since its inception in March 3, 2005, through late December 2006, the fund has gained 35%, beating all of its Morningstar large-value category peers. The fund's heavy exposure to the financial-services sector, one of the best performers over that time frame, is responsible for much of these returns.

This exposure was determined by the quantitative index the fund aims to match, the Amex Large Cap Value Intellidex. This index screens for stocks using 25 criteria including risk, momentum, current valuation, and fundamental growth prospects. It then ranks stocks based on their scores on each of such fields, attempting to identify those that are cheap.

The problem is that the Intellidex methodology is unknown and unproven. Because it is proprietary, we don't know how Amex uses their criteria to evaluate stocks. The current portfolio's huge stake in financial stocks shows that the model can make big sector bets, which can be risky. But because of the fund's brief track record, we don't know how it will behave over different periods.

Besides, the index remakes itself quarterly, so its turnover will be much higher than its peers'. This more frequent trading results in higher trading costs and higher tax liability. And the fund's lack of a long track record adds doubt to the effectiveness of the process.

Finally, this fund has the highest fees of any ETF in the large-value category. We don't know whether the index's quant approach will be able to beat the fund's peers in the long run. But we do know that high fees are a barrier to outperformance. We need to see proof of the model's worth before we recommend it. In the meantime, Vanguard Value ETF can add the same large-value zest in a cheap and more tax-efficient way.

Address:	301 West Roosevelt Road Wheaton, IL 60187 800-983-0903
Web Address:	www.powershares.com
Inception:	03-04-05 *
Advisor:	PowerShares Capital Management LLC

Management Fee:	0.50%		
Expense Projections:	3Yr:$280	5Yr:$501	10Yr:$1137
Income Distrib:	Quarterly		
Exchange:	AMEX		

Portfolio Analysis 11-30-06

Share change since 10-06 Total Stocks:51	Sector	PE	Tot Ret%	% Assets
� Chevron Corporation	Energy	9.3	33.75	3.64
⊕ ExxonMobil Corporation	Energy	11.7	39.07	3.49
� Johnson & Johnson	Health	17.4	12.44	3.47
⊕ AT&T, Inc.	Telecom	19.2	51.59	3.41
⊖ Pfizer Inc.	Health	15.1	15.22	3.37
⊕ Altria Group, Inc.	Goods	15.9	19.87	3.32
⊕ Verizon Communications	Telecom	16.1	34.88	3.31
⊕ Merck & Co., Inc.	Health	18.8	42.66	3.31
⊕ Wachovia Corporation	Financial	13.0	12.02	3.30
⊕ Wells Fargo Company	Financial	14.7	16.82	3.26
⊕ Bank of America Corporat	Financial	12.4	20.68	3.25
⊕ Citigroup, Inc.	Financial	13.3	19.55	3.24
⊖ American International G	Financial	17.1	6.05	3.23
⊕ J.P. Morgan Chase & Co.	Financial	13.7	25.60	3.22
⊖ IBM	Hardware	16.8	19.77	3.22
� Marathon Oil Corporation	Energy	6.5	54.68	1.54
⊕ Valero Energy Corporatio	Energy	6.5	-0.33	1.50
� Regions Financial Corpor	Financial	13.8	14.92	1.48
� General Mills, Inc.	Goods	19.2	19.94	1.47
⊕ PPL Corporation	Utilities	15.4	26.06	1.46

Current Investment Style

Value Blnd Growth — Large Mid Small

Market Cap	%
Giant	51.5
Large	48.5
Mid	0.0
Small	0.0
Micro	0.0

Avg $mil: 60,836

Value Measures		Rel Category
Price/Earnings	12.94	0.91
Price/Book	2.35	0.98
Price/Sales	1.52	1.14
Price/Cash Flow	8.07	1.04
Dividend Yield %	2.58	1.00

Growth Measures	%	Rel Category
Long-Term Erngs	9.26	0.92
Book Value	8.07	1.12
Sales	8.56	1.00
Cash Flow	3.83	0.45
Historical Erngs	14.30	0.92

Profitability	%	Rel Category
Return on Equity	20.08	1.15
Return on Assets	12.01	1.20
Net Margin	15.11	1.10

Sector Weightings	% of Stocks	Rel S&P 500	3 Year High Low
↷ Info	9.97	0.50	
🖥 Software	0.00	0.00	— —
💻 Hardware	3.23	0.35	— —
🎙 Media	0.00	0.00	— —
☎ Telecom	6.74	1.92	— —
☞ Service	56.48	1.22	
🩺 Health	10.17	0.84	— —
🏠 Consumer	2.85	0.37	— —
💼 Business	1.37	0.32	— —
$ Financial	42.09	1.89	— —
🏭 Mfg	33.56	0.99	
🏪 Goods	11.91	1.39	— —
⚙ Ind Mtrls	5.72	0.48	— —
⛽ Energy	10.20	1.04	— —
💡 Utilities	5.73	1.64	— —

Composition

● Cash	0.3	
● Stocks	99.8	
● Bonds	0.0	
● Other	0.0	
Foreign	0.0	
(% of Stock)		

Mᴏʀɴɪɴɢsᴛᴀʀ® ETFs 150

PowerShares Dyn Market PWC

	Market Price $49.96	**Mstar Category** Large Blend

Morningstar Fair Value

Price/Fair Value Ratio	Coverage Rate %
1.04 Fairly valued	85 Good

Management

John W. Southard Jr. is the lead portfolio manager. He is a former senior analyst of Chicago Investment Analytics, a quantitative research firm bought by Charles Schwab in 2000. He also worked as an analyst and portfolio manager at a unit investment trust firm, First Trust Portfolios of Lisle, Ill.

Methodology

This ETF tracks the AMEX Dynamic Market Intellidex, which uses a 25-factor quantitative model to select 100 stocks from the 2,000 largest U.S. companies listed on major U.S. exchanges. The factors employed include both technical (i.e. price and volume trends) and fundamental (P/E ratios and growth rates) datapoints. The bogy follows rules to make sure its sector weightings stay close to those of its selection universe. It also caps position sizes and employs a stratified weighting scheme to keep large stocks from dominating the portfolio. The Intellidex reconstitutes quarterly.

Morningstar Rating ★★★★★ Highest	**Return** Highest	**Risk** High	**Yield** 0.6%	**NAV** $50.31	**Avg Daily Vol. (k)** 60	**52 wk High/Low** $50.71 - $43.93

Growth of $10,000
- Investment Value of ETF
- Investment Value of Index S&P 500

Trading Volume Millions

1997	1998	1999	2000	2001	2002	2003	2004	2005	2006	History
—	—	—	—	—	—	34.10	40.34	45.31	50.31	NAV $
—	—	—	—	—	—	34.02	40.48	45.32	50.37	Market Price $
—	—	—	—	—	—	19.40*	19.08	13.12	11.73	NAV Return%
—	—	—	—	—	—	19.46*	19.77	12.76	11.84	Market Price Return%
—	—	—	—	—	—	-0.01	0.22	0.12	0.03	Avg Premium/Discount%
—	—	—	—	—	—	19.40	8.20	8.21	-4.06	NAV Rtrn% +/-S&P 500
—	—	—	—	—	—	19.40	7.68	6.85	-3.73	NAV Rtrn% +/-Russ 1000
—	—	—	—	—	—	—	16	21	30	NAV Return% Rank in Cat
—	—	—	—	—	—	—	0.72	0.78	0.67	Income Return %
—	—	—	—	—	—	—	18.36	12.34	11.06	Capital Return %
—	—	—	—	—	—	0.25	0.24	0.31	0.30	Income $
—	—	—	—	—	—	0.00	0.00	0.00	0.00	Capital Gains $
—	—	—	—	—	—	—	0.60	0.60	0.60	Expense Ratio %
—	—	—	—	—	—	—	0.46	0.68	0.76	Income Ratio %
—	—	—	—	—	—	—	58	94	103	Turnover Rate %
—	—	—	—	—	—	36	230	691	958	Net Assets $mil

Performance 12-31-06

Historic Quarterly NAV Returns

	1st Qtr	2nd Qtr	3rd Qtr	4th Qtr	Total
2002	—	—	—	—	—
2003	—	—	3.73	11.56	— *
2004	6.46	2.13	-1.08	10.70	19.08
2005	0.47	4.86	6.34	0.98	13.12
2006	5.73	-2.61	1.15	7.28	11.73

Trailing	NAV Return%	Market Return%	NAV Rtrn% +/-S&P 500	%Rank Cat.(NAV)
3 Mo	7.28	7.49	0.58	44
6 Mo	8.51	8.53	-4.23	38
1 Yr	11.73	11.84	-4.06	30
3 Yr Avg	14.60	14.73	4.16	15
5 Yr Avg	—	—	—	—
10 Yr Avg	—	—	—	—

Tax Analysis	Tax-Adj Return%	Tax-Cost Ratio
3 Yr (estimated)	14.33	0.24
5 Yr (estimated)	—	—
10 Yr (estimated)	—	—

Rating and Risk

Time Period	Morningstar Rtn vs Cat	Morningstar Risk vs Cat	Morningstar Risk-Adj Rating
3 Yr	High	High	★★★★★
5 Yr	—	—	—
10 Yr	—	—	—

Other Measures	Standard Index S&P 500	Best Fit Index S&P Mid 400
Alpha	2.6	2.7
Beta	1.18	0.86
R-Squared	73	86
Standard Deviation	9.51	
Mean	14.60	
Sharpe Ratio	1.14	

Portfolio Analysis 11-30-06

Share change since 10-06 Total Stocks:100	Sector	PE	Tot Ret%	% Assets
☼ ExxonMobil Corporation	Energy	11.7	39.07	3.44
⊖ Marathon Oil Corporation	Energy	6.5	54.68	3.35
☼ Anheuser-Busch Companies	Goods	19.0	17.41	3.25
⊕ PepsiCo, Inc.	Goods	21.4	7.86	3.15
⊕ TXU Corporation	Utilities	13.0	11.19	2.57
☼ Lockheed Martin Corporat	Ind Mtrls	17.0	46.98	2.52
☼ Raytheon Company	Ind Mtrls	19.7	34.18	2.50
☼ Equifax, Inc.	Business	19.4	7.26	2.48
☼ St. Paul Travelers Compa	Financial	12.0	22.90	2.40
☼ Metropolitan Life Insura	Financial	15.8	21.67	2.39
⊖ Nucor Corp.	Ind Mtrls	10.1	70.67	2.39
⊖ Principal Financial Grou	Financial	16.6	25.45	2.38
⊕ Aflac, Inc.	Financial	15.3	0.30	2.36
⊖ Chubb Corporation	Financial	9.0	10.53	2.36
☼ ACE, Ltd.	Financial	10.8	15.41	2.34
☼ VF Corporation	Goods	16.8	52.02	2.25
☼ Newell Rubbermaid, Inc.	Goods	19.3	25.66	2.18
☼ Pfizer Inc.	Health	15.1	15.22	2.17
☼ Lexmark International, I	Hardware	23.8	63.28	2.15
⊖ Cigna Corporation	Health	13.6	17.89	2.14

Current Investment Style

Value Blnd Growth — Large/Mid/Small

	Market Cap	%
	Giant	16.3
	Large	43.5
	Mid	30.0
	Small	10.3
	Micro	0.0

Avg $mil: 14,635

Value Measures		Rel Category
Price/Earnings	14.35	0.86
Price/Book	2.77	1.01
Price/Sales	1.23	0.97
Price/Cash Flow	9.30	0.98
Dividend Yield %	1.38	0.77

Growth Measures	%	Rel Category
Long-Term Erngs	11.28	0.98
Book Value	9.70	1.14
Sales	9.81	1.18
Cash Flow	3.29	0.44
Historical Erngs	21.66	1.29

Profitability	%	Rel Category
Return on Equity	24.13	1.25
Return on Assets	12.59	1.31
Net Margin	10.91	0.98

Sector Weightings

	% of Stocks	Rel S&P 500	3 Year High Low
↻ Info	11.65	0.58	
Software	0.83	0.24	7 1
Hardware	7.60	0.82	12 1
Media	0.00	0.00	3 0
Telecom	3.22	0.92	4 3
☞ Service	48.59	1.05	
Health	13.20	1.09	14 8
Consumer	6.50	0.85	16 4
Business	8.60	2.03	14 4
Financial	20.29	0.91	24 17
凸 Mfg	39.75	1.18	
Goods	14.91	1.74	15 6
Ind Mtrls	11.46	0.96	16 6
Energy	9.70	0.99	11 6
Utilities	3.68	1.05	4 1

Composition

		%
● Cash		0.0
● Stocks		100.0
● Bonds		0.0
○ Other		0.0
Foreign (% of Stock)		0.0

Morningstar's Take by Dan Culloton 12-31-06

There is no free lunch here.

PowerShares Dynamic OTC came to market more than three years ago, touting an index that was supposed to be better than traditional market-capitalization-weighted benchmarks. This exchange-traded fund's sponsors contended that market-cap weighted indexes were flawed because they ranked stocks by size rather than investment merit. Their answer was this fund's target benchmark, the Amex Dynamic Market Intellidex, which relied on a multifactor computer model to pick stocks for a portfolio designed to beat than broad market and traditional index funds.

The ETF roared out of the gate, trouncing the S&P 500 for three years. There has been a trade-off for that start, though. The ETF leans heavily toward mid- and small-cap stocks (40% of assets), which has helped for most of its life because small caps have led large caps in recent years. The ETF, however, has suffered in periods when large caps have rallied. It lagged both the broad market and the typical conventional large-blend fund in the second half of 2006.

That's too short a period to judge a fund, but the ETF also has shown a sharper downside than its peers. When the broad market fell 3% from May to July of 2006, this ETF dropped by more than 12%. The portfolios small-cap leanings had something to do with that, but the models behind the ETF's benchmark also let in some richly valued stocks that tanked in the spring, such as semiconductor equipment maker Lam Research (that stock is now gone, though) .

So this fund pays a price for being different. Its volatility as measured by standard deviation is higher than the conventional category average and the broad stock market. The ETF's 0.60% expense ratio, though cheaper than the typical traditional no-load large blend fund, also is higher than most rival ETFs, which is a disadvantage in a category where some rivals charge 0.07%.

Doubts about this ETF's durability remain.

Address:	301 West Roosevelt Road Wheaton, IL 60187 800-983-0903
Web Address:	www.powershares.com
Inception:	05-01-03*
Advisor:	PowerShares Capital Management LLC

Management Fee:	0.50%
Expense Projections:	3Yr:$200 5Yr:$349 10Yr:$784
Income Distrib:	Quarterly
Exchange:	AMEX

MORNINGSTAR® ETFs 150

PowerShares Dyn MidGrowth PWJ

Market Price $18.97	**Mstar Category** Mid-Cap Growth	

Morningstar Fair Value

Price/Fair Value Ratio	Coverage Rate %
1.02 Fairly valued	90 Good

Management

PowerShares Capital Management, founded in 2002, manages this fund. John W. Southard Jr. is the lead portfolio manager. He was a senior analyst of Chicago Investment Analytics, a quantitative research firm. He also worked as an analyst and portfolio manager at a unit investment trust firm.

Methodology

This ETF tracks the Amex Mid Cap Growth Intellidex, which uses a 25-factor quantitative model to select 75 stocks from a pool of companies with a market capitalization range of between $1.7 billion and $13 billion. The factors employed include both technical (price and volume trends) and fundamental (P/E ratios and growth rates) data points. The index follows rules to make sure its sector weights stay close to those of its selection universe. It also caps position sizes and employs a stratified weighting scheme to keep large stocks from dominating the portfolio. The Intellidex reconstitutes quarterly.

	Morningstar Rating — Not Rated	Return Not Rated	Risk —	Yield 0.6%	NAV $19.03	Avg Daily Vol. (k) 32	52 wk High/Low $19.51 - $16.33

Growth of $10,000
- Investment Value of ETF
- Investment Value of Index S&P 500

1997	1998	1999	2000	2001	2002	2003	2004	2005	2006	History
—	—	—	—	—	—	—	—	17.49	19.03	NAV $
—	—	—	—	—	—	—	—	17.50	19.02	Market Price $
—	—	—	—	—	—	—	—	13.45*	9.44	NAV Return%
—	—	—	—	—	—	—	—	13.39*	9.34	Market Price Return%
—	—	—	—	—	—	—	—	0.01	0.01	Avg Premium/Discount%
—	—	—	—	—	—	—	—	13.45	-6.35	NAV Rtrn% +/-S&P 500
—	—	—	—	—	—	—	—	13.45	-1.22	NAV Rtrn% +/-Russ MG
—	—	—	—	—	—	—	—	—	6	NAV Return% Rank in Cat
—	—	—	—	—	—	—	—	—	0.65	Income Return %
—	—	—	—	—	—	—	—	—	8.79	Capital Return %
—	—	—	—	—	—	—	—	0.00	0.11	Income $
—	—	—	—	—	—	—	—	0.00	0.00	Capital Gains $
—	—	—	—	—	—	—	—	0.63	0.65	Expense Ratio %
—	—	—	—	—	—	—	—	-0.20	1.56	Income Ratio %
—	—	—	—	—	—	—	—	1	86	Turnover Rate %
—	—	—	—	—	—	—	—	68	126	Net Assets $mil

Performance 12-31-06

Historic Quarterly NAV Returns

	1st Qtr	2nd Qtr	3rd Qtr	4th Qtr	Total
2002	—	—	—	—	—
2003	—	—	—	—	—
2004	—	—	—	—	—
2005	—	5.92	6.96	6.32	—*
2006	7.09	-3.05	0.09	5.31	9.44

Trailing	NAV Return%	Market Return%	NAV Rtrn% +/-S&P 500	%Rank Cat.(NAV)
3 Mo	5.31	5.26	-1.39	8
6 Mo	5.41	5.38	-7.33	7
1 Yr	9.44	9.34	-6.35	6
3 Yr Avg	—	—	—	—
5 Yr Avg	—	—	—	—
10 Yr Avg	—	—	—	—

Tax Analysis	Tax-Adj Return%	Tax-Cost Ratio
3 Yr (estimated)	—	—
5 Yr (estimated)	—	—
10 Yr (estimated)	—	—

Rating and Risk

Time Period	Morningstar Rtn vs Cat	Morningstar Risk vs Cat	Morningstar Risk-Adj Rating
3 Yr	—	—	—
5 Yr	—	—	—
10 Yr	—	—	—

Other Measures	Standard Index S&P 500	Best Fit Index
Alpha	—	—
Beta	—	—
R-Squared	—	—
Standard Deviation	—	
Mean	—	
Sharpe Ratio	—	

Morningstar's Take by Federico Cepeda 12-31-06

PowerShares Dynamic Mid Cap Growth is expensive and unproven.

This exchange-traded fund may be new, but it has had a very successful start. From its inception on March 4, 2005, through late December 2006, the fund has achieved 27% returns. These returns have beaten those of most of the fund's mid-cap growth category peers.

This ETF, like many other PowerShares offerings, tracks an enhanced index--the Amex Mid Cap Growth Intellidex. The benchmark uses 25 selection criteria that measure risk, momentum, current valuation, and fundamental growth prospects. It then ranks the stocks based on their scores.

The problem is that the Intellidex methodology is unknown and unproven. Because it is proprietary, we don't know how Amex uses its criteria to evaluate stocks. And because the fund lacks a long track record, we are not certain about how it will behave in different market environments or whether it will be successful over the long term.

What's more, because the index remakes itself quarterly, the fund will have much higher turnover than other ETFs in its category. Its 86% turnover for 2006 is twice its category average. High turnover means frequent transaction costs that nibble on the fund's returns. It also generates higher tax liability.

And as in other PowerShares offerings, expenses are too high. With a 0.65% expense ratio, this fund is the priciest ETF in the mid-cap growth category, sharing the honor with PowerShares Dynamic OTC. By comparison, the rest of the ETFs in the category, which are issued by other advisors, charge less than 0.35%.

Low turnover and expenses are two of the great advantages of ETFs that investors will not benefit from here. Given these issues and the fund's lack of a proven record, investors should stay away from this fund.

Address:	301 West Roosevelt Road Wheaton, IL 60187 800-983-0903	
Web Address:	www.powershares.com	
Inception:	03-04-05*	
Advisor:	PowerShares Capital Management LLC	

Management Fee:	0.50%	
Expense Projections:	3Yr:$270 5Yr:$482 10Yr:$1093	
Income Distrib:	Quarterly	
Exchange:	AMEX	

Portfolio Analysis 11-30-06

Share change since 10-06 Total Stocks:78

	Sector	PE	Tot Ret%	% Assets
⊕ Allegheny Technologies C	Ind Mtrls	17.6	152.95	3.43
⊕ MEMC Electronic Material	Hardware	30.8	76.54	3.33
⊖ Garmin, Ltd.	Hardware	29.1	69.45	3.28
⊕ Humana	Health	22.8	1.80	3.25
☼ Clear Channel Outdoor Ho	Business	—	—	3.24
⊕ Laboratory Corporation o	Health	23.9	36.43	3.24
⊖ Cognizant Technology Sol	Business	52.1	53.49	3.24
⊖ Ensco International, Inc	Energy	11.6	13.12	3.23
⊕ Express Scripts	Health	23.6	-14.56	3.22
⊕ Polo Ralph Lauren Corpor	Goods	24.8	38.77	3.20
⊖ NVIDIA Corporation	Hardware	36.5	102.46	3.16
⊖ C.R. Bard, Inc.	Health	26.9	26.81	3.16
⊖ Precision Castparts Corp	Ind Mtrls	24.0	51.40	3.15
⊕ Intuit	Software	22.1	14.48	3.13
⊕ T Rowe Price Group	Financial	24.4	23.27	3.11
⊖ Starwood Hotels & Resort	Consumer	13.1	21.75	3.10
☼ Nordstrom, Inc.	Consumer	21.0	33.35	3.10
☼ Xilinx, Inc.	Hardware	22.5	-4.28	3.07
☼ National Semiconductor	Hardware	16.6	-12.17	3.07
⊖ Expeditors International	Business	32.9	20.54	3.06

Current Investment Style

Value Blnd Growth — Large Mid Small

Market Cap	%
Giant	0.0
Large	15.8
Mid	84.2
Small	0.0
Micro	0.0

Avg $mil: 7,321

Value Measures		Rel Category
Price/Earnings	22.30	1.13
Price/Book	4.72	1.37
Price/Sales	2.05	1.20
Price/Cash Flow	13.97	1.26
Dividend Yield %	0.37	0.76

Growth Measures	%	Rel Category
Long-Term Erngs	16.97	1.08
Book Value	10.28	0.88
Sales	-4.79	NMF
Cash Flow	22.15	1.30
Historical Erngs	26.39	1.15

Profitability	%	Rel Category
Return on Equity	22.99	1.14
Return on Assets	12.32	1.19
Net Margin	13.09	1.15

Sector Weightings	% of Stocks	Rel S&P 500	3 Year High Low
☊ Info	25.76	1.29	
Software	4.83	1.40	— —
Hardware	19.84	2.15	— —
Media	0.54	0.14	— —
Telecom	0.55	0.16	— —
☞ Service	51.25	1.11	
Health	17.51	1.45	— —
Consumer	11.97	1.56	— —
Business	15.85	3.75	— —
Financial	5.92	0.27	— —
❐ Mfg	22.99	0.68	
Goods	4.33	0.51	— —
Ind Mtrls	13.03	1.09	— —
Energy	5.63	0.57	— —
Utilities	0.00	0.00	— —

Composition

	%
● Cash	0.5
● Stocks	99.5
● Bonds	0.0
● Other	0.0
Foreign (% of Stock)	0.0

PowerShares Dyn Mid Value PWP

	Market Price	Mstar Category
	$18.45	Mid-Cap Value

Morningstar Fair Value

Price/Fair Value Ratio	Coverage Rate %
0.97 Fairly valued	97 Good

Management

PowerShares Capital Management, founded in 2002, manages this fund. John W. Southard Jr. is the lead portfolio manager. He was a senior analyst of Chicago Investment Analytics, a quantitative research firm. He also worked as an analyst and portfolio manager at a unit investment trust firm.

Methodology

This ETF tracks the AMEX Mid Cap Value Intellidex, which uses a 25 factor quant model to pick 75 stocks from a pool of companies with a market capitalization range of between $2 billion and $16 billion. The factors used include both technical (that is, price and volume trends) and fundamental (P/E ratios and growth rates) data points. The index follows rules to make sure its sector weights stay close to those of its selection universe. It also caps position sizes and employs a stratified weighting scheme to keep large stocks from dominating the portfolio. The Intellidex reconstitutes quarterly.

Performance 12-31-06

Historic Quarterly NAV Returns

	1st Qtr	2nd Qtr	3rd Qtr	4th Qtr	Total
2002	—	—	—	—	—
2003	—	—	—	—	—
2004	—	—	—	—	—
2005	—	3.39	3.68	3.89	—*
2006	3.60	0.14	2.60	7.42	14.33

Trailing	NAV Return%	Market Return%	NAV Rtrn% +/-S&P 500	%Rank Cat.(NAV)
3 Mo	7.42	7.18	0.72	8
6 Mo	10.21	10.14	-2.53	7
1 Yr	14.33	14.33	-1.46	6
3 Yr Avg	—	—	—	—
5 Yr Avg	—	—	—	—
10 Yr Avg	—	—	—	—

Tax Analysis	Tax-Adj Return%	Tax-Cost Ratio
3 Yr (estimated)	—	—
5 Yr (estimated)	—	—
10 Yr (estimated)	—	—

	Morningstar Rating	Return	Risk	Yield	NAV	Avg Daily Vol. (k)	52 wk High/Low
—	Not Rated	Not Rated	—	1.3%	$18.57	21	$18.80 - $16.25

Growth of $10,000
— Investment Value of ETF
— Investment Value of Index S&P 500

Trading Volume Millions

	1997	1998	1999	2000	2001	2002	2003	2004	2005	2006	History
	—	—	—	—	—	—	—	—	16.46	18.57	NAV $
	—	—	—	—	—	—	—	—	16.45	18.56	Market Price $
	—	—	—	—	—	—	—	—	13.00*	14.33	NAV Return%
	—	—	—	—	—	—	—	—	12.88*	14.33	Market Price Return%
	—	—	—	—	—	—	—	—	-0.01	0.05	Avg Premium/Discount%
	—	—	—	—	—	—	—	—	13.00	-1.46	NAV Rtrn% +/-S&P 500
	—	—	—	—	—	—	—	—	13.00	-5.89	NAV Rtrn% +/-Russ MV
	—	—	—	—	—	—	—	—	—	6	NAV Return% Rank in Cat
	—	—	—	—	—	—	—	—	—	1.44	Income Return %
	—	—	—	—	—	—	—	—	—	12.89	Capital Return %
	—	—	—	—	—	—	—	—	0.24	0.24	Income $
	—	—	—	—	—	—	—	—	0.00	0.00	Capital Gains $
	—	—	—	—	—	—	—	—	0.63	0.67	Expense Ratio %
	—	—	—	—	—	—	—	—	6.34	1.33	Income Ratio %
	—	—	—	—	—	—	—	—	1	117	Turnover Rate %
	—	—	—	—	—	—	—	—	41	72	Net Assets $mil

Rating and Risk

Time Period	Morningstar Rtn vs Cat	Morningstar Risk vs Cat	Morningstar Risk-Adj Rating
3 Yr	—	—	—
5 Yr	—	—	—
10 Yr	—	—	—

Other Measures	Standard Index S&P 500	Best Fit Index
Alpha	—	—
Beta	—	—
R-Squared	—	—
Standard Deviation	—	
Mean	—	
Sharpe Ratio	—	

Portfolio Analysis 11-30-06

Share change since 10-06 Total Stocks:76	Sector	PE	Tot Ret%	% Assets
⊕ Sunoco, Inc.	Energy	7.2	-19.42	3.39
✕ Coventry Health Care, In	Health	15.3	-12.13	3.33
⊖ VF Corporation	Goods	16.8	52.02	3.26
⊕ Ambac Financial Group, I	Financial	10.9	16.52	3.23
✕ Freeport-McMoRan Copper	Ind Mtrls	8.2	13.07	3.23
⊕ Ameriprise Financial, In	Financial	—	—	3.22
⊖ Cigna Corporation	Health	13.6	17.89	3.21
✕ Sara Lee Corporation	Goods	23.0	10.03	3.20
⊖ Eaton Corporation	Ind Mtrls	13.0	14.39	3.20
✕ R.R. Donnelley & Sons Co	Business	46.8	7.19	3.18
⊖ Sherwin-Williams Company	Goods	15.9	42.73	3.18
✕ CIT Group, Inc.	Financial	11.3	9.45	3.17
⊕ Comerica Incorporated	Financial	11.8	7.78	3.16
⊕ Newell Rubbermaid, Inc.	Goods	19.3	25.66	3.16
⊖ United States Steel Corp	Ind Mtrls	7.7	53.62	3.15
✕ Genuine Parts Company	Consumer	17.6	11.39	3.15
⊕ UST, Inc.	Goods	18.6	49.53	3.15
✕ AutoZone, Inc.	Consumer	14.9	25.95	3.14
⊖ Rohm and Haas Company	Ind Mtrls	15.3	8.35	3.14
⊖ Nationwide Financial Ser	Financial	11.5	25.62	3.13

Current Investment Style

Value Blnd Growth — Large/Mid/Small

Market Cap	%
Giant	0.0
Large	19.2
Mid	80.8
Small	0.0
Micro	0.0

Avg $mil: 7,103

Value Measures		Rel Category
Price/Earnings	13.03	0.87
Price/Book	2.52	1.32
Price/Sales	0.96	1.08
Price/Cash Flow	7.50	1.01
Dividend Yield %	1.80	0.73

Growth Measures	%	Rel Category
Long-Term Erngs	10.76	1.14
Book Value	7.69	1.35
Sales	11.45	1.38
Cash Flow	7.14	5.25
Historical Erngs	16.35	1.48

Profitability	%	Rel Category
Return on Equity	23.78	1.82
Return on Assets	11.35	1.50
Net Margin	11.68	1.00

Sector Weightings	% of Stocks	Rel S&P 500	3 Year High Low
↻ Info	2.28	0.11	
📈 Software	0.56	0.16	— —
💻 Hardware	0.57	0.06	— —
🎤 Media	0.00	0.00	— —
📞 Telecom	1.15	0.33	— —
☞ Service	47.08	1.02	
🏥 Health	6.55	0.54	— —
🛒 Consumer	8.00	1.05	— —
🏢 Business	5.91	1.40	— —
💲 Financial	26.62	1.20	— —
⚒ Mfg	50.64	1.50	
🏭 Goods	26.08	3.05	— —
⚙ Ind Mtrls	20.02	1.68	— —
🔋 Energy	3.96	0.40	— —
💡 Utilities	0.58	0.17	— —

Composition

		%
●	Cash	0.2
●	Stocks	99.8
●	Bonds	0.0
○	Other	0.0
	Foreign	0.0
	(% of Stock)	

Morningstar's Take by Federico Cepeda 12-31-06

There's not much reason to pick PowerShares Dynamic Mid Cap Value over the alternatives.

Although this exchange-traded fund is officially an index fund, it has quant fund genes. It aims to match the returns of the Amex Mid Cap Value Intellidex, whose strategy lies between active and passive investing. The index uses computers to screen for certain qualities that, Amex believes, indicate the greatest appreciation potential.

The index is based on a complex quantitative model. It uses 25 selection criteria that measure risk, momentum, current valuation, and fundamental growth prospects. This index then ranks stocks based on their scores on each of such fields. The process is repeated quarterly.

The problem is that the Intellidex methodology is unknown and unproven. Because it is proprietary, we don't know how Amex uses its criteria to evaluate stocks. And because the fund lacks a long track record, we are not certain how it will behave in different market environments or whether it'll be successful over the long term.

Also, because the index remakes itself quarterly, it will have much higher turnover than other ETFs in its category. Its 117% turnover for 2006 is more than 3 times the average for mid-value ETFs. High turnover means frequent transaction costs that nibble away at the fund's returns. It also generates higher tax liability.

And as with other PowerShares offerings, expenses are too high. With a 0.60% expense ratio, this fund is the priciest ETF in the mid-value category. The rest of the ETFs in the category charge less than 0.35%, except for the other PowerShares offering in the group, PowerShares HighYield Dividend Achievers, which charges 0.50%. You can see the pattern here.

Low turnover and expenses are two of the great advantages of ETFs that investors don't get here. Given these issues and the fund's lack of a proven record, investors are better off elsewhere.

Address:	301 West Roosevelt Road Wheaton, IL 60187 800-983-0903	Management Fee:	0.50%
		Expense Projections:	3Yr:$329 5Yr:$593 10Yr:$1347
Web Address:	www.powershares.com	Income Distrib:	Quarterly
Inception:	03-04-05*	Exchange:	AMEX
Advisor:	PowerShares Capital Management LLC		

MORNINGSTAR® ETFs 150

PowerShares Dyn OTC PWO

	Market Price	Mstar Category
	$52.67	Mid-Cap Growth

Morningstar Fair Value

Price/Fair Value Ratio	Coverage Rate %
0.95 Undervalued	69 Fair

Management

John W. Southard Jr. has managed this fund since its inception. He is a former senior analyst of Chicago Investment Analytics, a quantitative research firm bought by Charles Schwab in 2000. He also worked as an analyst and portfolio manager at a unit investment trust firm, First Trust Portfolios of Lisle, Ill.

Methodology

This ETF tracks the AMEX Dynamic OTC Intellidex, which uses a 25-factor quantitative model to select 100 stocks from the 1,000 largest U.S. companies listed on the Nasdaq Stock Market. The factors employed include both technical (that is, price and volume trends) and fundamental (P/E ratios and growth rates) data points. The bogy follows rules to make sure its sector weightings stay close to those of its selection universe. It also caps position sizes and employs a stratified weighting scheme to keep large stocks from dominating the portfolio. The Intellidex reconstitutes quarterly.

Performance 12-31-06

Historic Quarterly NAV Returns

	1st Qtr	2nd Qtr	3rd Qtr	4th Qtr	Total
2002	—	—	—	—	—
2003	—	—	11.82	13.24	—*
2004	1.21	0.30	-6.29	18.67	12.88
2005	-1.34	3.86	3.38	3.60	9.76
2006	6.87	-5.57	0.13	5.02	6.12

Trailing	NAV Return%	Market Return%	NAV Rtrn% +/-S&P 500	%Rank Cat.(NAV)
3 Mo	5.02	4.93	-1.68	8
6 Mo	5.15	5.29	-7.59	7
1 Yr	6.12	6.04	-9.67	6
3 Yr Avg	9.55	9.53	-0.89	3
5 Yr Avg	—	—	—	
10 Yr Avg	—	—	—	

Tax Analysis	Tax-Adj Return%	Tax-Cost Ratio
3 Yr (estimated)	9.53	0.02
5 Yr (estimated)	—	—
10 Yr (estimated)	—	—

Morningstar's Take by Dan Culloton 12-31-06

There's nothing passive about PowerShares Dynamic OTC.

This exchange-traded fund looks like an index fund but doesn't act like one, at least not like traditional market-capitalization-weighted index funds. This one tracks Amex Dynamic OTC Intellidex. As the fancy name implies, this benchmark offers something different. Instead of ranking the stocks in its target universe--the Nasdaq stock market--by the value of available shares on the market (the usual market-cap weighted approach) the OTC Intellidex uses computer models to pick 100 stocks for a portfolio of Nasdaq stocks that's designed to outperform the broader benchmark. Furthermore, while most other index funds trade infrequently, this ETF buys and sells often because its index reconstitutes itself (often drastically) four times a year.

In this way, this ETF is more like a quantitatively managed fund that does most of its trading once per quarter. A computer model employs 25

measures of valuation, financial strength, momentum, and risk to build a 100-stock index. Sector weightings stay close to the Nasdaq's, and the bogy limits position sizes to de-emphasize big stocks. Indeed, bellwethers, such as Microsoft, Apple Computer, and Qualcomm, are absent.

The ETF's returns over the past three years have been strong versus the large-cap focused Nasdaq 100 and Nasdaq Composite indexes, but it has not looked hot compared with the typical conventional mid-cap growth fund. That implies much of this fund's advantage since its inception has come from leaning toward smaller-cap stocks when they were in favor. The fund will probably lag the indexes when big stocks lead the market. Sure enough, this ETF trailed the Nasdaq and its peer group in the second half of 2006 when large caps revived.

It also courts other risks. It devotes a large slice of its portfolio to technology, media, and telecom stocks, and it owns a few richly valued stocks such as NVIDIA. This fund is novel but unnecessary.

Address:	301 West Roosevelt Road
	Wheaton, IL 60187
	800-983-0903
Web Address:	www.powershares.com
Inception:	05-01-03*
Advisor:	Barclays Global Fund Advisers

Management Fee:	0.50%		
Expense Projections:	3Yr:$215	5Yr:$378	10Yr:$853
Income Distrib:	Quarterly		
Exchange:	AMEX		

Morningstar Rating	Return	Risk	Yield	NAV	Avg Daily Vol. (k)	52 wk High/Low
★★	Below Avg	High	—	$52.21	15	$54.23 - $45.42

Growth of $10,000
— Investment Value of ETF
— Investment Value of Index S&P 500

Trading Volume Millions

	1997	1998	1999	2000	2001	2002	2003	2004	2005	2006	History
	—	—	—	—	—	—	39.76	44.88	49.20	52.21	NAV $
	—	—	—	—	—	—	39.75	44.96	49.20	52.17	Market Price $
	—	—	—	—	—	—	17.83*	12.88	9.76	6.12	NAV Return%
	—	—	—	—	—	—	17.89*	13.11	9.56	6.04	Market Price Return%
	—	—	—	—	—	—	-0.24	0.26	-0.01	-0.08	Avg Premium/Discount%
	—	—	—	—	—	—	17.83	2.00	4.85	-9.67	NAV Rtrn% +/-S&P 500
	—	—	—	—	—	—	17.83	-2.60	-2.34	-4.54	NAV Rtrn% +/-Russ MG
	—	—	—	—	—	—	—	3	4	6	NAV Return% Rank in Cat
	—	—	—	—	—	—	—	0.00	0.13	0.00	Income Return %
	—	—	—	—	—	—	—	12.88	9.63	6.12	Capital Return %
	—	—	—	—	—	—	0.00	0.00	0.06	0.00	Income $
	—	—	—	—	—	—	0.00	0.00	0.00	0.00	Capital Gains $
	—	—	—	—	—	—	—	0.60	0.60	0.60	Expense Ratio %
	—	—	—	—	—	—	—	-0.10	-0.06	-0.04	Income Ratio %
	—	—	—	—	—	—	—	79	112	77	Turnover Rate %
	—	—	—	—	—	—	22	58	187	185	Net Assets $mil

Rating and Risk

Time Period	Morningstar Rtn vs Cat	Morningstar Risk vs Cat	Morningstar Risk-Adj Rating
3 Yr	Avg	High	★★
5 Yr	—	—	—
10 Yr	—	—	—

Other Measures	Standard Index S&P 500	Best Fit Index Mstar Mid Growth TR
Alpha	-5.2	-4.1
Beta	1.76	1.06
R-Squared	64	79
Standard Deviation	15.00	
Mean	9.55	
Sharpe Ratio	0.47	

Portfolio Analysis 11-30-06

Share change since 10-06 Total Stocks:101	Sector	PE	Tot Ret%	% Assets
⊖ Cognizant Technology Sol	Business	52.1	53.49	3.12
✸ CDW Corporation	Business	20.1	23.32	3.06
⊖ Cisco Systems, Inc.	Hardware	28.8	59.64	3.05
⊖ NVIDIA Corporation	Hardware	36.5	102.46	3.05
⊖ BEA Systems, Inc.	Software	34.0	33.83	3.02
✸ Cadence Design Systems	Software	47.1	5.85	3.01
✸ Fiserv, Inc.	Business	19.5	21.15	2.99
✸ QLogic Corporation	Hardware	31.3	34.85	2.99
✸ Oracle Corporation	Software	25.6	40.38	2.96
✸ Integrated Device Techno	Hardware	—	17.45	2.94
⊖ Atmel Corporation	Hardware	—	95.79	2.94
⊖ Novellus Systems, Inc.	Hardware	36.6	42.70	2.90
✸ Staples, Inc.	Consumer	20.4	18.58	2.52
⊖ Sears Holdings Corporati	Consumer	19.8	45.36	2.46
⊖ Dollar Tree Stores, Inc.	Consumer	17.7	25.73	2.46
⊖ American Eagle Outfitter	Consumer	20.7	105.48	2.41
⊖ VCA Antech, Inc.	Health	26.4	14.15	2.36
✸ Express Scripts	Health	23.6	-14.56	2.35
✸ Biogen Idec, Inc.	Health	NMF	8.64	2.34
✸ Idexx Laboratories	Health	29.5	10.17	2.31

Current Investment Style

Value Blnd Growth — Large Mid Small

	Market Cap	%
	Giant	6.0
	Large	18.5
	Mid	47.7
	Small	23.5
	Micro	4.3
	Avg $mil:	4,263

Value Measures		Rel Category
Price/Earnings	19.10	0.97
Price/Book	3.08	0.90
Price/Sales	1.64	0.96
Price/Cash Flow	6.93	0.63
Dividend Yield %	0.31	0.63

Growth Measures	%	Rel Category
Long-Term Erngs	14.67	0.93
Book Value	7.29	0.62
Sales	12.78	1.11
Cash Flow	9.93	0.58
Historical Erngs	20.18	0.88

Profitability	%	Rel Category
Return on Equity	18.00	0.89
Return on Assets	11.18	1.08
Net Margin	11.68	1.02

Sector Weightings	% of Stocks	Rel S&P 500	3 Year High Low
↻ Info	37.75	1.89	
🖥 Software	14.55	4.22	33 11
🖥 Hardware	21.52	2.33	34 9
🎤 Media	0.00	0.00	5 0
📞 Telecom	1.68	0.48	4 2
☞ Service	53.98	1.17	
🏥 Health	12.97	1.08	14 10
🛒 Consumer	13.21	1.73	16 10
💼 Business	16.79	3.97	17 8
$ Financial	11.01	0.49	12 8
☐ Mfg	8.27	0.24	
🏭 Goods	2.88	0.34	5 1
🔧 Ind Mtrls	4.16	0.35	8 1
🔋 Energy	1.23	0.13	1 0
💡 Utilities	0.00	0.00	0 0

Composition

● Cash	0.0
● Stocks	100.0
● Bonds	0.0
● Other	0.0
Foreign	0.5
(% of Stock)	

PowerShares Dyn Sm Growth PWT

	Market Price	Mstar Category
	$17.50	Small Growth

Morningstar Rating	Return	Risk	Yield	NAV	Avg Daily Vol. (k)	52 wk High/Low
— Not Rated	Not Rated	Not Rated	—	$17.68	29	$19.12 - $15.11

Morningstar Fair Value

Price/Fair Value Ratio	Coverage Rate %
—	—

Management

PowerShares Capital Management, founded in 2002, manages this fund. John W. Southard Jr. is the lead portfolio manager. He was a senior analyst of Chicago Investment Analytics, a quantitative research firm. He also worked as an analyst and portfolio manager at a unit investment trust firm.

Methodology

This ETF tracks the Amex Small Cap Growth Intellidex, which uses a 25-factor quant model to pick 100 stocks from a pool of companies with a market capitalization range of between $300 million and $2.1 billion. The factors include both technical (price and volume trends) and fundamental (P/E ratios and growth rates) data points. The index follows rules to make sure its sector weights stay close to those of its selection universe. It also caps position sizes and employs a stratified weighting scheme to keep large stocks from dominating the portfolio. The Intellidex reconstitutes quarterly.

Growth of $10,000
- Investment Value of ETF
- Investment Value of Index S&P 500

Trading Volume Millions

	1997	1998	1999	2000	2001	2002	2003	2004	2005	2006	History
	—	—	—	—	—	—	—	—	16.75	17.68	NAV $
	—	—	—	—	—	—	—	—	16.77	17.64	Market Price $
	—	—	—	—	—	—	—	—	8.74*	5.54	NAV Return%
	—	—	—	—	—	—	—	—	8.49*	5.19	Market Price Return%
	—	—	—	—	—	—	—	—	-0.01	-0.05	Avg Premium/Discount%
	—	—	—	—	—	—	—	—	8.74	-10.25	NAV Rtrn% +/-S&P 500
	—	—	—	—	—	—	—	—	8.74	-7.81	NAV Rtrn% +/-Russ 2000 Gr
	—	—	—	—	—	—	—	—	—	6	NAV Return% Rank in Cat
	—	—	—	—	—	—	—	—	—	0.00	Income Return %
	—	—	—	—	—	—	—	—	—	5.54	Capital Return %
	—	—	—	—	—	—	—	—	0.00	0.00	Income $
	—	—	—	—	—	—	—	—	0.00	0.00	Capital Gains $
	—	—	—	—	—	—	—	—	0.63	0.65	Expense Ratio %
	—	—	—	—	—	—	—	—	-0.48	0.65	Income Ratio %
	—	—	—	—	—	—	—	—	—	120	Turnover Rate %
	—	—	—	—	—	—	—	—	59	65	Net Assets $mil

Performance 12-31-06

Historic Quarterly NAV Returns

	1st Qtr	2nd Qtr	3rd Qtr	4th Qtr	Total
2002	—	—	—	—	—
2003	—	—	—	—	—
2004	—	—	—	—	—
2005	—	4.84	7.60	1.15	—*
2006	9.55	-8.28	-0.28	5.33	5.54

Trailing	NAV Return%	Market Return%	NAV Rtrn% +/-S&P 500	%Rank Cat.(NAV)
3 Mo	5.33	5.13	-1.37	7
6 Mo	5.04	5.00	-7.70	7
1 Yr	5.54	5.19	-10.25	6
3 Yr Avg	—	—	—	—
5 Yr Avg	—	—	—	—
10 Yr Avg	—	—	—	—

Tax Analysis	Tax-Adj Return%	Tax-Cost Ratio
3 Yr (estimated)	—	—
5 Yr (estimated)	—	—
10 Yr (estimated)	—	—

Rating and Risk

Time Period	Morningstar Rtn vs Cat	Morningstar Risk vs Cat	Morningstar Risk-Adj Rating
3 Yr	—	—	—
5 Yr	—	—	—
10 Yr	—	—	—

Other Measures	Standard Index S&P 500	Best Fit Index
Alpha	—	—
Beta	—	—
R-Squared	—	—
Standard Deviation	—	
Mean	—	
Sharpe Ratio	—	

Morningstar's Take by Federico Cepeda 12-31-06

PowerShares Dynamic Small Cap Growth's premium fees aren't justified.

Although this exchange-traded small-cap fund is officially an index fund, it has quant-fund genes. It aims to match the returns of the Amex Small Cap Growth Intellidex, whose strategy lies between active and passive investing. The index uses computers to screen for certain qualities that, Amex believes, indicate the greatest growth potential.

The index is based on a complex quantitative model. It uses 25 selection criteria that measure risk, momentum, current valuation, and fundamental growth prospects. This index then ranks small-cap stocks based on their scores. The process is repeated quarterly.

The problem is that the Intellidex methodology is unknown and unproven. Because it is proprietary, we don't know how Amex uses its criteria to evaluate stocks. And because the fund lacks a long track record, we are not certain about how it will behave in different market environments or whether it will be successful over the long term.

What's more, because the index remakes itself quarterly, it will have much higher turnover than other ETFs in its category. Its 120% turnover for 2006 is more than twice the average in its ETF peer group. High turnover means frequent transaction costs that nibble on the fund's returns. It also generates higher tax liability.

And as in other PowerShares offerings, expenses are too high. With a 0.6% expense ratio, this fund is the priciest ETF in the small-cap growth category, sharing the honor with another PowerShares ETF. By comparison, the rest of the ETFs in the category, which are issued by other advisors, charge less than 0.35%.

Low turnover and expenses are two of the great advantages of ETFs that investors will not benefit from here. Given these issues and the fund's lack of a proven record, investors should stay away from this fund.

Address:	301 West Roosevelt Road Wheaton, IL 60187 800-983-0903	
Web Address:	www.powershares.com	
Inception:	03-04-05 *	
Advisor:	PowerShares Capital Management LLC	

Management Fee:	0.50%		
Expense Projections:	3Yr:$270	5Yr:$482	10Yr:$1093
Income Distrib:	Quarterly		
Exchange:	AMEX		

Portfolio Analysis 11-30-06

Share change since 10-06 Total Stocks:100	Sector	PE	Tot Ret%	% Assets
DSW, Inc.	Goods			2.64
Global Industries, Ltd.	Energy	15.9	14.89	2.52
Dril-Quip, Inc.	Energy	25.3	65.93	2.44
ValueClick, Inc.	Business	47.3	30.48	2.43
THQ, Inc.	Software	83.4	36.35	2.42
AK Steel Holding Corpora	Ind Mtrls	89.0	112.58	2.40
Immucor, Inc.	Health	44.3	87.70	2.39
Owens-Corning, Inc.	Ind Mtrls	—	—	2.38
American Reprographics C	Business	—	31.09	2.36
Valeant Pharmaceuticals	Health	—	-3.43	2.36
Amerigroup Corporation	Health	21.0	84.43	2.36
DeVry, Inc.	Consumer	33.7	40.26	2.35
Belden CDT, Inc.	Hardware	27.5	60.98	2.35
TIBCO Software, Inc.	Software	31.5	26.37	2.35
Netflix, Inc.	Consumer	23.9	-4.43	2.34
WebEx Communications, In	Software	37.9	61.30	2.33
Tessera Technologies, In	Hardware	35.7	56.05	2.33
Rollins, Inc.	Business	27.6	13.52	2.32
Triarc Companies, Inc. B	Goods	—	—	2.32
Strayer Education, Inc.	Consumer	30.0	14.34	2.29

Current Investment Style

Value Blnd Growth — Large Mid Small

Market Cap	%
Giant	0.0
Large	0.0
Mid	9.7
Small	90.3
Micro	0.0
Avg $mil:	1,445

Value Measures		Rel Category
Price/Earnings	24.00	1.13
Price/Book	3.39	1.14
Price/Sales	1.34	0.91
Price/Cash Flow	2.30	0.33
Dividend Yield %	0.17	0.55

Growth Measures	%	Rel Category
Long-Term Erngs	19.59	1.12
Book Value	9.34	0.78
Sales	12.58	1.36
Cash Flow	33.59	1.58
Historical Erngs	17.90	0.89

Profitability	%	Rel Category
Return on Equity	15.84	1.08
Return on Assets	9.85	1.24
Net Margin	11.16	1.15

Sector Weightings	% of Stocks	Rel S&P 500	3 Year High Low
Info	21.00	1.05	
Software	9.25	2.68	— —
Hardware	8.66	0.94	— —
Media	2.25	0.59	— —
Telecom	0.84	0.24	— —
Service	53.44	1.16	
Health	11.39	0.94	— —
Consumer	13.97	1.83	— —
Business	21.91	5.18	— —
Financial	6.17	0.28	— —
Mfg	25.57	0.76	
Goods	9.77	1.14	— —
Ind Mtrls	7.75	0.65	— —
Energy	7.62	0.78	— —
Utilities	0.43	0.12	— —

Composition

Cash	0.0	
Stocks	100.0	
Bonds	0.0	
Other	0.0	
Foreign	0.4	
(% of Stock)		

MORNINGSTAR® ETFs 150

PowerShares FTSE RAFI1000 PRF

Market Price	Mstar Category
$57.70	Large Blend

Morningstar Fair Value

Price/Fair Value Ratio	Coverage Rate %
0.92 Undervalued	94 Good

Management

The fund is managed by PowerShares Capital Management, which was founded in 2002. The fund's index was created by Robert Arnott of Research Affiliates.

Methodology

This fund tracks the newly created FTSE Research Affiliates Fundamental Index US 1000. The FTSE RAFI US 1000 weights companies according to their sales, book values, cash flows, and dividends, while most other indexes rely on a company's market cap. Each factor carries equal weight, and the index is rebalanced once a year.

	Morningstar Rating	Return	Risk	Yield	NAV	Avg Daily Vol. (k)	52 wk High/Low
—	Not Rated	Not Rated	—	1.1%	$57.93	104	$58.32 - $49.74

Growth of $10,000
- Investment Value of ETF
- Investment Value of Index S&P 500

12.0
11.7
10.6
10.0

Trading Volume Millions

0.1
0.0

	1997	1998	1999	2000	2001	2002	2003	2004	2005	2006	History
	—	—	—	—	—	—	—	—	49.29	57.93	NAV $
	—	—	—	—	—	—	—	—	49.30	58.02	Market Price $
	—	—	—	—	—	—	—	—	17.41*	18.86	NAV Return%
	—	—	—	—	—	—	—	—	18.61*	19.02	Market Price Return%
	—	—	—	—	—	—	—	—	0.02	0.05	Avg Premium/Discount%
	—	—	—	—	—	—	—	—	17.41	3.07	NAV Rtrn% +/-S&P 500
	—	—	—	—	—	—	—	—	17.41	3.40	NAV Rtrn% +/-Russ 1000
	—	—	—	—	—	—	—	—		30	NAV Return% Rank in Cat
	—	—	—	—	—	—	—	—	—	1.24	Income Return %
	—	—	—	—	—	—	—	—	—	17.62	Capital Return %
	—	—	—	—	—	—	—	—	0.00	0.61	Income $
	—	—	—	—	—	—	—	—	0.00	0.00	Capital Gains $
	—	—	—	—	—	—	—	—	—	0.76	Expense Ratio %
	—	—	—	—	—	—	—	—	—	1.38	Income Ratio %
	—	—	—	—	—	—	—	—	—	2	Turnover Rate %
	—	—	—	—	—	—	—	—	—	620	Net Assets $mil

Performance 12-31-06

Historic Quarterly NAV Returns

	1st Qtr	2nd Qtr	3rd Qtr	4th Qtr	Total
2002	—	—	—	—	—
2003	—	—	—	—	—
2004	—	—	—	—	—
2005	—	—	—	—	—*
2006	5.11	0.06	5.47	7.16	18.86

Trailing	NAV Return%	Market Return%	NAV Rtrn% +/-S&P 500	%Rank Cat.(NAV)
3 Mo	7.16	7.23	0.46	44
6 Mo	13.02	13.06	0.28	38
1 Yr	18.86	19.02	3.07	30
3 Yr Avg	—	—	—	—
5 Yr Avg	—	—	—	—
10 Yr Avg	—	—	—	—

Tax Analysis	Tax-Adj Return%	Tax-Cost Ratio
3 Yr (estimated)	—	—
5 Yr (estimated)	—	—
10 Yr (estimated)	—	—

Rating and Risk

Time Period	Morningstar Rtn vs Cat	Morningstar Risk vs Cat	Morningstar Risk-Adj Rating
3 Yr	—	—	—
5 Yr	—	—	—
10 Yr	—	—	—

Other Measures	Standard Index S&P 500	Best Fit Index
Alpha	—	—
Beta	—	—
R-Squared	—	—
Standard Deviation	—	
Mean	—	
Sharpe Ratio	—	

Portfolio Analysis 11-30-06

Share change since 10-06 Total Stocks:985

	Sector	PE	Tot Ret%	% Assets
⊕ ExxonMobil Corporation	Energy	11.7	39.07	3.00
⊕ General Electric Company	Ind Mtrls	19.8	9.35	2.43
⊕ Citigroup, Inc.	Financial	13.3	19.55	1.90
⊕ Bank of America Corporat	Financial	12.4	20.68	1.71
⊕ Microsoft Corporation	Software	23.7	15.83	1.67
⊕ Chevron Corporation	Energy	9.3	33.75	1.60
⊕ J.P. Morgan Chase & Co.	Financial	13.7	25.60	1.44
⊕ General Motors Corporati	Goods	—	63.96	1.43
⊕ Altria Group, Inc.	Goods	15.9	19.87	1.42
⊕ AT&T, Inc.	Telecom	19.2	51.59	1.36
⊕ Wal-Mart Stores, Inc.	Consumer	16.6	0.13	1.35
⊕ Verizon Communications	Telecom	16.1	34.88	1.28
⊕ Pfizer Inc.	Health	15.1	15.22	1.16
⊕ Berkshire Hathaway Inc.	Financial	13.5	24.89	0.98
⊕ Ford Motor Company	Goods	—	0.57	0.97
⊕ Merck & Co., Inc.	Health	18.8	42.66	0.95
⊕ American International G	Financial	17.1	6.05	0.91
⊕ Johnson & Johnson	Health	17.4	12.44	0.84
⊕ IBM	Hardware	16.8	19.77	0.80
⊕ Wells Fargo Company	Financial	14.7	16.82	0.77

Morningstar's Take by Karen Dolan 12-31-06

PowerShares FTSE RAFI US 1000 tracks a compelling new index, but it has limitations.

This ETF tracks the FTSE Research Affiliates Fundamental Index (RAFI) US 1000, which emerged from Robert Arnott's belief that traditional market-cap-weighted bogies, such as the S&P 500 Index, are flawed. Arnott argues that market cap is not the best measure of a company's size. Instead, he proposes a combination of four other factors: sales, book value, cash flows, and dividends. Arnott's solution successfully removes volatile and potentially misleading stock prices from the equation, but in doing so introduces some other biases. The index has a value tilt and ends up placing more emphasis on stocks with smaller market caps. When plotted in the Morningstar Style Box, the RAFI 1000 portfolio lands in the large-value square, not in large-blend like the S&P 500. The RAFI also parks more assets in mid-cap stocks and less in giant-caps. Those biases have been favorable in recent years. Smaller-cap value stocks have outpaced mega-cap growth-leaning fare, so the fund will likely lag the S&P 500 when that trend reverses.

There's merit to the index's methodology, but costs can erode its advantage. The index is rebalanced once a year, which is costly to execute and can trigger taxable gains. What's more, the fund has fee waivers in place to cap expenses at 0.60% (though the fund is currently charging closer to 0.76% of assets because PowerShares is excluding many of the ETF's start-up costs from the waiver). The fund's levy is far higher than competing broad-market index options. For example, Vanguard Total Stock Market ETF charges a mere 0.07% of assets.

The fund is tracking an innovative new index that can add value over market-cap-weighted alternatives. Yet, the ETF's expenses threaten its advantage for investors. This ETF is intriguing, but investors should be aware of its shortfalls.

Address:	301 West Roosevelt Road
	Wheaton, IL 60187
	800-843-2639
Web Address:	www.powershares.com
Inception:	12-19-05*
Advisor:	PowerShares Capital Management LLC

Management Fee:	0.50%		
Expense Projections:	3Yr:$302	5Yr: —	10Yr: —
Income Distrib:	Quarterly		
Exchange:	NYSE		

Current Investment Style

Value Blnd Growth — Large Mid Small

Market Cap	%
Giant	41.7
Large	34.4
Mid	21.5
Small	2.4
Micro	0.1

Avg $mil: 33,167

Value Measures		Rel Category
Price/Earnings	14.78	0.89
Price/Book	2.33	0.85
Price/Sales	0.86	0.68
Price/Cash Flow	7.87	0.83
Dividend Yield %	2.13	1.19

Growth Measures	%	Rel Category
Long-Term Erngs	10.36	0.90
Book Value	4.58	0.54
Sales	5.25	0.63
Cash Flow	0.19	0.03
Historical Erngs	14.83	0.88

Profitability	%	Rel Category
Return on Equity	15.07	0.78
Return on Assets	9.21	0.96
Net Margin	12.06	1.08

Sector Weightings	% of Stocks	Rel S&P 500	3 Year High Low
☞ Info	16.19	0.81	
🖥 Software	2.44	0.71	— —
🖥 Hardware	5.43	0.59	— —
🎙 Media	3.90	1.03	— —
📞 Telecom	4.42	1.26	— —
⊂ Service	46.02	1.00	
🏥 Health	8.54	0.71	— —
🛒 Consumer	8.78	1.15	— —
🏢 Business	4.17	0.99	— —
💲 Financial	24.53	1.10	— —
🏭 Mfg	37.79	1.12	
⚙ Goods	10.44	1.22	— —
⚗ Ind Mtrls	12.00	1.01	— —
🔥 Energy	8.80	0.90	— —
💧 Utilities	6.55	1.87	— —

Composition

● Cash		0.1
● Stocks		100.0
● Bonds		0.0
● Other		0.0
Foreign		0.2
(% of Stock)		

MORNINGSTAR® ETFs 150

PowerShares Dyn Sm Value PWY

	Market Price	Mstar Category
	$17.88	Small Value

Morningstar Fair Value

Price/Fair Value Ratio	Coverage Rate %
—	—

Management

PowerShares Capital Management, founded in 2002, manages this fund. John W. Southard Jr. is the lead portfolio manager. He was a senior analyst of Chicago Investment Analytics, a quantitative research firm. He also worked as an analyst and portfolio manager at a unit investment trust firm.

Methodology

This ETF tracks the Amex Small Cap Value Intellidex, which uses a 25-factor quant model to pick 100 stocks from a pool of firms with a market capitalization range of between $550 million and $2 billion. The factors used include both technical (price and volume trends) and fundamental (P/E ratios and growth rates) data points. The index follows rules to make sure its sector weights stay close to those of its selection universe. It also caps position sizes and employs a stratified weighting scheme to keep large stocks from dominating the portfolio. The Intellidex reconstitutes quarterly.

Morningstar Rating	Return	Risk	Yield	NAV	Avg Daily Vol. (k)	52 wk High/Low
— Not Rated	Not Rated	—	0.6%	$18.08	39	$18.36 - $15.47

Growth of $10,000
- Investment Value of ETF
- Investment Value of Index S&P 500

Trading Volume Millions

	1997	1998	1999	2000	2001	2002	2003	2004	2005	2006	History
	—	—	—	—	—	—	—	—	15.50	18.08	NAV $
	—	—	—	—	—	—	—	—	15.51	18.11	Market Price $
	—	—	—	—	—	—	—	—	10.38*	17.44	NAV Return%
	—	—	—	—	—	—	—	—	10.43*	17.55	Market Price Return%
	—	—	—	—	—	—	—	—	0.03	0.02	Avg Premium/Discount%
	—	—	—	—	—	—	—	—	10.38	1.85	NAV Rtrn% +/-S&P 500
	—	—	—	—	—	—	—	—	10.38	-6.04	NAV Rtrn% +/-Russ 2000
	—	—	—	—	—	—	—	—	—	6	NAV Return% Rank in C
	—	—	—	—	—	—	—	—	—	0.74	Income Return %
	—	—	—	—	—	—	—	—	—	16.70	Capital Return %
	—	—	—	—	—	—	—	—	0.09	0.11	Income $
	—	—	—	—	—	—	—	—	0.00	0.00	Capital Gains $
	—	—	—	—	—	—	—	—	0.63	0.66	Expense Ratio %
	—	—	—	—	—	—	—	—	0.45	0.73	Income Ratio %
	—	—	—	—	—	—	—	—	—	118	Turnover Rate %
	—	—	—	—	—	—	—	—	40	83	Net Assets $mil

Performance 12-31-06

Historic Quarterly NAV Returns

	1st Qtr	2nd Qtr	3rd Qtr	4th Qtr	Total
2002	—	—	—	—	—
2003	—	—	—	—	—
2004	—	—	—	—	—
2005	—	5.57	2.42	-0.20	— *
2006	8.69	-2.90	0.89	10.30	17.44

Trailing	NAV Return%	Market Return%	NAV Rtrn% +/-S&P 500	%Rank Cat.(NAV)
3 Mo	10.30	10.47	3.60	7
6 Mo	11.28	11.32	-1.46	7
1 Yr	17.44	17.55	1.65	6
3 Yr Avg	—	—	—	—
5 Yr Avg	—	—	—	—
10 Yr Avg	—	—	—	—

Tax Analysis	Tax-Adj Return%	Tax-Cost Ratio
3 Yr (estimated)	—	—
5 Yr (estimated)	—	—
10 Yr (estimated)	—	—

Rating and Risk

Time Period	Morningstar Rtn vs Cat	Morningstar Risk vs Cat	Morningstar Risk-Adj Rating
3 Yr	—	—	—
5 Yr	—	—	—
10 Yr	—	—	—

Other Measures	Standard Index S&P 500	Best Fit Index
Alpha	—	—
Beta	—	—
R-Squared	—	—
Standard Deviation	—	
Mean	—	
Sharpe Ratio	—	

Portfolio Analysis 11-30-06

Share change since 10-06 Total Stocks:100	Sector	PE	Tot Ret%	% A
⊖ Seaboard Corporation	Goods	8.4	17.05	
✕ Western Refining, Inc.	Energy	—	—	
⊕ OM Group, Inc.	Ind Mtrls	8.3	141.36	
✕ NBTY, Inc.	Health	25.7	155.82	
✕ IPC Holdings Limited	Financial	10.4	17.68	
✕ Swift Transportation Co.	Business	12.7	29.41	
⊖ Chaparral Steel Company	Ind Mtrls	—	193.39	
✕ Magellan Health Services	Health	14.4	37.42	
⊕ Regal-Beloit Corporation	Ind Mtrls	16.3	50.14	
⊕ Ikon Office Solutions, I	Ind Mtrls	20.5	59.10	
⊖ Lennox International, In	Business	14.0	10.33	
⊖ Ohio Casualty Corporatio	Financial	8.7	6.59	
✕ Emulex Corporation	Hardware	44.3	-1.41	
⊕ Idacorp, Inc.	Utilities	25.8	36.51	
✕ Delphi Financial Group	Financial	14.9	33.00	
⊕ Proassurance Corporation	Financial	14.1	2.63	
⊖ Toro Company	Ind Mtrls	15.9	7.44	
✕ Trustmark Corporation	Financial	15.7	22.37	
⊖ Zenith National Insuranc	Financial	7.5	4.36	
✕ Bio-Rad Laboratories Inc	Health	22.2	26.10	

Current Investment Style

Value Blnd Growth			Market Cap	%
		Large Mid Small	Giant	0.0
			Large	0.0
			Mid	21.2
			Small	78.3
			Micro	0.4
			Avg $mil:	1,501

Value Measures		Rel Category
Price/Earnings	12.73	0.84
Price/Book	1.87	1.09
Price/Sales	0.98	1.32
Price/Cash Flow	4.93	0.82
Dividend Yield %	1.20	0.58

Growth Measures	%	Rel Category
Long-Term Erngs	10.73	1.00
Book Value	8.55	1.83
Sales	9.43	2.20
Cash Flow	15.47	4.22
Historical Erngs	17.07	1.80

Profitability	%	Rel Category
Return on Equity	16.55	1.57
Return on Assets	11.59	1.75
Net Margin	12.72	1.28

Sector Weightings	% of Stocks	Rel S&P 500
↻ Info	4.48	0.22
Software	0.43	0.12
Hardware	3.20	0.35
Media	0.00	0.00
Telecom	0.85	0.24
⊂ Service	64.84	1.40
Health	7.53	0.62
Consumer	6.28	0.82
Business	11.64	2.75
Financial	39.39	1.77
⊔ Mfg	30.68	0.91
Goods	4.99	0.58
Ind Mtrls	19.18	1.61
Energy	3.32	0.34
Utilities	3.19	0.91

Composition
- Cash
- Stock
- Bonds
- Other
- Foreign (% of

Morningstar's Take by Federico Cepeda 12-31-06

PowerShares Dynamic Small Cap Value is an expensive ETF in an overheated market area.

This exchange-traded fund has only been in existence since March 2005, but it has already gained quite a bit of money. Had it been around longer, its record would look even better.

Investors should realize that small value has been the best performing of the nine sections of the Morningstar Style Box over the trailing five-year period. Because small-value stocks have gotten so much attention from investors lately, bargains have become harder to find. Also, the market is cyclical. Leadership between different sectors and asset classes rotates frequently.

This fund has not impressed out of the gate, but there are deeper issues. Because the fund lacks a long track record, we are not certain about how it will behave in different market environments or whether it will be successful over the long term. The fund aims to match the returns of the Amex Small Cap Value Intellidex, whose strategy lies

between active and passive investing. The Intellidex methodology is unknown and unproven. Because it is proprietary, we don't know how Amex uses its criteria to evaluate stocks. Also, because the index remakes itself quarterly, it has much higher turnover than other ETFs in its category. High turnover means frequent transaction costs that nibble into the fund's returns. It also generates higher tax liability.

And as in other PowerShares offerings, expenses are too high. With a 0.60% expense ratio, this fund is the priciest ETF in the small-value category. All of the other small-value ETFs, which are issued by other advisors, charge less than 0.35%.

Low turnover and expenses are two of the great advantages of ETFs that investors will not benefit from here. Given these issues and the fund's lack of a track record, investors are better off elsewhere.

Address:	301 West Roosevelt Road Wheaton, IL 60187 800-983-0903	Management Fee:	0.50%
		Expense Projections:	3Yr:$311 5Yr:$559 10Yr:$1270
Web Address:	www.powershares.com	Income Distrib:	Quarterly
Inception:	03-04-05*	Exchange:	AMEX
Advisor:	PowerShares Capital Management LLC		

Morningstar® ETFs 150

PowerShares Halter USX PGJ

	Market Price $20.80	Mstar Category Pacific/Asia ex-Japan Stk

Morningstar Fair Value

Price/Fair Value Ratio	Coverage Rate %
1.04 Fairly valued	79 Fair

Management

The fund is managed by PowerShares Capital Management LLC, which was founded in 2002 and acquired by Amvescap in 2006. John W. Southard Jr. is primarily responsible for the day-to-day management of the fund.

Methodology

This fund tracks the Halter USX China Index. The benchmark is composed of U.S.-listed securities that derive a majority of their revenues from the People's Republic of China. The index includes stocks from across the market-cap spectrum. The index is rebalanced quarterly.

Morningstar Rating	Return	Risk	Yield	NAV	Avg Daily Vol. (k)	52 wk High/Low
— Not Rated	Not Rated	Not Rated	1.0%	$20.92	217	$21.95 - $14.28

Growth of $10,000
- Investment Value of ETF
- Investment Value of Index MSCI EAFE

Trading Volume Millions

	1997	1998	1999	2000	2001	2002	2003	2004	2005	2006	History
	—	—	—	—	—	—	—	14.49	13.85	20.92	NAV $
	—	—	—	—	—	—	—	14.51	13.87	21.15	Market Price $
	—	—	—	—	—	—	—	20.76*	-3.29	53.10	NAV Return%
	—	—	—	—	—	—	—	21.12*	-3.29	54.56	Market Price Return%
	—	—	—	—	—	—	—	0.14	0.14	0.27	Avg Premium/Discount%
	—	—	—	—	—	—	—	20.76	-16.83	26.76	NAV Rtrn% +/-MSCI EAFE
	—	—	—	—	—	—	—	20.76	-21.15	24.63	NAV Rtrn% +/-MSCIAC FExJ
	—	—	—	—	—	—	—	—	9	9	NAV Return% Rank in Cat
	—	—	—	—	—	—	—	—	1.13	1.52	Income Return %
	—	—	—	—	—	—	—	—	-4.42	51.58	Capital Return %
	—	—	—	—	—	—	—	0.00	0.16	0.21	Income $
	—	—	—	—	—	—	—	0.00	0.00	0.00	Capital Gains $
	—	—	—	—	—	—	—	—	0.70	0.71	Expense Ratio %
	—	—	—	—	—	—	—	—	1.24	1.18	Income Ratio %
	—	—	—	—	—	—	—	—	9	21	Turnover Rate %
	—	—	—	—	—	—	—	25	79	354	Net Assets $mil

Performance 12-31-06

Historic Quarterly NAV Returns

	1st Qtr	2nd Qtr	3rd Qtr	4th Qtr	Total
2002	—	—	—	—	—
2003	—	—	—	—	—*
2004	—	—	—	—	—
2005	-8.97	3.71	7.01	-4.28	-3.29
2006	19.21	-2.17	0.99	29.99	53.10

Trailing	NAV Return%	Market Return%+/-MSCI EAFE	NAV Rtrn%	%Rank Cat.(NAV)
3 Mo	29.99	31.16	19.64	9
6 Mo	31.28	32.64	16.59	9
1 Yr	53.10	54.56	26.76	9
3 Yr Avg	—	—	—	—
5 Yr Avg	—	—	—	—
10 Yr Avg	—	—	—	—

Tax Analysis	Tax-Adj Return%	Tax-Cost Ratio
3 Yr (estimated)	—	—
5 Yr (estimated)	—	—
10 Yr (estimated)	—	—

Rating and Risk

Time Period	Morningstar Rtn vs Cat	Morningstar Risk vs Cat	Morningstar Risk-Adj Rating
3 Yr	—	—	—
5 Yr	—	—	—
10 Yr	—	—	—

Other Measures	Standard Index S&P 500	Best Fit Index
Alpha	—	—
Beta	—	—
R-Squared	—	—
Standard Deviation	—	
Mean	—	
Sharpe Ratio	—	

Portfolio Analysis 11-30-06

Share change since 10-06 Total Stocks:53	Sector	Country	% Assets
⊖ China Mobile Ltd. ADR	Telecom	China	6.19
⊖ PetroChina Company, Ltd.	Energy	China	6.16
⊖ Sinopec	Business	China	4.97
⊖ China Telecom Corporatio	Telecom	China	4.96
⊖ China Life Insurance Com	Financial	China	4.83
⊖ Aluminum Corp of China,	Ind Mtrls	China	4.75
⊖ Suntech Power Holdings C	Ind Mtrls	China	4.68
⊖ Huaneng Power Internatio	Utilities	China	4.59
⊖ China Unicom, Ltd. ADR	Telecom	China	4.57
⊖ China Netcom Group Corp.	Telecom	China	4.32
⊖ Baidu.com, Inc. ADR	Media	China	4.31
⊖ Focus Media Holding, Ltd	Business	China	4.15
⊖ CNOOC, Ltd. ADR	Energy	China	4.14
⊖ Yanzhou Coal Mining Comp	Energy	China	3.91
⊖ Sinopec Shanghai Petroch	Energy	China	3.76
⊖ NetEase.com, Inc. ADR	Business	China	2.69
⊖ Guangshen Railway Compan	Business	China	2.48
⊖ Semiconductor Manufactur	Hardware	China	2.48
⊖ Ctrip.com International,	Business	China	1.97
⊖ China Southern Airlines	Business	China	1.85

Current Investment Style

Value Blnd Growth — Large Mid Small

Market Cap	%
Giant	35.9
Large	9.1
Mid	35.0
Small	14.8
Micro	5.2
Avg $mil:	8,653

Value Measures	Rel Category
Price/Earnings	—
Price/Book	—
Price/Sales	—
Price/Cash Flow	—
Dividend Yield %	—

Growth Measures	%	Rel Category
Long-Term Erngs	—	—
Book Value	—	—
Sales	—	—
Cash Flow	—	—
Historical Erngs	—	—

Composition

Cash	0.2	Bonds	0.0
Stocks	99.8	Other	0.0
Foreign (% of Stock)			96.2

Sector Weightings	% of Stocks	Rel MSCI EAFE	3 Year High	Low
↻ Info	34.85	2.95		
🖥 Software	0.36	0.64	2	0
💻 Hardware	5.81	1.51	10	5
🎙 Media	6.52	3.56	7	3
📶 Telecom	22.16	3.98	23	19
☞ Service	30.06	0.64		
⚕ Health	1.15	0.16	3	0
🛒 Consumer	0.00	0.00	0	0
📑 Business	24.00	4.73	26	20
💲 Financial	4.91	0.16	5	4
⚒ Mfg	35.09	0.86		
🏭 Goods	0.81	0.06	2	1
⚙ Ind Mtrls	11.34	0.73	13	8
🔥 Energy	18.27	2.56	24	17
💡 Utilities	4.67	0.89	5	4

Regional Exposure		% Stock
UK/W. Europe 0	N. America	4
Japan 0	Latn America	0
Asia X Japan 96	Other	0

Country Exposure		% Stock
China	94	South Korea 0
United States	4	
Hong Kong	2	

Morningstar's Take by William Samuel Rocco 12-31-06

Don't get too het up about PowerShares Golden Dragon Halter USX China.

This ETF is one of the most attractively priced China funds. While its 0.71% expense ratio is a bit higher than that of one of the three China-oriented ETFs, it is slightly lower than that of the third such ETF and much lower than those of all the mutual funds that focus on the Middle Kingdom. And its relatively low costs give this young ETF an enduring edge over its rivals.

This ETF also provides relatively broad exposure to its chosen country. While iShares FTSE/Xinhua China 25 Index has a pronounced giant-cap bias and several other China offerings focus on giant- and large-cap stocks, this ETF spreads its assets pretty evenly across the market-cap range. It also makes fuller use of the sector spectrum than do a number of its rivals.

However, while this relatively diversified portfolio may well make this young ETF somewhat less volatile than other China offerings over time,

it's crucial to recognize that there is quite a lot of risk here. This ETF may be less focused than many of its peers in certain respects, but it's really concentrated in absolute terms. (It has hefty stakes in three sectors; it has zero to minuscule stakes in four sectors; and it devotes about half its assets to its top 10 names.) Also, focusing on a single emerging market is always dangerous, and concentrating on China is no exception.

It's also important to understand that superior economic growth doesn't always translate into superior market performance. China funds lag the average Pacific/Asia ex-Japan offering over the trailing three-, five-, and 10-year periods, in fact, despite the success of the Chinese economy.

In short, while this young ETF does have its strengths, we remain wary of China funds in general and continue to believe that the vast majority of investors would be better off with broader emerging-markets offerings.

Address:	301 West Roosevelt Road Wheaton, IL 60187 800-983-0903
Web Address:	www.powershares.com
Inception:	12-09-04 *
Advisor:	Barclays Global Investors

Management Fee:	0.50%		
Expense Projections:	3Yr:$269	5Yr:$477	10Yr:$1074
Income Distrib:	Quarterly		
Exchange:	AMEX		

MORNINGSTAR® ETFs 150

PowerShares High Gr Div PHJ

Market Price $16.85	**Mstar Category** Large Blend		

Morningstar Fair Value

Price/Fair Value Ratio	Coverage Rate %
0.86 Undervalued	92 Good

Management

PowerShares Capital Management, founded in 2002, manages this fund. John W. Southard Jr. is the lead portfolio manager. He was a senior analyst of Chicago Investment Analytics, a quantitative research firm. He also worked as an analyst and portfolio manager at a unit investment trust firm.

Methodology

This ETF tracks the High Growth Rate Dividend Achievers Index, which is a subset of the Broad Dividend Achievers Index. The bogy holds the 100 stocks with the highest 10-year compound annualized dividend growth rate. Components are weighted by a modified market-capitalization methodology. The index also employs additional liquidity and investability screens. It is rebalanced quarterly and reconstituted annually.

Morningstar Rating	Return	Risk	Yield	NAV	Avg Daily Vol. (k)	52 wk High/Low
— Not Rated	Not Rated	—	1.7%	$16.73	12	$16.97 - $15.04

Growth of $10,000
— Investment Value of ETF
— Investment Value of Index S&P 500

Trading Volume Millions

	1997	1998	1999	2000	2001	2002	2003	2004	2005	2006	History
	—	—	—	—	—	—	—	—	15.25	16.73	NAV $
	—	—	—	—	—	—	—	—	15.25	16.85	Market Price $
	—	—	—	—	—	—	—	—	12.07*	11.67	NAV Return%
	—	—	—	—	—	—	—	—	12.66*	12.44	Market Price Return%
	—	—	—	—	—	—	—	—	0.08	0.09	Avg Premium/Discount%
	—	—	—	—	—	—	—	—	12.07	-4.12	NAV Rtrn% +/-S&P 500
	—	—	—	—	—	—	—	—	12.07	-3.79	NAV Rtrn% +/-Russ 1000
	—	—	—	—	—	—	—	—	—	30	NAV Return% Rank in Cat
	—	—	—	—	—	—	—	—	—	1.89	Income Return %
	—	—	—	—	—	—	—	—	—	9.78	Capital Return %
	—	—	—	—	—	—	—	—	0.09	0.29	Income $
	—	—	—	—	—	—	—	—	0.00	0.00	Capital Gains $
	—	—	—	—	—	—	—	—	—	0.66	Expense Ratio %
	—	—	—	—	—	—	—	—	—	1.59	Income Ratio %
	—	—	—	—	—	—	—	—	—	20	Turnover Rate %
	—	—	—	—	—	—	—	—	32	37	Net Assets $mil

Performance 12-31-06

Historic Quarterly NAV Returns

	1st Qtr	2nd Qtr	3rd Qtr	4th Qtr	Total
2002	—	—	—	—	—
2003	—	—	—	—	—
2004	—	—	—	—	—
2005	—	—	—	4.60	—*
2006	3.79	-1.01	4.83	3.69	11.67

Trailing	NAV Return%	Market Return%	NAV Rtrn% +/-S&P 500	%Rank Cat.(NAV)
3 Mo	3.69	4.31	-3.01	44
6 Mo	8.69	9.09	-4.05	38
1 Yr	11.67	12.44	-4.12	30
3 Yr Avg	—	—	—	—
5 Yr Avg	—	—	—	—
10 Yr Avg	—	—	—	—

Tax Analysis	Tax-Adj Return%	Tax-Cost Ratio
3 Yr (estimated)	—	—
5 Yr (estimated)	—	—
10 Yr (estimated)	—	—

Rating and Risk

Time Period	Morningstar Rtn vs Cat	Morningstar Risk vs Cat	Morningstar Risk-Adj Rating
3 Yr	—	—	—
5 Yr	—	—	—
10 Yr	—	—	—

Other Measures	Standard Index S&P 500	Best Fit Index
Alpha	—	—
Beta	—	—
R-Squared	—	—
Standard Deviation	—	
Mean	—	
Sharpe Ratio	—	

Portfolio Analysis 11-30-06

Share change since 10-06 Total Stocks:101	Sector	PE	Tot Ret%	% Assets
⊕ Medtronic, Inc.	Health	23.7	-6.29	4.29
⊕ American International G	Financial	17.1	6.05	4.18
⊕ Home Depot, Inc.	Consumer	13.7	1.01	4.10
⊕ McDonald's Corporation	Consumer	19.2	34.63	4.06
⊕ Pfizer Inc.	Health	15.1	15.22	4.05
⊕ Bank of America Corporat	Financial	12.4	20.68	4.02
⊕ Lowe's Companies Inc.	Consumer	15.4	-6.05	3.98
⊕ Citigroup, Inc.	Financial	13.3	19.55	3.95
⊕ Washington Mutual, Inc.	Financial	13.5	9.62	3.94
⊕ Freddie Mac	Financial	24.0	7.06	3.89
⊕ Wells Fargo Company	Financial	14.7	16.82	3.89
⊕ Johnson & Johnson	Health	17.4	12.44	3.87
⊕ Wal-Mart Stores, Inc.	Consumer	16.6	0.13	3.64
⊕ Illinois Tool Works, Inc	Ind Mtrls	15.7	6.69	2.51
⊕ Automatic Data Processin	Business	25.1	9.11	2.51
⊕ Archer Daniels Midland	Ind Mtrls	13.8	31.02	2.16
⊕ Sysco Corporation	Consumer	26.1	20.96	2.08
⊕ Fifth Third Bancorp	Financial	15.7	12.99	2.06
⊕ Aflac, Inc.	Financial	15.3	0.30	2.05
⊕ Stryker Corporation	Health	29.8	24.53	1.98

Current Investment Style

Value Blnd Growth — Large Mid Small

Market Cap	%
Giant	36.6
Large	47.4
Mid	12.5
Small	3.0
Micro	0.5

Avg $mil: 36,369

Value Measures		Rel Category
Price/Earnings	15.78	0.95
Price/Book	2.78	1.01
Price/Sales	1.90	1.50
Price/Cash Flow	10.12	1.07
Dividend Yield %	2.12	1.18

Growth Measures	%	Rel Category
Long-Term Erngs	11.75	1.02
Book Value	10.01	1.17
Sales	10.68	1.29
Cash Flow	-17.90	NMF
Historical Erngs	10.30	0.61

Profitability	%	Rel Category
Return on Equity	19.92	1.03
Return on Assets	13.54	1.41
Net Margin	18.22	1.63

Sector Weightings	% of Stocks	Rel S&P 500	3 Year High Low
⌖ Info	1.36	0.07	
🖥 Software	0.00	0.00	— —
💾 Hardware	0.96	0.10	— —
🎙 Media	0.40	0.11	— —
☎ Telecom	0.00	0.00	— —
⊜ Service	85.17	1.84	
⚕ Health	14.43	1.20	— —
🛒 Consumer	18.66	2.44	— —
💼 Business	6.50	1.54	— —
$ Financial	45.58	2.05	— —
⚒ Mfg	13.49	0.40	
🏭 Goods	3.88	0.45	— —
⚙ Ind Mtrls	9.47	0.79	— —
🔋 Energy	0.14	0.01	— —
💡 Utilities	0.00	0.00	— —

Composition

	%
● Cash	0.2
● Stocks	99.8
● Bonds	0.0
○ Other	0.0
Foreign	0.1
(% of Stock)	

Morningstar's Take by Federico Cepeda 12-31-06

PowerShares High Growth Rate Dividend Achievers is expensive and risky.

This exchange-traded fund seeks companies with high dividend growth potential. It holds the 100 stocks that make up the Broad Dividend Achievers Index. These companies have had decent growth rates and generate enough cash flow that they can afford to issue dividends. Prominent examples are Wal-Mart and McDonald's.

But we see the index's methodology as flawed. It only selects companies that have demonstrated 10 years of dividend growth--a backward-looking metric. The index ignores firms that lack such a track record but are likely to issue dividends in the future. For instance, Microsoft has a lot of cash that will likely be returned to investors. However, because it has not given out any dividends during most of the past decade, it wasn't among the fund's holdings as of September 30, 2006. What's more, the firms in the index, which have recorded 10 years of dividend growth, have likely reached a mature stage of their corporate lives. Their potential for future growth is, arguably, less than that of companies with a shorter dividend-issuing track record.

Also, the fund is heavily concentrated in a few sectors. Its heavy 19% exposure to consumer services looks tiny compared with the 48% of assets that stocks in the financial-services sector take up. If we add the 14% exposure to health care, a full 81% of the portfolio is committed to three sectors out of the 12 Morningstar identifies as comprising the market. This brings risk. When financials lag the market, this fund will suffer.

Finally, the fund's 0.66% expense ratio is one of the highest among ETFs in the large-blend category. Vanguard Large Cap ETF has a 0.07% expense ratio and provides a higher yield along with wider diversification. Consider other options before investing here.

Address:	301 West Roosevelt Road Wheaton, Il 60187 800-843-2639	Management Fee:	0.40%
		Expense Projections:	3Yr:$296 5Yr: — 10Yr: —
		Income Distrib:	Quarterly
Web Address:	www.powershares.com	Exchange:	AMEX
Inception:	09-15-05*		
Advisor:	PowerShares Capital Management LLC		

 **MORNINGSTAR® ETFs 150**

PowerShares HY Div Achiev PEY

Market Price $16.25	**Mstar Category** Mid-Cap Value	

Morningstar Fair Value

Price/Fair Value Ratio	Coverage Rate %
0.98 Fairly valued	69 Fair

Management

John W. Southard Jr. is the lead portfolio manager. He is a former senior analyst of Chicago Investment Analytics, a quantitative research firm bought by Charles Schwab in 2000. He also worked as an analyst and portfolio manager at a unit investment trust firm, First Trust Portfolios of Lisle, Ill.

Methodology

This ETF tracks the Mergent Dividend Achievers 50. The benchmark includes the 50 highest-yielding members of the Dividend Achievers, a list of stocks that have increased their dividends in each of the last 10 years. The index selects the 50 highest-yielding stocks from the Dividend Achiever universe of more than 300 stocks and weights them by the size of their yields. The index rebalances quarterly. The fund distributes income monthly.

	Morningstar Rating	Return	Risk	Yield	NAV	Avg Daily Vol. (k)	52 wk High/Low
—	Not Rated	Not Rated	—	2.5%	$16.16	97	$16.65 - $14.35

Growth of $10,000
— Investment Value of ETF
— Investment Value of Index S&P 500

Trading Volume Millions

1997	1998	1999	2000	2001	2002	2003	2004	2005	2006	History
—	—	—	—	—	—	—	15.27	14.95	16.16	NAV $
—	—	—	—	—	—	—	15.27	14.93	16.42	Market Price $
—	—	—	—	—	—	—	7.41*	1.13	10.97	NAV Return%
—	—	—	—	—	—	—	8.24*	0.99	12.90	Market Price Return%
—	—	—	—	—	—	—	0.00	0.05	0.08	Avg Premium/Discount%
—	—	—	—	—	—	—	7.41	-3.78	-4.82	NAV Rtrn% +/-S&P 500
—	—	—	—	—	—	—	7.41	-11.52	-9.25	NAV Rtrn% +/-Russ MV
—	—	—	—	—	—	—	—	4	6	NAV Return% Rank in Cat
—	—	—	—	—	—	—	—	3.25	2.71	Income Return %
—	—	—	—	—	—	—	—	-2.12	8.26	Capital Return %
—	—	—	—	—	—	—	0.00	0.49	0.40	Income $
—	—	—	—	—	—	—	0.00	0.00	0.00	Capital Gains $
—	—	—	—	—	—	—	—	0.60	0.61	Expense Ratio %
—	—	—	—	—	—	—	—	3.57	3.49	Income Ratio %
—	—	—	—	—	—	—	—	21	9	Turnover Rate %
—	—	—	—	—	—	—	102	492	431	Net Assets $mil

Performance 12-31-06

Historic Quarterly NAV Returns

	1st Qtr	2nd Qtr	3rd Qtr	4th Qtr	Total
2002	—	—	—	—	—
2003	—	—	—	—	—
2004	—	—	—	—	—*
2005	-4.02	4.30	1.08	-0.06	1.13
2006	1.22	-1.50	6.06	4.94	10.97

Trailing	NAV Return%	Market Return%	NAV Rtrn% +/-S&P 500	%Rank Cat.(NAV)
3 Mo	4.94	6.36	-1.76	8
6 Mo	11.29	13.39	-1.45	7
1 Yr	10.97	12.90	-4.82	6
3 Yr Avg	—	—	—	—
5 Yr Avg	—	—	—	—
10 Yr Avg	—	—	—	—

Tax Analysis	Tax-Adj Return%	Tax-Cost Ratio
3 Yr (estimated)	—	—
5 Yr (estimated)	—	—
10 Yr (estimated)	—	—

Rating and Risk

Time Period	Morningstar Rtn vs Cat	Morningstar Risk vs Cat	Morningstar Risk-Adj Rating
3 Yr	—	—	—
5 Yr	—	—	—
10 Yr	—	—	—

Other Measures	Standard Index S&P 500	Best Fit Index
Alpha	—	—
Beta	—	—
R-Squared	—	—
Standard Deviation	—	
Mean	—	
Sharpe Ratio	—	

Portfolio Analysis 11-30-06

Share change since 10-06 Total Stocks:50	Sector	PE	Tot Ret%	% Assets
Universal Corporation	Goods	—	18.22	2.92
F.N.B. Corporation	Financial	19.6	11.30	2.88
Progress Energy, Inc.	Utilities	16.7	18.07	2.72
First Commonwealth Finan	Financial	17.9	9.27	2.64
Peoples Energy Corp.	Utilities	—	34.37	2.62
FirstMerit Corporation	Financial	16.6	-2.24	2.49
Consolidated Edison Comp	Utilities	17.5	9.14	2.44
ServiceMaster Limited Pa	Consumer	21.5	14.21	2.42
Washington Mutual, Inc.	Financial	13.5	9.62	2.42
Arthur J. Gallagher & Co	Financial	25.9	-0.04	2.33
Atmos Energy Corporation	Utilities	17.5	27.57	2.31
Altria Group, Inc.	Goods	15.9	19.87	2.27
WPS Resources	Utilities	14.9	2.11	2.24
Pinnacle West Capital	Utilities	21.9	27.04	2.23
Vectren Corporation	Utilities	17.2	8.97	2.19
WGL Holdings, Inc.	Utilities	18.0	13.29	2.15
Old National Bancorp	Financial	15.6	-8.72	2.15
Susquehanna Bancshares	Financial	14.6	18.10	2.13
MGE Energy, Inc.	Utilities	18.8	12.48	2.10
Bank of America Corporat	Financial	12.4	20.68	2.06

Current Investment Style

Value Blnd Growth — Large Mid Small

Market Cap	%
Giant	9.9
Large	19.7
Mid	27.4
Small	41.1
Micro	1.9
Avg $mil:	4,024

Value Measures		Rel Category
Price/Earnings	16.00	1.07
Price/Book	1.89	0.99
Price/Sales	1.24	1.39
Price/Cash Flow	8.48	1.15
Dividend Yield %	4.00	1.63

Growth Measures	%	Rel Category
Long-Term Erngs	6.80	0.72
Book Value	5.10	0.89
Sales	9.79	1.18
Cash Flow	-9.65	NMF
Historical Erngs	-1.04	NMF

Profitability	%	Rel Category
Return on Equity	11.64	0.89
Return on Assets	8.26	1.09
Net Margin	16.12	1.38

Sector Weightings	% of Stocks	Rel S&P 500	3 Year High	Low
Info	1.99	0.10		
Software	0.00	0.00	0	0
Hardware	0.00	0.00	0	0
Media	0.00	0.00	0	0
Telecom	1.99	0.57	3	2
Service	56.76	1.23		
Health	1.72	0.14	3	2
Consumer	2.42	0.32	5	1
Business	0.00	0.00	2	0
Financial	52.62	2.36	53	38
Mfg	41.25	1.22		
Goods	9.57	1.12	11	7
Ind Mtrls	0.00	0.00	0	0
Energy	0.00	0.00	1	0
Utilities	31.68	9.05	41	30

Composition

● Cash	0.0
● Stocks	100.0
● Bonds	0.0
● Other	0.0
Foreign	0.0
(% of Stock)	

Morningstar's Take by Dan Culloton 12-31-06

PowerShares HighYield Dividend Achievers is interesting, but not compelling.

When launched nearly two years ago, this exchange-traded fund was one of two yield-centric ETFs on the market. Now it is one of dozens. Its distinguishing factor still is that its benchmark, the Mergent Dividend Achievers 50, included the 50 highest-yielding U.S. stocks among those that have increased their dividends 10 years in a row.

That sounds good in theory. It can be a sign of financial health and consistent cash-flow growth if a company pays a dividend and is able to increase it consistently. Indeed, the index and this portfolio include some companies that have boasted significant competitive advantages and profitability, such as tobacco giant Altria and financial-services titan Citigroup.

In practice, however, this approach has serious drawbacks. Paramount among those is sector concentration. The index doesn't make any effort to look like the broad market. That isn't necessarily a bad thing, but when this ETF's benchmark lets the chips fall, they land disproportionately in the financial-services and utilities sectors, which account for 53% and 32%, respectively, of this portfolio's assets. The fund's financial holdings are further clustered in small regional banks. The downside of these leanings has been apparent. Rate-sensitive banks have lagged most other industries and the market in 2006, and acted as a drag on this ETF's performance relative to the typical conventional mid-cap value fund and dividend ETF.

Those areas of the market won't stay out of favor, but this ETF's concentration still will make for lumpy performance. It comes at a higher price, too. The fund's 0.61% expense ratio is low relative to the typical no-load mid-cap value fund, but more than twice the levy of low-cost dividend-oriented ETFs, such as Vanguard Dividend Appreciation and WisdomTree Total Dividend.

Look elsewhere for dividend-stock exposure.

Address:	301 West Roosevelt Road Wheaton, IL 60187 800-983-0903
Web Address:	www.powershares.com
Inception:	12-09-04 *
Advisor:	PowerShares Capital Management LLC

Management Fee:	0.40%
Expense Projections:	3Yr:$205 5Yr:$360 10Yr:$808
Income Distrib:	Quarterly
Exchange:	AMEX

MORNINGSTAR® ETFs 150

125

Data through December 31, 2006

PowerShares Intl Div Ach PID

Market Price $18.52	**Mstar Category** Foreign Large Value

Morningstar Fair Value

Price/Fair Value Ratio	Coverage Rate %
0.97 Fairly valued	89 Good

Management

This fund's advisor, PowerShares Capital Management, has stormed the exchange-traded fund arena with scores of fund launches in just a few short years. John Southard, who has been with the firm since its 2002 inception, handles day-to-day management responsibilities here.

Methodology

This exchange-traded fund tracks an index of foreign stocks that have at least a 5-year streak of increasing dividends. It will own a fair number of emerging-markets names as well as long as such stocks are listed on the main U.S. exchanges. The resultant portfolio of 60-odd stocks is relatively compact and sports large sector concentrations as well.

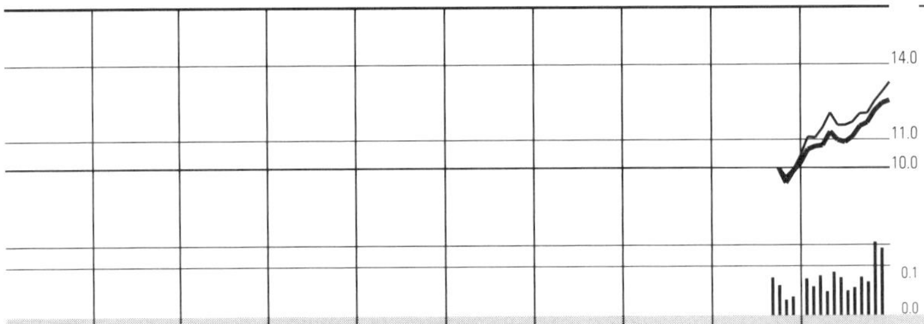

Morningstar Rating	Return	Risk	Yield	NAV	Avg Daily Vol. (k)	52 wk High/Low
— Not Rated	Not Rated		2.7%	$18.25	203	$19.03 - $15.61

Growth of $10,000
- Investment Value of ETF
- Investment Value of Index MSCI EAFE

Trading Volume Millions

	1997	1998	1999	2000	2001	2002	2003	2004	2005	2006	History
	—	—	—	—	—	—	—	—	15.38	18.25	NAV $
	—	—	—	—	—	—	—	—	15.38	18.96	Market Price $
	—	—	—	—	—	—	—	—	19.79*	22.15	NAV Return%
	—	—	—	—	—	—	—	—	23.37*	26.88	Market Price Return%
	—	—	—	—	—	—	—	—	0.08	0.62	Avg Premium/Discount%
	—	—	—	—	—	—	—	—	19.79	-4.19	NAV Rtrn% +/-MSCI EAFE
	—	—	—	—	—	—	—	—	19.79	-3.56	NAV Rtrn% +/-MSCI Wd xUS
	—	—	—	—	—	—	—	—	3		NAV Return% Rank in Cat
	—	—	—	—	—	—	—	—	—	3.26	Income Return %
	—	—	—	—	—	—	—	—	—	18.89	Capital Return %
	—	—	—	—	—	—	—	—	0.09	0.50	Income $
	—	—	—	—	—	—	—	—	0.00	0.00	Capital Gains $
	—	—	—	—	—	—	—	—	—	0.62	Expense Ratio %
	—	—	—	—	—	—	—	—	—	3.06	Income Ratio %
	—	—	—	—	—	—	—	—	—	8	Turnover Rate %
	—	—	—	—	—	—	—	—	27	323	Net Assets $mil

Performance 12-31-06

Historic Quarterly NAV Returns

	1st Qtr	2nd Qtr	3rd Qtr	4th Qtr	Total
2002	—	—	—	—	—
2003	—	—	—	—	—
2004	—	—	—	—	—
2005	—	—	—	1.63	—*
2006	5.78	1.00	6.47	7.38	22.15

Trailing	NAV Return%	Market Return%	NAV Rtrn% +/-MSCI EAFE	%Rank Cat.(NAV)
3 Mo	7.38	11.34	-2.97	3
6 Mo	14.32	18.75	-0.37	3
1 Yr	22.15	26.88	-4.19	3
3 Yr Avg	—	—	—	—
5 Yr Avg	—	—	—	—
10 Yr Avg	—	—	—	—

Tax Analysis	Tax-Adj Return%	Tax-Cost Ratio
3 Yr (estimated)	—	—
5 Yr (estimated)	—	—
10 Yr (estimated)	—	—

Rating and Risk

Time Period	Morningstar Rtn vs Cat	Morningstar Risk vs Cat	Morningstar Risk-Adj Rating
3 Yr	—	—	—
5 Yr	—	—	—
10 Yr	—	—	—

Other Measures	Standard Index S&P 500	Best Fit Index
Alpha	—	—
Beta	—	—
R-Squared	—	—
Standard Deviation	—	
Mean	—	
Sharpe Ratio	—	

Portfolio Analysis 11-30-06

Share change since 10-06 Total Stocks:60	Sector	Country	% Assets
⊕ Nam Tai Electronics Inc.	Hardware	Hong Kong	7.33
⊕ Provida ADR	Financial	Chile	4.41
⊕ Telstra Corporation, Ltd	Telecom	Australia	3.99
⊕ Endesa SA ADR	Utilities	Spain	3.41
⊕ Lloyds TSB Group PLC ADR	Financial	U.K.	3.39
⊕ National Australia Bank	Financial	Australia	2.58
⊕ Huaneng Power Internatio	Utilities	China	2.49
⊕ ABN AMRO Holding NV ADR	Financial	Netherlands	2.43
⊕ Gallaher Group PLC ADR	Goods	U.K.	2.39
⊕ Australia & New Zealand	Financial	Australia	2.34
⊕ National Grid PLC ADR	Utilities	U.K.	2.19
⊕ Barclays PLC ADR	Financial	U.K.	2.17
⊕ HSBC Holdings PLC ADR	Financial	U.K.	2.16
⊕ Volvo AB ADR	Ind Mtrls	Sweden	2.05
⊕ ENI SpA ADR	Energy	Italy	1.97
⊕ Bank of Ireland ADR	Financial	Ireland	1.96
⊕ Bank of Montreal	Financial	Canada	1.94
⊕ Unilever NV	Goods	Netherlands	1.93
⊕ Unilever PLC ADR	Goods	U.K.	1.93
⊕ BP PLC ADR	Energy	U.K.	1.85

Current Investment Style

Value Blnd Growth — Large Mid Small

Market Cap	%
Giant	50.5
Large	29.1
Mid	8.1
Small	11.7
Micro	0.5

Avg $mil: 20,334

Value Measures		Rel Category
Price/Earnings	12.34	0.89
Price/Book	2.14	0.97
Price/Sales	1.72	1.19
Price/Cash Flow	6.11	0.85
Dividend Yield %	2.63	0.97

Growth Measures	%	Rel Category
Long-Term Erngs	10.40	1.00
Book Value	5.92	0.82
Sales	10.93	1.13
Cash Flow	-5.04	NMF
Historical Erngs	20.53	1.00

Composition

Cash	0.1	Bonds	0.0
Stocks	99.9	Other	0.0
Foreign	(% of Stock)		94.9

Sector Weightings	% of Stocks	Rel MSCI EAFE	3 Year High Low
⌖ Info	16.02	1.36	
🅝 Software	0.81	1.45	— —
🅗 Hardware	7.33	1.90	— —
🅜 Media	3.88	2.12	— —
🅣 Telecom	4.00	0.72	— —
⌗ Service	46.06	0.98	
🅗 Health	3.72	0.52	— —
🅒 Consumer	0.00	0.00	— —
🅑 Business	1.52	0.30	— —
🅢 Financial	40.82	1.36	— —
⌐ Mfg	37.92	0.93	
🅖 Goods	13.47	1.03	— —
🅘 Ind Mtrls	5.24	0.34	— —
🅔 Energy	9.30	1.30	— —
🅤 Utilities	9.91	1.89	— —

Regional Exposure			% Stock
UK/W. Europe	51	N. America	21
Japan	1	Latn America	5
Asia X Japan	19	Other	3

Country Exposure			% Stock
U.K.	25	Hong Kong	7
Canada	16	Netherlands	6
Australia	9		

Morningstar's Take by Arijit Dutta 12-31-06

We don't think PowerShares International Dividend Achievers is such a great idea.

This ETF focuses on a rather narrow group of stocks. It is based on an index of foreign stocks that have a streak of increasing their dividends for at least 5 consecutive years. Further, the index only considers stocks that have American Depository Receipts, which means the companies' corporate governance standards must comply with U.S. regulations. Currently, this portfolio only has 60 stocks.

This is a far cry from more mainstream, diversified foreign benchmarks. The iShares MSCI EAFE Value Index, a rival foreign large-value ETF, owns 540 stocks, for example. Moreover, the approach can lead to inadequate diversification in terms of sectors.

We're not enthusiastic about investing in such a thin slice of the non-U.S. market. While dividends can be a good indicator of a company's health, this ETF's approach puts too much emphasis on a single characteristic. The fund may end up with stocks whose dividend outlook turns negative in a hurry. Indeed, the index lost 21% in 2002, compared with the MSCI EAFE benchmark's 16% loss that year (though the fund only launched in late 2005, the underlying index has backtested hypothetical returns going back several years). Also, the fund is likely to miss companies that are using their cash for future growth rather than on dividends. For example, the portfolio has virtually no exposure to technology stocks, which isn't a sector known for rich dividends.

Overall, we think investors have better choices. For those looking for an ETF option, the iShares fund offers far broader, and considerably lower-cost exposure to value stocks within the MSCI EAFE universe. Those who would rather not hazard a guess about the future performance of value or growth stocks have a number of exceptionally cheap index mutual-funds from which to choose.

Address:	301 West Roosevelt Road Wheaton, IL 60187 800-843-2639
Web Address:	www.powershares.com
Inception:	09-15-05 *
Advisor:	PowerShares Capital Management LLC

Management Fee:	0.40%
Expense Projections:	3Yr:$216 5Yr: — 10Yr: —
Income Distrib:	Quarterly
Exchange:	AMEX

126

MORNINGSTAR® ETFs 150

Expand Your Investing Horizons with These Other Morningstar Annuals!

Morningstar® Funds 500™

Reduce your portfolio's risk and benefit from the investment expertise of the best mutual fund managers in the business. Our fund reports cover the biggest and most popular mutual funds, and contain critical year-end information and written commentary by a Morningstar analyst. These reports are the industry standards—the same full-page reports relied upon by financial professionals.

► Analyst guidance in every report
► Best funds for 2007

January 2007. Softbound. 8 1/2" X 11". Approx. 600 pages. $35 ($4.95 S&H).

Morningstar® Stocks 500™

If you want to add stocks to your portfolio, this popular annual is a must-have. Follow our analysts' guidance on widely held stocks. Each report page contains the Morningstar Rating for stocks, a fair value estimate, Consider Buying/Selling prices, historical data, written analysis by a Morningstar stock analyst— everything you expect from Morningstar.

► Buy/sell guidance in every report
► Morningstar's picks for 2007

January 2007. Softbound. 8 1/2" x 11". Approx. 600 pages. $35 (plus $4.95 S&H).

Examine both annuals risk-free for 30 days.

Additional Reports Available Free!
Order either book now and gain access to additional Morningstar Fund Reports or Morningstar Stock Reports of your choice. Access up to 50 of our 2,000 Fund Reports or up to 50 of our 1,800 Stock Reports—you decide when!

016139-EI-7A

To order, call toll-free 866-608-9570
Mention code AE1-INS-7A

MORNINGSTAR®

Get Even More ETF Buy/Sell Ideas—Free!

Use the 30-day online ETF research pass any time in 2007. It's fast, easy, and completely free to you.

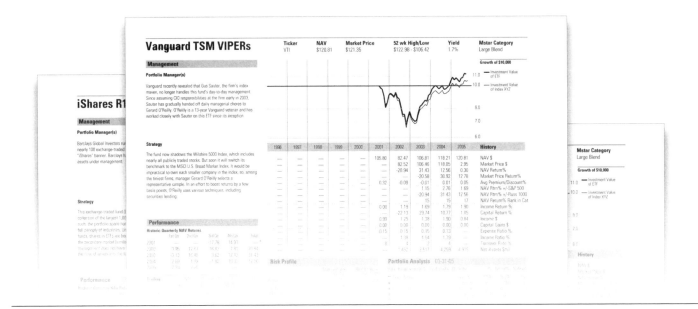

Thank you for purchasing *Morningstar ETFs 150*. In addition to the reports contained here, you have free access to our online ETF content for 30 days. You decide when!

Note that you will be asked to register if you are not already registered for one of Morningstar's online services. This process takes only a minute, does not require a credit card, and is absolutely free.

Online information includes:

▶ Prices updated throughout the trading day

▶ The latest Morningstar Ratings for ETFs

▶ The most current Morningstar analysis

▶ All the financial data you'll find in the print reports with up-to-date information

▶ Morningstar's exclusive ETF screener

▶ And more!

When you're ready to activate your free 30-day ETF Research Pass, visit this Web address:

www.morningstar.com/goto/2007ETFs150

Thank You for Choosing Morningstar!

PowerShares Val Line Time *PIV*

Market Price $16.19		**Mstar Category** Large Growth

Morningstar Fair Value

Price/Fair Value Ratio	Coverage Rate %
1.01 Fairly valued	73 Fair

Management

PowerShares Capital Management, founded in 2002, manages this fund. John W. Southard Jr. is the lead portfolio manager. He was a senior analyst of Chicago Investment Analytics, a quantitative research firm. He also worked as an analyst and portfolio manager at a unit investment trust firm.

Methodology

This ETF seeks to match the performance of the Value Line Index. This index represents the 50 highest-ranking common stocks between $650 million and $88 billion of market capitalization. The ranking is based on a proprietary methodology using different indicators that include momentum, investor expectations, and risk factors. Stocks are added to or removed from the portfolio as they move up or down the rank, which is updated daily.

Morningstar Rating	Return	Risk	Yield	NAV	Avg Daily Vol. (k)
— Not Rated	— Not Rated	—	—	$15.98	115

52 wk High/Low $17.87 - $13.88

Growth of $10,000
— Investment Value of ETF
— Investment Value of Index S&P 500

Trading Volume Millions

	1997	1998	1999	2000	2001	2002	2003	2004	2005	2006	History
	—	—	—	—	—	—	—	—	15.27	15.98	NAV $
	—	—	—	—	—	—	—	—	15.28	15.98	Market Price $
	—	—	—	—	—	—	—	—	2.75*	4.66	NAV Return%
	—	—	—	—	—	—	—	—	2.44*	4.58	Market Price Return%
	—	—	—	—	—	—	—	—	0.09	0.03	Avg Premium/Discount%
	—	—	—	—	—	—	—	—	2.75	-11.13	NAV Rtrn% +/-S&P 500
	—	—	—	—	—	—	—	—	2.75	-4.41	NAV Rtrn% +/-Russ 1000Gr
	—	—	—	—	—	—	—	—	—	13	NAV Return% Rank in Cat
	—	—	—	—	—	—	—	—	0.00	0.00	Income Return %
	—	—	—	—	—	—	—	—	—	4.66	Capital Return %
	—	—	—	—	—	—	—	—	0.00	0.00	Income $
	—	—	—	—	—	—	—	—	0.00	0.00	Capital Gains $
	—	—	—	—	—	—	—	—	0.71		Expense Ratio %
	—	—	—	—	—	—	—	—	-0.30		Income Ratio %
	—	—	—	—	—	—	—	—	39		Turnover Rate %
	—	—	—	—	—	—	—	—	179		Net Assets $mil

Performance 12-31-06

Historic Quarterly NAV Returns

	1st Qtr	2nd Qtr	3rd Qtr	4th Qtr	Total
2002	—	—	—	—	—
2003	—	—	—	—	—
2004	—	—	—	—	—
2005	—	—	—	—	—*
2006	9.19	-5.34	-5.62	7.28	4.66

Trailing	NAV Return%	Market Return%	NAV Rtrn% +/-S&P 500	%Rank Cat.(NAV)
3 Mo	7.28	7.39	0.58	15
6 Mo	1.26	1.46	-11.48	15
1 Yr	4.66	4.58	-11.13	13
3 Yr Avg	—	—	—	—
5 Yr Avg	—	—	—	—
10 Yr Avg	—	—	—	—

Tax Analysis	Tax-Adj Return%	Tax-Cost Ratio
3 Yr (estimated)	—	—
5 Yr (estimated)	—	—
10 Yr (estimated)	—	—

Rating and Risk

Time Period	Morningstar Rtn vs Cat	Morningstar Risk vs Cat	Morningstar Risk-Adj Rating
3 Yr	—	—	—
5 Yr	—	—	—
10 Yr	—	—	—

Other Measures	Standard Index S&P 500	Best Fit Index
Alpha	—	—
Beta	—	—
R-Squared	—	—
Standard Deviation	—	
Mean	—	
Sharpe Ratio	—	

Morningstar's Take by Federico Cepeda 12-31-06

There are several reasons to avoid PowerShares Value Line Timeliness Select.

This exchange-traded fund tracks the Value Line Index, which owns companies it believes will outperform the U.S. equity market. The index holds the 50 highest-ranking stocks on a variety of criteria, including stock price momentum, investor expectations, and risk factors. Although we place this fund in our large-growth category, it holds stocks of all market capitalizations. Its current portfolio's average market cap is 5 times smaller than the large-growth category average.

Given the fund's all-cap nature, its 2006 performance has been disappointing. Small and mid-cap growth stocks have generally outperformed their larger peers for the year to date through Nov. 21, 2006. Yet this fund has been in the wrong stocks, which might be due to the Value Line Index's methodology. The index is willing to buy very pricey stocks, a strategy which has not been rewarded this year. Several of the fund's top holdings as of Oct. 31, 2006, including Midwest Air Group, American Eagle Outfitters, and CommScope, were rated as overpriced by Morningstar equity analysts. The fund might look better in a different market environment, but we're skeptical about its chances for long-term success. A conventional mutual fund named Value Line has been following a strategy that takes into account similar factors, and it has badly underperformed its mid-growth peers over the trailing one-, three-, five-, and 10-year periods.

Another drawback is the fund's cost. Its 0.71% expense ratio is the highest among large-cap, mid-cap, and small-cap growth ETFs. Even some actively managed funds, such as Selected American Shares, charge less than that. The high price tag isn't surprising, given that many PowerShares ETFs charge much more than their peers.

In short, we'd look elsewhere for a growth fund.

Address:	301 West Roosevelt Road Wheaton, IL 60187 800-843-2639
Web Address:	www.powershares.com
Inception:	12-06-05*
Advisor:	PowerShares Capital Management LLC

Management Fee:	0.50%		
Expense Projections:	3Yr:$244	5Yr: —	10Yr: —
Income Distrib:	Quarterly		
Exchange:	AMEX		

Portfolio Analysis 11-30-06

Share change since 10-06 Total Stocks:50

	Sector	PE	Tot Ret%	% Assets
☆ PC Connection, Inc.	Consumer	41.2	175.65	2.19
☆ NBTY, Inc.	Health	25.7	155.82	2.09
☆ Digene Corporation	Health	88.7	64.28	2.08
⊖ Cognizant Technology Sol	Business	52.1	53.49	2.07
⊖ Kimball International, I	Goods	35.7	136.74	2.06
☆ BT Group PLC ADR	Telecom	18.4	63.56	2.06
☆ CSG Systems Internationa	Software	23.9	19.76	2.05
⊖ AT&T, Inc.	Telecom	19.2	51.59	2.05
☆ Gartner, Inc. A	Business	45.0	53.41	2.04
⊖ BMC Software, Inc.	Software	36.6	57.15	2.04
☆ Sepracor, Inc.	Health	NMF	19.34	2.04
☆ Schering-Plough Corporat	Health	36.9	14.63	2.04
☆ Lockheed Martin Corporat	Ind Mtrls	17.0	46.98	2.03
☆ Infosys Technologies, Lt	Software	54.6	36.82	2.03
☆ TeleTech Holdings, Inc.	Business	41.9	98.17	2.02
☆ Comcast Corporation	Media	—	—	2.02
☆ Coach, Inc.	Goods	31.4	28.85	2.02
☆ Safeway Inc.	Consumer	21.1	47.22	2.02
⊖ Synovus Financial Corp.	Financial	17.0	17.31	2.01
☆ AMN Healthcare Services,	Business	29.3	39.23	2.01

Current Investment Style

Value Blnd Growth / Large Mid Small

Market Cap	%
Giant	14.3
Large	32.5
Mid	34.5
Small	16.5
Micro	2.2

Avg $mil: 8,348

Value Measures		Rel Category
Price/Earnings	20.63	1.00
Price/Book	3.60	1.10
Price/Sales	1.28	0.72
Price/Cash Flow	14.84	1.33
Dividend Yield %	0.76	0.88

Growth Measures	%	Rel Category
Long-Term Erngs	14.54	0.97
Book Value	5.79	0.72
Sales	4.56	0.39
Cash Flow	3.35	0.23
Historical Erngs	15.58	0.55

Profitability	%	Rel Category
Return on Equity	20.88	1.04
Return on Assets	9.37	0.94
Net Margin	10.54	0.84

Sector Weightings	% of Stocks	Rel S&P 500	3 Year High Low
↻ Info	24.20	1.21	
↘ Software	8.10	2.35	— —
▣ Hardware	1.99	0.22	— —
▣ Media	8.00	2.11	— —
▣ Telecom	6.11	1.74	— —
⊂ Service	55.93	1.21	
▤ Health	16.10	1.33	— —
▤ Consumer	17.82	2.33	— —
▤ Business	16.07	3.80	— —
▤ Financial	5.94	0.27	— —
⊔ Mfg	19.85	0.59	
▤ Goods	8.01	0.94	— —
▤ Ind Mtrls	11.84	0.99	— —
▤ Energy	0.00	0.00	— —
▤ Utilities	0.00	0.00	— —

Composition

● Cash		0.0
● Stocks		100.0
● Bonds		0.0
● Other		0.0
Foreign		4.1
(% of Stock)		

PowerShares Zacks MicroCp PZI

Market Price $17.45	**Mstar Category** Small Blend	

Morningstar Fair Value

Price/Fair Value Ratio —

Coverage Rate % —

Management

The fund is managed by PowerShares Capital Management, which was founded in 2002. John W. Southard Jr. is the lead portfolio manager. He is a former senior analyst of Chicago Investment Analytics, a quantitative research firm bought by Charles Schwab in 2000.

Methodology

This ETF tracks the Zacks Micro Cap Index, which is a quasi-actively managed benchmark. The benchmark includes the 300 to 500 stocks with market capitalizations between $60 million and $600 million. Zacks uses a computer model to select the index's constituents based on several valuation and momentum factors. The index is equal weighted and rebalanced once per quarter, but Zacks will kick out benchmark members on a weekly basis if the stocks stop meeting the model's screens. The index omits stocks that trade over the counter or on the pink sheets. The advisor uses representative sampling.

	Morningstar Rating	Return	Risk	Yield	NAV	Avg Daily Vol. (k)	52 wk High/Low
—	Not Rated	Not Rated		0.1%	$17.73	56	$18.03 - $15.15

Growth of $10,000
— Investment Value of ETF
— Investment Value of Index S&P 500

1997	1998	1999	2000	2001	2002	2003	2004	2005	2006	History
—	—	—	—	—	—	—	—	15.16	17.73	NAV $
—	—	—	—	—	—	—	—	15.15	17.86	Market Price $
—	—	—	—	—	—	—	—	14.33*	17.11	NAV Return%
—	—	—	—	—	—	—	—	14.82*	18.03	Market Price Return%
—	—	—	—	—	—	—	—	-0.01	-0.06	Avg Premium/Discount%
—	—	—	—	—	—	—	—	14.33	1.32	NAV Rtrn% +/-S&P 500
—	—	—	—	—	—	—	—	14.33	-1.26	NAV Rtrn% +/-Russ 2000
—	—	—	—	—	—	—	—	—	8	NAV Return% Rank in Cat
—	—	—	—	—	—	—	—	—	0.14	Income Return %
—	—	—	—	—	—	—	—	—	16.97	Capital Return %
—	—	—	—	—	—	—	—	0.01	0.02	Income $
—	—	—	—	—	—	—	—	0.00	0.00	Capital Gains $
—	—	—	—	—	—	—	—	—	0.72	Expense Ratio %
—	—	—	—	—	—	—	—	—	0.01	Income Ratio %
—	—	—	—	—	—	—	—	—	78	Turnover Rate %
—	—	—	—	—	—	—	—	103	165	Net Assets $mil

Performance 12-31-06

Historic Quarterly NAV Returns

	1st Qtr	2nd Qtr	3rd Qtr	4th Qtr	Total
2002	—	—	—	—	—
2003	—	—	—	—	—
2004	—	—	—	—	—
2005	—	—	—	0.93	—*
2006	13.92	-5.21	-0.29	8.77	17.11

Trailing	NAV Return%	Market Return%	NAV Rtrn% +/-S&P 500	%Rank Cat.(NAV)
3 Mo	8.77	9.57	2.07	12
6 Mo	8.46	9.23	-4.28	10
1 Yr	17.11	18.03	1.32	8
3 Yr Avg	—	—	—	—
5 Yr Avg	—	—	—	—
10 Yr Avg	—	—	—	—

Tax Analysis	Tax-Adj Return%	Tax-Cost Ratio
3 Yr (estimated)	—	—
5 Yr (estimated)	—	—
10 Yr (estimated)	—	—

Rating and Risk

Time Period	Morningstar Rtn vs Cat	Morningstar Risk vs Cat	Morningstar Risk-Adj Rating
3 Yr	—	—	—
5 Yr	—	—	—
10 Yr	—	—	—

Other Measures	Standard Index S&P 500	Best Fit Index
Alpha	—	—
Beta	—	—
R-Squared	—	—
Standard Deviation	—	
Mean	—	
Sharpe Ratio	—	

Portfolio Analysis 11-30-06

Share change since 10-06 Total Stocks:399	Sector	PE	Tot Ret%	% Assets
Amrep Corporation	Consumer	22.3	380.14	0.42
Savient Pharmaceuticals	Health	31.1	199.73	0.41
CDC Corporation A	—	—	196.88	0.37
Alliance One Internation	Goods	—	81.03	0.37
Atlantic Tele-Network, I	Telecom	19.7	79.03	0.36
Medifast, Inc.	Health	31.4	139.89	0.35
Bolt Technology Corporat	Energy	21.6	59.06	0.35
Universal Stainless & Al	Ind Mtrls	14.3	123.20	0.34
☼ Primus Guaranty, Ltd.	Financial	7.1	-11.49	0.34
Zoll Medical Corporation	Health	71.0	131.20	0.33
Exploration Company of D	Energy	16.9	106.50	0.33
Innospec, Inc.	Energy	—	188.05	0.33
21st Century Holding Com	Financial	9.7	42.53	0.33
Brush Engineered Materia	Ind Mtrls	28.9	112.39	0.33
LB Foster Company A	Ind Mtrls	36.5	74.20	0.33
Rita Medical Systems, In	Health	—	17.65	0.33
Robbins & Myers, Inc.	Ind Mtrls	—	127.64	0.32
Buckeye Technologies, In	Ind Mtrls	74.9	48.82	0.32
Cogent Communications Gr	Telecom	—	195.45	0.32
Arena Resources, Inc.	Energy	29.7	54.75	0.31

Current Investment Style

Value Blnd Growth — Large Mid Small

Market Cap	%
Giant	0.0
Large	0.0
Mid	0.0
Small	19.5
Micro	80.5

Avg $mil: 335

Value Measures		Rel Category
Price/Earnings	16.90	0.96
Price/Book	1.67	0.81
Price/Sales	0.79	0.77
Price/Cash Flow	4.83	0.74
Dividend Yield %	1.29	0.81

Growth Measures	%	Rel Category
Long-Term Erngs	14.45	1.08
Book Value	1.40	0.26
Sales	6.65	2.93
Cash Flow	3.26	0.36
Historical Erngs	8.55	0.72

Profitability	%	Rel Category
Return on Equity	6.05	0.52
Return on Assets	3.93	0.60
Net Margin	7.02	0.71

Sector Weightings	% of Stocks	Rel S&P 500	3 Year High Low
☐ Info	19.86	0.99	
🖥 Software	5.15	1.49	— —
💽 Hardware	12.10	1.31	— —
🎬 Media	0.29	0.08	— —
📞 Telecom	2.32	0.66	— —
☎ Service	55.16	1.19	
🏥 Health	5.59	0.46	— —
🛒 Consumer	13.16	1.72	— —
💼 Business	13.53	3.20	— —
💲 Financial	22.88	1.03	— —
🏭 Mfg	24.97	0.74	
🏷 Goods	4.90	0.57	— —
⚙ Ind Mtrls	15.86	1.33	— —
🔥 Energy	3.99	0.41	— —
💡 Utilities	0.22	0.06	— —

Composition

● Cash		0.0
● Stocks		99.7
● Bonds		0.0
○ Other		0.2
Foreign		4.5
(% of Stock)		

Morningstar's Take by Annie Sorich 12-31-06

Don't be tempted by PowerShares Zacks Micro Cap's recent performance.

With a one-year return of 18.30% through Nov. 28, 2006, this ETF stands in the top quintile of its small-blend peers. Its small-cap value tilt has something to do with its success this year, as this section of the market continues to outperform almost all others.

Whether the fund will keep its value tilt is a mystery. It replicates the Zacks Microcap Index, a benchmark created by Zacks Investment Research that uses value and momentum factors to select stocks within the market cap range of $60 million to $600 million. Zacks doesn't disclose the specific factors to the public. Moreover, the fund and index lack long track records, and we aren't certain how the fund will behave in different market environments. While this lack of transparency about index construction is becoming more common and it's not unusual for quantitative funds to guard proprietary models, we think investors deserve

more information about its methodology.

Another way this fund separates itself from the rest of the ETF world is its high turnover. Every quarter the index is reconstituted, and so far, this has resulted in turnover of 78% during the fund's first eight months of existence. The average ETF has a turnover rate of 16% a year, and only a handful of ETFs top the fund's partial-year turnover. This does not bode well for the fund's tax efficiency or trading costs, both of which are usually touted as advantages of owning ETFs.

In addition, while the ETF may look cheap relative to other micro-cap focused offerings, there is a more proven mutual fund alternative. Bridgeway Ultra-Small Company Market has an expense ratio of 0.65%, which is only five basis points more expensive than this ETF, not to mention it has a time-tested, tax-efficient investment strategy. We think investing in a proven fund makes more sense in this turbulent asset class, and investors can pass on this ETF.

Address:	301 West Roosevelt Road Wheaton, IL 60187 800-843-2639
Web Address:	www.powershares.com
Inception:	08-18-05*
Advisor:	PowerShares Capital Management LLC

Management Fee:	0.50%
Expense Projections:	3Yr:$255 5Yr: — 10Yr: —
Income Distrib:	Quarterly
Exchange:	AMEX

 MORNINGSTAR® ETFs 150

PowerShares Zacks Sm Cap PZJ

	Market Price	Mstar Category
	$26.63	Small Blend

Morningstar Rating	Return	Risk	Yield	NAV	Avg Daily Vol.(k)	52 wk High/Low
— Not Rated	Nnt Rated	—	—	$26.88	14	$27.27 - $22.76

Management

The fund is managed by PowerShares Capital Management, which was founded in 2002. John W. Southard Jr. is the lead portfolio manager. He is a former senior analyst of Chicago Investment Analytics, a quantitative research firm bought by Charles Schwab in 2000.

Growth of $10,000
— Investment Value of ETF
— Investment Value of Index S&P 500

12.4
10.6
10.0
9.0

Trading Volume Millions
0.07
0.0

Methodology

This ETF tracks the Zacks Small Cap Index, which is a quasi-actively managed benchmark. The index tries to take advantage of swings in stock prices due to analyst revision estimates. A quantitative model ranks stocks based on these revisions, and the index contains the top 250 most-promising candidates. It is equal weighted and rebalanced once per quarter, but can be rebalanced when appropriate for timeliness of stock purchases.

1997	1998	1999	2000	2001	2002	2003	2004	2005	2006	History
—	—	—	—	—	—	—	—	—	26.88	NAV $
—	—	—	—	—	—	—	—	—	27.19	Market Price $
—	—	—	—	—	—	—	—	—	5.95*	NAV Return%
—	—	—	—	—	—	—	—	—	7.19*	Market Price Return%
—	—	—	—	—	—	—	—	—	-0.05	Avg Premium/Discount%
—	—	—	—	—	—	—	—	—	5.95	NAV Rtrn% +/-S&P 500
—	—	—	—	—	—	—	—	—	5.95	NAV Rtrn% +/-Russ 2000
—	—	—	—	—	—	—	—	—	—	NAV Return% Rank in Cat
—	—	—	—	—	—	—	—	—	—	Income Return %
—	—	—	—	—	—	—	—	—	—	Capital Return %
—	—	—	—	—	—	—	—	—	0.04	Income $
—	—	—	—	—	—	—	—	—	0.00	Capital Gains $
—	—	—	—	—	—	—	—	—	0.75	Expense Ratio %
—	—	—	—	—	—	—	—	—	0.30	Income Ratio %
—	—	—	—	—	—	—	—	—	1	Turnover Rate %
—	—	—	—	—	—	—	—	—	62	Net Assets $mil

Performance 12-31-06

Historic Quarterly NAV Returns

	1st Qtr	2nd Qtr	3rd Qtr	4th Qtr	Total
2002	—	—	—	—	—
2003	—	—	—	—	—
2004	—	—	—	—	—
2005	—	—	—	—	—
2006	—	-6.12	-2.15	10.64	—*

Trailing	NAV Return%	Market Return%	NAV Rtrn% +/-S&P 500	%Rank Cat.(NAV)
3 Mo	10.64	12.03	3.94	12
6 Mo	8.26	9.83	-4.48	10
1 Yr	—	—	—	—
3 Yr Avg	—	—	—	—
5 Yr Avg	—	—	—	—
10 Yr Avg	—	—	—	—

Tax Analysis	Tax-Adj Return%	Tax-Cost Ratio
3 Yr (estimated)	—	—
5 Yr (estimated)	—	—
10 Yr (estimated)	—	—

Rating and Risk

Time Period	Morningstar Rtn vs Cat	Morningstar Risk vs Cat	Morningstar Risk-Adj Rating
3 Yr	—	—	—
5 Yr	—	—	—
10 Yr	—	—	—

Other Measures	Standard Index S&P 500	Best Fit Index
Alpha	—	—
Beta	—	—
R-Squared	—	—
Standard Deviation	—	
Mean	—	
Sharpe Ratio	—	

Portfolio Analysis 11-30-06

Share change since 10-06 Total Stocks:250	Sector	PE	Tot Ret%	% Assets
✿ Omrix Biopharmaceuticals	Health	—	—	0.57
⊖ Dolby Laboratories, Inc.	Goods	—	81.94	0.56
⊕ Allis-Chalmers Energy, I	Business	24.0	84.76	0.55
✿ CorVel Corporation	Financial	59.0	275.75	0.54
✿ Green Mountain Coffee Ro	Goods	41.7	21.26	0.50
⊖ Goodrich Petroleum Corpo	Energy	32.6	43.86	0.50
⊖ MarketAxess Holdings, In	Financial	96.9	18.72	0.50
⊖ Gulf Island Fabrication,	Energy	37.3	53.58	0.49
✿ Exploration Company of D	Energy	16.9	106.50	0.48
⊖ Cascade Bancorp	Financial	25.7	70.66	0.48
✿ PharmaNet Development Gr		—	37.85	0.47
⊖ Rock-Tenn	Ind Mtrls	35.2	102.79	0.47
✿ Advanta B	Financial	16.2	37.83	0.47
⊖ Brown Shoe Company, Inc.	Consumer	20.9	70.25	0.47
✿ Bradley Pharmaceuticals,	Health	42.9	116.63	0.47
✿ Internap Network Service	Business	—	361.86	0.46
⊖ Isis Pharmaceuticals	Health	—	112.21	0.46
⊖ Faro Technologies, Inc.	Ind Mtrls	75.1	20.20	0.45
⊖ Horizon Lines, Inc.	Business	—	—	0.45
⊖ MIPS Technologies, Inc.	Hardware	69.2	46.13	0.45

Morningstar's Take by Annie Sorich 12-31-06

Despite PowerShares Zacks Small Cap's interesting approach, better options abound.

This ETF tracks a quasi-actively managed index: the Zacks Small Cap Index. The index is constructed by a quantitative model that tracks stocks by analyst earnings revision estimates. Zacks Investment Research believes that changes to stock analysts' earnings estimates are strong predictors of future stock movements. The quantitative model ranks stocks according to patterns of these changes, and the index is comprised of the top 250 ranking small-cap companies. The index is rebalanced quarterly, or as necessary, to ensure timely purchase of stocks.

While it's not uncommon for quantitative funds to closely guard their models, PowerShares' description of its index methodology is opaque. One benefit of most ETFs is transparency--investors know what they're buying. In this case, it's unclear how the stocks are ranked and what patterns of earnings estimate revisions the model favors.

We have some other concerns as well. The fund is non-diversified, meaning it can take additional sector risk based on where the fund finds opportunity. Plus, the fund will have higher-than-average turnover, given the model's dependence on timely information. Rapid-trading is uncommon among ETFs. In fact, turnover is generally very low, decreasing tax consequences and trading costs for investors.

Perhaps the best reason to refrain from buying this ETF is its fees. The stated goal of the index is to outperform both the Russell 2000 and professional small-cap managers. Yet the fund has an expense ratio of 0.6%, making it one of the most expensive ETFs around. For ETF investors looking for a small-cap option, Vanguard Small Cap ET offers tax-efficient exposure to more than 1,700 stocks and comes with an ultra-low expense ratio of 0.1%, making it one of the cheapest options out there.

Current Investment Style

Value Blnd Growth — Large Mid Small

Market Cap	%
Giant	0.0
Large	0.0
Mid	3.0
Small	59.8
Micro	37.1

Avg $mil: 733

Value Measures		Rel Category
Price/Earnings	18.86	1.07
Price/Book	2.15	1.04
Price/Sales	0.99	0.96
Price/Cash Flow	5.38	0.83
Dividend Yield %	0.91	0.57

Growth Measures	%	Rel Category
Long-Term Ergns	14.03	1.05
Book Value	6.54	1.20
Sales	7.57	3.33
Cash Flow	14.20	1.57
Historical Ergns	14.60	1.22

Profitability	%	Rel Category
Return on Equity	11.26	0.97
Return on Assets	6.20	0.94
Net Margin	7.24	0.74

Sector Weightings	% of Stocks	Rcl S&P 500	3 Year High Low
↻ Info	14.54	0.73	
🖥 Software	4.27	1.24	— —
💻 Hardware	6.74	0.73	— —
🎤 Media	1.21	0.32	— —
📱 Telecom	2.32	0.66	— —
☞ Service	49.86	1.08	
🩺 Health	10.04	0.83	— —
🛒 Consumer	9.45	1.24	— —
📋 Business	14.64	3.46	— —
💲 Financial	15.73	0.71	— —
🏭 Mfg	35.60	1.05	
🛍 Goods	6.62	0.77	— —
⚙ Ind Mtrls	19.87	1.66	— —
🔥 Energy	5.58	0.57	— —
💡 Utilities	3.53	1.01	— —

Composition

● Cash	0.0	
● Stocks	100.0	
● Bonds	0.0	
● Other	0.0	
Foreign	2.1	
(% of Stock)		

Address:	301 West Roosevelt Road Wheaton, IL 60187 800-843-2639	Management Fee: 0.50%
		Expense Projections: 3Yr:$344 5Yr: — 10Yr: —
		Income Distrib: Quarterly
Web Address:	www.powershares.com	Exchange: AMEX
Inception:	02-16-06*	
Advisor:	PowerShares Capital Management LLC	

Rydex Russell Top 50 XLG

Market Price $107.74	**Mstar Category** Large Blend

Morningstar Fair Value

Price/Fair Value Ratio	Coverage Rate %
0.87 Undervalued	99 Good

Morningstar Rating	Return	Risk	Yield	NAV	Avg Daily Vol. (k)	52 wk High/Low
—	Not Rated	Not Rated	—	1.7%	$107.82	57	$108.52 - $90.97

Growth of $10,000
- Investment Value of ETF
- Investment Value of Index S&P 500

Management

Key personnel involved in managing this and many other ETFs at Rydex include Michael Byrum, president and CIO; James King, director of portfolio management; and Michael Dellapa, director of investment research.

Methodology

This ETF tracks the Russell Top 50 Index, which invests in the biggest 50 names from the Russell 3000. The bogy's portfolio represents roughly 41% of the Russell 3000's total market capitalization and ensures that the fund is a slower mover than many other large-cap blend funds because of its mega-cap focus. It is reconstituted annually.

	1997	1998	1999	2000	2001	2002	2003	2004	2005	2006	History
	—	—	—	—	—	—	—	—	93.18	107.82	NAV $
	—	—	—	—	—	—	—	—	93.13	107.90	Market Price $
	—	—	—	—	—	—	—	—	13.10*	17.90	NAV Return%
	—	—	—	—	—	—	—	—	13.16*	18.06	Market Price Return%
	—	—	—	—	—	—	—	—	0.01	0.08	Avg Premium/Discount%
	—	—	—	—	—	—	—	—	13.10	2.11	NAV Rtrn% +/-S&P 500
	—	—	—	—	—	—	—	—	13.10	2.44	NAV Rtrn% +/-Russ 1000
	—	—	—	—	—	—	—	—	—	30	NAV Return% Rank in Cat
	—	—	—	—	—	—	—	—	—	2.01	Income Return %
	—	—	—	—	—	—	—	—	—	15.89	Capital Return %
	—	—	—	—	—	—	—	—	0.93	1.86	Income $
	—	—	—	—	—	—	—	—	0.00	0.00	Capital Gains $
	—	—	—	—	—	—	—	—	0.20	—	Expense Ratio %
	—	—	—	—	—	—	—	—	1.74	—	Income Ratio %
	—	—	—	—	—	—	—	—	1	—	Turnover Rate %
	—	—	—	—	—	—	—	—	140	544	Net Assets $mil

Performance 12-31-06

Historic Quarterly NAV Returns

	1st Qtr	2nd Qtr	3rd Qtr	4th Qtr	Total
2002	—	—	—	—	—
2003	—	—	—	—	—
2004	—	—	—	—	—
2005	—	—	2.00	1.20	—*
2006	2.44	-1.20	8.29	7.58	17.90

Trailing	NAV Return%	Market Return%	NAV Rtrn% +/-S&P 500	%Rank Cat.(NAV)
3 Mo	7.58	7.55	0.88	44
6 Mo	16.50	16.16	3.76	38
1 Yr	17.90	18.06	2.11	30
3 Yr Avg	—	—	—	—
5 Yr Avg	—	—	—	—
10 Yr Avg	—	—	—	—

Tax Analysis	Tax-Adj Return%	Tax-Cost Ratio
3 Yr (estimated)	—	—
5 Yr (estimated)	—	—
10 Yr (estimated)	—	—

Rating and Risk

Time Period	Morningstar Rtn vs Cat	Morningstar Risk vs Cat	Morningstar Risk-Adj Rating
3 Yr	—	—	—
5 Yr	—	—	—
10 Yr	—	—	—

Other Measures	Standard Index S&P 500	Best Fit Index
Alpha	—	—
Beta	—	—
R-Squared	—	—
Standard Deviation	—	
Mean	—	
Sharpe Ratio	—	

Morningstar's Take by Marta Norton 12-31-06

There are more reasons to avoid Rydex Russell Top 50 than to buy it.

At the very least, this exchange-traded fund is straightforward. It tracks the Russell Top 50 Index, which holds the 50 largest stocks in the Russell 3000 (the index may hold extra stocks from time to time because of company spin-offs). The ETF's holdings will change up once a year, when the index is reconstituted. But this doesn't spell major upheaval for the fund. Because the list of the biggest of the big doesn't change much, this fund's portfolio will likely stay relatively stable year over year. For example, at the May 31, 2006, reconstitution, the index dropped only seven stocks and added just five more. That kind of low turnover helps make the fund pretty tax-efficient.

There are also other attractions here. By focusing on giant-cap stocks, the fund invests only in well-established companies that aren't as volatile as their smaller peers. Also, because small-cap stocks have ruled the market for the past

several years, many giant-cap stocks boast attractive valuations. That puts this ETF in a good position: Of the 50 stocks in its portfolio that Morningstar stock analysts cover, 43 of them are considered either fairly priced or undervalued. And because of its low expenses, it looks like a good way to ride a resurgence of large caps.

But that's where this fund's strengths end. By limiting itself to such a narrow segment of the market, the fund has a poorly diversified portfolio. It usually devotes approximately 40% of its assets to its top 10 holdings, which makes it heavily dependent on stocks such as ExxonMobil (that stock claims about 7% of its assets). And the fund loads up in sectors filled with lots of big names, such as health care and financials. If those sectors tank, this fund will also suffer.

There's little reason to invest here. The fund will likely rally with a large-cap resurgence, but investors with core funds already have exposure there. You can pass on this one.

Address:	9601 Blackwell Rd Rockville, MD 20850 800-820-0888
Web Address:	www.rydex.com
Inception:	05-10-05*
Advisor:	Rydex Global Advisors, Inc.

Management Fee:	0.20%		
Expense Projections:	3Yr:$65	5Yr:$113	10Yr:$257
Income Distrib:	Quarterly		
Exchange:	AMEX		

Portfolio Analysis 12-31-06

Share change since 11-06 Total Stocks:51

	Sector	PE	Tot Ret%	% Assets
⊕ ExxonMobil Corporation	Energy	11.7	39.07	7.46
⊕ General Electric Company	Ind Mtrls	19.8	9.35	6.23
⊕ Citigroup, Inc.	Financial	13.3	19.55	4.46
⊕ Microsoft Corporation	Software	23.7	15.83	4.27
⊕ Bank of America Corporat	Financial	12.4	20.68	3.92
⊕ Procter & Gamble Company	Goods	24.2	13.36	3.39
⊕ Johnson & Johnson	Health	17.4	12.44	3.15
⊕ Pfizer Inc.	Health	15.1	15.22	3.05
⊕ Altria Group, Inc.	Goods	15.9	19.87	2.88
⊕ J.P. Morgan Chase & Co.	Financial	13.7	25.60	2.70
⊕ Cisco Systems, Inc.	Hardware	28.8	59.64	2.69
⊕ Chevron Corporation	Energy	9.3	33.75	2.62
⊕ American International G	Financial	17.1	6.05	2.54
⊕ IBM	Hardware	16.8	19.77	2.42
⊕ AT&T, Inc.	Telecom	19.2	51.59	2.24
⊕ Wells Fargo Company	Financial	14.7	16.82	1.92
⊕ ConocoPhillips	Energy	6.9	26.53	1.91
⊕ Intel Corporation	Hardware	20.3	-17.18	1.90
⊕ Hewlett-Packard Company	Hardware	18.9	45.21	1.86
⊕ Wal-Mart Stores, Inc.	Consumer	16.6	0.13	1.83

Current Investment Style

Market Cap	%
Giant	99.0
Large	0.9
Mid	0.1
Small	0.0
Micro	0.0
Avg $mil:	154,891

Value Measures		Rel Category
Price/Earnings	15.45	0.93
Price/Book	2.77	1.01
Price/Sales	1.87	1.47
Price/Cash Flow	10.34	1.09
Dividend Yield %	2.07	1.16

Growth Measures	%	Rel Category
Long-Term Erngs	10.66	0.93
Book Value	10.58	1.24
Sales	12.92	1.56
Cash Flow	12.20	1.61
Historical Erngs	17.98	1.07

Profitability	%	Rel Category
Return on Equity	21.68	1.13
Return on Assets	12.45	1.29
Net Margin	16.31	1.46

Sector Weightings	% of Stocks	Rel S&P 500	3 Year High Low
Info	27.16	1.36	
Software	5.36	1.55	— —
Hardware	10.82	1.17	— —
Media	4.74	1.25	— —
Telecom	6.24	1.78	— —
Service	41.99	0.91	
Health	14.14	1.17	— —
Consumer	3.20	0.42	— —
Business	2.33	0.55	— —
Financial	22.32	1.00	— —
Mfg	30.86	0.91	
Goods	9.53	1.11	— —
Ind Mtrls	9.33	0.78	— —
Energy	12.00	1.22	— —
Utilities	0.00	0.00	— —

Composition

● Cash	0.0	
● Stocks	100.0	
● Bonds	0.0	
● Other	0.0	
Foreign	0.0	
(% of Stock)		

MORNINGSTAR ETFs 150

Rydex S&P 500 Pure Growth RPG

Market Price $35.77	**Mstar Category** Large Growth		

Morningstar Fair Value

Price/Fair Value Ratio	Coverage Rate %
0.90 Undervalued	96 Good

Management

Key personnel involved in managing this, and other Rydex ETFs, include Michael Byrum, president and CIO, James King, director of portfolio management, and Michael Dellapa, director of investment research.

Methodology

This fund tracks the S&P 500/Citigroup Pure Growth Index, which weights stocks by their growth attributes. It starts out by ranking stocks from the S&P 500 Index by seven growth and value factors, including dividend yield and sales per share growth rate. Then it selects the stocks with the highest growth scores. The index is reconstituted annually in December.

Morningstar Rating	Return	Risk	Yield	NAV	Avg Daily Vol. (k)	52 wk High/Low
— Not Rated	— Not Rated	—	—	$35.86	13	$36.48 - $31.33

Growth of $10,000
- Investment Value of ETF
- Investment Value of Index S&P 500

Trading Volume Millions

	1997	1998	1999	2000	2001	2002	2003	2004	2005	2006	History
	—	—	—	—	—	—	—	—	—	35.86	NAV $
	—	—	—	—	—	—	—	—	—	35.87	Market Price $
	—	—	—	—	—	—	—	—	—	4.52*	NAV Return%
	—	—	—	—	—	—	—	—	—	—	Market Price Return%
	—	—	—	—	—	—	—	—	—	-0.01	Avg Premium/Discount%
	—	—	—	—	—	—	—	—	—	4.52	NAV Rtrn% +/-S&P 500
	—	—	—	—	—	—	—	—	—	4.52	NAV Rtrn% +/-Russ 1000Gr
	—	—	—	—	—	—	—	—	—	—	NAV Return% Rank in Cat
	—	—	—	—	—	—	—	—	—	—	Income Return %
	—	—	—	—	—	—	—	—	—	—	Capital Return %
	—	—	—	—	—	—	—	—	—	0.11	Income $
	—	—	—	—	—	—	—	—	—	0.00	Capital Gains $
	—	—	—	—	—	—	—	—	—	—	Expense Ratio %
	—	—	—	—	—	—	—	—	—	—	Income Ratio %
	—	—	—	—	—	—	—	—	—	—	Turnover Rate %
	—	—	—	—	—	—	—	—	—	22	Net Assets $mil

Performance 12-31-06

Historic Quarterly NAV Returns

	1st Qtr	2nd Qtr	3rd Qtr	4th Qtr	Total
2002	—	—	—	—	—
2003	—	—	—	—	—
2004	—	—	—	—	—
2005	—	—	—	—	—
2006	—	-5.04	4.31	4.89	—*

Trailing	NAV Return%	Market Return%	NAV Rtrn% +/-S&P 500	%Rank Cat.(NAV)
3 Mo	4.89	4.82	-1.81	15
6 Mo	9.42	9.39	-3.32	15
1 Yr	—	—	—	—
3 Yr Avg	—	—	—	—
5 Yr Avg	—	—	—	—
10 Yr Avg	—	—	—	—

Tax Analysis	Tax-Adj Return%	Tax-Cost Ratio
3 Yr (estimated)	—	—
5 Yr (estimated)	—	—
10 Yr (estimated)	—	—

Rating and Risk

Time Period	Morningstar Rtn vs Cat	Morningstar Risk vs Cat	Morningstar Risk-Adj Rating
3 Yr	—	—	—
5 Yr	—	—	—
10 Yr	—	—	—

Other Measures	Standard Index S&P 500	Best Fit Index
Alpha	—	—
Beta	—	—
R-Squared	—	—
Standard Deviation	—	
Mean	—	
Sharpe Ratio	—	

Morningstar's Take by Marta Norton 12-31-06

Rydex S&P 500 Pure Growth's new methodology introduces new problems.

This exchange-traded fund has several quirks. For one, the fund tracks the S&P 500/Citigroup Pure Growth Index, which practices a unique weighting methodology. Instead of weighting its constituents by market capitalization, as most of its competitors do, it weights its holdings by their growth attributes. Therefore, companies with the strongest growth rates, according to factors such as five-year earnings per share and sales per share growth rates, claim the most assets here.

This methodology tilts the ETF toward more growth-oriented sectors. For instance, the fund has almost twice as much in consumer services as iShares S&P 500 Growth Index, which tracks a market-cap-weighted version of the same index. That sector has seen tremendous growth over the past decade as consumer spending has increased significantly. And the fund also stores more in health care, as many of those stocks have strong long-term demand and are often highly profitable.

This ETF's focus on quickly growing sectors should appeal to aggressive investors, but there's more to consider. This ETF's benchmark gives it a smaller average market cap than its peers. That's because, unlike its market-cap-weighted contemporaries, its benchmark allows smaller-sized companies to compete with larger ones to hold the most assets in its portfolio. In fact, the fund has nearly 40% of its assets in mid-cap stocks, while its ETF competitors average around 25% there. Investors interested in this fund for exposure to large companies may find it a difficult fit for their portfolios.

We'd hold off on this ETF. Its quirky portfolio likely makes it difficult to use, and its unconventional construction methodology is untested in the market. Opt for one of its cheaper, more conventional competitors instead.

Address:	9601 Blackwell Rd Rockville, MD 20850 800-820-0888
Web Address:	www.rydex.com
Inception:	03-01-06 *
Advisor:	Rydex Global Advisors, Inc., Rydex Inves

Management Fee:	0.35%		
Expense Projections:	3Yr:$113	5Yr: —	10Yr: —
Income Distrib:	Annually		
Exchange:	AMEX		

Portfolio Analysis 12-31-06

Share change since 11-06   Total Stocks:146

	Sector	PE	Tot Ret%	% Assets
⊕ Caremark RX, Inc.	Health	23.8	10.89	1.32
⊕ Amazon.com, Inc.	Consumer	58.0	-16.31	1.27
⊖ Hospira, Inc.	Health	25.1	-21.51	1.26
⊖ Google, Inc.	Business	58.6	11.00	1.23
⊕ Coach, Inc.	Goods	31.4	28.85	1.23
⊖ XTO Energy, Inc.	Energy	9.2	12.16	1.21
⊖ Forest Laboratories, Inc	Health	22.6	24.39	1.17
⊕ Express Scripts	Health	23.6	-14.56	1.15
⊖ Coventry Health Care, In	Health	15.3	-12.13	1.13
⊕ Zimmer Holdings, Inc.	Health	24.6	16.22	1.12
⊕ Countrywide Financial Co	Financial	9.8	26.22	1.11
⊖ Cognizant Technology Sol	Software	52.1	53.49	1.10
⊕ Apollo Group, Inc. A	Consumer	15.3	-35.54	1.08
⊕ Gilead Sciences, Inc.	Health	41.1	23.51	1.07
⊕ Progressive Corporation	Financial	12.5	-16.93	1.06
⊕ Intuit	Software	22.1	14.48	1.05
⊕ D.R. Horton Incorporated	Consumer	6.8	-24.41	1.01
⊕ UnitedHealth Group, Inc.	Health	21.0	-13.49	1.00
⊕ eBay, Inc.	Consumer	40.6	-30.43	0.99
⊕ Apache Corporation	Energy	7.9	-2.30	0.97

Current Investment Style

Value Blnd Growth — Large Mid Small

Market Cap	%
Giant	11.7
Large	47.0
Mid	41.2
Small	0.0
Micro	0.0

Avg $mil: 16,076

Value Measures		Rel Category
Price/Earnings	18.62	0.90
Price/Book	3.52	1.08
Price/Sales	1.67	0.94
Price/Cash Flow	11.73	1.05
Dividend Yield %	0.74	0.86

Growth Measures	%	Rel Category
Long-Term Erngs	13.79	0.92
Book Value	17.81	2.23
Sales	14.93	1.27
Cash Flow	15.45	1.06
Historical Erngs	19.71	0.70

Profitability	%	Rel Category
Return on Equity	25.61	1.27
Return on Assets	12.46	1.25
Net Margin	13.98	1.11

Sector Weightings	% of Stocks	Rel S&P 500	3 year High	Low
↻ Info	14.88	0.74		
🗔 Software	6.48	1.88	—	—
🖥 Hardware	7.24	0.78	—	—
🎤 Media	1.16	0.31	—	—
☎ Telecom	0.00	0.00	—	—
🖴 Service	55.18	1.19		
⚕ Health	24.18	2.00	—	—
🛒 Consumer	17.48	2.28	—	—
📇 Business	5.05	1.19	—	—
💲 Financial	8.47	0.38	—	—
🏭 Mfg	29.94	0.89		
🏺 Goods	13.41	1.57	—	—
⚙ Ind Mtrls	6.95	0.58	—	—
🔥 Energy	9.17	0.94	—	—
💡 Utilities	0.41	0.12	—	—

Composition

● Cash	0.1	
● Stocks	99.9	
● Bonds	0.0	
○ Other	0.0	
Foreign	0.0	
(% of Stock)		

Rydex S&P 500 Pure Value RPV

Market Price	Mstar Category
$33.39	Large Value

Morningstar Fair Value

Price/Fair Value Ratio	Coverage Rate %
0.98 Fairly valued	94 Good

Management

Key personnel involved in managing this, and other Rydex ETFs, include Michael Byrum, president and CIO, James King, director of portfolio management, and Michael Dellapa, director of investment research.

Methodology

This fund tracks the S&P 500/Citigroup Pure Value Index, which weights stocks by their value attributes. It starts out by ranking stocks from the S&P 500 Index by seven growth and value factors, including dividend yield and price/book value. Then it selects the stocks with the highest value scores. The index is reconstituted annually in December.

Growth of $10,000
— Investment Value of ETF
— Investment Value of Index S&P 500

Trading Volume Millions

	1997	1998	1999	2000	2001	2002	2003	2004	2005	2006	History
	—	—	—	—	—	—	—	—	—	33.81	NAV $
	—	—	—	—	—	—	—	—	—	33.81	Market Price $
	—	—	—	—	—	—	—	—	—	14.83*	NAV Return%
	—	—	—	—	—	—	—	—	—	—	Market Price Return%
	—	—	—	—	—	—	—	—	—	-0.10	Avg Premium/Discount%
	—	—	—	—	—	—	—	—	—	14.83	NAV Rtrn% +/-S&P 500
	—	—	—	—	—	—	—	—	—	14.83	NAV Rtrn% +/-Russ 1000 Vl
	—	—	—	—	—	—	—	—	—	—	NAV Return% Rank in Cat
	—	—	—	—	—	—	—	—	—	—	Income Return %
	—	—	—	—	—	—	—	—	—	—	Capital Return %
	—	—	—	—	—	—	—	—	—	0.47	Income $
	—	—	—	—	—	—	—	—	—	0.00	Capital Gains $
	—	—	—	—	—	—	—	—	—	—	Expense Ratio %
	—	—	—	—	—	—	—	—	—	—	Income Ratio %
	—	—	—	—	—	—	—	—	—	—	Turnover Rate %
	—	—	—	—	—	—	—	—	—	25	Net Assets $mil

Performance 12-31-06

Historic Quarterly NAV Returns

	1st Qtr	2nd Qtr	3rd Qtr	4th Qtr	Total
2002	—	—	—	—	—
2003	—	—	—	—	—
2004	—	—	—	—	—
2005	—	—	—	—	—
2006	—	2.42	2.98	8.11	—*

Trailing	NAV Return%	Market Return%	NAV Rtrn% +/-S&P 500	%Rank Cat.(NAV)
3 Mo	8.11	8.02	1.41	16
6 Mo	11.33	11.28	-1.41	16
1 Yr	—	—	—	—
3 Yr Avg	—	—	—	—
5 Yr Avg	—	—	—	—
10 Yr Avg	—	—	—	—

Tax Analysis	Tax-Adj Return%	Tax-Cost Ratio
3 Yr (estimated)	—	—
5 Yr (estimated)	—	—
10 Yr (estimated)	—	—

Rating and Risk

Time Period	Morningstar Rtn vs Cat	Morningstar Risk vs Cat	Morningstar Risk-Adj Rating
3 Yr	—	—	—
5 Yr	—	—	—
10 Yr	—	—	—

Other Measures	Standard Index S&P 500	Best Fit Index
Alpha	—	—
Beta	—	—
R-Squared	—	—
Standard Deviation	—	
Mean	—	
Sharpe Ratio	—	

Morningstar's Take by Marta Norton 12-31-06

We're not convinced Rydex S&P 500 Pure Value's methodology is better than its peers'.

This exchange-traded fund strives to distinguish itself from other large-value ETFs with its weighting methodology. It tracks the S&P 500/Citigroup Pure Value Index, which weights its holdings by their value attributes. That means stocks that look the cheapest based on seven factors, including cash flow to price and dividend yield, get the most assets here. That's a noticeable difference from other ETFs in this category that track market-cap-weighted indexes that put the stocks with the largest market capitalizations on top.

The distinctive weighting of the fund's index structure leads it to stress some sectors more than others. For instance, areas where stocks tend to offer higher dividends will be well represented. The fund has more than three times as much in the high-yielding utilities sector as iShares S&P 500 Value Index, a rival ETF tracking the market-cap-weighted version of this fund's index.

Stocks that have suffered in recent times--such as SuperValu, a grocer that has struggled along with other traditional supermarkets--also get a fair amount of attention here.

We like the fund's efforts to offer undiluted value exposure, but its substantial stake in mid-cap stocks makes it difficult for investors to use. That's because, unlike its market-cap-weighted peers, the fund cares only about stocks' value characteristics, which gives smaller stocks a chance to compete with their larger peers for the fund's assets. Indeed, the fund keeps around 45% of its assets in midsized stocks, while its average ETF competitor has only 15% there.

The fund's style-pure exposure is valuable, but we think long-term investors may have trouble fitting its smaller market cap into their portfolios if they also own mid-cap funds. And given that its 0.35% expense ratio is above those of many of its more-established peers, investors should consider other options.

Address:	9601 Blackwell Rd Rockville, MD 20850 800-820-0888
Web Address:	www.rydex.com
Inception:	03-01-06*
Advisor:	Rydex Global Advisors, Inc., Rydex Inves

Management Fee:	0.35%		
Expense Projections:	3Yr:$113	5Yr: —	10Yr: —
Income Distrib:	Annually		
Exchange:	AMEX		

Portfolio Analysis 12-31-06

Share change since 11-06 Total Stocks:145	Sector	PE	Tot Ret%	% Assets
Ford Motor Company	Goods	—	0.57	2.32
Fannie Mae	Financial	—	24.34	1.84
Embarq Corporation	Telecom	—	—	1.81
Sanmina-SCI Corporation	Hardware	—	-19.01	1.68
SuperValu, Inc.	Consumer	25.7	12.44	1.38
Dillard's, Inc.	Consumer	14.9	41.62	1.30
General Motors Corporati	Goods	—	63.96	1.28
DTE Energy Holding Compa	Utilities	12.6	17.58	1.25
NiSource, Inc.	Utilities	22.3	20.51	1.21
KeySpan Corporation	Utilities	16.8	20.97	1.21
Windstream Corporation	Telecom	—	37.36	1.16
Tyson Foods, Inc. A	Goods	—	-2.78	1.14
Progress Energy, Inc.	Utilities	16.7	18.07	1.13
Pinnacle West Capital	Utilities	21.9	27.04	1.12
Verizon Communications	Telecom	16.1	34.88	1.11
AutoNation, Inc.	Consumer	15.3	-1.89	1.10
XL Capital, Ltd.	Financial	—	9.34	1.09
Xcel Energy, Inc.	Utilities	17.0	30.53	1.09
ConocoPhillips	Energy	6.9	26.53	1.04
Washington Mutual, Inc.	Financial	13.5	9.62	1.03

Current Investment Style

Value Blnd Growth — Large Mid Small

Market Cap	%
Giant	8.5
Large	41.5
Mid	47.3
Small	2.7
Micro	0.0

Avg $mil: 11,731

Value Measures		Rel Category
Price/Earnings	14.54	1.02
Price/Book	1.70	0.71
Price/Sales	0.56	0.42
Price/Cash Flow	5.02	0.65
Dividend Yield %	2.58	1.00

Growth Measures	%	Rel Category
Long-Term Erngs	8.77	0.87
Book Value	1.16	0.16
Sales	3.35	0.39
Cash Flow	0.01	0.00
Historical Erngs	12.11	0.78

Profitability	%	Rel Category
Return on Equity	8.95	0.51
Return on Assets	5.52	0.55
Net Margin	7.82	0.57

Sector Weightings	% of Stocks	Rel S&P 500	3 Year High Low
↻ Info	14.69	0.73	
Software	1.22	0.35	— —
Hardware	2.98	0.32	— —
Media	2.94	0.78	— —
Telecom	7.55	2.15	— —
☞ Service	37.95	0.82	
Health	3.40	0.28	— —
Consumer	7.82	1.02	— —
Business	2.79	0.66	— —
Financial	23.94	1.07	— —
Mfg	47.37	1.40	
Goods	11.70	1.37	— —
Ind Mtrls	12.81	1.07	— —
Energy	2.66	0.27	— —
Utilities	20.20	5.77	— —

Composition

● Cash	0.3	
● Stocks	99.7	
● Bonds	0.0	
○ Other	0.0	
Foreign	0.0	
(% of Stock)		

MORNINGSTAR® ETFs 150

Rydex S&P Equal Weight RSP

	Market Price	Mstar Category
	$47.23	Large Blend

Morningstar Rating	Return	Risk	Yield	NAV	Avg Daily Vol. (k)	52 wk High/Low
★★★★★ Highest	Highest	Above Avg	1.1%	$47.37	281	$47.84 - $41.02

Growth of $10,000
- Investment Value of ETF
- Investment Value of Index S&P 500

Morningstar Fair Value

Price/Fair Value Ratio	Coverage Rate %
0.93 Undervalued	95 Good

Management

Key personnel involved in managing this and other Rydex ETFs include Michael Byrum, president and CIO; James King, director of portfolio management; and Michael Dellapa, director of investment research.

Methodology

This fund allocates an equal amount of assets to each of the individual components of the S&P 500 Index instead of using a market weighting. That means that companies such as General Electric get a weighting of just 0.2% of assets, as opposed to the much larger position the stock gets in more common index offerings. Management rebalances the portfolio on a quarterly basis.

Trading Volume Millions

1997	1998	1999	2000	2001	2002	2003	2004	2005	2006	History
—	—	—	—	—	—	33.84	39.02	41.55	47.37	NAV $
—	—	—	—	—	—	33.86	39.04	41.48	47.34	Market Price $
—	—	—	—	—	—	19.90*	16.50	7.65	15.33	NAV Return%
—	—	—	—	—	—	—	16.48	7.41	15.46	Market Price Return%
—	—	—	—	—	—	0.03	0.02	-0.03	0.02	Avg Premium/Discount%
—	—	—	—	—	—	19.90	5.62	2.74	-0.46	NAV Rtrn% +/-S&P 500
—	—	—	—	—	—	19.90	5.10	1.38	-0.13	NAV Rtrn% +/-Russ 1000
—	—	—	—	—	—	—	16	21	30	NAV Return% Rank in Cat
—	—	—	—	—	—	—	1.09	1.12	1.26	Income Return %
—	—	—	—	—	—	—	15.41	6.53	14.07	Capital Return %
—	—	—	—	—	—	0.25	0.37	0.44	0.52	Income $
—	—	—	—	—	—	0.00	0.00	0.00	0.00	Capital Gains $
—	—	—	—	—	—	0.40	0.40	0.40	—	Expense Ratio %
—	—	—	—	—	—	1.13	1.09	1.11	—	Income Ratio %
—	—	—	—	—	—	42	55	22	—	Turnover Rate %
—	—	—	—	—	—	223	765	1,313	1,871	Net Assets $mil

Performance 12-31-06

Historic Quarterly NAV Returns

	1st Qtr	2nd Qtr	3rd Qtr	4th Qtr	Total
2002	—	—	—	—	—
2003	—	—	5.14	14.91	—*
2004	3.71	2.26	-2.09	12.19	16.50
2005	-2.27	2.68	4.73	2.43	7.65
2006	6.14	-2.16	3.82	6.96	15.33

Trailing	NAV Return%	Market Return%	NAV Rtrn% +/-S&P 500	%Rank Cat.(NAV)
3 Mo	6.96	6.95	0.26	44
6 Mo	11.05	11.02	-1.69	38
1 Yr	15.33	15.46	-0.46	30
3 Yr Avg	13.09	13.04	2.65	15
5 Yr Avg	—	—	—	—
10 Yr Avg	—	—	—	—

Tax Analysis	Tax-Adj Return%	Tax-Cost Ratio
3 Yr (estimated)	12.66	0.38
5 Yr (estimated)	—	—
10 Yr (estimated)	—	—

Rating and Risk

Time Period	Morningstar Rtn vs Cat	Morningstar Risk vs Cat	Morningstar Risk-Adj Rating
3 Yr	High	+Avg	★★★★★
5 Yr	—	—	—
10 Yr	—	—	—

Other Measures	Standard Index S&P 500	Best Fit Index Mstar Mid Core
Alpha	0.8	0.8
Beta	1.25	0.79
R-Squared	92	96
Standard Deviation	8.93	
Mean	13.09	
Sharpe Ratio	1.07	

Portfolio Analysis 12-31-06

Share change since 11-06 Total Stocks:500	Sector	PE	Tot Ret%	% Assets
⊖ Realogy Corporation	Financial			0.24
⊕ Caremark RX, Inc.	Health	23.8	10.89	0.23
⊖ Goodyear Tire & Rubber	Ind Mtrls	22.8	20.77	0.23
⊕ Viacom, Inc. B	Media		—	0.22
⊕ Qwest Communications Int	Telecom		48.14	0.22
⊖ UnitedHealth Group, Inc.	Health	21.0	-13.49	0.22
⊖ Monsanto Company	Ind Mtrls	41.4	36.78	0.22
⊕ Ford Motor Company	Goods		0.57	0.21
⊕ ITT Industries, Inc.	Ind Mtrls	36.9	11.45	0.21
⊖ Honeywell International,	Ind Mtrls	18.7	24.14	0.21
⊖ CIT Group, Inc.	Financial	11.3	9.45	0.21
⊖ Unisys Corporation	Software		34.48	0.21
⊕ Express Scripts	Health	23.6	-14.56	0.21
⊕ Alltel Corp.	Telecom	17.6	19.54	0.21
⊖ Harrah's Entertainment,	Consumer	43.5	18.55	0.21
⊕ Citigroup, Inc.	Financial	13.3	19.55	0.21
⊕ Boston Scientific Corpor	Health		-29.85	0.21
⊕ Northern Trust Corporati	Financial	20.9	19.11	0.21
⊕ Health Management Associ	Health	20.5	-2.74	0.21
⊖ NCR Corporation	Hardware	22.0	25.99	0.21

Current Investment Style

Value Blnd Growth — Large / Mid / Small

	Market Cap	%
	Giant	10.7
	Large	45.7
	Mid	42.8
	Small	0.8
	Micro	0.0

Avg $mil: 14,153

Value Measures		Rel Category
Price/Earnings	17.14	1.03
Price/Book	2.56	0.93
Price/Sales	1.18	0.93
Price/Cash Flow	8.75	0.92
Dividend Yield %	1.45	0.81

Growth Measures	%	Rel Category
Long-Term Erngs	11.84	1.03
Book Value	6.36	0.74
Sales	7.48	0.90
Cash Flow	8.09	1.07
Historical Erngs	16.20	0.97

Profitability	%	Rel Category
Return on Equity	17.68	0.92
Return on Assets	9.14	0.95
Net Margin	11.57	1.04

Sector Weightings	% of Stocks	Rel S&P 500	3 Year High	Low
⟳ Info	18.59	0.93		
Software	3.57	1.03	4	3
Hardware	9.52	1.03	11	10
Media	3.43	0.91	4	3
Telecom	2.07	0.59	2	2
⟲ Service	45.69	0.99		
Health	11.33	0.94	12	10
Consumer	11.33	1.48	11	10
Business	5.35	1.26	7	5
Financial	17.68	0.79	18	16
⟰ Mfg	35.73	1.06		
Goods	10.33	1.21	11	10
Ind Mtrls	13.08	1.10	16	13
Energy	6.08	0.62	7	5
Utilities	6.24	1.78	7	6

Composition

	%
● Cash	0.0
● Stocks	100.0
● Bonds	0.0
● Other	0.0
Foreign	0.0
(% of Stock)	

Morningstar's Take by Marta Norton 12-31-06

Rydex S&P Equal Weight's twist on conventional indexing solves some problems but creates others.

This exchange-traded fund uses a different methodology to provide exposure to the S&P 500. Many ETFs in this space track market-cap-weighted indexes, but this fund tracks the S&P Equal Weight Index, which spreads its assets evenly across the S&P 500 stocks. So, while most ETFs offer more weight to mammoth market leaders such as ExxonMobil, this fund puts smaller companies on equal footing with their larger peers. Also, at quarterly rebalances, stocks that clawed their way to the top of the index over the trailing three months due to performance once again drop to equal weight with the other holdings.

This approach has a couple of good effects. Because the fund doesn't allow the largest companies to grab the most assets, its portfolio is more diversified across its holdings. In fact, the fund's 10 largest holdings claim only about 2.5% of its assets, while its average ETF competitor stores roughly 25% in the top 10. We also like that the fund trims winners and adds to laggards quarterly, which helps keep it from storing too much in overvalued stocks.

There are some trouble spots, though. The fund's equal-weighted portfolio limits its mega-cap stake, but it also gives the fund an extra helping of mid-caps. The fund generally holds more than 40% of its assets in midsize companies, so investors may have trouble owning it alongside a mid-cap fund.

Also, because smaller stocks have had such a strong run in recent years, the time may not be right to buy a fund with a heavy mid-cap stake. Indeed, according to Morningstar equity analysts, at the end of November this ETF had more assets in overvalued stocks than its market-weighted competitor iShares S&P 500 Index.

Because of these concerns and the fund's relatively high fees, we'd recommend looking elsewhere.

Address:	9601 Blackwell Rd Rockville, MD 20850 800-820-0888	Management Fee:	0.40%
		Expense Projections:	3Yr:$129 5Yr:$225 10Yr:$508
Web Address:	www.rydex.com	Income Distrib:	Quarterly
Inception:	04-24-03*	Exchange:	AMEX
Advisor:	Rydex Global Advisors, Inc., Rydex Inves		

MORNINGSTAR ETFs 150

Rydex S&P Midcap 400 Gr RFG

	Market Price	Mstar Category
	$52.05	Mid-Cap Growth

Morningstar Fair Value

Price/Fair Value Ratio	Coverage Rate %
0.89 Undervalued	75 Fair

Management

Key personnel involved in managing this and other Rydex ETFs include Michael Byrum, president and CIO; James King, director of portfolio management; and Michael Dellapa, director of investment research.

Methodology

This fund tracks the S&P MidCap 400/Citigroup Pure Growth Index, which weights stocks by their growth attributes. It starts out by ranking stocks from the S&P MidCap 400 Index by seven growth and value factors, including dividend yield and sales per share growth rate. Then it selects the stocks with the highest growth scores. The index is reconstituted annually in December.

Morningstar Rating	Return	Risk	Yield	NAV	Avg Daily Vol. (k)	52 wk High/Low
— Not Rated	Not Rated	—	—	$51.73	2	$53.49 - $34.42

Growth of $10,000
- Investment Value of ETF
- Investment Value of Index S&P 500

13.2
12.0
10.7
10.0
8.0
0.004
0.0

Trading Volume Millions

	1997	1998	1999	2000	2001	2002	2003	2004	2005	2006	History
	—	—	—	—	—	—	—	—	—	51.73	NAV $
	—	—	—	—	—	—	—	—	—	51.76	Market Price $
	—	—	—	—	—	—	—	—	—	-1.64*	NAV Return%
	—	—	—	—	—	—	—	—	—	—	Market Price Return%
	—	—	—	—	—	—	—	—	—	-0.12	Avg Premium/Discount%
	—	—	—	—	—	—	—	—	—	-1.64	NAV Rtrn% +/-S&P 500
	—	—	—	—	—	—	—	—	—	-1.64	NAV Rtrn% +/-Russ MG
	—	—	—	—	—	—	—	—	—	—	NAV Return% Rank in Cat
	—	—	—	—	—	—	—	—	—	—	Income Return %
	—	—	—	—	—	—	—	—	—	—	Capital Return %
	—	—	—	—	—	—	—	—	—	0.02	Income $
	—	—	—	—	—	—	—	—	—	0.00	Capital Gains $
	—	—	—	—	—	—	—	—	—	—	Expense Ratio %
	—	—	—	—	—	—	—	—	—	—	Income Ratio %
	—	—	—	—	—	—	—	—	—	—	Turnover Rate %
	—	—	—	—	—	—	—	—	—	23	Net Assets $mil

Performance 12-31-06

Historic Quarterly NAV Returns

	1st Qtr	2nd Qtr	3rd Qtr	4th Qtr	Total
2002	—	—	—	—	—
2003	—	—	—	—	—
2004	—	—	—	—	—
2005	—	—	—	—	—
2006	—	-6.63	-2.65	7.72	—*

Trailing	NAV Return%	Market Return%	NAV Rtrn% +/-S&P 500	%Rank Cat.(NAV)
3 Mo	7.72	7.68	1.02	8
6 Mo	4.87	5.21	-7.87	7
1 Yr	—	—	—	—
3 Yr Avg	—	—	—	—
5 Yr Avg	—	—	—	—
10 Yr Avg	—	—	—	—

Tax Analysis	Tax-Adj Return%	Tax-Cost Ratio
3 Yr (estimated)	—	—
5 Yr (estimated)	—	—
10 Yr (estimated)	—	—

Rating and Risk

Time Period	Morningstar Rtn vs Cat	Morningstar Risk vs Cat	Morningstar Risk-Adj Rating
3 Yr	—	—	—
5 Yr	—	—	—
10 Yr	—	—	—

Other Measures	Standard Index S&P 500	Best Fit Index
Alpha	—	—
Beta	—	—
R-Squared	—	—
Standard Deviation	—	
Mean	—	
Sharpe Ratio	—	

Portfolio Analysis 12-31-06

Share change since 11-06 Total Stocks:94	Sector	PE	Tot Ret%	% Assets
⊖ Sepracor, Inc.	Health	NMF	19.34	1.66
⊖ Par Pharmaceutical Compa	Health	31.5	-28.62	1.58
⊖ Corinthian Colleges, Inc	Consumer	35.9	15.80	1.52
⊕ Gen-Probe, Inc.	Health	45.9	7.34	1.50
⊕ Aeropostale, Inc.	Consumer	18.6	17.38	1.50
⊕ Hovnanian Enterprises In	Consumer	5.0	-31.71	1.39
⊖ Western Digital Corporat	Hardware	10.7	9.94	1.37
⊕ Chico's FAS, Inc.	Consumer	19.3	-52.90	1.36
⊕ Career Education Corpora	Consumer	19.4	-26.51	1.33
⊕ Community Health Systems	Health	20.8	-4.75	1.32
⊖ Cytyc Corporation	Health	26.2	0.25	1.29
⊕ Silicon Laboratories, In	Hardware	47.5	-5.48	1.29
⊕ DST Systems, Inc.	Business	13.8	4.54	1.26
⊖ Pogo Producing Company	Energy	4.9	-2.16	1.24
☼ W.R. Berkley Corporation	Financial	10.4	9.20	1.23
⊕ Ryland Group, Inc.	Consumer	6.0	-23.60	1.23
⊕ Energizer Holdings, Inc.	Goods	17.1	42.58	1.19
⊕ Gamestop Corporation A	Goods	34.2	73.19	1.16
⊖ Brown & Brown, Inc.	Financial	23.1	-6.98	1.15
⊕ Lincare Holdings Inc.	Health	19.3	-4.94	1.13

Current Investment Style

Value Blnd Growth — Large Mid Small

Market Cap	%
Giant	0.0
Large	0.0
Mid	75.9
Small	24.1
Micro	0.0

Avg $mil: 2,937

Value Measures		Rel Category
Price/Earnings	17.89	0.90
Price/Book	3.02	0.88
Price/Sales	1.41	0.82
Price/Cash Flow	10.41	0.94
Dividend Yield %	0.37	0.76

Growth Measures	%	Rel Category
Long-Term Erngs	14.16	0.90
Book Value	15.87	1.36
Sales	18.01	1.56
Cash Flow	13.60	0.80
Historical Erngs	21.10	0.92

Profitability	%	Rel Category
Return on Equity	21.44	1.06
Return on Assets	11.39	1.10
Net Margin	11.03	0.97

Sector Weightings	% of Stocks	Rel S&P 500	3 Year High Low
↻ Info	10.55	0.53	
Software	2.51	0.73	— —
Hardware	5.31	0.57	— —
Media	2.73	0.72	— —
Telecom	0.00	0.00	— —
⊕ Service	68.75	1.49	
Health	19.79	1.64	— —
Consumer	26.95	3.52	— —
Business	14.62	3.46	— —
Financial	7.39	0.33	— —
⚒ Mfg	20.71	0.61	
Goods	6.06	0.71	— —
Ind Mtrls	7.84	0.66	— —
Energy	6.81	0.69	— —
Utilities	0.00	0.00	— —

Composition

● Cash	0.0	
● Stocks	100.0	
● Bonds	0.0	
● Other	0.0	
Foreign	0.0	
(% of Stock)		

Morningstar's Take by Marta Norton 12-31-06

We're not convinced Rydex S&P MidCap 400 Pure Growth is any better than its peers.

This exchange-traded fund operates with an unusual structure. It tracks the S&P MidCap 400/Citigroup Pure Growth Index, which weights its constituents by their growth attributes, as measured by factors such as five-year earnings and sales per share growth rates. That gives companies with the greatest rates of growth the most assets. Most of the fund's rivals, by contrast, track indexes that weight their holdings by market cap, which means their largest stocks hoard the most assets.

Because of its structure, investors can find more-targeted growth exposure with this ETF than with one of its competitors. Its top 20 holdings in its Nov. 30, 2006, portfolio grew their revenues an average of 176% over the past five years. IShares S&P MidCap 400 Growth's top 20 holdings averaged less--123% over the same period. And given that the fund offers a more concentrated portfolio than its peers (it typically owns less than 100 stocks, while its average ETF competitor holds around 216 stocks), its fastest-growing stocks have a greater impact on its performance.

The fund isn't quite as effective at targeting mid-cap stocks though. It's true that it generally stays out of the large-cap space, so it doesn't have the same large-cap bias as its average ETF peer. Unfortunately, it also generally keeps about 20% of its assets in small caps. By contrast, its typical ETF competitor holds less than 10% there. This larger small-cap stake gives it less pure exposure to mid-caps than iShares S&P MidCap 400 Growth and makes it a harder fit for investors who also own small-cap funds.

There are arguments on both sides for this ETF. But since it relies on a new methodology that has yet to be proven in the marketplace and because it charges a higher expense ratio than other mid-growth ETFs, we'd go with more proven competitors instead.

Address:	9601 Blackwell Rd	Management Fee:	0.35%
	Rockville, MD 20850	Expense Projections:	3Yr:$113 5Yr: — 10Yr: —
	800-820-0888	Income Distrib:	Annually
Web Address:	www.rydex.com	Exchange:	AMEX
Inception:	03-01-06*		
Advisor:	Rydex Global Advisors, Inc., Rydex Inves		

 MORNINGSTAR® ETFs 150

Rydex S&P Midcap 400 Val RFV

Market Price $34.32	**Mstar Category** Mid-Cap Value	

Morningstar Fair Value

Price/Fair Value Ratio	Coverage Rate %
0.96 Fairly valued	68

Management

Key personnel involved in managing this, and other ETFs at Rydex, include Michael Byrum, president and CIO, James King, director of portfolio management, and Michael Dellapa, director of investment research.

Methodology

This fund tracks the S&P MidCap 400/Citigroup Pure Value. The index ranks the constituents from the S&P MidCap 400 Index by their value attributes as determined by seven metrics, including book value to price, sales to price, and cash flow to price. It then selects the stocks with the strongest value characteristics. Expect an annual reconstitution here.

Morningstar Rating	Return	Risk	Yield	NAV	Avg Daily Vol. (k)	52 wk High/Low
— Not Rated	Not Rated	—	—	$34.61	8	$35.23 - $29.77

Growth of $10,000
- Investment Value of ETF
- Investment Value of Index S&P 500

Trading Volume Millions

	1997	1998	1999	2000	2001	2002	2003	2004	2005	2006	History
	—	—	—	—	—	—	—	—	—	34.61	NAV $
	—	—	—	—	—	—	—	—	—	34.69	Market Price $
	—	—	—	—	—	—	—	—	—	11.62*	NAV Return%
	—	—	—	—	—	—	—	—	—	—	Market Price Return%
	—	—	—	—	—	—	—	—	—	-0.04	Avg Premium/Discount%
	—	—	—	—	—	—	—	—	—	11.62	NAV Rtrn% +/-S&P 500
	—	—	—	—	—	—	—	—	—	11.62	NAV Rtrn% +/-Russ MV
	—	—	—	—	—	—	—	—	—	—	NAV Return% Rank in Cat
	—	—	—	—	—	—	—	—	—	—	Income Return %
	—	—	—	—	—	—	—	—	—	—	Capital Return %
	—	—	—	—	—	—	—	—	—	0.55	Income $
	—	—	—	—	—	—	—	—	—	0.00	Capital Gains $
	—	—	—	—	—	—	—	—	—	—	Expense Ratio %
	—	—	—	—	—	—	—	—	—	—	Income Ratio %
	—	—	—	—	—	—	—	—	—	—	Turnover Rate %
	—	—	—	—	—	—	—	—	—	16	Net Assets $mil

Performance 12-31-06

Historic Quarterly NAV Returns

	1st Qtr	2nd Qtr	3rd Qtr	4th Qtr	Total
2002	—	—	—	—	—
2003	—	—	—	—	—
2004	—	—	—	—	—
2005	—	—	—	—	—
2006	—	0.70	0.55	10.25	—*

Trailing	NAV Return%	Market Return%	NAV Rtrn% +/-S&P 500	%Rank Cat.(NAV)
3 Mo	10.25	10.40	3.55	8
6 Mo	10.86	11.43	-1.88	7
1 Yr	—	—	—	—
3 Yr Avg	—	—	—	—
5 Yr Avg	—	—	—	—
10 Yr Avg	—	—	—	—

Tax Analysis	Tax-Adj Return%	Tax-Cost Ratio
3 Yr (estimated)	—	—
5 Yr (estimated)	—	—
10 Yr (estimated)	—	—

Rating and Risk

Time Period	Morningstar Rtn vs Cat	Morningstar Risk vs Cat	Morningstar Risk-Adj Rating
3 Yr	—	—	—
5 Yr	—	—	—
10 Yr	—	—	—

Other Measures	Standard Index S&P 500	Best Fit Index
Alpha	—	—
Beta	—	—
R-Squared	—	—
Standard Deviation	—	
Mean	—	
Sharpe Ratio	—	

Morningstar's Take by Marta Norton 12-31-06

We're not sure Rydex S&P MidCap Pure Value's distinctive methodology makes it worthwhile.

This exchange-traded fund works a little differently than its mid-value peers. While most ETFs in this space track indexes that use market capitalization to weight stocks, this ETF tracks the S&P MidCap 400/Citigroup Pure Value Index, which gives the most weight to stocks with the strongest value attributes as measured by metrics such as book value to price and dividend yield.

We like some aspects of this methodology. Because the fund doesn't include stocks exhibiting growth attributes, its portfolio arguably offers a purer dose of value than those of its peers and, therefore, should do well when value stocks dominate the market. Also, the fund doesn't suffer from the same large-cap bias as its market-cap-weighted peers, which give the largest stocks the most assets. In fact, it usually doesn't hold any large-cap stocks. Its typical ETF peer, on the other hand, has had as much as 15% of its assets in large caps.

But while the fund addresses some of the shortcomings of its peers, it has its own set of difficulties. It has a larger stake in small-cap stocks. That makes the fund a hard fit for investors who already have small-value exposure. It is especially worrisome now, after small-value stocks have had such a long run. (They've beaten their larger peers for the past five years.) There's no telling when market winds will turn, but when they do, this fund will likely take a harder hit than its rivals will.

We'd take a pass on this ETF for now. Its unconventional methodology is new, and it's not clear how it will hold up over the long term. The fund is also handicapped by a higher expense ratio than rival ETFs', which is a significant setback in the indexing universe, where fund fees often differ by no more than a few hundredths of a percent. Invest in one of its cheaper, more established rivals instead.

Address:	9601 Blackwell Rd Rockville, MD 20850 800-820-0888
Web Address:	www.rydex.com
Inception:	03-01-06*
Advisor:	Rydex Global Advisors, Inc., Rydex Inves

Management Fee:	0.35%		
Expense Projections:	3Yr:$113	5Yr: —	10Yr: —
Income Distrib:	Annually		
Exchange:	AMEX		

Portfolio Analysis 12-31-06

Share change since 11-06 Total Stocks:115

	Sector	PE	Tot Ret%	% Assets
Avis Budget Group, Inc.	Business	5.9	-0.53	2.28
Furniture Brands Interna	Goods	10.9	-25.10	2.04
Lear Corporation	Ind Mtrls	—	4.93	2.00
WPS Resources	Utilities	14.9	2.11	1.83
Lyondell Chemical Compan	Energy	10.2	11.52	1.82
Energy East Corporation	Utilities	14.9	14.15	1.67
Westwood One, Inc.	Media	11.6	-55.10	1.64
YRC Worldwide, Inc.	Business	7.5	-15.42	1.64
Universal Corporation	Goods	—	18.22	1.63
Bowater Incorporated	Ind Mtrls	—	-24.19	1.56
Modine Manufacturing Com	Ind Mtrls	15.1	-20.99	1.52
Puget Energy, Inc.	Utilities	17.1	29.99	1.44
Olin Corporation	Ind Mtrls	7.4	-12.22	1.41
Black Hills Corporation	Utilities	34.5	10.84	1.40
Pepco Holdings, Inc.	Utilities	16.9	21.37	1.32
First American Corporati	Financial	8.4	-8.61	1.29
Kelly Services, Inc. A	Business	20.0	12.18	1.29
Avnet, Inc.	Business	15.4	6.64	1.23
Ferro Corporation	Ind Mtrls	55.9	13.73	1.22
Northeast Utilities	Utilities	33.9	47.76	1.22

Current Investment Style

Value Blnd Growth — Large Mid Small

Market Cap	%
Giant	0.0
Large	0.0
Mid	61.0
Small	39.0
Micro	0.0
Avg $mil:	2,140

Value Measures		Rel Category
Price/Earnings	15.13	1.01
Price/Book	1.29	0.68
Price/Sales	0.44	0.49
Price/Cash Flow	5.15	0.70
Dividend Yield %	3.20	1.30

Growth Measures	%	Rel Category
Long-Term Erngs	9.40	1.00
Book Value	3.94	0.69
Sales	10.07	1.21
Cash Flow	-2.28	NMF
Historical Erngs	6.78	0.61

Profitability	%	Rel Category
Return on Equity	6.14	0.47
Return on Assets	4.40	0.58
Net Margin	5.89	0.50

Sector Weightings	% of Stocks	Rel S&P 500	3 Year High Low	
Info	8.26	0.41		
Software	0.00	0.00	—	—
Hardware	2.15	0.23	—	—
Media	5.75	1.52	—	—
Telecom	0.36	0.10	—	—
Service	37.18	0.80		
Health	0.00	0.00	—	—
Consumer	6.37	0.83	—	—
Business	14.42	3.41	—	—
Financial	16.39	0.74	—	—
Mfg	54.57	1.61		
Goods	10.60	1.24	—	—
Ind Mtrls	17.57	1.47	—	—
Energy	2.32	0.24	—	—
Utilities	24.08	6.88	—	—

Composition

	%
Cash	0.5
Stocks	99.5
Bonds	0.0
Other	0.0
Foreign (% of Stock)	0.0

Rydex S&P Smallcap 600 Gr RZG

	Market Price	Mstar Category
	$39.82	Small Growth

Morningstar Rating	Return	Risk	Yield	NAV	Avg Daily Vol. (k)	52 wk High/Low
— Not Rated	Not Rated		—	$40.44	4	$41.71 - $35.81

Morningstar Fair Value

Price/Fair Value Ratio —   Coverage Rate % —

Management

Key personnel involved in managing this, and many other ETFs at Rydex, include Michael Byrum, president and CIO, James King, director of portfolio management, and Michael Dellapa, director of investment research.

Methodology

This fund tracks the S&P SmallCap 600/Citigroup Pure Growth Index, which weights stocks by their growth attributes. It starts out by ranking stocks from the S&P SmallCap 600 Index by seven growth and value factors, including five-year earnings per share growth rate. Then it selects the stocks with the highest growth scores. The index is reconstituted annually in December.

Growth of $10,000
- Investment Value of ETF
- Investment Value of Index S&P 500

Trading Volume Millions

1997	1998	1999	2000	2001	2002	2003	2004	2005	2006	History
—	—	—	—	—	—	—	—	—	40.44	NAV $
—	—	—	—	—	—	—	—	—	40.71	Market Price $
—	—	—	—	—	—	—	—	—	2.86*	NAV Return%
—	—	—	—	—	—	—	—	—	—	Market Price Return%
—	—	—	—	—	—	—	—	—	0.08	Avg Premium/Discount%
—	—	—	—	—	—	—	—	—	2.86	NAV Rtrn% +/-S&P 500
—	—	—	—	—	—	—	—	—	2.86	NAV Rtrn% +/-Russ 2000 Gr
—	—	—	—	—	—	—	—	—	—	NAV Return% Rank in Cat
—	—	—	—	—	—	—	—	—	—	Income Return %
—	—	—	—	—	—	—	—	—	—	Capital Return %
—	—	—	—	—	—	—	—	—	0.00	Income $
—	—	—	—	—	—	—	—	—	0.00	Capital Gains $
—	—	—	—	—	—	—	—	—	—	Expense Ratio %
—	—	—	—	—	—	—	—	—	—	Income Ratio %
—	—	—	—	—	—	—	—	—	—	Turnover Rate %
—	—	—	—	—	—	—	—	—	8	Net Assets $mil

Performance 12-31-06

Historic Quarterly NAV Returns
	1st Qtr	2nd Qtr	3rd Qtr	4th Qtr	Total
2002	—	—	—	—	—
2003	—	—	—	—	—
2004	—	—	—	—	—
2005	—	—	—	—	—
2006	—	-5.25	-3.57	8.70	—*

Trailing
	NAV Return%	Market Return%	NAV Rtrn% +/-S&P 500	%Rank Cat.(NAV)
3 Mo	8.70	8.50	2.00	7
6 Mo	4.81	5.85	-7.93	7
1 Yr	—	—	—	
3 Yr Avg	—	—	—	
5 Yr Avg	—	—	—	
10 Yr Avg	—	—	—	

Tax Analysis
	Tax-Adj Return%	Tax-Cost Ratio
3 Yr (estimated)	—	—
5 Yr (estimated)	—	—
10 Yr (estimated)	—	—

Rating and Risk

Time Period	Morningstar Rtn vs Cat	Morningstar Risk vs Cat	Morningstar Risk-Adj Rating
3 Yr	—	—	—
5 Yr	—	—	—
10 Yr	—	—	—

Other Measures
	Standard Index S&P 500	Best Fit Index
Alpha	—	—
Beta	—	—
R-Squared	—	—
Standard Deviation	—	
Mean	—	
Sharpe Ratio	—	

Morningstar's Take by Marta Norton 12-31-06

We're not convinced Rydex S&P Smallcap 600 Pure Growth will beat its rivals over the long haul.

This exchange-traded fund attempts to fill a hole in the market with its unique methodology. Instead of tracking an index using market capitalization to weight its stocks, it tracks the S&P SmallCap 600/Citigroup Pure Growth Index, which weights its holdings by their growth attributes. The index first ranks stocks from the S&P SmallCap 600 Index according to seven growth and value attributes, and then selects the ones with the highest growth scores. Stocks with the strongest growth attributes have the most weight.

This weighting scheme pushes the fund toward sectors considered to be traditional growth haunts. For instance, it shares many of its holdings with iShares S&P SmallCap 600 Growth, an ETF that tracks the market-cap-weighted version of the same index, but it stores more assets in health care. Health-care stocks have historically been less sensitive to the economy and can produce products

that can lead to periods of aggressive growth (consider drug companies with novel new treatments). The fund is also lighter in industrials, which often plod along at a more measured pace.

It also favors smaller stocks. When ETFs track market-cap-weighted indexes, bigger stocks tend to carry more weight than smaller ones. Since this fund's index instead ranks by growth attributes, smaller stocks have a better shot at claiming more assets. It usually holds more micro-cap stocks than almost all its peers. So it may appeal to investors interested in targeted small-cap growth exposure, but it'll also be more volatile, since tiny companies tend to face more challenges in their early stages.

It's too early to tell if the fund will deliver better results than a conventionally weighted small-growth ETF. What's more certain, though, is that its 0.35% expense ratio is higher than those of most rival ETFs. That's too much to pay for an unproven approach to tracking the small-growth market.

Portfolio Analysis 12-31-06

Share change since 11-06 Total Stocks:140

	Sector	PE	Tot Ret%	% Assets
⊖ Possis Medical, Inc.	Health	NMF	35.18	1.18
⊕ Vertrue, Inc.	Consumer	13.6	8.72	1.11
⊖ AMN Healthcare Services,	Business	29.3	39.23	1.09
⊕ Headwaters, Inc.	Energy	10.9	-32.39	1.09
⊖ PetMed Express, Inc.	Consumer	23.4	-5.79	1.09
☼ Infinity Property and Ca	Financial	10.4	30.99	1.09
⊕ Komag, Inc.	Hardware	8.6	9.29	1.09
⊕ Neoware, Inc.	Hardware	57.4	-43.30	1.08
⊕ Bankrate, Inc.	Business	65.4	28.56	1.08
⊖ FLIR Systems, Inc.	Ind Mtrls	28.7	42.54	1.07
⊖ J2 Global Communications	Telecom	26.2	27.52	1.07
⊖ Coinstar, Inc.	Business	39.7	33.90	1.07
⊖ Integra LifeSciences Hol	Health	43.9	20.11	1.05
⊖ NVR, Inc.	Consumer	6.7	-8.12	1.04
☼ Rewards Network, Inc.	Financial	30.2	8.59	1.04
⊕ Websense, Inc.	Software	29.3	-30.44	1.02
⊕ Biosite, Inc.	Health	21.0	-13.22	0.99
⊖ Portfolio Recovery Assoc	Business	17.6	0.54	0.98
⊖ Meritage Homes Corporati	Consumer	4.2	-24.16	0.97
⊖ Shuffle Master	Consumer	90.3	4.22	0.94

Current Investment Style

Value Blnd Growth — Large/Mid/Small

Market Cap	%
Giant	0.0
Large	0.0
Mid	18.5
Small	65.9
Micro	15.6

Avg $mil: 1,060

Value Measures		Rel Category
Price/Earnings	19.06	0.90
Price/Book	2.80	0.94
Price/Sales	1.51	1.02
Price/Cash Flow	8.95	1.27
Dividend Yield %	0.21	0.68

Growth Measures	%	Rel Category
Long-Term Erngs	15.89	0.91
Book Value	19.81	1.65
Sales	18.73	2.03
Cash Flow	20.40	0.96
Historical Erngs	17.36	0.86

Profitability	%	Rel Category
Return on Equity	17.90	1.22
Return on Assets	11.19	1.41
Net Margin	11.24	1.16

Sector Weightings
	% of Stocks	Rel S&P 500	3 Year High Low
↻ Info	15.36	0.77	
Software	7.83	2.27	— —
Hardware	5.12	0.55	— —
Media	0.00	0.00	— —
Telecom	2.41	0.69	— —
☞ Service	58.92	1.28	
Health	20.00	1.66	— —
Consumer	18.68	2.44	— —
Business	11.21	2.65	— —
Financial	9.03	0.41	— —
↦ Mfg	25.72	0.76	
Goods	5.52	0.65	— —
Ind Mtrls	11.20	0.94	— —
Energy	9.00	0.92	— —
Utilities	0.00	0.00	— —

Composition
● Cash	0.0
● Stocks	100.0
● Bonds	0.0
○ Other	0.0
Foreign	0.0
(% of Stock)	

Address:	9601 Blackwell Rd Rockville, MD 20850 800-820-0888	Management Fee:	0.35%
		Expense Projections:	3Yr:$113 5Yr: — 10Yr: —
Web Address:	www.rydex.com	Income Distrib:	Annually
Inception:	03-01-06*	Exchange:	AMEX
Advisor:	Rydex Global Advisors, Inc., Rydex Inves		

MORNINGSTAR® ETFs 150

Rydex S&P Smallcap 600 Va RZV

Market Price $41.25	**Mstar Category** Small Value	

Morningstar Fair Value

Price/Fair Value Ratio —   Coverage Rate % —

Management

Key personnel involved in managing this, and many other ETFs at Rydex, include Michael Byrum, president and CIO, James King, director of portfolio management, and Michael Dellapa, director of investment research.

Methodology

This fund tracks the S&P SmallCap 600/Citigroup Pure Value Index, which weights stocks by their value attributes. It starts out by ranking stocks from the S&P SmallCap 600 Index by seven growth and value factors, including dividend yield and price/book value. Then it selects the stocks with the highest value scores. The index is reconstituted annually in December.

Morningstar Rating	Return	Risk	Yield	NAV	Avg Daily Vol. (k)	52 wk High/Low
— Not Rated	Not Rated	—	—	$41.83	2	$42.39 - $35.47

Growth of $10,000
- Investment Value of ETF
- Investment Value of Index S&P 500

Trading Volume Millions

	1997	1998	1999	2000	2001	2002	2003	2004	2005	2006	History
	—	—	—	—	—	—	—	—	—	41.83	NAV $
	—	—	—	—	—	—	—	—	—	42.00	Market Price $
	—	—	—	—	—	—	—	—	—	10.01*	NAV Return%
	—	—	—	—	—	—	—	—	—	—	Market Price Return%
	—	—	—	—	—	—	—	—	—	0.05	Avg Premium/Discount%
	—	—	—	—	—	—	—	—	—	10.01	NAV Rtrn% +/-S&P 500
	—	—	—	—	—	—	—	—	—	10.01	NAV Rtrn% +/-Russ 2000 VL
	—	—	—	—	—	—	—	—	—	—	NAV Return% Rank in Cat
	—	—	—	—	—	—	—	—	—	—	Income Return %
	—	—	—	—	—	—	—	—	—	—	Capital Return %
	—	—	—	—	—	—	—	—	—	0.43	Income $
	—	—	—	—	—	—	—	—	—	0.00	Capital Gains $
	—	—	—	—	—	—	—	—	—	—	Expense Ratio %
	—	—	—	—	—	—	—	—	—	—	Income Ratio %
	—	—	—	—	—	—	—	—	—	—	Turnover Rate %
	—	—	—	—	—	—	—	—	—	10	Net Assets $mil

Performance 12-31-06

Historic Quarterly NAV Returns

	1st Qtr	2nd Qtr	3rd Qtr	4th Qtr	Total
2002	—	—	—	—	—
2003	—	—	—	—	—
2004	—	—	—	—	—
2005	—	—	—	—	—
2006	—	-4.06	0.21	10.67	—*

Trailing	NAV Return%	Market Return%	NAV Rtrn% +/-S&P 500	%Rank Cat.(NAV)
3 Mo	10.67	11.00	3.97	7
6 Mo	10.90	11.51	-1.84	7
1 Yr	—	—	—	—
3 Yr Avg	—	—	—	—
5 Yr Avg	—	—	—	—
10 Yr Avg	—	—	—	—

Tax Analysis	Tax-Adj Return%	Tax-Cost Ratio
3 Yr (estimated)	—	—
5 Yr (estimated)	—	—
10 Yr (estimated)	—	—

Rating and Risk

Time Period	Morningstar Rtn vs Cat	Morningstar Risk vs Cat	Morningstar Risk-Adj Rating
3 Yr	—	—	—
5 Yr	—	—	—
10 Yr	—	—	—

Other Measures	Standard Index S&P 500	Best Fit Index
Alpha	—	—
Beta	—	—
R-Squared	—	—
Standard Deviation	—	
Mean	—	
Sharpe Ratio	—	

Morningstar's Take by Marta Norton 12-31-06

Rydex S&P Smallcap 600 Pure Value's new approach solves some problems, but introduces others.

This exchange-traded fund comes at small-value stocks from a different angle than its peers. Instead of tracking an index that weights stocks by their market capitalizations, it tracks the S&P SmallCap 600/Citigroup Pure Value Index, which gives the most assets to stocks with the strongest value attributes. The index starts with the S&P SmallCap 600 Index and ranks stocks by seven growth and value factors, including five-year sales per share growth rate and price/book value. It then selects the stocks with the highest value scores. This approach is an attempt to provide undiluted value exposure and avoid the large-cap bias of its market-cap-weighted peers.

But we're not sure the methodology is better. Sure, this ETF has less mid-cap exposure than its peers. In fact, it typically only dedicates roughly 5% of its assets to mid-caps, while its average ETF peer allocates more than 20% there. But the fund also has a larger helping of micro-cap stocks (nearly 40%, compared with the 12% ETF category average). That means increased volatility, as tiny companies often face frequent challenges in their early stages of development.

Also, we're not crazy about the fund's sector weightings. The fund usually stores more than 30% of its assets in industrials, which is more than 10 percentage points more than what its average ETF peer put there. Many companies in that sector, particularly the smaller ones, are suppliers with limited pricing power and are less likely to have periods of outperformance. When they do perform well, as in recent years, they're likely headed for a correction due to their cyclical nature. There's no telling when that'll occur, but when it does, this fund will probably look worse than its peers.

Given these reservations, we'd advise investors to avoid the fund's higher-than-average ETF expense ratio and invest elsewhere.

Address:	9601 Blackwell Rd Rockville, MD 20850 800-820-0888
Web Address:	www.rydex.com
Inception:	03-01-06*
Advisor:	Rydex Global Advisors, Inc., Rydex Inves

Management Fee:	0.35%
Expense Projections:	3Yr:$113 5Yr: — 10Yr: —
Income Distrib:	Annually
Exchange:	AMEX

Portfolio Analysis 12-31-06

Share change since 11-06 Total Stocks:176

	Sector	PE	Tot Ret%	% Assets
⊕ Hancock Fabrics, Inc.	Consumer	—	-15.48	1.61
⊕ Chesapeake Corporation	Ind Mtrls	—	6.31	1.50
⊕ Nash-Finch Company	Consumer	21.8	10.25	1.40
⊕ Libbey Inc.	Ind Mtrls	—	22.00	1.35
⊕ Steel Technologies, Inc.	Ind Mtrls	15.3	-36.37	1.28
⊕ Stewart Information Serv	Financial	19.1	-9.18	1.27
⊕ La-Z-Boy, Inc.	Goods	NMF	-9.56	1.25
⊕ LandAmerica Financial Gr	Financial	8.9	2.40	1.22
⊕ Ryerson, Inc. A	Ind Mtrls	8.7	3.95	1.22
�֍ New Century Financial Co	Financial	4.7	4.91	1.19
⊕ C & D Technologies, Inc.	Ind Mtrls	—	-37.69	1.09
⊖ Standard Motor Products	Ind Mtrls	51.7	68.68	1.09
�֍ Flagstar Bancorp, Inc.	Financial	10.4	7.28	1.06
✖ Building Materials Holdi	Business	5.6	-26.55	1.06
✖ Mesa Air Group, Inc.	Business	7.9	-18.07	1.05
⊕ Wellman, Inc.	Ind Mtrls	—	-51.53	1.05
⊕ Spherion Corporation	Business	21.2	-25.77	1.04
⊖ Standard Register Compan	Business	—	-18.93	1.04
⊖ Central Vermont Public S	Utilities	20.8	36.54	1.02
⊕ Pope & Talbot, Inc.	Ind Mtrls	—	-34.33	1.01

Current Investment Style

Value Blnd Growth — Large Mid Small

Market Cap	%
Giant	0.0
Large	0.0
Mid	4.2
Small	50.0
Micro	45.8
Avg $mil:	544

Value Measures		Rel Category
Price/Earnings	15.12	1.00
Price/Book	1.29	0.75
Price/Sales	0.33	0.45
Price/Cash Flow	4.64	0.77
Dividend Yield %	2.47	1.19

Growth Measures	%	Rel Category
Long-Term Erngs	11.16	1.04
Book Value	0.91	0.19
Sales	8.52	1.99
Cash Flow	-1.36	NMF
Historical Erngs	—	—

Profitability	%	Rel Category
Return on Equity	5.68	0.54
Return on Assets	2.55	0.39
Net Margin	4.24	0.43

Sector Weightings	% of Stocks	Rel S&P 500	3 Year High Low
⊙ Info	4.42	0.22	
🖥 Software	0.00	0.00	— —
🖥 Hardware	2.43	0.26	— —
🎙 Media	0.36	0.09	— —
📶 Telecom	1.63	0.46	— —
ⓒ Service	48.20	1.04	
🩺 Health	4.22	0.35	— —
🛒 Consumer	15.27	2.00	— —
💼 Business	10.74	2.54	— —
$ Financial	17.97	0.81	— —
🏭 Mfg	47.37	1.40	
🛠 Goods	7.52	0.88	— —
⚙ Ind Mtrls	29.03	2.43	— —
🔋 Energy	1.29	0.13	— —
💡 Utilities	9.53	2.72	— —

Composition

● Cash	0.0
● Stocks	100.0
● Bonds	0.0
● Other	0.0
Foreign	0.6
(% of Stock)	

SPDR S&P Dividend SDY

	Market Price	**Mstar Category**
	$61.61	Large Value

Morningstar Fair Value

Price/Fair Value Ratio	Coverage Rate %
0.94 Undervalued	80 Fair

Management

A five-member team from SSgA manages this fund. All of them have at least a decade of industry experience and more than six years with SSgA. John A. Tucker is head of the team. He's assisted by Michael J. Feehily, David Chin, Karl Schneider, and John May.

Methodology

The fund tracks the S&P High Yield Dividend Aristocrats Index, which includes the 50 highest-yielding members of the S&P 1500 that have increased their dividends for at least 25 years in a row. Holdings are weighted by yield, capped at 4% of the portfolio, and required to have market capitalizations of $500 million and average monthly trading volume of 1.5 million shares. The index reweighs its holdings quarterly and reconstitutes itself once a year in December. It controls turnover by not kicking out holdings until their yield ranking drops below 60.

	Morningstar Rating	Return	Risk	Yield	NAV	Avg Daily Vol. (k)	52 wk High/Low
	Not Rated	Not Rated	—	2.9%	$61.79	18	$62.41 - $54.56

Growth of $10,000
— Investment Value of ETF
— Investment Value of Index S&P 500

Trading Volume Millions

	1997	1998	1999	2000	2001	2002	2003	2004	2005	2006	History
	—	—	—	—	—	—	—	—	54.09	61.79	NAV $
	—	—	—	—	—	—	—	—	54.15	61.85	Market Price $
	—	—	—	—	—	—	—	—	17.05*	17.74	NAV Return%
	—	—	—	—	—	—	—	—	—	17.71	Market Price Return%
	—	—	—	—	—	—	—	—	0.07	0.04	Avg Premium/Discount%
	—	—	—	—	—	—	—	—	17.05	1.95	NAV Rtrn% +/-S&P 500
	—	—	—	—	—	—	—	—	17.05	-4.51	NAV Rtrn% +/-Russ 1000 Vl
	—	—	—	—	—	—	—	—	—	14	NAV Return% Rank in Cat
	—	—	—	—	—	—	—	—	—	3.31	Income Return %
	—	—	—	—	—	—	—	—	—	14.43	Capital Return %
	—	—	—	—	—	—	—	—	0.31	1.77	Income $
	—	—	—	—	—	—	—	—	0.00	0.00	Capital Gains $
	—	—	—	—	—	—	—	—	—	0.30	Expense Ratio %
	—	—	—	—	—	—	—	—	—	3.45	Income Ratio %
	—	—	—	—	—	—	—	—	—	25	Turnover Rate %
	—	—	—	—	—	—	—	—	32	198	Net Assets $mil

Performance 12-31-06

Historic Quarterly NAV Returns

	1st Qtr	2nd Qtr	3rd Qtr	4th Qtr	Total
2002	—	—	—	—	—
2003	—	—	—	—	—
2004	—	—	—	—	—
2005	—	—	—	—	—*
2006	3.60	0.74	6.44	5.98	17.74

Trailing	NAV Return%	Market Return%	NAV Rtrn% +/-S&P 500	%Rank Cat.(NAV)
3 Mo	5.98	5.96	-0.72	16
6 Mo	12.81	12.70	0.07	16
1 Yr	17.74	17.71	1.95	14
3 Yr Avg	—	—	—	—
5 Yr Avg	—	—	—	—
10 Yr Avg	—	—	—	—

Tax Analysis	Tax-Adj Return%	Tax-Cost Ratio
3 Yr (estimated)	—	—
5 Yr (estimated)	—	—
10 Yr (estimated)	—	—

Rating and Risk

Time Period	Morningstar Rtn vs Cat	Morningstar Risk vs Cat	Morningstar Risk-Adj Rating
3 Yr	—	—	—
5 Yr	—	—	—
10 Yr	—	—	—

Other Measures	Standard Index S&P 500	Best Fit Index
Alpha	—	—
Beta	—	—
R-Squared	—	—
Standard Deviation	—	
Mean	—	
Sharpe Ratio	—	

Morningstar's Take by Dan Culloton 12-31-06

It's still too early to know what to do with SPDR Dividend ETF.

This exchange-traded fund has some promise. It tracks a benchmark of established companies with long histories of increasing their dividends. Like many other dividend-focused ETFs that have emerged in recent years, it weights its constituents by yield. It is, however, one of the cheaper yield-hungry funds, with a 0.30% expense ratio that's less than a third of that of the typical no-load large-cap value fund and lower than most yield-centric ETFs. Just WisdomTree Total Dividend and Vanguard Dividend Appreciation have lower levies at 0.28% apiece.

While it's difficult to compare this young ETF's portfolio with those slightly cheaper and even younger options, the fund does appear to be a bit more diversified than its more established peers. This ETF has big helpings of financial and utilities stocks, but not as big as those of iShares Dow Jones Select Dividend Index and PowerShares

HighYield Dividend Achievers. That's largely because the ETF's index caps individual holdings at 4% and requires companies to have minimum market caps of at least $500 million, which rules out many regional banks and savings and loans.

The methodology, however, rules in a few high-quality companies that Morningstar equity analysts think are priced well below their fair values, such as Coca-Cola and Johnson & Johnson. Overall, though, it's hard to call this portfolio undervalued. Its average price/cash and price/earnings ratios are higher than the average large-value fund. It also owns stakes in some arguably overvalued stocks, such as packaged food company ConAgra.

Not only is the fund not an obvious opportunity from a valuation perspective, but it and its benchmark also lack much of a track record. Low costs and diversification make it worth watching, but it still needs to prove itself before earning an endorsement.

Address:	State Street Bank & Tr, 225 Franklin St Boston MA 02210 866-787-2257	
Web Address:	www.advisors.ssga.com	
Inception:	11-08-05 *	
Advisor:	SSgA Funds Management Inc	

Management Fee:	0.35%	
Expense Projections:	3Yr:$113	5Yr:$197 10Yr:$446
Income Distrib:	Quarterly	
Exchange:	AMEX	

Portfolio Analysis 12-31-06

Share change since 11-06 Total Stocks:49	Sector	PE	Tot Ret%	% Assets
⊕ Consolidated Edison Comp	Utilities	17.5	9.14	3.05
⊖ First Horizon National C	Financial	17.4	13.71	3.02
⊕ WPS Resources	Utilities	14.9	2.11	2.89
⊕ Vectren Corporation	Utilities	17.2	8.97	2.76
⊕ Bank of America Corporat	Financial	12.4	20.68	2.70
⊕ Fifth Third Bancorp	Financial	15.7	12.99	2.68
⊖ US Bancorp	Financial	14.1	26.29	2.66
⊕ Altria Group, Inc.	Goods	15.9	19.87	2.64
⊕ Comerica Incorporated	Financial	11.8	7.78	2.57
⊕ KeyCorp	Financial	13.0	21.03	2.57
⊖ WGL Holdings, Inc.	Utilities	18.0	13.29	2.56
⊕ BB&T Corporation	Financial	14.0	8.92	2.52
⊕ La-Z-Boy, Inc.	Goods	NMF	-9.56	2.51
⊕ Regions Financial Corpor	Financial	13.8	14.92	2.49
⊕ Black Hills Corporation	Utilities	34.5	10.84	2.40
⊕ Pfizer Inc.	Health	15.1	15.22	2.32
⊕ Associated Banc-Corp	Financial	14.2	10.95	2.31
⊕ Northwest Natural Gas	Energy	19.8	28.90	2.25
⊕ RPM International, Inc.	Goods	—	24.55	2.25
⊖ Piedmont Natural Gas Com	Utilities	20.6	15.05	2.09

Current Investment Style

Value Blnd Growth — Large Mid Small

Market Cap	%
Giant	23.1
Large	25.3
Mid	38.7
Small	12.9
Micro	0.0
Avg $mil:	11,709

Value Measures		Rel Category
Price/Earnings	16.13	1.13
Price/Book	2.33	0.97
Price/Sales	1.29	0.97
Price/Cash Flow	11.52	1.49
Dividend Yield %	3.10	1.20

Growth Measures	%	Rel Category
Long-Term Erngs	8.31	0.83
Book Value	6.06	0.84
Sales	9.86	1.16
Cash Flow	-1.26	NMF
Historical Erngs	8.11	0.52

Profitability	%	Rel Category
Return on Equity	15.95	0.92
Return on Assets	10.04	1.01
Net Margin	15.33	1.12

Sector Weightings	% of Stocks	Rel S&P 500	3 Year High Low
⟳ Info	1.35	0.07	
📇 Software	0.00	0.00	— —
💻 Hardware	0.00	0.00	— —
📱 Media	1.35	0.36	— —
📞 Telecom	0.00	0.00	— —
⟳ Service	46.79	1.01	
🩺 Health	8.47	0.70	— —
🛒 Consumer	1.56	0.20	— —
📊 Business	1.49	0.35	— —
💲 Financial	35.27	1.58	— —
🏭 Mfg	51.87	1.54	
🏠 Goods	17.02	1.99	— —
⚙ Ind Mtrls	13.18	1.10	— —
🔋 Energy	2.26	0.23	— —
💡 Utilities	19.41	5.55	— —

Composition

● Cash	0.2	
● Stocks	99.8	
● Bonds	0.0	
○ Other	0.0	
Foreign	0.0	
(% of Stock)		

 MORNINGSTAR® ETFs 150

SPDR Trust Series 1 SPY

	Market Price $141.07	Mstar Category Large Blend

Morningstar Fair Value

Price/Fair Value Ratio	Coverage Rate %
0.91 Undervalued	97 Good

Management

State Street Global Advisors has managed this fund since its inception in 1993. State Street is one of the world's largest money managers. The organization has a lot of experience running index ETF portfolios.

Methodology

This fund owns and passively tracks the stocks in the S&P 500 Index in proportion to their weight in the benchmark. The offering is organized as a unit investment trust, so unlike open-ended mutual funds, it cannot use futures contracts or lend securities for a fee to close the expense gap between it and its bogy. It also cannot reinvest the dividends it receives until it pays them out to investors. It has to hold the payouts in a non-interest bearing account until they are distributed once a quarter.

Morningstar Rating ★★★ Neutral	Return Neutral	Risk Average	Yield 1.7%	NAV $141.64	Avg Daily Vol. (k) 64,801

52 wk High/Low $142.51 - $122.55

Growth of $10,000
— Investment Value of ETF
— Investment Value of Index S&P 500

38.0
31.0
15.0
10.0

Trading Volume Millions
67.8
1.6

	1997	1998	1999	2000	2001	2002	2003	2004	2005	2006	History
	97.07	123.00	147.08	132.21	115.05	88.21	111.45	121.10	124.70	141.64	NAV $
	97.06	123.31	146.88	131.19	114.23	88.23	111.28	120.87	124.51	142.21	Market Price $
	33.06	28.35	20.86	-9.15	-11.86	-22.12	28.39	10.75	4.79	15.69	NAV Return%
	33.48	28.69	20.39	-9.73	-11.81	-21.54	28.18	10.70	4.83	16.33	Market Price Return%
	-0.13	-0.12	-0.17	-0.08	-0.09	-0.21	0.00	0.02	-0.01	0.07	Avg Premium/Discount%
	-0.30	-0.23	-0.18	-0.05	0.03	-0.02	-0.29	-0.13	-0.12	-0.10	NAV Rtrn% +/-S&P 500
	0.21	1.33	-0.05	-1.36	0.59	0.47	-1.50	-0.65	-1.48	0.23	NAV Rtrn% +/-Russ 1000
	1	1	4	4	12	14	14	16	21	30	NAV Return% Rank in Cat
	1.87	1.47	1.18	1.03	1.08	1.31	1.86	1.99	1.79	1.98	Income Return %
	31.19	26.88	19.68	-10.18	-12.94	-23.43	26.53	8.76	3.00	13.71	Capital Return %
	1.38	1.42	1.44	1.51	1.42	1.50	1.63	2.20	2.15	2.45	Income $
	0.00	0.00	0.00	0.00	0.00	0.00	0.00	0.00	0.00	0.00	Capital Gains $
	0.18	0.18	0.17	0.13	0.11	0.11	0.12	0.11	0.10	—	Expense Ratio %
	1.63	1.35	1.18	1.01	1.14	1.40	1.67	1.63	2.02	—	Income Ratio %
	3	6	6	8	5	4	2	2	6	—	Turnover Rate %
	—	—	—	—	—	39,273	43,815	55,944	58,539	63,997	Net Assets $mil

Performance 12-31-06

Historic Quarterly NAV Returns

	1st Qtr	2nd Qtr	3rd Qtr	4th Qtr	Total
2002	0.24	-13.38	-17.24	8.39	-22.12
2003	-3.20	15.31	2.60	12.11	28.39
2004	1.67	1.69	-1.89	9.18	10.75
2005	-2.16	1.33	3.58	2.05	4.79
2006	4.18	-1.45	5.63	6.67	15.69

Trailing	NAV Return%	Market Return%	NAV Rtrn% +/-S&P 500	%Rank Cat.(NAV)
3 Mo	6.67	7.05	-0.03	44
6 Mo	12.68	12.89	-0.06	38
1 Yr	15.69	16.33	-0.10	30
3 Yr Avg	10.32	10.52	-0.12	15
5 Yr Avg	6.07	6.31	-0.12	13
10 Yr Avg	8.30	8.38	-0.12	1

Tax Analysis	Tax-Adj Return%	Tax-Cost Ratio
3 Yr (estimated)	9.61	0.64
5 Yr (estimated)	5.42	0.61
10 Yr (estimated)	7.70	0.55

Rating and Risk

Time Period	Morningstar Rtn vs Cat	Morningstar Risk vs Cat	Morningstar Risk-Adj Rating
3 Yr	Avg	-Avg	★★★
5 Yr	Avg	Avg	★★★
10 Yr	Avg	Avg	★★★

Other Measures	Standard Index S&P 500	Best Fit Index S&P 500
Alpha	-0.1	-0.1
Beta	1.00	1.00
R-Squared	100	100
Standard Deviation	6.90	
Mean	10.32	
Sharpe Ratio	1.00	

Morningstar's Take by Sonya Morris 12-31-06

The SPDR has a tough time measuring up against the competition.

Investors seeking exposure to the ubiquitous S&P 500 Index have several exchange-traded funds and conventional mutual funds to choose from. By mandate, all of these offerings must hold the exact same portfolio, so a fund has only a few ways to distinguish itself from its rivals. For the most part, they compete on costs and tax efficiency. This ETF does a respectable job on both counts, but there are challengers that do better.

Let's start with expenses. This ETF's 0.10% expense ratio is one of the lowest around, but it's not the cheapest way to get exposure to the S&P 500 Index. Its ETF rival, iShares S&P 500 Index is a tad cheaper at 0.09%. Meanwhile, a traditional fund, E*Trade S&P 500 Index, can be had for 0.09%, and Fidelity Spartan 500 Index charges just 0.10% in fees. These conventional funds wind up being cheaper because you don't have to pay brokerage commissions to trade them.

Another cost to consider is taxes if you plan on holding these in a taxable account. Although this is a relatively tax-efficient fund compared with other large-blend offerings, its rivals do a better job of limiting the tax man's bite. This ETF's five-year tax-cost ratio (which expresses tax costs in the form of an expense ratio) of 0.61% is one of the highest among funds that track the S&P 500 Index. And on average over the past five years, Vanguard 500 Index has picked up an extra 0.25% in post-tax returns each year thanks to its superior tax efficiency.

Still, this ETF is by no means fatally flawed. It's done a solid job of tracking its benchmark, and that's been enough to lift it past the majority of its actively managed rivals over time. Plus, this fund provides broad exposure to U.S. large caps at a very low price. But because it falls short of its rivals in terms of costs and tax efficiency, it's not our first choice among S&P 500 index funds.

Portfolio Analysis 12-31-06

Share change since 11-06 Total Stocks:501

	Sector	PE	Tot Ret%	% Assets
⊖ ExxonMobil Corporation	Energy	11.7	39.07	3.49
⊖ General Electric Company	Ind Mtrls	19.8	9.35	3.00
⊖ Citigroup, Inc.	Financial	13.3	19.55	2.14
⊖ Microsoft Corporation	Software	23.7	15.83	2.02
⊖ Bank of America Corporat	Financial	12.4	20.68	1.87
⊖ Procter & Gamble Company	Goods	24.2	13.36	1.59
⊖ Johnson & Johnson	Health	17.4	12.44	1.50
⊖ Pfizer Inc.	Health	15.1	15.22	1.46
⊖ American International G	Financial	17.1	6.05	1.46
⊖ Altria Group, Inc.	Goods	15.9	19.87	1.41
⊖ J.P. Morgan Chase & Co.	Financial	13.7	25.60	1.31
⊖ Cisco Systems, Inc.	Hardware	28.8	59.64	1.30
⊖ Chevron Corporation	Energy	9.3	33.75	1.26
⊖ IBM	Hardware	16.8	19.77	1.14
⊖ AT&T, Inc.	Telecom	19.2	51.59	1.07
⊖ Wells Fargo Company	Financial	14.7	16.82	0.94
⊖ ConocoPhillips	Energy	6.9	26.53	0.93
⊖ Intel Corporation	Hardware	20.3	-17.18	0.91
⊖ Wal-Mart Stores, Inc.	Consumer	16.6	0.13	0.89
⊖ Hewlett-Packard Company	Hardware	18.9	45.21	0.88

Current Investment Style

Value Blnd Growth — Large Mid Small

Market Cap	%
Giant	51.0
Large	38.2
Mid	10.7
Small	0.1
Micro	0.0

Avg $mil: 53,095

Value Measures		Rel Category
Price/Earnings	15.94	0.96
Price/Book	2.71	0.99
Price/Sales	1.52	1.20
Price/Cash Flow	9.33	0.99
Dividend Yield %	1.79	1.00

Growth Measures	%	Rel Category
Long-Term Erngs	11.41	0.99
Book Value	8.55	1.00
Sales	9.94	1.20
Cash Flow	10.76	1.42
Historical Erngs	17.92	1.07

Profitability	%	Rel Category
Return on Equity	19.79	1.03
Return on Assets	11.06	1.15
Net Margin	14.27	1.28

Sector Weightings

	% of Stocks	Rel S&P 500	3 Year High	Low
Info	20.30	1.02		
Software	3.77	1.09	5	3
Hardware	9.20	1.00	12	9
Media	3.81	1.01	4	3
Telecom	3.52	1.00	4	3
Service	45.93	0.99		
Health	12.05	1.00	14	12
Consumer	7.66	1.00	9	7
Business	3.92	0.93	5	4
Financial	22.30	1.00	22	20
Mfg	33.79	1.00		
Goods	8.55	1.00	10	8
Ind Mtrls	11.96	1.00	13	12
Energy	9.81	1.00	11	6
Utilities	3.47	0.99	4	3

Composition

● Cash	0.5
● Stocks	99.5
● Bonds	0.0
● Other	0.0
Foreign	0.0
(% of Stock)	

Address:	PDR Services, 86 Trinity Place New York NY 10006 800-843-2639	Management Fee:	0.06%
Web Address:	www.amex.com/spy	Expense Projections:	3Yr: — 5Yr: — 10Yr: —
Inception:	01-29-93	Income Distrib:	Quarterly
Advisor:	PDR Services	Exchange:	AMEX

SPDR DJ Global Titans DGT

Market Price $75.57	**Mstar Category** World Stock

Morningstar Fair Value

Price/Fair Value Ratio	Coverage Rate %
0.91 Undervalued	91 Good

Morningstar Rating	Return	Risk	Yield	NAV	Avg Daily Vol. (k)	52 wk High/Low
★ Lowest	Lowest	Below Avg	2.0%	$76.06	16	$76.45 - $64.55

Management

The fund is run by the ETF team at State Street Global Advisors. The team is made up of John Tucker, Karl Schneider, David Chin, and James May. Tucker is the head of the portfolio management team for the firm's ETFs. He's the former head of SSgA's structured-products group in the firm's London office.

Methodology

This fund tracks the Dow Jones Global Titans 50 Index. To create the index, Dow Jones ranks the 5,000 stocks in its global indexes by market cap, selects the 100 largest issues that meet certain quality and competitive standards and earn at least some of their revenue outside their home country, and rates those 100 names by size, assets, book value, sales/ revenue, and net profit. The top 50 stocks make the index.

Growth of $10,000
- Investment Value of ETF
- Investment Value of Index MSCI EAFE

Trading Volume Millions

1997	1998	1999	2000	2001	2002	2003	2004	2005	2006	History
—	—	—	76.96	66.32	50.02	61.22	64.40	64.89	76.06	NAV $
—	—	—	76.97	66.94	50.00	61.22	64.43	65.01	76.08	Market Price $
—	—	—	0.14*	-12.88	-23.37	24.92	7.34	2.82	19.84	NAV Return%
—	—	—	0.14*	-12.08	-24.11	24.97	7.36	2.97	19.65	Market Price Return%
—	—	—	-0.60	0.34	0.06	0.05	0.08	0.17	0.09	Avg Premium/Discount%
—	—	—	0.14	8.54	-7.43	-13.67	-12.91	-10.72	-6.50	NAV Rtrn% +/-MSCI EAFE
—	—	—	0.14	3.92	-3.48	-8.19	-7.38	-6.67	-0.23	NAV Rtrn% +/-MSCI World
—	—	—	—	2	2	2	2	2	2	NAV Return% Rank in Cat
—	—	—	—	0.93	1.25	2.28	2.06	2.06	2.39	Income Return %
—	—	—	—	-13.81	-24.62	22.64	5.28	0.76	17.45	Capital Return %
—	—	—	0.13	0.71	0.83	1.13	1.25	1.32	1.54	Income $
—	—	—	0.00	0.00	0.00	0.00	0.00	0.00	0.00	Capital Gains $
—	—	—	—	0.52	0.55	0.54	0.51	0.51	0.51	Expense Ratio %
—	—	—	—	0.87	1.07	1.77	1.84	2.47	2.11	Income Ratio %
—	—	—	—	16	12	13	15	36	9	Turnover Rate %
—	—	—	—	15	24	93	91	186		Net Assets $mil

Performance 12-31-06

Historic Quarterly NAV Returns

	1st Qtr	2nd Qtr	3rd Qtr	4th Qtr	Total
2002	-2.26	-13.14	-18.00	10.08	-23.37
2003	-4.66	14.79	1.53	12.43	24.92
2004	-0.32	1.48	-1.64	7.88	7.34
2005	-1.28	-0.06	4.00	0.21	2.82
2006	3.85	0.59	7.30	6.91	19.84

Trailing	NAV Return%	Market Return%	NAV Rtrn% +/-MSCI EAFE	%Rank Cat.(NAV)
3 Mo	6.91	6.68	-3.44	6
6 Mo	14.72	14.75	0.03	2
1 Yr	19.84	19.65	-6.50	2
3 Yr Avg	9.77	9.77	-10.16	2
5 Yr Avg	4.83	4.64	-10.15	2
10 Yr Avg	—	—	—	—

Tax Analysis	Tax-Adj Return%	Tax-Cost Ratio
3 Yr (estimated)	8.97	0.73
5 Yr (estimated)	4.10	0.70
10 Yr (estimated)	—	—

Rating and Risk

Time Period	Morningstar Rtn vs Cat	Morningstar Risk vs Cat	Morningstar Risk-Adj Rating
3 Yr	Low	Low	★★
5 Yr	Low	-Avg	★
10 Yr	—	—	—

Other Measures	Standard Index S&P 500	Best Fit Index Mstar Large Value
Alpha	-2.0	-3.2
Beta	0.54	0.84
R-Squared	66	82
Standard Deviation	6.34	
Mean	9.77	
Sharpe Ratio	1.02	

Portfolio Analysis 12-31-06

Share change since 11-06 Total Stocks:50

	Sector	Country	% Assets
⊕ ExxonMobil Corporation	Energy	United States	6.09
⊕ General Electric Company	Ind Mtrls	United States	5.27
⊕ Citigroup, Inc.	Financial	United States	3.77
⊕ Microsoft Corporation	Software	United States	3.56
⊕ Bank of America Corporat	Financial	United States	3.27
⊕ BP PLC ADR	Energy	U.K.	2.98
⊕ HSBC Holdings PLC ADR	Financial	U.K.	2.88
⊕ Procter & Gamble Company	Goods	United States	2.78
⊕ Toyota Motor Corporation	Goods	Japan	2.77
⊕ Johnson & Johnson	Health	United States	2.61
⊕ Pfizer Inc.	Health	United States	2.55
⊕ Altria Group, Inc.	Goods	United States	2.42
⊕ J.P. Morgan Chase & Co.	Financial	United States	2.29
⊕ Cisco Systems, Inc.	Hardware	United States	2.27
⊕ Total SA ADR	Energy	France	2.23
⊕ American International G	Financial	United States	2.23
⊕ Chevron Corporation	Energy	United States	2.20
⊕ GlaxoSmithKline PLC ADR	Health	U.K.	2.15
⊕ Vodafone Group PLC ADR	Telecom	U.K.	1.99
⊕ IBM	Hardware	United States	1.99

Current Investment Style

Value Blnd Growth — Large / Mid / Small

Market Cap	%
Giant	100.0
Large	0.0
Mid	0.0
Small	0.0
Micro	0.0

Avg $mil: 171,433

Value Measures		Rel Category
Price/Earnings	14.79	0.92
Price/Book	2.86	1.07
Price/Sales	1.80	1.45
Price/Cash Flow	10.42	1.08
Dividend Yield %	2.38	0.99

Growth Measures	%	Rel Category
Long-Term Erngs	10.01	0.80
Book Value	10.50	1.12
Sales	13.21	1.80
Cash Flow	11.13	1.31
Historical Erngs	18.65	0.90

Composition

Cash	0.1	Bonds	0.0
Stocks	99.9	Other	0.0
Foreign	(% of Stock)		38.0

Sector Weightings

	% of Stocks	Rel MSCI EAFE	3 Year High	Low
↻ Info	21.65	1.83		
Software	3.56	6.36	5	3
Hardware	10.33	2.68	13	9
Media	1.18	0.64	2	1
Telecom	6.58	1.18	7	4
⊆ Service	41.25	0.87		
Health	15.33	2.15	19	15
Consumer	1.63	0.33	3	2
Business	0.00	0.00	0	0
Financial	24.29	0.81	25	20
⊐ Mfg	37.09	0.91		
Goods	13.86	1.06	14	11
Ind Mtrls	5.27	0.34	6	5
Energy	17.96	2.51	20	14
Utilities	0.00	0.00	0	0

Regional Exposure

	% Stock		
UK/W. Europe	33	N. America	62
Japan	4	Latn America	0
Asia X Japan	1	Other	0

Country Exposure

	% Stock		
United States	62	Japan	4
U.K.	15	Netherlands	3
Switzerland	7		

Morningstar's Take by William Samuel Rocco 12-31-06

Giant-cap fans should consider StreetTracks Dow Jones Global Titan's cons as well as its pros.

There's no denying this ETF's dedication to the word's biggest and brightest. It tracks the Dow Jones Global Titans Index, which is a float-adjusted, market-cap-weighted index of 50 prominent blue chips that are selected based on their size, assets, book value, sales or revenue, and net profit. The result is a focused portfolio of household names with giant market caps. Indeed, stocks like ExxonMobil, General Electric, and Microsoft dominate this ETF's portfolio, and its average market cap, which is currently $169 billion, is by far the biggest of any fund in Morningstar's database and more than $40 billion larger than those of other global mega-cap vehicles.

Performance has been respectable here, all things considered. Thanks to the quality and durability of its holdings, this ETF, which opened in late 2000, has been less volatile then the typical world offering so far. It has lagged the two other global mega-cap offerings by a moderate amount and the typical world fund by a major amount over the past several years, but that's understandable given its commitment to giant caps and the dominance of small caps during most of the 2000s. And it has done a good job of aping the returns of its benchmark (after taking its costs into account).

While all this is likely to appeal to giant-cap fans, there are some caveats here. This ETF is especially vulnerable to blue-chip sell-offs. Because it always has a hefty U.S. weight and big stakes in certain sectors and names, it courts various risks and overlaps a lot with many domestic large-cap funds. And while it is cheap relative to actively run world funds, its 0.50% expense ratio is 10 basis points higher than that of the other global giant-cap ETF, iShares S&P Global 100.

Address:	State Street Bank & Tr, 225 Franklin St Boston MA 02210 866-787-2257
Web Address:	www.advisors.ssga.com
Inception:	09-25-00*
Advisor:	SSgA Funds Management Inc

Management Fee:	0.50%		
Expense Projections:	3Yr:$161	5Yr:$281	10Yr:$628
Income Distrib:	Quarterly		
Exchange:	AMEX		

Morningstar® ETFs 150

SPDR DJ Wilshire Large Cp ELR

	Market Price $64.71	Mstar Category Large Blend

Morningstar Fair Value

Price/Fair Value Ratio
0.91 Undervalued

Coverage Rate %
97 Good

Management

SSgA Funds Management is this ETF's advisor. The ETF group at SSgA is headed by John Tucker. He joined the firm in 1988.

Methodology

This fund tracks the Dow Jones Wilshire Large Cap Index. The bogy is float-adjusted and market-capitalization weighted. It invests in the 750 largest stocks in the Dow Jones Wilshire 5000. Buffer zones are employed during the review process to limit turnover. The index is reviewed in March and September; new stocks (IPOs) are added monthly as they are added to the Dow Jones Wilshire 5000.

Morningstar Rating	Return	Risk	Yield	NAV	Avg Daily Vol. (k)	52 wk High/Low
— Not Rated	Not Rated	—	2.1%	$64.86	2	$65.40 - $56.40

Growth of $10,000
— Investment Value of ETF
— Investment Value of Index S&P 500

12.0
11.7
10.6
10.0

Trading Volume Millions
0.006
0.0

	1997	1998	1999	2000	2001	2002	2003	2004	2005	2006	History
	—	—	—	—	—	—	—	—	57.47	64.86	NAV $
	—	—	—	—	—	—	—	—	57.93	64.88	Market Price $
	—	—	—	—	—	—	—	—	16.06*	15.38	NAV Return%
	—	—	—	—	—	—	—	—	—	14.53	Market Price Return%
	—	—	—	—	—	—	—	—	0.86	0.05	Avg Premium/Discount%
	—	—	—	—	—	—	—	—	16.06	-0.41	NAV Rtrn% +/-S&P 500
	—	—	—	—	—	—	—	—	16.06	-0.08	NAV Rtrn% +/-Russ 1000
	—	—	—	—	—	—	—	—	—	30	NAV Return% Rank in Cat
	—	—	—	—	—	—	—	—	—	2.34	Income Return %
	—	—	—	—	—	—	—	—	—	13.04	Capital Return %
	—	—	—	—	—	—	—	—	0.11	1.33	Income $
	—	—	—	—	—	—	—	—	0.00	0.00	Capital Gains $
	—	—	—	—	—	—	—	—	—	0.21	Expense Ratio %
	—	—	—	—	—	—	—	—	—	1.68	Income Ratio %
	—	—	—	—	—	—	—	—	—	4	Turnover Rate %
	—	—	—	—	—	—	—	—	14	13	Net Assets $mil

Performance 12-31-06

Historic Quarterly NAV Returns

	1st Qtr	2nd Qtr	3rd Qtr	4th Qtr	Total
2002	—	—	—	—	—
2003	—	—	—	—	—
2004	—	—	—	—	—
2005	—	—	—	—	—*
2006	4.27	-1.59	5.20	6.89	15.38

Trailing	NAV Return%	Market Return%	NAV Rtrn% +/-S&P 500	%Rank Cat.(NAV)
3 Mo	6.89	6.71	0.19	44
6 Mo	12.44	12.36	-0.30	38
1 Yr	15.38	14.53	-0.41	30
3 Yr Avg	—	—	—	—
5 Yr Avg	—	—	—	—
10 Yr Avg	—	—	—	—

Tax Analysis	Tax-Adj Return%	Tax-Cost Ratio
3 Yr (estimated)	—	—
5 Yr (estimated)	—	—
10 Yr (estimated)	—	—

Rating and Risk

Time Period	Morningstar Rtn vs Cat	Morningstar Risk vs Cat	Morningstar Risk-Adj Rating
3 Yr	—	—	—
5 Yr	—	—	—
10 Yr	—	—	—

Other Measures	Standard Index S&P 500	Best Fit Index
Alpha	—	—
Beta	—	—
R-Squared	—	—
Standard Deviation	—	
Mean	—	
Sharpe Ratio	—	

Portfolio Analysis 12-31-06

Share change since 11-06 Total Stocks:745	Sector	PE	Tot Ret%	% Assets
⊖ ExxonMobil Corporation	Energy	11.7	39.07	3.21
⊕ General Electric Company	Ind Mtrls	19.8	9.35	2.79
⊕ Citigroup, Inc.	Financial	13.3	19.55	2.00
⊖ Microsoft Corporation	Software	23.7	15.83	1.88
⊖ Bank of America Corporat	Financial	12.4	20.68	1.73
⊕ Procter & Gamble Company	Goods	24.2	13.36	1.47
⊖ Johnson & Johnson	Health	17.4	12.44	1.38
⊖ Pfizer Inc.	Health	15.1	15.22	1.34
⊕ Altria Group, Inc.	Goods	15.9	19.87	1.28
⊕ J.P. Morgan Chase & Co.	Financial	13.7	25.60	1.21
⊖ Cisco Systems, Inc.	Hardware	28.8	59.64	1.20
⊕ American International G	Financial	17.1	6.05	1.18
Chevron Corporation	Energy	9.3	33.75	1.16
⊖ IBM	Hardware	16.8	19.77	1.05
⊖ AT&T, Inc.	Telecom	19.2	51.59	0.99
Wal-Mart Stores, Inc.	Consumer	16.6	0.13	0.85
Berkshire Hathaway Inc.	Financial			0.85
Intel Corporation	Hardware	20.3	-17.18	0.84
⊕ Wells Fargo Company	Financial	14.7	16.82	0.81
⊖ Hewlett-Packard Company	Hardware	18.9	45.21	0.81

Current Investment Style

Value Blend Growth
Large Mid Small

	Market Cap	%
	Giant	46.9
	Large	36.1
	Mid	17.0
	Small	0.0
	Micro	0.0
	Avg $mil:	44,430

Value Measures		Rel Category
Price/Earnings	16.12	0.97
Price/Book	2.71	0.99
Price/Sales	1.53	1.20
Price/Cash Flow	9.39	0.99
Dividend Yield %	1.75	0.98

Growth Measures	%	Rel Category
Long-Term Erngs	11.53	1.00
Book Value	8.77	1.03
Sales	10.25	1.23
Cash Flow	11.25	1.49
Historical Erngs	17.95	1.07

Profitability	%	Rel Category
Return on Equity	19.50	1.01
Return on Assets	10.86	1.13
Net Margin	14.20	1.27

Sector Weightings	% of Stocks	Rel S&P 500	3 Year High Low
↻ Info	20.02	1.00	
Software	3.87	1.12	— —
Hardware	8.88	0.96	— —
Media	3.69	0.97	— —
Telecom	3.58	1.02	— —
⊆ Service	47.20	1.02	
Health	12.02	1.00	— —
Consumer	7.92	1.04	— —
Business	4.25	1.00	— —
Financial	23.01	1.03	— —
↵ Mfg	32.80	0.97	
Goods	8.19	0.96	— —
Ind Mtrls	11.21	0.94	— —
Energy	9.89	1.01	— —
Utilities	3.51	1.00	— —

Composition

Composition	
● Cash	0.1
● Stocks	99.9
● Bonds	0.0
● Other	0.0
Foreign	0.1
(% of Stock)	

Morningstar's Take by Marta Norton 12-31-06

StreetTRACKS Dow Jones Wilshire Large Cap is passable, but it's not our first choice.

We like how this exchange-traded fund is put together. Like many of its ETF peers, it's well diversified, holding more than 700 large-cap stocks from across all market sectors. Also, its index, the Dow Jones Wilshire Large Cap Index, uses buffer zones to slow stocks' movement across market-cap boundaries. That should keep a lid on turnover and may provide better tax efficiency over time, too.

Even with its good construction, the fund has slightly underperformed most of its ETF competitors since its late 2005 inception. That's partly due to its size characteristics. Its average market cap is one of the highest in its peer group, and large-cap stocks have continued to underperform their smaller peers. Market winds could be changing, though. Many behemoths stocks boast attractive valuations. For example, more than 76% of this fund's assets are tied up in fairly valued or undervalued stocks, according to Morningstar equity analysts'

estimates. And in recent months, large-cap stocks have rallied. As a result, this fund's recent returns look more competitive.

We wouldn't get too caught up in the short-term numbers. For one, indexing is made for the long term. Plus, even though it is more focused on the biggest of the big, investors can find most of this ETF's holdings in its competitors' portfolios. Thus, the deciding factor comes down to cost. That's where the fund comes up short. Its 0.21% expense ratio is a heavier levy than those of many of its rivals. Close competitor Vanguard Large Cap ETF charges 0.07%, and investors can get iShares S&P 500 Index for 0.10%. Plus, there are a few cheaper conventional index funds out there. Fidelity Spartan 500 Index comes with a low 0.10% expense ratio, for example. With so many rivals getting a head start out of the gate, it's hard to see how this ETF will keep pace over the long term. So, it's well built but not a top pick.

Address:	State Street Bank & Tr, 225 Franklin St Boston MA 02210 866-787-2257	Management Fee:	0.20%		
		Expense Projections:	3Yr:$65	5Yr:$113	10Yr:$257
Web Address:	www.advisors.ssga.com	Income Distrib:	Quarterly		
Inception:	11-08-05 *	Exchange:	AMEX		
Advisor:	SSgA Funds Management Inc				

SPDR DJ Wilshire Lg Value ELV

Market Price $82.70	**Mstar Category** Large Value

Management

SSgA Funds Management is this ETF's advisor. The ETF group at SSgA is headed by John Tucker. He joined the firm in 1988.

Methodology

This fund tracks the Dow Jones Wilshire Large Cap Value Index. The bogy uses six factors to sort the biggest stocks in the Dow Jones Wilshire 5000 into value or growth buckets. Stocks' style scores are based on their projected price/earnings, projected earnings growth, price/book, dividend yield, trailing revenue growth, and trailing earnings growth. Half the universe's float-adjusted market cap ends up in value and half in growth. Buffer zones keep constituents from jumping in and out of the index due to market cap or style score changes. It rebalances in March and September.

Morningstar Rating ★★★ Neutral	**Return** Neutral	**Risk** Average	**Yield** 2.1%	**NAV** $83.31	**Avg Daily Vol. (k)** 8	**52 wk High/Low** $83.86 - $70.44	

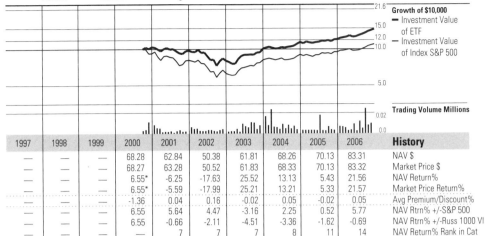

Growth of $10,000
— Investment Value of ETF
— Investment Value of Index S&P 500

Trading Volume Millions

	1997	1998	1999	2000	2001	2002	2003	2004	2005	2006	History
	—	—	—	68.28	62.84	50.38	61.81	68.26	70.13	83.31	NAV $
	—	—	—	68.27	63.28	50.52	61.83	68.33	70.13	83.32	Market Price $
	—	—	—	6.55*	-6.25	-17.63	25.52	13.13	5.43	21.56	NAV Return%
	—	—	—	6.55*	-5.59	-17.99	25.21	13.21	5.33	21.57	Market Price Return%
	—	—	—	-1.36	0.04	0.16	-0.02	0.05	-0.02	0.05	Avg Premium/Discount%
	—	—	—	6.55	5.64	4.47	-3.16	2.25	0.52	5.77	NAV Rtrn% +/-S&P 500
	—	—	—	6.55	-0.66	-2.11	-4.51	-3.36	-1.62	-0.69	NAV Rtrn% +/-Russ 1000 Vl
	—	—	—	—	7	7	7	8	11	14	NAV Return% Rank in Cat
	—	—	—	1.66	2.30	2.58	2.54	2.67	2.55		Income Return %
	—	—	—	-7.91	-19.93	22.94	10.59	2.76	19.01		Capital Return %
	—	—	—	0.29	1.12	1.43	1.29	1.55	1.81	1.77	Income $
	—	—	—	0.00	0.00	0.00	0.00	0.00	0.00	0.00	Capital Gains $
	—	—	—	—	0.21	0.24	0.23	0.21	0.21	0.21	Expense Ratio %
	—	—	—	—	1.61	1.81	2.54	2.72	2.51	2.52	Income Ratio %
	—	—	—	—	12	10	33	28	19	42	Turnover Rate %
	—	—	—	—	25	87	123	98	154		Net Assets $mil

Performance 12-31-06

Historic Quarterly NAV Returns

	1st Qtr	2nd Qtr	3rd Qtr	4th Qtr	Total
2002	1.55	-11.89	-16.48	10.23	-17.63
2003	-5.52	18.25	0.16	12.15	25.52
2004	1.62	1.23	1.27	8.60	13.13
2005	-0.78	1.16	3.21	1.76	5.43
2006	4.89	0.55	7.11	7.60	21.56

Trailing	NAV Return%	Market Return%	NAV Rtrn% +/-S&P 500	%Rank Cat.(NAV)
3 Mo	7.60	7.45	0.90	16
6 Mo	15.25	15.17	2.51	16
1 Yr	21.56	21.57	5.77	14
3 Yr Avg	13.18	13.18	2.74	8
5 Yr Avg	8.43	8.28	2.24	7
10 Yr Avg	—	—	—	—

Tax Analysis	Tax-Adj Return%	Tax-Cost Ratio
3 Yr (estimated)	12.22	0.85
5 Yr (estimated)	7.48	0.88
10 Yr (estimated)	—	—

Rating and Risk

Time Period	Morningstar Rtn vs Cat	Morningstar Risk vs Cat	Morningstar Risk-Adj Rating
3 Yr	+Avg	-Avg	★★★★
5 Yr	Avg	Avg	★★★
10 Yr	—	—	—

Other Measures	Standard Index S&P 500	Best Fit Index Russ 1000 Vl
Alpha	3.7	-0.3
Beta	0.81	0.87
R-Squared	84	92
Standard Deviation	6.16	
Mean	13.18	
Sharpe Ratio	1.55	

Morningstar's Take by Marta Norton 12-31-06

It's not the best available, but streetTRACKS DJ Wilshire Large Cap Value is a reasonable option nonetheless.

This exchange-traded fund's biggest handicap is its expense ratio. That might seem counterintuitive at first, given that its 0.21% expense ratio is much cheaper than that of the typical conventional large-value fund. It looks reasonably priced relative to most of its ETF large-value rivals, too. But indexing is a game of inches, and funds with the lowest expense ratios will always have the biggest advantage. So, with close rival Vanguard Value ETF charging only 0.11%, its unlikely this fund will keep pace over the long haul.

That said, we still see a lot of positives at this fund. We like that it tracks the Dow Jones Wilshire Large Cap Value Index. Besides being well diversified, that index uses buffer zones to slow stocks' movement between styles and market caps. That helps keep turnover low and may lead to greater tax efficiency over time, too. Plus, the bogy

relies on a six-factor model to zero in on value stocks, which, in turn, makes this fund a good representation of the large-value universe.

There are a few quirks worth noting. First, the ETF holds fewer stocks than many of its large-value ETF rivals and gives slightly more weight to its largest holdings. So, stocks like ExxonMobil and General Electric will have a bigger impact on the fund's performance. Also, the fund has a heavier stake in mega-cap stocks than its peers. It allocates nearly 60% of its assets to the market's behemoths. By contrast, its average peer keeps about 44% there. That'll give the fund a slight edge when mega caps rally, but, as has been the case in recent years, it'll hold the fund back when the market prefers smaller fare.

Overall, though, we think this ETF is a decent option for broad large-value exposure. It's not the cheapest of its peer group, but investors could do a lot worse. Keep it in mind.

Portfolio Analysis 12-31-06

Share change since 11-06 Total Stocks:318

	Sector	PE	Tot Ret%	% Assets
⊖ ExxonMobil Corporation	Energy	11.7	39.07	6.14
⊕ General Electric Company	Ind Mtrls	19.8	9.35	5.31
⊕ Citigroup, Inc.	Financial	13.3	19.55	3.81
⊖ Bank of America Corporat	Financial	12.4	20.68	3.30
⊖ Pfizer Inc.	Health	15.1	15.22	2.56
⊕ Altria Group, Inc.	Goods	15.9	19.87	2.44
⊕ J.P. Morgan Chase & Co.	Financial	13.7	25.60	2.31
⊕ American International G	Financial	17.1	6.05	2.25
⊕ Chevron Corporation	Energy	9.3	33.75	2.23
⊖ IBM	Hardware	16.8	19.77	2.01
⊖ AT&T, Inc.	Telecom	19.2	51.59	1.88
⊖ Intel Corporation	Hardware	20.3	-17.18	1.62
⊖ Hewlett-Packard Company	Hardware	18.9	45.21	1.55
⊕ Wells Fargo Company	Financial	14.7	16.82	1.54
⊕ ConocoPhillips	Energy	6.9	26.53	1.53
⊕ Wachovia Corporation	Financial	13.0	12.02	1.50
⊕ Verizon Communications	Telecom	16.1	34.88	1.49
⊕ Coca-Cola Company	Goods	21.5	23.10	1.43
⊕ Merck & Co., Inc.	Health	18.8	42.66	1.31
⊕ BellSouth Corporation	Telecom	—	—	1.19

Current Investment Style

Value Blnd Growth — Large Mid Small

Market Cap	%
Giant	57.2
Large	29.8
Mid	13.0
Small	0.0
Micro	0.0

Avg $mil: 60,831

Value Measures		Rel Category
Price/Earnings	14.13	0.99
Price/Book	2.46	1.02
Price/Sales	1.43	1.08
Price/Cash Flow	7.74	1.00
Dividend Yield %	2.47	0.95

Growth Measures	%	Rel Category
Long-Term Erngs	10.02	1.00
Book Value	6.93	0.96
Sales	8.71	1.02
Cash Flow	8.79	1.02
Historical Erngs	15.75	1.02

Profitability	%	Rel Category
Return on Equity	17.51	1.01
Return on Assets	10.53	1.06
Net Margin	14.57	1.06

Sector Weightings

	% of Stocks	Rel S&P 500	3 Year High	Low
⌂ Info	15.67	0.78		
🖳 Software	1.62	0.47	2	0
💻 Hardware	7.10	0.77	8	2
📶 Media	1.56	0.41	3	0
📞 Telecom	5.39	1.54	8	5
⛭ Service	44.26	0.96		
🩺 Health	6.70	0.56	12	7
🛒 Consumer	2.06	0.27	3	2
🏢 Business	1.53	0.36	2	1
💲 Financial	33.97	1.53	37	31
🏭 Mfg	40.07	1.19		
🏠 Goods	7.83	0.92	8	5
⚙ Ind Mtrls	14.46	1.21	17	14
🔥 Energy	11.86	1.21	17	11
💡 Utilities	5.92	1.69	6	4

Composition

● Cash	0.2	
● Stocks	99.8	
● Bonds	0.0	
○ Other	0.0	
Foreign	0.1	
(% of Stock)		

Address:	State Street Bank & Tr, 225 Franklin St Boston MA 02210 866-787-2257	Management Fee:	0.20%		
		Expense Projections:	3Yr:$65	5Yr:$113	10Yr:$257
Web Address:	www.advisors.ssga.com	Income Distrib:	Quarterly		
Inception:	09-25-00*	Exchange:	AMEX		
Advisor:	SSgA Funds Management Inc				

MORNINGSTAR® ETFs 150

SPDR DJ Wilshire Lg Grwth ELG

	Market Price	Mstar Category
	$53.47	Large Growth

Morningstar Fair Value

Price/Fair Value Ratio	Coverage Rate %
0.89 Undervalued	95 Good

Management

SSgA Funds Management is this ETF's advisor. The ETF group at SSgA is headed by John Tucker. He joined the firm in 1988.

Methodology

This fund tracks the Dow Jones Wilshire Large Cap Growth Index. The bogy uses six factors, including projected price/earnings ratio, projected earnings growth, price/book ratio, dividend yield, trailing revenue growth, and trailing earnings growth, to select growth stocks from the Dow Jones Wilshire 5000 Index. Buffer zones are employed during the review process to limit turnover. The index is reviewed semiannually in March and September.

Morningstar Rating	Return	Risk	Yield	NAV	Avg Daily Vol. (k)	52 wk High/Low
★★ Below Avg	Below Avg	Average	0.7%	$53.43	18	$54.18 - $46.91

Growth of $10,000
— Investment Value of ETF
— Investment Value of Index S&P 500

10.8
5.0
3.0

0.04
0.0

Trading Volume Millions

1997	1998	1999	2000	2001	2002	2003	2004	2005	2006	History
—	—	—	71.97	53.39	36.33	46.68	48.32	49.44	53.43	NAV $
—	—	—	73.12	54.09	36.55	46.65	48.45	49.42	53.46	Market Price $
—	—	—	-8.55*	-25.65	-31.66	29.19	4.94	3.00	8.93	NAV Return%
—	—	—	-8.54*	-25.86	-32.14	28.34	5.27	2.69	9.01	Market Price Return%
—	—	—	-0.18	0.81	0.14	0.28	0.12	0.01	0.02	Avg Premium/Discount%
—	—	—	-8.55	-13.76	-9.56	0.51	-5.94	-1.91	-6.86	NAV Rtrn% +/-S&P 500
—	—	—	-8.55	-5.23	-3.78	-0.56	-1.36	-2.26	-0.14	NAV Rtrn% +/-Russ 1000Gr
—	—	—	—	6	6	6	7	10	13	NAV Return% Rank in Cat
—	—	—	—	0.16	0.32	0.65	1.38	0.67	0.80	Income Return %
—	—	—	—	-25.81	-31.98	28.54	3.56	2.33	8.13	Capital Return %
—	—	—	0.02	0.12	0.17	0.23	0.64	0.32	0.40	Income $
—	—	—	0.00	0.00	0.00	0.00	0.00	0.00	0.00	Capital Gains $
—	—	—	—	0.22	0.25	0.23	0.21	0.21	0.21	Expense Ratio %
—	—	—	—	0.10	0.32	0.64	0.59	1.57	0.74	Income Ratio %
—	—	—	—	16	18	37	20	21	43	Turnover Rate %
—	—	—	—	15	35	82	143	214		Net Assets $mil

Performance 12-31-06

Historic Quarterly NAV Returns

	1st Qtr	2nd Qtr	3rd Qtr	4th Qtr	Total
2002	-4.61	-19.28	-17.18	7.15	-31.66
2003	0.62	12.40	3.02	10.88	29.19
2004	0.37	1.79	-5.28	8.43	4.94
2005	-4.96	1.08	3.47	3.62	3.00
2006	3.48	-3.79	3.12	6.10	8.93

Trailing	NAV Return%	Market Return%	NAV Rtrn% +/-S&P 500	%Rank Cat.(NAV)
3 Mo	6.10	6.05	-0.60	15
6 Mo	9.41	9.26	-3.33	15
1 Yr	8.93	9.01	-6.86	13
3 Yr Avg	5.59	5.63	-4.85	7
5 Yr Avg	0.78	0.52	-5.41	6
10 Yr Avg	—	—	—	—

Tax Analysis	Tax-Adj Return%	Tax-Cost Ratio
3 Yr (estimated)	5.25	0.32
5 Yr (estimated)	0.51	0.27
10 Yr (estimated)	—	—

Rating and Risk

Time Period	Morningstar Rtn vs Cat	Morningstar Risk vs Cat	Morningstar Risk-Adj Rating
3 Yr	-Avg	-Avg	★★★
5 Yr	-Avg	Avg	★★
10 Yr	—	—	

Other Measures	Standard Index S&P 500	Best Fit Index Russ 1000Gr
Alpha	-5.2	-1.1
Beta	1.11	0.96
R-Squared	86	96
Standard Deviation	8.28	
Mean	5.59	
Sharpe Ratio	0.31	

Morningstar's Take by Marta Norton 12-31-06

Investors have a decent, but not great, option in StreetTRACKS Dow Jones Wilshire Large Cap Growth.

An exchange-traded fund like this one makes a lot of sense right now. Large-growth stocks have suffered a multiyear slump. In fact, the typical open-end large-growth fund has returned only 3.3% for the trailing five years ending Dec. 13, 2006. By contrast, the typical small-value fund, its stylistic opposite, has been on a tear, gaining near 15% over the same period. Thus, it's not surprising that many large-growth stocks now sport attractive valuations. Indeed, 75% of this fund's assets are invested in fairly valued or undervalued stocks, according to Morningstar equity analysts' estimates. That could mean significant upside for investors here should large growth rally.

There are reasons beyond current market conditions to give this fund a look. Its well-constructed benchmark, the Dow Jones Wilshire Large Cap Growth Index, uses buffer zones to slow stocks' migration across style and market-cap borders. That keeps turnover down and may also improve tax efficiency over the long haul. Plus, because its index also uses six factors to sort stocks into value or growth buckets, this ETF is a good source for pure growth exposure.

But even with these advantages, this ETF isn't its category's best. Indexing is a game of inches, and the surest way to win is to keep expenses down. At 0.21%, the fund's expense ratio is much cheaper than those of most actively managed large-growth funds, but it looks expensive next to those of some of its similarly structured ETF rivals. For example, iShares S&P 500 Growth charges a 0.18% levy. Vanguard Growth ETF is even cheaper: It costs only 0.11%. It'll be next to impossible for this ETF to keep up with those competitors over the long haul, given their edge in expenses.

So, while this ETF will get the job done, we like its cheaper competitors more.

Address:	State Street Bank & Tr, 225 Franklin St Boston MA 02210 866-787-2257	Management Fee:	0.20%	
		Expense Projections:	3Yr:$65	5Yr:$113 10Yr:$257
Web Address:	www.advisors.ssga.com	Income Distrib:	Quarterly	
Inception:	09-25-00 *	Exchange:	AMEX	
Advisor:	SSgA Funds Management Inc			

Portfolio Analysis 12-31-06

Share change since 11-06 Total Stocks:427

	Sector	PE	Tot Ret%	% Assets
⊕ Microsoft Corporation	Software	23.7	15.83	3.94
⊕ Procter & Gamble Company	Goods	24.2	13.36	3.07
⊕ Johnson & Johnson	Health	17.4	12.44	2.89
⊕ Cisco Systems, Inc.	Hardware	28.8	59.64	2.51
⊕ Wal-Mart Stores, Inc.	Consumer	16.6	0.13	1.80
⊕ Berkshire Hathaway Inc.	Financial	—	—	1.70
⊕ PepsiCo, Inc.	Goods	21.4	7.86	1.57
⊕ Google, Inc.	Business	58.6	11.00	1.54
⊕ Time Warner, Inc.	Media	19.1	26.37	1.34
⊕ Comcast Corporation A	Media	45.0	63.31	1.27
⊕ Home Depot, Inc.	Consumer	13.7	1.01	1.25
⊕ Amgen, Inc.	Health	28.0	-13.38	1.20
⊕ Schlumberger, Ltd.	Energy	24.0	31.07	1.12
⊕ UnitedHealth Group, Inc.	Health	21.0	-13.49	1.09
⊕ Apple Computer, Inc.	Hardware	37.4	18.01	1.09
⊕ Wyeth	Health	17.0	12.88	1.03
⊕ American Express Company	Financial	21.2	19.09	0.99
⊕ US Bancorp	Financial	14.1	26.29	0.96
⊕ Qualcomm, Inc.	Hardware	26.2	-11.32	0.94
⊕ Medtronic, Inc.	Health	23.7	-6.29	0.93

Current Investment Style

Value Blend Growth — Large / Mid / Small

Market Cap	%
Giant	35.4
Large	43.0
Mid	21.6
Small	0.0
Micro	0.0

Avg $mil: 31,301

Value Measures		Rel Category
Price/Earnings	19.15	0.92
Price/Book	3.06	0.94
Price/Sales	1.66	0.94
Price/Cash Flow	11.74	1.05
Dividend Yield %	0.95	1.10

Growth Measures	%	Rel Category
Long-Term Erngs	13.87	0.93
Book Value	12.09	1.51
Sales	12.48	1.06
Cash Flow	14.55	0.99
Historical Erngs	21.96	0.78

Profitability	%	Rel Category
Return on Equity	21.64	1.08
Return on Assets	11.18	1.12
Net Margin	13.76	1.09

Sector Weightings

	% of Stocks	Rel S&P 500	3 Year High Low	
↻ Info	24.78	1.24		
Software	6.33	1.83	9	5
Hardware	10.83	1.17	21	11
Media	6.02	1.59	9	6
Telecom	1.60	0.46	2	0
⊑ Service	50.29	1.09		
Health	17.83	1.48	23	18
Consumer	14.38	1.88	16	12
Business	7.21	1.70	9	3
Financial	10.87	0.49	11	4
Mfg	24.93	0.74		
Goods	8.56	1.00	14	8
Ind Mtrls	7.71	0.65	8	3
Energy	7.77	0.79	10	1
Utilities	0.89	0.25	1	0

Composition

		%
● Cash		0.1
● Stocks		99.9
● Bonds		0.0
● Other		0.0
	Foreign	0.1
	(% of Stock)	

SPDR DJ Wilshire Mid Cap EMM

	Market Price	Mstar Category
	$56.22	Mid-Cap Blend

Morningstar Fair Value

Price/Fair Value Ratio 0.97 Fairly valued
Coverage Rate % 84

Management

SSgA Funds Management is this ETF's advisor. The ETF group at SSgA is headed by John Tucker. He joined the firm in 1988.

Methodology

This fund tracks the Dow Jones Wilshire U.S. Mid-Cap Index. The bogy invests in the 501st-largest to the 1,000th-largest stocks in the D.J. Wilshire 5000 universe. The float-adjusted, market-capitalization-weighted index is rebalanced semiannually in March and September. Buffer zones keep constituents from jumping in and out of the index due to market-cap changes.

	Morningstar Rating	Return	Risk	Yield	NAV	Avg Daily Vol. (k)	52 wk High/Low
	Not Rated	Not Rated	—	1.3%	$56.46	6	$58.19 - $49.87

Growth of $10,000
— Investment Value of ETF
— Investment Value of Index S&P 500

	1997	1998	1999	2000	2001	2002	2003	2004	2005	2006	History
	—	—	—	—	—	—	—	—	51.23	56.46	NAV $
	—	—	—	—	—	—	—	—	51.50	56.38	Market Price $
	—	—	—	—	—	—	—	—	15.75*	13.27	NAV Return%
	—	—	—	—	—	—	—	—	—	12.53	Market Price Return%
	—	—	—	—	—	—	—	—	0.28	-0.05	Avg Premium/Discount%
	—	—	—	—	—	—	—	—	15.75	-2.52	NAV Rtrn% +/-S&P 500
	—	—	—	—	—	—	—	—	15.75	2.95	NAV Rtrn% +/-S&P Mid 400
	—	—	—	—	—	—	—	—	—	8	NAV Return% Rank in Cat
	—	—	—	—	—	—	—	—	—	1.48	Income Return %
	—	—	—	—	—	—	—	—	—	11.79	Capital Return %
	—	—	—	—	—	—	—	—	0.09	0.76	Income $
	—	—	—	—	—	—	—	—	0.00	0.79	Capital Gains $
	—	—	—	—	—	—	—	—	—	0.26	Expense Ratio %
	—	—	—	—	—	—	—	—	—	1.24	Income Ratio %
	—	—	—	—	—	—	—	—	—	25	Turnover Rate %
	—	—	—	—	—	—	—	—	26	17	Net Assets $mil

Performance 12-31-06

Historic Quarterly NAV Returns

	1st Qtr	2nd Qtr	3rd Qtr	4th Qtr	Total
2002	—	—	—	—	—
2003	—	—	—	—	—
2004	—	—	—	—	—
2005	—	—	—	—	—*
2006	8.65	-3.95	0.07	8.46	13.27

Trailing	NAV Return%	Market Return%	NAV Rtrn% +/-S&P 500	%Rank Cat.(NAV)
3 Mo	8.46	7.97	1.76	10
6 Mo	8.54	8.75	-4.20	9
1 Yr	13.27	12.53	-2.52	8
3 Yr Avg	—	—	—	—
5 Yr Avg	—	—	—	—
10 Yr Avg	—	—	—	—

Tax Analysis	Tax-Adj Return%	Tax-Cost Ratio
3 Yr (estimated)	—	—
5 Yr (estimated)	—	—
10 Yr (estimated)	—	—

Rating and Risk

Time Period	Morningstar Rtn vs Cat	Morningstar Risk vs Cat	Morningstar Risk-Adj Rating
3 Yr	—	—	—
5 Yr	—	—	—
10 Yr	—	—	—

Other Measures	Standard Index S&P 500	Best Fit Index
Alpha	—	—
Beta	—	—
R-Squared	—	—
Standard Deviation	—	
Mean	—	
Sharpe Ratio	—	

Portfolio Analysis 12-31-06

Share change since 11-06 Total Stocks:497	Sector	PE	Tot Ret%	% Assets
⊕ Health Care Property	Financial	33.5	53.18	0.45
⊖ Sepracor, Inc.	Health	NMF	19.34	0.42
⊖ CB Richard Ellis Group,	Financial	30.3	69.24	0.42
⊕ Terex Corporation	Ind Mtrls	19.9	117.44	0.41
⊖ Realogy Corporation	Financial	—	—	0.41
⊖ Avaya, Inc.	Hardware	32.5	31.02	0.40
⊖ Manpower, Inc.	Business	20.6	62.53	0.40
⊖ Robert Half Internationa	Business	23.6	-1.17	0.39
⊖ Macerich Company	Financial	—	33.91	0.39
⊖ SL Green Realty Corporat	Financial	58.2	77.73	0.38
⊕ iStar Financial, Inc.	Financial	18.5	44.44	0.38
⊖ AMR Corporation	Business	—	35.99	0.38
⊖ VeriSign, Inc.	Software	54.7	9.82	0.37
⊕ IntercontinentalExchange	Financial	—	—	0.37
⊖ Mercantile Bankshares Co	Financial	20.0	27.85	0.37
⊖ Joy Global, Inc.	Ind Mtrls	15.5	22.11	0.36
⊖ CarMax, Inc.	Consumer	31.2	93.75	0.36
⊕ Health Net, Inc.	Health	17.9	-5.61	0.36
⊖ Dean Foods Company	Goods	22.3	12.27	0.36
⊕ Goodrich Corporation	Ind Mtrls	12.9	12.95	0.36

Current Investment Style

Value Blnd Growth — Large Mid Small

	Market Cap	%
	Giant	0.0
	Large	0.0
	Mid	99.2
	Small	0.8
	Micro	0.0

Avg $mil: 3,740

Value Measures		Rel Category
Price/Earnings	17.30	1.04
Price/Book	2.41	0.94
Price/Sales	1.10	0.98
Price/Cash Flow	8.95	0.98
Dividend Yield %	1.42	1.04

Growth Measures	%	Rel Category
Long-Term Erngs	11.77	0.96
Book Value	6.01	0.82
Sales	5.61	0.80
Cash Flow	10.59	1.07
Historical Erngs	15.48	0.81

Profitability	%	Rel Category
Return on Equity	15.80	0.92
Return on Assets	7.96	0.93
Net Margin	10.74	1.01

Sector Weightings	% of Stocks	Rel S&P 500	3 Year High Low
↻ Info	12.01	0.60	
🖥 Software	2.76	0.80	— —
🖥 Hardware	5.78	0.63	— —
📺 Media	1.46	0.39	— —
☎ Telecom	2.01	0.57	— —
☞ Service	54.31	1.18	
⚕ Health	10.99	0.91	— —
🛒 Consumer	8.21	1.07	— —
🏢 Business	11.35	2.68	— —
💲 Financial	23.76	1.07	— —
⟳ Mfg	33.70	1.00	
🏭 Goods	6.79	0.79	— —
⚙ Ind Mtrls	12.68	1.06	— —
🔋 Energy	7.67	0.78	— —
💡 Utilities	6.56	1.87	— —

Composition

● Cash	0.3	
● Stocks	99.7	
● Bonds	0.0	
● Other	0.0	
Foreign	0.6	
(% of Stock)		

Morningstar's Take by Marta Norton 12-31-06

StreetTRACKS Dow Jones Wilshire Mid Cap serves as a good building block for investors looking for mid-cap exposure.

This exchange-traded fund is market-cap purity at its finest. Its portfolio sticks almost exclusively to mid-cap stocks, such as Dean Foods and Level 3 Communications. By contrast, many of its peers, including the low-priced Vanguard Mid-Cap ETF, have sizable stakes in large- or small-cap stocks. The Vanguard offering, for instance, generally holds more than 15% in large caps. So, investors looking to fit a mid-cap fund into their portfolios will have an easier time with this fund than with one its competitors.

And, of course, the fund has other advantages that have become traditional fare for streetTRACKS ETFs. It provides wide diversification by owning approximately 500 stocks across market sectors. And because its benchmark, the Dow Jones Wilshire U.S. Mid Cap Index, uses buffer zones to slow the transition of growing stocks in and out of its portfolio, it offers low turnover. That keeps a lid on trading costs and should also help promote tax efficiency.

But given the increasing number of new, innovative competitors arriving on the scene, investors might wonder if these advantages are enough. And it's true that many of the recently launched ETFs offer attractive characteristics. For instance, WisdomTree MidCap Dividend, which weights holdings by a cash dividend, will likely provide a higher yield and may invest in more financially stable companies. Still, the new methodologies are untested in a dynamic marketplace and often come with higher expense ratios. Because costs are such an important element to ETF investing and considering the uncertainty surrounding many of the upstarts, we'd go with a more established offering like this fund instead.

Investors interested in cheap, mid-cap exposure have a good option in this ETF.

Address:	State Street Bank & Tr, 225 Franklin St Boston MA 02210 866-787-2257
Web Address:	www.advisors.ssga.com
Inception:	11-08-05 *
Advisor:	SSgA Funds Management Inc

Management Fee:	0.25%		
Expense Projections:	3Yr:$81	5Yr:$141	10Yr:$320
Income Distrib:	Quarterly		
Exchange:	AMEX		

MORNINGSTAR® ETFs 150

SPDR DJ Wilshire Mid Gr EMG

	Market Price	Mstar Category
	$60.91	Mid-Cap Growth

Morningstar Fair Value

Price/Fair Value Ratio	Coverage Rate %
0.96 Fairly valued	84

Management

SSgA Funds Management is this ETF's advisor. The ETF group at SSgA is headed by John Tucker. He joined the firm in 1988.

Methodology

This fund tracks the Dow Jones Wilshire Mid-Cap Growth Index. The bogy uses six factors, including projected price-to-earnings and dividend yield, to sort the 501st largest to the 1,000th largest stocks in the Dow Jones Wilshire 5000 Index into value or growth buckets. Half the universe's float-adjusted market cap ends up in value and half in growth. Buffer zones keep constituents from jumping in and out of the index due to market cap or style-score changes. It rebalances in March and September.

	Morningstar Rating	Return	Risk	Yield	NAV	Avg Daily Vol. (k)	52 wk High/Low
	Not Rated	Not Rated	—	0.5%	$60.83	2	$63.36 - $54.07

Growth of $10,000
— Investment Value of ETF
— Investment Value of Index S&P 500

Trading Volume Millions

	1997	1998	1999	2000	2001	2002	2003	2004	2005	2006	History
	—	—	—	—	—	—	—	—	56.28	60.83	NAV $
	—	—	—	—	—	—	—	—	56.31	60.83	Market Price $
	—	—	—	—	—	—	—	—	14.01*	11.31	NAV Return%
	—	—	—	—	—	—	—	—	—	11.26	Market Price Return%
	—	—	—	—	—	—	—	—	0.09	-0.18	Avg Premium/Discount%
	—	—	—	—	—	—	—	—	14.01	-4.48	NAV Rtrn% +/-S&P 500
	—	—	—	—	—	—	—	—	14.01	0.65	NAV Rtrn% +/-Russ MG
	—	—	—	—	—	—	—	—	—	6	NAV Return% Rank in Cat
	—	—	—	—	—	—	—	—	—	0.58	Income Return %
	—	—	—	—	—	—	—	—	—	10.73	Capital Return %
	—	—	—	—	—	—	—	—	0.03	0.33	Income $
	—	—	—	—	—	—	—	—	0.00	1.50	Capital Gains $
	—	—	—	—	—	—	—	—	0.26	Expense Ratio %
	—	—	—	—	—	—	—	—	0.30	Income Ratio %
	—	—	—	—	—	—	—	—	—	34	Turnover Rate %
	—	—	—	—	—	—	—	—	25	21	Net Assets $mil

Performance 12-31-06

Historic Quarterly NAV Returns

	1st Qtr	2nd Qtr	3rd Qtr	4th Qtr	Total
2002	—	—	—	—	—
2003	—	—	—	—	—
2004	—	—	—	—	—
2005	—	—	—	—	—*
2006	9.47	-5.39	-0.97	8.52	11.31

Trailing	NAV Return%	Market Return%	NAV Rtrn% +/-S&P 500	%Rank Cat.(NAV)
3 Mo	8.52	8.39	1.82	8
6 Mo	7.48	8.13	-5.26	7
1 Yr	11.31	11.26	-4.48	6
3 Yr Avg	—	—	—	—
5 Yr Avg	—	—	—	—
10 Yr Avg	—	—	—	—

Tax Analysis	Tax-Adj Return%	Tax-Cost Ratio
3 Yr (estimated)	—	—
5 Yr (estimated)	—	—
10 Yr (estimated)	—	—

Rating and Risk

Time Period	Morningstar Rtn vs Cat	Morningstar Risk vs Cat	Morningstar Risk-Adj Rating
3 Yr	—	—	—
5 Yr	—	—	—
10 Yr	—	—	—

Other Measures	Standard Index S&P 500	Best Fit Index
Alpha	—	—
Beta	—	—
R-Squared	—	—
Standard Deviation	—	
Mean	—	
Sharpe Ratio	—	

Morningstar's Take by Marta Norton 12-31-06

StreetTRACKS Dow Jones Wilshire Mid Cap Growth isn't perfect, but it's still a reasonable choice.

This exchange-traded fund has, until recently, been one of the cheapest of its kind in the mid-growth category. But in August 2006, Vanguard Mid-Cap Growth ETF entered the market with a 0.13% expense ratio, which is half the size of this fund's levy. A slight edge in expenses can mean the difference between a leader and laggard in the indexing world, especially among funds tracking similar asset classes and benchmarks, so this ETF is at a disadvantage to its cheaper Vanguard rival.

Even so, there are a number of things we like about this ETF. It serves as an excellent way to tap the mid-cap market. While most of its mid-cap ETF rivals hold heavy slugs of either large- or small-cap stocks (iShares S&P MidCap 400 Growth Index has a 10% small-cap stake, for instance), it keeps nearly 100% of its portfolio in mid-cap land. Because its index, the Dow Jones Wilshire Mid Cap

Growth Index, doesn't pull stocks from other market caps, it's easy to use alongside larger or smaller funds without much overlap.

The ETF also has the same structural strengths other streetTRACKS ETFs offer. Its index uses six growth and value factors to sort stocks into growth and value buckets. That's a more stringent style test than what many of its competitors offer (for instance, iShares Russell Midcap Growth relies on only two factors) and allows for this fund to offer purer exposure to growth stocks. Plus, the fund's bogy uses buffer zones to slow stocks' style and market-cap changes, which reduces turnover and, in turn, tax and trading costs.

Still, while its undiluted mid-cap portfolio and well-constructed index are attractive, the fund's higher expenses make it next to impossible to keep pace with the cheaper Vanguard rival over long stretches of time. We like what we see here, but the ETF's heavier levy damps our enthusiasm.

Address:	State Street Bank & Tr, 225 Franklin St
	Boston MA 02210
	866-787-2257
Web Address:	www.advisors.ssga.com
Inception:	11-08-05 *
Advisor:	SSgA Funds Management Inc

Management Fee:	0.25%		
Expense Projections:	3Yr:$81	5Yr:$141	10Yr:$320
Income Distrib:	Quarterly		
Exchange:	AMEX		

Portfolio Analysis 12-31-06

Share change since 11-06 Total Stocks:248

	Sector	PE	Tot Ret%	% Assets
⊖ Sepracor, Inc.	Health	NMF	19.34	0.84
⊖ CB Richard Ellis Group,	Financial	30.3	69.24	0.84
⊖ Terex Corporation	Ind Mtrls	19.9	117.44	0.82
⊖ Realogy Corporation	Financial	—	—	0.81
⊖ Avaya, Inc.	Hardware	32.5	31.02	0.80
⊖ Manpower, Inc.	Business	20.6	62.53	0.80
⊖ Robert Half Internationa	Business	23.6	-1.17	0.78
⊖ SL Green Realty Corporat	Financial	58.2	77.73	0.76
⊖ VeriSign, Inc.	Software	54.7	9.82	0.74
⊕ IntercontinentalExchange	Financial	—	—	0.74
⊖ Joy Global, Inc.	Ind Mtrls	15.5	22.11	0.72
⊖ CarMax, Inc.	Consumer	31.2	93.75	0.72
⊖ Dean Foods Company	Goods	22.3	12.27	0.71
⊖ Health Net, Inc.	Health	17.9	-5.61	0.71
⊖ Telephone and Data Syste	Telecom	20.2	52.10	0.70
⊖ Level 3 Communications,	Telecom	—	95.12	0.70
⊖ Amphenol Corporation	Hardware	24.4	40.57	0.68
⊖ Tiffany & Co.	Goods	22.3	3.58	0.68
⊖ Darden Restaurants, Inc.	Consumer	18.1	4.37	0.68
⊖ Monster Worldwide, Inc.	Business	45.7	14.26	0.67

Current Investment Style

Value Blnd Growth — Large Mid Small

Market Cap	%
Giant	0.0
Large	0.0
Mid	99.2
Small	0.8
Micro	0.0

Avg $mil: 3,897

Value Measures		Rel Category
Price/Earnings	19.36	0.98
Price/Book	3.08	0.90
Price/Sales	1.30	0.76
Price/Cash Flow	9.20	0.83
Dividend Yield %	0.49	1.00

Growth Measures	%	Rel Category
Long-Term Erngs	15.16	0.96
Book Value	9.49	0.81
Sales	11.15	0.97
Cash Flow	17.82	1.05
Historical Erngs	19.05	0.83

Profitability	%	Rel Category
Return on Equity	19.17	0.95
Return on Assets	8.88	0.86
Net Margin	9.76	0.85

Sector Weightings	% of Stocks	Rel S&P 500	3 Year High Low
↻ Info	15.39	0.77	
Software	3.74	1.08	— —
Hardware	6.95	0.75	— —
Media	1.88	0.50	— —
Telecom	2.82	0.80	— —
⊂ Service	58.68	1.27	
Health	19.10	1.58	— —
Consumer	12.04	1.57	— —
Business	15.22	3.60	— —
Financial	12.32	0.55	— —
Mfg	25.92	0.77	
Goods	6.78	0.79	— —
Ind Mtrls	8.56	0.72	— —
Energy	9.97	1.02	— —
Utilities	0.61	0.17	— —

Composition

		%
● Cash		0.5
● Stocks		99.5
● Bonds		0.0
○ Other		0.0
Foreign		1.0
(% of Stock)		

SPDR DJ Wilshire Mid Val EMV

Market Price $58.08	**Mstar Category** Mid-Cap Value	

Morningstar Fair Value

Price/Fair Value Ratio	Coverage Rate %
0.98 Fairly valued	84 Good

Management

SSgA Funds Management is this ETF's advisor. The ETF group at SSgA is headed by John Tucker. He joined the firm in 1988.

Methodology

This fund tracks the Dow Jones Wilshire Mid Cap Value Index. The bogy invests in value stocks ranging from the 501-largest to the 1,000-largest stocks in the Dow Jones Wilshire 5000 universe. Factors used to determine value include price-to-book ratios and dividend yield. The float-adjusted, market-capitalization-weighted index is rebalanced semiannually in March and September. Buffer zones keep constituents from jumping in and out of the index because of market-cap and style changes.

Morningstar Rating	Return	Risk	Yield	NAV	Avg Daily Vol. (k)	52 wk High/Low
— Not Rated	Not Rated	—	2.1%	$58.40	1	$60.20 - $52.28

Growth of $10,000
— Investment Value of ETF
— Investment Value of Index S&P 500

Trading Volume Millions

	1997	1998	1999	2000	2001	2002	2003	2004	2005	2006	History
	—	—	—	—	—	—	—	—	52.47	58.40	NAV $
	—	—	—	—	—	—	—	—	52.37	58.73	Market Price $
	—	—	—	—	—	—	—	—	17.67*	15.42	NAV Return%
	—	—	—	—	—	—	—	—		16.29	Market Price Return%
	—	—	—	—	—	—	—	—	0.10	-0.04	Avg Premium/Discount%
	—	—	—	—	—	—	—	—	17.67	-0.37	NAV Rtrn% +/-S&P 500
	—	—	—	—	—	—	—	—	17.67	-4.80	NAV Rtrn% +/-Russ MV
	—	—	—	—	—	—	—	—		6	NAV Return% Rank in Cat
	—	—	—	—	—	—	—	—		2.42	Income Return %
	—	—	—	—	—	—	—	—		13.00	Capital Return %
	—	—	—	—	—	—	—	—	0.16	1.26	Income $
	—	—	—	—	—	—	—	—	0.00	0.83	Capital Gains $
	—	—	—	—	—	—	—	—		0.26	Expense Ratio %
	—	—	—	—	—	—	—	—		2.20	Income Ratio %
	—	—	—	—	—	—	—	—		29	Turnover Rate %
	—	—	—	—	—	—	—	—	26	9	Net Assets $mil

Performance 12-31-06

Historic Quarterly NAV Returns

	1st Qtr	2nd Qtr	3rd Qtr	4th Qtr	Total
2002	—	—	—	—	—
2003	—	—	—	—	—
2004	—	—	—	—	—
2005	—	—	—	—	—*
2006	7.69	-2.35	1.26	8.40	15.42

Trailing	NAV Return%	Market Return%	NAV Rtrn% +/-S&P 500	%Rank Cat.(NAV)
3 Mo	8.40	8.72	1.70	8
6 Mo	9.76	10.61	-2.98	7
1 Yr	15.42	16.29	-0.37	6
3 Yr Avg	—	—	—	—
5 Yr Avg	—	—	—	—
10 Yr Avg	—	—	—	—

Tax Analysis	Tax-Adj Return%	Tax-Cost Ratio
3 Yr (estimated)	—	—
5 Yr (estimated)	—	—
10 Yr (estimated)	—	—

Rating and Risk

Time Period	Morningstar Rtn vs Cat	Morningstar Risk vs Cat	Morningstar Risk-Adj Rating
3 Yr	—	—	—
5 Yr	—	—	—
10 Yr	—	—	—

Other Measures	Standard Index S&P 500	Best Fit Index
Alpha	—	—
Beta	—	—
R-Squared	—	—
Standard Deviation	—	
Mean	—	
Sharpe Ratio	—	

Morningstar's Take by Marta Norton 12-31-06

StreetTRACKS DJ Wilshire Mid Cap Value is a good choice for dead-on mid-cap value exposure.

This exchange-traded fund focuses exclusively on the mid-cap market. That might seem like an obvious point, but all of its ETF competitors, including Vanguard Mid-Cap Value ETF and iShares S&P MidCap 400 Value Index, sprinkle in large- and small-cap stocks among their mid-cap holdings. In fact, iShares Russell Midcap Value Index has a 32% large-cap stake in companies like Ford Motor and Xerox Corporation. Because this ETF doesn't tilt toward larger- or smaller-market caps, investors will have an easier time fitting it into their portfolios.

We like other things about the ETF as well. Its index, the Dow Jones Wilshire Mid Cap Value, uses buffer zones to slowly shift stocks between market caps and styles. That keeps a lid on turnover, trading costs, and may help limit taxes on capital gains as well. Also, the index relies on a multifactor model with six growth and value factors, including price-to-book ratios and long-term projected earnings, to help ensure the fund invests in stocks with the clearest value characteristics.

Expenses are the only real detractor here. At 0.26%, this ETF's expense ratio is in line with those of its peers, but it's much higher than Vanguard Mid-Cap Value's 0.13% levy. That's a significant handicap because the returns of index funds' tracking the same market regions often vary by as little as hundredths of a percentage point.

That said, we still think there's plenty of good reasons to keep this fund in mind when looking for a mid-value fund. Its well-constructed index helps make it easy to use, and although it's more expensive than one of its ETF competitors, its accurate mid-value portfolio comes at a price that looks cheap relative to that of its typical conventional mid-value competitor and reasonable relative to that of its average ETF peer.

Portfolio Analysis 12-31-06

Share change since 11-06 Total Stocks:248

	Sector	PE	Tot Ret%	% Assets
⊕ Health Care Property	Financial	33.5	53.18	0.91
⊖ Macerich Company	Financial		33.91	0.79
⊕ iStar Financial, Inc.	Financial	18.5	44.44	0.77
⊖ AMR Corporation	Business		35.99	0.75
⊖ Mercantile Bankshares Co	Financial	20.0	27.85	0.74
Goodrich Corporation	Ind Mtrls	12.9	12.95	0.72
⊖ Wisconsin Energy Corpora	Utilities	17.3	24.21	0.70
American Power Conversio	Ind Mtrls	58.8	41.75	0.70
⊖ Duke Realty Corporation	Financial	75.7	28.98	0.70
⊖ Apartment Investment & M	Financial		55.18	0.69
⊖ MeadWestvaco Corporation	Ind Mtrls	49.3	10.94	0.69
⊖ Interpublic Group of Com	Business		26.84	0.69
⊖ Regency Centers Corporat	Financial	57.1	37.58	0.67
⊕ Fidelity National Financ	Financial			0.67
⊖ Sealed Air Corporation	Goods	23.1	16.85	0.66
AMB Property Corporation	Financial	30.9	23.30	0.66
⊖ MGIC Investment Corporat	Financial	9.4	-3.39	0.66
⊖ First Horizon National C	Financial	17.4	13.71	0.65
⊖ Equifax, Inc.	Business	19.4	7.26	0.65
⊖ Pinnacle West Capital	Utilities	21.9	27.04	0.64

Current Investment Style

Value Blnd Growth — Large Mid Small

Market Cap	%
Giant	0.0
Large	0.0
Mid	99.3
Small	0.8
Micro	0.0

Avg $mil: 3,591

Value Measures		Rel Category
Price/Earnings	15.64	1.04
Price/Book	2.01	1.05
Price/Sales	0.95	1.07
Price/Cash Flow	8.72	1.18
Dividend Yield %	2.36	0.96

Growth Measures	%	Rel Category
Long-Term Erngs	9.05	0.96
Book Value	4.29	0.75
Sales	2.29	0.28
Cash Flow	3.98	2.93
Historical Erngs	13.29	1.20

Profitability	%	Rel Category
Return on Equity	12.47	0.95
Return on Assets	7.04	0.93
Net Margin	11.71	1.00

Sector Weightings

	% of Stocks	Rel S&P 500	3 Year High Low
↻ Info	8.58	0.43	
Software	1.76	0.51	— —
Hardware	4.59	0.50	— —
Media	1.03	0.27	— —
Telecom	1.20	0.34	— —
☞ Service	49.86	1.08	
Health	2.75	0.23	— —
Consumer	4.33	0.57	— —
Business	7.43	1.76	— —
Financial	35.35	1.59	— —
Mfg	41.56	1.23	
Goods	6.80	0.80	— —
Ind Mtrls	16.83	1.41	— —
Energy	5.34	0.54	— —
Utilities	12.59	3.60	— —

Composition

● Cash	0.2
● Stocks	99.7
● Bonds	0.0
○ Other	0.1
Foreign	0.3
(% of Stock)	

Address:	State Street Bank & Tr, 225 Franklin St Boston MA 02210 866-787-2257	Management Fee:	0.25%	
		Expense Projections:	3Yr:$81 5Yr:$141 10Yr:$320	
Web Address:	www.advisors.ssga.com	Income Distrib:	Quarterly	
Inception:	11-08-05 *	Exchange:	AMEX	
Advisor:	SSgA Funds Management Inc			

MORNINGSTAR® ETFs 150

SPDR DJ Wilshire Small Cp DSC

	Market Price	Mstar Category
	$60.22	Small Blend

Morningstar Fair Value

Price/Fair Value Ratio	Coverage Rate %
0.98 Fairly valued	51 Poor

Management

SSgA Funds Management is this ETF's advisor. The ETF group at SSgA is headed by John Tucker. He joined the firm in 1988.

Methodology

This fund tracks the Dow Jones Wilshire U.S. Small Cap Index. The bogy invests in stocks ranked 751 to 2500 in the DJ Wilshire 5000 Composite Index. The float-adjusted, market-cap-weighted index is rebalanced semiannually in March and September. Buffer zones keep constituents from jumping in and out of the index due to changes in their market cap.

Morningstar Rating	Return	Risk	Yield	NAV	Avg Daily Vol. (k)	52 wk High/Low
— Not Rated	Not Rated	—	1.3%	$61.21	12	$63.49 - $54.00

Growth of $10,000
- Investment Value of ETF
- Investment Value of Index S&P 500

	1997	1998	1999	2000	2001	2002	2003	2004	2005	2006	History
	—	—	—	—	—	—	—	—	54.22	61.21	NAV $
	—	—	—	—	—	—	—	—	54.03	61.22	Market Price $
	—	—	—	—	—	—	—	—	17.93*	16.59	NAV Return%
	—	—	—	—	—	—	—	—	—	17.03	Market Price Return%
	—	—	—	—	—	—	—	—	0.17	-0.10	Avg Premium/Discount%
	—	—	—	—	—	—	—	—	17.93	0.80	NAV Rtrn% +/-S&P 500
	—	—	—	—	—	—	—	—	17.93	-1.78	NAV Rtrn% +/-Russ 2000
	—	—	—	—	—	—	—	—	—	8	NAV Return% Rank in Cat
	—	—	—	—	—	—	—	—	1.52	Income Return %
	—	—	—	—	—	—	—	—	—	15.07	Capital Return %
	—	—	—	—	—	—	—	—	0.08	0.82	Income $
	—	—	—	—	—	—	—	—	0.00	1.14	Capital Gains $
	—	—	—	—	—	—	—	—	0.26	Expense Ratio %
	—	—	—	—	—	—	—	—	—	1.35	Income Ratio %
	—	—	—	—	—	—	—	—	—	10	Turnover Rate %
	—	—	—	—	—	—	—	—	24	15	Net Assets $mil

Performance 12-31-06

Historic Quarterly NAV Returns

	1st Qtr	2nd Qtr	3rd Qtr	4th Qtr	Total
2002	—	—	—	—	—
2003	—	—	—	—	—
2004	—	—	—	—	—
2005	—	—	—	—	—*
2006	12.52	-4.34	-0.23	8.58	16.59

Trailing	NAV Return%	Market Return%	NAV Rtrn% +/-S&P 500	%Rank Cat.(NAV)
3 Mo	8.58	8.53	1.88	12
6 Mo	8.32	8.95	-4.42	10
1 Yr	16.59	17.03	0.80	8
3 Yr Avg	—	—	—	—
5 Yr Avg	—	—	—	—
10 Yr Avg	—	—	—	—

Tax Analysis	Tax-Adj Return%	Tax-Cost Ratio
3 Yr (estimated)	—	—
5 Yr (estimated)	—	—
10 Yr (estimated)	—	—

Rating and Risk

Time Period	Morningstar Rtn vs Cat	Morningstar Risk vs Cat	Morningstar Risk-Adj Rating
3 Yr	—	—	—
5 Yr	—	—	—
10 Yr	—	—	—

Other Measures	Standard Index S&P 500	Best Fit Index
Alpha	—	—
Beta	—	—
R-Squared	—	—
Standard Deviation	—	
Mean	—	
Sharpe Ratio	—	

Morningstar's Take by Marta Norton 12-31-06

While streetTRACKS Dow Jones Wilshire Small Cap ETF is not our first choice, investors could do worse than this exchange-traded fund.

There's a case to be made for streetTRACKS Dow Jones Wilshire Small Cap. For one, its more than 1,700 stock portfolio provides broad small-cap exposure. And because it uses buffer zones to slowly transition growing stocks out of its portfolio, it keeps a lid on turnover. That helps limit trading costs and could help enhance its tax efficiency.

ETFs like this one provide reasonable alternatives to capacity-constrained, active, small-blend funds. Because smaller stocks tend to trade less than their larger peers, many of the best small-cap funds quickly close to new investors so they don't push against liquidity constraints. In fact, Bogle Small Cap Growth and Third Avenue Small-Cap Value, two of our three small-blend Analyst Picks, have shut their doors. (The third, Vanguard Tax-Managed Small Cap, has a $10,000 investment minimum to limit inflows into the fund.)

But because this ETF trades infrequently and takes such small positions across so many stocks, it can handle more assets than most competing actively managed small-cap funds.

Some investors may be put off by the fund's larger mid-cap stake. The fund typically stashes about 40% of its assets in midsized companies, while its average ETF small-value competitor stores roughly 14% there. But while that might give rise to overlap issues for investors who hold mid-cap funds, it makes this ETF more comparable to actively managed rivals, which often hold on to stocks after they graduate to mid-cap land.

Others may legitimately criticize this ETF for its expense ratio. At 0.26%, it isn't the cheapest in its category. Vanguard Small Cap ETF gets that honor and will consistently have a built-in advantage over this fund. That said, this ETF's price tag is far from expensive, and it's a reasonable--if not perfect--choice for ETF investors seeking small-cap exposure.

Portfolio Analysis 12-31-06

Share change since 11-06 Total Stocks:1741	Sector	PE	Tot Ret%	% Assets
⊕ IntercontinentalExchange	Financial	—	—	0.30
⊖ PartnerRe, Ltd.	Financial	—	10.90	0.21
⊖ Plains All American Pipe	Energy	17.1	37.95	0.21
⊖ ResMed, Inc.	Health	39.4	28.48	0.19
⊖ Foster Wheeler, Ltd.	Business	—	49.92	0.19
⊖ Reckson Associates Realt	Financial	46.1	31.78	0.19
⊖ Renaissance Re Holdings,	Financial	12.5	38.30	0.19
⊖ Avnet, Inc.	Business	15.4	6.64	0.19
⊕ Sierra Pacific Resources	Utilities	12.5	29.06	0.19
⊖ CMS Energy Corporation	Utilities	—	15.09	0.19
⊖ Continental Airlines, In	Business	13.1	93.66	0.19
⊖ Manitowoc Company, Inc.	Business	28.6	137.42	0.10
⊕ OfficeMax, Inc.	Consumer	—	98.81	0.19
⊖ Gamestop Corporation A	Goods	34.2	73.19	0.19
⊖ OGE Energy Corp	Utilities	16.3	55.73	0.19
⊖ Celanese Corporation	Ind Mtrls	—	36.48	0.19
Intuitive Surgical, Inc.	Health	37.0	-18.22	0.18
⊖ HCC Insurance Holdings I	Financial	17.0	9.39	0.18
⊖ US Airways Group, Inc.	Business	—	44.99	0.18
⊖ Stericycle, Inc.	Business	45.5	28.23	0.17

Current Investment Style

Value Blnd Growth — Large Mid Small

Market Cap	%
Giant	0.0
Large	0.0
Mid	41.3
Small	52.7
Micro	6.0

Avg $mil: 1,578

Value Measures		Rel Category
Price/Earnings	17.75	1.01
Price/Book	2.14	1.03
Price/Sales	1.00	0.97
Price/Cash Flow	7.35	1.13
Dividend Yield %	1.38	0.87

Growth Measures	%	Rel Category
Long-Term Erngs	12.90	0.97
Book Value	5.96	1.09
Sales	-2.69	NMF
Cash Flow	7.41	0.82
Historical Erngs	12.97	1.09

Profitability	%	Rel Category
Return on Equity	12.65	1.10
Return on Assets	6.65	1.01
Net Margin	10.00	1.02

Sector Weightings	% of Stocks	Rel S&P 500	3 Year High Low
↻ Info	15.01	0.75	
Software	3.82	1.11	— —
Hardware	7.59	0.82	— —
Media	1.89	0.50	— —
Telecom	1.71	0.49	— —
⊆ Service	51.57	1.12	
Health	9.41	0.78	— —
Consumer	9.80	1.28	— —
Business	11.19	2.65	— —
Financial	21.17	0.95	— —
↰ Mfg	33.44	0.99	
Goods	6.16	0.72	— —
Ind Mtrls	15.20	1.27	— —
Energy	7.87	0.80	— —
Utilities	4.21	1.20	— —

Composition

● Cash	0.4	
● Stocks	99.6	
● Bonds	0.0	
● Other	0.0	
Foreign	0.9	
(% of Stock)		

Address:	State Street Bank & Tr, 225 Franklin St Boston MA 02210 866-787-2257	Management Fee:	0.25%
		Expense Projections:	3Yr:$81 5Yr:$141 10Yr:$320
Web Address:	www.advisors.ssga.com	Income Distrib:	Quarterly
Inception:	11-08-05 *	Exchange:	AMEX
Advisor:	SSgA Funds Management Inc		

SPDR DJ Wilshire Sm Value DSV

Market Price $69.89	**Mstar Category** Small Value	

Morningstar Fair Value

Price/Fair Value Ratio
0.98 Fairly valued

Coverage Rate %
53 Poor

Management

SSgA Funds Management is this ETF's advisor. The ETF group at SSgA is headed by John Tucker. He joined the firm in 1988.

Methodology

This fund tracks the Dow Jones Wilshire Small Cap Value Index. The bogy uses six factors to sort the small-cap stocks in the Dow Jones Wilshire 5000 into value or growth buckets. Stocks' style scores are based on their projected price/earnings, projected earnings growth, and price/book ratios; dividend yield, trailing revenue growth, and trailing earnings growth. Buffer zones keep constituents from jumping in and out of the index due to market cap or style score changes. It rebalances in March and September.

Performance 12-31-06

Historic Quarterly NAV Returns

	1st Qtr	2nd Qtr	3rd Qtr	4th Qtr	Total
2002	11.35	-2.42	-13.92	3.99	-2.74
2003	-5.69	22.69	5.16	17.52	43.00
2004	7.11	-1.01	-0.93	12.39	18.06
2005	-5.00	3.83	5.81	1.18	5.60
2006	11.32	-2.15	1.11	8.66	19.67

Trailing	NAV Return%	Market Return%	NAV Rtrn% +/-S&P 500	%Rank Cat.(NAV)
3 Mo	8.66	8.83	1.96	7
6 Mo	9.86	10.19	-2.88	7
1 Yr	19.67	19.80	3.88	6
3 Yr Avg	14.26	14.23	3.82	3
5 Yr Avg	15.72	15.60	9.53	3
10 Yr Avg	—	—	—	—

Tax Analysis	Tax-Adj Return%	Tax-Cost Ratio
3 Yr (estimated)	12.77	1.30
5 Yr (estimated)	14.17	1.34
10 Yr (estimated)	—	—

Morningstar's Take by Marta Norton 12-31-06

StreetTRACKS Dow Jones Wilshire Small Cap Value has its advantages, but it's not the best of its kind.

This exchange-traded fund takes its role as a broad proxy for its market segment seriously. It holds nearly 900 stocks and allocates only 5% of its assets to its top 10 holdings. In fact, its largest position size typically doesn't grow much larger than half a percentage point. This diversification helps keep a lid on volatility by limiting the fund's sensitivity to the movements of any one stock.

The ETF also works hard to mirror the traditional small-value fund. That may seem counterintuitive at first, given its mid-cap stake tends to run larger than that of its typical ETF peer. But plenty of small-cap fund managers buy a stock when it's under a certain market-cap range and hang on as it grows larger. In order to mimic that investing style, this fund's bogy of one year, the Dow Jones Wilshire Small Cap Value, won't automatically kick a small-cap stock out of its portfolio once it reaches

a certain size. Instead, it uses buffer zones to slowly transition stocks between styles and market caps. Besides allowing the fund to hang on to winners, the fund's slower turnover helps limit trading costs and promote tax efficiency.

That's not to say this ETF doesn't have any drawbacks. It keeps more than 30% of its assets in financial services, with about 10% of its assets devoted to real estate investment trusts (REITs) alone. After several years of outperformance, REITs look expensive. Morningstar stock analysts rate more than half of the REITs they cover as overvalued. Given its heavy stake there, should REITs' prices fall, this ETF may suffer.

This fund doesn't offer the best deal around, either. Vanguard Small Cap Value ETF has many of the same advantages, including buffer zones and a broad portfolio (it also has decent exposure to REITs). However, Vanguard ETF's expense ratio is less than half that of this ETF's. Given the fund's similarities, we'd go with the cheaper option.

Address:	State Street Bank & Tr, 225 Franklin St Boston MA 02210 866-787-2257	
Web Address:	www.advisors.ssga.com	
Inception:	09-25-00*	
Advisor:	SSgA Funds Management Inc	

Management Fee:	0.25%		
Expense Projections:	3Yr:$81	5Yr:$141	10Yr:$320
Income Distrib:	Quarterly		
Exchange:	AMEX		

Morningstar Rating ★★★★ Above Avg	**Return** Above Avg	**Risk** Below Avg	**Yield** 2.2%	**NAV** $70.81	**Avg Daily Vol. (k)** 6	**52 wk High/Low** $71.88 - $61.88

Growth of $10,000
■ Investment Value of ETF
— Investment Value of Index S&P 500

Trading Volume Millions

	1997	1998	1999	2000	2001	2002	2003	2004	2005	2006	History
	—	—	—	39.70	42.16	39.66	54.16	60.27	60.58	70.81	NAV $
	—	—	—	39.25	42.38	39.70	54.20	60.40	60.50	70.79	Market Price $
	—	—	—	17.21*	12.51	-2.74	43.00	18.06	5.60	19.67	NAV Return%
	—	—	—	17.21*	14.42	-3.15	42.98	18.23	5.24	19.80	Market Price Return%
	—	—	—	-1.29	0.22	0.03	0.04	-0.14	-0.13	-0.09	Avg Premium/Discount%
	—	—	—	17.21	24.40	19.36	14.32	7.18	0.69	3.88	NAV Rtrn% +/-S&P 500
	—	—	—	17.21	-1.51	8.69	-3.03	-4.19	0.89	-3.81	NAV Rtrn% +/-Russ 2000 VL
	—	—	—	—	3	3	3	3	5	6	NAV Return% Rank in Cat
	—	—	—	—	2.07	2.66	2.61	1.94	1.81	2.60	Income Return %
	—	—	—	—	10.44	-5.40	40.39	16.12	3.79	17.07	Capital Return %
	—	—	—	0.31	0.82	1.11	1.03	1.04	1.08	1.56	Income $
	—	—	—	0.00	1.58	0.30	1.18	2.49	1.99	0.01	Capital Gains $
	—	—	—	—	0.28	0.28	0.29	0.27	0.26	0.26	Expense Ratio %
	—	—	—	—	—	2.70	2.31	2.76	1.88	2.00	2.21	Income Ratio %
	—	—	—	—	47	29	43	54	33	97	Turnover Rate %
	—	—	—	—	—	42	57	99	97	96	Net Assets $mil

Rating and Risk

Time Period	Morningstar Rtn vs Cat	Morningstar Risk vs Cat	Morningstar Risk-Adj Rating
3 Yr	Avg	Avg	★★★
5 Yr	+Avg	-Avg	★★★★
10 Yr	—	—	—

Other Measures	Standard Index S&P 500	Best Fit Index Russ 2000 VL
Alpha	0.0	-1.6
Beta	1.56	0.97
R-Squared	75	96
Standard Deviation	12.35	
Mean	14.26	
Sharpe Ratio	0.89	

Portfolio Analysis 12-31-06

Share change since 11-06 Total Stocks:845

	Sector	PE	Tot Ret%	% Assets
⊕ Plains All American Pipe	Energy	17.1	37.95	0.41
PartnerRe, Ltd.	Financial	—	10.90	0.41
Foster Wheeler, Ltd.	Business	—	49.92	0.38
Reckson Associates Realt	Financial	46.1	31.78	0.38
Renaissance Re Holdings,	Financial	12.5	38.30	0.38
⊕ Sierra Pacific Resources	Utilities	12.5	29.06	0.38
Avnet, Inc.	Business	15.4	6.64	0.38
⊕ OfficeMax, Inc.	Consumer	—	98.81	0.38
⊖ CMS Energy Corporation	Utilities	—	15.09	0.37
⊖ Manitowoc Company, Inc.	Business	28.6	137.42	0.37
OGE Energy Corp	Utilities	16.3	55.73	0.37
⊕ Celanese Corporation	Ind Mtrls	—	36.48	0.36
⊖ BRE Properties, Inc.	Financial	73.1	48.20	0.33
⊖ Convergys Corporation	Business	23.1	50.03	0.33
⊖ Indymac Bancorp, Inc.	Financial	9.0	20.80	0.33
⊕ Southern Union Company	Energy	—	20.09	0.32
Harsco Corporation	Ind Mtrls	16.3	14.65	0.32
⊖ Cullen/Frost Bankers, In	Financial	16.5	6.45	0.32
⊖ Ryder System, Inc.	Business	13.1	26.29	0.32
Rayonier, Inc.	Ind Mtrls	18.0	7.95	0.32

Current Investment Style

Value Blnd Growth — Large Mid Small

Market Cap	%
Giant	0.0
Large	0.0
Mid	45.0
Small	49.5
Micro	5.5

Avg $mil: 1,620

Value Measures		Rel Category
Price/Earnings	15.66	1.03
Price/Book	1.79	1.05
Price/Sales	0.80	1.08
Price/Cash Flow	7.10	1.18
Dividend Yield %	2.34	1.13

Growth Measures	%	Rel Category
Long-Term Erngs	10.16	0.95
Book Value	4.15	0.89
Sales	-6.63	NMF
Cash Flow	1.34	0.37
Historical Erngs	9.73	1.02

Profitability	%	Rel Category
Return on Equity	10.53	1.00
Return on Assets	6.40	0.97
Net Margin	10.45	1.05

Sector Weightings	% of Stocks	Rel S&P 500	3 Year High Low
⟳ Info	9.63	0.48	
▣ Software	1.59	0.46	5 1
▣ Hardware	5.24	0.57	12 5
▣ Media	2.01	0.53	2 1
▣ Telecom	0.79	0.23	2 1
⟳ Service	50.44	1.09	
▣ Health	2.20	0.18	4 2
▣ Consumer	8.05	1.05	9 7
▣ Business	7.80	1.84	8 6
▣ Financial	32.39	1.45	37 29
⟳ Mfg	39.92	1.18	
▣ Goods	5.97	0.70	6 4
▣ Ind Mtrls	19.94	1.67	21 14
▣ Energy	6.04	0.62	6 2
▣ Utilities	7.97	2.28	14 7

Composition

● Cash	0.3	
● Stocks	99.6	
● Bonds	0.0	
● Other	0.1	
Foreign	1.0	
(% of Stock)		

MORNINGSTAR® ETFs 150

SPDR DJ Wilshire Sm Grwth DSG

	Market Price	Mstar Category
	$92.46	Small Growth

Morningstar Fair Value

Price/Fair Value Ratio —   Coverage Rate % —

Morningstar Rating	Return	Risk	Yield	NAV	Avg Daily Vol. (k)	52 wk High/Low
★★★ Neutral	Neutral	Average	0.1%	$92.83	6	$95.20 - $79.73

Growth of $10,000
- Investment Value of ETF
- Investment Value of Index S&P 500

Management

SSgA Funds Management is this ETF's advisor. The ETF group at SSgA is headed by John Tucker. He joined the firm in 1988.

Methodology

This fund tracks the Dow Jones Wilshire Small Cap Growth Index. The bogy uses six factors to sort the small-cap stocks in the Dow Jones Wilshire 5000 into value or growth buckets. Factors include projected price/earnings, projected earnings growth, and price/book ratios; dividend yield, trailing revenue growth, and trailing earnings growth. Half the universe's float-adjusted market cap ends up in value and half in growth. Buffer zones slow stocks' transition between styles and markets caps. It rebalances in March and December.

1997	1998	1999	2000	2001	2002	2003	2004	2005	2006	History
—	—	—	80.39	73.26	44.73	66.08	75.72	82.01	92.83	NAV $
—	—	—	80.38	73.37	44.96	66.31	75.75	82.07	92.92	Market Price $
—	—	—	-1.03*	-8.87	-38.94	47.96	15.19	8.75	13.37	NAV Return%
—	—	—	-1.01*	-8.72	-38.72	47.71	14.84	8.79	13.39	Market Price Return%
—	—	—	-1.14	0.01	0.25	0.04	-0.10	0.01	-0.04	Avg Premium/Discount%
—	—	—	-1.03	3.02	-16.84	19.28	4.31	3.84	-2.42	NAV Rtrn% +/-S&P 500
—	—	—	-1.03	0.36	-8.68	-0.58	0.88	4.60	0.02	NAV Rtrn% +/-Russ 2000 Gr
—	—	—	—	3	3	3	3	5	6	NAV Return% Rank in Cat
—	—	—	—	0.00	0.00	0.22	0.55	0.43	0.16	Income Return %
—	—	—	—	-8.87	-38.94	47.74	14.64	8.32	13.21	Capital Return %
—	—	—	0.00	0.00	0.00	0.10	0.36	0.32	0.13	Income $
—	—	—	0.00	0.00	0.00	0.00	0.00	0.00	0.00	Capital Gains $
—	—	—	—	0.30	0.30	0.29	0.27	0.26	0.26	Expense Ratio %
—	—	—	—	-0.22	-0.22	-0.04	0.59	0.46	0.26	Income Ratio %
—	—	—	—	34	46	60	63	37	84	Turnover Rate %
—	—	—	—	16	50	57	70	84	Net Assets $mil

Trading Volume Millions

Performance 12-31-06

Historic Quarterly NAV Returns

	1st Qtr	2nd Qtr	3rd Qtr	4th Qtr	Total
2002	-6.61	-20.93	-24.20	9.07	-38.94
2003	-2.77	23.13	9.80	12.56	47.96
2004	5.12	0.92	-3.87	12.95	15.19
2005	-2.82	3.44	5.34	2.69	8.75
2006	13.83	-6.60	-1.71	8.49	13.37

Trailing	NAV Return%	Market Return%	NAV Rtrn% +/-S&P 500	%Rank Cat.(NAV)
3 Mo	8.49	8.53	1.79	7
6 Mo	6.63	7.21	-6.11	7
1 Yr	13.37	13.39	-2.42	6
3 Yr Avg	12.40	12.31	1.96	3
5 Yr Avg	5.11	5.10	-1.08	3
10 Yr Avg	—	—	—	—

Tax Analysis	Tax-Adj Return%	Tax-Cost Ratio
3 Yr (estimated)	12.26	0.12
5 Yr (estimated)	5.02	0.09
10 Yr (estimated)	—	—

Rating and Risk

Time Period	Morningstar Rtn vs Cat	Morningstar Risk vs Cat	Morningstar Risk-Adj Rating
3 Yr	+Avg	-Avg	★★★★
5 Yr	Avg	Avg	★★★
10 Yr	—	—	—

Other Measures	Standard Index S&P 500	Best Fit Index Russ 2000 Gr
Alpha	-1.9	3.0
Beta	1.60	0.79
R-Squared	76	97
Standard Deviation	12.65	
Mean	12.40	
Sharpe Ratio	0.74	

Morningstar's Take by Marta Norton 12-31-06

If only streetTRACKS Dow Jones Wilshire Small Cap Growth were cheaper.

We like most things about this exchange-traded fund. The ETF typically holds approximately 900 stocks across all market sectors, with the largest position size constituting around half of a percentage point. It tracks the Dow Jones Wilshire Small Cap Growth Index, which uses six different metrics, including projected earnings growth and dividend yield, to sort stocks into growth and value camps. And the fund employs buffer zones, which slow the transition of stocks between styles and market caps. The sum total of these structural advantages is a well-diversified, low-turnover fund with targeted exposure to growth stocks.

It's worth noting the market-cap bias here. Because the fund targets a larger number of stocks than many of its closest competitors (its portfolio is nearly 2.5 times larger than that of iShares S&P Small Cap 600 Growth), it stores roughly 40% of its assets in midsized companies such as Continental

Airlines and Corrections Corporation of America. By comparison, its average small-growth ETF competitor has about 24% allocated to mid-caps. But while that heavier stake in bigger companies can make it a more difficult fit for investors' portfolios, it also helps the ETF better mirror actively managed funds that hold onto stocks long after they could technically be classified as mid-caps.

The fund's only real drawback is its expense ratio. While it is much cheaper than its open-end peers, the fund isn't the cheapest ETF in the category. Vanguard Small Cap Growth ETF offers many of the same advantages, but costs 0.12%, which makes this fund's 0.26% levy look expensive. This is an important distinction because low expenses are one of the biggest differences among ETFs that track similar market segments. With that in mind, take the Vanguard offering over this one.

Portfolio Analysis 12-31-06

Share change since 11-06 Total Stocks:896

	Sector	PE	Tot Ret%	% Assets
⊕ IntercontinentalExchange	Financial	—	—	0.62
⊕ ResMed, Inc.	Health	39.4	28.48	0.40
⊕ Continental Airlines, In	Business	13.1	93.66	0.39
⊕ Gamestop Corporation A	Goods	34.2	73.19	0.39
⊕ HCC Insurance Holdings I	Financial	17.0	9.39	0.38
⊕ Intuitive Surgical, Inc.	Health	37.0	-18.22	0.38
⊕ US Airways Group, Inc.	Business	—	44.99	0.37
⊕ Jones Lang LaSalle, Inc.	Financial	18.9	84.32	0.35
⊕ Stericycle, Inc.	Business	45.5	28.23	0.35
⊕ First Marblehead Corpora	Financial	13.7	152.12	0.35
⊕ Denbury Resources, Inc.	Energy	16.6	21.99	0.35
⊕ Goodyear Tire & Rubber	Ind Mtrls	22.8	20.77	0.35
⊕ Agere Systems, Inc.	Hardware	—	48.60	0.35
⊕ NAVTEQ Corporation	Business	35.3	-20.29	0.34
⊕ Frontier Oil Corporation	Energy	8.4	53.75	0.34
⊕ Affiliated Managers Grou	Financial	32.5	31.00	0.33
⊕ Mettler-Toledo Internati	Health	22.0	42.84	0.33
⊕ Energen Corporation	Energy	14.7	30.75	0.33
⊕ Cimarex Energy Company	Energy	6.4	-14.79	0.32
⊕ Nasdaq Stock Market, Inc	Financial	46.6	-12.48	0.32

Current Investment Style

Value Blnd Growth — Large Mid Small

Market Cap	%
Giant	0.0
Large	0.0
Mid	37.6
Small	55.7
Micro	6.7

Avg $mil: 1,536

Value Measures		Rel Category
Price/Earnings	20.78	0.98
Price/Book	2.79	0.94
Price/Sales	1.34	0.91
Price/Cash Flow	7.67	1.08
Dividend Yield %	0.38	1.23

Growth Measures	%	Rel Category
Long-Term Erngs	16.69	0.95
Book Value	9.82	0.82
Sales	12.39	1.34
Cash Flow	16.04	0.76
Historical Erngs	20.42	1.02

Profitability	%	Rel Category
Return on Equity	14.80	1.01
Return on Assets	6.89	0.87
Net Margin	9.45	0.97

Sector Weightings

	% of Stocks	Rel S&P 500	3 Year High	Low
⌖ Info	20.62	1.03		
🖥 Software	6.13	1.78	8	4
💾 Hardware	10.05	1.09	14	6
🔊 Media	1.75	0.46	4	2
📶 Telecom	2.69	0.77	3	0
☞ Service	52.79	1.14		
🏥 Health	16.99	1.41	23	16
🛒 Consumer	11.68	1.53	16	11
📋 Business	14.73	3.48	15	7
$ Financial	9.39	0.42	17	9
⚒ Mfg	26.58	0.79		
🏭 Goods	6.32	0.74	8	4
⚙ Ind Mtrls	10.21	0.86	17	9
🔥 Energy	9.75	0.99	12	5
💡 Utilities	0.30	0.09	0	0

Composition

● Cash	0.3	
● Stocks	99.7	
● Bonds	0.0	
● Other	0.0	
Foreign	0.7	
(% of Stock)		

Address:	State Street Bank & Tr, 225 Franklin St Boston MA 02210 866-787-2257
Web Address:	www.advisors.ssga.com
Inception:	09-25-00*
Advisor:	SSgA Funds Management Inc

Management Fee:	0.25%		
Expense Projections:	3Yr:$81	5Yr:$141	10Yr:$320
Income Distrib:	Quarterly		
Exchange:	AMEX		

Data through December 31, 2006

streetTRACKS DJ STOXX 50 FEU

Market Price $47.87	**Mstar Category** Europe Stock

Morningstar Fair Value

Price/Fair Value Ratio — | Coverage Rate % —

Management

The advisor is SSgA Funds Management, which is a subsidiary of State Street Global Advisors and State Street. SSgA manages more than $1 trillion in institutional, mutual fund, and separate accounts and is a major player in the ETF field.

Methodology

The fund tracks the Dow Jones Stoxx 50, which is an index of the largest stocks from each sector in 17 European countries with developed economies. As a result, this index and fund cover a bit less than 60% of the total market capitalization of the stocks traded on major European exchanges. It's a free-float market-capitalization-weighted index that rebalances annually in September.

Morningstar Rating ★★ Below Avg	**Return** Below Avg	**Risk** Low	**Yield** 3.0%	**NAV** $48.21	**Avg Daily Vol. (k)** 23

52 wk High/Low $48.80 - $40.22

Growth of $10,000
— Investment Value of ETF
— Investment Value of Index MSCI EAFE

Trading Volume Millions

	1997	1998	1999	2000	2001	2002	2003	2004	2005	2006	History
	—	—	—	—	—	25.49	33.62	37.80	39.34	48.21	NAV $
	—	—	—	—	—	24.80	33.98	37.72	39.47	48.34	Market Price $
	—	—	—	—	—	19.87*	35.50	15.26	7.39	26.76	NAV Return%
	—	—	—	—	—	19.18*	40.75	13.79	7.97	26.67	Market Price Return%
	—	—	—	—	—	-1.21	0.02	0.67	0.21	0.26	Avg Premium/Discount%
	—	—	—	—	—	19.87	-3.09	-4.99	-6.15	0.42	NAV Rtrn% +/-MSCI EAFE
	—	—	—	—	—	19.87	-3.04	-5.62	-2.03	-6.96	NAV Rtrn% +/-MSCI Eur
	—	—	—	—	—	—	15	15	15	16	NAV Return% Rank in Cat
	—	—	—	—	—	—	2.98	2.49	2.82	3.70	Income Return %
	—	—	—	—	—	—	32.52	12.77	4.57	23.06	Capital Return %
	—	—	—	—	—	0.00	0.75	0.83	1.05	1.44	Income $
	—	—	—	—	—	0.00	0.00	0.00	0.15	0.01	Capital Gains $
	—	—	—	—	—	—	0.35	0.33	0.32	—	Expense Ratio %
	—	—	—	—	—	—	2.96	2.98	2.75	—	Income Ratio %
	—	—	—	—	—	—	6	7	9	—	Turnover Rate %
	—	—	—	—	—	31	9	28	31	92	Net Assets $mil

Performance 12-31-06

Historic Quarterly NAV Returns

	1st Qtr	2nd Qtr	3rd Qtr	4th Qtr	Total
2002	—	—	—	—	—*
2003	-9.25	21.53	1.65	20.87	35.50
2004	-1.80	1.01	1.88	14.05	15.26
2005	-0.55	-0.09	7.30	0.74	7.39
2006	8.12	3.14	4.54	8.74	26.76

Trailing	NAV Return%	Market Return%+/-	NAV Rtrn% MSCI EAFE	%Rank Cat.(NAV)
3 Mo	8.74	8.45	-1.61	19
6 Mo	13.67	14.16	-1.02	19
1 Yr	26.76	26.67	0.42	16
3 Yr Avg	16.20	15.89	-3.73	15
5 Yr Avg	—	—	—	—
10 Yr Avg	—	—	—	—

Tax Analysis	Tax-Adj Return%	Tax-Cost Ratio
3 Yr (estimated)	15.02	1.02
5 Yr (estimated)	—	—
10 Yr (estimated)	—	—

Rating and Risk

Time Period	Morningstar Rtn vs Cat	Morningstar Risk vs Cat	Morningstar Risk-Adj Rating
3 Yr	-Avg	Low	★★
5 Yr	—	—	—
10 Yr	—	—	—

Other Measures	Standard Index S&P 500	Best Fit Index MSCI Eur
Alpha	-1.1	-2.8
Beta	0.86	0.92
R-Squared	81	96
Standard Deviation	9.11	
Mean	16.20	
Sharpe Ratio	1.36	

Morningstar's Take by Gregg Wolper 12-31-06

It's tough to make a case for StreetTracks Dow Jones Stoxx 50 Fund.

One reason is its focus on big European companies. There's no reason such companies won't prosper, of course, but an investor who owns broad international funds most likely already has substantial exposure to such firms--in fact, to the very stocks in this portfolio. Those funds commonly have roughly two thirds of their assets in Europe.

Even if you don't face a problem of overlap on that front, it's not clear why you'd want this fund. Compared with broader funds, its Europe-only focus cuts it off from companies in any other area of the world. And if you do decide you specifically want a Europe fund, this one has its shortcomings. Most notably, it is not as broadly diversified as others. Top holdings BP and HSBC each get more than 5% of assets, and six other companies get more than 3% each. The fund has 39% of assets in the financials sector, roughly 10 percentage points more than a similar offering not limited to the

biggest of the big, Vanguard European Stock Index. It is also overweighted by several percentage points versus that fund (which tracks the MSCI Europe Index) in energy and health care.

Another reason for caution with this fund is its low trading volume. If you want to buy or sell 100 shares, that shouldn't be a problem, but at higher levels, trading could be more difficult. On a typical day, fewer than 25,000 shares of this fund change hands; the ETF version of the Vanguard Europe fund typically has more than double that volume.

This fund does have an low expense ratio (though not as low as the Vanguard ETF's), and its focus on the biggest blue chips from large markets should protect against the volatility inherent in small caps or Eastern European stocks. It also has a higher-than-average yield. But other alternatives have more overall appeal.

Portfolio Analysis 12-31-06

Share change since 11-06 Total Stocks:50	Sector	Country	% Assets
⊕ BP	Energy	U.K.	4.98
⊕ HSBC Hldgs	Financial	U.K.	4.82
⊕ Total SA	Energy	France	3.76
⊕ GlaxoSmithKline	Health	U.K.	3.61
⊕ Vodafone Grp	Telecom	U.K.	3.35
⊕ Novartis	Health	Switzerland	3.28
⊕ Nestle	Goods	Switzerland	3.26
⊕ Royal Dutch Shell	Energy	U.K.	3.01
⊕ Roche Holding	Health	Switzerland	2.88
⊕ Royal Bank Of Scotland G	Financial	U.K.	2.84
⊕ Banco Santander Central	Financial	Spain	2.67
⊕ UBS AG	Financial	Switzerland	2.65
⊕ BNP Paribas	Financial	France	2.19
⊕ E. On Ag Npv	Utilities	Germany	2.15
⊕ Barclays	Financial	U.K.	2.13
⊕ ING Groep	Financial	Netherlands	2.12
⊕ Telefonica	Telecom	Spain	2.10
⊕ UniCredito Italiano Grp	Financial	Italy	2.09
⊕ Allianz	Financial	Germany	2.02
⊕ BBVA	Financial	Spain	1.96

Current Investment Style

Value Blnd Growth — Large/Mid/Small

Market Cap	%
Giant	99.0
Large	1.0
Mid	0.0
Small	0.0
Micro	0.0
Avg $mil:	96,515

Value Measures		Rel Category
Price/Earnings	12.78	0.94
Price/Book	2.35	1.05
Price/Sales	1.32	1.17
Price/Cash Flow	8.73	1.03
Dividend Yield %	3.32	0.96

Growth Measures	%	Rel Category
Long-Term Erngs	11.03	0.99
Book Value	7.64	0.89
Sales	8.02	1.05
Cash Flow	5.66	2.11
Historical Erngs	22.64	1.01

Composition

Cash	0.1	Bonds	0.0
Stocks	99.9	Other	0.0
Foreign (% of Stock)			100.0

Sector Weightings	% of Stocks	Rel MSCI EAFE	3 Year High Low
⊙ Info	15.28	1.29	
Software	1.08	1.93	1 1
Hardware	5.20	1.35	6 5
Media	0.00	0.00	0 0
Telecom	9.00	1.62	13 8
⊂ Service	54.41	1.15	
Health	11.69	1.64	14 12
Consumer	2.30	0.46	2 2
Business	0.00	0.00	0 0
Financial	40.42	1.34	40 32
Mfg	30.30	0.74	
Goods	7.91	0.60	10 8
Ind Mtrls	5.19	0.34	5 2
Energy	13.66	1.91	21 14
Utilities	3.54	0.68	4 2

Regional Exposure	% Stock
UK/W. Europe	100
N. America	0
Japan	0
Latn America	0
Asia X Japan	0
Other	0

Country Exposure	% Stock		
U.K.	39	Germany	12
Switzerland	14	Spain	7
France	13		

Address:	State Street Bank & Tr, 225 Franklin St, Boston MA 02210, 866-787-2257
Web Address:	www.advisors.ssga.com
Inception:	10-21-02*
Advisor:	SSgA Funds Management Inc

Management Fee:	0.29%
Expense Projections:	3Yr:$103 5Yr:$180 10Yr:$406
Income Distrib:	Quarterly
Exchange:	NYSE

© 2007 Morningstar, Inc. All rights reserved. The information herein is not represented or warranted to be accurate, correct, complete or timely. Past performance is no guarantee of future results. Activate your free 30-day research pass at http://www.morningstar.com/goto/2007ETFs150

MORNINGSTAR® ETFs 150

streetTRACKS Gold Shares GLD

Market Price $60.85	**Mstar Category** Specialty-Precious Metals

Morningstar Fair Value

Price/Fair Value Ratio	Coverage Rate %
—	—

Management

This fund is sponsored by the World Gold Council. Administration is handled by the Bank of New York as Trustee and the gold is held by HSBC in London.

Methodology

This fund issues shares equal to roughly one tenth of an ounce of gold, at current market prices.

Morningstar Rating	Return	Risk	Yield	NAV	Avg Daily Vol. (k)	52 wk High/Low
— Not Rated	Not Rated	Not Rated	—	$63.04	4,229	$71.12 - $52.34

Growth of $10,000
- Investment Value of ETF
- Investment Value of Index MSCI EAFE

Trading Volume Millions

	1997	1998	1999	2000	2001	2002	2003	2004	2005	2006	History
	—	—	—	—	—	—	—	43.78	51.07	63.04	NAV $
	—	—	—	—	—	—	—	43.80	51.58	62.90	Market Price $
	—	—	—	—	—	—	—	18.27*	16.65	23.44	NAV Return%
	—	—	—	—	—	—	—	17.91*	17.76	21.95	Market Price Return%
	—	—	—	—	—	—	—	-0.21	-0.04	0.40	Avg Premium/Discount%
	—	—	—	—	—	—	—	18.27	3.11	-2.90	NAV Rtrn% +/-MSCI EAFE
	—	—	—	—	—	—	—	18.27	-17.01	-11.12	NAV Rtrn% +/-MSCI W Me&M
	—	—	—	—	—	—	—	1	1	2	NAV Return% Rank in Cat
	—	—	—	—	—	—	—	—	0.00	0.00	Income Return %
	—	—	—	—	—	—	—	—	16.65	23.44	Capital Return %
	—	—	—	—	—	—	—	0.00	0.00	0.00	Income $
	—	—	—	—	—	—	—	0.00	0.00	0.00	Capital Gains $
	—	—	—	—	—	—	—	—	—	—	Expense Ratio %
	—	—	—	—	—	—	—	—	—	—	Income Ratio %
	—	—	—	—	—	—	—	—	—	—	Turnover Rate %
	—	—	—	—	—	—	—	1,335	4,341	9,261	Net Assets $mil

Performance 12-31-06

Historic Quarterly NAV Returns

	1st Qtr	2nd Qtr	3rd Qtr	4th Qtr	Total
2002	—	—	—	—	—
2003	—	—	—	—	— *
2004	—	—	—	—	—
2005	-2.49	2.13	8.17	8.29	16.65
2006	13.35	5.30	-2.42	5.98	23.44

Trailing	NAV Return%	Market Return%	NAV Rtrn% +/-MSCI EAFE	%Rank Cat.(NAV)
3 Mo	5.98	5.77	-4.37	4
6 Mo	3.41	2.73	-11.28	4
1 Yr	23.44	21.95	-2.90	2
3 Yr Avg	—	—	—	—
5 Yr Avg	—	—	—	—
10 Yr Avg	—	—	—	—

Tax Analysis	Tax-Adj Return%	Tax-Cost Ratio
3 Yr (estimated)	—	—
5 Yr (estimated)	—	—
10 Yr (estimated)	—	—

Rating and Risk

Time Period	Morningstar Rtn vs Cat	Morningstar Risk vs Cat	Morningstar Risk-Adj Rating
3 Yr	—	—	—
5 Yr	—	—	—
10 Yr	—	—	—

Other Measures	Standard Index S&P 500	Best Fit Index
Alpha	—	—
Beta	—	—
R-Squared	—	—
Standard Deviation	—	
Mean	—	
Sharpe Ratio	—	

Portfolio Analysis 09-30-06

Share change since 09-05 Total Stocks:0	Sector	Country	% Assets
⊕ Gold Bullion	—	—	100.00

Morningstar's Take by Karen Wallace 12-31-06

StreetTRACKS Gold Trust has merits as a long-term holding, but we wouldn't use it to speculate on gold prices.

Gold's rise over the past six years has piqued many investors' interests. In fact, this fund and its similarly structured rival, iShares COMEX Gold Trust, have arguably fueled gold's rise. Together they have attracted more than $10 billion in assets since they launched just over a year ago.

This ETF offers direct exposure to gold price fluctuations in a more liquid and convenient format than taking physical delivery of the metal itself. Unlike most precious-metals funds, this one does not invest in the stocks of gold producers. Rather, each share of the trust represents one tenth of an ounce of gold bullion at current market prices, less the fund's 0.40% expense ratio. (Another important difference: This investment is taxed differently than other gold-linked investments, so it's a good idea to consult your tax advisor before buying in.)

Rolling three-month returns since the fund's inception show that it has been less volatile than the average fund that invests in the stocks of gold producers over the same time period. (This makes sense because the price of bullion tends not to be as volatile as gold producers' stock prices.)

But that's not to say that this is a tame investment: Gold prices have historically fluctuated wildly. If we were to see another period of flat to falling gold prices, as we saw in much of the 1990s, this fund would languish. In addition, the amount of gold represented by each share will continue to decrease due to the sales necessary to pay the sponsor's fee and trust expenses.

A gold investment makes the most sense as part of a long-term asset-allocation plan. A speculator buying into this fund now, with gold trading near 25-year highs, could be in for a disappointment. Many factors could negatively impact gold prices going forward, including a strengthening dollar and increased selling by speculators. Handle this fund with care.

Address:	444 Madison Ave, 3rd Fl New York NY 10022 866-320-4053
Web Address:	www.streettracksgoldshares.com
Inception:	11-18-04 *
Advisor:	Bank of New York

Management Fee:	0.40%			
Expense Projections:	3Yr: —	5Yr: —	10Yr: —	
Income Distrib:	None			
Exchange:	NYSE			

Current Investment Style

Value Blnd Growth — Large Mid Small

Market Cap	%
Giant	—
Large	—
Mid	—
Small	—
Micro	—

Avg $mil: —

Value Measures	Rel Category
Price/Earnings	—
Price/Book	—
Price/Sales	—
Price/Cash Flow	—
Dividend Yield %	—

Growth Measures	% Rel Category
Long-Term Erngs	—
Book Value	—
Sales	—
Cash Flow	—
Historical Erngs	—

Composition

Cash	0.0	Bonds	0.0
Stocks	0.0	Other	100.0
Foreign (% of Stock)			0.0

Sector Weightings

		% of Rel MSCI Stocks	EAFE	3 Year High Low
☁	Info	0.00	0.00	
▩	Software	—	0.00	— —
▤	Hardware	—	0.00	— —
♫	Media	—	0.00	— —
☎	Telecom	—	0.00	— —
☞	Service	0.00	0.00	
✚	Health	—	0.00	— —
▨	Consumer	—	0.00	— —
▤	Business	—	0.00	— —
$	Financial	—	0.00	— —
⚒	Mfg	0.00	0.00	
▦	Goods	—	0.00	— —
✿	Ind Mtrls	—	0.00	— —
◔	Energy	—	0.00	— —
♨	Utilities	—	0.00	— —

Regional Exposure % Stock

UK/W. Europe	0	N. America	0
Japan	0	Latn America	0
Asia X Japan	0	Other	100

Country Exposure % Stock

Morningstar ETFs 150

SPDR DJ Wilshire Tot Mkt TMW

Market Price $101.50	**Mstar Category** Large Blend	

Morningstar Fair Value

Price/Fair Value Ratio
0.92 Undervalued

Coverage Rate %
90 Good

Management

SSgA Funds Management is this ETF's advisor. The ETF group at SSgA is headed by John Tucker. He joined the firm in 1988.

Methodology

This fund tracks the Dow Jones Wilshire 5000 Index. The bogy is designed to represent the broad U.S. market. Its only requirement is that the stock is the primary equity issue of a U.S. company. That means this ETF will hold companies that have been proven profitable and ones that are more speculative. It is reviewed monthly.

Morningstar Rating ★★★ Neutral	**Return** Neutral	**Risk** Average	**Yield** 1.5%	**NAV** $101.80	**Avg Daily Vol. (k)** 3

52 wk High/Low $102.60 - $88.12

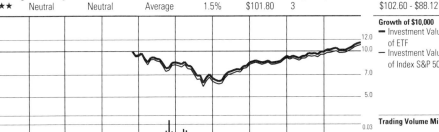

Growth of $10,000
— Investment Value of ETF
— Investment Value of Index S&P 500

Trading Volume Millions

	1997	1998	1999	2000	2001	2002	2003	2004	2005	2006	History
	—	—	—	92.42	81.86	63.61	79.30	85.62	90.02	101.80	NAV $
	—	—	—	92.42	81.93	63.36	79.20	85.94	90.16	101.83	Market Price $
	—	—	—	2.20*	-10.18	-21.22	26.62	10.03	6.78	14.92	NAV Return%
	—	—	—	2.20*	-10.11	-21.59	26.97	10.57	6.54	14.78	Market Price Return%
	—	—	—	-0.49	0.11	-0.05	-0.05	0.04	-0.01	0.02	Avg Premium/Discount%
	—	—	—	2.20	1.71	0.88	-2.06	-0.85	1.87	-0.87	NAV Rtrn% +/-S&P 500
	—	—	—	2.20	2.27	0.43	-3.27	-1.37	0.51	-0.54	NAV Rtrn% +/-Russ 1000
	—	—	—	—	12	14	14	16	21	30	NAV Return% Rank in Cat
	—	—	—	—	1.19	1.15	1.78	1.96	1.60	1.72	Income Return %
	—	—	—	—	-11.37	-22.37	24.84	8.07	5.18	13.20	Capital Return %
	—	—	—	0.22	1.09	0.94	1.13	1.55	1.36	1.54	Income $
	—	—	—	0.00	0.00	0.00	0.00	0.00	0.00	0.00	Capital Gains $
	—	—	—	—	0.21	0.23	0.24	0.22	0.21	0.21	Expense Ratio %
	—	—	—	—	1.06	1.25	1.65	1.59	2.05	1.62	Income Ratio %
	—	—	—	—	6	6	6	5	32	2	Turnover Rate %
	—	—	—	—	—	83	103	120	104	112	Net Assets $mil

Performance 12-31-06

Historic Quarterly NAV Returns

	1st Qtr	2nd Qtr	3rd Qtr	4th Qtr	Total
2002	0.75	-12.65	-16.73	7.52	-21.22
2003	-3.43	14.77	2.30	11.68	26.62
2004	1.35	1.32	-1.68	8.98	10.03
2005	-1.32	1.61	4.21	2.20	6.78
2006	4.90	-2.02	4.60	6.89	14.92

Trailing	NAV Return%	Market Return%	NAV Rtrn% +/-S&P 500	%Rank Cat.(NAV)
3 Mo	6.89	6.85	0.19	44
6 Mo	11.81	11.73	-0.93	38
1 Yr	14.92	14.78	-0.87	30
3 Yr Avg	10.52	10.58	0.08	15
5 Yr Avg	6.14	6.12	-0.05	13
10 Yr Avg	—	—	—	—

Tax Analysis	Tax-Adj Return%	Tax-Cost Ratio
3 Yr (estimated)	9.88	0.58
5 Yr (estimated)	5.54	0.57
10 Yr (estimated)	—	—

Rating and Risk

Time Period	Morningstar Rtn vs Cat	Morningstar Risk vs Cat	Morningstar Risk-Adj Rating
3 Yr	Avg	Avg	★★★
5 Yr	Avg	Avg	★★★
10 Yr	—	—	—

Other Measures	Standard Index S&P 500	Best Fit Index Russ 1000
Alpha	0.1	-0.1
Beta	0.99	0.96
R-Squared	98	98
Standard Deviation	6.94	
Mean	10.52	
Sharpe Ratio	1.02	

Portfolio Analysis 12-31-06

Share change since 11-06 Total Stocks:982

Sector		PE	Tot Ret%	% Assets
⊖ ExxonMobil Corporation	Energy	11.7	39.07	2.82
General Electric Company	Ind Mtrls	19.8	9.35	2.38
Citigroup, Inc.	Financial	13.3	19.55	1.72
Microsoft Corporation	Software	23.7	15.83	1.69
Bank of America Corporat	Financial	12.4	20.68	1.46
Procter & Gamble Company	Goods	24.2	13.36	1.26
Pfizer Inc.	Health	15.1	15.22	1.21
Johnson & Johnson	Health	17.4	12.44	1.17
Cisco Systems, Inc.	Hardware	28.8	59.64	1.07
Altria Group, Inc.	Goods	15.9	19.87	1.06
J.P. Morgan Chase & Co.	Financial	13.7	25.60	1.02
American International G	Financial	17.1	6.05	1.01
Chevron Corporation	Energy	9.3	33.75	0.97
IBM	Hardware	16.8	19.77	0.97
AT&T, Inc.	Telecom	19.2	51.59	0.85
Intel Corporation	Hardware	20.3	-17.18	0.78
Hewlett-Packard Company	Hardware	18.9	45.21	0.76
Wal-Mart Stores, Inc.	Consumer	16.6	0.13	0.70
Berkshire Hathaway Inc.	Financial	—	—	0.69
ConocoPhillips	Energy	6.9	26.53	0.68

Current Investment Style

Value Blnd Growth — Large Mid Small

Market Cap	%
Giant	40.6
Large	33.2
Mid	19.8
Small	3.3
Micro	3.1

Avg $mil: 29,245

Value Measures		Rel Category
Price/Earnings	16.30	0.98
Price/Book	2.65	0.96
Price/Sales	1.45	1.14
Price/Cash Flow	9.19	0.97
Dividend Yield %	1.74	0.97

Growth Measures	%	Rel Category
Long-Term Erngs	11.75	1.02
Book Value	7.91	0.93
Sales	10.08	1.21
Cash Flow	11.45	1.51
Historical Erngs	17.92	1.07

Profitability	%	Rel Category
Return on Equity	18.63	0.97
Return on Assets	10.24	1.06
Net Margin	13.74	1.23

Sector Weightings	% of Stocks	Rel S&P 500	3 Year High	Low
↗ Info	20.11	1.01		
🖥 Software	4.16	1.21	4	3
💻 Hardware	9.01	0.98	10	8
🎤 Media	3.68	0.97	4	3
☎ Telecom	3.26	0.93	4	3
☞ Service	47.51	1.03		
🏥 Health	11.90	0.99	14	12
🛒 Consumer	8.50	1.11	10	8
💼 Business	4.69	1.11	6	4
💲 Financial	22.42	1.01	23	19
📐 Mfg	32.39	0.96		
🏭 Goods	7.87	0.92	10	7
⚙ Ind Mtrls	11.40	0.95	13	11
🔋 Energy	9.72	0.99	11	6
🔌 Utilities	3.40	0.97	4	3

Composition

● Cash	0.1	
● Stocks	99.9	
● Bonds	0.0	
● Other	0.0	
Foreign	0.0	
(% of Stock)		

Morningstar's Take by Marta Norton 12-31-06

In an increasingly competitive marketplace, the run-of-the-mill streetTRACKS Total Market ETF's greatest threat comes from an old rival.

This ETF relies on traditional indexing methodology to offer investors broad market exposure. It tracks the Dow Jones Wilshire 5000, which weights stocks by market capitalization (a stock's market price times the total number of shares available for trading). So, the largest U.S. companies, such as ExxonMobil (this ETF's biggest holding as of Nov. 30, 2006), grab the most assets, while small stocks, such as NeoMagic Corporation, a computer supplier with $59 million in market capitalization, sink to the bottom of its portfolio.

Lately, this cap-weighted approach to indexing seems almost antiquated. More and more ETFs hitting the marketplace today offer new ways to tap the same broad market. WisdomTree Total Dividend, for example, mimics an index that ranks stocks by dividends. And PowerShares Dynamic OTC tracks a benchmark with strict rules designed to provide broad market exposure while muting the influence of larger-cap stocks. These newer methodologies aren't entirely without merit, but they remain untested, and it remains to be seen whether the alternatively weighted ETFs will outperform more traditional ETFs like this one over the long haul. Plus, many of the upstart ETFs are more expensive. Because low costs are one of the major selling points in the ETF universe, that's a significant strike against them.

We think this fund's greatest competition comes from another cap-weighted ETF: Vanguard Total Stock Market ETF, which tracks the MSCI U.S. Broad Market Index. It offers much the same profile as this fund, but at a third of the price. That said, investors could certainly do worse than this ETF. Although it's not the cheapest option, its 0.21% expense ratio is by no means expensive. While it's not our first choice, it still provides broad-market exposure at a reasonable price.

Address:	State Street Bank & Tr, 225 Franklin St Boston MA 02210 866-787-2257
Web Address:	www.advisors.ssga.com
Inception:	10-04-00*
Advisor:	SSgA Funds Management Inc

Management Fee:	0.20%
Expense Projections:	3Yr:$65 5Yr:$113 10Yr:$257
Income Distrib:	Quarterly
Exchange:	AMEX

Morningstar® ETFs 150

DJ Wilshire REIT ETF RWR

Market Price $87.62	**Mstar Category** Specialty-Real Estate	

Morningstar Fair Value

Price/Fair Value Ratio	Coverage Rate %
1.22 Overvalued	91 Good

Management

The Tuckerman Group, a subsidiary of SSgA, runs this fund. Managers Amos Rogers III and Murat Sensoy, have worked for the Tuckerman Group since 2003. Prior to then Rogers worked in Citigroup's real estate division and Sensoy was an international credit analysts for State Street Bank.

Methodology

This exchange-traded fund tracks the Wilshire REIT Index. It's a benchmark of about 90 stocks that derive at least three fourths of their revenue from the equity ownership or operation of real estate. The bogey rebalances monthly but makes additions quarterly and deletions at year-end.

	Morningstar Rating ★★★ Neutral	Return Neutral	Risk High	Yield 3.2%	NAV $87.86	Avg Daily Vol. (k) 72	52 wk High/Low $92.23 - $70.40

Growth of $10,000
— Investment Value of ETF
— Investment Value of Index S&P 500

Trading Volume Millions

	1997	1998	1999	2000	2001	2002	2003	2004	2005	2006	History
	—	—	—	—	39.38	38.67	49.83	62.54	67.52	87.86	NAV $
	—	—	—	—	39.56	38.76	49.93	62.53	67.50	87.85	Market Price $
	—	—	—	—	22.88*	2.88	35.58	32.75	13.12	35.50	NAV Return%
	—	—	—	—	22.85*	2.65	35.52	32.45	13.10	35.53	Market Price Return%
	—	—	—	—	0.07	0.23	0.06	0.05	0.09	0.02	Avg Premium/Discount%
	—	—	—	—	22.88	24.98	6.90	21.87	8.21	19.71	NAV Rtrn% +/-S&P 500
	—	—	—	—	22.88	-0.72	-0.48	-0.39	-0.88	-0.63	NAV Rtrn% +/-DJ Wilshire REIT
	—	—	—	—	—	3	3	3	4	4	NAV Return% Rank in Cat
	—	—	—	—	—	4.93	5.43	6.41	4.33	4.22	Income Return %
	—	—	—	—	—	-2.05	30.15	26.34	8.79	31.28	Capital Return %
	—	—	—	—	1.71	1.91	2.06	3.12	2.67	2.81	Income $
	—	—	—	—	0.23	0.00	0.16	0.00	0.45	0.54	Capital Gains $
	—	—	—	—	0.32	0.30	0.28	0.26	0.26	0.26	Expense Ratio %
	—	—	—	—	6.88	6.74	6.95	5.23	5.06	3.57	Income Ratio %
	—	—	—	—	2	15	10	5	12	11	Turnover Rate %
	—	—	—	—	87	284	535	807	1,323		Net Assets $mil

Performance 12-31-06

Historic Quarterly NAV Returns

	1st Qtr	2nd Qtr	3rd Qtr	4th Qtr	Total
2002	8.26	4.43	-9.11	0.11	2.88
2003	1.20	11.96	9.77	9.02	35.58
2004	11.99	-5.38	8.17	15.82	32.75
2005	-7.23	14.50	3.88	2.51	13.12
2006	15.65	-1.21	9.04	8.76	35.50

Trailing	NAV Return%	Market Return%	NAV Rtrn% +/-S&P 500	%Rank Cat.(NAV)
3 Mo	8.76	8.67	2.06	5
6 Mo	18.59	18.58	5.85	5
1 Yr	35.50	35.53	19.71	4
3 Yr Avg	26.72	26.62	16.28	3
5 Yr Avg	23.20	23.08	17.01	3
10 Yr Avg	—	—	—	

Tax Analysis	Tax-Adj Return%	Tax-Cost Ratio
3 Yr (estimated)	24.70	1.59
5 Yr (estimated)	21.17	1.65
10 Yr (estimated)	—	—

Rating and Risk

Time Period	Morningstar Rtn vs Cat	Morningstar Risk vs Cat	Morningstar Risk-Adj Rating
3 Yr	Avg	High	★★★
5 Yr	Avg	High	★★★
10 Yr	—	—	—

Other Measures	Standard Index S&P 500	Best Fit Index DJ Wilshire REIT
Alpha	13.2	-0.4
Beta	1.27	0.99
R-Squared	27	100
Standard Deviation	16.67	
Mean	26.72	
Sharpe Ratio	1.33	

Portfolio Analysis 12-31-06

Share change since 11-06 Total Stocks:85	Sector	PE	Tot Ret%	% Assets
⊕ Simon Property Group, In	Financial	59.2	36.97	6.86
⊕ Equity Office Properties	Financial	—	64.28	5.17
⊕ Vornado Realty Trust	Financial	38.2	51.13	4.90
⊕ ProLogis Trust	Financial	34.3	34.02	4.61
⊕ Equity Residential	Financial	NMF	34.64	4.53
⊕ Boston Properties, Inc.	Financial	15.1	62.75	4.01
⊕ Host Hotels & Resorts, I	Financial	53.4	33.95	3.92
⊕ Archstone-Smith Trust	Financial	60.0	43.93	3.91
⊕ Public Storage, Inc.	Financial	46.2	47.46	3.84
⊕ General Growth Propertie	Financial	—	15.09	3.63
⊕ Kimco Realty Corporation	Financial	30.8	44.91	2.99
⊕ AvalonBay Communities, I	Financial	67.7	49.69	2.96
⊕ Developers Diversified R	Financial	41.1	39.65	2.12
⊕ Macerich Company	Financial	—	33.91	1.90
⊕ SL Green Realty Corporat	Financial	58.2	77.73	1.86
⊕ Duke Realty Corporation	Financial	75.7	28.98	1.69
⊕ Apartment Investment & M	Financial	—	55.18	1.67
⊕ Regency Centers Corporat	Financial	57.1	37.58	1.63
⊕ AMB Property Corporation	Financial	30.9	23.30	1.61
⊕ Federal Realty Investmen	Financial	55.6	44.88	1.44

Current Investment Style

Value Blnd Growth — Large Mid Small

Market Cap	%
Giant	0.0
Large	45.4
Mid	41.4
Small	12.3
Micro	0.9
Avg $mil: 6,565	

Value Measures	Rel Category
Price/Earnings	19.14	1.11
Price/Book	3.28	1.17
Price/Sales	4.36	1.15
Price/Cash Flow	15.98	0.98
Dividend Yield %	3.99	1.22

Growth Measures	%	Rel Category
Long-Term Erngs	6.70	0.86
Book Value	-1.89	NMF
Sales	10.92	0.94
Cash Flow	—	—
Historical Erngs	3.24	0.34

Profitability	%	Rel Category
Return on Equity	10.55	0.74
Return on Assets	9.50	0.85
Net Margin	23.74	1.07

Sector Weightings	% of Stocks	Rel S&P 500	3 Year High Low
↻ Info	0.00	0.00	
🖥 Software	0.00	0.00	0 0
💻 Hardware	0.00	0.00	0 0
🎙 Media	0.00	0.00	0 0
📶 Telecom	0.00	0.00	0 0
⚙ Service	100.00	2.16	
⚕ Health	0.00	0.00	0 0
🛒 Consumer	0.00	0.00	0 0
📁 Business	0.00	0.00	0 0
💲 Financial	100.00	4.49	100 100
🏭 Mfg	0.00	0.00	
🛋 Goods	0.00	0.00	0 0
⚙ Ind Mtrls	0.00	0.00	0 0
🔥 Energy	0.00	0.00	0 0
💡 Utilities	0.00	0.00	0 0

Composition

	%
● Cash	0.1
● Stocks	99.9
● Bonds	0.0
● Other	0.0
Foreign (% of Stock)	0.0

Morningstar's Take by Dan Culloton 12-31-06

StreetTracks Dow Jones Wilshire REIT offers decent exposure to an increasingly risky sector.

This ETF offers cheap and convenient exposure to the REIT market. It tracks the Wilshire REIT Index, which includes a substantial portion of the U.S. REIT market and charges an expense ratio that is a fraction of the typical no-load sector fund. The 0.26% levy also is one of the lowest among real estate ETFs, which have an average expense ratio of about 0.33%. It's not the cheapest REIT ETF, though. Vanguard REIT Index ETF charges 0.12%.

The fund's subadvisor, the Tuckerman Group, has done a decent job over time of tracking the returns of the ETF's benchmark. Its returns from its April 23, 2001, inception through the end of November 2006 lag those of its index by less than the ETF's expense ratio. But there have been periods, the trailing three-year period ending in November 2006, for instance, in which the ETF's results have fallen behind those of the benchmark by more than the fund's expense ratio. So, it's not a cinch this ETF will always give you the returns of its index minus its expenses.

The ETF concentrates its assets in a narrow and arguably richly valued sector. REITs have enjoyed an extremely strong run in the last six years. As a result this portfolio looks pricey by several measures. Its average valuation measures are higher than the typical conventional real estate mutual fund as well as the broad stock market, as defined by the Morningstar U.S. Market Index. The ETF's dividend yield is lower than those of less risky 10-year Treasury bonds. Nearly three fourths of the 61 REITs in this fund that are covered by Morningstar stock analysts were trading above their fair value estimates at December 2006's end.

There are good reasons to set aside a small portion of your portfolio for real estate. Given the sector's valuations, though, we'd tread cautiously, if at all. Even then, there are cheaper vehicles than this one, such as Vanguard REIT Index and its ETF cousin.

Address:	State Street Bank & Tr, 225 Franklin St, Boston MA 02210, 866-787-2257
Web Address:	www.advisors.ssga.com
Inception:	04-23-01 *
Advisor:	SSgA Funds Management Inc

Management Fee:	0.25%		
Expense Projections:	3Yr:$81	5Yr:$141	10Yr:$320
Income Distrib:	Quarterly		
Exchange:	AMEX		

MORNINGSTAR® ETFs 150

Technology SPDR XLK

	Market Price	Mstar Category
	$23.60	Specialty-Technology

Morningstar Fair Value

Price/Fair Value Ratio	Coverage Rate %
0.84 Undervalued	99 Good

Management

State Street Global Advisors serves as advisor to the trust. Michael Feehily, head of U.S. Equity in SSgA's global structured products group, and John Tucker, head of SSgA's ETF management effort, lead a team that runs all of SSgA's ETFs. They both have 15 years or more of experience at SSgA.

Methodology

This fund contains all the technology companies in the S&P 500 Index, which screens its components for profitability, industry leadership, and certain trading criteria. The index is limited to U.S. companies, which eliminates some big international technology players, including Nokia. The fund holds 90 stocks, giving it some diversification, but it keeps one third of its assets in its top five stocks. S&P's index committee controls which stocks are included in the broader S&P 500, but Merrill Lynch Pierce Fenner & Smith decides what stocks belong here.

Morningstar Rating	Return	Risk	Yield	NAV	Avg Daily Vol. (k)	52 wk High/Low
★★★ Neutral	Neutral	Below Avg	0.8%	$23.28	1,676	$23.81 - $19.00

Growth of $10,000
- Investment Value of ETF
- Investment Value of Index S&P 500

Trading Volume Millions

	1997	1998	1999	2000	2001	2002	2003	2004	2005	2006	History
	—	32.64	54.19	31.32	24.13	14.82	20.47	21.12	20.92	23.28	NAV $
	—	32.62	53.88	31.31	24.00	14.80	20.38	21.11	20.90	23.26	Market Price $
	—	-3.37*	66.03	-42.20	-22.96	-38.42	39.08	5.26	-0.26	12.12	NAV Return%
	—	-3.39*	65.18	-41.89	-23.35	-38.17	38.68	5.65	-0.32	12.15	Market Price Return%
	—	-0.06	-0.05	0.02	0.09	-0.04	-0.07	0.00	-0.05	0.00	Avg Premium/Discount%
	—	-3.37	44.99	-33.10	-11.07	-16.32	10.40	-5.62	-5.17	-3.67	NAV Rtrn% +/-S&P 500
	—	-3.37	-50.37	-25.98	-7.37	-5.09	-13.06	-6.47	-7.62	7.44	NAV Rtrn% +/-ArcaEx Tech 100
	—	—	1	1	4	8	8	8	9	14	NAV Return% Rank in Cat
	—	—	0.00	0.00	0.00	0.17	0.95	2.04	0.70	0.85	Income Return %
	—	—	66.03	-42.20	-22.96	-38.59	38.13	3.22	-0.96	11.27	Capital Return %
	0.00	0.00	0.00	0.00	0.00	0.04	0.14	0.42	0.15	0.18	Income $
	0.00	0.00	0.00	0.00	0.00	0.00	0.00	0.00	0.00	0.00	Capital Gains $
	—	—	—	0.56	0.42	0.28	0.27	0.28	0.26	0.26	Expense Ratio %
	—	—	—	-0.15	-0.16	-0.05	0.12	0.65	0.68	2.33	Income Ratio %
	—	—	—	21	24	11	18	10	3	8	Turnover Rate %
	—	—	—	—	—	972	1,101	1,236	1,541	2,018	Net Assets $mil

Performance 12-31-06

Historic Quarterly NAV Returns

	1st Qtr	2nd Qtr	3rd Qtr	4th Qtr	Total
2002	-9.90	-26.95	-25.44	25.50	-38.42
2003	-3.24	18.76	7.18	12.92	39.08
2004	-1.22	2.12	-7.46	12.76	5.26
2005	-7.52	2.01	4.86	0.82	-0.26
2006	5.81	-8.36	8.65	6.43	12.12

Trailing	NAV Return%	Market Return%	NAV Rtrn% +/-S&P 500	%Rank Cat.(NAV)
3 Mo	6.43	6.33	-0.27	18
6 Mo	15.64	15.30	2.90	18
1 Yr	12.12	12.15	-3.67	14
3 Yr Avg	5.59	5.71	-4.85	8
5 Yr Avg	0.16	0.25	-6.03	8
10 Yr Avg	—	—	—	—

Tax Analysis	Tax-Adj Return%	Tax-Cost Ratio
3 Yr (estimated)	5.16	0.41
5 Yr (estimated)	-0.15	0.31
10 Yr (estimated)	—	—

Rating and Risk

Time Period	Morningstar Rtn vs Cat	Morningstar Risk vs Cat	Morningstar Risk-Adj Rating
3 Yr	Avg	Low	★★★
5 Yr	Avg	-Avg	★★★
10 Yr	—	—	—

Other Measures	Standard Index S&P 500	Best Fit Index ArcaEx Tech 100
Alpha	-8.5	-1.7
Beta	1.65	0.89
R-Squared	76	92
Standard Deviation	13.03	
Mean	5.59	
Sharpe Ratio	0.24	

Morningstar's Take by Dan Culloton 12-31-06

Technology Select Sector SPDR has a little surprise.

This large-cap technology fund has its positives. This exchange-traded fund is cheap. Its 0.26% expense ratio is lower than those of all but one rival (Vanguard Information Technology ETF) conventional or exchange-traded fund in the technology category. That gives it a big head start against most of its peers.

The ETF is also ostensibly simple. It tracks an index of tech stocks in the S&P 500. So, it is full of sector bellwethers such as Microsoft and Intel. The offering has one of the highest average market caps in the category, and its focus on established, profitable tech leaders can buoy it when the sector's more speculative denizens falter.

There is more to this ETF than meets the eye, though. A preponderance of large-cap stocks doesn't immunize it from risk. It's very concentrated, with just 90 stocks and about one third of its assets in its top five holdings. It also isn't all tech. It

includes a huge shot of telecommunications stocks, such as AT&T. Indeed, its more than 17% stake in telecom is bigger than any other tech fund's. That was a boon for the ETF in 2006 as service providers like AT&T and BellSouth rallied. But it could leave the fund a step or two behind its contemporaries when telecom stocks are hurting.

By some measures, such as standard deviation, this fund has been less volatile than the typical technology fund. But its record shows it can still pack a wallop. It lost money in 44% of the 93 rolling three-month periods from January 1999 through November 2006. And it fell by double digits in more than half of the down periods.

It's not clear the ETF has compensated investors for its risks. Returns versus the typical conventional fund are mixed. This ETF might work for a low-cost play on giant tech and telecom stocks, but there are other options that do a better job of capturing the return of the broad tech sector, such as Vanguard Information Technology ETF.

Portfolio Analysis 12-31-06

Share change since 11-06 Total Stocks:89	Sector	PE	Tot Ret%	% Assets
⊕ Microsoft Corporation	Software	23.7	15.83	10.85
⊕ Cisco Systems, Inc.	Hardware	28.8	59.64	6.97
⊖ IBM	Hardware	16.8	19.77	6.15
⊕ Intel Corporation	Hardware	20.3	-17.18	4.91
⊕ Hewlett-Packard Company	Hardware	18.9	45.21	4.76
⊕ Verizon Communications	Telecom	16.1	34.88	4.57
⊖ AT&T, Inc.	Telecom	19.2	51.59	4.40
⊕ Google, Inc.	Business	58.6	11.00	4.15
⊖ BellSouth Corporation	Telecom	—	—	3.63
⊕ Apple Computer, Inc.	Hardware	37.4	18.01	3.19
⊕ Oracle Corporation	Software	25.6	40.38	2.89
⊕ Qualcomm, Inc.	Hardware	26.2	-11.32	2.65
⊕ Dell, Inc.	Hardware	17.7	-16.23	2.40
⊖ Sprint Nextel Corporatio	Telecom	29.1	-10.44	2.34
⊖ Motorola, Inc.	Hardware	13.0	-8.17	2.12
⊖ Texas Instruments, Inc.	Hardware	16.8	-9.82	1.81
⊖ eBay, Inc.	Consumer	40.6	-30.43	1.46
⊖ Yahoo, Inc.	Media	32.3	-34.81	1.35
⊕ Corning Inc.	Hardware	25.6	-4.83	1.32
⊖ EMC Corporation	Hardware	30.7	-3.08	1.25

Current Investment Style

Value Blnd Growth — Large/Mid/Small

Market Cap	%
Giant	60.1
Large	27.3
Mid	12.4
Small	0.3
Micro	0.0
Avg $mil:	59,192

Value Measures		Rel Category
Price/Earnings	20.70	0.83
Price/Book	2.81	0.89
Price/Sales	2.33	0.87
Price/Cash Flow	10.40	0.99
Dividend Yield %	1.08	1.71

Growth Measures	%	Rel Category
Long-Term Erngs	12.92	0.85
Book Value	10.47	1.51
Sales	8.63	0.92
Cash Flow	11.20	0.58
Historical Erngs	22.03	0.72

Profitability	%	Rel Category
Return on Equity	21.12	1.24
Return on Assets	11.26	1.18
Net Margin	16.18	1.16

Industry Weightings	% of Stocks	Rel Cat
Software	19.8	0.9
Hardware	21.3	1.9
Networking Eq	10.3	1.4
Semis	13.2	0.7
Semi Equip	1.9	0.4
Comp/Data Sv	7.8	0.8
Telecom	13.6	4.6
Health Care	0.0	0.0
Other	12.3	0.7

Composition

● Cash	0.1	
● Stocks	99.9	
● Bonds	0.0	
● Other	0.0	
● Foreign	0.0	
(% of Stock)		

Address:	c/o State Street Bk&Tr, 225 Franklin St Boston MA 02210 800-843-2639
Web Address:	www.spdrindex.com
Inception:	12-22-98*
Advisor:	SSgA Funds Management Inc

Management Fee:	0.05%		
Expense Projections:	3Yr:$81	5Yr:$141	10Yr:$320
Income Distrib:	Quarterly		
Exchange:	AMEX		

MORNINGSTAR® ETFs 150

Utilities SPDR XLU

	Market Price $36.12	Mstar Category Specialty-Utilities

Morningstar Fair Value

Price/Fair Value Ratio	Coverage Rate %
1.03 Fairly valued	99 Good

Management

State Street Global Advisors serves as advisor to the trust. Michael Feehily, head of U.S. Equity in SSgA's global structured products group; and John Tucker, head of SSgA's ETF management effort, lead a team that runs all of SSgA's ETFs. They both have 15 years or more of experience at SSgA.

Methodology

This exchange-traded fund owns and passively tracks the utilities-sector stocks in the S&P 500 in proportion to their weight in the utilities sector. The fund includes companies providing water, electric, and natural-gas service. S&P's index committee controls what stocks are included in the broader S&P 500, but Merrill Lynch Pierce Fenner & Smith decides what stocks belong here.

Morningstar Rating ★★ Below Avg	Return Below Avg	Risk Above Avg	Yield 3.0%	NAV $36.71	Avg Daily Vol. (k) 2,434	52 wk High/Low $37.31 - $30.21

Growth of $10,000
- Investment Value of ETF
- Investment Value of Index S&P 500

Trading Volume Millions

1997	1998	1999	2000	2001	2002	2003	2004	2005	2006	History
—	30.13	28.18	33.11	27.94	19.21	23.29	27.86	31.44	36.71	NAV $
—	30.23	28.14	33.19	28.03	19.15	23.33	27.85	31.39	36.73	Market Price $
—	6.32*	-3.33	22.02	-13.05	-28.31	25.80	23.86	16.53	20.65	NAV Return%
—	6.26*	-3.79	22.50	-12.99	-28.77	26.44	23.58	16.37	20.93	Market Price Return%
—	0.33	-0.04	0.07	-0.11	0.02	0.11	-0.01	-0.02	0.01	Avg Premium/Discount%
—	6.32	-24.37	31.12	-1.16	-6.21	-2.88	12.98	11.62	4.86	NAV Rtrn% +/-S&P 500
—	6.32	2.69	-28.74	13.22	-4.93	-3.59	-6.38	-8.61	4.02	NAV Rtrn% +/-DOWJNS UTIL
—	—	1	1	2	2	2	2	3	5	NAV Return% Rank in Cat
—	—	2.62	3.26	2.69	3.34	4.21	3.81	3.67	3.61	Income Return %
—	—	-5.95	18.76	-15.74	-31.65	21.59	20.05	12.86	17.04	Capital Return %
—	0.00	0.78	0.91	0.88	0.92	0.80	0.87	1.01	1.12	Income $
—	0.00	0.18	0.25	0.00	0.00	0.00	0.00	0.00	0.00	Capital Gains $
—	—	0.57	0.40	0.29	0.27	0.27	0.27	0.26	—	Expense Ratio %
—	—	2.62	3.45	2.87	3.60	4.02	3.64	3.33	—	Income Ratio %
—	—	39	45	12	57	6	10	4	—	Turnover Rate %
—	—	—	—	—	534	1,284	1,686	1,752	2,982	Net Assets $mil

Performance 12-31-06

Historic Quarterly NAV Returns

	1st Qtr	2nd Qtr	3rd Qtr	4th Qtr	Total
2002	1.13	-12.65	-22.51	4.73	-28.31
2003	-3.26	21.20	-0.54	7.87	25.80
2004	5.07	-1.36	6.64	12.08	23.86
2005	5.36	9.22	7.17	-5.52	16.53
2006	-1.22	5.63	6.04	9.05	20.65

Trailing	NAV Return%	Market Return%	NAV Rtrn% +/-S&P 500	%Rank Cat.(NAV)
3 Mo	9.05	9.04	2.35	7
6 Mo	15.64	15.71	2.90	5
1 Yr	20.65	20.93	4.86	5
3 Yr Avg	20.31	20.26	9.87	2
5 Yr Avg	9.45	9.39	3.26	2
10 Yr Avg	—	—	—	—

Tax Analysis	Tax-Adj Return%	Tax-Cost Ratio
3 Yr (estimated)	18.92	1.16
5 Yr (estimated)	8.06	1.27
10 Yr (estimated)	—	—

Rating and Risk

Time Period	Morningstar Rtn vs Cat	Morningstar Risk vs Cat	Morningstar Risk-Adj Rating
3 Yr	Avg	+Avg	★★★
5 Yr	Avg	+Avg	★★
10 Yr	—	—	—

Other Measures	Standard Index S&P 500	Best Fit Index DOWJNS UTIL
Alpha	13.9	0.0
Beta	0.27	0.84
R-Squared	4	92
Standard Deviation	8.84	
Mean	20.31	
Sharpe Ratio	1.78	

Morningstar's Take by Dan Culloton 12-31-06

The risks of Utilities Select Sector SPDR outweigh the rewards.

This exchange-traded fund succeeds at providing cheap and convenient exposure to large-cap utilities stocks. It tracks a custom-made index of the utilities stocks in the S&P 500 and charges a low price. Its 0.26% expense ratio is one of the cheapest available to retail investors in the utilities category. Only Vanguard Utilities ETF beats it and then only by the narrowest of margins.

Low costs help a great deal, but this ETF still has drawbacks for long-term investors. It remains too narrow and concentrated for most investors. It owns about 30 stocks and packs nearly 60% of its assets in its top holdings. Indeed, more than a third of the fund's money is in three companies: Exelon, Duke Energy, and TXU. So, the ETF is prone to sharp losses in short periods of time. The ETF has lost money in 44% of the 93 rolling three-month periods since its 1998 inception. (Its worst loss among those periods was more than 38% between Sept. 1,

2000, and Nov. 30, 2000.)

Furthermore, many of this fund's holdings are not the highest-quality stocks. On average, the companies in this portfolio have heavier debt burdens and lower returns on equity and assets than the stocks in the average utility fund. A good example is emerging-markets power supplier AES, which carries a big debt load and is at the mercy of emerging-market politics and regulatory systems.

Finally, after three years of strong performance, utility stocks are no bargains. Some of this portfolio's average valuation measures, such as price/prospective earnings, were above the category average and on par with or higher than those of the S&P 500, as of December 2006. According to Morningstar's equity analysts, all of the ETF's holdings were trading at or above their fair values, including TXU, whose stock looks pricey despite slipping in 2006's fourth quarter. This concentrated ETF doesn't seem to offer much potential upside or much of a margin of safety.

Address:	c/o State Street Bk&Tr, 225 Franklin St Boston MA 02210 800-843-2639
Web Address:	www.spdrindex.com
Inception:	12-22-98*
Advisor:	Barclays Global Fund Advisers

Management Fee:	0.05%		
Expense Projections:	3Yr:$81	5Yr:$141	10Yr:$320
Income Distrib:	Quarterly		
Exchange:	AMEX		

Portfolio Analysis 12-31-06

Share change since 11-06 Total Stocks:31	Sector	PE	Tot Ret%	% Assets
⊕ Exelon Corporation	Utilities	—	19.78	9.20
⊖ Duke Energy Corporation	Utilities	14.6	30.15	8.86
⊕ Dominion Resources, Inc.	Utilities	18.3	12.56	6.57
⊕ Southern Company	Utilities	17.8	11.69	6.07
⊕ TXU Corporation	Utilities	13.0	11.19	5.52
⊕ FPL Group	Utilities	17.7	35.49	4.88
⊕ FirstEnergy Corporation	Utilities	16.6	27.31	4.27
⊕ Entergy Corporation	Utilities	19.9	38.40	4.23
⊕ American Electric Power	Utilities	18.6	19.58	3.73
⊕ Public Service Enterpris	Utilities	21.4	5.72	3.71
⊕ PG & E Corporation	Utilities	16.8	31.58	3.66
⊕ Edison International	Utilities	13.5	7.02	3.28
⊕ Sempra Energy	Utilities	10.9	28.10	3.26
⊕ AES Corporation	Utilities	35.0	39.23	3.24
⊕ PPL Corporation	Utilities	15.4	26.06	3.03
⊕ Progress Energy, Inc.	Utilities	16.7	18.07	2.77
⊕ Constellation Energy Gro	Utilities	17.4	22.70	2.75
⊕ Consolidated Edison Comp	Utilities	17.5	9.14	2.74
⊕ Ameren Corporation	Utilities	21.3	10.14	2.46
⊕ Xcel Energy, Inc.	Utilities	17.0	30.53	2.08

Current Investment Style

Value Blnd Growth — Large/Mid/Small

	Market Cap	%
	Giant	0.0
	Large	84.3
	Mid	15.3
	Small	0.4
	Micro	0.0
	Avg $mil: 17,933	

Value Measures		Rel Category
Price/Earnings	17.06	0.97
Price/Book	2.26	1.04
Price/Sales	1.39	1.09
Price/Cash Flow	11.78	1.17
Dividend Yield %	3.06	0.96

Growth Measures	%	Rel Category
Long-Term Erngs	7.40	0.90
Book Value	1.92	0.56
Sales	5.12	1.09
Cash Flow	-14.16	NMF
Historical Erngs	4.39	0.60

Profitability	%	Rel Category
Return on Equity	10.83	0.86
Return on Assets	3.10	0.85
Net Margin	7.95	0.95

Industry Weightings	% of Stocks	Rel Cat
Telecom Srv	0.0	0.0
Electric Utls	93.7	1.5
Nat Gas Utls	6.3	0.7
Wireless Srv	0.0	0.0
Energy	0.0	0.0
Media	0.0	0.0
Network Eq	0.0	0.0
Water	0.0	0.0
Other	0.0	0.0

Composition

● Cash	0.1	
● Stocks	99.9	
● Bonds	0.0	
Other	0.0	
Foreign	0.0	
(% of Stock)		

Vanguard Div Appr ETF VIG

	Market Price	Mstar Category
	$53.86	Large Blend

Morningstar Fair Value

Price/Fair Value Ratio —   Coverage Rate % —

Management

The fund is run by Ryan Ludt, a member of Vanguard's Quantitative Equity Group. He's been with Vanguard for nearly 10 years and has managed equity funds for the family since 2000. He also runs the Vanguard Telecom Services, Vanguard Health Care, and Vanguard Large Cap index funds and ETFs.

Methodology

The fund tracks the Dividend Achievers Select Index, which is a subset of the broad Dividend Achievers Index. Dividend Achievers are stocks that have increased their dividends in each of the last 10 years. The index's author, Mergent, crafted this fund's benchmark specially for Vanguard, applying proprietary screens that weed out nonliquid stocks and companies that don't have good prospects for continued dividend growth from the broad Dividend Achievers universe. The benchmark is a modified market-cap-weighted index that includes more than 200 stocks of mostly large U.S. companies.

Performance 12-31-06

Historic Quarterly NAV Returns

	1st Qtr	2nd Qtr	3rd Qtr	4th Qtr	Total
2002	—	—	—	—	—
2003	—	—	—	—	—
2004	—	—	—	—	—
2005	—	—	—	—	—
2006	—	—	4.93	5.25	—*

Trailing	NAV Return%	Market Return%	NAV Rtrn% +/-S&P 500	%Rank Cat.(NAV)
3 Mo	5.25	5.22	-1.45	44
6 Mo	10.43	10.29	-2.31	38
1 Yr	—	—	—	
3 Yr Avg	—	—	—	
5 Yr Avg	—	—	—	
10 Yr Avg	—	—	—	

Tax Analysis	Tax-Adj Return%	Tax-Cost Ratio
3 Yr (estimated)	—	—
5 Yr (estimated)	—	—
10 Yr (estimated)	—	—

	Morningstar Rating	Return	Risk	Yield	NAV	Avg Daily Vol. (k)	52 wk High/Low
	— Not Rated	Not Rated	—	—	$53.77	21	$54.25 - $47.77

Growth of $10,000
- Investment Value of ETF
- Investment Value of Indox S&P 500

Trading Volume Millions

	1997	1998	1999	2000	2001	2002	2003	2004	2005	2006	History
	—	—	—	—	—	—	—	—	—	53.77	NAV $
	—	—	—	—	—	—	—	—	—	53.80	Market Price $
	—	—	—	—	—	—	—	—	—	8.46*	NAV Return %
	—	—	—	—	—	—	—	—	—	—	Market Price Return%
	—	—	—	—	—	—	—	—	—	0.05	Avg Premium/Discount%
	—	—	—	—	—	—	—	—	—	8.46	NAV Rtrn% +/-S&P 500
	—	—	—	—	—	—	—	—	—	8.46	NAV Rtrn% +/-Russ 1000
	—	—	—	—	—	—	—	—	—	—	NAV Return% Rank in Cat
	—	—	—	—	—	—	—	—	—	—	Income Return %
	—	—	—	—	—	—	—	—	—	—	Capital Return %
	—	—	—	—	—	—	—	—	—	0.53	Income $
	—	—	—	—	—	—	—	—	—	0.00	Capital Gains $
	—	—	—	—	—	—	—	—	—	—	Expense Ratio %
	—	—	—	—	—	—	—	—	—	—	Income Ratio %
	—	—	—	—	—	—	—	—	—	—	Turnover Rate %
	—	—	—	—	—	—	—	—	—	109	Net Assets $mil

Rating and Risk

Time Period	Morningstar Rtn vs Cat	Morningstar Risk vs Cat	Morningstar Risk-Adj Rating
3 Yr	—	—	—
5 Yr	—	—	—
10 Yr	—	—	—

Other Measures	Standard Index S&P 500	Best Fit Index
Alpha	—	—
Beta	—	—
R-Squared	—	—
Standard Deviation	—	
Mean	—	
Sharpe Ratio	—	

Portfolio Analysis 09-30-06

Share change since 06-06 Total Stocks:214

	Sector	PE	Tot Ret%	% Assets
⊕ Johnson & Johnson	Health	17.4	12.44	4.37
⊕ General Electric Company	Ind Mtrls	19.8	9.35	4.17
⊕ Wal-Mart Stores, Inc.	Consumer	16.6	0.13	4.14
⊕ ExxonMobil Corporation	Energy	11.7	39.07	4.14
⊕ Procter & Gamble Company	Goods	24.2	13.36	4.05
⊕ American International G	Financial	17.1	6.05	3.92
⊕ IBM	Hardware	16.8	19.77	3.90
⊕ PepsiCo, Inc.	Goods	21.4	7.86	3.69
⊕ Coca-Cola Company	Goods	21.5	23.10	3.62
⊕ Home Depot, Inc.	Consumer	13.7	1.01	2.62
⊕ Abbott Laboratories	Health	23.6	26.88	2.56
⊕ Eli Lilly & Company	Health	17.4	-5.16	2.21
⊕ United Technologies	Ind Mtrls	17.6	13.65	2.20
⊕ Medtronic, Inc.	Health	23.7	-6.29	1.91
⊕ 3M Company	Ind Mtrls	16.8	2.98	1.91
⊕ McDonald's Corporation	Consumer	19.2	34.63	1.67
⊕ Target Corporation	Consumer	19.1	4.65	1.65
⊕ Freddie Mac	Financial	24.0	7.06	1.56
⊕ Walgreen Company	Consumer	26.7	4.35	1.53
⊕ Caterpillar Inc.	Ind Mtrls	12.0	7.86	1.53

Current Investment Style

Value Blend Growth — Large Mid Small

Market Cap	%
Giant	49.5
Large	34.4
Mid	13.9
Small	2.1
Micro	0.2

Avg $mil: 45,402

Value Measures		Rel Category
Price/Earnings	16.06	0.97
Price/Book	3.11	1.13
Price/Sales	1.56	1.23
Price/Cash Flow	4.50	0.48
Dividend Yield %	1.79	1.00

Growth Measures	%	Rel Category
Long-Term Erngs	11.31	0.98
Book Value	12.64	1.48
Sales	11.31	1.36
Cash Flow	8.44	1.12
Historical Erngs	13.44	0.80

Profitability	%	Rel Category
Return on Equity	22.47	1.17
Return on Assets	11.37	1.18
Net Margin	12.86	1.15

Sector Weightings

	% of Stocks	Rel S&P 500	3 Year High Low
↻ Info	6.79	0.34	
🖰 Software	0.00	0.00	— —
🖥 Hardware	4.34	0.47	— —
🗔 Media	1.55	0.41	— —
📶 Telecom	0.90	0.26	— —
☰ Service	49.94	1.08	
✚ Health	13.07	1.08	— —
🛒 Consumer	14.63	1.91	— —
🗎 Business	2.70	0.64	— —
$ Financial	19.54	0.88	— —
↥ Mfg	43.25	1.28	
🗀 Goods	17.58	2.06	— —
✹ Ind Mtrls	20.74	1.74	— —
⬡ Energy	4.65	0.47	— —
🔌 Utilities	0.28	0.08	— —

Composition

Cash	0.1
Stocks	100.0
Bonds	0.0
Other	0.0
Foreign	0.0
	(% of Stock)

Morningstar's Take by Dan Culloton 12-31-06

More than low costs set this dividend-focused exchange-traded fund apart.

While not cheap for a conventional index fund or ETF, Vanguard Dividend Appreciation ETF's 0.28% expense ratio is lower than all but a few rival dividend-oriented ETFs. Notably this ETF's levy is less than half that of rival PowerShares Dividend Achievers, which tracks a different version of the same index, research firm Mergent's Dividend Achievers Index.

But you don't get the same thing for less here. First, it's closer to a traditional index fund because the ETF's benchmark, the Dividend Achievers Select Index, ranks its constituents by market caps, not their yields or the size of their cash payouts like other dividend ETFs. This means you'll always find the largest-cap companies, rather than those with the highest yields or biggest dividend checks, at the top of the portfolio, which should make it easier for the fund to trade its holdings.

There are other differences. The Dividend Achievers Select Index still focuses on domestic stocks that have increased their total annual payouts for at least 10 consecutive years, but it has been customized for Vanguard. It holds 100 fewer stocks than the broad Dividend Achievers Index due to liquidity screens, which weed out smaller stocks that are harder and more expensive to trade. Other screens that Vanguard considers proprietary exclude large dividend payers such as Citigroup, J.P. Morgan Chase, Verizon, and Altria, which are staples in other dividend funds.

Therein lies this ETFs objective. It doesn't aim to deliver a high yield but rather exposure to businesses that have proven they can steadily increase their dividends. Such stocks are capable of delivering decent long-term appreciation and holding up well in bear markets.

This ETF and its benchmark have short records, but it's an ETF worth watching.

Address:	PO Box 2600
	Valley Forge PA 19482
	866-499-8473
Web Address:	www.vanguard.com
Inception:	04-27-06 *
Advisor:	The Vanguard Group

Management Fee:	0.26%
Expense Projections:	3Yr:$90 5Yr: — 10Yr: —
Income Distrib:	Quarterly
Exchange:	AMEX

MØRNINGSTAR® ETFs 150

Vanguard EmergMkts ETF VWO

Market Price $73.91	**Mstar Category** Diversified Emerging Mkts

Morningstar Fair Value

Price/Fair Value Ratio —   Coverage Rate % —

Management

Vanguard's Duane F. Kelly is manager of this fund. He has been a manager of its identical mutual fund version since that fund's 1994 inception. For much of that time, he worked closely with Gus Sauter, Vanguard's indexing chief.

Methodology

This exchange-traded fund tries to mirror the performance of the MSCI Emerging Markets Index. Prior to August 2006, it tracked a custom-made version of that index. One difference between the two had been that this fund's benchmark excluded Russia, but now Russia is included. The fund does not engage in currency hedging. Vanguard uses fair-value pricing on occasion when it deems it necessary.

Morningstar Rating	Return	Risk	Yield	NAV	Avg Daily Vol. (k)	52 wk High/Low
— Not Rated	— Not Rated	—	1.8%	$76.69	219	$77.90 - $56.31

Growth of $10,000
— Investment Value of ETF
— Investment Value of Index MSCI EAFE

Trading Volume Millions

	1997	1998	1999	2000	2001	2002	2003	2004	2005	2006	History
	—	—	—	—	—	—	—	—	60.40	76.69	NAV $
	—	—	—	—	—	—	—	—	60.88	77.39	Market Price $
	—	—	—	—	—	—	—	—	29.02*	29.23	NAV Return%
	—	—	—	—	—	—	—	—	29.57*	29.36	Market Price Return%
	—	—	—	—	—	—	—	—	0.53	0.56	Avg Premium/Discount%
	—	—	—	—	—	—	—	—	29.02	2.89	NAV Rtrn% +/-MSCI EAFE
	—	—	—	—	—	—	—	—	29.02	0.05	NAV Rtrn% +/-MSCI EmrMkt
	—	—	—	—	—	—	—	—		4	NAV Return% Rank in Cat
	—	—	—	—	—	—	—	—	—	2.22	Income Return %
	—	—	—	—	—	—	—	—	—	27.01	Capital Return %
	—	—	—	—	—	—	—	—	1.08	1.34	Income $
	—	—	—	—	—	—	—	—	0.00	0.00	Capital Gains $
	—	—	—	—	—	—	—	—	0.30	0.30	Expense Ratio %
	—	—	—	—	—	—	—	—	2.59	2.32	Income Ratio %
	—	—	—	—	—	—	—	—	15	26	Turnover Rate %
	—	—	—	—	—	—	—	—	553	2,055	Net Assets $mil

Performance 12-31-06

Historic Quarterly NAV Returns

	1st Qtr	2nd Qtr	3rd Qtr	4th Qtr	Total
2002	—	—	—	—	—
2003	—	—	—	—	—
2004	—	—	—	—	—
2005	—	3.73	17.22	7.15	—*
2006	11.23	-4.54	4.07	16.95	29.23

Trailing	NAV Return%	Market Return%	NAV Rtrn% +/-MSCI EAFE	%Rank Cat.(NAV)
3 Mo	16.95	17.27	6.60	4
6 Mo	21.71	22.52	7.02	4
1 Yr	29.23	29.36	2.89	4
3 Yr Avg	—	—	—	—
5 Yr Avg	—	—	—	—
10 Yr Avg	—	—	—	—

Tax Analysis	Tax-Adj Return%	Tax-Cost Ratio
3 Yr (estimated)	—	—
5 Yr (estimated)	—	—
10 Yr (estimated)	—	—

Rating and Risk

Time Period	Morningstar Rtn vs Cat	Morningstar Risk vs Cat	Morningstar Risk-Adj Rating
3 Yr	—	—	—
5 Yr	—	—	—
10 Yr	—	—	—

Other Measures	Standard Index S&P 500	Best Fit Index
Alpha	—	—
Beta	—	—
R-Squared	—	—
Standard Deviation	—	
Mean	—	
Sharpe Ratio	—	

Portfolio Analysis 09-30-06

Share change since 06-06 Total Stocks:803

	Sector	Country	% Assets
☼ GAZ OAO	Goods	Russia	5.19
⊕ Samsung Electronics	Goods	Korea	3.94
⊕ America Movil S.A. de C.	Telecom	Mexico	1.84
☼ Lukoil ADR	Energy	Russia	1.78
⊖ Taiwan Semiconductor Mfg	Hardware	Taiwan	1.77
⊖ China Mobile	Telecom	Hong Kong	1.77
⊖ Petroleo Brasileiro Sa P	Energy	Brazil	1.41
⊕ Kookmin Bank	Financial	Korea	1.27
⊕ Hon Hai Precision Indust	Hardware	Taiwan	1.22
⊖ Teva Pharmaceutical Indu	Health	Israel	1.21
⊖ Petroleo Brasileiro	Energy	Brazil	1.15
⊖ PetroChina	Energy	Hong Kong	1.03
⊕ CEMEX	Financial	Mexico	0.98
⊖ Sasol Ltd	Energy	South Africa	0.97
⊕ Infosys Technologies Ltd	Software	India	0.89
⊖ Cia Vale Rio Doce	—	Brazil	0.86
⊕ POSCO	Ind Mtrls	Korea	0.82
⊖ Reliance Industries Ltd	Ind Mtrls	India	0.81
☼ Surgutneftegaz	Energy	Russia	0.77
⊖ Bco Itau Hldg F	—	Brazil	0.77

Current Investment Style

Value Blnd Growth — Large / Mid / Small

Market Cap	%
Giant	37.2
Large	35.9
Mid	17.4
Small	9.1
Micro	0.4

Avg $mil: 8,934

Value Measures		Rel Category
Price/Earnings	12.62	0.93
Price/Book	1.93	0.75
Price/Sales	1.02	0.85
Price/Cash Flow	5.52	0.60
Dividend Yield %	3.98	1.04

Growth Measures	%	Rel Category
Long-Term Erngs	14.26	0.96
Book Value	11.56	0.98
Sales	15.16	0.89
Cash Flow	11.00	0.87
Historical Erngs	16.31	0.64

Composition

Cash	0.4	Bonds	0.3
Stocks	94.1	Other	5.1
Foreign (% of Stock)			99.5

Sector Weightings	% of Stocks	Rel MSCI EAFE	3 Year High	Low
↻ Info	21.19	1.79		
🖥 Software	1.58	2.82	2	2
💾 Hardware	7.57	1.96	10	5
🎬 Media	1.28	0.70	2	1
📞 Telecom	10.76	1.93	13	11
☞ Service	30.33	0.64		
🏥 Health	2.36	0.33	4	2
🛒 Consumer	3.87	0.78	4	3
🏢 Business	4.96	0.98	6	4
💲 Financial	19.14	0.64	21	16
🏭 Mfg	48.47	1.18		
🏗 Goods	18.39	1.40	18	14
⚙ Ind Mtrls	16.08	1.04	24	16
🔋 Energy	11.16	1.56	11	8
💡 Utilities	2.84	0.54	3	2

Regional Exposure	% Stock		
UK/W. Europe	0	N. America	0
Japan	0	Latn America	18
Asia X Japan	55	Other	27

Country Exposure	% Stock		
South Korea	18	Hong Kong	9
Taiwan	14	South Africa	8
Russia	11		

Morningstar's Take by Gregg Wolper 12-31-06

Vanguard Emerging Markets Stock ETF has become more inclusive, which has both pros and cons.

Rather than following MSCI's standard emerging markets index, this exchange-traded vehicle, along with its much older mutual fund version, had been tracking a custom-made version that excluded countries in which trading was difficult. Over time, as those markets matured--at least in terms of trading--more were added, until only one major difference between the two indexes remained: Russia. Then, in August 2006, Vanguard announced it would dispense with the customized benchmark, and this fund would simply track the actual MSCI Emerging Markets Index. So Russia is now included in the fund.

This is not a trivial change. In the past few years, Russia's market has soared in market capitalization, powered by strong prices in energy and global investors' search for new destinations. Thus, the fund's Russian stake went from 0% in June 2006 to 10% at the end of September. It's now the fund's third-biggest country weighting. Energy giant Gazprom is the number-one holding.

So is this fund more appealing now? That depends on what you're looking for. Its new benchmark is a more accurate reflection of the way most active emerging-markets managers invest these days; Russian companies have become common in such portfolios. Excluding Russia made this fund an odd duck.

However, Russia is also more volatile than some more mature emerging markets, and its heavy energy focus makes it vulnerable to declines in those commodities' prices. As a cheap, straightforward choice for broad emerging-markets exposure, this fund still has appeal. But it does also carry new risks--on top of the risks it already carried as an emerging-markets play at a time when such markets already have enjoyed a long and powerful rally.

Address:	PO Box 2600 Valley Forge PA 19482 866-499-8473	Management Fee:	0.17%
		Expense Projections:	3Yr:$97 5Yr:$169 10Yr:$381
Web Address:	www.vanguard.com	Income Distrib:	Annually
Inception:	03-10-05*	Exchange:	AMEX
Advisor:	The Vanguard Group, Inc.		

Vanguard Energy ETF VDE

Market Price $79.88	**Mstar Category** Specialty-Natural Res

Morningstar Fair Value

Price/Fair Value Ratio	Coverage Rate %
1.04 Fairly valued	92 Good

Management

Corey Holeman is a member of Vanguard's indexing team, which has a strong record of closely tracking benchmarks.

Methodology

This ETF is tethered to the MSCI US Investable Market Energy Index, a market-cap-weighted index that focuses on firms involved in the U.S. energy sector, including those in exploration and production, oil service, natural gas, and coal. The fund invests across the market-cap spectrum, but it is dominated by major U.S. oil firms. It does not have exposure to energy firms headquartered overseas.

Morningstar Rating — Not Rated	Return — Not Rated	Risk — Not Rated	Yield 1.1%	NAV $84.94	Avg Daily Vol. (k) 40	52 wk High/Low $90.50 - $72.00

Growth of $10,000
- Investment Value of ETF
- Investment Value of Index S&P 500

Trading Volume Millions

	1997	1998	1999	2000	2001	2002	2003	2004	2005	2006	History
	—	—	—	—	—	—	—	52.39	72.16	84.94	NAV $
	—	—	—	—	—	—	—	52.41	72.19	85.01	Market Price $
	—	—	—	—	—	—	—	27.89*	39.05	18.98	NAV Return%
	—	—	—	—	—	—	—	27.97*	39.05	19.03	Market Price Return%
	—	—	—	—	—	—	—	0.02	0.01	0.04	Avg Premium/Discount%
	—	—	—	—	—	—	—	27.89	34.14	3.19	NAV Rtrn% +/-S&P 500
	—	—	—	—	—	—	—	27.89	2.57	2.16	NAV Rtrn% +/-GS NATR RES
	—	—	—	—	—	—	—	—	6	9	NAV Return% Rank in Cat
	—	—	—	—	—	—	—	—	1.34	1.29	Income Return %
	—	—	—	—	—	—	—	—	37.71	17.69	Capital Return %
	—	—	—	—	—	—	—	0.22	0.70	0.93	Income $
	—	—	—	—	—	—	—	0.00	0.00	0.00	Capital Gains $
	—	—	—	—	—	—	—	—	0.26	0.25	Expense Ratio %
	—	—	—	—	—	—	—	—	1.97	1.23	Income Ratio %
	—	—	—	—	—	—	—	—	16	21	Turnover Rate %
	—	—	—	—	—	—	—	31	209	391	Net Assets $mil

Performance 12-31-06

Historic Quarterly NAV Returns

	1st Qtr	2nd Qtr	3rd Qtr	4th Qtr	Total
2002	—	—	—	—	—
2003	—	—	—	—	—
2004	—	—	—	4.34	—*
2005	17.43	3.61	21.57	-5.99	39.05
2006	8.84	4.34	-4.99	10.27	18.98

Trailing	NAV Return%	Market Return%	NAV Rtrn% +/-S&P 500	%Rank Cat.(NAV)
3 Mo	10.27	10.31	3.57	21
6 Mo	4.77	4.79	-7.97	18
1 Yr	18.98	19.03	3.19	9
3 Yr Avg	—	—	—	—
5 Yr Avg	—	—	—	—
10 Yr Avg	—	—	—	—

Tax Analysis	Tax-Adj Return%	Tax-Cost Ratio
3 Yr (estimated)	—	—
5 Yr (estimated)	—	—
10 Yr (estimated)	—	—

Rating and Risk

Time Period	Morningstar Rtn vs Cat	Morningstar Risk vs Cat	Morningstar Risk-Adj Rating
3 Yr	—	—	—
5 Yr	—	—	—
10 Yr	—	—	—

Other Measures	Standard Index S&P 500	Best Fit Index
Alpha	—	—
Beta	—	—
R-Squared	—	—
Standard Deviation	—	
Mean	—	
Sharpe Ratio	—	

Portfolio Analysis 09-30-06

Share change since 06-06 Total Stocks:147	Sector	PE	Tot Ret%	% Assets
⊕ ExxonMobil Corporation	Energy	11.7	39.07	22.26
⊕ Chevron Corporation	Energy	9.3	33.75	11.90
⊕ ConocoPhillips	Energy	6.9	26.53	7.94
⊕ Schlumberger, Ltd.	Energy	24.0	31.07	6.64
⊕ Occidental Petroleum Cor	Energy	8.6	24.32	3.12
⊕ Valero Energy Corporatio	Energy	6.5	-0.33	2.41
⊕ Halliburton Company	Energy	12.0	1.11	2.22
⊕ Marathon Oil Corporation	Energy	6.5	54.68	2.13
⊕ Devon Energy Corporation	Energy	9.4	8.06	2.03
⊕ Transocean, Inc.	Energy	29.3	16.07	1.82
⊕ Baker Hughes Inc.	Energy	10.8	23.67	1.78
⊕ Apache Corporation	Energy	7.9	-2.30	1.60
⊕ Anadarko Petroleum Corp.	Energy	5.5	-7.44	1.50
⊕ EOG Resources	Energy	10.1	-14.62	1.23
⊕ XTO Energy, Inc.	Energy	9.2	12.16	1.14
⊕ Weatherford Internationa	Energy	16.9	16.56	1.13
⊕ Williams Companies, Inc.	Energy	65.3	14.41	1.12
⊕ GlobalSantaFe Corporatio	Energy	17.2	24.06	0.93
⊕ Chesapeake Energy Corp.	Energy	6.3	-7.74	0.91
⊕ Kinder Morgan, Inc.	Energy	20.7	19.22	0.89

Current Investment Style

Value Blnd Growth — Large/Mid/Small

Market Cap	%
Giant	48.8
Large	26.8
Mid	17.8
Small	5.9
Micro	0.7

Avg $mil: 40,788

Value Measures		Rel Category
Price/Earnings	9.95	0.80
Price/Book	2.28	0.89
Price/Sales	0.86	0.63
Price/Cash Flow	5.93	0.82
Dividend Yield %	1.42	1.27

Growth Measures	%	Rel Category
Long-Term Erngs	11.13	0.77
Book Value	18.58	1.34
Sales	23.69	1.46
Cash Flow	29.96	1.00
Historical Erngs	51.21	1.02

Profitability	%	Rel Category
Return on Equity	26.01	1.12
Return on Assets	13.00	1.18
Net Margin	14.72	1.00

Industry Weightings	% of Stocks	Rel Cat
Oil & Gas	58.2	1.9
Oil/Gas Products	11.6	1.1
Oil & Gas Srv	24.1	0.8
Pipelines	3.0	2.9
Utilities	0.0	0.0
Hard Commd	0.1	0.0
Soft Commd	0.0	0.0
Misc. Indstrl	0.2	0.0
Other	2.8	0.3

Composition

Cash	0.0	
Stocks	100.0	
Bonds	0.0	
Other	0.0	
Foreign	0.0	(% of Stock)

Morningstar's Take by Sonya Morris 12-31-06

Don't be tempted to chase Vanguard Energy ETF's high-octane returns.

Since this ETF's launch two years ago, it has generated sizable double-digit gains. But even with those impressive results, its performance is only about middling for a natural-resources fund. Because it dedicates most of its assets to industry giants like ExxonMobil and Chevron, this fund hasn't done quite as well as competing offerings with more exposure to smaller industry players, which have benefited the most from rising commodity prices and the increased pace of exploration.

Still, just because this fund keeps the bulk of its assets in financially solid industry leaders, it can't be considered a tame option by any stretch of the imagination. Energy stocks can be extremely volatile, and even the largest names in the sector aren't immune to the turbulence that comes with the territory. For example, from April through June 2002, ExxonMobil plunged more than 26%.

And if you're thinking the fund's diversification will help blunt the blow of a downturn in any single stock, think again. Just because this fund holds over 150 individual equities doesn't mean it diversifies its risk. Its top 10 holdings soak up more than 60% of assets, and ExxonMobil and Chevron combined consume more than 30% of the portfolio. If any of these top holdings tank, this fund would likely follow suit.

Finally, given energy stocks' strong multiyear rally, the stocks in this ETF's portfolio don't look particularly cheap. In fact, nine of the fund's top 10 holdings are trading at or above their fair values, according to Morningstar stock analysts.

We think this fund's risks outweigh its potential rewards, particularly at present. Furthermore, investors who own a diversified core fund probably already have plenty of exposure to the vast majority of the stocks in this fund's portfolio. In short, we think investors should take a pass on this offering.

Address:	PO Box 2600, Valley Forge PA 19482
	866-499-8473
Web Address:	www.vanguard.com
Inception:	09-29-04 *
Advisor:	Vanguard Advisers, Inc.

Management Fee:	0.22%
Expense Projections:	3Yr:$84 5Yr:$146 10Yr:$331
Income Distrib:	Annually
Exchange:	AMEX

MORNINGSTAR® ETFs 150

Vanguard Euro Stk ETF VGK

	Market Price $67.02	Mstar Category Europe Stock

Morningstar Fair Value

Price/Fair Value Ratio — Coverage Rate % —

Management

Vanguard's index-tracking quantitative-equity group manages this offering. Duane Kelly oversees this fund on a day-to-day basis. Former manager Gus Sauter, now the company's chief investment officer, is still involved in an oversight capacity.

Methodology

This exchange-traded fund is designed to mirror the performance of the MSCI Europe Index, a capitalization-weighted benchmark of the region's largest markets and stocks. The portfolio is dominated by familiar global leaders such as BP, Nestle, and Novartis, but the large number of holdings dilutes exposure to individual names. The fund has a fair amount of mid-cap exposure but does not own stocks from Central or Eastern Europe. Vanguard does not hedge foreign currency exposure.

Morningstar Rating	Return	Risk	Yield	NAV	Avg Daily Vol. (k)	52 wk High/Low
— Not Rated	Not Rated	—	2.7%	$67.54	220	$69.90 - $53.82

Growth of $10,000
— Investment Value of ETF
— Investment Value of Index MSCI EAFE

Trading Volume Millions

	1997	1998	1999	2000	2001	2002	2003	2004	2005	2006	History
	—	—	—	—	—	—	—	—	52.05	67.54	NAV $
	—	—	—	—	—	—	—	—	52.60	68.16	Market Price $
	—	—	—	—	—	—	—	—	20.71*	33.26	NAV Return%
	—	—	—	—	—	—	—	—	20.96*	33.06	Market Price Return%
	—	—	—	—	—	—	—	—	0.54	0.66	Avg Premium/Discount%
	—	—	—	—	—	—	—	—	20.71	6.92	NAV Rtrn% +/-MSCI EAFE
	—	—	—	—	—	—	—	—	20.71	-0.46	NAV Rtrn% +/-MSCI Eur
	—	—	—	—	—	—	—	—	—	16	NAV Return% Rank in Cat
	—	—	—	—	—	—	—	—	—	3.48	Income Return %
	—	—	—	—	—	—	—	—	—	29.78	Capital Return %
	—	—	—	—	—	—	—	—	1.38	1.81	Income $
	—	—	—	—	—	—	—	—	0.00	0.00	Capital Gains $
	—	—	—	—	—	—	—	—	0.18	0.18	Expense Ratio %
	—	—	—	—	—	—	—	—	2.93	3.44	Income Ratio %
	—	—	—	—	—	—	—	—	5	6	Turnover Rate %
	—	—	—	—	—	—	—	—	277	1,507	Net Assets $mil

Performance 12-31-06

Historic Quarterly NAV Returns

	1st Qtr	2nd Qtr	3rd Qtr	4th Qtr	Total
2002	—	—	—	—	—
2003	—	—	—	—	—
2004	—	—	—	—	—
2005	—	-1.10	8.18	1.78	—*
2006	10.61	2.69	5.72	10.98	33.26

Trailing	NAV Return%	Market Return%+/-MSCI EAFE	NAV Rtrn% +/-MSCI EAFE	%Rank Cat.(NAV)
3 Mo	10.98	10.90	0.63	19
6 Mo	17.32	16.98	2.63	19
1 Yr	33.26	33.06	6.92	16
3 Yr Avg	—	—	—	—
5 Yr Avg	—	—	—	—
10 Yr Avg	—	—	—	—

Tax Analysis	Tax-Adj Return%	Tax-Cost Ratio
3 Yr (estimated)	—	—
5 Yr (estimated)	—	—
10 Yr (estimated)	—	—

Rating and Risk

Time Period	Morningstar Rtn vs Cat	Morningstar Risk vs Cat	Morningstar Risk-Adj Rating
3 Yr	—	—	—
5 Yr	—	—	—
10 Yr	—	—	—

Other Measures

	Standard Index S&P 500	Best Fit Index
Alpha	—	—
Beta	—	—
R-Squared	—	—
Standard Deviation	—	
Mean	—	
Sharpe Ratio	—	

Portfolio Analysis 09-30-06

Share change since 06-06 Total Stocks:598	Sector	Country	% Assets
⊕ HSBC Hldgs	Financial	U.K.	2.61
⊕ BP	Energy	U.K.	2.54
⊕ GlaxoSmithKline	Health	U.K.	1.93
⊕ Total SA	Energy	France	1.81
⊕ Nestle	Goods	Switzerland	1.75
⊕ Novartis	Health	Switzerland	1.69
⊕ Royal Dutch Shell	Energy	U.K.	1.58
⊕ UBS AG	Financial	Switzerland	1.54
⊕ Roche Holding	Health	Switzerland	1.51
⊖ Vodafone Grp	Telecom	U.K.	1.39
⊕ Royal Bank Of Scotland G	Financial	U.K.	1.37
⊕ AstraZeneca	Health	U.K.	1.22
⊕ Banco Santander Central	Financial	Spain	1.17
⊕ Royal Dutch Shell	Energy	U.K.	1.17
⊕ Sanofi-Synthelabo	Health	France	1.13
⊕ BNP Paribas	Financial	France	1.12
⊕ ING Groep	Financial	Netherlands	1.03
⊕ Barclays	Financial	U.K.	1.02
⊕ Nokia	Hardware	Finland	1.01
⊕ BBVA	Financial	Spain	0.98

Current Investment Style

Value Blnd Growth — Large/Mid/Small

	Market Cap	%
	Giant	56.5
	Large	29.8
	Mid	13.2
	Small	0.5
	Micro	0.0

Avg $mil: 37,478

Value Measures		Rel Category
Price/Earnings	12.93	0.95
Price/Book	2.21	0.99
Price/Sales	1.03	0.91
Price/Cash Flow	7.94	0.94
Dividend Yield %	3.60	1.04

Growth Measures	%	Rel Category
Long-Term Erngs	11.34	1.02
Book Value	6.68	0.78
Sales	6.46	0.85
Cash Flow	5.28	1.97
Historical Erngs	20.76	0.92

Composition

Cash	0.6	Bonds	0.0
Stocks	97.6	Other	1.7
Foreign	(% of Stock)		100.0

Sector Weightings

	% of Stocks	Rel MSCI EAFE	3 Year High	Low
↻ Info	12.73	1.08		
▣ Software	0.67	1.20	1	0
▣ Hardware	3.48	0.90	4	3
▣ Media	2.33	1.27	3	2
▣ Telecom	6.25	1.12	10	6
⊆ Service	49.10	1.04		
▣ Health	9.20	1.29	11	9
▣ Consumer	5.00	1.01	5	4
▣ Business	3.98	0.79	4	4
▣ Financial	30.92	1.03	31	25
↻ Mfg	38.17	0.93		
▣ Goods	10.64	0.81	12	11
▣ Ind Mtrls	11.96	0.78	12	9
▣ Energy	10.44	1.46	13	10
▣ Utilities	5.13	0.98	5	4

Regional Exposure

	% Stock		
UK/W. Europe	100	N. America	0
Japan	0	Latn America	0
Asia X Japan	0	Other	0

Country Exposure

	% Stock		
U.K.	36	Germany	10
France	14	Italy	6
Switzerland	11		

Morningstar's Take by Dan Lefkovitz 12-31-06

Even if Vanguard European Stock ETF can't keep up its current pace, it's still the best Europe ETF for the long run.

This exchange-traded fund continues to soar. While countries like China and India capture all the headlines, European markets have quietly posted years of stellar gains. The MSCI Europe Index, which this fund tracks, has climbed on the back of low interest rates, corporate restructuring, merger and acquisition activity, and, perhaps most importantly, strong companies benefiting from global growth. European currencies have also been appreciating. That has translated into gains for U.S. investors who bought this fund with dollars. In dollar terms, the fund has gained nearly 32% for the trailing one-year period through Dec. 15, 2006. Vanguard European Stock, the older, traditional mutual fund of which it is a share class, has recorded an average annual gain of 22% for the trailing three years.

Investors shouldn't get too accustomed to these sorts of numbers. This fund is bound to cool off eventually, whether because of rising interest rates, valuations, or currency effects.

That said, for investors looking for a Europe fund· koop in mind that most broad foreign funds devote two thirds of assets to Europe--this fund is a long-term winner. It provides very broad-based exposure to Western Europe, with diversification by market cap, geography, and sector. This gives it a leg up over single-country funds such as iShares MSCI Austria Index, geographically limited funds such as iShares MSCI EMU Index, and the mega-cap-dominated streetTRACKS Dow Jones Euro Stoxx 50, BLDRS Europe 100 ADR Index, and iShares S&P Europe 350 Index. It is also cheaper than all its rivals, and fees are a key predictor of long-term success.

It's true that over the past five years, Vanguard European Stock Index has lagged narrow offerings that focus on Eastern Europe or small-cap stocks. But that trend can only last so long.

Address:	PO Box 2600 Valley Forge PA 19482 866-499-8473	Management Fee:	0.14%
		Expense Projections:	3Yr:$58 5Yr:$101 10Yr:$230
Web Address:	www.vanguard.com	Income Distrib:	Annually
Inception:	03-10-05*	Exchange:	AMEX
Advisor:	The Vanguard Group, Inc.		

MORNINGSTAR® ETFs 150

Vanguard ExMkt ETF VXF

	Market Price	Mstar Category
	$101.58	Mid-Cap Blend

Morningstar Fair Value

Price/Fair Value Ratio	Coverage Rate %
0.98 Fairly valued	61 Poor

Management

Vanguard's indexing guru, Gus Sauter, will take on a supportive role at this offering. He recently handed over day-to-day managerial responsibilities to Donald Butler, who has been with Vanguard since 1992 and has worked with Sauter on this offering since 1997.

Methodology

This ETF tracks the S&P Completion Index. The benchmark owns companies not included in the S&P 500. It makes a good fit next to a fund tracking that well-known index, as it relies on the same committee-based approach and also screens for profitable companies.

Morningstar Rating	Return	Risk	Yield	NAV	Avg Daily Vol. (k)	52 wk High/Low
★★★★ Above Avg	Above Avg	Average	1.4%	$102.06	17	$104.86 - $88.85

Growth of $10,000

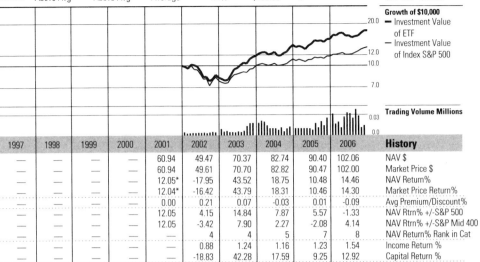
— Investment Value of ETF
— Investment Value of Index S&P 500

Trading Volume Millions

	1997	1998	1999	2000	2001	2002	2003	2004	2005	2006	History
	—	—	—	—	60.94	49.47	70.37	82.74	90.40	102.06	NAV $
	—	—	—	—	60.94	49.61	70.70	82.82	90.47	102.00	Market Price $
	—	—	—	—	12.05*	-17.95	43.52	18.75	10.48	14.46	NAV Return%
	—	—	—	—	12.04*	-16.42	43.79	18.31	10.46	14.30	Market Price Return%
	—	—	—	—	0.00	0.21	0.07	-0.03	0.01	-0.09	Avg Premium/Discount%
	—	—	—	—	12.05	4.15	14.84	7.87	5.57	-1.33	NAV Rtrn% +/-S&P 500
	—	—	—	—	12.05	-3.42	7.90	2.27	-2.08	4.14	NAV Rtrn% +/-S&P Mid 400
	—	—	—	—	—	4	4	5	7	8	NAV Return% Rank in Cat
	—	—	—	—	—	0.88	1.24	1.16	1.23	1.54	Income Return %
	—	—	—	—	—	-18.83	42.28	17.59	9.25	12.92	Capital Return %
	—	—	—	—	0.00	0.54	0.61	0.81	1.02	1.39	Income $
	—	—	—	—	0.00	0.00	0.00	0.00	0.00	0.00	Capital Gains $
	—	—	—	—	—	0.20	0.20	0.20	0.08	—	Expense Ratio %
	—	—	—	—	—	1.04	1.07	1.12	1.29	—	Income Ratio %
	—	—	—	—	20	17	8	17	27	—	Turnover Rate %
	—	—	—	—	—	107	231	368	409		Net Assets $mil

Performance 12-31-06

Historic Quarterly NAV Returns

	1st Qtr	2nd Qtr	3rd Qtr	4th Qtr	Total
2002	1.94	-10.00	-15.51	5.84	-17.95
2003	-3.32	21.33	7.55	13.76	43.52
2004	5.93	0.12	-1.82	14.05	18.75
2005	-3.28	5.52	5.47	2.63	10.48
2006	9.83	-3.89	-0.28	8.74	14.46

Trailing	NAV Return%	Market Return%	NAV Rtrn% +/-S&P 500	%Rank Cat.(NAV)
3 Mo	8.74	8.79	2.04	10
6 Mo	8.43	8.44	-4.31	9
1 Yr	14.46	14.30	-1.33	8
3 Yr Avg	14.51	14.31	4.07	5
5 Yr Avg	12.08	12.06	5.89	4
10 Yr Avg	—	—	—	—

Tax Analysis	Tax-Adj Return%	Tax-Cost Ratio
3 Yr (estimated)	14.26	0.22
5 Yr (estimated)	11.79	0.26
10 Yr (estimated)	—	—

Rating and Risk

Time Period	Morningstar Rtn vs Cat	Morningstar Risk vs Cat	Morningstar Risk-Adj Rating
3 Yr	+Avg	+Avg	★★★★
5 Yr	+Avg	Avg	★★★★
10 Yr	—	—	—

Other Measures	Standard Index S&P 500	Best Fit Index DJ Wilshire 4500
Alpha	0.7	-0.6
Beta	1.48	1.02
R-Squared	79	100
Standard Deviation	11.40	
Mean	14.51	
Sharpe Ratio	0.97	

Morningstar's Take by Marta Norton 12-31-06

Vanguard Extended Market Index ETF is a cheap and effective way to tap the mid- and small-cap markets.

This exchange-traded fund is still the cheapest of its kind. A price war between its cousin, Vanguard Extended Market Index, and close competitor Fidelity Spartan Extended Market Index blunted Vanguard's expense edge in the open-end universe, but at 0.08%, rivals will find it much harder to rob this ETF of its low-cost status. And because even slightly lower fees can have a big impact in the indexing world, its miniscule expense ratio has been the fund's greatest weapon. Since its late 2001 inception, it has edged past Vanguard's open-end share class and the conventional Fidelity index fund. (Don't forget, however, that frequent trading, or even dollar-cost averaging, can increase costs, as ETF investors must pay commissions to buy and sell.)

This ETF has other advantages beyond its attractive price tag. In 2005 it switched its benchmark from the Dow Jones Wilshire 4500 Index to the S&P Completion Index. That didn't mean dramatic changes, as its new index still owns domestic stocks not included in the S&P 500 Index. But investors wanting a cheaply constructed, well-diversified portfolio may have an easier time keeping things under the same roof by pairing this ETF with Vanguard 500 Index. All Standard & Poor's indexes rely on the same committee-governed approach. Further, because S&P screens out unprofitable companies, the fund theoretically should have a higher-quality bent than it historically has had. That may help correct some of the volatility issues it has had in years past, and may also mean steadier returns than those of Fidelity's conventional offering, which still tracks the Dow Jones Wilshire 4500 Index.

We think this cheap, well-diversified ETF can get the job done. Investors interested in mid- and small-cap exposure should consider it a viable option.

Address:	PO Box 2600 Valley Forge PA 19482 866-499-8473
Web Address:	www.vanguard.com
Inception:	12-27-01 *
Advisor:	Vanguard Advisers, Inc.

Management Fee:	0.06%		
Expense Projections:	3Yr:$26	5Yr:$45	10Yr:$103
Income Distrib:	Annually		
Exchange:	AMEX		

Portfolio Analysis 09-30-06

Share change since 06-06   Total Stocks:3383

	Sector	PE	Tot Ret%	% Assets
⊕ Genentech, Inc.	Health	47.2	-12.29	1.26
⊕ American Tower Corporati	Telecom	—	37.56	0.51
⊕ Celgene Corporation	Health	—	77.56	0.50
⊕ DirecTV, Inc.	Media	27.1	76.63	0.50
⊕ Host Hotels & Resorts, I	Financial	53.4	33.95	0.39
⊕ GlobalSantaFe Corporatio	Energy	17.2	24.06	0.39
⊕ NYSE Group	Financial	—	94.40	0.38
⊕ General Growth Propertie	Financial	—	15.09	0.38
⊖ Cognizant Technology Sol	Business	52.1	53.49	0.34
⊖ Peabody Energy Corporati	Energy	18.4	-1.48	0.32
⊕ NII Holdings, Inc.	Telecom	47.0	47.53	0.32
⊕ Expeditors International	Business	32.9	20.54	0.31
⊕ Las Vegas Sands, Inc.	Consumer	72.8	126.70	0.31
⊖ AvalonBay Communities, I	Financial	67.7	49.69	0.30
⊖ Precision Castparts Corp	Ind Mtrls	24.0	51.40	0.29
⊖ Noble Energy, Inc.	Energy	11.9	22.48	0.26
⊖ Akamai Technologies, Inc	Software	26.0	166.53	0.26
⊖ CH Robinson Worldwide, I	Business	28.4	11.88	0.25
⊖ Kraft Foods, Inc.	Goods	18.4	30.52	0.25
⊖ Ultra Petroleum Corporat	Energy	30.6	-14.44	0.24

Current Investment Style

Value Blnd Growth — Large Mid Small

Market Cap	%
Giant	1.5
Large	4.1
Mid	52.3
Small	31.0
Micro	11.0

Avg $mil: 2,127

Value Measures		Rel Category
Price/Earnings	16.94	1.02
Price/Book	2.21	0.86
Price/Sales	1.12	1.00
Price/Cash Flow	7.40	0.81
Dividend Yield %	1.23	0.90

Growth Measures	%	Rel Category
Long-Term Erngs	13.62	1.12
Book Value	6.06	0.83
Sales	7.23	1.03
Cash Flow	12.14	1.23
Historical Erngs	16.00	0.83

Profitability	%	Rel Category
Return on Equity	12.65	0.74
Return on Assets	6.74	0.79
Net Margin	10.58	1.00

Sector Weightings	% of Stocks	Rel S&P 500	3 Year High	Low
↗ Info	15.51	0.78		
Software	3.76	1.09	4	3
Hardware	6.50	0.70	8	6
Media	2.76	0.73	6	3
Telecom	2.49	0.71	2	1
⌒ Service	56.15	1.22		
Health	12.15	1.01	12	11
Consumer	9.65	1.26	12	9
Business	11.17	2.64	12	8
Financial	23.18	1.04	27	23
⊡ Mfg	28.33	0.84		
Goods	5.25	0.61	7	5
Ind Mtrls	11.18	0.94	12	8
Energy	7.81	0.80	9	5
Utilities	4.09	1.17	4	3

Composition

	%
● Cash	0.2
● Stocks	99.8
● Bonds	0.0
○ Other	0.0
Foreign	0.0
(% of Stock)	

MORNINGSTAR® ETFs 150

Vanguard Financial ETF VFH

Market Price $64.98	**Mstar Category** Specialty-Financial

Morningstar Fair Value

Price/Fair Value Ratio	Coverage Rate %
0.91 Undervalued	90 Good

Management

Vanguard chief investment officer George Sauter and a team of quantitative analysts have managed this offering since its 2003 inception. The team manages many of index funds, including other sector funds and the widely held Vanguard 500 Index. They closely follow each fund's designated benchmark.

Methodology

This portfolio includes all of the financials stocks included in the MSCI US Investable Market 2500 Index, which represents 98% of the capitalization of the U.S. equity market. That turns out to be more than 540 financial companies, ranging from global financial-services firms to tiny community banks. The fund is market-cap-weighted, so the market's biggest players have larger positions in the portfolio. About one quarter of the fund's assets are in mid- and small-cap stocks.

Morningstar Rating	Return	Risk	Yield	NAV	Avg Daily Vol. (k)
— Not Rated	Not Rated	—	2.0%	$65.33	21

52 wk High/Low $65.92 - $55.76

Growth of $10,000
- Investment Value of ETF
- Investment Value of Index S&P 500

Trading Volume Millions

	1997	1998	1999	2000	2001	2002	2003	2004	2005	2006	History
	—	—	—	—	—	—	—	53.75	55.95	65.33	NAV $
	—	—	—	—	—	—	—	53.81	56.01	65.50	Market Price $
	—	—	—	—	—	—	—	11.28*	5.53	19.25	NAV Return%
	—	—	—	—	—	—	—	11.38*	5.53	19.43	Market Price Return%
	—	—	—	—	—	—	—	0.03	-0.02	0.09	Avg Premium/Discount%
	—	—	—	—	—	—	—	11.28	0.62	3.46	NAV Rtrn% +/-S&P 500
	—	—	—	—	—	—	—	11.28	-0.93	-0.17	NAV Rtrn% +/-DJ Finance
	—	—	—	—	—	—	—	—	5	9	NAV Return% Rank in Cat
	—	—	—	—	—	—	—	—	1.40	2.32	Income Return %
	—	—	—	—	—	—	—	—	4.13	16.93	Capital Return %
	—	—	—	—	—	—	—	1.15	0.75	1.29	Income $
	—	—	—	—	—	—	—	0.00	0.00	0.00	Capital Gains $
	—	—	—	—	—	—	—	0.28	0.26	0.25	Expense Ratio %
	—	—	—	—	—	—	—	2.38	2.61	2.52	Income Ratio %
	—	—	—	—	—	—	—	9	6	6	Turnover Rate %
	—	—	—	—	—	—	—	27	62	209	Net Assets $mil

Performance 12-31-06

Historic Quarterly NAV Returns

	1st Qtr	2nd Qtr	3rd Qtr	4th Qtr	Total
2002	—	—	—	—	—
2003	—	—	—	—	—
2004	—	-2.53	1.37	8.95	—*
2005	-6.60	5.33	0.23	7.04	5.53
2006	4.52	-0.50	7.14	7.03	19.25

Trailing	NAV Return%	Market Return%	NAV Rtrn% +/-S&P 500	%Rank Cat.(NAV)
3 Mo	7.03	7.23	0.33	14
6 Mo	14.66	14.88	1.92	13
1 Yr	19.25	19.43	3.46	9
3 Yr Avg	—	—	—	—
5 Yr Avg	—	—	—	—
10 Yr Avg	—	—	—	—

Tax Analysis	Tax-Adj Return%	Tax-Cost Ratio
3 Yr (estimated)	—	—
5 Yr (estimated)	—	—
10 Yr (estimated)	—	—

Rating and Risk

Time Period	Morningstar Rtn vs Cat	Morningstar Risk vs Cat	Morningstar Risk-Adj Rating
3 Yr	—	—	—
5 Yr	—	—	—
10 Yr	—	—	—

Other Measures	Standard Index S&P 500	Best Fit Index
Alpha	—	—
Beta	—	—
R-Squared	—	—
Standard Deviation	—	
Mean	—	
Sharpe Ratio	—	

Portfolio Analysis 09-30-06

Share change since 06-06 Total Stocks:549	Sector	PE	Tot Ret%	% Assets
⊕ Citigroup, Inc.	Financial	13.3	19.55	7.40
⊕ Bank of America Corporat	Financial	12.4	20.68	7.32
⊕ J.P. Morgan Chase & Co.	Financial	13.7	25.60	4.89
⊕ American International G	Financial	17.1	6.05	4.38
⊕ Wells Fargo Company	Financial	14.7	16.82	3.46
⊕ Wachovia Corporation	Financial	13.0	12.02	2.74
⊕ Morgan Stanley	Financial	12.3	45.93	2.11
⊕ Merrill Lynch & Company,	Financial	14.1	39.27	2.05
⊕ Goldman Sachs Group, Inc	Financial	12.1	57.41	1.98
⊕ American Express Company	Financial	21.2	19.09	1.86
⊕ US Bancorp	Financial	14.1	26.29	1.77
⊕ Fannie Mae	Financial	—	24.34	1.62
⊕ Freddie Mac	Financial	24.0	7.06	1.37
⊕ Metropolitan Life Insura	Financial	15.8	21.67	1.29
⊕ Washington Mutual, Inc.	Financial	13.5	9.62	1.25
⊕ Allstate Corporation	Financial	8.7	23.38	1.14
⊕ Prudential Financial, In	Financial	16.1	18.70	1.12
⊕ Lehman Brothers Holdings	Financial	12.2	22.74	1.01
⊕ St. Paul Travelers Compa	Financial	12.0	22.90	0.98
⊕ Berkshire Hathaway Inc.	Financial	13.5	24.89	0.81

Current Investment Style

Value Blnd Growth — Large Mid Small

Market Cap	%
Giant	42.9
Large	31.7
Mid	18.5
Small	6.0
Micro	0.9

Avg $mil: 29,647

Value Measures		Rel Category
Price/Earnings	12.76	0.94
Price/Book	1.99	0.97
Price/Sales	2.34	0.90
Price/Cash Flow	3.13	0.40
Dividend Yield %	2.77	1.20

Growth Measures	%	Rel Category
Long-Term Erngs	10.61	0.99
Book Value	6.71	0.83
Sales	7.30	0.95
Cash Flow	35.91	7.72
Historical Erngs	13.11	0.86

Profitability	%	Rel Category
Return on Equity	15.23	0.96
Return on Assets	14.75	1.07
Net Margin	21.62	1.01

Industry Weightings	% of Stocks	Rel Cat
Intl Banks	22.7	1.3
Banks	19.0	0.9
Real Estate	10.8	3.5
Sec Mgmt	12.4	1.0
S & Ls	3.9	0.6
Prop & Reins	13.3	0.8
Life Ins	5.7	1.1
Misc. Ins	3.1	1.0
Other	9.2	0.7

Composition

● Cash	0.5	
● Stocks	99.5	
● Bonds	0.0	
○ Other	0.0	
Foreign	0.1	(% of Stock)

Morningstar's Take by Andrew Gunter 12-31-06

Vanguard Financials ETF competes well, but investors still probably don't need it.

Among a handful of niche ETFs indexed to financial-services companies, this one certainly holds its own. In charging an expense ratio of just 0.28% annually, it nicely follows Vanguard's tradition of low-cost offerings. In contrast, several financial-services category ETFs from iShares all carry expense ratios of 0.48% per year. Additionally, this fund's diversification differentiates it from the equally cheap Financials Select Sector SPDR from State Street Global Advisors. State Street's ETF indexes a subset of financial institutions found in the large-cap-only S&P 500 Index, whereas Vanguard's ETF also tracks many small- and mid-sized names in its 550-plus-company bogy, the MSCI Investable Market Financials Index.

That's not to say, however, that this fund should be used as a core holding. Though it indexes a broader set of financials stocks, nearly 75% of fund assets are tied to large- and mega-cap institutions such as Citigroup and its few conglomerate peers. During times when these financial heavyweights underperform the broader market, returns here will suffer with the rest of the category. The fund also serves little purpose as a diversification tool, since most investors' large-cap mutual funds already hold hefty exposure to financial institutions.

Still, we think this fund holds some merit as an opportunistic sector play. While its index lacks exposure to some global banks based outside the U.S., such as HSBC or Mitsubishi UFJ, it is an adequate proxy for the broad U.S. financials market. Should these stocks fall deeply out of favor, investors wishing to bet on their comeback with a small portion of assets will find this to be a useful ETF.

All told, this ETF beats its financial-services category rivals on a number of measures. Investors must use it wisely, however, and in small doses.

Address:	PO Box 2600, Valley Forge PA 19482, 866-499-8473
Web Address:	www.vanguard.com
Inception:	01-26-04*
Advisor:	Vanguard Advisers, Inc.

Management Fee:	0.15%		
Expense Projections:	3Yr:$90	5Yr:$157	10Yr:$356
Income Distrib:	Quarterly		
Exchange:	AMEX		

Vanguard Growth ETF VUG

	Market Price $58.11	Mstar Category Large Growth

Morningstar Fair Value

Price/Fair Value Ratio	Coverage Rate %
0.88 Undervalued	95 Good

Management

In April 2005, Gerard O'Reilly assumed control of this offering, replacing longtime manager Gus Sauter. O'Reilly, who has been with Vanguard since 1992, also manages Vanguard REIT Index and Vanguard Total Stock Market Index.

Methodology

This exchange-traded fund, or ETF, is tethered to the MSCI U.S. Prime Market Growth Index, which contains the 750 largest companies--in terms of free-float market capitalization--in the U.S. MSCI defines style (growth versus value) using an eight-factor model that includes measures ranging from dividend yield to long-term historical sales per share. MSCI employs buffer zones to limit the migration of stocks between the growth and value camps. This should serve to limit turnover.

Morningstar Rating	Return	Risk	Yield	NAV	Avg Daily Vol. (k)	52 wk High/Low
— Not Rated	Not Rated	—	0.9%	$57.85	221	$58.72 - $50.42

Growth of $10,000
- Investment Value of ETF
- Investment Value of Index S&P 500

Trading Volume Millions

1997	1998	1999	2000	2001	2002	2003	2004	2005	2006	History
—	—	—	—	—	—	—	51.33	53.52	57.85	NAV $
—	—	—	—	—	—	—	51.40	53.50	57.86	Market Price $
—	—	—	—	—	—	—	5.75*	5.20	9.13	NAV Return%
—	—	—	—	—	—	—	5.76*	5.02	9.19	Market Price Return%
—	—	—	—	—	—	—	0.14	0.14	0.03	Avg Premium/Discount%
—	—	—	—	—	—	—	5.75	0.29	-6.66	NAV Rtrn% +/-S&P 500
—	—	—	—	—	—	—	5.75	-0.06	0.06	NAV Rtrn% +/-Russ 1000Gr
—	—	—	—	—	—	—	—	10	13	NAV Return% Rank in Cat
—	—	—	—	—	—	—	—	0.90	0.99	Income Return %
—	—	—	—	—	—	—	—	4.30	8.14	Capital Return %
—	—	—	—	—	—	—	0.61	0.46	0.53	Income $
—	—	—	—	—	—	—	0.00	0.00	0.00	Capital Gains $
—	—	—	—	—	—	—	0.15	0.11	—	Expense Ratio %
—	—	—	—	—	—	—	1.22	0.86	—	Income Ratio %
—	—	—	—	—	—	—	24	23	—	Turnover Rate %
—	—	—	—	—	—	—	104	324	1,336	Net Assets $mil

Performance 12-31-06

Historic Quarterly NAV Returns

	1st Qtr	2nd Qtr	3rd Qtr	4th Qtr	Total
2002	—	—	—	—	—
2003	—	—	—	—	—
2004	—	1.51	-4.85	9.41	—*
2005	-3.53	2.17	3.58	3.05	5.20
2006	3.34	-3.92	3.83	5.87	9.13

Trailing	NAV Return%	Market Return%	NAV Rtrn% +/-S&P 500	%Rank Cat.(NAV)
3 Mo	5.87	5.81	-0.83	15
6 Mo	9.92	9.75	-2.82	15
1 Yr	9.13	9.19	-6.66	13
3 Yr Avg	—	—	—	—
5 Yr Avg	—	—	—	—
10 Yr Avg	—	—	—	—

Tax Analysis	Tax-Adj Return%	Tax-Cost Ratio
3 Yr (estimated)	—	—
5 Yr (estimated)	—	—
10 Yr (estimated)	—	—

Rating and Risk

Time Period	Morningstar Rtn vs Cat	Morningstar Risk vs Cat	Morningstar Risk-Adj Rating
3 Yr	—	—	—
5 Yr	—	—	—
10 Yr	—	—	—

Other Measures	Standard Index S&P 500	Best Fit Index
Alpha	—	—
Beta	—	—
R-Squared	—	—
Standard Deviation	—	
Mean	—	
Sharpe Ratio	—	

Morningstar's Take by Reginald Laing 12-31-06

Vanguard Growth ETF makes a fine long-term holding, and now may be a good time to buy it.

This exchange-traded fund tracks the MSCI U.S. Prime Market Growth Index--a good representation of the large-growth universe. Thus, it gives you exposure to all the mid- to mega-cap stocks that fit MSCI's criteria for growth, and it does so for the very reasonable expense ratio of 0.11%.

Now may be an opportune time to buy this index offering, too, as this ETF and the large-growth universe it approximates have been down-and-out for so long relative to the broader market. For the trailing five years through Dec. 27, 2006, this fund's older, open-end share class delivered a 3.2% annualized gain. That outpaced the 2.8% return of the typical large-growth fund, but it's well shy of the 14% return of the average small-value fund, its stylistic opposite. Morningstar's equity analysts estimate that nine out of this index's top 10 holdings are presently trading at discounts to their fair value--with retailer Wal-Mart and biotech firm

Amgen trading at steep discounts. That means these stocks might have some upside potential (though they could stay undervalued, too) and is another measure of this ETF's potential attractiveness.

If market leadership rotates back to large-growth stocks--and it's bound to happen eventually--it will be a boon to this ETF. That's because style-specific indexes generally look best (not only relative to the market, but to their category) when the portion of the Morningstar Style Box they represent leads all others. When that happens, this ETF--which is almost fully invested in large-growth and charges far less than its typical peer--will have a chance to stand out.

There are other reasons beyond a potentially bright immediate future to own this ETF, though. It's a good long-term holding. Low costs, attentive management, broad diversification, and high tax efficiency give it enduring appeal for those looking for growth exposure.

Portfolio Analysis 09-30-06

Share change since 06-06 Total Stocks:421

	Sector	PE	Tot Ret%	% Assets
⊖ Microsoft Corporation	Software	23.7	15.83	3.84
⊕ Procter & Gamble Company	Goods	24.2	13.36	3.22
⊕ Johnson & Johnson	Health	17.4	12.44	3.05
⊕ Cisco Systems, Inc.	Hardware	28.8	59.64	2.22
⊕ Wal-Mart Stores, Inc.	Consumer	16.6	0.13	1.95
⊕ Intel Corporation	Hardware	20.3	-17.18	1.90
⊕ PepsiCo, Inc.	Goods	21.4	7.86	1.71
⊕ American International G	Financial	17.1	6.05	1.51
⊕ Google, Inc.	Business	58.6	11.00	1.37
⊕ Amgen, Inc.	Health	28.0	-13.38	1.34
⊕ Oracle Corporation	Software	25.6	40.38	1.20
⊖ Home Depot, Inc.	Consumer	13.7	1.01	1.19
⊕ Schlumberger, Ltd.	Energy	24.0	31.07	1.16
⊕ UnitedHealth Group, Inc.	Health	21.0	-13.49	1.05
⊕ Goldman Sachs Group, Inc	Financial	12.1	57.41	1.04
⊕ Apple Computer, Inc.	Hardware	37.4	18.01	1.04
⊕ Walt Disney Company	Media	20.9	44.26	1.02
⊕ IBM	Hardware	16.8	19.77	1.01
⊕ American Express Company	Financial	21.2	19.09	0.99
⊕ Motorola, Inc.	Hardware	13.0	-8.17	0.98

Current Investment Style

Value Blnd Growth — Large Mid Small

Market Cap	%
Giant	42.6
Large	40.0
Mid	17.4
Small	0.0
Micro	0.0

Avg $mil: 35,871

Value Measures		Rel Category
Price/Earnings	18.91	0.91
Price/Book	3.22	0.98
Price/Sales	1.71	0.97
Price/Cash Flow	11.62	1.04
Dividend Yield %	0.97	1.13

Growth Measures	%	Rel Category
Long-Term Erngs	14.45	0.97
Book Value	11.70	1.46
Sales	11.78	1.00
Cash Flow	15.00	1.03
Historical Erngs	22.94	0.81

Profitability	%	Rel Category
Return on Equity	21.82	1.08
Return on Assets	11.25	1.13
Net Margin	13.41	1.07

Sector Weightings	% of Stocks	Rel S&P 500	3 Year High Low	
⟳ Info	30.75	1.54		
Software	7.00	2.03	8	6
Hardware	16.55	1.79	21	16
Media	5.63	1.49	6	4
Telecom	1.57	0.45	2	1
⟲ Service	46.20	1.00		
Health	17.19	1.43	22	17
Consumer	12.43	1.62	14	12
Business	7.89	1.87	9	6
Financial	8.69	0.39	10	6
⟰ Mfg	23.05	0.68		
Goods	8.33	0.97	11	8
Ind Mtrls	8.67	0.73	10	3
Energy	5.73	0.58	7	2
Utilities	0.32	0.09	1	0

Composition

		%
● Cash		0.0
● Stocks		100.0
● Bonds		0.0
○ Other		0.0
	Foreign	0.0
	(% of Stock)	

Address:	PO Box 2600 Valley Forge PA 19482 866-499-8473	Management Fee:	0.09%		
		Expense Projections:	3Yr:$35	5Yr:$62	10Yr:$141
		Income Distrib:	Quarterly		
Web Address:	www.vanguard.com	Exchange:	AMEX		
Inception:	01-26-04*				
Advisor:	Vanguard Advisers, Inc.				

MORNINGSTAR® ETFs 150

Vanguard HealthCar ETF VHT

Market Price $57.26	**Mstar Category** Specialty-Health	

Morningstar Fair Value

Price/Fair Value Ratio	Coverage Rate %
0.93 Undervalued	91 Good

Management

Gus Sauter has been at the helm of this offering since its January 2004 inception. Sauter is a highly capable, experienced index fund manager who also runs Vanguard 500 Index among other index funds.

Methodology

This exchange-traded fund tracks the MSCI U.S. Investable Market Health Care Index. Large-cap drug names dominate the benchmark, though biotechnology, medical-equipment, and health-care services stocks play supporting roles. The ETF is concentrated in its largest holdings, with more than half of its assets in its top 10. Given the MSCI index's domestic focus, the fund has no international exposure.

Morningstar Rating Not Rated	**Return** Not Rated	**Risk** —	**Yield** 1.1%	**NAV** $56.96	**Avg Daily Vol. (k)** 56		

52 wk High/Low $57.97 - $50.97

Growth of $10,000
— Investment Value of ETF
— Investment Value of Index S&P 500

Trading Volume Millions

History

	1997	1998	1999	2000	2001	2002	2003	2004	2005	2006	
	—	—	—	—	—	—	—	50.24	54.00	56.96	NAV $
	—	—	—	—	—	—	—	50.28	54.02	56.94	Market Price $
	—	—	—	—	—	—	—	4.89*	8.24	6.62	NAV Return%
	—	—	—	—	—	—	—	4.88*	8.20	6.54	Market Price Return%
	—	—	—	—	—	—	—	0.07	0.06	0.03	Avg Premium/Discount%
	—	—	—	—	—	—	—	4.89	3.33	-9.17	NAV Rtrn% +/-S&P 500
	—	—	—	—	—	—	—	4.89	-0.08	-0.26	NAV Rtrn% +/-DJ Hlthcare
	—	—	—	—	—	—	—	—	5	7	NAV Return% Rank in Cat
	—	—	—	—	—	—	—	—	0.77	1.14	Income Return %
	—	—	—	—	—	—	—	—	7.47	5.48	Capital Return %
	—	—	—	—	—	—	—	0.13	0.39	0.62	Income $
	—	—	—	—	—	—	—	0.00	0.00	0.00	Capital Gains $
	—	—	—	—	—	—	—	0.28	0.26	0.25	Expense Ratio %
	—	—	—	—	—	—	—	1.09	1.13	1.15	Income Ratio %
	—	—	—	—	—	—	—	8	9	11	Turnover Rate %
	—	—	—	—	—	—	—	55	238	342	Net Assets $mil

Performance 12-31-06

Historic Quarterly NAV Returns

	1st Qtr	2nd Qtr	3rd Qtr	4th Qtr	Total
2002	—	—	—	—	—
2003	—	—	—	—	—
2004	—	2.62	-5.60	6.30	—*
2005	-0.86	5.14	2.21	1.59	8.24
2006	2.07	-5.13	8.26	1.70	6.62

Trailing	NAV Return%	Market Return%	NAV Rtrn% +/-S&P 500	%Rank Cat.(NAV)
3 Mo	1.70	1.63	-5.00	14
6 Mo	10.11	9.94	-2.63	13
1 Yr	6.62	6.54	-9.17	7
3 Yr Avg	—	—	—	—
5 Yr Avg	—	—	—	—
10 Yr Avg	—	—	—	—

Tax Analysis	Tax-Adj Return%	Tax-Cost Ratio
3 Yr (estimated)	—	—
5 Yr (estimated)	—	—
10 Yr (estimated)	—	—

Rating and Risk

Time Period	Morningstar Rtn vs Cat	Morningstar Risk vs Cat	Morningstar Risk-Adj Rating
3 Yr	—	—	—
5 Yr	—	—	—
10 Yr	—	—	—

Other Measures	Standard Index S&P 500	Best Fit Index
Alpha	—	—
Beta	—	—
R-Squared	—	—
Standard Deviation	—	
Mean	—	
Sharpe Ratio	—	

Morningstar's Take by Christopher Davis 12-31-06

Vanguard Health Care ETF is cheap, but that's not enough.

If you're looking for low-cost exposure to health-care stocks, this exchange-traded fund is about as cheap as they come. The fund's 0.26% annual expense ratio ranks among the health-care group's lowest. With the average no-load health care offering charging 1.90% per year, the fund's built-in edge over the competition is formidable.

To be sure, the fund boasts some advantages over other health-care ETFs in addition to low costs. For one, it's less concentrated in large-cap stocks. Its $29.9 billion average market cap is roughly half that of ETF rival iShares S&P Global Healthcare Sector, for instance. Moreover, the fund is better diversified across health-care subsectors. The iShares offering is more dependent upon pharmaceutical stocks and keeps a scant 7% of assets in biotech stocks. This fund's stake, by contrast, weighs in at 17%.

While comparing favorably in the ETF arena, the fund suffers from some big shortcomings. Its market cap is less than other ETFs', but it still clocks in at 70% above the health-care category average. And at 42% of assets, its weighting in drug stocks is well above the category norm. That means the fund will fare well when large caps and pharma lead the way, but that makes it less suited to make a broad bet on the health-care sector. Finally, because the fund's bogy includes only U.S.-based firms, it has no exposure to major foreign drug companies like AstraZeneca and Novartis. With the health-care industry becoming increasingly global, that's a major flaw.

We'd be a little more sanguine on the fund if its holdings were especially attractive, but that's not the case. Morningstar's equity analysts think most of the fund's top stocks are fairly valued. That suggests the potential for outsized gains is limited.

All told, you can do without this offering.

Address:	PO Box 2600 Valley Forge PA 19482 866-499-8473	
Web Address:	www.vanguard.com	
Inception:	01-26-04 *	
Advisor:	Vanguard Advisers, Inc.	

Management Fee:	0.20%		
Expense Projections:	3Yr:$90	5Yr:$157	10Yr:$356
Income Distrib:	Annually		
Exchange:	AMEX		

Portfolio Analysis 09-30-06

Share change since 06-06 Total Stocks:276	Sector	PE	Tot Ret%	% Assets
⊕ Pfizer Inc.	Health	15.1	15.22	11.15
⊕ Johnson & Johnson	Health	17.4	12.44	10.33
⊕ Merck & Co., Inc.	Health	18.8	42.66	4.91
⊕ Amgen, Inc.	Health	28.0	-13.38	4.53
⊕ Abbott Laboratories	Health	23.6	26.88	3.99
⊕ Wyeth	Health	17.0	12.88	3.67
⊕ UnitedHealth Group, Inc.	Health	21.0	-13.49	3.57
⊕ Eli Lilly & Company	Health	17.4	-5.16	3.11
⊕ Medtronic, Inc.	Health	23.7	-6.29	3.01
⊕ WellPoint, Inc.	Health	17.2	-1.38	2.70
⊕ Bristol-Myers Squibb Com	Health	23.3	19.93	2.62
⊕ Genentech, Inc.	Health	47.2	-12.29	2.10
⊕ Schering-Plough Corporat	Health	36.9	14.63	1.76
⊕ Gilead Sciences, Inc.	Health	41.1	23.51	1.70
⊕ Baxter International Inc	Health	24.0	24.81	1.60
⊕ Cardinal Health, Inc.	Health	20.9	-5.81	1.48
⊕ Caremark RX, Inc.	Health	23.8	10.89	1.35
⊕ Aetna, Inc.	Health	14.6	-8.34	1.20
⊕ Hca	Health	—	—	0.98
⊕ Medco Health Solutions,	Health	28.3	-4.23	0.98

Current Investment Style

Value Blnd Growth — Large Mid Small

Market Cap	%
Giant	50.4
Large	27.5
Mid	15.7
Small	5.6
Micro	0.9

Avg $mil: 32,824

Value Measures		Rel Category
Price/Earnings	19.14	0.93
Price/Book	3.39	0.96
Price/Sales	1.79	0.60
Price/Cash Flow	14.62	1.00
Dividend Yield %	1.31	1.30

Growth Measures	%	Rel Category
Long-Term Erngs	12.38	0.87
Book Value	11.08	1.39
Sales	9.97	0.83
Cash Flow	5.32	0.47
Historical Erngs	10.42	0.70

Profitability	%	Rel Category
Return on Equity	18.02	1.27
Return on Assets	8.94	1.54
Net Margin	13.92	1.23

Industry Weightings	% of Stocks	Rel Cat
Biotech	15.2	0.5
Drugs	47.7	1.5
Mgd Care	13.1	1.2
Hospitals	1.3	1.1
Other HC Srv	1.4	0.9
Diagnostics	1.5	1.1
Equipment	14.8	1.1
Good/Srv	4.0	1.1
Other	1.1	0.4

Composition

● Cash	0.0	
● Stocks	100.0	
● Bonds	0.0	
Other	0.0	
Foreign	0.0	
(% of Stock)		

Vanguard InfoTech ETF VGT

	Market Price $53.54	Mstar Category Specialty-Technology

Morningstar Fair Value

Price/Fair Value Ratio	Coverage Rate %
0.83 Undervalued	93 Good

Management

Michael Perre has run this since its 2004 inception. He's been with Vanguard since 1990 and has managed the equity portion of Vanguard Tax-Managed Balanced since 1999.

Methodology

This ETF tracks the MSCI U.S. Investable Information Technology Index, a subset of the market-cap-weighted MSCI U.S. Investable Market 2500 Index. The MSCI IT Index holds more than 400 stocks in the software, hardware, semiconductor, IT consulting, Internet, data processing, and outsourcing industries. The fund takes a more diversified approach than many tech portfolios, but it's still pretty concentrated.

Morningstar Rating	Return	Risk	Yield	NAV	Avg Daily Vol. (k)	52 wk High/Low
— Not Rated	Not Rated	Not Rated	0.3%	$52.50	36	$54.13 - $42.60

Growth of $10,000
— Investment Value of ETF
— Investment Value of Index S&P 500

14.8
11.0
10.0
8.0

Trading Volume Millions
0.04
0.0

	1997	1998	1999	2000	2001	2002	2003	2004	2005	2006	History
	—	—	—	—	—	—	—	47.04	48.31	52.50	NAV $
	—	—	—	—	—	—	—	47.06	48.38	52.53	Market Price $
	—	—	—	—	—	—	—	1.67*	2.89	8.95	NAV Return%
	—	—	—	—	—	—	—	1.69*	2.99	8.86	Market Price Return%
	—	—	—	—	—	—	—	0.11	0.00	0.03	Avg Premium/Discount%
	—	—	—	—	—	—	—	1.67	-2.02	-6.84	NAV Rtrn% +/-S&P 500
	—	—	—	—	—	—	—	1.67	-4.47	4.27	NAV Rtrn% +/-ArcaEx Tech 100
	—	—	—	—	—	—	—	—	9	14	NAV Return% Rank in Cat
	—	—	—	—	—	—	—	—	0.19	0.28	Income Return %
	—	—	—	—	—	—	—	—	2.70	8.67	Capital Return %
	—	—	—	—	—	—	—	0.61	0.09	0.14	Income $
	—	—	—	—	—	—	—	0.00	0.00	0.00	Capital Gains $
	—	—	—	—	—	—	—	0.28	0.26	0.25	Expense Ratio %
	—	—	—	—	—	—	—	0.12	1.28	0.36	Income Ratio %
	—	—	—	—	—	—	—	9	7	8	Turnover Rate %
	—	—	—	—	—	—	—	19	106	247	Net Assets $mil

Performance 12-31-06

Historic Quarterly NAV Returns

	1st Qtr	2nd Qtr	3rd Qtr	4th Qtr	Total
2002	—	—	—	—	—
2003	—	—	—	—	—
2004	—	1.41	-10.56	14.08	—*
2005	-7.63	1.96	6.34	2.74	2.89
2006	5.28	-9.34	7.31	6.38	8.95

Trailing	NAV Return%	Market Return%	NAV Rtrn% +/-S&P 500	%Rank Cat.(NAV)
3 Mo	6.38	6.50	-0.32	18
6 Mo	14.15	13.92	1.41	18
1 Yr	8.95	8.86	-6.84	14
3 Yr Avg	—	—	—	—
5 Yr Avg	—	—	—	—
10 Yr Avg	—	—	—	—

Tax Analysis	Tax-Adj Return%	Tax-Cost Ratio
3 Yr (estimated)	—	—
5 Yr (estimated)	—	—
10 Yr (estimated)	—	—

Rating and Risk

Time Period	Morningstar Rtn vs Cat	Morningstar Risk vs Cat	Morningstar Risk-Adj Rating
3 Yr	—	—	—
5 Yr	—	—	—
10 Yr	—	—	—

Other Measures	Standard Index S&P 500	Best Fit Index
Alpha	—	—
Beta	—	—
R-Squared	—	—
Standard Deviation	—	
Mean	—	
Sharpe Ratio	—	

Portfolio Analysis 09-30-06

Share change since 06-06 Total Stocks:394	Sector	PE	Tot Ret%	% Assets
⊕ Microsoft Corporation	Software	23.7	15.83	10.61
⊕ Cisco Systems, Inc.	Hardware	28.8	59.64	6.15
⊕ IBM	Hardware	16.8	19.77	5.56
⊕ Intel Corporation	Hardware	20.3	-17.18	5.24
⊕ Hewlett-Packard Company	Hardware	18.9	45.21	4.48
⊕ Google, Inc.	Business	58.6	11.00	3.78
⊕ Oracle Corporation	Software	25.6	40.38	3.32
⊕ Apple Computer, Inc.	Hardware	37.4	18.01	2.87
⊕ Motorola, Inc.	Hardware	13.0	-8.17	2.70
⊕ Qualcomm, Inc.	Hardware	26.2	-11.32	2.67
⊕ Texas Instruments, Inc.	Hardware	16.8	-9.82	2.27
⊕ Dell, Inc.	Hardware	17.7	-16.23	2.19
⊕ Corning Inc.	Hardware	25.6	-4.83	1.67
⊕ First Data Corporation	Business	12.3	9.88	1.41
⊕ Yahoo, Inc.	Media	32.3	-34.81	1.40
⊕ eBay, Inc.	Consumer	40.6	-30.43	1.31
⊕ EMC Corporation	Hardware	30.7	-3.08	1.24
⊕ Automatic Data Processin	Business	25.1	9.11	1.20
⊖ Applied Materials	Hardware	19.0	3.89	1.08
⊕ Adobe Systems Inc.	Software	49.0	11.26	0.98

Current Investment Style

Value Blnd Growth — Large / Mid / Small

	Market Cap	%
	Giant	49.9
	Large	22.7
	Mid	19.5
	Small	6.9
	Micro	1.0
	Avg $mil:	31,013

Industry Weightings	% of Stocks	Rel Cat
Software	23.1	1.1
Hardware	21.3	1.9
Networking Eq	10.0	1.3
Semis	16.2	0.9
Semi Equip	2.9	0.6
Comp/Data Sv	9.5	1.0
Telecom	0.3	0.1
Health Care	0.1	0.0
Other	16.5	0.9

Value Measures		Rel Category
Price/Earnings	21.28	0.85
Price/Book	3.52	1.11
Price/Sales	2.20	0.82
Price/Cash Flow	10.90	1.04
Dividend Yield %	0.64	1.02

Growth Measures	%	Rel Category
Long-Term Erngs	14.48	0.96
Book Value	5.38	0.77
Sales	8.84	0.94
Cash Flow	14.75	0.76
Historical Erngs	21.39	0.70

Profitability	%	Rel Category
Return on Equity	20.52	1.21
Return on Assets	11.24	1.18
Net Margin	16.10	1.16

Composition

	%
● Cash	0.1
● Stocks	99.9
● Bonds	0.0
○ Other	0.0
Foreign	0.3
(% of Stock)	

Morningstar's Take by Dan Culloton 12-31-06

Vanguard Information Technology ETF may be the best of a volatile lot.

This ETF is a sector fund, so it comes with all the attendant perils. It's focused on just a few industries, so there isn't anywhere to hide when its stocks are out of favor. It's concentrated with nearly half of its assets in its top 10 holdings. So, it can lose money in a hurry; the fund has fallen in value in about a third of the 31 rolling three-month periods since its inception.

Still, this ETF has redeeming characteristics, namely, strong management, low costs, and broad diversification. Michael Perre, a member of Vanguard's quantitative equity team, has done a good job tracking this fund's benchmark, the MSCI U.S. Investible Information Technology Index. Its annualized returns since inception trailed the index by less than the ETF's expense ratio through the end of November 2006.

This fund's expense hurdle also is lower than those of its peers. Its levy dropped in 2006 one hundredth of a percent to 0.25%, solidifying its place as one of the cheapest tech funds, exchange-traded or otherwise, that retail investors can buy.

Though this fund has its share of risks, it does own more stocks than any of its ETF peers do and is less concentrated than a lot of its rivals, such as the Technology Select Sector SPDR. That should keep a lid on volatility, at least relative to other tech funds, over time.

Finally, like many other tech ETFs, many of this fund's top holdings (Microsoft, Dell, and EMC) were trading below Morningstar equity analysts' estimates of their fair values at the end of December. That doesn't mean these stocks can't get cheaper or that tech stocks are due for an imminent, extended rally, but it does indicate that there could be some upside here. The same could be said for a lot of tech ETFs, but this one gets the nod over the rest due to its low costs, diversification, and credible management.

Address:	PO Box 2600 Valley Forge PA 19482 866-499-8473	Management Fee:	0.18%
		Expense Projections:	3Yr:$90 5Yr:$157 10Yr:$356
Web Address:	www.vanguard.com	Income Distrib:	Annually
Inception:	01-26-04 *	Exchange:	AMEX
Advisor:	Vanguard Advisers, Inc.		

MORNINGSTAR® ETFs 150

Vanguard Large Cap ETF VV

	Market Price	Mstar Category
	$62.80	Large Blend

Morningstar Fair Value

Price/Fair Value Ratio	Coverage Rate %
0.91 Undervalued	95 Good

Management

Ryan Ludt, who has been with Vanguard since 1997, handles the day-to-day operations of this fund. Vanguard's indexing pro, Gus Sauter, serves in a supervisory role.

Methodology

This index fund tracks the MSCI U.S. Prime Market 750 Index, which gives investors exposure to the 750 largest U.S. stocks. Unlike the S&P 500 Index, the ubiquitous large-cap bogy, its methodology is purely quantitative and transparent. It also dips down a bit further on the market cap ladder, pulling in a passel of mid-cap stocks.

Morningstar Rating	Return	Risk	Yield	NAV	Avg Daily Vol. (k)	52 wk High/Low
— Not Rated	Not Rated		1.7%	$62.92	202	$63.67 - $54.47

Growth of $10,000
- Investment Value of ETF
- Investment Value of Index S&P 500

Trading Volume Millions

	1997	1998	1999	2000	2001	2002	2003	2004	2005	2006	History
	—	—	—	—	—	—	—	52.99	55.40	62.92	NAV $
	—	—	—	—	—	—	—	53.19	55.49	62.93	Market Price $
	—	—	—	—	—	—	—	10.14*	6.26	15.61	NAV Return%
	—	—	—	—	—	—	—	10.14*	6.03	15.44	Market Price Return%
	—	—	—	—	—	—	—	-0.14	0.02	0.03	Avg Premium/Discount%
	—	—	—	—	—	—	—	10.14	1.35	-0.18	NAV Rtrn% +/-S&P 500
	—	—	—	—	—	—	—	10.14	-0.01	0.15	NAV Rtrn% +/-Russ 1000
	—	—	—	—	—	—	—		21	30	NAV Return% Rank in Cat
	—	—	—	—	—	—	—		1.66	1.91	Income Return %
	—	—	—	—	—	—	—		4.60	13.70	Capital Return %
	—	—	—	—	—	—	—	0.96	0.87	1.05	Income $
	—	—	—	—	—	—	—	0.00	0.00	0.00	Capital Gains $
	—	—	—	—	—	—	—	0.12	0.07	—	Expense Ratio %
	—	—	—	—	—	—	—	2.00	1.84	—	Income Ratio %
	—	—	—	—	—	—	—	5	23	—	Turnover Rate %
	—	—	—	—	—	—	—	48	178	587	Net Assets $mil

Performance 12-31-06

Historic Quarterly NAV Returns

	1st Qtr	2nd Qtr	3rd Qtr	4th Qtr	Total
2002	—	—	—	—	—
2003	—	—	—	—	—
2004	—	1.53	-1.78	9.59	—*
2005	-1.93	1.93	3.86	2.35	6.26
2006	4.33	-1.47	5.26	6.85	15.61

Trailing	NAV Return%	Market Return%	NAV Rtrn% +/-S&P 500	%Rank Cat.(NAV)
3 Mo	6.85	6.81	0.15	44
6 Mo	12.47	12.35	-0.27	38
1 Yr	15.61	15.44	-0.18	30
3 Yr Avg	—	—	—	—
5 Yr Avg	—	—	—	—
10 Yr Avg	—	—	—	—

Tax Analysis	Tax-Adj Return%	Tax-Cost Ratio
3 Yr (estimated)	—	—
5 Yr (estimated)	—	—
10 Yr (estimated)	—	—

Rating and Risk

Time Period	Morningstar Rtn vs Cat	Morningstar Risk vs Cat	Morningstar Risk-Adj Rating
3 Yr	—	—	—
5 Yr	—	—	—
10 Yr	—	—	—

Other Measures	Standard Index S&P 500	Best Fit Index
Alpha	—	—
Beta	—	—
R-Squared	—	—
Standard Deviation	—	
Mean	—	
Sharpe Ratio	—	

Portfolio Analysis 09-30-06

Share change since 06-06 Total Stocks:752

	Sector	PE	Tot Ret%	% Assets
⊕ ExxonMobil Corporation	Energy	11.7	39.07	3.07
⊕ General Electric Company	Ind Mtrls	19.8	9.35	2.77
⊕ Citigroup, Inc.	Financial	13.3	19.55	1.87
⊕ Bank of America Corporat	Financial	12.4	20.68	1.85
⊕ Microsoft Corporation	Software	23.7	15.83	1.83
⊕ Pfizer Inc.	Health	15.1	15.22	1.57
⊕ Procter & Gamble Company	Goods	24.2	13.36	1.54
⊕ Johnson & Johnson	Health	17.4	12.44	1.45
⊕ J.P. Morgan Chase & Co.	Financial	13.7	25.60	1.23
⊕ Altria Group, Inc.	Goods	15.9	19.87	1.21
⊕ American International G	Financial	17.1	6.05	1.11
⊕ Chevron Corporation	Energy	9.3	33.75	1.09
⊕ Cisco Systems, Inc.	Hardware	28.8	59.64	1.06
⊕ IBM	Hardware	16.8	19.77	0.96
⊕ AT&T, Inc.	Telecom	19.2	51.59	0.96
⊕ Wal-Mart Stores, Inc.	Consumer	16.6	0.13	0.93
⊕ Intel Corporation	Hardware	20.3	-17.18	0.90
⊕ Wells Fargo Company	Financial	14.7	16.82	0.87
⊕ Verizon Communications	Telecom	16.1	34.88	0.82
⊕ PepsiCo, Inc.	Goods	21.4	7.86	0.82

Current Investment Style

Value Blnd Growth — Large Mid Small

	Market Cap	%
	Giant	47.3
	Large	35.8
	Mid	16.9
	Small	0.0
	Micro	0.0
	Avg $mil:	42,617

Value Measures		Rel Category
Price/Earnings	15.31	0.92
Price/Book	2.56	0.93
Price/Sales	1.45	1.14
Price/Cash Flow	7.27	0.77
Dividend Yield %	1.87	1.04

Growth Measures	%	Rel Category
Long-Term Erngs	11.33	0.98
Book Value	8.87	1.04
Sales	10.22	1.23
Cash Flow	9.74	1.29
Historical Erngs	17.43	1.04

Profitability	%	Rel Category
Return on Equity	19.33	1.00
Return on Assets	10.60	1.10
Net Margin	14.01	1.26

Sector Weightings	% of Stocks	Rel S&P 500	3 Year High Low	
☊ Info	20.12	1.01		
Software	3.53	1.02	4	3
Hardware	9.36	1.01	11	9
Media	3.71	0.98	5	4
Telecom	3.52	1.00	4	3
☞ Service	47.56	1.03		
Health	12.86	1.07	14	12
Consumer	7.82	1.02	9	8
Business	4.52	1.07	5	4
Financial	22.36	1.00	22	20
Mfg	32.32	0.96		
Goods	8.25	0.96	9	8
Ind Mtrls	11.15	0.93	12	11
Energy	9.50	0.97	11	6
Utilities	3.42	0.98	3	3

Composition

	%
● Cash	0.9
● Stocks	99.1
● Bonds	0.0
○ Other	0.0
Foreign	0.1
(% of Stock)	

Morningstar's Take by Reginald Laing 12-31-06

Vanguard Large Cap ETF is a viable exchange-traded alternative to the more famous Vanguard 500.

In its construction, this ETF isn't radically different from sibling Vanguard 500. It does track a different index, the MSCI U.S. Prime Market 750 Index--but 19 of its top 20 holdings are the same as the S&P 500's, and are held in similar proportions. For that reason, the performance of the two indexes shouldn't differ markedly over time. In fact, for the trailing 12 months through Dec. 22, 2006, this offering's return (gross of fees) trailed the S&P 500's by only a hundredth of a percentage point.

Still, there are differences between this ETF and its S&P-tracking peers. First, the MSCI index includes 250 mid-cap stocks omitted from the S&P 500, so its average weighted market cap is a bit lower than the S&P's. Also, its portfolio includes equities that the S&P omits, such as holding companies (Warren Buffett's Berkshire Hathaway) and domestically listed offshore firms

(Bermuda-based consultancy Accenture). And MSCI's methodology is based purely on quantitative measures, whereas S&P's index committee approves all additions, excluding what it deems more-speculative fare and companies with limited operating histories. That's why this ETF owned search engine Google more than a year before it was added to the S&P--thus capturing about $200 per share worth of price appreciation that S&P investors missed out on. (Of course, the S&P's screen can work in the S&P's favor at times, because it will help prevent exposure to lower-quality, volatile companies.)

This ETF's main advantage is its 0.07% expense ratio, which makes it one of retail investors' cheapest large-blend options. (Avoid buying and selling it too frequently, though, as brokerage commissions can erase its expense advantage.)

All in all, this is a fine ETF with which to anchor a portfolio.

Address:	PO Box 2600		Management Fee:	0.01%		
	Valley Forge PA 19482		Expense Projections:	3Yr:$23	5Yr:$40	10Yr:$90
	866-499-8473		Income Distrib:	Quarterly		
Web Address:	www.vanguard.com		Exchange:	AMEX		
Inception:	01-27-04*					
Advisor:	Vanguard Advisers, Inc.					

MORNINGSTAR® ETFs 150

Vanguard Mid Cap ETF VO

	Market Price	Mstar Category
	$72.24	Mid-Cap Blend

Morningstar Fair Value

Price/Fair Value Ratio	Coverage Rate %
0.98 Fairly valued	92 Good

Management

Donald Butler, who has been with Vanguard since 1992, runs this ETF. Butler also handles the day-to-day management of Vanguard Extended Market Index and Vanguard Institutional Index. As Vanguard's chief investment officer, Gus Sauter serves a supervisory role here.

Methodology

The ETF tracks the MSCI U.S. Mid-Cap 450 Index, which spans the 301st to 750th largest stocks by market capitalization. The index's quantitative methodology should limit turnover and provide a close approximation of the mid-cap universe.

	Morningstar Rating	Return	Risk	Yield	NAV	Avg Daily Vol. (k)	52 wk High/Low
	— Not Rated	Not Rated		1.3%	$72.48	59	$74.54 - $63.45

Growth of $10,000
- Investment Value of ETF
- Investment Value of Index S&P 500

Trading Volume Millions

	1997	1998	1999	2000	2001	2002	2003	2004	2005	2006	History
	—	—	—	—	—	—	—	57.32	64.61	72.48	NAV $
	—	—	—	—	—	—	—	57.35	64.61	72.63	Market Price $
	—	—	—	—	—	—	—	14.66*	14.03	13.69	NAV Return%
	—	—	—	—	—	—	—	14.74*	13.97	13.93	Market Price Return%
	—	—	—	—	—	—	—	0.11	0.04	0.07	Avg Premium/Discount%
	—	—	—	—	—	—	—	14.66	9.12	-2.10	NAV Rtrn% +/-S&P 500
	—	—	—	—	—	—	—	14.66	1.47	3.37	NAV Rtrn% +/-S&P Mid 400
	—	—	—	—	—	—	—	—	7	8	NAV Return% Rank in Cat
	—	—	—	—	—	—	—	—	1.31	1.51	Income Return %
	—	—	—	—	—	—	—	—	12.72	12.18	Capital Return %
	—	—	—	—	—	—	—	0.64	0.75	0.97	Income $
	—	—	—	—	—	—	—	0.00	0.00	0.00	Capital Gains $
	—	—	—	—	—	—	—	0.18	0.13	—	Expense Ratio %
	—	—	—	—	—	—	—	1.30	1.45	—	Income Ratio %
	—	—	—	—	—	—	—	16	18	—	Turnover Rate %
	—	—	—	—	—	—	—	58	1,044	1,582	Net Assets $mil

Performance 12-31-06

Historic Quarterly NAV Returns

	1st Qtr	2nd Qtr	3rd Qtr	4th Qtr	Total
2002	—	—	—	—	—
2003	—	—	—	—	—
2004	—	1.05	-0.86	14.79	—*
2005	-0.38	4.41	6.41	3.03	14.03
2006	7.60	-2.88	1.30	7.39	13.69

Trailing	NAV Return%	Market Return%	NAV Rtrn% +/-S&P 500	%Rank Cat.(NAV)
3 Mo	7.39	7.57	0.69	10
6 Mo	8.79	9.15	-3.95	9
1 Yr	13.69	13.93	-2.10	8
3 Yr Avg	—	—	—	—
5 Yr Avg	—	—	—	—
10 Yr Avg	—	—	—	—

Tax Analysis	Tax-Adj Return%	Tax-Cost Ratio
3 Yr (estimated)	—	—
5 Yr (estimated)	—	—
10 Yr (estimated)	—	—

Rating and Risk

Time Period	Morningstar Rtn vs Cat	Morningstar Risk vs Cat	Morningstar Risk-Adj Rating
3 Yr	—	—	—
5 Yr	—	—	—
10 Yr	—	—	—

Other Measures	Standard Index S&P 500	Best Fit Index
Alpha	—	—
Beta	—	—
R-Squared	—	—
Standard Deviation	—	
Mean	—	
Sharpe Ratio	—	

Morningstar's Take by Sonya Morris 12-31-06

The fine Vanguard Mid Capitalization ETF has a long list of pleasing attributes.

An inventory of this ETF's many strengths should begin at the expense line. With a price tag of just 0.13%, this is the cheapest pure mid-blend fund available to retail investors. Low costs are crucial to the success of index funds because they use their expense advantage to edge past rivals over time.

Furthermore, this ETF's low fee structure helps make management's job of tracking the benchmark (MSCI U.S. MidCap 450 Index) easier. But Vanguard's indexing team is a skillful lot, and they've demonstrated their capabilities here by making up some of the ground lost to expenses. Since this ETF's January 2004 inception, it has generated average annual returns that fall just 0.04% shy of the index's. That's been enough to lift this fund to the top of the category. Its average annual returns since its inception rank in the category's top 20%.

This ETF looks good from an aftertax perspective as well. Its posttax returns over the past two calendar years were better than 75% of the competition. And the fund's conventional share class, Vanguard Mid Capitalization Index, boasts a three-year tax-cost ratio (which expresses tax costs in the form of an expense ratio) of just 0.17%, which ranks among the lowest 10% in the category. Indexing is an inherently tax-efficient strategy because trading is kept to a minimum. Plus, this ETF's benchmark uses buffer zones to limit the migration of stocks in and out of the mid-cap universe, which further damps turnover. Management also attempts to enhance the fund's tax-friendliness by employing tactics such as tax-loss harvesting (when it can do so without venturing too far from its benchmark). Indeed, Vanguard's indexing team is one of the best around when it comes to dodging the tax man.

All told, this fund's low costs, skillful management, and fine, tax-efficient record make it easy to recommend.

Address:	PO Box 2600 Valley Forge PA 19482 866-499-8473
Web Address:	www.vanguard.com
Inception:	01-26-04 *
Advisor:	Vanguard Advisers, Inc.

Management Fee:	0.11%		
Expense Projections:	3Yr:$42	5Yr:$73	10Yr:$166
Income Distrib:	Annually		
Exchange:	AMEX		

Portfolio Analysis 09-30-06

Share change since 06-06 Total Stocks:450

	Sector	PE	Tot Ret%	% Assets
⊕ American Tower Corporati	Telecom	—	37.56	0.66
⊕ CSX Corporation	Business	15.3	37.05	0.63
⊕ Qwest Communications Int	Telecom	—	48.14	0.61
⊕ ProLogis Trust	Financial	34.3	34.02	0.61
⊕ AES Corporation	Utilities	35.0	39.23	0.58
⊕ Micron Technology, Inc.	Hardware	24.5	4.88	0.55
⊕ Seagate Technology	Hardware	24.3	34.47	0.53
⊕ GlobalSantaFe Corporatio	Energy	17.2	24.06	0.53
⊕ T Rowe Price Group	Financial	24.4	23.27	0.52
⊕ Sempra Energy	Utilities	10.9	28.10	0.51
⊕ Archstone-Smith Trust	Financial	60.0	43.93	0.51
⊕ Chesapeake Energy Corp.	Energy	6.3	-7.74	0.50
⊕ Office Depot, Inc.	Consumer	23.1	21.56	0.50
⊕ Host Hotels & Resorts, I	Financial	53.4	33.95	0.49
⊕ Kinder Morgan, Inc.	Energy	20.7	19.22	0.49
⊕ Liberty Capital A	Media	—		0.49
⊕ Boston Properties, Inc.	Financial	15.1	62.75	0.49
⊕ Humana	Health	22.8	1.80	0.47
⊕ Public Storage, Inc.	Financial	46.2	47.46	0.47
⊕ Constellation Energy Gro	Utilities	17.4	22.70	0.46

Current Investment Style

Value Blnd Growth — Large Mid Small

	Market Cap	%
	Giant	0.0
	Large	13.2
	Mid	86.8
	Small	0.0
	Micro	0.0

Avg $mil: 6,334

Value Measures		Rel Category
Price/Earnings	15.90	0.95
Price/Book	2.41	0.94
Price/Sales	1.17	1.04
Price/Cash Flow	9.07	0.99
Dividend Yield %	1.37	1.00

Growth Measures	%	Rel Category
Long-Term Erngs	12.57	1.03
Book Value	8.50	1.16
Sales	9.91	1.41
Cash Flow	10.66	1.08
Historical Erngs	19.13	1.00

Profitability	%	Rel Category
Return on Equity	16.66	0.97
Return on Assets	8.45	0.99
Net Margin	12.05	1.13

Sector Weightings	% of Stocks	Rel S&P 500	3 Year High	Low
↻ Info	17.32	0.87		
Software	2.73	0.79	3	3
Hardware	9.19	0.99	13	9
Media	1.94	0.51	3	2
Telecom	3.46	0.99	3	1
⊂ Service	50.66	1.10		
Health	10.33	0.86	11	10
Consumer	10.31	1.35	12	10
Business	8.97	2.12	10	7
Financial	21.05	0.95	21	18
Mfg	32.03	0.95		
Goods	7.25	0.85	8	7
Ind Mtrls	9.07	0.76	12	9
Energy	9.80	1.00	12	7
Utilities	5.91	1.69	6	6

Composition

● Cash	0.1	
● Stocks	99.9	
● Bonds	0.0	
● Other	0.0	
Foreign (% of Stock)	0.3	

MORNINGSTAR® ETFs 150

Vanguard Pacif Stk ETF VPL

	Market Price $66.02	Mstar Category Japan Stock

Morningstar Fair Value

Price/Fair Value Ratio —   Coverage Rate % —

Morningstar Rating	Return	Risk	Yield	NAV	Avg Daily Vol. (k)	52 wk High/Low
— Not Rated	Not Rated	—	2.2%	$65.73	77	$70.12 - $56.20

Growth of $10,000
- Investment Value of ETF
- Investment Value of Index MSCI EAFE

14.4 / 11.0 / 10.0

Trading Volume Millions 0.08 / 0.0

Management

This ETF is run by Vanguard's quantitative equity group, which has exceptional indexing experience and expertise. Gus Sauter, who has a long and successful history managing index offerings and is Vanguard's chief investment officer, headed all index funds. But now he is in a supervisory role, and this ETF's manager is Michael Buek.

Methodology

This ETF tracks the MSCI Pacific Index, a capitalization-weighted benchmark of the region's largest stocks in developed markets, as defined by MSCI. Although its 70%-80% Japan stake lands it in the Japan-stock category, it puts the remainder of its assets in Australia, Hong Kong, Singapore, and New Zealand. It does not have any exposure to other popular Asian markets such as Taiwan, Korea, India, or Thailand. Its bogy gives it hefty exposure to its markets' biggest stocks. It does not hedge its currency exposure.

1997	1998	1999	2000	2001	2002	2003	2004	2005	2006	History
—	—	—	—	—	—	—	—	60.03	65.73	NAV $
—	—	—	—	—	—	—	—	60.89	66.47	Market Price $
—	—	—	—	—	—	—	—	17.79*	11.97	NAV Return%
—	—	—	—	—	—	—	—	18.13*	11.61	Market Price Return%
—	—	—	—	—	—	—	—	0.81	0.51	Avg Premium/Discount%
—	—	—	—	—	—	—	—	17.79	-14.37	NAV Rtrn% +/-MSCI EAFE
—	—	—	—	—	—	—	—	17.79	5.73	NAV Rtrn% +/-MSCI JP NDT
—	—	—	—	—	—	—	—	—	3	NAV Return% Rank in Cat
—	—	—	—	—	—	—	—	—	2.45	Income Return %
—	—	—	—	—	—	—	—	—	9.52	Capital Return %
—	—	—	—	—	—	—	—	0.93	1.47	Income $
—	—	—	—	—	—	—	—	0.00	0.00	Capital Gains $
—	—	—	—	—	—	—	—	0.18	0.18	Expense Ratio %
—	—	—	—	—	—	—	—	1.89	1.82	Income Ratio %
—	—	—	—	—	—	—	—	7	2	Turnover Rate %
—	—	—	—	—	—	—	—	312	816	Net Assets $mil

Performance 12-31-06

Historic Quarterly NAV Returns

	1st Qtr	2nd Qtr	3rd Qtr	4th Qtr	Total
2002	—	—	—	—	—
2003	—	—	—	—	—
2004	—	—	—	—	—
2005	—	-1.58	17.33	8.21	—*
2006	6.55	-2.78	0.37	7.70	11.97

Trailing	NAV Return%	Market Return%	NAV Rtrn% +/-MSCI EAFE	%Rank Cat.(NAV)
3 Mo	7.70	8.59	-2.65	6
6 Mo	8.09	8.57	-6.60	6
1 Yr	11.97	11.61	-14.37	3
3 Yr Avg	—	—	—	—
5 Yr Avg	—	—	—	—
10 Yr Avg	—	—	—	—

Tax Analysis	Tax-Adj Return%	Tax-Cost Ratio
3 Yr (estimated)	—	—
5 Yr (estimated)	—	—
10 Yr (estimated)	—	—

Rating and Risk

Time Period	Morningstar Rtn vs Cat	Morningstar Risk vs Cat	Morningstar Risk-Adj Rating
3 Yr	—	—	—
5 Yr	—	—	—
10 Yr	—	—	—

Other Measures

	Standard Index S&P 500	Best Fit Index
Alpha	—	—
Beta	—	—
R-Squared	—	—
Standard Deviation	—	
Mean	—	
Sharpe Ratio	—	

Portfolio Analysis 09-30-06

Share change since 06-06 Total Stocks:554

	Sector	Country	% Assets
⊕ Toyota Motor	Goods	Japan	4.26
⊕ Mitsubishi UFJ Financial	Financial	Japan	3.00
⊕ Mizuho Financial Grp	Financial	Japan	2.02
⊕ BHP Billiton, Ltd.	Ind Mtrls	Australia	1.79
⊕ Sumitomo Mitsui Financia	Financial	Japan	1.75
⊕ Canon	Goods	Japan	1.51
⊕ Takeda Chemical Industri	Health	Japan	1.50
⊕ Honda Motor	Goods	Japan	1.42
⊕ Commonwealth Bank of Aus	Financial	Australia	1.19
⊕ National Australia Bank	Financial	Australia	1.19
⊕ Matsushita Electric Indu	Ind Mtrls	Japan	1.12
⊕ Sony	Goods	Japan	1.10
⊕ Australia & New Zealand	Financial	Australia	0.99
⊕ Tokyo Elec Pwr	Utilities	Japan	0.95
⊕ Nomura Hldgs	Financial	Japan	0.84
⊕ Westpac Banking	Financial	Australia	0.84
⊕ NTT DoCoMo	Telecom	Japan	0.78
⊕ Seven & I Holdings	Consumer	Japan	0.72
⊕ Mitsubishi Estate	Financial	Japan	0.69
⊕ Mitsubishi	Ind Mtrls	Japan	0.69

Current Investment Style

Value Blnd Growth — Large / Mid / Small

Market Cap	%
Giant	53.4
Large	35.5
Mid	10.7
Small	0.0
Micro	0.3

Avg $mil: 16,611

Value Measures		Rel Category
Price/Earnings	6.89	0.42
Price/Book	1.70	1.08
Price/Sales	1.06	1.25
Price/Cash Flow	8.48	1.06
Dividend Yield %	2.20	1.27

Growth Measures	%	Rel Category
Long-Term Erngs	10.07	0.87
Book Value	10.19	0.99
Sales	4.97	0.98
Cash Flow	2.42	121.00
Historical Erngs	12.70	0.66

Composition

Cash	0.6	Bonds	0.0
Stocks	98.4	Other	1.0
Foreign (% of Stock)			100.0

Sector Weightings

	% of Stocks	Rel MSCI EAFE	3 Year High	Low
☎ Info	9.22	0.78		
🖥 Software	0.43	0.77	1	0
💾 Hardware	4.63	1.20	6	4
🎤 Media	0.94	0.51	3	1
📱 Telecom	3.22	0.58	5	3
☞ Service	46.10	0.98		
🏥 Health	4.82	0.68	5	4
🛒 Consumer	5.27	1.06	6	5
💼 Business	6.85	1.35	7	6
$ Financial	29.16	0.97	29	24
🏭 Mfg	44.68	1.09		
🏠 Goods	17.39	1.33	21	17
⚙ Ind Mtrls	21.72	1.41	23	19
🔋 Energy	1.30	0.18	2	1
💡 Utilities	4.27	0.81	5	4

Regional Exposure % Stock

UK/W. Europe	0	N. America	0
Japan	75	Latn America	0
Asia X Japan	25	Other	0

Country Exposure % Stock

Japan	75	Singapore	3
Australia	17	New Zealand	0
Hong Kong	5		

Morningstar's Take by William Samuel Rocco 12-31-06

This ETF has its strengths, but it has only limited appeal.

Vanguard Pacific Stock is likely to accomplish its mission of replicating the performance of the MSCI Pacific Index. This young ETF is managed by the skilled indexers in Vanguard's quantitative equity group and has an expense ratio of just 0.18%. It has done a nice job of matching the MSCI Pacific Index's returns so far. The mutual fund clone of this ETF, which was launched in 1990, has tracked the performance of the index well over time.

But it's important to recognize that this ETF, like its mutual fund clone, has a distinctive makeup. The MSCI Pacific Index is a market-cap-weighted set of the bigger stocks in its region's major markets, so it sports a marked large-cap bias and devotes roughly 75% of its assets to Japan, 17% to Australia, 5% to Hong Kong, 2% to Singapore, and 1% to New Zealand. This ETF has the same large-cap bias and country weightings as its target index, of course, which means that it stands out both from Japan funds and diversified Pacific/Asia funds.

This ETF's atypical country stance makes it tough to compare its performance with that of other offerings. We put this ETF in with Japan funds, but it's at a major disadvantage relative to such funds whenever Japan leads the way in Asia, and it enjoys a major advantage relative to such funds whenever Japan lags its neighbors. (And the opposite is true when comparing this ETF with diversified Pacific/Asia funds, which invest around half of their assets in Japan and readily consider opportunities in Asia's smaller markets.)

This ETF's unusual makeup also makes it hard to use. Most foreign large-cap funds have ample exposure to blue chips from Japan and elsewhere in the region, so overlap is a real issue. And this ETF's betwixt-and-between status means it's not a good fit for those who'd like to double up on Japan or those who'd like to double up on Asia overall.

Despite its low costs and Vanguard's indexing skill, this ETF lacks broad appeal.

Address:	PO Box 2600 Valley Forge PA 19482 866-499-8473	
Web Address:	www.vanguard.com	
Inception:	03-10-05*	
Advisor:	The Vanguard Group, Inc.	

Management Fee:	0.14%	
Expense Projections:	3Yr:$58	5Yr:$101 10Yr:$230
Income Distrib:	Annually	
Exchange:	AMEX	

MORNINGSTAR® ETFs 150   167

Vanguard REIT Index ETF VNQ

Market Price $76.86	**Mstar Category** Specialty-Real Estate	

Management

Gerard O'Reilly is the day-to-day manager of this fund, although Gus Sauter oversees Vanguard's quantitative equity group. O'Reilly has been with Vanguard since 1992, and he runs several of Vanguard's other index funds.

Methodology

This fund attempts to track the MCSI U.S. REIT Index, a broad benchmark that includes REITs of all property types. Investing exclusively in REITs and lows costs help drive a fairly high dividend yield relative to other real estate funds, but that restriction can be a limitation when non-REITs shine. The REIT universe is fairly stable, so the fund has few challenges on the trading front. Mortgage REITs are excluded from the index.

Morningstar Rating	Return	Risk	Yield	NAV	Avg Daily Vol. (k)	52 wk High/Low
— Not Rated	Not Rated	Not Rated	3.7%	$76.98	120	$80.77 - $62.05

Growth of $10,000
- Investment Value of ETF
- Investment Value of Index S&P 500

18.0
16.4
12.0
10.0

Trading Volume Millions
0.2
0.0

	1997	1998	1999	2000	2001	2002	2003	2004	2005	2006	History
	—	—	—	—	—	—	—	56.55	59.59	76.98	NAV $
	—	—	—	—	—	—	—	56.55	59.56	77.00	Market Price $
	—	—	—	—	—	—	—	28.67*	12.00	35.20	NAV Return%
	—	—	—	—	—	—	—	—	11.94	35.29	Market Price Return%
	—	—	—	—	—	—	—	0.06	0.02	0.01	Avg Premium/Discount%
	—	—	—	—	—	—	—	28.67	7.09	19.41	NAV Rtrn% +/-S&P 500
	—	—	—	—	—	—	—	28.67	-2.00	-0.93	NAV Rtrn% +/-DJ Wilshire REIT
	—	—	—	—	—	—	—	—	4	4	NAV Return% Rank in Cat
	—	—	—	—	—	—	—	—	5.22	4.93	Income Return %
	—	—	—	—	—	—	—	—	6.78	30.27	Capital Return %
	—	—	—	—	—	—	—	0.68	2.89	2.89	Income $
	—	—	—	—	—	—	—	0.59	0.68	0.36	Capital Gains $
	—	—	—	—	—	—	—	—	0.18	0.12	Expense Ratio %
	—	—	—	—	—	—	—	—	3.60	3.00	Income Ratio %
	—	—	—	—	—	—	—	7	13	17	Turnover Rate %
	—	—	—	—	—	—	—	171	410	1,476	Net Assets $mil

Performance 12-31-06

Historic Quarterly NAV Returns

	1st Qtr	2nd Qtr	3rd Qtr	4th Qtr	Total
2002	—	—	—	—	—
2003	—	—	—	—	—
2004	—	—	—	15.00	—*
2005	-7.31	14.65	3.59	1.73	12.00
2006	14.82	-1.37	9.42	9.10	35.20

Trailing	NAV Return%	Market Return%	NAV Rtrn% +/-S&P 500	%Rank Cat.(NAV)
3 Mo	9.10	9.24	2.40	5
6 Mo	19.38	19.56	6.64	5
1 Yr	35.20	35.29	19.41	4
3 Yr Avg	—	—	—	—
5 Yr Avg	—	—	—	—
10 Yr Avg	—	—	—	—

Tax Analysis	Tax-Adj Return%	Tax-Cost Ratio
3 Yr (estimated)	—	—
5 Yr (estimated)	—	—
10 Yr (estimated)	—	—

Rating and Risk

Time Period	Morningstar Rtn vs Cat	Morningstar Risk vs Cat	Morningstar Risk-Adj Rating
3 Yr	—	—	—
5 Yr	—	—	—
10 Yr	—	—	—

Other Measures	Standard Index S&P 500	Best Fit Index
Alpha	—	—
Beta	—	—
R-Squared	—	—
Standard Deviation	—	
Mean	—	
Sharpe Ratio	—	

Portfolio Analysis 09-30-06

Share change since 06-06 Total Stocks:106

Sector		PE	Tot Ret%	% Assets
⊕ Simon Property Group, In	Financial	59.2	36.97	5.93
⊕ Equity Residential	Financial	NMF	34.64	4.36
⊖ Equity Office Properties	Financial	—	64.28	4.31
⊕ ProLogis Trust	Financial	34.3	34.02	4.14
⊕ Vornado Realty Trust	Financial	38.2	51.13	4.11
⊕ Archstone-Smith Trust	Financial	60.0	43.93	3.45
⊕ Host Hotels & Resorts, I	Financial	53.4	33.95	3.34
⊕ Boston Properties, Inc.	Financial	15.1	62.75	3.32
⊕ Public Storage, Inc.	Financial	46.2	47.46	3.21
⊕ General Growth Propertie	Financial	—	15.09	3.06
⊕ Kimco Realty Corporation	Financial	30.8	44.91	2.75
⊕ AvalonBay Communities, I	Financial	67.7	49.69	2.65
⊕ Developers Diversified R	Financial	41.1	39.65	1.81
⊕ Macerich Company	Financial	—	33.91	1.62
⊕ Apartment Investment & M	Financial	—	55.18	1.57
⊕ Duke Realty Corporation	Financial	75.7	28.98	1.49
⊕ AMB Property Corporation	Financial	30.9	23.30	1.44
⊕ SL Green Realty Corporat	Financial	58.2	77.73	1.43
⊕ Regency Centers Corporat	Financial	57.1	37.58	1.40
⊕ Liberty Property Trust	Financial	19.4	20.84	1.26

Morningstar's Take by John Coumarianos 12-31-06

We'd pass on Vanguard REIT Index ETF.

This exchange-traded fund benefits from many of the same features that assist other index funds. Its expense ratio, which has come down over the years, is the lowest among real estate ETFs. Moreover, its turnover typically trends below 20%. This minimizes trading costs and capital gains distributions, which can cut into returns. Because REITs (real estate investment trusts) are typically high-yielding stocks, with a large percentage of their total return coming from dividends, a low expense ratio ensures that most of its yield flows through to shareholders.

Unfortunately, this ETF's structural advantages have been negated in the recent climate, while some of its disadvantages have been as salient as ever. This has allowed some of the better actively managed funds to outpace this ETF's benchmark. First, yield hasn't mattered that much, with REITs appreciating dramatically in recent years. In other words, yield has been a much smaller part of total return over the last five years than in the past, minimizing this fund's low-cost advantage.

Second and more importantly, because this fund is limited to a REIT index, it cannot invest in real estate operating companies, such as Starwood Hotels, Marriott International, Brookfield Properties, and St. Joe. Not being organized as REITs allows these businesses to keep their earnings in order to finance future growth, and many of them have posted strong returns over the past few years. This ETF, which tracks the MSCI REIT Index, has not been able to own them.

Finally, the REIT rally is growing long in the tooth, so now's a good time to consider easing into the sector by dollar cost averaging. That also argues against this ETF since you must pay a brokerage commission each time you trade it. Those who'd like to dollar-cost average would be better off in this ETF's conventional fund twin, Vanguard REIT Index.

Current Investment Style

Value Blnd Growth — Large Mid Small

Market Cap	%
Giant	0.0
Large	40.1
Mid	43.9
Small	15.2
Micro	0.9

Avg $mil: 5,395

Value Measures		Rel Category
Price/Earnings	17.19	1.00
Price/Book	2.90	1.03
Price/Sales	4.17	1.10
Price/Cash Flow	14.95	0.91
Dividend Yield %	4.37	1.34

Growth Measures	%	Rel Category
Long-Term Erngs	6.51	0.83
Book Value	-2.84	NMF
Sales	9.95	0.86
Cash Flow	—	—
Historical Erngs	2.67	0.28

Profitability	%	Rel Category
Return on Equity	10.82	0.76
Return on Assets	9.77	0.88
Net Margin	26.47	1.19

Sector Weightings	% of Stocks	Rel S&P 500	3 Year High Low	
⟳ Info	0.00	0.00		
📈 Software	0.00	0.00	0	0
💻 Hardware	0.00	0.00	0	0
🎙 Media	0.00	0.00	0	0
📞 Telecom	0.00	0.00	0	0
⟲ Service	100.00	2.16		
🏥 Health	0.00	0.00	0	0
🛒 Consumer	0.00	0.00	0	0
💼 Business	0.00	0.00	0	0
$ Financial	100.00	4.49	100	100
⚒ Mfg	0.00	0.00		
🔧 Goods	0.00	0.00	0	0
⚙ Ind Mtrls	0.00	0.00	0	0
🔋 Energy	0.00	0.00	0	0
💡 Utilities	0.00	0.00	0	0

Composition

● Cash		2.1
● Stocks		97.9
● Bonds		0.0
○ Other		0.0
Foreign		0.0
(% of Stock)		

Address:	PO Box 2600
	Valley Forge PA 19482
	866-499-8473
Web Address:	www.vanguard.com
Inception:	09-23-04 *
Advisor:	Vanguard Advisers, Inc.

Management Fee:	0.09%
Expense Projections:	3Yr:$39 5Yr:$68 10Yr:$154
Income Distrib:	Quarterly
Exchange:	AMEX

 **M**ORNINGSTAR® ETFs 150

Vanguard Small Cap ETF VB

Market Price $67.60	**Mstar Category** Small Blend

Morningstar Fair Value

Price/Fair Value Ratio	Coverage Rate %
—	—

Management

In 2005, Michael Buek became this fund's listed manager, taking over from Gus Sauter, Vanguard's chief investment officer. Buek has been with Vanguard since 1987 and has helped manage this fund since 1991. Buek also manages the venerable Vanguard 500.

Methodology

This ETF tracks the MSCI U.S. Small Cap 1750 Index, which contains the smallest 1,750 of the top 2,500 publicly traded companies in the United States (ranked by market capitalization). Because it pulls in a passel of mid-cap names, its median market cap is a tad higher than that of the typical small-blend fund.

Morningstar Rating	Return	Risk	Yield	NAV	Avg Daily Vol. (k)
— Not Rated	Not Rated	Not Rated	1.2%	$68.16	42

52 wk High/Low $69.99 - $59.32

Growth of $10,000
- Investment Value of ETF
- Investment Value of Index S&P 500

Trading Volume Millions

	1997	1998	1999	2000	2001	2002	2003	2004	2005	2006	History
	—	—	—	—	—	—	—	56.05	59.59	68.16	NAV $
	—	—	—	—	—	—	—	56.16	59.55	68.10	Market Price $
	—	—	—	—	—	—	—	11.99*	7.53	15.79	NAV Return%
	—	—	—	—	—	—	—	11.96*	7.25	15.77	Market Price Return%
	—	—	—	—	—	—	—	-0.10	-0.08	-0.09	Avg Premium/Discount%
	—	—	—	—	—	—	—	11.99	2.62	0.00	NAV Rtrn% +/-S&P 500
	—	—	—	—	—	—	—	11.99	2.98	-2.58	NAV Rtrn% +/-Russ 2000
	—	—	—	—	—	—	—	—	4	8	NAV Return% Rank in Cat
	—	—	—	—	—	—	—	—	1.22	1.40	Income Return %
	—	—	—	—	—	—	—	—	6.31	14.39	Capital Return %
	—	—	—	—	—	—	—	0.62	0.68	0.83	Income $
	—	—	—	—	—	—	—	0.00	0.00	0.00	Capital Gains $
	—	—	—	—	—	—	—	0.18	0.10	—	Expense Ratio %
	—	—	—	—	—	—	—	1.19	1.20	—	Income Ratio %
	—	—	—	—	—	—	—	19	18	—	Turnover Rate %
	—	—	—	—	—	—	—	186	265	670	Net Assets $mil

Performance 12-31-06

Historic Quarterly NAV Returns

	1st Qtr	2nd Qtr	3rd Qtr	4th Qtr	Total
2002	—	—	—	—	—
2003	—	—	—	—	—
2004	—	1.01	-2.26	13.93	—*
2005	-3.74	4.86	5.25	1.22	7.53
2006	12.22	-4.68	-0.25	8.53	15.79

Trailing	NAV Return%	Market Return%	NAV Rtrn% +/-S&P 500	%Rank Cat.(NAV)
3 Mo	8.53	8.52	1.83	12
6 Mo	8.26	8.50	-4.48	10
1 Yr	15.79	15.77	0.00	8
3 Yr Avg	—	—	—	—
5 Yr Avg	—	—	—	—
10 Yr Avg	—	—	—	—

Tax Analysis	Tax-Adj Return%	Tax-Cost Ratio
3 Yr (estimated)	—	—
5 Yr (estimated)	—	—
10 Yr (estimated)	—	—

Rating and Risk

Time Period	Morningstar Rtn vs Cat	Morningstar Risk vs Cat	Morningstar Risk-Adj Rating
3 Yr	—	—	—
5 Yr	—	—	—
10 Yr	—	—	—

Other Measures	Standard Index S&P 500	Best Fit Index
Alpha	—	—
Beta	—	—
R-Squared	—	—
Standard Deviation	—	
Mean	—	
Sharpe Ratio	—	

Morningstar's Take by Reginald Laing 12-31-06

Vanguard Small Cap ETF doesn't rank in the category elite, but it's better than most of its peers.

This exchange-traded fund, which charges only 0.10%, is among the cheapest in the small-blend category. Expenses are especially important here, as this offering passively owns roughly 1,500 of the stocks in its MSCI index and relies on low fees to edge past a majority of competitors.

For the trailing three years through Dec. 21, 2006, this fund's older, conventional share class--Vanguard Small Cap Index--has delivered a 14.8% annualized gain, which outpaced the returns of two thirds of its peers. While investors can't expect such strong absolute gains every year, this ETF's ultralow fees should pave the way to a competitive category ranking over time. Moreover, its broad exposure limits stock- and sector-specific risk, which should keep volatility below the average for this somewhat volatile category.

The ETF's high tax efficiency gives it a further leg up versus its peer group. Because the index employs buffer zones--which limit stocks' migration into and out of the fund--its turnover should be even lower than that of comparable ETFs. That means taxable investors here will be able to keep a greater percentage of their profits than will owners of higher-turnover funds. Low turnover also controls trading costs, which aren't reflected in an ETF's expense ratio but erode returns nonetheless.

Last, although active managers historically have taken advantage of small caps' relative inefficiency to outpace their indexing peers, finding a good small-cap manager (whose fund is still open and not already swamped with assets) is a tall order, now that small caps have been on a multiyear run and investors have flooded into the hottest performing of these funds.

By its passive nature, this ETF won't likely top the small-blend category in any given calendar year--or even over long stretches of time. But it's still a good option for investors seeking no-frills exposure to small caps.

Address:	PO Box 2600 Valley Forge PA 19482 866-499-8473
Web Address:	www.vanguard.com
Inception:	01-26-04*
Advisor:	Vanguard Advisers, Inc.

Management Fee:	0.08%
Expense Projections:	3Yr:$32 5Yr:$56 10Yr:$128
Income Distrib:	Annually
Exchange:	AMEX

Portfolio Analysis 09-30-06

Share change since 06-06 Total Stocks:1728	Sector	PE	Tot Ret%	% Assets
⊕ Level 3 Communications,	Telecom	—	95.12	0.31
⊕ Camden Property Trust	Financial	33.3	32.17	0.25
⊕ Covance, Inc.	Health	27.8	21.34	0.24
⊕ Federal Realty Investmen	Financial	55.6	44.88	0.24
⊕ Roper Industries, Inc.	Ind Mtrls	25.6	27.83	0.22
⊕ FMC Technologies, Inc.	Energy	21.2	43.59	0.21
⊕ HCC Insurance Holdings I	Financial	17.0	9.39	0.21
⊕ Ventas, Inc.	Financial	33.1	38.19	0.21
⊕ Northeast Utilities	Utilities	33.9	47.76	0.21
⊕ Reckson Associates Realt	Financial	46.1	31.78	0.21
⊕ Denbury Resources, Inc.	Energy	16.6	21.99	0.20
⊕ Plains Exploration & Pro	Energy	—	19.63	0.19
⊕ Range Resources Corporat	Energy	17.5	4.62	0.19
⊕ OGE Energy Corp	Utilities	16.3	55.73	0.19
⊕ Harsco Corporation	Ind Mtrls	16.3	14.65	0.19
⊕ Mack-Cali Realty Corpora	Financial	34.7	24.56	0.19
⊕ Integrated Device Techno	Hardware	—	17.45	0.19
⊕ O'Reilly Automotive, Inc	Consumer	20.7	0.16	0.18
⊕ CMS Energy Corporation	Utilities	—	15.09	0.18
⊕ Conseco, Inc.	Financial	23.8	-13.77	0.18

Current Investment Style

Value Blnd Growth		
		Large/Mid/Small

	Market Cap	%
	Giant	0.0
	Large	0.0
	Mid	40.3
	Small	52.7
	Micro	6.9
	Avg $mil: 1,467	

Value Measures		Rel Category
Price/Earnings	16.62	0.94
Price/Book	2.06	1.00
Price/Sales	0.99	0.96
Price/Cash Flow	6.72	1.04
Dividend Yield %	1.45	0.91

Growth Measures	%	Rel Category
Long-Term Erngs	13.03	0.98
Book Value	5.81	1.06
Sales	5.50	2.42
Cash Flow	8.29	0.92
Historical Erngs	13.75	1.15

Profitability	%	Rel Category
Return on Equity	11.94	1.03
Return on Assets	6.48	0.98
Net Margin	9.84	1.00

Sector Weightings

	% of Stocks	Rel S&P 500	3 Year High	Low
↻ Info	14.62	0.73		
🖥 Software	3.88	1.12	5	4
💻 Hardware	7.35	0.80	9	7
🎙 Media	1.52	0.40	2	1
📶 Telecom	1.87	0.53	2	1
☞ Service	53.78	1.16		
🏥 Health	10.11	0.84	12	10
🛒 Consumer	10.13	1.32	12	10
🏢 Business	11.14	2.63	11	10
💲 Financial	22.40	1.01	23	22
🏭 Mfg	31.60	0.94		
🏷 Goods	5.91	0.69	6	4
⚙ Ind Mtrls	15.02	1.26	16	13
🔥 Energy	6.33	0.65	8	5
💡 Utilities	4.34	1.24	5	4

Composition

● Cash	0.2	
● Stocks	99.8	
● Bonds	0.0	
○ Other	0.0	
Foreign (% of Stock)	0.4	

Mᴏʀɴɪɴɢsᴛᴀʀ® ETFs 150

Vanguard Sm Cap Gr ETF VBK

	Market Price	Mstar Category
	$64.91	Small Growth

Morningstar Rating	Return	Risk	Yield	NAV	Avg Daily Vol. (k)	52 wk High/Low
— Not Rated	Not Rated	—	0.4%	$65.24	40	$67.68 - $56.19

Morningstar Fair Value

Price/Fair Value Ratio — 　Coverage Rate % —

Management

Gerard O'Reilly, who has been with Vanguard since 1992, was named lead manager of this fund in May 2005. He also skippers Vanguard Total Stock Market Index, Vanguard Value Index, and Vanguard Growth Index.

Methodology

This ETF tracks the MSCI U.S. Small Cap Growth Index, which uses an eight-pronged classification system to identify small-growth stocks. The index also employs buffer zones, which limit the migration of stocks into and out of the index. The buffers should help keep portfolio turnover and trading costs low and tax efficiency high.

Growth of $10,000
— Investment Value of ETF
— Investment Value of Index S&P 500

Trading Volume Millions

	1997	1998	1999	2000	2001	2002	2003	2004	2005	2006	History
	—	—	—	—	—	—	—	53.95	58.47	65.24	NAV $
	—	—	—	—	—	—	—	53.94	58.40	65.25	Market Price $
	—	—	—	—	—	—	—	9.29*	8.77	12.03	NAV Return%
	—	—	—	—	—	—	—	9.29*	8.66	12.19	Market Price Return%
	—	—	—	—	—	—	—	-0.21	-0.06	-0.10	Avg Premium/Discount%
	—	—	—	—	—	—	—	9.29	3.86	-3.76	NAV Rtrn% +/-S&P 500
	—	—	—	—	—	—	—	9.29	4.62	-1.32	NAV Rtrn% +/-Russ 2000 Gr
	—	—	—	—	—	—	—	—	5	6	NAV Return% Rank in Cat
	—	—	—	—	—	—	—	—	0.40	0.45	Income Return %
	—	—	—	—	—	—	—	—	8.37	11.58	Capital Return %
	—	—	—	—	—	—	—	0.09	0.21	0.27	Income $
	—	—	—	—	—	—	—	0.00	0.00	0.00	Capital Gains $
	—	—	—	—	—	—	—	0.22	0.12	—	Expense Ratio %
	—	—	—	—	—	—	—	0.15	0.37	—	Income Ratio %
	—	—	—	—	—	—	—	41	39	—	Turnover Rate %
	—	—	—	—	—	—	—	92	206	518	Net Assets $mil

Performance 12-31-06

Historic Quarterly NAV Returns

	1st Qtr	2nd Qtr	3rd Qtr	4th Qtr	Total
2002	—	—	—	—	—
2003	—	—	—	—	—
2004	—	1.11	-5.73	14.85	— *
2005	-4.19	4.43	6.45	2.13	8.77
2006	13.29	-6.69	-2.35	8.53	12.03

Trailing	NAV Return%	Market Return%	NAV Rtrn% +/-S&P 500	%Rank Cat.(NAV)
3 Mo	8.53	8.60	1.83	7
6 Mo	5.98	6.50	-6.76	7
1 Yr	12.03	12.19	-3.76	6
3 Yr Avg	—	—	—	—
5 Yr Avg	—	—	—	—
10 Yr Avg	—	—	—	—

Tax Analysis	Tax-Adj Return%	Tax-Cost Ratio
3 Yr (estimated)	—	—
5 Yr (estimated)	—	—
10 Yr (estimated)	—	—

Rating and Risk

Time Period	Morningstar Rtn vs Cat	Morningstar Risk vs Cat	Morningstar Risk-Adj Rating
3 Yr	—	—	—
5 Yr	—	—	—
10 Yr	—	—	—

Other Measures	Standard Index S&P 500	Best Fit Index
Alpha	—	—
Beta	—	—
R-Squared	—	—
Standard Deviation	—	
Mean	—	
Sharpe Ratio	—	

Portfolio Analysis 09-30-06

Share change since 06-06 Total Stocks:936	Sector	PE	Tot Ret%	% Assets
⊕ Level 3 Communications,	Telecom	—	95.12	0.64
⊕ Covance, Inc.	Health	27.8	21.34	0.51
⊕ Roper Industries, Inc.	Ind Mtrls	25.6	27.83	0.47
⊕ FMC Technologies, Inc.	Energy	21.2	43.59	0.44
⊕ Denbury Resources, Inc.	Energy	16.6	21.99	0.41
⊕ Range Resources Corporat	Energy	17.5	4.62	0.40
⊕ O'Reilly Automotive, Inc	Consumer	20.7	0.16	0.38
⊕ Dade Behring Holdings, I	Health	26.4	-2.13	0.38
⊖ Affiliated Managers Grou	Financial	32.5	31.00	0.38
⊕ Crown Holdings, Inc.	Goods	—	7.12	0.37
⊕ Ametek, Inc.	Ind Mtrls	19.4	12.94	0.37
⊕ Jones Lang LaSalle, Inc.	Financial	18.9	84.32	0.37
⊕ ResMed, Inc.	Health	39.4	28.48	0.36
⊕ VCA Antech, Inc.	Health	26.4	14.15	0.36
⊕ Thomas & Betts Corporati	Hardware	19.5	12.68	0.36
⊕ Global Payments, Inc.	Business	27.9	-0.49	0.36
⊕ Stericycle, Inc.	Business	45.5	28.23	0.35
⊖ ITT Educational Services	Consumer	25.8	12.59	0.35
⊕ Helix Energy Solutions G	Energy	11.3	-12.59	0.35
⊕ Idexx Laboratories	Health	29.5	10.17	0.34

Current Investment Style

Value Blnd Growth — Large Mid Small

	Market Cap	%
	Giant	0.0
	Large	0.0
	Mid	38.6
	Small	54.5
	Micro	6.9
	Avg $mil:	1,463

Value Measures		Rel Category
Price/Earnings	19.67	0.93
Price/Book	2.83	0.95
Price/Sales	1.30	0.88
Price/Cash Flow	7.15	1.01
Dividend Yield %	0.28	0.90

Growth Measures	%	Rel Category
Long-Term Erngs	17.41	0.99
Book Value	9.65	0.80
Sales	2.04	0.22
Cash Flow	17.65	0.83
Historical Erngs	22.18	1.10

Profitability	%	Rel Category
Return on Equity	14.24	0.97
Return on Assets	6.87	0.87
Net Margin	8.47	0.87

Sector Weightings	% of Stocks	Rel S&P 500	3 Year High Low	
↻ Info	20.61	1.03		
▣ Software	6.37	1.85	8	6
▣ Hardware	9.96	1.08	15	9
◉ Media	1.29	0.34	3	1
▤ Telecom	2.99	0.85	3	2
☞ Service	50.89	1.10		
◪ Health	18.36	1.52	21	18
▤ Consumer	11.21	1.47	14	11
▣ Business	14.52	3.43	15	13
$ Financial	6.80	0.31	8	6
▥ Mfg	28.51	0.84		
▦ Goods	6.23	0.73	6	4
✦ Ind Mtrls	13.17	1.10	14	8
♨ Energy	8.85	0.90	11	5
◘ Utilities	0.26	0.07	1	0

Composition

● Cash		0.5
● Stocks		99.5
● Bonds		0.0
○ Other		0.0
Foreign		0.4
(% of Stock)		

Morningstar's Take by Reginald Laing 12-31-06

Vanguard Small Cap Growth ETF is a relatively tame way to own a volatile corner of the style box.

Small-growth is an inherently volatile corner of Morningstar's style box. Small companies are less diversified across different lines of business, and have less heft with which to weather lean economic times, than their larger counterparts. And growth companies tend to have high valuation multiples, which can compress quickly if revenue or earnings growth fails to keep up with market expectations. That translates to volatility: For the trailing 10 years through Nov. 30, 2006, the standard deviation (a common measure of volatility) of the typical small-growth fund was 25.9, versus 16.6 for the average small-value offering.

This Vanguard exchange-traded fund is a sensible way to gain exposure to small-growth stocks, though. Its broad diversification ensures the fund isn't overallocated to a particular company or sector. That should help limit volatility here a bit. Another virtue is the fund's use of buffer zones,

which keep stocks from migrating out of the index when they leave the index's market-cap and style range. That keeps portfolio turnover and trading fees low--and tax efficiency high: The fund's trailing three-year (through Dec. 12, 2006) annualized gain ranks in the category's top 25%, but its aftertax gains rank in the top 20%.

A side effect of the buffer zones is this ETF's sizable mid-cap stake, which stands at 38.6% of assets. But what it loses in style purity it gains in stability, as midsized firms should provide ballast if the economy and financial markets hit turbulence--further tempering the volatility associated with small-growth funds. The buffer zones also allow the fund to more fully capture the upside of former small caps when they rally into mid-cap territory.

The ETF's biggest draw, however, is its ultralow 0.12% expense ratio (frequent trading can rack up brokerage fees and erode that expense advantage, though). This is an appealing option.

Address:	PO Box 2600 Valley Forge PA 19482 866-499-8473
Web Address:	www.vanguard.com
Inception:	01-26-04 *
Advisor:	Vanguard Advisers, Inc.

Management Fee:	0.09%		
Expense Projections:	3Yr:$39	5Yr:$68	10Yr:$154
Income Distrib:	Annually		
Exchange:	AMEX		

MORNINGSTAR® ETFs 150

Data through December 31, 2006

Vanguard Sm Cp Val ETF VBR

Market Price $70.33	**Mstar Category** Small Value

Morningstar Fair Value

Price/Fair Value Ratio	Coverage Rate %
0.99 Fairly valued	51 Poor

Management

In 2005, Michael Buek became this fund's listed manager, taking over from Gus Sauter, Vanguard's chief investment officer. Buek has been with Vanguard since 1987 and has helped manage this fund since 1991. Buek also manages Vanguard Small Cap Index and the venerable Vanguard 500.

Methodology

This exchange-traded fund is tethered to the MSCI U.S. Small Cap Value Index, which consists of the cheapest stocks (as determined by its eight-pronged classification scheme) in the small-cap universe. The index uses bands to limit the migration of stocks between market-cap and style boundaries, thus limiting turnover.

Morningstar Rating	Return	Risk	Yield	NAV	Avg Daily Vol. (k)	52 wk High/Low
— Not Rated	Not Rated	—	1.9%	$71.16	61	$73.15 - $62.01

Growth of $10,000
- Investment Value of ETF
- Investment Value of Index S&P 500

Trading Volume Millions

History	1997	1998	1999	2000	2001	2002	2003	2004	2005	2006
NAV $	—	—	—	—	—	—	—	58.31	60.76	71.16
Market Price $	—	—	—	—	—	—	—	58.30	60.69	71.13
NAV Return%	—	—	—	—	—	—	—	14.53*	6.20	19.40
Market Price Return%	—	—	—	—	—	—	—	14.51*	6.09	19.49
Avg Premium/Discount%	—	—	—	—	—	—	—	-0.03	-0.14	-0.04
NAV Rtrn% +/-S&P 500	—	—	—	—	—	—	—	14.53	1.29	3.61
NAV Rtrn% +/-Russ 2000 VL	—	—	—	—	—	—	—	14.53	1.49	-4.08
NAV Return% Rank in Cat	—	—	—	—	—	—	—		5	6
Income Return %	—	—	—	—	—	—	—		2.00	2.26
Capital Return %	—	—	—	—	—	—	—		4.20	17.14
Income $	—	—	—	—	—	—	—	0.97	1.17	1.37
Capital Gains $	—	—	—	—	—	—	—	0.00	0.00	0.00
Expense Ratio %	—	—	—	—	—	—	—	0.22	0.12	—
Income Ratio %	—	—	—	—	—	—	—	2.16	2.07	—
Turnover Rate %	—	—	—	—	—	—	—	30	28	—
Net Assets $mil	—	—	—	—	—	—	—	47	188	510

Performance 12-31-06

Historic Quarterly NAV Returns

	1st Qtr	2nd Qtr	3rd Qtr	4th Qtr	Total
2002	—	—	—	—	—
2003	—	—	—	—	—
2004	—	0.93	1.06	13.04	—*
2005	-3.28	5.23	4.06	0.27	6.20
2006	11.11	-2.68	1.74	8.54	19.40

Trailing	NAV Return%	Market Return%	NAV Rtrn% +/-S&P 500	%Rank Cat.(NAV)
3 Mo	8.54	8.54	1.84	7
6 Mo	10.42	10.48	-2.32	7
1 Yr	19.40	19.49	3.61	6
3 Yr Avg	—	—	—	—
5 Yr Avg	—	—	—	—
10 Yr Avg	—	—	—	—

Tax Analysis	Tax-Adj Return%	Tax-Cost Ratio
3 Yr (estimated)	—	—
5 Yr (estimated)	—	—
10 Yr (estimated)	—	—

Rating and Risk

Time Period	Morningstar Rtn vs Cat	Morningstar Risk vs Cat	Morningstar Risk-Adj Rating
3 Yr	—	—	—
5 Yr	—	—	—
10 Yr	—	—	—

Other Measures	Standard Index S&P 500	Best Fit Index
Alpha	—	—
Beta	—	—
R-Squared	—	—
Standard Deviation	—	
Mean	—	
Sharpe Ratio	—	

Morningstar's Take by Reginald Laing 12-31-06

Vanguard Small Cap Value ETF is decent, though it will have trouble keeping up its recent pace.

This exchange-traded fund has benefited in recent years from a favorable market. For the past several years, small-value equities have posted double-digit yearly gains and led all other style categories. For that reason, this offering--which invests in more than 900 micro- to mid-cap value stocks and charges an extremely cheap expense ratio--has posted strong absolute and relative returns: For the trailing three years through Dec. 22, 2006, its older, conventional mutual fund share class delivered a 16.1% annualized gain--a better record than 77% of its peers.

However, market conditions won't always be so favorable, and it's unlikely that this fund will maintain its recent pace indefinitely. If, in the coming years, its small-value universe falters relative to the rest of the market, this ETF's absolute returns could be far less impressive. Its relative returns might suffer, too, as actively managed peers could outmaneuver the index by investing in bigger and more growth-oriented stocks that this ETF forsakes.

That doesn't mean you should avoid this offering. It remains one of the lowest-cost options in the category, and its broad exposure limits stock- and sector-specific risk. Moreover, this ETF's use of buffer zones, which limit the migration of stocks into and out of the index, should limit portfolio turnover, making it tax-efficient and keeping trading costs (which come out of assets but aren't included in a fund's published expense ratio) low. And as money has flowed into hot-performing small-value funds in recent years, finding a good active manager with capacity can now be a challenge. Last, because this ETF tracks a less commonly followed index, management can add and delete holdings without worrying about front-runners, who buy stocks in anticipation of their being added to the bogy (and bid up by indexers) and can hurt investors' returns.

Address:	PO Box 2600, Valley Forge PA 19482, 866-499-8473
Web Address:	www.vanguard.com
Inception:	01-26-04*
Advisor:	Vanguard Advisers, Inc.

Management Fee:	0.09%
Expense Projections:	3Yr:$39 5Yr:$68 10Yr:$154
Income Distrib:	Annually
Exchange:	AMEX

Portfolio Analysis 09-30-06

Share change since 06-06 Total Stocks:973

	Sector	PE	Tot Ret%	% Assets
Camden Property Trust	Financial	33.3	32.17	0.47
Federal Realty Investmen	Financial	55.6	44.88	0.45
Ventas, Inc.	Financial	33.1	38.19	0.40
Northeast Utilities	Utilities	33.9	47.76	0.39
Reckson Associates Realt	Financial	46.1	31.78	0.39
Plains Exploration & Pro	Energy	—	19.63	0.37
OGE Energy Corp	Utilities	16.3	55.73	0.36
Harsco Corporation	Ind Mtrls	16.3	14.65	0.36
Mack-Cali Realty Corpora	Financial	34.7	24.56	0.36
Integrated Device Techno	Hardware		17.45	0.36
CMS Energy Corporation	Utilities		15.09	0.35
Conseco, Inc.	Financial	23.8	-13.77	0.35
Sierra Pacific Resources	Utilities	12.5	29.06	0.35
Ryder System, Inc.	Business	13.1	26.29	0.35
Lubrizol Corporation	Ind Mtrls	16.7	18.17	0.34
BRE Properties, Inc.	Financial	73.1	48.20	0.34
Ann Taylor Stores Corpor	Consumer	16.1	-4.87	0.34
Brandywine Realty Trust	Financial	—	24.09	0.33
Energen Corporation	Energy	14.7	30.75	0.32
OfficeMax, Inc.	Consumer		98.81	0.32

Current Investment Style

Value Blend Growth — Large Mid Small

Market Cap	%
Giant	0.0
Large	0.0
Mid	41.9
Small	51.1
Micro	7.0
Avg $mil:	1,470

Value Measures		Rel Category
Price/Earnings	14.66	0.97
Price/Book	1.67	0.98
Price/Sales	0.81	1.09
Price/Cash Flow	6.38	1.06
Dividend Yield %	2.54	1.23

Growth Measures	%	Rel Category
Long-Term Erngs	10.25	0.96
Book Value	4.19	0.90
Sales	7.70	1.80
Cash Flow	2.10	0.57
Historical Erngs	9.95	1.05

Profitability	%	Rel Category
Return on Equity	9.88	0.94
Return on Assets	6.12	0.93
Net Margin	11.09	1.11

Sector Weightings	% of Stocks	Rel S&P 500	3 Year High Low
Info	9.14	0.46	
Software	1.60	0.46	2 1
Hardware	4.95	0.54	6 3
Media	1.74	0.46	2 1
Telecom	0.85	0.24	1 0
Service	56.43	1.22	
Health	2.50	0.21	4 2
Consumer	9.12	1.19	9 8
Business	8.03	1.90	8 6
Financial	36.78	1.65	39 36
Mfg	34.44	1.02	
Goods	5.61	0.66	6 5
Ind Mtrls	16.72	1.40	20 17
Energy	4.01	0.41	6 3
Utilities	8.10	2.31	9 8

Composition

	%
Cash	0.6
Stocks	99.4
Bonds	0.0
Other	0.0
Foreign (% of Stock)	0.5

MORNINGSTAR ETFs 150

171

Vanguard TelcomSrv ETF VOX

Market Price $72.25	**Mstar Category** Specialty-Communications	

Morningstar Fair Value

Price/Fair Value Ratio	Coverage Rate %
1.03 Fairly valued	79 Fair

Management

Ryan Ludt is the manager of this and other Vanguard sector offerings. He is supported by Vanguard's Quantitative Equity Group. Gus Sauter, Vanguard's chief investment officer and indexing pro, oversees the group.

Methodology

This ETF tracks the MSCI U.S. Investable Telecommunications Services Index, a subset of the market-cap-weighted MSCI U.S. Investable Market 2500 Index. The MSCI Telecom index holds fewer than 50 stocks that offer communications services through fixed-line, cellular, wireless, high-bandwidth, or fiber-optic cable networks. The index and ETF don't include equipment makers, such as Qualcomm. The index is so concentrated, the ETF has to modify the weightings of its largest holdings to comply with IRS diversification rules. So, the fund won't exactly mimic its bogy.

Morningstar Rating	Return	Risk	Yield	NAV	Avg Daily Vol. (k)	52 wk High/Low
— Not Rated	Not Rated		1.3%	$73.47	31	$74.02 - $55.80

Growth of $10,000
- Investment Value of ETF
- Investment Value of Index S&P 500

Trading Volume Millions

	1997	1998	1999	2000	2001	2002	2003	2004	2005	2006	History
	—	—	—	—	—	—	—	54.93	54.45	73.47	NAV $
	—	—	—	—	—	—	—	54.90	54.46	73.51	Market Price $
	—	—	—	—	—	—	—	21.18*	1.92	36.65	NAV Return%
	—	—	—	—	—	—	—	21.91*	2.00	36.70	Market Price Return%
	—	—	—	—	—	—	—	0.02	-0.07	-0.01	Avg Premium/Discount%
	—	—	—	—	—	—	—	21.18	-2.99	20.86	NAV Rtrn% +/-S&P 500
	—	—	—	—	—	—	—	21.18	5.92	-0.18	NAV Rtrn% +/-DJ Telecom
	—	—	—	—	—	—	—	—	3	5	NAV Return% Rank in Cat
	—	—	—	—	—	—	—	—	2.83	1.70	Income Return %
	—	—	—	—	—	—	—	—	-0.91	34.95	Capital Return %
	—	—	—	—	—	—	—	0.41	1.56	0.93	Income $
	—	—	—	—	—	—	—	0.00	0.00	0.00	Capital Gains $
	—	—	—	—	—	—	—	—	0.26	0.25	Expense Ratio %
	—	—	—	—	—	—	—	—	2.72	3.31	Income Ratio %
	—	—	—	—	—	—	—	—	41	32	Turnover Rate %
	—	—	—	—	—	—	—	16	22	147	Net Assets $mil

Performance 12-31-06

Historic Quarterly NAV Returns

	1st Qtr	2nd Qtr	3rd Qtr	4th Qtr	Total
2002	—	—	—	—	—
2003	—	—	—	—	—
2004	—	—	—	11.91	—*
2005	-6.55	4.75	2.57	1.52	1.92
2006	14.82	-0.74	10.15	8.85	36.65

Trailing	NAV Return%	Market Return%	NAV Rtrn% +/-S&P 500	%Rank Cat.(NAV)
3 Mo	8.85	8.89	2.15	6
6 Mo	19.90	19.96	7.16	5
1 Yr	36.65	36.70	20.86	5
3 Yr Avg	—	—	—	—
5 Yr Avg	—	—	—	—
10 Yr Avg	—	—	—	—

Tax Analysis	Tax-Adj Return%	Tax-Cost Ratio
3 Yr (estimated)	—	—
5 Yr (estimated)	—	—
10 Yr (estimated)	—	—

Rating and Risk

Time Period	Morningstar Rtn vs Cat	Morningstar Risk vs Cat	Morningstar Risk-Adj Rating
3 Yr	—	—	—
5 Yr	—	—	—
10 Yr	—	—	—

Other Measures	Standard Index S&P 500	Best Fit Index
Alpha	—	—
Beta	—	—
R-Squared	—	—
Standard Deviation	—	
Mean	—	
Sharpe Ratio	—	

Morningstar's Take by Andrew Gogerty 12-31-06

Vanguard Telecom Services ETF is one of the few Vanguard offerings we don't recommend.

Vanguard index offerings typically deliver a compelling one-two punch of low costs and low tracking error versus their respective benchmarks. With regard to fees, this fund is true to its family heritage. Its 0.26% expense ratio is not only the cheapest levy for a communications ETF, but also ranks among the least expensive of all ETFs.

Tracking error is a different story, but blame rests with the index, not fund management. The fund's portfolio can't directly mirror its MSCI telecom benchmark because it would violate diversification rules that cap any single fund position at 25% of assets. In addition, half of the portfolio's holdings must be less than 5% each. So the fund has modified positions in the index's biggest constituents, such as AT&T and Verizon. Because of these construction limitations, investors have seen gaps of more than 2 percentage points in returns versus the index in the past, and are likely to see more of the same.

Even if the fund's portfolio was able to mirror its index, we still wouldn't invest here. Although this ETF's assets are spread more evenly than its benchmark, it's still extremely tilted toward a select few. More than 60% of the fund's assets are stashed in its top five holdings, including a 30% stake in just AT&T and Verizon combined. So this fund is far from an all-weather choice, but rather will sink or swim based on its top holdings. AT&T and Verizon's strong gains have led to one of the category's best showings in 2006.

In addition, the regional bell operating companies (RBOCs) that dominate this portfolio, such as AT&T, Verizon, and Qwest Communications International, face big competitive challenges and must make massive capital outlays to offer the same services as rival cable companies. Any offering with a top-heavy portfolio focused on a volatile area of the market is best avoided. We'd look elsewhere.

Address:	PO Box 2600 Valley Forge PA 19482 866-499-8473
Web Address:	www.vanguard.com
Inception:	09-29-04 *
Advisor:	Vanguard Advisers, Inc.

Management Fee:	0.26%		
Expense Projections:	3Yr:$84	5Yr:$146	10Yr:$331
Income Distrib:	Annually		
Exchange:	AMEX		

Portfolio Analysis 09-30-06

Share change since 06-06 Total Stocks:44	Sector	PE	Tot Ret%	% Assets
⊕ AT&T, Inc.	Telecom	19.2	51.59	18.77
⊕ Verizon Communications	Telecom	16.1	34.88	14.05
⊕ BellSouth Corporation	Telecom	—	—	8.55
⊕ Sprint Nextel Corporatio	Telecom	29.1	-10.44	5.18
⊕ Alltel Corp.	Telecom	17.6	19.54	4.09
⊕ American Tower Corporati	Telecom	—	37.56	3.93
⊕ Qwest Communications Int	Telecom	—	48.14	3.65
⊕ Windstream Corporation	Telecom	—	37.36	3.26
⊕ NII Holdings, Inc.	Telecom	47.0	47.53	2.61
⊕ Crown Castle Internation	Telecom	—	20.94	2.35
⊕ Embarq Corporation	Telecom	—	—	2.16
⊕ Level 3 Communications,	Telecom	—	95.12	2.02
⊕ Citizens Communications	Telecom	17.1	26.56	1.72
⊕ Centurytel, Inc.	Telecom	14.4	32.52	1.68
⊕ Time Warner Telecom, Inc	Telecom	—	102.34	1.26
⊕ Leap Wireless Internatio	Telecom	79.3	57.00	1.25
⊕ SBA Communications Corpo	Telecom	—	53.63	1.18
⊕ NeuStar, Inc.	Telecom	—	—	1.12
⊕ Commonwealth Telephone E	Telecom	12.7	31.08	1.04
⊕ Broadwing Corporation	Telecom	—	—	1.04

Current Investment Style

Value Blnd Growth — Large Mid Small

Market Cap	%
Giant	42.4
Large	17.3
Mid	22.9
Small	12.7
Micro	4.6
Avg $mil:	17,028

Value Measures		Rel Category
Price/Earnings	17.71	1.02
Price/Book	1.48	0.81
Price/Sales	1.77	1.03
Price/Cash Flow	6.60	0.90
Dividend Yield %	3.00	1.06

Growth Measures	%	Rel Category
Long-Term Erngs	7.87	0.81
Book Value	16.14	1.54
Sales	-1.21	NMF
Cash Flow	4.59	0.93
Historical Erngs	5.52	0.50

Profitability	%	Rel Category
Return on Equity	8.19	0.59
Return on Assets	2.74	0.53
Net Margin	5.93	0.78

Industry Weightings	% of Stocks	Rel Cat
Telecom Srv	71.9	2.2
Wireless Srv	25.8	0.9
Network Eq	0.0	0.0
Semis	0.0	0.0
Big Media	0.0	0.0
Cable TV	0.0	0.0
Other Media	0.0	0.0
Soft/Hardwr	0.0	0.0
Other	2.3	0.3

Composition

● Cash	0.1	
● Stocks	99.8	
● Bonds	0.0	
○ Other	0.0	
Foreign (% of Stock)	0.0	

MORNINGSTAR® ETFs 150

Vanguard TSM ETF VTI

	Market Price $139.63	**Mstar Category** Large Blend

Morningstar Fair Value

Price/Fair Value Ratio	Coverage Rate %
0.91 Undervalued	89 Good

Management

Day-to-day managerial chores at this fund are handled by Gerard O'Reilly, a member of Vanguard's vaunted indexing team. O'Reilly has worked on this ETF since its inception and has been with Vanguard since 1992.

Methodology

The fund shadows the MSCI U.S. Broad Market Index. It would be impractical to own each smaller company in the index, so, among the tiniest firms, manager Gerard O'Reilly selects a representative sample.

Morningstar Rating	Return	Risk	Yield	NAV	Avg Daily Vol. (k)	52 wk High/Low
★★★★ Above Avg	Above Avg	Average	1.6%	$140.08	148	$141.69 - $121.31

Growth of $10,000
— Investment Value of ETF
— Investment Value of Index S&P 500

Trading Volume Millions

	1997	1998	1999	2000	2001	2002	2003	2004	2005	2006	History
	—	—	—	—	105.80	82.47	106.81	118.21	123.25	140.08	NAV $
	—	—	—	—	105.39	82.52	106.46	118.05	123.33	140.21	Market Price $
	—	—	—	—	5.30*	-20.94	31.43	12.55	6.10	15.66	NAV Return%
	—	—	—	—	5.34*	-20.58	30.93	12.77	6.31	15.69	Market Price Return%
	—	—	—	—	0.32	-0.09	-0.01	0.01	0.04	0.02	Avg Premium/Discount%
	—	—	—	—	5.30	1.16	2.75	1.67	1.19	-0.13	NAV Rtrn% +/-S&P 500
	—	—	—	—	5.30	0.71	1.54	1.15	-0.17	0.20	NAV Rtrn% +/-Russ 1000
	—	—	—	—	—	14	14	16	21	30	NAV Return% Rank in Cat
	—	—	—	—	—	1.19	1.69	1.79	1.77	1.88	Income Return %
	—	—	—	—	—	-22.13	29.74	10.76	4.33	13.78	Capital Return %
	—	—	—	—	0.99	1.25	1.38	1.90	2.08	2.30	Income $
	—	—	—	—	0.00	0.00	0.00	0.00	0.00	0.00	Capital Gains $
	—	—	—	—	0.15	0.15	0.15	0.13	0.07	—	Expense Ratio %
	—	—	—	—	1.26	1.38	1.54	1.79	1.74	—	Income Ratio %
	—	—	—	—	7	4	11	4	12	—	Turnover Rate %
	—	—	—	—	—	1,452	2,517	4,259	5,612	6,885	Net Assets $mil

Performance 12-31-06

Historic Quarterly NAV Returns

	1st Qtr	2nd Qtr	3rd Qtr	4th Qtr	Total
2002	0.95	-12.67	-16.82	7.81	-20.94
2003	-3.13	16.46	3.62	12.43	31.43
2004	2.59	1.29	-1.83	10.33	12.55
2005	-2.38	2.20	4.05	2.19	6.10
2006	5.38	-1.94	4.52	7.09	15.66

Trailing	NAV Return%	Market Return%	NAV Rtrn% +/-S&P 500	%Rank Cat.(NAV)
3 Mo	7.09	7.19	0.39	44
6 Mo	11.93	12.02	-0.81	38
1 Yr	15.66	15.69	-0.13	30
3 Yr Avg	11.37	11.52	0.93	15
5 Yr Avg	7.49	7.60	1.30	13
10 Yr Avg	—	—	—	—

Tax Analysis	Tax-Adj Return%	Tax-Cost Ratio
3 Yr (estimated)	11.03	0.31
5 Yr (estimated)	7.14	0.33
10 Yr (estimated)	—	—

Rating and Risk

Time Period	Morningstar Rtn vs Cat	Morningstar Risk vs Cat	Morningstar Risk-Adj Rating
3 Yr	+Avg	Avg	★★★★
5 Yr	+Avg	Avg	★★★★
10 Yr	—	—	—

Other Measures	Standard Index S&P 500	Best Fit Index Russ 1000
Alpha	0.1	-0.2
Beta	1.11	1.08
R-Squared	98	99
Standard Deviation	7.72	
Mean	11.37	
Sharpe Ratio	1.03	

Morningstar's Take by Dan Culloton 12-31-06

Vanguard Total Stock Market ETF has it all, literally.

This exchange-traded fund delivers exposure to the broad domestic stock market at a price that is hard for retail investors to beat. Its index, the MSCI U.S. Broad Market Index, encompasses virtually every domestic stock, so it's suitable as a core (or sole) U.S. equity holding. For that, it charges an ultralow expense ratio of 0.07%, which makes it not only one of the lowest-cost ETFs in the large-blend category (the other is sibling Vanguard Large Cap ETF), but also one of the lowest-cost ETFs in existence. (Remember, though, that commission costs incurred to buy and sell this ETF could quickly negate that advantage.)

Those two traits, diversification and low costs, give this ETF an enduring advantage in a category crowded with competitive conventional and exchange-traded funds. A lot of new funds touting purportedly better ways to track the market have emerged in recent years. They range from funds

tracking indexes that weight their constituents by fundamental factors, such as dividends, to offerings that use quantitative stock-picking models to beat traditional benchmarks. It's hard to rival this ETF's cost, but some newcomers come close to matching its diversification.

Nevertheless, this ETF has other advantages that help it stand up to the competition. It is run by an experienced indexer, Gerard O'Reilly, who knows how to control tax and transaction costs. Indeed, the fund's tracking error, or the amount by which it trails its benchmark, is usually no more than the size of its expense ratio, which indicates its manager does a good job aping the index.

Finally, the ETF's long-term track record looks strong on a pre- and post-tax basis. Because this fund owns more small caps than other core funds, it may look a bit sluggish in the future if small stocks surrender the market leadership they've enjoyed in recent years. This fund can still serve as an excellent core holding, though.

Address:	PO Box 2600 Valley Forge PA 19482 866-499-8473
Web Address:	www.vanguard.com
Inception:	05-31-01 *
Advisor:	Vanguard Advisers, Inc.

Management Fee:	0.05%		
Expense Projections:	3Yr:$23	5Yr:$40	10Yr:$90
Income Distrib:	Quarterly		
Exchange:	AMEX		

Portfolio Analysis 09-30-06

Share change since 06-06 Total Stocks:3727	Sector	PE	Tot Ret%	% Assets
⊕ ExxonMobil Corporation	Energy	11.7	39.07	2.68
⊕ General Electric Company	Ind Mtrls	19.8	9.35	2.43
⊕ Citigroup, Inc.	Financial	13.3	19.55	1.63
⊕ Bank of America Corporat	Financial	12.4	20.68	1.62
⊖ Microsoft Corporation	Software	23.7	15.83	1.60
⊕ Pfizer Inc.	Health	15.1	15.22	1.37
⊕ Procter & Gamble Company	Goods	24.2	13.36	1.34
⊕ Johnson & Johnson	Health	17.4	12.44	1.27
⊕ J.P. Morgan Chase & Co.	Financial	13.7	25.60	1.08
⊕ Altria Group, Inc.	Goods	15.9	19.87	1.06
⊕ American International G	Financial	17.1	6.05	0.97
⊕ Chevron Corporation	Energy	9.3	33.75	0.95
⊕ Cisco Systems, Inc.	Hardware	28.8	59.64	0.93
⊕ IBM	Hardware	16.8	19.77	0.84
⊕ AT&T, Inc.	Telecom	19.2	51.59	0.84
⊕ Wal-Mart Stores, Inc.	Consumer	16.6	0.13	0.82
⊕ Intel Corporation	Hardware	20.3	-17.18	0.79
⊕ Wells Fargo Company	Financial	14.7	16.82	0.76
⊕ Verizon Communications	Telecom	16.1	34.88	0.72
⊕ PepsiCo, Inc.	Goods	21.4	7.86	0.71

Current Investment Style

Value Blnd Growth — Large / Mid / Small

	Market Cap	%
	Giant	41.1
	Large	31.2
	Mid	19.5
	Small	6.1
	Micro	2.1
	Avg $mil: 26,900	

Value Measures		Rel Category
Price/Earnings	15.48	0.93
Price/Book	2.49	0.91
Price/Sales	1.37	1.08
Price/Cash Flow	7.18	0.76
Dividend Yield %	1.81	1.01

Growth Measures	%	Rel Category
Long-Term Erngs	11.50	1.00
Book Value	8.26	0.97
Sales	9.28	1.12
Cash Flow	9.64	1.28
Historical Erngs	16.90	1.01

Profitability	%	Rel Category
Return on Equity	18.25	0.95
Return on Assets	9.97	1.04
Net Margin	13.43	1.20

Sector Weightings	% of Stocks	Rel S&P 500	3 Year High	Low
↻ Info	19.47	0.97		
🖥 Software	3.59	1.04	4	3
💻 Hardware	9.14	0.99	10	9
🔊 Media	3.42	0.90	5	3
☎ Telecom	3.32	0.95	3	3
⊂ Service	48.45	1.05		
🏥 Health	12.61	1.05	13	12
🛒 Consumer	8.08	1.06	10	8
📋 Business	5.36	1.27	6	5
💲 Financial	22.40	1.01	23	20
🔧 Mfg	32.09	0.95		
🏭 Goods	7.93	0.93	9	8
🔩 Ind Mtrls	11.61	0.97	12	10
🔥 Energy	9.05	0.92	10	6
💡 Utilities	3.50	1.00	4	3

Composition

● Cash	0.5	
● Stocks	99.5	
● Bonds	0.0	
○ Other	0.0	
Foreign	0.1	
(% of Stock)		

Vanguard Utilities ETF VPU

	Market Price $75.53	Mstar Category Specialty-Utilities

Morningstar Fair Value

Price/Fair Value Ratio	Coverage Rate %
1.03 Fairly valued	87 Good

Management

Gus Sauter has managed this fund since its January 2004 inception. He also manages many other Vanguard index funds, including the other sector ETFs, though his name is no longer on the flagship Vanguard 500 Index.

Methodology

This exchange-traded fund tracks the MSCI U.S. Investable Market Utilities Index, an index of 89 domestic utility stocks. This index consists almost entirely of electric and natural-gas utilities, and thus doesn't contain the telecom and energy stocks found in the portfolios of most actively managed utilities-sector funds.

Morningstar Rating	Return	Risk	Yield	NAV	Avg Daily Vol. (k)	52 wk High/Low
— Not Rated	Not Rated	—	2.9%	$76.77	12	$78.09 - $63.43

Growth of $10,000
- Investment Value of ETF
- Investment Value of Index S&P 500

16.8
12.0
10.0

0.04
0.0

Trading Volume Millions

1997	1998	1999	2000	2001	2002	2003	2004	2005	2006	History
—	—	—	—	—	—	—	58.46	65.15	76.77	NAV $
—	—	—	—	—	—	—	58.56	65.14	76.81	Market Price $
—	—	—	—	—	—	—	19.53*	14.75	21.58	NAV Return%
—	—	—	—	—	—	—	19.54*	14.54	21.64	Market Price Return%
—	—	—	—	—	—	—	-0.02	-0.01	0.05	Avg Premium/Discount%
—	—	—	—	—	—	—	19.53	9.84	5.79	NAV Rtrn% +/-S&P 500
—	—	—	—	—	—	—	19.53	-10.39	4.95	NAV Rtrn% +/-DOWJNS UTIL
—	—	—	—	—	—	—	—	3	5	NAV Return% Rank in Cat
—	—	—	—	—	—	—	—	3.29	3.40	Income Return %
—	—	—	—	—	—	—	—	11.46	18.18	Capital Return %
—	—	—	—	—	—	—	1.55	1.90	2.19	Income $
—	—	—	—	—	—	—	0.00	0.00	0.00	Capital Gains $
—	—	—	—	—	—	—	0.28	0.26	0.25	Expense Ratio %
—	—	—	—	—	—	—	3.82	3.36	3.29	Income Ratio %
—	—	—	—	—	—	—	7	7	9	Turnover Rate %
—	—	—	—	—	—	—	53	105	163	Net Assets $mil

Performance 12-31-06

Historic Quarterly NAV Returns

	1st Qtr	2nd Qtr	3rd Qtr	4th Qtr	Total
2002	—	—	—	—	—
2003	—	—	—	—	—
2004	—	-0.86	6.00	11.79	—*
2005	4.41	9.41	6.88	-6.02	14.75
2006	-0.16	5.47	5.49	9.46	21.58

Trailing	NAV Return%	Market Return%	NAV Rtrn% +/-S&P 500	%Rank Cat.(NAV)
3 Mo	9.46	9.46	2.76	7
6 Mo	15.47	15.37	2.73	5
1 Yr	21.58	21.64	5.79	5
3 Yr Avg	—	—	—	—
5 Yr Avg	—	—	—	—
10 Yr Avg	—	—	—	—

Tax Analysis	Tax-Adj Return%	Tax-Cost Ratio
3 Yr (estimated)	—	—
5 Yr (estimated)	—	—
10 Yr (estimated)	—	—

Rating and Risk

Time Period	Morningstar Rtn vs Cat	Morningstar Risk vs Cat	Morningstar Risk-Adj Rating
3 Yr	—	—	—
5 Yr	—	—	—
10 Yr	—	—	—

Other Measures	Standard Index S&P 500	Best Fit Index
Alpha	—	—
Beta	—	—
R-Squared	—	—
Standard Deviation	—	
Mean	—	
Sharpe Ratio	—	

Morningstar's Take by David Kathman 12-31-06

Vanguard Utilities ETF is a decent option for ETF investors wanting pure utility exposure.

This niche exchange-traded fund tracks the MSCI U.S. Investable Market Utilities Index, which consists of around 90 utility stocks drawn from the broader MSCI U.S. Investable Market 2500 Index. Because it doesn't have any holdings in other areas such as energy or telecom, it provides purer utilities exposure than most actively managed utility funds. That can be both a good thing and a bad thing; the lack of energy stocks hurt the fund relative to its actively managed peers in 2005 and 2006, but this was partly canceled out by the lack of poorly performing telecom stocks.

This fund has a significantly smaller asset base than its two main ETF rivals, Utilities Select SPDR and iShares Dow Jones U.S. Utilities, and it also differs from each of them in other ways. The SPDR tracks the 31 utility stocks in the S&P 500 Index, and thus is more concentrated and has more large caps than this fund (86% versus 62%). The iShares

fund, which tracks the Dow Jones U.S. Utilities Index, is much more similar in construction to this fund, but is significantly more expensive, with a 0.60% expense ratio compared with this fund's 0.26%. (The SPDR also costs 0.26%.)

For investors seeking broad utility exposure in an ETF, this fund is marginally more attractive than its rivals: It's cheap like the SPDR, and diversified like the iShares fund. However, as with any ETF, only long-term investors who don't plan to trade much should consider this fund; otherwise, brokerage commissions will quickly erode any cost advantages.

Portfolio Analysis 09-30-06

Share change since 06-06 Total Stocks:89	Sector	PE	Tot Ret%	% Assets
⊕ Exelon Corporation	Utilities	—	19.78	7.46
⊕ Duke Energy Corporation	Utilities	14.6	30.15	6.91
⊕ TXU Corporation	Utilities	13.0	11.19	5.00
⊕ Dominion Resources, Inc.	Utilities	18.3	12.56	4.90
⊕ Southern Company	Utilities	17.8	11.69	4.72
⊕ FirstEnergy Corporation	Utilities	16.6	27.31	3.40
⊕ FPL Group	Utilities	17.7	35.49	3.19
⊕ Entergy Corporation	Utilities	19.9	38.40	3.00
⊕ Public Service Enterpris	Utilities	21.4	5.72	2.84
⊕ PG & E Corporation	Utilities	16.8	31.58	2.71
⊕ American Electric Power	Utilities	18.6	19.58	2.64
⊕ AES Corporation	Utilities	35.0	39.23	2.48
⊕ Edison International	Utilities	13.5	7.02	2.38
⊕ PPL Corporation	Utilities	15.4	26.06	2.31
⊕ Consolidated Edison Comp	Utilities	17.5	9.14	2.18
⊕ Sempra Energy	Utilities	10.9	28.10	2.16
⊕ Progress Energy, Inc.	Utilities	16.7	18.07	2.01
⊕ Ameren Corporation	Utilities	21.3	10.14	2.00
⊕ Constellation Energy Gro	Utilities	17.4	22.70	1.95
⊕ Xcel Energy, Inc.	Utilities	17.0	30.53	1.54

Current Investment Style

Value Blnd Growth — Large Mid Small

	Market Cap	%
	Giant	0.0
	Large	62.4
	Mid	32.4
	Small	5.2
	Micro	0.0
	Avg $mil:	11,022

Industry Weightings	% of Stocks	Rel Cat
Telecom Srv	0.0	0.0
Electric Utls	85.5	1.4
Nat Gas Utls	10.4	1.1
Wireless Srv	0.0	0.0
Energy	3.2	0.4
Media	0.0	0.0
Network Eq	0.0	0.0
Water	0.8	1.3
Other	0.0	0.0

Value Measures		Rel Category
Price/Earnings	16.06	0.91
Price/Book	1.98	0.91
Price/Sales	1.10	0.86
Price/Cash Flow	10.29	1.02
Dividend Yield %	3.18	1.00

Growth Measures	%	Rel Category
Long-Term Erngs	6.88	0.83
Book Value	1.87	0.55
Sales	7.17	1.53
Cash Flow	-11.93	NMF
Historical Erngs	5.10	0.70

Profitability	%	Rel Category
Return on Equity	10.94	0.87
Return on Assets	3.00	0.82
Net Margin	7.32	0.87

Composition

		%
● Cash		0.2
● Stocks		99.8
● Bonds		0.0
○ Other		0.0
Foreign (% of Stock)		0.0

Address:	PO Box 2600
	Valley Forge PA 19482
	866-499-8473
Web Address:	www.vanguard.com
Inception:	01-26-04 *
Advisor:	Vanguard Advisers, Inc.

Management Fee:	0.16%
Expense Projections:	3Yr:$90 5Yr:$157 10Yr:$356
Income Distrib:	Quarterly
Exchange:	AMEX

MORNINGSTAR® ETFs 150

Vanguard Value ETF VTV

	Market Price	Mstar Category
	$67.46	Large Value

Morningstar Fair Value

Price/Fair Value Ratio	Coverage Rate %
0.93 Undervalued	95 Good

Management

Gerard O'Reilly, the fund's day-to-day manager, has been with Vanguard since 1992. He has helped manage this fund's open-end version, Vanguard Value Index, since 1994. He also runs Vanguard Total Stock Market Index, Vanguard Growth Index, and Vanguard Small-Cap Growth Index.

Methodology

This ETF tracks the MSCI U.S. Prime Market Value Index, which consists of the value stocks within a universe of the 750 largest U.S. companies. MSCI classifies stocks as growth or value using an eight-factor model and also employs "buffer zones" to limit the migration of stocks between the growth and value camps and, thus, turnover.

Morningstar Rating	Return	Risk	Yield	NAV	Avg Daily Vol. (k)	52 wk High/Low
— Not Rated	Not Rated	—	2.3%	$68.14	154	$68.72 - $57.97

Growth of $10,000
— Investment Value of ETF
— Investment Value of Index S&P 500

Trading Volume Millions

	1997	1998	1999	2000	2001	2002	2003	2004	2005	2006	History
	—	—	—	—	—	—	—	54.74	57.14	68.14	NAV $
	—	—	—	—	—	—	—	54.75	57.17	68.23	Market Price $
	—	—	—	—	—	—	—	13.77*	7.19	22.28	NAV Return%
	—	—	—	—	—	—	—	13.82*	7.22	22.37	Market Price Return%
	—	—	—	—	—	—	—	0.02	0.08	0.06	Avg Premium/Discount%
	—	—	—	—	—	—	—	13.77	2.28	6.49	NAV Rtrn% +/-S&P 500
	—	—	—	—	—	—	—	13.77	0.14	0.03	NAV Rtrn% +/-Russ 1000 Vl
	—	—	—	—	—	—	—	—	11	14	NAV Return% Rank in Cat
	—	—	—	—	—	—	—	—	2.73	2.79	Income Return %
	—	—	—	—	—	—	—	—	4.46	19.49	Capital Return %
	—	—	—	—	—	—	—	1.22	1.48	1.58	Income $
	—	—	—	—	—	—	—	0.00	0.00	0.00	Capital Gains $
	—	—	—	—	—	—	—	0.15	0.11	—	Expense Ratio %
	—	—	—	—	—	—	—	2.46	2.72	—	Income Ratio %
	—	—	—	—	—	—	—	18	21	—	Turnover Rate %
	—	—	—	—	—	—	—	406	600	1,646	Net Assets $mil

Performance 12-31-06

Historic Quarterly NAV Returns

	1st Qtr	2nd Qtr	3rd Qtr	4th Qtr	Total
2002	—	—	—	—	—
2003	—	—	—	—	—
2004	—	1.55	1.24	9.79	—*
2005	-0.37	1.73	4.08	1.60	7.19
2006	5.32	0.97	6.64	7.83	22.28

Trailing	NAV Return%	Market Return%	NAV Rtrn% +/-S&P 500	%Rank Cat.(NAV)
3 Mo	7.83	7.92	1.13	16
6 Mo	14.99	14.91	2.25	16
1 Yr	22.28	22.37	6.49	14
3 Yr Avg	—	—	—	—
5 Yr Avg	—	—	—	—
10 Yr Avg	—	—	—	—

Tax Analysis	Tax-Adj Return%	Tax-Cost Ratio
3 Yr (estimated)	—	—
5 Yr (estimated)	—	—
10 Yr (estimated)	—	—

Rating and Risk

Time Period	Morningstar Rtn vs Cat	Morningstar Risk vs Cat	Morningstar Risk-Adj Rating
3 Yr	—	—	—
5 Yr	—	—	—
10 Yr	—	—	—

Other Measures	Standard Index S&P 500	Best Fit Index
Alpha	—	—
Beta	—	—
R-Squared	—	—
Standard Deviation	—	
Mean	—	
Sharpe Ratio	—	

Portfolio Analysis 09-30-06

Share change since 06-06 Total Stocks:413

	Sector	PE	Tot Ret%	% Assets
⊕ ExxonMobil Corporation	Energy	11.7	39.07	5.97
⊕ General Electric Company	Ind Mtrls	19.8	9.35	5.39
⊕ Citigroup, Inc.	Financial	13.3	19.55	3.63
⊕ Bank of America Corporat	Financial	12.4	20.68	3.59
⊕ Pfizer Inc.	Health	15.1	15.22	3.05
⊕ J.P. Morgan Chase & Co.	Financial	13.7	25.60	2.40
⊕ Altria Group, Inc.	Goods	15.9	19.87	2.35
⊕ Chevron Corporation	Energy	9.3	33.75	2.11
⊕ AT&T, Inc.	Telecom	19.2	51.59	1.86
⊕ Wells Fargo Company	Financial	14.7	16.82	1.70
⊕ Verizon Communications	Telecom	16.1	34.88	1.59
⊕ Wachovia Corporation	Financial	13.0	12.02	1.57
⊕ Coca-Cola Company	Goods	21.5	23.10	1.39
⊕ ConocoPhillips	Energy	6.9	26.53	1.37
⊕ Merck & Co., Inc.	Health	18.8	42.66	1.34
⊕ BellSouth Corporation	Telecom	—	—	1.14
⊕ Time Warner, Inc.	Media	19.1	26.37	1.12
⊕ Abbott Laboratories	Health	23.6	26.88	1.09
⊕ Morgan Stanley	Financial	12.3	45.93	1.03
⊕ Merrill Lynch & Company,	Financial	14.1	39.27	1.01

Current Investment Style

Value Blnd Growth — Large Mid Small

Market Cap	%
Giant	51.5
Large	32.0
Mid	16.5
Small	0.0
Micro	0.0

Avg $mil: 49,881

Value Measures		Rel Category
Price/Earnings	13.02	0.91
Price/Book	2.17	0.90
Price/Sales	1.28	0.96
Price/Cash Flow	5.17	0.67
Dividend Yield %	2.70	1.04

Growth Measures	%	Rel Category
Long-Term Erngs	9.39	0.93
Book Value	7.53	1.05
Sales	9.24	1.08
Cash Flow	5.98	0.70
Historical Erngs	14.56	0.94

Profitability	%	Rel Category
Return on Equity	17.07	0.98
Return on Assets	10.02	1.00
Net Margin	14.62	1.07

Sector Weightings

	% of Stocks	Rel S&P 500	3 Year High Low	
☊ Info	10.27	0.51		
Software	0.31	0.09	2	0
Hardware	2.69	0.29	4	2
Media	1.94	0.51	4	2
Telecom	5.33	1.52	5	4
⊂ Service	48.78	1.06		
Health	8.85	0.73	9	5
Consumer	3.56	0.47	4	3
Business	1.39	0.33	2	1
Financial	34.98	1.57	36	33
⊿ Mfg	40.96	1.21		
Goods	8.19	0.96	8	7
Ind Mtrls	13.46	1.13	20	12
Energy	13.00	1.33	16	11
Utilities	6.31	1.80	6	5

Composition

● Cash	0.2	
● Stocks	99.8	
● Bonds	0.0	
Other	0.0	
Foreign	0.1	
	(% of Stock)	

Morningstar's Take by Reginald Laing 12-31-06

Vanguard Value ETF has benefited from a strong market in large-value stocks, but remains attractive.

Style-specific index offerings tend to have their best relative performance when the segment of the market they track is in favor. That's been the case with this exchange-traded fund. As large-value has comfortably outpaced the other squares of the Morningstar Style Box in the past year, this ETF's nearly pure large-value exposure and low fees have lifted it relative to its category: For the trailing 12 months through Dec. 20, 2006, its 20.9% gain far outpaced the 17.1% gain of its average peer.

Of course, recent performance isn't a strong predictor of future returns, and one can't expect this ETF to trounce its peer group indefinitely. In particular, when market leadership rotates elsewhere, this fund may have difficulty keeping up: Its actively managed peers will be able to drift into more growth-oriented stocks or down the market-cap ladder when those segments of the market pull ahead, while this passive fund will mostly have to stick to its corner of the style box.

But the case for this ETF is as compelling as ever. First, it represents retail investors' cheapest option in the category. (It costs money to buy and sell it, though, and frequent trading can erase that expense advantage.) So, while active managers might outpace this ETF over short periods by chasing this or that hot area of the market, its sizable expense advantage should make it tough to beat over long stretches of time. Also, though this ETF has posted strong gains recently, there's reason to think it still has room to appreciate. Of its top 10 holdings, nine are trading at discounts to what Morningstar's stock analysts consider a discount to their fair value--financial-services company J.P. Morgan Chase at a sizable discount--which should at least give investors here a decent margin of safety.

We think this ETF has enduring merit for value-leaning investors in search of a core offering.

Address:	PO Box 2600
	Valley Forge PA 19482
	866-499-8473
Web Address:	www.vanguard.com
Inception:	01-26-04 *
Advisor:	Vanguard Advisers, Inc.

Management Fee:	0.09%
Expense Projections:	3Yr:$35 5Yr:$62 10Yr:$141
Income Distrib:	Quarterly
Exchange:	AMEX

MORNINGSTAR® ETFs 150

WisdomTree DIEFA DWM

Market Price $61.16	**Mstar Category** Foreign Large Blend	

Morningstar Fair Value

Price/Fair Value Ratio	Coverage Rate %
—	—

Management

WisdomTree Asset Management is the advisor. According to the prospectus, the firm doesn't manage any other investment companies and doesn't have much advisor experience. The Bank of New York has subadvisory responsibilities.

Methodology

This exchange-traded fund tracks the WisdomTree DIEFA Index, which emphasizes dividend payments more than market capitalization in its weightings. (Most index funds weight by market capitalization.) The index includes developed European markets and Japan and several other countries, but excludes the United States, Canada, and emerging markets.

	Morningstar Rating	Return	Risk	Yield	NAV	Avg Daily Vol. (k)	52 wk High/Low
	— Not Rated	— Not Rated	—	—	$61.53	21	$62.08 - $49.46

Growth of $10,000
- Investment Value of ETF
- Investment Value of Index MSCI EAFE

12.0
11.7
10.6
10.0

Trading Volume Millions
0.01
0.0

	1997	1998	1999	2000	2001	2002	2003	2004	2005	2006	History
	—	—	—	—	—	—	—	—	—	61.53	NAV $
	—	—	—	—	—	—	—	—	—	61.75	Market Price $
	—	—	—	—	—	—	—	—	—	23.68*	NAV Return%
	—	—	—	—	—	—	—	—	—	23.89*	Market Price Return%
	—	—	—	—	—	—	—	—	—	0.52	Avg Premium/Discount%
	—	—	—	—	—	—	—	—	—	23.68	NAV Rtrn% +/-MSCI EAFE
	—	—	—	—	—	—	—	—	—	23.68	NAV Rtrn% +/-MSCI Wd xUS
	—	—	—	—	—	—	—	—	—	—	NAV Return% Rank in Cat
	—	—	—	—	—	—	—	—	—	—	Income Return %
	—	—	—	—	—	—	—	—	—	—	Capital Return %
	—	—	—	—	—	—	—	—	—	0.21	Income $
	—	—	—	—	—	—	—	—	—	0.02	Capital Gains $
	—	—	—	—	—	—	—	—	—	—	Expense Ratio %
	—	—	—	—	—	—	—	—	—	—	Income Ratio %
	—	—	—	—	—	—	—	—	—	—	Turnover Rate %
	—	—	—	—	—	—	—	—	—	62	Net Assets $mil

Performance 12-31-06

Historic Quarterly NAV Returns

	1st Qtr	2nd Qtr	3rd Qtr	4th Qtr	Total
2002	—	—	—	—	—
2003	—	—	—	—	—
2004	—	—	—	—	—
2005	—	—	—	—	—
2006	—	—	5.23	12.09	—*

Trailing	NAV Return%	Market Return%	NAV Rtrn% +/-MSCI EAFE	%Rank Cat.(NAV)
3 Mo	12.09	11.50	1.74	7
6 Mo	17.95	18.00	3.26	6
1 Yr	—	—	—	—
3 Yr Avg	—	—	—	—
5 Yr Avg	—	—	—	—
10 Yr Avg	—	—	—	—

Tax Analysis	Tax-Adj Return%	Tax-Cost Ratio
3 Yr (estimated)	—	—
5 Yr (estimated)	—	—
10 Yr (estimated)	—	—

Rating and Risk

Time Period	Morningstar Rtn vs Cat	Morningstar Risk vs Cat	Morningstar Risk-Adj Rating
3 Yr	—	—	—
5 Yr	—	—	—
10 Yr	—	—	—

Other Measures	Standard Index S&P 500	Best Fit Index
Alpha	—	—
Beta	—	—
R-Squared	—	—
Standard Deviation	—	
Mean	—	
Sharpe Ratio	—	

Portfolio Analysis 11-30-06

Share change since 10-06 Total Stocks:609

	Sector	Country	% Assets
⊕ HSBC Hldgs	Financial	U.K.	2.25
⊕ BP	Energy	U.K.	1.88
⊕ Eni	Energy	Italy	1.78
⊕ Total SA	Energy	France	1.72
⊕ Vodafone Grp	Telecom	U.K.	1.29
⊕ France Telecom	Telecom	France	1.24
⊕ GlaxoSmithKline	Health	U.K.	1.17
⊕ Royal Dutch Shell	Energy	U.K.	1.16
⊕ Royal Bank Of Scotland G	Financial	U.K.	1.06
⊕ Deutsche Telekom	Telecom	Germany	1.05
⊕ Lloyds TSB Grp	Financial	U.K.	1.05
⊕ Barclays	Financial	U.K.	0.97
⊕ Banco Santander Central	Financial	Spain	0.96
⊕ UniCredito Italiano Grp	Financial	Italy	0.91
⊕ Telefonica	Telecom	Spain	0.89
⊕ China Mobile	Telecom	Hong Kong	0.83
⊕ Nestle	Goods	Switzerland	0.83
⊕ Royal Dutch Shell	Energy	U.K.	0.83
⊕ ING Groep	Financial	Netherlands	0.82
⊕ BNP Paribas	Financial	France	0.82

Current Investment Style

Value Blnd Growth — Large Mid Small

Market Cap	%
Giant	57.2
Large	35.0
Mid	7.3
Small	0.5
Micro	0.0

Avg $mil: 36,211

Value Measures		Rel Category
Price/Earnings	13.38	0.95
Price/Book	2.17	1.00
Price/Sales	1.07	1.10
Price/Cash Flow	7.65	1.01
Dividend Yield %	3.74	0.99

Growth Measures	%	Rel Category
Long-Term Erngs	10.42	0.92
Book Value	7.98	1.04
Sales	6.32	1.07
Cash Flow	1.89	0.77
Historical Erngs	19.94	1.04

Composition

Cash	0.2	Bonds	0.0
Stocks	99.6	Other	0.2
Foreign (% of Stock)			100.0

Sector Weightings	% of Stocks	Rel MSCI EAFE	3 Year High Low
☎ Info	14.82	1.25	
Software	0.30	0.54	— —
Hardware	1.78	0.46	— —
Media	2.47	1.35	— —
Telecom	10.27	1.84	— —
Service	46.86	0.99	
Health	4.61	0.65	— —
Consumer	4.07	0.82	— —
Business	4.35	0.86	— —
Financial	33.83	1.12	— —
Mfg	38.32	0.94	
Goods	10.58	0.81	— —
Ind Mtrls	11.15	0.72	— —
Energy	9.78	1.37	— —
Utilities	6.81	1.30	— —

Regional Exposure	% Stock		
UK/W. Europe 77	N. America	0	
Japan 8	Latn America	0	
Asia X Japan 14	Other	1	

Country Exposure	% Stock		
U.K.	27	Australia	8
France	13	Italy	7
Japan	8		

Morningstar's Take by Gregg Wolper 12-31-06

Don't think you're getting the MSCI EAFE Index from WisdomTree DIEFA Fund.

This offering aims to match the performance of a specially constructed WisdomTree Index that includes the same countries as the popular MSCI EAFE Index, the most well-known foreign-stock benchmark. Thus, it is restricted to markets generally recognized as developed markets, excluding Canada but including Hong Kong and Singapore. Also like EAFE, it leans heavily toward large companies. Not surprisingly, this exchange-traded fund's top 10 looks much like those of mutual funds and ETFs that track EAFE.

However, this fund has definite contrasts with EAFE and EAFE-trackers. In its index methodology, WisdomTree emphasizes the payment of dividends, and that leads to sharp differences. Most notably, its country weightings are vastly different. For example, Fidelity Spartan International Index, a conventional mutual fund, and iShares MSCI EAFE Index, an exchange-traded fund, currently both have nearly 24% of assets in Japan, while this offering has just 8.8% of assets in that large market, because so many Japanese companies pay paltry dividends, if any. Conversely, Australia gets nearly 8% of assets here and Italy 7.2%, each significantly more than in the EAFE trackers. In addition, this fund's stake in mid-caps is only about half the 12% position found in the EAFE trackers.

Whether these distinctions will give this fund better performance over the long run is open to question. WisdomTree's research shows that using dividend weighting rather than the market-cap weighting of regular index funds has provided stronger performance in the past, but whether that will be true in the future remains to be seen. What we do know for sure is that, with a projected expense ratio of 0.48%, this fund is costlier than several EAFE funds--another factor to consider.

Address:	48 Wall Street New York NY 10005 866-909-9473	Management Fee:	0.48%
		Expense Projections:	3Yr:$154 5Yr: — 10Yr: —
Web Address:	www.wisdomtree.com	Income Distrib:	Annually
Inception:	06-16-06*	Exchange:	NYSE
Advisor:	Wisdomtree Asset Management, Inc.		

 **ETFs 150**

WisdomTree DIEFA HiYld Eq DTH

	Market Price	Mstar Category
	$61.34	Foreign Large Blend

Morningstar Rating	Return	Risk	Yield	NAV	Avg Daily Vol. (k)	52 wk High/Low
— Not Rated	Not Rated	—	$61.56	21		$62.15 - $49.31

Morningstar Fair Value

Price/Fair Value Ratio — Coverage Rate % —

Management

WisdomTree Asset Management is the advisor. According to the prospectus, the firm doesn't manage any other investment companies and doesn't have much advisor experience. The Bank of New York has subadvisory responsibilities.

Methodology

This exchange-traded fund tracks the WisdomTree DIEFA High-Yielding Equity Index, which emphasizes dividend payments more than market capitalization in its weightings. (Most index funds weight by market capitalization.) The index includes developed European markets and Japan and several other countries, but excludes the United States, Canada, and emerging markets. This index takes the top 30% of companies, ranked by dividend yield, in the WisdomTree DIEFA Index.

Growth of $10,000
- Investment Value of ETF
- Investment Value of Index MSCI EAFE

Trading Volume Millions

	1997	1998	1999	2000	2001	2002	2003	2004	2005	2006	History
	—	—	—	—	—	—	—	—	—	61.56	NAV $
	—	—	—	—	—	—	—	—	—	61.75	Market Price $
	—	—	—	—	—	—	—	—	—	24.26*	NAV Return%
	—	—	—	—	—	—	—	—	—	24.46*	Market Price Return%
	—	—	—	—	—	—	—	—	—	0.64	Avg Premium/Discount%
	—	—	—	—	—	—	—	—	—	24.26	NAV Rtrn% +/-MSCI EAFE
	—	—	—	—	—	—	—	—	—	24.26	NAV Rtrn% +/-MSCI Wd xUS
	—	—	—	—	—	—	—	—	—	—	NAV Return% Rank in Cat
	—	—	—	—	—	—	—	—	—	—	Income Return %
	—	—	—	—	—	—	—	—	—	—	Capital Return %
	—	—	—	—	—	—	—	—	—	0.28	Income $
	—	—	—	—	—	—	—	—	—	0.00	Capital Gains $
	—	—	—	—	—	—	—	—	—	—	Expense Ratio %
	—	—	—	—	—	—	—	—	—	—	Income Ratio %
	—	—	—	—	—	—	—	—	—	—	Turnover Rate %
	—	—	—	—	—	—	—	—	—	92	Net Assets $mil

Performance 12-31-06

Historic Quarterly NAV Returns

	1st Qtr	2nd Qtr	3rd Qtr	4th Qtr	Total
2002	—	—	—	—	—
2003	—	—	—	—	—
2004	—	—	—	—	—
2005	—	—	—	—	—
2006	—	—	5.87	12.45	—*

Trailing	NAV Return%	Market Return%	NAV Rtrn% +/-MSCI EAFE	%Rank Cat.(NAV)
3 Mo	12.45	12.45	2.10	7
6 Mo	19.06	19.20	4.37	6
1 Yr	—	—	—	—
3 Yr Avg	—	—	—	—
5 Yr Avg	—	—	—	—
10 Yr Avg	—	—	—	—

Tax Analysis	Tax-Adj Return%	Tax-Cost Ratio
3 Yr (estimated)	—	—
5 Yr (estimated)	—	—
10 Yr (estimated)	—	—

Rating and Risk

Time Period	Morningstar Rtn vs Cat	Morningstar Risk vs Cat	Morningstar Risk-Adj Rating
3 Yr	—	—	—
5 Yr	—	—	—
10 Yr	—	—	—

Other Measures	Standard Index S&P 500	Best Fit Index
Alpha	—	—
Beta	—	—
R-Squared	—	—
Standard Deviation	—	
Mean	—	
Sharpe Ratio	—	

Morningstar's Take by Gregg Wolper 12-31-06

Like some of its siblings, WisdomTree DIEFA High-Yielding Equity has pronounced sector and country tilts that will turn off many potential buyers.

This exchange-traded offering aims to match the performance of a specially constructed WisdomTree index that includes the same countries as the MSCI EAFE Index, the most well-known foreign-stock benchmark. Thus, this fund is restricted to those markets generally recognized as developed, excluding Canada but including Hong Kong and Singapore. Also like EAFE, it leans toward large firms. Not surprisingly, this fund s top 10 looks much like those of mutual funds and ETFs that simply track EAFE.

Unlike the EAFE trackers, though, the WisdomTree offerings put much more emphasis on dividend payments than market capitalization in weighting their holdings. That leads to sharp differences with the EAFE trackers. Most notably, in this fund's case it leads to a strong bias toward the financials sector. This fund has 43% of assets in that field, compared with just under 30% in a prominent EAFE-tracking ETF, iShares MSCI EAFE (and roughly 34% in a similar sibling, WisdomTree DIEFA Fund). Meanwhile, this fund has remarkably low allocations of just 0.3% of assets in Japan and 0.5% in Switzerland. That compares with the 23% and 7% stakes in those countries, respectively, in the EAFE tracker.

It's impossible to know if such distinctions will benefit this fund over the long run. WisdomTree's research shows that using dividend weighting rather than the market-cap weighting of regular index funds has provided stronger returns in the past, but there's no telling if that will be true in the future. What we do know is that, with a projected expense ratio of 0.58%, this fund is costlier than several EAFE-tracking mutual funds and ETFs.

Portfolio Analysis 11-30-06

Share change since 10-06 Total Stocks:367	Sector	Country	% Assets
⊕ HSBC Hldgs	Financial	U.K.	3.67
⊕ BP	Energy	U.K.	3.06
⊕ Eni	Energy	Italy	2.91
⊕ Total SA	Energy	France	2.82
⊕ Vodafone Grp	Telecom	U.K.	2.10
⊕ France Telecom	Telecom	France	2.03
⊕ GlaxoSmithKline	Health	U.K.	1.90
⊕ Royal Dutch Shell	Energy	U.K.	1.89
⊕ Royal Bank Of Scotland G	Financial	U.K.	1.73
⊕ Lloyds TSB Grp	Financial	U.K.	1.71
⊕ Deutsche Telekom	Telecom	Germany	1.62
⊕ Banco Santander Central	Financial	Spain	1.60
⊕ Barclays	Financial	U.K.	1.58
⊕ ING Groep	Financial	Netherlands	1.34
⊕ BNP Paribas	Financial	France	1.33
⊕ HBOS	Financial	U.K.	1.32
⊕ Enel	Utilities	Italy	1.28
⊕ Commonwealth Bank of Aus	Financial	Australia	1.19
⊕ AXA	Financial	France	1.16
⊕ National Australia Bank	Financial	Australia	1.16

Current Investment Style

Value Blnd Growth — Large Mid Small

Market Cap	%
Giant	60.9
Large	25.6
Mid	12.0
Small	1.4
Micro	0.1

Avg $mil: 35,538

Value Measures		Rel Category
Price/Earnings	12.85	0.92
Price/Book	2.10	0.96
Price/Sales	1.07	1.10
Price/Cash Flow	6.92	0.91
Dividend Yield %	4.84	1.29

Growth Measures	%	Rel Category
Long-Term Erngs	9.01	0.80
Book Value	5.94	0.78
Sales	6.24	1.06
Cash Flow	3.33	1.36
Historical Erngs	19.92	1.04

Composition

Cash	0.3	Bonds	0.0
Stocks	99.6	Other	0.0
Foreign (% of Stock)			100.0

Sector Weightings	% of Stocks	Rel MSCI EAFE	3 Year High Low
⟳ Info	15.90	1.35	
▸ Software	0.06	0.11	— —
▪ Hardware	0.06	0.02	— —
▪ Media	3.43	1.87	— —
▪ Telecom	12.35	2.22	— —
☞ Service	52.14	1.10	
▪ Health	2.12	0.30	— —
▪ Consumer	4.01	0.81	— —
▪ Business	3.17	0.63	— —
▪ Financial	42.84	1.42	— —
▫ Mfg	31.97	0.78	
▪ Goods	6.14	0.47	— —
▪ Ind Mtrls	4.95	0.32	— —
▪ Energy	12.20	1.71	— —
▪ Utilities	8.68	1.66	— —

Regional Exposure

	% Stock		% Stock
UK/W. Europe	83	N. America	0
Japan	0	Latn America	0
Asia X Japan	17	Other	0

Country Exposure

	% Stock		% Stock
U.K.	35	Italy	10
France	12	Spain	5
Australia	12		

Address:	48 Wall Street New York NY 10005 866-909-9473	Management Fee:	0.58%
		Expense Projections:	3Yr:$186 5Yr: — 10Yr: —
Web Address:	www.wisdomtree.com	Income Distrib:	Annually
Inception:	06-16-06 *	Exchange:	NYSE
Advisor:	Wisdomtree Asset Management, Inc.		

WisdomTree Div Top 100 DTN

Market Price $57.74	**Mstar Category** Large Blend	

Morningstar Fair Value

Price/Fair Value Ratio —   Coverage Rate % —

Morningstar Rating	Return	Risk	Yield	NAV	Avg Daily Vol. (k)	52 wk High/Low
— Not Rated	Not Rated	—	—	$58.04	23	$58.51 - $49.58

Management

WisdomTree Asset Management is the advisor to this ETF. But the daily management of the fund is handled by BNY Investment Advisors, a division of Bank of New York. A five-person team from BNY handles the managerial chores: Kurt Zyla, Lloyd Buchanan, Denise Krisko, Robert McCormack, and Todd Rose.

Growth of $10,000
— Investment Value of ETF
— Investment Value of Index S&P 500

Trading Volume Millions

Methodology

This ETF mimics the WisdomTree Dividend Top 100 Index, which is a subset of the WisdomTree Dividend Large-Cap Index. Unlike most other WisdomTree indexes, this ETF's benchmark does not rank its constituents by cash dividends; rather, it weights its holdings based on their dividend yields (dividends divided by earnings). That means it winds up emphasizing sectors that are home to high-yielding stocks, like utilities and financials, and ignoring low-yielding industries, such as technology.

1997	1998	1999	2000	2001	2002	2003	2004	2005	2006	History
—	—	—	—	—	—	—	—	—	58.04	NAV $
—	—	—	—	—	—	—	—	—	58.06	Market Price $
—	—	—	—	—	—	—	—	—	17.16*	NAV Return%
—	—	—	—	—	—	—	—	—	17.24*	Market Price Return%
—	—	—	—	—	—	—	—	—	0.07	Avg Premium/Discount%
—	—	—	—	—	—	—	—	—	17.16	NAV Rtrn% +/-S&P 500
—	—	—	—	—	—	—	—	—	17.16	NAV Rtrn% +/-Russ 1000
—	—	—	—	—	—	—	—	—	—	NAV Return% Rank in Cat
—	—	—	—	—	—	—	—	—	—	Income Return %
—	—	—	—	—	—	—	—	—	—	Capital Return %
—	—	—	—	—	—	—	—	—	0.66	Income $
—	—	—	—	—	—	—	—	—	0.00	Capital Gains $
—	—	—	—	—	—	—	—	—	—	Expense Ratio %
—	—	—	—	—	—	—	—	—	—	Income Ratio %
—	—	—	—	—	—	—	—	—	—	Turnover Rate %
—	—	—	—	—	—	—	—	—	116	Net Assets $mil

Performance 12-31-06

Historic Quarterly NAV Returns

	1st Qtr	2nd Qtr	3rd Qtr	4th Qtr	Total
2002	—	—	—	—	—
2003	—	—	—	—	—
2004	—	—	—	—	—
2005	—	—	—	—	—
2006	—	—	7.17	7.37	—*

Trailing	NAV Return%	Market Return%	NAV Rtrn% +/-S&P 500	%Rank Cat.(NAV)
3 Mo	7.37	7.27	0.67	44
6 Mo	15.06	14.84	2.32	38
1 Yr	—	—	—	—
3 Yr Avg	—	—	—	—
5 Yr Avg	—	—	—	—
10 Yr Avg	—	—	—	—

Tax Analysis	Tax-Adj Return%	Tax-Cost Ratio
3 Yr (estimated)	—	—
5 Yr (estimated)	—	—
10 Yr (estimated)	—	—

Rating and Risk

Time Period	Morningstar Rtn vs Cat	Morningstar Risk vs Cat	Morningstar Risk-Adj Rating
3 Yr	—	—	—
5 Yr	—	—	—
10 Yr	—	—	—

Other Measures	Standard Index S&P 500	Best Fit Index
Alpha	—	—
Beta	—	—
R-Squared	—	—
Standard Deviation	—	
Mean	—	
Sharpe Ratio	—	

Portfolio Analysis 11-30-06

Share change since 10-06   Total Stocks:94

	Sector	PE	Tot Ret%	% Assets
⊕ Southern Copper Corporat	Ind Mtrls	8.8	79.47	4.39
⊕ Regions Financial Corpor	Financial	13.8	14.92	2.16
⊕ Lincoln National Corp.	Financial	13.2	28.58	1.80
⊕ General Motors Corporati	Goods	—	63.96	1.70
⊕ AT&T, Inc.	Telecom	19.2	51.59	1.60
⊕ Xcel Energy, Inc.	Utilities	17.0	30.53	1.57
⊕ Progress Energy, Inc.	Utilities	16.7	18.07	1.56
⊕ Consolidated Edison Comp	Utilities	17.5	9.14	1.53
⊕ Reynolds American, Inc.	Goods	16.1	43.87	1.50
⊕ Equity Office Properties	Financial	—	64.28	1.46
⊕ Ameren Corporation	Utilities	21.3	10.14	1.45
⊕ Merck & Co., Inc.	Health	18.8	42.66	1.40
⊕ Altria Group, Inc.	Goods	15.9	19.87	1.39
⊕ American Electric Power	Utilities	18.6	19.58	1.37
⊕ Bank of America Corporat	Financial	12.4	20.68	1.36
⊕ Southern Company	Utilities	17.8	11.69	1.33
⊕ FPL Group	Utilities	17.7	35.49	1.30
⊕ Washington Mutual, Inc.	Financial	13.5	9.62	1.26
⊕ Verizon Communications	Telecom	16.1	34.88	1.25
⊕ US Bancorp	Financial	14.1	26.29	1.24

Current Investment Style

Value Blend Growth — Large/Mid/Small

Market Cap	%
Giant	20.1
Large	71.2
Mid	8.7
Small	0.0
Micro	0.0

Avg $mil: 26,155

Value Measures		Rel Category
Price/Earnings	15.64	0.94
Price/Book	2.41	0.88
Price/Sales	1.38	1.09
Price/Cash Flow	11.72	1.24
Dividend Yield %	3.37	1.88

Growth Measures	%	Rel Category
Long-Term Erngs	8.31	0.72
Book Value	0.64	0.07
Sales	2.55	0.31
Cash Flow	-11.95	NMF
Historical Erngs	5.25	0.31

Profitability	%	Rel Category
Return on Equity	12.96	0.67
Return on Assets	8.25	0.86
Net Margin	15.22	1.36

Sector Weightings

	% of Stocks	Rel S&P 500	3 Year High Low
↻ Info	5.86	0.29	
🖥 Software	0.00	0.00	— —
💾 Hardware	0.00	0.00	— —
🎙 Media	2.45	0.65	— —
☎ Telecom	3.41	0.97	— —
🛋 Service	44.71	0.97	
🏥 Health	5.22	0.43	— —
🛒 Consumer	1.69	0.22	— —
📋 Business	0.68	0.16	— —
💲 Financial	37.12	1.67	— —
🔧 Mfg	49.43	1.46	
📦 Goods	12.73	1.49	— —
⚙ Ind Mtrls	12.08	1.01	— —
🔥 Energy	2.12	0.22	— —
💡 Utilities	22.50	6.43	— —

Composition

● Cash	0.3
● Stocks	99.7
● Bonds	0.0
○ Other	0.0
Foreign	4.4
(% of Stock)	

Morningstar's Take by Sonya Morris 12-31-06

This ETF's quirks limit its appeal.

WisdomTree Dividend Top 100 is the only domestic ETF in the WisdomTree family that does not rank its holdings by cash dividends. Instead, it weights stocks based on their dividend yields. That methodology gives rise to certain biases. For example, because the utility sector is home to many high-yielding stocks, that sector soaks up 21% of this portfolio. That's the highest utility weighting in the large-blend category and well above the category average of 2%. Financial stocks also lay claim to 36% of assets, which is well above the typical rival's 21% allocation. On the other hand, this fund holds no software and hardware names, since few firms in those sectors pay dividends. These sector biases could cause this ETF to behave quite differently than its peers. For example, if the utility sector--which has enjoyed a lengthy rally--cools off, this fund's relative performance could suffer.

There are other risks here as well. This ETF's exclusive focus on yield means it could end up favoring tired industry giants, and give short shrift to growing firms that are reinvesting in their businesses rather than issuing dividends. It's telling that GM is among this ETF's top holdings. And its presence here also illustrates that the existence of a dividend doesn't guarantee financial health.

In exchange for these risks, shareholders here are likely to receive a hefty dividend payout. Although this ETF has a very limited track record (it debuted in June 2006), historical data indicates that its yield should be well north of 3%, which is more than twice that of the S&P 500 Index. And because this fund has a relatively low expense ratio of 0.38%, most of that payout should flow through to shareholders.

But given this fund's idiosyncratic profile and short history, we're not convinced that the rewards outweigh the risks. In short, we think this untested ETF needs more time to prove itself.

Address:	48 Wall Street New York NY 10005 866-909-9473
Web Address:	www.wisdomtree.com
Inception:	06-16-06*
Advisor:	Wisdomtree Asset Management, Inc.

Management Fee:	0.38%
Expense Projections:	3Yr:$122 5Yr: — 10Yr: —
Income Distrib:	Annually
Exchange:	NYSE

MORNINGSTAR® ETFs 150

WisdomTree Euro Hi-Yld Eq DEW

Market Price $61.69	**Mstar Category** Europe Stock	

Management

WisdomTree Asset Management is the advisor. According to the prospectus, the firm doesn't manage any other investment companies and doesn't have much advisor experience. The Bank of New York has subadvisory responsibilities.

Methodology

This exchange-traded fund tracks the WisdomTree Europe High-Yielding Equity Index, which like other WisdomTree indexes, emphasizes dividend payments more than market capitalization in its weightings. (Most index funds weight by market capitalization.) This index includes the top 30% of the dividend-paying companies included in the WisdomTree Europe Dividend Index. It is much more heavily weighted toward financials and toward the U.K. than most other Europe funds.

	Morningstar Rating	Return	Risk	Yield	NAV	Avg Daily Vol. (k)
	Not Rated	Not Rated		—	$61.60	17

52 wk High/Low $62.30 - $49.38

Growth of $10,000
- Investment Value of ETF
- Investment Value of Index MSCI EAFE

Trading Volume Millions

	1997	1998	1999	2000	2001	2002	2003	2004	2005	2006	History
	—	—	—	—	—	—	—	—	—	61.60	NAV $
	—	—	—	—	—	—	—	—	—	61.86	Market Price $
	—	—	—	—	—	—	—	—	—	24.26*	NAV Return%
	—	—	—	—	—	—	—	—	—	23.60*	Market Price Return%
	—	—	—	—	—	—	—	—	—	0.63	Avg Premium/Discount%
	—	—	—	—	—	—	—	—	—	24.26	NAV Rtrn% +/-MSCI EAFE
	—	—	—	—	—	—	—	—	—	24.26	NAV Rtrn% +/-MSCI Eur
	—	—	—	—	—	—	—	—	—	—	NAV Return% Rank in Cat
	—	—	—	—	—	—	—	—	—	—	Income Return %
	—	—	—	—	—	—	—	—	—	—	Capital Return %
	—	—	—	—	—	—	—	—	—	0.32	Income $
	—	—	—	—	—	—	—	—	—	0.00	Capital Gains $
	—	—	—	—	—	—	—	—	—	—	Expense Ratio %
	—	—	—	—	—	—	—	—	—	—	Income Ratio %
	—	—	—	—	—	—	—	—	—	—	Turnover Rate %
	—	—	—	—	—	—	—	—	—	37	Net Assets $mil

Performance 12-31-06

Historic Quarterly NAV Returns

	1st Qtr	2nd Qtr	3rd Qtr	4th Qtr	Total
2002	—	—	—	—	—
2003	—	—	—	—	—
2004	—	—	—	—	—
2005	—	—	—	—	—
2006	—	—	6.48	11.75	—*

Trailing	NAV Return%	Market Return%	NAV Rtrn% +/-MSCI EAFE	%Rank Cat.(NAV)
3 Mo	11.75	11.58	1.40	19
6 Mo	18.99	19.05	4.30	19
1 Yr	—	—	—	—
3 Yr Avg	—	—	—	—
5 Yr Avg	—	—	—	—
10 Yr Avg	—	—	—	—

Tax Analysis	Tax-Adj Return%	Tax-Cost Ratio
3 Yr (estimated)	—	—
5 Yr (estimated)	—	—
10 Yr (estimated)	—	—

Rating and Risk

Time Period	Morningstar Rtn vs Cat	Morningstar Risk vs Cat	Morningstar Risk-Adj Rating
3 Yr	—	—	—
5 Yr	—	—	—
10 Yr	—	—	—

Other Measures	Standard Index S&P 500	Best Fit Index
Alpha	—	—
Beta	—	—
R-Squared	—	—
Standard Deviation	—	
Mean	—	
Sharpe Ratio	—	

Portfolio Analysis 11-30-06

Share change since 10-06 Total Stocks:150	Sector	Country	% Assets
HSBC Hldgs	Financial	U.K.	5.52
BP	Energy	U.K.	4.60
Eni	Energy	Italy	4.38
Vodafone Grp	Telecom	U.K.	3.16
France Telecom	Telecom	France	3.05
Royal Dutch Shell	Energy	U.K.	2.85
Royal Bank Of Scotland G	Financial	U.K.	2.60
Lloyds TSB Grp	Financial	U.K.	2.58
Deutsche Telekom	Telecom	Germany	2.43
Barclays	Financial	U.K.	2.38
Banco Santander Central	Financial	Spain	2.37
ING Groep	Financial	Netherlands	2.02
BNP Paribas	Financial	France	2.01
HBOS	Financial	U.K.	1.98
Enel	Utilities	Italy	1.92
⊖ UniCredito Italiano Grp	Financial	Italy	1.71
Fortis	Financial	Belgium	1.68
Societe Generale Grp	Financial	France	1.52
ABN AMRO Holding	Financial	Netherlands	1.51
Telecom Italia	Telecom	Italy	1.50

Morningstar's Take by Gregg Wolper 12-31-06

In order to like WisdomTree Europe High-Yielding Equity, you've got to like British companies--a lot.

This exchange-traded fund offers a new slant on European investing. Like other Europe index-trackers, it favors the region's biggest companies and biggest markets. It has differences, though, owing to the fact that this fund takes the WisdomTree approach--which emphasizes dividend payments quite heavily--even further than most of its siblings.

One result of this bias is that the portfolio is stuffed even more full of stocks from the United Kingdom than are most Europe funds. As by far the largest market in Europe by market capitalization, the U.K. naturally takes up the largest chunk of most Europe funds, whether actively managed or index-trackers. (One exception is iShares MSCI EMU Index, which entirely excludes the U.K.) For example, other Europe-focused ETFs--including sibling WisdomTree Europe Total Dividend--commonly have roughly 37% of assets

devoted to the U.K. (or roughly 34% to 35% if one excludes the Hong Kong/U.K. financial giant HSBC). By contrast, this fund has 47% of assets in the U.K. (41% if HSBC is excluded). That's not its only unusual weighting: The fund has nearly 45% of assets devoted to the financials sector, much more than other Europe offerings.

Those overweightings might help this fund outperform--or they might not. There's little reason to believe strongly either way. And while WisdomTree's research shows that using dividend weighting rather than the market-cap weighting of regular index funds has provided stronger performance in the past, there's no telling if that will be true in the future. Moreover, the fund's 0.58% projected expense ratio isn't bargain-basement for an indexer. For these reasons, it's hard to make a case for this new fund over broader-based--and cheaper--alternatives.

Current Investment Style

Value Blnd Growth		Market Cap	%
(Large/Mid/Small)		Giant	63.2
		Large	28.3
		Mid	7.0
		Small	1.5
		Micro	0.0
		Avg $mil: 45,349	

Value Measures		Rel Category
Price/Earnings	12.30	0.91
Price/Book	1.96	0.87
Price/Sales	0.90	0.80
Price/Cash Flow	6.12	0.73
Dividend Yield %	5.08	1.47

Growth Measures	%	Rel Category
Long-Term Erngs	9.14	0.82
Book Value	7.02	0.82
Sales	5.37	0.71
Cash Flow	2.80	1.04
Historical Erngs	22.42	1.00

Composition

Cash	0.0	Bonds	0.0
Stocks	100.0	Other	0.0
Foreign (% of Stock)			100.0

Sector Weightings	% of Stocks	Rel MSCI EAFE	3 Year High Low
↻ Info	18.86	1.60	
ℕ Software	0.00	0.00	— —
🖥 Hardware	0.01	0.00	— —
🎙 Media	3.23	1.77	— —
📱 Telecom	15.62	2.80	— —
☞ Service	47.49	1.01	
🏥 Health	0.02	0.00	— —
Consumer	3.46	0.70	— —
Business	1.86	0.37	— —
$ Financial	42.15	1.40	— —
🔧 Mfg	33.64	0.82	
Goods	7.62	0.58	— —
Ind Mtrls	3.64	0.24	— —
◇ Energy	13.20	1.85	— —
Utilities	9.18	1.75	— —

Regional Exposure % Stock

UK/W. Europe	100	N. America	0
Japan	0	Latn America	0
Asia X Japan	0	Other	0

Country Exposure % Stock

U.K.	45	Netherlands	7
Italy	14	Spain	6
France	10		

Address:	48 Wall Street New York NY 10005 866-909-9473	Management Fee:	0.58%
		Expense Projections:	3Yr:$186 5Yr: — 10Yr: —
Web Address:	www.wisdomtree.com	Income Distrib:	Annually
Inception:	06-16-06*	Exchange:	NYSE
Advisor:	Wisdomtree Asset Management, Inc.		

MORNINGSTAR ETFs 150

WisdomTree Eur Total Div DEB

	Market Price	Mstar Category
	$61.36	Europe Stock

Morningstar Rating	Return	Risk	Yield	NAV	Avg Daily Vol. (k)	52 wk High/Low
— Not Rated	Not Rated		—	$61.64	9	$62.14 - $49.49

Morningstar Fair Value

Price/Fair Value Ratio —   Coverage Rate % —

Management

WisdomTree Asset Management is the advisor and developed this fund's benchmark index. According to the fund's prospectus, the firm doesn't manage any other investment companies and doesn't have much advisor experience. The Bank of New York has subadvisory responsibilities here, as well as at all other WisdomTree ETF funds.

Methodology

This exchange-traded fund tracks the WisdomTree Europe Dividend Index, which like other WisdomTree indexes, emphasizes dividend payments rather than market capitalization in its weightings. (Most index funds weight by market capitalization.)

Growth of $10,000
- Investment Value of ETF
- Investment Value of Index MSCI EAFE

Trading Volume Millions

	1997	1998	1999	2000	2001	2002	2003	2004	2005	2006	History
	—	—	—	—	—	—	—	—	—	61.64	NAV $
	—	—	—	—	—	—	—	—	—	61.72	Market Price $
	—	—	—	—	—	—	—	—	—	23.84*	NAV Return%
	—	—	—	—	—	—	—	—	—	23.22*	Market Price Return%
	—	—	—	—	—	—	—	—	—	0.49	Avg Premium/Discount%
	—	—	—	—	—	—	—	—	—	23.84	NAV Rtrn% +/-MSCI EAFE
	—	—	—	—	—	—	—	—	—	23.84	NAV Rtrn% +/-MSCI Eur
	—	—	—	—	—	—	—	—	—	—	NAV Return% Rank in Cat
	—	—	—	—	—	—	—	—	—	—	Income Return %
	—	—	—	—	—	—	—	—	—	—	Capital Return %
	—	—	—	—	—	—	—	—	—	0.21	Income $
	—	—	—	—	—	—	—	—	—	0.00	Capital Gains $
	—	—	—	—	—	—	—	—	—	—	Expense Ratio %
	—	—	—	—	—	—	—	—	—	—	Income Ratio %
	—	—	—	—	—	—	—	—	—	—	Turnover Rate %
	—	—	—	—	—	—	—	—	—	25	Net Assets $mil

Performance 12-31-06

Historic Quarterly NAV Returns

	1st Qtr	2nd Qtr	3rd Qtr	4th Qtr	Total
2002	—	—	—	—	—
2003	—	—	—	—	—
2004	—	—	—	—	—
2005	—	—	—	—	—
2006	—	—	5.52	11.50	—*

Trailing	NAV Return%	Market Return%	NAV Rtrn% +/-MSCI EAFE	%Rank Cat.(NAV)
3 Mo	11.50	11.01	1.15	19
6 Mo	17.66	17.74	2.97	19
1 Yr	—	—	—	—
3 Yr Avg	—	—	—	—
5 Yr Avg	—	—	—	—
10 Yr Avg	—	—	—	—

Tax Analysis	Tax-Adj Return%	Tax-Cost Ratio
3 Yr (estimated)	—	—
5 Yr (estimated)	—	—
10 Yr (estimated)	—	—

Rating and Risk

Time Period	Morningstar Rtn vs Cat	Morningstar Risk vs Cat	Morningstar Risk-Adj Rating
3 Yr	—	—	—
5 Yr	—	—	—
10 Yr	—	—	—

Other Measures	Standard Index S&P 500	Best Fit Index
Alpha	—	—
Beta	—	—
R-Squared	—	—
Standard Deviation	—	
Mean	—	
Sharpe Ratio	—	

Portfolio Analysis 11-30-06

Share change since 10-06 Total Stocks:322	Sector	Country	% Assets
HSBC Hldgs	Financial	U.K.	2.90
BP	Energy	U.K.	2.42
Eni	Energy	Italy	2.30
Total SA	Energy	France	2.22
Royal Bank Of Scotland G	Financial	U.K.	1.98
Vodafone Grp	Telecom	U.K.	1.66
France Telecom	Telecom	France	1.60
GlaxoSmithKline	Health	U.K.	1.50
Royal Dutch Shell	Energy	U.K.	1.50
⊕ Deutsche Telekom	Telecom	Germany	1.43
Lloyds TSB Grp	Financial	U.K.	1.36
Barclays	Financial	U.K.	1.25
⊖ Banco Santander Central	Financial	Spain	1.24
Nestle	Goods	Switzerland	1.08
ING Groep	Financial	Netherlands	1.06
Royal Dutch Shell	Energy	U.K.	1.06
BNP Paribas	Financial	France	1.06
HBOS	Financial	U.K.	1.04
⊖ Telefonica	Telecom	Spain	1.02
Enel	Utilities	Italy	1.01

Current Investment Style

Value Blnd Growth — Large Mid Small

Market Cap	%
Giant	57.9
Large	34.4
Mid	7.3
Small	0.4
Micro	0.0

Avg $mil: 44,116

Value Measures		Rel Category
Price/Earnings	12.74	0.94
Price/Book	2.18	0.97
Price/Sales	1.11	0.98
Price/Cash Flow	7.27	0.86
Dividend Yield %	3.74	1.08

Growth Measures	%	Rel Category
Long-Term Erngs	10.62	0.95
Book Value	8.89	1.04
Sales	6.07	0.80
Cash Flow	5.43	2.03
Historical Erngs	22.43	1.00

Sector Weightings

	% Stocks	Rel MSCI EAFE	3 Year High Low
Info	14.21	1.20	
Software	0.17	0.30	— —
Hardware	1.76	0.46	— —
Media	2.79	1.52	— —
Telecom	9.49	1.70	— —
Service	46.90	0.99	
Health	5.17	0.73	— —
Consumer	3.76	0.76	— —
Business	4.16	0.82	— —
Financial	33.81	1.12	— —
Mfg	38.89	0.95	
Goods	9.21	0.70	— —
Ind Mtrls	10.35	0.67	— —
Energy	12.13	1.70	— —
Utilities	7.20	1.37	— —

Regional Exposure % Stock

UK/W. Europe	100	N. America	0
Japan	0	Latn America	0
Asia X Japan	0	Other	0

Composition

Cash	0.0	Bonds	0.0
Stocks	99.7	Other	0.3
Foreign (% of Stock)			100.0

Country Exposure % Stock

U.K.	35	Germany	9
France	16	Spain	7
Italy	9		

Morningstar's Take by Gregg Wolper 12-31-06

WisdomTree Europe Total Dividend is more balanced than some of its siblings, but that doesn't mean it has tremendous appeal.

Like WisdomTree's other exchange-traded funds, this offering is a passive portfolio that tracks a special WisdomTree index. These indexes--unlike most--emphasize dividend payments rather than market capitalization in ranking stocks.

That trait, plus some added quirks in some of the indexes, has in some cases resulted in portfolios that are quite heavily tilted toward specific sectors or countries. Take this fund's most similar sibling, WisdomTree Europe High-Yielding Equity. That fund dedicates 45% of assets to the United Kingdom, which is much higher than its typical sibling's 35% allocation to the U.K. That offering also has a 45% stake in the financials sector, much higher than the category norm. By contrast, this ETF has more typical weightings for the U.K. and financials--indeed, they're pretty closely in line with those of a popular rival, Vanguard European Stock ETF.

However, that doesn't mean this fund is like that one in all respects. For example, this ETF has a smaller health-care weighting and a larger telecom stake--nearly 10% of assets in the latter case. And most notably, this fund is costlier: Its projected expense ratio of 0.48% is significantly higher than the 0.18% charged by the Vanguard ETF.

WisdomTree's research shows that using dividend weighting rather than the market-cap weighting has provided stronger performance in the past. But there's no telling if that will be true in the future. Plus, because of its higher cost structure, it's at a disadvantage to its chief rival right out of the gate. Given this ETF's untested benchmark and higher expense ratio, investors have good reason to approach it with caution.

Address:	48 Wall Street New York NY 10005 866-909-9473	Management Fee:	0.48%
		Expense Projections:	3Yr:$154 5Yr: — 10Yr: —
Web Address:	www.wisdomtree.com	Income Distrib:	Annually
Inception:	06-16-06*	Exchange:	NYSE
Advisor:	Wisdomtree Asset Management, Inc.		

MORNINGSTAR® ETFs 150

WisdomTree High-Yld Eqty DHS

	Market Price $57.50	Mstar Category Large Blend

	Morningstar Rating	Return	Risk	Yield	NAV	Avg Daily Vol. (k)	52 wk High/Low
	— Not Rated	— Not Rated	—	—	$57.77	25	$58.21 - $49.65

Morningstar Fair Value

Price/Fair Value Ratio	Coverage Rate %
—	—

Management

This fund's advisor, WisdomTree Asset Management, outsources the daily management of this fund to BNY Investment Advisors, a division of Bank of New York. The day-to-day management of the fund is handled by a five-person team from BNY: Kurt Zyla, Lloyd Buchanan, Denise Krisko, Robert McCormack, and Todd Rose.

Methodology

This ETF is tethered to the WisdomTree High-Yielding Equity Index. To construct the index, WisdomTree ranks the stocks in the WisdomTree Dividend Index by dividend yield and isolates the top 30%. It then ranks those highest-yielding stocks by projected cash dividends. That means it emphasizes traditionally high-yielding sectors like utilities and financials and ignores low-yielding industries like technology.

Growth of $10,000
- Investment Value of ETF
- Investment Value of Index S&P 500

Trading Volume Millions

1997	1998	1999	2000	2001	2002	2003	2004	2005	2006	History
—	—	—	—	—	—	—	—	—	57.77	NAV $
—	—	—	—	—	—	—	—	—	57.73	Market Price $
—	—	—	—	—	—	—	—	—	16.77*	NAV Return%
—	—	—	—	—	—	—	—	—	16.64*	Market Price Return%
—	—	—	—	—	—	—	—	—	0.04	Avg Premium/Discount%
—	—	—	—	—	—	—	—	—	16.77	NAV Rtrn% +/-S&P 500
—	—	—	—	—	—	—	—	—	16.77	NAV Rtrn% +/-Russ 1000
—	—	—	—	—	—	—	—	—	—	NAV Return% Rank in Cat
—	—	—	—	—	—	—	—	—	—	Income Return %
—	—	—	—	—	—	—	—	—	—	Capital Return %
—	—	—	—	—	—	—	—	—	0.62	Income $
—	—	—	—	—	—	—	—	—	0.00	Capital Gains $
—	—	—	—	—	—	—	—	—	—	Expense Ratio %
—	—	—	—	—	—	—	—	—	—	Income Ratio %
—	—	—	—	—	—	—	—	—	—	Turnover Rate %
—	—	—	—	—	—	—	—	—	136	Net Assets $mil

Performance 12-31-06

Historic Quarterly NAV Returns

	1st Qtr	2nd Qtr	3rd Qtr	4th Qtr	Total
2002	—	—	—	—	—
2003	—	—	—	—	—
2004	—	—	—	—	—
2005	—	—	—	—	—
2006	—	—	8.29	6.14	—*

Trailing	NAV Return%	Market Return%	NAV Rtrn% +/-S&P 500	%Rank Cat.(NAV)
3 Mo	6.14	6.08	-0.56	44
6 Mo	14.93	14.56	2.19	38
1 Yr	—	—	—	—
3 Yr Avg	—	—	—	—
5 Yr Avg	—	—	—	—
10 Yr Avg	—	—	—	—

Tax Analysis	Tax-Adj Return%	Tax-Cost Ratio
3 Yr (estimated)	—	—
5 Yr (estimated)	—	—
10 Yr (estimated)	—	—

Rating and Risk

Time Period	Morningstar Rtn vs Cat	Morningstar Risk vs Cat	Morningstar Risk-Adj Rating
3 Yr	—	—	—
5 Yr	—	—	—
10 Yr	—	—	—

Other Measures	Standard Index S&P 500	Best Fit Index
Alpha	—	—
Beta	—	—
R-Squared	—	—
Standard Deviation	—	
Mean	—	
Sharpe Ratio	—	

Portfolio Analysis 11-30-06

Share change since 10-06 Total Stocks:407	Sector	PE	Tot Ret%	% Assets
⊕ Bank of America Corporat	Financial	12.4	20.68	6.79
⊕ General Electric Company	Ind Mtrls	19.8	9.35	6.52
⊕ Citigroup, Inc.	Financial	13.3	19.55	6.33
⊕ Altria Group, Inc.	Goods	15.9	19.87	4.89
⊕ Pfizer Inc.	Health	15.1	15.22	4.80
⊕ AT&T, Inc.	Telecom	19.2	51.59	3.99
⊕ J.P. Morgan Chase & Co.	Financial	13.7	25.60	3.26
⊕ Chevron Corporation	Energy	9.3	33.75	3.07
⊕ Verizon Communications	Telecom	16.1	34.88	2.99
⊕ Merck & Co., Inc.	Health	18.8	42.66	2.58
⊕ Wells Fargo Company	Financial	14.7	16.82	2.38
⊕ Coca-Cola Company	Goods	21.5	23.10	2.02
⊕ Wachovia Corporation	Financial	13.0	12.02	1.99
⊕ US Bancorp	Financial	14.1	26.29	1.62
⊕ Bristol-Myers Squibb Com	Health	23.3	19.93	1.37
⊕ Southern Copper Corporat	Ind Mtrls	8.8	79.47	1.29
⊕ Washington Mutual, Inc.	Financial	13.5	9.62	1.25
⊕ Abbott Laboratories	Health	23.6	26.88	1.23
⊕ Eli Lilly & Company	Health	17.4	-5.16	1.08
⊕ E.I. du Pont de Nemours	Ind Mtrls	18.6	18.64	0.93

Current Investment Style

Value Blend Growth — Large / Mid / Small

Market Cap	%
Giant	57.0
Large	23.7
Mid	13.4
Small	4.8
Micro	1.1

Avg $mil: 47,750

Value Measures		Rel Category
Price/Earnings	14.36	0.86
Price/Book	2.32	0.84
Price/Sales	1.79	1.41
Price/Cash Flow	10.41	1.10
Dividend Yield %	3.94	2.20

Growth Measures	%	Rel Category
Long-Term Erngs	8.53	0.74
Book Value	5.76	0.67
Sales	5.98	0.72
Cash Flow	-8.48	NMF
Historical Erngs	7.14	0.43

Profitability	%	Rel Category
Return on Equity	15.79	0.82
Return on Assets	10.11	1.05
Net Margin	18.38	1.65

Sector Weightings	% of Stocks	Rel S&P 500	3 Year High Low
↻ Info	7.58	0.38	
⬚ Software	0.00	0.00	— —
⬚ Hardware	0.00	0.00	— —
⬚ Media	0.13	0.03	— —
⬚ Telecom	7.45	2.12	— —
⬚ Service	55.57	1.20	
⬚ Health	11.17	0.93	— —
⬚ Consumer	0.27	0.04	— —
⬚ Business	0.28	0.07	— —
⬚ Financial	43.85	1.97	— —
⬚ Mfg	36.84	1.09	
⬚ Goods	10.90	1.27	— —
⬚ Ind Mtrls	10.98	0.92	— —
⬚ Energy	3.65	0.37	— —
⬚ Utilities	11.31	3.23	— —

Composition

● Cash	0.4	
● Stocks	99.6	
● Bonds	0.0	
● Other	0.0	
Foreign	1.3	(% of Stock)

Morningstar's Take by Sonya Morris 12-31-06

Investors shouldn't let this ETF's fat yield obscure its risks.

WisdomTree High-Yielding Equity ETF screens for the highest-yielding stocks in the WisdomTree Dividend Index with a market cap of at least $200 million. Then the ETF ranks the stocks based on their projected cash dividends over the next 12 months. By placing the focus on yield, this ETF is able to boost its dividend payout. The fund was only recently launched, but based on historical data, it should yield somewhere in the neighborhood of 3.9%. That ranks among the highest payouts in the large-blend category and is significantly higher than the S&P 500 Index, which yields just 1.5%.

But that hefty payout comes with certain risks. Because fast-growing technology firms tend to reinvest in their businesses rather than issue dividends, this ETF has no exposure at all to software and hardware names. By the same token, this fund loads up on high-yielding areas of the market like utilities and financials (it has an especially big stake in banks). Its utility stake of 10.6% is almost 5 times that of its typical rival. Similarly, its 43.9% weighting in financials is twice the category average.

Clearly, this fund is vulnerable to a downturn in those sectors, and we think these risks make it inappropriate as a core holding. Furthermore, this fund was only recently launched, and its methodology is untested in the real world. So there's reason to exercise caution.

Nevertheless, income-hungry sorts might wish to keep this ETF on their radar screen. It could serve as a useful supplemental holding for investors seeking to goose their portfolio's yield. Plus, because this fund has a low 0.38% expense ratio, most of its hefty payout flows through to shareholders. But keep in mind that you must pay a brokerage commission each time you trade an ETF, and those costs can add up quickly and override this fund's expense advantage.

Address:	48 Wall Street New York NY 10005 866-909-9473	Management Fee:	0.38%
		Expense Projections:	3Yr:$122 5Yr: — 10Yr: —
Web Address:	www.wisdomtree.com	Income Distrib:	Annually
Inception:	06-16-06 *	Exchange:	NYSE
Advisor:	Wisdomtree Asset Management, Inc.		

WisdomTree IntDiv Top 100 DOO

Market Price $63.32	**Mstar Category** Foreign Large Blend	

Morningstar Fair Value

Price/Fair Value Ratio — | Coverage Rate % —

Morningstar Rating — Not Rated	Return Not Rated	Risk Not Rated	Yield —	NAV $63.48	Avg Daily Vol. (k) 39	52 wk High/Low $64.18 - $49.81

Management

WisdomTree Asset Management is the advisor. The Bank of New York has subadvisory responsibilities here, as well as at all other WisdomTree ETF funds. Kurt Zyla, Lloyd Buchanan, Denise Krisko, Robert McCormack, and Todd Rose are senior members in charge of this fund at the subadvisor.

Growth of $10,000
- Investment Value of ETF
- Investment Value of Index MSCI EAFE

13.0 / 12.2 / 10.6 / 10.0

Trading Volume Millions
0.03 / 0.0

Methodology

This exchange-traded fund tracks the WisdomTree International Dividend Top 100 Index, which focuses on high-yielding stocks from Europe, Far East Asia, and Australia. The index skims off the 100 highest-yielding stocks from the WisdomTree International LargeCap Dividend Index and then weights them by their annual dividend yield as compared with the sum total of all annual dividend yields for the entire group. It reconstitutes annually.

1997	1998	1999	2000	2001	2002	2003	2004	2005	2006	History
—	—	—	—	—	—	—	—	—	63.48	NAV $
—	—	—	—	—	—	—	—	—	63.67	Market Price $
—	—	—	—	—	—	—	—	—	28.00*	NAV Return%
—	—	—	—	—	—	—	—	—	27.29*	Market Price Return%
—	—	—	—	—	—	—	—	—	0.58	Avg Premium/Discount%
—	—	—	—	—	—	—	—	—	28.00	NAV Rtrn% +/-MSCI EAFE
—	—	—	—	—	—	—	—	—	28.00	NAV Rtrn% +/-MSCI Wd xUS
—	—	—	—	—	—	—	—	—	—	NAV Return% Rank in Cat
—	—	—	—	—	—	—	—	—	—	Income Return %
—	—	—	—	—	—	—	—	—	—	Capital Return %
—	—	—	—	—	—	—	—	—	0.22	Income $
—	—	—	—	—	—	—	—	—	0.01	Capital Gains $
—	—	—	—	—	—	—	—	—	—	Expense Ratio %
—	—	—	—	—	—	—	—	—	—	Income Ratio %
—	—	—	—	—	—	—	—	—	—	Turnover Rate %
—	—	—	—	—	—	—	—	—	140	Net Assets $mil

Performance 12-31-06

Historic Quarterly NAV Returns

	1st Qtr	2nd Qtr	3rd Qtr	4th Qtr	Total
2002	—	—	—	—	—
2003	—	—	—	—	—
2004	—	—	—	—	—
2005	—	—	—	—	—
2006	—	—	7.32	14.05	*

Trailing	NAV Return%	Market Return%	NAV Rtrn% +/-MSCI EAFE	%Rank Cat.(NAV)
3 Mo	14.05	14.00	3.70	7
6 Mo	22.39	21.60	7.70	6
1 Yr	—	—	—	—
3 Yr Avg	—	—	—	—
5 Yr Avg	—	—	—	—
10 Yr Avg	—	—	—	—

Tax Analysis	Tax-Adj Return%	Tax-Cost Ratio
3 Yr (estimated)	—	—
5 Yr (estimated)	—	—
10 Yr (estimated)	—	—

Rating and Risk

Time Period	Morningstar Rtn vs Cat	Morningstar Risk vs Cat	Morningstar Risk-Adj Rating
3 Yr	—	—	—
5 Yr	—	—	—
10 Yr	—	—	—

Other Measures	Standard Index S&P 500	Best Fit Index
Alpha	—	—
Beta	—	—
R-Squared	—	—
Standard Deviation	—	
Mean	—	
Sharpe Ratio	—	

Portfolio Analysis 11-30-06

Share change since 10-06 Total Stocks:95

	Sector	Country	% Assets
⊕ QBE Insurance Grp Ltd	Financial	Australia	2.38
⊕ Telstra Corporation, Ltd	Telecom	Australia	2.18
⊕ Scottish Power UK	Utilities	U.K.	1.86
⊕ Lloyds TSB Grp	Financial	U.K.	1.75
⊕ Enel	Utilities	Italy	1.63
⊕ St. George Bank Ltd	Financial	Australia	1.62
⊕ Belgacom	Telecom	Belgium	1.61
⊕ BT Grp	Telecom	U.K.	1.59
⊕ France Telecom	Telecom	France	1.50
⊕ Telecom Italia	Telecom	Italy	1.50
⊕ Fortum Oyj	Energy	Finland	1.47
⊕ Commonwealth Bank of Aus	Financial	Australia	1.46
⊕ Australia & New Zealand	Financial	Australia	1.43
⊕ Westpac Banking	Financial	Australia	1.43
⊕ National Australia Bank	Financial	Australia	1.42
⊕ Credit Agricole	Financial	France	1.39
⊕ National Grid Transco	Utilities	U.K.	1.32
⊕ Volvo	Ind Mtrls	Sweden	1.29
⊕ Deutsche Telekom	Telecom	Germany	1.28
⊕ Scottish and Southern En	Utilities	U.K.	1.26

Current Investment Style

Value Blnd Growth — Large / Mid / Small

Market Cap	%
Giant	58.3
Large	41.7
Mid	0.0
Small	0.0
Micro	0.0

Avg $mil: 37,126

Value Measures		Rel Category
Price/Earnings	13.08	0.93
Price/Book	2.30	1.06
Price/Sales	0.95	0.98
Price/Cash Flow	7.13	0.94
Dividend Yield %	5.00	1.33

Growth Measures		Rel Category
Long-Term Erngs	8.58	0.76
Book Value	6.26	0.82
Sales	8.76	1.49
Cash Flow	-0.31	NMF
Historical Erngs	20.68	1.08

Composition

Cash	0.3	Bonds	0.0
Stocks	99.7	Other	0.0
Foreign (% of Stock)			100.0

Sector Weightings

	% of Stocks	Rel MSCI EAFE	3 Year High Low
↻ Info	18.01	1.52	
🖥 Software	0.00	0.00	— —
💾 Hardware	0.00	0.00	— —
🎙 Media	1.52	0.83	— —
📶 Telecom	16.49	2.96	— —
☞ Service	52.74	1.12	
🏥 Health	0.63	0.09	— —
🛒 Consumer	2.00	0.40	— —
🏢 Business	0.77	0.15	— —
💲 Financial	49.34	1.64	— —
⚙ Mfg	29.26	0.71	
📦 Goods	5.63	0.43	— —
✿ Ind Mtrls	4.41	0.29	— —
🔋 Energy	4.92	0.69	— —
💡 Utilities	14.30	2.73	— —

Regional Exposure % Stock

UK/W. Europe	78	N. America	0
Japan	0	Latn America	0
Asia X Japan	23	Other	0

Country Exposure % Stock

U.K.	26	Italy	8
Australia	15	Spain	7
France	9		

Morningstar's Take by Marta Norton 12-31-06

We have reservations about WisdomTree International Dividend Top 100.

This exchange-traded fund is part of the fundamental indexing movement. Instead of tracking a market-cap-weighted index, it follows the WisdomTree International Dividend Top 100 Index, which carves out the 100 highest-yielding stocks from the WisdomTree International LargeCap Dividend Index. The bogy then weights by dividend yield and reconstitutes annually.

Investors attracted to the current income this ETF throws off should be aware of its sector and country bias. Nearly half its assets fall in the financial sector, which is filled with dividend-paying large caps. Telecom and utilities, two other sectors loaded with high-yielding stocks, claim 17% and 14%, respectively. Meanwhile, although the ETF's index works off an investment universe similar to that of the MSCI EAFE Index, it leans toward countries where lots of companies pay dividends and ignores countries where most don't. For

example, the typical MSCI EAFE tracker has about 18% in Japan, but because dividend-paying firms are scarce there, this ETF avoids the nation.

We're wary of that kind of concentration. Not only does it leave the fund vulnerable to downturns in just a handful of market segments, it means the fund runs the risk of sitting out rallies in the sectors or countries it ignores, like Japan. Also, we're worried about the fund's short-term focus. Because its index screens for companies that paid dividends over the past 12 months and disregards longer-term trends, it may invest in companies whose current high yields are unsustainable.

To be fair, the ETF is young and it's not clear how it will perform over the long haul. With a 0.58% expense ratio, we don't think it is worth the test drive, though. Investors can find cheaper, better diversified large-cap international exposure from more-proven indexing options, such as iShares MSCI EAFE or conventional fund Fidelity Spartan International Index.

Address:	48 Wall Street New York NY 10005 866-909-9473	Management Fee: Expense Projections: Income Distrib: Exchange:	0.58% 3Yr:$186 Annually NYSE	5Yr: —	10Yr: —
Web Address:	www.wisdomtree.com				
Inception:	06-16-06*				
Advisor:	Wisdomtree Asset Management, Inc.				

MORNINGSTAR® ETFs 150

WisdomTree Intl LgCap Div DOL

	Market Price	Mstar Category
	$60.45	Foreign Large Blend

Morningstar Fair Value

Price/Fair Value Ratio — Coverage Rate % —

Morningstar Rating	Return	Risk	Yield	NAV	Avg Daily Vol. (k)	52 wk High/Low
Not Rated	Not Rated	—	—	$60.75	9	$61.41 - $50.19

Management

WisdomTree Asset Management is the advisor. According to the prospectus, the firm doesn't manage any other investment companies and doesn't have much advisor experience. The Bank of New York has subadvisory responsibilities.

Growth of $10,000
- Investment Value of ETF
- Investment Value of Index MSCI EAFE

12.0 / 11.7 / 10.6 / 10.0

Trading Volume Millions 0.008 / 0.0

Methodology

This exchange-traded fund tracks the WisdomTree LargeCap Dividend Index, which emphasizes dividend payments more than market capitalization in its weightings. (Most index funds weight by market capitalization.) The index includes developed European markets, Japan, and several other countries, but excludes the United States, Canada, and emerging markets. The fund's special emphasis on large companies means that, unlike sibling WisdomTree DIEFA Fund, which it otherwise closely resembles, this fund essentially has no exposure to mid-caps.

1997	1998	1999	2000	2001	2002	2003	2004	2005	2006	History
—	—	—	—	—	—	—	—	—	60.75	NAV $
—	—	—	—	—	—	—	—	—	60.98	Market Price $
—	—	—	—	—	—	—	—	—	22.45*	NAV Return%
—	—	—	—	—	—	—	—	—	22.10*	Market Price Return%
—	—	—	—	—	—	—	—	—	0.53	Avg Premium/Discount%
—	—	—	—	—	—	—	—	—	22.45	NAV Rtrn% +/-MSCI EAFE
—	—	—	—	—	—	—	—	—	22.45	NAV Rtrn% +/-MSCI Wd xUS
—	—	—	—	—	—	—	—	—	—	NAV Return% Rank in Cat
—	—	—	—	—	—	—	—	—	—	Income Return %
—	—	—	—	—	—	—	—	—	—	Capital Return %
—	—	—	—	—	—	—	—	—	0.30	Income $
—	—	—	—	—	—	—	—	—	0.00	Capital Gains $
—	—	—	—	—	—	—	—	—	—	Expense Ratio %
—	—	—	—	—	—	—	—	—	—	Income Ratio %
—	—	—	—	—	—	—	—	—	—	Turnover Rate %
—	—	—	—	—	—	—	—	—	43	Net Assets $mil

Performance 12-31-06

Historic Quarterly NAV Returns

	1st Qtr	2nd Qtr	3rd Qtr	4th Qtr	Total
2002	—	—	—	—	—
2003	—	—	—	—	—
2004	—	—	—	—	—
2005	—	—	—	—	—
2006	—	—	4.98	11.09	—*

Trailing	NAV Return%	Market Return%	NAV Rtrn% +/-MSCI EAFE	%Rank Cat.(NAV)
3 Mo	11.09	11.10	0.74	7
6 Mo	16.63	16.13	1.94	6
1 Yr	—	—	—	—
3 Yr Avg	—	—	—	—
5 Yr Avg	—	—	—	—
10 Yr Avg	—	—	—	—

Tax Analysis	Tax-Adj Return%	Tax-Cost Ratio
3 Yr (estimated)	—	—
5 Yr (estimated)	—	—
10 Yr (estimated)	—	—

Rating and Risk

Time Period	Morningstar Rtn vs Cat	Morningstar Risk vs Cat	Morningstar Risk-Adj Rating
3 Yr	—	—	—
5 Yr	—	—	—
10 Yr	—	—	—

Other Measures	Standard Index S&P 500	Best Fit Index
Alpha	—	—
Beta	—	—
R-Squared	—	—
Standard Deviation	—	
Mean	—	
Sharpe Ratio	—	

Morningstar's Take by Gregg Wolper 12-31-06

WisdomTree International LargeCap Dividend Fund's approach to broad international indexing is distinctive, but whether it's better remains to be seen.

Like WisdomTree DIEFA Fund, this exchange-traded offering aims to match the performance of a specially constructed WisdomTree index that includes the same countries as the MSCI EAFE Index, the most well-known foreign-stock benchmark. Thus, this fund is restricted to markets generally recognized as developed markets, excluding Canada but including Hong Kong and Singapore. Also like EAFE, it leans heavily toward large companies. Not surprisingly, this fund's top 10 looks much like those of mutual funds and ETFs that track EAFE.

Unlike the EAFE trackers, though, the WisdomTree offerings, in weighting their holdings, put much more emphasis on dividend payments than market capitalization. That leads to sharp differences with the EAFE trackers. For example,

Fidelity Spartan International Index, a conventional mutual fund, has nearly 24% of assets in Japan, while this offering has just 7.1% of assets in that large market, where dividends typically are paltry or nonexistent. In addition, this fund has essentially no money in mid-caps or small caps; the Fidelity EAFE tracker lacks small stocks but has roughly 13% in mid-caps. Meanwhile, this fund has about 37% of assets in financials while the Fidelity fund has 29%.

The bottom line? WisdomTree's research shows that using dividend-weighting rather than the market-cap weighting of regular index funds has provided stronger performance in the past, but there's no telling if that will be true in the future. What we do know is that, with a projected expense ratio of 0.48%, this fund is costlier than several EAFE funds, and is inappropriate for investors who want a more conventionally sized stake in Japan's market.

Address:	48 Wall Street, New York NY 10005, 866-909-9473
Web Address:	www.wisdomtree.com
Inception:	06-16-06*
Advisor:	Wisdomtree Asset Management, Inc.

Management Fee:	0.48%
Expense Projections:	3Yr:$154 5Yr: — 10Yr: —
Income Distrib:	Annually
Exchange:	NYSE

Portfolio Analysis 11-30-06

Share change since 10-06 Total Stocks:260

Sector	Country	% Assets
⊕ HSBC Hldgs	Financial	U.K.	3.08
⊕ BP	Energy	U.K.	2.57
⊕ Eni	Energy	Italy	2.45
⊕ Total SA	Energy	France	2.36
⊕ Vodafone Grp	Telecom	U.K.	1.76
⊕ France Telecom	Telecom	France	1.70
⊕ GlaxoSmithKline	Health	U.K.	1.60
⊕ Royal Dutch Shell	Energy	U.K.	1.59
⊕ Royal Bank Of Scotland G	Financial	U.K.	1.45
⊕ Lloyds TSB Grp	Financial	U.K.	1.44
⊕ Banco Santander Central	Financial	Spain	1.43
⊕ Deutsche Telekom	Telecom	Germany	1.38
⊕ Barclays	Financial	U.K.	1.33
⊕ China Mobile	Telecom	Hong Kong	1.15
⊕ Nestle	Goods	Switzerland	1.14
⊕ Royal Dutch Shell	Energy	U.K.	1.13
⊕ ING Groep	Financial	Netherlands	1.13
⊕ Commonwealth Bank of Aus	Financial	Australia	1.13
⊕ BNP Paribas	Financial	France	1.12
⊕ HBOS	Financial	U.K.	1.11

Current Investment Style

	Market Cap	%
	Giant	74.3
	Large	25.6
	Mid	0.0
	Small	0.0
	Micro	0.0
	Avg $mil:	58,209

Value Measures		Rel Category
Price/Earnings	12.94	0.92
Price/Book	2.15	0.99
Price/Sales	1.09	1.12
Price/Cash Flow	7.31	0.96
Dividend Yield %	3.94	1.05

Growth Measures	%	Rel Category
Long-Term Erngs	10.07	0.89
Book Value	8.25	1.08
Sales	6.72	1.14
Cash Flow	5.01	2.05
Historical Erngs	20.19	1.05

Composition

Cash	0.5	Bonds	0.0
Stocks	99.4	Other	0.1
Foreign (% of Stock)			100.0

Sector Weightings	% of Stocks	Rel MSCI EAFE	3 Year High Low
↻ Info	15.65	1.32	
Software	0.19	0.34	— —
Hardware	1.35	0.35	— —
Media	1.26	0.69	— —
Telecom	12.85	2.31	— —
☞ Service	46.75	0.99	
Health	5.24	0.74	— —
Consumer	2.60	0.53	— —
Business	1.57	0.31	— —
Financial	37.34	1.24	— —
Mfg	37.61	0.92	
Goods	10.29	0.78	— —
Ind Mtrls	7.28	0.47	— —
Energy	12.38	1.73	— —
Utilities	7.66	1.46	— —

Regional Exposure % Stock

UK/W. Europe	83	N. America	0
Japan	7	Latn America	0
Asia X Japan	11	Other	0

Country Exposure % Stock

U.K.	28	Italy	8
France	15	Japan	7
Germany	8		

WisdomTree Japan Tot Div DXJ

			Market Price $55.25		**Mstar Category** Japan Stock

Morningstar Fair Value

Price/Fair Value Ratio —   Coverage Rate % —

Management

The index fund management division of BNY Investment Advisors, a division of The Bank of New York, has subadvisory responsibilities here, as well as at all other WisdomTree ETFs. Kurt Zyla, Lloyd Buchanan, Denise Krisko, Robert McCormack, and Todd Rose are the senior members of the team.

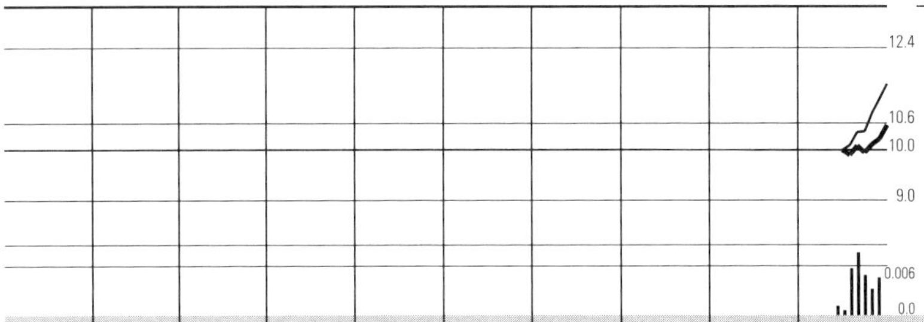

Methodology

This ETF is constructed in a different manner than most of the other ETFs and index funds in the Japan category that are dedicated to larger caps. While the two iShares ETFs and the Vanguard mutual fund/ETF tracks market-cap-weighted indexes, it, like all WisdomTree offerings, replicates an index that uses dividend payments rather than market caps to rank stocks. Specifically, it replicates the Wisdom Tree Japan Dividend Index, which includes dividend-paying stocks that trade on the Tokyo Stock Exchange and weights those stocks on their annual payouts.

Morningstar Rating	Return	Risk	Yield	NAV	Avg Daily Vol. (k)
— Not Rated	— Not Rated	—	—	$54.89	5

52 wk High/Low $55.95 - $47.89

Growth of $10,000
- Investment Value of ETF
- Investment Value of Index MSCI EAFE

12.4
10.6
10.0
9.0

Trading Volume Millions
0.006
0.0

	1997	1998	1999	2000	2001	2002	2003	2004	2005	2006	History
	—	—	—	—	—	—	—	—	—	54.89	NAV $
	—	—	—	—	—	—	—	—	—	55.34	Market Price $
	—	—	—	—	—	—	—	—	—	9.51*	NAV Return%
	—	—	—	—	—	—	—	—	—	10.57*	Market Price Return%
	—	—	—	—	—	—	—	—	—	0.40	Avg Premium/Discount%
	—	—	—	—	—	—	—	—	—	9.51	NAV Rtrn% +/-MSCI EAFE
	—	—	—	—	—	—	—	—	—	9.51	NAV Rtrn% +/-MSCI JP NDT
	—	—	—	—	—	—	—	—	—	—	NAV Return% Rank in Cat
	—	—	—	—	—	—	—	—	—	—	Income Return %
	—	—	—	—	—	—	—	—	—	—	Capital Return %
	—	—	—	—	—	—	—	—	—	0.21	Income $
	—	—	—	—	—	—	—	—	—	0.00	Capital Gains $
	—	—	—	—	—	—	—	—	—	—	Expense Ratio %
	—	—	—	—	—	—	—	—	—	—	Income Ratio %
	—	—	—	—	—	—	—	—	—	—	Turnover Rate %
	—	—	—	—	—	—	—	—	—	27	Net Assets $mil

Performance 12-31-06

Historic Quarterly NAV Returns

	1st Qtr	2nd Qtr	3rd Qtr	4th Qtr	Total
2002	—	—	—	—	—
2003	—	—	—	—	—
2004	—	—	—	—	—
2005	—	—	—	—	—
2006	—	—	-0.58	5.87	—*

Trailing	NAV Return%	Market Return%	NAV Rtrn% +/-MSCI EAFE	%Rank Cat.(NAV)
3 Mo	5.87	6.58	-4.48	6
6 Mo	5.26	4.71	-9.43	6
1 Yr	—	—	—	—
3 Yr Avg	—	—	—	—
5 Yr Avg	—	—	—	—
10 Yr Avg	—	—	—	—

Tax Analysis	Tax-Adj Return%	Tax-Cost Ratio
3 Yr (estimated)	—	—
5 Yr (estimated)	—	—
10 Yr (estimated)	—	—

Rating and Risk

Time Period	Morningstar Rtn vs Cat	Morningstar Risk vs Cat	Morningstar Risk-Adj Rating
3 Yr	—	—	—
5 Yr	—	—	—
10 Yr	—	—	—

Other Measures	Standard Index S&P 500	Best Fit Index
Alpha	—	—
Beta	—	—
R-Squared	—	—
Standard Deviation	—	
Mean	—	
Sharpe Ratio	—	

Portfolio Analysis 11-30-06

Share change since 10-06 Total Stocks:271

	Sector	Country	% Assets
Toyota Motor	Goods	Japan	7.58
NTT DoCoMo	Telecom	Japan	3.30
Nissan Motor	Goods	Japan	2.84
Canon	Goods	Japan	2.42
Nippon Telegraph & Telep	Telecom	Japan	2.38
The Tokyo Electric Power	Utilities	Japan	2.34
Takeda Chemical Industri	Health	Japan	2.16
Mitsubishi UFJ Financial	Financial	Japan	1.92
Honda Motor	Goods	Japan	1.86
Chubu Electric Power	Utilities	Japan	1.30
The Kansai Electric Powe	Utilities	Japan	1.27
Matsushita Electric Indu	Ind Mtrls	Japan	1.10
Nippon Steel	Ind Mtrls	Japan	1.01
Mizuho Financial Grp	Financial	Japan	0.97
Nomura Hldgs	Financial	Japan	0.89
Mitsubishi	Ind Mtrls	Japan	0.88
Denso	Ind Mtrls	Japan	0.85
Japan Tobacco	Goods	Japan	0.83
Kyushu Electric Power	Utilities	Japan	0.81
The Sumitomo Trust & Ban	Financial	Japan	0.81

Current Investment Style

Value Blnd Growth — Large Mid Small

Market Cap	%
Giant	45.2
Large	39.1
Mid	15.7
Small	0.0
Micro	0.0
Avg $mil:	17,332

Value Measures		Rel Category
Price/Earnings	17.42	1.05
Price/Book	1.64	1.04
Price/Sales	0.86	1.01
Price/Cash Flow	7.56	0.94
Dividend Yield %	1.74	1.01

Growth Measures	%	Rel Category
Long-Term Erngs	8.08	0.69
Book Value	11.25	1.09
Sales	4.63	0.91
Cash Flow	0.50	25.00
Historical Erngs	21.84	1.14

Composition

Cash	0.4	Bonds	0.0
Stocks	99.6	Other	0.0
Foreign	(% of Stock)		100.0

Sector Weightings

		% of Stocks	Rel MSCI EAFE	3 Year High Low
⟳ Info	11.56	0.98		
Software	0.87	1.55	—	—
Hardware	3.93	1.02	—	—
Media	1.06	0.58	—	—
Telecom	5.70	1.02	—	—
Service	30.56	0.65		
Health	5.53	0.78	—	—
Consumer	3.71	0.75	—	—
Business	7.31	1.44	—	—
Financial	14.01	0.47	—	—
Mfg	57.86	1.41		
Goods	26.02	1.98	—	—
Ind Mtrls	21.44	1.39	—	—
Energy	1.40	0.20	—	—
Utilities	9.00	1.72	—	—

Regional Exposure % Stock

UK/W. Europe	0	N. America	0
Japan	100	Latn America	0
Asia X Japan	0	Other	0

Country Exposure % Stock

Japan	100

Morningstar's Take by William Samuel Rocco 12-31-06

WisdomTree Japan Total Dividend differs from the other passive Japanese large-cap vehicles in subtle but significant respects.

This ETF is slightly more attractively priced than the other ETFs and index funds in the Japan category that are dedicated to larger caps. This ETF, which opened in June 2006, has a projected expense ratio of 0.48%, while iShares S&P/Topix 150 Index, WisdomTree Japan High-Yielding Equity, and iShares MSCI Japan Index have expense ratios of 0.50% to 0.59%. And although the mutual fund and ETF versions of Vanguard Pacific Stock are much cheaper, they devote about 25% of their assets to non-Japanese issues and thus may not satisfy those seeking pure Japan exposure.

This ETF is also constructed in a different manner than most of its rivals. While the two iShares ETFs and the Vanguard mutual fund/ETF track market-cap-weighted indexes, it, like all WisdomTree offerings, replicates an index that uses dividend payments rather than market caps to rank stocks. Specifically, it replicates the Wisdom Tree Japan Dividend Index, which includes dividend-paying stocks that trade on the Tokyo Stock Exchange and weights those stocks on their annual payouts.

This ETF is still quite young, and it's too soon to tell what type of performer it will be over time. (WisdomTree data indicate that this and its other dividend-weighted indexes have outpaced their market-cap-weighted peers in the past, but that outperformance may not persist.) That said, it does provide slightly broader market-cap and sector exposure than the other passive Japanese large-cap vehicles (although it's more focused than the typical actively run Japan fund on both counts). And that little bit of extra breadth and its relatively attractive cost structure mean index fans who are set on a pure-Japan play should keep their eye on this ETF.

Address:	48 Wall Street New York NY 10005 866-909-9473	
Web Address:	www.wisdomtree.com	
Inception:	06-16-06*	
Advisor:	Wisdomtree Asset Management, Inc.	
Management Fee:	0.48%	
Expense Projections:	3Yr:$154 5Yr: — 10Yr: —	
Income Distrib:	Annually	
Exchange:	NYSE	

MORNINGSTAR® ETFs 150

WisdomTree LargeCap Div DLN

	Market Price $57.58	Mstar Category Large Blend

Morningstar Fair Value

Price/Fair Value Ratio	Coverage Rate %
—	—

Morningstar Rating Not Rated	Return Not Rated	Risk Not Rated	Yield —	NAV $57.88	Avg Daily Vol. (k) 28	52 wk High/Low $58.45 - $50.02

Management

This ETF is advised by WisdomTree Asset Management. However, day-to-day management of the fund is farmed out to a subadvisor, BNY Investment Advisors, a unit of Bank of New York. A five-person team from BNY runs the fund: Kurt Zyla, Lloyd Buchanan, Denise Krisko, Robert McCormack, and Todd Rose.

Methodology

This ETF tracks the newly minted WisdomTree LargeCap Dividend Index, which includes the 300 largest companies, as measured by market capitalization, in the WisdomTree Dividend Index. The index isn't weighted by market capitalization though. Instead, the stocks are ranked by cash dividends.

Growth of $10,000
- Investment Value of ETF
- Investment Value of Index S&P 500

Trading Volume Millions

	1997	1998	1999	2000	2001	2002	2003	2004	2005	2006	History
	—	—	—	—	—	—	—	—	—	57.88	NAV $
	—	—	—	—	—	—	—	—	—	57.89	Market Price $
	—	—	—	—	—	—	—	—	—	16.10*	NAV Return%
	—	—	—	—	—	—	—	—	—	15.92*	Market Price Return%
	—	—	—	—	—	—	—	—	—	0.07	Avg Premium/Discount%
	—	—	—	—	—	—	—	—	—	16.10	NAV Rtrn% +/-S&P 500
	—	—	—	—	—	—	—	—	—	16.10	NAV Rtrn% +/-Russ 1000
	—	—	—	—	—	—	—	—	—	—	NAV Return% Rank in Cat
	—	—	—	—	—	—	—	—	—	—	Income Return %
	—	—	—	—	—	—	—	—	—	—	Capital Return %
	—	—	—	—	—	—	—	—	—	0.55	Income $
	—	—	—	—	—	—	—	—	—	0.00	Capital Gains $
	—	—	—	—	—	—	—	—	—	—	Expense Ratio %
	—	—	—	—	—	—	—	—	—	—	Income Ratio %
	—	—	—	—	—	—	—	—	—	—	Turnover Rate %
	—	—	—	—	—	—	—	—	—	203	Net Assets $mil

Performance 12-31-06

Historic Quarterly NAV Returns

	1st Qtr	2nd Qtr	3rd Qtr	4th Qtr	Total
2002	—	—	—	—	—
2003	—	—	—	—	—
2004	—	—	—	—	—
2005	—	—	—	—	—
2006	—	—	7.15	6.58	—*

Trailing	NAV Return%	Market Return%	NAV Rtrn% +/-S&P 500	%Rank Cat.(NAV)
3 Mo	6.58	6.54	-0.12	44
6 Mo	14.20	13.89	1.46	38
1 Yr	—	—	—	—
3 Yr Avg	—	—	—	—
5 Yr Avg	—	—	—	—
10 Yr Avg	—	—	—	—

Tax Analysis	Tax-Adj Return%	Tax-Cost Ratio
3 Yr (estimated)	—	—
5 Yr (estimated)	—	—
10 Yr (estimated)	—	—

Rating and Risk

Time Period	Morningstar Rtn vs Cat	Morningstar Risk vs Cat	Morningstar Risk-Adj Rating
3 Yr	—	—	—
5 Yr	—	—	—
10 Yr	—	—	—

Other Measures	Standard Index S&P 500	Best Fit Index
Alpha	—	—
Beta	—	—
R-Squared	—	—
Standard Deviation	—	
Mean	—	
Sharpe Ratio	—	

Portfolio Analysis 11-30-06

Share change since 10-06 Total Stocks:288	Sector	PE	Tot Ret%	% Assets
⊕ Bank of America Corporat	Financial	12.4	20.68	4.78
⊕ General Electric Company	Ind Mtrls	19.8	9.35	4.60
⊕ Citigroup, Inc.	Financial	13.3	19.55	4.46
⊕ ExxonMobil Corporation	Energy	11.7	39.07	4.29
⊕ Altria Group, Inc.	Goods	15.9	19.87	3.46
⊕ Pfizer Inc.	Health	15.1	15.22	3.39
⊕ AT&T, Inc.	Telecom	19.2	51.59	2.83
⊕ J.P. Morgan Chase & Co.	Financial	13.7	25.60	2.29
⊕ Chevron Corporation	Energy	9.3	33.75	2.18
⊕ Verizon Communications	Telecom	16.1	34.88	2.12
⊕ Procter & Gamble Company	Goods	24.2	13.36	1.93
⊕ Johnson & Johnson	Health	17.4	12.44	1.90
⊕ Merck & Co., Inc.	Health	18.8	42.66	1.83
⊕ Microsoft Corporation	Software	23.7	15.83	1.75
⊕ Wells Fargo Company	Financial	14.7	16.82	1.67
⊕ Wachovia Corporation	Financial	13.0	12.02	1.43
⊕ Coca-Cola Company	Goods	21.5	23.10	1.43
⊕ Wal-Mart Stores, Inc.	Consumer	16.6	0.13	1.19
⊕ US Bancorp	Financial	14.1	26.29	1.14
⊕ Intel Corporation	Hardware	20.3	-17.18	1.13

Current Investment Style

Value Blnd Growth — Large Mid Small

Market Cap	%
Giant	62.5
Large	34.5
Mid	3.0
Small	0.0
Micro	0.0

Avg $mil: 77,110

Value Measures		Rel Category
Price/Earnings	14.56	0.88
Price/Book	2.59	0.94
Price/Sales	1.64	1.29
Price/Cash Flow	10.42	1.10
Dividend Yield %	2.78	1.55

Growth Measures	%	Rel Category
Long-Term Erngs	9.76	0.85
Book Value	7.65	0.90
Sales	8.41	1.01
Cash Flow	-2.10	NMF
Historical Erngs	12.84	0.77

Profitability	%	Rel Category
Return on Equity	19.32	1.00
Return on Assets	11.14	1.16
Net Margin	15.93	1.43

Sector Weightings	% of Stocks	Rel S&P 500	3 Year High Low
⌾ Info	12.02	0.60	
⬛ Software	1.78	0.52	— —
⬛ Hardware	3.23	0.35	— —
⬛ Media	1.73	0.46	— —
⬛ Telecom	5.28	1.50	— —
⬛ Service	47.38	1.03	
⬛ Health	11.23	0.93	— —
⬛ Consumer	4.37	0.57	— —
⬛ Business	1.71	0.40	— —
⬛ Financial	30.07	1.35	— —
⬛ Mfg	40.59	1.20	
⬛ Goods	11.92	1.39	— —
⬛ Ind Mtrls	13.33	1.12	— —
⬛ Energy	9.30	0.95	— —
⬛ Utilities	6.04	1.73	— —

Composition

● Cash		0.4
● Stocks		99.6
● Bonds		0.0
○ Other		0.0
Foreign		0.9
(% of Stock)		

Morningstar's Take by Sonya Morris 12-31-06

WisdomTree LargeCap Dividend ETF is worth watching.

Unlike most index funds, which rank stocks based on their market capitalization (which is a stock's market price times the shares freely available for trading), this brand new ETF weights stocks based on the cash dividends they will pay over the next 12 months. It's among a new breed of index funds that seek to correct a perceived problem with cap-weighted indexes--namely, that they emphasize expensive stocks while underweighting value-priced stocks.

However, this ETF comes with biases of its own. For example, it sports a notable value tilt since growth companies generally reinvest in their businesses rather than pay dividends. For the same reason, this fund holds few technology stocks, while accentuating financial and utility sectors, which are home to some big dividend payers. This ETF also favors large firms. Its aggregative market cap is about 55% higher than the S&P 500, which

means it could lag when smaller, growthier stocks pace the market.

Plus, this ETF could see higher turnover--and thus higher trading costs--than a traditional index fund. The market does much of the work for cap-weighted index funds: When a stock's price goes up, so does its index ranking. But this fund must ditch stocks that stop paying dividends and admit new stocks that do. What's more, it may not be as tax-efficient as competing index funds. If it doesn't meet certain holding-period requirements, not all of its dividends will qualify for the lower 15% dividend rate. These concerns may prove to be overblown, but only time will tell.

That said, this fund holds promise. It's loaded with financially sturdy industry leaders, which look particularly cheap now. And its above-average yield might appeal to income-oriented sorts. Still, there's no reason to ditch an old cap-weighted index fund for this new ETF until it gets some real-world experience.

Address:	48 Wall Street New York NY 10005 866-909-9473	Management Fee:	0.28%
		Expense Projections:	3Yr:$90 5Yr: — 10Yr: —
Web Address:	www.wisdomtree.com	Income Distrib:	Annually
Inception:	06-16-06*	Exchange:	NYSE
Advisor:	Wisdomtree Asset Managment, Inc.		

WisdomTree MidCap Div DON

	Market Price	Mstar Category
	$56.40	Mid-Cap Blend

© 2007 Morningstar, Inc. All rights reserved. The information herein is not represented or warranted to be accurate, correct, complete or timely. Past performance is no guarantee of future results. Activate your free 30-day research pass at http://www.morningstar.com/goto/2007ETFs150

Morningstar Fair Value

Price/Fair Value Ratio —
Coverage Rate % —

Management

This ETF is advised by WisdomTree Asset Management. However, the management of the fund is outsourced to a subadvisor, BNY Investment Advisors, a division of Bank of New York. A five-person team from BNY is responsible for the day-to-day management of the fund.

Methodology

This ETF tracks WisdomTree MidCap Dividend Index. To create the index, WisdomTree ranks the stocks in the WisdomTree Dividend Index by market cap, removes the top 300 companies, and takes the remaining 75%. Then the index is ranked based on its constituents' planned cash dividends over the next 12 months. The index includes a large slug of REITs and utilities stocks.

Top data row

Morningstar Rating	Return	Risk	Yield	NAV	Avg Daily Vol. (k)	52 wk High/Low
— Not Rated	Not Rated	—	—	$56.80	12	$57.62 - $49.65

Growth of $10,000
- Investment Value of ETF
- Investment Value of Index S&P 500

12.0
11.7
10.6
10.0

Trading Volume Millions
0.007
0.0

History

	1997	1998	1999	2000	2001	2002	2003	2004	2005	2006	History
	—	—	—	—	—	—	—	—	—	56.80	NAV $
	—	—	—	—	—	—	—	—	—	56.84	Market Price $
	—	—	—	—	—	—	—	—	—	14.65*	NAV Return%
	—	—	—	—	—	—	—	—	—	14.77*	Market Price Return%
	—	—	—	—	—	—	—	—	—	0.03	Avg Premium/Discount%
	—	—	—	—	—	—	—	—	—	14.65	NAV Rtrn% +/-S&P 500
	—	—	—	—	—	—	—	—	—	14.65	NAV Rtrn% +/-S&P Mid 400
	—	—	—	—	—	—	—	—	—	—	NAV Return% Rank in Cat
	—	—	—	—	—	—	—	—	—	—	Income Return %
	—	—	—	—	—	—	—	—	—	—	Capital Return %
	—	—	—	—	—	—	—	—	—	0.73	Income $
	—	—	—	—	—	—	—	—	—	0.01	Capital Gains $
	—	—	—	—	—	—	—	—	—	—	Expense Ratio %
	—	—	—	—	—	—	—	—	—	—	Income Ratio %
	—	—	—	—	—	—	—	—	—	—	Turnover Rate %
	—	—	—	—	—	—	—	—	—	48	Net Assets $mil

Performance 12-31-06

Historic Quarterly NAV Returns

	1st Qtr	2nd Qtr	3rd Qtr	4th Qtr	Total
2002	—	—	—	—	—
2003	—	—	—	—	—
2004	—	—	—	—	—
2005	—	—	—	—	—
2006	—	—	4.29	7.70	—*

Trailing

	NAV Return%	Market Return%	NAV Rtrn% +/-S&P 500	%Rank Cat.(NAV)
3 Mo	7.70	7.67	1.00	10
6 Mo	12.32	12.37	-0.42	9
1 Yr	—	—	—	—
3 Yr Avg	—	—	—	—
5 Yr Avg	—	—	—	—
10 Yr Avg	—	—	—	—

Tax Analysis

	Tax-Adj Return%	Tax-Cost Ratio
3 Yr (estimated)	—	—
5 Yr (estimated)	—	—
10 Yr (estimated)	—	—

Rating and Risk

Time Period	Morningstar Rtn vs Cat	Morningstar Risk vs Cat	Morningstar Risk-Adj Rating
3 Yr	—	—	—
5 Yr	—	—	—
10 Yr	—	—	—

Other Measures

	Standard Index S&P 500	Best Fit Index
Alpha	—	—
Beta	—	—
R-Squared	—	—
Standard Deviation	—	
Mean	—	
Sharpe Ratio	—	

Morningstar's Take by Sonya Morris 12-31-06

WisdomTree MidCap Dividend's biases and risks limit its appeal.

This new ETF, like most of its siblings in the WisdomTree family, ranks the stocks in its portfolio based on cash dividends projected over the next 12 months. As you might expect, that structure gooses this ETF's dividend yield. It only recently launched, but based on historical data, it should yield roughly 3.6%. That's well ahead of the typical mid-blend fund, which has a tiny 0.40% payout.

You might also assume that a focus on dividends means this ETF would be dominated by financially resilient firms, but that's not necessarily true. This ETF's benchmark, the WisdomTree MidCap Dividend Index, simply screens for companies that have paid dividends over the past 12 months. That doesn't ensure that a company has grown its dividend or that its dividend is sustainable, nor does it guarantee a portfolio of sturdy balance sheets. In fact, this ETF's aggregate debt/capital ratio of 44% is higher than the category norm of 34%.

The ETF's dividend focus also results in substantial sector biases that leave this ETF vulnerable to downturns in its favored areas. Financials soak up nearly half of this fund's assets, well above the category average of 19%. Much of that financial exposure is composed of REIT stocks, which account for 21% of the portfolio. REITs have been on a major multiyear run, and it wouldn't be surprising to see them cool down soon, and if they do, this ETF is likely to suffer. What's more, REIT dividends don't qualify for the beneficial tax treatment that other dividends receive. Specifically, if investors meet certain holding requirements, most stock dividends are taxed at a 15% rate. REIT dividends, however, are taxed at higher rate, typically the shareholder's ordinary income-tax rate.

While this ETF's yield might appeal to income-hungry sorts, its quirks significantly damp our enthusiasm for it.

Address:	48 Wall Street New York NY 10005 866-909-9473	
Web Address:	www.wisdomtree.com	
Inception:	06-16-06*	
Advisor:	Wisdomtree Asset Maidmanagement, Inc.	

Management Fee:	0.38%			
Expense Projections:	3Yr:$122	5Yr: —	10Yr: —	
Income Distrib:	Annually			
Exchange:	NYSE			

Portfolio Analysis 11-30-06

Share change since 10-06 Total Stocks:431

	Sector	PE	Tot Ret%	% Assets
⊕ American Capital Strateg	Financial	8.9	39.34	1.57
⊕ UST, Inc.	Goods	18.6	49.53	1.50
⊕ DTE Energy Holding Compa	Utilities	12.6	17.58	1.33
⊕ iStar Financial, Inc.	Financial	18.5	44.44	1.27
⊕ CapitalSource, Inc.	Financial	16.2	32.16	1.10
⊕ Citizens Communications	Telecom	17.1	26.56	1.05
⊕ KeySpan Corporation	Utilities	16.8	20.97	0.98
⊕ New Century Financial Co	Financial	4.7	4.91	0.93
⊕ NiSource, Inc.	Utilities	22.3	20.51	0.92
⊕ Developers Diversified R	Financial	41.1	39.65	0.92
⊕ Plum Creek Timber Compan	Financial	23.6	15.65	0.89
⊕ Health Care Property	Financial	33.5	53.18	0.87
⊕ Apartment Investment & M	Financial	—	55.18	0.87
⊕ Duke Realty Corporation	Financial	75.7	28.98	0.85
⊕ Newell Rubbermaid, Inc.	Goods	19.3	25.66	0.82
⊕ Lyondell Chemical Compan	Energy	10.2	11.52	0.81
⊕ CenterPoint Energy, Inc.	Utilities	12.0	34.84	0.80
⊕ Thornburg Mortgage, Inc.	Financial	9.7	6.52	0.80
⊕ Pinnacle West Capital	Utilities	21.9	27.04	0.76
⊕ Cincinnati Financial Cor	Financial	8.1	4.39	0.75

Current Investment Style

Value Blnd Growth — Large Mid Small

Market Cap	%
Giant	0.3
Large	0.2
Mid	94.4
Small	5.1
Micro	0.0

Avg $mil: 4,146

Value Measures		Rel Category
Price/Earnings	15.55	0.93
Price/Book	2.19	0.85
Price/Sales	1.25	1.12
Price/Cash Flow	9.69	1.06
Dividend Yield %	3.25	2.37

Growth Measures	%	Rel Category
Long-Term Erngs	8.88	0.73
Book Value	4.56	0.62
Sales	10.28	1.46
Cash Flow	0.78	0.08
Historical Erngs	10.98	0.57

Profitability	%	Rel Category
Return on Equity	14.58	0.85
Return on Assets	9.45	1.10
Net Margin	16.14	1.52

Sector Weightings

	% of Stocks	Rel S&P 500	3 Year High Low
↻ Info	3.35	0.17	
🖬 Software	0.06	0.02	— —
🖵 Hardware	0.78	0.08	— —
🎙 Media	1.19	0.31	— —
🖀 Telecom	1.32	0.38	— —
☞ Service	58.75	1.27	
✚ Health	2.37	0.20	— —
🛒 Consumer	5.81	0.76	— —
📋 Business	3.71	0.88	— —
$ Financial	46.86	2.10	— —
⊔ Mfg	37.89	1.12	
⚒ Goods	10.10	1.18	— —
⚙ Ind Mtrls	10.41	0.87	— —
🔥 Energy	2.95	0.30	— —
💡 Utilities	14.43	4.12	— —

Composition

● Cash	0.5	
● Stocks	99.5	
● Bonds	0.0	
○ Other	0.0	
Foreign	0.0	
(% of Stock)		

WisdomTree Pac ex-Jp HYEq DNH

Market Price $60.97	**Mstar Category** Diversified Pacific/Asia	

Morningstar Fair Value

Price/Fair Value Ratio	Coverage Rate %
—	—

Management

This fund's advisor, WisdomTree Asset Management, uses a new approach to indexing. Using studies and methods endorsed by prominent academics such as Jeremy Siegel (who is a professor at the University of Pennsylvania's Wharton School), the firm's indexes weight stocks in proportion to their dividends.

Methodology

This exchange-traded fund ranks stocks incorporated in Australia, Hong Kong, Singapore, and New Zealand by their dividend payouts. The portfolio then selects the top 30% of the names and weights them by the size of their payouts.

Morningstar Rating	Return	Risk	Yield	NAV	Avg Daily Vol. (k)	52 wk High/Low
— Not Rated	Not Rated	—	—	$61.62	21	$62.07 - $48.00

Growth of $10,000
- Investment Value of ETF
- Investment Value of Index MSCI EAFE

13.0 / 12.2 / 10.6 / 10.0

Trading Volume Millions

1997	1998	1999	2000	2001	2002	2003	2004	2005	2006	History
—	—	—	—	—	—	—	—	—	61.62	NAV $
—	—	—	—	—	—	—	—	—	61.80	Market Price $
—	—	—	—	—	—	—	—	—	26.80*	NAV Return%
—	—	—	—	—	—	—	—	—	27.46*	Market Price Return%
—	—	—	—	—	—	—	—	—	0.32	Avg Premium/Discount%
—	—	—	—	—	—	—	—	—	26.80	NAV Rtrn% +/-MSCI EAFE
—	—	—	—	—	—	—	—	—	26.80	NAV Rtrn% +/-MSCI Pac
—	—	—	—	—	—	—	—	—	—	NAV Return% Rank in Cat
—	—	—	—	—	—	—	—	—	—	Income Return %
—	—	—	—	—	—	—	—	—	—	Capital Return %
—	—	—	—	—	—	—	—	—	0.52	Income $
—	—	—	—	—	—	—	—	—	0.00	Capital Gains $
—	—	—	—	—	—	—	—	—	—	Expense Ratio %
—	—	—	—	—	—	—	—	—	—	Income Ratio %
—	—	—	—	—	—	—	—	—	—	Turnover Rate %
—	—	—	—	—	—	—	—	—	49	Net Assets $mil

Performance 12-31-06

Historic Quarterly NAV Returns

	1st Qtr	2nd Qtr	3rd Qtr	4th Qtr	Total
2002	—	—	—	—	—
2003	—	—	—	—	—
2004	—	—	—	—	—
2005	—	—	—	—	—
2006	—	—	5.61	17.88	—*

Trailing	NAV Return%	Market Return%	NAV Rtrn%+/-MSCI EAFE	%Rank Cat.(NAV)
3 Mo	17.88	18.18	7.53	3
6 Mo	24.50	24.66	9.81	3
1 Yr	—	—	—	—
3 Yr Avg	—	—	—	—
5 Yr Avg	—	—	—	—
10 Yr Avg	—	—	—	—

Tax Analysis	Tax-Adj Return%	Tax-Cost Ratio
3 Yr (estimated)	—	—
5 Yr (estimated)	—	—
10 Yr (estimated)	—	—

Rating and Risk

Time Period	Morningstar Rtn vs Cat	Morningstar Risk vs Cat	Morningstar Risk-Adj Rating
3 Yr	—	—	—
5 Yr	—	—	—
10 Yr	—	—	—

Other Measures	Standard Index S&P 500	Best Fit Index
Alpha	—	—
Beta	—	—
R-Squared	—	—
Standard Deviation	—	
Mean	—	
Sharpe Ratio	—	

Morningstar's Take by Arijit Dutta 12-31-06

We'd choose its sibling over WisdomTree Pacific ex-Japan High-Yielding Equity.

This ETF strikes a distinct stance among both its index and actively managed peers. Unlike most diversified Asia-Pacific ex-Japan offerings, this one limits itself to stocks listed in just four countries: Australia, Hong Kong, Singapore, and New Zealand. The fund also takes a different approach to indexing. Instead of using the traditional method of weighting each stock in the index by its market cap, this ETF weights stocks by the size of their dividend payouts. While it shares this same approach with the firm's other offering in this category, WisdomTree Pacific ex-Japan Total Dividend, High-Yielding Equity limits itself to the top 30% of stocks ranked by their dividend payouts.

Prominent academic Jeremy Siegel, who endorsed the index strategy here, has some sensible arguments in its favor. Markets are often given to excess, and cap-weighted indexes, due to their very construction, tend to bulk up on the priciest stocks. Siegel's research has shown that weighting stocks by a fundamental measure such as dividend payout (rather than by stock price) results in better index performance as well as lower downside risk during bear markets. Though this ETF launched only in June 2006, its underlying index's backtested long-term returns are indeed superior to those of traditional indexes.

However, it's worth noting that the fund doesn't provide any exposure to many promising, fast-growing companies in the region (especially in emerging markets) that reinvest a lot of their cash instead of paying dividends. Moreover, this fund's added emphasis on just the top dividend-paying names can lead to extreme country bets. For example, the portfolio currently has an 87% stake in Australia alone (the category average is only 5%). For those drawn to the income-rich, developed-market-focused mandate here, we think Total Dividend is a better choice. That fund is better diversified and is also cheaper.

Address:	48 Wall Street New York NY 10005 866-909-9473	
Web Address:	www.wisdomtree.com	
Inception:	06-16-06*	
Advisor:	Wisdomtree Asset Management, Inc.	

Management Fee:	0.58%			
Expense Projections:	3Yr:$186	5Yr: —	10Yr: —	
Income Distrib:	Annually			
Exchange:	NYSE			

Portfolio Analysis 11-30-06

Share change since 10-06 Total Stocks:90

	Sector	Country	% Assets
⊕ National Australia Bank	Financial	Australia	8.36
⊕ Commonwealth Bank of Aus	Financial	Australia	8.32
⊕ Telstra Corporation, Ltd	Telecom	Australia	7.79
⊕ Australia & New Zealand	Financial	Australia	7.66
⊕ Westpac Banking	Financial	Australia	7.25
⊕ St. George Bank Ltd	Financial	Australia	3.74
⊕ Wesfarmers Ltd	Ind Mtrls	Australia	3.42
⊕ Qantas Airways Ltd.	Business	Australia	2.98
⊕ Telecom Corp. of New Zea	Telecom	New Zealand	2.96
⊕ Suncorp-Metway Ltd	Financial	Australia	2.60
⊕ Insurance Australia Grp	Financial	Australia	2.33
⊕ Tabcorp Holdings Limited	Consumer	Australia	2.29
⊕ Bluescope Steel Ltd	Ind Mtrls	Australia	1.67
⊕ Lend Lease	Financial	Australia	1.57
⊕ Promina Grp Ltd	Financial	Australia	1.45
⊕ Coca-Cola Amatil Ltd	Goods	Australia	1.35
⊕ Amcor Ltd	Goods	Australia	1.33
⊕ Fairfax (John) Hldgs Ltd	Media	Australia	1.30
⊕ Alinta Ltd	Utilities	Australia	1.15
⊕ Fletcher Building Ltd	Ind Mtrls	New Zealand	0.96

Current Investment Style

Value Blnd Growth — Large Mid Small

Market Cap	%
Giant	40.3
Large	30.3
Mid	24.4
Small	5.0
Micro	0.0

Avg $mil: 8,409

Value Measures		Rel Category
Price/Earnings	14.48	0.98
Price/Book	2.50	1.02
Price/Sales	1.38	0.88
Price/Cash Flow	6.99	0.87
Dividend Yield %	6.15	1.14

Growth Measures	%	Rel Category
Long-Term Erngs	8.06	0.84
Book Value	0.05	0.04
Sales	9.31	0.86
Cash Flow	1.17	0.22
Historical Erngs	7.43	0.55

Composition

Cash	0.8	Bonds	0.0
Stocks	98.8	Other	0.4
Foreign (% of Stock)			100.0

Sector Weightings

	% of Stocks	Rel MSCI EAFE	3 Year High Low
☎ Info	16.95	1.43	
Software	0.06	0.11	— —
Hardware	0.00	0.00	— —
Media	4.82	2.63	— —
Telecom	12.07	2.17	— —
☞ Service	64.29	1.36	
Health	0.38	0.05	— —
Consumer	6.36	1.28	— —
Business	8.75	1.73	— —
Financial	48.80	1.62	— —
Mfg	18.76	0.46	
Goods	5.63	0.43	— —
Ind Mtrls	10.16	0.66	— —
Energy	1.36	0.19	— —
Utilities	1.61	0.31	— —

Regional Exposure % Stock

UK/W. Europe	0	N. America	0
Japan	0	Latn America	0
Asia X Japan	100	Other	0

Country Exposure % Stock

Australia	87	Hong Kong	0
New Zealand	8		
Singapore	5		

WisdomTree Pac ex-Jp TDiv DND

	Market Price $62.20	Mstar Category Diversified Pacific/Asia

Morningstar Rating	Return	Risk	Yield	NAV	Avg Daily Vol. (k)	52 wk High/Low
— Not Rated	Not Rated		—	$62.80	11	$63.24 - $49.01

Morningstar Fair Value

Price/Fair Value Ratio	Coverage Rate %
—	—

Management

This fund's advisor, WisdomTree Asset Management, uses a new approach to indexing. Using studies and methods developed by prominent academics such as Jeremy Siegel (who is a professor at the University of Pennsylvania's Wharton School), the firm's indexes weight stocks in proportion to their dividends.

Methodology

This exchange-traded fund tracks a diversified index of stocks incorporated in Australia, Hong Kong, Singapore, and New Zealand. Instead of weighting the stocks by their market caps, the practice here is to own stocks in proportion to their annual cash dividends.

Growth of $10,000
■ Investment Value of ETF
— Investment Value of Index MSCI EAFE

Trading Volume Millions

1997	1998	1999	2000	2001	2002	2003	2004	2005	2006	History
—	—	—	—	—	—	—	—	—	62.80	NAV $
—	—	—	—	—	—	—	—	—	63.09	Market Price $
—	—	—	—	—	—	—	—	—	27.14*	NAV Return%
—	—	—	—	—	—	—	—	—	28.09*	Market Price Return%
—	—	—	—	—	—	—	—	—	0.28	Avg Premium/Discount%
—	—	—	—	—	—	—	—	—	27.14	NAV Rtrn% +/-MSCI EAFE
—	—	—	—	—	—	—	—	—	27.14	NAV Rtrn% +/-MSCI Pac
—	—	—	—	—	—	—	—	—	—	NAV Return% Rank in Cat
—	—	—	—	—	—	—	—	—	—	Income Return %
—	—	—	—	—	—	—	—	—	—	Capital Return %
—	—	—	—	—	—	—	—	—	0.39	Income $
—	—	—	—	—	—	—	—	—	0.00	Capital Gains $
—	—	—	—	—	—	—	—	—	—	Expense Ratio %
—	—	—	—	—	—	—	—	—	—	Income Ratio %
—	—	—	—	—	—	—	—	—	—	Turnover Rate %
—	—	—	—	—	—	—	—	—	31	Net Assets $mil

Performance 12-31-06

Historic Quarterly NAV Returns

	1st Qtr	2nd Qtr	3rd Qtr	4th Qtr	Total
2002	—	—	—	—	—
2003	—	—	—	—	—
2004	—	—	—	—	—
2005	—	—	—	—	—
2006	—	—	5.43	17.22	—*

Trailing	NAV Return%	Market Return%+/-	NAV Rtrn% +/-MSCI EAFE	%Rank Cat.(NAV)
3 Mo	17.22	17.75	6.87	3
6 Mo	23.58	24.18	8.89	3
1 Yr	—	—	—	—
3 Yr Avg	—	—	—	—
5 Yr Avg	—	—	—	—
10 Yr Avg	—	—	—	—

Tax Analysis	Tax-Adj Return%	Tax-Cost Ratio
3 Yr (estimated)	—	—
5 Yr (estimated)	—	—
10 Yr (estimated)	—	—

Rating and Risk

Time Period	Morningstar Rtn vs Cat	Morningstar Risk vs Cat	Morningstar Risk-Adj Rating
3 Yr	—	—	—
5 Yr	—	—	—
10 Yr	—	—	—

Other Measures	Standard Index S&P 500	Best Fit Index
Alpha	—	—
Beta	—	—
R-Squared	—	—
Standard Deviation	—	
Mean	—	
Sharpe Ratio	—	

Portfolio Analysis 11-30-06

Share change since 10-06 Total Stocks:237

	Sector	Country	% Assets
⊕ China Mobile	Telecom	Hong Kong	5.94
⊕ Commonwealth Bank of Aus	Financial	Australia	5.32
⊕ National Australia Bank	Financial	Australia	5.16
⊕ Australia & New Zealand	Financial	Australia	4.14
⊕ Telstra Corporation, Ltd	Telecom	Australia	3.68
⊕ Westpac Banking	Financial	Australia	3.61
⊕ BHP Billiton, Ltd.	Ind Mtrls	Australia	2.56
⊕ Hang Seng Bank	Financial	Hong Kong	2.24
⊕ Bank of China (Hong Kong)	Financial	Hong Kong	1.96
⊕ Hutchison Whampoa Ltd	Telecom	Hong Kong	1.58
⊕ Singapore Telecommunicat	Telecom	Singapore	1.53
⊕ DBS Grp Hldgs Ltd	Financial	Singapore	1.52
⊕ St. George Bank Ltd	Financial	Australia	1.51
⊕ Woolworths Ltd	Consumer	Australia	1.43
⊕ Wesfarmers Ltd	Ind Mtrls	Australia	1.38
⊕ CLP Holdings Limited	Utilities	Hong Kong	1.34
⊕ Sun Hung Kai Properties	Financial	Hong Kong	1.27
⊕ Telecom Corp. of New Zea	Telecom	New Zealand	1.25
⊕ United Overseas Bank Ltd	Financial	Singapore	1.21
⊕ Qantas Airways Ltd.	Business	Australia	1.15

Current Investment Style

Value Blnd Growth — Large Mid Small

Market Cap	%
Giant	52.6
Large	29.5
Mid	16.4
Small	1.4
Micro	0.0

Avg $mil: 13,540

Value Measures		Rel Category
Price/Earnings	15.10	1.02
Price/Book	2.40	0.98
Price/Sales	1.73	1.11
Price/Cash Flow	9.05	1.13
Dividend Yield %	4.60	0.86

Growth Measures	%	Rel Category
Long-Term Erngs	11.18	1.16
Book Value	2.43	1.96
Sales	12.26	1.14
Cash Flow	9.41	1.78
Historical Erngs	13.15	0.98

Sector Weightings

	% of Stocks	Rel MSCI EAFE	3 Year High Low
↻ Info	18.57	1.57	
🖥 Software	0.34	0.61	— —
📟 Hardware	0.35	0.09	— —
🎤 Media	3.04	1.66	— —
📞 Telecom	14.84	2.66	— —
☞ Service	59.06	1.25	
🛡 Health	1.38	0.19	— —
🛒 Consumer	4.84	0.98	— —
📋 Business	7.83	1.54	— —
💲 Financial	45.01	1.50	— —
⚒ Mfg	22.36	0.55	
🏭 Goods	3.53	0.27	— —
⚙ Ind Mtrls	12.82	0.83	— —
🔋 Energy	3.00	0.42	— —
💡 Utilities	3.01	0.57	— —

Composition

Cash	0.1	Bonds	0.0
Stocks	99.6	Other	0.3
Foreign	(% of Stock)		100.0

Regional Exposure % Stock

UK/W. Europe	0	N. America	0
Japan	0	Latn America	0
Asia X Japan	100	Other	0

Country Exposure % Stock

Australia	59	New Zealand	3
Hong Kong	27		
Singapore	11		

Morningstar's Take by Arijit Dutta 12-31-06

WisdomTree Pacific ex-Japan Total Dividend doesn't quite cover all bases, but it's still worth a look.

This ETF strikes a distinct stance among both its index and actively managed peers. Unlike most diversified Asia-Pacific ex-Japan offerings, this one limits itself to stocks listed in just four countries: Australia, Hong Kong, Singapore, and New Zealand. (Most rivals in this category tend to have large stakes in the region's emerging markets such as South Korea and Taiwan.) The fund also takes a different approach to indexing. Instead of using the traditional method of weighting each stock in the index by its market cap, this ETF weights stocks by the size of their dividend payouts.

Prominent academic Jeremy Siegel, who has endorsed the index strategy here, has some sensible arguments in its favor. Markets are often given to excess, and cap-weighted indexes, due to their very construction, tend to bulk up on the priciest stocks. Siegel's research and this index's

backtested results show that weighting stocks by a fundamental measure such as dividend payout (rather than by stock price) results in better index performance as well as lower downside risk during bear markets.

We would caution against relying too much on backtested data. The dividend-strategy tends to induce a value bias in the portfolio, which has been in the market's favor in recent years (and can therefore distort long-term performance). Also, the fund doesn't provide any exposure to many promising, fast-growing companies in the region (especially in emerging markets) that reinvest a lot of their cash instead of paying dividends.

That criticism aside, focusing on a fundamental measure of a firm's worth is inherently appealing. This income-rich, developed-market-focused portfolio is also likely to moderate the volatility that comes with any regional offering. Finally, the 0.48% expense ratio here is cheaper than the category median by miles.

Address:	48 Wall Street New York NY 10005 866-909-9473	Management Fee:	0.48%		
		Expense Projections:	3Yr:$154	5Yr: —	10Yr: —
		Income Distrib:	Annually		
Web Address:	www.wisdomtree.com	Exchange:	NYSE		
Inception:	06-16-06*				
Advisor:	Wisdomtree Asset Management, Inc.				

MORNINGSTAR® ETFs 150

WisdomTree SmallCap Div DES

| | Market Price $56.78 | Mstar Category Small Blend |

Morningstar Fair Value

Price/Fair Value Ratio — Coverage Rate % —

Management

WisdomTree Asset Management is this ETF's advisor. However, the daily management of the fund is handled by its subadvisor, BNY Investment Advisors, a division of Bank of New York. Managerial duties are performed by a five-person team from BNY: Kurt Zyla, Lloyd Buchanan, Denise Krisko, Robert McCormack, and Todd Rose.

Methodology

This ETF tracks the WisdomTree SmallCap Dividend Index, which includes the smallest stocks (as measured by market capitalization) in the WisdomTree Dividend Index. The stocks in the index are ranked by the projected cash dividend they are expected to pay out over the next 12 months. That results in substantial sector biases, since many of the biggest dividend payers in the small-cap arena reside in the financial sector, specifically in the REIT and regional banking industries.

| Morningstar Rating — Not Rated | Return — Not Rated | Risk — | Yield — | NAV $57.42 | Avg Daily Vol. (k) 18 | 52 wk High/Low $58.24 - $49.61 |

Growth of $10,000
— Investment Value of ETF
— Investment Value of Index S&P 500

12.4 / 10.6 / 10.0 / 9.0

Trading Volume Millions 0.01 / 0.0

	1997	1998	1999	2000	2001	2002	2003	2004	2005	2006	History
	—	—	—	—	—	—	—	—	—	57.42	NAV $
	—	—	—	—	—	—	—	—	—	57.36	Market Price $
	—	—	—	—	—	—	—	—	—	16.45*	NAV Return%
	—	—	—	—	—	—	—	—	—	16.40*	Market Price Return%
	—	—	—	—	—	—	—	—	—	-0.03	Avg Premium/Discount%
	—	—	—	—	—	—	—	—	—	16.45	NAV Rtrn% +/-S&P 500
	—	—	—	—	—	—	—	—	—	16.45	NAV Rtrn% +/-Russ 2000
	—	—	—	—	—	—	—	—	—	—	NAV Return% Rank in Cat
	—	—	—	—	—	—	—	—	—	—	Income Return %
	—	—	—	—	—	—	—	—	—	—	Capital Return %
	—	—	—	—	—	—	—	—	—	1.04	Income $
	—	—	—	—	—	—	—	—	—	0.00	Capital Gains $
	—	—	—	—	—	—	—	—	—	—	Expense Ratio %
	—	—	—	—	—	—	—	—	—	—	Income Ratio %
	—	—	—	—	—	—	—	—	—	—	Turnover Rate %
	—	—	—	—	—	—	—	—	—	69	Net Assets $mil

Performance 12-31-06

Historic Quarterly NAV Returns

	1st Qtr	2nd Qtr	3rd Qtr	4th Qtr	Total
2002	—	—	—	—	—
2003	—	—	—	—	—
2004	—	—	—	—	—
2005	—	—	—	—	—
2006	—	—	3.80	8.66	—*

Trailing	NAV Return%	Market Return%	NAV Rtrn% +/-S&P 500	%Rank Cat.(NAV)
3 Mo	8.66	8.53	1.96	12
6 Mo	12.79	12.78	0.05	10
1 Yr	—	—	—	—
3 Yr Avg	—	—	—	—
5 Yr Avg	—	—	—	—
10 Yr Avg	—	—	—	—

Tax Analysis	Tax-Adj Return%	Tax-Cost Ratio
3 Yr (estimated)	—	—
5 Yr (estimated)	—	—
10 Yr (estimated)	—	—

Rating and Risk

Time Period	Morningstar Rtn vs Cat	Morningstar Risk vs Cat	Morningstar Risk-Adj Rating
3 Yr	—	—	—
5 Yr	—	—	—
10 Yr	—	—	—

Other Measures	Standard Index S&P 500	Best Fit Index
Alpha	—	—
Beta	—	—
R-Squared	—	—
Standard Deviation	—	
Mean	—	
Sharpe Ratio	—	

Portfolio Analysis 11-30-06

Share change since 10-06 Total Stocks:777	Sector	PE	Tot Ret%	% Assets
American Home Mortgage I	Financial	10.2	20.59	1.45
Apollo Investment Corpor	Financial	—	—	1.29
Novastar Financial, Inc.	Financial	8.5	12.81	1.18
Nationwide Health Proper	Financial	30.5	50.74	1.04
Newcastle Investment Cor	Financial	12.3	38.77	1.00
American Financial Realt	Financial	—	3.69	0.98
Saxon Capital, Inc.	Financial	—	—	0.93
MCG Capital Corporation	Financial	11.9	54.30	0.86
Senior Housing Prop Trus	Financial	32.6	55.23	0.77
Entertainment Properties	Financial	23.2	51.98	0.74
Friedman Billings Ramsey	Financial	—	-15.04	0.74
Peoples Energy Corp.	Utilities	—	34.37	0.72
Trustreet Properties, In	Financial	NMF	25.27	0.68
Duquesne Light Holdings,	Utilities	18.9	28.59	0.66
Redwood Trust, Inc.	Financial	11.2	56.92	0.66
RAIT Investment Trust	Financial	13.9	45.67	0.61
Regal Entertainment Grou	Goods	36.1	19.27	0.59
Washington REIT	Financial	42.5	37.76	0.57
Lexington Corporate Prop	Financial	—	15.94	0.56
Municipal Mortgage & Equ	Financial	17.4	34.12	0.56

Current Investment Style

Value Blnd Growth — Large / Mid / Small

Market Cap	%
Giant	0.0
Large	0.0
Mid	3.3
Small	74.9
Micro	21.8

Avg $mil: 878

Value Measures		Rel Category
Price/Earnings	16.04	0.91
Price/Book	1.80	0.87
Price/Sales	1.22	1.18
Price/Cash Flow	7.72	1.19
Dividend Yield %	6.12	3.85

Growth Measures	%	Rel Category
Long-Term Erngs	8.48	0.64
Book Value	1.89	0.35
Sales	-4.13	NMF
Cash Flow	0.29	0.03
Historical Erngs	6.62	0.56

Profitability	%	Rel Category
Return on Equity	11.32	0.98
Return on Assets	7.75	1.18
Net Margin	16.97	1.72

Sector Weightings	% of Stocks	Rel S&P 500	3 Year High Low
Info	6.51	0.33	
Software	0.12	0.03	— —
Hardware	0.70	0.08	— —
Media	2.97	0.78	— —
Telecom	2.72	0.77	— —
Service	68.01	1.47	
Health	1.29	0.11	— —
Consumer	3.75	0.49	— —
Business	4.23	1.00	— —
Financial	58.74	2.64	— —
Mfg	25.50	0.75	
Goods	7.06	0.83	— —
Ind Mtrls	9.59	0.80	— —
Energy	1.43	0.15	— —
Utilities	7.42	2.12	— —

Composition

	%
Cash	0.5
Stocks	99.2
Bonds	0.0
Other	0.2
Foreign	0.0
(% of Stock)	

Morningstar's Take by Sonya Morris 12-31-06

We're wary of WisdomTree SmallCap Dividend.

This small-blend exchange-traded fund differs substantially from its peers thanks to its benchmark's unique system for ranking stocks. Unlike most indexes, which weight stocks based on market capitalization (a stock's market price times the shares available for trading), this ETF's bogy, the WisdomTree Small Cap Dividend Index, ranks its constituents based on cash dividends.

There's something intuitively appealing about concentrating on companies with the ability to pay dividends, particularly among riskier small-sized firms. But this ETF's benchmark only screens for firms that have paid dividends in the past 12 months. It doesn't make any assessments about sustainability or trends in those dividends. Indeed, 51 of the ETF's 781 holdings have seen their dividends decline over the past five years, and 69 do not have five years of dividend-paying history. True, that's just a small portion of the overall portfolio, but it indicates that this fund's dividend

criteria won't necessarily guarantee a portfolio of financially sturdy fare.

What's more, this ETF's methodology brings about certain biases. It loads up on areas that traditionally pay high dividends. Many of the dividend-paying stocks in small-cap land reside in the financial sector, which soaks up a whopping 58% of this ETF's portfolio. That's far more than its typical rival, which dedicates 19% to that sector. Most of the portfolio's financial exposure is clustered in REIT stocks and regional banks and savings & loans, which comprise 22% and 19% of assets, respectively. That leaves this fund vulnerable to downturns in those industries. That may be a relevant concern at the moment: REIT stocks have staged a scorching multiyear rally, but they're looking quite pricey, according to Morningstar equity analysts, and it wouldn't be surprising to see them take a breather.

All told, these risks detract from this ETF's appeal.

Address:	48 Wall Street, New York NY 10005
	866-909-9473
Web Address:	www.wisdomtree.com
Inception:	06-16-06*
Advisor:	Wisdomtree Asset Management, Inc.

Management Fee:	0.38%
Expense Projections:	3Yr:$122 5Yr: — 10Yr: —
Income Distrib:	Annually
Exchange:	NYSE

WisdomTree Total Dividend DTD

Market Price $57.33	**Mstar Category** Large Blend	

Morningstar Fair Value

Price/Fair Value Ratio —   Coverage Rate % —

Management

WisdomTree Asset Management is the advisor. The Bank of New York has subadvisory responsibilities here, as well as at all other WisdomTree ETF funds. Kurt Zyla, Lloyd Buchanan, Denise Krisko, Robert McCormack, and Todd Rose are senior members in charge of this fund at the subadvisor.

Methodology

This exchange-traded fund tracks the WisdomTree Dividend Index, which looks for companies that paid regular dividends over the 12 months prior to its annual December reconstitution. It then weights the selected stocks according to their projected dividends for the next 12 months as compared with the sum total of the projected dividends for the entire group. And although the index reconstitutes annually, it will cut companies that stop paying dividends throughout the year. As of Oct. 31, 2006, the ETF held 758 stocks.

	Morningstar Rating	Return	Risk	Yield	NAV	Avg Daily Vol. (k)	52 wk High/Low
	— Not Rated	— Not Rated	—	—	$57.62	10	$58.10 - $49.85

Growth of $10,000
- Investment Value of ETF
- Investment Value of Index S&P 500

12.0
11.7
10.6
10.0

Trading Volume Millions
0.005
0.0

1997	1998	1999	2000	2001	2002	2003	2004	2005	2006	History
—	—	—	—	—	—	—	—	—	57.62	NAV $
—	—	—	—	—	—	—	—	—	57.61	Market Price $
—	—	—	—	—	—	—	—	—	15.73*	NAV Return%
—	—	—	—	—	—	—	—	—	15.50*	Market Price Return%
—	—	—	—	—	—	—	—	—	0.06	Avg Premium/Discount%
—	—	—	—	—	—	—	—	—	15.73	NAV Rtrn% +/-S&P 500
—	—	—	—	—	—	—	—	—	15.73	NAV Rtrn% +/-Russ 1000
—	—	—	—	—	—	—	—	—	—	NAV Return% Rank in Cat
—	—	—	—	—	—	—	—	—	—	Income Return %
—	—	—	—	—	—	—	—	—	—	Capital Return %
—	—	—	—	—	—	—	—	—	0.60	Income $
—	—	—	—	—	—	—	—	—	0.00	Capital Gains $
—	—	—	—	—	—	—	—	—	—	Expense Ratio %
—	—	—	—	—	—	—	—	—	—	Income Ratio %
—	—	—	—	—	—	—	—	—	—	Turnover Rate %
—	—	—	—	—	—	—	—	—	63	Net Assets $mil

Performance 12-31-06

Historic Quarterly NAV Returns

	1st Qtr	2nd Qtr	3rd Qtr	4th Qtr	Total
2002	—	—	—	—	—
2003	—	—	—	—	—
2004	—	—	—	—	—
2005	—	—	—	—	—
2006	—	—	6.54	6.75	—*

Trailing	NAV Return%	Market Return%	NAV Rtrn% +/-S&P 500	%Rank Cat.(NAV)
3 Mo	6.75	6.64	0.05	44
6 Mo	13.73	13.28	0.99	38
1 Yr	—	—	—	—
3 Yr Avg	—	—	—	—
5 Yr Avg	—	—	—	—
10 Yr Avg	—	—	—	—

Tax Analysis	Tax-Adj Return%	Tax-Cost Ratio
3 Yr (estimated)	—	—
5 Yr (estimated)	—	—
10 Yr (estimated)	—	—

Rating and Risk

Time Period	Morningstar Rtn vs Cat	Morningstar Risk vs Cat	Morningstar Risk-Adj Rating
3 Yr	—	—	—
5 Yr	—	—	—
10 Yr	—	—	—

Other Measures	Standard Index S&P 500	Best Fit Index
Alpha	—	—
Beta	—	—
R-Squared	—	—
Standard Deviation	—	
Mean	—	
Sharpe Ratio	—	

Morningstar's Take by Marta Norton 12-31-06

Let WisdomTree Total Dividend prove itself.

This fund has a different mandate than other total-market ETFs. Its peers track market-cap-weighted indexes that blanket the entire market, but it tracks the WisdomTree Dividend Index, which screens the U.S. market for stocks paying regular dividends in the 12 months prior to its annual December reconstitution. It then weights them by their projected cash dividends as compared with the sum total for the group.

This methodology has a lot of arguments in its favor. The ETF's dividend focus offers exposure to companies showing signs of financial health while offering broad market representation. So, in theory, the fund is more selective about which stocks get the most assets, while its market-cap-weighted peers load up on the biggest stocks, regardless of whether they are financially strong. Investors here will also likely get more current income than at other ETFs, where companies that pay dividends are mixed in with those that don't.

Still, we have reservations. Because the ETF focuses only on the last 12 months and doesn't screen for historical dividend growth, its portfolio likely includes stocks whose current dividend rates are not sustainable. As of Oct. 31, 2006, the fund's more-than-700-stock portfolio had 61 stocks with negative dividend growth over the past five years, 34 stocks with 0% growth over that same period, and 161 stocks that didn't even have five years of dividend-paying history. To be sure, these stocks didn't grab too much of the fund's portfolio, but they still suggest that some of the fund's companies may not be as financially healthy as they first appear. Also, the ETF could have higher turnover, as its index will drop stocks that stop paying dividends. For instance, the benchmark recently dropped Ford after the automaker cut its dividend.

This ETF has some strengths, but there are enough questions about its methodology to give us pause. Wait for it to prove itself before jumping in.

Address:	48 Wall Street New York NY 10005 866-909-9473	
Web Address:	www.wisdomtree.com	
Inception:	06-16-06*	
Advisor:	Wisdomtree Asset Management, Inc.	

Management Fee:	0.28%
Expense Projections:	3Yr:$90 5Yr: — 10Yr: —
Income Distrib:	Annually
Exchange:	NYSE

Portfolio Analysis 11-30-06

Share change since 10-06 Total Stocks:775

	Sector	PE	Tot Ret%	% Assets
⊕ Bank of America Corporat	Financial	12.4	20.68	3.97
⊕ General Electric Company	Ind Mtrls	19.8	9.35	3.81
⊕ Citigroup, Inc.	Financial	13.3	19.55	3.71
⊕ ExxonMobil Corporation	Energy	11.7	39.07	3.56
⊕ Altria Group, Inc.	Goods	15.9	19.87	2.86
⊕ Pfizer Inc.	Health	15.1	15.22	2.81
⊕ AT&T, Inc.	Telecom	19.2	51.59	2.33
⊕ J.P. Morgan Chase & Co.	Financial	13.7	25.60	1.90
⊕ Chevron Corporation	Energy	9.3	33.75	1.80
⊕ Verizon Communications	Telecom	16.1	34.88	1.75
⊕ Procter & Gamble Company	Goods	24.2	13.36	1.60
⊕ Johnson & Johnson	Health	17.4	12.44	1.57
⊕ Merck & Co., Inc.	Health	18.8	42.66	1.51
⊕ Microsoft Corporation	Software	23.7	15.83	1.43
⊕ Wells Fargo Company	Financial	14.7	16.82	1.37
⊕ Coca-Cola Company	Goods	21.5	23.10	1.18
⊕ Wachovia Corporation	Financial	13.0	12.02	1.17
⊕ Wal-Mart Stores, Inc.	Consumer	16.6	0.13	0.97
⊕ Intel Corporation	Hardware	20.3	-17.18	0.93
⊕ US Bancorp	Financial	14.1	26.29	0.93

Current Investment Style

Value Blnd Growth — Large Mid Small

Market Cap	%
Giant	51.6
Large	28.3
Mid	16.6
Small	3.5
Micro	0.0

Avg $mil: 44,390

Value Measures		Rel Category
Price/Earnings	14.67	0.88
Price/Book	2.49	0.91
Price/Sales	1.56	1.23
Price/Cash Flow	10.21	1.08
Dividend Yield %	2.88	1.61

Growth Measures	%	Rel Category
Long-Term Erngs	9.67	0.84
Book Value	7.33	0.86
Sales	8.75	1.05
Cash Flow	-1.27	NMF
Historical Erngs	12.74	0.76

Profitability	%	Rel Category
Return on Equity	18.46	0.96
Return on Assets	10.85	1.13
Net Margin	15.93	1.43

Sector Weightings

	% of Stocks	Rel S&P 500	3 Year High Low
⊙ Info	10.65	0.53	
Software	1.47	0.43	— —
Hardware	2.81	0.30	— —
Media	1.72	0.45	— —
Telecom	4.65	1.32	— —
⊙ Service	50.04	1.08	
Health	9.64	0.80	— —
Consumer	4.73	0.62	— —
Business	2.10	0.50	— —
Financial	33.57	1.51	— —
⊙ Mfg	39.31	1.16	
Goods	11.40	1.33	— —
Ind Mtrls	12.68	1.06	— —
Energy	8.18	0.83	— —
Utilities	7.05	2.01	— —

Composition

● Cash	0.5	
● Stocks	99.5	
● Bonds	0.0	
○ Other	0.0	
	Foreign	0.8
	(% of Stock)	

M RNINGSTAR® ETFs 150

Tables and Charts

This section breaks down the performance of all exchange-traded funds and lists the best and worst ETFs in a variety of categories.

Performance Summary

Morningstar's ETF Universe

Page	Name	Cat	Style Box	NAV ($)	Market Price ($)	2006 Avg. Prem. Discount%	NAV Return% through 12-29-06 1Yr	Annualized 3Yr	5Yr	Mkt Price Rtn% through 12-29-06 1Yr	Annualized 3Yr	5Yr	Morningstar Rating	Standard Deviation	Sharpe Ratio
—	BLDRS Asia 50 ADR Index	DP	▣	32.95	33.00	0.04	22.29	16.97	—	22.52	16.30	—	★	13.46	1.00
—	BLDRS Dev Mkts 100 ADR	FB	▣	29.37	29.43	0.01	25.52	16.11	—	25.80	14.40	—	★★	9.69	1.28
—	BLDRS Emerg Mkts 50 ADR	EM	▣	38.94	38.93	0.00	37.69	31.28	—	37.54	29.96	—	★★★	18.77	1.39
—	BLDRS Europe 100 ADR	ES	▣	29.75	29.78	−0.03	27.95	16.66	—	27.94	16.63	—	★★	9.75	1.32
—	Claymore MACRO Oil Dn Tr	SN	—	58.99	56.92	−1.59	—	—	—	—	—	—	—	—	—
—	Claymore MACRO Oil Up Tr	SN	—	61.09	63.90	2.19	—	—	—	—	—	—	—	—	—
—	Claymore/BNY BRIC ETF	FB	—	31.68	32.00	0.37	—	—	—	—	—	—	—	—	—
—	Claymore/Sabrient Ins ETF	MB	—	27.10	27.12	0.10	—	—	—	—	—	—	—	—	—
—	Claymore/Sabrient Stealth	SB	—	27.83	27.87	0.05	—	—	—	—	—	—	—	—	—
—	Claymore/Zacks Sector ETF	LB	—	27.72	27.73	0.18	—	—	—	—	—	—	—	—	—
—	Claymore/Zacks Yld Hog	LB	—	26.44	26.43	0.08	—	—	—	—	—	—	—	—	—
—	Consumer Discr SPDR	LB	▦	38.38	38.36	0.02	18.45	7.71	6.77	18.41	7.69	6.86	★★★	11.01	0.44
—	Consumer Staple SPDR	LB	▦	26.13	26.12	0.04	14.49	8.27	2.41	14.49	8.22	2.40	★	6.71	0.74
—	CurrencyShares Aus Dollar	IB	—	78.86	79.41	0.41	—	—	—	—	—	—	—	—	—
—	CurrencyShares BP Strlng	IB	—	195.91	196.50	0.16	—	—	—	—	—	—	—	—	—
—	CurrencyShares Can Dollar	IB	—	85.84	85.96	0.13	—	—	—	—	—	—	—	—	—
—	CurrencyShares Euro Trust	IB	—	131.99	131.99	0.04	13.65	—	—	14.03	—	—	—	—	—
—	CurrencyShares Mex Peso	IB	—	92.63	93.06	0.25	—	—	—	—	—	—	—	—	—
—	CurrencyShares Swe Krona	IB	—	146.34	146.03	−0.04	—	—	—	—	—	—	—	—	—
—	CurrencyShares Swi Franc	IB	—	82.01	82.13	0.12	—	—	—	—	—	—	—	—	—
42	DIAMONDS Trust	LV	▦	124.45	124.41	0.07	18.81	8.55	6.81	18.91	8.57	6.90	★★	7.14	0.75
43	Energy SPDR	SN	▦	58.75	58.63	0.02	18.40	30.37	18.98	18.08	30.39	18.93	★★★	19.76	1.28
—	Fidelity Nasdaq Comp Trac	LG	▦	94.97	95.06	−0.01	10.18	6.81	—	10.28	6.96	—	★★★	13.26	0.32
44	Financial SPDR	SF	▦	36.77	36.74	0.01	18.90	11.77	9.19	18.89	11.86	9.26	★★	8.32	1.01
—	First Tr NASDAQ-100 Eq Id	LB	▦	20.12	20.15	0.02	—	—	—	—	—	—	—	—	—
—	First Tr NASDAQ100 Tech	ST	▦	19.97	20.00	−0.04	—	—	—	—	—	—	—	—	—
—	First Trust AMEX Bio Indx	SH	▦	23.55	23.54	0.04	—	—	—	—	—	—	—	—	—
—	First Trust DJ Intrnt Idx	ST	▦	22.57	22.58	0.06	—	—	—	—	—	—	—	—	—
45	First Trust DJ S MicroCap	SB	▦	23.92	23.95	−0.08	15.70	—	—	15.89	—	—	—	—	—
—	First Trust IPOX-100 Indx	LG	▦	22.20	22.19	−0.15	—	—	—	—	—	—	—	—	—
—	First Trust MStar Div Ld	LV	▦	23.51	23.52	0.04	—	—	—	—	—	—	—	—	—
46	Health Care Sel SPDR	SH	▦	33.50	33.49	0.02	7.10	4.96	5.47	7.05	4.88	5.64	★★★	8.76	0.23
—	Industrial SPDR	LB	▦	35.05	35.01	−0.02	13.61	11.09	6.43	13.51	11.15	6.43	★★★	9.50	0.82
—	iPath DJ-AIGCom Id TR ETN	SN	—	48.65	48.94	0.31	—	—	—	—	—	—	—	—	—
—	iPath GS CrOil TR Idx ETN	SN	—	38.12	38.06	−0.09	—	—	—	—	—	—	—	—	—
—	iPath GSCI TotRet Idx ETN	SN	—	40.29	40.40	0.25	—	—	—	—	—	—	—	—	—
—	iPath MSCI India Index	PJ	—	52.37	52.45	0.15	—	—	—	—	—	—	—	—	—
—	iShares Australia	PJ	▣	23.63	23.50	0.21	31.42	26.12	24.55	30.84	25.47	24.31	★★★★	13.82	1.53
—	iShares Austria Index	ES	▣	36.50	36.99	0.31	35.83	41.30	39.28	36.76	42.07	40.07	★★★★★	15.21	2.16
—	iShares Belgium Indx	ES	▣	25.60	25.61	0.38	36.35	28.35	22.00	35.62	28.65	22.31	★★★	11.13	2.03
—	iShares Brazil Index	LS	▦	46.87	46.85	0.03	44.27	43.43	32.63	43.30	42.98	32.15	★	29.01	1.29
47	iShares C&S Realty	SR	▦	100.51	100.30	−0.03	39.04	28.98	24.75	38.52	28.81	24.72	★★★★	17.22	1.39
—	iShares Canada Index	FV	▦	25.32	25.32	0.29	17.45	22.50	19.60	16.91	22.33	20.11	★★★	14.44	1.26
48	iShares COMEX Gold Trust	SP	—	63.03	63.25	0.30	22.35	—	—	22.27	—	—	—	—	—
—	iShares DJ BMaterial	LV	▦	59.09	59.08	0.03	16.99	11.09	11.01	17.06	11.02	10.91	★★★	14.71	0.57
—	iShares DJ Cons Services	LG	▦	67.40	67.42	0.00	13.81	7.06	4.26	13.80	7.16	4.22	★★★	10.05	0.41
—	iShares DJ Consumer Goods	LB	▦	59.66	59.68	0.04	14.32	8.91	8.21	14.31	9.13	8.19	★★★	8.42	0.68
51	iShares DJ Fin Sectr	SF	▦	117.80	117.67	0.00	18.79	12.32	10.17	18.74	12.37	9.95	★★★	8.33	1.06
52	iShares DJ Fin Svcs	SF	▦	133.75	133.69	0.06	19.32	11.37	10.15	19.19	11.28	9.97	★★★	8.71	0.92
53	iShares DJ Health	SH	▦	66.42	66.32	0.00	6.46	6.00	2.18	6.16	6.00	2.10	★★★	8.34	0.36
—	iShares DJ Industry	LB	▦	65.22	65.20	−0.03	13.21	11.15	6.41	13.20	11.07	6.28	★★★	9.45	0.83
54	iShares DJ RE Index	SR	▦	83.83	83.35	−0.12	35.24	24.40	21.91	34.91	24.13	21.78	★★	16.36	1.23
49	iShares DJ Sel Dividend	LV	▦	70.76	70.73	0.02	19.41	13.18	—	19.44	13.14	—	★★★★	6.64	1.43
55	iShares DJ Tech	ST	▦	54.43	54.45	0.01	9.56	4.41	0.83	9.68	4.53	0.82	★★★	15.60	0.15
56	iShares DJ Telecom	SC	▦	29.62	29.65	0.08	32.38	15.13	1.28	32.57	15.17	1.18	★★★	8.89	1.28

Performance Summary

Morningstar's ETF Universe

Portfolio				Costs		Trading Information					Contact
Top 3 Sectors	Avg. Mkt. Cap. ($mil)	P/E Ratio	P/B Ratio	Expense Ratio %	Tax-Cost Ratio	52-week High/Low	Avg. Daily Vol.	Exchange	Ticker	Phone	Web Address
[icons]	53864.41	17.47	2.09	0.30	0.46	33.61–26.51	27,068	XNMS	ADRA	888-627-3837	www.bldrsfunds.com
[icons]	77730.13	15.00	2.53	0.30	0.67	29.42–24.42	25,271	XNMS	ADRD	888-627-3837	www.bldrsfunds.com
[icons]	35171.40	15.15	3.05	0.30	0.57	38.95–27.01	175,899	XNMS	ADRE	888-627-3837	www.bldrsfunds.com
[icons]	73436.85	14.53	2.70	0.30	0.74	29.89–24.54	17,061	XNMS	ADRU	888-627-3837	www.bldrsfunds.com
—	—	—	—	—	—	59.67–56.02	39,895	AMEX	DCR	866-889-3828	www.claymore.com
—	—	—	—	—	—	64.20–60.35	76,752	AMEX	UCR	866-889-3828	www.claymore.com
—	—	—	—	—	—	31.82–24.18	131,245	AMEX	EEB	800-345-7999	www.claymore.com
—	—	—	—	—	—	27.69–24.62	13,854	AMEX	NFO	800-345-7999	www.claymore.com
—	—	—	—	—	—	28.20–24.45	16,354	AMEX	STH	800-345-7999	www.claymore.com
—	—	—	—	—	—	28.15–24.71	30,880	AMEX	XRO	800-345-7999	www.claymore.com
—	—	—	—	—	—	26.94–24.75	35,151	AMEX	CVY	800-345-7999	www.claymore.com
[icons]	24363.70	19.30	2.60	0.26	0.29	38.74–31.36	1,322,677	AMEX	XLY	800-843-2639	www.spdrindex.com
[icons]	57699.17	20.13	3.89	0.26	0.65	26.24–23.06	1,668,882	AMEX	XLP	800-843-2639	www.spdrindex.com
—	—	—	—	—	—	79.18–72.92	6,705	NYSE	FXA	800-820-0888	www.currencyshares.com
—	—	—	—	—	—	198.01–181.26	9,737	NYSE	FXB	800-820-0888	www.currencyshares.com
—	—	—	—	—	—	90.57–85.84	8,728	NYSE	FXC	800-820-0888	www.currencyshares.com
—	—	—	—	—	—	133.32–118.75	100,085	NYSE	FXE	800-820-0888	www.rydex.com
—	—	—	—	—	—	93.85–87.48	1,393	NYSE	FXM	800-820-0888	www.currencyshares.com
—	—	—	—	—	—	147.79–134.86	3,700	NYSE	FXS	800-820-0888	www.currencyshares.com
—	—	—	—	—	—	83.81–78.44	14,077	NYSE	FXF	800-820-0888	www.currencyshares.com
[icons]	109033.83	17.33	3.30	0.18	0.85	124.93–106.59	6,567,691	AMEX	DIA	800-843-2639	www.amex.com
[icons]	65263.81	10.43	2.64	0.26	0.48	61.86–50.24	18,952,214	AMEX	XLE	800-843-2639	www.spdrindex.com
[icons]	8875.35	22.23	3.21	0.45	—	97.06–79.34	93,527	XNMS	ONEQ	800-544-6666	www.fidelity.com
[icons]	57375.69	14.16	2.05	0.26	0.81	37.11–31.32	5,646,217	AMEX	XLF	800-843-2639	www.spdrindex.com
[icons]	12133.51	27.72	3.83	—	—	20.68–16.67	23,616	XNMS	QQEW	800-621-1675	www.ftportfolios.com
[icons]	16163.33	30.41	4.15	—	—	21.04–15.69	30,814	XNMS	QTEC	800-621-1675	www.ftportfolios.com
[icons]	5413.74	—	3.20	—	—	24.43–19.49	16,074	AMEX	FBT	800-621-1675	www.ftportfolios.com
[icons]	10959.51	31.82	3.75	—	—	23.75–18.68	12,420	AMEX	FDN	800-621-1675	www.ftportfolios.com
[icons]	535.96	20.37	2.24	0.60	—	24.23–20.17	11,465	AMEX	FDM	800-621-1675	www.ftportfolios.com
[icons]	6966.83	20.01	2.78	—	—	22.31–17.98	26,705	AMEX	FPX	800-621-1675	www.ftportfolios.com
[icons]	68121.16	14.97	2.36	—	—	23.64–20.01	35,917	AMEX	FDL	800-621-1675	www.ftportfolios.com
[icons]	51542.07	20.01	3.74	0.26	0.44	33.91–29.51	1,185,200	AMEX	XLV	800-843-2639	www.spdrindex.com
[icons]	44708.99	18.32	3.13	0.25	0.57	35.73–30.95	1,130,108	AMEX	XLI	800-843-2639	www.spdrindex.com
—	—	—	—	—	—	51.56–45.14	198,211	NYSE	DJP	877-764-7284	www.ishares.com
—	—	—	—	—	—	50.00–36.85	127,605	NYSE	OIL	877-764-7284	www.ishares.com
—	—	—	—	—	—	52.16–40.05	105,562	NYSE	GSP	877-764-7284	www.ishares.com
—	—	—	—	—	—	52.43–50.00	253,371	NYSE	INP	877-764-7284	www.barclays.com
[icons]	16047.85	15.40	3.68	0.54	1.32	24.16–19.13	534,791	NYSE	EWA	800-474-2737	www.ishares.com
[icons]	8455.90	16.39	3.46	0.54	0.40	37.01–27.31	116,591	NYSE	EWO	800-474-2737	www.ishares.com
[icons]	17156.52	12.89	2.14	0.54	0.86	25.93–19.62	87,185	NYSE	EWK	800-474-2737	www.ishares.com
[icons]	16708.91	12.29	2.99	0.70	0.68	47.00–32.07	2,854,782	NYSE	EWZ	800-474-2737	www.ishares.com
[icons]	10079.41	38.77	3.63	0.35	1.42	104.70–77.78	360,588	NYSE	ICF	800-474-2737	www.ishares.com
[icons]	17370.33	18.94	3.88	0.54	0.34	26.11–22.18	303,994	NYSE	EWC	800-474-2737	www.ishares.com
—	—	—	—	0.40	—	71.61–52.43	171,497	AMEX	IAU	800-474-2737	www.ishares.com
[icons]	12566.72	14.50	2.87	0.60	0.63	61.84–50.81	72,460	NYSE	IYM	800-474-2737	www.ishares.com
[icons]	20972.69	20.67	2.83	0.60	0.13	68.33–57.07	55,368	NYSE	IYC	800-474-2737	www.ishares.com
[icons]	34169.90	18.45	3.52	0.60	0.59	60.01–52.03	42,537	NYSE	IYK	800-474-2737	www.ishares.com
[icons]	35994.95	14.85	2.11	0.60	0.69	118.77–100.52	21,151	NYSE	IYF	800-474-2737	www.ishares.com
[icons]	54023.89	14.27	2.18	0.60	0.72	135.21–113.12	101,948	NYSE	IYG	800-474-2737	www.ishares.com
[icons]	37547.19	21.10	3.83	0.60	0.27	67.07–58.86	149,260	NYSE	IYH	800-474-2737	www.ishares.com
[icons]	26467.19	18.44	3.05	0.60	0.37	66.28–57.54	23,817	NYSE	IYJ	800-474-2737	www.ishares.com
[icons]	6885.28	32.18	3.09	0.60	1.50	86.90–66.96	1,972,962	NYSE	IYR	800-474-2737	www.ishares.com
[icons]	14885.62	15.33	2.14	0.40	1.12	71.42–61.47	365,882	NYSE	DVY	800-474-2737	www.ishares.com
[icons]	43006.97	23.93	4.05	0.60	0.20	56.05–43.94	323,237	NYSE	IYW	800-474-2737	www.ishares.com
[icons]	33622.61	19.74	2.09	0.60	0.94	29.62–23.13	379,561	NYSE	IYZ	800-474-2737	www.ishares.com

Performance Summary

Morningstar's ETF Universe

Page	Name	Cat	Style Box	NAV ($)	Market Price ($)	2006 Avg. Prem. Discount%	NAV Return% through 12-29-06			Mkt Price Rtn% through 12-29-06			Risk Statistics		
							1Yr	Annualized 3Yr	5Yr	1Yr	Annualized 3Yr	5Yr	Morningstar Rating	Standard Deviation	Sharpe Ratio
57	iShares DJ Total Mkt	LB		68.72	68.69	−0.02	15.31	11.01	6.79	15.30	11.00	6.71	★★★★	7.48	1.02
50	iShares DJ US Energy	SN		101.85	101.85	0.01	20.47	28.69	18.02	20.14	28.69	17.95	★★★	19.10	1.25
—	iShares DJ US Health Prov	SH		54.28	54.30	0.01	—	—	—	—	—	—	—	—	—
—	iShares DJ US Medical Dev	SH		51.06	51.05	0.01	—	—	—	—	—	—	—	—	—
—	iShares DJ US Oil & Gas	SN		47.77	47.75	0.04	—	—	—	—	—	—	—	—	—
—	iShares DJ US Oil Equip	SN		45.20	45.20	0.00	—	—	—	—	—	—	—	—	—
—	iShares DJ US Pharma	SH		53.11	53.08	0.03	—	—	—	—	—	—	—	—	—
58	iShares DJ Utilities	SU		89.82	89.87	0.02	20.71	19.48	10.66	20.79	19.41	10.53	★★★	8.68	1.73
—	iShares Dow Jones TransAv	MB		81.76	81.78	−0.07	8.92	15.64	—	8.98	15.60	—	★★★★	15.64	0.80
—	iShares Dow Jones US Aero	ST		53.45	53.44	0.01	—	—	—	—	—	—	—	—	—
—	iShares Dow Jones US BrDI	SF		53.77	53.81	−0.05	—	—	—	—	—	—	—	—	—
—	iShares Dow Jones US Home	SR		42.35	42.37	0.07	—	—	—	—	—	—	—	—	—
—	iShares Dow Jones US Insr	SF		54.25	54.24	−0.05	—	—	—	—	—	—	—	—	—
—	iShares Dow Jones US RegB	SF		51.89	51.90	0.03	—	—	—	—	—	—	—	—	—
74	iShares EMU Index	ES		103.05	103.35	0.15	35.84	21.33	14.80	35.50	21.16	14.78	★★	10.92	1.56
—	iShares France Index	ES		34.20	34.23	0.11	34.00	20.24	14.20	33.57	20.38	14.27	★★★	10.44	1.53
59	iShares FTSE/Xinhua China	PJ		111.14	111.45	0.48	83.19	—	—	83.17	—	—	—	—	—
—	iShares Germany Indx	ES		26.92	26.90	0.07	35.66	19.96	13.77	34.96	19.83	13.59	★★	12.77	1.26
60	iShares GS Nat Res	SN		101.35	101.60	0.05	16.30	25.19	17.93	16.41	25.34	17.83	★★★	18.99	1.11
—	iShares GS Network	ST		32.14	32.17	−0.04	3.54	5.26	0.98	3.77	5.23	0.94	★	29.02	0.20
—	iShares GS Software	ST		44.59	44.58	0.00	10.73	5.75	−0.24	10.76	5.90	−0.30	★★★	17.09	0.22
62	iShares GS Tech	ST		51.35	51.42	0.06	8.46	4.03	0.55	8.69	4.22	0.48	★★★	16.12	0.12
—	iShares GSCI Commodity Id	SN	—	39.84	40.07	0.40	—	—	—	—	—	—	—	—	—
—	iShares Hong Kong	PJ		16.06	16.00	−0.15	29.69	20.14	13.96	29.30	19.70	14.11	★★	13.84	1.17
63	iShares iBoxx$ Corp Bd	CL		106.21	106.68	0.12	3.96	3.60	—	4.22	3.68	—	★★	4.86	0.09
—	iShares Italy Index	ES		33.18	33.21	0.22	32.85	21.24	18.21	32.48	21.57	18.41	★★★	11.20	1.50
75	iShares Japan Index	JS		14.12	14.21	−0.13	5.49	14.71	12.87	5.85	14.39	13.36	★★★	14.93	0.78
—	iShares KLD 400 Social	LB	—	50.96	51.15	0.37	—	—	—	—	—	—	—	—	—
64	iShares KLD Sel Soc Idx	LB		59.02	59.05	0.04	12.85	—	—	12.84	—	—	—	—	—
65	iShares Lehman 1-3 T	GS		79.86	79.96	0.01	3.83	2.03	—	3.89	2.02	—	★★★	1.27	−1.0
66	iShares Lehman 20+	GL		88.42	88.43	−0.20	0.83	5.99	—	0.71	5.94	—	★★★★	8.98	0.33
67	iShares Lehman 7-10	GL		82.35	82.44	−0.02	2.65	3.11	—	2.52	3.09	—	★★	5.24	0.00
68	iShares Lehman Aggregate	CI		99.45	99.70	0.23	4.13	3.42	—	3.90	3.31	—	★★★	3.28	0.06
69	iShares Lehman TIPS Bond	IP	—	98.79	98.80	0.04	0.29	3.66	—	0.28	3.63	—	★★★	5.21	0.10
—	iShares Malaysia	PJ		9.17	9.10	−0.05	36.19	16.53	14.78	36.35	15.38	14.56	★	12.85	1.01
—	iShares Mexico Index	LS		51.06	51.25	0.06	44.02	45.96	29.77	44.84	45.85	29.75	★★	18.76	1.97
71	iShares MSCI EAFE	FB		72.95	73.22	0.29	26.00	19.60	14.86	25.81	19.25	14.93	★★★★	9.42	1.63
70	iShares MSCI EAFE Growth	FG		67.94	68.23	0.40	21.88	—	—	21.78	—	—	—	—	—
72	iShares MSCI EAFE Value	FV		71.58	72.20	0.47	29.96	—	—	30.34	—	—	—	—	—
73	iShares MSCI Emerg Mkts	EM		114.09	114.17	0.08	30.71	29.96	—	31.19	29.43	—	★★★	18.22	1.37
76	iShares MSCI ex-Japn	PJ		124.86	125.24	0.08	32.07	24.67	21.63	32.30	24.56	21.85	★★★★	12.30	1.61
—	iShares MSCI South Africa	EM		114.54	115.02	0.50	19.52	29.50	—	19.70	29.34	—	★	25.91	1.01
—	iShares MstarLargeCore	LB		75.54	75.60	0.08	15.28	—	—	15.35	—	—	—	—	—
—	iShares MstarLargeGrowth	LG		64.11	64.10	0.03	5.40	—	—	5.30	—	—	—	—	—
—	iShares MstarLargeValue	LV		83.75	83.77	0.05	25.19	—	—	25.28	—	—	—	—	—
—	iShares MstarMidCore	MB		82.21	82.25	−0.04	14.31	—	—	14.23	—	—	—	—	—
—	iShares MstarMidGrowth	MG		84.14	84.03	−0.03	9.35	—	—	9.17	—	—	—	—	—
—	iShares MstarMidValue	MV		85.89	85.87	−0.01	18.42	—	—	18.39	—	—	—	—	—
—	iShares MstarSmallCore	SB		86.25	86.36	−0.08	20.79	—	—	21.04	—	—	—	—	—
—	iShares MstarSmallGrowth	SG		73.96	73.91	−0.05	9.68	—	—	9.77	—	—	—	—	—
—	iShares MstarSmallValue	SV		82.70	82.62	−0.04	19.60	—	—	19.60	—	—	—	—	—
77	iShares NASD Biotech	SH		77.90	77.76	−0.12	0.57	2.55	−3.05	0.67	2.62	−3.11	★	15.42	0.03
—	iShares Netherlands	ES		26.26	26.31	0.12	32.06	19.12	11.05	31.73	19.32	11.29	★★	11.20	1.35
78	iShares NYSE 100 Index	LV		74.91	74.94	0.09	16.96	—	—	16.85	—	—	—	—	—
—	iShares NYSE Composite	LB		83.66	83.83	0.09	20.17	—	—	20.48	—	—	—	—	—

Performance Summary

Morningstar's ETF Universe

Portfolio				Costs		Trading Information				Contact	
Top 3 Sectors	Avg. Mkt. Cap. ($mil)	P/E Ratio	P/B Ratio	Expense Ratio %	Tax-Cost Ratio	52-week High/Low	Avg. Daily Vol.	Exchange	Ticker	Phone	Web Address
	33361.45	17.08	2.82	0.20	0.56	69.47–59.56	26,117	NYSE	IYY	800-474-2737	www.ishares.com
	67332.14	10.40	2.66	0.60	0.40	107.23–85.41	106,440	NYSE	IYE	800-474-2737	www.ishares.com
	13671.74	19.86	2.88	—	—	55.14–47.95	128,791	NYSE	IHF	800-474-2737	www.ishares.com
	7004.48	28.57	3.61	—	—	51.57–44.54	20,608	NYSE	IHI	800-474-2737	www.ishares.com
	9343.45	8.89	2.11	—	—	51.97–42.04	21,694	NYSE	IEO	800-474-2737	www.ishares.com
	13528.41	15.54	3.56	—	—	53.49–39.32	53,494	NYSE	IEZ	800-474-2737	www.ishares.com
	16643.81	20.90	3.70	—	—	54.26–46.96	14,437	NYSE	IHE	800-474-2737	www.ishares.com
	12542.80	16.86	2.19	0.60	1.01	91.34–74.19	28,051	NYSE	IDU	800-474-2737	www.ishares.com
	8792.54	14.14	2.27	0.60	0.19	89.77–73.21	507,791	NYSE	IYT	800-474-2737	www.ishares.com
	9205.92	19.47	2.89	—	—	53.86–45.09	17,960	NYSE	ITA	800-474-2737	www.ishares.com
	14417.52	15.46	2.77	—	—	55.77–41.07	61,665	NYSE	IAI	800-474-2737	www.ishares.com
	2041.79	6.13	1.25	—	—	49.80–33.04	210,194	NYSE	ITB	800-474-2737	www.ishares.com
	27769.10	13.24	1.67	—	—	54.68–46.73	4,074	NYSE	IAK	800-474-2737	www.ishares.com
	14014.65	14.65	2.06	—	—	52.54–47.60	4,185	NYSE	IAT	800-474-2737	www.ishares.com
	35945.84	14.98	3.10	0.54	0.61	104.20–79.45	112,271	NYSE	EZU	800-474-2737	www.ishares.com
	44636.91	14.79	3.57	0.54	0.44	34.39–26.88	80,994	NYSE	EWQ	800-474-2737	www.ishares.com
	45989.56	20.50	3.46	0.74	—	111.81–65.75	1,246,700	NYSE	FXI	800-474-2737	www.ishares.com
	40456.58	15.75	2.74	0.54	0.41	27.19–20.61	536,894	NYSE	EWG	800-474-2737	www.ishares.com
	36376.20	11.72	2.75	0.50	0.40	106.98–88.19	74,828	AMEX	IGE	800-474-2737	www.ishares.com
	13096.02	26.86	3.36	0.50	0.00	37.22–25.56	136,077	AMEX	IGN	800-474-2737	www.ishares.com
	11895.76	34.21	3.76	0.50	0.07	46.19–35.60	184,620	AMEX	IGV	800-474-2737	www.ishares.com
	34734.01	24.40	3.91	0.50	0.11	52.62–41.32	64,028	AMEX	IGM	800-474-2737	www.ishares.com
—	—	—	—	—	—	51.43–39.76	176,408	NYSE	GSG	800-474-2737	www.ishares.com
	13944.71	16.07	2.28	0.54	0.80	16.06–12.69	2,440,811	NYSE	EWH	800-474-2737	www.ishares.com
—	—	—	—	0.15	1.67	108.13–102.33	104,911	AMEX	LQD	800-474-2737	www.ishares.com
	38047.86	15.51	2.72	0.54	0.74	33.66–26.20	65,300	NYSE	EWI	800-474-2737	www.ishares.com
	19641.60	18.51	2.03	0.54	0.18	15.49–12.41	16,005,508	NYSE	EWJ	800-474-2737	www.ishares.com
—	—	—	—	—	—	51.47–49.86	1,673	AMEX	DSI	800-474-2737	www.ishares.com
	37480.87	17.57	3.01	0.50	—	59.76–51.85	5,441	AMEX	KLD	800-474-2737	www.ishares.com
—	—	—	—	0.15	1.06	80.44–79.26	814,414	AMEX	SHY	800-474-2737	www.ishares.com
—	—	—	—	0.15	1.61	92.45–82.60	987,217	AMEX	TLT	800-474-2737	www.ishares.com
—	—	—	—	0.15	1.37	84.20–79.61	289,551	AMEX	IEF	800-474-2737	www.ishares.com
—	—	—	—	0.20	1.41	100.78–96.66	316,422	AMEX	AGG	800-474-2737	www.ishares.com
—	—	—	—	0.20	1.57	103.41–98.19	228,905	NYSE	TIP	800-474-2737	www.ishares.com
	3526.25	17.23	2.28	0.54	0.98	9.34–6.95	1,213,865	NYSE	EWM	800-474-2737	www.ishares.com
	21294.57	17.75	4.27	0.54	0.39	51.06–31.84	1,722,948	NYSE	EWW	800-474-2737	www.ishares.com
	32619.35	16.35	3.07	0.35	0.63	74.19–60.01	4,850,645	AMEX	EFA	800-474-2737	www.ishares.com
	25727.28	20.20	3.99	0.40	—	68.39–56.31	73,605	NYSE	EFG	800-474-2737	www.ishares.com
	41245.17	13.79	2.56	0.40	—	72.42–57.01	131,257	NYSE	EFV	800-474-2737	www.ishares.com
	15829.62	16.08	2.68	0.77	0.43	114.09–82.61	5,053,537	AMEX	EEM	800-474-2737	www.ishares.com
	14696.11	16.54	3.26	0.50	1.28	126.86–100.74	147,320	AMEX	EPP	800-474-2737	www.ishares.com
	8232.54	13.95	3.97	0.70	0.66	124.31–88.54	75,008	AMEX	EZA	800-474-2737	www.ishares.com
	80061.60	17.61	3.14	0.20	—	76.14–65.16	9,960	NYSE	JKD	800-474-2737	www.ishares.com
	38962.34	23.64	4.16	0.25	—	65.24–55.78	16,271	NYSE	JKE	800-474-2737	www.ishares.com
	89365.05	13.01	2.22	0.25	—	84.32–69.83	44,874	NYSE	JKF	800-474-2737	www.ishares.com
	5240.46	19.79	2.76	0.25	—	83.63–70.53	16,940	NYSE	JKG	800-474-2737	www.ishares.com
	5552.57	24.63	4.00	0.30	—	87.44–73.01	9,737	NYSE	JKH	800-474-2737	www.ishares.com
	5160.08	13.73	1.90	0.30	—	87.01–74.92	4,880	NYSE	JKI	800-474-2737	www.ishares.com
	1307.12	19.41	2.37	0.25	—	87.65–73.45	11,771	NYSE	JKJ	800-474-2737	www.ishares.com
	1243.61	27.49	3.48	0.30	—	78.12–63.56	8,122	NYSE	JKK	800-474-2737	www.ishares.com
	1238.67	13.41	1.73	0.30	—	83.78–71.37	10,925	NYSE	JKL	800-474-2737	www.ishares.com
	4050.07	30.71	4.60	0.50	0.00	85.52–68.10	960,994	AMEX	IBB	800-474-2737	www.ishares.com
	27431.77	13.00	2.61	0.54	0.63	26.52–20.41	58,971	NYSE	EWN	800-474-2737	www.ishares.com
	105476.08	15.39	2.80	0.20	—	75.53–64.79	19,674	NYSE	NY	800-474-2737	www.ishares.com
	41613.56	15.90	2.66	0.25	—	84.06–71.06	5,465	NYSE	NYC	800-474-2737	www.ishares.com

Disclosure: Morningstar licenses its indexes to certain ETF providers, including Barclays Global Investors (BGI) and First Trust, for use in exchange-traded funds. These ETFs are not sponsored, issued, or sold by Morningstar. Morningstar does not make any representation regarding the advisability of investing in ETFs that are based on Morningstar indexes.

Performance Summary

Morningstar's ETF Universe

Page	Name	Cat	Style Box	NAV ($)	Market Price ($)	2006 Avg. Prem. Discount%	NAV Return% through 12-29-06 1Yr	Annualized 3Yr	5Yr	Mkt Price Rtn% through 12-29-06 1Yr	Annualized 3Yr	5Yr	Morningstar Rating	Standard Deviation	Sharpe Ratio
90	iShares R. Midcap	MB		99.93	99.84	−0.04	15.04	15.82	12.72	15.13	15.71	12.54	★★★★	9.74	1.23
89	iShares R. Midcap Gr	MG		103.12	103.07	−0.01	10.44	12.46	7.97	10.51	12.40	7.88	★★★	11.35	0.81
91	iShares R. Midcap Vl	MV		146.56	146.43	−0.02	19.95	18.54	15.68	20.00	18.43	15.57	★★★★★	8.74	1.63
79	iShares R1000 Growth	LG		55.10	55.03	0.01	8.86	6.67	2.50	8.94	6.60	2.49	★★★	8.42	0.43
80	iShares R1000 Index	LB		76.85	76.84	−0.03	15.29	10.84	6.68	15.41	10.85	6.52	★★★★	7.13	1.04
81	iShares R1000 Value	LV		82.60	82.70	0.03	22.00	14.90	10.65	22.48	14.89	10.74	★★★★	6.76	1.64
82	iShares R2000 Growth	SG		78.77	78.58	−0.19	13.13	10.34	6.77	13.18	10.26	6.81	★★★	15.78	0.50
83	iShares R2000 Index	SB		78.13	78.03	−0.08	18.17	13.41	11.24	18.27	13.40	11.38	★★★	13.93	0.74
84	iShares R2000 Value	SV		80.05	80.04	−0.07	23.18	16.24	15.14	23.48	16.31	15.13	★★★	12.49	1.02
85	iShares R3000 Growth	LG		44.90	44.93	−0.01	9.19	6.91	2.78	9.34	6.92	2.78	★★★	8.90	0.44
86	iShares R3000 Index	LB		81.93	82.04	0.04	15.52	11.01	6.99	15.66	11.07	7.01	★★★★	7.59	1.00
87	iShares R3000 Value	LV		107.81	107.79	−0.02	22.01	14.92	10.93	21.90	14.89	10.78	★★★★	7.09	1.56
88	iShares Russell Microcap	SB		58.56	58.45	−0.14	14.75	—	—	14.89	—	—	—	—	—
92	iShares S&P 100 Ind.	LB		66.08	66.08	0.09	18.22	8.25	4.31	18.13	8.30	4.20	★★	6.54	0.77
93	iShares S&P 1500 Index	LB		125.84	125.78	0.02	15.13	—	—	15.12	—	—	—	—	—
95	iShares S&P 500	LB		141.92	142.00	0.06	15.69	10.34	6.09	15.94	10.44	6.23	★★★	6.91	1.01
97	iShares S&P Euro-350	ES		104.32	104.97	0.46	32.77	20.07	14.31	32.56	20.22	14.44	★★★	9.46	1.67
98	iShares S&P Glb 100	WS		74.04	74.12	0.22	19.84	11.17	6.40	19.91	10.84	6.29	★★	7.57	1.03
—	iShares S.Korea Indx	PJ		49.30	49.40	−0.33	11.10	26.74	23.62	11.13	26.09	23.40	★★★	21.19	1.08
61	iShares Semiconductor	ST		61.03	61.01	0.00	0.20	−0.95	−1.67	0.23	−0.86	−1.67	★★	23.00	−0.1
110	iShares Silver Trust	SP	—	128.57	128.64	1.84	—	—	—	—	—	—	—	—	—
—	iShares Singapore	PJ		11.22	11.20	0.07	46.06	27.44	20.53	45.79	27.40	20.51	★★	11.86	1.86
104	iShares SP 400 Growth	MG		79.77	79.71	−0.08	5.75	10.86	7.49	5.82	10.88	7.40	★★★★	10.44	0.73
106	iShares SP 400 Value	MV		79.22	79.24	−0.01	14.33	14.78	13.64	14.54	14.66	13.58	★★★★	10.54	1.06
94	iShares SP 500 Growth	LG		64.93	64.92	0.06	10.81	6.80	3.11	10.89	6.81	3.14	★★★	7.54	0.49
96	iShares SP 500 Value	LV		76.92	76.89	0.02	20.59	13.75	8.87	20.65	13.80	8.86	★★★	6.82	1.47
107	iShares SP 600 Growth	SG		128.05	127.96	−0.13	10.30	13.50	11.09	10.55	13.45	11.12	★★★★★	13.04	0.79
109	iShares SP 600 Value	SV		75.42	75.34	−0.14	19.29	15.82	13.13	19.37	15.76	13.22	★★★	12.93	0.96
—	iShares SP Glb Cons Discr	WS		57.73	57.83	0.28	—	—	—	—	—	—	—	—	—
—	iShares SP Glb Cons Stpls	WS		53.10	53.26	0.26	—	—	—	—	—	—	—	—	—
99	iShares SP Glb Enrgy	SN		110.90	111.47	0.24	20.89	25.80	19.27	20.99	25.60	19.42	★★★	17.80	1.20
100	iShares SP Glb Fincl	SF		89.32	90.55	0.44	23.80	17.18	13.05	24.83	17.45	13.37	★★★★	8.36	1.58
101	iShares SP Glb Hlth	SH		57.11	57.18	0.26	10.34	7.45	3.70	10.47	7.05	3.66	★★★	7.40	0.58
—	iShares SP Glb Industrial	WS		55.68	55.84	0.38	—	—	—	—	—	—	—	—	—
—	iShares SP Glb Materials	WS		56.70	56.69	0.15	—	—	—	—	—	—	—	—	—
102	iShares SP Glb Tech	ST		57.97	58.32	0.33	9.43	5.34	1.30	9.81	5.30	1.19	★★★	14.35	0.21
103	iShares SP Glb Tele	SC		62.87	63.31	0.55	33.26	14.02	5.96	33.25	13.92	6.10	★★★	9.31	1.13
—	iShares SP Glb Utilities	SU		56.97	57.10	0.24	—	—	—	—	—	—	—	—	—
—	iShares SP Latin 40	LS		169.89	169.93	0.06	40.85	45.10	31.05	41.06	44.56	31.06	★★	21.68	1.70
105	iShares SP MidCap400	MB		80.25	80.17	0.00	10.13	12.94	10.71	9.96	12.95	10.78	★★★	10.34	0.92
108	iShares SP Small 600	SB		66.01	65.99	−0.02	14.94	14.80	12.33	15.09	14.85	12.45	★★★	12.86	0.89
—	iShares SP TOPIX 150	JS		124.54	125.08	0.03	8.22	15.14	12.70	8.49	14.86	13.02	★★★	14.85	0.81
—	iShares Spain Index	ES		53.48	53.60	0.17	49.53	26.45	22.30	49.25	26.63	22.55	★★★	11.91	1.79
—	iShares Sweden Index	ES		32.06	32.28	0.27	43.32	28.93	19.85	43.73	28.97	20.23	★★★	15.20	1.56
—	iShares Switzerland	ES		24.73	24.90	0.34	29.41	19.61	15.08	29.96	19.86	15.29	★★★	9.32	1.65
—	iShares Taiwan Index	PJ		14.50	14.51	0.05	18.94	10.64	7.10	18.73	10.30	6.99	★	18.18	0.47
—	iShares U.K. Index	ES		23.19	23.41	0.70	29.82	17.96	12.71	30.40	17.78	12.84	★★	8.73	1.59
—	Market Vectors Gld Miners	SP		40.57	39.91	1.44	—	—	—	—	—	—	—	—	—
—	Materials Sel SPDR	LV		34.84	34.81	−0.05	18.34	11.73	12.56	18.26	11.78	12.68	★★★	13.75	0.64
111	MidCap SPDR Trust	MB		146.46	146.35	−0.04	10.05	12.66	10.24	9.99	12.67	10.59	★★★★	10.30	0.90
112	Nasdaq 100 Trust	LG		43.17	43.16	0.01	6.82	6.26	1.65	6.93	6.28	2.39	★	14.35	0.27
—	PowerShares Aero&Defense	LG		18.55	18.57	−0.01	19.75	—	—	20.01	—	—	—	—	—
41	PowerShares DB Com Idx Fd	SN		24.55	24.58	0.24	—	—	—	—	—	—	—	—	—
113	PowerShares Div Achievers	LV		16.81	17.13	0.33	14.27	—	—	16.48	—	—	—	—	—
—	PowerShares Dyn Bio&Genom	SH		17.69	17.70	−0.01	2.06	—	—	2.31	—	—	—	—	—

Performance Summary

Morningstar's ETF Universe

Top 3 Sectors	Avg. Mkt. Cap. ($mil)	P/E Ratio	P/B Ratio	Expense Ratio %	Tax-Cost Ratio	52-week High/Low	Avg. Daily Vol.	Exchange	Ticker	Phone	Web Address
	7009.44	18.48	2.73	0.20	0.47	101.59–86.93	166,454	NYSE	IWR	800-474-2737	www.ishares.com
	7013.47	21.47	3.93	0.25	0.19	105.47–89.04	101,505	AMEX	IWP	800-474-2737	www.ishares.com
	6996.08	15.92	2.03	0.25	0.66	148.40–126.61	151,505	NYSE	IWS	800-474-2737	www.ishares.com
	34261.32	20.81	4.04	0.20	0.35	55.81–48.05	1,345,822	NYSE	IWF	800-474-2737	www.ishares.com
	39952.77	16.97	2.86	0.15	0.63	77.64–66.71	265,997	NYSE	IWB	800-474-2737	www.ishares.com
	46597.21	14.28	2.20	0.20	0.79	83.22–70.21	1,007,517	NYSE	IWD	800-474-2737	www.ishares.com
	1027.12	23.05	3.49	0.25	0.13	81.32–67.09	1,616,971	NYSE	IWO	800-474-2737	www.ishares.com
	1027.05	19.23	2.36	0.20	0.41	79.34–66.80	44,709,402	NYSE	IWM	800-474-2737	www.ishares.com
	1027.55	16.82	1.82	0.25	0.58	81.09–67.78	1,492,934	NYSE	IWN	800-474-2737	www.ishares.com
	25549.27	20.95	3.99	0.25	0.33	45.46–39.08	57,579	NYSE	IWZ	800-474-2737	www.ishares.com
	29002.03	17.12	2.81	0.20	0.59	82.73–71.00	398,782	NYSE	IWV	800-474-2737	www.ishares.com
	32934.62	14.45	2.16	0.25	0.74	108.58–91.58	36,757	NYSE	IWW	800-474-2737	www.ishares.com
	356.80	20.96	2.18	0.60	—	59.15–50.08	79,677	NYSE	IWC	800-474-2737	www.ishares.com
	114320.43	16.36	2.95	0.20	0.67	66.71–56.25	701,208	CBOE	OEF	800-474-2737	www.ishares.com
	36754.50	16.98	2.81	0.20	—	127.18–109.32	21,428	NYSE	ISI	800-474-2737	www.ishares.com
	53061.98	16.82	2.87	0.10	0.63	143.40–122.97	980,248	NYSE	IVV	800-474-2737	www.ishares.com
	49533.23	15.50	3.67	0.60	0.70	106.27–82.62	146,457	NYSE	IEV	800-474-2737	www.ishares.com
	125226.00	15.39	3.26	0.40	0.62	75.41–62.46	33,448	NYSE	IOO	800-474-2737	www.ishares.com
	13088.11	11.15	1.76	0.70	0.19	51.90–41.12	732,200	NYSE	EWY	800-474-2737	www.ishares.com
	13414.24	22.37	3.04	0.50	0.03	68.53–50.93	291,342	AMEX	IGW	800-474-2737	www.ishares.com
	—	—	—	—	—	149.37–97.13	493,351	AMEX	SLV	800-474-2737	www.ishares.com
	9013.46	18.03	2.67	0.54	1.18	11.34–8.12	2,187,188	NYSE	EWS	800-474-2737	www.ishares.com
	3768.23	19.53	3.14	0.25	0.17	82.39–70.85	68,165	NYSE	IJK	800-474-2737	www.ishares.com
	3084.14	17.01	2.04	0.25	0.57	80.72–70.30	88,397	NYSE	IJJ	800-474-2737	www.ishares.com
	59192.12	18.28	3.70	0.18	0.50	65.83–56.70	327,444	NYSE	IVW	800-474-2737	www.ishares.com
	47789.84	15.58	2.35	0.18	0.68	77.45–65.74	320,677	NYSE	IVE	800-474-2737	www.ishares.com
	1473.94	19.74	2.99	0.25	0.15	132.06–113.61	50,374	NYSE	IJT	800-474-2737	www.ishares.com
	1106.85	17.58	1.95	0.25	0.40	76.55–64.76	130,174	NYSE	IJS	800-474-2737	www.ishares.com
	27181.62	18.78	2.66	—	—	57.84–51.03	2,486	NYSE	RXI	800-474-2737	www.ishares.com
	50690.24	20.40	4.38	—	—	53.32–50.27	2,908	NYSE	KXI	800-474-2737	www.ishares.com
	97648.98	11.08	2.96	0.65	0.52	115.92–94.98	31,385	AMEX	IXC	800-474-2737	www.ishares.com
	51895.29	14.39	2.43	0.65	0.50	90.33–73.46	24,271	AMEX	IXG	800-474-2737	www.ishares.com
	60240.69	21.18	4.39	0.65	0.26	58.27–51.31	72,482	AMEX	IXJ	800-474-2737	www.ishares.com
	33406.26	18.49	3.17	—	—	56.07–50.25	1,787	NYSE	EXI	800-474-2737	www.ishares.com
	21841.57	15.01	3.34	—	—	56.81–48.42	22,488	NYSE	MXI	800-474-2737	www.ishares.com
	48647.29	24.11	3.97	0.66	0.17	58.98–47.38	22,560	AMEX	IXN	800-474-2737	www.ishares.com
	62979.72	16.15	2.82	0.65	0.71	64.35–48.17	28,671	AMEX	IXP	800-474-2737	www.ishares.com
	28077.55	18.75	2.86	—	—	57.30–49.99	7,135	NYSE	IXI	800-474-2737	www.ishares.com
	31771.98	17.28	4.36	0.50	0.52	170.47–113.94	164,020	AMEX	ILF	800-474-2737	www.ishares.com
	3405.24	18.21	2.46	0.20	0.39	82.08–71.27	248,780	NYSE	IJH	800-474-2737	www.ishares.com
	1272.33	18.59	2.35	0.20	0.29	67.18–57.58	844,582	NYSE	IJR	800-474-2737	www.ishares.com
	30194.07	19.39	2.14	0.50	0.15	134.95–108.35	17,228	AMEX	ITF	800-474-2737	www.ishares.com
	32918.23	18.65	4.62	0.54	0.51	54.62–36.98	219,671	NYSE	EWP	800-474-2737	www.ishares.com
	17490.86	16.69	3.87	0.54	0.42	32.06–22.53	202,532	NYSE	EWD	800-474-2737	www.ishares.com
	46460.10	20.16	4.82	0.54	0.22	24.96–19.78	94,960	NYSE	EWL	800-474-2737	www.ishares.com
	8790.35	16.24	2.25	0.85	0.45	14.86–11.70	2,972,054	NYSE	EWT	800-474-2737	www.ishares.com
	50882.80	14.01	3.88	0.54	0.97	24.07–19.10	293,725	NYSE	EWU	800-474-2737	www.ishares.com
	6529.54	26.51	4.45	—	—	42.06–32.21	746,788	AMEX	GDX	888-658-8287	www.vaneck.com
	17419.68	14.51	2.93	0.26	0.79	35.54–29.55	2,675,757	AMEX	XLB	800-843-2639	www.spdrindex.com
	3441.10	18.48	2.44	0.25	0.35	149.89–130.07	2,672,877	AMEX	MDY	800-843-2639	www.amex.com/mdy/index.ht
	30779.97	29.80	4.51	0.20	0.17	44.74–35.68	98,950,595	XNMS	QQQQ	800-843-2639	www.nasdaq.com/QQQQ
	12611.48	21.46	3.09	0.68	—	18.68–15.44	55,025	AMEX	PPA	800-843-2639	www.powershares.com
	—	—	—	—	—	27.03–22.25	239,037	AMEX	DBC	877-369-4617	www.dbfunds.db.com
	69979.63	16.26	2.98	0.67	—	16.84–14.97	23,522	AMEX	PFM	800-843-2639	www.powershares.com
	3931.75	25.46	3.76	0.64	—	19.30–15.29	137,648	AMEX	PBE	800-843-2639	www.powershares.com

Page	Name	Cat	Style Box	NAV ($)	Market Price ($)	2006 Avg. Prem. Discount%	NAV Return% through 12-29-06			Mkt Price Rtn% through 12-29-06			Morningstar Rating	Standard Deviation	Sharpe Ratio
							1Yr	Annualized 3Yr	5Yr	1Yr	Annualized 3Yr	5Yr			
—	PowerShares Dyn Building	LB		16.50	16.49	−0.11	1.75	—	—	1.63	—	—	—	—	—
—	PowerShares Dyn Cons Disc	MB		25.95	26.75	1.80	—	—	—	—	—	—	—	—	—
—	PowerShares Dyn Cons Stpl	LB		25.44	26.31	1.58	—	—	—	—	—	—	—	—	—
—	PowerShares Dyn Energy	SN		18.82	18.85	0.12	12.67	—	—	12.85	—	—	—	—	—
—	PowerShares Dyn Food&Bev	LB		16.46	16.42	−0.01	15.57	—	—	15.38	—	—	—	—	—
—	PowerShares Dyn Health	SH		25.04	25.92	1.29	—	—	—	—	—	—	—	—	—
—	PowerShares Dyn Hlth Svcs	SH		24.44	25.47	1.98	—	—	—	—	—	—	—	—	—
—	PowerShares Dyn Indust	MB		25.61	26.82	2.95	—	—	—	—	—	—	—	—	—
—	PowerShares Dyn Insurance	SF		18.40	18.43	0.08	13.37	—	—	13.54	—	—	—	—	—
—	PowerShares Dyn Leisr&Ent	LB		17.94	17.97	0.08	18.37	—	—	18.56	—	—	—	—	—
—	PowerShares Dyn Lg Cp	LB		25.61	25.71	0.28	—	—	—	—	—	—	—	—	—
114	PowerShares Dyn Lg Growth	LG		16.71	16.72	0.05	5.47	—	—	5.56	—	—	—	—	—
115	PowerShares Dyn Lg Value	LV		19.75	19.77	0.17	24.42	—	—	24.44	—	—	—	—	—
116	PowerShares Dyn Market	LB		50.31	50.37	0.03	11.73	14.60	—	11.84	14.73	—	★★★★★	9.51	1.14
—	PowerShares Dyn Media	SC		16.15	16.17	−0.06	12.97	—	—	13.13	—	—	—	—	—
—	PowerShares Dyn Mid Cap	MB		25.58	25.71	0.01	—	—	—	—	—	—	—	—	—
118	PowerShares Dyn Mid Value	MV		18.57	18.56	0.05	14.33	—	—	14.33	—	—	—	—	—
117	PowerShares Dyn MidGrowth	MG		19.03	19.02	0.01	9.44	—	—	9.34	—	—	—	—	—
—	PowerShares Dyn Network	ST		17.51	17.53	−0.02	12.25	—	—	12.16	—	—	—	—	—
—	PowerShares Dyn Oil & Gas	SN		19.87	19.88	0.23	10.01	—	—	9.83	—	—	—	—	—
119	PowerShares Dyn OTC	MG		52.21	52.17	−0.08	6.12	9.55	—	6.04	9.53	—	★★	15.00	0.47
—	PowerShares Dyn Pharma	SH		18.18	18.18	0.13	10.83	—	—	10.82	—	—	—	—	—
—	PowerShares Dyn Retail	LB		19.57	19.58	−0.03	21.43	—	—	21.52	—	—	—	—	—
—	PowerShares Dyn Semicond	ST		17.20	17.19	0.02	4.69	—	—	4.63	—	—	—	—	—
120	PowerShares Dyn Sm Growth	SG		17.68	17.64	−0.05	5.54	—	—	5.19	—	—	—	—	—
121	PowerShares Dyn Sm Value	SV		18.08	18.11	0.02	17.44	—	—	17.55	—	—	—	—	—
—	PowerShares Dyn Small Cap	SB		25.47	25.71	0.53	—	—	—	—	—	—	—	—	—
—	PowerShares Dyn Software	ST		19.24	19.22	0.03	10.81	—	—	10.40	—	—	—	—	—
—	PowerShares Dyn Tech	ST		25.51	25.87	1.13	—	—	—	—	—	—	—	—	—
—	PowerShares Dyn Utilities	SU		18.90	18.92	−0.06	23.56	—	—	23.80	—	—	—	—	—
—	PowerShares Finc Prefer	SF	—	24.94	25.00	0.15	—	—	—	—	—	—	—	—	—
123	PowerShares Halter USX	PJ	—	20.92	20.98	0.20	53.10	—	—	53.32	—	—	—	—	—
124	PowerShares High Gr Div	LB		16.73	16.85	0.09	11.67	—	—	12.44	—	—	—	—	—
125	PowerShares HY Div Achiev	MV		16.16	16.42	0.08	10.97	—	—	12.90	—	—	—	—	—
126	PowerShares Intl Div Ach	FV		18.25	18.96	0.62	22.15	—	—	26.88	—	—	—	—	—
—	PowerShares Lux Nanotech	ST		17.55	17.23	−0.16	7.53	—	—	5.06	—	—	—	—	—
—	PowerShares Val Line Indu	LB	—	25.91	25.96	0.15	—	—	—	—	—	—	—	—	—
—	PowerShares WilderHill	SN		17.34	17.32	0.02	7.54	—	—	7.26	—	—	—	—	—
128	PowerShares Zacks MicroCp	SB		17.73	17.86	−0.06	17.11	—	—	18.03	—	—	—	—	—
129	PowerShares Zacks Sm Cap	SB		26.88	26.89	−0.15	—	—	—	—	—	—	—	—	—
130	Rydex Russell Top 50	LB		107.82	107.90	0.08	17.90	—	—	18.06	—	—	—	—	—
131	Rydex S&P 500 Pure Growth	LG		35.86	35.87	−0.01	—	—	—	—	—	—	—	—	—
132	Rydex S&P 500 Pure Value	LV		33.81	33.81	−0.10	—	—	—	—	—	—	—	—	—
133	Rydex S&P Equal Weight	LB		47.37	47.34	0.02	15.33	13.09	—	15.46	13.04	—	★★★★★	8.93	1.07
—	Rydex S&P EqWght Cons Dis	LB		46.83	46.94	−0.18	—	—	—	—	—	—	—	—	—
—	Rydex S&P EqWght Cons Stp	LB		49.12	49.40	0.24	—	—	—	—	—	—	—	—	—
—	Rydex S&P EqWght Energy	SN		50.05	50.31	0.54	—	—	—	—	—	—	—	—	—
—	Rydex S&P EqWght Financls	SF		50.78	50.77	−0.06	—	—	—	—	—	—	—	—	—
—	Rydex S&P EqWght HlthCare	SH		50.96	51.10	−0.12	—	—	—	—	—	—	—	—	—
—	Rydex S&P EqWght Industr	LB		50.64	50.63	−0.76	—	—	—	—	—	—	—	—	—
—	Rydex S&P EqWght Material	LB		51.62	51.67	0.09	—	—	—	—	—	—	—	—	—
—	Rydex S&P EqWght Tech	ST		49.31	49.67	0.22	—	—	—	—	—	—	—	—	—
—	Rydex S&P EqWght Util	SU		57.03	57.13	−0.78	—	—	—	—	—	—	—	—	—
134	Rydex S&P Midcap 400 Gr	MG		51.73	51.76	−0.12	—	—	—	—	—	—	—	—	—
135	Rydex S&P Midcap 400 Val	MV		34.61	34.69	−0.04	—	—	—	—	—	—	—	—	—

Performance Summary

Morningstar's ETF Universe

Top 3 Sectors	Avg. Mkt. Cap. ($mil)	P/E Ratio	P/B Ratio	Expense Ratio %	Tax-Cost Ratio	52-week High/Low	Avg. Daily Vol.	Exchange	Ticker	Phone	Web Address
	3985.06	14.70	2.68	0.67	—	18.81–13.72	15,491	AMEX	PKB	800-843-2639	www.powershares.com
	4061.24	20.10	3.49	—	—	26.17–25.43	8,268	AMEX	PEZ	800-843-2639	www.powershares.com
	8562.23	20.42	3.21	—	—	25.64–25.19	3,103	AMEX	PSL	800-843-2639	www.powershares.com
	11063.59	9.55	2.35	0.66	—	20.04–15.80	62,797	AMEX	PXE	800-843-2639	www.powershares.com
	9007.41	20.23	3.32	0.69	—	16.58–14.48	9,705	AMEX	PBJ	800-843-2639	www.powershares.com
	6013.21	20.39	3.32	—	—	25.28–24.94	6,561	AMEX	PTH	800-843-2639	www.powershares.com
	5839.93	19.31	3.02	—	—	25.06–24.44	15,648	AMEX	PTJ	800-843-2639	www.powershares.com
	4273.38	18.21	3.09	—	—	26.36–25.61	3,622	AMEX	PRN	800-843-2639	www.powershares.com
	5807.28	11.83	1.63	0.68	—	18.56–15.75	25,214	AMEX	PIC	800-843-2639	www.powershares.com
	6586.30	22.16	2.54	0.68	—	18.10–14.44	31,477	AMEX	PEJ	800-843-2639	www.powershares.com
	50139.96	16.05	2.93	—	—	25.79–25.18	2,225	AMEX	PJF	800-983-0903	www.powershares.com
	46238.29	22.94	3.87	0.64	—	16.90–14.71	72,880	AMEX	PWB	800-983-0903	www.powershares.com
	60836.36	13.84	2.34	0.65	—	19.88–16.33	163,888	AMEX	PWV	800-983-0903	www.powershares.com
	14634.82	15.06	2.96	0.60	0.24	50.67–43.97	59,511	AMEX	PWC	800-983-0903	www.powershares.com
	6539.01	23.71	2.68	0.68	—	16.28–13.23	25,765	AMEX	PBS	800-843-2639	www.powershares.com
	7234.32	17.68	3.17	—	—	25.79–25.26	1,488	AMEX	PJG	800-983-0903	www.powershares.com
	7103.19	13.73	2.55	0.67	—	18.79–16.23	20,770	AMEX	PWP	800-983-0903	www.powershares.com
	7321.33	24.74	4.91	0.65	—	19.51–16.35	31,531	AMEX	PWJ	800-983-0903	www.powershares.com
	2627.03	27.90	3.17	0.68	—	18.12–13.42	26,674	AMEX	PXQ	800-843-2639	www.powershares.com
	4624.78	14.85	3.11	0.64	—	23.09–17.23	114,328	AMEX	PXJ	800-843-2639	www.powershares.com
	4262.60	22.54	3.32	0.60	0.02	54.19–45.40	14,705	AMEX	PWO	800-983-0903	www.powershares.com
	12020.25	21.65	3.41	0.66	—	18.39–15.47	31,917	AMEX	PJP	800-843-2639	www.powershares.com
	5041.11	19.50	3.10	0.70	—	19.91–16.18	37,682	AMEX	PMR	800-843-2639	www.powershares.com
	4843.47	22.63	2.96	0.65	—	20.91–14.76	121,277	AMEX	PSI	800-843-2639	www.powershares.com
	1444.80	25.10	3.90	0.65	—	19.10–15.21	29,451	AMEX	PWT	800-983-0903	www.powershares.com
	1501.07	14.28	1.94	0.66	—	18.36–15.45	38,788	AMEX	PWY	800-983-0903	www.powershares.com
	1516.89	15.96	2.37	—	—	25.85–25.17	1,129	AMEX	PJM	800-983-0903	www.powershares.com
	4299.57	26.05	4.20	0.67	—	20.06–16.04	98,657	AMEX	PSJ	800-843-2639	www.powershares.com
	4373.09	21.02	3.50	—	—	25.89–25.43	11,242	AMEX	PTF	800-843-2639	www.powershares.com
	5541.67	16.86	2.27	0.69	—	19.33–15.86	29,962	AMEX	PUI	800-843-2639	www.powershares.com
	—	—	—	—	—	25.12–24.86	56,042	AMEX	PGF	800-983-0903	www.powershares.com
	8652.65	16.11	2.44	0.71	—	21.10–14.25	216,537	AMEX	PGJ	800-983-0903	www.powershares.com
	36368.88	17.01	2.92	0.66	—	16.77–15.03	11,962	AMEX	PHJ	800-843-2639	www.powershares.com
	4024.06	16.74	2.00	0.61	—	16.16–14.38	96,925	AMEX	PEY	800-983-0903	www.powershares.com
	20333.66	14.07	2.76	0.62	—	18.27–15.59	203,382	AMEX	PID	800-843-2639	www.powershares.com
	1536.62	23.54	2.93	0.73	—	19.81–15.95	64,008	AMEX	PXN	800-843-2639	www.powershares.com
	—	—	—	—	—	26.18–25.19	14,155	AMEX	PYH	800-983-0903	www.powershares.com
	1405.05	—	2.92	0.71	—	23.81–16.47	372,974	AMEX	PBW	800-983-0903	www.powershares.com
	335.17	10.00	1.69	0.72	—	17.88–15.18	55,858	AMEX	PZI	800-843-2639	www.powershares.com
	733.47	18.01	2.35	0.75	—	27.23–22.71	14,222	AMEX	PZJ	800-843-2639	www.powershares.com
	150645.54	16.49	3.00	0.20	—	108.40–91.44	57,062	AMEX	XLG	800-820-0888	www.rydex.com
	15096.11	18.99	3.68	—	—	36.46–31.32	12,534	AMEX	RPG	800-820-0888	www.rydex.com
	11333.66	14.30	1.85	—	—	34.06–29.34	3,934	AMEX	RPV	800-820-0888	www.rydex.com
	14012.27	17.69	2.68	0.40	0.38	47.99–41.07	281,382	AMEX	RSP	800-820-0888	www.rydex.com
	10511.62	17.83	2.65	—	—	47.34–44.59	9,502	AMEX	RCD	800-820-0888	www.rydex.com
	18028.60	21.74	3.44	—	—	49.42–47.42	6,330	AMEX	RHS	800-820-0888	www.rydex.com
	21001.29	11.49	2.75	—	—	53.51–48.35	2,019	AMEX	RYE	800-820-0888	www.rydex.com
	19061.05	15.41	2.09	—	—	51.16–48.21	27,953	AMEX	RYF	800-820-0888	www.rydex.com
	14631.64	22.44	3.47	—	—	51.27–48.79	4,876	AMEX	RYH	800-820-0888	www.rydex.com
	14763.70	18.40	2.99	—	—	51.57–48.93	4,000	AMEX	RGI	800-820-0888	www.rydex.com
	9916.04	13.28	2.92	—	—	52.35–48.43	12,417	AMEX	RTM	800-820-0888	www.rydex.com
	11763.65	25.21	3.00	—	—	51.13–47.80	2,092	AMEX	RYT	800-820-0888	www.rydex.com
	12494.01	17.27	2.09	—	—	57.33–54.57	12,382	AMEX	RYU	800-820-0888	www.rydex.com
	3056.96	20.05	3.53	—	—	53.57–45.43	1,634	AMEX	RFG	800-820-0888	www.rydex.com
	2433.01	16.77	1.71	—	—	36.69–29.96	8,340	AMEX	RFV	800-820-0888	www.rydex.com

Performance Summary

Morningstar's ETF Universe

Page	Name	Cat	Style Box	NAV ($)	Market Price ($)	2006 Avg. Prem. Discount%	NAV Return% through 12-29-06 1Yr	Annualized 3Yr	5Yr	Mkt Price Rtn% through 12-29-06 1Yr	Annualized 3Yr	5Yr	Morningstar Rating	Standard Deviation	Sharpe Ratio
136	Rydex S&P Smallcap 600 Gr	SG		40.44	40.71	0.08	—	—	—	—	—	—	—	—	—
137	Rydex S&P Smallcap 600 Va	SV		41.83	42.00	0.05	—	—	—	—	—	—	—	—	—
—	SPDR Biotech	SH		46.15	46.14	−0.01	—	—	—	—	—	—	—	—	—
138	SPDR Dividend ETF	LV		61.79	61.85	0.04	17.74	—	—	17.71	—	—	—	—	—
—	SPDR Homebuilders	LB		37.35	37.39	0.01	—	—	—	—	—	—	—	—	—
—	SPDR Metals & Mining	SN		49.09	49.08	−0.16	—	—	—	—	—	—	—	—	—
—	SPDR Oil & Gas Expl & Pro	SN		38.15	38.07	−0.17	—	—	—	—	—	—	—	—	—
—	SPDR Oil&Gas Equip & Serv	SN		29.40	29.43	−0.05	—	—	—	—	—	—	—	—	—
—	SPDR Pharmaceuticals	SH		34.50	34.42	0.05	—	—	—	—	—	—	—	—	—
—	SPDR Retail	LB		40.70	40.61	−0.04	—	—	—	—	—	—	—	—	—
—	SPDR Semiconductor	ST		49.19	49.20	−0.06	—	—	—	—	—	—	—	—	—
139	SPDR Trust Series 1	LB		141.64	141.62	0.04	15.69	10.32	6.07	15.85	10.37	6.22	★★★	6.90	1.00
149	streetTRACK DJ Small Gr	SG		92.83	92.92	−0.04	13.37	12.40	5.11	13.39	12.31	5.10	★★★	12.65	0.74
140	streetTRACK Global T	WS		76.06	76.08	0.09	19.84	9.77	4.83	19.65	9.77	4.64	★	6.34	1.02
—	streetTRACKS DJ Euro 50	ES		54.15	54.30	0.08	32.07	18.84	—	31.86	18.66	—	★★	10.84	1.37
—	streetTRACKS DJ Int RlEst	SR		62.70	63.26	0.89	—	—	—	—	—	—	—	—	—
141	streetTRACKS DJ Large Cap	LB		64.86	64.88	0.05	15.38	—	—	14.53	—	—	—	—	—
143	streetTRACKS DJ Lg Growth	LG		53.43	53.46	0.02	8.93	5.59	0.78	9.01	5.63	0.52	★★	8.28	0.31
142	streetTracks DJ Lg Value	LV		83.31	83.32	0.05	21.56	13.18	8.43	21.57	13.18	8.28	★★★	6.16	1.55
144	streetTRACKS DJ Mid Cap	MB		56.46	56.38	−0.05	13.27	—	—	12.53	—	—	—	—	—
146	streetTRACKS DJ Mid Value	MV		58.40	58.73	−0.04	15.42	—	—	16.29	—	—	—	—	—
145	streetTRACKS DJ MidGrowth	MG		60.83	60.83	−0.18	11.31	—	—	11.26	—	—	—	—	—
153	streetTRACKS DJ REIT	SR		87.86	87.85	0.02	35.50	26.72	23.20	35.53	26.62	23.08	★★★	16.67	1.33
148	streetTRACKS DJ Small Val	SV		70.81	70.79	−0.09	19.67	14.26	15.72	19.80	14.23	15.60	★★★★	12.35	0.89
150	streetTRACKS DJ STOXX 50	ES		48.21	48.34	0.26	26.76	16.20	—	26.67	15.89	—	★★	9.11	1.36
151	streetTRACKS Gold Shares	SP		63.04	63.21	0.44	23.44	—	—	22.55	—	—	—	—	—
—	streetTRACKS KBW Reg Bank	SF		50.24	50.12	−0.12	—	—	—	—	—	—	—	—	—
—	streetTRACKS MS Tech	ST		56.49	56.60	0.05	8.83	6.05	2.17	9.15	6.13	2.13	★★★	16.94	0.24
—	streetTRACKS Rus/Nom PRJp	JS		55.36	55.69	0.10	—	—	—	—	—	—	—	—	—
—	streetTRACKS Rus/Nom SmJp	JS		50.71	51.41	0.53	—	—	—	—	—	—	—	—	—
152	streetTRACKS Total Market	LB		101.80	101.83	0.02	14.92	10.52	6.14	14.78	10.58	6.12	★★★	6.94	1.02
154	Technology SPDR	ST		23.28	23.26	0.00	12.12	5.59	0.16	12.15	5.71	0.25	★★★	13.03	0.24
—	United States Oil	SN		51.87	51.60	−0.16	—	—	—	—	—	—	—	—	—
155	Utilities SPDR	SU		36.71	36.72	0.01	20.65	20.31	9.45	20.90	20.25	9.38	★★	8.84	1.78
—	Vanguard Cons Disc ETF	LG		60.69	60.80	0.05	16.52	—	—	16.51	—	—	—	—	—
—	Vanguard Cons Stap ETF	LB		63.82	63.84	0.05	15.81	—	—	15.86	—	—	—	—	—
156	Vanguard Div Appr ETF	LB		53.77	53.80	0.05	—	—	—	—	—	—	—	—	—
157	Vanguard EmergMkts ETF	EM		76.69	77.39	0.56	29.23	—	—	29.36	—	—	—	—	—
158	Vanguard Energy ETF	SN		84.94	85.01	0.04	18.98	—	—	19.03	—	—	—	—	—
159	Vanguard Euro Stk ETF	ES		67.54	68.16	0.66	33.26	—	—	33.06	—	—	—	—	—
160	Vanguard ExMkt ETF	MB		102.06	102.00	−0.09	14.46	14.51	12.08	14.30	14.31	—	★★★★	11.40	0.97
161	Vanguard Financial ETF	SF		65.33	65.50	0.09	19.25	—	—	19.43	—	—	—	—	—
162	Vanguard Growth ETF	LG		57.85	57.86	0.03	9.13	—	—	9.19	—	—	—	—	—
163	Vanguard HealthCar ETF	SH		56.96	56.94	0.03	6.62	—	—	6.54	—	—	—	—	—
—	Vanguard High Dividend Yi	LV		51.70	51.71	0.07	—	—	—	—	—	—	—	—	—
—	Vanguard Indstrls ETF	LB		65.34	65.43	0.05	15.15	—	—	15.16	—	—	—	—	—
164	Vanguard InfoTech ETF	ST		52.50	52.53	0.03	8.95	—	—	8.86	—	—	—	—	—
165	Vanguard Large Cap ETF	LB		62.92	62.93	0.03	15.61	—	—	15.44	—	—	—	—	—
—	Vanguard Materials ETF	SN		70.60	70.51	0.01	19.50	—	—	19.52	—	—	—	—	—
166	Vanguard Mid Cap ETF	MB		72.48	72.63	0.07	13.69	—	—	13.93	—	—	—	—	—
—	Vanguard Mid Growth ETF	MG		55.35	55.44	−0.06	—	—	—	—	—	—	—	—	—
—	Vanguard Mid Value ETF	MV		56.67	56.69	0.04	—	—	—	—	—	—	—	—	—
167	Vanguard Pacif Stk ETF	JS		65.73	66.47	0.51	11.97	—	—	11.61	—	—	—	—	—
168	Vanguard REIT Index ETF	SR		76.98	77.00	0.01	35.20	—	—	35.29	—	—	—	—	—
170	Vanguard Sm Cap Gr ETF	SG		65.24	65.25	−0.10	12.03	—	—	12.19	—	—	—	—	—

Performance Summary

Morningstar's ETF Universe

Portfolio Top 3 Sectors	Avg. Mkt. Cap. ($mil)	P/E Ratio	P/B Ratio	Costs Expense Ratio %	Tax-Cost Ratio	Trading Information 52-week High/Low	Avg. Daily Vol.	Exchange	Ticker	Phone	Contact Web Address
[icons]	1021.02	20.19	3.19	—	—	41.70–35.62	4,240	AMEX	RZG	800-820-0888	www.rydex.com
[icons]	650.99	18.38	1.62	—	—	42.42–35.50	1,797	AMEX	RZV	800-820-0888	www.rydex.com
[icons]	3566.97	—	5.47	0.36	—	54.35–42.46	16,788	AMEX	XBI	866-787-2257	www.advisors.ssga.com
[icons]	11584.38	17.57	2.37	0.30	—	62.37–54.48	17,811	AMEX	SDY	866-787-2257	www.advisors.ssga.com
[icons]	3919.07	6.64	1.50	0.36	—	46.92–29.34	1,527,840	AMEX	XHB	866-787-2257	www.advisors.ssga.com
[icons]	4083.98	13.66	3.11	0.36	—	53.19–39.57	41,274	AMEX	XME	866-787-2257	www.advisors.ssga.com
[icons]	6899.65	10.61	2.37	0.36	—	41.36–33.63	28,817	AMEX	XOP	866-787-2257	www.advisors.ssga.com
[icons]	6905.32	15.08	3.03	0.36	—	31.75–25.01	26,952	AMEX	XES	866-787-2257	www.advisors.ssga.com
[icons]	12924.21	21.76	3.57	0.36	—	35.44–30.92	17,070	AMEX	XPH	866-787-2257	www.advisors.ssga.com
[icons]	5293.82	20.85	3.16	0.36	—	41.87–34.90	355,631	AMEX	XRT	866-787-2257	www.advisors.ssga.com
[icons]	7696.05	27.43	2.86	0.36	—	56.73–40.24	63,982	AMEX	XSD	866-787-2257	www.advisors.ssga.com
[icons]	52400.78	16.89	2.86	0.10	0.64	143.05–122.80	64,801,008	AMEX	SPY	800-843-2639	www.amex.com/spy
[icons]	1548.93	20.91	3.20	0.26	0.12	95.19–79.79	6,345	AMEX	DSG	866-787-2257	www.advisors.ssga.com
[icons]	168672.73	14.95	2.87	0.51	0.73	76.39–64.35	15,900	AMEX	DGT	866-787-2257	www.advisors.ssga.com
[icons]	67910.94	13.13	2.65	0.32	0.90	54.21–42.94	110,834	NYSE	FEZ	866-787-2257	www.advisors.ssga.com
	—	—	—	—	—	62.70–59.98	187,466	AMEX	RWX	—	www.advisors.ssga.com
[icons]	43858.01	17.11	2.86	0.21	—	65.47–56.45	1,544	AMEX	ELR	866-787-2257	www.advisors.ssga.com
[icons]	31188.79	20.33	3.52	0.21	0.32	54.23–46.84	18,468	AMEX	ELG	866-787-2257	www.advisors.ssga.com
[icons]	59662.91	14.95	2.44	0.21	0.85	83.84–70.47	8,302	AMEX	ELV	866-787-2257	www.advisors.ssga.com
[icons]	3718.04	17.96	2.53	0.26	—	58.13–49.85	6,436	AMEX	EMM	866-787-2257	www.advisors.ssga.com
[icons]	3575.63	16.81	2.06	0.26	—	60.20–52.23	1,157	AMEX	EMV	866-787-2257	www.advisors.ssga.com
[icons]	3868.85	19.23	3.25	0.26	—	63.31–53.63	1,829	AMEX	EMG	866-787-2257	www.advisors.ssga.com
[icons]	6829.69	39.18	3.25	0.26	1.59	92.37–70.30	71,637	AMEX	RWR	866-787-2257	www.advisors.ssga.com
[icons]	1619.01	16.28	1.86	0.26	1.30	71.85–61.86	6,148	AMEX	DSV	866-787-2257	www.advisors.ssga.com
[icons]	94899.41	13.54	3.38	0.32	1.02	48.54–40.26	22,525	NYSE	FEU	866-787-2257	www.advisors.ssga.com
	—	—	—	0.40	—	72.08–52.24	4,228,620	NYSE	GLD	866-320-4053	www.streettracksgoldshare
[icons]	2244.33	16.51	2.04	0.36	—	50.97–46.81	247,208	AMEX	KRE	866-787-2257	www.advisors.ssga.com
[icons]	33856.94	25.41	4.24	0.51	0.04	58.17–44.86	49,500	AMEX	MTK	866-787-2257	www.advisors.ssga.com
	—	—	—	—	—	55.47–50.92	5,037	AMEX	JPP	866-787-2252	www.advisors.ssga.com
	—	—	—	—	—	51.79–46.65	6,822	AMEX	JSC	866-787-2257	www.advisors.ssga.com
[icons]	28742.09	17.41	2.79	0.21	0.58	102.85–88.32	3,477	AMEX	TMW	866-787-2257	www.advisors.ssga.com
[icons]	59259.22	23.50	3.59	0.26	0.41	23.78–19.00	1,675,637	AMEX	XLK	800-843-2639	www.spdrindex.com
	—	—	—	—	—	73.41–50.68	1,887,814	AMEX	USO	800-920-0259	www.unitedstatesoilfund.c
[icons]	18031.78	16.68	2.26	0.26	1.16	37.35–30.22	2,433,900	AMEX	XLU	800-843-2639	www.spdrindex.com
[icons]	12560.33	17.68	2.42	0.25	—	61.58–49.82	8,311	AMEX	VCR	866-499-8473	www.vanguard.com
[icons]	34820.67	19.92	3.58	0.25	—	64.65–55.65	27,102	AMEX	VDC	866-499-8473	www.vanguard.com
[icons]	45402.35	17.90	3.39	—	—	54.18–47.74	21,037	AMEX	VIG	866-499-8473	www.vanguard.com
[icons]	8933.71	14.45	2.45	0.30	—	76.89–56.87	219,022	AMEX	VWO	866-499-8473	www.vanguard.com
[icons]	40788.11	10.09	2.49	0.25	—	90.44–72.11	40,262	AMEX	VDE	866-499-8473	www.vanguard.com
[icons]	37478.19	14.62	3.42	0.18	—	69.52–53.48	220,097	AMEX	VGK	866-499-8473	www.vanguard.com
[icons]	2127.27	18.14	2.42	0.08	0.22	104.81–88.92	17,000	AMEX	VXF	866-499-8473	www.vanguard.com
[icons]	29646.55	15.04	2.06	0.25	—	65.87–55.69	20,962	AMEX	VFH	866-499-8473	www.vanguard.com
[icons]	35871.35	20.88	3.72	0.11	—	58.68–50.35	221,380	AMEX	VUG	866-499-8473	www.vanguard.com
[icons]	32824.10	21.56	3.78	0.25	—	58.01–50.90	55,734	AMEX	VHT	866-499-8473	www.vanguard.com
	—	—	—	—	—	52.04–49.86	12,293	AMEX	VYM	866-499-8473	www.vanguard.com
[icons]	24009.72	18.14	2.91	0.25	—	66.57–57.03	10,065	AMEX	VIS	866-499-8473	www.vanguard.com
[icons]	31012.75	23.42	3.71	0.25	—	54.11–42.58	36,474	AMEX	VGT	866-499-8473	www.vanguard.com
[icons]	42616.82	16.91	2.79	0.07	—	63.66–54.44	202,371	AMEX	VV	866-499-8473	www.vanguard.com
[icons]	9398.57	14.33	2.55	0.25	—	72.71–58.85	12,382	AMEX	VAW	866-499-8473	www.vanguard.com
[icons]	6333.79	17.39	2.56	0.13	—	74.54–63.51	58,577	AMEX	VO	866-499-8473	www.vanguard.com
[icons]	6459.12	20.89	3.71	—	—	56.97–50.82	12,255	AMEX	VOT	866-499-8473	www.vanguard.com
[icons]	6196.95	15.09	2.00	—	—	57.51–50.65	13,794	AMEX	VOE	866-499-8473	www.vanguard.com
[icons]	16610.76	17.34	2.19	0.18	—	69.66–56.54	77,380	AMEX	VPL	866-499-8473	www.vanguard.com
[icons]	5394.91	35.49	2.85	0.12	—	80.79–61.68	120,111	AMEX	VNQ	866-499-8473	www.vanguard.com
[icons]	1462.69	20.00	3.16	0.12	—	67.64–56.14	39,571	AMEX	VBK	866-499-8473	www.vanguard.com

Performance Summary

Morningstar's ETF Universe

Page	Name	Cat	Style Box	NAV ($)	Market Price ($)	2006 Avg. Prem. Discount%	NAV Return% through 12-29-06 1Yr	Annualized 3Yr	5Yr	Mkt Price Rtn% through 12-29-06 1Yr	Annualized 3Yr	5Yr	Morningstar Rating	Standard Deviation	Sharpe Ratio
171	Vanguard Sm Cp Val ETF	SV		71.16	71.13	−0.04	19.40	—	—	19.49	—	—	—	—	—
169	Vanguard Small Cap ETF	SB		68.16	68.10	−0.09	15.79	—	—	15.77	—	—	—	—	—
172	Vanguard TelcomSrv ETF	SC		73.47	73.51	−0.01	36.65	—	—	36.70	—	—	—	—	—
173	Vanguard TSM ETF	LB		140.08	140.21	0.02	15.66	11.37	7.49	15.69	11.52	7.60	★★★★	7.72	1.03
174	Vanguard Utilities ETF	SU		76.77	76.81	0.05	21.58	—	—	21.64	—	—	—	—	—
175	Vanguard Value ETF	LV		68.14	68.23	0.06	22.28	—	—	22.37	—	—	—	—	—
176	WisdomTree DIEFA	FB		61.53	61.75	0.52	—	—	—	—	—	—	—	—	—
177	WisdomTree DIEFA HiYld Eq	FB		61.56	61.75	0.64	—	—	—	—	—	—	—	—	—
178	WisdomTree Div Top 100	LB		58.04	58.06	0.07	—	—	—	—	—	—	—	—	—
—	WisdomTree Eur SmCap Div	ES		65.10	65.25	0.62	—	—	—	—	—	—	—	—	—
180	WisdomTree Eur Total Div	ES		61.64	61.72	0.49	—	—	—	—	—	—	—	—	—
179	WisdomTree Euro Hi-Yld Eq	ES		61.60	61.66	0.58	—	—	—	—	—	—	—	—	—
181	WisdomTree High-Yld Eqty	LB		57.77	57.73	0.04	—	—	—	—	—	—	—	—	—
182	WisdomTree IntDiv Top 100	FB		63.48	63.67	0.58	—	—	—	—	—	—	—	—	—
—	WisdomTree Intl Basic Mat	FB		28.60	28.59	0.46	—	—	—	—	—	—	—	—	—
—	WisdomTree Intl Comm	SC		28.58	28.52	0.07	—	—	—	—	—	—	—	—	—
—	WisdomTree Intl Con Cycl	FB		28.32	28.31	0.18	—	—	—	—	—	—	—	—	—
—	WisdomTree Intl Con NonCy	FB		26.65	26.79	0.71	—	—	—	—	—	—	—	—	—
—	WisdomTree Intl Energy	SN		27.83	28.03	0.54	—	—	—	—	—	—	—	—	—
—	WisdomTree Intl Financial	SF		27.27	27.42	0.52	—	—	—	—	—	—	—	—	—
—	WisdomTree Intl Hlth Care	SH		26.29	26.49	0.61	—	—	—	—	—	—	—	—	—
—	WisdomTree Intl Indust	FB		28.37	28.55	0.49	—	—	—	—	—	—	—	—	—
183	WisdomTree Intl LgCap Div	FB		60.75	60.98	0.53	—	—	—	—	—	—	—	—	—
—	WisdomTree Intl MdCap Div	FA		63.58	63.76	0.54	—	—	—	—	—	—	—	—	—
—	WisdomTree Intl SmCap Div	FA		62.71	62.95	0.70	—	—	—	—	—	—	—	—	—
—	WisdomTree Intl Tech	ST		26.61	26.72	0.53	—	—	—	—	—	—	—	—	—
—	WisdomTree Intl Utilities	SU		28.42	28.66	0.70	—	—	—	—	—	—	—	—	—
—	WisdomTree Japan HiYld Eq	JS		57.31	57.65	−0.49	—	—	—	—	—	—	—	—	—
—	WisdomTree Japan SmCp Div	JS		50.42	50.80	0.22	—	—	—	—	—	—	—	—	—
184	WisdomTree Japan Tot Div	JS		54.89	55.34	0.40	—	—	—	—	—	—	—	—	—
185	WisdomTree LargeCap Div	LB		57.88	57.89	0.07	—	—	—	—	—	—	—	—	—
186	WisdomTree MidCap Div	MB		56.80	56.84	0.03	—	—	—	—	—	—	—	—	—
187	WisdomTree Pac ex-Jp HYEq	DP		61.62	61.80	0.32	—	—	—	—	—	—	—	—	—
188	WisdomTree Pac ex-Jp TDiv	DP		62.80	62.93	0.25	—	—	—	—	—	—	—	—	—
189	WisdomTree SmallCap Div	SB		57.42	57.36	−0.03	—	—	—	—	—	—	—	—	—
190	WisdomTree Total Dividend	LB		57.62	57.61	0.06	—	—	—	—	—	—	—	—	—
122	PowerShares FTSE RAFI US 1000	LB		57.93	57.70	0.05	18.86	—	—	19.02	—	—	—	—	—
127	PowerShares Value Line Timeliness Sel	LG		15.98	16.19	0.03	4.66	—	—	4.58	—	—	—	—	—
147	SPDR DJ Wilshire Small Cap	SB		61.21	60.22	−0.10	16.59	—	—	17.03	—	—	—	—	—

Fund Categories

CI	Intermediate-Term Bond	GI	Intermediate-Term Government Bond
CL	Long-Term Bond	GL	Long-Term Government Bond
CS	Short-Term Bond	GS	Short-Term Government Bond
CV	Convertible Bond	HY	High-Yield Bond
DH	Domestic Hybrid	IB	International Bond
DP	Diversified Pacific Stock	IH	International Hybrid
EB	Emerging Markets Bond	JS	Japan Stock
EM	Diversified Emerging Markets	LB	Large-Cap Blend
ES	Europe Stock	LG	Large-Cap Growth
FS	Foreign Stock	LS	Latin America Stock

LV	Large-Cap Value	SH	Specialty–Health
MB	Mid-Cap Blend	SP	Specialty–Precious Metals
MG	Mid-Cap Growth	SN	Specialty–Natural Resources
MU	Multisector Bond	SR	Specialty–Real Estate
MV	Mid-Cap Value	SS	Specialty–Unaligned
PJ	Pacific ex-Japan Stock	ST	Specialty–Technology
SB	Small-Cap Blend	SU	Specialty–Utilities
SC	Specialty–Communications	SV	Small-Cap Value
SF	Specialty–Financials	UB	Ultrashort Bond
SG	Small-Cap Growth	WS	World Stock

Performance Summary

Morningstar's ETF Universe

Portfolio — Top 3 Sectors	Avg. Mkt. Cap. ($mil)	P/E Ratio	P/B Ratio	Expense Ratio %	Tax-Cost Ratio	52-week High/Low	Avg. Daily Vol.	Exchange	Ticker	Phone	Web Address
(sectors)	1469.60	16.06	1.78	0.12	—	73.05–62.09	61,165	AMEX	VBR	866-499-8473	www.vanguard.com
(sectors)	1466.75	17.68	2.24	0.10	—	69.94–59.31	41,542	AMEX	VB	866-499-8473	www.vanguard.com
(sectors)	17027.82	19.33	2.37	0.25	—	74.01–55.43	30,957	AMEX	VOX	866-499-8473	www.vanguard.com
(sectors)	26899.58	17.02	2.70	0.07	0.31	141.66–121.38	147,537	AMEX	VTI	866-499-8473	www.vanguard.com
(sectors)	11021.95	17.31	2.04	0.25	—	78.14–63.43	12,020	AMEX	VPU	866-499-8473	www.vanguard.com
(sectors)	49880.65	14.34	2.27	0.11	—	68.71–57.96	154,491	AMEX	VTV	866-499-8473	www.vanguard.com
(sectors)	36211.46	15.06	3.13	—	—	61.53–48.71	20,951	NYSE	DWM	866-909-9473	www.wisdomtree.com
(sectors)	35537.74	13.54	3.17	—	—	61.56–48.88	20,970	NYSE	DTH	866-909-9473	www.wisdomtree.com
(sectors)	26154.67	17.10	2.43	—	—	58.51–49.35	23,170	NYSE	DTN	866-909-9473	www.wisdomtree.com
(sectors)	1108.64	14.65	2.78	—	—	65.10–48.53	11,702	NYSE	DFE	866-909-9473	www.wisdomtree.com
(sectors)	44116.30	14.42	3.38	—	—	61.77–48.83	9,148	NYSE	DEB	866-909-9473	www.wisdomtree.com
(sectors)	45349.45	12.64	2.97	—	—	61.88–48.90	16,811	NYSE	DEW	866-909-9473	www.wisdomtree.com
(sectors)	47749.67	15.51	2.39	—	—	58.13–49.32	24,811	NYSE	DHS	866-909-9473	www.wisdomtree.com
(sectors)	37126.22	13.88	3.25	—	—	63.48–48.81	38,802	NYSE	DOO	866-909-9473	www.wisdomtree.com
(sectors)	16273.27	15.31	2.93	—	—	28.60–25.26	1,652	NYSE	DBN	866-909-9473	www.wisdomtree.com
(sectors)	38997.81	14.65	5.11	—	—	28.81–25.30	2,991	NYSE	DGG	866-909-9473	www.wisdomtree.com
(sectors)	13038.08	16.09	2.30	—	—	28.32–25.18	392	NYSE	DPC	866-909-9473	www.wisdomtree.com
(sectors)	30440.13	19.52	5.48	—	—	26.71–24.89	9,714	NYSE	DPN	866-909-9473	www.wisdomtree.com
(sectors)	41779.66	11.95	2.94	—	—	28.00–25.16	6,779	NYSE	DKA	866-909-9473	www.wisdomtree.com
(sectors)	33163.97	13.15	2.59	—	—	27.27–25.02	2,775	NYSE	DRF	866-909-9473	www.wisdomtree.com
(sectors)	19169.93	23.68	5.51	—	—	26.29–24.93	8,012	NYSE	DBR	866-909-9473	www.wisdomtree.com
(sectors)	8486.77	17.05	3.13	—	—	28.37–25.37	579	NYSE	DDI	866-909-9473	www.wisdomtree.com
(sectors)	58209.02	14.29	3.22	—	—	60.83–48.78	9,225	NYSE	DOL	866-909-9473	www.wisdomtree.com
(sectors)	7819.83	16.94	2.83	—	—	63.58–48.57	14,431	NYSE	DIM	866-909-9473	www.wisdomtree.com
(sectors)	1485.96	16.56	2.41	—	—	62.71–48.55	28,162	NYSE	DLS	866-909-9473	www.wisdomtree.com
(sectors)	10041.92	23.75	3.61	—	—	26.61–24.88	1,704	NYSE	DBT	866-909-9473	www.wisdomtree.com
(sectors)	28173.37	19.05	3.27	—	—	28.42–24.96	13,808	NYSE	DBU	866-909-9473	www.wisdomtree.com
(sectors)	21665.33	15.32	1.83	—	—	57.31–47.86	3,911	NYSE	DNL	866-909-9473	www.wisdomtree.com
(sectors)	1010.71	17.90	1.31	—	—	51.84–46.21	18,754	NYSE	DFJ	866-909-9473	www.wisdomtree.com
(sectors)	17332.31	17.58	1.96	—	—	54.92–47.44	4,654	NYSE	DXJ	866-909-9473	www.wisdomtree.com
(sectors)	77110.13	15.43	2.67	—	—	58.30–49.44	20,237	NYSE	DLN	866-909-9473	www.wisdomtree.com
(sectors)	4145.56	17.00	2.28	—	—	57.57–49.28	12,494	NYSE	DON	866-909-9473	www.wisdomtree.com
(sectors)	8409.49	15.45	3.41	—	—	61.62–48.19	20,571	NYSE	DNH	866-909-9473	www.wisdomtree.com
(sectors)	13540.16	16.57	3.14	—	—	62.80–48.57	10,642	NYSE	DND	866-909-9473	www.wisdomtree.com
(sectors)	877.85	17.41	1.93	—	—	58.15–49.46	18,200	NYSE	DES	866-909-9473	www.wisdomtree.com
(sectors)	44390.00	15.63	2.57	—	—	58.05–49.42	9,571	NYSE	DTD	866-909-9473	www.wisdomtree.com
(sectors)	33,167.33	15.63	2.40	0.76	—	58.32–49.74	104,000	AMEX	PRF	800-843-2639	www.powershares.com
(sectors)	8,347.98	24.39	3.58	0.71	—	17.87–13.88	115,000	AMEX	PIV	800-843-2639	www.powershares.com
(sectors)	1,577.77	18.18	2.36	0.26	—	63.49–54.00	12,000	AMEX	DSC	866-787-2257	www.advisors.ssga.com

Equity Style Box

Val Blnd Grth / Lrg Mid Sm

Sectors

- Information
- Software
- Hardware
- Media
- Telecom
- Service
- Healthcare
- Consumer Svs
- Business Svs
- Financial
- Manufacturing
- Consumer Goods
- Industrial Materials
- Energy
- Utilities

Performance Summary

Indexes

Index	2006 Total Return % 1st Qrt	2nd Qrt	3rd Qrt	4th Qrt	2006	Annualized Total Return% 3 Yr	5 Yr	10 Yr	Annual Total Return % 2005	2004	2003	2002	2001	2000	1999	1998	1997
Domestic Stock																	
DJ Wilshire 4500	9.26	−3.43	0.48	9.48	16.07	14.92	12.38	9.74	10.27	18.57	43.72	−17.81	−9.30	−15.77	35.49	8.63	25.69
DJ Wilshire 5000	5.61	−1.91	4.31	7.32	15.97	11.54	7.65	8.67	6.24	12.62	31.64	−20.86	−10.97	−10.89	23.56	23.43	31.29
DJ Wilshire REIT	15.79	−1.20	9.20	8.97	36.13	27.37	23.84	15.29	14.00	33.14	36.06	3.60	12.36	31.04	−2.57	−17.00	19.67
Dow Jones Financials Sector	4.38	−0.45	7.43	6.97	19.42	12.97	10.81	12.43	6.46	13.39	32.23	−12.35	−6.38	26.94	1.52	7.51	48.94
Dow Jones Health Care Sector	1.45	−4.81	8.82	1.71	6.88	6.58	2.74	9.65	8.32	4.55	19.43	−20.81	−12.84	37.84	−4.03	39.09	36.88
Dow Jones Industrial Average TR	4.25	0.94	5.35	7.39	19.05	8.44	6.81	8.91	1.72	5.31	28.28	−15.01	−5.44	−4.85	27.21	18.13	24.87
Dow Jones Large Growth	2.03	−4.19	4.92	4.81	7.50	5.06	0.55	3.42	2.56	5.18	29.52	−31.58	−25.46	−32.41	36.38	45.77	36.01
Dow Jones Large Value	4.76	0.70	7.14	8.25	22.34	13.41	8.68	9.77	5.12	13.41	25.88	−17.41	−6.12	10.35	1.36	15.41	38.16
Dow Jones Small Growth	11.35	−6.98	−1.43	6.83	9.07	11.07	4.45	6.75	8.78	15.47	48.48	−38.89	−8.50	−14.91	61.48	6.43	15.49
Dow Jones Small Value	11.55	−2.89	2.31	9.12	20.95	15.16	16.46	13.53	6.68	18.37	43.66	−2.37	12.78	24.00	−5.06	−6.51	33.75
Dow Jones Telecommunications Sector	15.08	−0.75	10.35	8.55	36.83	15.96	1.84	3.73	−4.00	18.70	7.33	−34.55	−12.77	−40.27	18.41	51.82	40.64
Dow Jones Transportation Average TR	9.12	8.17	−9.40	2.68	9.81	16.13	12.82	8.66	11.65	27.73	31.84	−11.48	−9.30	0.40	−4.52	−2.45	48.07
Dow Jones Utilities Sector	−0.38	5.45	5.67	9.26	21.28	20.17	11.30	9.57	15.35	24.04	24.91	−21.19	−26.18	56.07	−13.19	13.32	28.76
Goldman Sachs Natural Resources	9.03	4.46	−6.39	9.57	16.82	25.70	18.21	9.72	36.48	24.57	34.01	−13.26	−15.59	15.81	27.22	−24.67	16.94
MSCI US Mid Cap 450 Index	7.57	−2.84	1.32	7.42	13.75	16.03	12.65	12.14	13.94	20.52	39.05	−16.46	−6.38	−1.86	34.32	9.26	28.58
MSCI US Prime Market 750 Index	4.34	−1.47	5.30	6.87	15.68	11.05	6.72	8.57	6.26	11.41	29.45	−21.93	−12.84	−11.89	24.56	28.90	33.38
MSCI US Prime Market Value Index	5.34	0.98	6.67	7.84	22.37	14.86	10.30	10.81	7.26	15.44	29.72	−16.95	−3.33	9.02	6.25	14.63	33.25
MSCI US Prime Market Growth Index	3.35	−3.92	3.85	5.89	9.20	7.27	3.00	6.05	5.25	7.38	29.20	−27.30	−22.14	−27.79	43.96	43.62	33.57
MSCI US Small Cap Growth Index	13.27	−6.68	−2.38	8.57	12.03	12.25	8.49	8.97	8.71	16.13	50.37	−29.31	−6.29	−8.25	49.55	6.63	14.56
MSCI US Small Cap Value Index	11.09	−2.67	1.74	8.58	19.44	16.24	16.18	13.74	6.28	23.72	44.34	−6.63	12.95	21.22	−2.17	−5.12	34.73
MSCI US Small Cap 1750 Index	12.19	−4.69	−0.26	8.55	15.77	14.30	12.43	11.88	7.48	20.01	47.38	−18.37	3.22	8.67	21.94	0.58	24.34
Morningstar Large Cap TR	3.75	−1.13	5.94	6.67	15.91	10.02	5.30	7.59	4.87	9.54	27.04	−23.47	−15.10	−11.38	21.05	30.74	34.78
Morningstar Large Core TR	4.05	−1.91	6.55	6.24	15.54	11.00	5.37	—	3.82	13.99	24.71	−23.82	−14.35	4.24	17.81	23.18	—
Morningstar Large Growth TR	1.49	−4.56	3.34	5.58	5.68	3.08	−0.89	—	3.43	0.19	30.65	−33.15	−29.07	−33.51	42.59	51.23	—
Morningstar Large Value TR	5.50	2.71	7.47	8.02	25.78	15.37	10.50	—	7.05	14.05	26.26	−15.05	−3.38	5.66	0.57	17.85	—
Morningstar Mid Cap TR	7.93	−3.00	1.08	8.02	14.32	15.52	11.82	10.44	12.70	19.66	38.38	−18.06	−4.63	6.94	15.55	6.01	23.65
Morningstar Mid Core TR	7.77	−3.93	2.34	8.28	14.72	14.55	12.79	—	10.05	19.05	38.68	−12.42	6.05	14.77	1.89	2.87	—
Morningstar Mid Growth TR	9.52	−4.65	−1.78	6.89	9.63	13.75	6.81	—	16.27	15.45	40.02	−32.54	−21.59	−11.10	52.46	9.49	—
Morningstar Mid Value TR	6.43	−0.14	2.65	8.90	18.81	18.10	15.04	—	11.54	24.30	35.94	−10.00	5.06	24.59	−6.83	5.85	—
Morningstar Small Growth TR	13.78	−7.99	−1.94	7.19	10.04	9.72	4.94	—	5.77	13.48	52.65	−36.87	−12.92	−12.10	46.80	−6.55	—
Morningstar Small Value TR	10.86	−3.60	3.08	8.96	20.03	16.10	16.41	—	5.12	24.03	48.87	−8.24	18.58	18.65	−5.19	−3.67	—
Morningstar Small Cap TR	12.99	−5.03	0.74	8.28	17.05	14.24	11.89	10.25	5.76	20.44	47.70	−20.36	5.26	7.66	17.78	−6.01	20.58
Morningstar Small Core TR	14.22	−3.51	1.17	8.67	21.16	16.77	14.28	—	6.30	23.61	42.59	−14.16	14.60	23.21	16.74	−7.55	—
Morningstar US Core TR	5.54	−2.53	5.39	6.77	15.76	12.08	7.38	—	5.19	15.62	28.63	−21.18	−9.31	7.10	14.67	17.75	—
Morningstar US Growth TR	4.04	−4.86	1.85	5.97	6.83	5.87	1.23	—	6.41	4.37	34.12	−33.20	−26.32	−28.45	44.51	39.76	—
Morningstar US Market TR	5.22	−1.81	4.63	7.03	15.70	11.46	7.10	8.48	6.52	12.35	30.73	−22.17	−11.88	−7.02	19.79	23.86	31.78
Morningstar US Value TR	6.02	1.75	6.29	8.23	24.10	16.06	11.86	—	7.82	16.85	29.75	−13.68	−0.68	10.06	−1.27	14.13	—
NASDAQ Composite	6.10	−7.17	3.97	6.95	9.52	6.43	4.37	6.46	1.37	8.59	50.01	−31.53	−21.05	−39.29	85.59	39.63	21.64
NYSE Composite	6.18	−0.78	3.68	7.90	17.86	12.24	7.94	8.22	6.95	12.16	29.28	−19.83	−10.21	1.01	9.15	16.55	30.31
Russell 1000	4.49	−1.66	5.06	6.95	15.46	10.98	6.82	8.64	6.27	11.40	29.89	−21.65	−12.45	−7.79	20.91	27.02	32.85
Russell 1000 Growth	3.09	−3.90	3.94	5.93	9.07	6.87	2.69	5.44	5.26	6.30	29.75	−27.88	−20.42	−22.42	33.16	38.71	30.49
Russell 1000 Value	5.93	0.59	6.22	8.00	22.25	15.09	10.86	11.00	7.05	16.49	30.03	−15.52	−5.59	7.01	7.35	15.63	35.18
Russell 2000	13.94	−5.02	0.44	8.90	18.37	13.56	11.39	9.44	4.55	18.33	47.25	−20.48	2.49	−3.02	21.26	−2.55	22.36
Russell 2000 Growth	14.36	−7.25	−1.76	8.77	13.35	10.51	6.93	4.88	4.15	14.31	48.54	−30.26	−9.23	−22.43	43.09	1.23	12.95
Russell 2000 Value	13.51	−2.70	2.55	9.03	23.48	16.48	15.37	13.27	4.71	22.25	46.03	−11.43	14.02	22.83	−1.49	−6.45	31.78
Russell 3000	5.31	−1.98	4.64	7.12	15.72	11.19	7.17	8.64	6.12	11.95	31.06	−21.54	−11.46	−7.46	20.90	24.14	31.78
Russell Midcap	7.61	−2.58	2.11	7.67	15.26	16.00	12.88	12.14	12.65	20.22	40.06	−16.19	−5.62	8.25	18.23	10.09	29.01
Russell Midcap Growth	7.61	−4.69	0.89	6.96	10.66	12.73	8.22	8.62	12.10	15.48	42.71	−27.41	−20.15	−11.75	51.29	17.86	22.54
Russell Midcap Value	7.62	−0.56	3.53	8.50	20.22	18.77	15.88	13.65	12.65	23.71	38.07	−9.64	2.33	19.18	−0.11	5.08	34.37
Standard & Poor's Midcap 400 TR	7.63	−3.14	−1.08	6.99	10.32	13.09	10.89	13.47	12.56	16.48	35.62	−14.53	−0.61	17.51	14.72	19.12	32.25
Standard & Poor's 500 - Cons. Discretion	2.96	−0.47	4.99	10.27	18.64	7.96	5.66	9.90	−6.36	13.25	37.42	−23.82	2.79	−20.00	25.18	41.14	34.35
Standard & Poor's 500 - Consumer Staples	1.56	2.92	5.69	3.52	14.36	8.62	6.48	6.93	3.58	8.18	11.57	−4.26	−6.40	16.78	−15.09	15.76	32.89
Standard & Poor's 500 - Energy	9.05	4.28	−1.74	11.17	24.21	29.00	19.11	14.03	31.37	31.56	25.64	−11.13	−10.40	15.68	18.73	0.63	25.28
Standard & Poor's 500 - Financials	3.24	−0.13	7.99	7.04	19.19	12.07	9.52	11.98	6.48	10.91	31.13	−14.64	−8.95	25.70	4.12	11.42	48.15
Standard & Poor's 500 - Health Care	1.25	−4.99	10.22	1.41	7.53	5.22	1.70	9.27	6.46	1.76	15.06	−18.82	−11.95	37.05	−10.66	43.88	43.73

Performance Summary

Indexes

Index	2006 Total Return %					Annualized Total Return%			Annual Total Return %								
	1st Qrt	2nd Qrt	3rd Qrt	4th Qrt	2006	3 Yr	5 Yr	10 Yr	2005	2004	2003	2002	2001	2000	1999	1998	1997
Standard & Poor's 500 - Information Tech	4.17	−9.63	8.52	6.12	8.42	3.94	0.69	6.38	0.99	2.56	47.23	−37.41	−25.87	−40.90	78.74	78.14	28.53
Standard & Poor's 500 - Industrials	7.04	0.01	−0.10	5.93	13.29	11.02	5.91	8.57	2.32	18.04	32.20	−26.34	−5.74	5.88	21.50	10.87	27.04
Standard & Poor's 500 - Materials	7.43	−0.43	−0.49	11.44	18.63	11.93	12.87	7.37	4.42	13.20	38.20	−5.46	3.48	−15.72	25.26	−6.18	8.41
Standard & Poor's 500 - Telecomm Serv	14.45	−0.57	10.60	8.69	36.80	15.66	1.77	4.16	−5.63	19.85	7.08	−34.11	−12.25	−38.81	19.14	52.37	41.24
Standard & Poor's 500 - Utilities	−1.16	5.69	6.11	9.15	20.99	20.69	9.23	8.25	16.87	24.32	26.34	−29.99	−30.44	57.19	−9.18	14.84	24.65
Standard & Poor's 500 Equal Weighted	6.24	−2.07	3.95	7.08	15.80	13.53	11.04	11.57	8.06	16.95	40.97	−18.18	−0.39	9.64	12.03	12.19	29.05
Standard & Poor's 500 TR	4.21	−1.44	5.67	6.70	15.79	10.44	6.19	8.42	4.91	10.88	28.68	−22.10	−11.89	−9.10	21.04	28.58	33.36
S&P 500/Citigroup Growth	2.61	−3.46	6.06	5.65	11.01	6.29	1.87	6.65	1.14	6.97	27.08	−28.10	−16.12	−19.14	37.38	38.16	34.73
S&P 500/Citigroup Value	5.87	0.61	5.27	7.72	20.80	14.74	10.43	9.45	8.71	15.03	30.36	−16.59	−8.18	−0.51	4.88	18.91	31.87
S&P Mid Cap 400/Citigroup Growth	6.17	−4.37	−1.67	5.98	5.81	11.91	9.11	15.51	14.42	15.78	37.32	−19.67	−2.55	15.77	36.10	37.19	29.83
S&P Mid Cap 400/Citigroup Value	9.07	−2.02	−0.57	7.87	14.62	14.16	12.51	11.52	10.77	17.18	33.80	−9.43	1.43	19.51	−2.63	3.71	34.84
S&P Small Cap 600/Citigroup Growth	11.34	−5.11	−2.45	7.26	10.54	13.73	11.19	10.19	7.06	24.29	38.50	−16.57	3.00	7.59	19.72	−0.08	17.11
S&P Small Cap 600/Citigroup Value	14.28	−4.04	0.59	8.40	19.57	16.20	13.71	12.73	8.36	21.09	39.20	−12.93	9.52	15.77	4.91	−2.63	34.53
Standard & Poor's Smallcap 600 TR	12.84	−4.56	−0.88	7.84	15.12	14.99	12.49	11.57	7.68	22.65	38.79	−14.63	6.54	11.80	12.40	−1.31	25.58
Standard & Poor's 100 TR	3.68	−0.84	7.58	7.12	18.47	8.45	4.51	8.01	1.17	6.43	26.25	−22.59	−13.81	−12.55	32.79	33.21	30.01

Bond

Index	2006 Total Return %					Annualized Total Return%			Annual Total Return %								
	1st Qrt	2nd Qrt	3rd Qrt	4th Qrt	2006	3 Yr	5 Yr	10 Yr	2005	2004	2003	2002	2001	2000	1999	1998	1997
Lehman Brothers 1-3 Year Government	0.42	0.66	2.01	0.98	4.12	2.30	2.97	4.79	1.73	1.07	2.01	6.01	8.53	8.17	2.97	6.97	6.65
Lehman Brothers Aggregate Bond	−0.65	−0.08	3.81	1.24	4.33	3.70	5.06	6.24	2.43	4.34	4.10	10.25	8.44	11.63	−0.82	8.69	9.65
Lehman Brothers Intermediate Gove Bond	−0.30	0.30	2.92	0.89	3.84	2.62	3.92	5.48	1.68	2.33	2.29	9.64	8.42	10.47	0.49	8.49	7.72
Lehman Brothers Intermediate Treasury	−0.48	0.28	2.92	0.77	3.51	2.36	3.66	5.30	1.56	2.02	2.10	9.28	8.16	10.26	0.41	8.62	7.69
Lehman Brothers Long Term Govt Bond	−3.52	−1.22	6.48	0.57	2.06	5.51	7.11	7.75	6.61	7.94	2.61	16.99	4.34	20.29	−8.73	13.41	15.12
Lehman Brothers Long Term Treasury Bond	−3.62	−1.19	6.43	0.49	1.85	5.32	6.94	7.65	6.50	7.70	2.48	16.79	4.21	20.27	−8.74	13.52	15.08

International

Index	2006 Total Return %					Annualized Total Return%			Annual Total Return %								
	1st Qrt	2nd Qrt	3rd Qrt	4th Qrt	2006	3 Yr	5 Yr	10 Yr	2005	2004	2003	2002	2001	2000	1999	1998	1997
MSCI Argentina ID	27.63	4.37	−6.72	33.65	66.07	48.93	26.30	7.86	59.68	24.57	98.53	−50.99	−22.11	−26.09	30.03	−27.28	21.84
MSCI Australia Ndtr_D	5.85	3.71	2.59	16.19	30.86	25.55	23.89	11.56	16.02	30.34	49.46	−1.34	1.76	−10.05	17.66	6.05	−10.44
MSCI Austria Ndtr_D	13.46	−2.04	3.36	18.85	36.54	42.91	39.80	15.18	24.64	71.52	56.96	16.55	−5.65	−11.93	−9.13	0.34	1.57
MSCI BRAZIL ID	20.18	−3.41	−1.70	23.15	40.52	40.10	29.87	10.71	49.96	30.49	102.85	−33.78	−21.75	−14.17	61.64	−44.11	23.46
MSCI Belgium Ndtr_D	10.52	0.84	11.34	10.13	36.66	28.84	19.74	11.53	9.05	43.53	35.33	−14.97	−10.88	−16.81	−14.26	67.66	13.55
MSCI Canada Ndtr_D	8.40	0.42	1.14	7.01	17.80	22.70	19.91	12.96	28.31	22.20	54.60	−13.19	−20.40	5.30	53.82	−6.19	12.80
MSCI EAFE Gr ND	9.01	0.26	2.31	9.40	22.33	17.18	12.27	—	13.28	16.12	31.99	−16.02	−24.54	−24.52	29.49	—	—
MSCI EAFE NDTR_D	9.40	0.70	3.93	10.35	26.34	19.93	14.98	7.71	13.54	20.25	38.59	−15.94	−21.42	−14.19	27.03	19.93	1.78
MSCI EAFE Val ND	9.77	1.13	5.53	11.29	30.38	22.64	17.65	—	13.80	24.33	45.30	−15.91	−18.52	−3.16	24.14	—	—
MSCI EM ID	11.51	−5.11	4.10	17.28	29.18	27.26	23.52	6.73	30.31	22.45	51.59	−7.97	−4.68	−31.90	64.09	−27.67	−13.45
MSCI EMU ID	12.66	−0.44	6.13	11.73	33.00	18.80	12.45	9.13	6.22	18.68	39.88	−23.34	−23.42	−9.84	17.68	37.82	19.00
MSCI France Ndtr_D	13.23	2.50	4.87	10.49	34.48	20.53	14.11	11.40	9.88	18.48	40.22	−21.18	−22.34	−4.32	29.31	41.48	11.94
MSCI Germany Ndtr_D	13.80	−0.34	4.84	14.37	35.99	20.20	13.70	9.19	9.92	16.17	63.80	−33.18	−22.38	−15.61	20.08	29.41	24.57
MSCI Hong Kong Ndtr_D	7.09	−0.07	6.34	14.54	30.35	20.87	14.93	5.15	8.40	24.98	38.10	−17.79	−18.61	−14.43	59.44	−3.23	−23.29
MSCI Italy Ndtr_D	8.73	4.21	4.46	11.95	32.49	21.39	17.97	13.05	1.90	32.48	37.83	−7.33	−26.53	−1.27	−0.13	52.11	35.48
MSCI Japan NDTR_D	6.78	−4.56	−0.72	5.01	6.24	15.61	13.51	2.15	25.52	15.86	35.91	−10.28	−29.39	−28.17	61.53	5.05	−23.67
MSCI KOREA ID	3.97	−3.07	5.34	4.75	11.20	27.20	24.00	12.15	54.28	19.96	32.60	7.43	47.23	−50.63	90.36	137.14	−67.29
MSCI MALYSI ID	7.88	−1.92	5.01	19.79	33.11	13.59	11.93	−3.95	−1.52	11.81	23.12	−2.66	2.71	−17.53	113.19	−32.59	−68.75
MSCI MEXICO ID	6.91	−4.74	15.66	18.04	39.04	43.05	26.42	17.95	45.22	44.98	29.82	−15.04	16.00	−21.54	78.56	−34.52	51.71
MSCI Netherlands Ndtr_D	11.63	−0.82	10.75	7.14	31.38	18.85	11.23	7.56	13.85	12.24	28.09	−20.83	−22.09	−4.08	6.91	23.17	23.77
MSCI Pacific ex Japan ID	5.69	1.42	2.99	15.98	28.03	20.71	17.72	3.35	10.23	24.63	41.26	−9.00	−12.13	−17.42	39.33	−9.56	−32.74
MSCI Singapore Ndtr_D	11.07	0.25	6.86	23.30	46.71	27.07	20.22	5.38	14.37	22.27	37.60	−11.05	−23.41	−27.46	99.58	−13.28	−30.05
MSCI South Africa ID	17.37	−15.56	−7.35	27.70	17.25	26.94	28.67	8.12	24.03	40.67	39.88	23.26	−19.98	−19.90	54.33	−30.22	−10.34
MSCI Spain Ndtr_D	12.76	3.30	12.20	14.27	49.36	26.21	21.97	14.77	4.41	28.93	58.46	−15.29	−11.33	−15.80	4.77	49.83	25.41
MSCI Sweden Ndtr_D	14.23	−2.03	6.88	19.87	43.39	29.17	19.77	12.57	10.31	36.28	64.53	−30.49	−27.18	−21.40	79.94	13.99	12.92
MSCI Switzerland Ndtr_D	7.10	2.66	7.44	7.85	27.40	19.44	15.43	10.94	16.33	14.96	34.08	−10.31	−21.37	6.04	−7.04	23.33	44.25
MSCI Taiwan ID	2.62	0.17	0.18	12.94	16.30	8.57	5.98	−1.24	3.28	6.54	40.01	−25.38	9.19	−45.43	51.52	−21.43	−6.96
MSCI United Kingd Ndtr_D	8.28	4.92	4.24	10.28	30.61	18.80	13.42	8.77	7.35	19.57	32.06	−15.23	−14.04	−11.66	12.44	17.97	22.62
S&P Global 100	4.61	0.52	6.32	7.70	20.42	11.84	6.95	8.82	5.47	10.15	30.93	−23.59	−14.02	−14.33	25.84	34.69	33.29

NDTR_D=the index is listed in US dollars, with net dividends reinvested.   ID=the index is listed in dollars, without net dividends reinvested.   TR=Total Return

Largest & Smallest ETFs

Morningstar's ETF Universe

Largest ETFs

Page	Name	Assets ($mil)
	Domestic ETFs	
139	SPDR Trust Series 1	63997.00
95	iShares S&P 500	17982.00
112	Nasdaq 100 Trust	17957.00
83	iShares R2000 Index	12392.00
81	iShares R1000 Value	9177.00
111	MidCap SPDR Trust	8558.00
49	iShares DJ Sel Dividend	7770.00
79	iShares R1000 Growth	7675.00
173	Vanguard TSM ETF	6885.00
42	DIAMONDS Trust	6733.00
65	iShares Lehman 1-3 T	5662.00
68	iShares Lehman Aggregate	4913.00
108	iShares SP Small 600	4660.00
96	iShares SP 500 Value	4530.00
84	iShares R2000 Value	4375.00
94	iShares SP 500 Growth	4360.00
105	iShares SP MidCap400	4189.00
43	Energy SPDR	3808.00
92	iShares S&P 100 Ind.	3182.00
80	iShares R1000 Index	3051.00
	International ETFs	
71	iShares MSCI EAFE	37076.00
73	iShares MSCI Emerg Mkts	15694.00
75	iShares Japan Index	13787.00
151	streetTRACKS Gold Shares	9261.00
59	iShares FTSE/Xinhua China	5696.00
—	iShares Brazil Index	2958.00
76	iShares MSCI ex-Japn	2497.00
97	iShares S&P Euro-350	2384.00
74	iShares EMU Index	2221.00
—	iShares Taiwan Index	2146.00
157	Vanguard EmergMkts ETF	2055.00
—	iShares S.Korea Indx	1619.00
—	iShares SP Latin 40	1580.00
110	iShares Silver Trust	1562.00
159	Vanguard Euro Stk ETF	1507.00
—	iShares Hong Kong	1359.00
—	iShares Mexico Index	1317.00
—	iShares Canada Index	1076.00
—	iShares Singapore	1074.00
—	iShares U.K. Index	992.00

Smallest ETFs

Page	Name	Assets ($mil)
	Domestic ETFs	
—	Rydex S&P EqWght Util	3.00
—	WisdomTree Intl Financial	5.00
—	WisdomTree Intl Tech	5.00
—	Rydex S&P EqWght Financls	5.00
—	Rydex S&P EqWght Material	5.00
—	WisdomTree Intl Comm	6.00
—	Rydex S&P EqWght Cons Stp	7.00
—	Rydex S&P EqWght Tech	7.00
136	Rydex S&P Smallcap 600 Gr	8.00
—	Rydex S&P EqWght Energy	8.00
—	Rydex S&P EqWght HlthCare	8.00
—	Rydex S&P EqWght Industr	8.00
146	streetTRACKS DJ Mid Value	9.00
—	CurrencyShares Mex Peso	9.00
137	Rydex S&P Smallcap 600 Va	10.00
141	streetTRACKS DJ Large Cap	13.00
—	PowerShares Dyn Building	15.00
—	PowerShares Dyn Cons Stpl	15.00
—	PowerShares Dyn Health	15.00
—	PowerShares Dyn Indust	15.00
	International ETFs	
—	WisdomTree Intl Basic Mat	6.00
—	WisdomTree Intl Con Cycl	6.00
—	WisdomTree Intl Indust	6.00
—	streetTRACKS Rus/Nom SmJp	8.00
—	WisdomTree Intl Con NonCy	21.00
180	WisdomTree Eur Total Div	25.00
184	WisdomTree Japan Tot Div	27.00
—	iShares SP Glb Cons Stpls	27.00
—	iShares SP Glb Industrial	28.00
—	iShares SP Glb Materials	28.00
—	WisdomTree Japan HiYld Eq	29.00
—	iShares SP Glb Cons Discr	29.00
—	WisdomTree Japan SmCp Div	30.00
188	WisdomTree Pac ex-Jp TDiv	31.00
—	WisdomTree Eur SmCap Div	33.00
179	WisdomTree Euro Hi-Yld Eq	37.00
—	BLDRS Europe 100 ADR	39.00
183	WisdomTree Intl LgCap Div	43.00
187	WisdomTree Pac ex-Jp HYEq	49.00
—	WisdomTree Intl MdCap Div	57.00

Best & Worst Performing ETFs

Morningstar's ETF Universe

Best Performing

Page	Name	Market Return %*
	One Year (12-29-2006)	
59	iShares FTSE/Xinhua China	83.17
123	PowerShares Halter USX	53.32
0	iShares Spain Index	49.25
0	iShares Singapore	45.79
0	iShares Mexico Index	44.84
0	iShares Sweden Index	43.73
0	iShares Brazil Index	43.30
0	iShares SP Latin 40	41.06
47	iShares C&S Realty	38.52
0	BLDRS Emerg Mkts 50 ADR	37.54
0	iShares Austria Index	36.76
172	Vanguard TelcomSrv ETF	36.70
0	iShares Malaysia	36.35
0	iSharcs Belgium Indx	35.62
153	streetTRACKS DJ REIT	35.53
	Three Year (12-29-2006)	
0	iShares Mexico Index	45.85
0	iShares SP Latin 40	44.56
0	iShares Brazil Index	42.98
0	iShares Austria Index	42.07
43	Energy SPDR	30.39
0	BLDRS Emerg Mkts 50 ADR	29.96
73	iShares MSCI Emerg Mkts	29.43
0	iShares MSCI South Africa	29.34
0	iShares Sweden Index	28.97
47	iShares C&S Realty	28.81
50	iShares DJ US Energy	28.69
0	iShares Belgium Indx	28.65
0	iShares Singapore	27.40
0	iShares Spain Index	26.63
153	streetTRACKS DJ REIT	26.62
	Five Year (12-29-2006)	
0	iShares Austria Index	40.07
0	iShares Brazil Index	32.15
0	iShares SP Latin 40	31.06
0	iShares Mexico Index	29.75
47	iShares C&S Realty	24.72
0	iShares Australia	24.31
0	iShares S.Korea Indx	23.40
153	streetTRACKS DJ REIT	23.08
0	iShares Spain Index	22.55
0	iShares Belgium Indx	22.31
76	iShares MSCI ex-Japn	21.85
54	iShares DJ RE Index	21.78
0	iShares Singapore	20.51
0	iShares Sweden Index	20.23
0	iShares Canada Index	20.11

Worst Performing

Page	Name	Market Return %*
	One Year (12-29-2006)	
61	iShares Semiconductor	0.23
69	iShares Lehman TIPS Bond	0.28
77	iShares NASD Biotech	0.67
66	iShares Lehman 20+	0.71
0	PowerShares Dyn Building	1.63
0	PowerShares Dyn Bio&Genom	2.31
67	iShares Lehman 7-10	2.52
0	iShares GS Network	3.77
65	iShares Lehman 1-3 T	3.89
68	iShares Lehman Aggregate	3.90
63	iShares iBoxx$ Corp Bd	4.22
127	PowerShares Val Line Time	4.58
0	PowerShares Dyn Semicond	4.63
0	PowerShares Lux Nanotech	5.06
120	PowerShares Dyn Sm Growth	5.19
	Three Year (12-29-2006)	
61	iShares Semiconductor	−0.86
65	iShares Lehman 1-3 T	2.02
77	iShares NASD Biotech	2.62
67	iShares Lehman 7-10	3.09
68	iShares Lehman Aggregate	3.31
69	iShares Lehman TIPS Bond	3.63
63	iShares iBoxx$ Corp Bd	3.68
62	iShares GS Tech	4.22
55	iShares DJ Tech	4.53
46	Health Care Sel SPDR	4.88
0	iShares GS Network	5.23
102	iShares SP Glb Tech	5.30
143	streetTRACKS DJ Lg Growth	5.63
154	Technology SPDR	5.71
0	iShares GS Software	5.90
	Five Year (12-29-2006)	
77	iShares NASD Biotech	−3.11
61	iShares Semiconductor	−1.67
0	iShares GS Software	−0.30
154	Technology SPDR	0.25
62	iShares GS Tech	0.48
143	streetTRACKS DJ Lg Growth	0.52
55	iShares DJ Tech	0.82
0	iShares GS Network	0.94
56	iShares DJ Telecom	1.18
102	iShares SP Glb Tech	1.19
53	iShares DJ Health	2.10
0	streetTRACKS MS Tech	2.13
112	Nasdaq 100 Trust	2.39
0	Consumer Staple SPDR	2.40
79	iShares R1000 Growth	2.49

* Three- and five-year returns are annualized.

Most & Least Costly ETFs

Morningstar's ETF Universe

Highest Expense Ratio

Page	Name	Expense Ratio %
—	iShares Taiwan Index	0.85
73	iShares MSCI Emerg Mkts	0.77
122	PowerShares FTSE RAFI1000	0.76
129	PowerShares Zacks Sm Cap	0.75
59	iShares FTSE/Xinhua China	0.74
—	PowerShares Lux Nanotech	0.73
128	PowerShares Zacks MicroCp	0.72
123	PowerShares Halter USX	0.71
—	PowerShares WilderHill	0.71
127	PowerShares Val Line Time	0.71
—	iShares S.Korea Indx	0.70
—	iShares Brazil Index	0.70
—	iShares MSCI South Africa	0.70
—	PowerShares Dyn Retail	0.70
—	PowerShares Dyn Food&Bev	0.69
—	PowerShares Dyn Utilities	0.69
—	PowerShares Dyn Leisr&Ent	0.68
—	PowerShares Dyn Media	0.68
—	PowerShares Dyn Network	0.68
—	PowerShares Aero&Defense	0.68

Lowest Expense Ratio

Page	Name	Expense Ratio %
173	Vanguard TSM ETF	0.07
165	Vanguard Large Cap ETF	0.07
160	Vanguard ExMkt ETF	0.08
139	SPDR Trust Series 1	0.10
95	iShares S&P 500	0.10
169	Vanguard Small Cap ETF	0.10
175	Vanguard Value ETF	0.11
162	Vanguard Growth ETF	0.11
170	Vanguard Sm Cap Gr ETF	0.12
171	Vanguard Sm Cp Val ETF	0.12
168	Vanguard REIT Index ETF	0.12
166	Vanguard Mid Cap ETF	0.13
80	iShares R1000 Index	0.15
65	iShares Lehman 1-3 T	0.15
67	iShares Lehman 7-10	0.15
66	iShares Lehman 20+	0.15
63	iShares iBoxx$ Corp Bd	0.15
42	DIAMONDS Trust	0.18
94	iShares SP 500 Growth	0.18
96	iShares SP 500 Value	0.18

Highest Tax Cost Ratio

Page	Name	Tax Cost Ratio %
63	iShares iBoxx$ Corp Bd	1.67
66	iShares Lehman 20+	1.61
153	streetTRACKS DJ REIT	1.59
69	iShares Lehman TIPS Bond	1.57
54	iShares DJ RE Index	1.50
47	iShares C&S Realty	1.42
68	iShares Lehman Aggregate	1.41
67	iShares Lehman 7-10	1.37
—	iShares Australia	1.32
148	streetTRACKS DJ Small Val	1.30
76	iShares MSCI ex-Japn	1.28
—	iShares Singapore	1.18
155	Utilities SPDR	1.16
49	iShares DJ Sel Dividend	1.12
65	iShares Lehman 1-3 T	1.06
150	streetTRACKS DJ STOXX 50	1.02
58	iShares DJ Utilities	1.01
—	iShares Malaysia	0.98
—	iShares U.K. Index	0.97
56	iShares DJ Telecom	0.94

Lowest Tax Cost Ratio

Page	Name	Tax Cost Ratio %
77	iShares NASD Biotech	0.00
—	iShares GS Network	0.00
119	PowerShares Dyn OTC	0.02
61	iShares Semiconductor	0.03
—	streetTRACKS MS Tech	0.04
—	iShares GS Software	0.07
62	iShares GS Tech	0.11
149	streetTRACK DJ Small Gr	0.12
—	iShares DJ Cons Services	0.13
82	iShares R2000 Growth	0.13
107	iShares SP 600 Growth	0.15
—	iShares SP TOPIX 150	0.15
112	Nasdaq 100 Trust	0.17
104	iShares SP 400 Growth	0.17
102	iShares SP Glb Tech	0.17
75	iShares Japan Index	0.18
—	iShares S.Korea Indx	0.19
89	iShares R. Midcap Gr	0.19
—	iShares Dow Jones TransAv	0.19
55	iShares DJ Tech	0.20

Most & Least Concentrated ETFs

Morningstar's ETF Universe

Highest % of Assets in Top 10 Holdings

Page	Name	%
41	PowerShares DB Com Idx Fd	88.47
—	iShares Belgium Indx	81.62
—	iShares Austria Index	80.88
56	iShares DJ Telecom	77.73
—	iShares Spain Index	77.60
—	iShares Mexico Index	77.38
—	iShares Netherlands	75.23
—	PowerShares Dyn Network	72.63
—	iShares Switzerland	72.38
—	iShares Singapore	71.86
50	iShares DJ US Energy	71.06
—	First Trust DJ Intrnt Idx	70.62
—	Market Vectors Gld Miners	70.01
—	iShares Italy Index	69.70
43	Energy SPDR	68.35
—	PowerShares FTSE RAFI Ene	68.27
—	iShares GS Network	68.13
—	iShares Brazil Index	67.57
—	Consumer Staple SPDR	67.17
—	iShares DJ US Health Prov	66.88

Lowest % of Assets in Top 10 Holdings

Page	Name	%
83	iShares R2000 Index	1.99
147	streetTRACKS DJ Small Cap	2.00
169	Vanguard Small Cap ETF	2.31
133	Rydex S&P Equal Weight	2.50
—	PowerShares FTSE RAFI1500	2.62
88	iShares Russell Microcap	2.68
84	iShares R2000 Value	3.30
82	iShares R2000 Growth	3.47
128	PowerShares Zacks MicroCp	3.64
148	streetTRACKS DJ Small Val	3.79
171	Vanguard Sm Cp Val ETF	3.91
149	streetTRACK DJ Small Gr	3.97
144	streetTRACKS DJ Mid Cap	3.98
170	Vanguard Sm Cap Gr ETF	4.38
90	iShares R. Midcap	4.49
160	Vanguard ExMkt ETF	4.97
129	PowerShares Zacks Sm Cap	5.17
108	iShares SP Small 600	5.41
166	Vanguard Mid Cap ETF	5.73
—	iShares MstarSmallCore	5.83

Most Total Holdings

Page	Name	# of Holdings
173	Vanguard TSM ETF	3746.00
160	Vanguard ExMkt ETF	3394.00
86	iShares R3000 Index	2962.00
—	Fidelity Nasdaq Comp Trac	2031.00
85	iShares R3000 Growth	1977.00
83	iShares R2000 Index	1975.00
87	iShares R3000 Value	1924.00
147	streetTRACKS DJ Small Cap	1748.00
169	Vanguard Small Cap ETF	1735.00
57	iShares DJ Total Mkt	1633.00
93	iShares S&P 1500 Index	1500.00
—	iShares NYSE Composite	1495.00
88	iShares Russell Microcap	1453.00
—	PowerShares FTSE RAFI1500	1360.00
84	iShares R2000 Value	1314.00
82	iShares R2000 Growth	1294.00
80	iShares R1000 Index	988.00
122	PowerShares FTSE RAFI1000	987.00
152	streetTRACKS Total Market	983.00
171	Vanguard Sm Cp Val ETF	978.00

Fewest Total Holdings

Page	Name	# of Holdings
—	United States Oil	3.00
41	PowerShares DB Com Idx Fd	7.00
—	First Trust AMEX Bio Indx	20.00
—	SPDR Pharmaceuticals	21.00
—	SPDR Homebuilders	22.00
—	iShares Dow Jones TransAv	23.00
—	SPDR Semiconductor	23.00
—	iShares Dow Jones US Home	23.00
—	iShares Belgium Indx	24.00
—	iShares Austria Index	25.00
—	PowerShares Lux Nanotech	25.00
—	streetTRACKS KBW Bank ETF	25.00
—	streetTRACKS KBWInsurance	25.00
—	streetTRACKS KBW Cap Mkt	25.00
56	iShares DJ Telecom	27.00
59	iShares FTSE/Xinhua China	27.00
—	SPDR Metals & Mining	27.00
—	iShares Netherlands	28.00
—	iShares Dow Jones US BrDl	28.00
—	SPDR Oil&Gas Equip & Serv	28.00

Most & Least Volatile ETFs

Morningstar's ETF Universe

Highest Standard Deviation

Page	Name	Standard Deviation
—	iShares GS Network	29.02
—	iShares Brazil Index	29.01
—	iShares MSCI South Africa	25.91
61	iShares Semiconductor	23.00
—	iShares SP Latin 40	21.68
—	iShares S.Korea Indx	21.19
43	Energy SPDR	19.76
50	iShares DJ US Energy	19.10
60	iShares GS Nat Res	18.99
—	BLDRS Emerg Mkts 50 ADR	18.77
—	iShares Mexico Index	18.76
73	iShares MSCI Emerg Mkts	18.22
—	iShares Taiwan Index	18.18
99	iShares SP Glb Enrgy	17.80
47	iShares C&S Realty	17.22
—	iShares GS Software	17.09
—	streetTRACKS MS Tech	16.94
153	streetTRACKS DJ REIT	16.67
54	iShares DJ RE Index	16.36
62	iShares GS Tech	16.12

Lowest Standard Deviation

Page	Name	Standard Deviation
65	iShares Lehman 1-3 T	1.27
68	iShares Lehman Aggregate	3.28
63	iShares iBoxx$ Corp Bd	4.86
69	iShares Lehman TIPS Bond	5.21
67	iShares Lehman 7-10	5.24
142	streetTracks DJ Lg Value	6.16
140	streetTRACK Global T	6.34
92	iShares S&P 100 Ind.	6.54
49	iShares DJ Sel Dividend	6.64
—	Consumer Staple SPDR	6.71
81	iShares R1000 Value	6.76
96	iShares SP 500 Value	6.82
139	SPDR Trust Series 1	6.90
95	iShares S&P 500	6.91
152	streetTRACKS Total Market	6.94
87	iShares R3000 Value	7.09
80	iShares R1000 Index	7.13
42	DIAMONDS Trust	7.14
101	iShares SP Glb Hlth	7.40
57	iShares DJ Total Mkt	7.48

Highest Beta

Page	Name	Beta
—	iShares GS Network	3.00
61	iShares Semiconductor	2.69
66	iShares Lehman 20+	2.63
—	iShares MSCI South Africa	2.36
—	iShares Brazil Index	2.15
—	streetTRACKS MS Tech	2.12
62	iShares GS Tech	2.03
82	iShares R2000 Growth	1.99
55	iShares DJ Tech	1.93
—	iShares GS Software	1.88
112	Nasdaq 100 Trust	1.83
102	iShares SP Glb Tech	1.82
—	iShares SP Latin 40	1.79
83	iShares R2000 Index	1.76
119	PowerShares Dyn OTC	1.76
—	Fidelity Nasdaq Comp Trac	1.74
73	iShares MSCI Emerg Mkts	1.71
—	BLDRS Emerg Mkts 50 ADR	1.68
154	Technology SPDR	1.65
149	streetTRACK DJ Small Gr	1.60

Lowest Beta

Page	Name	Beta
155	Utilities SPDR	0.27
65	iShares Lehman 1-3 T	0.34
58	iShares DJ Utilities	0.37
—	Consumer Staple SPDR	0.48
101	iShares SP Glb Hlth	0.50
140	streetTRACK Global T	0.54
46	Health Care Sel SPDR	0.60
53	iShares DJ Health	0.62
—	iShares Malaysia	0.67
98	iShares S&P Glb 100	0.71
56	iShares DJ Telecom	0.72
—	iShares Singapore	0.73
49	iShares DJ Sel Dividend	0.76
52	iShares DJ Fin Svcs	0.78
—	iShares U.K. Index	0.79
142	streetTracks DJ Lg Value	0.81
44	Financial SPDR	0.82
—	iShares Switzerland	0.84
150	streetTRACKS DJ STOXX 50	0.86
—	iShares DJ Consumer Goods	0.88

New ETFs in 2006

Morningstar's ETF Universe

Page	Name	Category	Inception Date	Ticker	Family	Phone	Web Address
—	Claymore MACRO Oil Dn Tr	SN	11/29/2006	DCR	Claymore Securities	866-889-3828	www.claymore.com
—	Claymore MACRO Oil Up Tr	SN	11/29/2006	UCR	Claymore Securities	866-889-3828	www.claymore.com
—	Claymore/BNY BRIC ETF	FB	09/21/2006	EEB	Claymore Securities	800-345-7999	www.claymore.com
—	Claymore/Sabrient Ins ETF	MB	09/21/2006	NFO	Claymore Securities	800-345-7999	www.claymore.com
—	Claymore/Sabrient Stealth	SB	09/21/2006	STH	Claymore Securities	800-345-7999	www.claymore.com
—	Claymore/Zacks Sector ETF	LB	09/21/2006	XRO	Claymore Securities	800-345-7999	www.claymore.com
—	Claymore/Zacks Yld Hog	LB	09/21/2006	CVY	Claymore Securities	800-345-7999	www.claymore.com
—	CurrencyShares Aus Dollar	IB	06/21/2006	FXA	Rydex	800-820-0888	www.currencyshares.com
—	CurrencyShares BP StrIng	IB	06/21/2006	FXB	Rydex	800-820-0888	www.currencyshares.com
—	CurrencyShares Can Dollar	IB	06/21/2006	FXC	Rydex	800-820-0888	www.currencyshares.com
—	CurrencyShares Mex Peso	IB	06/21/2006	FXM	Rydex	800-820-0888	www.currencyshares.com
—	CurrencyShares Swe Krona	IB	06/21/2006	FXS	Rydex	800-820-0888	www.currencyshares.com
—	CurrencyShares Swi Franc	IB	06/21/2006	FXF	Rydex	800-820-0888	www.currencyshares.com
—	First Tr NASDAQ-100 Eq Id	LB	04/25/2006	QQEW	First Trust	800-621-1675	www.ftportfolios.com
—	First Tr NASDAQ100 Tech	ST	04/25/2006	QTEC	First Trust	800-621-1675	www.ftportfolios.com
—	First Trust AMEX Bio Indx	SH	06/23/2006	FBT	First Trust	800-621-1675	www.ftportfolios.com
—	First Trust DJ Intrnt Idx	ST	06/23/2006	FDN	First Trust	800-621-1675	www.ftportfolios.com
—	First Trust IPOX-100 Indx	LG	04/13/2006	FPX	First Trust	800-621-1675	www.ftportfolios.com
—	First Trust MStar Div Ld	LV	03/15/2006	FDL	First Trust	800-621-1675	www.ftportfolios.com
—	iPath DJ-AIGCom Id TR ETN	SN	06/06/2006	DJP	Barclays	877-764-7284	www.ishares.com
—	iPath GS CrOil TR Idx ETN	SN	08/15/2006	OIL	Barclays	877-764-7284	www.ishares.com
—	iPath GSCI TotRet Idx ETN	SN	06/06/2006	GSP	Barclays	877-764-7284	www.ishares.com
—	iPath MSCI India Index	PJ	12/19/2006	INP	Barclays	877-764-7284	www.barclays.com
—	iShares DJ US Health Prov	SH	05/01/2006	IHF	Barclays	800-474-2737	www.ishares.com
—	iShares DJ US Medical Dev	SH	05/01/2006	IHI	Barclays	800-474-2737	www.ishares.com
—	iShares DJ US Oil & Gas	SN	05/01/2006	IEO	Barclays	800-474-2737	www.ishares.com
—	iShares DJ US Oil Equip	SN	05/01/2006	IEZ	Barclays	800-474-2737	www.ishares.com
—	iShares DJ US Pharma	SH	05/01/2006	IHE	Barclays	800-474-2737	www.ishares.com
—	iShares Dow Jones US Aero	ST	05/01/2006	ITA	Barclays	800-474-2737	www.ishares.com
—	iShares Dow Jones US BrDl	SF	05/01/2006	IAI	Barclays	800-474-2737	www.ishares.com
—	iShares Dow Jones US Home	SR	05/01/2006	ITB	Barclays	800-474-2737	www.ishares.com
—	iShares Dow Jones US Insr	SF	05/01/2006	IAK	Barclays	800-474-2737	www.ishares.com
—	iShares Dow Jones US RegB	SF	05/01/2006	IAT	Barclays	800-474-2737	www.ishares.com
—	iShares GSCI Commodity Id	SN	07/21/2006	GSG	Barclays	800-474-2737	www.ishares.com
—	iShares KLD 400 Social	LB	11/14/2006	DSI	Barclays	800-474-2737	www.ishares.com
110	iShares Silver Trust	SP	04/28/2006	SLV	Barclays	800-474-2737	www.ishares.com
—	iShares SP Glb Cons Discr	WS	09/12/2006	RXI	Barclays	800-474-2737	www.ishares.com
—	iShares SP Glb Cons Stpls	WS	09/12/2006	KXI	Barclays	800-474-2737	www.ishares.com
—	iShares SP Glb Industrial	WS	09/12/2006	EXI	Barclays	800-474-2737	www.ishares.com
—	iShares SP Glb Materials	WS	09/12/2006	MXI	Barclays	800-474-2737	www.ishares.com
—	iShares SP Glb Utilities	SU	09/12/2006	JXI	Barclays	800-474-2737	www.ishares.com
—	Market Vectors Gld Miners	SP	05/22/2006	GDX	Van Eck	888-658-8287	www.vaneck.com
41	PowerShares DB Com Idx Fd	SN	02/03/2006	DBC	Powershares	877-369-4617	www.dbfunds.db.com
—	PowerShares Dyn Cons Disc	MB	10/12/2006	PEZ	Powershares	800-843-2639	www.powershares.com
—	PowerShares Dyn Cons Stpl	LB	10/12/2006	PSL	Powershares	800-843-2639	www.powershares.com
—	PowerShares Dyn Health	SH	10/12/2006	PTH	Powershares	800-843-2639	www.powershares.com
—	PowerShares Dyn Hlth Svcs	SH	10/12/2006	PTJ	Powershares	800-843-2639	www.powershares.com
—	PowerShares Dyn Indust	MB	10/12/2006	PRN	Powershares	800-843-2639	www.powershares.com
—	PowerShares Dyn Lg Cp	LB	12/01/2006	PJF	Powershares	800-983-0903	www.powershares.com
—	PowerShares Dyn Mid Cap	MB	12/01/2006	PJG	Powershares	800-983-0903	www.powershares.com
—	PowerShares Dyn Small Cap	SB	12/01/2006	PJM	Powershares	800-983-0903	www.powershares.com
—	PowerShares Dyn Tech	ST	10/12/2006	PTF	Powershares	800-843-2639	www.powershares.com
—	PowerShares Finc Prefer	SF	12/01/2006	PGF	Powershares	800-983-0903	www.powershares.com
—	PowerShares FTSE RAFI Bas	LB	09/20/2006	PRFM	Powershares	800-983-0903	www.powershares.com
—	PowerShares FTSE RAFI CGo	LB	09/20/2006	PRFG	Powershares	800-983-0903	www.powershares.com

New ETFs in 2006

Morningstar's ETF Universe

Page	Name	Category	Inception Date	Ticker	Family	Phone	Web Address
—	PowerShares FTSE RAFI CSe	LB	09/20/2006	PRFS	Powershares	800-983-0903	www.powershares.com
—	PowerShares FTSE RAFI Ene	SN	09/20/2006	PRFE	Powershares	800-983-0903	www.powershares.com
—	PowerShares FTSE RAFI Fin	SF	09/20/2006	PRFF	Powershares	800-983-0903	www.powershares.com
—	PowerShares FTSE RAFI Hth	SH	09/20/2006	PRFH	Powershares	800-983-0903	www.powershares.com
—	PowerShares FTSE RAFI Ind	LB	09/20/2006	PRFN	Powershares	800-983-0903	www.powershares.com
—	PowerShares FTSE RAFI Tel	SC	09/20/2006	PRFQ	Powershares	800-983-0903	www.powershares.com
—	PowerShares FTSE RAFI Utl	SU	09/20/2006	PRFU	Powershares	800-983-0903	www.powershares.com
—	PowerShares FTSE RAFI1500	SB	09/20/2006	PRFZ	Powershares	800-983-0903	www.powershares.com
—	PowerShares Val Line Indu	LB	12/01/2006	PYH	Powershares	800-983-0903	www.powershares.com
129	PowerShares Zacks Sm Cap	SB	02/16/2006	PZJ	Powershares	800-843-2639	www.powershares.com
131	Rydex S&P 500 Pure Growth	LG	03/01/2006	RPG	Rydex	800-820-0888	www.rydex.com
132	Rydex S&P 500 Pure Value	LV	03/01/2006	RPV	Rydex	800-820-0888	www.rydex.com
—	Rydex S&P EqWght Cons Dis	LB	11/01/2006	RCD	Rydex	800-820-0888	www.rydex.com
—	Rydex S&P EqWght Cons Stp	LB	11/01/2006	RHS	Rydex	800-820-0888	www.rydex.com
—	Rydex S&P EqWght Energy	SN	11/01/2006	RYE	Rydex	800-820-0888	www.rydex.com
—	Rydex S&P EqWght Financls	SF	11/01/2006	RYF	Rydex	800-820-0888	www.rydex.com
—	Rydex S&P EqWght HlthCare	SH	11/01/2006	RYH	Rydex	800-820-0888	www.rydex.com
—	Rydex S&P EqWght Industr	LB	11/01/2006	RGI	Rydex	800-820-0888	www.rydex.com
—	Rydex S&P EqWght Material	LB	11/01/2006	RTM	Rydex	800-820-0888	www.rydex.com
—	Rydex S&P EqWght Tech	ST	11/01/2006	RYT	Rydex	800-820-0888	www.rydex.com
—	Rydex S&P EqWght Util	SU	11/01/2006	RYU	Rydex	800-820-0888	www.rydex.com
134	Rydex S&P Midcap 400 Gr	MG	03/01/2006	RFG	Rydex	800-820-0888	www.rydex.com
135	Rydex S&P Midcap 400 Val	MV	03/01/2006	RFV	Rydex	800-820-0888	www.rydex.com
136	Rydex S&P Smallcap 600 Gr	SG	03/01/2006	RZG	Rydex	800-820-0888	www.rydex.com
137	Rydex S&P Smallcap 600 Va	SV	03/01/2006	RZV	Rydex	800-820-0888	www.rydex.com
—	SPDR Biotech	SH	01/31/2006	XBI	State Street Global Advisors	866-787-2257	www.advisors.ssga.com
—	SPDR Homebuilders	LB	01/31/2006	XHB	State Street Global Advisors	866-787-2257	www.advisors.ssga.com
—	SPDR Metals & Mining	SN	06/22/2006	XME	State Street Global Advisors	866-787-2257	www.advisors.ssga.com
—	SPDR Oil & Gas Expl & Pro	SN	06/22/2006	XOP	State Street Global Advisors	866-787-2257	www.advisors.ssga.com
—	SPDR Oil&Gas Equip & Serv	SN	06/22/2006	XES	State Street Global Advisors	866-787-2257	www.advisors.ssga.com
—	SPDR Pharmaceuticals	SH	06/22/2006	XPH	State Street Global Advisors	866-787-2257	www.advisors.ssga.com
—	SPDR Retail	LB	06/22/2006	XRT	State Street Global Advisors	866-787-2257	www.advisors.ssga.com
—	SPDR Semiconductor	ST	01/31/2006	XSD	State Street Global Advisors	866-787-2257	www.advisors.ssga.com
—	streetTRACKS DJ Int RlEst	SR	12/19/2006	RWX	State Street Global Advisors	—	www.advisors.ssga.com
—	streetTRACKS KBW Reg Bank	SF	06/22/2006	KRE	State Street Global Advisors	866-787-2257	www.advisors.ssga.com
—	streetTRACKS Rus/Nom PRJp	JS	11/09/2006	JPP	State Street Global Advisors	866-787-2252	www.advisors.ssga.com
—	streetTRACKS Rus/Nom SmJp	JS	11/09/2006	JSC	State Street Global Advisors	866-787-2257	www.advisors.ssga.com
—	United States Oil	SN	04/10/2006	USO	United States Oil	800-920-0259	www.unitedstatesoilfund.c
156	Vanguard Div Appr ETF	LB	04/27/2006	VIG	Vanguard	866-499-8473	www.vanguard.com
—	Vanguard High Dividend Yi	LV	11/10/2006	VYM	Vanguard	866-499-8473	www.vanguard.com
—	Vanguard Mid Growth ETF	MG	08/17/2006	VOT	Vanguard	866-499-8473	www.vanguard.com
—	Vanguard Mid Value ETF	MV	08/17/2006	VOE	Vanguard	866-499-8473	www.vanguard.com
176	WisdomTree DIEFA	FB	06/16/2006	DWM	WisdomTree	866-909-9473	www.wisdomtree.com
177	WisdomTree DIEFA HiYld Eq	FB	06/16/2006	DTH	WisdomTree	866-909-9473	www.wisdomtree.com
178	WisdomTree Div Top 100	LB	06/16/2006	DTN	WisdomTree	866-909-9473	www.wisdomtree.com
—	WisdomTree Eur SmCap Div	ES	06/16/2006	DFE	WisdomTree	866-909-9473	www.wisdomtree.com
180	WisdomTree Eur Total Div	ES	06/16/2006	DEB	WisdomTree	866-909-9473	www.wisdomtree.com
179	WisdomTree Euro Hi-Yld Eq	ES	06/16/2006	DEW	WisdomTree	866-909-9473	www.wisdomtree.com
181	WisdomTree High-Yld Eqty	LB	06/16/2006	DHS	WisdomTree	866-909-9473	www.wisdomtree.com
182	WisdomTree IntDiv Top 100	FB	06/16/2006	DOO	WisdomTree	866-909-9473	www.wisdomtree.com
—	WisdomTree Intl Basic Mat	FB	10/13/2006	DBN	WisdomTree	866-909-9473	www.wisdomtree.com
—	WisdomTree Intl Comm	SC	10/13/2006	DGG	WisdomTree	866-909-9473	www.wisdomtree.com
—	WisdomTree Intl Con Cycl	FB	10/13/2006	DPC	WisdomTree	866-909-9473	www.wisdomtree.com
—	WisdomTree Intl Con NonCy	FB	10/13/2006	DPN	WisdomTree	866-909-9473	www.wisdomtree.com
—	WisdomTree Intl Energy	SN	10/13/2006	DKA	WisdomTree	866-909-9473	www.wisdomtree.com

New ETFs in 2006

Morningstar's ETF Universe

Page	Name	Category	Inception Date	Ticker	Family	Phone	Web Address
—	WisdomTree Intl Financial	SF	10/13/2006	DRF	WisdomTree	866-909-9473	www.wisdomtree.com
—	WisdomTree Intl Hlth Care	SH	10/13/2006	DBR	WisdomTree	866-909-9473	www.wisdomtree.com
—	WisdomTree Intl Indust	FB	10/13/2006	DDI	WisdomTree	866-909-9473	www.wisdomtree.com
183	WisdomTree Intl LgCap Div	FB	06/16/2006	DOL	WisdomTree	866-909-9473	www.wisdomtree.com
—	WisdomTree Intl MdCap Div	FA	06/16/2006	DIM	WisdomTree	866-909-9473	www.wisdomtree.com
—	WisdomTree Intl SmCap Div	FA	06/16/2006	DLS	WisdomTree	866-909-9473	www.wisdomtree.com
—	WisdomTree Intl Tech	ST	10/13/2006	DBT	WisdomTree	866-909-9473	www.wisdomtree.com
—	WisdomTree Intl Utilities	SU	10/13/2006	DBU	WisdomTree	866-909-9473	www.wisdomtree.com
—	WisdomTree Japan HiYld Eq	JS	06/16/2006	DNL	WisdomTree	866-909-9473	www.wisdomtree.com
—	WisdomTree Japan SmCp Div	JS	06/16/2006	DFJ	WisdomTree	866-909-9473	www.wisdomtree.com
184	WisdomTree Japan Tot Div	JS	06/16/2006	DXJ	WisdomTree	866-909-9473	www.wisdomtree.com
185	WisdomTree LargeCap Div	LB	06/16/2006	DLN	WisdomTree	866-909-9473	www.wisdomtree.com
186	WisdomTree MidCap Div	MB	06/16/2006	DON	WisdomTree	866-909-9473	www.wisdomtree.com
187	WisdomTree Pac ex-Jp HYEq	DP	06/16/2006	DNH	WisdomTree	866-909-9473	www.wisdomtree.com
188	WisdomTree Pac ex-Jp TDiv	DP	06/16/2006	DND	WisdomTree	866-909-9473	www.wisdomtree.com
189	WisdomTree SmallCap Div	SB	06/16/2006	DES	WisdomTree	866-909-9473	www.wisdomtree.com
190	WisdomTree Total Dividend	LB	06/16/2006	DTD	WisdomTree	866-909-9473	www.wisdomtree.com

ETFs by Family

Morningstar's ETF Universe

ETF Family	Page	Name	Ticker	Category	Inception Date	Expense Ratio %
BLDRS	—	BLDRS Asia 50 ADR Index	ADRA	DP	11/08/2002	0.30
	—	BLDRS Dev Mkts 100 ADR	ADRD	FB	11/08/2002	0.30
	—	BLDRS Emerg Mkts 50 ADR	ADRE	EM	11/08/2002	0.30
	—	BLDRS Europe 100 ADR	ADRU	ES	11/08/2002	0.30
Barclays	—	iPath DJ-AIGCom Id TR ETN	DJP	SN	06/06/2006	—
	—	iPath GS CrOil TR Idx ETN	OIL	SN	08/15/2006	—
	—	iPath GSCI TotRet Idx ETN	GSP	SN	06/06/2006	—
	—	iPath MSCI India Index	INP	PJ	12/19/2006	—
	—	iShares Australia	EWA	PJ	03/12/1996	0.54
	—	iShares Austria Index	EWO	ES	03/12/1996	0.54
	—	iShares Belgium Indx	EWK	ES	03/12/1996	0.54
	—	iShares Brazil Index	EWZ	LS	07/10/2000	0.70
	47	iShares C&S Realty	ICF	SR	01/29/2001	0.35
	—	iShares Canada Index	EWC	FV	03/12/1996	0.54
	48	iShares COMEX Gold Trust	IAU	SP	01/21/2005	0.40
	—	iShares DJ BMaterial	IYM	LV	06/12/2000	0.60
	—	iShares DJ Cons Services	IYC	LG	06/12/2000	0.60
	—	iShares DJ Consumer Goods	IYK	LB	06/12/2000	0.60
	51	iShares DJ Fin Sectr	IYF	SF	05/22/2000	0.60
	52	iShares DJ Fin Svcs	IYG	SF	06/12/2000	0.60
	53	iShares DJ Health	IYH	SH	06/12/2000	0.60
	—	iShares DJ Industry	IYJ	LB	06/12/2000	0.60
	54	iShares DJ RE Index	IYR	SR	06/12/2000	0.60
	49	iShares DJ Sel Dividend	DVY	LV	11/03/2003	0.40
	55	iShares DJ Tech	IYW	ST	05/15/2000	0.60
	56	iShares DJ Telecom	IYZ	SC	05/22/2000	0.60
	57	iShares DJ Total Mkt	IYY	LB	06/12/2000	0.20
	50	iShares DJ US Energy	IYE	SN	06/12/2000	0.60
	—	iShares DJ US Health Prov	IHF	SH	05/01/2006	—
	—	iShares DJ US Medical Dev	IHI	SH	05/01/2006	—
	—	iShares DJ US Oil & Gas	IEO	SN	05/01/2006	—
	—	iShares DJ US Oil Equip	IEZ	SN	05/01/2006	—
	—	iShares DJ US Pharma	IHE	SH	05/01/2006	—
	58	iShares DJ Utilities	IDU	SU	06/12/2000	0.60
	—	iShares Dow Jones TransAv	IYT	MB	10/06/2003	0.60
	—	iShares Dow Jones US Aero	ITA	ST	05/01/2006	—
	—	iShares Dow Jones US BrDl	IAI	SF	05/01/2006	—
	—	iShares Dow Jones US Home	ITB	SR	05/01/2006	—
	—	iShares Dow Jones US Insr	IAK	SF	05/01/2006	—
	—	iShares Dow Jones US RegB	IAT	SF	05/01/2006	—
	74	iShares EMU Index	EZU	ES	07/25/2000	0.54
	—	iShares France Index	EWQ	ES	03/12/1996	0.54
	59	iShares FTSE/Xinhua China	FXI	PJ	10/05/2004	0.74
	—	iShares Germany Indx	EWG	ES	03/12/1996	0.54
	60	iShares GS Nat Res	IGE	SN	10/22/2001	0.50
	—	iShares GS Network	IGN	ST	07/10/2001	0.50
	—	iShares GS Software	IGV	ST	07/10/2001	0.50
	62	iShares GS Tech	IGM	ST	03/13/2001	0.50
	—	iShares GSCI Commodity Id	GSG	SN	07/21/2006	—
	—	iShares Hong Kong	EWH	PJ	03/12/1996	0.54
	63	iShares iBoxx$ Corp Bd	LQD	CL	07/22/2002	0.15
	—	iShares Italy Index	EWI	ES	03/12/1996	0.54
	75	iShares Japan Index	EWJ	JS	03/12/1996	0.54
	—	iShares KLD 400 Social	DSI	LB	11/14/2006	—
	64	iShares KLD Sel Soc Idx	KLD	LB	01/24/2005	0.50
	65	iShares Lehman 1-3 T	SHY	GS	07/22/2002	0.15
	66	iShares Lehman 20+	TLT	GL	07/22/2002	0.15
	67	iShares Lehman 7-10	IEF	GL	07/22/2002	0.15
	68	iShares Lehman Aggregate	AGG	CI	09/22/2003	0.20
	69	iShares Lehman TIPS Bond	TIP	IP	12/04/2003	0.20
	—	iShares Malaysia	EWM	PJ	03/12/1996	0.54
	—	iShares Mexico Index	EWW	LS	03/12/1996	0.54
	71	iShares MSCI EAFE	EFA	FB	08/14/2001	0.35

Disclosure: Barclays Global Investors (BGI), which is owned by Barclays, currently licenses Morningstar's 16 style-based indexes for use in BGI's iShares exchange-traded funds. iShares are not sponsored, issued, or sold by Morningstar. Morningstar does not make any representation regarding the advisability of investing in iShares that are based on Morningstar indexes.

ETFs by Family

Morningstar's ETF Universe

ETF Family	Page	Name	Ticker	Category	Inception Date	Expense Ratio %
	70	iShares MSCI EAFE Growth	EFG	FG	08/01/2005	0.40
	72	iShares MSCI EAFE Value	EFV	FV	08/01/2005	0.40
	73	iShares MSCI Emerg Mkts	EEM	EM	04/07/2003	0.77
	76	iShares MSCI ex-Japn	EPP	PJ	10/25/2001	0.50
	—	iShares MSCI South Africa	EZA	EM	02/03/2003	0.70
	—	iShares MstarLargeCore	JKD	LB	06/28/2004	0.20
	—	iShares MstarLargeGrowth	JKE	LG	06/28/2004	0.25
	—	iShares MstarLargeValue	JKF	LV	06/28/2004	0.25
	—	iShares MstarMidCore	JKG	MB	06/28/2004	0.25
	—	iShares MstarMidGrowth	JKH	MG	06/28/2004	0.30
	—	iShares MstarMidValue	JKI	MV	06/28/2004	0.30
	—	iShares MstarSmallCore	JKJ	SB	06/28/2004	0.25
	—	iShares MstarSmallGrowth	JKK	SG	06/28/2004	0.30
	—	iShares MstarSmallValue	JKL	SV	06/28/2004	0.30
	77	iShares NASD Biotech	IBB	SH	02/05/2001	0.50
	—	iShares Netherlands	EWN	ES	03/12/1996	0.54
	78	iShares NYSE 100 Index	NY	LV	03/29/2004	0.20
	—	iShares NYSE Composite	NYC	LB	03/30/2004	0.25
	90	iShares R. Midcap	IWR	MB	07/17/2001	0.20
	89	iShares R. Midcap Gr	IWP	MG	07/17/2001	0.25
	91	iShares R. Midcap Vl	IWS	MV	07/17/2001	0.25
	79	iShares R1000 Growth	IWF	LG	05/22/2000	0.20
	80	iShares R1000 Index	IWB	LB	05/15/2000	0.15
	81	iShares R1000 Value	IWD	LV	05/22/2000	0.20
	82	iShares R2000 Growth	IWO	SG	07/24/2000	0.25
	83	iShares R2000 Index	IWM	SB	05/22/2000	0.20
	84	iShares R2000 Value	IWN	SV	07/24/2000	0.25
	85	iShares R3000 Growth	IWZ	LG	07/24/2000	0.25
	86	iShares R3000 Index	IWV	LB	05/22/2000	0.20
	87	iShares R3000 Value	IWW	LV	07/24/2000	0.25
	88	iShares Russell Microcap	IWC	SB	08/12/2005	0.60
	92	iShares S&P 100 Ind.	OEF	LB	10/23/2000	0.20
	93	iShares S&P 1500 Index	ISI	LB	01/20/2004	0.20
	95	iShares S&P 500	IVV	LB	05/15/2000	0.10
	97	iShares S&P Euro-350	IEV	ES	07/25/2000	0.60
	98	iShares S&P Glb 100	IOO	WS	12/05/2000	0.40
	—	iShares S.Korea Indx	EWY	PJ	05/09/2000	0.70
	61	iShares Semiconductor	IGW	ST	07/10/2001	0.50
	110	iShares Silver Trust	SLV	SP	04/28/2006	—
	—	iShares Singapore	EWS	PJ	03/12/1996	0.54
	104	iShares SP 400 Growth	IJK	MG	07/24/2000	0.25
	106	iShares SP 400 Value	IJJ	MV	07/24/2000	0.25
	94	iShares SP 500 Growth	IVW	LG	05/22/2000	0.18
	96	iShares SP 500 Value	IVE	LV	05/22/2000	0.18
	107	iShares SP 600 Growth	IJT	SG	07/24/2000	0.25
	109	iShares SP 600 Value	IJS	SV	07/24/2000	0.25
	—	iShares SP Glb Cons Discr	RXI	WS	09/12/2006	—
	—	iShares SP Glb Cons Stpls	KXI	WS	09/12/2006	—
	99	iShares SP Glb Enrgy	IXC	SN	11/12/2001	0.65
	100	iShares SP Glb Fincl	IXG	SF	11/12/2001	0.65
	101	iShares SP Glb Hlth	IXJ	SH	11/13/2001	0.65
	—	iShares SP Glb Industrial	EXI	WS	09/12/2006	—
	—	iShares SP Glb Materials	MXI	WS	09/12/2006	—
	102	iShares SP Glb Tech	IXN	ST	11/12/2001	0.66
	103	iShares SP Glb Tele	IXP	SC	11/12/2001	0.65
	—	iShares SP Glb Utilities	JXI	SU	09/12/2006	—
	—	iShares SP Latin 40	ILF	LS	10/25/2001	0.50
	105	iShares SP MidCap400	IJH	MB	05/22/2000	0.20
	108	iShares SP Small 600	IJR	SB	05/22/2000	0.20
	—	iShares SP TOPIX 150	ITF	JS	10/23/2001	0.50
	—	iShares Spain Index	EWP	ES	03/12/1996	0.54
	—	iShares Sweden Index	EWD	ES	03/12/1996	0.54
	—	iShares Switzerland	EWL	ES	03/12/1996	0.54
	—	iShares Taiwan Index	EWT	PJ	06/20/2000	0.85
	—	iShares U.K. Index	EWU	ES	03/12/1996	0.54

ETFs by Family

Morningstar's ETF Universe

ETF Family	Page	Name	Ticker	Category	Inception Date	Expense Ratio %
Claymore Securities	—	Claymore MACRO Oil Dn Tr	DCR	SN	11/29/2006	—
	—	Claymore MACRO Oil Up Tr	UCR	SN	11/29/2006	—
	—	Claymore/BNY BRIC ETF	EEB	FB	09/21/2006	—
	—	Claymore/Sabrient Ins ETF	NFO	MB	09/21/2006	—
	—	Claymore/Sabrient Stealth	STH	SB	09/21/2006	—
	—	Claymore/Zacks Sector ETF	XRO	LB	09/21/2006	—
	—	Claymore/Zacks Yld Hog	CVY	LB	09/21/2006	—
Fidelity Investments	—	Fidelity Nasdaq Comp Trac	ONEQ	LG	09/25/2003	0.45
First Trust	—	First Tr NASDAQ-100 Eq Id	QQEW	LB	04/25/2006	—
	—	First Tr NASDAQ100 Tech	QTEC	ST	04/25/2006	—
	—	First Trust AMEX Bio Indx	FBT	SH	06/23/2006	—
	—	First Trust DJ Intrnt Idx	FDN	ST	06/23/2006	—
	45	First Trust DJ S MicroCap	FDM	SB	09/30/2005	0.60
	—	First Trust IPOX-100 Indx	FPX	LG	04/13/2006	—
	—	First Trust MStar Div Ld	FDL	LV	03/15/2006	—
Nasdaq-Amex Investment Prod Svcs	112	Nasdaq 100 Trust	QQQQ	LG	03/10/1999	0.20
PDR SERVICES LLC	111	MidCap SPDR Trust	MDY	MB	05/04/1995	0.25
Powershares	—	PowerShares Aero&Defense	PPA	LG	10/26/2005	0.68
	41	PowerShares DB Com Idx Fd	DBC	SN	02/03/2006	—
	113	PowerShares Div Achievers	PFM	LV	09/15/2005	0.67
	—	PowerShares Dyn Bio&Genom	PBE	SH	06/23/2005	0.64
	—	PowerShares Dyn Building	PKB	LB	10/26/2005	0.67
	—	PowerShares Dyn Cons Disc	PEZ	MB	10/12/2006	—
	—	PowerShares Dyn Cons Stpl	PSL	LB	10/12/2006	—
	—	PowerShares Dyn Energy	PXE	SN	10/26/2005	0.66
	—	PowerShares Dyn Food&Bev	PBJ	LB	06/23/2005	0.69
	—	PowerShares Dyn Health	PTH	SH	10/12/2006	—
	—	PowerShares Dyn Hlth Svcs	PTJ	SH	10/12/2006	—
	—	PowerShares Dyn Indust	PRN	MB	10/12/2006	—
	—	PowerShares Dyn Insurance	PIC	SF	10/26/2005	0.68
	—	PowerShares Dyn Leisr&Ent	PEJ	LB	06/23/2005	0.68
	—	PowerShares Dyn Lg Cp	PJF	LB	12/01/2006	—
	114	PowerShares Dyn Lg Growth	PWB	LG	03/04/2005	0.64
	115	PowerShares Dyn Lg Value	PWV	LV	03/04/2005	0.65
	116	PowerShares Dyn Market	PWC	LB	05/01/2003	0.60
	—	PowerShares Dyn Media	PBS	SC	06/23/2005	0.68
	—	PowerShares Dyn Mid Cap	PJG	MB	12/01/2006	—
	118	PowerShares Dyn Mid Value	PWP	MV	03/04/2005	0.67
	117	PowerShares Dyn MidGrowth	PWJ	MG	03/04/2005	0.65
	—	PowerShares Dyn Network	PXQ	ST	06/23/2005	0.68
	—	PowerShares Dyn Oil & Gas	PXJ	SN	10/26/2005	0.64
	119	PowerShares Dyn OTC	PWO	MG	05/01/2003	0.60
	—	PowerShares Dyn Pharma	PJP	SH	06/23/2005	0.66
	—	PowerShares Dyn Retail	PMR	LB	10/26/2005	0.70
	—	PowerShares Dyn Semicond	PSI	ST	06/23/2005	0.65
	120	PowerShares Dyn Sm Growth	PWT	SG	03/04/2005	0.65
	121	PowerShares Dyn Sm Value	PWY	SV	03/04/2005	0.66
	—	PowerShares Dyn Small Cap	PJM	SB	12/01/2006	—
	—	PowerShares Dyn Software	PSJ	ST	06/23/2005	0.67
	—	PowerShares Dyn Tech	PTF	ST	10/12/2006	—
	—	PowerShares Dyn Utilities	PUI	SU	10/26/2005	0.69
	—	PowerShares Finc Prefer	PGF	SF	12/01/2006	—
	123	PowerShares Halter USX	PGJ	PJ	12/09/2004	0.71
	124	PowerShares High Gr Div	PHJ	LB	09/15/2005	0.66
	125	PowerShares HY Div Achiev	PEY	MV	12/09/2004	0.61
	126	PowerShares Intl Div Ach	PID	FV	09/15/2005	0.62
	—	PowerShares Lux Nanotech	PXN	ST	10/26/2005	0.73
	—	PowerShares Val Line Indu	PYH	LB	12/01/2006	—
	—	PowerShares WilderHill	PBW	SN	03/04/2005	0.71
	128	PowerShares Zacks MicroCp	PZI	SB	08/18/2005	0.72
	129	PowerShares Zacks Sm Cap	PZJ	SB	02/16/2006	0.75

ETFs by Family

Morningstar's ETF Universe

ETF Family	Page	Name	Ticker	Category	Inception Date	Expense Ratio %
Rydex	—	CurrencyShares Aus Dollar	FXA	IB	06/21/2006	—
	—	CurrencyShares BP StrIng	FXB	IB	06/21/2006	—
	—	CurrencyShares Can Dollar	FXC	IB	06/21/2006	—
	—	CurrencyShares Euro Trust	FXE	IB	12/12/2005	—
	—	CurrencyShares Mex Peso	FXM	IB	06/21/2006	—
	—	CurrencyShares Swe Krona	FXS	IB	06/21/2006	—
	—	CurrencyShares Swi Franc	FXF	IB	06/21/2006	—
	130	Rydex Russell Top 50	XLG	LB	05/10/2005	0.20
	131	Rydex S&P 500 Pure Growth	RPG	LG	03/01/2006	—
	132	Rydex S&P 500 Pure Value	RPV	LV	03/01/2006	—
	133	Rydex S&P Equal Weight	RSP	LB	04/24/2003	0.40
	—	Rydex S&P EqWght Cons Dis	RCD	LB	11/01/2006	—
	—	Rydex S&P EqWght Cons Stp	RHS	LB	11/01/2006	—
	—	Rydex S&P EqWght Energy	RYE	SN	11/01/2006	—
	—	Rydex S&P EqWght Financls	RYF	SF	11/01/2006	—
	—	Rydex S&P EqWght HlthCare	RYH	SH	11/01/2006	—
	—	Rydex S&P EqWght Industr	RGI	LB	11/01/2006	—
	—	Rydex S&P EqWght Material	RTM	LB	11/01/2006	—
	—	Rydex S&P EqWght Tech	RYT	ST	11/01/2006	—
	—	Rydex S&P EqWght Util	RYU	SU	11/01/2006	—
	134	Rydex S&P Midcap 400 Gr	RFG	MG	03/01/2006	—
	135	Rydex S&P Midcap 400 Val	RFV	MV	03/01/2006	—
	136	Rydex S&P Smallcap 600 Gr	RZG	SG	03/01/2006	—
	137	Rydex S&P Smallcap 600 Va	RZV	SV	03/01/2006	—
State Street Global Advisors	—	Consumer Discr SPDR	XLY	LB	12/22/1998	0.26
	—	Consumer Staple SPDR	XLP	LB	12/22/1998	0.26
	42	DIAMONDS Trust	DIA	LV	01/20/1998	0.18
	43	Energy SPDR	XLE	SN	12/22/1998	0.26
	44	Financial SPDR	XLF	SF	12/22/1998	0.26
	46	Health Care Sel SPDR	XLV	SH	12/22/1998	0.26
	—	Industrial SPDR	XLI	LB	12/22/1998	0.25
	—	Materials Sel SPDR	XLB	LV	12/22/1998	0.26
	—	SPDR Biotech	XBI	SH	01/31/2006	0.36
	138	SPDR Dividend ETF	SDY	LV	11/08/2005	0.30
	—	SPDR Homebuilders	XHB	LB	01/31/2006	0.36
	—	SPDR Metals & Mining	XME	SN	06/22/2006	0.36
	—	SPDR Oil & Gas Expl & Pro	XOP	SN	06/22/2006	0.36
	—	SPDR Oil&Gas Equip & Serv	XES	SN	06/22/2006	0.36
	—	SPDR Pharmaceuticals	XPH	SH	06/22/2006	0.36
	—	SPDR Retail	XRT	LB	06/22/2006	0.36
	—	SPDR Semiconductor	XSD	ST	01/31/2006	0.36
	139	SPDR Trust Series 1	SPY	LB	01/29/1993	0.10
	149	streetTRACK DJ Small Gr	DSG	SG	09/25/2000	0.28
	140	streetTRACK Global T	DGT	WS	09/25/2000	0.51
	—	streetTRACKS DJ Euro 50	FEZ	ES	10/21/2002	0.32
	—	streetTRACKS DJ Int RIEst	RWX	SR	12/19/2006	—
	141	streetTRACKS DJ Large Cap	ELR	LB	11/08/2005	0.21
	143	streetTRACKS DJ Lg Growth	ELG	LG	09/25/2000	0.21
	142	streetTracks DJ Lg Value	ELV	LV	09/25/2000	0.21
	144	streetTRACKS DJ Mid Cap	EMM	MB	11/08/2005	0.26
	146	streetTRACKS DJ Mid Value	EMV	MV	11/08/2005	0.26
	145	streetTRACKS DJ MidGrowth	EMG	MG	11/08/2005	0.26
	153	streetTRACKS DJ REIT	RWR	SR	04/23/2001	0.26
	148	streetTRACKS DJ Small Val	DSV	SV	09/25/2000	0.26
	150	streetTRACKS DJ STOXX 50	FEU	ES	10/21/2002	0.32
	—	streetTRACKS KBW Reg Bank	KRE	SF	06/22/2006	0.36
	—	streetTRACKS MS Tech	MTK	ST	09/25/2000	0.51
	—	streetTRACKS Rus/Nom PRJp	JPP	JS	11/09/2006	—
	—	streetTRACKS Rus/Nom SmJp	JSC	JS	11/09/2006	—
	152	streetTRACKS Total Market	TMW	LB	10/04/2000	0.21
	154	Technology SPDR	XLK	ST	12/22/1998	0.26
	155	Utilities SPDR	XLU	SU	12/22/1998	0.26

ETF Family	Page	Name	Ticker	Category	Inception Date	Expense Ratio %
United States Oil	—	United States Oil	USO	SN	04/10/2006	—
Van Eck	—	Market Vectors Gld Miners	GDX	SP	05/22/2006	—
Vanguard	—	Vanguard Cons Disc ETF	VCR	LG	01/26/2004	0.25
	—	Vanguard Cons Stap ETF	VDC	LB	01/26/2004	0.25
	156	Vanguard Div Appr ETF	VIG	LB	04/27/2006	—
	157	Vanguard EmergMkts ETF	VWO	EM	03/10/2005	0.30
	158	Vanguard Energy ETF	VDE	SN	09/29/2004	0.25
	159	Vanguard Euro Stk ETF	VGK	ES	03/10/2005	0.18
	160	Vanguard ExMkt ETF	VXF	MB	12/27/2001	0.08
	161	Vanguard Financial ETF	VFH	SF	01/26/2004	0.25
	162	Vanguard Growth ETF	VUG	LG	01/26/2004	0.11
	163	Vanguard HealthCar ETF	VHT	SH	01/26/2004	0.25
	—	Vanguard High Dividend Yi	VYM	LV	11/10/2006	—
	—	Vanguard Indstrls ETF	VIS	LB	09/29/2004	0.25
	164	Vanguard InfoTech ETF	VGT	ST	01/26/2004	0.25
	165	Vanguard Large Cap ETF	VV	LB	01/27/2004	0.07
	—	Vanguard Materials ETF	VAW	SN	01/26/2004	0.25
	166	Vanguard Mid Cap ETF	VO	MB	01/26/2004	0.13
	—	Vanguard Mid Growth ETF	VOT	MG	08/17/2006	—
	—	Vanguard Mid Value ETF	VOE	MV	08/17/2006	—
	167	Vanguard Pacif Stk ETF	VPL	JS	03/10/2005	0.18
	168	Vanguard REIT Index ETF	VNQ	SR	09/23/2004	0.12
	170	Vanguard Sm Cap Gr ETF	VBK	SG	01/26/2004	0.12
	171	Vanguard Sm Cp Val ETF	VBR	SV	01/26/2004	0.12
	169	Vanguard Small Cap ETF	VB	SB	01/26/2004	0.10
	172	Vanguard TelcomSrv ETF	VOX	SC	09/29/2004	0.25
	173	Vanguard TSM ETF	VTI	LB	05/31/2001	0.07
	174	Vanguard Utilities ETF	VPU	SU	01/26/2004	0.25
	175	Vanguard Value ETF	VTV	LV	01/26/2004	0.11
WisdomTree	176	WisdomTree DIEFA	DWM	FB	06/16/2006	—
	177	WisdomTree DIEFA HiYld Eq	DTH	FB	06/16/2006	—
	178	WisdomTree Div Top 100	DTN	LB	06/16/2006	—
	—	WisdomTree Eur SmCap Div	DFE	ES	06/16/2006	—
	180	WisdomTree Eur Total Div	DEB	ES	06/16/2006	—
	179	WisdomTree Euro Hi-Yld Eq	DEW	ES	06/16/2006	—
	181	WisdomTree High-Yld Eqty	DHS	LB	06/16/2006	—
	182	WisdomTree IntDiv Top 100	DOO	FB	06/16/2006	—
	—	WisdomTree Intl Basic Mat	DBN	FB	10/13/2006	—
	—	WisdomTree Intl Comm	DGG	SC	10/13/2006	—
	—	WisdomTree Intl Con Cycl	DPC	FB	10/13/2006	—
	—	WisdomTree Intl Con NonCy	DPN	FB	10/13/2006	—
	—	WisdomTree Intl Energy	DKA	SN	10/13/2006	—
	—	WisdomTree Intl Financial	DRF	SF	10/13/2006	—
	—	WisdomTree Intl Hlth Care	DBR	SH	10/13/2006	—
	—	WisdomTree Intl Indust	DDI	FB	10/13/2006	—
	183	WisdomTree Intl LgCap Div	DOL	FB	06/16/2006	—
	—	WisdomTree Intl MdCap Div	DIM	FA	06/16/2006	—
	—	WisdomTree Intl SmCap Div	DLS	FA	06/16/2006	—
	—	WisdomTree Intl Tech	DBT	ST	10/13/2006	—
	—	WisdomTree Intl Utilities	DBU	SU	10/13/2006	—
	—	WisdomTree Japan HiYld Eq	DNL	JS	06/16/2006	—
	—	WisdomTree Japan SmCp Div	DFJ	JS	06/16/2006	—
	184	WisdomTree Japan Tot Div	DXJ	JS	06/16/2006	—
	185	WisdomTree LargeCap Div	DLN	LB	06/16/2006	—
	186	WisdomTree MidCap Div	DON	MB	06/16/2006	—
	187	WisdomTree Pac ex-Jp HYEq	DNH	DP	06/16/2006	—
	188	WisdomTree Pac ex-Jp TDiv	DND	DP	06/16/2006	—
	189	WisdomTree SmallCap Div	DES	SB	06/16/2006	—
	190	WisdomTree Total Dividend	DTD	LB	06/16/2006	—
World Gold Trust Services, LLC	151	streetTRACKS Gold Shares	GLD	SP	11/18/2004	0.40

Highest and Lowest Star Rating
Morningstar's ETF Universe

Highest Morningstar Rating

Page	Name	Morningstar Rating				Morningstar Return			Morningstar Risk		
		Overall	3Yr	5Yr	10Yr	3Yr	5Yr	10Yr	3Yr	5Yr	10Yr
107	iShares SP 600 Growth	★★★★★	★★★★	★★★★★	—	Above Avg	Above Avg	—	Below Avg	Low	—
—	iShares Austria Index	★★★★★	★★★★★	★★★★★	★★★★	Above Avg	Above Avg	Above Avg	Above Avg	Avg	Avg
91	iShares R. Midcap VI	★★★★★	★★★★★	★★★★★	—	High	High	—	Avg	Avg	—
133	Rydex S&P Equal Weight	★★★★★	★★★★★	—	—	High	—	—	Above Avg	—	—
116	PowerShares Dyn Market	★★★★★	★★★★★	—	—	High	—	—	High	—	—
111	MidCap SPDR Trust	★★★★	★★★	★★★	★★★★	Avg	Avg	Above Avg	Avg	Avg	Avg
104	iShares SP 400 Growth	★★★★	★★★	★★★★	—	Avg	Avg	—	Below Avg	Below Avg	—
106	iShares SP 400 Value	★★★★	★★★	★★★★	—	Avg	Above Avg	—	Above Avg	Avg	—
57	iShares DJ Total Mkt	★★★★	★★★★	★★★★	—	Above Avg	Above Avg	—	Avg	Above Avg	—
86	iShares R3000 Index	★★★★	★★★★	★★★★	—	Above Avg	Above Avg	—	Avg	Above Avg	—
87	iShares R3000 Value	★★★★	★★★★	★★★★	—	Above Avg	Above Avg	—	Avg	Avg	—
80	iShares R1000 Index	★★★★	★★★★	★★★★	—	Above Avg	Above Avg	—	Avg	Avg	—
81	iShares R1000 Value	★★★★	★★★★	★★★★	—	Above Avg	Above Avg	—	Avg	Avg	—
—	iShares Australia	★★★★	★★★★	★★★★	★★★★★	Above Avg	Above Avg	Above Avg	Below Avg	Below Avg	Low
148	streetTRACKS DJ Small Val	★★★★	★★★	★★★★	—	Avg	Above Avg	—	Avg	Below Avg	—
47	iShares C&S Realty	★★★★	★★★★	★★★★	—	Above Avg	Above Avg	—	High	High	—
173	Vanguard TSM ETF	★★★★	★★★★	★★★★	—	Above Avg	Above Avg	—	Avg	Avg	—
90	iShares R. Midcap	★★★★	★★★★	★★★★	—	Above Avg	Above Avg	—	Avg	Avg	—
71	iShares MSCI EAFE	★★★★	★★★★	★★★★	—	Avg	Above Avg	—	Below Avg	Avg	—
76	iShares MSCI ex-Japn	★★★★	★★★★	★★★★	—	Above Avg	Avg	—	Low	Low	—

Lowest Morningstar Rating

Page	Name	Morningstar Rating				Morningstar Return			Morningstar Risk		
		Overall	3Yr	5Yr	10Yr	3Yr	5Yr	10Yr	3Yr	5Yr	10Yr
112	Nasdaq 100 Trust	★	★★	★	—	Avg	Below Avg	—	High	High	—
—	Consumer Staple SPDR	★	★★	★	—	Below Avg	Low	—	Below Avg	Low	—
—	iShares Taiwan Index	★	★	★	—	Low	Low	—	Above Avg	Above Avg	—
—	iShares Brazil Index	★	★	★	—	Below Avg	Avg	—	High	Above Avg	—
—	iShares Malaysia	★	★	★	★	Low	Low	Low	Low	Below Avg	Above Avg
140	streetTRACK Global T	★	★★	★	—	Low	Low	—	Low	Below Avg	—
77	iShares NASD Biotech	★	★	★	—	Low	Low	—	Above Avg	High	—
—	iShares GS Network	★	★★	★	—	Avg	Avg	—	High	High	—
—	iShares MSCI South Africa	★	★	—	—	Avg	—	—	High	—	—
—	BLDRS Asia 50 ADR Index	★	★	—	—	Below Avg	—	—	Below Avg	—	—
42	DIAMONDS Trust	★★	★	★★	—	Low	Below Avg	—	Avg	Avg	—
44	Financial SPDR	★★	★★★	★★	—	Avg	Below Avg	—	Avg	Avg	—
155	Utilities SPDR	★★	★★★	★★	—	Avg	Avg	—	Above Avg	Above Avg	—
54	iShares DJ RE Index	★★	★★	★★	—	Avg	Below Avg	—	Above Avg	Above Avg	—
—	iShares U.K. Index	★★	★★	★★	★★	Below Avg	Below Avg	Low	Low	Low	Low
—	iShares Singapore	★★	★★★★★	★★★	★	Above Avg	Avg	Low	Low	Below Avg	Above Avg
—	iShares Netherlands	★★	★★	★	★★	Below Avg	Below Avg	Low	Avg	Above Avg	Avg
—	iShares Mexico Index	★★	★★★	★★★	★	Avg	Below Avg	Low	Low	Low	Low
—	iShares Hong Kong	★★	★★	★	★★	Below Avg	Low	Low	Below Avg	Below Avg	Avg
—	iShares Germany Indx	★★	★★★	★	★★	Avg	Below Avg	Below Avg	Avg	Above Avg	Above Avg

Highest and Lowest Valuation

Morningstar's ETF Universe

Highest Vauation

Page	Name	Price/Cash Flow	Price/Prospective Earnings	Price/Book	Price/Sales	Dividend Yield
—	SPDR Biotech	24.13	33.27	4.33	7.82	—
—	iShares Hong Kong	20.73	16.58	1.91	3.23	3.19
47	iShares C&S Realty	19.77	20.74	3.63	6.47	3.38
—	iShares DJ US Medical Dev	19.68	24.44	3.45	2.84	0.26
54	iShares DJ RE Index	17.10	19.01	3.08	3.56	3.68
77	iShares NASD Biotech	16.96	23.80	3.90	5.74	0.01
—	First Tr NASDAQ100 Tech	16.65	26.72	3.61	3.76	0.42
153	streetTRACKS DJ REIT	16.51	19.71	3.41	4.53	3.89
53	iShares DJ Health	16.15	18.97	3.55	2.35	1.35
—	iShares Switzerland	15.54	16.64	2.86	1.86	2.25
112	Nasdaq 100 Trust	15.49	26.09	4.16	2.86	0.45
—	iShares GS Software	15.22	24.35	2.98	4.37	0.20
46	Health Care Sel SPDR	15.17	18.09	3.48	1.76	1.52
168	Vanguard REIT Index ETF	14.95	17.19	2.90	4.17	4.37
—	PowerShares FTSE RAFI Hth	14.92	17.77	3.37	1.92	1.88
127	PowerShares Val Line Time	14.84	20.63	3.60	1.28	0.76
—	iShares DJ US Pharma	14.82	19.26	3.72	3.17	1.54
—	First Trust AMEX Bio Indx	14.75	28.15	4.17	4.11	—
163	Vanguard HealthCar ETF	14.62	19.14	3.39	1.79	1.31
—	iShares MstarMidGrowth	14.57	22.87	3.59	2.48	0.41

Lowest Vauation

Page	Name	Price/Cash Flow	Price/Prospective Earnings	Price/Book	Price/Sales	Dividend Yield
120	PowerShares Dyn Sm Growth	2.30	24.00	3.39	1.34	0.17
—	PowerShares Dyn Software	2.44	23.46	4.06	3.36	0.13
—	PowerShares Dyn Small Cap	3.10	14.97	2.25	1.08	0.76
161	Vanguard Financial ETF	3.13	12.76	1.99	2.34	2.77
—	iShares DJ BMaterial	3.24	13.79	2.80	1.05	1.82
—	BLDRS Dev Mkts 100 ADR	3.66	13.28	1.81	0.75	3.31
—	BLDRS Europe 100 ADR	3.66	13.28	1.81	0.75	3.31
—	PowerShares Dyn Tech	3.72	19.44	3.31	1.57	0.20
—	iShares DJ US Oil & Gas	4.18	10.51	1.96	1.06	0.76
—	iShares Taiwan Index	4.35	14.73	1.96	1.03	5.07
—	iShares S.Korea Indx	4.36	12.03	1.40	0.65	1.87
—	SPDR Oil & Gas Expl & Pro	4.42	12.55	2.16	1.23	0.47
—	PowerShares FTSE RAFI CGo	4.47	14.25	2.15	0.29	3.11
—	SPDR Metals & Mining	4.48	13.13	3.18	1.05	0.76
—	PowerShares Lux Nanotech	4.49	27.41	2.83	2.66	0.50
156	Vanguard Div Appr ETF	4.50	16.06	3.11	1.56	1.79
137	Rydex S&P Smallcap 600 Va	4.59	17.66	1.55	0.43	1.90
—	iShares Brazil Index	4.67	11.46	2.11	1.44	6.73
—	PowerShares Dyn Energy	4.78	10.61	2.19	0.71	0.84
128	PowerShares Zacks MicroCp	4.83	16.90	1.67	0.79	1.29

Ranked by price to cash flow and cash flow growth.

Highest and Lowest Growth
Morningstar's ETF Universe

Highest Growth

Page	Name	Cash Flow Growth	Projected Earnings Growth	Historical Earnings Growth	Book Value Growth	Sales Growth
—	PowerShares Dyn Oil & Gas	53.70	67.51	23.56	15.24	−30.91
—	SPDR Metals & Mining	53.32	49.31	13.83	7.37	14.33
—	Market Vectors Gld Miners	44.75	33.31	17.54	13.67	20.31
—	iShares DJ BMaterial	39.73	30.64	13.67	7.32	11.91
—	iShares Dow Jones US Insr	37.30	21.40	11.05	6.46	6.12
161	Vanguard Financial ETF	35.91	13.11	10.61	6.71	7.30
—	SPDR Oil&Gas Equip & Serv	35.66	71.77	25.31	13.30	17.50
—	iShares GS Network	35.57	24.62	16.46	0.45	8.81
—	iShares DJ US Oil & Gas	35.04	53.22	10.08	22.57	28.60
—	PowerShares Dyn Energy	34.03	55.46	9.25	21.50	31.92
—	SPDR Oil & Gas Expl & Pro	33.83	50.76	11.12	22.42	30.62
120	PowerShares Dyn Sm Growth	33.59	17.90	19.59	9.34	12.58
—	iShares DJ US Oil Equip	33.07	73.19	24.77	8.88	9.39
—	PowerShares Dyn Network	31.66	7.24	14.25	11.90	9.21
—	PowerShares Lux Nanotech	31.23	23.51	14.75	5.21	11.09
158	Vanguard Energy ETF	29.96	51.21	11.13	18.58	23.69
—	iShares Mexico Index	29.09	34.82	19.51	16.17	23.94
50	iShares DJ US Energy	29.03	48.64	11.19	17.64	22.18
43	Energy SPDR	28.08	52.41	10.67	18.50	22.51
—	iShares SP Latin 40	27.81	38.25	23.62	14.99	27.27

Lowest Growth

Page	Name	Cash Flow Growth	Projected Earnings Growth	Historical Earnings Growth	Book Value Growth	Sales Growth
—	iShares Dow Jones US BrDI	−46.94	23.55	13.71	13.20	12.63
124	PowerShares High Gr Div	−17.90	10.30	11.75	10.01	10.68
—	iShares Dow Jones US Home	−15.15	34.53	11.91	23.54	18.63
155	Utilities SPDR	−14.55	4.37	7.46	1.83	4.91
44	Financial SPDR	−13.66	14.04	10.86	6.70	6.82
—	PowerShares FTSE RAFI Utl	−13.35	4.46	6.86	0.79	6.54
58	iShares DJ Utilities	−12.74	4.97	7.23	1.96	7.02
—	PowerShares FTSE RAFI Fin	−12.08	11.41	10.36	5.63	5.76
178	WisdomTree Div Top 100	−11.95	5.25	8.31	0.64	2.55
174	Vanguard Utilities ETF	−11.93	5.10	6.88	1.07	7.17
125	PowerShares HY Div Achiev	−9.65	−1.04	6.80	5.10	9.79
—	Rydex S&P EqWght Financls	−9.13	13.79	10.61	6.72	5.61
—	streetTRACKS KBW Bank ETF	−9.12	9.92	9.84	7.65	4.69
138	SPDR Dividend ETF	−8.64	5.67	8.02	5.65	8.61
—	streetTRACKS KBW Reg Bank	−8.58	9.53	9.26	9.50	5.98
181	WisdomTree High-Yld Eqty	−8.48	7.14	8.53	5.76	5.98
—	Rydex S&P EqWght Util	−8.02	1.52	6.90	4.40	4.15
—	iShares SP Glb Utilities	−7.84	12.19	9.94	6.37	3.09
—	First Trust MStar Div Ld	−7.64	6.85	8.11	8.33	6.84
—	streetTRACKS KBWInsurance	−5.68	19.52	10.61	6.24	6.13

Ranked by price to cash flow and cash flow growth.

Profitability Measures

Morningstar's ETF Universe

Highest Profitability

Page	Name	ROE %	ROA %	Net Margin %	Debt to Capital %
—	iShares SP Latin 40	30.36	14.45	17.47	33.73
—	iShares Brazil Index	30.06	11.09	18.24	28.52
99	iShares SP Glb Enrgy	27.94	12.97	13.30	18.57
50	iShares DJ US Energy	27.78	13.91	15.20	18.74
—	iShares Mexico Index	27.66	11.03	15.58	36.61
—	PowerShares Dyn Energy	27.57	12.45	16.30	26.50
43	Energy SPDR	27.44	13.51	14.70	20.52
—	WisdomTree Intl Con NonCy	27.09	9.47	12.45	27.94
—	iShares MSCI South Africa	26.99	9.94	13.56	18.59
—	iShares Spain Index	26.77	5.38	15.43	44.49
—	iShares DJ US Oil Equip	26.76	14.13	19.28	25.71
—	iShares U.K. Index	26.70	7.26	12.22	30.53
—	iShares Dow Jones US Home	26.17	15.68	8.42	46.15
—	SPDR Homebuilders	26.11	13.36	7.95	40.14
158	Vanguard Energy ETF	26.01	13.00	14.72	21.18
—	PowerShares FTSE RAFI Ene	25.68	12.61	13.01	21.87
—	Rydex S&P EqWght Energy	25.51	11.58	17.26	28.72
131	Rydex S&P 500 Pure Growth	25.47	12.02	14.74	33.00
—	iShares Netherlands	25.45	5.54	13.15	43.78
—	WisdomTree Intl Energy	25.16	10.80	11.56	19.70

Lowest Profitability

Page	Name	ROE %	ROA %	Net Margin %	Debt to Capital %
—	SPDR Biotech	−6.03	−11.35	2.02	38.84
—	PowerShares Lux Nanotech	−4.69	−6.14	−7.19	27.70
—	PowerShares WilderHill	−4.47	−4.05	−5.73	26.69
—	First Trust AMEX Bio Indx	−1.97	−1.95	7.68	42.97
77	iShares NASD Biotech	−1.88	−7.09	7.94	35.86
—	PowerShares FTSE RAFI CGo	−0.14	6.61	6.48	50.07
88	iShares Russell Microcap	4.11	1.23	6.79	—
—	Market Vectors Gld Miners	4.27	1.86	9.89	20.66
137	Rydex S&P Smallcap 600 Va	5.57	2.50	2.52	34.37
—	PowerShares Dyn Bio&Genom	5.93	−3.82	14.90	27.88
128	PowerShares Zacks MicroCp	6.05	3.93	7.02	24.24
135	Rydex S&P Midcap 400 Val	7.96	4.29	5.26	37.97
—	WisdomTree Japan SmCp Div	8.07	3.72	5.47	15.86
172	Vanguard TelcomSrv ETF	8.19	2.74	5.93	45.15
84	iShares R2000 Value	8.87	5.99	10.66	35.15
132	Rydex S&P 500 Pure Value	9.10	5.55	7.45	43.18
—	PowerShares Dyn Network	9.76	5.87	9.88	—
171	Vanguard Sm Cp Val ETF	9.88	6.12	11.09	37.04
—	PowerShares FTSE RAFI Utl	10.02	2.66	6.72	53.89
83	iShares R2000 Index	10.18	5.53	9.37	34.20

Tables and Charts

Morningstar Most & Least Traded

Morningstar's ETF Universe

Highest Daily Volume

Page	Name	Category	Average Daily Volume
112	Nasdaq 100 Trust	Large Growth	98,950,595
139	SPDR Trust Series 1	Large Blend	64,801,008
83	iShares R2000 Index	Small Blend	44,709,402
43	Energy SPDR	Specialty-Natural Res	18,952,214
75	iShares Japan Index	Japan Stock	16,005,508
42	DIAMONDS Trust	Large Value	6,567,691
44	Financial SPDR	Specialty-Financial	5,646,217
73	iShares MSCI Emerg Mkts	Diversified Emerg Mkts	5,053,537
71	iShares MSCI EAFE	Foreign Large Blend	4,850,645
151	streetTRACKS Gold Shares	Specialty-Precious Mtls	4,228,620
—	iShares Taiwan Index	Pacific/Asia ex-Jpn Stk	2,972,054
—	iShares Brazil Index	Latin America Stock	2,854,782
—	Materials Sel SPDR	Large Value	2,675,757
111	MidCap SPDR Trust	Mid-Cap Blend	2,672,877
—	iShares Hong Kong	Pacific/Asia ex-Jpn Stk	2,440,811
155	Utilities SPDR	Specialty-Utilities	2,433,900
—	iShares Singapore	Pacific/Asia ex-Jpn Stk	2,187,188
54	iShares DJ RE Index	Specialty-Real Estate	1,972,962
—	United States Oil	Specialty-Natural Res	1,887,814
—	iShares Mexico Index	Latin America Stock	1,722,948
154	Technology SPDR	Specialty-Technology	1,675,637
—	Consumer Staple SPDR	Large Blend	1,668,882
82	iShares R2000 Growth	Small Growth	1,616,971
—	SPDR Homebuilders	Large Blend	1,527,840
84	iShares R2000 Value	Small Value	1,492,934
79	iShares R1000 Growth	Large Growth	1,345,822
—	Consumer Discr SPDR	Large Blend	1,322,677
59	iShares FTSE/Xinhua China	Pacific/Asia ex-Jpn Stk	1,246,700
—	iShares Malaysia	Pacific/Asia ex-Jpn Stk	1,213,865
46	Health Care Sel SPDR	Specialty-Health	1,185,200
—	Industrial SPDR	Large Blend	1,130,108
81	iShares R1000 Value	Large Value	1,007,517
66	iShares Lehman 20+	Long Government	987,217
95	iShares S&P 500	Large Blend	980,248
77	iShares NASD Biotech	Specialty-Health	960,994
108	iShares SP Small 600	Small Blend	844,582
05	IShares Lehman 1-3 T	Short Government	814,414
—	Market Vectors Gld Miners	Specialty-Precious Mtls	746,788
—	iShares S.Korea Indx	Pacific/Asia ex-Jpn Stk	732,200
92	iShares S&P 100 Ind.	Large Blend	701,208

Lowest Daily Volume

Page	Name	Category	Average Daily Volume
—	WisdomTree Intl Con Cycl	Foreign Large Blend	392
—	PowerShares FTSE RAFI Utl	Specialty-Utilities	486
—	PowerShares FTSE RAFI CGo	Large Blend	516
—	WisdomTree Intl Indust	Foreign Large Blend	579
—	PowerShares Dyn Small Cap	Small Blend	1,129
146	streetTRACKS DJ Mid Value	Mid-Cap Value	1,157
—	PowerShares FTSE RAFI Tel	Specialty-Com	1,173
—	PowerShares FTSE RAFI Ene	Specialty-Natural Res	1,211
—	CurrencyShares Mex Peso	World Bond	1,393
—	PowerShares FTSE RAFI Fin	Specialty-Financial	1,443
—	PowerShares Dyn Mid Cap	Mid-Cap Blend	1,488
141	streetTRACKS DJ Large Cap	Large Blend	1,544
134	Rydex S&P Midcap 400 Gr	Mid-Cap Growth	1,634
—	WisdomTree Intl Basic Mat	Foreign Large Blend	1,652
—	iShares KLD 400 Social	Large Blend	1,673
—	WisdomTree Intl Tech	Specialty-Technology	1,704
—	iShares SP Glb Industrial	World Stock	1,787
137	Rydex S&P Smallcap 600 Va	Small Value	1,797
145	streetTRACKS DJ MidGrowth	Mid-Cap Growth	1,829
—	Rydex S&P EqWght Energy	Specialty-Natural Res	2,019
—	Rydex S&P EqWght Tech	Specialty-Technology	2,092
—	PowerShares Dyn Lg Cp	Large Blend	2,225
—	iShares SP Glb Cons Discr	World Stock	2,486
—	WisdomTree Intl Financial	Specialty-Financial	2,775
—	iShares SP Glb Cons Stpls	World Stock	2,908
—	WisdomTree Intl Comm	Specialty-Com	2,991
—	PowerShares Dyn Cons Stpl	Large Blend	3,103
—	PowerShares FTSE RAFI Hth	Specialty-Health	3,258
152	streetTRACKS Total Market	Large Blend	3,477
—	PowerShares Dyn Indust	Mid-Cap Blend	3,622
—	CurrencyShares Swe Krona	World Bond	3,700
—	WisdomTree Japan HiYld Eq	Japan Stock	3,911
132	Rydex S&P 500 Pure Value	Large Value	3,934
—	Rydex S&P EqWght Industr	Large Blend	4,000
—	iShares Dow Jones US Insr	Specialty-Financial	4,074
—	iShares Dow Jones US RegB	Specialty-Financial	4,185
136	Rydex S&P Smallcap 600 Gr	Small Growth	4,240
184	WisdomTree Japan Tot Div	Japan Stock	4,654
—	PowerShares FTSE RAFI Ind	Large Blend	4,709
—	Rydex S&P EqWght HlthCare	Specialty-Health	4,876

Morningstar Price/Fair Value

Morningstar's ETF Universe

Highest Price/Fair Value

Page	Name	Coverage Rate*	Premium	Price/Fair Value	Price per Share	Fair Value per Share
—	iShares DJ US Oil Equip	85.39	28.66	1.40	47.85	34.13
47	iShares C&S Realty	99.06	19.49	1.24	51.84	41.74
153	streetTRACKS DJ REIT	90.64	18.18	1.22	44.97	36.79
54	iShares DJ RE Index	88.58	17.07	1.21	42.96	35.63
168	Vanguard REIT Index ETF	85.39	17.06	1.21	43.76	36.30
—	BLDRS Asia 50 ADR Index	89.46	13.73	1.16	26.96	23.26
—	BLDRS Emerg Mkts 50 ADR	80.87	11.81	1.13	24.80	21.87
—	iShares DJ US Health Prov	92.16	9.84	1.11	46.01	41.49
60	iShares GS Nat Res	92.09	8.61	1.09	49.62	45.35
—	streetTRACKS KBW Cap Mkt	100.00	8.04	1.09	45.16	41.53
43	Energy SPDR	100.00	6.13	1.07	59.00	55.38
50	iShares DJ US Energy	98.92	4.72	1.05	60.88	58.00
—	iShares Dow Jones US BrDl	96.50	5.20	1.05	40.25	38.15
116	PowerShares Dyn Market	85.31	3.40	1.04	39.07	37.75
158	Vanguard Energy ETF	92.14	3.73	1.04	58.16	55.99
155	Utilities SPDR	98.85	3.07	1.03	39.71	38.49
58	iShares DJ Utilities	94.02	3.01	1.03	37.91	36.77
174	Vanguard Utilities ETF	87.02	3.23	1.03	38.14	36.91
—	BLDRS Dev Mkts 100 ADR	85.93	1.93	1.02	36.50	35.79
117	PowerShares Dyn MidGrowth	90.14	1.61	1.02	34.08	33.54

Lowest Price/Fair Value

Page	Name	Coverage Rate*	Premium	Price/Fair Value	Price per Share	Fair Value per Share
—	iShares Dow Jones US Home	89.18	−61.02	0.62	28.30	45.58
—	SPDR Homebuilders	92.06	−47.53	0.68	33.41	49.28
—	iShares GS Network	94.52	−29.49	0.77	7.77	10.06
—	streetTRACKS MS Tech	100.00	−20.79	0.83	19.58	23.65
62	iShares GS Tech	95.25	−19.77	0.83	20.22	24.22
164	Vanguard InfoTech ETF	92.69	−19.93	0.83	21.07	25.27
112	Nasdaq 100 Trust	95.23	−18.98	0.84	27.22	32.39
154	Technology SPDR	98.68	−18.65	0.84	22.28	26.44
55	iShares DJ Tech	94.76	−18.50	0.84	20.94	24.82
—	iShares DJ Cons Services	90.03	−17.24	0.85	29.18	34.21
—	Vanguard Cons Disc ETF	82.20	−17.93	0.85	27.35	32.26
—	First Tr NASDAQ100 Tech	93.70	−17.49	0.85	17.57	20.65
—	First Tr NASDAQ-100 Eq Id	90.85	−17.61	0.85	22.35	26.28
61	iShares Semiconductor	90.29	−16.44	0.86	19.28	22.44
124	PowerShares High Gr Div	92.28	−16.25	0.86	40.83	47.47
—	SPDR Semiconductor	84.76	−15.84	0.86	17.56	20.34
92	iShares S&P 100 Ind.	99.96	−14.50	0.87	37.65	43.11
130	Rydex Russell Top 50	99.18	−14.80	0.87	40.89	46.94
—	Consumer Discr SPDR	91.88	−14.09	0.88	30.80	35.14
—	Industrial SPDR	96.08	−14.05	0.88	45.06	51.38

*This ranking only includes ETFs with coverage rates of 80% or more.

Glossary

This section explains how to use the data found in this publication to make better investment decisions.

Glossary

A

90-Day Treasury Bill

see U.S. 90-Day Treasury Bill

Address

Usually the location of the fund's distributor, this is where to write to receive a prospectus.

Advisor

This is the company that takes primary responsibility for managing the fund.

Alpha

see Modern Portfolio Theory Statistics

Analysis

see Morningstar's Take

Arbitrage Mechanism

This is the market mechanism that allows an ETF's market price to trade roughly in line with the net asset values of its underlying portfolio. ETFs create and redeem shares in-kind. That means they exchange ETF shares for baskets of their underlying stocks and vice versa. When ETF shares trade at a discount to their net asset values, institutional investors can assemble 50,000-share blocks in the open market at the discounted price, redeem them for the underlying stocks, and sell those stocks at a profit. The actual transaction isn't quite that simple, but the idea is the same: The arbitrage opportunity generates sufficient demand for the discounted ETF shares to close the gap between their market price and the net asset value of the underlying portfolio.

Authorized Participant

see also Creation Unit

Typically large institutional investors or intermediaries (specialists, market makers, or broker dealers, for example), authorized participants directly enter participation agreements with ETF sponsors to purchase or redeem creation units of ETF shares. Authorized participants transfer a portfolio of stocks to a fund manager or trustee, who then places these stocks into a trust and issues creation units back to the authorized participant in exchange for the underlying securities. The authorized participant can then sell these creation units on a secondary market and redeem the units for its underlying securities.

Average Credit Quality

see also Credit Analysis

Average credit quality gives a snapshot of the portfolio's overall credit quality. It is an average of each bond's credit rating, adjusted for its relative weighting in the portfolio. For the purposes of Morningstar's calculations, U.S. government securities are considered AAA bonds, nonrated municipal bonds generally are classified as BB, and other nonrated bonds generally are considered B.

Average Daily Volume

The average number of shares of an ETF traded per day, usually measured over the previous 12 months. This number, in addition to total net assets, can be a rough gauge of an ETF's popularity in the market.

Average Effective Duration

Average effective duration provides a measure of a fund's interest-rate sensitivity. The longer a fund's duration, the more sensitive the fund is to shifts in interest rates. The relationship among funds with different durations is straightforward: A fund with a duration of 10 years is expected to be twice as volatile as a fund with a five-year duration. Duration also gives an indication of how a fund's net asset value (NAV) will change as interest rates change. A fund with a five-year duration would be expected to lose 5% of its NAV if interest rates rose by 1 percentage point, or gain 5% if interest rates fell by 1 percentage point. Morningstar surveys fund companies for this information.

Average Effective Maturity

Average effective maturity is a weighted average of all the maturities of the bonds in a portfolio, computed by weighting each bond's effective maturity by the market value of the security. Average effective maturity takes into consideration all mortgage prepayments, puts, and adjustable coupons. (Because Morningstar uses fund company calculations for this figure and because different companies use varying interest-rate assumptions in determining call likelihood and timing, we ask that companies not adjust for call provisions.) Funds with longer maturity are generally considered more interest-rate sensitive than their shorter counterparts.

Average Return
see also Total Return and Market Return
The annualized return of the ETF over a multiyear period, such as three or five years. This represents the annual return that an investor would have received if the fund's returns were evenly spread across the time period.

Average Stock Percentage
see also Composition
For stock-oriented funds, we provide a yearly average stock position calculated by averaging all reported composition numbers for the year. These averages provide a valuable complement to the current composition numbers; investors can compare a fund's current level of market participation with its historical averages.

Average Weighted Coupon
see also Coupon Range
Average weighted coupon is computed by averaging each bond's coupon rate adjusted for its relative weighting in the portfolio. This figure indicates whether the fund is opting for a high- or low-coupon strategy, and it may serve as an indicator of interest-rate sensitivity, particularly for mortgage-backed funds or other funds with callable bonds. A high coupon frequently indicates less sensitivity to interest rates; a low coupon, the opposite.

Average Weighted Price
Average weighted price is computed for most bond funds by weighting the price of each bond by its relative size in the portfolio. This number reveals whether the fund favors bonds selling at prices above or below face value (premium or discount securities, respectively) and can also serve as an indicator of interest-rate sensitivity. This statistic is expressed as a percentage of par (face) value. This statistic is not calculated for international-bond funds, because their holdings are often expressed in terms of foreign currencies.

B

Bear Market
see also Bull Market
A period when stock prices fall and investors are pessimistic about market returns. Bear markets usually are not labeled as such until stock prices have slipped by at least 15%. The opposite of a bear market is a bull market.

Best Fit Index
see also Modern Portfolio Theory Statistics
The Best Fit Index is the market index whose monthly returns have correlated the most closely with a given fund's in the most recent 36 consecutive months. Morningstar regresses the fund's monthly excess returns against monthly excess returns of several well-known market indexes. Best Fit signifies the index that provides the highest R-squared, or correlation with a given fund.

Beta
see Modern Portfolio Theory Statistics

Bid/Ask Spread
The difference in the price at which an investor can buy and sell ETF shares. A wide bid/ask spread allows market makers to buy at a lower price and sell at a higher price.

Bull Market
see also Bear Market
A period when stock prices rise and investors are optimistic about market returns. Bull markets usually are not labeled as such until stock prices have risen by at least 15%. The opposite of a bull market is a bear market.

C

Capital Gains
Capital gains are the profits received and distributed from the sale of securities within a portfolio. This line shows a summary of the ETF's annual capital gains distributions expressed in per-share dollar amounts. Both short- and long-term gains are included, as are options premiums and distributions from paid-in capital. Most ETFs realize and distribute fewer capital gains than conventional mutual funds because ETFs do not have to sell securities to satisfy redemptions.

As a result, ETFs are often considered to be more tax-efficient than mutual funds.

Capital Return %

see also Income Return % and Total Return
Morningstar provides the portion of a fund's total returns that was generated by realized and unrealized increases in the value of securities in the portfolio. Frequently, a stock fund's returns will be derived entirely from capital return. By looking at capital return and income return, an investor can see whether the fund's returns come from capital, from income, or from a combination of both. Adding capital and income return will produce the fund's total return.

Category

see Morningstar Category

Commission

The fee paid to a broker to buy or sell a security on behalf of an investor. Like stock trades, commissions for ETFs are typically assessed on a per-trade basis. As a result, it can be more cost-effective for frequent traders to purchase no-load indexed mutual funds in lieu of an ETF with a similar portfolio. Brokerage commissions vary greatly according to account size, individual trading frequency, and the brokerage company used.

Composition

see also Average Stock Percentage
The composition percentages provide a simple breakdown of the fund's portfolio holdings, as of the date listed, into general investment classes at the bottom of the Portfolio Analysis section. Cash encompasses both the actual cash and the cash equivalents (fixed-income securities with maturities of one year or less) held by the portfolio. A negative percentage of cash indicates that the portfolio is leveraged, meaning it has borrowed against its own assets to buy more securities or that it has used other techniques to gain additional exposure to the market. The percentage listed as Stocks incorporates only the portfolio's straight common stocks. Bonds include every fixed-income security with a maturity of more than one year, from government notes to high-yield corporate bonds. Other includes preferred stocks (equity securities that pay dividends at a specified rate), as well as convertible bonds and convertible preferreds, which are corporate securities that are exchangeable

for a set amount of another form of security (usually shares of common stock) at a prestated price. Other also includes all those not-so-neatly categorized securities, such as warrants and options.

Country Exposure

For each international portfolio the country exposure information displays the top five countries in which the ETF is invested. This information is gathered directly from the portfolios given by the fund companies.

Coupon Range

see also Average Weighted Coupon
Taxable-bond funds feature a table listing the breakdown of each portfolio's bond coupons, or rates of interest payments. The coupon range is designed to help an investor complete the picture suggested by the average weighted coupon statistic. These ranges differ according to Morningstar category and, due to changing interest rates, are subject to alteration over time. Whatever the breakdown may be, the first number is always exclusive and the second number is always inclusive. A range of 8% to 10% for example, would exclude bonds that have a weighted coupon rate of exactly 8% but would include bonds with a weighted coupon rate of 10%. High-yield bond funds include PIKs in their coupon breakdown, which are payment-in-kind issues that make interest payments in the form of additional securities rather than cash.

The overall percentage of bond assets that fall within each coupon range is noted in the % of Bonds column. The Rel Cat column compares a fund with others in its Morningstar Category. The category average is set at 1.0.

Creation Unit

see also Authorized Participant
The smallest block of ETF shares that can be bought or sold from the ETF at net asset value, usually 50,000. These are only bought and sold "in-kind." For example, when you sell one, you receive a portfolio of securities that approximates the ETF's holdings, not cash. Creation units' size means that only market makers and institutions can afford to buy or sell them. Such investors are referred to as authorized participants. All other investors can buy or sell ETF shares in any size lot at the market price, rather than at NAV, over an exchange.

Credit Analysis

see also Average Credit Quality

This section depicts the quality of bonds in a bond fund's portfolio. The credit analysis shows the percentage of fixed-income securities that fall within each credit-quality rating as assigned by Standard & Poor's or Moody's.

At the top of the ratings are U.S. government bonds. Bonds issued and backed by the government, as well as those backed by government-linked organizations such as Fannie Mae and Freddie Mac, are of extremely high quality and thus are considered equivalent to bonds rated AAA, which is the highest possible rating a corporate issue can receive. Morningstar gives U.S. government bonds a credit rating separate from AAA securities to allow for a more accurate credit analysis of a portfolio's holdings. Bonds with a BBB rating are the lowest grade that are still considered to be investment grade. Bonds that are rated BB or lower (often called junk bonds or high-yield bonds) are considered to be speculative. Any bonds that appear in the NR/NA category are either not rated by Standard & Poor's or Moody's, or did not have a rating available at the time of publication.

Current Investment Style

see also Investment Style Box

For equity funds, this section lists a fund portfolio's current averages for various portfolio statistics, including price/earnings, price/cash flow, and historical earnings growth. To provide perspective, we compare these measures with the funds' category average.

For bond funds, this section lists a portfolio's current duration, as well as averages for effective maturity, credit quality, weighted coupon, and price. These numbers are helpful in determining how much interest-rate and credit risk the portfolio currently has. For example, funds with high durations typically are very sensitive to changes in interest rates, whereas those with durations of just a year or two tend to be relatively insensitive to interest-rate changes. Funds with AAA or AA average credit-quality rankings take on less credit risk than those with, for example, B ratings, which indicate the portfolio holds a lot of high-yield (or junk) debt.

Morningstar currently uses price/cash flow, price/book, and median market capitalization to categorize foreign funds. This section also compares international-stock funds' current valuations with those of the MSCI EAFE Index, which is the most widely used benchmark for international offerings. Funds with low valuations typically hold stocks that aren't expected to grow rapidly, and therefore land in one of the value style boxes. By contrast, portfolios with high valuations typically hold fast-growing issues.

D

Diamonds

see also Unit Investment Trust, Dow Jones Industrial Average

Shares in the Diamonds Trust Series I DIA, an ETF that tracks the Dow Jones Industrial Average. The fund is structured as a unit investment trust.

Discount to NAV

Unlike regular open-end mutual funds, which are bought and sold directly from the fund company at the net asset value (NAV) of their portfolio securities, ETFs and closed-end funds trade at prices determined by the market forces of supply and demand. A fund that trades at a price less than its NAV is said to trade at a discount to its NAV. Any discount or premium should be small and short-lived due to the arbitrage mechanisms inherent in ETF structures.

Dividend

The portion of a company's profit paid directly to shareholders, generally expressed in a per-share amount. Most ETFs pay dividends at least semiannually or annually. Some ETFs such as the iShares Dow Jones Select Dividend Index, actively mimic indexes that identify high dividend-paying stocks. The way in which an ETF pays out its dividends depends on the legal structure of the ETF. The open-end index ETFs automatically reinvest dividends and pay shareholders through a quarterly cash distribution; unit investment trust ETFs do not reinvest dividends, instead putting them in a non-interest-bearing account until quarterly payout; and grantor trust ETFs allow investors to receive dividends directly from the companies of the underlying securities, instead of from the authorized participant. For an ETF's specific distribution policy, you must read the ETF's prospectus or consult with your financial advisor.

Dollar-Cost Averaging

The practice of making investments in fixed amounts at regular intervals, such as monthly, quarterly, semiannually, or annually. The process allows investors to lower their average costs by forcing them to buy more shares at low prices and fewer at high prices. Also referred to as systematic investing or constant-dollar plan. Conventional fund companies often will waive normal minimum investments for investors to commit to make direct deposits from their savings or checking accounts into such regular investment plans. However, because investors must pay brokerage commissions each time they purchase or redeem ETF shares, investing small sums of money at regular intervals for ETFs may not be very cost-efficient.

Dow Jones Industrial Average

The Dow Jones Industrial Average, or Dow, is the most widely known stock market index. The index is composed of 30 companies selected by the editors of the *Wall Street Journal*. The prices of the companies are added together and divided by a divisor that changes when a new company replaces an old one in the index, or when any company in the index splits its stock. While the Dow is not an accurate measure of the market, it is still popular because it is so well known and the companies in it are generally well-established blue chips. Other indexes, such as Standard & Poor's 500 (S&P 500) or the Wilshire 5000, are considered to be more accurate representations of the market.

Duration

see Average Effective Duration

E

ETF

see also Open-Index ETF, Unit Investment Trust, and Grantor Trust
An abbreviation for exchange-traded funds. ETFs are baskets of securities that are traded on an exchange and, unlike open-end mutual funds, can be bought and sold throughout the trading day. They can also be sold short and bought on margin. In brief, anything you might do with a stock, you can do with an ETF. Currently most ETFs are index funds and are composed of holdings that mimic a given index or specialize in certain commodities. They offer diversification, low costs, and trading flexibility to investors. Unlike mutual funds, there are options available on many ETFs. There are three different legal structures for ETFs: open-end funds, unit investment trusts, and grantor trusts. The first two structures are registered with the SEC under the Investment Company Act of 1940, while the third is not. The primary differences among these three structures regard their dividend distribution schedules and purchase/redemption policies.

ETF Star Rating

see Historical Profile, Rating, and Risk

Equity Style

see Investment Style Box

Exchange

Where ETFs are traded, including the American Stock Exchange (AMEX), New York Stock Exchange (NYSE), and Nasdaq Stock Market. Exchanges are formal organizations approved and regulated by the Securities and Exchange Commission and whose members use the facilities to trade securities. Because ETFs' shares are traded on an exchange, their prices will fluctuate according to supply and demand and offer investors the kind of real-time flexibility not available with traditional mutual funds.

Exchange Traded Notes (ETNs)

Exchange Traded Notes are 30-year senior, unsecured debt securities that track indexes and can be bought and sold on the New York Stock Exchange through a broker at market prices that are set throughout the day by supply and demand. ETNs don't necessarily invest in the indexes they track, but their issuers promise to pay investors what they would have gained or lost if they had invested directly in the index (minus commission costs and the ETNs' fees). As such, there is little risk that the ETN will not track its index, but there is credit risk, or the possibility that the issuer will go bankrupt before it has to meet its obligations to ETN holders.

ETNs are not ETFs, but like ETFs they have an arbitrage mechanism that theoretically should keep their market prices close to the intrinsic value of their benchmarks. Large institutional investors who can amass 50,000 notes can redeem them directly back to the issuer once per week, which gives them a chance to take advantage of premiums or discounts.

ETNs, like their ETF cousins, could offer tax advantages because they don't make income or capital gains distributions. Investors have to pay capital gains taxes only when they sell their notes in the secondary market or accept payment when the securities mature (Note that the Internal Revenue Service has never actually opined on how this kind of structured product should be taxed and could rule ETNs need to be taxed differently in the future.)

Expense Projections (Three-, Five-, and 10-Year)
The SEC mandates that each fund administered by a registered investment company list its expense projections. Found in the fund's prospectus, these figures show how much an investor would expect to pay in expenses, sales charges (loads), and fees over the next three, five, and 10 years, assuming a $10,000 investment that grows by 5% per year with redemption at the end of each time period. Expense projections are commonly based on the past year's incurred fees or an estimate of the current fiscal year's fees, should a portion of the overall fee structure change as of the printing of the fund's most current prospectus. Newer funds are required to print expense projections for only one- and three-year time periods, as longer-term projections may not be possible to estimate.

Expense Ratio
The annual fee that all ETFs charge their shareholders. It is taken from the ETF's annual report and expressed as a percentage of the ETF's average daily net assets deducted each fiscal year for fund expenses. It may include such items as the management fee, trustee's fee, and license fee, among others. The expense ratio is deducted from the ETF's average net assets and accrued on a daily basis. It does not include the commissions paid to trade ETF shares, or the costs incurred by the fund in trading its underlying securities. If the ETF's assets are small, its expense ratio can be quite high because the ETF must meet its expenses from a restricted asset base.

Conversely, as the net assets of the fund grow, the expense percentage should ideally diminish because expenses are spread across the wider base. To note, HOLDRs do not express their fees as expense ratios, but instead charge a flat quarterly fee per 100 shares.

F

Fixed-Income Style
see Investment Style Box

Fair Value
see also Morningstar Price/Fair Value Measure
Morningstar stock analysts estimate a stock's fair value using a discounted cash flow model that takes into account their estimates of the company's growth, profitability, risk, and many other factors over the next five years. This fair value is then compared with the stock's market price to figure its Morningstar Rating.

Morningstar uses the fair values its analysts set for stocks to help determine if an ETF's portfolio holdings are over- or undervalued.

G

Grantor Trust
An ETF structure not registered under the Investment Company Act of 1940. Grantor trusts create shares in lots of 100 and can be purchased or redeemed only in multiples of these units. They are unique in structure because investors retain the voting rights to the underlying securities of the shares and can receive dividends immediately. Merrill Lynch's HOLDRs are examples of ETFs structured as grantor trusts.

Growth
see also Investment Style Box
Often contrasted with a value approach to investing, the term growth is used to describe an investment style in which a manager looks for equity securities with high rates of revenue or earnings growth. A company's valuations are generally not emphasized as much as they are in value-style investing.

Growth of $10,000

The Growth of $10,000 graph shows an ETF's perform-ance based on how $10,000 invested in the fund would have grown over time. The returns used in the graph are not load-adjusted. The growth of $10,000 begins at the date of the fund's inception, or the first year listed on the graph, whichever is appropriate. Located alongside the ETF's graph line is a line that represents the growth of $10,000 in either the S&P 500 Index (for stock funds and hybrid funds) or the LB Aggregate Index (for bond funds). The third line represents the fund's Morningstar category average (see definition below). These lines allow investors to compare the performance of the fund with the performance of a benchmark index and the ETF's Morningstar category. Both lines are plotted on a logarithmic scale, so that identical percent-age changes in the value of an investment have the same vertical distance on the graph. For example, the vertical distance between $10,000 and $20,000 is the same as the distance between $20,000 and $40,000 because both represent a 100% increase in investment value. This provides a more accurate representation of performance than would a simple arithmetic graph. The graphs are scaled so that the full length of the vertical axis represents a tenfold increase in investment value. For securities with returns that have exhibited greater than a tenfold increase over the period shown in the graph, the vertical axis has been compressed accordingly.

Growth Measures

Long-Term Earnings Growth

Earnings are what are left of a firm's revenues after it pays all of its expenses, costs, and taxes. Companies whose earnings grow faster than those of their industry peers usually see better price performance for their stocks. Projected earnings growth is an estimate of a company's expected long-term growth in earnings, derived from all polled analysts' estimates. When report-ed for an ETF, it shows the weighted average of the projected growth in earnings for each stock in the ETF's portfolio. This measure helps determine Morningstar's growth score for each stock and the overall growth orientation of the ETF.

Historical Earnings Growth

Historical earnings growth shows the rate of increase in a company's earnings per share, based on up to four time periods. When reported for an ETF, it shows the weighted average of the growth in earnings for each stock in the ETF's portfolio. This measure helps deter-mine Morningstar's growth score for each stock and the overall growth orientation of the ETF.

Sales Growth

Sales growth shows the rate of increase in a company's sales per share, based on up to four time periods, and it is considered the best gauge of how rapidly a compa-ny's core business is growing. When reported for an ETF, it shows the weighted average of the sales-growth rates for each stock in the ETF's portfolio. This measure helps determine Morningstar's growth score for each stock and the overall growth orientation of the ETF.

Cash Flow Growth

Cash flow tells you how much cash a business is actually generating—in other words, its earnings before depreciation, amortization, and noncash charges. Sometimes called cash earnings, it's considered a gauge of liquidity and solvency. Cash flow growth shows the rate of increase in a company's cash flow per share, based on up to four time periods. When reported for an ETF, it shows the weighted average of the growth in cash flow for each stock in the ETF's portfolio. This measure helps determine Morningstar's growth score for each stock and the overall growth orientation of the ETF.

Book Value Growth

Book value is, in theory, what would be left over for shareholders if a company shut down its operations, paid off all its creditors, collected from all its debtors, and liquidated itself. In practice, however, the value of assets and liabilities can change substantially from when they are first recorded. Book value growth shows the rate of increase in a company's book value per share, based on up to four time periods. When reported for an ETF it shows the weighted average of the growth rates in book value for each stock in the ETF's portfolio. This measure helps determine Morningstar's growth score for each stock and the overall growth orientation of the ETF.

H

Historical Profile, Star Rating, and Risk

see also Morningstar Category

The star rating displayed in the Historical Profile section is an ETF's overall risk-adjusted star rating. The star ratings for the three time periods in the Rating and Risk section are combined here. In ascending order, these categories are Lowest (★), Below Average (★★), Neutral (★★★), Above Average (★★★★), and Highest (★★★★★). ETFs less than three years old are listed as Not Rated.

HOLDR

An abbreviation for Holding Company Depository Receipts. Unlike other ETFs, HOLDRs can be bought and sold only in 100-share increments and are structured as grantor trust ETFs. As such, they have unique characteristics regarding voting rights and distributions (as compared with open-end index ETFs and unit investment trusts). HOLDRs are currently offered by Merrill Lynch and the ones that currently exist focus on narrow industry groups.

I

Inception

The date on which the ETF commenced operations by offering its shares for sale to investors.

Income $

Income reflects the dividends and interest generated by an ETF's holdings. This area shows a fund's yearly income distribution expressed in per-share dollar amounts.

Income Distribution

The number of times per year that an ETF intends to make income payments (from either dividends or interest). This will differ according to the legal structure of the ETF and is specified in the ETF's prospectus or marketing documents.

Income Ratio %

The fund's income ratio reveals the percentage of current income earned per share. It is calculated by dividing the ETF's net investment income by its average net assets. (Net investment income is the total income of the ETF, less expenses.) An income ratio can be nega-tive if an ETF's expenses exceed its income, which can occur with funds that have high costs or that tend to emphasize capital gains rather than income. Because the income ratio is based on an ETF's fiscal year and is taken directly from the fund's annual shareholder report, it may not exactly correspond with other calendar-year information on the page.

Income Return %

see also Capital Return % and Total Return

Income return is that portion of an ETF's total returns that was derived from income distributions. Income return will often be higher than capital return for bond-tracking ETFs, and typically lower for equity-tracking ETFs. Adding the income return and the capital return together will produce the fund's total return.

Index Fund

A fund type that attempts to passively track the composition and returns of a given index, rather than actively trying to select securities to beat the bogy. The portfolios of index funds provide a complete or near complete representation of their benchmark indexes. Their performance should be similar the performance of the benchmark. All ETFs are currently index funds, though there are plans for actively managed ETFs.

Industry Weightings

see also Relative Comparisons and Sector Weightings

For specialty ETFs (also called sector ETFs), we replace the standard sector weightings, which include broad industry classifications such as hardware, with a breakdown of the ETF's weightings in the sector's sub-industries, or subsectors. Each sector has its own breakdown of subsectors, which can help investors decide which specific areas of an industry the ETF invests in, and how pure its focus is. The industry weightings show at a glance whether an ETF is conservatively diversified across a sector, betting on just a couple of risky subsectors to charge up returns, or crouching defensively in the mildest corner of the specialty. The ETF's weightings relative to its category average are also shown.

Each specialty ETF's breakdown also includes an Other classification, but a large weighting there shouldn't be interpreted as meaning the ETF is investing outside of its specialty. This is merely a catchall designation to classify the stocks that don't meet the exact criteria for any specific subsector. It's impossible to capture every nook and cranny of the sprawling technology category, for example, in the eight subsectors included on the page. Thus, a fair number of tech stocks fall into Other.

In-Kind Redemption
When redeeming investors receive the underlying securities of an ETF instead of cash.

Institutional Investor
An entity, company, or firm that manages assets on behalf of other investors (individual or otherwise). Some examples of institutional investors include mutual fund companies, insurance companies, and brokerage firms. Because of the large volume of assets traded by institutional investors, they can act as market makers and also often qualify for lower expense charges. Institutional investors often can enter into authorized participation agreements with ETF sponsors.

Investment Company (Open-End Fund)
see also Open-End ETF
A company regulated under the Investment Company Act of 1940 whose primary business is to invest, reinvest, or trade in securities. The investment company offers its own securities to the public and must comply with the specified regulations.

Investment Style Box
see also Current Investment Style, Growth, Market Capitalization, Morningstar Category, and Value
To help investors cut through the confusion and profusion of mutual funds and ETFs, Morningstar designed the style box, a visual tool for better understanding a fund's true investment strategy. Based on an analysis of a fund's portfolio, the Morningstar style box is a snapshot of the types of securities held by the fund. The style box is calculated with methodology similar to that used to assign the Morningstar Categories. By providing an easy-to-understand visual representation of stock and fund characteristics, the Morningstar style box allows for informed comparisons and portfolio construction based on actual holdings, as opposed to assumptions based on a fund's name or how it is marketed. The style box also forms the basis for Morningstar's style-based fund categories and market indexes.

Stock Style Box

Risk	Investment Style			Average Weighted Market Capitalization
	Value	Blend	Growth	
Low ○	Large-cap Value	Large-cap Blend	Large-cap Growth	Large
Moderate ○	Mid-cap Value	Mid-cap Blend	Mid-cap Growth	Mid
High ○	Small-cap Value	Small-cap Blend	Small-cap Growth	Small

Within the stock style box grid, nine possible combinations exist, ranging from large-cap value for the safest funds to small-cap growth for the riskiest.

Domestic-Stock Style Box
The Morningstar domestic-stock style box is a nine-square grid that provides a graphical representation of the "investment style" of stocks, mutual funds, and ETFs. It classifies securities according to market capitalization (the vertical axis) and growth and value factors (the horizontal axis). Note: Fixed-income funds are classified according to credit quality (the vertical axis) and sensitivity to changes in interest rates (the horizontal axis).

How It Works
Style box assignments begin at the individual stock level. Morningstar determines the investment style of each individual stock in its database. The style attributes of individual stocks are then used to determine the style classification of stock ETFs.

The Horizontal Axis
The scores for a stock's value and growth characteristics determine its placement on the horizontal axis of the stock style box:

Value Score Components and Weights

Forward-looking measures	
Price/projected earnings	50.0%

Historical-based measures	
Price/book	12.5%
Price/sales	12.5%
Price/cash flow	12.5%
Dividend yield	12.5%

Growth Score Components and Weights

Forward-looking measures

Long-term projected earnings growth	50.0%

Historical-based measures

Historical earnings growth	12.5%
Sales growth	12.5%
Cash flow growth	12.5%
Book value growth	12.5%

Growth and value characteristics for each individual stock are compared with those of other stocks within the same capitalization band and are scored from zero to 100 for both value and growth. To determine the overall style score, the value score is subtracted from the growth score.

The resulting number can range from 100 (for low-yield, extremely growth-oriented stocks) to -100 (for high-yield, low-growth stocks). A stock is classified as growth if the net score equals or exceeds the "growth threshold" (normally about 25 large-cap stocks). It is deemed value if its score equals or falls below the "value threshold" (normally about -15 for large-cap stocks). And if the score lies between the two thresholds, the stock is classified as "core."

The thresholds between value, core, and growth stocks vary to some degree over time, as the distribution of stock styles changes in the market. However, on average, the three stock styles each account for approximately one third of the total free float in each size category.

The Vertical Axis
Rather than a fixed number of large-cap or small-cap stocks, Morningstar uses a flexible system that isn't adversely affected by overall movements in the market to classify stocks as small, medium, or large. Large-cap stocks are defined as the group that accounts for the top 70% capitalization of the Morningstar domestic-stock universe; mid-cap stocks represent the next 20%; and small-cap stocks represent the balance. The Morningstar stock universe represents approximately 99% of the U.S. market for actively traded stocks.

Moving from Individual Stocks to Funds
A stock-tracking ETF is an aggregation of individual stocks and its style is determined by the style assignments of the stocks it owns. By plotting all of an ETF's stocks on the stock style grid, the range of stock styles included in the fund immediately becomes apparent. An asset-weighted average of the stocks' net value/growth scores determines a fund's horizontal placement-value, growth, or blend.

A fund's vertical placement is determined by its "market cap," which is defined as the geometric mean of the market capitalization (or average weighted market cap) for the stocks it owns.

$Cap1$ = the capitalization of stock 1 and $W1$ = the % weight in the portfolio and the geometric mean of market capitalization

$$= (Cap1^{W1})(Cap2^{W2})(Cap3^{W3})(Cap4^{W4})\dots(CapN^{WN})$$

For a simple example, consider a fund that owns just three stocks:

25% stake in Stock A, market cap = $1.85 Billion
35% stake in Stock B, market cap = $3.56 Billion
40% stake in Stock C, market cap = $8.58 Billion

Its geometric mean of market capitalization would equal:

$$(\$1.85\ bil^{.25})(\$3.56\ bil^{.35})(\$8.58\ bil^{.40}) = \$4.30\ Billion$$

Note that this number is larger than the fund's median market cap-the capitalization of the median stock in its portfolio. That's because stock C, with a relatively higher market cap, occupies the biggest slice of the portfolio. The geometric mean better identifies the portfolio's "center of gravity." In other words, it provides more accurate insight into how market trends (as defined by capitalization) might affect the portfolio.

Style box assignments for stocks are updated each month. Assignments for ETFs are recalculated whenever Morningstar receives updated portfolio holdings for the ETF.

Using the Style Box

In general, a growth-oriented ETF will hold the stocks of companies that the portfolio manager believes will increase earnings faster than the rest of the market. A value-oriented ETF contains mostly stocks the manager thinks are currently undervalued in price and will eventually see their worth recognized by the market. A blend fund might be a mix of growth stocks and value stocks, or it may contain stocks that exhibit both characteristics.

Understanding how different types of stocks behave is crucial for building a diversified, style-controlled portfolio of stocks, mutual funds, or ETFs. The Morningstar style box helps investors construct portfolios based on the characteristics, or style factors, of all the stocks and funds that portfolio includes.

International-Stock Style Box

These style boxes are similar to the domestic-stock style boxes described above, although the methodology is different.

On the vertical axis, international-stock ETFs are grouped as small, medium, or large. ETFs with median market capitalizations of less than $1 billion are grouped in the small-cap box. ETFs with median market caps equal to or greater than $1 billion but less than or equal to $5 billion are labeled as mid-cap offerings. ETFs with median market caps exceeding $5 billion are large cap. On the horizontal axis, international-stock ETFs, like their domestic counterparts, are separated into value, blend, or growth ETFs. We take the stock portfolio's average price/cash-flow ratio relative to the MSCI EAFE Index and add it to the portfolio's average price/book figure relative to the MSCI EAFE Index. (The MSCI EAFE average in each case is set equal to 1.00.) If the sum of the relative price/cash flow and the relative price/book is less than 1.75, the ETF is defined as a value offering if the sum lands from 1.75 to 2.25 the ETF is classified as a blend vehicle; if the sum is greater than 2.25 the ETF falls into the growth column.

Bond Style Box

Domestic- and international-bond ETFs feature their own Morningstar style box, which focuses on two pillars of bond performance: interest-rate sensitivity and credit quality. Morningstar splits bond ETFs into three groups of rate sensitivity as determined by duration (short,

Bond Style Box

Risk		Duration			Quality
		Value	Blend	Growth	
Low	○	Short-term High Quality	Interm-term High Quality	Long-term High Quality	High
Moderate	○	Short-term Medium Quality	Interm-term Medium Quality	Long-term Medium Quality	Medium
High	◉	Short-term Low Quality	Interm-term Low Quality	Long-Term Low Quality	Low

Within the bond style box grid, nine possible combinations exist, ranging from short duration or maturity/high quality for the safest funds to long duration or maturity/low quality for the riskiest.

intermediate, and long) and three credit-quality groups (high, medium, and low). These groupings graphically display a portfolio's average effective duration and credit quality. As with stock funds, nine possible combinations exist, ranging from short duration/high quality for the safest funds to long duration/low quality for the most volatile.

Along the horizontal axis of the style box lies the interest-rate sensitivity of an ETF's bond portfolio based on average effective duration. This figure, which is calculated by the ETF sponsors, weights each bond's duration by its relative size within the portfolio. Duration provides a more accurate description of a bond's true interest-rate sensitivity than does maturity because it takes into consideration all mortgage prepayments, puts and call options, and adjustable coupons. ETFs with an average effective duration of less than 3.5 years qualify as short term. ETFs with an average effective duration of greater than or equal to 3.5 years and less than or equal to six years are classified as intermediate. ETFs with an average effective duration of greater than six years are considered long term.

Along the vertical axis of a bond style box lies the average credit-quality rating of a bond portfolio. ETFs that have an average credit rating of AAA or AA are categorized as high quality. Bond portfolios with average ratings of A or BBB are medium quality, and those rated BB and below are categorized as low quality. For the purposes of Morningstar's calculations, U.S. government securities are considered AAA bonds, nonrated municipal bonds generally are classified as BB, and all other non-rated bonds generally are considered B.

L

Lehman Brothers Aggregate Index

An index that measures the value of a wide variety of investment-grade government and corporate bonds, as well as asset-backed and mortgage-backed securities. This is one of the most popular benchmarks for bonds, bond funds, and bond-tracking ETFs.

Lehman Brothers Corporate Index

An index that measures the value of a wide variety of U.S. corporate bonds and is commonly used as a benchmark for corporate bonds and corporate bond funds.

Leverage

An investment technique that involves investing borrowed money to increase returns. Certain financial instruments, such as options, also are said to have leverage relative to the underlying stock or ETF because price changes in the stock can cause larger increases or decreases in the value of the option.

Limit Order

A price order that stipulates the maximum price at which a buyer is willing to purchase shares or the minimum price at which he or she is willing to sell shares.

M

Management

The portfolio manager is the individual or individuals responsible for the overall ETF strategy, as well as the buying and selling decisions for the securities in an ETF's portfolio. To help investors know who is running an ETF, we detail management with a brief biography. We note the manager's background, experience, analytical support, other funds managed, and whether the manager invests in his or her own fund. Because ETFs are often passively managed, the portfolio manager may take a less forthright role than would a mutual fund manager.

Management Fee

The management fee is the maximum percentage deducted from a ETF's average net assets to pay an advisor or subadvisor. Often, as the ETF's net assets grow, the percentage deducted for management fees decreases. Alternatively, the ETF may compute the fee as a flat percentage of average net assets. Management fees for ETFs should be relatively low compared with mutual funds, with most being well under 1.00%.

Market Cap

see also Market Capitalization
Shown for domestic-stock ETFs, this section gives investors a view of the different sizes of companies in a fund's portfolio. Every month, we break down a stock portfolio into five different sizes of companies by their market capitalization and show what percentage of a fund's stock assets is devoted to each. Instead of using stationary market-cap cut-offs, we base our boundaries on percentiles: We call the largest 1% of U.S. companies Giant, the next 4% Large, the next 15% Medium, the next 30% Small, and the bottom 50% Micro. The Market Cap section is designed to help investors complete the picture suggested by the median market cap statistic. While average weighted market cap pinpoints the size of the average holding, this section allows investors to see the whole range of companies held by the fund.

Market Capitalization (Average Weighted)

see also Market Cap, Relative Comparisons, and Investment Style Box
For domestic-stock offerings, this measures the portfolio's "center of gravity," in terms of its market-cap exposure. A market capitalization is calculated for each stock. Its weight in the average weighted market cap calculation is then determined by the percentage of stocks it consumes in the overall portfolio. For example, a stock that is a 10% position in a fund will have twice as much influence on the calculation than a stock that is a 5% stake.

Market Maker

A dealer, such as a brokerage or bank, who fulfills buy and sell orders from investors for particular stocks. Market makers display a publicly offered price for securities in their inventory and the number of securities offered for sale. They have an important role in providing liquidity and efficiency for the securities in which they traffic.

Market Order

A price order executed with no specified price maximum or minimum. Instead, brokers buy or sell securities at the best price available on the market at the time.

Market Price

An ETF's share price as determined by market supply and demand. The market price can be expressed as the bid or offer price, the midpoint between the bid/offer spread, or the last sale price. Its expression depends on the policy of the quoting entity.

Market Return

see also Total Return and NAV Return
The total return of an ETF based on its market price at the beginning and end of the holding period. This may differ from the ETF's NAV return. The market return is the return earned by ETF investors, except for those who hold creation units (authorized participants).

Maturity

see Average Effective Maturity and Average Nominal Maturity

Mean

see Standard Deviation

Methodology

While the Morningstar Category gives investors an idea of what sorts of investments an ETF makes, it does not fully capture the nuances of the construction methodology of the ETF's underlying index. In this section, Morningstar analysts explain the criteria ETF bogies use in selecting securities and how risky a given methodology may be. On the equity side, the strategy description often focuses on what size and type of company an index keys on, or a discussion regarding how a style-based benchmark, for instance, defines growth and value stocks. With bond ETFs, the strategy section explains how the ETF manager goes about tracking the often wide-ranging fixed-income indexes. Strategy section also often notes whether an ETF manager uses representative sampling to track the underlying index and the benchmarks rebalancing schedule.

Modern Portfolio Theory (MPT) Statistics

see also Benchmark Index
Developed in the 1950s by Harry Markowitz, Modern Portfolio Theory statistics (or MPT statistics) are standard financial and academic statistical tools for assessing the risk and return of a portfolio relative to its benchmark. The main theory behind MPT is that a certain risk level will produce a certain corresponding return. Its statistical tools are best-fit beta, alpha, and R-squared. Morningstar bases alpha, beta, and R-squared on a least-squares regression of the portfolio's excess return over Treasury bills compared with the excess returns of the fund's benchmark index. These calculations are computed for the trailing 36-month period. For ETFs, the benchmark index should have a high R-squared, because index-tracking ETF's underlying portfolio should replicate the composition of its target index.

Alpha
Alpha represents the amount by which a portfolio has outperformed or underperformed what was expected based on its risk (beta). If alpha is positive, it means the portfolio's returns were higher than its regression line predicted. With mutual funds, investors often view alpha as a measurement of the value added or subtracted by active fund managers. With index-tracking ETFs, the alpha should correlate with the accepted beta of the benchmark. There are limitations to alpha's ability to accurately depict a fund's added or subtracted value. In some cases, a negative alpha can result from the expenses that are present in the fund figures but are not present in the figures of the comparison index. Alpha is completely dependent on the accuracy of beta: If the investor accepts beta as a conclusive definition of risk, a positive alpha would be a conclusive indicator of good fund performance.

Beta
Beta is a measure of a fund's sensitivity to market movements. It measures the relationship between a fund's excess return over T-bills and the excess return of the benchmark index. Morningstar calculates beta using the same regression equation as the one used for alpha, which regresses excess return for the fund against excess return for the index. This approach differs slightly from other methodologies that rely on a regression of raw returns. By definition, the beta of the benchmark (in this case, an index) is 1.00. Accordingly, a fund with

beta 1.10 has performed 10% better than its benchmark index after deducting the T-bill rate in up markets and 10% worse in down markets, assuming all other factors remain constant. Conversely, a beta of 0.85 indicates that the fund has performed 15% worse than the index in up markets and 15% better in down markets. A low beta does not imply that the fund has a low level of volatility, though; rather, a low beta means only that the fund's market-related risk is low. A specialty fund that invests primarily in gold, for example, will usually have a low beta (and a low R-squared), as its performance is tied more closely to the price of gold and gold-mining stocks than to the overall stock market. Thus, although the specialty fund might fluctuate wildly because of rapid changes in gold prices, its beta will remain low. With index-tracking ETFs, the beta coefficient should not deviate greatly from 1.00 because the portfolio aims to replicate the composition of the underlying benchmark. Hence, its volatility should also approximate that of the benchmark.

R-Squared

R-squared ranges from zero to 100 and reflects the percentage of an ETF's movements that are explained by movements in its benchmark index. An R-squared of 100 means that all movements of an ETF are completely correlated with movements in the index. Thus, index ETFs that invest only in S&P 500 stocks will have an R-squared very close to 100. Conversely, a low R-squared indicates that very few of the ETF's movements are explained by movements in its benchmark index. An R-squared measure of 25, for example, means that only 25% of the ETF's movements can be explained by movements in its benchmark index. Therefore, R-squared can be used to ascertain the significance of a particular beta or alpha. Generally, a high R-squared will indicate a more reliable beta figure. If the R-squared is low, then the beta explains less of the ETF's performance.

Morningstar Category

see also Investment Style Box

While the investment objective stated in a fund's prospectus may or may not reflect how the ETF actually invests, the Morningstar Category is assigned based on the underlying securities in each portfolio. Morningstar assigns categories based on three years of composition

and style boxes. For ETFs that are not yet three years old an average of the portfolios since the ETF's inception is used.

The Morningstar Category helps investors make meaningful comparisons between mutual funds and ETFs. The categories make it easier to build well-diversified portfolios, assess potential risk, and identify the top-performing mutual funds and ETFs.

The following is a list and explanation of the categories. We place funds in a given category based on their portfolio statistics and compositions over the past three years. If the fund is new and has no portfolio history, we estimate where it will fall before giving it a more permanent category assignment. When necessary, we may change a category assignment based on recent changes to the portfolio.

Stock ETFs

Domestic-Stock ETFs

ETFs with at least 70% of assets in domestic stocks are categorized based on the style and size of the stocks they typically own. The style and size divisions reflect those used in the investment style box: value, blend, or growth style and small, medium, or large. Based on their investment style over the past three years, diversified domestic-stock funds are placed in one of the nine categories shown below:

Large Growth	Mid-cap Growth	Small Growth
Large Blend	Mid-cap Blend	Small Blend
Large Value	Mid-cap Value	Small Value

Morningstar also includes several other domestic-stock categories: Communications, Financial, Health Care, Natural Resources, Precious Metals, Real Estate, Technology, Utilities, Convertible Bond (convertible-bond funds have at least 50% of their assets invested in convertible securities), Conservative Allocation (conservative-allocation funds invest in both stocks and bonds, with just 20% to 50% of assets in stocks), and Moderate Allocation (moderate-allocation funds invest in both stocks and bonds, with more than 50% in stocks).

International-Stock ETFs

Stock funds and ETFs that have invested 40% or more of their equity holdings in foreign stocks (on average over the past three years) are placed in an international-stock category, based on the following parameters:

Europe: at least 75% of stocks invested in Europe.

Latin America: at least 75% of stocks invested in Latin America.

Diversified Emerging Markets: at least 50% of stocks invested in emerging markets.

Diversified Asia/Pacific: at least 65% of stocks invested in Pacific countries, with at least an additional 10% of stocks invested in Japan.

Asia/Pacific ex-Japan: at least 75% of stocks in Pacific countries, with less than 10% of stocks invested in Japan.

Japan: at least 75% of stocks invested in Japan.

Foreign Large Value: a majority of assets invested in large-cap foreign stocks that are value-oriented (based on low price/book and price/cash flow ratios, relative to the MSCI EAFE Index).

Foreign Large Blend: a majority of assets invested in large-cap foreign stocks, where neither growth nor value characteristics predominate.

Foreign Large Growth: a majority of assets invested in large-cap foreign stocks that are growth-oriented (based on high price/book and price/cash flow ratios, relative to the MSCI EAFE Index).

Foreign Small/Mid-Cap Value: a majority of assets invested in small- and mid-cap foreign stocks that are value-oriented (based on low price/book and price/cash flow ratios, relative to the MSCI EAFE Index).

Foreign Small/Mid-Cap Growth: a majority of assets invested in small- and mid-cap foreign stocks that are growth-oriented (based on high price/book and price/cash flow ratios, relative to the MSCI EAFE Index).

World : at least 40% of stock holdings invested in foreign stocks, with at least 10% of stocks invested in the United States.

World Allocation: a fund with stock holdings of greater than 20% but less than 70% of the portfolio where 40% of the stocks and bonds are foreign. Also, must have at least 10% of assets invested in bonds.

Bond ETFs

ETFs with 80% or more of their assets invested in bonds are classified as bond ETFs. Note: For all bond funds, maturity figures are used only when duration figures are unavailable.

Taxable-Bond ETFs

Long-Term Government: at least 90% of bond portfolio invested in government issues with a duration of greater than six years, or an average effective maturity of greater than 10 years.

Intermediate-Term Government: at least 90% of bond portfolio invested in government issues with a duration of greater than or equal to 3.5 years and less than or equal to six years, or an average effective maturity of greater than or equal to four years and less than or equal to 10 years.

Short-Term Government: at least 90% of bond portfolio invested in government issues with a duration of greater than or equal to one year and less than 3.5 years, or an average effective maturity of greater than or equal to one year and less than four years.

Long-Term Bond: focuses on corporate and other investment-grade issues with an average duration of more than six years, or an average effective maturity of more than 10 years.

Intermediate-Term Bond: focuses on corporate and other investment-grade issues with an average duration of greater than or equal to 3.5 years but less than or equal to six years, or an average effective maturity of greater than or equal to four but less than or equal to 10 years.

Short-Term Bond: focuses on corporate and other investment-grade issues with an average duration of greater than or equal to one but less than 3.5 years, or an average effective maturity of greater than or equal to one but less than four years.

Ultrashort Bond: used for ETFs with an average duration or an average effective maturity of less than one year. This category includes general corporate and government bond funds, and excludes any international, convertible, multisector, and high-yield bond funds.

High-Yield Bond: at least 65% of assets in bonds rated below BBB.

Multisector Bond: seeks income by diversifying assets among several fixed-income sectors, usually U.S. government obligations, foreign bonds, and high-yield domestic debt securities.

Morningstar Return vs. Category

An assessment of a fund's excess return over a risk-free rate (the return of the 90-day Treasury bill) in comparison to similar ETFs and conventional open-end funds after adjusting for an assumed 0.20% commission. (ETF commissions are treated like front- and back-end loads. The 0.20% commission represents Morningstar's $20 estimate of the average retail commission paid and the $10,000 average investment amount, per SEC guidelines for expense projections.) Morningstar uses NAVs to calculate returns rather than market prices. ETF market prices are set throughout the day by supply and demand, and tend to stick close to their NAVs, which are set at the end of the trading day. NAVs are a better measure of performance because if ETFs don't trade often, their market prices grow stale.

In each Morningstar Category, the top 10% of funds earn a High Morningstar Return, the next 22.5% Above Average, the middle 35% Average, the next 22.5% Below Average, and the bottom 10% Low. Morningstar Return is measured for up to three time periods (three, five, and 10 years). These separate measures are then weighted and averaged to produce an overall measure for the fund. Funds with less than three years of performance history are not rated.

Morningstar Risk vs. Category

As assessment of the variations in a fund's monthly returns in comparison to similar ETFs and conventional open-end funds, with an emphasis on downward variation. The greater the variation, the higher the risk score. If two funds have precisely the same return, the one with the greater variations in its return is given the larger risk score.

In each Morningstar Category, the 10% of funds with the lowest measure of risk are described as Low Risk, the next 22.5% Below Average, the middle 35% Average, the next 22.5% Above Average, and the top 10% High. Morningstar Risk is measured for up to three time periods (three, five, and 10 years). These separate measures are then weighted and averaged to produce an overall measure for the fund. Funds with less than three years of performance history are not rated.

Morningstar Price/Fair Value Measure

A ratio that offers a bottom-up assessment of whether an ETF portfolio is cheap or expensive by gauging if its holdings, on average, are trading above or below their Morningstar fair value estimates. The process draws on the research of Morningstar's stable of 90 in-house equity analysts who research and estimate fair values for more than 1,700 stocks. Morningstar calculates the market value of all the holdings in a given ETF for which it has fair value estimates. Then it uses the fair value estimates of those stocks to calculate a fair value of the same portfolio. Lastly, Morningstar compares the two numbers and calculates the percentage premium or discount of the market value compared to the fair value. The result is expressed as a ratio. A measure higher than 1.0 means the ETF is overvalued, according to Morningstar estimates. A reading lower than 1.0 means the offering is undervalued. Because Morningstar does not estimate a fair value for every stock an ETF might own, the relevance of the results of the price/fair value depends on how many stocks in a given portfolio have received a fair value estimate and the percentage of that portfolio's assets these stocks represent.

Coverage Rate

The percentage of stocks in an ETF's portfolio under coverage by Morningstar stock analysts. These stocks for which Morningstar equity analysts have researched and estimated fair values. The coverage rate helps investors determine the relevance of an ETF's Price/Fair Value Measure. Coverage rates of less than 50% are not relevant. Coverage rates of 50% to 66% are considered poor and only somewhat relevant. Coverage rates of more than 66% to 83% are considered fair and moderately relevant. Coverage rates of more than 83% are considered good and relevant.

Fair Value Per Share

The aggregate fair value of the stocks in an ETF portfolio that are under coverage by Morningstar equity analysts, divided by the ETF's shares outstanding. Depending on the coverage rate, the fair value may not include all of the stocks in the ETF portfolio.

Price/Fair Value Premium/Discount

The percent by which the aggregate fair value of an ETF's portfolio exceeds or trails the aggregate market price of the stocks in the portfolio for which Morningstar has estimated fair values.

Price Per Share

The aggregate market price of the stocks in an ETF portfolio that are under coverage by Morningstar equity analysts divided by the ETF's shares outstanding. Depending on the coverage rate, the price per share may not comprise all of the stocks in the ETF portfolio and will not match the ETF's market price or NAV.

Morningstar Style Box

see Investment Style Box

Morningstar's Take

Morningstar's analysis of a fund that interprets and enhances the numerical data in an effort to provide an assessment of an ETF's worth. To accomplish this, a Morningstar analyst scrutinizes past shareholder reports, puts historical performance into the perspective of market trends, and whenever possible, interviews an ETF manager or other fund official. Although many people are involved in producing this Morningstar page, the analyst is ultimately responsible for its content.

MSCI EAFE (Morgan Stanley Capital International Europe, Australasia, Far East)

An index that measures the combined market value of a selected group of stocks from Europe, Australasia, and the Far East. This is one of the most widely used benchmarks for international stocks, funds, and ETFs.

MSCI Emerging Markets

An index maintained by Morgan Stanley Capital International that measures the combined market value of a selected group of stocks from 26 emerging markets including Latin America, Eastern Europe, and most of Asia except for Japan and Australia. It is commonly used as a benchmark for emerging-markets stocks, funds, and ETFs.

N

Nasdaq Composite

An index that measures the cumulative market cap of all of the stocks traded on the Nasdaq stock market exchange. Because the Nasdaq exchange is heavily weighted with technology stocks, the Nasdaq Composite is often used as a proxy for the performance of the technology sector.

NAV

see Net Asset Value

NAV Return

see also Total Return, Market Return

The total return of an ETF, based on its NAV at the beginning and end of the holding period and assuming reinvested dividends. This may be different from the ETF's market return. The market return, not the NAV return, is the return actually earned by ETF investors, except for those who hold creation units (authorized participants).

Net Assets

see Total Net Assets

Net Asset Value

An ETF's net asset value (NAV) represents its per-share price. An ETF's NAV is derived by dividing the total net assets of the ETF by the number of shares outstanding. Note that the Net Asset Value of ETFs may differ from the market price, which is the price at which the ETF shares are traded on an intraday market.

O

Open-End ETF

The most common type of ETF structure and registered under the Investment Act of 1940, open-end ETFs automatically reinvest dividends and pay them out to shareholders through a quarterly cash distribution. Open-end ETFs are authorized to use derivatives and generate income by loaning securities of its underlying portfolio.

Options

The right, but not the obligation, to buy or sell a specific number of securities at a set price until a specified date. Like stocks and unlike traditional mutual funds, many ETFs offer options trading. Because options offer the right and not the obligation to buy shares, they can buffer price fluctuations for investors and are often profitably traded on the rise and fall of their premium prices. Call options allow the buyer to buy 100 shares of the underlying security by a certain date in the future for a certain price; put options allow the buyer to sell a certain number of shares within a certain time period for a certain price.

P

Percentile Rank (% Rank)

see also Performance

Located in the Performance and History sections these rankings allow investors to compare a fund's total returns with those of other funds.

In the Performance section we compare the fund's total return for various time periods against the same Morningstar Category (% Rank Cat). In the History section, we compare a fund's calendar-year total returns with its category's (Total Rtn % Rank Cat). In both sections, a fund's total returns are ranked on a scale from 1 to 100 where 1 represents the highest-returning 1% of funds and 100 represents the lowest-returning 1% of funds. Thus, in the performance section, a Percentile rank of 15 under the % Rank Cat column for the trailing three-month period indicates that the fund's three-month return placed in the top 15% of all funds in its category for that time period.

Performance

see also Percentile Rank, Tax Analysis, and Total Return

A fund's total return figures for various time periods.

Investment Value Graph

The Investment Value graph line shows a fund's performance trend, derived from the fund's historical growth of $10,000. It provides a visual depiction of how a fund has amassed its returns, including the performance swings its shareholders have endured along the way. The growth of $10,000 begins at the date of the fund's inception; if the fund has been in existence for more than 12 years, the growth of $10,000 begins at the first year listed on the graph. Also, featured in the graph is the performance of an index (S&P 500 or MSCI EAFE) that allows investors to compare the performance of the fund with the performance of the benchmark index.

Quarterly Returns

The first section provides the fund's quarterly and year-end total returns for the past five years. The quarterly returns are compounded to obtain the year-end total return shown on the right. (Calculating the sum of the four quarterly returns will not produce the year-end total return because simple addition does not take into account the effects of compounding.)

Total Return %

This figure is calculated by taking the change in net asset value, reinvesting all income and capital-gains distributions during the period, and dividing by the starting net asset value.

+/- S&P 500

This statistic measures the difference between a stock ETF's total return and the total return of the S&P 500 Index. A negative number indicates that the ETF underperformed the index by the given amount, while a positive number indicates that the ETF outperformed the index by the given amount. For example, a listing of -2.0 indicates that the fund underperformed the index by 2 percentage points. The difference between each stock ETF's performance and the S&P 500 Index is listed. Bond ETFs are compared with the Lehman Brothers Aggregate Bond Index. The next column shows the same performance figure relative to another more specialized benchmark index.

% Rank Cat:

see also Percentile Rank

Morningstar lists each ETF's total return for various time periods against the funds in the same Morningstar Category (% Rank Cat). One is the highest or best percentile ranking and 100 is the lowest, or worst.

Portfolio Analysis

Occupying much of the right side of the Morningstar page is the Portfolio Analysis section. Prominent in this section are an ETF's most recently reported top securities (excluding cash and cash equivalents for all but short-term bond funds), ranked in descending order by the percentage of the portfolio's net assets they occupy. With this information, investors can more clearly identify what drives the fund's performance.

Morningstar makes every effort to gather the most up-to-date portfolio information from a fund. By law, however, funds need only report this information four times during a calendar year, and they have two months after the report date to actually release the shareholder report and portfolio. Therefore, it is possible that a fund's portfolio could be up to five months old or more at the time of publication. We print the date the portfolio was reported. Older portfolios should not be disregarded, however; although the list may not represent the exact current holdings of the fund, it may still provide a good picture of the overall nature of the fund's management style.

Total Stocks/Total Fixed-Income

Total Stock indicates the total number of stock securities in a fund's portfolio, and Total Fixed-Income denotes the number of bond securities a fund holds. Theses do not simply refer to the stocks or bonds listed on the page; rather, they represent all stocks and bonds in the portfolio. These listings can be quite useful for gaining greater insight into the portfolio's diversification.

Share Change

Applied only to common stocks, the share change entry indicates the change in the number of shares of each stock from the previously reported portfolio. If the change column shows a minus sign for one of the portfolio's stocks, that means the ETF's manager sold shares of that stock since the previous portfolio was reported. Similarly, a plus sign next to the holding means that management added shares of that stock to the portfolio. The sunshine symbol indicates that the stock is a new addition to the portfolio. We list the date of the previously reported portfolio in the column heading, so that you know how much time has passed between the current portfolio and the previously reported portfolio.

Security

This column lists the names of the stock or bond securities held as of the portfolio date. For stock holdings, this line typically displays just the name of the issuing company. Other stock labels are included where appropriate, such as ADR, which distinguishes an American Depository Receipt. Bond holdings, however, will usually include more information to differentiate among the many types of bonds available. For most bonds, the coupon rate is listed as a percentage figure after the name of the bond. Adjustable-rate mortgages and floating-rate notes will have ARM or FRN (or IFRN for inverse-floating rate notes) listed after the name of the bond to indicate that the coupon rate is variable. Some adjustable-rate bond listings will include the formula by which the coupon rate is calculated, which is usually a fixed percentage plus some benchmark value. Securities followed by the abbreviation IO are interest-only securities, or those that consist only of the interest

portion of a security, not the principal portion. PO indicates a principal-only security that sells at a discount to par and carries a coupon rate of zero.

Sector: see also Sector Weighting and Industry Weightings

The industry sector of each stock holding is reported in this column this gives investors greater insight into where an ETF's top holdings are concentrated and where its vulnerabilities lie.

P/E: see also Price/Earnings Ratio and Value Measures

To add depth to the average P/E number for the entire portfolio (listed under Current Investment Style), the P/E ratio for each stock is reported here. NMF means the stock's p/e is 100 or more. A minus sign means the company has no earnings or the figure is not available.

YTD Return %

The year-to-date stock returns show whether one or two big winners (or losers) are driving fund performance, or a lot of little successes. In some cases, losses in top holdings can suggest a bargain-hunting strategy if a position in a losing stock is new or expanded.

% Assets

The % Assets column indicates what percentage of the portfolio's net assets a given security constitutes. Morningstar calculates the percentage of net assets figure by dividing the market value of the security by the ETF's total net assets. If a given security makes up a large percentage of the fund's net assets, the fund uses a concentrated portfolio strategy, at least with respect to the security in question. If, however, the percentage figures are low, then the manager is simply not willing to bet heavily on a particular security.

Date of Maturity

Maturity, located in the portfolio section for bond ETFs only, indicates the date on which a bond or note comes due. This information can be used in determining the portfolio's basic fixed-income strategy. For example, if most of these dates are a year or two away, the fund is taking a conservative, short-term approach. The maturity dates listed here, however, are not adjusted for calls (rights an issuer may have to redeem outstanding bonds before their scheduled maturity) or for the likelihood of mortgage prepayments. Thus, they might not accurately state the actual time to repayment of a bond, and might overstate a portfolio's sensitivity to interest-rate changes.

Amount

Found on bond ETF pages, the amount column refers to the size of the fund's investment in a given security as to the portfolio dates listed above. This figure reflects the principal value of the security in thousands of dollars.

Value

Value simply gives the market value of a particular security in thousands of dollars as of the portfolio date. The value column allows investors to gauge whether a fixed-income security is selling at a premium or a discount to its face value, as reflected in the amount column.

Premium

see also NAV and Discount to NAV

The amount by which an ETF's market price is greater than its net asset value (NAV). Any discount or premium is usually small and short-lived because ETFs' in-kind redemption process allows market makers to arbitrage away the difference.

Profitability Measures

Return on Assets (ROA)

This measures how effectively companies use their assets to generate profits. The formula for an individual firm is net income divided by assets. Companies with high returns on assets include software firms and beverage companies. Both types of companies frequently generate high profits but have relatively small investments in plant, equipment, and other assets. Firms with low returns on assets are typically in manufacturing or other capital-intensive industries. Companies with low returns on assets tend to have low valuations and are mostly held by value ETFs; by contrast, growth managers favor firms with high returns on assets. An ETF's ROA is equal to the weighted average ROA of its individual holdings.

Return on Equity (ROE)

This calculation reveals how effectively management has invested shareholders' equity, which is the amount of money initially invested in the business plus retained earnings. ROE is simply net income divided by average shareholder equity. A high ROE is often a

sign that a company's management uses its resources wisely, and the company is often located in a growing industry with high barriers to entry. For example, thanks to its dominance of the software operating-systems market, Microsoft usually has high ROEs. By contrast, companies with low ROEs frequently operate in stagnant industries in which there is overcapacity. For example, automakers frequently earn low returns on equity. Companies with high ROEs generally have better business models, but as a reflection of that, their share prices are often expensive. Growth managers typically prefer companies with high and rising ROEs, while valuation concerns may lead value managers to buy firms with low ROEs. A fund's ROE is the weighted average of its individual holdings' ROEs.

Net Margin

We arrive at net margin by dividing a firm's net income (after all expenses, including taxes) by its sales. This measures how effective a company is at wringing profits out of each dollar of revenues. Companies with high net margins tend to have strong competitive positions, while those with low net margins often operate in highly price-competitive industries such as retailing. Companies that consistently earn high net margins include pharmaceuticals and successful software companies.

Low-margin businesses include supermarkets and other retailers. High-margin firms earn superior returns but also garner premium valuations, so the stocks are often too expensive for value managers. At the ETF level, net margin represents the weighted average of the individual stocks' net margins.

Q

Qube

Shares in the ETF that tracks the Nasdaq 100 Index. The name Qube is derived from its old ticker symbol, QQQ. The fund is the most heavily invested ETF by volume. Qubes have a unit investment trust structure. In 2005 the fund switched from the American Stock Exchange to the Nasdaq Stock Market and changed its ticker symbol to QQQQ.

R

Rank
see Percentile Rank

Rating and Risk
see also Historical Profile
In this section, Morningstar includes commission-adjusted returns and several risk measures and proprietary statistics.

Regional Exposure
All international stock funds feature a regional exposure listing. This table displays the percentage of the fund's total net assets invested in the U.K./Western Europe, Japan, Asia ex-Japan, North America, and Latin America. Below the regional information on each page we list the five largest country exposures. The information in this section is gathered from portfolios and is the most recent available.

Relative Comparisons
see also Market Capitalization, Price/Book Ratio, Price/Cash Flow, Price/Earnings Ratio, and Industry Weightings
At various places in the Portfolio Analysis section, Morningstar shows how an individual ETF compares with the average of all ETFs within its category (Rel Cat) or a benchmark index (Rel S&P 500). The category average (or index) is always set equal to 1.00. For example, a domestic-stock ETF with a utilities weighting of 1.50 relative to its category has 50% more in utilities issues than its average peer. Stock statistics are displayed in comparison with the S&P Index. In this case, 1.00 represents the index. A relative price/book ratio of 0.43, for example, indicates that the fund's price/book is 57% lower than that of the index.

Restricted/Illiquid Securities
see Special Securities

Return
see Total Return

Risk
see Modern Portfolio Theory Statistics and Standard Deviation

Russell 2000
An index, updated annually by the Frank Russell Company, that is composed of the 1,001st through 3,000th largest companies in the United States in terms of market capitalization. This is one of the most commonly used benchmarks for measuring the performance of small-cap stocks, and numerous funds and ETFs mimic all or portions of this index.

S

S&P 500 Index (Standard & Poor's 500 Index)
Also known simply as the "S&P," this is one of the most common indexes used to represent the U.S. stock market. Contrary to popular belief, it does not consist of the 500 largest U.S. companies, but is composed of a range of small capitalization to large capitalization companies selected by the Standard & Poor's Index Committee. The S&P 500 is a market-cap-weighted index, however, and the largest companies have more influence on its performance than the smaller-cap companies. Many stocks, funds, and ETFs are measured against this benchmark.

Sector Breakdown for Fixed-Income Funds
The fixed-income sector illustrates the type of bonds a fund owns. These sectors help investors compare and understand the sector exposure of each mutual fund. These data are especially useful for comparing two funds that may be in the same Morningstar Category. The fixed-income sectors are calculated for all domestic taxable-bond portfolios. It is based on the securities in the most recent portfolio. This information shows the percentage of bond and cash assets invested in each of the 14 fixed-income sectors.

Morningstar groups all fixed-income assets into the following sectors:

U.S. Government
U.S. Treasuries
This sector includes all conventional fixed-rate debt issued by the Treasury department of the United States government (i.e. this sector excludes tips). Some examples of this type of debt are Treasury bonds and Treasury notes. Treasury bills are included under % Cash, because they mature in less than 12 months.

TIPS

TIPS are inflation-indexed debt issued by the U.S. Treasury. (The term TIPS derives from their former name, Treasury Inflation-Protected Securities.) These bonds have principal and coupon payments that are linked to movements in the Consumer Price Index. They are a defensive measure against expectations of inflation, which typically erodes the real yield of conventional bonds. Even if inflation fears are in check, these bonds can benefit when the yields fall on traditional Treasuries. These unique securities act very differently than any other fixed-rate bond, and their volatility can change over time, depending on the level of interest rates.

U.S. Agency

This sector includes debt securities issued by government agencies-such as the Federal National Mortgage Association (FNMA), also known as Fannie Mae, or the Federal Home Loan Mortgage Corporation (FHLMC), also known as Freddie Mac-to raise capital and finance their operations. These "debentures" are not secured by physical assets, so they differ from most of the mortgage bonds that are issued by these agencies.

Mortgage

Mortgage Pass-Throughs

These are fixed-income securities that represent a claim to the cash flows associated with a pool of mortgages. The bondholders are entitled to a share of the principal and interest payments paid by the homeowners. The majority of these bonds are issued by a government agency such as FNMA, GNMA, or FHLMC. A few private corporations and banks also securitize and package mortgages in this way, and those are also included in this sector.

Mortgage CMO

Collateralized mortgage obligations (CMO) are similar to pass-through mortgage securities, but investors have more control over whether they will be paid sooner or later. CMOs are structured by time, so that some investors can line up for the first series of cash flow payments, while others may choose to put themselves at the end of the line. A fund manager would buy a late-paying CMO if he or she believed that there would be a lot of mortgage refinancing in the near term. This would protect the fund from getting its money back too early, which would require it to be reinvested at a lower interest rate. Most CMOs are based on mortgages from government agencies, such as FNMA or GNMA.

Mortgage ARM

Adjustable-rate mortgage (ARM) securities are backed by residential home mortgages where the interest rate is reset periodically in relation to a benchmark. Most ARMs are from government agencies, such as FNMA and GNMA.

Credit

U.S. Corporate

This sector includes all fixed-income securities that are issued by corporations domiciled in the United States. Corporate bonds are issued with a wide range of coupon rates and maturity dates.

Asset-Backed

Asset-backed securities are based on the expected cash flow from such things as auto loans, credit-card receivables, and computer leases. The cash flows for asset-backed securities can be fixed (e.g. auto loans have a defined payment schedule and a fixed maturity) or variable (credit-card debt is paid at random intervals). These securities typically range in maturity from two to seven years.

Convertible

Convertible bonds give the owner an opportunity to convert the bond to a certain number of shares of common stock at a certain price. As the stock approaches that price, the option to convert becomes more valuable and the price of the convertible bond also rises. These securities usually provide lower interest payments, because the option to convert to stock could potentially be quite valuable at some point in the future.

Municipal

Local and state governments issue municipal bonds in order to raise money for operations and development. This financing is sometimes used to build or upgrade hospitals, sewer systems, schools, housing, stadiums, or industrial complexes. Some municipal bonds are backed by the issuing entity while others are linked to a revenue stream, such as from a tollway or a utility. Municipal bonds are exempt from federal tax and often from state and local taxes, too. The tax break allows municipal governments to sell the bonds at a lower interest rate, because the investor gets an additional tax benefit. Currently there are no municipal-bond ETFs.

Corporate Inflation-Protected

Inflation-protected securities are similar to TIPS, but they are issued by a private entity rather than by the U.S. government. These bonds are linked to an index of inflation, and the principal and coupon payments increase when inflation increases. As with TIPS, these securities behave quite differently from conventional bonds.

Foreign

Foreign Corporate

These fixed-income securities are issued by corporations that are based outside of the United States.

Foreign Government

These fixed-income securities are issued by governments outside the United States.

Cash

Cash can be cash in the bank, certificates of deposit, currency, or money market holdings. Cash can also be any fixed-income securities that mature in less than 12 months. Cash also includes commercial paper and any repurchase agreements held by the ETF. Because this data point is based on only the cash and bond assets in the ETF, it can be different than the % Cash in the composition breakdown, which is expressed as a percent of total assets.

Sector Weightings/Economic Spheres

see also Subsector Weightings

Morningstar divides the stock market into three broad "economic spheres," each of which contains four specific industry sectors. Sectors are based on what companies actually do. That is, unlike some other sector classification systems, sectors aren't based on expected behavior of the stocks of these companies.

The economic spheres with their major inclusive sectors are as follows:

ⓣ Information Sphere
Made up of the Software, Hardware, Media, and Telecommunications sectors.

☞ Service Sphere
Made up of the Health Care, Consumer Services, Business Services, and Financial Services sectors.

⬏ Manufacturing Sphere
Made up of the Consumer Goods, Industrial Materials, Energy, and Utilities sectors.

The sectors with their major inclusive industries are as follows:

▣ Software
Companies engaged in the design and marketing of computer operating systems and applications. Examples include Microsoft, Oracle, and Siebel Systems.

▣ Hardware
Manufacturers of computer equipment, communication equipment, semiconductors, and components. Examples include IBM, Cisco Systems, and Intel.

▣ Media
Companies that own and operate broadcast networks and those that create content or provide it for other media companies. Examples include Time Warner, Walt Disney, and Washington Post.

▣ Telecommunications
Companies that provide communication services using fixed-line networks or those that provide wireless access and services. Examples include, AT&T, and Alltel.

▣ Health Care
Includes biotechnology, pharmaceuticals, research services, HMOs, home health, hospitals, assisted living, and medical equipment and supplies. Examples include Abbott Laboratories, Merck, and Cardinal Health.

▣ Consumer Services
Includes retail stores, personal services, home builders, home supply, travel and entertainment companies, and educational providers. Examples include Wal-Mart, Home Depot, and Expedia.

Business Services

Includes advertising, printing, publishing, business support, consultants, employment, engineering and construction, security services, waste management, distributors, and transportation. Examples include Manpower, R.R. Donnelley, and Southwest Airlines.

Financial Services

Includes banks, finance companies, money-management firms, savings and loans, securities brokers, and insurance companies. Examples include Citigroup, Washington Mutual, and Fannie Mae.

Consumer Goods

Companies that manufacture or provide food, beverages, household and personal products, apparel, shoes, textiles, autos and auto parts, consumer electronics, luxury goods, packaging, and tobacco. Examples include PepsiCo, Ford Motor, and Kraft Foods.

Industrial Materials

Includes aerospace and defense firms, companies that provide or manufacture chemicals, machinery, building materials, and commodities. Examples include Boeing, DuPont, and Alcoa.

Energy

Companies that produce or refine oil and gas, oilfield services and equipment companies, and pipeline operators. Examples include ExxonMobil, Schlumberger, and BP.

Utilities

Electric, gas, and water utilities. Examples include Duke Energy, Exelon, and El Paso.

SEC Yield

see also Yield

SEC yield is a standardized figure that the Securities and Exchange Commission requires funds to use to calculate rates of income return on a fund's capital investment. SEC yield is an annualized calculation that is based on a trailing 30-day period. This figure will often differ significantly from Morningstar's other yield figure, which reflects trailing 12-month distributed yield, because of differing time periods as well as differing accounting policies. For example, SEC yield is based on a bond's yield to maturity, which takes into account amortization of premiums and discounts, while Morningstar's distributed yield is based on what funds actually pay out.

Share Change

see Portfolio Analysis

Sharpe Ratio

The Sharpe ratio is a risk-adjusted measure developed by Nobel Laureate William Sharpe. It is calculated using standard deviation and excess return to determine reward per unit of risk. First, the average monthly return of the 90-day Treasury bill (over a 36-month period) is subtracted from the fund's average monthly return. The difference in total return represents the fund's excess return beyond that of the 90-day Treasury bill, a risk-free investment. An arithmetic annualized excess return is then calculated by multiplying this monthly return by 12. To show a relationship between excess return and risk, this number is then divided by the standard deviation of the ETF's annualized excess returns. The higher the Sharpe ratio, the better the ETF's historical risk-adjusted performance.

Short Sale

Selling a borrowed security with the intention of buying it back at a lower price in the future and pocketing the difference. In essence, short sales are bets that a ETF will fall. To sell short, an investor borrows ETF shares from one party and then sells them to another on the open market. The investor hopes the ETF drops, because he or she would be able to buy the shares back at a lower price and then return them to the lender. The difference between the original price and the price the investor pays to buy the shares back is the profit or loss. Short sales can slow returns in a rising market, but reduce losses or even produce gains in a falling market. One of the risks of short sales is that the maximum gain is 100%, but potential losses are unlimited.

SPDR

An abbreviation for Standard & Poor's Depository Receipts. SPDRs are ETFs that track a variety of S&P indexes. For example, the popular SPDR Trust Series 1 tracks the S&P 500 Index. Select Sector SPDRs track various sector indexes that carve up the S&P 500 Index into separate industry groups. SPDR Trust, Series 1 is structured as a unit investment trust, but Select Sector SPDRs are open-end funds.

Specialist

see also Market Maker

A member of a given stock exchange (an individual or a firm) who maintains an inventory of specific securities and is responsible for executing limit orders and buying or selling to maintain the specialist's own account.

Special Securities

This section shows an ETF's exposure to a variety of complex or illiquid securities, including derivatives. The percentage of total net assets represented by each type of security is listed to the right of each group. Some securities may fall under more than one type.

Restricted/Illiquid Securities

Restricted and illiquid securities are issues that may be hard to accurately price and difficult to sell because an investor may be unable to find a buyer quickly. Private placement issues and 144(a) securities are both included here. Both types have varying degrees of liquidity and are exempt from some of the cumbersome registration and disclosure requirements that public offerings usually face.

Exotic Mortgage-Backed Securities

This section indicates how much of an ETF's net assets are held in unusual mortgage-backed derivatives. Specifically, we delineate those securities that see their price changes magnified when interest rates or mortgage-prepayment speeds change. Because not all mortgage-backed derivatives have these traits, we include the following: interest-only (IOs) and principal-only paper (POs), inverse floating-rate securities (IFRNs), and Z-tranche collateralized mortgage obligation issues, all of which are fairly clearly labeled in a fund's shareholder reports. Kitchen-sink bonds, a complex mix of interest-only, principal-only bonds, and cast-off CMO tranches, are also tallied here. For stock funds, which rarely hold mortgage-backed issues of any kind, we combine exotic mortgage-backed securities with structured notes.

Emerging-Markets Securities

Debt or equity securities from emerging markets are listed here. These figures are calculated from the most recently available portfolio. Morningstar classifies as an emerging market anything aside from the following developed markets: Australia, Austria, Belgium, Canada, Denmark, Finland, France, Germany, Greece, Hong Kong, Ireland, Italy, Japan, the Netherlands, New Zealand, Norway, Portugal, Singapore, South Korea, Spain, Sweden, Switzerland, Taiwan, the United Kingdom, and the United States. This list is subject to change as markets become more developed or vice versa.

Options/Futures/Warrants

Options and futures may be used speculatively, to leverage a portfolio, or cautiously, as a hedge against risk. We don't show the percentage of assets devoted to options or futures because it is difficult to determine from shareholder reports how much of a portfolio is affected by an options or futures contract. We also include forward contracts and warrants in this area.

Standard Deviation

A statistical measure of the range of an ETF's performance. When an ETF has a high standard deviation, its range of performance has been very wide, indicating greater volatility. Investors use the standard deviation of historical performance to try to predict the range of returns that are most likely for a given portfolio. Standard deviation is based on a bell-curve distribution, so approximately 68% of the time, returns will fall within one standard deviation of the mean return for the portfolio, and 95% within two standard deviations. The most important thing to note is that the greater the standard deviation, the greater the fund's volatility has been.

For example, an investor can compare two ETFs with the same average monthly return of 5%, but with different standard deviations. The first ETF has a standard deviation of 2, which means that its range of returns for the past 36 months has typically remained between 1% and 9%. On the other hand, assume that the second ETF has a standard deviation of 4 for the same period. This higher deviation indicates that this ETF has experienced returns fluctuating between -3% and 13%. With the second ETF, an investor can expect greater volatility.

Mean

The mean represents the annualized average monthly return from which the standard deviation is calculated. The mean will be the same as the annualized trailing, three-year return figure for the same time period.

Stop Loss Order

A trading technique designed to limit losses by designating a specified threshold at which shares must be sold.

Strategic Asset Allocation

see also Tactical Asset Allocation

A passive investment strategy or portfolio construction model by which investments are selected according to a fixed asset allocation model. This asset allocation model is defined by broad asset class (stocks, bonds, cash, or alternative instruments). Strategic asset allocators often rebalance portfolios under management on a monthly or quarterly basis and strictly adhere to the preordained asset allocation model. This investment model can be used in conjunction with tactical asset allocation model, but is sometimes viewed as its opposite.

Style Box

see Investment Style Box

T

Tactical Asset Allocation

see also Strategic Asset Allocation

An active investment strategy or portfolio construction model by which investments are selected with deference to a particular asset-allocation model but is regularly rebalanced to benefit from favorable investment climates, sectors, or subgroups. Tactical asset allocators will also shift their strategies in accordance with fundamental investment principles such as returns, various measures of volatility, and risk while keeping in mind the original asset-allocation strategy. Tactical asset-allocation models are sometimes used in conjunction with strategic asset-allocation models, though the two strategies are also considered to be opposites.

Tax-Adjusted Return %

see Tax Analysis

Tax Analysis

The information provided in the Tax Analysis section can be used to evaluate an ETF's aftertax returns and its efficiency in achieving them. Additionally, the potential capital gains exposure figure can provide a glimpse at a shareholder's vulnerability to taxation. All these figures can help an investor judge which ETFs have been tax-friendly.

Tax-Adjusted Return

The Tax-Adj Rtn % column shows an estimate of an ETF's annualized aftertax total return for the three-, five-, and 10-year periods, excluding any capital gains effects that would result from selling the ETF at the end of the period. Consistent with SEC guidance regarding tax-adjusted returns, these figures reflect the maximum load paid by fund shareholders. To determine this figure, all income and short-term (less than one year) capital-gain distributions are taxed at the maximum federal rate at the time of distribution. Long-term (more than one year) capital gains are taxed at a 20% rate. The aftertax portion is then reinvested in the fund. The category percentile rank (% Rank Cat) for each fund's tax-adjusted return is also listed. This ranking helps investors compare a fund's estimated aftertax performance with that of other funds in the category.

Tax-Cost Ratio

This represents the estimated percentage-point reduction in an annualized return that has resulted from income taxes over the past three-, five-, and 10-year periods. The calculation assumes investors pay the maximum federal rate on capital gains and ordinary income.

Telephone Numbers

These are the local and toll-free (if available) numbers that an investor may use to contact the fund, call for a prospectus, or get marketing information.

Ticker

A ticker is the symbol assigned to the ETF based on the exchange on which it's sold. ETF tickers range from three to four characters and are commonly used to locate a fund on electronic price-quoting systems.

Total Net Assets (TNA)

see also Average Trading Volume

This figure gives the ETF's asset base, net of fees and any expenses, at year end of past calendar years and at month end for the current year. Both total net assets and average trading volume can indicate the popularity of an ETF with investors.

Total Return

see also Capital Return %, Income Return %, and Market Return

All references to total return represent an ETF's gains over a specified period of time. Total return includes both income (in the form of dividends or interest payments) and capital gains or losses (the increase or decrease in the value of a security). Morningstar calculates total return by taking the change in an ETF's NAV, assuming the reinvestment of all income and capital-gains distributions (on the actual reinvestment date used by the ETF) during the time period, and then dividing the initial NAV. The quarterly returns, listed in the Performance section, express the ETF's return for each individual quarter; the total shown on the right is the compounded return for the four quarters of that year. An asterisk next to the total return number indicates that the return is calculated for a partial quarter or partial year because the ETF began operations during that time period.

Note that market return calculates total return by using market prices in place of the ETF's net asset value (NAV). Thus, the market total return and NAV total return may differ slightly.

Total Stocks/Total Fixed-Income

see Portfolio Analysis

Tracking Error

As applied to index exchange-traded funds, this refers to the amount by which the ETF portfolio's returns differ from that of the benchmark it tries to follow. In general, an index ETF's tracking error should be no greater than its expense ratio. That shows the fund is doing a good job tracking its underlying index before expenses are deducted. Tracking error greater than an ETF's expense ratio could indicate the fund's manager isn't doing a good job running the fund, or that the fund has selected an inefficient index to follow.

Turnover Rate

The rate that represents, roughly, the percentage of the portfolio's holdings that have changed over the past year, this number provides a rough measure of the ETF's level of trading activity. This publicly reported figure is calculated by funds in accordance with SEC regulations, and Morningstar gathers the information

from fund shareholder reports. An ETF divides the lesser of purchases or sales (expressed in dollars and excluding all securities with maturities of less than one year) by the ETF's average monthly assets. The resulting percentage can be loosely interpreted to represent the percentage of the portfolio's holdings that have changed over the past year. The turnover ratio is most accurate, however, when an ETF's asset base remains stable. A low turnover figure (typically less than 30%) might indicate that the manager is following a buy-and-hold strategy. High turnover (more than 100%) could be an indication of an investment strategy involving considerable buying and selling of securities. For index-tracking ETFs, the turnover ratio should be low (ie. generally in single digits) because they are not actively managed; however, the turnover rate can be greater based on the methodology of the particular index tracked.

U

Unit Investment Trust

An ETF structure registered under the Investment Company Act of 1940. Unit investment trusts replicate their benchmark but cannot invest greater than 25% of its assets in any single issuer. Unlike open-end funds, unit investment trusts do not reinvest dividends immediately. Instead, dividends are placed in a non-interest-bearing account until they are paid out on a quarterly basis. This can create a slight drag on the performance of these ETFs.

U.S. 90-Day Treasury Bill

Also known as the 90-day "T-bill", these debt securities, issued by the U.S. government, are used as a common measure of short-term interest rates.

V

Value

see also Growth and Investment Style Box

The investment style commonly referred to as a value approach focuses on stocks that an investor or fund manager thinks are currently undervalued in price and will eventually have their worth recognized by the market. It is often contrasted with a growth style approach to investing.

Value Measures

Price/Projected Earnings

Projected earnings are the consensus analyst opinion of how much a company will earn during its next fiscal year. Price/projected earnings represents the amount investors are paying for each dollar of expected earnings per share. When reported for an ETF, it shows the weighted average of the price/projected earnings ratio for each stock in the ETF's portfolio. This measure helps determine Morningstar's value score for each stock and the overall value orientation of the ETF.

Price/Book Value

Book value is, in theory, what would be left over for shareholders if a company shut down its operations, paid off all of its creditors, collected from all of its debtors, and liquidated itself. In practice, however, the value of assets and liabilities can change substantially from when they are first recorded. Many investors use the price/book ratio-the ratio of a company share price to its total book value per share-as a way to value a stock. If the share price is less than total equity per share, the company is selling for less than its break-up value. When reported for an ETF, it shows the weighted average of the price/book ratio for each stock in the ETF's portfolio. This measure helps determine Morningstar's value score for each stock and the overall value orientation of the ETF.

Price/Sales

Price/sales represents the amount investors are paying for each dollar of sales generated by the company. Price/sales is usually a less volatile measure than either price/earnings or price/book and can be especially useful when evaluating companies with volatile earnings. When reported for an ETF, it shows the weighted average of the price/sales ratio for each stock in the ETF's portfolio. This measure helps determine Morningstar's value score for each stock and the overall value orientation of the ETF.

Price/Cash Flow

Cash flow tells you how much cash a business is actually generating-its earnings before depreciation, amortization, and noncash charges. Sometimes called cash earnings, it's considered a gauge of liquidity and solvency. Price/cash flow represents the amount investors are paying for each dollar generated from a company's operations. When reported for an ETF, it shows the weighted

average of the price/cash flow ratio for each stock in the ETF's portfolio. This measure helps determine Morningstar's value score for each stock and the overall value orientation of the ETF.

Dividend Yield

Dividends are the per-share amount taken from a company's profits and paid to shareholders. Dividend yield is equal to a company's annual dividend divided by its share price. It works as a kind of valuation measure-the lower the yield, the more investors have to pay for each dollar of dividends. Investors often consider stocks with high dividend yields potentially undervalued investments. When reported for an ETF, it shows the weighted average of the dividend yield for each stock in the ETF's portfolio.

This measure helps determine Morningstar's value score for each stock and the overall value orientation of the ETF.

Y

YTD

An abbreviation for year to date, or since the beginning of the current calendar or fiscal year. When evaluating YTD total returns, for example, the beginning price is the first day of the current calendar or last day of the current calendar (usually December 31 or January 1) to the present date.

Yield

see also SEC Yield

Yield, expressed as a percentage, represents a fund's income return on capital investment for the past 12 months. This figure refers only to interest distributions from fixed-income securities and dividends from stocks. Money generated from the sale of securities, from options and futures transactions, and from currency transactions are considered capital gains, not income. Return of capital is also not considered income. NMF (No Meaningful Figure) appears in this space for ETFs that do not properly label distributions. N/A appears if an ETF is less than one year old, in which case we cannot calculate yield. Morningstar computes yield by dividing the sum of the fund's income distributions for the past 12 months by the previous month's NAV (adjusted upward for any capital gains distributed over the same period).